Way of Death

A page of an inventory of slaves that was turned over to the colonial government after a military expedition against Caconda in 1736. This first page of the four-page inventory gives the names, descriptions, and prices for male and female slaves. A translation of the inventory appears on pages xii-xiii.

Way of Death

*Merchant Capitalism and the
Angolan Slave Trade
1730–1830*

Joseph C. Miller

The University of Wisconsin Press

This publication has been supported by the National Endowment for the Humanities, a federal agency which supports the study of such fields as history, philosophy, literature, and languages.

The University of Wisconsin Press
114 North Murray Street
Madison, Wisconsin 53715

Table 10.2 is from Herbert S. Klein, *The Middle Passage: Comparative Studies in the Atlantic Slave Trade,* copyright © 1978 by Princeton University Press, table 2.6. Reprinted with permission of Princeton University Press.

Library of Congress Cataloging-in-Publication Data
Miller, Joseph Calder.
    Way of death.
    Bibliography: pp. 717–745.
    Includes index.
    1. Slave trade—Portugal—History. 2. Slave trade—
Angola—History. 3. Slave trade—Brazil—History.
4. Slave traders—Angola—History. 5. Portugal—
Commercial policy—History. 6. Brazil—Commerce—
History. I. Title.
HT1221.M55   1988   382'.44'09469   87–40368
ISBN 0–299–11560–7

For Janet

Contents

Part **3** Brazil: The Last Stop

Part **4** Portugal: Merchants of Death

Part 5 Conclusion

Maps

Tables and Figures

Translation of a Slave Inventory

Evaluation of the Slaves That Arrived
from Benguela on the . . . of April 1738

Negroes

Sunba		4$000
Cabeto		20$000
Camumo		6$000
Caputto	small boy	1$000
Caita		25$000
Quitte		5$000
Quipallaca	wounded in the right eye	6$000
		67$000
Sunba		5$000
Bindando		4$000
Cangullo	small boy	$500
Gallo		4$000
Cahiuca		6$000
		86$500
Suba	old man, with injured left leg	3$000
Canhungo		8$000
Quellengue		28$000
		125$500

Old Women

Quepigi		16$000
Calhoca		4$000
Quicoco		6$000
Zumba		12$000
Matunbo		8$000
Catunbo		14$000
Ussoa		5$000
Catunbo		10$000
Cayeco		9$000
Quicunbo		12$000
Ussoa		3$000
		224$500/
Catua		3$000
Muco	lame in the left knee, from a burn in the fire	$500
Iaballa		3$000
Catumbo		9$000
Candunbo		5$000
Ussôa		6$000
Ussôa		12$000
		263$000

Young Women and Children

Mama/Cambia	with the child dying	6$000
Bissoa/Bivalla	with the child walking	8$000
Camia	child already evaluated among the males, named Cangullo	3$000
Biabo/Catunba		7$000
Banba/Caceyo	child dying	4$000
Tembo/Cabeto		8$000
Camia/Ligongo	child walking (dying)	4$000
Tundo		3$000
Quimano	no child—died on the path	3$000
Banba/Sonbi	child at the breast—almost dead	3$000
Canengo	no child—died on the path	1$000
Nangonbe		6$000
Oongo		5$000
		324$000/
Marongo	lame in a toe on the left foot	3$000
Nhâma	open sores on both legs	$500
Camia		5$000
Cahunda	no child—died in the bush	5$000
Sungo	small girl	1$000
Sungo	girl	2$000
Ullunga		6$000
Catana	girl	4$000
Ussoa		2$000
Eraô		1$000
Tembo	old woman	12$000
		365$500
Singa	defects on the toes of both feet	3$000
Lanta	small girl	1$500
Callunbo	huge wound on left leg	1$000
Sonbe	small girl	1$000
Bienba/Sungu	child at the breast	7$000
Sanga/Bienba	child walking—dying	3$000
Ussoa	girl	3$000
Ullunga	girl	1$000
		386$000

Child, name unknown as she is dying and cannot speak, / male without value, and a small girl Callenbo, no value because she is dying; one small girl Catunbe, no value because she is dying

68 head	901$000

Summary of an inventory of slaves turned over to the government in the aftermath of a military expedition against Caconda in 1736; enclosed in João Jacques de Magalhães (governor, Angola), 29 April 1738, AHU, Angola cx. 30. The war was described and authenticated as a "just war" in Rodrigo Cezar de Menezes (governor, Angola), 8 Jan. 1737, AHU, Angola cx. 30. The first page of this inventory is reproduced as the frontispiece.

Preface

In growing from a short study originally conceived much in the statistical style of the early 1970s into the present longer and rather more complex manuscript, *Way of Death* has acquired so many nuances that a preliminary outline of what I have tried to accomplish may make its many pages somewhat easier for the reader to follow. The initial challenge came implicitly from the National Endowment for the Humanities, whose guidelines rightly emphasize the humanistic content of projects they support. Could one portray the meaning of the unevenly documented trade in slaves, particularly from the virtually unrecorded perspectives of the slaves themselves, in warmer tones than the coldly quantitative and theoretical terms then current in the literature? I have assembled the evidence I could find to convey some sense of the meanings of southern Atlantic slaving, and not just from the point of view of the slaves but also from the viewpoints of other eighteenth-century worlds that gradually became apparent to me as I proceeded. The bare statistics of the Angolan trade appear elsewhere in studies by Herbert Klein and myself, as cited in the footnotes. This text concentrates on eliciting how people recorded themselves as feeling about what they did, insofar as expressions or actions suggest why they behaved as they did, and it tries hard to avoid confusing those remote and sometimes surprising *mentalités* with modern notions, particularly the easy moral outrage that arises when liberal humanist sentiments confront the brutal facts of slavery and the slave trade. I have tried to understand, not merely to condemn.

What began as an economic history of Angola also expanded to present Angolan slaving as an aspect of the entire Atlantic economy in the eighteenth century. As a result, half the book deals with Brazil and Portugal. Only my respect for the intricacy of events in northern Europe in that century (and my awareness of the limits of the not-quite-infinite patience of family and colleagues, not to mention weary readers) has deterred me from adding the obviously required chapter on the British and French roles in the Portuguese empire. I fear that the product of this evolution is an uneasy balance between a study that has not escaped its primary research basis in documents from and about Angola but strains to sketch influences of three or four continents from faint traces visible at Luanda. I could not resist the temptation to express in footnotes to later chapters my hope that Brazilianists and specialists in Portuguese and European history will treat my naiveté about their fields as stimulating rather than disrespectful or disruptive.

Writing, even secondarily, on the Atlantic scale of course brought me face to face with an enormous theoretical literature of many stripes. Though the considerable length of the study as I have written it may not immediately suggest the restraint that the author feels he has exercised, the absence of systematic commentary on the theoretical implications of Angolan slaving, as I have reconstructed it, is a particularly glaring example of the many holes I made no attempt to fill in the end. Perhaps others will wish to reflect on how I have incorporated insights from world-systems theory, Marxism, liberal economics, anthropology, and probably other things as well, but here I have settled for the privilege of eclecticism that historians sometimes claim. Unargued is a case for coherence among the various perspectives conditioning the book that is not entirely unconsidered. Just as I hope the book shows how it required a multiplicity of valid, if contradictory, perspectives on slaving to produce the southern Atlantic trade in human beings, so also are the plural and conflicting viewpoints of abstract social science necessary to elicit even a part of the full human content of the past.

It is in large part a consequence of the necessary effort to see events from more than a single point of view that situations occasionally come up in more than one chapter. I hope that their multiple and intersecting meanings will thus become apparent, without at the same time leaving a sense of repetitiousness.

The organization of the book is thus only secondarily chronological, though several different senses of time are meant to inform the various points of view expressed, from the long and very slow changes in ecology, African ideological systems, and societal institutions underlying the early chapters to more familiar calendars and sequences as Europeans come on the scene in Luanda, Brazil, and Portugal. In the end, nonetheless, the book remains historical in its underlying focus on the profound alterations on every level of commerce in the southern Atlantic between the early eighteenth and the early nineteenth centuries.

This study of perceptions and motivations falls well outside the value-neutral parameters of the formal statistical and economic analysis that has informed much recent work on the Atlantic slave trade, including the elegant study by David Eltis that appeared as these words were being written. Although I hope that my conclusions are consistent with conventional economics, the numerical data available for Angola and Brazil before the nineteenth century are too few, and too unreliable in that dark age of statistics, to base the presentation on the sort of quantification that such analysis would require. Some of the bits and pieces, prices, volume of slaving, and the like, that I have been able to assemble I have discussed at length in technical studies appearing elsewhere in support of this work (see the bibliography).

Further, an analysis that begins deep within Africa and retains an emphasis on the uncountable African contribution to events would not proceed far even with better statistics on the European side than in fact exist, as prices in European currencies, for example, may have had very little relevance to values and costs in other currency zones inland from the coast. Slaving responded to so wide a range of institutional factors that may be reconstructed with some confidence—climate, changing geography, technological developments, and most prominently the fraility of the people being bought and sold—that it seemed efficient to examine southern Atlantic slaving on the basis of all these influences. I have no reservations about the value of a contextualized application of formal statistics and economics; here, however, the numbers remain mostly in the background to buttress arguments made also on other grounds. That is probably appropriate, too, in view of the limited formal training in these admirably technical fields that I have managed to acquire.

The more prominent levels of quasi-economic analysis employed in the book concern structural differences between capitalist and other sorts of economies, how people functioned along the margins between different economic systems, and how one sort of economy became transformed into another. The principal example here concerns what strikes me as a transition from earlier African values centering on production for use and on people, with practice reflecting that sort of theory to a significant extent, to something much closer to an exchange economy of material goods by the eighteenth century. It is important to remember that Brazil, too, possessed whole economic sectors not at all well integrated into the bullion-based currency zones of the Atlantic in the eighteenth century. There is also recurrent concern here with the behavior of firms—African traders, the organizers of a slaving venture, or royally chartered Portuguese companies. Some of these microeconomic levels of the study contain elements of a business history of slaving, with emphasis on questions of financing operations in an environment of scarce capital. The scattered documentation from the southern Atlantic reveals the optimizing strategies of these individuals more clearly than would available data on the aggregate behavior necessary to support other kinds of economic analysis.

In terms of history, the book considers one or two aspects of how people experienced the great change that divided early modern times from the modern world, mostly using economic metaphors to get at limited social and economic facets of the same transformation. It concludes that the dominant precapitalist institutions in Africa trembled under challenges discernibly similar to the emergence of mercantilism in northern Europe at about the same time, though the balance of nonmodern and modern elements was very different on the two continents, both at the beginning and at the end of the century. Portugal, Brazil, and Angola were following parallel tracks, but each of them at different points along the continuum between the two extremes, and central Africa itself contained areas at various moments of the common movement. The final chapter tries to explain why so many and disparate parts of the Atlantic world seemed to be moving, though unequally, in the same direction; it may not have been inevitable, but it did happen.

History thus moved at differing paces. Chapter 1, which introduces readers unfamiliar with the geography of central Africa to the outlines of it necessary to understand where the slaves came from, avoids presenting a static "traditional" background; rather, ethnic identities changed with majestic slowness, and demographic patterns tended to oscillate back and forth around levels relatively stable in the long run. Chapter 2 explores an ideological framework of communal use-values that seems readily inferable from what we know about economic behavior in nonliterate, low-technology environments in general; that framework did not change much between 1730 and 1830 in the sense of becoming its modern contrast, exchange-valued individualism, but its interesting historical feature was how old ideas in Africa accommodated far-reaching and novel changes in behavior with resiliency. Chapter 3 identifies the subtle sources of those changes in the imported goods that reached coastal western central Africa beginning in the seventeenth century and spread much more widely in the interior in the eighteenth. What did change dramatically in Africa was politics, and Chapter 4 examines the decline of old polities based on keeping people as dependents and the rise of a new type of state that thrived on enslaving some and selling others abroad. The demographic correlates of these revolutions, as Chapter 5 argues, mostly resettled people within Africa without causing widespread depopulation from exporting people to America. These sketches of the people, ideology, economics, politics, and societies of eighteenth-century western central Africa complete the background to the slave trade set out in Part 1.

Part 2 takes up the traders. A prominent and permanent aspect of the political and economic transformation in Africa was the emergence of a commercial economy and society within the African use-value environment, as Chapter 6 suggests through an examination of the institutions that composed it. At this level of the story something closer to what we usually think of as historical change becomes apparent, and Chapter 7 takes up this story by going back over the ground of the preceding chapter in terms of the expanding geography of trade and the growth in the numbers of people moving along the slaving trails of Africa. Europeans begin to appear in this largely African scene at this point, and so Chapter 8 begins to take account of events near, on, and beyond the Atlantic by reviewing how Euro-African traders in the Portuguese colony of Angola fit into the broader African transport sector. One distinctive feature of these "Luso-Africans" was their involvement simultaneously in very different African and Portuguese economic and political systems. Thus, their eighteenth-century history leads inevitably to the European merchants on whose commercial capital they often relied. Chapter 9 examines these immigrant traders from Europe in Luanda, capital of Angola and virtually the only port on the entire coast that functioned solidly within the capitalist economy of the Atlantic. Also present there, but playing a role, outlined in Chapter 10, very different from Portuguese expatriates, were Brazilian shippers, who, for most of the history of the trade, carried most Angolan slaves across the middle passage to America. Finally, with the conflicting interests of African traders, Luso-Africans, Brazilian slavers, and metropolitan merchants sketched in structural terms, it is possible to illuminate the experiences of the slaves they handled, mostly in terms of how and why so many died. Chapter 11 reconstructs what may be known of the slaves' sufferings and establishes the incidence of mortality that profoundly influenced the strategies of the traders fighting over the captives.

The following chapters take up the relatively familiar narrative of Brazilian colonial history and the history of the Portuguese empire in terms that indicate how southern Atlantic slaving fit into the mercantilist currents flowing out from Lisbon in the eighteenth century. Chapters 12, 13, and 14 indicate how the marginality of the trade to the main economic and political issues of the period may explain the three phases of capital-short Brazilian participation in it, each to the detriment of the slaves, as Europe and Portugal made new demands on the American colony for sugar, specie, and cotton and other industrial raw materials. At the same time, Portugal's quest for silver and gold was relatively constant, though Britain's priorities began to change from stimulating trade to stimulating production by the 1790s. In Part 3, America, though the last stop for the slaves, emerges as the departure point of wealth for Portugal, if not Europe.

The chapters on Portugal, 15 through 18, trace the waxing and waning influence of the nominal European imperial authority over all these remote developments in the southern Atlantic as Lisbon merchants tried and ultimately failed to gain some advantage from their king's imperial possessions in Africa. Commercial capital—faintly visible as far away, and as early in the book, as the growing imports spreading throughout western central Africa; prominent, of course, in the history of the traders; and essential for understanding Brazilian slaving, though more by its scarcity than by its plentitude—inevitably becomes the explicit theme in Part 4. Lisbon's frustrated efforts to draw advantage from southern Atlantic slaving fell into four distinct periods, the first led by brokers of foreign goods from Britain and Asia; a second featuring nationalistic efforts to develop domestic industry and trade under the famous prime minister, the marquis of Pombal; a third in which metropolitan investment in Angola languished while planners in Portugal focused similar plans on Brazil; and finally a fourth in which Portuguese investors in slaving transferred themselves to Brazil while the trade drifted toward abolition. Behind these ebbs and flows of Lisbon's direct involvement in the slave trade, indirect British commercial support for Portuguese slave trading grew without cease, right through the early nineteenth century, when the government in London was simultaneously exerting itself to abolish slaving.

The concluding chapter attempts to draw some unity out of the diversity of viewpoints—European and African, metropolitan and colonial, slavers and enslaved, modern and medieval—explored in the body of the book. The very divergences of values that came together in the trade explain how each class of participants got something of what it treasured out of slaving, except for the slaves—even though some of them may have survived starvation in Africa by living through the journey to America. In the end, Africans' unwavering view of wealth as people, if increasingly also as trade goods, complemented an equally set Portuguese view of wealth as money, specie and currencies, in the eighteenth century.

The focus on merchant capital, I hope, adequately justifies the period studied, 1730 to 1830. Despite scattered earlier antecedents, some of which are mentioned, that was the hundred years in which commercialization spread deep into central Africa, in which merchants in Lisbon tried and failed to take over slaving from Angola, in which British mercantilism suffused the Portuguese empire, and in which the southern Atlantic slave trade passed from an earlier militaristic and planter-dominated phase into condemnation, illegality, and, belatedly, termination in the nineteenth century. I have restricted my discussion of earlier institutions in Africa and on the Atlantic to the outline necessary to understand why merchants chose the ways they did to overwhelm them. Already by the 1820s, capitalists from industrializing Britain were making demands on the southern Atlantic basin that were beginning to restructure production as well as exchange, and Africans were shifting from slaving to commodity extraction, and the Angolan economy was diversifying to include plantations as well as people, and I have no more than hinted at what happened then. Fortunately, Portuguese and Angolan history for those alien eras is the capable hands of other scholars.

Thus, there was no animate expanding capitalism that overwhelmed Africa, benignly or malignantly, during the slaving era or later. Rather, there were only merchant capitalists and traders, most of them short of capital, even desperately so on the Angolan end. The scarcity of capital is a point of some analytical significance. While capitalist relations, or exchange economies, have subsequently come to characterize much economic activity in Africa, they still have not done so uniformly. It is hopelessly historicist to write about earlier centuries as if merchants and governments in Europe were about to seize control then. Overemphasis on animate, even animistic, capital further obscures the vital analytical significance of the domestic use-value economy, the modern "peasant" sector, to the profits of traders and producers in the economies of Africa and Brazil. In fact, the very shortness of credit was what made capital so valuable and led Africans and Europeans alike to devise the ways of controlling it for themselves that they did. By the eighteenth century, capital stocks were enormous compared to past standards in Europe and even more so according to recent experience in Africa, but it was an era of extremely rapid economic growth and development on both continents, and the available funds were insufficient to enable everyone to do everything they wanted, or even just to keep up with the accelerating pace. One understands mercantilism more fully by using as one's point of departure what ordinary people, of the most diverse sorts, thought they were doing.

The comprehensiveness of the metaphor of death—physical for some slaves but sociological for others, financial as well as physical for European traders in Africa, political for many ambitious Africans, and paradoxically philosophical as mercantilism and industrialism coalesced in the Atlantic—occurred to me in 1977 as I moved beyond horrified fascination with the fate awaiting the slaves and began to realize the extent to which the slavers made their money by passing dying slaves off to other owners. The image infused other levels of the study as it took shape, and I was gratified later to find a parallel emphasis on death in Mary Karasch's penetrating reconstruction of the lives of the same slaves I was studying after they settled in Rio de Janeiro and to discover the universality of the theme in Orlando Patterson's grand synthesis. It seemed to further my original goal of infusing abstract theories of colonialism, demography, development and underdevelopment, world systems, and the like with human values: the slaves could have thought of little else, and it turned out that the slavers shared the concern, though from a very different angle. Thus, it ultimately also unified the diffuse contents of the book.

Readers may wish to consider for themselves other levels on which the story seems to make sense also: change accelerates from start to finish, as the geographical scene shifts from the center of Africa to Portugal and Europe. Writing on this intercontinental scale has forced me to simplify the variety of individual experiences into relatively stereotyped groups of people, with racial and ethnic features that also enter into the history; each of these groups emphasized one or another of the several specialized economic functions necessary to link commercial flows from all around the Atlantic. There is expansion in scale, from a single captive youth in a small village to the global stage on which capitalism appears to work. Only some of the distinctiveness of the Portuguese trade in relation to that of the British, French, and others emerges from the analysis here, though I hope to comment more explicitly on the contrasts in another context. Central Africa strikes me as significantly less commercialized than West Africa, the other major area from which slaves came to the Atlantic, and I hope that specialists in that field will explain to me exactly how. The evidence behind my conclusions drifts from what may verge dangerously close on sheer speculation in some of the early chapters to detail confirmed in such expressive abundance for some later sections that I was willing to suspend inferences about the African side of the story from it, like a cantilever bridge leaning out over the chasm. But all that must stand or fall by itself, without further commentary from me here.

I am most of all uncomfortable with my inability to research the chapters on Brazil and Portugal in anything like the detail managed for the Angolan end of the study. In some ways, the evidence for the argument therefore sways precariously on a very small pivot centered at Luanda, an obscure corner of the world by anyone's standards, including those of many people who ended up there in the eighteenth century. Benguela is already relatively blurred, owing to a quite deliberate lack of documentation from that southern center of subterfuge. The African interior retains much of its well-known enigmatic paucity of evidence. For Brazil, I have taken the broad outline of the colony's history for granted and have tried to use recent specialized monographs and published documents to explore what strikes me as a neglected local commercial sector there, one about which specialists concerned with issues more central to Brazilian history have not researched systematically. Portugal is even less thoroughly investigated here, but then, Angola was even less significant to Lisbon than it was to Rio. Accordingly, I found very little of direct relevance to the southern Atlantic in the abundant literature on Portuguese history and decided to content myself with inferring broader patterns in the metropole from their specific manifestations in remote Angola. That sort of strategy is a tail wagging a dog and may not commend the result to Brazilianists and historians of Portugal whose favorite questions I do not raise, but it may be an unavoidable first step toward opening a subject significant precisely for its inherent marginality to those wealthier parts of the world.

I have otherwise tried to document what I argue, but the historical record is not often explicit on points as subtle as some it is necessary to introduce or on changes as slow as those under way. Africans said much that turned out to be important in their distinctive oral idioms, and ethnographers have described other aspects of life in Africa that informed the analysis. Most of the primary documentation comes from colonial officials in Angola, but competent Portuguese bureaucrats knew better than to set down on paper very much about the reality of politics and economics in the empire. Thus, it has sometimes been necessary to adopt inferences as working hypotheses and then proceed to build other conclusions on that less than absolutely solid basis. In the interest of readability, I have tended to take these initial reservations, once mentioned, as givens and have not weighted down the prose with subsequent technical qualifications of the argument or with repeated acknowledgements of stated uncertainties. Interested readers may consult the supporting studies published elsewhere for more discussion of the method behind conclusions stated rather baldly here. Doubt is a method of inquiry for all historians, but it is also an unavoidable aspect of one's conclusions. In the end, even starting points as tenuous as these gain enormously in plausibility and probability from the coherence of the entire set of conclusions to which they lead—what has been aptly called a "wigwam" method of historical documentation, or "united we stand, divided we fall."

Carlos Couto has noticed what he alludes to as "a conspiracy of silence" in official records, and I found the silence deafening indeed. It is almost axiomatic that the most important things were discussed least. Hence the most profound dilemma for a historian: what becomes most obvious is never documented explicitly and potentially hardest of all to render plausible to a reader who has not spent years immersed in the eloquent silences of governors' letters from Luanda. Portuguese Minister for the Colonies Martinho de Mello e Castro wrote to Angolan Governor Manuel de Almeida e Vasconcelos on 7 August 1791, deploring "the extremely common, pernicious, and inveterate abuse in Angola of telling this Court not what it should know but only what it seems convenient there ought to be known here." The historian of the Angolan slave trade can only sympathize with the sentiment expressed but then, like the minister, plunge on anyway.

Charlottesville, Virginia
August 1987

Acknowledgments

A book is more a collective enterprise than anyone but its author—really only the "front man"—ever knows. I would begin by acknowledging the material support that has allowed the researching and writing of this one. Beyond the leave from teaching responsibilities that the University of Virginia gave me through Sesquicentennial Associateships in 1978–79 and 1985, a Wilson Gee Institute Summer Grant from the university permitted me to begin preliminary computer analyses of shipping data in 1974 and to develop other technical aspects of the study under similar support in 1976 and 1980. The National Endowment for the Humanities initiated its consistent support of the project in 1977 with a Summer Stipend for Younger Humanists. Research that summer—intended for Angola but confined by political developments in Luanda to Britain, France, Portugal, and Brazil—proceeded under an Africa Research Grant from the Joint Committee on Africa of the Social Science Research Council and the American Council of Learned Societies. The Fundação Calouste Gulbenkian of Lisbon aided in allowing me to consult materials in the Lisbon archives at that stage. Research in Portugal, Britain, and elsewhere in Europe advanced in 1978, and most of the original draft was written under the Fellowship for Independent Study and Research that the NEH awarded in 1978–79. The National Library of Medicine provided a translation grant in 1979–80 that permitted me to return to Portugal and to develop medical aspects of the slaves' experience much farther than I would have had the time to do otherwise. And, of course, there is no telling how long it might have taken me to revise the manuscript in hand as of late 1984 had the NEH not come to the rescue with a second Fellowship for Independent Study and Research in 1985. The Carter G. Woodson Institute of the University of Virginia supported the cartography that now graces the volume. To these generous sponsors I am more than grateful. According to custom, I absolve them publicly here of any responsibility for what they have enabled me to decide about the history of the Angolan slave trade.

No historian can make any headway whatsoever without the expert professionals who care for the libraries and archives holding the source materials that he or she consults. For almost twenty years now I have worked in the Arquivo Histórico Ultramarino in Lisbon, the core collection of colonial records underlying this study. Since 1975 I have greatly appreciated the professionalism of the staff of the archive, led by its director Dr. Isaú Santos and several members of the staff of its reading room, who have facilitated access to that unique assemblage of documents and who patiently tolerated the sometimes erratic haste of a foreign researcher forced to compress consultation of the collection into months, or sometimes days, when he ought to have given it the years of attention that it deserves, and that resident researchers have often lavished on it. Years ago, in quite another era, the personnel of the Arquivo Histórico de Angola in Luanda organized and accorded me access to the documentary riches of that collection. I always received cordial and efficient welcomes at other archives where I spent even less time, and I wish here to express my gratitude especially to colleagues at the Arquivo Histórico do Ministério das Finanças (João Duarte de Carvalho, director), the Biblioteca da Sociedade de Geografia de Lisboa, the Biblioteca e Arquivo do Palácio da Ajuda (Lisbon), the Arquivo Histórico do Tribunal de Contas (Lisbon), the Biblioteca Nacional do Rio de Janeiro, the Arquivo Nacional (Rio de Janeiro), the Instituto Histórico e Geográfico do Brasil (Rio de Janeiro), and the National Library of Medicine (Bethesda, Maryland).

In Portuguese African studies, beyond those who preserve the documents, are those who publish them. Everyone who works on Angola starts with the monumental collection of "*monumenta*" of the late Father António Brásio, fourteen volumes of documents running from the fifteenth century through 1699. Other documentary studies appear in the bibliography appended to this volume, and I wish that Father Graziano Saccardo's three-volume compilation of data from his career devoted to the Angolan Capuchines, *Congo e Angola: con la storia dell'antica missione dei cappuccini* (Venice: Curia Provinciale dei Cappuccini, 1982), had reached me in time for the use I could have made of it. A new generation of scholars is now beginning to take documentary criticism and publication seriously, as the collection of papers in *Paideuma* 33 (1987) amply demonstrates, and Angolan historians are very fortunate to have the exemplary study of Governor Fernão de Sousa's papers (c. 1626–30) by Beatrix Heintze already in hand, with the welcome prospect of another volume yet to come. Brazilian historians deserve similar recognition, with the most prominent example of documentary editing there for this study the five volumes in Luís Lisanti's *Negócios coloniaes*. Without these editors, historical interpretation on the level I have attempted would be much, much more laborious, if not impossible.

My list of personal debts is even longer, and no less important. My footnotes acknowledge some of my scholarly predecessors who have written works that I have appropriated shamelessly for my own purposes; if I sometimes appear to give less than full consideration to worthy arguments they chose to make, it is not often because I disagree with their skilled presentations but rather because I have had to get on with making my own case. Among those who have not only tolerated my private musings on elements of the book but have also spurred me on with trenchant comments are Dauril Alden, David Birmingham, Larissa Brown, Gervase Clarence-Smith, Philip D. Curtin, Jill R. Dias, Beatrix Heintze, Jan Hogendorn, Kenneth F. Kiple, Paul Lovejoy, Patrick Manning, Phyllis Martin, Joel Mokyr, John Thornton, Leroy Vail, and, especially, Jan Vansina. Students, in wondering whatever I could be trying to say, also helped me understand. Either Duane Osheim or I came up with the title one fall afternoon in 1978 as we ran through the hills of central Virginia, but it has been so long that I cannot recall which of us it was; perhaps it was both. Dedicated staff of the Faculty of Arts and Sciences, the Carter G. Woodson Institute for Afro-American and African Studies, and especially the Department of History at the University of Virginia instructed me in using word processing equipment and somehow transformed my messy yellow drafts into electronic orderliness, over and over again. Barbara Hanrahan, of the University of Wisconsin Press, moved matters forward with breathtaking despatch. Claudine Vansina has drawn the maps with exceptional expertise and skill. Carolyn Moser smoothed the prose and uncovered an impressive range of details requiring further attention in copyediting. Martin Hyatt verified the bibliography, and Carey Goodman read the proofs with a sharp and experienced eye.

After nearly ten years at a succession of desks, an author can only be grateful for the patient tolerance he has enjoyed: most of all from spouse and children, some of whom may not recognize their husband or father without "the book" looming behind every free moment. Julie, John, and Laura grew up as the project matured, and their inquiring spirits were also inspiring in keeping me at my own search for understanding something about the African past. Janet has been unfailing, and in ways beyond what either of us understand very clearly, even after all these years. She and they will presumably find their rewards in having it over and done with. Colleagues here at the university and Angola specialists elsewhere always managed to give me the impression that they believed I would one day finish. And, indeed, without all of the above—and others too numerous to mention here—I well might not have. Mere thanks can never convey my gratitude. Writing this book has been more than worth the while, and not only because completing it reminds me so forcefully of how much I owe to so many.

Abbreviations Used in Notes

AHA   Arquivo Histórico de Angola (Luanda)[1]

AHCML   Arquivo Histórico da Câmara Municipal de Luanda

AHMAE   Archives Historiques du Ministère des Affaires Etrangères (Paris)

AHMF   Arquivo Histórico do Ministério de Finanças (Lisbon)

AHTC   Arquivo Histórico do Tribunal de Contas (Lisbon)

AHU   Arquivo Histórico Ultramarino (Lisbon)[2]

ANRJ   Arquivo Nacional do Rio de Janeiro

ANTT   Arquivo Nacional da Torre do Tombo (Lisbon)

1. The designations of the holdings of the AHA refer to the collection as it existed in 1969–72, before its relocation and presumed reorganization in the wake of political independence in Angola in 1975. The holdings as they then were catalogued were listed in Arquivo Histórico de Angola, *Roteiro topográfico dos códices* (Angola: Instituto de Investigação Científica de Angola, 1966) and in five volumes of a *Roteiro topográfico dos avulsos* (Angola: Instituto de Investigação Científica de Angola, 1969–71), for the *concelhos* (alphabetically) from Alto Dande through Luanda. See further discussion in Joseph C. Miller, "The Archives of Luanda, Angola," *International Journal of African Historical Studies*, 7, no. 4 (1974):551–90.

2. The locations of the documents from the AHU are those prior to the recent reorganization of the archive's contents; for the only available information on this reorganization and the new file numbers, see José C. Curto, "The Angolan Manuscript Collection of the AHU, Lisbon: Toward a Working Guide," *History in Africa* (forthcoming). A typescript of this guide exists in the archive.

APB   Arquivo Público da Bahia

BAL   Biblioteca e Arquivo da Ajuda (Lisbon)

BAPP   Biblioteca e Arquivo Público do Pernambuco

BNL   Biblioteca Nacional de Lisboa

BNRJ   Biblioteca Nacional do Rio de Janeiro

cod.   *códice* (codex)

cx.   *caixa* (box) (document series in AHU)

FO   Foreign Office series, PRO

D.O.   *documentos em organização* (documents being organized)

IHGB   Instituto Histórico e Geográfico Brasileiro (Rio de Janeiro)

PRO   Public Record Office (London)

Part 1

Africa

Births and Deaths

1

The People of Western Central Africa

About 1775, near a village called Kisuka kya Laseta, a fifteen-year-old youth found himself unexpectedly in the power of some of the local men of his country. The boy's captors marched him upstream along the river that flowed past his home, famed for its seven large baobab trees and more recently known also for the local market where foreigners came to sell exotic goods for prisoners whom the local people brought in to them. The lord of his village restricted this fair to the bank of the river opposite the dwellings of the people in an evident effort to limit the violence emanating from the unsavory business these strangers conducted, but their influence had spread far beyond the confines of the marketplace anyway to provoke kidnappings like the one that sent the youth, later baptized as Domingos, off into the wilderness to the west.

The moon passed through three full cycles from the start of Domingos's trek before he and a number of other similarly captive companions reached the sea at the mouth of the Kikombo River. At the Kikombo, Domingos became the property of a European. An alert and promising young man, he later worked his way up to a not-uncomfortable or un-appreciated position as the slave valet of a ship captain, João Ignacio Coelho, who worked the shipping lanes of the southern Atlantic taking other slaves from western central Africa to Brazil.

A certain justice, or at least punishment, ultimately arose from the original kidnapping somewhere near the sources of the Zambezi, in the very heart of central Africa. The local man who had stolen young Domingos returned from his venture in the west to find his victim's father waiting in the village of the seven baobabs, authorized by his lord to repay the abductor in kind. The old man's anger, and perhaps his greed as well, led him to multiply the degree of retribution. In addition to the kidnapper he seized no less than six people from among the kidnapper's relatives or associates, sending four of them off to the west, and keeping two others at home for himself. Those who went west fell into the hands of a profes-sional slave dealer at one of the huge markets held there. Finally embarked on a slave ship at Benguela, the kidnapper found himself set ashore in the

Brazilian viceregal capital of Rio de Janeiro. Having apparently learned little from the misfortunes flowing thus far from his original theft of the boy who became Domingos, he constructed a new life out of his old habits of theft and crime as a slave in Brazil. The Portuguese variety of justice then caught up with him and condemned him to penal servitude pulling an oar in the lighters of the city's harbor. It was there that Domingos, evidently already sailing with Captain Coelho, encountered him eight years later and had the satisfaction of learning of the misfortunes greater than his own that had befallen his captor.[1]

Domingos's later recollections of his seizure and westward journey,[2] perhaps dimmed by his more recent accomplishments as a slave in Brazil, or softened for the ears of his Portuguese masters, did not emphasize the horrors of his experience of enslavement in Africa. In fact, bleaching human bones marked the trails along which he and other dazed, shackled, and abandoned people stumbled westward through African woodlands two and three centuries ago. For these thousands of men, women, and children, the dry-season, reddening late afternoon sun they followed dropped toward smoky horizons leading to unknown regions they dreaded as lands of death.

There to the west, so the elders and wise tellers of tales had confided in happier times at home, lay the boundary between the lands of the living and the domain of the dead. There beyond the mountains and dry, low coastlands, others had recounted, lay a great water so broad that no living person could cross it.[3] From beyond the water, some alleged, came the strangers who drove captive people from the cool highlands and the sandy plains relentlessly onward to the west, where other blood-red-skinned followers of the great Lord of the Dead, Mwene Puto, awaited them. These people of Mwene Puto, it was well known, were cannibals who took their nourishment from the flesh of the blacks they so avidly sought.[4]

1. "Memória de Brant Pontes sôbre a communicação das duas costas (9/9/800)," in Alfredo de Albuquerque Felner, *Angola: apontamentos sôbre a colonização dos planaltos e litoral do sul de Angola* (Lisbon: Agência Geral das Colónias, 1940), 1: 240–50.

2. The story was told and recorded about 1800.

3. Wyatt MacGaffey, "The West in Congolese Experience," in Philip D. Curtin, ed., *Africa and the West: Intellectual Responses to European Culture* (Madison: University of Wisconsin Press, 1972), pp. 49–74; idem, "Kongo and the King of the Americans," *Journal of Modern African Studies* 6, no. 2 (1968): 171–81; idem, "Cultural Roots of Kongo Prophetism," *History of Religion* 17, no. 2 (1977): 186–87.

4. E.g., for the 1750s, see Manuel Correia Leitão, in Gastão Sousa Dias, ed., "Uma viagem a Cassange nos meados do século XVIII," *Boletim da Sociedade de geografia de Lisboa* 56, nos. 1–2 (1938): 20–21. The story was ubiquitous throughout Africa: see William D. Piersen, "White Cannibals, Black Martyrs: Fear, Depression, and Religious Faith as Causes of Suicide among New Slaves," *Journal of Negro History* 62, no. 2 (1977): 147–50; Gabriel Debien, "La traite nantaise vue par un Nantais," in *Enquêtes et documents* (Centre de Recherches sur l'Histoire de la France Atlantique) 2 (1972): 210; Katia M. de Queirós Mattoso, *Être esclave au Brésil XVIe–XIXe siècle* (Paris: Hachette, 1979), p. 58; Mary C. Karasch, *Slave Life in Rio de Janeiro, 1808–1850* (Princeton: Princeton University Press, 1987), p. 39 et

People had in fact seen the certain evidence of this horrible truth: huge copper kettles on the great vessels that carried the condemned off across the Styx-like seas.[5] The salted meat fed to the beings who lived in those vessels confirmed the stories. The bodies of the blacks taken off to those regions of the dead far beyond the water Mwene Puto pressed to extrude the cooking oil that his subjects brought back to Africa for their own use in settlements at the edge of the ocean where they lived. The blood of Mwene Puto's black victims also returned to Africa as the deep red wine the strangers sold.[6] The foreigners' cheeses, it was further said, were made from blacks' brains.[7] The fires of Hell flared also in the Land of the Dead, where the followers of Mwene Puto burned the bones of the blacks to yield the ashlike, lethal gray powder that, when placed in iron tubes, transformed itself back into the flames from which it had come and spewed pain and destruction against any who tried, unprepared, to resist their demands.[8] These fears, and the violent and unpredictable behavior of the strangers who collected the blacks and drove them to the west, struck terror in the hearts of all who met them.[9]

Mercifully, many of the people sent off down the twisting paths dropped before meeting their Charons of the sea, leaving their bones and wooden shackles to whiten, stark against the vermillion clay, beside those of uncounted predecessors. Of those who survived to stare dully at the towns where the red people of Mwene Puto flavored their cooking with oils pressed from black bodies, very much as did reputed African cannibals back in the lands to the east,[10] perhaps 20,000 lived to begin their crossing of the great water each year in the early decades of Mwene Puto's eighteenth century. Even larger numbers would follow in the succeeding 150 years.

passim. Also see Gabriel Debien, "Le journal de traite de la *Licorne* au Mozambique, 1787–1788," in *Etudes africaines offertes à Henri Brunschwig* (Paris: Editions de l'Ecole des Hautes Etudes en Sciences Sociales, 1982), pp. 105–6.

5. Cf. Jay Coughtry, *The Notorious Triangle: Rhode Island and the African Slave Trade, 1700–1807* (Philadelphia: Temple University Press, 1981), p. 147, citing Equiano, who recorded his fears upon being taken aboard a British slaver off the lower Guinea Coast in 1756.

6. Debien, "Traite nantaise vue par un Nantais," p. 210; Debien, "Journal de traite de la *Licorne*," pp. 105–6.

7. Dr. Francisco Damião Cosme, in Luis de Pina, ed., "Tractado das queixas endemicas, e mais fataes nesta Conquista (Luanda, 1770)," *Studia* 20–22 (1967): 264.

8. Pina, ed. (Cosme), "Tractado," p. 264. Cf. Affonso Escragnolle de Taunay, *Subsídios para a história do tráfico africano no Brasil* (São Paulo: Anais do Museu Paulista, 1941), pp. 139–40.

9. Franciso Inocêncio de Sousa Coutinho (governor, Angola), 26 Nov. 1772, AHU, Angola *papeis avulsos*, cx. 36; João Alvares Ferreira, *memória*, 25 June 1762, AHU, Angola cx. 29; Pina, ed. (Cosme), "Tractado," p. 264.

10. Compare these African beliefs about the cannibalism of the Europeans with ideas about local anthropophagi, e.g., the so-called "Jaga"; Joseph C. Miller, *Kings and Kinsmen: Early Mbundu States in Angola* (Oxford: Clarendon Press, 1976), esp. pp. 244–49.

Most of those who embarked endured the month or more of confinement aboard the ships that carried them through the Middle Passage to find that the lands beyond the water—which they learned to call Brazil, from the red wood that had first drawn the attention of Europeans to the place—were no less a place of death than they had imagined, though perhaps not in the ways they had foreseen. Epidemics periodically ravaged the black people of these lands.[11] Some of the Africans, taken in as forced laborers by powerful masters, worked themselves to early deaths, shivering knee-deep in icy water beneath the lashes of wildcat miners. Other slaves endured the heat and monotonous travail of sugar, tobacco, or cotton fields for a few years before exhaustion, deprivation, and sheer physical abuse left them too weakened to carry on.

Only a tiny minority of the new arrivals, like Domingos, lived to acquire the manners and privileges of life close to the masters, mostly in towns and in the Big Houses of the rural plantations. By no means all of the black people fell, but enough died that the mines, plantations, and cities of Brazil consumed another two million or so African lives in the century and a half after 1700.

Few of the people of Mwene Puto—or Portugal, as the slaves discovered the Land of the Dead was known in the wider world ringing the Atlantic Ocean they had crossed—noted the human suffering of those caught up in what they viewed in narrowly economic terms as a trade in slave labor. As the eighteenth century wore on, the Portuguese preserved their trade in African captives into an age that their European neighbors knew as an Enlightened one. Enlightenment elsewhere around the Atlantic came to imply, among many other things, a growing sensitivity to the injustices to which enslavement subjected human beings, even those from western central Africa, and deepening revulsion at its attendant cruelties and deaths. However, only peripheral eddies from these humanitarian currents stirring in northern Europe washed up on Portuguese shores around the southern Atlantic.

The Portuguese slave trade from western central Africa to Brazil survived, even thrived, as a matter of economics more than of ethics, where Enlightenment took the form of doctrines of "free trade" that effectively concealed what others viewed as moral wrongs to the slaves behind a screen of the masters' enlightened self-interest. But economic changes brought profound changes to the trade between 1730 and 1830, particularly after 1760, as liberalizing influences emanating from Lisbon sub-

11. Karasch, *Slave Life in Rio*, develops the theme of slave mortality and the slaves' awareness of death; for smallpox epidemics, see Dauril Alden and Joseph C. Miller, "Unwanted Cargoes: The Origins and Dissemination of Smallpox via the Slave Trade from Africa to Brazil, c. 1560–c. 1830," in Kenneth F. Kiple, ed., *The African Exchange: Toward a Biological History of the Black People* (Durham, N.C.: Duke University Press, forthcoming).

stituted new monopolies for old ones in Portugal's African colony in Angola and as Brazilian mineral and agricultural booms and busts altered the organization of the trade on its American side. The southern Atlantic commerce in human beings finally ended only gradually and belatedly after 1830, its final two decades concealed in the obscurity of the illegality to which it had been condemned by British Enlightenment and self-interest, cruisers off the coasts of southern Africa, and diplomats in the chancelleries of Lisbon and Rio de Janeiro. Behind the humanitarian rhetoric of the English and the economics of the Portuguese empire, the slaves continued to march westward in Africa according to an internal economic and demographic logic resting on the stark and unavoidable specter of death that had stalked the farmers of western central Africa since long before caravans of captives started moving toward the coast, crowded and stinking "death traps" plied the Middle Passage, or raw new slaves died as they "seasoned" in Brazil.

The Land and the Rains

The lands from which the slaves came, though extensive, were not populous. Captives who were embarked along the 1,200 kilometers of western African coasts south of Cape Lopes, the equatorial promontory at the mouth of the Ogowe River, came from pockets of population scattered unevenly throughout an area that by 1830 extended up to 2,500 kilometers eastward into forests, clearings, woods, grassy savannas, and semidesert. On its northern flank, this region included much of the western equatorial forest of the central basin of the Zaire (or Congo) River and at its peak probably touched the edges of the northern savannas beyond.[12] In the woodlands and savannas to the south of the forest, the eastern fringes of the slave catchment zone had passed the Kasai River to reach the undulating plains cut by northward-flowing tributaries of the central part of the Zaire River system. The headwaters of the Zambezi, still farther to the south, also felt the impact of Atlantic slaving by the late eighteenth century. The boundaries of the zone drained by the European traders' hunt for human labor dissipated in the far south only where arable land withered into the nearly deserted dry scrub of the Kalahari Desert. The interior deltas of the Kubango and the lower Kunene rivers at the edges of that

---

12. Jan Vansina, *The Tio Kingdom of the Middle Congo, 1880–1892* (London: Oxford University Press, for the International African Institute, 1973), p. 448; Robert W. Harms, *River of Wealth, River of Sorrow: The Central Zaire Basin in the Era of the Slave and Ivory Trade, 1500–1891* (New Haven: Yale University Press, 1981), pp. 27–32; Jan Vansina, "The Peoples of the Forest," in David Birmingham and Phyllis Martin, eds., *History of Central Africa* (London: Longmans, 1983), 1:79 ff.

desert probably marked the extreme southern limits of the lands that sent people off into the slave trade. Altogether, the areas affected may have amounted to about 2.5 million square kilometers, an area roughly the extent of the modern Sudan, 30 percent the size of Brazil, larger than the United States east of the Mississippi River, and five times the territory of France (see Map 1.1).

No one knows how many farmers, fishermen, herders, and others—nearly all speakers of closely related, though not mutually intelligible, Bantu languages—may have occupied those lands in the eighteenth century. Two hundred years later, a rough estimate of the inhabitants of a larger area of environmentally similar forest and grasslands suggested a population density of around five persons per square kilometer. Similar densities before 1830 would have meant that 12.5 million people lived in the area on which Atlantic slaving drew at its greatest extent before 1830.[13] If the population densities of around four per square kilometer prevailing between 1650 and 1700 in the region near the coast and just south of the lower Zaire River—the only documented estimate for the entire region before the twentieth century—were representative, around 10 million people would have been present.[14] By 1970, a slightly differently shaped block of western central African territory of about the same extent contained an estimated 19,319,640 persons, an average density of nearly eight per square kilometer.[15] The two lower estimates may have undercounted the people present, while the later, higher figure represents the fruits of both improved

13. John D. Fage, "The Effect of the Export Slave Trade on African Populations," in R. P. Moss and R. J. A. R. Rathbone, eds., *The Population Factor in African Studies* (London: University of London Press, 1975), p. 21. John K. Thornton, "The Demographic Effect of the Slave Trade on Western Africa, 1500–1850," in *African Historical Demography: II* (Edinburgh: Centre of African Studies, 1981), pp. 691–720, has worked out estimates of population in this range for an area somewhat smaller than the one on which my calculations are based. His estimates for the central highlands are, for example, only 10–20 persons/km².

14. John K. Thornton, "Demography and History in the Kingdom of Kongo, 1550–1750," *Journal of African History* 18, no. 4 (1977): 521–26, but see the entire essay for methodology and caveats. Two contemporary estimates for the populous central highlands concur in suggesting densities of a much higher order, 78.1 persons/km² in 1799. Alexandre José Botelho de Vasconcelos, "Descrição da Capitania de Benguella, suas provincias, povos, rios mais caudalosos, minas de ferro e enxofre, e outras particularidades que tem, mais consideraveis (1799)," *Annaes marítimos e coloniaes* (parte não oficial) 4 (1844): 161, gives population estimates for Mbailundo, Ngalangi, and the Bihe areas in the 1790s; and László Magyar, *Reisen in Sud-Afrika in den Jahren 1849 bis 1857*, trans. Johann Hunfalvy (Pest and Leipzig: Lauffer and Stolp, 1859), pp. 125, 238, 362, etc., provides figures for the 1850s that are similar in magnitude to (and plausibly larger than) those of Vasconcelos two generations earlier: Magyar's global estimate was 98.3 persons/km². The areas used to calculate the densities from Vasconcelos are those employed in Merran McCulloch, *The Ovimbundu of Angola* (London: International African Institute, 1952), p. 4; also see Gladwyn M. Childs, *Umbundu Kinship and Character* (London: Oxford University Press, International African Institute, 1949), p. 24.

15. Roger T. Anstey, *The Atlantic Slave Trade and British Abolition, 1760–1810* (London: Macmillan, 1975), p. 79–82.

(if still seriously deficient) modern statistical procedures and the population growth of recent years. A range of between 10 and 20 million western central Africans subject at any single time before 1830 to sale to slavers seems a reasonable beginning conjecture in a field of history notoriously "short on hard evidence and abound[ing] in analogically derived reasoning, backward projection and sheer speculation."[16]

If the absolute number of western central Africans is unknown, the unevenness of their distribution over the land surface is more certain and of greater importance for the quality of their lives and the effects of slaving on them. The terrain varied enormously, both locally and on a larger scale, in terms of topography, soils, rainfall, vegetation, resources, ease of transportation and communication, and safety from slaving raids. Farmers, traders, raiders, herders, and fugitives grouped themselves according to the advantages they could draw from these features of the land. Their

16. Ibid., p. 79. Cf. William Allan, *The African Husbandsman* (Edinburgh: Oliver and Boyd, 1965), p. 218; he cites a "critical population density," beyond which existing agricultural technology could not sustain a population, at 15 persons/km² for long-fallow systems of the sort common in western central Africa. This figure is the midpoint of the estimated range adopted here. Colin Clark and Margaret Haswell, *The Economics of Subsistence Agriculture* (New York: St. Martin's Press, 1967), p. 21, cite an estimated carrying capacity of 10–15 persons/km² in zones of "poor soil, scanty rainfall" and 20 persons/km² as "average for forest zone." Vansina, "Peoples of the Forest," pp. 79 ff., projects a general forest population of 3.75/km² as of about 1875 indefinitely back into the past, but pockets of dense population up to 15 persons/km² along its heavily slaved southern margins. For these areas, see Muzong Wanda Kodi, "A Pre-Colonial History of the Pende People (Republic of Zaire) from 1620 to 1900" (Ph.D. diss., Northwestern University, 1976), pp. 73–75 (locally up to 40 persons/km²), and Jan Vansina, *The Children of Woot: A History of the Kuba Peoples* (Madison: University of Wisconsin Press, 1978), pp. 179 and 347 (n. 31) (6–8/km²). For the drier savannas, in addition to Kongo (see n. 14 above), Jeffrey J. Hoover, "The Seduction of Ruwej: Reconstructing Ruund History [The Nuclear Lunda: Zaire, Angola, Zambia]" (Ph.D. diss., Yale University, 1978), p. 7, has the dry and sandy Lunda area at 2 persons/km² (modern), with inhabited areas at 3–15/km²; but Andrew D. Roberts, *A History of Zambia* (New York: Africana, 1976), pp. 11–12, puts the savanna woodlands there at 4–10 persons/km², and Jean-Luc Vellut, "Africa central do oeste, em vésperas da partilha colonial: um esboço histórico do séc. XIX," *Africa* (São Paulo) 3 (1980): 77, allows for up to 8/km². David Birmingham, *Central Africa to 1870* (Cambridge: Cambridge University Press, 1981), p. 108, has 6/km² for the region as a whole, but Colin McEvedy and Richard Jones, *Atlas of World Population History* (Harmondsworth: Penguin Books, 1978), p. 249, estimate only about 2/km² for the period of the slave trade. Other estimates run higher, often in the context of demonstrating depopulation from the slave trade, e.g., Marie-Louise Diop, "Le sous-peuplement de l'Afrique noire," *Bulletin de l'Institut fondamental de l'Afrique noire*, sér. B, 40, no. 4 (1978): 807, map.

For central Africa, at least, direct projections from twentieth-century census counts, which usually produce lower estimates for earlier periods, have only very limited value. The droughts and epidemics that coincided with colonial occupation occasioned substantial depopulation between ca. 1880 and 1920; I have remarked on the point in "Paradoxes of Impoverishment in the Atlantic Zone," in Birmingham and Martin, *History of Central Africa*, 1:158. Jill R. Dias, "Famine and Disease in the History of Angola, c. 1830–1930," *Journal of African History* 22, no. 3 (1981): 349–78, and elsewhere, conveys the same impression. For Kongo, Wyatt MacGaffey, "The Closing of the Frontier in Lower Congo, 1885–1921" (paper presented to the African Studies Association, New Orleans, 1985), p. 10.

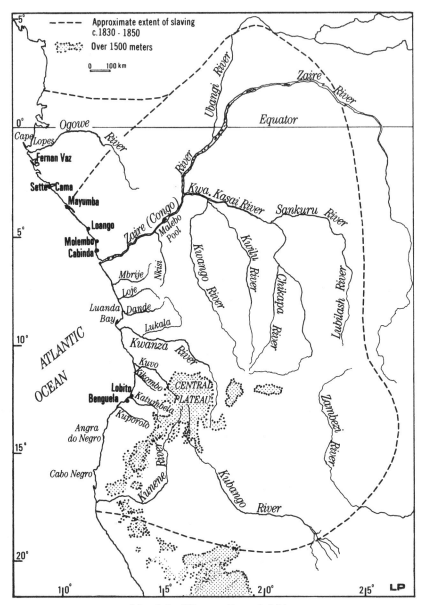

Map 1.1. Western Central Africa

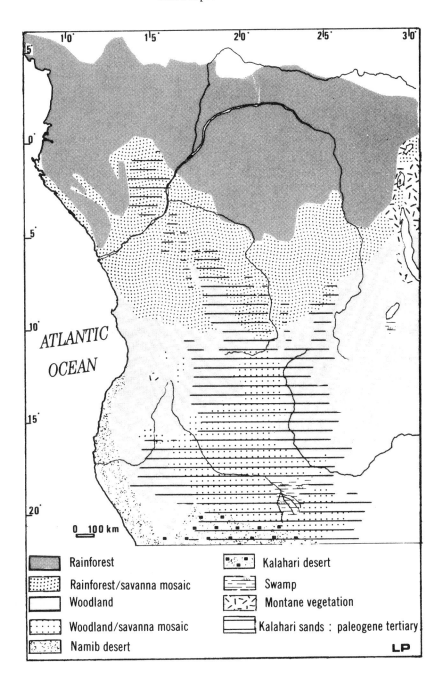

ATLANTIC
OCEAN

0   100 km

	Rainforest		Kalahari desert
	Rainforest/savanna mosaic		Swamp
	Woodland		Montane vegetation
	Woodland/savanna mosaic		Kalahari sands : paleogene tertiary
	Namib desert		

LP

tendencies to congregate or disperse, while on the individual level often products of idiosyncratic preferences for closer contact or greater isolation from neighbors and kin, also derived in the aggregate from the basic opportunities offered by the physical environment.

Though not many of the captives trudging toward the ocean could have comprehended more than a few aspects of the unfamiliar countryside through which they moved, varying elevations and soil compositions caused most of the occupants of western central Africa to cluster in the best watered, and therefore often the lowest, valleys. Viewed in terms of hydrology, the bulk of western central Africa consisted of an elevated rolling surface, a thousand meters or more in altitude. Most of its rivers drained from raised outer rims down into the vast, shallow depression of the central Zaire River basin, taking their sources along its wooded southern edge in the so-called southern savannas. The soils of the western parts of this savanna—roughly the plains drained by the Kasai River and its tributaries and by the streams flowing into the Lubilash and the Sankuru farther east—consisted of porous and infertile overlays of sands blown in over the ages from the Kalahari Desert to the south. The highest of these plains crested along an east-west watershed in the latitude of 10° to 12° south. To the south flowed the headwaters of the upper Zambezi.

Captives moving west on the north side of this divide thus forded or boarded canoes to cross numerous rivers flowing to their right through moist, narrow, forested valleys. They climbed again and again up onto long, narrow, sandy ridges between the rivers, uneroded remains of ancient plateaux that descended like a series of wide, shallow stairsteps toward the north. As the rivers dropped through falls and rapids leading on to each lower level, they repeatedly cut canyons and gorges back into the north-facing edge of each plain and then spread out into widened alluvial valleys in the next plain below.[17] Toward the latitude of 6° or 7° south, the rivers finally carved their way down into the more fertile underlying clay soils of the central Zaire basin and there gradually arched westward toward the Atlantic Ocean through forest-savanna mosaics that presented near-ideal ranges of complementing ecological regimes. If later population distributions provide a reliable guide to the residential preferences of people in the eighteenth century, western central African farmers congregated by choice in the wider valleys at the lower edge of each plain, and particularly on the moister soils of those along the edge of the forest.[18]

Still nearer the equator, dense forests covered much of the land and crowded in over the rivers that structured human occupation there. Wood-

17. As usefully described in Hoover, "Seduction of Ruwej," p. 6.
18. E.g., Kodi, "Pre-Colonial History of the Pende People," p. 80.

lands and clearings allowed people to spread out only along the mid-Zaire, particularly on the tongue of sandy plateau west of the river and along the Kwa (the lower Kasai just before it reaches the Zaire). In the latitudes below 4° south the remaining clearings intruded only intermittently on a vast expanse of heavier forests that covered the center of the Zaire River basin. Although extensive patches of secondary forest cover testified to the industry of earlier occupants who had cleared the virgin trees, cultivators and fishing people lived principally along the main watercourses, and so population densities deep within the forest were generally lower than around its edges.[19]

South of the main Zaire-Zambezi watershed, travelers plodded through nearly deserted expanses of scrub and open woods occupied mostly by cautious bands of hunter-gatherers who spoke in the soft staccato accents of the San people of the desert. Millet-raising and Bantu-speaking farmers like Domingos's father clustered along the banks of the larger streams, where they also fished and sometimes watered a few head of cattle. Surprisingly, the only populations of numerical significance lived on the very edges of the desert, in three isolated oases where the greatest rivers—the Zambezi itself, the Kubango, and the Kunene—flowed through floodplains or dispersed their waters onto the sands of interior deltas that would support seasonal agriculture.[20] Everywhere else in those dry southern latitudes people concentrated on building up herds of livestock, particularly cattle, that they could drive out in wide-ranging transhumant cycles to remote grazing lands that greened for a few months each year with the coming of the rains and then head back to the river bottoms when the vegetation withered with the return of the dry season. Their mobility, frequent dispersal over broad, empty ranges, and martial inclinations made these nomads difficult targets for would-be captors, and so they generally escaped the ravages that the slave trade brought to more densely-populated areas. Thus, viewing the slaved regions of western central Africa as a whole, people tended to congregate in the wetter woodlands and forest-savanna

19. Vansina, "Peoples of the Forest."
20. E.g., for the upper Zambezi, Robert J. Papstein, "The Upper Zambezi: A History of the Luvale People, 1000–1900" (Ph.D. diss., University of California, Los Angeles, 1978), and Gwyn Prins, *The Hidden Hippopotamus: Reappraisal in African History: The Early Colonial Experience in Western Zambia* (New York: Cambridge University Press, 1980), citing much earlier literature on the Lozi, including Mutumba Mainga, *Bulozi under the Luyana Kings: Political Evolution and State Formation in Pre-Colonial Zambia* (London: Longmans, 1973). For the lower Kubango, Gordon D. Gibson, Thomas J. Larson, and Cecilia R. McGurk, *The Kavango Peoples* (Wiesbaden: Franz Steiner Verlag, 1981). For the Kunene, Carlos Estermann, *The Ethnography of Southwestern Angola*, trans. and ed. Gordon D. Gibson, 2 vols. (New York: Africana, 1976–79); also Joseph C. Miller, "Central and Southern Angola," draft manuscript (1979) for publication in Franz-Wilhelm Heimer, ed., *The Formation of Angolan Society* (forthcoming).

mosaics of the inland plateaux between 4° and 12° south, with additional pockets of relatively concentrated population in the better-watered high-lands and river valleys and in the grassier areas around the middle Zaire.

Increasing rains from south to north contributed profoundly to the transitions in vegetation and population from the desert of the higher southern latitudes to the equatorial forest. The sandy plains south of the Zaire-Zambezi watershed defied settled occupation because a short and unreliable rainy season lasting only from November through March left them too dry to farm for nine months of the year and subjected parts of them to annual inundations for much of the rest.[21] To the north of the main watershed the rains normally began earlier—in October, or even in September—and lasted well into April. There they failed much less fre-quently. These longer rainy seasons tended to divide into two segments, separated by a break between late November and early February that permitted farmers in the savanna and woodlands near the forest to bring in two crops in good years. If the rains did not arrive on time, they tended to fail only in the earlier of the two wet seasons.[22] Farmers reaped two crops where the two rainy seasons merged into the single one only in the best years and only as far south as the latitude of the Kwanza. In the areas further south, they made do with a single harvest.[23] The favored forest-savanna mosaics in the latitude of the mouth of the Zaire received eight months or more of rain in most years, although its intensity could vary to the extent that localized shortages of food appeared from time to time.[24] The rains fell reliably throughout the year—some would say incessantly—where people lived in the coolness of the equatorial forest and keyed their seasons to annual pulsations in the flood of the great rivers flowing there rather than to precipitation.[25]

21. Alvin W. Urquhart, *Patterns of Settlement and Subsistence in Southwestern Angola* (Washington: National Academy of Sciences, National Research Council, 1963), in addition to authorities cited in n. 20, above.

22. In addition to Joseph C. Miller, "The Significance of Drought, Disease, and Famine in the Agriculturally Marginal Zones of West-Central Africa," *Journal of African History* 23, no. 1 (1982): 17–61, John K. Thornton, *The Kingdom of Kongo: Civil War and Transition, 1641–1718* (Madison: University of Wisconsin Press, 1983), pp. 36–37, is careful on early agriculture; also see Mario Maestri Filho, *A agricultura africana nos séculos XVI e XVII no litoral angolano* (Porto Alegre: Instituto de Filosofia e Ciências Humanas, Universidade Federal do Rio Grande do Sul, 1978), esp. p. 52.

23. For the mid-eighteenth century, Francisco Antonio Pita Bezerra (e Alpoim e Castro), "Convenção dos dizimos," 1796, AHU, Angola cx. 42.

24. Vansina, *Children of Woot*, esp. 174–79, describes the richest agricultural system in this zone, but even there, famine was not "wholly unknown" (pp. 94, 176, 182). Phyllis Martin, *The External Trade of the Loango Coast, 1576–1870* (Oxford: Clarendon Press, 1972), p. 134, refers to Sonyo oral traditions that emphasize a history of overpopulation in that relatively wet region; Thornton, "Demography and History," cites evidence from the sev-enteenth century.

25. E.g., Harms, *River of Wealth, River of Sorrow,* esp. chap. 1. Also Robert W. Harms, *Games against Nature* (New York: Cambridge University Press, forthcoming).

Slaves who survived to reach the ocean descended down toward it through the most striking topographical feature of the entire region, the mountainous western edge of the plateaux from which they had come. These ranges of hills, often rocky and rugged, heavily forested in the north but more barren toward the south, ran parallel to the coast all the way from the forests southeast of Cape Lopes to the deserts beyond the Black Cape (Cabo Negro). The peaks of the range generally increased in altitude from maximums of a thousand meters in the north to a crest approaching three thousand meters that towered above even the huge central plateau lying between 12° and 15° south. In this entire stretch of nearly eight hundred kilometers, only the Zaire River broke through cleanly to release the rivers of the central basin to the Atlantic, tumbling down through three hundred kilometers of cataracts below Malebo Pool, where the waters of the interior rivers paused before beginning their rush to the sea. The Kwanza River, which flowed into the ocean at about 10° south, drained the northeastern slopes of the central highlands into a great northwest-curving arc but left the sandy plains to its east mostly to the westernmost tributaries of the Zaire. The lower Kwanza received its major affluents from smaller plateaux on its right, northern bank. The southeastern parts of the central highlands declined toward the Kunene River, which, like the Kwanza, rose on the inland side of the central massif before turning westward through a gap in the mountains to reach the ocean at the very southern limit of the regions afflicted with the slave trade. All the other, smaller rivers reaching the Atlantic drained only the western slopes of the coastal ranges.

The slaves ended their journey from the interior by crossing a narrow plain, some fifteen to two hundred kilometers in width, that descended from an altitude around four hundred meters at the foothills of the mountains down to the level of the sea. Conditions along the coast everywhere south of the mouth of the Zaire were much drier than in the mountains behind, since cool southwesterly winds blowing off cold antarctic ocean currents dominated the maritime climate and, warming and drying as they overspread the littoral, could prevent rainfall for years on end, even as far north as Luanda Bay. As a result, the coastlands were a remote and alien periphery to most western central African farmers, who lived in the more reliable climate zones east of the mountains. Only a few impoverished herders clustered around the beds of seasonal rivers in the far south. The people who chose to live in the lowlands as far north as Luanda Bay concentrated themselves around the good fishing sites in the river mouths, in the fertile riverain bottomlands, and around coastal salt flats and shell fisheries producing marine commodities prized in the inland areas back to the east. Only toward the Zaire River and beyond did the higher rainfall of the equatorial latitudes support relatively dense populations of farmers within a few kilometers of the ocean and put people of the interior in close and regular contact with the coast. Paths running down the smaller rivers of the western slopes of the mountains converged on a dozen or so bays and river mouths where the oceangoing craft of the Portuguese and other Europeans could find safe anchorage and take on supplies of food, firewood, and fresh water in addition to their human cargoes.[26]

From the point of view of a ship captain trying to reach these slaving termini by sail, the barren Kunene mouth, or the coasts south of it, was the part of the coast closest to both Brazil and Europe. Steady south-westerly winds and the north-flowing current then carried ships on down the coast past a series of embarkation points, the individual significance of which varied over the decades, but whose general distribution along the coast reflected the generally increasing frequencies of safe harbors and inland population densities from south to north. Closely crowded near the equator, sometimes even lying within sight of one another, they became less frequent toward the south until they disappeared into sandy nonexistence beyond the Kunene.

In the far north, these harbors included three minor ones at bays formed by long, northward-extending spits of land between Cape Lopes and 4° south: Fernan Vaz at Nkomi and Iguela lagoons, Sette Cama at Ndugu Lagoon, and Mayumba at Banya Lagoon. Although prevented by the thinness of the forest populations just behind them from becoming major slaving harbors, these three ports lay slightly less than one hundred kilometers from one another. Next to the south, and nearer the principal belt of population in the forest-savanna mosaic, much larger numbers of slaves converged on a second set of three bays more open to the sea: Loango, Molembo (or Malemba in some sources), and Cabinda, all on the coast immediately north of the Zaire River mouth. Canoes filled with slaves crossed the Zaire at numerous coves along the river estuary, and several of these coves from time to time became secondary points for embarking captives for the ocean passage.

South of the Zaire, river mouths, especially the Mbrije, the Loje, and the Dande, took over the role of providing convenient points of embarkation from the bays and lagoons nearer the equator. The Dande offered the special attraction of shelter behind a protruding headland. Next came the Kwanza River, which, although the largest stream south of the Zaire, never became a focal point for the slave routes wending through its valley owing to a treacherous sandbar blocking its mouth. But the tons of silt that constantly renewed the Kwanza bar contributed directly to the prominence of the nearby bay at Luanda as a slaving center. The strong north-

---

26. For the phrase, Colin Palmer, *Human Cargoes: The British Slave Trade to Spanish America, 1700–1739* (Urbana: University of Illinois Press, 1981).

flowing coastal currents pulled the Kwanza sediments up into a long sandy spit sheltering a bay there, guarded on its landward side by rocky, defensible sites at both its openings to the sea. As if following the alluvium of the river, slaves eroded from populations all around the Kwanza basin and from far beyond washed up onto the beach there. Luanda Bay in fact became the focal point of a network of coastwise schooner and canoe traffic bringing captives from all along the adjacent coasts, some from the Bengo River, just to the north of the bay, and others from the mouths of the Kikombo, where Domingos had first glimpsed the ocean, and the Kuvo, to the south of the Kwanza. The established points of embarkation along the four hundred kilometers of shoreline between Loango and Luanda averaged more than one each forty kilometers and handled most of the captives descending from the interior plateaux.

Farther to the south the river mouths became less commodious, the bays less sheltered, and the coastlands drier and less hospitable. A single enduring termination point, the exposed bay at Benguela, received slaves coming down from the southern parts of the central highlands, like Domingos's unfortunate captor. The Katumbela River, just to its north, and a sheltered lagoon at Lobito, just beyond, were outlying subsidiary receptacles for this flow of captives. For five hundred kilometers south of Benguela to the mouth of the Kunene, traders gathered slaves only in small numbers for transfer to ships making occasional calls along exposed shores and at small bays, mostly at the Angra do Negro and Cabo Negro (the modern Moçâmedes, or Namibe, and Porto Alexandre).[27]

The People

The human geography—the distribution of farmers and herders in the varied landscape of savanna western central Africa—resembled an archipelago of populous nodes clustered in the best-watered corners of the land, which were in turn scattered through seas of barren sands and hills.[28] Well-populated lowlands, small valleys, and the central highlands, all dotted with fields and habitations, alternated with vast expanses of almost uninhabited mountains, woodland, or desert.[29] Nearer the forests the con-

27. Moçâmedes and Porto Alexandre in the colonial period.
28. An emphasis developed, e.g., in Hoover, "Seduction of Ruwej," p. 7, and in Miller, "Central and Southern Angola." For the same point in more general terms, Jean-Luc Vellut, "Notes de cours: histoire de l'Afrique Centrale" (unpublished lecture notes, Université de Louvain, 1977–78), esp. pp. 21–22.
29. Thornton, *Kingdom of Kongo*, pp. 4, 6, 12–13; Dias, ed. (Leitão), "Viagem a Cassange," pp. 13, 14, 23, 28; also "Reflexão anonimo sobre o comercio de Angola," n.d. (ca. 1780s), AHU, Sala 12, cx. 1, for "deserts between Ambaca and Kasanje" (with thanks to Dr. Jill R. Dias for this reference), and reference to the same deserted areas in John K.

straints of aridity operated with the least draconian effect, and so the people of the lower Kasai, the Kwa, and the lower Kwango lived in relatively even distributions all through that region. Small groups could move easily from one place to another, drifting from generation to generation according to opportunities presented by commerce, political protection, or marriage alliance, as they responded to news of opportunities spread far and wide by the intense movement of canoe-borne traders on the rivers.[30]

As soon, however, as one moved west into the drier coastlands or south into the Kalahari sand country, populations grouped themselves into isolated pockets anchored to the islands of heavier rainfall or better ground moisture. Along the rivers of the Kasai system most people lived within the shelter of the gallery forests lining the streams. People inhabiting the western slopes of the mountains and the coastal plain clustered, insofar as space permitted, along the larger rivers south of the Zaire: the Loje, the Dande, the Bengo, the Kuvo, and the Kuporolo, and particularly the lower valleys of the lower Kwanza and its principal northern affluent, the Lukala. Farther inland, the valley of the Nkisi (the main tributary of the lower Zaire) and the broad, flat, low plains along the middle reaches of the Kwango sheltered two of the larger concentrations of people in those latitudes.

South of the Kwanza, agriculture remained most dependable on the higher elevations of the great central plateau, where heavier rains produced by the altitude of the land and the better soils rising out of the surrounding sands permitted communities of farmers to prosper in the valleys of all the major rivers flowing down from its crest. The upper Kuvo in the northwest and the headwaters of the Kunene and the Kubango in the southeast, as well as the highest plains just above them, together supported one of the largest populations of the entire region.[31] On the southern flanks of the highlands more widely dispersed populations mixed herding with farming along the margins of seasonal water courses feeding the middle Kunene and, on the fringes of the Kalahari, in the deltas of the

---

Thornton, "The Slave Trade in Eighteenth-Century Angola: Effects on Demographic Structures," *Canadian Journal of African Studies* 14, no. 3 (1980): 425 (though the lack of inhabitants is ascribed to slaving rather than ecology). See the report of the *pombeiros* (the first recorded transcontinental travelers, 1804–14) for the territories east of the Kwango, most recently studied with references to earlier literature by François Bontinck, "Le voyage des pombeiros: essai de réinterpretation," *Cultures au Zaïre et en Afrique* 5 (1974): 39–70; see also Joaquim Rodrigues Graça, "Viagem feita de Loanda com destino às cabeceiras do Rio Sena, ou aonde for mais conveniente pelo interior do continente, de que as tribus são senhores, principada em 24 de abril de 1845," *Annaes do Conselho Ultramarino* (parte não oficial) ser. 1 (1854–58), passim. For the central highlands, see Miller, "Central and Southern Angola."

30. A pattern of movement convincingly described by Jan Vansina, "Probing the Past of the Lower Kwilu Peoples (Zaire)," *Paideuma* 19–20 (1973–74): 332–64.

31. Miller, "Central and Southern Angola."

main rivers.[32] Where the lower Kunene and the Kuvelai divided into numerous shallow courses seasonally watered by runoff from the highlands above, the most numerous of the southern herders added agriculture to their pastoralism to produce an oasis of people isolated in the wilderness of the desert edge.[33] The lower Kubango and the swamps through which it flowed as it spread out to reach Lake Ngami supported a similarly isolated, though less numerous, cluster of people.[34] Finally, the floodplains of the upper Zambezi attracted settlement, particularly south from the confluence of the Kabompo and Lungwebungu rivers to Victoria Falls, where the river dropped from its broad upper valley to the narrow gorge of its middle course.[35] Domingos had almost surely been born into this last community.

More scattered populations occupied the ridges between these low-lying centers, but they often lived precariously on the frontiers of survival, threatened by both drought and human predators. Farmers on these higher plains distributed their lands up and down the hillsides above the small streams flowing there as a measure of insurance, in the hope that they would reap from one level what they might lose to drought or flood at others.[36] By the eighteenth century, many of these people had acquired an added measure of security from the adoption of manioc, or cassava, a tuber of New World origins that grew as well in the sandy soils of most of the savannas as in the moister clays of the river valleys. Mature tubers in the ground could survive two years or more of failed rains that would have devastated the staple grains, sorghums and millets, of the region. The crop required less labor to plant and to tend than did the bananas and pulses that supplemented cereal agriculture in the wetter areas nearer the forest. Manioc therefore encouraged more intensive settlement of less desirable lands, permitted larger numbers of people to survive in the river

32. Urquhart, *Patterns of Settlement*.

33. In addition to Estermann, *Ethnography*, for the logic of settlement see Gervase Clarence-Smith, *Slaves, Peasants, and Capitalists in Southern Angola, 1840–1926* (New York: Cambridge University Press, 1979), and Clarence-Smith and Richard Moorsom, "Underdevelopment and Class Formation in Ovamboland, 1845–1915," *Journal of African History* 16, no. 3 (1975): 365–67.

34. Gibson, Larson, and McGurk, *Kavango Peoples*. The ups and downs of the rainfall from decade to decade in this region produced varying lake, and presumably also population, levels. Lake Ngami was desiccated before about 1750, high during the years that saw the region begin to produce slaves from 1775 to 1825, and irregularly declining through the mid-nineteenth century to its present swampy condition: Sharon E. Nicholson, "Climate, Drought, and Famine in Africa," in Art Hansen and Della E. McMillan, eds., *Food in Sub-Saharan Africa* (Boulder, Colo.: Lynne Rienner Publishers, 1986), p. 114.

35. Papstein, "Upper Zambezi"; Mainga, *Bulozi under the Luvana Kings*.

36. Manuscript reports of the Missão de Inquéritos Agrícolas de Angola, ca. 1960s. Francisco de Sousa Guerra de Araujo Godinho, 23 Oct. 1804, AHU, Angola cx. 55, described agriculture in essentially equivalent terms. Also see Elias Alexandre da Silva Corrêa, *História de Angola* (Lisbon: Editorial Atica, 1937), 2:14.

valleys, and reduced the mortality that had resulted from drought and famine in the centuries before its arrival in western central Africa.

This revolution in agriculture had begun to spread over western central Africa in the early seventeenth century and probably advanced eastward from the coast with the trade in slaves, thus permitting population to grow to levels previously unattainable, particularly in the belt running from the Zaire and the Kwanza east between 7° and 9°–10° south.[37] Population increase resulting from the introduction of manioc seems to have produced its most striking effects on the sandy steppes of the upper Lulua and its tributaries, near the very center of the continent, where settlers moved up from the lower reaches of these rivers with the imported crop to form a new late-seventeenth-century population nucleus on the infertile sands of that region.[38]

A second agricultural revolution, based on maize, another immigrant cultigen from the New World, eventually enriched the diets of people in better-watered areas where the rains were sufficient to meet its higher moisture requirements. Since it exhausted the fragile soils of western central Africa more rapidly than did manioc or other grains, it needed greater inputs of labor, principally for the frequent clearing of new fields. It therefore tended to appeal to farmers in the more lightly wooded southerly regions, where cutting the trees demanded less labor than in the more densely forested areas to the north.[39] People who could afford the time to plant the crop preferred maize to sorghum also because its husks tended to protect the grain from theft by birds.[40] Its lesser resistance to drought slowed its adoption in the sandy woodland, but it became particularly well established as an important food crop in the central highlands. Elsewhere, it tended to remain a secondary crop fed primarily to poultry and small livestock, but not of little importance, since it thereby increased supplies of scarce animal protein in the starch-heavy diets of most people in the region.[41] The geography of maize thus complemented that of manioc to

37. An early history of manioc is sketched in José Redinha, "Subsídio para a história e cultura da mandioca entre os povos do nordeste de Angola," *Boletim do Instituto de investigação científica de Angola* 5, no. 1 (1968): 95–108. See also Maestri Filho, *Agricultura africana,* pp. 85–91. For the Kongo, Anne Wilson, "The Kongo Kingdom to the Mid-Seventeenth Century" (Ph.D. diss., University of London, 1977), pp. 95–96; Papstein, "Upper Zambezi," pp. 219–20; Vansina, *Children of Woot,* pp. 175–76.

38. Hoover, "Seduction of Ruwej," pp. 336–38.

39. Wilson, "Kongo Kingdom," pp. 95–96; also for Kongo, Thornton, *Kingdom of Kongo,* pp. 1, 23.

40. Papstein, "Upper Zambezi," p. 219–20; Vansina, *Children of Woot,* p. 17.

41. References to *milho* in the central highlands are common but of uncertain significance, since the term could refer generically to maize or to the African millets and sorghums. The most likely explicit reference to maize is José Maria de Lacerda, "Observações sobre a viagem da costa d'Angola á Costa de Moçambique," *Annaes marítimos e coloniaes* (parte não oficial) 5 (1844): 191–92; but see also João Carlos Feo Cardoso de Castello Branco e Torres, *Memórias contendo a biographia do vice almirante Luis da Motta Feo e Torres, a História dos*

add calories to the diet (if at the expense of nutritional balance), reduce infant mortality, increase survival rates during droughts, permit occupation of areas previously too marginal to inhabit on a continuous basis, and thus stabilize general population levels even in areas giving up many of their inhabitants to the slave trade.

Despite the aggregate sparseness of the population, by the late sixteenth century at least, the numbers of people in much of western central Africa had grown beyond the long-term capacity of the locations in which they preferred to live to support them. Undependable rains, heavy vegetation cover, and infertile soils combined to limit the amount of land susceptible to occupation and utilization with the techniques of agriculture and husbandry available to residents of the region. In western central Africa's forested wetter zones, scattered clearings and riverbanks held most of the population, and it took only a little pressure on the confined living space there to prompt dislocations spreading over large areas.

In the drier parts of the region, for several hundred years farmers had been moving up out of moist river valleys in times of plentiful rains to occupy higher lands incapable of sustaining agriculture if the rains should fail. Serious droughts, which occurred at least once each decade through the eighteenth century, exposed the hardy folk who had opened these marginal farming areas to famine and left them vulnerable to ensuing outbreaks of epidemic disease. General population levels outside the forest thus tended to expand out from the main agricultural cores as farmers moved up to open new lands while good rains lasted and then collapse during major droughts, particularly during prolonged periods of aridity like the one that parched the land in 1784–95.[42] The alternation of demographic growth and contraction probably produced population levels that tended to oscillate widely around a relatively stable long-term average in the savannas.[43]

---

governadores e capitaens generaes de Angola desde 1575 até 1825, e a Descripção geographica e politica dos reinos de Angola e Benguella (Paris: Fantin, 1825), p. 369; Ralph Delgado, *Ao sul do Cuanza (ocupação e aproveitamento do antigo reino de Benguela)* (Lisbon: n.p., 1944), 1:597 (for 1798); idem, *A famosa e histórica Benguela: Catalogo dos governadores (1779–1940)* (Lisbon: Edições Cosmos, 1940), p. 484 (1828); idem, *O reino de Benguela: do descobrimento à criação do governo subalterno* (Lisbon: Imprensa Beleza, 1945). See also Antonio José Pimental de Castro e Mesquita (governor, Benguela), 8 Dec. 1781, AHU, Angola cx. 38, for his report of distributing *milho* seed in the interior, which the Africans planted but sold rather than consumed. In general, for use as cattle feed, see Georg Tams, *A Visit to the Portuguese Possessions in South-Western Africa,* trans. H. Evans Lloyd (London: T. C. Newby, 1845), 1:150, 2:101.

42. Miller, "Significance of Drought, Disease, and Famine," esp. pp. 29–30, 51–54.

43. Joseph C. Miller, "Lineages, Ideology, and the History of Slavery in Western Central Africa," in Paul E. Lovejoy, ed., *The Ideology of Slavery in Africa* (Beverly Hills: Sage Publications, 1981), pp. 41–71. Dias, "Famine and Disease," pp. 8, 25–26, cites evidence of the process for the nineteenth century; also for the Angolan central highlands ca. 1915, see

Conflicts that arose from drought and population pressure, and by the eighteenth century frequently also raids for slaves, drove refugees from the good farm lands into defensible sites hidden in the fastnesses of the highest elevations and in thickets "so thorny that one could barely make one's way along the paths." It struck at least one European observer as "difficult to believe that these savages, for fear of the Portuguese, live in places that the very beasts avoid because of their harshness."[44] The thick forests of the northern mountains paralleling the coast provided good cover south to the headwaters of the Lukala and in patches beyond to the northeastern slopes of the central highlands. These harbored fugitives of all sorts, some of whom played important roles in the slave trade as raiders. To the south along the western edge of the central highlands, the highest mountain peaks in the entire region contained labyrinthine caves and offered good supplies of water that could sustain large numbers of people through periods of warfare in the plains below. Similar refuges were to be had on huge inselbergs dotting the surface of the highlands to the east, and the spine of mountains terminated in the south in dramatically high cliffs and tablelands offering good protection from raiding to the cattle herders of the surrounding semideserts.[45] These refugee communities, however swollen by the disorders of the eighteenth century, had roots reaching far back into the times when farmers and herders had first filled the lands most suited to agriculture and thus condemned late arrivals to struggle for survival on the margins of their societies.[46]

Linda Heywood and John Thornton, "Portuguese Colonial Policies and Demographic Change in Central Angola, 1900–1950" (paper presented to the annual conference of the Canadian African and Latin American and Caribbean Studies Associations, Montreal, May 1985), p. 5. Timothy Matthews, "The Historical Tradition of the Peoples of the Gwembe Valley, Middle Zambezi" (Ph.D. diss., University of London, 1976), pp. 46–47, has similar movements for the Zambezi valley. John Janzen, *Lemba, 1650–1930: A Drum of Affliction in Africa and the New World* (New York: Garland, 1982), p. 38, has an example of migration owing to famine as far north as Mayombe, and Jan Vansina (personal communication, 20 Sept. 1986) adds that migrations to flee famine commonly dislocated people in the densely inhabited and relatively wet Kasai as well.

44. This flight was noted as early as 1631: Maestri Filho, *Agricultura africana*, pp. 69–70, citing António Brásio, ed., *Monumenta missionaria africana: África occidental (Série I)*, 14 vols. to date (Lisbon: Agência Geral do Ultramar, 1952–), 8:65. Also see Susan Herlin Broadhead, "Slave Wives, Free Sisters: Bakongo Women and Slavery, c. 1700–1850," in Claire C. Robertson and Martin A. Klein, eds., *Women and Slavery in Africa* (Madison: University of Wisconsin Press, 1983), p. 168, on Kongo.

45. Miller, "Central and Southern Angola."

46. For Kongo in general, see Thornton, *Kingdom of Kongo*, pp. 6–8; eighteenth-century general allusions to this pattern include Dias, ed., (Leitão), "Viagem a Cassange," p. 21, and D. António de Vasconcelos (governor, Angola), 22 April 1762, AHU, Angola cx. 29.

Community and Polity

Captives plodding along the slave trails of west central Africa felt the crushing isolation of cast-offs from tight local communities defined most often by descent and, secondarily, by local co-residence in small villages. Such small-scale notions of community predominated for people from much of the forest and the lower Kasai. Only in the third instance did others, mostly in the savannas, identify with distinct, overarching political authorities of broader proportions. Some of those from the drier areas also possessed less precisely defined senses of commonality based on general linguistic and cultural habits shared with neighbors in the widely separated river basins, plateaux, and refuge sites in which the inhabitants of the woodlands and grasslands clustered. However, for the enslaved all of these notions of belonging must have faded as their pasts receded behind the hills and valleys behind them and as the shared suffering of the slave trails and markets through which they passed overwhelmed the condemned. New identities in terms that their new masters understood better, more relevant to the slaves' present and future lives, were simultaneously forming to bind people according to the markets where slavers assembled them in coffles, where they boarded ships, and the individual ships that carried them to the New World.[47]

The general linguistic and cultural identities of western central Africa—familiar outside of Africa because a few of them became bases for stereotyped ethnic or "tribal" labels familiar in twentieth-century colonial ethnography—derived mainly from the concentrations of population in isolated fertile localities and from the distinctive habits such groups developed to utilize the ecological advantages of the regions they shared (see Map 1.2). Thus, the people of the upper Lulua plains known as Ruund (or Lunda) were originally descendants of those who had introduced manioc to the region and who thus inhabited it in adequate numbers and on a sufficiently settled basis to acquire a distinct identity.[48] The varied peoples scattered more thinly over the western tributaries of the upper Zambezi, and originally perhaps anyone in the Kalahari sand country east of the upper Kwanza and Kunene, acquired their Ngangela ethnonym from a term for the flat, sandy grasslands in which they lived. Others living on the red soils exposed from place to place amidst the whitish Kalahari sands took the name Mbunda from the special coloration of the land from

---

47. For these identities, and still others, in Rio at the beginning of the nineteenth century, see Karasch, *Slave Life in Rio*. Generally on the historicity and fluidity of ethnic identities, see forthcoming proceedings of the Conference on the History of Ethnic Awareness in Southern Africa (Charlottesville, Virginia, 1983): H. Leroy Vail, ed., *The Creation of Tribalism in South and Central Africa: Studies in the Political Economy of Ideology* (London: James Currey).

48. Hoover, "Seduction of Ruwej," pp. 336–38.

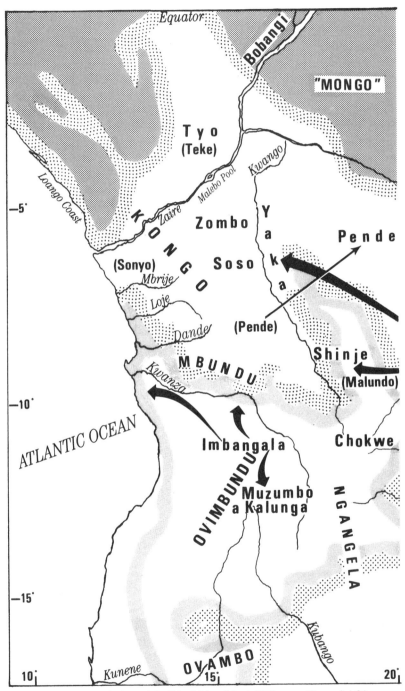

Map 1.2. Major Ethnic and Political Identities of Western Central Africa, Eighteenth Century

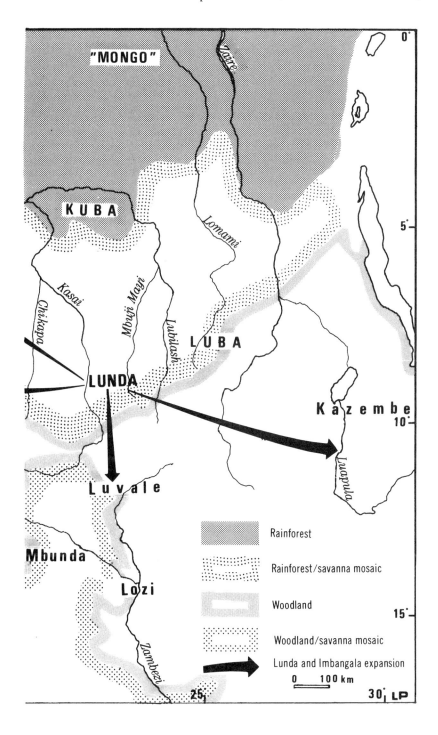

which they drew their living.[49] The early Pende, who had lived in the upper parts of the lower Kwango River valley before falling to intrusive warlords in the 1620s, had taken their shared identity from co-residence in a region topographically set sharply off from the highlands around them.[50] The people of some of the regions south of the lower Zaire River, like those of the valley of the Nkisi, had shared ancient and strong senses of community based similarly on geography, and the Teke (or Tio) distinguished themselves as the occupants of the sandy plateau intruding on the forests north and east of Malebo Pool.[51] The congruence of ecology and ethnicity could not have been clearer than among the agro-pastoralists of the south, where the Kuvelai-Kunene people were grouped as Ovambo, or where herders near the sea derived their collective labels from the names of the rivers on which they centered their transhumant movement.[52]

By the eighteenth century, better-defined political systems of lordship and tribute overlaid some of these vague ancient commonalities and provided new primary identities for many people of the savannas, for some highland dwellers, and for some coastland and forest dwellers. Slaves from everywhere east of the Kwango would have remembered, many with bitterness, the Lunda imperial network centered on great lords of the Ruund known as the *mwaant yaav*. These *mwaant yaav* ruled directly over the Ruund from capitals near the Kalanyi affluent of the upper Mbuji Mayi (Sankuru) and claimed tribute from subordinate lords ruling riverain population nuclei, each separated from the others by less-populated wildernesses, along an axis paralleling the movement of the slaves to the west. These Lunda chiefs maintained courts in valleys from the Kwango in the far west to the Luapula in the east.[53] The wealthiest and most powerful subordinates of the *mwaant yaav* were the *kazembe* of the rich fishing and agricultural lands in the lower Luapula and the *kiamfu* who ruled and raided the "Yaka" people of the lower Kwango River valley.[54] The "Lunda" subjects of these two rulers shared little with the Ruund of the Kalanyi except for the political culture of the lords who ruled them. Farther up the east bank of the Kwango, three other Lunda lords, of whom Malundo

49. Papstein, "Upper Zambezi," pp. 5, 7.

50. Miller, *Kings and Kinsmen*, pp. 70–73.

51. Wilson, "Kongo Kingdom," pp. 29 ff.; Vansina, *Tio Kingdom*, p. 443.

52. João Pilarte da Silva, 9 Dec. 1770, *relação*, published, AHU, Angola maço 13 (D.O.) published in *Arquivos de Angola* 1, no. 2 (1933), doc. 18, and in Felner, *Angola*, 1:177 ff.

53. Hoover, "Seduction of Ruwej," is the most detailed study of the Ruund. For a recent survey of the Luba see Thomas Q. Reefe, "The Societies of the Eastern Savanna," Birmingham and Martin, *History of Central Africa* 1:189–92.

54. In addition to Reefe, "Societies of the Eastern Savanna," see Jan Vansina, *Kingdoms of the Savanna* (Madison: University of Wisconsin Press, 1966), pp. 165–74, 203–7; also Thomas Q. Reefe, *The Rainbow and the Kings: A History of the Luba Empire to 1891* (Berkeley and Los Angeles: University of California Press, 1981), pp. 133–44.

waxed strongest in the eighteenth century, commanded subjects who acquired the collective designation of Shinje.[55]

Numerous other minor leaders throughout the sandy country east of the upper Kwanza and north of the watershed pretended to similar connections with the great Lunda lords at the Kalanyi, but they had only small and dispersed followings by the grand standards of the central Ruund court. Even so, several managed at one time or another during the century to assemble locally powerful retinues for a lifetime or so.[56] This network of Lunda rulers—really a chain of political islands in a sea of woodlands occupied mostly by dispersed villagers recognizing no overlord at all—collectively constituted an integrated commercial, tribute-collecting, and intelligence-gathering network by the early nineteenth century, when it acquired its modern designation as the "Lunda empire." For most of the eighteenth century, the *mwaant yaav* had struggled militarily to impose a degree of coherence on the congeries of tributary lords east of the Kwango. The homelands of many persons enslaved in the eighteenth century felt the impact of the demands for tribute, the armies, and the Ruund court styles of the *mwaant yaav* and their emulators. People on the western fringes of this consolidating state knew the *mwaant yaav* and their commercial and military emissaries as Mulua.[57]

The influence of the Ruund *mwaant yaav* extended north and south of their eighteenth-century courts in still less structured ways. Lunda political culture and perhaps a few Ruund emigrés advanced southward beyond the Zambezi watershed, where *kazembe* and other characteristically Lunda titles became political reference points for the scattered populations of these grasslands.[58] Lunda influence spilled over into the valley of the upper Zambezi, where people living under a variety of local grandees radiated the ideas and symbols of the imperial system outward through a small court or two. These people collectively acquired a regional designation as Luvale (or Lovar in the orthography of contemporary Portuguese) by the latter part of the eighteenth century.[59] The more densely populated lands to the north of the Ruund attracted the attention of the

55. Vansina, *Kingdoms of the Savanna*, p. 93; Dias, ed. (Leitão), "Viagem a Cassange," pp. 16, 19; Jean-Luc Vellut, "Relations internationales du Moyen-Kwango et de l'Angola dans la deuxième moitié du XVIIIe siècle," *Etudes d'histoire africaine* 1 (1970): 75–135.

56. Also on the Lunda, Jean-Luc Vellut, "Notes sur le Lunda et la frontière luso-africaine (1700–1900)," *Etudes d'histoire africaine* 3 (1972): 61–166.

57. Dias, ed. (Leitão), "Viagem a Cassange," pp. 25–26; D. Miguel António de Mello (governor, Angola), 21 Oct. 1801, AHU, Angola cx. 50.

58. Robert E. Schecter, "History and Historiography on a Frontier of Lunda Expansion: The Origins and Early Development of the Kanongesha" (Ph.D. diss., University of Wisconsin, 1976).

59. Papstein, "Upper Zambezi," revising earlier attributions of much greater and earlier Lunda influence.

mwaant yaav principally as slave-raiding grounds, rather than as arenas for political assimilation. Lunda emperor after Lunda emperor in the eighteenth century tested the valor of his armies against the populous regions downriver from their courts.[60] Relatively little Lunda influence penetrated the northeastern lands beyond the Lubilash, where a distinct political culture, different languages, and a north-south regional trading system centered on the Lomami and Lubilash rivers formed a world largely impervious to the Lunda political and economic shock waves emanating from the west.[61]

The farmers of the central highlands, collectively known later as Ovimbundu, shared similar linguistic traits, but none of them in the eighteenth century would have claimed much unity at the scale of the entire plateau. Although they possessed a single general constellation of political ideas and practices, they claimed much less centralization in theory than the Lunda of the same period. Their traditions looked back to a combination of ancient rainmaking kings, warlords rich in cattle, and a late-sixteenth-century military cult recalled in the eighteenth century as that of the "Jaga."[62] The Jaga movement, known to its participants as Imbangala, had spilled down in every direction over the flanks of the plateau. The inhabitants of the upper Kunene valley had fallen subjects to Jaga lords known as Muzumbo a Kalunga, whose power had waxed in the seventeenth century but waned thereafter, even though echoes of their reputation still inspired awe hundreds of kilometers to the north in the eighteenth century.[63]

To the north and along the ridges and mountains of the western crest of the main plateau, a number of fiercely independent Ovimbundu lords also claiming descent from seventeenth-century Jaga, or Imbangala, warlords commanded competing domains from stone-walled fortresses located on rocky eminences overlooking the surrounding plains. Wambu in the center and Mbailundu in the north ranked among the largest and most powerful of these kingdoms (Map 1.3). The easterly lordship of Bihe, which cited direct descent from the earliest Jaga lords among its credits, faced east out over the upper Kwanza toward the Ngangela lands beyond. It grew to importance only later in the eighteenth century and had then not yet become so imposing a power as Mbailundu and Wambu. The ordinary people of these regions shared little beyond their need of the

60. Hoover, "Seduction of Ruwej," pp. 348 ff.; for the other side of these raids, see William Pruitt, "An Independent People: A History of the Sala Mpasu of Zaire and Their Neighbors" (Ph.D. diss., Northwestern University, 1973), and John Yoder, "A People on the Edge of Empires: A History of the Kanyok of Central Zaire" (Ph.D. diss., Northwestern University, 1977), esp. chap. 4, though for defenses against Luba rather than Lunda raiders.
61. Reefe, *Rainbow and the Kings.*
62. Miller, *Kings and Kinsmen,* esp. pp. 167–75; idem, "Central and Southern Angola."
63. Miller, *Kings and Kinsmen,* pp. 155–61; Vellut, "Relations internationales," pp. 98–99; and for the eighteenth century, Dias, ed. (Leitão), "Viagem a Cassange," p. 18.

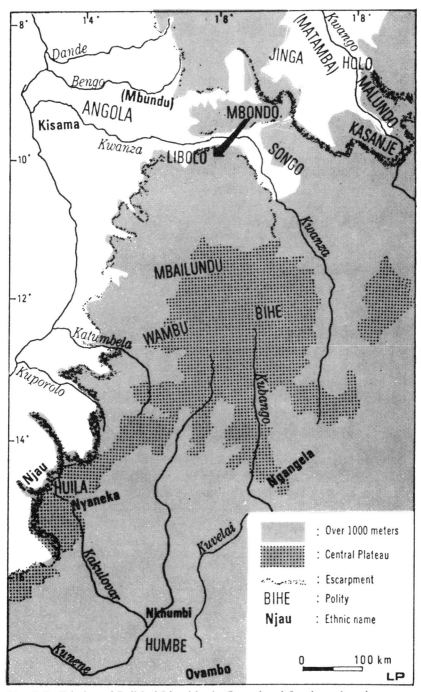

Map 1.3. Ethnic and Political Identities in Central and Southern Angola, Eighteenth Century

great military lords for protection against the armies of the others. The frequent raiding made agriculture difficult, although fields of maize must have been spreading through the areas protected by major lords like those of Mbailundu and Wambu. Scattered among these Ovimbundu states also lived a number of traders, Europeans and others of Afro-European descent, often products of marriages between immigrants and the women of the Ovimbundu aristocracies.

The agro-pastoralists of the floodplain where the Kakulovar River joined the Kunene, and perhaps also some of their neighbors in the interior delta of the Kuvelai, just to the southeast, obeyed a lord with the title of Humbe. These isolated dwellers on the edge of the desert divided themselves into the Nkhumbi of the Kunene valley and the Ovambo (Ambo, Hambo) of the regions to the southeast. The transhumant movements of the Nkhumbi cattle had spawned outlying colonies on the western tributaries of the Kunene all the way to the crest of the plateau and also down the lower river almost to the sea.[64] In the highlands, which rose at the southern tip of the main body of the plateau and cradled the upper basin of the Kakulovar, well-watered and sheltered valleys cut back into the eastern face of the mountains and provided opportunities for agriculture in the alluvial deposits along the streambeds. The valleys' occupants, collectively designated later as Nyaneka, grew in numbers during the eighteenth century, in part by taking in refugees from the more exposed plains rolling eastward toward the Kunene, and drew together under lords of the plateau known as Huila. Some of them eventually spilled back up onto the plateau of Humpata behind them, where initially subordinate lords called Njau grew wealthy and powerful and by the 1760s extended their authority down the dry mountain slopes to the west.[65]

If Lunda overrule gave a certain political identity to the woodland people living east of the Kwango, and if the Ovimbundu shared a different, more diffuse political heritage within the bends of the Kwanza and Kunene, residents of the hills and river valleys to the northwest claimed a common heritage in yet another, entirely different set of traditions of rule that had come originally from the equatorial forests (Map 1.2). Relatively

64. Pilarte da Silva, 9 Dec. 1770; Pedro José Correa de Quevedo Homem e Magalhães (governor, Benguela), 16 Sept. 1785, AHU, Angola maço 13 (D.O.); Barão de Moçâmedes (former governor, Angola), *parecer* on a *consulta* (16 June 1796) of the Conselho Ultramarino (Lisbon), 24 Feb. 1796, AHU, Angola maço 6; António José Valente, 8 Feb. 1791, AHU, Angola cx. 41.

65. Gervase Clarence-Smith, "Capitalist Penetration among the Nyaneka of Southern Angola, 1760s to 1920s," *African Studies* 37, no. 2 (1978): 166; sources cited in note 64, and Boaventura José de Mello, *requerimento*, n.d. (minuted 12 Aug. 1807), AHU, Angola maço 6; Sousa Coutinho, 18 Oct. 1769, AHU, Angola cx. 32 (published in *Arquivos de Angola* 1, no. 1 [1933]: n.p., and in Felner, *Angola*, 1:163–69); also Sousa Coutinho *bando*, 23 Sept. 1768, AHU, Angola cx. 31 (published in *Arquivos de Angola* 1, no. 6 [1936]: n.p.), and related documentation.

sparse populations of maize and manioc farmers, who became known as Teke in the south but who carried a number of other designations toward the north, had developed the forest political traditions in the direction of centralized political institutions on the high grassy plains to the west of the middle Zaire. They were nominally subject to a lord, Ngobila, heir to a loosely structured network of political titles known to Europeans since the sixteenth century, when a predecessor, the Great Makoko, had claimed primacy and had initiated the flow of slaves from the equatorial regions westward to the Atlantic.[66] By the late eighteenth and early nineteenth centuries, Teke loyalty to the plateau king had yielded to much more localized allegiances to other lords living along the main river, who supervised the active riverain trade.

Elsewhere, in the equatorial latitudes ethnic and political identities of this sort assumed only muted forms. People living in the forests of the Zaire basin knew no unity at all. Aggregated as Mongo by colonial ethnographers because of similarities in their languages, their eighteenth-century ancestors had developed only small federations of villages connected to one another by the canoe traffic that moved slaves down the rivers and brought imports back up.[67] By the eighteenth century, this trade was encouraging the inhabitants of the main rivers to form extended trading networks. One such group, known as Bobangi, in fact dominated the commerce of the Zaire from the confluence of the Ubangi down to Malebo Pool. Like traders everywhere, they steered well clear of entanglements with the political systems of their farming neighbors.[68]

Great concentrations of people lived around Malebo Pool itself, where quantities of slaves, forest products, dried fish, vegetable foods, and imports changed hands in marketplaces huge by western central African standards. Unlike their neighbors in the grasslands, these people lived as much from commerce as from farming. They bore a number of designations similar in appearance to the community labels common in the farming communities around them, but their loyalties were less permanent, less subject to the determinants of birth and co-residence, and more the products of temporary association for business purposes than those of the farmers. The banks of the Pool contained the most cosmopolitan, and probably also the densest, population in eighteenth-century western central Africa. The only groups of similar size, heterogeneity, and concentration elsewhere congregated around the capitals of the Lunda *mwaant yaav*.[69]

---

66. Vansina, *Tio Kingdom*, pp. 451–67.
67. Jan Vansina et al., *Introduction à l'ethnographie du Congo* (Kinshasa/Lubumbashi/Kisangani: Editions Universitaires du Congo, [ca. 1965]), pp. 79–92.
68. Harms, *River of Wealth, River of Sorrow*.
69. Vansina, *Tio Kingdom*, pp. 255–56, says 10,000 people in all at Malebo Pool; Hoover, "Seduction of Ruwej," p. 7, estimates tens of thousands for the major Ruund courts of the nineteenth century.

Even the swarms of refugees who gathered from time to time in some of the most defensible centers did not approach the size or complexity of the settlements ringing the Pool.

Upriver from Malebo Pool along the Kwa and lower Kasai lived the small groupings of mobile clan segments of the forest-savanna mosaic. Their mobility scattered their ethnonyms discontinuously over broad areas and left individual groups with multiple names that presented a bewildering kaleidoscope to outsiders accustomed to viewing Africans in terms of simplistic "tribal" labels. In fact, the apparent confusion reflected the extremely local perspectives and fluid mobility of the inhabitants along the banks of those rivers.

South of the Zaire, the middle reaches of the Kwango River separated the sand-country people of remotely Lunda connections from others in the west whose lords, by 1700 or so, had worked out a political geography based in significant part on the exigencies of forwarding slaves on through the mountains to the coast (Map 1.3). There, no less than three major merchant-kings in the middle valley of the Kwango presided over trading centers at which captives left the control of African slavers and entered the hands of Europeans or their African agents. It would have been in such slave markets as those along the Kwango that most captives caught their first glimpse of the red-skinned strangers who would dominate their lives from that moment on.

The "Jaga" Kasanje were proprietors of the southernmost market and lords over the people who lived in the upper parts of the Kwango valley and portions of the surrounding high plains to the south and west. These Kasanje lords preserved political ideas and practices centered on warfare and cannibalism that derived from Jaga origins like those of the highland Ovimbundu rulers. The rudeness of their manners was in jarring contrast to the air of cosmopolitanism and luxury that flowed from recent wealth acquired from the slave trade between the Ruund and western Lunda chiefs and the Europeans from the west. The riches they accumulated around their court—supplemented in no small part by local wealth in salt, manioc, and cattle, and the superior agricultural reserves of the valley in time of drought—attracted a flow of immigrants from the more vulnerable highlands all around. Westerners also fled down into Kasanje to escape slaving raids and labor impressment in their homelands, and easterners who had been brought in as slaves congregated there as well. The upper part of the Kwango valley thus constituted one of the most important concentrations of people in the west.[70] The material sophistication of

---

70. In addition to Jean-Luc Vellut, "Le Royaume de Cassange et les réseaux luso-africains (ca. 1750–1810)," *Cahiers d'études africaines* 15, 1 (no. 57) (1975): 117–36, I base my comments on Kasanje on still-unpublished research, except as summarized in my "Formation

Kasanje would have impressed slaves coming from the more provincial court of the *mwaant yaav,* and the power of its kings would have awed traders from Malebo Pool. A mixture of languages and cultures brought by recent immigrants from both east and west would have attenuated the ancient Pende substratum of the local population deriving from the early seventeenth century.

Just down the Kwango, to the north, lay a similar but smaller and briefer-lived trading state known as Holo. The lords of Holo probably broke off from Kasanje at the end of the seventeenth century to take control over river crossings leading into the central and western parts of the Kwango valley. They grew powerful during the first stages of trade to Lunda, from the 1730s to the 1760s, but then succumbed to pressures emanating from the Lunda lords of the Yaka in the north and from others in the west, who squeezed them out of the mature commerce of the end of the eighteenth century.[71]

The people of the western parts of the Kwango valley lived under monarchs claiming the ancient title of the Ngola a Kiluanje, sixteenth-century rulers of the middle Kwanza and the surrounding plateaux. That honorific had become the name, Angola, that the Europeans used for the lands between the lower Kwanza and the Dande that they had seized from the Ngola of the seventeenth century. The eighteenth-century lords of this line ruled the valley area two hundred kilometers northeast of their ances-tors' lost domains. They also retained among their titles that of "Jinga," after the seventeenth-century queen who had succeeded the Ngola and reconstituted this later version of their polity in the part of the valley then known as Matamba.[72] Eighteenth-century Europeans knew these Jinga lords as brokers in charge of a slaving market similar to that in Kasanje and great competitors of it. Their influence extended down the valley to the north, roughly to the Kwale River, or as far as the population spoke Kimbundu, and at times west up to the upper Lukala. In the south they controlled a narrow and largely uninhabited corridor to the Kwanza islands of Kindonga, and they often threatened to cut the road to Kasanje that ran through the corridor.[73]

---

and Transformation of the Mbundu States from the Sixteenth to the Eighteenth Centuries" (1977), forthcoming in Heimer, *The Formation of Angolan Society,* and in "The Paradoxes of Impoverishment."

71. There is no full study of Holo, but see A. Maesen, "Les Holo du Kwango," *Reflets du Monde* 9 (1956): 3–16, 31–44.

72. Again, no adequate study exists for Matamba/Jinga; for occasional references for the eighteenth century, as for other regions adjoining Portuguese Angola, see David Bir-mingham, *Trade and Conflict in Angola: The Mbundu and Their Neighbours under the Influence of the Portuguese, 1453–1790* (Oxford: Clarendon Press, 1966).

73. E.g., António de Lencastre (governor, Angola) to Francisco Mattozo de Menezes (*capitão-mor,* Ambaca), 11 Dec. 1778, AHA, códice 81, fols. 111–13v; Joaquim Xavier (*capitão-mor,* Pungo Andongo) to Gov. de Mello, AHA, códice 3018, fols. 13–13v.

Thousands of slaves from the east beyond the Kwango, from the slopes of the central highlands to the south, and also from the northeast, poured each year into the basin of the Kwanza, mostly in Kasanje and Jinga. By the eighteenth century the area contained people of highly diverse origins, the progeny of unions between immigrants from Europe, the old Mbundu substratum of the area, and captured women from all over western central Africa. The language they spoke was Kimbundu. Portuguese was heard only in a few centers, like the towns on the coast, and then mostly among European immigrants or native-born Afro-Europeans, here termed Luso-Africans. Even there, only the tiny minority of men who had come from Portugal or Brazil spoke it at all fluently.

Between the lower Dande and Kwanza rivers lay an area that government ministers in distant Lisbon regarded as a Portuguese colony, or a conquered realm (*reino*) or *conquista* in the terminology of the time. Lisbon, in fact, exercised only a loose influence over its claimed dominion. Instead, an independent-minded military gentry of mostly Euro-African complexion dominated some hundred or so petty African squires, or *sobas,* in part descended from Mbundu nobles of the seventeenth century and acting as local headmen in the rural villages of the colony. The Europeans and Euro-Africans also employed immigrant African mercenary leaders (*kilambas* and others) in military capacities to maintain "Portuguese" authority in the *conquista*. Around the fringes of the area thus partially controlled by the Portuguese lived other Kimbundu-speaking people organized under autonomous local princes, mostly the Songo in the power vacuum between Kasanje and the easternmost Portuguese outposts and in the Kimbundu-speaking region south of the Kwanza known as Libolo and integrated into the highland world of the Ovimbundu beyond.

Other slaves coming from east of the lower Kwango through the Yaka and most of those who stepped ashore from canoes at Malebo Pool began the four- to five-hundred-kilometer hike leading finally down to the coast amidst people speaking dialects of Kikongo, a tongue many slaves had first encountered as a trade language spreading eastward with Kongo merchants between 8° and 9° south. The eastern Kikongo-speakers living in the hills between the Kwango and the mountains were in the process of acquiring distinct senses of community based on the local hydrography and on their respective commercial orientations toward the east. Soso (or Nsonso) lived toward the south along the Kwilu and looked east toward the Yaka for trade. The Zombo on the Nkisi in the north had their main contacts on the lower Kwango and at Malebo Pool (see Map 1.4).

As the slaves ascended to the passes through the main range of mountains, they passed through a band of montane refugee Kongo principalities, running from the Kanda Mountains in the north to the Ndembu (Dembos) hills in the south, where both Kongo and Mbundu populations flocked in time of distress. Some veered toward their right, toward the northwest and the hills where the largely deserted capitals of the sixteenth- and seventeenth-century Kongo kingdom had once attracted slaves and politicians by the thousands. Although little remained of the former political unity of the area by the eighteenth century, provincial Kongo lords claiming Christian titles of nobility (counts, dukes, marquises, and so on) descending from earlier periods of more extensive Portuguese influence in Kongo still fought one another for a Christian Kongo royal title (in Kongo terms, the *mani* Kongo) that they had somehow preserved through the political fragmentation and internecine wars of later years. Victorious pretenders rarely remained long in authority and even less often wielded significant power from the tarnished throne they claimed, yet challengers from mountaintop principalities and from all over the hills south of the Zaire nonetheless continued their struggles to possess it. In the meanwhile, merchants with fewer pretensions to aristocracy grew wealthy from the caravans of slaves and imports that passed through their lands.[74] If the traders enjoyed less prestige, they exercised a greater power through their retinues of slaves.

The real powers among the eighteenth-century speakers of Kikongo, who inhabited the coastlands from well north of the mouth of the Zaire to the Dande in the south, were merchant princes residing at courts located just inland from the main embarkation points for slaves. Many of those south of the Zaire retained Portuguese-style titles of nobility, but few bothered to compete for the insignificant position of king in the hills behind them. Instead they faced squarely west, toward the sea, and grew eminent as brokers between the ship-borne Europeans and their eastern woodland Kongo neighbors.

The largest of these domains in area was the Sonyo principality, controlling the coast north of the Mbrije River and the southern banks of the lower Zaire. Its "counts" mastered much of the trade that crossed the great river to slaving ports on its north bank and along the coast beyond. They traded north of the river principally through the kingdoms of Ngoyo, which commanded the bay at Cabinda, and Kakongo, doing business at Molembo. To the north of these two lay Loango, where traders known as Vili (or Mubire) mediated between European slavers and a partially distinct network of trading villages dispersed eastward toward Malebo Pool and southward across the Zaire as far as the Ndembu region.[75]

74. For the eighteenth-century trade, Anne (Wilson) Hilton, "Political and Social Change in the Kingdom of Kongo to the late Nineteenth Century," in Heimer, *The Formation of Angolan Society*. Also for politics, Susan Herlin Broadhead, "Beyond Decline: The Kingdom of Kongo in the Eighteenth and Nineteenth Centuries," *International Journal of African Historical Studies* 12, no. 4 (1979): 615–50.

75. Martin, *External Trade*, esp. p. 85. Also Martin, "Cabinda and Cabindans: Some Aspects of an African Maritime Society," in Jeffrey C. Stone, ed., *Africa and the Sea* (Aberdeen: Aberdeen University African Studies Group, 1985), pp. 80–96, and idem, "Family Strategies in Nineteenth-Century Cabinda," *Journal of African History* 28, no. 1 (1987): 65–86.

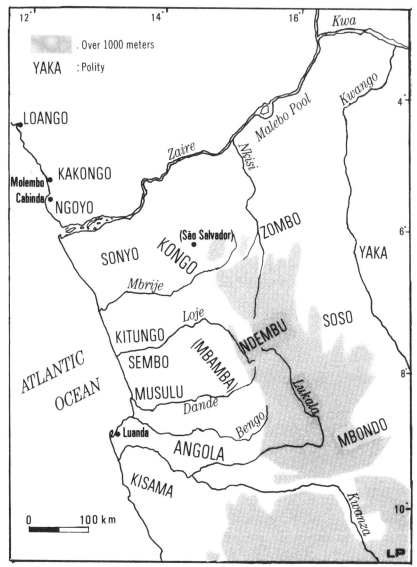

Map 1.4. Kongo and Adjoining Regions, ca. Eighteenth Century

To the south, other Kongo lords at the Mbrije supervised trading at that river's mouth, mostly as a secondary outlet for captives coming from Malebo Pool and through Sonyo. Tidal salt marshes at the mouth of the Loje, still farther up the coast, drew traders from the interior, and its sheltered bay attracted the Europeans. Two lords at the mouth of the

Loje, Kitungo and Sembo, both professed fealty to the kings of Kongo and conducted a thriving trade through the old southern Kongo province of Mbamba. At the extreme southern limit of the Kikongo-speaking peoples lay the marquisate of Musulu in the plains between the Dande and the Loje. Though less populous than its neighbors to the north and the east, since it occupied mostly dry bushland, its control over trade flowing down the Dande from the Ndembu region made it a formidable southern anchor to the Kongo coastal trading states north of Luanda Bay.[76] Imports circulated plentifully in these regions, and foreign culture had spread among the trading specialists on the coast to the extent that prominent merchants and officials in places like Cabinda spoke good French and practiced European manners with an aplomb that impressed at least the rough sea captains who dealt with them.[77] The atmosphere, at least to the malcomprehending eyes of slaves arriving from the east, would not have differed much from that in most of the Portuguese *conquista*.

South of the Dande, the coastlands became noticeably drier and less densely inhabited. Almost no one lived in the thorny scrub just east of the Bay of Luanda. Fishermen occupied the banks of the Kwanza estuary, where a steady parade of canoes and sailing launches moved upstream and downstream between the city on the bay and a string of Portuguese trading posts along the river. The land on the south bank of the Kwanza constituted a sanctuary for hundreds, perhaps thousands, of slaves fleeing captivity among the Portuguese and Euro-Africans of the *conquista*. Powerful lords there, in the lands known as Kisama, welcomed these refugees and employed them in quarrying and carrying salt from rock salt deposits that constituted the otherwise barren region's only source of wealth. Agriculture in Kisama, as elsewhere to the south, was possible only on the margins of the rivers.[78]

Finally, flight and the search for protection from bandits, political warfare, and enslavement had developed many refugee polities and communities of the Kisama sort in eighteenth-century western central Africa. Raiding and bloodshed by no means predominated at all times or in most places, but the dangers of capture and exile loomed sufficiently large that

76. For the coastal principalities, António Maximo de Souza Magalhães, *relatório* of 16 March 1780, AHU, Angola cx. 37.

77. This was evident as early as 1702–3: Gilberto Ferrez, "Diario anônime de uma viagem às costas d'Africa e às Indias Espanholas (1702–1703)," *Revista do Instituto histórico e geografico brasileiro* 267 (April–June 1965): 8; also, among other descriptions, Luiz Candido Cordeiro Pinheiro Furtado, 13 Aug. 1783, AHU, Angola cx. 40. Not long after, at least one seven-year-old son of a notable at Cabinda accompanied a slaving captain to Rio for an education in Portuguese culture: Karasch, *Slave Life in Rio*, p. 217. Also see Martin, "Family Strategies," pp. 72–74, 80.

78. For Kisama generally, Beatrix Heintze, "Historical Notes on the Kisama of Angola," *Journal of African History* 13, no. 3 (1972): 407–18.

many people abandoned the general search for agricultural security to seek the safety of the barely habitable rocky outcrops, squeezed themselves into narrow canyons like those on the western edge of the central highlands, or simply vanished into the remote high forests of Kongo or the woodlands of the Zaire-Zambezi watershed.[79]

By the eighteenth century, the fame of mountain warriors from Kimbangu in Kongo, of the Ndembu at the headwaters of the Dande and Lukala, of Wambu and Kiyaka in the central highlands, and of Huila and Njau in the far south testified to the extent to which retreat for protection from marauders had become the means by which many escaped enslavement. Wars had ravaged the Ovimbundu with particular ferocity, with the flames there fanned by the accessibility of defensible sites in their highlands. The people east of the Kwango River who retreated into the deep woods covering the crest from which sprang the Kwango, the Kasai and most of its major tributaries, and the major western affluents of the Zambezi—one of the wildest regions in all of the western savanna—became known as Kioko, or Chokwe: "those who fled (or left)."[80] Nearer the Portuguese *conquista* and its concentration of unwilling captives, the frequency of fugitive communities increased. In addition to the slaves who fled to Kisama, others regularly crossed the Dande to seek asylum in Musulu. The kingdom of Mbondo, perched on flat-topped hills with steep, eroded sides dropping five or six hundred meters down to the floor of the Kwango valley, had attracted refugees at least since the early seventeenth century, and it doubtless continued to fulfill its historic role as shelter for escapees from Jinga, Kasanje, and the eastern parts of the Portuguese *conquista*. The thickly forested summits of the Ndembu region held virtually impregnable wooden palisades within which fugitives from barracoons found freedom as subjects of powerful lords there.

Communities thus coalesced out of heterogeneous groups of refugees on all sides. Flight from the slaving of the *mwaant yaav* certainly contributed to the formation of the so-called Sala Mpasu, who lived just beyond the slave-hunting grounds on the north flank of the Lunda empire, and the (Luba) Kanyok similarly found unity in their shared sufferings under Luba assault.[81] Not far east of the Ndembu, the Hungu—a mixture of Kongo and Mbundu refugees since the eighteenth century, who have stymied ethnographers trying to identify them in terms of discrete and immutable ethnic identities—probably also originated in flights from the slaving wars of the late seventeenth and early eighteenth centuries. In the

79. Cf. notes 44–46 above; also Miller, "Central and Southern Angola," for the central highlands.

80. Joseph C. Miller, "Cokwe Expansion, 1850–1900," occasional paper, no. 1, 2d ed. rev. (Madison: African Studies Program, University of Wisconsin, 1974).

81. Pruitt, "Independent People," and Yoder, "People on the Edge of Empires."

unstable universe of community and polity of western central Africa, by the eighteenth century a significant proportion of the population of those who remained behind, limited only by the scarcity of defensible yet still habitable sites in the generally open terrain, had also come to identify themselves in terms of their efforts to escape capture and the long, deadly march west to the coast. An even larger proportion of the others had become members of older communities and polities modified and geared to enslaving and keeping those whom they did not have to sell.

Conclusion

If, by the eighteenth century, communities and politics in western central Africa had come to reflect slaving and the commercial currents swirling over the land from the Atlantic trade, other background features of the physical ecology imposed established limits that people could not escape in the longer term. Productive land was not plentiful, whether from the difficulty of clearing away the heavy vegetation cover nearer the equator or from the uncertainty of the rainfall farther to the south. Technology had not advanced in the spheres of medicine, food production, or trans-portation to an extent that would permit saving the lives threatened by violent conflict over scarce living space, or avoid the subordination of those who had no land to those who did, or provide nourishment to starving sufferers from drought, or combat the parasites and viruses in-festing the sick. It was a geography over which human mortality loomed large by modern standards, one in which populations might relocate them-selves from place to place but not one in which their aggregate numbers could grow very much in the long run. Western central Africa thus featured economies and societies in which alert and ambitious survivors always took careful account of the omnipresence of death.

2

The Value of Material Goods and People in African Political Economies

An Interpretation

If Mwene Puto lured enslaved Africans off to a land of the dead, his agents and the material wealth they offered were sirens beckoning ambitious youths and frustrated minor lords away from the networks of personal obligation surrounding local lineage elders, patrons, and kings.[1] Much of the history of Angolan slaving from before 1500 A.D. through the nineteenth century arose from the interaction of African societies and economies, conceived essentially in terms of interpersonal relationships, with an Atlantic economy of material wealth, and from the volatile mixture of the distinct values of each, people and products. The political and economic changes associated with slaving in the eighteenth century are thus largely explicable in terms of Africans' perceptions of the relationship between goods and people.

To the modern Western mind, how and why Africans could have exchanged other Africans for a collection of what some regarded as bric-a-brac cast off from industrializing Europe presents an overwhelming paradox. But the paradox arises not from African behavior but rather from misplaced projections of a modern liberal civilization's individualistic ethic into a time and place where people, quite sensibly in view of the immediacy of death all around them, apparently calculated value in forms more enduring than fragile individual human lives. From the point of view attributable to eighteenth-century Africans, the true paradox arose from the contradiction between the high productivity of the human hand in their low-energy-technology environment and the vulnerability to drought and disease of the people on whom that productivity depended. But the Africans' ironies were not more profound than other incongruities inherent in Western industrial ideologies that celebrate individualism even as they

1. Janzen, *Lemba*, p. xiii, reports the image.
The subtitle of the chapter is intended to indicate its admittedly speculative character; perhaps the hypotheses advanced will stimulate discussion in the directions outlined here, to verify or reject my perception of the issues. For similar sentiments, and a highly stimulating discussion, see T. C. McCaskie, "Accumulation, Wealth, and Belief in Asante History," *Africa* 53, no. 1 (1983): 23–43, endorsing what is advanced as "conjectural history." McCaskie (p. 33) notes a transition similar to the one evident in central Africa.

sacrifice it to acquiring the material goods and abstract forms of capital that undergird modern abilities to preserve human life, without comparable insistence on its quality. Western central Africans had numerous sensible reasons to sell people, and often for purposes that paralleled the development strategies of modern entrepreneurs, but they pursued these strategies according to a thoroughly political-economic logic that drew a less absolute distinction between economic maximization and human relations than do the separated ethics and economics of the liberal Western world. An African ethno-political-economic thought[2] structured the production and exchange of the people who eventually entered the trade of the southern Atlantic as slaves.

Political economy must, as the term implies, consider simultaneously and explicitly the interaction of human beings and the material goods that sustain their lives and structure relationships among them. The approach explored here is economic to the extent that it studies material goods and strategies of utilizing them efficiently to achieve specified social ends. It is also political in the degree that it traces contests among people rendered unequal by maximizing actions of the successful that also deprive the less efficient or less fortunate of a proportional share of the limited material goods available in the short run. Modern Marxist concepts like the "[human] relations of [material] production" and the "[political] struggle of [economically defined] classes" capture much of the bivalent essence of this emphasis. Political economy thus reveals how control of necessary and scarce material goods mediates authority over people and, conversely, how those with power and authority use their power to channel access to material wealth.

Understanding the slave trade of western central Africa forces attention to this abstract level because it turned on an exchange of human

---

2. The term, however awkward, is offered by analogy to the endeavors of anthropologists to grasp non-Western "ethno-medical" systems on their own terms, or of historians to elicit "ethno-histories" premised on the concepts and assumptions of the nonmodern people who created them. Need for emphasis on the relativism of the political-economic aspect of human life arises from the equally strong and erroneous insistence of both "formalist" economics and most Marxism, paleo- or neo-, on the supracultural objectivity of their working axioms: Caroline Neale, "The Idea of Progress in the Revision of African History, 1960–1970," in Bogumil Jewsiewicki and David Newbury, eds., *African Historiographies: What History for Which Africa?* (Beverly Hills: Sage, 1986), pp. 112–22. Though the historical dialectics of both—whether individualistic competition or class struggle— contain certain valuable truths, the technologies and value systems of the people seeking advantage at the expense of others in each must receive prior consideration through the relativistic lens of cultural, symbolic, and structural analysis. I agree, for example, with Mary Douglas and Baron Isherwood, *The World of Goods: Towards an Anthropology of Consumption* (New York: Basic Books, 1979); the point applies to modern as well as nonmodern economies and societies. See also the conclusion of Philip D. Curtin, *Cross-Cultural Trade in World History* (New York: Cambridge University Press, 1984), p. 14 et passim, on the coexistence of both cultural metaphors and abstract economic principles in all behavior.

wealth for material goods in its starkest form and thus revealed fundamental characteristics of political economy usually well hidden elsewhere
in human society behind layers of ideology and the mediating goods and
currencies. Such a direct exchange explicitly violated the moral and economic axioms separating humans and material goods into ostensibly distinct spheres of exchange that have taken over Western ways of thinking
since the eighteenth century. Liberal economic thought has (perhaps only
until recently) triumphed so completely that it has virtually excluded systematic examination of the ways in which goods inevitably mediate control
over people and how control over people is necessary to acquire goods,
so long as human welfare remains dependent on material wealth. With
respect to African economic history, liberal assumptions have all but pre-
cluded penetrating analysis of slavery and the slave trade. But the separation
of goods and people characteristic of liberal economics was by no means
as common in eighteenth-century western central Africa as it has become
among modern Europeans, and not exclusively among the African sellers
of slaves, since late-medieval or early-modern Portuguese "fatalism" (so
called by more progressive European detractors) shared significant features
with African thought. Hence, the African processes that produced the
people who became slaves gain intelligibility for the twentieth-century
mind when rethought from the political-economic premises held by the
people who offered other people for sale.

Ethno-Political Economics

Eighteenth-century western central African producers and traders tried to
accumulate what they regarded as "capital" no less than did their European
counterparts, but they understood the notion more broadly, in its true
sense of any resource productive of wealth in the future, than the restricted
sense of buildings, machines, and financial instruments usually left as the
content of the depoliticized concept common in modern liberal thought.
And the Africans quite correctly stressed people as sources of productivity,
for they knew none of the hydraulic, fossil-fuel, and nuclear sources of
energy that have multiplied water-, hydrocarbon-, and atomic-powered
productivity in modern industrial societies for three hundred years, at rates
far exceeding even the high rates of population increase of the last century,
astronomical by the long-term standards of preceding eras. This modern
limitation of the sense of "capital" to such technological wonders and to
abstract representations of it in the form of financial instruments[3] is un-

3. Though forced to concede, by a kind of awkward analogy, the notion of "human
capital" to refer to the training and expertise of the people required to operate complicated
technology. This conceptualization of "human capital," however, specifically excludes the
broader physical strength of the human arm or back, consigned in modern economic thought
to the residual category of "unskilled labor."

derstandable in view of the fact that these have recently been the most productive components of Western economies and societies by a long way.

However, non-Westerners defining "capital" by the same implicit standard of "maximum productivity" in the low-energy-technology economies of Africa would have found this same essential quality also in livestock and particularly in human beings, as well as—but only secondarily—in material tools that gave their users a mechanical advantage over the bare hand but relied entirely upon human energy for their effectiveness. Because control of animate capital gave African owners no less of an advantage over others than does material and abstract modern "capital," economic wealth and political power and authority were frequently indistinguishable in Africa, where capital was people. A wealthy man increased productivity by organizing and controlling people, and African entrepreneurs, by acquiring dependent persons, sought productive and constructive aims similar to those that modern "capitalists" pursue by buying and selling mechanical or financial assets. Hierarchical social and political institutions, rather than individualistic and egalitarian ones, were axiomatic, unquestioned features of such a political economy, no more anomalous there than are the notions of private property and individual egalitarianism in an ideology founded on an implicit definition of "capital" as material.

Getting ahead by means of aggregating human dependents possessed severe limitations that amounted to profound and chronic insufficiencies of (human) capital in the political economies of much of western central Africa, particularly in the areas committed to more labor-intensive forms of agricultural production. Shortages of dependents, owing in significant part to background ecological and technological limits on the ability of the population to survive, limited both general economic growth in the abstract and individual opportunity in immediate personal terms. Junior kin, boys and girls, the ideal source of dependents in farming villages, reproduced more junior kin, but only at stately rates governed by the female reproductive cycle, nutritional insufficiencies, high losses to infant mortality, delays in conception arising from the needs of small children to nurse for lengthy periods of time, and accidents and diseases afflicting older youths.

In addition, the independence and superiority that some few gained by controlling junior kinsmen necessarily implied the dependence of many others. In most areas, ambitious superiors tried to overcome these limitations by recruiting affines and even strangers as clients, subjects, or slaves. Those who were left behind in the competition quite reasonably desired to emulate neighbors who had got ahead as lords, patrons, elders, or masters, and they could become rebellious or restless and hard to control.[4]

4. I am aware of the shortcomings of structural and social anthropological models predicated on kinship as descriptions of historical social realities in Africa, but it is analytically significant that Africans' ideological representations of their various strategies remained un-

Nonetheless, in the minds of virtually all western central Africans loomed the assumption, visible in the ideology of kinship that they employed in structuring and discussing human relations of all sorts, that wealth was people and that its sources resided in the propagation of descendants owing proper respect to their elders.[5] At least people spoke that way, whether or not their practice approximated what they preached.

Most western central Africans had in fact diverged rather far from the ideal productive strategies expressed in the logic of kinship and descent long before slaving spread over the land in the eighteenth century. By then, relatives still actually resided together in the descent-defined lineages that fascinated a later generation of Western anthropologists only in the woodlands recently opened to intensive settlement by the planting of manioc, or in higher sandy elevations newly reoccupied in the wake of recent droughts. There land was cheap, often free to its first occupants. Ambitious homesteading men could take their wives and children out to open fresh fields in the Kalahari sand country as the first step in attracting clusters of dependents of other sorts who would one day raise them to the status of petty Ngangela and Mbunda gentry.

Elsewhere, in the moist, fertile, and continuously occupied valleys, the lineage ideal still thrived, but largely because it identified advantaged descendants of the first settlers on land that had long since grown scarce and justified their primacy over a majority of more recent arrivals, whom

---

deniably phrased in terms of descent. Their notions provide the appropriate point of departure for this chapter's ethnocentric analysis of the content of African political economy. For general critiques of "lineage theory" of the exclusivist variety, see Adam Kuper, "Lineage Theory: A Critical Retrospect," *Annual Review of Anthropology* 11 (1982): 71–95, and Jan Vansina, "Lignage, idéologie, et histoire en Afrique Equatoriale," *Enquêtes et documents d'histoire africaine* 4 (1980): 133–55. Vansina, "Towards a History of Lost Corners in the World," *Economic History Review* 35, no. 2 (1982): 165–78, has applied the general point to the forested parts of central Africa; see also his "Peoples of the Forest." I have developed some of the applications of the logic of kinship to politics in *Kings and Kinsmen* and, more generally, in "Listening for the African Past," in Miller, ed., *The African Past Speaks: Essays in Oral Tradition and History* (Folkestone: Wm. Dawson and Sons, 1980), pp. 1–59.

5. The equivalence of "capital" to people in African political economies is becoming general in the literature, and one finds occasional references to African statements of the point in these terms: e.g., Théophile Conneau, in Brantz Mayer, *Captain Canot, An African Slaver* (New York: Arno Press, 1968), pp. 127–28: "The financial genius of Africa . . . has from time immemorial declared that a human creature—*the true representative and embodiment of labor*—is the most valuable article on earth"; or a Wagenya trader on the upper Zaire to Verney Lovett Cameron, *Across Africa* (New York: Harper and Brothers, 1877), p. 267, who refused cowries in payment for a canoe, saying that "the cowries would be lying idle and bringing him in nothing until he managed to buy slaves with them . . . he did not want his capital to lie idle." It is becoming apparent—at least for areas of mobile populations, perhaps for others disrupted by slaving in the nineteenth century, and for those characterized by intensive commerce—that the "kinship" and "lineage" institutions of colonial ethnography are modern creations; for the forest, see Jan Vansina, "Knowledge and Perceptions of the African Past," in Bogumil Jewsiewicki and David Newbury, eds., *African Historiographies: What History for Which Africa?* (Beverly Hills: Sage, 1986), p. 34.

they accepted only on condition of subordination to the heirs of the original occupants. There, access to land had supplemented the recruitment of dependents as the key component of production. In turn, these "guests" appropriated the same rules of descent to defend the lesser privileges they retained over other groups of still more recent arrivals. Even the latter defended the kinship principle as a means of elevating themselves above the isolated and despised people of slave origins, people defined as lacking descent entirely. The resulting hierarchical lineage systems developed most elaborately where reliable agriculture attracted groups of relatives fleeing famine in the more marginal zones. Isolated individuals fleeing similar conditions might offer themselves as slaves to gain asylum in these same favored regions. All these variants of the ideology of descent prevailed in the farming areas of western central Africa, generally in the savannas, and in the western fringes of the mountains and valleys, where the prime economic resource remained human labor put to work in the fields and where control of people thus opened the road to wealth.[6]

Cattle in the desert south and, on the rivers of the forest to the north, more elaborate fishing and transportation equipment, scarce cleared land, and good fishing grounds advanced nonhuman sources of productivity to a point where canoes, fishing weirs and dams, or trade goods supplemented techniques focused on recruiting human labor in the pursuit of economic advancement. In the forest, luxuriant tropical vegetation and the seasonal inundations of the rivers sharply reduced arable spaces. People possessing cleared dry land tended to dispense access to it as a kind of currency mediating the acquisition of dependents, allowing strangers to farm for their livelihoods on condition of subordinating themselves as clients to land-holding village patrons. Along the rivers themselves, life revolved around an elaborate material technology of fishing nets, traps, dams, and canoes, with big river canoes also used, increasingly, for transportation of slaves and goods.

In extreme cases, these sorts of material equipment—"capital" in a form more easily recognized by the standards of industrial societies—assumed productive functions that enabled their possessors to assemble heterogeneous "canoe houses" of unrelated paddlers and warriors and other groupings of followers that relegated kinship to a pure fiction. If the restricted supplies of land available as capital in the forest limited possibilities for agricultural growth, other than through improved yields from new crops like maize or manioc, the relative ease of fabricating fishing and transport equipment allowed modest economic and political growth up to the limits of the people—usually clients—available to fabricate and operate it.[7]

6. Argued in greater detail in Miller, "Lineages, Ideology, and History."
7. In addition to Vansina, "Peoples of the Forest," for economy and society in the forest, see Harms, *River of Wealth, River of Sorrow,* and P. van Leynseele, "Les transformations

In the south the ability of cattle to reproduce with no more than slight human intervention gave much greater buoyancy to the political economies of the desert fringes and made livestock the focus of intense intellectual concentration and economic competition among the herders living there. Boys worked for their fathers by managing the herds in their annual transhumant grazing cycles, and wealthy men with many head of livestock established themselves as patrons to networks of cattle-clients by lending their animals to less fortunate neighbors and to kin. Prosperity reigned as long as the cattle increased in numbers, but never for very long, since enlarged herds crowded the restricted rangeland on the margins of the Kalahari and led to overgrazing and loss of bovine assets. Frequent drought along the desert edges repeatedly killed off the herds and frustrated the ambitions of men trying to extend their political influence through loans of cattle.

Like herders everywhere, these cattle barons also relied on agriculture, where the rivers permitted it, to support the majority of their dependents. Accordingly, most people actually lived along the Kunene or the Kubango, but none of them grew wealthy from hoeing millet fields. Cattle technology held far greater opportunity, if also greater risks, than agriculture, and the constant mobility that herd management entailed kept interest in bulky material equipment to a minimum. Hence, cattle remained the nearly exclusive means through which men structured their relations with their fellows, though often expressed also, as elsewhere, through an ideology of more or less fictive descent.

Though people always remained at the heart of the matter, as they do in the relations of production even in industrial economies, the extent of clientage as a relation of production thus increased north and south of the agricultural savannas in rough proportion to the importance of non-human forms of capital in political economies where fishing, herding, and trading supplemented farming as the most productive form of activity. But in all cases, successful entrepreneurs in the end turned their material "profits" back into people: dependent kin, clients, and slaves.

The analogies between the western central Africans' treatment of people and modern Western economies' treatment of material "capital" extended beyond strategies of maximization to analytical distinctions, expressed in their modern forms as differences between "commercial," "industrial," and "financial" capital. Abstract "financial capital" is often superior to its physical counterparts in goods and machines under stable environmental conditions, since its value derives from ineradicable legal guarantees rather than from its perishable concrete substance, and its value is absolute,

des systèmes de production et d'échanges de populations ripuaires du Haut-Zaire," *African Economic History* 7 (1979): 117–29, and other studies by all three authors.

not affected by deterioration in the physical condition of the assets it represents: the owner of a factory destroyed by fire (or his insurer) still owes the bank for the mortgage he had given on his vanished material assets.

Similarly, given the centrality of human life to the political economy of western central Africa, but also its fragility amidst the high mortality there, abstract claims to future labor from a general category of people that continually renewed itself were worth more in the long run than immediate control over the physical exertions of specific individuals, junior kinsmen, clients, or slaves, who might desert, disobey, or die at any time. Deaths or dispersal of clients could leave powerful patrons abandoned old men, and infertility among nieces or daughters-in-law cast even headmen of theoretically perpetual corporate lineages onto hard times. On the other hand, political warlords holding more abstract forms of authority over refugees who renewed themselves through continuing flights toward the safety of the warlords' fortresses, or dynasties of rainmaking kings who commanded tribute from anyone dependent on timely rains to farm in their agricultural domains, attained more enduring, impersonal kinds of power.

What ambitious men struggled to achieve was therefore not direct supervision over others, and still less stocks of the physical products of their labor beyond immediate needs, since both people and their fabrications were all too perishable, but rather a general claim to unspecified future labor and its product at whatever moment need for them might arise. Without the obligation to cover significant maintenance (or overhead) costs of the material equipment characteristic of high-energy economies by commanding the continuous services of dependents, they valued people more in their potential than in their presence and gave greater worth to their loyalty than to their labor. Hence, although many rich and powerful men surrounded themselves with living followers, the wealthiest and grandest refined their demands to the prospective and the intermittent, requiring primarily the "symbolic" tribute usually glossed in modern Western languages as "respect." Exploitation in such a system was disguised from Western eyes as rights to the future service of dependents rather than appearing clearly as extractions of immediate material surpluses from their labor. Control over the "means of production" in its highest human form brought deference rather than storehouses filled with spoiling fish or rotting grain.

"Exchange" in the modern sense of definitively separating oneself from a product of one's personal labor was literally inconceivable in this African political economy. People did not think in terms of the potential worth of an object in the context of exchange but, rather, saw its immediate value in terms of concrete use. Objects of a person's fabrication could be loaned, entrusted to the possession and utilization of another, but not parted with. It was the indissoluble association of a person with the things he or she had created, even after they might have passed into the hands of another, that produced the bond that always united givers and receivers, a reciprocal connection in personal terms of the association in material terms that arose out of possessing some material extension of another's labor. The loans of cattle common among herding communities were merely the manifestation most obvious to modern ethnographers of the inalienability of the product of one's efforts fundamental to Africans' thinking of the material world in terms of use-values.

Transactions in material goods nonetheless occupied a central position in this political economy of rights over people, a position not very different from their "social" role in modern economies, though the ideology of respect and deference concealed their significance in Africa no less than tributes to individual human rights hide their role in capitalist political economies. Most western central Africans personally produced a much higher percentage of what they consumed than do modern people, and their cultural heritage conveyed corresponding assumptions that they should and could do so that liberal economic theories based on exchanges lack. Their economic assumptions made it appear easier to fabricate what they desired for themselves than to acquire it from others, although that sometimes required extending the concept of the "self" to include assemblages of the kinspeople and dependents necessary to accomplish the tasks at hand. Even enormously expensive investments like the fifty- and sixty-foot trade canoes used in the commercialized economy of the central Zaire basin most people assumed they could make for themselves, if need be.[8] If this attitude of self-sufficiency prevailed long after the eighteenth century even along the Zaire, where practice had moved far indeed from the approximation of the independence and sharing within isolated lineages more common on the agricultural frontiers that had given rise to the ideology, axioms of production for use by oneself and one's own must have profoundly influenced the ways that people generally thought about material goods throughout western central Africa.

Hence, exchange as a means of acquiring material goods was a derived notion rather than a primary one. Where exchanges occurred, they were a practice to be explained and conducted in terms of producing for one's own use rather than understood as axiomatic first principles, as they are in Western thought, from which such related economic ideas as "consumption" might flow. Methods of gaining access to material goods thus subordinated "exchange" of goods to acquiring of rights over the producers responsible for making them. Transfers of goods became a means

---

8. A revealing assumption mentioned in Harms, *River of Wealth, River of Sorrow*, p. 22.

to another end, a mediating procedure with the more basic purpose of acquiring people, or productive potential. Successful headmen therefore exchanged dependents, often in marriage alliances between their lineages according to structures well described by anthropologists, to surround themselves with a variety of kin and affines who could produce the entire range of foods, crafts, clothing, wood, and skins they desired without having to seek the materials themselves outside the primary communities they thus created. They provided for these dependents by distributing the product of each within the community according to standards of patronage, redistribution, gifts and largesse, or communal "sharing." Such a distribution fell outside any conceptual field of "exchange" that would be limited, as in liberal economics, to transactions among autonomous equals. Patrons ideally duplicated this sharing within their villages of clients, and kings and lords managed it on a larger scale, at least symbolically, through redistributive tribute systems operating at the level of their political domains.[9]

Thus, before the advent of slaving and commercialism, goods were not generally viewed as made for exchange. The purpose of production was for use within a community, with the ordinary distribution of products handled under the rubrics of inheritance, redistribution, or sharing. One provided for the future by asserting rights to respect, expressed by occasional contributions of the product of the dependents assembled, whether clients, kin, or slaves. Although farmers might plant extra manioc, which kept well in the ground, for future use in the event of drought,[10] no one stocked surpluses with much thought to the value of unused portions of it if sold to strangers. In practice, of course, extra food was often transferred to those in need, but sellers negotiated the transfer in terms of the human obligations of the receiver to the giver rather than in terms of an abstract commodity "price" that was worth denoting by some intermediary material token or standard of value, like a currency. The fortunate possessors of food reserves in time of famine simply fed the needy as members of their communities—as new slaves and clients—more often than they sold their stores to strangers for material tokens. People and subordination, not

9. Among the seminal thinkers contributing elements to this analysis, see e.g., Marshall Sahlins, *Stone-Age Economics* (Chicago: Aldine-Atherton, 1972), the works of Karl Polanyi, and studies by Claude Meillassoux. Formal derivation of these notions from the rich and varied literature in economics, political economy, and economic anthropology awaits an appropriate opportunity, although I can acknowledge immediate inspiration and encouragement from Michael Taussig, *The Devil and Commodity Fetishism in South America* (Chapel Hill: University of North Carolina Press, 1980), and unpublished work on Melanesia by my colleague Frederick Damon.

10. Paulo Martins Pinheiro de Lacerda, "Noticia da cidade de S. Filippe de Benguella e dos costumes dos gentios habitantes daquelle sertão," *Annaes marítimos e coloniaes* (parte não oficial) 5, no. 12 (1845): 489, confirmed in [Alexandre da Silva Teixeira?], "Derrota de Benguella para o sertão," in Felner, *Angola*, 2:22.

goods, were what moved or were exchanged. These acquisitions of people confirmed in practice what African political-economic thought assumed in theory: the value of material goods resided in their use for, or consumption by, members of the group rather than in their potential for future exchanges with outsiders.

The hypothetical, but not improbable, transaction imagined here illustrates also the connotations of superiority and inferiority that arose when material goods changed hands in violation of the axiom that each person or group produced for its own use, not for that of any other. Every transfer of material goods confirmed the fundamentally hierarchical character of social relations in western central Africa, and in doing so such exchanges reinforced the desires of every subordinated recipient to avoid having to resort to such transactions whenever possible. Although men acknowledged the biological necessity of exchanging women to reproduce capital assets in the form of human dependents, either children to be born or sisters to be returned as future wives, by doing so they mainly strived to attain self-sufficiency in shared material things for themselves and their retinue. To accept material goods was, at base, to acknowledge one's dependence on the owner, as, in the extreme case of famine, refugees submitted to slavery in return for food. Less extreme need brought less abject subordination, but patrons who offered gifts thereby reconfirmed their superiority over their clients.

Lineages that gave their daughters and nieces as wives claimed precedence over other lineages that received their women, although return flows of material bridewealth or future wives lessened the obligation in time, except where one-way flows of females expressed interlineage relations of dominance and subordination. Typically in practice, only occasional strangers, often semiprofessional traders from far away, had accepted material goods in direct exchange for material goods in confined spheres of luxuries, thus neutralizing the implied reciprocal bonds of superiority/inferiority and leaving the parties to the transaction separate, theoretically equal, and autonomous. Still more rare in the background from which western central African notions of political economy had descended were generalized exchanges common enough to make it worth anyone's while to work out currency tokens that could be returned to cancel the human debt created by acceptance of a material good.

Material exchanges and the bonds of obligation they formed assumed vital importance in a political economy where human dependence was the most efficacious means of increasing production. Givers initiated transactions to confirm the inferiority of receivers. Translating the material prestations of this hierarchical society into modern concepts derived from assumptions of individualism and equality, gifts constituted loans confirming the subordinated borrower's general obligation to repay at some unstated future time and in some other, as yet unspecified, material form. They thus constituted "capital" in the sense of being an investment in future human productivity, consumption forgone now in the expectation of a return later. Characteristically, relations of human dependency rather than material currency or financial instruments intermediated the delayed returns in material goods. Everyone tried to avoid the humiliation of receiving rather than giving such obligations, or "gifts" as they were termed. But those who had material goods spread them as widely as they could among their dependents, disposing of fundamentally perishable material objects to accumulate the enduring values of personal debt, extended on through the generations to heirs of the debtors by the ideology of descent. The relationship thus created differed from what modern economics calls "credit" only in its conceptual stress on immediate human relationships rather than on the abstract financial instruments that disguise them in a capitalist economy.

On the other hand, giving material goods in return for loyalty also contained an element of relativity in the degrees of dependence it could create. High and powerful dependents might demand material goods from a patron, even when they could afford not to accept them, to the extent that they retained alternatives to clientage or juniority in their benefactor's lineage. Powerful regional lords in segmentary kingdoms thus merited grand largesse from their sovereigns; lesser royal gifts would only invite wavering devotion to the superior's cause. Only the lowliest of clients would give their respect in return for basic food or shelter. The greater the degree of choice remaining to the recipient, the larger the quantities and the higher the quality of the gifts necessary to indebt, as well as the greater the degree of autonomy and prestige thereby left to a subordinate able to mitigate his debt by sending tribute in return.

Slavery in western central Africa represented the qualitatively different status left to helpless persons able to demand no goods at all for themselves as the condition of their subordination. Theirs was dependence without recourse. Slaves often originated in practice as humble outsiders, taken in circumstances that saved them from sheer starvation, from harm at the hands of pursuers, or from death by judicial condemnation. It was not that slaves could never repay their debt to a lord and master who had quite literally saved their lives but rather that they lacked the autonomy to do so. They were pure extensions of their master, and what they had was already his. Pure slavery, and thus the formal ideology of the institution, originated from inability to give anything but a life for a life; slaves only later became recipients of material gifts that confirmed their continuing total subservience.

From that ideal model of the abject slave came the assumption, later appropriated by European slaveowners to rationalize their purchase of these unfortunates to an enlightened world that had forgotten how to think in terms of paternal obligation, that the alternative to enslavement was death. It was, but primarily in a figurative sense.[11] Similarly, as Africans explained to later malcomprehending European buyers, slaves born into a household and thus not obtained for material goods should not be "sold" in the sense of being exchanged for imported wares. Such slaves were totally passive recipients of material support from their masters in the short run and completely abased providers of loyalty, respect, and future labor in the long run: thus the ideal, highly productive form of human capital. They could circulate, however, in the capital sphere in which women moved from lineage to lineage as wives, in which prominent subjects felt honored to send a son or nephew to their monarch's court, or in which enemies evened an outstanding score by transferring a pawned person from the offender to the offended. The dominant tendency in western central Africa was to take in such outsiders as slaves, rather than to dispose of them, since they filled out and enlarged the followings that made men powerful.

One could also "buy" a slave with material goods, but the logic of African political economics represented such a transaction as a gift to the seller of the slave (or receiver of the goods), who thereby assigned his compensating dependency onto a substitute, a member of his kin group or a dependent in his entourage, the person who became the slave. By the same criterion of substitution within the sphere of collective responsibility, debtors owing for goods sent their dependents off to settle their accounts with their creditors. Such delegation of obligation was both sensible and desirable for anyone who had dependents on hand with whom he could share his debts as well as his wealth. So long as the recipient of the goods showed no prospect of repaying his debt with other material assets, the obligation he transferred to the slave remained total in its quality and indefinite in its duration. Such an absolute transfer, amounting to outright sale of a slave, arose most often in transactions between passing strangers and merged there with offers initiated to acquire goods, not people. On the other hand, to the extent that buyers and sellers of slaves under these circumstances stayed in touch with one another and regarded their relationship as subject to continued adjustment through future exchanges of people or material goods, the dependent's subjugation could remain conditional and revocable. In instances where this transfer of dependency was undertaken with the explicit intention of canceling it by future repayment of other material goods, the resulting assignment of dependency conveyed the contingent status distinguished by anthropologists as "pawnship."

---

11. See the elaboration of this insight in Orlando Patterson, *Slavery as Social Death* (Cambridge: Harvard University Press, 1982).

In practice, of course, this assimilative and paternalistic slavery constituted an ideal honored as often in the breach as in its observance. Refugees from drought arrived helpless, physically weakened, and vulnerable to abuses of all kinds. Criminals condemned to slavery found themselves sent beyond the borders of their judge's realm to strangers willing to accept them, without obligation to the enslaver, in return for material wealth. There the slaves had to carve out new places in alien communities of people speaking a language they did not comprehend. The larger the political domain from which they came, the more distant the penal transportation and the greater the disabilities attending their incorporation in the society of their new masters. The practical disabilities afflicting new slaves lessened over time, as the once-defenseless outsiders learned the ways of their masters, acquired knowledge of their language, and applied their skills and wits to winning a measure of their respect. And so, depending on how far slaves had come and how recently they had arrived to live with their owners, their origins as isolated defenseless recent arrivals imposed fewer and less onerous burdens in practice, although their ineradicable origin as slaves never ceased to convey a lowly status compared to the prestige of first arrivals and of the locally born. In most of western central Africa before the rise of the Atlantic commerce, the distance and regularity of such transactions scarcely amounted to an institutionalized "trade" in slaves.

The political-economic maximizers of western central Africa therefore made their ways in a world where the material realities of modern economics faded intellectually toward abstractions, an accurate enough reflection of how the soft iron of their hoes wore away and rusted, the wood of their houses yielded to tropical rot and termites, salt blocks dissolved in the rains, and stores of food decomposed in their bins. Similarly, the greater but still relatively ephemeral substance of living dependents dissipated all too often before desertions, drought, disease, and death. Permanent, real wealth resided in dependents' abstract collective obligations to provide future material goods upon command, in respect, and in prestige. Success came to those who headed autonomous communities, small or large, within which material goods circulated for immediate use as gifts given and largesse redistributed to create subordination. "Exchange" in the sense of material transactions between independent and equal partners, as understood in Western economics, occupied a logically secondary place. In practice, even in the eighteenth century in most parts of western central Africa, exchange still occurred less frequently than did sharing within relatively self-sufficient groups of dependents.

Exchange

Exchanges between strangers were far from unknown, however, though such transactions hardly threatened to challenge the logic of a political economy focused on the transfers of people and on material production only for use within the community. Foods and luxuries moved everywhere across ecological boundaries separating forest and savanna, seashore and interior, dry woodlands and moist valleys, clay river banks and the sandy hills above them, cattle ranges and arable lands, and around concentrations of copper, salt, and iron—the primary minerals necessary to standards of living that western central Africans struggled to maintain in the eighteenth century.

Farmers living in the clearings of the equatorial forest had for a long time routinely sold products of their agriculture to often alien water people, and the canoemen of the rivers and dwellers in the swamps caught and dried fish to sell inland. The water people also carried dyewoods and other forest products out to river ports like Malebo Pool, where they sold them to strangers who carried them on to consumers in remote savannas.[12] Residents of the forest-savanna mosaic, favored with raffia palms in their lands, stripped fibers from their fronds and wove squares of fine textiles that circulated widely in the grasslands and woodlands to the south, where similar raw materials were rare.[13] Fishermen working the bays along the coast sent dried fish to protein-short cereal farmers in the interior and satisfied anonymous desires there for rare items of personal adornment and distinctions of wealth by sending marine shells as well.[14] Leathers and hides, as well as occasional livestock on the hoof, came out of the dry scrub of the south in a desert-side exchange economy that could not have differed in structure very much from better-known counterparts along the edge of the Sahara.[15] Pioneers who braved the rigors of farming in the dry sandy plains of the upper Kasai could supplement their unreliable and

12. Harms, *River of Wealth, River of Sorrow*; Vansina, *Tio Kingdom*, pp. 247–312, for a later period; more generally Vansina, "Peoples of the Forest," and Thornton, *Kingdom of Kongo*, p. 34.

13. See Anne Hilton, *The Kingdom of Kongo* (Oxford: Clarendon Press, 1985), pp. 6, 7 ff., and 75–78, for the height of this trade through Kongo in the seventeenth century. Also Martin, *External Trade*, pp. 36–39 ff. In more remote areas, imported raffia textiles merely supplemented local bark cloths; Lacerda, "Noticia da cidade de Benguella," p. 489, for Ngangela in the 1780s.

14. The most famous example was the *nzimbu* shell currency taken out of Luanda Bay and circulated through the old Kongo kingdom; see Hilton, *Kingdom of Kongo*, pp. 7 ff., and Thornton, *Kingdom of Kongo*, pp. 23–25.

15. David Birmingham, "Early African Trade in Angola and Its Hinterland," in Richard Gray and David Birmingham, eds., *Pre-Colonial African Trade* (London: Oxford University Press, 1970), pp. 163–73. Cf. Paul E. Lovejoy and Steven Baier, "The Desert-Side Economy of the Central Sudan," *International Journal of African Historical Studies* 8, no. 4 (1975): 351–81.

low-yielding agriculture by selling honey from hives of bees they encouraged in the woods there and meat and skins from game they hunted in their wilderness homelands for bananas and grains from intensively farmed bottomlands and for cooking oil from palm groves nurtured there, very much as the Pygmies of the forests gave meat to the farmers of the forest clearings in exchange for starch.[16]

These continual but diffuse exchanges of ecologically specialized food products, minerals, cloths, and luxuries slid easily into the prevailing concepts of production for use rather than exchange. They tended to occur along lengthy ecological boundaries and thus to flow through small capillaries linking close neighbors to close neighbors among customary patrons and clients. Exchanges of goods thus became mixed, in the manner of African political economy, with exchanges of people given to signify the permanence of such gift and tributary relations between regular trading partners. Although strangers might buy from and sell to one another on an occasional basis in the more remote and infrequent manifestations of this trade, in most instances local political relations of clientage and tribute channeled even this systematic trade into the gulleys scored by sharing of foodstuffs within the primary communities of the neighborhood.

Only slightly less susceptible to comprehension in terms of personal hierarchies were distributions of minerals from deposits scattered relatively infrequently over the landscape, or metal products useful only after technically complicated processing by trained and experienced specialists to a much wider range of stranger-consumers. Iron, basic to the agricultural and hunting technologies of the region, occurred with some frequency in the forests and in the western mountains but less commonly in the sandy plains to the south and east. The fine ironwares of the forest and its fringes, tempered in the hot fires of tropical hardwoods, flowed toward Kongo, Mbundu, and Ovimbundu areas to the west and south across the Kwango and Kwanza, and within the Kongo, Mbundu, and Ovimbundu areas regional suppliers also distributed their ferrous products.[17] Whatever the exact geography of early iron manufacturing, so long as such objects moved

16. Especially the Chokwe woodsmen of the Kwango-Kasai headwaters; see, e.g., "Derrota de Benguela," in Felner, *Angola*, 2:23, 25; also Pontes letter of 9 Oct. 1800, ibid., 1:253. For the general economy of the woodlands, especially wax, see Jean-Luc Vellut, "Diversification de l'économie de cueillette: miel et cire dans les sociétés de la forêt claire d'Afrique centrale (c. 1750–1950)," *African Economic History* 7 (1979): 93–112.

17. Although information on African iron production is scattered through many sources, no systematic study on its technology and trade has yet been attempted for western central Africa. For early sources of iron in the forested river valleys inland from Luanda, see Maestri Filho, *Agricultura africana*, pp. 57–60, and Miller, *Kings and Kinsmen*, pp. 36, 67, 74–75. By the 1750s, Kasanje and presumably much of the Kwango valley were buying iron hoes from the Kwanza-Kasai watershed, as per Dias, ed. (Leitão), "Viagem a Cassange," p. 24. For a major eighteenth-century iron-working center on the central highlands, "Derrota para o sertão," in Felner, *Angola*, 2:15–16, 19.

in relatively small quantities from neighbor to neighbor, they passed easily through the local networks of interpersonal obligation, prestations, and gifts.

Copper artifacts circulated even more widely from at least four main outcroppings of cuprous ores, one north of the lower Zaire at Mindouli, a second just inland from the mouths of the Kuvo and Kikombo rivers, a third in the desert far south at Tsumeb, and the fourth and most famous in the easterly plains of Katanga.[18] The products of smiths working near these deposits traveled hundreds of kilometers, often in standardized bracelets and cross-shaped ingots appropriate for handling by strangers ignorant of their makers and thus reliant on recognizable standard qualities of the depersonalized objects themselves, rather than on acquaintance with their producers, to assess their value. Copper, and in some cases marine shells as well, possessed the essential characteristics of durability and uniformity that allowed central Africans to attribute standardized value to them rather than to rights over people and thereby to exchange them as the closest western central African approximations to modern currencies—stores of value and media of exchange.[19] However, their rarity and the tenuousness and intermittence of the exchange channels along which such items escaped far from the hands of their producers still left them minor features of a political economy resting squarely on its attribution of fundamental value to rights over people.

Salt was another scarce and valuable mineral resource that circulated widely but seldom strained by economic logic based on production for use rather than for exchange. Marine salt pans predated European trade at most of the coastal bays and river mouths that later became major boarding areas for slaves: Loango, the Loje River, Kakwako near Luanda Bay, Lobito near Benguela Bay, and the mouth of the Kuporolo at Dombe just to the south.[20] Distinctively high-quality rock-salt deposits at Kisama

18. In general, for copper, see Eugenia W. Herbert, *Red Gold of Africa: Copper in Precolonial History and Culture* (Madison: University of Wisconsin Press, 1984), and for the antiquity of the Katanga mining complex, Pierre de Maret, "L'évolution monétaire du Shaba Central entre le 7e et le 18e siècle," *African Economic History* 10 (1981): 117–49. For more detail on Kongo copper sources, see Wilson, *Kingdom of Kongo*, pp. 6, 7, 32–34, 53–55; Martin, *External Trade*, pp. 41–42; also Janzen, *Lemba*, pp. 32, 61–70. On Sumbe copper south of the Kwanza, Delgado, *Reino*, pp. 20–21, 29–30, 78, 82, 116, 146–50, 307–17.

19. Though see de Maret, "Evolution monétaire," pp. 134 et passim, on the long-term shifts in value and size of the copper crosses from the Zaire-Zambezi watershed. Marion Johnson, "Art and Patronage in Ashanti" (unpublished paper, n.d.), offers a sensitive analysis of the conceptual distinctions between producing for a known patron—i.e., for "use" within the community—and for an anonymous "mass" market.

20. Birmingham, "Early African Trade in Angola," in general; Phyllis Martin, "The Making of Cabindan Society, Seventeenth to Nineteenth Century," in Heimer, *Formation of Angolan Society*; also idem, *External Trade*, p. 14, which stresses the importance of early trade in salt from the Loango Coast to the interior. For the Kongo Coast, Thornton, *Kingdom of Kongo*, p. 33, and Wilson, *Kingdom of Kongo*, pp. 6, 29, 33–34, etc., and (though later)

made the barren southern bank of the lower Kwanza a commercial center widely known throughout the basin of the upper river.[21] Inland salt pans on the lower Kuvo and particularly along the Lui affluent in the valley of the middle Kwango attracted farmers from distant regions.[22] Even the bland, dirty product they could scrape from the dried mud of receded rivers in the dry season was superior to the alternative of using ash from burned marsh grasses along rivers flowing through salty sediments.[23] Where salt consumers depended on highly perishable scrapings from the banks of springs and pans, they congregated during the dry season to wrap the precious mineral in leaves and thus avoided exchanging it at all beyond the confines of the communities they recognized. But where better marine salts, and especially the hard salt blocks of Kisama, could withstand the cost and wear and tear of transportation, exchanges between strangers bearing them became more frequent. In the extreme case of the Kisama salt, such blocks acquired features of a currency that strangers could use to mediate generalized exchange systems.

As commercialization increased relative to production for use in western central African economies, goods moved through at least four different sorts of channels defined in terms of the transactions in people presumed to prevail in the region's political-economic ideology, distinguished according to volume and the concentration of trade among specialists. The lines of marital alliance, patronage, and tribute allowed nearly everyone to acquire sufficient goods for immediate consumption by sharing, gifts, and redistribution within defined and relatively inflexible spheres, the existing communities of kinship, co-residence, and hierarchy. Such "domestic" circuits of exchange could also move significant amounts of luxury commodities, even distributing a few items, like copper, over great distances, though only in small quantities, through repeated transfers along long chains of these local links.

A second type of distribution system, one less fully integrated into local social and political institutions, arose when unrelated parties with goods to exchange, or producers with market opportunities among distant

---

specifically for the Loje, Souza Magalhães, 25 Jan. 1773, AHU, Angola cx. 36. The salt pans at Kakwako near Luanda, at Lobito just north of Benguela, and at the mouth of the Kuporolo are well known, as they were later developed by the Portuguese. For early references, see Delgado, *Reino*, pp. 98, 102, 117, 164–65.

21. On Kisama in general, Heintze, "Kisama of Angola." Early references to circulation of salt up into the Kwanza basin include the anonymous Jesuit history, 1 May 1954, in Brásio, *Monumenta missionaria africana*, 4:550; Manoel Gomes de Avellar (*ouvidor geral*), 20 May 1731, AHU, Angola maço 18-A; ibid., 28 May 1732, AHU, Angola cx. 21; Rodrigo Cezar de Meneses (governor, Angola), 12 June 1734, AHU, Angola cx. 21.

22. Miller, *Kings and Kinsmen*, pp. 70 ff.

23. Harms, *River of Wealth, River of Sorrow*, pp. 57–58, discusses the difficulties of salt production in the moist central basin of the Zaire.

populations with whom they shared no prior connections, deliberately created relationships of alliance, patronage, or tribute to route new trading opportunities. Some swore a bond of "blood brotherhood" that extended the language of descent to cover the novel connection they had made and fleshed out a guarded and risky commercial relationship to include some of the trust, rights, and responsibilities of kinsmen, though modified to emphasize equality rather than the subordination of junior to elder common in the lineage. Others expressed political tribute as a manifestation of the old institutional forms, as for example, the "kin" relations claimed by political lords in the Lunda and other state systems. Such techniques preserved the conventional view of production as being for use within a community, political or kin-based, but in practice created new bonds to facilitate exchanges between former strangers by converting them into presumed relatives or clients.

Only a few traders took the further step toward the third type: explicit acknowledgment at rare trade centers like Malebo Pool of open exchanges of material goods between autonomous equals, unbalanced by personal obligation. There, regular transactions between people from far away and acknowledged as strangers so eclipsed occasional encounters between people linked by ties of familiarity that traders had to devise formal and public market institutions to handle direct exchanges of material products without countervailing transfers of people and bonds of dependence. Yet western central Africans still conducted even this trade in terms of concepts and assumptions focused on people that derived from the old and still dominant ideological premises of production for use rather than for exchange.[24]

Only a very few became so committed to living by commerce that they took the fourth step toward a modern commercial economy: shedding the assumptions of the old political economy for an ideology that attributed basic value to useless tokens of exchange rather than to people. In these latter two instances, commerce had become large enough in volume and the difference between costs of acquisition and sales prices great enough that specialists found it advantageous to commit themselves to trade as a way of life, no longer using dependents to grow food or fabricate goods for home consumption but, rather, investing in goods, stocking commodities, employing followers, and using material things to acquire what they needed for consumption and even for dependents. Such professional traders had begun to divert their investment strategies from reproducing people, through wives and children, to acquiring goods that would bring in other goods and followers through commerce.

---

24. Janzen, *Lemba*, is absolutely clear on the intellectual gyrations necessary to express new ideas in terms of old concepts in the highly commercialized area between the Pool and the Loango Coast; for the Bobangi, see Harms, *River of Wealth, River of Sorrow*.

These four exchange strategies differed also in economic terms, according to how much material wealth practitioners of each committed to supporting trading activities in themselves. The first two techniques of acquiring others' goods from far away, through interpersonal links designed to generate more people and dependence, involved little additional wealth to supplement local sharing and gifts with occasional small-scale peddling of goods. The latter two involved substantial material investment—goods to buy slave canoemen, stocks of wares in transit, gifts for local contacts through whom peripatetic merchants contacted local communities of consumers, and third-party judicial institutions to regulate disputes arising from the intense contacts and conflicts among strangers. The inexpensive options could spread widely, if diffusely, because their informality as commercial systems erected almost no barriers to participation and because almost everyone had social contacts which they could enlarge to include systematic reciprocal gift-giving.

The latter two, on the other hand, could expand no more rapidly than the asset base available to support them. Since the ability to reproduce dependents was inherently limited, so long as people remained the prime form of capital trading profits had to supply the wealth to support the growth of specialized commerce. The value of material goods, like that of slaves, increased with distance from their origin, but it was expensive to move them far. Such profits, to judge from the rudimentary extent of specialized trade in western central Africa before the sixteenth century, were insufficient to support significant commercial growth much of anywhere beyond the low-cost canoe-transport network of the forest. Much less did they provide wealth adequate to finance backward integration of mercantile investment into the production process or its forward integration into links of political superiority over consumers rendered subjects by continual offers of commodities as "gifts," on credit. Rather, professional traders managed to become no more than just that: middlemen putting all their accumulated assets just into supporting the institutions of their trade. Nonetheless, they whetted consumer appetites for exotic cloth and other luxuries that were capable of significant expansion if and when adequate capital resources—that is, credit—might become available.

Accelerated flows of goods presented no less attractive opportunities to political lords with established networks of dependence, who could use them for converting material things directly into larger followings. More goods allowed them to subordinate not only helpless refugees but also powerful lords with significant followings of their own. But since the highly dispersed local exchanges of food across extended ecological boundaries spread movements of even large aggregate quantities of goods, like a river running slow and shallow across a wide plain, trade currents rarely built up enough force through the hands of any one man that he could use them to indebt many of his fellows. Farmers who converged seasonally on salt pans concentrated the gains through local owners of the marshes somewhat more, and these last accordingly seem to have become cores of dependency networks large enough and permanent enough to be recalled in much later oral traditions.[25] Copper and developed centers of iron-working depended on the smelting skills of small, self-contained, and inward-looking groups of trained, full-time producers, especially slaves, rather than on assembling large numbers of part-time producers. The monetary qualities of these metal products offered less potential for po-litical consolidation, since owners of the mines distributed bars, hoes, and crosses of metal in open exchanges through professional traders and did not tax strangers as users of the resource or indebt them to create political ties.

In only one or two exceptional cases did flows of goods from com-plementing sources overlap—with the direct exchanges intensified further by low-cost transportation narrowed to river channels—to support the growth of trade-based centralized monarchical power. In the very heart of the continent, on the eastern fringe of western central Africa, north-south trade between forest and savanna, copper from the Zaire/Zambezi watershed, local supplies of iron, salt, and fish, and the Lualaba River came together in the Upemba depression. What appears to have been centralized political power, or at least commercial wealth that was consid-erable by local standards, emerged there as early as the end of the first millenium.[26] In the far west, similar convergences underlay the growing power claimed by the fifteenth century by *mani* Kongo lords positioned astride trade routes from forest to savanna and from the sea to the interior, adjacent to the copper mines at Mindouli, and in contact also with the enormous transportation potential of the interior Zaire River system at Malebo Pool.[27] Elsewhere, trade remained diffused through too many local communities to promote, by itself, centralized political authority beyond the intermediate scale on which farmers living in moist valleys had long before joined beneath kings who, they believed, brought them the rains from which they derived bounteous harvests and the numerous dependents whom plentiful food allowed them to support.

The political economy of these more common, fundamentally agri-cultural polities rested only minimally on "tribute" flows of material goods from subordinated regional and local lords to a central court. Comple-menting royal "gifts" of goods sent back out to the provinces consumed most of what the center received and primarily left tokens symbolic of the

25. Miller, *Kings and Kinsmen*, pp. 70 ff. Reefe, *Rainbow and Kings*, pp. 80–85, offers a similar hypothesis for the origins of Luba polities in the Upemba Depression (Shaba).

26. De Maret, "Evolution monétaire"; Reefe, *Rainbow and Kings*.

27. Wilson, *Kingdom of Kongo*, chap. 1.

court's control of these trade flows rather than substantially supporting its population. What the king did not send back out, his retinue consumed—a fact that may account for the habit of expressing the idea of political power in terms of "eating." The more significant forms of political integration and surplus extraction in these cases came in the people sent to the court: daughters and nieces offered to the king as wives, sons and nephews loaned to the court as pages, and a few dependents and unwanted kin conceded as criminals and slaves to work in the fields and craft industries that constituted the modest "public works" of the realm.

The human retinue residing at the capital represented its lord's wealth and power more than did the modest physical contents of its treasuries and storehouses. Its material splendor derived from the skilled human labor that royal dependents lavished on its monuments and decoration.[28] Kings returned smaller portions of their wealth in human dependents to their subjects than they redistributed from the material possessions that came into their hands. Gifts of goods honored their subject recipients, but the king's messengers and mercenaries brought royal power to bear on nobles and gentry throughout the realm, forced into obedience despite the tokens of recognition by the king that bedecked them. The possession of physical wealth assumed less significance in politics of this sort than where power derived from regional trade flows had raised material goods to the status of a currency that took primacy in accumulating new followers.

Exchanges and political expansion of these sorts meant that persons of slave origin could not have been uncommon in central Africa before commercialized slaving began to spread from the Atlantic in the sixteenth century. These slaves would have been distributed no less unevenly than the general population, though in different patterns, and would have been found more commonly in areas of concentrated habitation than in regions of dispersed settlement. People cast directly into the pure form of abject slavery through flight from drought, war, or other historical circumstances producing overpopulation tended to become dependents of the owner-occupants of good, moist farmlands.[29] Traders or politicians with material goods to offer would have converted those goods, insofar as practicable, into wealth held in dependent humans of all sorts, including many slaves. The centers in which such conversions had built up the largest followings must have been the royal courts, particularly those, like Kongo, that supported themselves from commerce in material goods, but also the domains of rain kings, who assembled consumable tribute in foods and home crafts

28. See Vansina, *Children of Woot*, for an epitome among the Kuba.
29. For an example documented from the central highlands of Angola at the end of the nineteenth century, see Heywood and Thornton, "Portuguese Colonial Policies." An analogous situation and similar result appears in Robert Ross, "Ethnic Identity, Demographic Crises, and Xhosa-Khoikhoi Interaction," *History in Africa* 7 (1980): 259–71.

from their agriculturalist subjects.[30] Certain centers of production for exchange, such as the major shell fishery at Luanda Bay or some of the mineral smelting industries, would also have offered opportunities to build up concentrations of slave workers. Professional traders in the forest may also have taken on a few employees or slaves. But throughout the region, subordination, clientage, and kinship remained the main currencies of dependence held by the powerful and the rich.

The fundamental ideology of producing people for exchange and goods for use thus did not prevent widespread circulation of material wealth. It merely accomplished distribution by means uncommon in modern market economies. Co-resident communities shared among themselves on a face-to-face basis. Administered transfers of "tribute" and "largesse" moved significant quantities of goods within politically unified communities. Elsewhere, consumers traveled to acquire salt directly rather than waiting for specialized producers or merchants with inventories of the commodity to contact them. Strangers created pseudo communities of blood brotherhood and affinity, and "friends" transferred goods in private rather than publicly in open markets.[31] Even the most commercialized institutions cloaked trade in notions of familiarity: foreign merchants lived as nominal "guests" of landholding "hosts," and trading states converted personal genealogies into permanent political structures. But human relations obscured trade relations, fabricated goods were inseparable from their fabricators, and a consequent presumed directness of transactions between producer and final consumer left utterly no logical space for the notion of living from trade alone.

Explicit Institutions of Trade in a Political Economy of Use-Values

Anomalous widespread exchanges of good against good between strangers, as those in rock salt and copper or in many commodities along the main streams of the Zaire system, nonetheless sometimes overwhelmed the assumptions prevailing in the African political economy. Though one ideally acquired material goods not by exchange but rather by aggregating dependents and then sharing their production through networks of personal obligation, most people also bought things. Though outright commercial exchange fit only awkwardly into concepts of labor that viewed production as primarily for use, some people made things for sale. Though iron

30. Thornton, *Kingdom of Kongo*, esp. pp. 18–19.
31. G. Michael La Rue, "Khabir 'Ali at Home in Kubayh: A Brief Biography of a Dar Fur Caravan Leader," *African Economic History* 13 (1984): 60, notes the phenomenon in the much more commercialized environment of the trans-Saharan trade.

commodity-currencies tended to circulate in such ready-to-use forms as hoes, salt distributors from Kisama and copper miners on the Zaire-Zambezi watershed produced minerals and metal in quantities far greater than their personal needs dictated and in shapes other than readily useful ones. They did so, of course, in order to acquire the food and other necessities of life that their devotion to specialized production left them unable to make for themselves.

Since exchanges of these sorts brought together people who had never seen one another before and who could not count on renewing the contact at any certain time in the future, the conventional ideas of distributing material possessions to accumulate personal obligations hardly applied. It was possible, as many did, to create fictive kinship relations of the familiar sort between unrelated traders even where they came in repeated contact with one another. But where trading encounters between strangers developed into repeated similar exchanges, people began to calculate the value of what they had in terms of such an exchange, and it made more sense to establish direct material equivalencies between the goods traded, standard exchange ratios that allowed each party to calculate the value of a good in terms of another he or she hoped to acquire: so many bars of Kisama salt for so many copper crosses, so many marine shells for a specified type of raffia textile from the lower Kwango valley, so many yams for so much fish. Direct barter of material good given for the material good received concluded the relationship between the traders, cancelled the paired subordinations of receiver to giver, and left no outstanding credit or dependency.

The obvious notions of value available for constructing such barter equivalencies derived from the objects' respective uses. These values remained absolute because usefulness did not vary, and the worth of every item remained fixed with regard to a finished unit of every other commodity so long as people exchanged items for their personal consumption. The equivalences adopted arose from *ad hoc* direct exchanges of such usable, whole concrete items, and more generalized patterns of exchange merely extended these fixed exchange ratios to larger quantities marketed in bulk, far beyond the consumption needs of the trader or even his community. Traders did not alter these established use-equivalencies within normal ranges of fluctuating supplies and demand. The accepted ratios represented unquestioned community judgments about the inherent relative usefulness of two specific sorts of items, and it would not occur to many to alter these merely because of ephemeral changes in availability, as quantities offered rose or fell with the season, or with warfare, or with illness on one side or the other. Variations in the probabilities of exchanges occurring had no effect on the usefulness of items actually traded or, for that reason, on the ratio at which such transactions were accomplished.

Quantity varied instead as additional potential buyers brought more producers onto the scene and the volume of exchanges rose at the existing barter ratio.[32] Accounting and calculations of gain, or loss, without the aid of written records and fractional values remained easy to remember and efficient to visualize in terms of the physical objects at hand. Inducements to attract goods at times of scarcity took the form of "gifts" offered over and above the stable equivalency ratio, which remained unquestioned over large temporary disjunctions between supply and demand. Long-term imbalances between supply and demand for established sorts of transactions altered quality and quantity behind an unchanging facade of set equivalency ratios. The size of raffia palm cloths shrank when they became scarce relative to their fixed equivalents in shells, for example.[33] Sellers filled the accepted measure of grain obtainable for a chicken more fully in times of plenty than in times of scarcity, or over the longer term the volume of the measure itself would decrease while traders proclaimed its strict equality.[34] Kisama salt blocks were cut and subdivided as they became increasingly scarce in inland regions farther from their source, and less carefully refined wax could find more willing buyers when it was scarce than where it was plentiful.[35] Thus, adjustments in the quantity and quality

32. I am here extending the notion of "quantity bargaining" developed in Philip D. Curtin, *Economic Change in Pre-Colonial Africa: Senegambia in the Era of the Slave Trade* (Madison: University of Wisconsin Press, 1975), pp. 239–40, 249–50, and Marion Johnson, "Cloth Strip Currencies" (paper presented to the annual meeting of the African Studies Association, Houston, 1977). See my further discussion of "prices" and equivalency ratios in "Slave Prices in the Portuguese Southern Atlantic, 1600–1830," in Paul E. Lovejoy, ed., *Africans in Bondage: Studies in Slavery and the Slave Trade* (Madison: African Studies Program, University of Wisconsin, 1986), pp. 43–77, and "Quantities and Currencies: Bargaining for Slaves on the Fringes of the World Capitalist Economy" (forthcoming). Janzen, *Lemba*, p. 31, terms the fixed standards of measurement "natural values" and provides illustrative detail for the area just north of the Zaire estuary.

33. E.g., Wilson, "Kongo Kingdom," pp. 126–29, 131, 207. The long-term shrinkage of the Shaba copper crosses is well known, and see Vansina, *Tio Kingdom,* pp. 285–86 ff., 294, for copper rods in the Zaire trade at the end of the nineteenth century.

34. E.g., the various *cazongueis* (a measure of volume; see the Glossary of Foreign Terms) in use in 1816, *memória* on the Kwanza canal, n.d. (ca. 1816), AHU, Angola cx. 64. There were also repeated official efforts to regulate theoretically standard weights and measures, usually at times of pressure on prices: Sousa Coutinho *bando* of 9 Apr. 1766, enclosure in de Mello letter of 29 Aug. 1801, AHU, Angola cx. 50, on the same issue; Sousa Continho *regimento* (charter) for the public granary in Luanda, 26 Nov. 1766, AHU, Angola cx. 31.

35. There is also evidence of shrinkage in the size of the salt block standard in the trade from as early as the late sixteenth century; e.g., António Mendes, 9 May 1563, in Brásio, *Monumenta Missionaria africana*, 2:551 (noting a salt-block size of 3 *palmos quadrados* [a *palmo quadrado* equaled ca. 20 cm on a side]); cf. "Informação acerca dos escravos de Angola," n.d. (ca. 1582–83), ibid., 3:227–29; Jesuit history, 1 May 1594, ibid., 4:550 (2½ *palmos quadrados*); Conde de Oeyras, *paracer,* 20 Nov. 1760, AHU, Angola cx. 28 (1 ½ *palmo* in length by 4 *dedos,* or about a half *palmo* [?], in width and height), confirmed in draft *regimento* for José Gonçalo da Câmara (governor, Angola), 22 June 1779, AHU, Angola maço 3 (D.O.); Nicolau de Abreu Castelobranco (governor, Angola), 16 May 1828, AHU, Angola cx. 72 (noting a size of 8–10 *polegadas* [in length?], i.e., approximately 1 *palmo*). Cf. Vasconcelos *bando,* 18 April 1762, AHU, Angola cx. 29, ordering that measures not be altered. On wax, the point is inferred from the Africans' refusal to deliver a pure product; see Ferreira,

of concrete goods that were maintained at fixed use-value equivalencies assumed all the adjusting functions that variation in abstract currency prices performs in capitalist economies for goods assumed there to be of standardized sizes, qualities, and form, and usually exchanged without accompanying gratuities. In this habit one senses the origins of fixed nominal "asking prices" in modern exchange economies that generously conceal the real values of goods to buyers and sellers. "Bargaining" then allows the parties to an exchange to determine the actual worth of an item and to effect a sale according to supply and demand functions created by the individuals' perceived needs.

These techniques, based on modifying quantities and qualities of nominally standard use-values bartered at fixed equivalency ratios, applied more to occasional exchanges and less to specialized African traders fully committed to commerce or to politicians bent on acquiring goods to invest in networks of dependency that extended beyond the consumption needs of their personal retinue. For such merchants, patrons, or monarchs, the notion of "use" expanded to include functions that goods could perform if given to anonymous distant consumers through a marketplace, or if offered to attract the loyalty of neighboring provincial nobles. For men like these, it became feasible to adjust equivalency ratios in the abstract, with an eye less on the final use of the items changing hands than on their productivity in terms of aggregate abstract dependency or stocks of goods held for general resale.

African merchants in some parts of the Zaire River trading system had probably explored techniques of adjusting equivalency ratios in ways that resembled modern price mechanisms long before Europeans appeared on the scene, though they still expressed the adjustable ratios in terms of concrete goods rather than in a generalized abstract currency.[36] But contact with Europe and Asia via the Atlantic trade gradually, and in the longer run very profoundly, allowed African merchants to expand the commercialized fringes of local economies relative to the spheres within which most farmers, or herders, continued to produce food and dependency for their own use. However, the African political economy remained the basis of production and survived until the nineteenth century as the ideological framework within which traders worked these changes, even though com-

---

memória, 25 June 1762, AHU, Angola cx. 29; Câmara, draft *regimento,* 22 June 1779, AHU, Angola maço 3 (D.O.). Balls of rubber and wax cakes sold in the nineteenth century were similarly adulterated and reduced in size: Joseph C. Miller, "Cokwe Trade and Conquest," in Gray and Birmingham, *Pre-Colonial African Trade,* p. 185. Linda Heywood, "Production, Trade, and Power: The Politics of Labor in the Central Highlands of Angola, 1850–1930" (Ph.D. diss., Columbia University, 1984), pp. 74–75, presents data that make the point for iron axes and hoes in the central highlands between about 1800 and 1850.

36. Robert W. Harms, "The Genesis of the Commercial Economy along the Middle Zaire River," *Enquêtes et documents d'histoire africaine* 4 (1980): 101–13, explains prices there in terms partly similar to those suggested here.

mercialized economic activities retained fewer and fewer of the old features that had once made the idea of use-values approximate more closely what people ordinarily did. The old strategies, in fact, continued to prevail to the extent that even African merchants and trading kings remained primarily committed to accumulating people rather than goods. The Africans, in turn, imposed practices arising from their political economy of people and use-values on the Europeans and their agents, everywhere beyond the most Atlantic-oriented counting houses in the commercial lower town in the single city of Luanda, rather than accepting currency-based concepts of Western capitalist economics. The capitalist world economy instead introduced a vast, long-term inflation in the quantities of imported goods available in Africa relative to people, since the exchange between the two consisted essentially of Africans' dependents for Europeans' wares.

Though only glimpses of the changes in African perceptions that must have accompanied this transformation over the centuries of the slave trade have yet been drawn out of Africa's intellectual history, the consequences of the political economy of people and use-values were painfully and bewilderingly obvious to European traders operating at the juncture of the two contrasting systems. They found African methods of negotiating difficult to predict or understand in the terms in which their mercantile capitalist background led them to try to conduct their business.

Price changes of considerable refinement, for example, took place in terms of the African calculus of fixed concrete use-equivalencies, accumulating increment by increment around nominally stable core exchange ratios, and in particular for large items like the slaves and ivory that dominated international trade. But nominal "prices" seldom varied, even when demand placed pressures on supplies.[37] The long-term results of such gradual adjustments were evident in the complex composition of the "bundle" of goods conceived of as a single unit that Europeans were already paying for slaves by the early seventeenth century.[38] The terminology for the slave traded on the Angolan coast, as elsewhere in Africa—the *peça* (or *pièce*, or "piece") early on, and later a *cabeça*, or "head"—retained the original elementary exchange ratio established when Africans had first begun to offer one adult male slave for a cut, or piece, of imported textile

37. For pressure on units of slaves, see "Capitulaçoens" (of D. Veronica, queen in Matamba), 24 Nov. 1684, AHU, Angola cx. 10; Francisco Xavier de Lobão Machado Peçanha (*ouvidor*), 27 June 1785, AHU, Angola cx. 40; Manoel Almeida e Vasconcelos (governor, Angola) to Manoel da Fonseca Coutinho (*capitão-mor*, Ambaca), 17 Nov. 1790, AHU, códice 1627, fols. 23–24v; "Directorio para o Capitão Chagas com o estabelecimento da nova Regulação do Commercio," 22 Aug. 1792, *Arquivos de Angola* 1, no. 6 (1936): doc. 6; de Mello, 29 Aug. 1801, AHU, Angola cx. 50; and many other indications.

38. For references to the *banzo*, or bundle of goods, offered for a slave, see *petição* from D. Maria de Tavora (widow of former governor Manuel Pereira Forjaz, 1607–11) in AHU, Angola cx. 1; the *banzo* is defined in António de Oliveira de Cadornega, *História geral das guerras angolanas* (*1680*), ed. José Matias Delgado (Lisbon: Agência Geral das Colónias, 1940), 1:143; in general, see Carlos Couto, *Os capitães-mores em Angola no século XVIII*

cut to a standard length determined roughly by the amount of fabric judged appropriate to garb a person, usually about two meters but sometimes more.[39] At that early time, probably still in the sixteenth century, imported silks and other fine cloths had been so rare and dependents relatively so plentiful that African lords had been willing to part with people for no more than that. By the eighteenth century, the exchange ratios had shifted dramatically against the common woolens and cottons then employed in the commerce.[40] Reflecting these changes in the terms of trade in favor of slaves, the concept of the standard adult male slave, originally restricted to fully postpubertal individuals fifteen to eighteen years or older, had broadened to include youths and even larger children.[41] On the import side of the transaction, quantity-equivalents in imported goods included not only prime multiples of the basic "piece" of cloth but also short lengths of it and a whole "bundle" of highly divisible ancillary items—wine, cane brandy, Dutch knives, mirrors, beads, shells, and often gunpowder—appropriate for making subtle adjustments as necessary.[42]

It is not hard to imagine how, over a century or more of declining offerings of slaves and rising quantities of goods, price increases took this

---

(*subsídios para o estudo da sua actuação*) (Luanda: Instituto de Investigação Científica de Angola, 1972), p. 223. Further discussion in Miller, "Slave Prices."

39. Similarly, Martin, *External Trade,* p. 106; Debien, "Traite nantaise vue par un nantais," p. 206. Johnson, "Cloth Strip Currencies," describes the comparable West African *paign,* similar in terms of its intended use(s). Lengths of cloth ranged from six to two meters at Loango, according to Martin, *External Trade,* p. 106; see price data for the Luanda hinterland discussed in Miller, "Slave Prices."

40. A general discussion of rising prices everywhere in Africa (though in terms of European currency equivalents marginal to the effective "prices" in Africa) is contained in Richard Bean, *The British Trans-Atlantic Slave Trade, 1650–1775* (New York: Arno Press, 1975), pp. 137–57, table A6.

41. The growing emphasis, throughout the trade, on the youth of the slaves being transported is mentioned in David L. Chandler, *Health and Slavery in Colonial Columbia* (New York: Arno Press, 1981), p. 146. Beatrix Heintze, "Das Ende des unabhängigen Staates Ndongo (Angola)," *Paideuma* 27 (1981): 246, senses a reduction in the quality of slaves as early as the 1620s; see Fernão de Sousa, 7 Dec. 1631, BAL, 51-IX-20, fols. 370–71v. By the late eighteenth century, inventories of slave holdings typically showed no, or very few, adult males; e.g., *processo* of Belchior Clemente Domingos Martins (accused smuggler), 1774, AHU, Angola cx. 36; *auto de devassa* regarding the ship *São João Deligente, auto de avaliação* (Domingos de Araujo e Azevedo and João da Silva Guimarães, 1 Mar. 1799), AHU, Angola cx. 48; *auto* (4 Oct. 1784) regarding the ship *Nossa Senhora de Belém e S. José,* ANRJ, cx. 388, pac. 2. A *consulta* of the Lisbon Junta do Comércio, 19 Aug. 1782, ANTT, Junta do Comércio, maço 62, macete 122, put the average proportion of full *peça* slaves in a ship at ca. 12.5%. Cf. Karl Polanyi, "Sortings and 'Ounce Trade' in the West African Slave Trade," *Journal of African History* 5, no. 3 (1964): 381–94, who reported the average West African "adult" slave by 1793 at only 4'4" for males and 4' for females.

42. For typical composition of the Angolan *banzo,* e.g., João Jacques de Magalhães (governor, Angola), 29 Apr. 1738, AHU, Angola cx. 21; further discussion in Miller, "Slave Prices." The "bundle" was, of course, similar in composition and function to the bars, manillas, ounces, and other equivalents in use in West Africa. In addition to Polanyi, "Sortings and 'Ounce Trade,'" see Curtin, *Economic Change,* pp. 237 ff., and Marion Johnson, "The Ounce in Eighteenth-Century West African Trade," *Journal of African History* 7, no. 2 (1966): 197–214.

form. Buyers first defined additional units of slaves to reflect the lesser qualities of the individuals offered for sale as supplies tightened. Hence, a whole set of categories less than the ideal adult male slave came into use, mostly derivations according to Portuguese linguistic forms from the Kimbundu term, *muleke,* for a dependent.[43] Each category possessed its distinct equivalency ratio in African marketplaces, no less fixed than that of the *peça,* but lower according to the age, health, and strength of the labor power it implied.[44]

The inflationary effects of the influx of goods appeared also in reductions of the quality of individuals accepted as meeting the theoretical standards of each category. Slave buyers faced with a sellers' market would have been tempted to regard one or two marginally healthy youths as nominal *peças.* Exceptions of this order gradually came to overwhelm the rule as shortages continued, with the category of *peça* expanding in practice to include younger and weaker individuals until most slaves were traded as *peças,* even though the actual proportion of strong healthy adult males among them dropped steadily over the years. In acknowledgment of the reality of the inflation, the Portuguese tended to abandon the technical term *peça,* which they inherited from early buying to fulfill sixteenth- and seventeenth-century Spanish *asiento* contracts and from Spanish administration of the trade from 1580 to 1640,[45] in favor of the less explicit standard designation of *cabeça* ("head"). It was a human application of the African practice of adulterating the quality or reducing the quantity of physical goods transferred at single unalterable fixed ratios of exchange.

On the buyers' side of the fixed slave-goods exchange ratio, a similar long series of small increases must have led to "prices" constructed in terms

43. Thornton, "Kongo Kingdom," pp. 21–22, cites *nleke* as the Kikongo term for freed slave wards of the Catholic church and for "children" (i.e., dependents) in general. Ferreira, *memória,* 26 June 1762, AHU, Angola cx. 29, describes the categories in use in the Angolan interior, ca. 1760s; see the inventories in note 41, above, for application of the categories at the coast; the same terminology was employed in Brazil. The Kimbundu term, *muleke* (Port. *moleque*) appears to have entered official discourse shortly after Portugal's separation from Spanish rule (1640) and its loss of the Spanish *asiento* contracts based on the *peça* (*pieza*) as the unit of slaves delivered to the American colonies; for further references see Miller, "Slave Prices," table XI. The same terminology spread to the Spanish trade by the late eighteenth century; cf. Palmer, *Human Cargoes,* pp. 98–99, who does not mention it, and Chandler, *Health and Slavery,* pp. 83–87 ff., who found it in use by the 1750s–60s. A parallel African set of categories was also employed throughout the central Sudan in the nineteenth century: Dennis D. Cordell, *Dar Al-Kuti and the Last Years of the Trans-Saharan Slave Trade* (Madison: University of Wisconsin Press, 1985), pp. 117–21.

44. Vasconcelos, *bando,* 10 Nov. 1759, AHU, Angola cx. 28; "Directorio para o Capitão Chagas."

45. José Gonçalves Salvador, *Os magnatas do trafico negreiro (séculos XVI e XVII)* (São Paulo: Livraria Pioneira Editora, 1981); Pierre Chaunu and Hugette Chaunu, *Séville et l'Atlantique (1594–1650),* 8 vols. (Paris: Institute des Hautes Etudes de l'Amérique Latine, 1955–59); Frédéric Mauro, *Le Portugal et l'Atlantique au XVIIIe siècle, 1570–1670* (Paris: S.E.V.P.E.N., 1960).

of large assortments of many individually useful items. European buyers of slaves would have begun to bid up the "price" of slaves by adding extra small "gifts" in the African manner to negotiations surrounding a basic transaction nominally maintained at the established import equivalent of one "piece" of cloth. The extra sweetener that one seller of a slave was able to obtain, all his competitors would soon demand also. Since the African sellers thought in terms of use-values, they had none of the means of comparing alternative "dashes" available to Europeans in the form of their money values in Europe, and so there was a tendency to insist on increments in precisely similar physical forms: a dozen Dutch knives, for example. Thus, the value of increasingly scarce slaves rose in the form of increasingly complex assortments of goods, the basic "piece" supplemented by the specific gratuities and inducements fortuitously on hand as buyers bid up prices by offering gifts.

Slave buyers would eventually have conceded these prestations as parts of the formal exchange ratio with which negotiations began, adding more gifts and more components as gratuities, and finally even multiplying the core "piece" of cloth when the differential between nominal and market prices became great enough to absorb increases of so large a magnitude.[46] The length of the useful "piece" could not be increased incrementally to cover gradual exchange-ratio changes in less than whole-number multiples, at least not legitimately, since African buyers wanted only cloths of the functionally useful standard lengths and had no precedent or need to calculate in divisible abstract units of measure like the ells or fathoms in which European cloth wholesalers might deal. Hence, proliferating physical components of the "price" of slaves reflected long-run changes in terms of trade as they accumulated out of shorter-term price adjustments, rather than modulations of standardized abstract equivalents like a currency.

In a system based on use-values rather than on currency equivalents, short-term price negotiations took place as bargaining over the extent to which the goods and captives actually offered approximated the abstract standards of the ideal equivalency.[47] The use-value of the ideal standard *peça* slave was clear: the laboring capacity of a healthy, strong adult male. The inferred original African standard for a "piece" of cloth would have been bodily covering for a person of noble rank, though it gradually depreciated to become clothing—even a loincloth—suited to ordinary in-

46. Thus the multiple "piece" prices found on the Loango coast, as opposed to retention of a unitary "bundle" (of multiplying contents) at Luanda; cf. Martin, *External Trade*, pp. 107–11, and further discussion in Miller, "Slave Prices."

47. Ferreira, *memória*, 26 June 1762, AHU, Angola cx. 29, and all records of actual slave transactions. The Angolan trade did not differ in this respect from slaving anywhere else in West Africa; for a recent, clear, and documented description for the Gold Coast, see George Metcalf, "Gold, Assortments, and the Trade Ounce: Fante Merchants and the Problem of Supply and Demand in the 1770s," *Journal of African History* 28, no. 1 (1987): 39.

dividuals. By that standard, several of the highly varied textiles that Europeans offered in African markets could be fundamentally interchangeable, depending on fashion. The variation that the Europeans saw—usually based on physical or financial aspects of the cloth itself and on production techniques, quality, sources of supply, and especially currency costs—seldom approximated the use-valuations that Africans perceived. Thus, African consumers might treat fabrics of distinct costs, origins, durabilities, or weights as equally suitable for the standard wearer of cloth, while singling out a single color or pattern from a range Europeans regarded as insignificantly differentiated as denoting distinctive status, and thus not at all equivalent to others that Europeans placed in the same class.

Portuguese and other traders on the coast, fully immersed in the currency values of a capitalist world economy, seldom arrived in Angola with much appreciation of African unconcern for their textiles' abstract monetary equivalents or for the African vision of an exchange-ratio "price" as a set of physically defined components. They accepted but seldom grasped why they could buy slaves only for complex, seemingly arbitrary, and unalterably specific assortments of wares hard to assemble and impossible to keep in balance in that remote corner of the world economy. The Europeans saw minor African increases or decreases in price as incomprehensible substitutions of one good for another, perhaps of no significant difference in money cost price but evidently critically distinguished in terms of the uses to which Africans put them. Slave sellers could not be persuaded to substitute one pattern for another and would walk hundreds of kilometers to obtain an item available on one part of the coast but not along portions of it much closer to home.

African methods of varying exchange ratios in terms of physical quantities and qualities, grouped according to their uses in consumption or in attracting followers, were only the most superficial implication of increasing rates of exchange of people against imports, though the one most visible, and frustrating, to Europeans. In a political economy like that of western central Africa, based on production for use and on aggregating followers, the introduction of material goods had profound implications beyond the senses of ethnic community that formed by the eighteenth century, as wealthy importers transformed the new goods into abstract human obligations.[48] Quantities of imports, huge by African standards, introduced into such an environment could not help but inflate dependency, and that in turn had further consequences that touched all participants in the African commerce in goods and people as it became reoriented toward the Angolan trade in slaves.

48. Janzen, *Lemba*, pp. 37–38, grasps the extent to which ethnic identity itself became a product of the exchange circuits along which the vast quantities of imports moved. See also Vansina, *Tio Kingdom*, pp. 306–7.

3

Foreign Imports and Their Uses in the Political Economy of Western Central Africa

Western central Africans, from their earliest contacts with the Atlantic economy in the fifteenth century, seemed to exhibit unquenchable thirsts for foreign imports. By the eighteenth century they still seemed ready to buy as many European, Asian, and American goods as, and at times more goods than, their means of payment allowed. The desire to satisfy these ambitions arose from the contradictions in the political economies of their lands, and the opportunity to invest allowed them to alter politics and economics in ways that left locally powerful groups heavily dependent for their prestige on closer integration with a changing world economy. Leaving aside for the moment the fact that slaves paid much of the intercontinental debt that such purchases created abroad, within Africa imports themselves allowed the primary historical changes associated with contact with European merchant capitalism.

From the point of view of the men struggling to improve their positions in the competitive networks of hierarchy and wealth of eighteenth-century western central Africa, imported wares brought unprecedented opportunities to scramble up a rung or two on the local ladders of prestige and obligation.[1] The textiles, alcohol, and weapons—which together accounted for three-fourths of the European values of the imported goods—possessed advantages over the competing products of local industry principally in securing the rights over dependents that everyone sought to create. Insofar as luxury consumption items also figured in the import ledgers, the initial rarity and later the variety of certain goods added to their convertibility into capital stocks of human dependents. More important, imports of any sort came in huge quantities, on easy credit terms, and from outside the established networks of prestations and politics. They thus attracted ambitious upstarts, men marginal to the regional trade systems that had previously been the primary routes to wealth and power, and allowed them to get ahead in the game of people and products. Imports, in short, made it easier to attract followers. The irony, and the

---

1. See Hoover, "Seduction of Ruwej," p. 346, for this emphasis for the Lunda.

tragedy, was that many of these new men found it possible in the long run to maintain access to the goods that gave the power they had won only by sacrificing the very dependents they had set out to keep.

Although one cannot appreciate the motivations of the Africans who invested in foreign imports by examining their strategies exclusively in terms of productive efficiency, any more than viewing them solely in Western materialist terms as consumers tells the entire story, many imports were in fact also productive in this narrow economic sense. The initial imports filtering inland from the coast stimulated material production for local and regional exchanges, though usually by intensifying existing technologies, and in the longer term Africans concentrated their imports in items arguably productive by the human standards of their own political economies. It is unlikely that local artisanal or industrial output fell in western central Africa in the period before 1830, though that was not the only point that would have assumed significance in a political economy centered more on people than on products.

The ideological effects of buying extensively from the Atlantic were, as the peculiarities of trade in western central Africa suggest, far from overwhelming—an extension of exchange theories already emerging from the underlying political economy of use-values to cover practices in the new commercial sphere. The demographic consequences of paying for the imports with people, it will be shown, were rather more profound for populations in Africa, though still less than the increased political stratification and not of a magnitude to compare with the personal sufferings of the enslaved.

The key exchanges of goods for slaves along African shores, or at inland extensions of the coastal marketplaces, thus make it difficult to sustain any simple judgment on their consequences for "economic development" in Africa. Because they brought together African, Euro-African, and European merchants from vastly different political economies, the direct participants could all gain from their dealings with the others. The Europeans concentrated on earning returns in specie they could earn from selling slave labor in the Americas above the currency costs of the goods they sold, and they hardly bothered to notice the rather different values, in terms of human followings, that the same goods brought to their customers in Africa. The distinct calculations of value rendered the inequality of the exchange irrelevant to the traders, since the relationship was also in fact one of complementarity, in which both parties to the exchange gained from it in their own terms, in contrasting ways that a single shared standard of value would not have permitted.

On the other hand, complementing interests across the divide between the Atlantic and the African systems allowed neither Europeans nor Africans to escape from the zero-sum constraints of exchange within their respective political economies, where everyone competed in terms of similar priorities. The traders on the African side displaced the costs of their exchanges of goods for people to others who had less direct contact with the import-export interface of the two economies. Farmers fell subject, often as slaves, to newly powerful kings in Africa. The zero-sum calculus on the side of the African political economy also turned on gains in adherents made at the expense of depleting the followings of local rivals. Though the livestock of the herders and the alternative commercial opportunities open to fishermen on the Zaire significantly lessened their need for imported goods to accomplish similar ends, new products from abroad gave such enormous advantages to their recipients in the agricultural zones that the inflows there drove competitors of those first to receive these products to copy the same policies. The quest for imports, once begun, thus tended to gain uncontrollable momentum in these areas, and the rate of importing, while not destroying local production, created a kind of political dependence on foreign trade. It accelerated to the benefit of a few African masters and merchant princes, at the expense of reducing many people to resettlement and dependency in Africa and of sending thousands of others each year to death or to enslavement in the Americas.

The Import Ledger

From the Kunene in the south to the equatorial ports of Loango, ships of the Portuguese, Dutch, British, French, and Brazilians combined to discharge similarly balanced ranges of imports. Their cargoes reflected relatively constant African consumer and investment preferences that arose from widespread features of their political economy of goods and people. Contrary to the misimpressions of critics in Europe, who caricatured African demand mostly from hearsay, worthless knickknacks and gewgaws made up only a small portion of the bundles and boxes hoisted over the gunwales of vessels anchored along the western central African coastline. Rather, deckhands and stevedores wrestled mostly bales packed with textiles of every variety, European and Asian, into lighters and onto the beaches. Throughout the entire history of slaving these long bolts and shorter cuts of cloth gave considerable substance to the traders' manner of calculating slave prices in the "pieces" of woven goods changing hands.[2]

2. Details in Joseph C. Miller, "Imports at Luanda, Angola: 1785–1823," in Gerhard Liesegang, Helma Pasch, and Adam Jones, eds., *Figuring African Trade: Proceedings of the Symposium on the Quantification and Structure of the Import and Export and Long-Distance Trade of Africa in the Nineteenth Century (c. 1800–1913) (St. Augustin, 3–6 January 1983)*, Kölner Beiträge zur Afrikanistik, no. 11 (Berlin: Dietrich Reimer Verlag, 1986), and in idem, "Capitalism and Slaving: The Financial and Commercial Organization of the Angolan Slave Trade, According to the Accounts of António Coelho Guerreiro (1684–1692)," *International Journal of African Historical Studies* 17, no. 1 (1984): 1–56.

Among the textiles, cottons—originally from Asia but later copied in Portugal and by the 1810s overwhelmingly British imitations of the Asian prototypes—predominated in quantity and diversity. Their types and sources in China and India varied from decade to decade with the vicissitudes of remote European warfare and politics, but the general category of cotton goods never lost its central place in the trade, probably amounting to a third or more of the total by European currency values and to much more by the African use-value. The Asian goods ranged from fine, expensive weaves with threads of gold or silver to coarse stuffs for sacking or for slaves' or common laborers' loincloths. The mainstays of the selection were plain, dyed, lightweight cottons; but woven patterns— mostly blue-and-white and red-and-white striped goods and checked ginghams, and small-patterned printed calicoes and chintzes—were other long-term staples. Among the plain fabrics, indigo-dyed blues were prominent, but strong reds, greens, and other colors, especially yellows, would fill out a well-diversified selection. Although some of the basic types endured throughout the eighteenth century, others changed constantly and were sought mainly for their novelty. Overall, the variety of color and pattern obtainable from Asian weavers and dyers was probably the most attractive feature of these fabrics.

European textiles came in similar, if less spectacular, diversity. They tended to center more than their Asian counterparts on a relatively few basic weaves, mostly British light woolens or their Continental imitations. The standard cloth of this category was a plain-finished wool baize, light in weight compared to counterparts intended for sale in chilly northern Europe, and sold in a range of solid dark colors, usually reds, blues, and greens. Patterned weaves—twilled druggets and others—offered limited variation on the basic fabric. Other parts of northern Europe, particularly Brittany, contributed linens and, later from northern Germany, linen imitations; and captains of different nationalities competed for distinctiveness with their own country's regional specialties in wool, linen, or blends of the two. Silks, both woven patterns and printed, arrived in lesser, though still significant, quantities. Altogether, at a guess, European woolens, linens, and blends before the nineteenth century accounted for a third of the value of the cottons from Asia. Both categories, European and Asian, represented half or more of the total value stowed in the holds of the ships reaching western central Africa.[3]

3. Martin, *External Trade*, pp. 112–13, put the proportion of "Asian" textiles alone on French ships at Loango at 75%–80% in the 1750s–60s. For the (later) French trade in general, David Eltis, draft appendix on mortality to *Economic Growth and the Ending of the Transatlantic Slave Trade* (New York: Oxford University Press, 1987), puts the percentage of all textiles at around 55%; Marion Johnson, "To Barter for Slaves" (unpublished paper), shows the British trade in general running between 60% and 70% textiles (by value) throughout the eighteenth century (with India goods accounting for about 85% of the volume

As crews cleared the ships' holds of these fabrics, they turned next to bulky casks, or "pipes," of 500 liters' capacity, filled with spirits or wine. The exact character of the booze unloaded depended on the Europeans' varying techniques of fermentation and distillation, from grapes, grain, sugarcane, or potatoes. Whether Portuguese wine or Brazilian rum, it usually arrived in forty or fifty or more of those huge casks on a ship, each weighing two-thirds to three-quarters of a metric ton.[4] French brandies, other wines, Dutch gin, and the like could flow from smaller barrels and flasks. Altogether, the range of liquid intoxicants accounted for a large minority of the ships' cargoes. It was the second most significant general category, perhaps 20 percent by Portuguese valuation at Luanda between 1784 and 1823, and not greatly different elsewhere.[5]

Crates of muskets and kegs of powder came in a strong third at not much more than 10 percent only along the Loango coast, particularly from British ships calling there.[6] Guns may have assumed a comparable impor-

---

before 1750 but only 44.4% after that date); also Marion Johnson, "The Atlantic Slave Trade and the Economy of West Africa," in Roger Anstey and P.E.H. Hair, eds., *Liverpool, the African Slave Trade, and Abolition* (Liverpool: Historic Society of Lancashire and Cheshire, 1976), pp. 14–38. David Richardson, "West African Consumption Patterns and Their Influence in the Eighteenth-Century English Slave Trade," in Henry A. Gemery and Jan S. Hogendorn, eds., *The Uncommon Market: Essays in the Economic History of the Atlantic Slave Trade* (New York: Academic Press, 1979), esp. table 12.2, pp. 312–15, suggests that textiles comprised an unusually large percentage of shipments to central (as opposed to western) Africa.

4. For the Portuguese, a *pipa*, of varying actual sizes but usually defined in Angola as consisting of 300–360 *canadas* (a small unit of liquid measure equal to about 1 2/3 liters), 6 *barris* (barrels, each of 50 or so *canadas*), 120 *garrafas* (each of about 3 *canadas*), or 20–25 *almudes* (a widely varying abstract measure of ca. 20 liters). The *canada* could be further subdivided into 4 *quartilhos* (not much smaller than the English pint). For sources: letter from Sousa Coutinho, 21 Aug. 1770, AHU, Angola cx. 32; *auto de dezobediencia* (Senado da Câmara, Luanda), 3 April 1782, AHU, Angola maço 2; "Memoria" on the Kwanza canal, 1816, AHU, Angola cx. 64; Eulalia Maria Lahmeyer Lobo, "Economia do Rio de Janeiro nos séculos XVIII e XIX," in Paulo Neuhaus, ed., *Economia brasileira: uma visão histórica* (Rio de Janeiro: Editora Campus, 1980), p. 153, citing Celso Furtado, *Formação econômica,* pp. 89–92; Peçanha, *relatório,* 27 June 1785, AHU, Angola, cx. 40. Andrew Grant, *History of Brazil* (London: H. Colburn, 1809), p. 169, described the *pipa* standard for tax purposes in early-nineteenth-century Rio de Janeiro as 180 British gallons, i.e., as rather larger (ca. 50%?) than Portuguese reports.

5. Detailed figures in Miller, "Imports at Luanda." The Portuguese estimated intoxicating beverages at 28.4% by value at Luanda and Benguela in the 1760s: Vellut, "Royaume de Cassange," pp. 133–34.

6. For the British munitions trade, which apparently ran only 10%–20% by value, and in the low end of that range for central Africa (Richardson, "West African Consumption Patterns," pp. 312–15, and Johnson, "To Barter for Slaves"), see W. A. Richards, "The Import of Firearms into West Africa in the Eighteenth Century," *Journal of African History* 21, no. 1 (1980): 43–59, and Joseph E. Inikori, "The Import of Firearms into West Africa, 1750–1807: A Quantitative Analysis," *Journal of African History* 18, no. 3 (1977): 339–68. Martin, *External Trade,* pp. 110–11, emphasizes how important firearms were to negotiations but presents figures suggesting only modest numbers of weapons being sold before the 1720s. Proyart, as translated and quoted in Pinkerton, and reprinted in Elizabeth Donnan,

tance at some times and places among the French off-loading further south, but they never did at the government-supervised Portuguese ports.[7] Portuguese captains directing their cargoes into the storerooms of merchants' houses near Luanda's waterfront had to evade official prohibitions against these weapons and so diverted crates of firearms on small lighters and canoes to hidden bays not far from the port. Powder came more directly off the ships as "rice," "flour," "pepper," or other "dry goods." Merchants concealed both the guns and the powder in private homes and other secret storage places throughout the city.[8]

The remainder of the bales and boxes deposited on beaches up and down the coast, and then lugged on the backs of slave stevedores to storehouses to await prospective buyers, contained often hundreds of additional products, but mostly in small quantities that together amounted to no more than 20 percent of the total. This miscellaneous sample of European technology included hats and other fabricated items of apparel, glassware, metalwares, and, at Luanda, not inconsiderable quantities of the Portuguese delicacies and food specialties that brought the tastes of a distant homeland to nostalgic emigrants living in the city.

For political and economic reasons on the European, supply side of the trade, the availability of particular items in each category of goods varied considerably from one part of the coast to another for African buyers. Textiles from Asia were easiest to find anywhere, since traders could acquire them from any of the three major eighteenth-century suppliers, the British, the French, and the Portuguese.[9] Before 1790, Asian

---

Documents Illustrative of the History of the Slave Trade to America, 4 vols. (Washington: Carnegie Institution of Washington, 1930–35), 2:555, confirms these modest figures for the 1760s–70s. Richards, "Import of Firearms," p. 51, misquotes Proyart in attributing to him the figure of 30 guns per slave, apparently by calculating the full European currency price of the slave in terms of its equivalent in guns. Putting muskets at about 10% of the entire bundle of goods exchanged for a slave, Richards' 30 would approximate the 2 or 3 guns in fact given. Phyllis Martin, "The Trade of Loango in the Seventeenth and Eighteenth Centuries," in Gray and Birmingham, *Pre-Colonial African Trade,* pp. 152–53, raises the calculation to 3 guns per slave.

7. For the French in very general terms, see Robert Stein, *The French Slave Trade in the Eighteenth Century: An Old Regime Business* (Madison: University of Wisconsin Press, 1979), pp. 59, 71–72, 85. The details of a French voyage to Loango in 1702–3 are found in Ferrez, "Diário anônimo de uma viagem," pp. 9–11, and one of 1777 in Debien, "Traite nantaise vue par un Nantais," pp. 206–7. Cf. Martin's conclusions, *External Trade,* pp. 112–13.

8. Câmara, 22 Feb. 1780, AHU, Angola cx. 38; Vasconcelos, 19 May 1759, AHU, Angola cx. 28; Lencastre, *bando* of 18 March 1776, AHU, Angola cx. 37.

9. The Dutch, while participants of major significance along the Loango coast in the seventeenth century and into the 1770s or so, became less prominent after the 1720s and ceased to influence trading patterns; see, e.g., Martin, *External Trade,* p. 86. For overviews, Johannes Postma, "The Dimension of the Dutch Slave Trade from Western Africa," *Journal of African History* 13, no. 2 (1972): 237–48; idem, "The Origin of African Slaves: The Dutch Activities on the Guinea Coast, 1675–1795," in Stanley L. Engerman and Eugene D. Genovese, eds., *Race and Slavery in the Western Hemisphere: Quantitative Studies* (Princeton:

cottons were probably most important to the French, who had the fewest alternatives to offer in the African markets, and who apparently had unsatisfactory domestic imitations of the goods made in India and China.[10] In European textiles, the edge went to the British, who had the most advanced woolen-manufacturing capacity, but northern French ports and even the Portuguese also had domestic looms on which they could draw. But the French and particularly the Portuguese nonetheless reexported British woolens in significant quantities. All three countries had to reexport Belgian and North German linens, and so they could provide these goods on an approximately equal basis. As British textile designers learned to duplicate the Asian cottons in the second half of the eighteenth century, the Portuguese and Brazilians added these goods to the reexports they sent to Africa from Britain.

The British, who held their great advantage in their firearms earlier in the eighteenth century, set most of them ashore directly from British ships anchored off Loango ports. Their "Angola gun," an inexpensive, unproved long-barreled flintlock musket (blunderbuss?), dominated the weapons trade in western central Africa. Though French and Portuguese merchants tried vainly to compete by offering others, even at a loss, from coastal bases further south, Africans in need of firearms had to preserve contacts along the northern parts of the coast to obtain weapons in acceptable quality and quantity.

In alcohol, the Brazilians' cheap, highly alcoholic rum undercut all the wines and other inebriants of Europe. The French offered similarly strong *eau de vie,* and the Portuguese managed to sell brandies and wines from Porto as well as from Madeira, though at notably higher prices and in much more limited quantities. In alcohol, the British, for once at a competitive disadvantage, countered only with expensive reexports of Jamaican rum. Ordinary African drinkers, wherever they lived, acquired purchases of Brazilian rum through Benguela and Luanda.

Though the plethora of other items was distributed comparably from supplier to supplier, none attained much individual significance. Each trader filled out his cargo manifests with miscellaneous manufactured items from suppliers all over Europe: glass beads from Venice, or their Dutch imitations; Indian Ocean shells reexported through London or Amsterdam; steel knives and cutlasses, copper pans and basins from northern Germany; and much else besides.[11]

Princeton University Press, 1975), pp. 33–49; and idem, "The Dutch Slave Trade: A Quantitative Assessment," *Revue française d'histoire d'outre-mer* 62, 1–2 (nos. 226–27) (1975): 232–44.

10. Richardson, "West African Consumption Patterns," p. 324; also on textiles in Senegambia, Curtin, *Economic Change,* pp. 312 ff.

11. Martin, *External Trade,* p. 110, introduces the African distinction between "large" goods—cloth, firearms, alcohol—and "small" goods such as these.

African buyers demanded roughly constant proportions of textiles, alcohol, and firearms up and down the coast, no matter where the final consumers lived in relation to the positions of specific European and American suppliers. Thus, British muskets and French brandies off-loaded at Loango only partially satisfied hunters and chiefs in the interior near that part of the coast; buyers there also demanded secondary contacts with traders who could deliver Portuguese gunpowder and Brazilian rum from Luanda or Benguela. The Africans in closest contact with Luanda, where British guns were scarce and expensive, conversely had to keep their commercial relations open also with the Loango coast. South of Luanda, the inability of Portuguese traders to supply firearms left an unmet demand that encouraged French to "smuggle," as frustrated Luanda governors perceived the situation, along a part of the coast where they did not have to confront British superiority in the weapons trade. At Benguela, Brazilians managed to exclude most metropolitan Portuguese sources of Asian textiles and European manufactures, thus leaving the door wide open there for the French to introduce their European glass beads and Asian shells and textiles. The partially specialized European suppliers combined at each point along the coast to fill only part of the complete range of products demanded, and so complex African networks of supply lines crisscrossed the interior to spread the entire spectrum of desired goods from their separate debarkation points at the coast.

African Applications

European and Asian goods acquired general advantages in the eyes of African buyers only partly because of production and transportation technologies beyond the Atlantic that, by 1700 or so, had advanced beyond comparable western central African sectors. If the Europeans could not make products better, at least they could make more of them. European ship and sail design and navigational techniques synthesized from around the Eurasian land mass had created maritime transportation systems that, from the late fifteenth century, inexpensively delivered what they could make to every corner of the globe by sea.[12] At least as important, Europe had also mobilized capital resources capable of financing the great expenses and long-delayed returns from so far-flung and risky a commerce, and even the costs of buying and stocking large quantities of goods. These elementary facts put the growing productive capabilities of eastern and southern Asia, the Mediterranean world, northern Europe, and the slaves

---

12. For a recent global synthesis of this familiar story, see Eric Wolf, *Europe and the People without History* (Berkeley and Los Angeles: University of California Press, 1982).

laboring in the Americas, as well as these continents' reserves of a few raw materials in demand in Africa, for the first time at the service of potential African consumers.

In western central Africa, further, the Europeans encountered little Muslim or Asian mercantile competition. The African regions in and south of the equatorial forest had no significant contact with competing trans-Saharan routes leading from the Mediterranean to northerly parts of the continent nearer the desert. The considerable canoe trade of the forested zone of West Africa only peripherally touched the coast north of the Zaire. Asian wares long available on Africa's eastern Indian Ocean coast occasionally filtered as far as the center of the continent, but only in highly attenuated streams that did not begin to have the effects of the much more plentiful goods that appeared on the Atlantic side. The efficiency of the Europeans in assembling and delivering cloth, intoxicants, items of personal adornment, and—by the end of the seventeenth century—firearms in modest quantities, and their ignorance of the returns in dependency that these goods gave to African buyers, meant that they could and would offer the wares on terms superior to the local alternatives. In other products in which local industry retained technological or price advantage—especially ironworking in western central Africa, but also tobacco, dyestuffs, and foods—the Africans bought very little from Europeans. In every case, the capital resources of the European suppliers, especially the British, made the imports available on easy terms to African buyers unwilling, and sometimes unable, to resist the opportunities that they seemed to promise for getting ahead.

Apparel constituted western central Africa's greatest single under-developed technology relative to its population's needs and desires. Irrelevant questions of Victorian modesty aside, few highland central Africans knew the consistently warm climate that European visitors, confined to the often steamy coasts and debilitated by the diseases endemic there, generalized to the entire continent and used to explain both the occasional nakedness and what they regarded as the indolence of its natives.[13] The higher elevations of the mountains and the Kasai plains sometimes experienced frost in the dry season,[14] and the nights and the rainy season then surely, as now, brought uncomfortably cool temperatures everywhere outside the forests near the equator. Only near the equator did the insulating blanket of foliage maintain the closest approximation to the con-

13. In general, Philip D. Curtin, *The Image of Africa: British Ideas and Action, 1780–1850* (Madison: University of Wisconsin Press, 1964); specifically for the Portuguese at Luanda, José Pinto de Azeredo, *Ensaios sobre algumas enfermidades d'Angola* (Lisbon: Regia Oficina Typografica, 1799), pp. 46–47 et passim.

14. "Derrota de Benguella," in Felner, *Angola,* 2:25. Cf. Childs, *Umbundu Kinship and Character,* p. 54.

tinuously comfortable tropical temperatures that Europeans imagined. Much more important than physical comfort were the aesthetic effects attainable from bodily adornment and the ability of clothing to designate personal rank in a highly status-conscious society that used material symbols to express status.

It was the ability rather than the desire to clothe that was lacking. Domestic goats in most areas offered a limited capacity to produce skins for needed cover. Trade with cattle herders in the pastoral zones of the south, or with hunters in the game-rich woodlands, similarly satisfied only a small proportion of the widespread demand for skins, hides, and leathers. Local bark pounded to spread its fibers out thinly and give it pliability and woven raffia cloth squares available through trade from the palm belt fringing the forests added modest quantities of textiles of vegetable origin, but all of these together hardly came near meeting the sheer material demand for warmth and prestige. Nor did many dyestuffs achieve the clarity of hue known in Europe and Asia. Instead, the scarcity of bodily coverings, especially of the rarer skins and the more finely made raffia squares, available only through trade, as opposed to inferior home-grown substitutes, meant that such products confirmed the importance of attire as a mark of wealth and power more than they contributed to physical comfort.

Even in their coarsest forms products of northern European and Asian looms offered covering to people who had little, and in their finer manifestations, they added brighter colors, novelty, and especially the availability achieved only rarely by African technologies and methods of distribution. Wealthy princes bedecked themselves and their retainers in the finest and most stylish fabrics obtainable, with scarlet silks occupying a favored position, displayed their countenances beneath broad-brimmed hats, and had themselves transported from place to place in palanquins lined with fine taffetas.[15] Lesser dignitaries wrapped themselves in lengths of imported

15. For Kasanje in the 1750s, Dias, ed. (Leitão), "Viagem a Cassange," pp. 16, 18. Paulo Martins Pinheiro de Lacerda, "Noticia da campanha, e paiz do Mosul, que conquistou o Sargento Mór Paulo Martins Pinheiro de Lacerda, no anno de 1790, até principio do anno de 1791," *Annaes marítimos e coloniaes* (parte não oficial), sér. 6, no. 4 (1846): 131, so describes the audience chamber of a petty chief near the coast. Capt. William F. Owen, *Narrative of Voyages to Explore the Shores of Africa, Arabia, and Madagascar* (London: Richard Bentley, 1833), 2:296, reports "native grass-cloth" from the interior still used to clothe slaves and "for common purposes" at Cabinda in the 1820s. Unlike the much more developed West African weaving industry, which continued to supply fine textiles, leaving the cheap mass consumption goods to the European sources, imported goods seem to have redirected local cloth production to the far interior by the early eighteenth century; cf. Marion Johnson, "Technology, Competition, and African Crafts," in Clive Dewey and A. G. Hopkins, eds., *The Imperial Impact: Studies in the Economic History of Africa and India* (London: Athlone Press, 1978), pp. 259–69; also Vansina, *Children of Woot*, pp. 189–94, for regional trade in raffia cloths centering on the Kuba. Tams, *Visit to the Portuguese Possessions*, 2:136, reported that even the slave-trading areas of Matamba (Jinga) and Kasanje were known in the 1840s for their "manufacture of woven articles of clothing, mats, and baskets."

cottons in all their lively colors and patterns, competing with one another to set the fashions that others might follow. Ordinary people made do with whatever coarse woolens or flimsy cottons they could acquire, and the lowly—the newest slaves and the impoverished—contented themselves with squares of unbleached burlap worn as loincloths drawn between the legs and knotted in front. In the longer run, imported textiles covered common folk with quantities of stuffs that only the wealthiest and most powerful had once worn, and the wealthy kept ahead of the generally rising standards of sartorial display by adding length upon length of foreign fabric to their costume until they could hardly move about.[16]

In the more commercialized areas, imported cloth became not only an item of consumption in the narrow sense but also, because of its value, a means of storing wealth, whether piled in the storerooms of a rich man's compound or worn around the hips or on the backs of his dependents. It thus became a form of material capital in itself, one that confirmed and generated dependency in the political economy of human followers. The truly rich hoarded stocks of textiles and demonstrated their affluence by distributing lengths of fabrics among their wives and followings. Where cloth was most plentiful, it took on attributes of a specialized currency circulating in the export sector of the economy among those wealthy enough to deal in the substantial values that people and most imported fabrics represented. The "piece" of finely woven India goods, for which Africans would originally give a healthy adult male and which long remained the unit of account in the Atlantic trade, symbolized the intimacy of the connection between cloths and people in the terminological and presumably conceptual equivalency it established. Squares of other imported textiles about a meter on a side—a "kerchief" known as a *makuta* or a *folhinha* (literally, "a small piece of paper") in Angola—and pieces of two or three meters' length, finished or cut, provided the "small change" of this commodity currency system inserted in the basic exchanges of people in the African political economy.[17]

The origins of the textiles imported into western central Africa, whether British woolens or Indian cottons, and their European currency costs of production mattered less to African buyers than their uses in the interplay of dress and dominance through which they circulated. Since Africans conceptualized value in terms of human uses for goods, as opposed to the Europeans' abstract measures of material dimensions, buyers visualized

16. Owen, *Narrative of Voyages,* 2:283, 293, and Tams, *Visit to the Portuguese Possessions,* 1:121–22, describe male and female basic wraps at the coast. For Lunda, see Hoover, "Seduction of Ruwej," p. 342. Conspicuous consumption of imported cloth was highly developed at Luanda: Magalhães, 29 April 1738, AHU, Angola cx. 22; Peçanha, 20 March 1784, AHU, Angola cx. 39. Harms, *River of Wealth, River of Sorrow,* p. 43, notes that wealthy men were buried in rolls and rolls of imported fabric.

17. These small pieces of cloth are visible as kerchiefs—*panos,* or *paigns* in French—in the import ledgers; see Miller, "Capitalism and Slaving" and "Imports at Luanda."

cloth in units of its immediate usefulness and in terms of its social significance. The original "piece" in the textile currency system, equivalent to the "big bills" of European paper currencies, was a *beirame*, or *birama*, originally a length suitable for wrapping a human form of noble bearing, or about five meters, but less thereafter as imported cloths came to cover common shapes as well.[18] Since a cloth of this length greatly surpassed local equivalents in size and function, it understandably became the early standard by which Africans sold people for imported goods. The European woolens became blanketlike wraps, cloaks by day and bedding by night. The "smaller change" of cuts similar in sizes to local raffia squares or bark cloths become wrappings for the head or, if more coarsely woven, *tangas* or loincloths for a servant or a slave.[19] Like palm cloths of similar dimensions, several of them could be sewed together to make full waistcloths. Great quantities of such cloth squares entered western central Africa in the eighteenth century.

Given the considerable significance that Africans placed on apparel and adornment as signifiers of rank, intensified beyond the parallel functions of European fashion by more explicit emphasis on hierarchy and by fewer alternative means of expressing superiority, they developed variation in color, texture, and pattern of the imported cloths as ends in themselves.[20] The wealthy and powerful sought constantly to corner the circulation of novelties that conferred status because of their rarity and to make them private marks of their personal distinction.[21] But success in making them so inevitably spread such innovations widely, since the owners of a new style had to distribute it among their followers to create the dependence that they sought, and competitors could imitate the trend with goods from alternative sources of supply. Spreading circulation soon devalued the new goods' prestige, and they lost some, or even most, of their social value. Rejection of these outmoded patterns or colors then followed as suddenly and absolutely as hemlines now rise and fall in Europe or the United States, regardless of the goods' remaining functional value as bodily cov-

18. Taunay, *Subsídios,* pp. 135, 140–41, noted a length of 5 *varas* (5.5 meters) in 1668; "Capitulaçoens" (of D. Veronica of Matamba), 24 Nov. 1684, AHU, Angola cx. 10, notes still 5 *varas*; but Custódio Simões da Silva, 26 June 1762, AHU, Angola cx. 24, notes only 3 *covados* (or less than 2 meters, calculated from the *folhinha* in de Mello, 21 May 1801, AHU, Angola cx. 50). Cf. Martin, *External Trade,* p. 107, who finds the "piece" at Loango remained constant at 6 yards (i.e., 5 *varas*) until at least 1873.

19. Martin, *External Trade,* p. 106, has the *makuta* at Loango equivalent to 2 meters.

20. Portuguese sumptuary laws of the same period, which severely restricted the right of wearing elaborate garb and jewelry, expressed a close European equivalent of these African concerns with status and its signifiers; see Mattoso, *Etre esclave au Brésil,* p. 253; *parecer* of the Conselho Ultramarino (Lisbon), 12 May 1741, AHU, Angola cx. 22.

21. Cf. the theory of "primitive rationing," developed by Mary Douglas, "Primitive Rationing: A Study in Controlled Exchange," in Raymond Firth, ed., *Themes in Economic Anthropology* (London: Tavistock, 1967), pp. 119–47.

ering. The almost infinite modifications that European and Asian weavers could work from cotton, wool, linen, silks, and metallic threads lent the imported textiles the distinctiveness that local weavers achieved with pattern and texture in their own cloths. Basic plain dyed goods suitable for lowly dependents were significantly more plentiful, if not always more durable, than their African predecessors.

Alcohol, the second largest category of African imports, allowed prodigiously increased consumption of the psychoactive substances that intensified communication with the spiritual component of power in Africa. Intoxicants also carried strong connotations of status in the political economy of goods and people, confirming the mundane prestige of those able to distribute them liberally among dependents and guests.[22] Beyond the local mood-altering "weed," *hamba* or *dihamba*,[23] wealthy lords in the wetter regions maintained groves of palms from which they drew sap that fermented rapidly into wine.[24] Residents of the wooded uplands prepared mead from the honey they collected from the hives of wild bees, and farmers in the drier zones brewed millet beers.[25] The imported distillates contained a much higher alcoholic content than these fermented local alternatives and were often sharp in taste, which African drinkers took as a sign of strength and quality.

At a rough correlation of ten slaves exported per *pipa* of imported Brazilian rum, and allowing the 50 percent slave mortality between sale of the alcohol in the interior and embarkation at the coast to offset consumption in the taverns of the coast towns, by pilferage from the caravans, and for other purposes not productive of slaves, a chief would have received two or three of the large *garrafas,* or demijohns, in which traders carried the booze for each dependent he sold. These would have approximated twelve to fifteen liters, or a case and a half of the 750-milliliter bottles

22. E.g., reports of the great drunkenness of the Kasanje kings in Vellut, "Royaume de Cassange," p. 124. See also the general symbolism in Luc de Heusch, *Le roi ivre (ou l'origine de l'état)* (Paris: Gallimard, 1972), and the comment in Jan Vansina, "Equatorial Africa and Angola: Migrations and the Emergence of the First States," in D. T. Niane, ed., *Africa from the Twelfth to the Sixteenth Century,* vol. 4 of *General History of Africa* (Paris: UNESCO, 1984), p. 558.

23. Brian M. du Toit, "Man and Cannabis in Africa: A Study of Diffusion," *African Economic History* 1 (1976): 17–35, seems to vacillate on the probable antiquity of cannabis in western central Africa; cf. pp. 24–25 and 28. António de Saldanha da Gama, *Memoria historica e politica sobre o commércio da escravatura entregue no dia 2 de Novembro de 1816 ao Conde Capo d'Istria ministro do Imperador da Russia* (Lisbon: Imprensa Nacional, 1880), p. 73, seems to assume that the plant was widespread early in the nineteenth century and notes that a European plantation had attained some success with commercial production of it in 1803.

24. For early references, Gastão Sousa Dias, *Relações de Angola* (Coimbra: Imprensa da Universidade, 1934), pp. 58–59, 154, 179.

25. Vansina, *Tio Kingdom,* pp. 151, 279, mentions other possibilities, nearly all based on crops spreading with the slave trade: sugarcane wine, cassava wine, maize beer, etc.

standard in the sale of modern spirits, though watering probably raised the quantity by 50 percent while reducing its proof. At an assumed rate of two cases per slave, if Africans drank the same daily one-pint ration allowed sailors in the Royal Navy, sale of a slave would enable a chief to drink alone for three to four weeks, to share a pint with one honored guest per day for less than two weeks, or to lavish the entire proceeds on a one-time gathering of two dozen followers. By this hypothetical projection from estimated imports, serious politicians could entertain entirely with foreign liquors only by selling about 400 or more slaves per year and leaving everyone else in their realms to support a thriving industry in local intoxicants.[26]

Increased quantities of European brandies and American rums at first enhanced the powers of lords and elders to contact ancestors or other spirits they engaged on behalf of the communities they represented. Later, these beverages presumably helped the new men grown wealthy by trade to imitate the supernatural abilities of their predecessors. It made little sense to trade without also drinking and distributing alcohol in the large quantities commensurate with their status. By the nineteenth century, still greater quantities of imported inebriants had cheapened these beliefs, noble in their origins and acceptable then for the selectivity of their application, into the valueless dependence into which the fallen heirs of these men sank, left behind by further economic and political changes as the stereotyped drunken sots, sitting alone in their deserted compounds and condemned by temperate Victorians. Nobles who had managed human relations with other-worldly forces had lost out to successors possessing more mundane contacts with guns and in the trade of later eras. In the meanwhile, pipe after pipe of rum, *eau de vie,* and brandy, their sharp taste sometimes enhanced by the addition of hot American peppers, had burned the throats of African men who thus ardently aspired to greatness. Lesser folk, cast off from changing societies and abandoned to humble lives in the towns of the Europeans, concealed their failures by mimicking the drinking habits of their superiors in taverns in the seaports.[27]

26. E.g., a gift of two *ancoretas* of sugarcane brandy, in letter to Dom Hui a Quissua Quiateca, Soba Ndalla Quissua, Manoel Bernardo Vidal, 13 July 1838, AHA, códice 101, fols. 48–48v. For equivalencies, see note 4 above. The mortality estimate is rationalized in Joseph C. Miller, "Mortality in the Atlantic Slave Trade: Statistical Evidence on Causality," *Journal of Interdisciplinary History* 11, no. 3 (1981): 385–434. For more on the rum-slaves ratio, see Miller, "Overcrowded and Undernourished: The Techniques and Consequences of Tight-Packing in the Portuguese Southern Atlantic Slave Trade" (paper presented to the Colloque International sur la Traite des Noirs, Nantes, 1985). The assumed (minimalist) entertainment standard is the sale of 15 slaves for continual inebriation of a chief, the sale of 15 slaves for one guest per day, and the sale of 12 slaves for one assembly per month, converted to total slaves sold at the 20% proportion of rum to all goods imported (and used to buy slaves), assuming redistribution of half the proceeds.

27. The *tavernas* of Luanda, not untypical of seaports anywhere in the world, were a constant theme in descriptions of the city; e.g., Azeredo, *Ensaios sobre algumas enfermidades;*

Hardwares of all kinds formed less significant components of the western central African import ledger than did the bars of iron important in Africa north of the equator, where they became the basis of a trading currency known as the "bar."[28] Central African sales of cross-shaped copper ingots and rings (termed "bracelets") made the region a net exporter of metal on balance. Although Africans south of the Zaire River mouth sold only small quantities of iron to Europeans, they seldom bought raw iron ingots. Iron seems to have found somewhat greater acceptance at more northerly ports, particularly toward the end of the eighteenth century, when the trade routes inland from Loango began to supply the middle reaches of the great river. The clayey soils of the central equatorial basin may have been less abundantly endowed with iron than the southern uplands, even though the high quality of the iron smelted at the high temperatures attainable in that area from forest hardwood charcoals still kept reliance on imports there to a minimum.[29]

Prior to the late eighteenth century, only a limited range of finished metal products found widespread acceptance, particularly bush knives, and secondarily cutlasses and swords, of the finest Dutch and North German makers. These imported blades may not have kept their edges longer than the best steels from the forest, but they must have been better than much local iron, less expensive to buy, and more plentiful from relatively early times in the trade.[30] Fishhooks figured prominently in the goods entering through the port at Luanda, probably for similar reasons of superiority over the local bone equivalents. Brass pans and vessels, not alloyed from the African copper, which was mostly cast into rings and drawn into wire,

---

Corrêa, *Historia de Angola,* 2:168; Conde de Lavradio to Diogo de Mendonça Corte Real, 6 Aug. 1752, AHU, Angola cx. 25; Vasconcelos *bando,* 30 Oct. 1759, AHU, Angola cx. 28; Luiz da Motta Feo e Torres (governor, Angola), 7 Sept. 1816, AHU, Angola cx. 67.

28. Especially in Senegambia; see Curtin, *Economic Change,* pp. 312–14, and Johnson, "Economy of West Africa." Africans had imported iron bars there since the sixteenth century; see John Vogt, *Portuguese Rule on the Gold Coast, 1489–1682* (Athens: University of Georgia Press, 1979), pp. 60–70, for the Gold Coast.

29. Vansina, *Tio Kingdom,* pp. 140–41, 272–73, 442–43, 465. Smelting of the metal had been a key attribute of the early political authorities in the region, the famous "smith-kings" of Kongo and adjoining regions. The list of "Fazendas q são precisas pᵃ compra dos escravos nesta costa" (i.e., Cabinda), n.d. (but ca. 1770), AHU, Angola cx. 38, specified iron bars. Debien, "Traite nantaise vue par un Nantais," p. 207, also mentions them at Cabinda in 1765. Harms, *River of Wealth, River of Sorrow,* p. 46, says that imported iron ruined Tsaayi producers (living well west of the Zaire River, near the coast) by 1800. On the other hand, K. G. Davies, *The Royal African Company* (London: Longmans Green, 1957), p. 234, found that the RAC iron trade included "none at all" to Angola (meaning the Loango coast area).

30. These metal products were near-constants of the import lists from the seventeenth century onwards; see Miller, "Capitalism and Slaving," for the 1680s–90s, and later lists reproduced in Miller, "Imports at Luanda." Vansina, *Tio Kingdom,* p. 266, notes the presence of ironwares, e.g., knives, but also the absence of iron bars. On earlier African smelting and forging of relatively soft irons south of the forests, Maestri Filho, *Agricultura africana,* pp. 57–60, and sources cited there.

and a few similar items of tin seem to have been preferred over gourds and wooden bowls by those who could afford to import them.[31] Aside from assorted metal items of little significance beyond their novelty, other hardwares in continuing demand included mirrors, which had uses both for grooming and for communication with the spirit worlds they seemed to hold within their frames.[32] Small bells supplemented drums, rattles, and the larger local "bells of kings" as noisemaking instruments of magical efficacy, and others helped hunters keep track of the belled dogs they sent searching through the bush.[33]

Finally, marine shells from the coasts of Brazil and from the Indian Ocean and beads from around the Mediterranean and from Amsterdam added color or varied shape to the available selection of local mollusks, beads of ostrich shell, carved bone, and other decorative and valuable items.[34] In general, all of these imports supplemented older domestic equivalents, and they no more replaced the prestige accorded the original items than trendy plastic furniture substitutes for an heirloom oak chest today. In fact, as in the modern analogy, the spread of inexpensive substitutes for the masses may have stimulated demand among the wealthy for the authentic local equivalents. The African ancien régime there, too, surely never confused the ostentatious display of imported novelties, acquired by exchange, with the genuine products of a personal entourage of craftsmen and craftswomen.[35]

Muskets, gunpowder, and lead for shot transformed the political economy of goods and people somewhat more profoundly by putting previously undreamt-of power in the hands of a few armed individuals, particularly ones who would have had little claim to such eminence according to the older standards of kinship, rainmaking skills, or personal following. The Africans' notion that the ashes of the bones of people sent off as slaves to Mwene Puto's Land of the Dead returned as gunpowder gave chillingly direct expression to the efficacy of exchanging a single unskilled youth for weapons that, properly lodged in the hands of a trained marksman, could

31. Ferrez, "Diário anônimo de uma viagem," p. 9; Debien, "Traite nantaise vue par un Nantais," p. 206. But brass and copper items were generally not as prominent as they became in parts of West Africa; cf. Curtin, *Economic Change*, p. 315. For the prestige of copper generally, Herbert, *Red Gold of Africa*.

32. As reported for the Kwango valley, at least, by Sousa Kalunga, interview 10 Sept. 1969. Cf. de Mello, 21 Oct. 1801, AHU, Angola cx. 50, who confirmed the importance of mirrors in the same area a century and a half earlier. Vansina, *Tio Kingdom*, p. 270, mentions them in passing.

33. Jan Vansina, "The Bells of Kings," *Journal of African History* 10, no. 2 (1969): 187–97.

34. Miller, "Capitalism and Slaving" and "Imports at Luanda, Angola."

35. Cf. Harms, *River of Wealth, River of Sorrow*, pp. 45–47, for a parallel formal economic argument applied to the forest; also arguments made for local iron in West Africa by L. M. Pole, "Decline or Survival? Iron Production in West Africa from the Seventeenth to the Twentieth Centuries," *Journal of African History* 23, no. 4 (1982): 503–13.

intimidate hundreds of subjects and dependents. In a direct sense, the gun interposed European technology between rulers and their subjects. It transferred real power from kings exalted for the numbers of people they commanded to the hands of upstarts, poor in followers, who sold the masses of adherents of the older rulers for European firearms. Guns made these new men into a distinct genre of warlords who typically thrived by preying on the large populations of the settled valleys from fortified rocky heights or dense woods. More than any other category of import, muskets undermined the humane political economy of western central Africa by rendering large, loyal followings of people superfluous to the exercise of power. Henceforth small bands of armed brigands could rule.

On the other hand, the revolutionary effects of guns should not be overestimated. The physical ability of the guns to mete out death and destruction was seldom greater than the magical powers they gave their owners to command the respect and loyalty of armies still composed mostly of spearmen and archers in the eighteenth century.[36] African lords armed and trained small corps of musketeers to supplement the large numbers of conventionally armed warriors of the sort that powerful kings had always had massed in western central African warfare. For kings who ruled through the supernatural powers that their subjects attributed to them—omniscience, the knack of calling the rains, and especially the ability to empower the weapons that their followers wielded—firearms became an extension of the rulers' supernatural powers, a means of attracting forces in numbers sufficient to overpower opponents in the conventional manner and of instilling in them the morale that enabled them to cow enemies by intimidation at the outset of massed confrontations.[37] The symbolic single volley that began battles of this sort could matter more than all the stones, iron slag, and lead shot fired in the course of ensuing struggles actually conducted mostly with bows, spears, and daggers. The gun became a bond linking liege to lord, not unlike the mystical union of medieval knights to their kings.[38] European weapons, adorned and decorated for their magical as well as their chemical charges, need not have been fired with accuracy

36. For the seventeenth century, John K. Thornton, "The Art of War in Angola, 1575–1680" (unpublished paper, Carter G. Woodson Institute, University of Virginia, 1984).

37. The importance of the implications of "ritual" as the equivalent of modern technology is developed in Randall M. Packard, *Chiefship and Cosmology: An Historical Study of Political Competition* (Bloomington: Indiana University Press, 1981). See Raymundo José da Cunha Matos, *Compêndio histórico das possessões portuguesas na África* (Rio de Janeiro: Arquivo Nacional, 1963), p. 247, for the late eighteenth and early nineteenth centuries in Angola.

38. For eighteenth-century warfare, see Corrêa, *Historia de Angola*, 2:48–61 et passim, for the same structure of Portuguese government armies in Angola. Harms, *River of Wealth, River of Sorrow*, pp. 44–45, confirms for the forest; also see Cordell, *Dar Al-Kuti*, p. 109. In general, Gerald M. Berg, "The Sacred Musket: Tactics, Technology, and Power in Eighteenth-Century Madagascar," *Comparative Studies in Society and History* 27, no. 2 (1985): 261–79.

to achieve effects comparable to the legendary knives and spears wielded by the African kings of old.[39] Even in Kasanje, the premier slave-selling state of the middle Kwango valley, which was in touch with British sources of firearms at the Loango coast and notoriously well armed by local standards, the reportedly huge army of the king still preferred to fight with bows, arrows, spears, and swords of local manufacture in the 1750s.[40] The Lunda, perhaps the most militaristic of central African polities, had no significant quantities of firearms as late as the latter part of the nineteenth century. They fought only with daggers and spears, forging the barrels of enemy muskets they captured in their wars into the bladed weapons they preferred.[41] The gun, too, thus became a part of the African political economy in which force, like power, was exercised through people.

Northern European armorers developed cheap, if unreliable, flintlock muskets in the latter half of the seventeenth century. The subsequent perfection of techniques of producing these plausible imitations of working weapons added significant quantities of firearms to African arsenals just after the turn of the eighteenth century.[42] The British "Angola gun" then became an essential component of every transaction negotiated along the Loango coast north of the mouth of the Zaire River, and not long afterwards British arms dealers developed alternative outlets for the same guns through Lisbon to Luanda.[43] Only a small percentage of these weapons survived the first few attempts to fire them, and a good many were unusable from the start. An official check of the trade guns stocked in Luanda in 1759 revealed that 200 of the 4,000 on hand, or only 5 percent, met the government's standards of military reliability.[44]

39. See also the fame of the Lunda sacred *mukwale* knife: Miller, *Kings and Kinsmen,* p. 139.

40. E.g., Dias, ed. (Leitão), "Viagem a Cassange," pp. 18, 25.

41. Hoover, "Seduction of Ruwej," p. 342, n. 31; Dias, ed. (Leitão), "Viagem a Cassange," p. 25.

42. Richards, "Import of Firearms." Cf. the rising concern of Portuguese officials at Luanda in the 1720s, as British suppliers began to deliver substantial quantities of guns and powder to Loango: (copy) *provizão* of 17 Oct. 1724, AHU, Angola cx. 16; Francisco Pereira da Costa (*provedor da Fazenda*), 7 April 1727, AHU, Angola cx. 17; cf. Birmingham, *Trade and Conquest in Angola,* p. 140. Guns had earlier been introduced by the Dutch from the 1620s and 1630s but only in small numbers; see Wilson, "Kongo Kingdom," pp. 84, 170–71, citing prohibition of imports by the Portuguese (Fajardo, in Brásio, *Monumenta missionaria africana,* 7:210); Thornton, *Kongo Kingdom,* pp. 42, 75–76; Heintze, "Ende des unabhängigen Staates Ndongo," p. 199. Modern assertions that Africans earlier possessed firearms "in abundance" (e.g., Vellut, "Relations internationales," pp. 92–93, for the 1680s) turn out to exaggerate the claims actually made in sources, all of which center on a small palace guard armed with imported weapons surrounded by "innumerable bowmen and spearmen" (Cadornega, *História geral,* 3:216).

43. Inikori, "Import of Firearms," pp. 360–61; Richards, "Import of Firearms," p. 44; Martin, *External Trade,* p. 111.

44. Vasconcelos, 19 May 1759, AHU, Angola cx. 28; idem, 26 April 1762, AHU, Angola cx. 29.

Such deficiencies by European standards of lethality seem not to have greatly dampened African enthusiasm for firearms that also served, with different effect, as ceremonial tokens of homage, power, and obligation. As the Africans employed the weapons, noise and smoke, in which eighteenth-century muskets were far from wanting, were as efficacious as accuracy. The use-value of the product in the hands of the African consumer, too, mattered little to coastal purveyors of the guns, who acquired them only for their further value in exchange. It may be argued with some force that gunrunners had every reason to peddle worthless muskets to customers who otherwise might have turned superior weapons against their suppliers and who might then have to buy fewer replacements. If the warlord owners of the guns were held responsible for their magical functioning in the hands of their men, no one could have blamed the sellers for the instruments' failings.

For hunting, especially for hunters who were also smithies and able to repair or improve the faulty mechanisms they bought from the coast, functioning guns must have assumed a growing importance in the production of food.[45] Though the utility of imported firearms in this respect is disputed in the Portuguese evidence on the uses of European munitions in Africa, interested parties on both sides acknowledged the centrality of the issue. The chief defenders of the gun trade in Angola—self-serving metropolitan arms dealers and proponents of eighteenth-century programs to promote industrialization in Portugal through domestic powder manufacturies—of course consistently claimed that their customers employed the weapons mostly in pursuit of game and not against other people, whether their local enemies, villages they raided for slaves, or the Portuguese troops and traders.[46] Competing local merchants, who bought weapons through British smugglers, usually raised alarms about attacks from armed African enemies to limit imports of the Lisbon guns[47] but sometimes admitted as much as well.[48] To the extent that European demand for ivory increased African hunting for elephant, guns surely assumed some significance, if, again, only in the hands of specialized hunters trained in their use and maintenance, since local methods of trapping and killing the beasts were notably inferior.[49]

45. See Janzen, *Lemba*, p. 28, for the hinterland of the Loango Coast. Tams, *Visit to the Portuguese Possessions*, 1:136–37, says that as late as the 1840s Africans used guns mainly for ivory hunting and that people near Benguela remained quite independent of imports for most weapons (bows, arrows, spears, javelins, etc.).

46. Manoel da Silva *requerimento*, n.d. (ca. 1778), AHU, Angola maço 17 (D.O); Moçâmedes *apontamentos* (notes) (ca. 1784), AHU, Angola maço 2–A. For further notes on guns and powder at Luanda, see Miller, "Imports at Luanda," and Chapters 16–18 below.

47. E.g., Lencastre, 9 Oct. 1779, AHU, Angola cx. 37; *instruções* to Gov. Lencastre, n.d. (ca. 1772), AHU, Angola maço 11; Manoel da Silva *requerimento*, n.d. (ca. 1784), AHU, Angola maço 17 (D.O.).

48. Oeyras *parecer*, 21 Nov. 1760, AHU, Angola cx. 28.

49. Martin, *External Trade*, p. 111.

Although firearms had thus become as vital to western central African life by the middle of the eighteenth century as had textiles, if only in limited ways, they probably circulated far less widely. At Loango, where a single gun and the powder to fire it had become essential to the purchase of a slave early in the century, the full price that the buyer paid still included a large assortment of other goods, mainly textiles. Later in the century, still only two guns figured in the computation of the cost of a slave there, or about 10 percent of the full price by European currency values.[50]

The dispute at Luanda between metropolitan merchants hoping to push guns and powder from Portugal and local traders with ostensible interests in excluding them to preserve the security of the trading routes provides an even lower estimate of the volume of the gun trade south of the Zaire. In the 1760s, a proposed compromise between the two contending groups of traders put the level of imports capable of allowing metropolitan gun dealers to compete with British firearms coming in through Loango while not disrupting the tranquility of the colonial interior at 1,500 guns per year.[51] Adding a generous estimate for smuggling at three or four times that number would still leave actual imports at slightly less than one gun per slave exported. Such a guess would be consistent with reports that the British, then supplying two or three guns per slave, generally gave twice the price in goods that the Portuguese paid for slaves. It would also be plausibly consistent with the 4,000 guns reported stocked in Luanda at that time, thus according merchants the half year's average inventory needed to keep adequate supplies on hand between annual shipments from Lisbon. These converging indications of actual imports of guns through Luanda would put the figure at 6,000 to 7,000 per year in the last half of the eighteenth century. Almost certainly, far fewer had arrived in preceding decades. The unknown quantities of firearms the French also sold south of Luanda for awhile in the 1760s and 1770s probably never approached those of the British at Loango.[52]

The official government records of firearms imports at Luanda, which must have missed a significant portion of the contraband guns, run plausibly less than this estimate of 6,000 to 7,000 per year. Between 1785 and

50. Ibid.

51. *Certidão*, 12 Dec. 1767, AHU, Angola cx. 31.

52. The case is circumstantial but compelling. Corrêa, *Historia de Angola*, 2:36–37, places the French near the mouth of the Kuvo at the time, and other sources link foreign gunrunners with the contemporaneous bellicosity of Mbailundu kings in the central highlands that led to a major confrontation between government troops and the highland lords in the "Bailundo war" of 1774–76; see, e.g., Lencastre, 1 June 1776, in Candido de Almeida Sandoval, "Noticia do sertão do Balundo (1837)," *Annaes do Conselho Ultramarino* (parte não oficial), sér. 1 (1858), pp. 519–21; see also the oblique allusion in the file on "Extinção do Prezidio das Pedras," n.d. (ca. 1772), AHU, Angola cx. 37, which misleadingly and quite improbably attributes the arms supplies to British sources to the north, at the mouths of the Bengo and Dande rivers.

1794, approximately 40,000 guns passed legally through the rather loose customs inspections then in effect at the Luanda port, or an average of less than 4,000 per year.[53] Only 2,838 firearms arrived in the following three years, from 1795 to 1797, or less than 1,000 per year on the average; and about the same low rate of imports still obtained in 1823.[54]

Combining these scattered indications from Loango, Luanda, and beyond yields a generous estimate of the average number of guns brought in all along the coast at 60,000 per year, roughly twice the number of the slaves exported at the peak of the trade at the end of the eighteenth century.[55] In earlier decades, and after 1810 or so, the totals were rather less.

With similarly generous methods of estimation, one-third of those guns may have proved more than minimally serviceable in the hands of African musketeers, for an average useful life of about a year. Under tropical conditions of maintenance and taking account of irregularities in the supply of gunpowder and deterioration of stocks on hand, perhaps 20,000 guns were functioning at any one time. This number would have left less than 1 percent of the two to four million adult males in the region who were in touch with the Atlantic trade able to raise an operable weapon on any given day.[56] The brief useful life of these trade muskets—not widespread arming of the population—necessitated the continuous rearmament that made African traders so insistent on obtaining more weapons. Real militarization and disruption spawned directly by imported firearms awaited improvements in the guns sold to Africans later in the nineteenth century.[57]

53. "Balanço da importação e exportação deste Reino de Angola desde o anno de 1785, em que teve principio o estabelecimento da alfandega, até o anno de 1794, inclusive," IHGB, lata 77, no. 1.

54. "Balanço da importação e exportação deste Reino de Angola nos annos de 1795, 1796, 1797," BNRJ, 13–3–33. See also T. Edward Bowdich, *An Account of the Discoveries of the Portuguese in the Interior of Angola and Mozambique* (London: J. Booth, 1824), p. 151, who has Lisbon exports for 1803 at 2,159 muskets, or 1.8% of total value of exports. For the figures by value in the early nineteenth century, see Miller, "Imports at Luanda"; some have been excerpted in Manoel dos Anjos da Silva Rebelo, *Relações entre Angola e Brasil (1808–1830)* (Lisbon: Agência Geral do Ultramar, 1970), quadro 5, which gives 1,088 "armas sortidas."

55. Cf. Martin, "Trade of Loango," p. 153, who guesses at 50,000 guns per year for the Loango Coast alone in the late eighteenth century. Ferreira, 25 June 1762, AHU, Angola cx. 29, put the figure at 30,000 in about 1760. Vansina, *Tio Kingdom*, p. 448, n. 23, is properly suspicious of the 50,000 figure.

56. Compare the numbers of handguns alone in the United States, ca. 1980, estimated at "tens of millions" (*U.S. News and World Report*, 22 Dec. 1980, p. 23), which would put the proportion of these weapons, taking no account of long-barreled hunting guns or military hardware, several times higher at least. The annual production and import of civilian firearms in the U.S. ran at 5 to 6 million in the 1970s (*Statistical Abstract of the United States*, 1981 ed., p. 830), or more than 20 per 1,000 residents of the nation, compared to late-eighteenth-century western central African imports in the range of 3–6 per 1,000.

57. Lacerda, "Noticia da campanha," pp. 130–31, describes the entire Kongo area north of Luanda—in the 1790s long reliant on British trade—as only partially armed with muskets (on one occasion, without powder) but generally reliant on precisely the weapons reported

In the eighteenth century, Africans preferred the weak domestic Portuguese gunpowder above the more powerful British product because it wrought less damage to the shoddy guns in which they discharged it and because it killed fewer of its users, or at least so its proponents claimed.[58]

Stocks of firearms, even if not held widely throughout western central Africa, could have had greater effects than their overall scarcity would imply.[59] Allowing for concentrations of half the estimated arsenal of 20,000 functioning weapons in the hands of trained musketeers stationed around the defensive stockades of a relatively few warlords, 1,000 guns each would have serviced only five or so of the greatest warlords. Alternatively, they might have supported one hundred or so commanders of less well-armed forces bearing 100 guns each. The actual circumstances of the eighteenth century might plausibly have included fifty or so primary concentrations of firearms, in forces numbering somewhere between the extremes of these hypothetical cases. Each would then have had to have used the guns to intimidate 200,000 people spread over domains averaging about 140 kilometers on a side, or with radii of 75 kilometers, plausibly within the range of a day's forced march. It need not have taken many guns, particularly when employed in conjunction with more conventional weaponry, to produce a pervasive atmosphere of danger in limited areas, particularly the main slaving trails, where European visitors, against whom such violence was often selectively directed and who left the only direct testimony to the circumstances, passed.[60]

This qualified evaluation of the eighteenth-century arms race in western central Africa is consistent with the general picture of huge masses of conscripted nonprofessional bowmen and spear-throwers employed for offensive military operations, who literally protected small standing armies

----

from the seventeenth century: machetes, sharp stabbing spears, and shields that did not resist gunshot. The inhabitants also relied on a woman priest, who assured an army about to face the Portuguese that her charms had coverted the European firepower into water. Susan Herlin Broadhead, "Luso-Kongolese Armed Conflict in Northern Angola: An Historical Perspective," *Etudes d'histoire africaine* (forthcoming), cites a missionary report that Kongo guns had "only two or three charges each" in 1793.

58. Merchants' petition of 20 Jan. 1803, in Francisco Infante de Sequeira e Correa da Silva (governor, Benguela), 9 March 1803, AHU, Angola cx. 54. Martin, *External Trade*, p. 111, notes the same preference on the Loango Coast. Raymond Kea, "Firearms and Warfare on the Gold and Slave Coasts from the Sixteenth to the Nineteenth Centuries," *Journal of African History* 12, no. 2 (1971): 204–5, notes similar African demand for powder with low saltpeter content.

59. Cf. the trenchant observation of Jean Suret-Canale, "Refléxions sur quelques problèmes d'histoire de l'Afrique," *La Pensée*, no. 212 (May 1980): 110–11, that the surprising feature of the munitions trade to Africa was not how many guns were imported but how much damage was done with the few that were.

60. Though the reports of violence tended to concentrate in periods of distress from drought; see, for examples, Mesquita, 20 July 1781, AHU, Angola cx. 38; Corrêa, *Historia de Angola*.

of elite troops with muskets (and, in the case of the Portuguese, often also the artillery) at the center of the army. Reasonable estimates of African armed forces at the time, taking the reported adult male populations as men available for military service, run higher than the numbers of guns available to them by a factor of twenty or more. Compared to a rough mean of perhaps 250 functioning guns in the magazines of the more powerful lords, the Ndembu lords Mbwila and Mbwela, probably among the best-armed warlords of the region, in 1755 could call out an estimated 5,000 men-at-arms, who must therefore have included a vast majority trained to fight with bladed hand weapons.[61] Powerful kings in the highlands east of Benguela were said to mobilize 10,000 to 12,000 men during a period of great drought and distress in 1792.[62] The largest Kikongo-speaking principalities along the coast north of Luanda mustered military forces of an estimated 30,000 (Sonyo) to 40,000 (Loango) men in the 1780s. An exceptionally powerful *mani* Kongo, D. José I, could call out about 30,000 partisans in 1781. Kakongo and Ngoyo could each raise about 12,000 men, Musulu 10,000, and the smaller remaining states only some 2,000 to 2,500.[63] In the 1750s, the king at Kasanje was reported, rather less plausibly, to be able to field 120,000 men of his own and to have the power to summon another 235,000 allies in time of need.[64] Allowing the obviously exaggerated estimate for Kasanje to stand for the collective forces of all other firearms-importers for whom there are no estimates and combining the reports on other Kongo and Ovimbundu forces, a generous guess could put roughly 300,000 men available for military service to the major polities of the region.[65] Arsenals of guns estimated to total 10,000 would not have put muskets in the hands of 4 percent of that number.

However rare and ineffective firearms may have been in eighteenth-century western central Africa, they were still the "very soul of commerce" in the exchange of people for goods with the Europeans.[66] No Africans dealing with the foreigners could pass up the opportunity to acquire a gun and a supply of powder, and Africans would refuse all other wares and withdraw from negotiations if the assortment of goods offered lacked these essential components. But their significance as instruments of death

61. *Parecer* of the Conselho Ultramarino (Lisbon), 7 May 1755, AHU, Angola cx. 26.
62. Vasconcelos, 17 March 1792, AHU, Angola cx. 42.
63. Souza Magalhães report, 16 March 1790, AHU, Angola cx. 37; Broadhead, "Luso-Kongolese Armed Conflict," MS p. 6.
64. Dias, ed. (Leitão), "Viagem a Cassange," p. 18, implying a population in the central valley of over 500,000, with another 1.1 million in the immediate surrounding areas, even at normal population distributions (age/sex), and perhaps twice as much if the probable preponderance of women in the overall population is taken into account.
65. Thus ca. 10% of the region's total adult male population.
66. Ferreira, 26 June 1762, AHU, Angola cx. 29.

and warfare is less certain than the strong African demand for them might make them appear. They may have been as directly productive of elephant ivory as of human captives. Guards of caravans carrying imports or accompanying slave coffles down to the coast may have protected their human property with them as much as brigands used them to steal people.[67] Kings of refugee states may have used guns as often to protect their subjects as to lead them in retaliatory raids. Even monarchs committed to the slave trade for the revenues of their court, like those in Kasanje, may have used guns to defend their subjects while drawing slaves from them by other, peaceful, means, as much or more than they employed their guns in slave-hunting expeditions around the fringes of their domains. The "guns-slaves cycle" in western central Africa was a much more complicated affair than the sheer unbridled violence sometimes inferred from the data on imports.[68]

Dependency, "Development," and Structural Change

Though firearms, liquor, and textiles thus had discernible applications for western central Africans as items of consumption and even for production in the narrow economic sense, their greater appeal lay in the crucial gains they gave their possessors in converting material goods into the fundamental values of the African political economy, into dependents and dependency. Beyond the obvious coercive potential of muskets and the political prestige of strong drink, the sheer circulation of imports of any sort nurtured social and political stratification in Africa. Goods from the Atlantic accelerated the rates at which the powerful dislocated the weak and at which people of all sorts were uprooted from their home communities and moved to those of new lords or masters, from villages to kings' courts, from old patrons to new patrons, or from lineage leaders to merchants. In the time-conscious societies of western central Africa, where antiquity meant prestige and power brought seniority, these displacements and reintegrations weakened the growing majority of the newcomers and consolidated the dominance of the few earlier arrivals at the tops of the hierarchies.

Increasing stratification manifested itself principally in the spread of enslavement in Africa and in a greater degree of disability brought by the condition of slavery. Kings used imports to buy captives rather than to honor the lords of their realms, and the goods allowed monarchs to build up larger retinues of slave retainers, more isolated and more dependent than had been the wives and pages, sisters and sons of their own subjects,

---

67. E.g., the famous government elite troops armed with guns, the *empacasseiros* or "buffalo hunters."
68. See Chapters 4 and 5, following.

whom they had previously assembled only on more limited terms of reciprocity and indenture. Ordinary farmers borrowed material goods and bought slave wives from strangers rather than exchanging sisters and nieces with their nearby affines as spouses, and the women from far away they took in as slaves lacked the protection and refuge that accessible and loyal kin guaranteed to women from neighboring communities. Creditors in the credit-scarce economy of use-values had once exercised only limited rights over the "pawns" whom they took as pledges against debts that their neighbors owed them, but more goods and greater indebtedness shaded those mild relationships into the absolute authority of a harsh master over a slave abandoned by her kinsmen.

Since the hardships of the African assimilative slave systems fell most heavily on recent arrivals, the increased velocity with which slaves circulated as the flows of material goods intensified meant that slave dependents moved more frequently and spent greater portions of their lives beginning over and over again as helpless, culturally disabled aliens in a succession of new communities. Whether males at the royal courts, or young women in rural villages, such new slaves were subject to greater demands from their masters to work harder. To the extent that their masters took up less laborious pursuits or that the growing merchant sector of the economy provided opportunities to sell local food and craft products, the slave artisans and fieldhands who produced them came under pressures to make continuous contributions of material products rather than only to accord the abstract right to such occasional labor time as masters might demand in some indefinite future. Adding the obligation to work longer and harder to the dishonor and subordination of enslavement multiplied the burdens imposed on the expanding numbers of people in this humble position. Even the institution of slavery itself changed to accent its assimilative aspects, since the speed with which masters allowed bought slaves and their descendants gradually to become members of the new community came mostly from the ease and frequency of replacing them with debased successors.

The kings, of course, often gained first from the opportunity to convert imports into dependent followers in these ways. Among the primary responsibilities generally conceded to African superiors was mediation of relationships between the subordinate members of the community and all beings from outside it, divided only indistinctly, by Western standards at least, into the categories of strangers and spirits that modern ethnography has contrasted so strongly. For example, every indication from the early contacts between the Portuguese messengers of Mwene Puto and the Kongo, the western central Africans who first received the outsiders in the 1480s along the banks of the lower Zaire River, suggests the supernatural aura the foreigners carried and the consequent propriety, if not prudence, of directing them to their chief priest and lord protector, the *mani* Kongo.[69] The reasons behind the eagerness of the kings' welcome lay in the fragility of the political institutions they nominally headed. Kings of those savannas—even those, like the *mani* Kongo and the "Great Makoko" of the Tio in control of Malebo Pool, who used commercial flows through their domains to set themselves most effectively apart from the agricultural bases on which most, still weaker, western central African political authorities rose—stood only precariously above the regional gentry of their realms.[70] The provincial rulers had larger followings and greater wealth in people than did kings, whose power rested only on the attenuated early exchanges of material goods.[71]

Such direct influence as these trader-kings could achieve depended on their ability to assemble court entourages, not always of slave origins, through the exchange of their commodity assets for the people of their nominal subordinates. From the point of view of an early-sixteenth-century *mani* Kongo, the exotic European wares offered an enormous opportunity to shift the political balance within his kingdom in favor of his court, since these wares added extremely rare goods, lacked the political encumbrances of tribute collected from reluctant subjects, and were available in quantities vastly greater than the local products that such kings usually offered as largesse to the regional and village potentates who repaid these gifts with wives, court attendants, slaves, and provisions for the royal compound.

Trade goods also aided lineage leaders and land-holding patrons in building clienteles of their own. A monopoly over the fertility and the reproductive capabilities of female kin and affines formed the essential strength of these minor gentry but also imposed strict limitations on their ability to enlarge the communities around them. Infants died at high rates, clients fled, and women spaced and aborted their pregnancies. The minor

69. Rather than extend an already lengthy presentation with detailed documentation of my interpretation of the much-debated history of Kongo, I refer readers generally to the work of Wyatt MacGaffey, conveniently listed recently in *Modern Kongo Prophets: Religion in a Plural Society* (Bloomington: Indiana University Press, 1983); to Kajsa Ekholm, *Power and Prestige: The Rise and Fall of the Old Kongo Kingdom* (Uppsala: Skriv Service AG, 1972), and "External Exchange and the Transformation of Central African Social Systems," in Jonathan Friedman and Michael J. Rowlands, eds., *The Evolution of Social Systems* (Pittsburgh: University of Pittsburgh Press, 1978), pp. 115–36; and to the several studies, listed in previous notes, by John Thornton and Anne (Wilson) Hilton. The interpretation is my own, based on tendencies evident throughout western central Africa, and the Kongo material is offered more as illustration of a generalized process than as detailed proof of the circumstances in Kongo.

70. Vansina, *Tio Kingdom*, pp. 442–45, emphasizing copper.

71. This model seems to fit the earliest recoverable periods in both the Kwango valley and the Angolan central highlands: Miller, *Kings and Kinsmen* and "Central and Southern Angola." For Kongo, Wilson, "Kongo Kingdom," chap. 1, is best. Also see John K. Thornton, "The Kingdom of Kongo, ca. 1390–1680: The Development of an African Social Formation," *Cahiers d'études africaines* 22, 3–4 (nos. 87–88) (1982): 325–42.

gentry also controlled only restricted amounts of good land that they might offer to attract new clients without undertaking land-grabs that engendered conflict with their neighbors. Heads of such farming communities who got access to trade goods could find these goods a bonanza permitting accumulation of greatly increased numbers of dependents through trade and allowing them to encroach with impunity on the lands of their neighbors. They could buy slaves faster than their women could or would bear children by themselves, and the clients to whom they distributed other imports would endure greater degrees of subservience than young relatives or affines had to accept.

If imported silks, cottons, or firearms in part reinforced the established wealth and authority of kings and elders, they held even stronger attractions for men outside the existing circuits of goods and obligation. Locally dominant monopolists who distributed the limited output of African brewers, weavers, and artisans could not compete with the plenty in which new men could obtain Mwene Puto's rum, mirrors, and woolens by trade and with them create competing networks of human dependency. Former underlings of any sort could benefit from independent contact with the merchants and could turn up in any societal context: minor lineages that expanded at the expense of larger ones, warlords surrounded by slaves and gunmen who threatened older communities of farmers, provincial lords who challenged old royalty, or new groups of merchants with contacts at the coast who intruded with their imports on the less well-financed specialists in the regional trade. In these cases, though the enormous volume in which the imports arrived helped to support the upstarts, the critical boost came from the willingness and ability of the foreigners to sell to persons of no social standing or creditworthiness, and to cover such hard-up customers' inability to provide immediate payment for goods by delaying a settlement of debts for long enough that even the obscure could get both feet positioned firmly on the local ladders of status and power. A subtle evolution is detectable from the earliest trade, African-financed for the most part and therefore conducted by established authorities of substantial means, to later importing, pushed by European lenders through the eager hands of obscure figures aiming to ride borrowed goods to positions of eminence and respect. People of less exalted status, who stood little chance of acquiring dependents through exchanges of the tightly controlled local tokens, could thus subjugate their superiors by importing goods even faster than they could pay for them.

The fact that the agents of Mwene Puto would deal on such generous terms and would do it with anyone was only the first of several features of buying imports from the Atlantic that was distinctively attractive to beginners. The liberal credit represented a pure windfall in African terms of respect and duty, since it came from nearly powerless traders, usually so distant from their own overlords and sponsors in Europe and so few that they could demand no bonds of dependency analogous to the great homage imposed by local creditors, lords, and patrons. Only in the immediate vicinity of Portuguese Angola did the king in Lisbon aspire to a more formal sort of vassalage, accompanied by respect for his Christian god, and by a limited political fealty.[72]

But even there, the obligation imposed by the Portuguese in practice hardly exceeded equivalent duties customary in the western central African political economy. African kings rendered a great deal of lip service to Lisbon, contributed warriors of their own to the military campaigns of the Angolan Portuguese, and, somewhat more reluctantly, sent human dependents to Portuguese governors at Luanda in exchange for material wealth they expected, and usually received, in return from abroad. Kasanje kings, for example, for all their disputes with individual foreign traders at their courts, petitioned the Luanda governors for representatives of the Crown "to dominate them."[73] And for good reason, since the commercial disputes arose from Portuguese inability to collect the undelivered slaves that Kasanje kings owed them for goods received: Kasanje protestations of fealty could partially cover the outstanding debt. In effect, the evident relationship of the Kasanje kings to their Portuguese overlords exactly duplicated the indefinite obligation at the heart of African political ties to send dependents one day, as needed. African lords nominally tributary to the Angola colony generally remained in perpetual debt to the foreigners, accepting loans of trade goods in the spirit of largesse, and regarding their unpaid obligations as tokens of a continuing clientship to not entirely unwelcome distant patrons.

Further, foreign traders worked exclusively in the exchange sphere and demanded no loyalty at all comparable to those sought by African superiors bargaining their goods for respect. The strangers' willingness to terminate a potentially hierarchical relationship with an equalizing transfer of even the lowliest dependent, some relatively valueless individual unwanted by his neighbors and certainly not the sort of client on whom one would choose to build local prestige, made transactions with such people extremely cheap in terms of the currencies of obligation that African buyers sought to accumulate. Everyone preferred discharging a debt with sale of a slave over the alternatives, political clientage or lineage juniority, since it displaced the subordination incurred from receiving material goods onto

---

72. For details, since early in the history of the Portuguese conquests, Beatrix Heintze, "Der portugiesisch-afrikanische Vasallenvertrag in Angola im 17. Jahrhundert," *Paideuma* 25 (1979): 195–223, or idem, "The Angolan Vassal Tributes of the Seventeenth Century," *Revista de história económica e social* 6 (1980): 57–78.

73. Fran⁰⁰ Jozé Franco (escrivão das Terras de Cassangi), 25 Aug. 1739, AHU, Angola, cx. 21; and the tone of much later correspondence.

a third party. The "buyer" of goods discharged his debt to the "seller" by putting the onus of hierarchy implicit in the transaction onto a third party, the slave. To the extent that such slaves were finally exported out of Africa, the relatively egalitarian and individualistic relationships of an exchange-based political economy built up in Africa, while abject dependency accumulated in America, were borne entirely by the slaves.

Best of all from the point of view of the lineages, the foreigners would supply valuable trade goods in exchange for males, who performed only secondary functions in the essential reproduction of dependents. The males' primary contribution to the agricultural regime was in clearing land for the women to cultivate, but the bush knives prominent in import ledgers all along the coast must have enhanced the effectiveness of the men in Africa who remained at this task.[74] Goods obtainable for a young male could buy a slave wife capable, in time, of bearing children who would more than replace the youth lost. The long-run reproductive potential of the women, even discounted for infant mortality, was worth more than an exposed and vulnerable young man on hand, particularly when the threat of famine hung over the land. The logic of this trade-off carried the African politicians' risk-averting strategies of preferring abstract obligation over active subjects into the realm of human fertility. To the extent that elders and patrons could retain the women that material goods enabled them to acquire, they had improved the efficiency with which their community could grow through human reproduction, precisely the sphere in which lay their primary sources of autonomy, and still supply clients to the overlords or traders through whom they received their goods. Dependent junior kinsmen subjected to these pressures found relief by taking imported goods themselves, investing them in slave women, and thus bypassing the long delay before the elders would negotiate a wife or before one's descendants might reproduce followers.

All these attractive aspects applied most forcefully to agricultural economies based on hoe cultivation and lacking the mechanical advantages of the ox-drawn plough. Livestock breeders and fishermen had relatively less to gain from imported material wealth as a new means of achieving the old ends of accumulating followings.[75] Cattle already enabled the herders

74. Broadhead, "Slave Wives, Free Sisters," pp. 160–81, explores some of the economic implications of the selective export of males, including the replacement of male weaving skills with imported textiles. I would place the emphasis on the efficiency of imported bush knives in the hands of the remaining males rather than emphasizing the imports of iron or hoes as she does, for which I find little evidence. In any case, the significant aspect of the transaction was the female reproductive capacity retained rather than the economic productivity of tools or techniques.

75. Also emphasized by Steven Feierman, "Political Culture and Political Economy in Early East Africa," in Philip D. Curtin et al., *African History* (Boston: Little, Brown, 1978), p. 174.

of the south to broker their political and labor relations through livestock loans, and their herds had the ability to multiply faster than people reproduced, thus allowing successful herd owners to convert them into power and prestige. The relative availability and cheapness of hides for clothing and the disadvantages of trying to integrate bulky, if durable, imported goods into pastoral lives keyed on frequent movement further diminished the utility of goods from the Atlantic. The herders turned to imports, particularly guns, only much later, when improved European weapons and rising nineteenth-century opportunities for exporting hides and beef made firearms an efficient means of generating both more cattle by raiding and more dependents by redistributing the cattle seized. The herders' fundamental disinterest in building up large stocks of imported goods, other than beads and small luxuries, and later guns, was matched on the side of the foreign traders by the inefficiency of trying to build up markets among sparse desert-side populations of mobile and martial people.

Imported goods presented similarly fewer new opportunities to the fishers and transporters of the great equatorial river system and to many of the forest people as well. Canoes, nets, dams, sun-dried or smoked fish, traps, and commercial inventories of other goods gave the fishing and trading peoples of the river material capital to attract many of the clients and slaves they might need without embracing the new commercial wares from the Atlantic. At modest levels of volume, the new goods mostly supplemented established trades in local products, and the buyers could draw on their existing commercial contacts to supply ivory or other commodities to pay for the foreign luxuries they might require without resorting to debt or having to sell dependents.[76] Precedents involving material goods of local origin presumably existed also among the farmers, where marriage-exchange circuits may already have incorporated exotic goods, palm cloths, or copper bracelets in bridewealth payments. Politics, too, surely included largesse distributed in the material form of prestige metals and marine shells. But the commodity component of human relations in the agricultural zone had previously remained relatively more subordinated to direct exchanges of people and loyalties.[77]

Imports, finally, attracted western central African buyers because they permitted capital formation and economic growth at rates exceeding the limited pace at which one could accumulate wealth from local resources. "Credit," or human "capital," was difficult to conceive of in the African political economy, since it would logically have taken the form of voluntary and total subordination in advance of receiving material largesse—that is,

---

76. Vansina, *Tio Kingdom,* pp. 256–57; generally, Harms, *River of Wealth, River of Sorrow.*

77. And significantly less than the much more commercialized economies of contemporaneous West Africa.

precisely the submission that everyone sought to avoid. Overpopulation and droughts could create a certain concentration of human wealth and corresponding political strength of this sort, but the elevated death rates accompanying these sources of dependency retarded accumulation of human capital over the longer run.

Africans concentrated wealth and power not by borrowing but by collaboration among large numbers of small contributors of assets, mobilizing resources collectively but not placing them in the hands of a minority. Segmentary lineages cooperated to attain shared ends, but they never sacrificed their separate identities and formal equality. Rather than maintaining centralized armies, kings raised military forces by inviting local leaders to invest men and materiel in joint expeditions, but they did not merge multiple contingents into a single force. Chain-link trading networks and even diasporas of specialized merchant communities combined the commercial resources of a great number of individual traders. Even caravans, later in the nineteenth century, were composed of multiple small traders who pooled their own goods and efforts for a common mercantile purpose. Production was conducted largely by individual miners or farmers. In the African political economy, people raised "capital" and coordinated their efforts toward the same shared ends that centralized financing accomplishes under modern capitalism but without credit and without separating wealth from its owners.

However, imported goods were more efficient and productive development strategies than reproducing people, if only for the minority able to take advantage of them. Though material production remained technologically limited, when overlords used imported goods to enlarge their followings of increasingly subordinated dependents, they "developed" by expanding productivity, putting the communities of people to work producing more for domestic use, and by consolidating the autonomy of the group—both conventional aims in the African political economy. The general point applied equally to lineage or patron villages, to "states" on a larger scale, and to the slave-staffed "houses" of traders developing trade along the Zaire River. Bringing vast quantities of material imports into the African political economy was analogous to the release of new money into a modern economy based on finance capitalism. More goods supported more exchanges involving more people over greater geographical ranges, and they thus increased dependency in both senses relevant to Africa: assembling more people and working them more intensely. To the extent that slave wives might have been forced to bear more children than women who had local relatives or affines to back up their reluctance to do so, they contributed to political economic growth and to human capital formation in the most direct sense possible in an African political economy, both individually through the children they reared for their husbands and masters and in the aggregate through the renewed pressures that their more numerous progeny collectively placed on the land.

Imported goods also "developed" western central Africa in the distinct structural sense of moving the region a step away from its historic emphasis on production only for domestic use and closer to a political economy including a significant component of material exchanges and of currencies. At a further level of structural change, goods improved access to slaves, who could replace deceased dependents or departed followers, and thus made it cheaper to buy and utilize living labor than to continue to stockpile abstract obligations: direct control over labor began to supplement respect as a central objective of the powerful and wealthy. At still another level, though the imported commodity currencies often promoted old methods of amassing human dependents and seldom became plentiful enough to add wages to the bonds of personal dependence that generally organized work and relations among people, they made much more prominent the material component of such exchanges of people and/or obligation. Imported material capital goods thus added a vital restructuring element of dynamism and growth to a political economy formerly able to expand no faster than its population could grow, which by the eighteenth century had long lingered, with repeatedly fatal consequences, at the ecological limits of its environment and technology.

Imports did not encourage the possible further structural transformation toward wage workers and high-energy technologies precisely because the enslavement and clientage achieved through redistributing new goods so enhanced the old African strategies of amassing human dependents that they reduced incentives to lessen the reliance of basic agricultural and craft sectors on human labor. They thereby eliminated significant tendencies to "develop" in the specifically Western sense of adopting costly, high-energy forms of technology. Technological development along the lines of contemporaneous industrialization in Britain would, in any case, have required capital investments inconceivable from African resources and far in excess also of the modest amounts that European slavers were prepared to provide. Capital equipment would also have carried opportunity costs in Europe much higher than the goods, often otherwise unsalable, actually shipped and would therefore have been impossibly expensive from the African point of view.

Reorganization of the African client and slave labor force as "free" workers paid in currency wages would hardly have increased its mobility compared to the dislocations of enslavement, and further monetization of the economy would have consumed commodity currencies and credit in quantities much greater than those actually available. An inexpensive transportation infrastructure, a vital further precondition of expanding material productivity, likewise lay far beyond the capacity of anyone, European or otherwise, to finance in the eighteenth century, except for the Zaire system, where African rivermen in fact developed a viable transport network from local resources. Many of these conditions of "development" in this industrializing sense still await fulfillment in Africa at the end of the twentieth century, despite substantial commitments of funds and enthusiastic rhetoric devoted to them. The African method of "development" via increased social and political stratification was the logical, lowest-cost strategy of increasing productivity to adopt.

The most important increases in African productivity during the era of import growth, and the major technological transformations in the African political economy, took the form of incorporating new American food crops, principally manioc (cassava) and maize, into the agricultural systems of the area crossed by the slaving trails. These exceptions eloquently demonstrated the general rule that otherwise limited "development" in the technological sense. Manioc and maize were "appropriate" technology in their negligible acquisition cost to farmers, required virtually no long-term capital investment to implement, and fit well into the existing strategy of raising dependents at home, within the autoconsuming communities of western central Africa, since they enabled landowners to feed more people from the same area than the old crops would have supported. It was more than a little ironic that they also nourished children, captives, and slaves to ages at which they could be sold profitably to Europeans. Like the imported trade goods, which arrived in quantities adequate only to expand the exchange sphere but not to support further structural transformations, these food crops added just enough to African agricultural productivity to replace the population lost to slaving, but they did not permit farmers to overcome the nutritional and ecological crises of drought and famine and thus the occasional need to sell people who could not be fed at home. Merchant capitalism brought Africa to an unstable halfway station between its old political economy of use and the more thoroughly monetized exchange economy of the Atlantic.

Conclusion: Disadvantages

Since African technology could not produce the imported goods that became the new media of dependency, the men who rode their contacts with the coast to local power became dependent on the Atlantic economy to retain the respect they had gained, at virtually any cost. Most soon found it necessary to supply even highly prized dependents to Mwene Puto, who knew the magic of transforming those African bodies into the exotic commodities his agents returned to sell at Luanda, Loango, or Benguela. The stories circulating about the bones of the vanished Africans yielding the gunpowder of the new trade thus expressed the essence of the fatal and tragic exchange of people for power in a strikingly accurate metaphor, if one innocent of the technological details of the process. And one attained power and personal autonomy from one's neighbors by selling dependents off into the Atlantic trade only at the cost of dependence on remote strangers behind the traders who supplied the imports. But it was an impersonal dependence, and therefore not fully perceived.

The greatest disadvantage, of course, emerges from the point of view of the farmers, women, and others whose humiliation and labor as slaves in Africa sustained processes that appear as "development" when viewed through more abstract optics. The greatest drawbacks of all afflicted the slaves who died along the path on their way down to the coast, or during the Middle Passage, or who survived to endure the suffering that prosperous sellers transferred out of Africa to the mines and plantations of the Americas.

4

The Production of People

Political Consolidation and the Release
of Dependents for Export

Most slaves from western central Africa, and nearly all of them from outside the limited area under direct Portuguese control, reached the coast as by-products of political-economic strategies that African kings and lineage leaders followed to attract dependents. These men distributed imports to build up retinues, not to sell people. The history of how and why these men came also to give up dependents whom all but the most commercialized middlemen traders fundamentally hoped to retain thus posed a deep dilemma. To attain their primary goal of enlarging entourages of clients, subjects, kin, and slaves, leaders had to meet the antithetical necessity of releasing a portion of their hard-won gains in people to the foreigners whose imports made them powerful. It was these reluctantly conceded dependents who became the slaves of the Atlantic trade.

African producers of slaves calculated the advantages they gained from goods-people exchanges of this sort in terms of the number of dependents who remained with them and the degree of their dependency. Their human "profits" corresponded to the "retained (cash) earnings" of the modern firm's balance sheet, or to positive balances of international trade flows calculated in currencies in national income accounts, and they accordingly represented the increase in the productive capital of an African political economy based primarily on the strength of the human hand and back. Two distinct sets of "terms of trade," neither precisely quantifiable from the evidence at hand, determined the final profitability to African producers whose by-products finally became prisoners of the Europeans: first, and the subject of this chapter, the rate of return in new dependents from imports they deployed among lineage elders or anyone else with people, and second, the quantity of imported goods obtained from traders for a given individual released into Atlantic slaving.

With respect to the first set of terms of trade, imported goods had a high initial efficiency in generating dependency in Africa, but their value almost inevitably declined through time, since the very profitability of the first exchanges encouraged further imports in such large quantities that goods became common and lost much of their value. The struggles of thousands of individuals in varying social, political, economic, and historical circumstances to protect the gains they made from those highly profitable initial contacts, to maximize the numbers and vulnerability of the dependents each could claim for himself, resulted in the wars, the new social and political formations, and the intra-African population movements, as well as all the people exported as slaves, of the eighteenth-century production of dependents in western central Africa.

The First Imports and Commodity Exports

This outpouring of western central African slaves originated only after the early advantageous terms of trade had made kings, patrons, or elders wealthy in human obligations at home, as they intended, but had then turned against them. The lords, to whom the first foreigners bearing imports directed themselves, initially attempted to discharge the obligation incurred in accepting these goods in wholly conventional ways, by offering members of their personal entourages. They then regularized these contacts by adding prestations of locally produced commodities—usually copper, ivory, wax, and tropical skins and vegetable products.[1] They found the Europeans' wares so exceedingly productive of dependents that they took those goods in quantities beyond what the limited commodity-production capacities of their followers could cover, and then, only after they had expanded trade in goods, and with evident reluctance, began to give up a portion of human wealth they would have preferred to keep to cover the debts they had incurred. Although by the eighteenth century eager, if guarded, welcomes were turning into grudging concessions of human dependents in unrecorded instances far east of the Kwango River, the prototypical shifts from commodity exports to people had followed much-better-known contacts between African political economies near the coast and the commercial economy of the Atlantic in the late fifteenth century. The pattern set by the Kongo kings would continue until the stage of first encounters finally dissipated in the late nineteenth century in the very center of the continent.

It had not taken long for the Kongo kings who received Portuguese emissaries in the 1480s to begin trading along lines that set the initial precedents. These *mani* Kongo, presumably mindful of the implications of hierarchy involved in accepting largesse from the distant European lord who offered the goods, disclaimed theoretical subordination to him but acknowledged the Christian god whom the Portuguese kings claimed to

---

1. Initial contact recorded in detail only for Kongo in 1482–85; e.g., Birmingham, *Trade and Conflict in Angola*, pp. 21–22; also Hilton, *Kingdom of Kongo*, pp. 50–68, esp. p. 57.

serve. They also, logically, tried to incorporate production of things European within their own followings to the point of importing foreign artisans, including priests, who knew how to fabricate the new objects and promised to teach the king's own men the secrets of their crafts. In return, they offered relatives as wards to the Portuguese and supplied commodities from the existing commercial networks they commanded, principally copper but also dyewoods, ivory, and other tropical products rare and valuable in temperate Europe.[2] They deployed the imports and the foreign clients in standard ways to enhance their own power, in part through gifts to the ancient agricultural gentry of their realm, but also through appointed officials of their own, new men who lacked personal followings but who were correspondingly eager to do the king's bidding.[3]

Kongo kings discovered the long-term costs of the expansionary course they had chosen within a generation after accepting the first imports. Segments of the agricultural gentry and their priests and emissaries at the Christian Kongo court resisted the loss of influence over the monarchy that the kings' riches in foreign goods threatened. This resistance forced the kings to intensify their efforts at political centralization, which in turn meant accepting more imports. Already by 1510 or so the *mani* Kongo would no longer provide tropical exotica, minerals, and Christian converts in quantities sufficient to support the political institutions they had created, or to meet their obligations to the Portuguese king, even by attempting to seize direct control of the sources of much of their commodity trade at Malebo Pool.[4]

Almost at once the kings also encountered declining returns in dependents from the exotic goods they distributed throughout their realm. As imports from the court became more common, the high value of the first goods to enter a rural region quickly drained the available populations of troublesome kinsmen and slaves whom village leaders could send off to the court without disrupting local economies and societies. The inelasticity of the supplies of dependents whom elders in agricultural areas could recruit through kinship and alliance forced the ratios at which kings could convert goods into people sharply up. A growing volume of goods thus simply inflated against relatively fixed numbers of the unwanted dependents sent off at the start. As the *mani* Kongo Afonso I wrote to the

2. Wilson, "Kongo Kingdom," pp. 51–52. C. Ivana Elbl, "The Portuguese Trade with West Africa, 1440–1521" (Ph.D. diss., University of Toronto, 1986), pp. 612, 623, and 645, n. 110, documents the same reluctance to part with people in the early phases of Portuguese trading along West African coasts.

3. See the revealing conflict summarized in Vansina, *Kingdoms of the Savanna*, p. 46. Thus the origins of the court-centric aristocracy that Thornton, *Kingdom of Kongo*, pp. 38 ff., describes for the seventeenth century.

4. Wilson, "Kongo Kingdom," p. 56. Note also the longer-term Kongo emphasis on supplying palm cloths, not slaves, to the Portuguese at Luanda.

Portuguese king in 1526, "Formerly we would have given [provincial governors and tributary chiefs] these things [European goods] in order to satisfy them and keep them under our suzerainty and jurisdiction."[5] The result was that the *mani* Kongo found themselves forced to buy imports in increasing amounts just to maintain the domestic power their initial distributions of goods had won them. However, the terms of trade demanded by the foreign traders who supplied the imports did not necessarily improve when returns of captives fell on the African side of the kings' two political economies. African importers thus found themselves facing the impossible task of extracting people and commodities from a capital-short local political economy, unable to increase its production either of goods or of people. As investment in imports rapidly lost its ability to generate returns that would cover its cost, their first way out of the impasse was typically to expand the search for commodities acceptable to the Europeans into new areas.

Lacking even the inferential testimony available for Kongo as to the motivations of men who later became involved in importing and exporting elsewhere in western central Africa, the circumstantial evidence most expressive of the universal reluctance to release dependents comes from the fact that others also attempted first to cover their foreign debts with commodities rather than people. It is sometimes difficult to perceive those early, and in the long run feeble, efforts to pay in local products behind the teleological tone of modern historical interpretations, which concentrate far too narrowly on early tendencies toward slaving, long before the later trend to selling people had become dominant and when it was probably not yet even an eventuality anticipated by anyone on the scene.

Successful avoidance of selling slaves elsewhere in far more commercially developed parts of Africa—for almost the entire history of contact at Benin, for more than a century along the Gold Coast, later in Senegambia, and at least until 1750 also in southeastern Africa[6]—may be taken as generally consistent with similar intentions in western central Africa. This widespread response to the Atlantic trade was not absent there but rather was merely truncated by enthusiastic commitments to foreign buying that the autoconsuming political economies of that part of the continent could not sustain without resorting to destructive sales of people. Historians therefore cannot ignore the compelling suggestion of the high

5. Hilton, *Kingdom of Kongo*, p. 237, n. 5.

6. In addition to Birmingham, "Early African Trade," for Angola, see Eugenia W. Herbert, "Portuguese Adaptation to Trade Patterns: Guinea to Angola (1443–1640)," *African Studies Review* 17, no. 2 (1974): 411–23; A. F. C. Ryder, *Benin and the Europeans, 1485–1897* (New York: Humanities Press, 1969); Ray A. Kea, *Settlement, Trade, and Politics in the Seventeenth-Century Gold Coast* (Baltimore: Johns Hopkins University Press, 1982); Curtin, *Economic Change*; Edward A. Alpers, *Ivory and Slaves in East Central Africa: Changing Patterns of Trade to the Later Nineteenth Century* (London: Heinemann, 1975).

value Africans placed on people in even their modest sales of commodities into the world economy. Tendencies to offer goods marked the first stages of importing all up and down the western central African coasts. African producers managed to cover their import debts with local commodity exports for the longest time where commercialization had proceeded furthest before the foreign goods arrived. North of the mouth of the Zaire, thriving deliveries of forest products through small sixteenth-century trading principalities already linked maritime salt pans along the Loango coast to sources of ivory, copper, raffia cloth, and forest products at Malebo Pool and beyond into the trading system of the Zaire basin, and this trade achieved the most sustained postponement of the shift to selling people.[7] The traders and canoemen of Loango began to handle slaves in significant quantities only much later, in the seventeenth century, when the commitment to world commerce acquired a momentum beyond the capacity of even this developed regional trading system to maintain.[8] Even then, slaves supplied to European buyers there at first came largely from Kongo sources well to the southeast, beyond the lower Zaire, zones well outside the main networks of the established commodity trade directly east toward the forest and areas far beyond the vicinity where coastal merchants would experience burdensome reductions in their own dependents.

In the far south near Benguela, in the early stages of trade with Europeans Africans provided significant quantities of coastal salt, cattle, hides, copper, and feathers from an existing interior trade with the Humpata Plateau and beyond.[9] A probable severe drought at the end of the sixteenth century introduced starving refugees into these transactions much earlier than slaves became prominent at relatively moist Loango.[10] Near the Kwanza in the sixteenth century, coastal Kongo and Mbundu authorities had alternative means of buying imports with salt from Kisama and with the saline and shell wealth of Luanda Bay. They showed little initial enthusiasm for the growing interests of the Portuguese in buying labor. Their failure to supply slaves, supported by Kongo state efforts to exclude Europeans from the kings' important sources of shell currency at Luanda, forced traders seeking slaves to bypass them, ascending the Kwanza to obtain captives instead from the Mbundu lords of its middle reaches and its Lukala tributary, mainly the Ngola a Kiluanje. This early Portuguese commitment to African slaving partners located far enough inland to lack commodities that could stand the costs of transport to the coast, supported

7. Martin, *External Trade*, pp. 33–52.
8. Ibid., pp. 53–72.
9. For the trade route, Cadornega, *História geral*, 3:172 ff. For the nonslave emphasis in early trade at Benguela, Delgado, *Reino*, pp. 28–29, 100, et passim.
10. Miller, "Significance of Drought, Disease, and Famine," pp. 24, 36–40.

by expectations that substantial wealth in silver would cover the expenses of conquest, led them to take possession of territories there that, after a sequence of conflicts, droughts, and epidemics between about 1575 and 1630, became the Portuguese colony of Angola. The failure of initial Portuguese hopes of an African Potosí on the Kwanza prompted them to refound the colony on the basis of slave exporting.

In the longer run, the originally rich variety of tropical commodities with which Africans paid for imported goods dwindled into a trickle of wax and ivory, the only two items of African production that commanded prices sufficient to cover the high costs of their transport to the coast. Transportation costs became a major obstacle because the later wax and ivory exports continued to come mainly from the peripheries of the area in touch with the Atlantic economy, that is, from the parts of western central Africa where goods had only just begun to enter and where they still circulated in quantities so limited as not yet to have exceeded the capacity of the local economies to pay for them with something other than people. The sources of ivory and wax therefore moved steadily inland, and their aggregate volume failed to keep pace with the rapid growth in exports of slaves.

Africans found ivory a profitable means of paying for European textiles and alcohol, since they had few or no uses for the unwieldy tusks of elephant, and to a lesser extent also of hippopotamus. Though expensive to carry down to the coast, the tusks frequently originated as nearly costless by-products of hunting expeditions undertaken to dispose of animals that had intruded on gardens or to obtain meat or bristles prized for their alleged aphrodisiac powers. The proceeds of such hunts went in part to land chiefs, who claimed the first tusk to hit the ground as the stricken animal fell. In regions where firearms became part of the technology of ivory production, the importer of the weapons could also demand an additional share as the provider of the means, both physical and magical, that brought the elephant to earth. Once the tusks acquired value in goods, hunters organized themselves systematically to pursue for their ivory beasts that they had formerly killed mostly to protect villages and fields.[11]

By the eighteenth century, the principal ivory-producing areas of central Africa lay in savannas and gallery forests hundreds of kilometers inland from the coast. In the equatorial latitudes, cheap water transportation and the developed commercial contacts along the Zaire allowed intensified ivory hunting to spread widely but thinly over a huge area of

11. Martin, *External Trade*, p. 40; Manoel da Silva Ribeiro *requerimento*, n.d., AHU, Angola maço 17 (D.O.). Hilton, *Kingdom of Kongo*, p. 108, appears to grasp the critical distinction between early low-cost sales of ivory stocks accumulated over decades and even centuries, and the much higher cost of later systematic production of ivory with attendant investment of capital resources.

the central river basin without diverting the resources of other economic sectors. The combination of inexpensive canoe transport and the large bulking center at Malebo Pool kept the cost of heavy tusks delivered at the coast not far above the costs of the sixteenth and seventeenth centuries, when ivory supplies had originated much nearer the sea.[12] Ivory therefore remained an important item of commerce relative to slaves north of the mouth of the Zaire, even after its sources receded far into the interior.

Farther to the south, where no similar advantages in transportation or commercial organization reduced the cost of ivory delivered at the coast, most tusks came from the sandy plains beyond the Kunene by the last third of the eighteenth century, just before slaving broke out in force in those distant areas.[13] In general, the pursuit of ivory there encouraged hardy hunters to spread out in greater numbers than before through the wilder woodland regions where elephants flourished. For people fleeing slaving and political oppression in densely inhabited regions subject to overbearing lords, hunting elephants in wilderness areas probably became an important way of achieving self-protection without sacrificing access to Atlantic imports available otherwise only at the cost of a significant loss of autonomy. Ivory from less populated fringe zones thus complemented exports of labor from densely inhabited centers both geographically and economically.

Only much later, by the mid-nineteenth century, did improved guns supplement time-consuming pit-traps and spears to facilitate the growing commercial production of ivory by skilled specialists. Firearm-wielding professionals organized in guilds must have profited most, though ordinary villagers would also have occasionally encountered the ground ivory of animals that had died of natural causes and must have killed a few elephant through the continued use of the older devices of local manufacture.[14] Land-owning lineage leaders would have used the half of the ivory given to them as tribute or as payoffs to protect the kin and clients they had carefully assembled from demanding kings and from dangerous bands of hunters camped in the vicinity. Trained and armed dependents of the lords must have killed elephant also, but most ivory came from areas so removed from the populous domains of kings, and it commanded so few goods in the far interior, that organized hunting offered rulers fewer long-term advantages, in terms of avoiding having to commit dependents to cover deficits in their balance of payments, than it afforded the frontiersmen of the woodlands.

12. Martin, *External Trade*, p. 94; Harms, *River of Wealth, River of Sorrow*, pp. 39–43, for ivory production in the Zaire basin.

13. Mesquita, 20 July 1781, AHU, Angola cx. 38.

14. Cf. the Chokwe in the nineteenth century: see Miller, "Cokwe Expansion," pp. 25–27 ff. Also Harms, *River of Wealth, River of Sorrow*, pp. 41–42; Tams, *Visit to the Portuguese Possessions*, 1:138.

The high volume of ivory exported late in the seventeenth century, when trade routes had not yet extended far into the interior, declined as the tusks came from ever more distant hunting grounds and as costs of transporting them rose.[15] Exports of ivory remained sluggish through the growth of the Atlantic trading zone during the first half of the 1700s. The fixed monopoly purchase price offered at the Portuguese ports stayed low, and the lethargic value of ivory in Europe depressed the trade elsewhere along the coast. World prices turned upward again only after about 1780, and quantities of ivory delivered began to increase almost at once outside the ports at Luanda and Benguela.[16] Ivory from perhaps two or three thousand animals reached the coast in peak years toward the end of the eighteenth century,[17] not an impressive amount compared to the hundreds of thousands of elephants roaming the land or in comparison to the much larger numbers of tusks sold in the nineteenth century at much higher prices. Although African traders and others retained additional numbers of tusks, sometimes burying them for safekeeping and in other instances displaying them ostentatiously before traders at their compounds (particularly the largest ones, too bulky to transport to the coast),[18] ivory production before 1830 could not have occupied more than a few thousand part-time hunters working mostly in areas with only slight contact with the world economy.

If the currency cost (14.223$824 *réis*) of the ivory shipped legally at Luanda and Benguela in 1771 represented the same balance of imports as Africans received for the 13,000 slaves boarded through those ports

15. One small trader in Luanda acquired 1,230(?) tusks in just two or three years in the 1680s: Miller, "Capitalism and Slaving," pp. 41–44, 47. But Martin, *External Trade*, p. 149, implies that ivory shipments from Loango had all but ceased after the rise of slaving, and François Gaulme, "Un document sur le Ngoyo et ses voisins en 1784: l' 'Observation sur la navigation et le commerce de la côte d'Angole' du comte de Capellis," *Revue française d'histoire d'outre-mer* 64, 3 (no. 236) (1977): 368, confirms for Cabinda.

16. Curtin, *Economic Change*, p. 224, traces a tenfold increase from the 1780s to the 1830s; Marion Johnson, "Elephants' Teeth in the Age of Elegance" (unpublished paper, n.d.) follows European demand and West African sources of ivory through the nineteenth century.

17. Extrapolation from recorded Luanda-Benguela exports in the 1770s of ca. 2,500 tusks delivered annually to the Portuguese royal treasury, and allowing for an equal amount of unreported contraband sales to foreign buyers: annual reports in AHU, Angola cxs. 32, 33. Compare the 7,000–8,000 tusks delivered each year in the 1640s to the main ivory port on the Loango Coast: Martin, *External Trade*, p. 57. The tone of the Portuguese documentation begins to imply more significant amounts in the 1780s: *provisão* of 26 May 1780, livro no. 1 de registo das provisões e cartas régias expedidas para Angola, AHTC, fols. 233–34; Câmara draft *regimento*, 21 June 1779, AHU, Angola maço 3 (D.O.); *provisão*, 8 Aug. 1790, livro no. 2, AHTC, fols. 122–23; João Victo da Silva, n.d. (ca. 1792), AHU, Angola cx. 42, for the French at Benguela; Gov. D. Miguel António de Mello, "Angola no começo do século," *Boletim da Sociedade de geografia de Lisboa* 5 (1885): 559, n. 2; Godinho, 23 Oct. 1804, AHU, Angola cx. 55.

18. Matos, *Compêndio histórico*, pp. 330–31.

that year and for the wax also sent out, it would have represented less than 2 percent of the value of African production for export.[19] Between 1784 and 1794, the value of ivory exports from Luanda dropped to less than 1 percent of the total, and between 1795 and 1797 it climbed back to hardly more than 1.3 percent.[20] Only by the 1820s did ivory begin to show signs of strength in the Portuguese ports, increasing to a still-modest 3.7 percent of the value of slaves in 1823.[21] The insignificance of these quantities resulted in part from the uncompetitively low government prices offered at Luanda compared to larger British and French purchases elsewhere along the coast, but the low volume also resulted from the speed with which ivory production retreated into distant corners of the interior and drove African kings nearer the coast to buying their imports with people.[22]

European demand for beeswax offered few similar opportunities to acquire imports, since African apiculturalists less commonly sold their product for foreign goods. Though wax seems not to have become integrated into the grand trade circuits that converted imports into dependents before 1830, like ivory it came from the sparsely inhabited woodlands. Also like ivory, beeswax was originally a low-cost by-product of enterprises undertaken for local purposes. In this case, it had been a residue boiled off the contents of hives in the process of refining honey and mead for eating and drinking purposes. Producers normally subjected the waxy remainder to only minimal further purification, and so their marginal cost of selling it was relatively low.

Beeswax thus began its course from central African woodlands to the coastal ports as highly impure loaves and cakes of varying sizes that producers exchanged for palm oil, salt, or local cotton threads, but seldom for imported textiles.[23] Unlike the gains from firearms in ivory-hunting efficiency, imported technologies added nothing to the production process for wax. Honey gatherers placed hollow tubes of bark high in trees to attract swarms of bees and then drove them out destructively by burning

---

19. Ivory *relação*, AHU, Angola maço 6 (D.O.), assuming the proportion of ivory hoarded to be equal to mortality losses of slaves before embarkation; cf. Vellut, "Royaume de Cassange," pp. 133–34, estimating annual exports of ivory at 9.000$000 in the 1760s, also 2% by currency value.

20. Miller, "Imports at Luanda," table IX.

21. Miller, "Imports at Luanda," table IX; also Rebelo, *Relações*, Quadro 1.

22. Traders offered much of the ivory sold at Benguela and Luanda only because it qualified for slave duties payable in liquid assets, cash, or bills of exchange, which were in extremely short supply: Delgado, *Famosa e histórica Benguela*, p. 442 (1796 *regimento* of Benguela governor).

23. Ferreira, *memória*, 26 June 1762, AHU, Angola cx. 29. Cf. Luiz António de Oliveira Mendes, *Memória a respeito dos escravos e tráfico da escravatura entre a costa d'Africa e o Brazil*, (ed. José Capela) (Porto: Escorpião, 1977), p. 30; "Reflexão anonima sobre o comercio de Angola," n.d. (ca. 1780s?) AHU, Sala 12 diversos, cx. 1.

the hive to retrieve the comb and its contents. They lacked the labor to refine the wax into a form vendible at the coast and resolutely rejected more labor-intensive but less wasteful methods of production. Their obstinacy later became a source of profound frustration to nineteenth-century Portuguese merchants hoping to conserve a bee population expected to make up losses they anticipated from the ending of their trade in slaves.[24] Eighteenth-century wax gatherers engaged in the intercontinental trade at all only because the opportunity cost of preparing their product was so low. The natural resources of their uninhabited surroundings also left them with fewer needs for imports than people in some of the more populous areas. Hunting communities tended to dress in skins rather than in cottons and woolens. The origin of wax as a by-product of a local intoxicant reduced demand for imported alcohols among its producers. Wax therefore entered into the exchange sphere mostly for local commodities, especially foodstuffs not plentiful in the wooded uplands, and insulated its frontier producers from the later trade in slaves.

The Portuguese currency value of wax delivered at Angolan ports in the course of the eighteenth century, sometimes after further refinement by petty traders and resale to European buyers, rose much higher than the value of ivory exports. At Luanda alone, wax amounted to a nearly constant volume of more than a hundred metric tons per year, nearly a fourth of the depressed value of slaves in the 1760s and still more than 5 percent of much larger exports of higher-priced captives early in the nineteenth century.[25] At the prevailing casual levels of production, a woodland honey gatherer could presumably maintain a dozen or so hives by himself. At that rate, perhaps 10,000 to 15,000 producers (or 0.1% of the total population) would have engaged regularly in producing wax for sale in the late eighteenth century.[26] The big commercial production of wax from hundreds of hives under the care of specialist apiculturalists came only later with enormous rises in price and quantity after 1830, though even then mostly from frontier areas rather than from the big slave-producing kingdoms.[27]

24. E.g., de Mello, "Angola no começo do século," p. 560; Godinho, 23 Oct. 1804, AHU, Angola cx. 55; Castelobranco, 6 June 1825, AHU, Angola cx. 69. On wax in general, Vellut, "Diversification de l'économie de cueillette."

25. For the 1760s, Vellut, "Royaume de Cassange," pp. 133–34; Miller, "Imports at Luanda," table IX; Rebelo, *Relações,* Quadro 13 and p. 189; also ibid., Quadro 8, for Benguela (1825), which then ran slightly less than Luanda in quantity shipped.

26. But these producers were concentrated in areas of low population density, so that as many as 10% of the people—i.e., half of the adult males—might have been involved there. Cf. Vellut, "Diversification de l'économie de cueillette," pp. 102–3.

27. E.g., the Chokwe highlanders; see Miller, "Cokwe Trade and Conquest," pp. 178–79 ff.; also Vellut, "Diversification de l'économie de cueillette," pp. 97–103.

Thus, in the long run African monarchs grown powerful by distributing new imports through their realms had no chance to consolidate their regimes by selling ivory or wax. Rulers like those of Kongo, whose primary power and wealth derived from managing regional commercial systems, had no preemptive claim to elephant ivory even within their own domains, since they had to collect it as tribute from the land-owning headmen, who claimed one-half of it, and by exchange with the hunters in possession of the other half. In any event, tusks came primarily from regions peripheral to areas with a significant flow of imports, except for the Zaire basin. The low world price of ivory before the 1780s left producers little margin of profit beyond the high costs of transporting it to the coast. Volume consequently also remained low relative to the kings' need to pay. Beeswax, in the limited quantities exchanged in the eighteenth century, came from small individual producers and moved mostly through decentralized petty trade circuits beyond the authority of kings. Hence, the lords who could have assembled labor to produce refined wax on a commercial scale had no chance of matching the low marginal costs of part-time sellers of honey and brewers of mead, whose products were for their own use or for exchange in the local circuits of alliance and dependency.

Tragically, the only, and distinctly secondary, alternatives to payment in people came in the form of these commodities in the production of which lords wealthy in dependents could not employ the labor they controlled. As a result, royal African importers turned, one after another, to releasing some of their hard-won dependents to satisfy European creditors and developed a whole range of novel strategies to replace the followers they lost. Dependency increased within Africa, and the transition to the export of slaves to America began.

Political Methods of Generating Dependents

The kings' turn to large-scale concessions of dependents derived much of its rationale from the willingness, toward the end of the sixteenth century, of a new rank of foreigners, of American more than European connections, to offer premium quantities of imports to Africans who would pay in captives rather than commodities. These foreign buyers wished to populate vast territorial possessions in the New World with productive Africans. The late-fifteenth-century Portuguese had sought ivory and copper from Kongo in part because their Lisbon monarchs as yet possessed little land and were still more interested in precious metals than in labor. In fact, their first modest purchases of central African slaves in the early sixteenth century went to the Gold Coast mines that supplied the Portuguese kings with bullion.

The market for Kongo labor then expanded to supply sixteenth-century sugar plantations on the Portuguese Atlantic islands just off the African shore, in particular on nearby São Tomé, and to meet needs for labor in a mother country drained of its own population by far-flung overseas enterprises in Asia. Between about the 1520s and the 1540s São Tomé planters extended slaving from Kongo ports to the Mbundu area east of Luanda. The ranks of traders in humans then grew further to include Lisbon merchants licensed to replace decimated Amerindian populations in the Spanish Indies with slaves from Africa. With the transfer of sugar cultivation from the Atlantic islands to Brazil after the 1560s and 1570s, and later with the expansion of American cane plantations to the Dutch and English islands of the Caribbean in the seventeenth century, New World markets for African labor vastly exceeded European demand for commodities from Africa and also the ability of central African lords and patrons to supply dependents from their existing reserves. European buyers of slaves consequently spread out north of the equator in the eighteenth century to develop slaving in West Africa.[28]

By 1700 in western central Africa, slavers presented buyers of imports with effectively unlimited opportunities to pay for these goods with people. Kings therefore sent off whomever they could spare from the fringes of their retinues and set about replacing those sold in a series of distinguishable stages that revealed their continued initial reluctance to release more than a few clients or slaves of their own and then changed to deliberate use of imports to increase the numbers of dependents they retained under their own control in Africa by deliberately conceding others to the export trade in slaves.

The kings' first and relatively costless strategy of meeting debts for foreign imports centered on releasing surplus dependents from existing stocks of undesirables. Criminals, disobedient and disruptive slaves, and refugees from drought who could not be fed from stores of grain on hand would have intermittently supplied modest numbers of such victims. The departures of troublemakers and intruders of that sort would have occasioned so little loss that patrons and kings must have resorted readily to such strategies from the very outset, soon after each area's trade with the Atlantic exceeded its ability to pay with commodities. Though the numbers of these surplus people were small, and their contributions to the local political economies so marginal that their absence would not have been

---

28. For general surveys, see Philip D. Curtin, *The Atlantic Slave Trade: A Census* (Madison: University of Wisconsin Press, 1969), and James A. Rawley, *The Transatlantic Slave Trade: A History* (New York: Norton, 1981), chap. 2, pp. 21–50. Curtin's volume estimates are updated, and a great deal of the literature on the subject cited, in Paul E. Lovejoy, "The Volume of the Atlantic Slave Trade: A Synthesis," *Journal of African History* 23, no. 4 (1982): 473–502.

noticed, selling them confirmed the kings' dependence on imports and tied them to slave-buyers under precedents that later kings could not reverse. European sellers of goods were quick to exploit these openings in ways less supportive of the established order.

Indeed, the disposal of those marginal people would have confirmed, rather than disrupted, established ways of doing things. A skilled politician would have condemned criminal offenders to banishment to America in ways that legitimated the judicial and commercial institutions under his control. Even if famine led kings to consign refugees to foreign creditors in disruptive numbers, such losses would hardly have added to dislocations from drought already afflicting the land. In the Kongo case, the kings' first exchanges of honored followers as ambassadors and hostages with the Portuguese monarch in the 1480s and 1490s must have drifted through an almost imperceptible transition to the banishment of a few convicts aboard vessels bound for São Tomé and its sugar estates. In the heart of central Africa, in the 1840s, after 150 years of systematic slaving, penal transportation remained the official ideology of Lunda emperors grown arrogantly powerful through sales of much less deserving people to the Atlantic trade. They countered Portuguese explanations of the impending end of the Atlantic slave trade, and therefore also of the Europeans' ability to continue to accept Lunda prisoners as slaves for export, with accurate objections that Lisbon had similarly populated its colony of Angola for centuries with its own political and criminal exiles.[29]

Since African kings who fell short of superfluous dependents also had often grown powerful through distributing the foreign goods for which they owed, their obvious next step in paying for the goods lay in marshaling their new institutions of coercion to draw more lineage members out of the village systems of kinship, clientage, and alliance. European creditors, eager to help these Africans find means to pay their debts, frequently encouraged and assisted this resort to compulsion. In terms of the African political economy of goods and people, the kings applied their enhanced power to intrude more directly on the monopoly over human reproduction left to the lineages, though still without altering the direct exchanges of people, unmediated by material goods, through which the lineage headmen and village big men managed their recruitment and reproduction of dependents.

Throughout the history of slaving in western central Africa, the kings' first efforts to tap the reproductive resources of the lineages took the form

29. A comment reported by Joaquim Rodrigues Graça (ca. 1845), cited in Birmingham, *Central Africa to 1870*, p. 114. For Portuguese penal transportation in general, Dauril Alden, " 'Rogues, Vagabonds, Sturdy Beggars,' and Other Undesirables: The Practice of Banishment in the Portuguese Empire" (Unpublished paper, University of Washington, Seattle, 1981), and to Angola, Gerald J. Bender, *Angola under the Portuguese: The Myth and the Reality* (Berkeley and Los Angeles: University of California Press, 1978), pp. 60–64.

of military campaigns sent out beyond the domain within which they owed subjects protection, rather than direct exploitation.[30] Earlier, in the sixteenth century, the Kongo kings mounted these wars of expansion specifically to gain slaves, but in no more than a few instances did they enlist the participation of Portuguese mercenaries wielding the crude arquebuses and cannon of the period.[31] They then seem to have abandoned guns, either because they found them ineffective or because arms imports increased the very foreign debts they meant such warfare to reduce. Elsewhere, Kongo kings seem to have mounted effective campaigns in search of foreign captives in the Kwango valley or in the remote Mbundu regions to the south without guns or European mercenaries, and thus to have temporarily spared their own subjects from capture.[32] *Ndembu* lords in the southern Kongo highlands and the Ngola a Kiluanje kings, who originally grew powerful by organizing Mbundu defenses against early Kongo intrusions and who were in touch with European merchants, likewise placed little reliance on firearms in the hands of their own armies.

Throughout most of the seventeenth century, later Mbundu warlords mounted joint expeditions with tiny minorities of Portuguese musketeers and artillerymen. They surely viewed these Europeans primarily as mercenaries in the African wars of expansion for capturing slaves, no less than the Portuguese perceived the hordes of African bowmen and spearthrowers who formed the bulk of these armies as contributing to the European "wars of conquest" in and around Angola. The Africans' willingness to engage the Portuguese, rather than fighting autonomously, probably confirms that they had few firearms of their own at that time. This working misunderstanding, which united masses of African assault troops around a small nucleus of European firepower, partially dissolved with the incorporation of inexpensive and more efficient "Angola guns" into African arsenals in the late seventeenth and early eighteenth centuries.

---

30. A principle identified as a generalized "African mode of production" with respect to slaving states by Catherine Coquery-Vidrovitch in "Research on the African Mode of Production," in Martin A. Klein and G. Wesley Johnson, eds., *Perspectives on the African Past* (Boston: Little, Brown, 1972), pp. 33–54, and applied in a more historical form to the Sudan by Claude Meillassoux, "The Role of Slavery in the Economic and Social History of Sahelo-Sudanic Africa," in Joseph E. Inikori, ed., *Forced Migration: The Impact of the Export Slave Trade on African Societies* (London: Hutchinson, 1981), pp. 74–99. In central Africa, with some exceptions (see my discussion of Lunda, below), this raiding style of slave production occurred in any given region mostly as an initial brief phase.

31. E.g., the early wars against the Tio; see Wilson, "Kongo Kingdom," pp. 55–57. Thornton, "Kingdom of Kongo, ca. 1390–1678," p. 335, mentions one other instance in the south in 1513.

32. The prominence of the principal exception to the general rarity of guns—Mbata in the 1580s in the wake of the "Jaga" disturbances of 1568–71—would seem to prove their rarity elsewhere before the 1700s.

The weapons evident in the hands of the Africans by the eighteenth century ended the early military collaboration between Portuguese and Mbundu, since powerful lords could by then train slave warriors at their courts as the core of marksmen in their armies and consequently became less dependent on European mercenaries. With this modest revolution in African military technology, warfare in Angola turned from European "wars of conquest" and direct quests for slaves into African assaults on armed Portuguese merchant caravans to steal the trade goods they carried. Since guns also lessened the kings' crucial dependence on the lineages by making warlords with modern arms less reliant on direct control of people for their power, state-sponsored raiding around the borders of the realm for slaves to retain at home may have declined as muskets became widely available. Bandits instead used guns to capture goods, not people only, and to enforce domestic subservience more than to capture foreigners for sale.[33] For these reasons, too, the "guns-slaves cycle" only indirectly linked imports of muskets to exports of captive people.

Though firearms may have enhanced the destructiveness of such border raids by the eighteenth century, they never made them particularly efficient methods of producing slaves. In fact, for kings bent on centralizing their political and economic power in segmentary African states, frontier warfare with or without firearms had severe longer-term limitations as a means of generating dependents to replace others lost to the Europeans. Far from least among these drawbacks was the tendency of military campaigns to strengthen the kings' challengers in the segmentary political systems. Royally sponsored armies depended on sheer numbers of followers for their effectiveness, and they necessarily drew into the fray those regional lords who exercised direct command over most of the populations of the realm—the very rivals whom the monarchs meant to contain. While opportunities to share in gains from foreign plunder as field commanders of such expeditions might retrieve the wavering loyalties of nobles otherwise chafing against the increased power of the central court, a successful raid conducted on these terms also left a share of the captives in the hands of the king's most dangerous political opponents. Such victories also produced far-flung and poorly integrated new provinces that offered little political advantage to lords with only limited administrative capacities to keep them under control. Raiding the borders of the domain for captives thus solved the monarchy's external payments problems only at the expense

---

33. Thornton's emphasis on the small number of musketeers surrounding earlier African lords, in "Art of War in Angola," is not inconsistent with the stress here on the subtle shift in the balance of power that attended new and more efficacious military technology after the 1680s.

of compromising the very domestic superiority that kings sought from the imports for which they owed payment.[34]

The strategy of seizing captives through foreign conquests also presented logistical difficulties when applied across the widely separated gaps between the nodes of dense population in most of savanna western central Africa. Massed forces of foot soldiers large enough to be effective inevitably strained the ecological resources of the regions through which they passed. The common tendency to fight during the dry months, for example, must have derived its rationale as much from the ripening fields and full granaries available for plunder during that season as from the relative ease of crossing shrunken rivers and moving through open, dry woodlands.[35] Captives taken by such an army also were weakened physically by the arduousness of the trek from the scene of their seizure to their place of resettlement or sale, and many of them died.[36] The army's escape back home with a rabble of captives, many wounded or stunned, unaccustomed to long marches through difficult terrain, uncooperative, and liable to escape or death, could not have brought many through alive to a point of sale. Estimates of deaths at this stage of the enslavement process ran over 50 percent.[37] As a result of all these inefficiencies, systematic and organized raiding for captives after the Angolan wars of the seventeenth century probably figured larger in the heroic tales of those who indulged in it occasionally than it did as a regular source of the vast numbers of people sold as slaves.

---

34. With regard to Kongo, I adopt the much less centralized depiction of Wilson, "Kongo Kingdom," over the court-centric model presented in Thornton, *Kingdom of Kongo,* for the mid-seventeenth century and projected back to at least 1500 in "Kingdom of Kongo, ca. 1390–1678." See the general political anthropology literature on the difficulty of integrating outlying provinces and powerful provincial rulers.

For techniques of raising armed forces through according spoils to participants see the fascinating passage in Heywood, "Production, Trade, and Power," pp. 67–69.

35. One must compare Thornton's conclusion ("Art of War in Angola") that armies carried their own supplies before 1680 against the pervasive evidence of Angolan armies' stealing food, of continual movement into new, unplundered areas, and of starvation: for the general rule, Corrêa, *História de Angola,* 2:54–55, note. Cf. the Imbangala of the early seventeenth century: Miller, *Kings and Kinsmen,* pp. 248–49, and "Significance of Drought, Disease, and Famine," pp. 25–28.

36. Also see Curtin, *Economic Change,* pp. 154–68, on the difficulty and expense of maintaining a horde of dependents in the midst of a military campaign; also Jan S. Hogendorn, "Slave Acquisition and Delivery in Precolonial Hausaland," in Raymond E. Dumett and Ben K. Schwartz, eds., *West African Culture Dynamics: Archaeological and Historical Perspectives* (The Hague: Mouton, 1980), pp. 477–93.

37. See the description in Vasconcelos, 12 June 1762, AHU, Angola cx. 29, which puts mortality at 50%–90%. Leitão's account of Lunda slave-raiding across the Kwango, in Dias, ed. (Leitão), "Viagem a Cassange," pp. 19–20, says 90% losses. Corrêa, *História de Angola,* 2:61, note, emphasizes the lack of means to support captives taken in battle. See also similar estimates of losses in the northern savannas in Cordell, *Dar Al-Kuti,* and the slave inventory translated in the front matter, above.

Outright organized assaults burned themselves out also because they tended to provoke victimized populations to reorganize in self-defense, often in locations inaccessible to raiding parties. Retreats from warfare frequently lay at the origin of the new ethnic and political identities that formed during the seventeenth century, particularly in the mountains near the coast. The *ndembu* lords in the heavily forested peaks at the headwaters of the Lukala, Bengo, and Dande rivers grew from minor figures to major powers as people fled to their protection from Kongo slaving raids mounted in the vicinity. Similar border raids for slaves south of the Kwanza by the Ngola a Kiluanje provoked highland Ovimbundu to regroup under lords holding the rocky redoubts from Kibala on the north face of the plateau, through Wambu above Benguela, to Huila at its southern extremity.[38] By the mid-seventeenth century, several important provinces of the Kongo kingdom no longer centered on the lush valleys once preferred by peaceful farmers but, rather, occupied the defensible plateaux of the central spine of mountains.[39] Mbondo, on an inaccessible corner of the high plains above Kasanje and Jinga, represented another ethnicity created by immigrants fleeing the slave raids of surrounding major kingdoms.[40] The ubiquity and durability of these refugee communities clearly indicates the futility of relying on border wars to capture enough slaves to support the foreign debt of a consolidating state.

Systematic royal raids at the boundaries of the state, finally, tended to produce people more suitable for retention than for sale. Captive aliens brought in from remote regions gained in value to their new masters because of the great distances that separated them from their homes and prevented them from fleeing back to their relatives, and also because resettlement in their new communities left them severely disabled culturally as a result of their ignorance of distinctive local ways. Since the main population centers in western central Africa lay far from potential aggressors, regions populous enough to repay the trouble and expense of systematic raiding often yielded advantageously displaced captives. Kings would have been correspondingly reluctant to release such prized new dependents to Europeans. Though a conquering monarch who put foreign slaves to work in the royal fields around his court could make his capital virtually independent of the surrounding provinces,[41] he had not solved the problem of his debt to the Atlantic economy.

38. Miller, "Central and Southern Angola."
39. Thornton, *Kingdom of Kongo*, pp. 6–7, 44.
40. Miller, *Kings and Kinsmen*, pp. 95–111, for origins of Mbondo. Dias, ed. (Leitão), "Viagem a Cassange," p. 14, and Vellut, "Royaume de Cassange," pp. 129–31, for the 1750s–60s.
41. Thornton, *Kingdom of Kongo*, discusses this strategy at some length, though presenting it as a more regular and stable feature of the state than it appears to me; cf., for the Lunda, Hoover, "Seduction of Ruwej," or Vellut, "Notes sur le Lunda," pp. 77–78.

External slave raiding successfully replenished royal dependents over the long term only where dense populations, lacking good defensive sites around which to cluster for protection, lived within easy reach of the warriors of a warlord's capital—circumstances not common in western central Africa. The Ovimbundu warlords, for example, collectively must have lost as many followers as they gained in the internecine conflicts of the central plateau. Only the warlike Lunda emperors of the eighteenth century demonstrated the potential yield of this unusual combination of circumstances, since the Lunda *mwaant yaav* regularly harvested slaves from large but defenseless populations living in the open valleys of the forest fringes north of their capitals. They thus made sustained warfare a major source of captives, who, retained, made them powerful and who also made them wealthy in imported goods when exported. The uniqueness of the Lunda court's continuing reliance on border raids in the southern savannas proved the more general limitations of prolonged reliance on external war to replace well-dressed and armed residents of royal towns threatened with reduction in numbers to pay foreign debts.[42]

The inefficiencies and potential domestic strains nourished by border wars soon forced most kings to look closer to home for the captives they needed to sell abroad. They did so by converting the coercive institutions of their realms from the collection of material tribute, which did not threaten the lineages' control over the reproductive powers of the population, to direct extractions of people from among their own subjects. Seizing and selling inhabitants of the kingdom, even lowly ones, drained away dangerously large concentrations of dependents building up around the compounds of a regional nobility that the kings had just cowed into submission and debilitated provincial resistance to the growing power of the center.

Exporting slaves taken within the realm also protected the kings' domestic power because local people were considerably less dependent than foreigners from beyond its borders. Subjects often reached the court with links to provincial factions who could defend their interests even after their removal to the court. They also knew the language and the culture of their royal masters. Thus, though kings might increase the number of dependents arriving at their courts through domestic tribute and trials, they sacrificed the degree of dependency they could impose on

---

42. Thornton, "Kingdom of Kongo, ca. 1390–1678," pp. 334–35, presents the phase of external slave raids as "maturation" rather than a step in a continuously changing process that brought on its own obsolescence. Central African border wars were unlike the much more persistent, systematic raiding in analogous ecological circumstances in the West African savannas, with the aggressors from the Sudan there having the additional—and probably decisive—advantage of the horse, though see the limitations emphasized there in Meillassoux, "Role of Slavery."

the people they gained. This relative independence of local people reduced the opportunity cost of using them to pay traders for imports.

As border raids lost their efficacy as a way of obtaining salable slaves, kings grown powerful from the Atlantic trade faced the choice of declining to powerless figureheads or strengthening domestic institutions to deprive the provincial aristocracies of their followings. They therefore converted judicial institutions from courts of arbitration to tribunals condemning accused thieves, witches, and sorcerers from rural areas to sale and exile.[43] They dispatched details of slave mercenary police from their courts throughout the provinces to seize recalcitrants who resisted the harsh judgments they handed down.[44] The kings' strategy of using their own subjects for export as slaves had thus drifted from giving up unwanted outcasts to systematic extortion of their own subjects. Rule through sheer force replaced the old links of interdependency within a segmentary state.

State violence and robbery in turn reduced a ruler's need to redistribute imported goods domestically, beyond those consumed at the court, for use rather than in exchange for people. The resort to force in itself lessened the kings' obligations to foreign suppliers of textiles and guns because they did not have to invest goods in costly purchases, but African importers trapped between goods of lowered value at home and unpayable debts abroad devised still other strategies to restore the imports' power to generate dependent followers. Their most elementary tactic rested on simple deferral of payment for goods they had received. To judge from the widespread and persistent indebtedness of African importers throughout the history of their trading with Europeans, most developed techniques of delayed payment to a high art.[45] In increasing borrowing by this in-

43. The best-known example of a tribunal converted to creating slaves for sale is the *ndua* poison ordeal of the Kasanje kings; e.g., Dias, ed. (Leitão), "Viagem a Cassange," pp. 19–20; cf. Felner, *Angola,* 2:14, for contemporary reference to the *ndua,* a bird whose gall was believed to be highly poisonous. See Broadhead, "Slave Wives, Free Sisters," p. 167, for Kongo. Also see Silva, 25 June 1762, AHU, Angola cx. 42, for the generality of the practice; and Luiz António de Oliveira Mendes, "Discurso academico ao programma . . . ," in António Carreira, "As companhias pombalinas de navegação, comércio, e tráfico de escravos entre a costa africana e o nordeste brasileiro," *Boletim cultural da Guiné portuguesa* 24, no. 94 (1969): 420, and an anonymous *memória,* n.d. (ca. 1790s), in de Mello, 7 Dec. 1798, AHU, Angola cx. 46.

44. The classic example is the Lunda *tukwata:* Hoover, "Seduction of Ruwej," p. 105 (*kakwat*).

45. This indebtedness is not generally emphasized, though pervasively noted; see, for Angola, Wilson, *Kingdom of Kongo,* pp. 113, 116, 164, and 166–67, in reference to the cloth trade in Kongo (1630s–40s), and for Kongo, Broadhead, "Slave Wives, Free Sisters," pp. 167, 175. Martin, "Family Strategies," p. 81, refers to credit at Loango. The problem of unpaid debt in Portuguese Angola is discussed more fully below, but for the present cf. Vellut, "Royaume de Cassange"; Maria Emília Madeira dos Santos, "Perspectiva do comércio sertanejo do Bié na segunda metade do século XIX," *Studia* 45 (1981): 65–129, which is excellent on the pervasiveness of the problem. Salvador, *Magnatas do tráfico negreiro,* pp. 164–65 et passim, discusses debt generally for the Atlantic trade. Fritz Hoppe, *A África oriental*

formal "float," they managed to retain a fair number of the dependents they had acquired, even at high costs.

But prolonged indebtedness carried to extremes could eventually cost the African importer the support of his European suppliers and—given his dependence on their goods—also his political title. At a minimum, even where European power was weak and the African central lord overwhelmingly strong, excessive debt could drive unsatisfied creditors to boycott the offender. Portuguese merchants frustrated by the unpaid debts of the Kasanje kings withdrew from the main marketplace near the Kasanje court early in the nineteenth century. Within a generation after this boycott, the line of Kasanje rulers dominant in the upper Kwango valley since the 1650s had lost power to the regional nobles of their realm.[46] Where the balance of forces was less favorable to the African lords, European creditors could collaborate with pretenders at the time of regular succession crises or interregna to place a man with a better credit rating on the throne, as happened time after time around the fringes of the Portuguese *conquista* of Angola.[47] Though the limited military power backing the European creditors after the Angolan wars of the seventeenth century and before the final Portuguese conquests of the late nineteenth century made the extreme step of direct seizure of offending debtors an infrequent—but not entirely unknown—event, outright refusals to pay had definite limits even

---

portuguesa no tempo do Marquês de Pombal (1750–1777) (Lisbon: Agência Geral do Ultramar, 1970), pp. 30, 125–26, 176–83, 184–87, and Alpers, *Ivory and Slaves,* pp. 85–94, place some emphasis on the problem in Mozambique. African indebtedness was general. Kwame Yeboa Daaku, *Trade and Politics on the Gold Coast, 1600–1720: A Study of the African Reaction to European Trade* (Oxford: Clarendon Press, 1970), p. 41, and Metcalf, "Gold, Assortments, and the Ounce Trade," esp. p. 32, note that credit characterized trade even on the Gold Coast, where African producers of bullion frequently had a ready supply of the metallic basis of the currencies of their European creditors. See also Charles Becker and Victor Martin, "Kayor and Baol: Senegalese Kingdoms and the Slave Trade in the Eighteenth Century," in Inikori, *Forced Migration,* p. 112; Ernst van den Boogaart and Pieter C. Emmer, "The Dutch Participation in the Atlantic Slave Trade, 1595–1650," in Gemery and Hogendorn, *The Uncommon Market,* p. 360 (Gold Coast in the 1640s); Elbl, "Portuguese Trade," pp. 222, 594–96; A. J. H. Latham, *Old Calabar, 1600–1891: The Impact of the International Economy upon a Traditional Society* (Oxford: Clarendon Press, 1973); idem, "Currency, Credit, and Capitalism on the Cross River in the Precolonial Era," *Journal of African History* 12, no. 4 (1971): 602–3; Carole P. MacCormack, "Slaves, Slave Owners, and Slave Dealers: Sherbro Coast and Hinterland," in Robertson and Klein, *Women and Slavery in Africa*; Cordell, *Dar Al-Kuti,* p. 138; Jan S. Hogendorn, "The Economics of the African Slave Trade" (review essay), *Journal of American History* 70, no. 4 (1984), p. 856. All of these are couched in terms of neoclassical assumptions about individuals and currency profits, rather than in terms of the social implications of credit in the African context. For a sense of the worldwide importance and generality of the phenomenon, see Wolf, *Europe and the People without History,* pp. 140–41 et passim.

46. Vellut, "Royaume de Cassange," for a chronology of some of these events; see also Chapter 17 below.

47. Beatrix Heintze, "Luso-African Feudalism in Angola? The Vassal Treaties of the Sixteenth to the Eighteenth Century," *Revista portuguesa de história* 18 (1980): 124–25.

for the most powerful African monopolists. Lesser buyers of imports, who operated in a competitive environment where European suppliers could afford to refuse to sell to unreliable customers, professed an almost Protestant ethic of capitalist responsibility for making good on the funds they, or their subjects, borrowed.[48]

In the new times of plentiful goods, African kings and nobles usually devised ways to turn the internal terms of the goods-for-captives exchanges back in their favor long before nonpayment of debt led to open conflict, thus firming their own positions in the local political game while also satisfying foreign creditors. If they could not limit the quantities of goods inundating their domains, they could selectively restore rarity to styles they controlled by promoting novelty and changing fashion. Aristocrats and royalty thus took advantage of the variety in the arriving imports to reserve rights of first selection from the traders' stocks for themselves and to appropriate fresh and attractive colors and designs of fabrics, headgear with novel decorations, beads of style not seen before, and any other sort of innovation to generate new, if inevitably ephemeral, monopolies over chosen goods they thus declared to be distinctive marks of style and authority. At the same time they abandoned old symbols of wealth and power that had lost their value because they had become too common. Over the decades, kings repeatedly consigned the majority of imports to the category of vulgar staple consumer goods for the mass market, worthless in terms of prestige, while they endowed a smaller and constantly shifting set of new items with the critical function of creating power and wealth. Given the great significance that Africans, preoccupied with status and hierarchy, placed on apparel and adornment as signifiers of rank, much stronger than corresponding dictates of "fashion" among Europeans, arbitrary prescribed shifts in style assumed the serious tones of a struggle for dominance waged with pattern, weaves, finishes, and hue.

The wealthy and powerful also restored a measure of political-economic worth to common goods by sending them into remote areas where there were still material scarcities similar to those closer to home at the outset of the importers' own original contacts with the Atlantic economy. There, the rarity of European wares gave them a high value in exchange for surplus dependents in small numbers. In practice, kings nearer the coast opened up trade routes to the east and initially had to restrict access to those regions in order to preserve the value of imports they sent there. Caravans of goods sent to far-off locations brought in helplessly alien dependents of the most desirable sort without the political and economic costs of military conflict. High people-goods exchange ratios in the east allowed kings to avoid having to underwrite the opening of this trade with credit

48. Santos, "Perspectiva do comércio sertanejo," pp. 82 ff.

and to retain substantial portions of their imports for domestic consumption and even redistribution at home. In addition, contacts in the east initially enabled them to add limited ivory, sometimes copper, and, in the sandier savannas, wax to their foreign debt payments. All of these advantages allowed kings to keep a significant portion of the captives who arrived from those remote regions for themselves.

The structural significance of this peaceful "economic" tactic resided in its extension of the initial low-cost exchanges of goods for people into far larger regions than the pedestrian and hand-projectile military technology of western central Africa could have subjected to organized slaving raids. It placed a premium on commercial skills and institutions abroad, even as militarism and violence were on the increase at home. Since its success depended on putting only small quantities of goods in the hands of a great many minor lords dispersed over a huge area, it created an expansive geographical trading frontier and propelled it hundreds of kilometers east of the growing political turmoil in the western kingdoms. By the late seventeenth century, when local tensions had already erupted in fighting west of the Kwango, the first European goods had already begun to stimulate political centralization east of the Kasai among the Bushoong and the Lunda.[49] Farther south, traders from the warring kingdoms of the central plateau contacted the upper Zambezi in the 1760s, well before the domestic conflict of slaving had died down in their highland homes.[50] Their largely peaceful eastern commerce, of course, also planted seeds of violence in fertile economic and political terrain that would eventually also yield bitter fruit.

Civil War and the New Order

In the end, the abundant contradictions of kings losing power to once-tributary nobles, of importers holding stocks of trade goods of depreciating value relative to the people they sought, of Europeans and their commercial agents meddling in local politics to milk payment from indebted rulers and to promote the causes of pretenders too weak in local supporters to resist collaboration with outsiders, of overextended military and administrative institutions, and of royal traders sent off into remote areas where they could expect little security or protection for themselves or their baggage could hardly fail to transform the western states fallen into dependency on imports. Indebtedness to the Atlantic economy grew on all sides,

---

49. Vansina, *Children of Woot.* See Hoover, "Seduction of Ruwej," and John K. Thornton, "The Chronology and Causes of Lunda Expansion to the West, 1700–1852," *Zambia Journal of History* 1 (1981): 6, for a rationalization of the date.

50. Miller, "Central and Southern Angola."

as imports lost their efficiency as claims on the people necessary to pay for them and eventually declined to inconsequential use mostly as items of personal consumption. Foreign trade and debts drew area after area toward chaotic violence as the politicians sought to generate the people necessary to pay for imports. While the economic transformation proceeded on stage, a paroxysm of social and political revolution waited in the wings.

The revolution moved into the spotlight when the shortcomings of foreign conquests and the kings' resort to internal pressure sucked the peripheral violence back into the heart of the large states. Provincial lords sought direct access to the foreign traders for themselves, and they had the people with whom to pay. Insofar as they had shared in the human fruits of the period of frontier fighting, they had assembled colonies of dependents, or had become independent of their local followers. From either group they could offer people directly to the foreign traders at exchange ratios better than the grudging terms on which their royal overlords distributed foreign wares through largesse. Even favored subordinates with license to sell the human booty of the border raids through markets held at the royal court would have wanted to avoid the taxes and obligations imposed there.

The foreign merchants, for their part, recognized the regional lords as sources of prompt payment in slaves for goods delivered, and they could expect better exchange ratios from isolated and competing gentry than from a royal monopolist in charge of a single marketplace. They therefore hastened to extend credit directly into the provinces, spreading once-rare imports even more widely. The kings, financially bankrupt and politically discredited, lost the support of their erstwhile creditors, who turned as actively to supporting the provincial factions as they had once engaged in the politics of the royal compound. The arms Europeans had formerly lent the kings they began to raise in support of ambitious nobles seeking the royal emblems for themselves. Conflict over successions at the center intensified accordingly, and the frequency of assassinations and interregna increased, while the duration of reigns tended to fall.

Not only had copious flows of imports reduced the power of goods to produce dependency by the old rules of largesse, but the demographic distribution of dependents between the center and the outlying regions had also ceased to favor the monarchy. Clients and slaves clustered around rising regional nobles or marginal royal pretenders, or even new men without aristocratic pedigree of any sort, rather than at the kings' courts. The initial centralizing tendencies generated by the arrival of imports in small quantities through a single monopolist lord had dissipated into massive quantities of goods underwriting impending political fragmentation.

The outbreak of these conflicts assumed the aspect of "civil wars" most clearly in the large kingdoms, since the largest military forces there usually followed the banners of regional lords, provincial governors, and royal pretenders who continued to fight in terms of the ideologies of the crumbling ancien régime that gave them their personal legitimacy as politicians, unaware that they were thereby contributing to its demise. In the Kongo, hostile regional aristocracies of this ilk contested possession of the Christian title adopted by the Kongo kings of the seventeenth century. Though most *mani* Kongo had been powerless figureheads since the early eighteenth century, the Christian ideology behind their throne survived, since it alone transcended the parochialism of pretenders trying to raise followings to secure the title.[51] Struggles like these in Kongo intermittently produced significant numbers of captives for the victors, but such wars probably made relatively minor overall contributions to the export trade. The contenders certainly had good reason to exchange their enemies' adherents for guns and goods of their own, but they also needed to keep every captive they could seize.

Kasanje aristocrats channeled similar conflicts through three relatively stable political alliances and confined warfare to the occasion of royal successions for most of the eighteenth century. Their battles appeared different from those in the Kongo only because of the greater political centralization achieved in the upper parts of the Kwango valley. Possession of the Kasanje title brought privileged access to a steady stream of traders from Luanda. When the old king died or was assassinated, the factions temporarily expelled foreign merchants and closed the roads to the west in order to resolve the succession among themselves. With the domestic issue settled, the winning party reopened the markets and consolidated its victory by releasing hundreds of captives seized from the losers into the Atlantic trade. Their unchallenged domestic power gave them the freedom to sell off more of the human profits of their triumph.

Elsewhere, particularly in the wildernesses where refugees escaped the violence spreading in the populous valleys of the old kingdoms, upstarts claiming little or no connection with the old political aristocracies took the lead in fomenting other disorders. On the central highlands, where most Ovimbundu farmers resettled under the protection of such warlords, a plurality of military kingdoms settled into a none-too-peaceful coexistence of more or less continuous low-level hostilities.[52] The refugee communities gradually became new states that foretold political, social, and economic reorganization in response to systematic slaving still only dimly

---

51. Hilton, "Political and Social Change"; Broadhead, "Beyond Decline"; idem, "Luso-Kongolese Armed Conflict."
52. Miller, "Central and Southern Angola."

glimpsed by most people. The Ovimbundu antagonists, of roughly comparable population and power, fought one other to draws in wars and warily eyed their opponents across the deserts separating their fortified settlements. Though their armed forces were partially converted to foreign military technologies, these warlords still relied primarily on masses of unskilled, spear-wielding farmers. Each kept as many captives as he could from raiding parties dispatched into the territories of his neighbors, settling most of the captives to repopulate his own lands, and sent on to the coast only those necessary to replenish munitions and stocks of foreign textiles and alcohol.

Outright bandits and "maroon" colonies of fugitive slaves thrived on the fringes of this chaos. Occasionally, in times of severe drought, bands of men forced off desiccated farmlands took up raiding almost as a way of life. Marauding was a resort of ancient precedent in itself, but the opportunity to sell stolen people prolonged it long after returning rains would formerly have drawn erstwhile farmers back to their fields.[53] Whether political struggles deriving from greed for imported goods took place in the name of competition for a powerful and wealthy merchant title like that of the Kasanje rulers, for a relic of former aristocratic grandeur like the Christian *mani* Kongo, among Ovimbundu warlords with palpably contrived claims to noble origin, or by admitted renegades, all were sustained by a rough parity that the contenders maintained by disposing of their opponents' followers to the foreign slavers.

Though the flames of violence flared brightly, they seldom burned for long in any one area, since conflict in any of these forms regrouped people in ways that snuffed them out within a generation or two. All who could escape simply abandoned disordered homelands in the time-honored manner of independent rural folk the world over. Most refugees found a measure of protection in adjoining regions by giving their allegiance to the warlords, secure in citadels built around the caves and rocks of mountain fastnesses and protected by trained cadres of mercenaries bearing imported firearms in their defense. Others who failed to escape found themselves seized and evacuated, either handed over to foreign traders or kept to reside in relatively safe subordination at the towns of trading nobles. Flights, seizures, and killings thus drove off the populations of the war zones and left the survivors too exhausted and weakened to maintain the fighting at the intensity it attained at its peak. Empty expanses in between the compact settlements were abandoned to all but outlaw bands and heavily defended trading caravans. Many of the refugees, even the enslaved, would have noted a modest recovery from the immediately preceding era of anarchy rather than the privations they had suffered relative

53. See sources cited in notes 79–80 to Chapter 1, above.

to the half-forgotten times before the violence, and some could even have counted themselves fortunate.

Whatever low-level fighting and aggrandizement continued, lords who survived the disorder used their commercial contacts with the Atlantic traders to evolve steadily toward more peaceful, mercantilistic methods of extracting the captives needed to buy imports. Most prominent eighteenth-century polities west of the Kwango-Kwanza-Kubango line based themselves not on open violence but rather on conversions of their trading contacts to the east to slaving. With these commercial strategies, not outright terrorism, war leaders extended their rule from defensible hideouts to the habitable farmlands in the river valleys below and set about repopulating domains devastated in the preceding cycle of border raids and civil wars.

Commercial contacts in the distant east, where goods still produced advantageous returns in the form of people, brought back valuable, vulnerable dependents whom the lords settled around their own courts and elsewhere under the authority of loyal lieutenants rewarded with those newly imported followers. These kings separated returning caravans of alien dependents into two streams, one mostly of males destined for slavery among the Europeans and the other of females sent out to populate the villages of their realms. By retaining the women, they gained reproductive capacities that would found lines of future dependency, and they paid off their suppliers with males ranked low in terms of the underlying strategy of multiplying dependency. In practice, the need for male warriors and headbearers compelled Africans to retain the most promising men brought in for themselves, and the pressures of indebtedness forced them to concede less-wanted females to the Atlantic trade in numbers that produced the approximately two-to-one ratio of male to female slaves eventually sent to the Americas.

In the new polities these second-generation kings ruled as merchant princes supervising distribution of goods among their own subjects and on to the east. Although they maintained formidable military capacities to protect themselves from jealous rivals, domestic and foreign, and to back their commercial strategies with an implicit threat of coercion, they had become monarchs of primarily mercantile regimes in the sense that imported trade goods mediated nearly all their institutionalized sources of dependents. If the lords of these realms generated people externally by sending imports on to the eastern regions, internally they used goods in addition to captives to fix the loyalty of their principal courtiers and to keep the provincial gentry in line. They could accord their favorites priority in the crucial selection of the most fashionable and valuable wares from the stocks of imports they controlled, guarantee the foreign debts of faithful followers in the name of the kingdom, and permit privileged subordinates to invest goods and people in the commercial expeditions sent off under royal sponsorship.[54] All these transactions they channeled through a new version of the single central marketplace, close by their capitals and under their strict supervision.

These kings also extended the commercial credit they obtained from the coast on to their subjects in the compelling form of forced loans that lesser nobles and gentry found it awkward, if not fatal, to refuse. They distributed imports throughout the provinces, superficially in the familiar style of royal largesse, to create debt among the elders and patrons who held the dependents available in their realms. But unlike the kings of old, who had cherished these obligations for the abstract respect they brought in return, the new princes called in debts by demanding living people when they needed captives to satisfy insistent European creditors at their court. They converted institutions of royal justice, however unjust, into debtors' courts, in which they presided as chief judges and doubled also as commanders of the police and effective agents of the creditors. They used these overlapping powers to foreclose on insolvent subject borrowers of their trade goods, imposing draconian seizures of their dependents in numbers that added ruinous penalties for default to the burden of the original loan.[55]

Debt to European traders, originally the trap forcing the royalty and aristocracies of the new states into releasing dependents for sale, also

---

54. These arrangements are evident in the detailed reports from Kasanje in the 1790s; see *requerimento* and attached documents enclosed in de Mello, 30 May 1801, AHU, Angola cx. 51. Also, more generally, Santos, "Perspectiva do comércio sertanejo."

55. For Kasanje, interviews conducted in 1969; contemporary allusion to the same practice just east of Kasanje in the 1750s is in Dias, ed. (Leitão), "Viagem a Cassange," pp. 20–21. For Kongo in the early eighteenth century, Broadhead, "Slave Wives, Free Sisters," pp. 167–68; in general, from a contemporary, Mendes (Carreira ed.), "Discurso academico ao programma," pp. 420–21; see also Carreira, "Companhias pombalinas de navegação," pp. 74–75, 76. The practice dated to the seventeenth century near the coast: João António Cavazzi de Montecucculo, *Descrição histórica dos três reinos de Congo, Matamba e Angola*, trans. and ed. Graciano Maria de Luguzzano (Lisbon: Junta de Investigações do Ultramar, 1965), 2:160.

P.E.H. Hair, "The Enslavement of Koelle's Informants," *Journal of African History* 6, no. 2 (1965): 193–203, notes only 7% of the early-nineteenth-century West African slaves interviewed by Koelle had been sold because of "debts," though several others of his categories could have included debt behind the perceived or proximate causes of enslavement—e.g., "sold by relatives or superiors" (7%), "kidnapping" (43%), "judicial process" (11%), and unspecified (11%).

E. Adeniyi Oroge, "Iwofa: An Historical Survey of the Yoruba Institution of Indenture," *African Economic History* 14 (1985): 75–106, has an excellent and detailed description of parallel uses of debt in nineteenth-century West Africa. Gwyn R. Campbell, "The Monetary and Financial Crisis of the Merina Empire, 1810–1826," *South African Journal of Economic History* 1, no. 1 (1986): 116, estimates that half of the 300,000 slaves in central Madagascar by 1830 were bankrupts. McCaskie, "Accumulation, Wealth, and Belief," pp. 33, 35, and 36, notes the same transition in late-eighteenth- and early-nineteenth-century Asante in West Africa.

became the means by which kings pried immigrant women and children away from the villages of their patrons and masters. The lesser men at the heads of these villages, who surely sought to protect their dependents to preserve their personal wealth in people and their power, if not also for reasons of sentiment, contradictorily owed their modest prominence largely to their willingness to deliver these same dependents over to the overlords at the central courts. The irreconcilable goals of surrounding themselves with dependents and simultaneously holding them available for powerful central kings produced political conflict in these mercantile states no less than parallel contradictions had animated struggles between regional lords and the monarchs in the older sort of African kingdom. But in the re-populated areas, dependents whose fates hung on the outcome of struggles among their patrons and masters tended to be slaves of relatively recent arrival, much less able to protect themselves against the cruelties of the new regimes than kinsmen had been earlier. Vulnerable to seizure and abuse, they consequently became the sources of most of the captives generated for shipment abroad from the regions where the violence of the civil wars had subsided.

Debts for trade goods the mercantile kings had received, or credits the people of their states owed in people, enforced by the institutions of law and coercion, thus produced a significant proportion of the slaves handed over to European merchants. Other trade goods sent on to the east brought in alien men and women at ratios that enabled the lineages and villages to replace the losses of resident slaves and clients, and more, keeping the females and releasing the males whenever possible. The relatively high proportion of women of child-bearing ages left in the rural areas made possible rates of reproduction that, even allowing for the possibly reduced fertility of polygynous unions and lost reproductivity through resettlement, produced small boys, youths, and girls whom their older male relatives, masters, and patrons could send off to the kings' marketplaces in time of need.[56] There at the central courts, storehouses filled with trade goods, pens jammed with abandoned people of all origins and descriptions, and the camps of traders from far away to the west stood as symbols of the broker regimes' dependence on systematic and largely peaceful, if brutally efficient, conversions of goods into slaves through commercialized debt. A portion of the human "profits" the kings skimmed

---

56. Reduced fertility addressed in John C. Caldwell, Comment, *Canadian Journal of African Studies* 16, no. 1 (1982): 128, and Manning response, ibid., pp. 133–34. The village residence of slave women in western central Africa may have muted the limitations on fertility that other residence patterns and types of slavery imposed in, e.g., the western Sudan or the Americas; cf. Claude Meillassoux, "Female Slavery," in Robertson and Klein, *Women and Slavery in Africa*, pp. 51–55, and numerous comments by other authors throughout this volume.

from their control of credit occupied the servants' quarters, barracks, and villages of field hands settled around the royal compound. Others roamed the domain as armed messengers summoning tribute in people. Most lived in the outlying villages as slave dependents, where the lesser beneficiaries of the imports from the Atlantic ruled as compromised patrons and masters.

The Kongo had been the first to redevelop their war-torn lands along these mercantile lines, though without centralized political authority, in the wake of the old kingdom's shattering defeat at Ambuila in 1665 by Portuguese-led forces from Angola.[57] Thereafter, while the old elite continued to play out the Christian politics of the defunct central kingdom, the trading Zombo and Soso in the far east, princes of Sonyo and other smaller trading principalities along the coast, and new men with slave retinues everywhere often held economic and de facto political power.

Angolan Portuguese, or Luso-Africans, similarly replaced the old Mbundu aristocracy not long after. The valley of Kasanje became perhaps the epitome of the general pattern in the eighteenth century, owing to its rare combination of rich agricultural potential and direct access to eastern sources of slaves beyond the Kwango. It was simultaneously a major importer of slaves through trade and a producer of captives for export through tribute its kings claimed from their villages.[58] Commercially oriented rulers in Mbailundu and Wambu and their allied states in the central highlands replaced the old warlord elites during the 1770s, after an armed Portuguese intervention ended the military standoff of the preceding decades. Trading lords at Bihe on the eastern slopes of the plateau made their fertile plains, previously valueless because they were exposed to the warlords' raiding, into a populous and powerful kingdom in the decades after 1780.[59] All these rulers rebuilt local populations by bringing new captives in from east of the Kwanza and Kunene. The Bihe kings' close association with foreign importers of goods, the open geography of their realm, and their trade to the east made them symbols of the features that distinguished the mercantile regimes, fully integrated into the Atlantic economy, from their warrior predecessors.

In terms of the African political economy of dependency, the new rulers' use of foreign goods and credit had reversed the conventional exchanges between kings and subjects, or between lineages and lords. Kings formerly had honored the lineages with titles and women, supple-

---

57. Thornton, *Kingdom of Kongo*, pp. 69 ff.; for aspects of the interpretation stressed here, Vansina, *Kingdoms of the Savanna*, pp. 152–54.

58. For the general circumstances, Vellut, "Relations internationales" and "Royaume de Cassange."

59. Miller, "Central and Southern Angola." Lacerda, "Noticia da cidade de Benguella," p. 110, makes the distinction, as observed by eighteenth-century Portuguese, in these terms: "Quimbundo" commercialized polities relied on the legal techniques of enslavement for trivial offenses, while "Quimbangala" warrior states did not.

mented by prestige goods, in return for material tribute of domestic origin to support the entourage at the court, backed by respect. The new merchant princes, grown powerful from the Atlantic trade, turned the flow of material goods outward and in return expected personnel. The portion of these dishonored captives sold as slaves generated more goods that brought alien captives in from remote regions, who were kept to produce the local consumption goods that sustained the court. Where earlier kings had left lineage intermediaries and others in charge of the inhabitants of their realms, the merchant princes used the imported goods to create direct access to subject debtors and to buy slaves. By transferring the real productive power of the African political economy—its human beings—from the villages to the royal compound and by rendering the kings relatively autonomous of domestic political opposition, this reversal in the vectors of the flows of goods and people substantially centralized political authority.

Where the trading kings substituted peaceful, institutionalized coercion for the erratic, large-scale violence of earlier states' or nobles' seizures of one another's followings, overt force became the outlawed last resort of losers impoverished by the spread of new commercial forms of wealth. Violence no longer raged over possessing good, populous agricultural lands and their inhabitants but focused rather on thefts of goods. Men facing loss of their dependents fled into the uninhabited wildernesses, where they gathered followings to strike back at the owners of commercial wealth who had victimized them. Slaves escaped to join them and received ready welcomes from leaders eager to attract followers, particularly from their oppressors' entourages, and willing to accord them a measure of status superior to the captivity they had formerly endured. Other fugitives formed maroon colonies of their own, some of which, like Kisama just across the lower Kwanza from Portuguese Angola, became large and powerful enough to mount attacks against the masters from whom they had fled. Others, without goods but nonetheless hopeful of forcing their way into the new game rather than retreating from it, became highway robbers who stole imports from caravans moving along the roads. Still others, thugs lacking the new forms of wealth but determined to assume the status that came from holding them, took up systematic kidnapping around the fringes of the Atlantic zone, perhaps of the sort that started Domingos on his way toward slavery in Brazil.

Conviction and exile into slavery became preferred punishments for crimes committed by people denied access to the commercial goods that had come to constitute wealth and power in the new regimes, and thus supported the new bases of political power. Ambitious village headmen who borrowed beyond their eventual ability to repay found themselves forced to part with the children whom they had acquired with the goods. Embittered losers in the competition for dependents sent off their last remaining nephew in return for strong drink to wash away the humiliation of the defeat they felt. All these—and doubtless others with similar dreams and failures—added to the rising tide of dependents leaving the areas where the early exchanges of goods to acquire people had somehow become a sell-off of people to get goods.

Conclusions: The Great Transformation

Imports had enabled kings in the old agricultural states to transform fragile segmentary polities into centralizing monarchies that were able, briefly, to concentrate dependent people, mainly slaves, around the royal courts. At the same time, the monarchs' need to pay for the foreign goods inspired expansionist methods of taking captives with whom they could settle up their debts. The frontier wars of this early stage of slaving quickly proved counterproductive because they extended state borders outward beyond the abilities of a central authority to defend, or else enriched and embold-ened nobles to mount domestic resistance a monarch could not contain. Out of these ephemeral achievements frequently leaped the conflagration of civil war, and from the ashes of these conflicts arose new mercantile regimes that peacefully, if coercively, distributed imported goods widely on credit and collected on the debt with greater productivity in terms of amassing the dependencies and people valued in the African political economies.

Village headmen and gentry took trade goods on loan from overlords in the new states to buy the new slaves who enabled them to create and enlarge the autonomous communities of dependents they sought. In doing so they transformed the populations of the regions in touch with the Atlantic trade into unusually heavy concentrations of enslaved alien women and their children, constantly renewed in their dependency by the arrival of additional helpless female immigrants and the departure of acculturated and hence more assertive (usually male) offspring of their predecessors. The offspring of these women covered their masters' debts if all went according to plan. To the extent that these harems of wives reproduced at rates able to cover their masters' obligations, credit in trade goods enabled lineage elders, patrons, obscure newcomers, and royal appointees to remake themselves as masters of enslaved human capital in unprece-dented numbers.[60]

The characteristics of the imports matched the changing quality of this western central African political and economic "development": textiles

---

60. Harms, *River of Wealth, River of Sorrow,* describes the extreme form of this tendency among the highly commercialized Bobangi.

and other prestige goods, new, scarce, and valuable in their nearly infinite variety, created opportunities when they first arrived but then turned into burdens that borrowers had to repay in people. Guns backed coercive methods of claiming dependents whom masters would rather have retained at home. Criminals employed firearms to seize other goods directly for themselves. Alcohol allowed new men who ruled by sheer force to foster the illusion that they communed with the spirits of the land or with honored ancestors no less than had the lords and elders of old. But they in fact ruled from lending textiles widely throughout their domains.

Their new powers were rooted in dislocations, often forced, that transformed the lives of tens of thousands of people each year. Not without importance was the minority of the uprooted, perhaps a third or a half, mostly men, whose seizure led to a wearisome trek toward the coast, or to death along the way. But of greater significance for western central Africa was the probable majority, mostly young women resettled as newly dependent slaves in societies and economies more hierarchical than the communities of local-born folk they had left behind. Agricultural technologies and the bulk of the labor for the use of the community must have been redirected, though adaptations to the new American crops, into the hands of the numerous females available to hoe the fields. Even domestic criminality changed to center on persecuting younger men and traders who violated the sexual monopoly that the few wealthy older males asserted over the dependent majority of women.

Paradoxically, the key features of this economic transformation in western central Africa were the weakness of the credit and goods from the Atlantic and the exquisite sensitivity of finely balanced African social and political institutions to its faint emanations. Relative to the size of the African economies and societies, this transformation did not require many imports or the sale of a substantial proportion of them very far in advance of payment to set off intricate and irreversible chains of actions and reactions that culminated in political conquests, resistance, and resettlement. The power of the Atlantic commerce to reshape came in part from the European loans of trade goods that converted long-standing relationships of cherished debt left outstanding in the African political economy to forced collections of people for exchange to obtain further credit from the Europeans. It also gained force from the African importers' pervasive resort to violence in the initial stages of the conversion, perhaps because the goods they had were so meager compared to the magnitude of the political centralization they prompted. Warfare brought slaves into the transaction with very little investment of commercial resources. To the extent that credit, currencies, and exchanges of material commodities became prominent methods of reorganizing human relationships in western central Africa, the political economy had become more "capitalistic" in the conventional European sense.

In fact, the economic transformation bore an arguable family resemblance to the first stirrings of forces elsewhere in the world that later became merchant capitalism, the very system that was bringing imports to western central Africa in such unprecedented volume by the eighteenth century. The violence of the fall of the old kingdoms, or the rise of the new regimes, was analogous to the forced appropriation of wealth sometimes termed "primitive accumulation" in the context of northern Europe. Though in western central Africa's manual political economy, kings seized people rather than the lands that were taken in the feudal environment of late medieval England, the process was the same: powerful men hastened an incipient conversion to exchange and credit by seizing the most productive assets of their respective economies, and they used force to accomplish the task at very low expenditures of the still-scarce assets of a barely nascent commercial sector.

The debt-slaving techniques of the trading kings represented a degree of capitalized production in Africa comparable to the early modern European "putting-out" system of merchant-financed cottage industry. Mercantile-owned raw materials enabled cottagers and craftsmen in Europe to fabricate woolens and guns that, loaned by African merchant princes to villagers in a political economy of people, became sources of slaves sent to America. The process made slaves of western central African farmers, not wage-earning "free" workers, because the credit and commodity currencies available there remained too scarce to monetize the economy fully. Peasants and artisans in northern Europe fell ultimately into dependency on currency wages, because the stock of commercial capital grew large enough there to finance the expensive further transition to industrial capitalism. Industrial capital reached Africa in a similarly weak form only with the advent of colonial rule.

In a further parallel, the African princes in possession of commercial capital advanced to formal political authority at a pace not far behind their English counterparts' seizure of the state in London, a once-peripheral area of Europe undergoing its own "bourgeois revolution" at the end of the seventeenth century. It required far fewer goods to overcome the weak rain kings of central Africa than it took commercial capital to tame the powerful and heavily armed monarchies of western Europe. Without pushing the odd contemporaneity to speculative excess, woolens then flowing out from the British Isles and other London-financed goods reaching Loango and Luanda, slaves from Africa laboring in the cane fields of the West Indies, gold retrieved by Angolan slaves from the hills and streams of Minas Gerais in Brazil, and silver extracted by other slaves from Spain's

American mines were transatlantic analogs of the imported textiles and the brass basins that inflated the economies of western central Africa. Allowing fully for the many other sources of capital in early modern Britain, including profits from reselling slave-grown New World commodities to continental Europe through England and Scotland, the tokens of wealth peculiar to each supported parallel political mercantilisms in Kongo, Kasanje, the highlands warrior kingdoms, London, and Lisbon.

If western central Africans began to reorient their economies and societies toward slaving in large part because the required initial investment was so modest, completion of the process proceeded from the subsequently rapid and unexpected rises in costs. The first imports lost their value as they became common, though they also became common because they were initially so valuable. African monarchs repeatedly entered the Atlantic trade at virtually no political or economic start-up expense to themselves, owing to the credit they obtained from Europeans in part, but more importantly because of the small losses entailed in releasing criminals or launching raids on accessible neighboring populations. Ivory and wax for exchange, not to mention the surplus people, were low-cost by-products of productive activities Africans pursued for their use-values alone. The first trading occurred through existing institutions, commercial and political.

The feebleness of the capital available to cover these rising needs in the longer term drove nearly everyone involved to resort to violence when in every case, and in fact as a direct consequence of the marginal first engagements, the costs became excessive. Ivory production retreated toward the interior. Armed pursuit of people provoked resistance. Military and administrative expenses grew beyond the capability of existing kingdoms to afford, and peaceful sales of surplus ivory turned into violent seizures of people whom no one wished to lose. This unintended outcome had the unforeseen, gradual, and tragic quality of a similarly "unthinking decision" behind the simultaneous emergence of slavery in North America.[61] Thus the entire historical process, the reasons for making the decisions, the methods adopted, and the identities of the leading actors make sense only when viewed in terms of change itself.

Geographical dislocations and consequent enslavement created coercive labor institutions in Africa that would enable African entrepreneurs in the era of "legitimate trade" in wax, ivory, and rubber exports that succeeded slaves after about 1850 to mobilize young males, no longer directly converted to imported goods through sale abroad, as processors of beehives and latex-bearing creepers and as hunters of elephant. These youths also served as headbearers and guards of caravans that carried

---

61. Winthrop D. Jordan, *White over Black: American Attitudes toward the Negro, 1550–1812* (Chapel Hill: University of North Carolina Press, 1968), chap. 2, pp. 44–98.

commodities over lengthened trails of a vastly expanded commercial sector and performed other activities productive of the commodities in demand in a later Atlantic economy. The structural changes—"development" in African terms—flowing from the new communities of dependents assembled via the first rare and valuable imports thus set the African stage for the nineteenth-century boom in commodity exports and, ultimately, for the colonial conquest that came hard on the heels of its crash in the 1870s.

5

The Demography of Slaving

Because the richest returns from converting goods into people came from spreading textiles and imports widely into areas where they remained rare, or from employing guns to capture slaves in the regions farthest from home, the transformation of the African political economies acquired an expansive geographical momentum that drove its violence off toward the east. From the earliest period of slave exporting in western central Africa, the political revolutions thus moved toward the interior, leaving behind them a growing commercialized area under new regimes oriented toward the Atlantic trade. In geographical terms, the areas of greatest violence formed a kind of frontier zone, as well as a transitional period, within which the initial recipients of imported goods had acquired enough dependents to overwhelm older institutions but had not yet spread imports in quantities sufficient to bring social and political order based on debt out of the chaos. The movement of this slaving frontier slowed only after it had drawn the wealthy and the poor of all of western central Africa into new relations of production and reproduction underwritten by exchanges of neighbors, kin, and dependents for foreign goods. The demographic consequences of the attendant resettlement and exile varied according to where people lived in relation to the opening phases of the trade, its cataclysmic transitional stage, and the reconstruction of states based on mercantile principles.

The Slaving Frontier

The violence of the revolution—from a political economy in which kings commanded the respect and occasional material tribute of their subjects to one in which warlords drew strength from imported slave mercenaries and guns and in which indebted patrons, elders, and dependent gentry stocked immigrant slaves against future payments on forced loans from powerful merchant princes—probably drove more western central Africans into hiding in the long run than it exposed to seizure and shipment off to the west. Leaving the sufferings of the enslaved aside for the moment, the demographic significance of the transformation for Africa lay less in aggregate population losses than in profound changes in settlement patterns, epidemiological exposure, and the reproductive capabilities of the populations who remained behind.

The entire series of local transformations, viewed over the three centuries of the Angolan slave trade, resembled a moving frontier zone of slaving violence.[1] It took shape with the first border raids of the newly centralized Kongo kingdom shortly after 1500 and continued in the shudders that ran through that state in the late sixteenth century. After several distinct eastward advances these wars of slaving finally died down in the very heart of the continent with the advent of colonial rule at the end of the nineteenth century. The Kongo violence fed the initial Portuguese purchases of slaves in western central Africa. The sixteenth-century growth of the Mbundu kingdom of the Ngola a Kiluanje and a similar collapse of its conquered domains into partisan struggles in the 1620s, though complicated by the interference of Portuguese armies in the internal politics of the African state in the "Angolan Wars" of the seventeenth century, advanced the slaving frontier south from Kongo beyond the Kwanza. It also set Luanda-based slaving on the war footing it featured for the first half of the seventeenth century.[2]

1. I employ the term *slaving frontier* in a different sense than the cultural syncretic one used by Vellut in "Notes sur le Lunda" and elsewhere. Some readers will note that the phrase turns up also in Paul E. Lovejoy, *Transformations in Slavery: A History of Slavery in Africa* (New York: Cambridge University Press, 1983), pp. 80, 84, et passim, in several senses, some of them broadly consistent with the specific concept developed in this chapter. Birmingham, *Trade and Conflict in Angola*, pp. 133–54, outlines much of the basic geography.

European slave buyers were acutely aware of these movements, at least insofar as they periodically had to meet the increased transport costs that each further retreat imposed on merchants attempting to stay in touch with more and more remote sources of slaves. For the early seventeenth century, Fernão de Sousa, 7 Dec. 1631, BAL, 52-IX-20, fols. 370–71v; letter from Padre Gonçalo de Sousa, ca. 1633, as cited in Couto, *Capitães-mores*, p. 217 (see also Brásio, *Monumenta missionaria africana*, 8:91–100, 237–39, 241–44); *aviso*, Bastos Viana, 31 July 1757, AHU, Angola cx. 27; *memória*, n.d. (ca. 1762), AHU, Angola cx. 29; João Joseph de Lima, *memória*, 10 June 1762, AHU, Angola cx. 29. See also H. Capello and R. Ivens, *From Benguella to the Territory of Yacca*, trans. A. Elwes (London: S. Low, Marston, Searle, and Rivington, 1982), 1:290: "The [slave] market, rather than being fixed, moved slowly and gradually in the direction of the productive regions, and as those are toward the east . . ."

2. Miller, *Kings and Kinsmen*, and "Nzinga of Matamba in a New Perspective," *Journal of African History* 16, no. 2 (1975): 201–16. Beatrix Heintze has written extensively on this period, especially "Angola nas garras do tráfico de escravos: as guerras do Ndongo (1611–1630)," *Revista international de estudos africanos* 1 (1984): 11–59, and "Ende des unabhängigen Staates Ndongo." I summarize the period in this vein in "Paradoxes of Impoverishment." Fernão de Sousa (governor, Angola), 7 Dec. 1631, BAL, 51-IX-20, fols. 370–71v (published in Beatrix Heintze, *Fontes para a história de Angola do século XVII* [Weisbaden: Franz Steiner Verlag, 1985], pp. 379–82), described the destruction left by these wars north of the Bengo and south of the Kwanza River.

The seventeenth-century spread of raiding out from Portuguese-conquered lands east of Luanda, the Angolan *conquista*, provides another relatively well-documented example between 1650 and 1680 of the slaving frontier's movement into new regions. When the struggles subsided within this region around 1630, the Portuguese had consolidated the military institutions of their *conquista* at a level supportable only through continued access to the inexpensive slaves that came from outright warfare. Though mercantile methods of skimming slaves, mostly by making forced loans of trade goods within the conquered area, soon appeared also, the local Luso-African Portuguese continued to slave mostly by extending violence into the hundred or two hundred kilometers of territory surrounding their comparatively calm center.

The wars in the area immediately around Angola began in the 1620s and 1630s, when militaristic Portuguese governors at Luanda employed African mercenary allies, the Imbangala or "Jaga," to raid north into southern Kongo and bought slaves from others south of the Kwanza on the slopes of the central highlands.[3] These Imbangala, very much like warriors who helped African warlords to consolidate their power elsewhere, brought slaves in from raids conducted around the borders of the Portuguese domain. Some of these incursions north of the Dande culminated in defeat of the Kongo royal forces at Ambuila in 1665.[4] This crisis of the old Kongo monarchy left the way open for Vili traders—a northern Kongo slave-trading gentry from Loango supported by French, Dutch, and English goods—and heirs of the old provincial nobility of the once-united realm to consolidate commercial slaving networks in Kongo that lasted into the nineteenth century. They largely excluded the militaristic Angolan Portuguese from this relatively peaceful trade.

Instead, slaves generated from violence in the middle and later seventeenth century continued to flow toward Luanda from the northern slopes of the central highlands through Portuguese outposts along the middle Kwanza. This raiding drove the inhabitants of the plateau to regroup themselves around Ovimbundu warlords, whose successors would dominate the history of the region for the century to come.[5] The Kwango valley, at about the same distance in the east from the colonial core, particularly the central portions of it then falling under the influence of Im-

3. Fernão de Sousa papers, 7 Dec. 1631, BAL, 51-IX-20, fols. 370–71v (published in Heintze, *Fontes,* pp. 379–82); *relação,* BAL, 51-IX-21, fols. 19–29v; anonymous report, n.d. (ca. 1650s), BAL, 50-V-37, fols. 245–47v. In general for these wars, see Miller, *Kings and Kinsmen,* pp. 176–223. Also see Heintze, "Ende des unabhängigen Staates Ndongo" and "Angola nas garras do tráfico de escravos."
4. Thornton, *Kingdom of Kongo,* pp. 73–77ff.; Birmingham, *Trade and Conflict in Angola,* pp. 117–22.
5. Miller, "Central and Southern Angola."

bangala bands led by the famous queen Nzinga of Matamba, began contributing slaves from local wars in the same decades.[6]

The Kwango zone of violent slaving consolidated into stable warlord states during the 1650s and 1660s, when Portuguese and Brazilian buyers disentangled themselves from Spanish overrule (1580–1640), ended Dutch interference in Angola (1641–48) and Brazil (1654), and began to seek labor. Nzinga signed a treaty in 1656 admitting Christian missionaries and Portuguese traders to Matamba, thus securing a reliable outlet for the captives that her armies seized through Luanda traders of no particular financial strength.[7] Similarly formalized contacts with Kasanje in the 1650s allowed these traders from Luanda to tap the stream of inexpensive captives generated by the military adventures of kings there in the following decade or two. African warfare on the frontier, not the economic strength of European merchants, generally determined the geography of slaving at that early period in the Angolan trade.[8]

The slaving frontier's advance into the Kwango valley and up the mountains ringing the central highlands thus established a set of economically specialized concentric rings surrounding the conquered lands of Angola between 1650 and 1680.[9] At the center, a warlord-dominated Portuguese core directed the skimming of slaves, largely by military means, from around its borders, though secondarily also by making forced loans of trade goods within colonial territories. Outside this nucleus merchants invested few goods, usually passively awaiting the arrival of slaves produced in the violence in the encircling disrupted areas and paying for them on receipt.[10] Late-seventeenth-century Portuguese at Luanda had thus duplicated the slaving strategies on which Kongo kings had fallen back a hundred years earlier: slaving wars conducted at the limits of their military capability, backed up by commercial consolidation at the center. Other African states would recapitulate the same sequence as they later expanded the slaving frontier into regions to the east.

In areas just beyond this tumultuous frontier, trade patterns showed the preference for commodity exports evident in earlier phases of importing elsewhere in western central Africa. Slaves were taken mostly on a relatively unsystematic basis there, as cast-offs from droughts, wars, and trading not directly related to the slaving frontier. The less mature Portuguese outpost at Benguela, for example, at that time remained largely a supplier of salt,

6. Miller, "Nzinga of Matamba."

7. Cavazzi, *Descrição histórica dos três reinos,* docs. 45–48, 2:330–36; also *Arquivos de Angola* 2, nos. 7–8 (1936): 9–14.

8. See the absolute stability in slave prices at Luanda throughout the period, during a sharp rise in the value of new slaves in Brazil: Miller, "Slave Prices."

9. Birmingham, *Trade and Conflict in Angola.*

10. Further details of this structure in Chapters 6–7 below.

copper, and cattle to the main base of the Portuguese slaving operations inland from Luanda, although slaves also emerged from its hinterland on the western slopes of the great plateau in the wake of drought and associated warfare, African and European.[11] The Loango Coast, with its greater commercial resources and lesser susceptibility to ecological distress, stayed committed for a longer time to supplying palm cloths, dyewoods, and other forest products also useful to the Portuguese at Luanda, as well as ivory sold for direct shipment off to Europe.[12] The trans-Kwango sent raffia cloths through Kongo and copper through the middle Kwango valley. But these commodity trades into the areas beyond the frontier created the networks of contacts and infrastructure that subsequent ecological crises and investments of trade goods would all too soon convert to handling slaves.

Violence in the Kwango valley ebbed after only a generation or so, since warlord-rulers in Matamba and Kasanje exhausted the local sources of war captives, quickly made contact with Lunda suppliers of slaves from beyond the Kasai, and transformed themselves into merchant princes busy brokering slaves who arrived from beyond the river and repopulating their fertile lands with the human profits of this trade. A civil war marked Matamba's transition from militarism to mercantilism in the 1680s. The heirs of the queen Nzinga, committed to Catholicism and thus also to slave buyers from Luanda, lost control of the kingdom's Kambamba marketplace to other factions in the kingdom. The usurpers, although identified in the sources only superficially in relation to the domestic politics of the state, but parties certainly hostile to the Portuguese, must have acquired slaves from new sources in the east and then sold them off through more commercialized outlets through the *ndembu* to the northern coast. The Portuguese militarists from Angola lost their position as principal buyers of Matamba war captives, and the new regime, known henceforward as Jinga, probably drifted from that time onward into the orbit of the more commercialized outlets to the northwest.[13]

The same commercial expansion from Loango fanned flames of civil warfare in neighboring Kasanje, just to the south, during the general distress of the 1680s. There, factions favorable to Portuguese merchants in the upper parts of the valley seem to have won out against others in northerly portions of the realm under the influence of adjacent Matamba. The victorious southerners accepted Christian baptism, as well as agents of slavers from Angola and settled in to buy refugees from east of the

11. Miller, "Central and Southern Angola."
12. Martin, *External Trade,* pp. 53–72.
13. In addition to Miller, "Nzinga of Matamba," and unpublished field notes on late-seventeenth-century Kasanje, see Fernando Campos, "A data da morte da Rainha Jinga D. Verónica I," *Africa* (São Paulo), no. 4 (1981): 79–103, and no. 5 (1982): 72–104.

Kwango in a marketplace near their new royal court under the supervision of Portuguese residents appointed by the government at Luanda. The warlord Kasanje kings of the preceding generation were doomed, as were their methods of supplying slaves from raids mounted from the valley up into the surrounding highlands, since both the northern and the southern factions represented the new forces of mercantilist slaving. Commerce thus replaced conquest in the greatest warrior kingdom of them all, and the violence of the slaving frontier passed from the Kwango valley after 1700.[14] For the remainder of the eighteenth century the mercantile lords of Jinga sent their slaves northwest toward the southern Kongo, while the Kasanje rulers sold directly west toward Angola.

These two, plus the trading chiefs of Kongo just to the north, prospered as agents for the emergent Lunda, from whom they acquired many slaves from the east beginning in the first decades after 1700. The Lunda *mwaant yaav*, thus put in touch with the coast, then carried the violent phase of slaving east by raiding the wetter and densely inhabited latitudes north of their capitals. Related political centralization among western Lunda nobles convulsed the regions just east of the Kwango in warfare during the 1740s and 1750s.[15] This advance of the slaving frontier probably drove many earlier inhabitants of the river valleys there away from their homes and up into the dense thickets crowning the watershed of the Kwango and Kasai, where, by the end of the century, the first generation of their locally born descendants became known as Chokwe.

On the central highlands the accessibility of good defensive sites and the greater difficulty of drawing large numbers of new alien dependents from the sparsely inhabited woodlands and deserts east and south of the plateau by commercial means kept the slaving frontier, with its Ovimbundu warlords and their more institutionalized forms of violence, stationary there well into the eighteenth century.[16] Other disorders that continued to disturb the commercial states west of the upper Kwango River in the 1730s and 1740s stemmed not from deep structural transformations connected with movements of the slaving frontier but rather from relatively superficial maneuvers by competing merchant regimes, mainly Kasanje and Jinga, to control resale of the captives reaching their markets from the east.

Consolidation of the traders at Loango, the markets in the Kwango valley, and the warlords of the central highlands connected the coast with the violence of a new slaving frontier located, by the end of the seventeenth century, squarely in the two most densely inhabited parts of western central

14. Miller, unpublished field notes (1969–70).
15. Vellut, "Relations internationales."
16. Miller, "Central and Southern Angola."

Africa. These populations would support the violent portion of the trade for the half century from about 1730 to 1780. Wars in the central highlands sent slaves both west to Benguela and north to Luanda in this period. The eastern slaves came from similarly militaristic pressures placed by early Lunda warlords on the hospitable band of woodland and gallery forest running east from the middle Kwango between 6° and 8° south latitude.

But pressures were simultaneously building in the west to expand the zone of Atlantic-financed slaving southeastward once again, beyond its mid-eighteenth-century perimeter. The consequences appeared first on the southern flanks of the area from Luanda to Loango that was already fully committed to commercial slaving. The French, active south of the Kwanza, initiated the change on the central plateau by contributing to the consolidation of Mbailundu in the 1760s, and the Portuguese at Luanda completed the transformation there by expelling the Mbailundu kings and their neighboring warlords in the 1770s. This consolidation of mercantilism on the highlands extended commercial slaving through Bihe in the 1780s to the populations of the upper Zambezi, including Domingos's village. Increased funding from Portuguese merchants also strained the centralized commercial regime in Kasanje by the 1760s, bypassing its market to contact the trans-Kwango through Songo and by distributing goods to its regional nobles later in the century.

Centralized regimes of the old sort drew the slaving frontier to the center of the continent early in the nineteenth century. By the middle third of the nineteenth century, the Luvale aristocracy near the upper tributaries of the Zambezi had fallen into the internecine wars characteristic of the slaving frontier.[17] The central Lunda, with the population resources of the forest-savanna mosaics conveniently nearby and available for plunder, postponed the outbreak of civil disorder until after the middle of the nineteenth century, but then even they, the most long-lived of the dynasties of border-raiding kings, too fell into civil conflicts that culminated in indiscriminate slaving by the 1880s.[18] Enriched western provincial Lunda lords were emboldened to dispute the succession to the imperial power in the 1850s, and by the following decades Lunda was accelerating into domestic strife. Though the precise role that trade goods and merchants from the west played in these events in the far interior is not fully documented, the similarity of what transpired there to earlier and better-known destabilizing consequences of commercialization in the west leaves little doubt that these

17. Papstein, "Upper Zambezi," pp. 180–81.

18. Miller, "Cokwe Trade and Conquest," pp. 197–98; Jean-Luc Vellut, "Les grands tournants dans l'histoire de l'est du Kwanza du XIXᵉ siècle," *Revista do Departamento de Biblioteconomia e História* (da Fundação Universidade do Rio Grande do Sul) 1, no. 2 (1979): 93–111; also Edouard N'dua, "L'installation des Tutshokwe dans l'Empire Lunda, 1850–1903" (Mémoire de licence, Histoire, Université Lovanium de Kinshasa, 1971).

wars represented the last movement of the slaving frontier. The full violence of this eruption merged into the quite different invasive disturbances of the eve of colonial conquest, backed by nineteenth-century weaponry and the great armed caravans of the period.

Only on the extremities did the pattern of violence differ. In the far south, along the fringes of the Kalahari desert, the agro-pastoralists of the lower Kunene floodplain sufficiently limited the quantities of goods they received to forestall the advance of the slaving frontier. Since their herds gave them means to create clients by lending livestock, they could assimilate the imports through established patron-client networks of exchange. The disorders that meddlesome foreign traders and inflated exchange networks brought everywhere else in western central Africa arose there only after 1850.[19] In the forest to the north, inexpensive river transport allowed slaving to expand without gathering momentum from an initial phase of warfare entailing no expense to the merchants.

The continuity of the process in the savannas seems amply demonstrated by striking resemblances among the eighteenth-century disorders beyond the Kwango, others reported simultaneously from slaving wars in the Ovimbundu highlands, and the extreme seventeenth-century disruptions recorded in detail when the slaving frontier lay nearer Luanda.[20] In the 1750s, organized bands of desperate brigands roamed a countryside east of the Kwango laid waste by utterly unrestrained conflict raging on all sides. The bandits lived in fortresses of pointed stakes, from which they ventured forth to attack any agricultural populations they could find. They lived by pillage alone, grew no food for themselves, and quite literally survived from eating lizards, snakes, monkeys, or whatever game they could kill, no matter how despised under normal circumstances; crops they could steal, supplies bought from importers; and occasionally the flesh of people who fell in their raids, particularly the elderly folk not exchangeable for foodstuffs. Raiders of this sort had reached a point of such abject poverty that they could not afford to fight with imported firearms, relying instead on bows, arrows, and other weapons of their own manufacture.[21] In the cattle areas southeast of Benguela similar raiding for people became intertwined with livestock rustling.

Reports from Kasanje in the 1750s described in what must have been only slightly exaggerated terms the same desperation in areas into which refugees fled east of the Kwango. There, people termed "Mucutibas,"

19. Miller, "Central and Southern Angola."

20. Miller, *Kings and Kinsmen,* pp. 242–51, with the argument refined in idem, "Significance of Drought, Disease, and Famine," pp. 24–28.

21. Dias, ed. (Leitão), "Viagem a Cassange," pp. 17–21. For the warfare inland from Benguela, Mesquita, 20 Aug. 1781 and 8 Dec. 1781, AHU, Angola cx. 38; also Miller, "Central and Southern Angola."

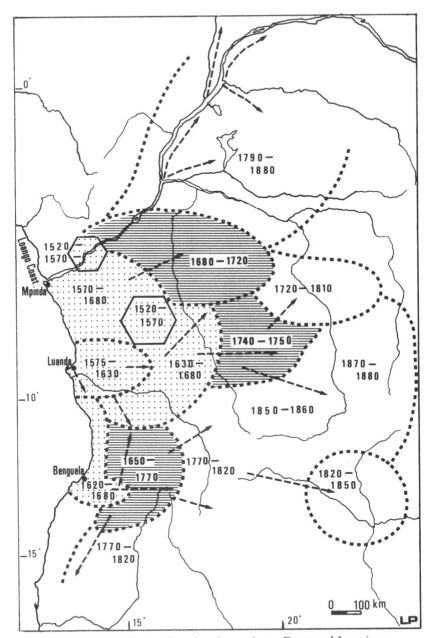

Map 5.1. The Slaving Frontier: Approximate Dates and Locations

probably archetypal Chokwe, killed and were killed as if life had become totally meaningless. They possessed no clothes, ate nothing but human flesh and raw insects, and hoped to ward off famished marauders by throwing their dead out on the roads for the bandits to consume. They hid out from strangers by climbing trees, again, surely out of fear of any stranger, and attacked intruders whom they thought they could overcome.[22] Wars, probably exacerbated by drought in the extreme cases that came to European notice, brought devastation so absolute that young males survived only by living off the capture, consumption, and sale of others. This phase necessarily ended when deaths, estimated as high as 90 percent of those involved in the fighting, seizures, and flight, so depopulated afflicted regions that the warrior bands had to disperse or take up systematic hunting for game or, when better rains allowed, keep females they captured and settle down again to agriculture.

The slaving frontier zone thus washed inland in the sixteenth century and surged east like a demographic wave bearing the sea-borne goods of the Europeans on its crest. It tossed people caught in its turbulence about in wildly swirling currents of political and economic change. Like an ocean swell crashing on a beach, it dragged some of its victims out to sea in the undertow of slave exports that flowed from it, but it set most of the people over whom it washed down again in Africa, human flotsam and jetsam exposed to slavers combing the sands of the African mercantile realms left by the receding waters in the west, displaced from their birthplaces but not distantly so compared to the faraway destinations of the slaves carried off to America. By the middle third of the nineteenth century, the wave had tumbled populations all the way to the center of the continent. There it rose to towering heights of chaos as its force combined with a similar demographic surge flooding the area from the Indian Ocean. Behind it, toward the Atlantic to the west, the turbulence subsided into relatively still demographic pools where quiet-flowing currents of reproduction and debt carried off most of the people sent into slaving, and where only eddies of periodic succession struggles and banditry from the distant sweeping tide continued to disturb the calm surface of politics.

Despite the stability of this frontier zone pattern, its movements were by no means mechanical or regular. The resourcefulness of the old rulers, the survival of the agricultural way of life that they represented, and the resiliency of the institutions they created often held back the wave's advance for years after commercialization and depopulation had built up pressures for an eastward advance, and so violence usually surged eastward only

22. Dias, ed. (Leitão), "Viagem a Cassange," p. 21. See also reports of similarly savage "Hungu" near the Kwango at about this time: Vasconcelos, 12 June 1762, AHU, Angola cx. 29; Sousa Coutinho, 18 Dec. 1765, AHU, Angola cx. 30; Birmingham, *Trade and Conflict in Angola,* pp. 150–51.

after fortuitous events or external intervention bent the retarding polities past their breaking points in particular localities. The Christian kings of Kongo maintained the militaristic posture they assumed during their period of expansion in the early sixteenth century and sometimes repelled Portuguese armies looking for slaves long after provincial lords involved with the Atlantic trade and the mercantile gentry had claimed most of the people living there. A good portion of the conflict that divided the Luanda Portuguese from kings in Kasanje between 1750 and 1790 derived from the stubborn refusal of the Kwango valley rulers to yield their monopoly over the trade on to the east. Ovimbundu warlords survived close to the coast for decades after their Mbundu and Kongo counterparts had fallen, as the slaving frontier moved on.

In frequent instances, drought added the straw that broke the camel's back. The well-documented spread of slaving from Kongo south to the Mbundu living above the Kwanza provided the first instance of the correlation of ecological stress, warfare, and exports of refugees as slaves. Slave exports from Luanda jumped with the onset of drought at the end of the sixteenth and at the beginning of the seventeenth centuries.[23] The seventeenth-century "Angolan Wars" between the Bengo and the Kwanza flared during subsequent periods of aridity. The next major inland movement of the slaving frontier in the early 1680s, when the upper Kwango valley and much of the sandy Ngangela woodlands east of the upper Kwanza and Kunene erupted in warfare, coincided with severe drought.

The same drought pushed the southern wing of the slaving frontier inland from Benguela to the central highlands. The modest numbers of slaves reaching the southern Portuguese outpost in the early seventeenth century had come mostly from wars on the western slopes of the highlands, very near the coast. The resulting tensions there boiled over onto the high plateau amidst the widespread ecological distress after 1680. Africans on its western rim then regrouped themselves under the warlords holding the best defensive sites there, while the Benguela Portuguese established a market center just below the mountainous crest at Caconda to forward the slaves captured as the conflicts spread. Recurrent drought between 1715 and 1725 provoked more African warfare on the highlands and drew Portuguese military expeditions east over the plateau surface as far as the upper reaches of the Kubango. By that time, the Portuguese were fighting founding lords of the eighteenth-century highland warrior states and driving populations from their earlier homes in the valleys of the rivers into the refuges they later inhabited.[24] Slaving east of the Kwanza in the 1750s

23. For the upsurge in exports, see Curtin, *Atlantic Slave Trade,* p. 112; for the circumstances, Miller, "Significance of Drought, Disease, and Famine," pp. 24–28. Heintze, "Ende des unabhängigen Staates Ndongo," p. 208, remarks on the increase ca. 1617–21.

24. Miller, "Central and Southern Angola."

and 1760s seemed to reach its chaotic peaks with lesser failures of the rains in those decades.

In the 1780s and 1790s ecological disaster and slaving once again spread together over western central Africa, this time at a juncture when commercial ventures mounted from Bihe and the Kwango valley had just introduced the commercial wealth of the Atlantic economy beyond the Kasai from central Lunda to the headwaters of the Zambezi. The Ovimbundu then consolidated their trading east of the Kwanza and Kunene as the most severe drought of the eighteenth century threw the marginal farming settlements of the Kalahari sand country into dire straits. Slavers from Portuguese Angola undertook their direct initiatives to Lunda, bypassing the broker state of Kasanje, as the distress continued through further epidemics and reversions to drought after 1800.

Starvation and disease forced these expansions of the slave catchment zones in part because they reduced populations near the coast so severely—one report claimed 50 percent losses east of Luanda on the occasion of the 1680s drought—that the coastal areas could no longer support existing levels of slave exports.[25] Widespread drought also discredited ancien régime rulers by puncturing a political legitimacy that often depended more on claims to rainmaking than on the force of the weapons they controlled. When their subjects dispersed to survive the drought, they lost bearers of these arms as well as the faith of their followers. In addition, failed rains drew traders out to the east, particularly to pick up starving refugees and abandoned kin in the areas of porous soil beyond the Kwango, whom they could resettle as slaves in the moister confines of valleys like the middle Kwango or whom they could take back up to relatively well-watered plains on the central highlands. The alternation of ample and failed rains itself fed the tragic economics that lured headmen and kings from importing goods to exporting slaves, in a real sense prolonging the natural disasters of drought into commercially stimulated raids and warfare. Lords welcomed the faint pulses of commodity trade that grew up in drought-stricken regions when starving people were cheap. Then when returning rains again permitted patrons and elders to feed and retain larger numbers of dependents, they found that their initial nearly costless acceptance of imports had become an overcommitment that they had to fight and steal to repay.

Portuguese armies also sometimes pushed the slaving frontier eastward by hastening the collapse of tottering military regimes within reach of Angola and replacing them with merchant princes more willing to rule through the loans of trade goods that European traders and camp followers extended to them. European-led armies had consolidated the power of

25. Miller, "Significance of Drought, Disease, and Famine," pp. 45–46.

trading kings in Kongo in the 1570s. The "Angolan Wars" saw militaristic Portuguese governors destroy the old kingdom of the Ngola a Kiluanje in the 1610s and 1620s, as well as Kongo royal power at Ambuila in 1665. The military expedition from Luanda that defeated Mbailundu and its allied highland warrior states in the 1770s offered the only clear eighteenth-century example of this interventionist tendency, since the slaving frontier elsewhere had retreated far beyond the reach of Portuguese arms. The Portuguese victory on the central plateau produced a dramatic and immediate collapse there of militarist regimes that had already outlived their time. The fact that revolution brought down the old regimes only with the added impetus of ecological collapse or foreign intervention, and frequently both, meant that the slaving frontier lurched eastward in uneven leaps, exaggerated near the desert all the more by the substantial distances separating pockets of population dense enough to support new eruptions of prolonged violence.

The contrasting institutions of trade on either side of this slaving frontier clearly expressed the revolution from earlier local political economies to later ones dependent on the Atlantic trade, as the zone in touch with the world economy expanded. To the east of the frontier, chiefs and local notables increased their followings of dependents with small quantities of goods and consolidated existing regimes by consigning a few unwanted individuals to slave merchants from the west. The seven baobabs symbolic of ancient authority still shaded the village of Domingos, while its chief confined the foreign traders, harbingers of the future, to a camp pointedly located on the opposite bank of the river. His effort to keep his people safely removed from the foreign wares had already drained the vitality of the old ways, as the transgressions of Domingos's kidnapper revealed all too clearly. Yet agriculture and regional trade still retained their vitality there in the 1770s, since the chief and Domingos's father eventually brought the kidnappers to heel and emerged from the confrontation with increased numbers of dependents for themselves—even though those dependents were slaves. Their very successes foretold the violence that would befall that area in the following decades.

To the west of the frontier zone, traders congregated at the royal courts, intermarried with local aristocracies, and sometimes sent their agents directly into outlying villages. Gifts of trade goods became pretexts for demanding immediate repayment in dependents rather than establishing some indefinite future obligation that in the meanwhile bound patron and client together in a continuing relationship of dependency. Where imports had become the basis of wealth, firearms helped creditors collect the debts they had created, and a seemingly endless plenty of new wares available on easy credit terms allowed African importers to replace obligations that their dependents managed to pay off with new debt. In the seventeenth-century Kongo, an ancient word for "slave" carried the connotation of "captured," while a new term implied that the notion of "buying" a person was recent and novel.[26] Modern linguistic research indicates similarly contrasting terms distributed in patterns that outline the boundaries of the Atlantic trade at its height.[27] The heat of the slaving frontier had reforged the old links of hierarchy culminating in ancient authorities, who brokered rare and hence valuable imports of African origin to selected subordinates, into chains binding nearly everyone to *nouveaux-riches* lords spreading masses of cheapened imported goods everywhere to impose new and greater degrees of subordination and dependency.

The Demography of Dependency

Increased dependency west of the slaving frontier had its principal demographic correlates in forced relocations of many inhabitants and in increased reproductive capacities of the population left behind by slaving. Relocation imposed general nutritional costs in addition to the losses individuals suffered in subjugation to powerful lords or masters. Farmers often abandoned good farmlands as they regrouped in isolated forest camps or mountain refuges to escape spreading violence, with only partial compensation from the yield of the hardy manioc tubers they adopted to coax harvests from plots confined to small clearings or sandy or rocky soils. They must have permanently sacrificed nourishment well beyond the temporary losses of harvests laid waste by war. General depopulation seems less likely.

An assumed range of ten to twenty million inhabitants in western central Africa is both general enough to be probable and sufficiently precise to gauge the impact of war, malnutrition, and epidemic contagion in relation to losses from slave exporting as the frontier of violence advanced eastward through the region. Working back from estimated levels of exports[28] and making the worst-case assumption that deaths among captives en route to the coast equaled the number of their companions who survived to board the slave ships, perhaps 50,000 to 60,000 individuals, 2.5 to 6 per 1,000 per annum, or one-fourth to one-half of one percent of the entire population, began the long westward walk each year at the command of masters who intended to remove them from Africa.

Adding fully as many more people seized as slaves but left to reside in other parts of western central Africa to those counted as killed or destined for the New World would approximate the overall impact of the

26. Hilton, *Kingdom of Kongo,* p. 21 and n. 86.
27. Jan Vansina, personal communication and sketch map, 25 April 1986.
28. See Chapter 7 below.

trade on people's daily lives. A hypothetically average farming hamlet of one hundred people could thus expect to suffer the disappearance of one of its twenty or so young men once in the course of each agricultural cycle or two. Rephrasing the probabilities to reflect the highly uneven geographical incidence of violent slaving in the frontier zone, two-thirds or more of all the villages in the region would experience such a single loss to slavers in a given year, though not all of that portion every year. For every village of that size wiped out by raiders, more than one hundred others of comparable population would have escaped unscathed. One may intuitively compare these rates of loss with the deaths and disabilities owing to continuing causes unrelated to slaving that regularly depleted all communities.

On the other hand, a warlord with five thousand followers would have to plan to replace perhaps sixty more of them in a year's time, or something above 1 percent, than he would otherwise have had to do. A community of ten or so settlements linked by economic and affinal ties would mourn the abduction of six to a dozen neighbors and kin every year. Every individual settlement would have been touched in this way, some more than once, before the two generations or so of warfare associated with the passage of the slaving frontier had died away. If a young male faced a roughly equal risk of capture for his twenty years between the ages of ten and thirty, his lifetime odds of enslaved exile rose above 12 percent during the period. It became virtually inevitable that a close relative or friend would vanish without trace during one's adulthood. Still, that individual's chances of escaping seizure and exile were still about five times better than those of avoiding a crime reported to police in American cities in 1980, more than half the odds of escaping assault involving personal violence in a U.S. urban area, one-eighth as good as those of avoiding a fatality on U.S. highways, and much less than half those of steering clear of physical injury in an automobile accident.[29] These comparisons may, of course, comment as eloquently on the hazards of modern Western society as on perils under slaving in Africa. Though the similarities excuse neither, they may convey an accurate sense of the demographic implications of slaving.

The threat of capture and resettlement stemming from the commercial revolution in western central Africa thus approached the level of endemic violence in modern industrial cities, where all the twentieth-century dangers just mentioned, and others, loom simultaneously. Slaving would have overwhelmed individual perceptions to the point of dulling the senses in

29. Crime statistics from *Statistical Abstract of the United States* (1981 ed.), pp. 74, 173; the *Washington Post,* 2 June 1982, gave figures of 1 in 60 and 2 in 3, respectively, for highway death and injury.

any given area only for four to six or eight decades during the passage of the slaving frontier, though an entire generation there, or two, would have lived and died without knowing an existence unburdened by such afflictions. What bitter lessons they drew from the experience and passed on to their children, with a lingering fatalism in the culture, can only be surmised. On the other hand, it is not difficult to imagine how survivors might have rationalized the concrete instances of these abstract processes that they witnessed as products of routine personal failings, unremarkable local conflicts, and other circumstances not linked clearly to what hindsight reveals as a widespread and systematic trade in slaves. In any case, as throughout the world's history, "human societies . . . displayed an immense capacity for living with violence."[30]

Great as must have been individual grief and resignation at the loss of loved ones to the trade in slaves, Atlantic and African, their disappearance hardly overshadowed other sources of personal tragedy, violence, and death in the lives of most western central African farmers. Nor did slaving in itself probably deplete the population of the region in the long run. Only half of the losses hypothesized for individual villages resulted in death or removal from Africa and thus in net demographic loss for the area as a whole. Year in and year out, overall mortality beyond losses from slaving surely fell near the approximately 50 per 1,000 reported for modern populations lacking Western medical technology and usually projected back for African populations before recent times, well above the 2 to 6 per 1,000 permanent losses to slaving.[31] Parents must have grown inured to seeing newborn offspring perish at rates up to ten times higher than kidnappings and captures.

Farming populations in all but the wettest areas lived at the margin of their agricultural technologies, with death rates repeatedly rising higher than the 50 per 1,000 norm in times undisturbed by slaving. A serious drought usually forced these people to abandon their homelands and disperse throughout the surrounding wilderness in search of whatever they could scavenge to eat, and led to the starvation of many.[32] Some withdrew

30. William B. Taylor, *Drinking, Homicide, and Rebellion in Colonial Mexican Villages* (Stanford: Stanford University Press, 1979), p. 74. Taylor estimated the incidence of homicides in colonial Mexican villages at 0.12/1,000, a twentieth or less of estimated rates of enslavement in western central Africa.

31. John C. Caldwell, ed., *Population Growth and Socio-Economic Change in West Africa* (New York: Columbia University Press, 1975), p. 4. Thornton, "Demography and History," p. 518, uses 47.2/1,000 as an overall mortality rate, a figure accepted by Inikori, Introduction to *Forced Migration*, p. 32.

32. Sousa Coutinho, 18 Dec. 1765, AHU, Angola cx. 30. Hilton, *Kingdom of Kongo*, p. 219, gives population figures for the Kongo capital town in contrasting periods of plentiful rains (5,000 people in 1774) and drought (only 100 people in the 1790s) that dramatically illustrate the strategy of dispersal.

to plant in the few remaining sites moist enough for agriculture, even banks of pure sand exposed in the beds of shrunken streams.[33] But with slavers in the vicinity, these conventional solutions to famine presented many with the dilemma of also exposing themselves to substantial risk of capture.

Smallpox added to the damages following famine, since survivors compressed in better-watered areas communicated the infecting virus to each other at epidemic rates. Under the constraints of slaving, the passage of the disease accelerated further among refugees clustered together for protection, through massed armies, and along trails where the captives and their captors moved through the interior.[34] At least once each century during the slaving era ecological and epidemiological crises reached intensities sufficient to eliminate perhaps a third to a half or more of local populations.[35] The commercial revolution surely increased hunger and contagion among the dependents of powerful importers of goods at the same time that it encouraged these masters of followers they could not feed, or who fell ill, to use them to pay debts owed to the Europeans. But the fact that villagers generally continued to scatter to survive in times of drought and epidemics even in the eighteenth century, thus risking capture and enslavement, may mean that slaving merely removed people who would otherwise have starved.

Wars in areas where slaving had not yet set in also put entire groups of people to flight and temporarily disrupted settlements, as populations fought each other to survive drought. Even if formal confrontations between armies did not always cause widespread loss of life, the dislocations that the campaigns imposed on the general populace could be destructive. Earlier possibilities of attack from neighbors or the passage of a friendly army must have preoccupied people as much as later fears of kidnapping by thugs seeking captives to sell. Twentieth-century descendants of the villagers who had endured the tribulations of the eighteenth century themselves managed to survive the departure of able-bodied male relatives to mines and factories in percentages greater than the probable losses to slaving earlier, demographically if not economically.

Slaving wars in western central Africa probably intensified dislocations of individual dependents, but they did not create mobility or initiate resettlement. Recurring serious drought had always forced people to aban-

---

33. Field notes, Angola, 1972; Motta Feo e Torres, *edital,* 2 March 1817, AHU, Angola cx. 64, for the early nineteenth century; Maestri Filho, *Agricultura africana,* pp. 44–45, for the seventeenth century.

34. Alden and Miller, "Unwanted Cargoes."

35. Vansina, *Kingdoms of the Savanna,* p. 149, notes a reference to halving of the Kongo population during an "epidemic of pestilence" between 1655 and 1657; and see Miller, "Significance of Drought, Disease, and Famine," pp. 45–46 for the 1680s east of Luanda; Estermann, *Ethnography,* 2:96.

don their homes and with sufficient regularity that few bothered to construct commodious or permanent dwellings which they knew they might have to abandon at any time. They frequently moved village sites in response to failure of the rains, or to escape the sickness that succeeded famine, attributing both drought and disease to the displeasure of local spirits whose wrath they expected to escape by moving. Individual settlements moved constantly in a slow transhumant rhythm, even among the farming populations that in the aggregate tended to concentrate permanently in hospitable latitudes and in moist river valleys. Individuals kept on the move in response to the seasonality of the rains, annually gathering in villages to plant when the rains fell and dispersing to pursue hunting and gathering or other activities during the dry months. Communities also regrouped themselves from time to time for defense and regularly abandoned village sites when accumulating refuse spread vermin among their inhabitants. Most savanna agriculture involved techniques of shifting cultivation that required periodic movement of living sites to keep near new fields opened up in fertile bush. Drought forced the herders to exaggerate their seasonal transhumant movements and in extreme cases provoked them to send formidable parties of raiders ranging hundreds of kilometers in search of food.

When drought became so extensive that it drove people out of the best-watered corners of their domains, as it did every second or third generation even before slaving, or when it persisted so long that relative deprivations became absolute, then desperately hungry people threw aside the social contract and became marauders preying callously on one another in order to survive. Suffering at such times easily approached that of the slaving frontier. Mobility, which farmers reluctantly accepted in normal times only as a necessary retreat from preferred sedentary ways, became an end in itself and formed the basis of new kinds of social and political organization no less revolutionary than those attending the incorporation of new areas in the Atlantic zone. People caught in such straits raised cannibalism, prohibitions against reproduction, infanticide, murder, and destruction from abhorred aberrations to the level of philosophical ideals, all notions based on disdain for the human lives that, suddenly rendered superfluous by failure of the rains, they implicitly viewed as the source of their widespread suffering.[36] Cannibalism, of course, was the idiom in

36. Beyond the seventeenth-century Imbangala and the trans-Kwango disturbances of the 1750s, one finds echoes of similarly extreme practices in the lower Kubango region: see Thomas J. Larson, "The Significance of Rain-Making for the Mbukushu," *African Studies* 25, no. 1 (1966): 24, 28, 32, 35, and R. K. Hitchcock, "The Traditional Response to Drought in Botswana," in Madalon T. Hinchey, ed., *Proceedings of the Symposium on Drought in Botswana* (Hanover, N.H.: Clark University Press, 1979), pp. 91, 96, both in areas not (yet) affected by intensive slaving. For parallel structural changes following drought in the western Sudan, see Richard Roberts, "Production and Reproduction of Warrior States: Segu

which western central Africans also understood the aims of the European slavers.

On a scale only slightly less desperate than the resort of refugees from major drought to such marauding, communities sometimes elected to survive shortages of food by disposing, however reluctantly, of their least integrated and productive members, usually children. By giving them up, they hoped to spread scarce provisions more adequately among the reduced group left behind. Consigning relatives and dependents under these circumstances might perhaps even bring food in exchange or secure protection from the powerful and wealthy recipients against the bandits overspreading the land. Starving parents extended these practices to African merchant princes and even to European slavers by the eighteenth century, and so droughts contributed captives to the trade in human beings independently of the other deliberate modes of enslavement, whether by direct sale or indirectly through the disruptions of the wars and banditry that they provoked.[37]

Bambara and Segu Tokolor, c. 1712–1890," *International Journal of African Historical Studies* 13, no. 3 (1980): 21 et passim. Nor was cannibalism a purely local, or even African, response to famine: Peter H. Freeman et al., *Cape Verde: Assessment of the Agricultural Sector* (McLean, Va.: General Research Corp., 1978), table II.1. Jan Vansina, in a personal communication (20 Sept. 1986), notes that some practices may represent extensions of normal practices of abortion and infanticide.

37. Eighteenth-century references for Angola include Oeyras *parecer,* 20 Nov. 1760, AHU, Angola cx. 28, and de Mello, "Angola no começo do século," pp. 552–53. For the nineteenth century, Dias, "Famine and Disease in the History of Angola," pp. 349–78. Also Clarence-Smith, *Slaves, Peasants, and Capitalists,* p. 84. The sale of children, and sometimes of oneself, into the slave trade in time of famine is widely noted in the primary sources from all parts of Africa but is only recently beginning to receive the general theoretical acknowledgment it merits; e.g., Mattoso, *Etre esclave au Brésil,* p. 45; Martin A. Klein, "Women in Slavery in the Western Sudan," in Robertson and Klein, *Women and Slavery in Africa,* p. 78. For theoretical background see Robert Dirks, "Social Responses during Severe Food Shortages and Famine," *Current Anthropology* 21, no. 1 (1980): 30. For specific references, John D. Fage, "Slaves and Society in Western Africa, c. 1445–c. 1700," *Journal of African History* 21, no. 3 (1980): 308; Frédéric Mauro, "L'Atlantique portugais et les esclaves (1570–1670)," *Revista da Faculdade de letras* (Universidade de Lisboa) 22, no. 2 (1956): 28 (citing Dapper for Senegambia); Daniel P. Mannix and Malcolm Cowley, *Black Cargoes: A History of the Atlantic Slave Trade, 1518–1865* (New York: Viking Press, 1962), p. 42 (citing Barbot on Gorée, 1681, and Bosman on the Gold Coast); David Beach, "The Shona Economy, Branches of Production," in Robin Palmer and Neil Parsons, eds., *The Roots of Rural Poverty in Central and Southern Africa* (London: Heinemann, 1977), pp. 43–44, 45, 56; Gerald Hartwig, "Social Consequences of Epidemic Diseases: The Nineteenth Century in Eastern Africa," in Gerald Hartwig and David Patterson, eds., *Disease in African History: An Introductory Survey and Case Studies* (Durham, N.C.: Duke University Press, 1978), p. 38; John Tosh, *Clan Leaders and Colonial Chiefs in Lango* (Oxford: Clarendon Press, 1978), pp. 57, 269. Especially graphic on the classic combination of debt and famine is Edward A. Alpers, "The Story of Swema: Female Vulnerability in Nineteenth-Century East Africa," in Robertson and Klein, *Women and Slavery in Africa,* pp. 190, 195, et passim. Phillips, *Slavery from Roman Times,* pp. 46, 62–63, notes a resort to slavery as an alternative to starvation among the ancient Germanic kingdoms and Lombards, who sold themselves to Byzantines for enslavement among the Muslims ca. 770.

One early shipload of slaves sent by the Angolan governor João Correa de Souza (1621–23) provides a glimpse of the debility of dependents boarded on the slave ships in time of drought, and in this case (as so frequently) also in time of war: of 195 slaves sent aboard one of the governor's vessels, 85 died (43.6%), and the survivors, presumably among the stronger of the captives originally embarked, included 25 sick old men, 55 elderly women, and 30 youths and children.[38] If the governor's advantages in the Luanda trade could bring him slaves no stronger or healthier than those, one can imagine the extreme youth, advanced age, and gross infirmities of the captives ordinary traders shipped at such times. The major eighteenth-century drought from 1784 to 1795 coincided with the all-time peak volume of slaves sent off into the Atlantic trade from the drier latitudes of western central Africa, surely not entirely by chance.[39] The majority of the slaves by then were children, mostly boys.[40]

Where the slaving frontier had passed, long-term resettlement of abandoned fertile lands with highly reproductive populations of women and children, under the protection of the new generation of trading kings, was at least as common as the temporary and localized depopulation of the frontier zone. The resulting population structure in the most densely inhabited areas—which by the eighteenth century contained the great majority of the inhabitants of western central Africa—would have tended in the direction of a striking preponderance of females, owing to kidnappings of the boys, the removal of men through judicial condemnations, and the importation of enslaved women.

A remarkable Portuguese colonial census taken in the late 1770s[41] revealed an African population in the *conquista* with precisely the sex and age imbalances that such African demographic processes would usually produce: approximately normal rates of female fertility and a relatively standard female age structure coupled with a significant absence of young male adults, the apparent result of the slavers' tendency to retain women and to release the able-bodied youths into slaving. A population unaffected by such policies would have contained roughly equal numbers of men and women in each age cohort, with only slight tendencies for older men to outnumber older women owing to female deaths in childbirth and a pos-

38. Cited in Mattoso, *Etre esclave au Brésil,* p. 52.

39. As observed by a visitor to Angola, João Victo da Silva, n.d. (ca. 1792, i.e., during the great drought of the late eighteenth century), AHU, Angola cx. 42, and confirmed by de Mello, 8 Nov. 1799, to the Conde de Rezende, AHU, Angola cx. 47. Also see Miller, "Significance of Drought, Disease, and Famine."

40. For the evidence in detail, Miller, "Slave Prices"; also see below, Chapter 11.

41. "Mappa de todos os moradores, e habitantes deste reino de Angola, e suas conquistas, tirado no fim do anno de 1778, em que entrão todos os dembos potentados, e sovas vassallos de sua Magestade Fidelissima," in Lencastre, 26 June 1779, AHU, Angola cx. 37; published in *Arquivo das Colónias* (Lisbon) 3, no. 16 (1918): 175–78, and discussed at length by Thornton, "Slave Trade in Angola," pp. 417–27.

sible offsetting decrease of adult men from accidental death rates higher than those affecting adult women. In this case, the African population of the colony, the so-called free blacks shown in Table 5.1, showed more females already in the age cohort of small children (1.2 males to every 1.5 females, or a sex ratio of 80 to 100). The excess of women increased to 65 to 100 (1.02 males to 1.56 females) among youths, and it reached the extraordinary disproportion of 50 to 100 (0.47 to 0.93), only half as many men as women, in the adult years of life, when slightly more men than women would have survived under other circumstances.

Though the disproportionately large number of women could conceivably have resulted in part from census anomalies, the probability of distortion to this extreme degree is not high. For example, males might

Table 5.1. Angolan Population Structure, 1777–1778: Index of Age Cohorts by Sex

	"Free blacks"[b]		"Slave blacks"[c]	
Age cohort[a]	Males	Females	Males	Females
Children, age 1–7	1.20	1.50	1.36	1.63
Youths (boys age 7–15, girls age 7–14)	1.02	1.56	1.18	1.19
Adults (men age 15–60, women age 14–40)	0.47	0.93	0.40	1.13
Elders (men above 60, women more than 40)[d]	0.18	0.14	0.08	0.16

SOURCE: "Mappa de todos os moradores, e habitantes deste reino de Angola, e suas conquistas, tirado no fim do anno de 1778 . . . ," in letter from Governor Lencastre, 26 June 1778, AHU, Angola cx. 37. Published in *Arquivo das Colonias* 3 (1918): 175–78.

Note: The unequal sizes of the age categories employed in the census make it necessary to develop an abstract standard by which to render them comparable to one another in terms of sex ratios. The figures represent the number of people in the average yearly cohort calculable from each age category relative to a standard population of 100 persons. Thus, the proportions hold vertically as well as horizontally on the table.

[a] The varying age ranges of the categories employed derive from definitions imposed for an empirewide population census ordered from Lisbon at that time. They presumably reflect rough distinctions between newborns (less than one year of age), fully dependent children, children and youths capable of making some economic contribution, women of reproductive age and men eligible for military service, and older people. The standards were European and not African in origin.

[b] A category including nearly all of the African population, "free" in the sense of not being directly owned by a European subject of the Portuguese colony, but not necessarily of local birth (and hence "free" in African terms). This category, 89.3% of the total, reflected the effects of importation of dependents by the African population of the *conquista*.

[c] "Slaves" of the European population only; 8.6% of the total.

[d] Assuming average attained ages of 70 years for women and men.

have absented themselves temporarily from the oppressed villages where the count was taken, since Portuguese colonial forced-labor policies in fact drove men subject to impressment as head porters away from their villages.[42] On the other hand, the shortage of males that drove Portuguese labor recruiters to impress bearers could itself have arisen in part from actual small numbers of adult men, as reported in the census. Further, the census could equally well have undercounted the females within the colony, since headmen had good reason to hide the women in their villages. They were subject to a hut tax that amounted to a levy on females, the primary form in which the Africans held their wealth, since they housed each adult female dependent in her own dwelling.[43] On the assumption that complementing evasions reduced the counts of males and females about equally, the low number of men must have resulted from elders sending younger male dependents off into slavery and, secondarily, from slaving-related male flight into surrounding warrior states and maroon colonies to avoid seizure. Such losses began to reduce the population of small boys below that of little girls before the age of seven, increased the disproportion during the next eight or nine years of their prepubertal lives, and left its cumulative impact in the young adult years of primary male laboring capacity and greatest female fertility.[44]

The large numbers of females found in the colonial Angolan census could have arisen from the estimated overall 6 percent incidence of enslavement under a series of plausible assumptions that demonstrate the

42. Governor Lencastre's covering letter with the 1778 census expressed his reservations about the numbers assembled, owing to the African authorities' distrust of Portuguese intentions in asking them the size of their followings; also Lencastre to Menezes, 11 Dec. 1778, AHA, códice 81, fols. 111–13v; for other doubts about the early colonial census counts, de Mello, 14 April 1800, AHU, Angola cx. 48.

43. For the hut tax and the religious tithe, or *dizimo,* D. António Alvares da Cunha (governor, Angola), 4 March 1756, with *bando* of 11 Dec. 1755, AHU, Angola maço 18 (D.O.); "Convenção dos dizimos," with accompanying report from Bezerra de Alpoim e Castro, 1796, AHU, Angola cx. 42; D. Fernando António Soares Noronha (governor, Angola), 1 Jan. 1804, AHU, Angola cx. 54.

44. Numerous other counts tend to confirm the large numbers of females in the Angolan population during the slave trade. A more detailed survey, district by district, taken in 1771, shows a consistently similar pattern, with the sex ratio at 91.5/100 in a height category taken to be equivalent to the "7–14 years" age category used in 1778 (*muleques/raparigas* of 5–6 *palmos*) and 36.9/100 in the adult category ("pretos machos capazes para todo o serviço/femeas capazes de terem filhos"); in "Convençao dos dizimos," AHU, Angola cx. 42. Also see population *mappa,* n.d., AHU, Angola maço 22 (54.5/100), and "Mappa da população do Reino de Angola," 1827, AHU, Angola cx. 71 (85.8/100 in the "free black" category). Tito Omboni, *Viaggi nell'Africa occidentale* (Milan: Civelli, 1845), pp. 408–9, gave figures of 79.6/100 for "free blacks" and 86.2/100 among slaves; also in José Joaquim Lopes de Lima, *Ensaios sobre a statistica das possessões portuguezas* (Lisbon: Imprensa Nacional, 1846), 3:4–A. Matos, *Compêndio histórico,* p. 143, has 57.4/100 for free males/females in São Tomé in 1814. For West Africa, Daryll Forde, *Marriage and Family among the Yakö in South-Eastern Nigeria* (London: Percy Humphries, 1951), pp. 81–89, has reconstructed the same 2:1 female-male ratio for the early colonial period in a heavily slaved region.

highly profitable human returns from the political-economic strategies presumed for eighteenth-century western central Africa. Two-to-one losses of males to females to the Atlantic trade should have meant that the risk of export for males was about 8 percent and that for females about 4 percent. If elders who sent their slave sons and nephews off into captivity replaced every two males lost with a single new young wife taken from the women retained, the resulting sex ratio in their villages would have reached 92 to 104, or 88.4 to 100. The reported ratio of 50 to 100, or 184 females for every 92 males, implies that reproduction and further imports brought the long-term return in human dependents to almost ten to one (80 additional females above the 4 replacements for the 8 males lost).[45] Allowing for surviving births of two boys and two girls to each of the women retained, with the young males later sent off and replaced with an additional female and the girls to be kept through their reproductive years, would account for about half of the reported surplus of females through reproduction alone, leaving the other half attributable to further imports of young women generated through sales of imported goods.[46]

The census gives no indication that precisely this balance of imports and reproduction produced the sex ratios observed, but the hypothetical calculation gives an approximate indication of strategies that would have been necessary to produce twice as many women as men in the years of prime adulthood. These inferred strategies would also suggest how many people remained behind to be counted in these censuses, consequences of their masters' having adapted western central African political economies to imports from the Atlantic. The people kept were more numerous than the people exported, and their numbers indicate something of the order of increased dependency in Africa produced by transfers of people from the locale of their birth to other regions of the continent. Even many of the males left behind and counted in their youthful and adult years would have been brought into the enumerated region as slaves born elsewhere.

The increase in the proportion of females between the category of small children (1–7 years) and that of youths (7–14 years) resulted from importation and retention of little slave girls. The reduced numbers of adult women relative to the girls reflect both the female mortality of childbirth and the export of older women in, say, their thirties, mostly those past their years of prime fertility. But to judge from the census,

45. With appropriate modifications for the other estimates listed in note 44, none of which would alter the essential point: the profitability of the exchange in terms of returns of human dependents.

46. Assuming 2 boys lost to slavery for every girl in the 1–7 and 7–14/15 age cohorts in Table 5.1 would in fact give 3.9 males and/or females per 0.93 women of reproductive ages, or more than twice the estimate conservatively adopted: Thornton, "Slave Trade in Angola," pp. 423–25.

African men sold off far fewer adult women than they did potential rivals among younger men. The wars of the slaving frontier zone—in fact, wars generally—supplied the additional females, since warriors captured mainly women and children, killing the elderly and leaving them for the consumption of starving marauders and driving the male survivors into flight in the hills and woods.[47] The age and sex structure of the resulting agricultural populations also reflected the assimilative logic of African slavery, in which older slave women and their children, who had learned the local culture and who had begun to establish local ties lessening their dependency, would have been the first to be sold off. Men may have continued to sell off older women as useless for agricultural labor or childbearing, since the numbers of elderly women dropped half again as fast as those of old men (0.47 to 0.18, or a drop of 62% for the men, and 0.93 to 0.14, or a decline of 85% for the women).

In areas west of the slaving frontier, like the Portuguese territories surveyed for the census, visitors would have gotten the impression of villages filled with women and children, with the prepubertal girls outnumbering the boys. Men would have been striking only by their absence. The numbers of young wives surrounding older males in fact astonished visitors to the interior of Angola, unaccustomed to such demographic imbalances.[48] Commercial pressure from the Atlantic twisted local marriage systems into parodies of the older exchanges of women among lineages. Near Massangano, a district in the Portuguese *conquista* along the lower Kwanza pervaded by the commercial economy since at least the 1620s, a man desiring a young woman as his wife often had to pay her relatives

47. Dias, ed. (Leitão), "Viagem a Cassange," p. 20; and see the frontispiece. Compare also the 25:55 sex ratio of the older slaves surviving the 1621–23 voyage cited in note 38 above. See also for an earlier period the patterns reported in Fernão de Sousa, 7 Dec. 1631, published in Heintze, *Fontes,* pp. 379–82.

48. Wilson, "Kongo Kingdom," p. 68, reported late-sixteenth-century Kongo men possessing from 4 or 5 to 20 or 30 wives; Gaulme, "Document sur le Ngoyo," p. 372, says that the "princes" there had 30 or 40 wives and slave women, with 4 or 5 not unusual among commoners; Broadhead, "Slave Wives, Free Sisters," adds documentation for eighteenth-century Kongo; da Cunha, 4 March 1756, AHU, Angola cx. 26 and maço 18 (D.O.), puts the figure at 30 women for gentry in the Luanda hinterland, 10–15 for most males, and at least 2 for even the poorest adult male; for nineteenth-century references, Thornton, "Slave Trade in Angola," p. 425. Vansina, "Peoples of the Forest," p. 108, points out that the spread of cassava cultivation, which required greater inputs of female labor for processing, was consistent with the heavily female population left behind by the slave trade; cf. Broadhead, "Slave Wives, Free Sisters," pp. 171 et passim. Wyatt MacGaffey, "Lineage Structure, Marriage, and the Family amongst the Central Bantu," *Journal of African History* 24, no. 2 (1983): 184, wonders if the modern matrilineal emphasis in central African descent systems may not have resulted from the period of the trade. For another line of argument associating "a large immigrant and alien labor force" of the sort found as slaves in western central Africa with matrilinearity, see Ivor Wilks, "Land, Labour, Capital, and the Forest Kingdom of Asante: A Model of Early Change," in J. Friedman and M. J. Rowlands, eds., *The Evolution of Social Systems* (Pittsburgh: University of Pittsburgh Press, 1978), pp. 522–25 (phrase quoted on p. 523).

nearly twice the cost of a slave, in trade goods, to keep them from sending her off to Luanda. When he tired of the woman, or needed cash, he sent her back, demanding the return of his investment. The woman then languished as a prisoner in the colonial jail until her relatives came up with the payment.[49] Women without men turned to adulterous relationships to satisfy their natural desires. Unscrupulous elders and patrons forced some of their female dependents into whoredom and then seized their young male partners and condemned them to enslavement and exile as adulterers.[50] Even the social definition of domestic crime had come to reflect the commercialization of human dependency prevalent within the Atlantic zone. The youthful and female population of these regions formed an exact complement to the rural immigrant slave populations of the Americas, heavy on able-bodied men but short on women and children.[51] The two groups of Africans, reunited across the seas that separated them, would have showed age and sex distributions not far out of line with normal premodern populations subject to high risks of death.

A population containing such large numbers of fertile women possessed enormous abilities to produce children, great enough in fact to replace fully the demographic losses attributable to slaving. Births during the year preceding the Angolan census had numbered 313 per 1,000 women of childbearing age (for all racial and civil categories, of whom 98.7% were "black" Africans), indicating both the probable youthfulness of the women in the residual population of "adult females" that resulted from disposal of older members of that category and the extreme dependence of immigrant girls forced to give birth at frequencies that may have attained rates of one child born every third year.[52] Overall, these women were bearing children at a relatively normal rate of one every 3.2 years for the entire period that they remained in Africa. The western central African males' tendency to retain these children and the females of childbearing age helps to explain the extremely low proportions of infants embarked on Portuguese ships leaving Luanda and Benguela, relative to the higher proportions of births recorded in the census and the numbers of children found also among captives taken in wars.[53]

49. "Convenção dos dizimos," AHU, Angola cx. 42.

50. Mendes (Carreira ed.), "Discurso academico ao programma," p. 420, reported "adultery" as the main source of slaves for the trade; female prostitutes along the commercial trails of the nineteenth century are common in the sources.

51. Cf. Michael Craton, *Sinews of Empire: A Short History of British Slavery* (Garden City, N.Y.: Anchor Press, 1974), p. 198.

52. Assumed from surviving births, allowing for a 50/1,000 infant mortality rate and a reproductive career of about 16 years; cf. the nearly identical rate (56.2/1,000) calculated on an entirely different basis in Thornton, "Slave Trade in Angola," pp. 423–24.

53. On the "children" exported, see Miller, "Overcrowded and Undernourished," refining the impression given by Herbert S. Klein, *The Middle Passage: Comparative Studies in the Atlantic Slave Trade* (Princeton: Princeton University Press, 1978), pp. 35–37, 49–50, 57–58, 254–56.

Table 5.2. Western Central African Populations: Alternative Assumptions

Assumed total population	10,000,000	20,000,000
1. Projected normal growth rate of 25/1,000/year would add, per year	250,000	500,000
2. Assumed 50% loss of people in wars and other destructive aspects of exposing dependents to sale in interior, above normal mortality[a]	60,000	60,000
3. Population increase remaining[b]	190,000	440,000
4. Working estimate of persons handed over as slaves in interior markets[c]	60,000	60,000
5. Assumed 50% survivors reaching the coast for embarkation[d]	30,000	30,000
6. Residual population increase[e]	130,000	380,000
7. Net rate of population growth[f]	13/1,000	19/1,000

Level of population necessary to produce known levels of exports under the conditions assumed, without long-term loss: 4,800,000

[a]Equal to (4)	[d]Estimated from export data
[b](1) less (2)	[e](3) less (4)
[c]Twice (5)	[f](6) / (1)

These births, combined with a relatively high death rate of 55 per 1,000,[54] allowed the enumerated population to grow by reproduction at a rate of more than 25 per 1,000 per annum. Such rapid increase, projected over an estimated population of ten to twenty million in the area within the slaving frontier by the late eighteenth century would have produced enough children to replace young adults lost through exports even at the minimum assumed level of demographic density, allowing for mortality of 50 percent for losses to violence and disease attending the export of individuals surviving to youth and adulthood before they reached the coast (see Table 5.2).[55] Under the less restrictive assumption of a total population of twenty million, the women remaining had the ability to increase the population at a long-term rate of 1.7 percent per year, almost exactly than the rate of a normal population (1.6%), assuming ecological sufficiency and/or technological progress probably absent in western central Africa, but greater than that inferred for parts of Kongo in the second half of the seventeenth century (0.09% per year).[56] The Kongo population had en-

54. Thornton, "Demography and History," p. 518, for example, assumes a death rate of 45/1,000.
55. The last is an assumption conservative by comparison to parallel guesstimations; Thornton, "Demographic Effect," p. 695, uses 15%, and Patrick Manning, "The Enslavement of Africans: A Demographic Model," *Canadian Journal of African Studies* 15, no. 3 (1981): 509, has only 10%. The documentation for central Africa supports the higher estimate employed here; see Chapter 11 below. Thornton, "Demographic Effect," p. 527, calculates the long-term growth rate, net of (implicit) losses to famine, disease, and slaving, at 2/1,000.
56. Thornton, "Demography and History," pp. 79–82.

tered the phase of importing females at the time it exhibited that estimated growth rate and had presumably attained an age and sex structure tending toward those observed a century later in Angola.

A population growing at 0.4 percent for a century would increase by about 49 percent or roughly the dimension of demographic losses attributed to the catastrophic droughts that occurred every hundred or so years, and thus account for the long-term stability assumed for western central African populations from about 1200–1400 A.D. until the *pax colonial,* modern medicine, and famine relief capabilities. Significantly higher growth rates (compounding at only 0.7% per annum would have more than doubled the population in a century) would clearly have strained the region's agricultural technologies to their breaking point. The low growth rate in late-seventeenth-century Kongo—well below the purely biological capacity of the population to increase—could have resulted from losses to disease and starvation in the droughts and epidemics recorded between 1650 and about 1700. The slight medium-term increase observed there hardly differed from the overall stability assumed to have resulted in the long run from populations physically able to reproduce at rates well beyond the ability of their technology to sustain the resulting numbers of people through times of ecological collapse. These crude demographic estimates thus conform to the impression, conveyed by other sorts of sources, that losses to slaving were far from the major determinant of the total number of people living in western central Africa in 1700, 1800, or 1850.

The numbers of women must have been even greater in the uncounted majority populations of western central Africa outside Angola than in the colonial regions enumerated in the Portuguese census, since generally greater prosperity beyond the pressures of European rule would have taken the form of more women and other dependents than those left to the beleaguered villagers reached by census takers in the Angolan *conquista.* Assuming only negligible losses from the areas east of the slaving frontier and allowing temporary local depopulation in the zones of violence to account for occasional export levels above those attributable to peaceful methods of generating slaves, the females of the repopulated regions could have reproduced at rates adequate to avoid demographic collapse in the long run.

By the eighteenth century, circumstances approximating this heavily female slave-producing population structure existed throughout the area immediately around the Portuguese-ruled territory along the Kwanza. They probably also prevailed in most of the Kwango valley, in most parts of Kongo, mainly the principality of Sonyo but also among the Soso and Zombo in the east and elsewhere, and along the coast to the north of the Zaire River. They may also have appeared in the parts of the central Zaire basin most adapted to transferring people, around Malebo Pool and in the Kwa–lower Kasai regions, at the heart of the Lunda empire, all over the Ovimbundu plateau, and to a lesser extent in southern population nuclei like Humbe. In the eastern regions still relatively untouched by repopulation, the numbers of males would have been decreasing only to a lesser extent. Adult men would have predominated in the refugee areas, in warrior bands, and in bandit lairs.[57]

Conclusion

Even discounting the roughness of the statistical evidence and the speculativeness of the assumptions necessary to assess its probable significance, selective exports of youths, adult men, and older females raised the fertility of western central Africa's population so high that the women remaining could easily have increased its numbers at rates that exceeded their abilities as cultivators to feed. Either a total population lower than that assumed or birth rates lower than those recorded, though not both, would still have supported known levels of slave exports under the stated assumptions without demographic decline. On the whole, slave exports slowed people's ability to recover from ecological collapse and thus may have postponed conflicts that inevitably followed drought. Population stability ensued not so much in spite of the localized destruction wrought by the violence of the commercial revolution but rather because of the unbalanced sex ratio and the increased dependency of the general population that violence left behind.[58] The highest fertility would have appeared in the regions of densest population and more intensive agriculture, where lords and elders aggregated young women and in effect bred children with whom they hoped to surround themselves in an honored old age. Surely, few planned to find themselves constrained to release these youths when they neared the age of puberty, but in fact they sometimes were. The young women taken from them went to other central African regions, while most of the males became the boys and young men whom Europeans bought and embarked at the coast for America.

57. At the calculated birthrates, a total population of 10 million averaging the sex ratios listed below would produce births as shown; note that reducing the male-female disproportion by 50% lowers the births by only about 25%, so that the estimate is not particularly sensitive to the accuracy of this figure.

58. I have deliberately allowed my assumptions to stand without detailed criticism of the alternatives proposed by Thornton and Manning, to acknowledge the large component of guesswork in all such analysis. The fact that my conclusions converge with those of Thornton, though reached along a different route, may prompt further analysis of the assumptions made by Manning, who doubts that the western central African population could have sustained the losses reported from slave exports. My principal difference with Thornton is the limited role that I accord to warfare in generating slaves and hence the larger area that I include in the slave catchment zone.

Such differences in the age and sex distributions of the overall population reflected, as logic would suggest they should, the contrasting types of political economy that arose from the spread of imports in western central Africa. In the populous zones west of the slaving frontier, wealthy males converted their guns and textiles into families of women and children, seizing and selling the men and older boys, who brought larger quantities of imports, by coercive but generally nonviolent means. Males fearing capture and sale fled into the wildernesses, where they took up banditry, ivory hunting, and wax gathering to supplement the marginal agricultural production of the relatively few women who accompanied them there at first. Other men fought back from the security of the rocky outcrops, caves, and canyons, stealing the women and children they desired from their richer competitors in the farming areas and robbing the caravans that moved slaves and imports to and from the marketplaces. The farther east the slaving frontier advanced, the larger the areas of peacefully reproducing populations grew, and the greater became the availability of western African women to bear the human wealth of their lords and the slaves of the Europeans.

The uses and abuses of foreign goods as capital would surely rank at the top of the scale of the several ways in which western central Africans fell captive or into domestic slavery. Violence stemming from import-driven political centralization and consequent disintegration may have taken first place early in the history of Angolan slaving, when most captives came from areas near the coast, but it faded over time in relation to the less chaotic, if ultimately not much less forceful, methods based on lending and foreclosure. The proportion of slaves generated by commercial techniques increased as the Atlantic zone expanded in size and population, while the extent and inhabitants of the areas disrupted by the moving slaving frontier at any one time remained relatively fixed. Sales of refugees from drought would probably have finished third, though starvation and attendant struggles over food and fertile land might locally have produced more slaves than other means in bad times like the 1780s and 1790s. Drought also interacted in complex ways with capital goods from the Atlantic trade both to intensify the effects of foreign commerce on unstable kingdoms and to enable merchant princes indebted to the world economy to pay off their obligations with refugees. Finally, judicial condemnations and exiles arising from purely African circumstances beyond the range of the Atlantic commerce gave the trade in people its initial impetus in locality after locality, but these sources of people soon diminished to insignificance compared to the later pressures from debt, discord, and drought.

The demographic shift to high rates of reproduction, once the Atlantic slave trade ceased to relieve the pressures of growth after the middle of the nineteenth century, produced a "bubble" of rapid population increase in the post-1850 generation.[59] Overpopulation—the ancient affliction of people in western central Africa paradoxically intensified by the centuries of slaving and "development" in the vein of the African political economy—in turn exacerbated the ecological collapse attending the return of drought at the end of the nineteenth century. The epidemics and warfare of that era left weakened populations vulnerable to defeat by European forces that displaced the last of the slaving era's wealthy warlords and merchant princes in favor of colonial "chiefs," who powerlessly resumed their predecessors' habit of sending their young men off, this time to the cities and mines of modern Africa rather than to America as slaves.

59. For the population "bubble," see Vansina, *Tio Kingdom,* p. 308, n. 47; Miller, "Cokwe Trade and Conquest"; Thornton, "Slave Trade in Angola," p. 426.

Part 2

Traders
On the Way

6

Bridging the Gap

The Structure of the African Commercial and Transport Sector

Merchant and transport specialists enlarged the nascent western central African sphere of commerce and transport in the 1600s so that by the eighteenth century it had acquired an integrity of its own, with distinctive organizational forms and a complex geography of crisscrossing caravan trails. The participants in this growing commercial sphere ranged from small-scale petty traders, who culled slaves singly or in pairs from a narrow circle of villages, up through far-flung merchant diaspora sometimes thousands of people strong who collected captives by the hundreds over tens of thousands of square kilometers. Together, these and other commercial specialists kept western central Africa's Atlantic ports in touch with the retreating slaving frontier and consolidated new commercialized slaving systems in its wake.

This transport sphere also bridged the structural gap between two political economies of remote and incompatible characteristics: the African one of use-values, where exchanges depended so heavily on enduring face-to-face relationships that they resembled "sharing" more than "buying and selling," and the much more thoroughly commercialized and anonymous trade from the Atlantic. In institutional terms, the traders grafted intermittent long-distance commercial contacts between strangers onto a trunk that remained rooted firmly in continuous local exchanges among neighbors. Though the distinctly alien flavors of each system repelled participants from the other side, and though each side viewed their partners across the divide in terms of their own assumptions and rationalized the other's anomalous behavior in terms of sickness and savagery, traders developed working misunderstandings that allowed business to continue as usual.

The African traders adapted their institutional forms to the demography and the existing commercial resources of their territories. Where merchants were able to build on established exchange systems, as they could near the Loango Coast and in the Zaire River basin, and where they could distribute themselves thinly and evenly among the denser populations of the equatorial river valleys and the forest fringe, they tended to settle in decentralized diaspora of permanent villages. In the drier and less evenly inhabited lands to the south and east, where interregional exchange systems were less developed, the commerce in imports and the transport of slaves depended more on long-distance caravans moving between the widely separated population nuclei. Most slaves emerged in an irregular rhythm from scattered and sporadic violence, and that irregularity made mobility, in the form of caravans, an efficient way of managing their evacuation toward the coast.

The commercial capital necessary to expand the originally small exchange sectors of the African political economy came in varying degrees from European trade goods supplied on credit. The regional trade systems inland from the northerly parts of the coast thrived on the greater amounts of African commercial capital already available, and so some traders there relied less on outside borrowing for their working assets. Farther south, the caravan system made the transition from warfare to commercialized slaving based on debt only with a substantial influx of European capital. The wealthy British and other northern Europeans active at Loango thus bought slaves through African commercial agents at the coast itself in a manner not unlike the prevailing mode in West Africa, while the less well financed Portuguese managed to compete for slaves from Luanda only by injecting large quantities of credit in trade goods to build up slaving networks from scratch, making their purchases far into the interior at the end of dependent branches of the world economy. Farther still to the south, the combination of dense local populations on the central highlands and the prolongation of violent slaving there allowed poor immigrant Portuguese traders and their African affines to finance caravans sent down to Benguela largely out of profits made from selling very low-cost captives taken in African wars. Without the implicitly African financing behind this trade, undercapitalized Brazilian buyers at Benguela would have competed at disadvantages even greater than those under which they in fact labored.

Though these communities of specialized merchants meshed elements of the two independent economic and social systems—African sources of slaves with credit originating in the capitalist economy of the Atlantic— they also constituted a third, increasingly autonomous world of their own. They traded largely in terms of African ideological precedents, and though unlike the lineages in their virtual unconcern with biological reproduction of people and less involved than the kings in the creation of abstract loyalties and dependency, they still belonged to the African political economy to the extent that they invested most of their commercial profits in living human dependents, slaves, agents, affines, and pawns. On the other hand, they belonged to the Atlantic economy to the degree that they also held inventories of trade goods, obtained these dependents by exchange rather than through reproduction, employed some of the people they bought to staff growing commercial networks rather than employing them in agriculture, and exchanged others for more foreign goods to trade. The traders thus constructed an exchange sector distinct from that of the royal courts and the villages, one with its own forms of assets, its distinctive institutions, and its own currencies, all of material rather than human form. Over time, this commercial and transport system expanded into new areas and absorbed the older political economy of which it had once formed only a minor appendage.

Commercial Centers and Credit

The keystones of the trading sector were specialized commercial settlements, sometimes described as towns and at other times as marketplaces (or *feiras* in the Portuguese literature). These centers served as more than just physical locations where producers gathered to exchange goods directly with consumers, whether by barter or on a monetized basis. Rather, they were wholesale and financial centers where commercial credit in European trade goods filtered through foreign merchants and local brokers to the kings and other specialists, who redeployed them in the local political economies to generate slaves. The market centers thus served as the partially permeable membranes that permitted goods and people, imports and slaves, to pass between the commercialized Atlantic economy and the less exchange-oriented African users of goods. By a process of economic osmosis the *feiras* allowed the capital resources of each, human of the one and material of the other, to pass through while keeping separate the distinct and incompatible features of the two economies.

Depending on whether a marketplace lay on the African or the Atlantic side of the economic interface, its physical form could vary from a compact commercial ghetto to a dispersed set of compounds, each with attached fields, barracks, and storehouses, distributed through an extensive district. The economics of holding slaves favored scattering the population of captives near the fields that provided their food and separating them from one another to minimize losses to contagious disease. Where the African sellers still retained control, they dispersed their own reserves of slaves in surrounding villages in this fashion but forced the traders to concentrate in dangerously compact, costly, and dependent settlements. Where the foreign traders had gained the upper hand, they followed the more efficient strategy and spread their trading stations thinly over the terrain.[1] The economics of slave mortality gave a significant advantage to

1. Vellut, "Royaume de Cassange," p. 128, notes the shift in Kasanje, evident by at least 1812. Eighteenth-century correspondence between Luanda and Kasanje was predicated on concentrating traders in a single site. The mid-nineteenth-century descriptions of the Portuguese *feira* in Kasanje all indicate a diffuse settlement spread out over perhaps 1,000

African sellers able to crowd foreign buyers of slaves together in a compact dependent ghetto.

The physical isolation of marketplaces dominated by the strong African states, even when it harmed slaves awaiting forwarding on to the coast or onto the ships waiting offshore, insulated the kings' domains from the commercial economy at the same time that they depended heavily on its capital. The status of these large markets as alien enclaves of credit and exchange thus reiterated on a much grander scale the separation of Domingos's village from the traders' camp located on the opposite bank of the river. The expanse of water between the beach at Cabinda and the slave ships anchored at a distance from it expressed in the strongest terms of all this physical division between the worlds of use and of exchange.

The central markets in the interior, though seldom described in detail by contemporaries, probably contained clusters of straw-roofed huts, each with a high-walled pen of rough stakes to hold slaves, and all facing inward on an irregular square or boulevard some distance from the town of the supervising African lord. In these settlements resided almost exclusively immigrant traders, most of them there only on a temporary basis to transact business during a single wet season while they waited for the rains to abate before departing back to the west. Each merchant occupied his own compound of this sort, which provided rudimentary living quarters for himself and his crew of slave guards and bearers, a reasonably secure storehouse for his goods, and a means of confining his trade slaves between the time he acquired them and the day he eventually marched them westward or boarded them on his ship.

On the coast north of the Zaire, ship captains set up flimsy sheds on shore while their vessels road at anchor in the bay, though traders might remain on the beach on that temporary basis for months. At some points along the northern coast and throughout the Luanda hinterland, slave traders could make use of more substantial facilities maintained by the African market authorities and rented from them. These authorities were usually brokers delegated by the political lord behind the marketplace to represent him and his followers to the traders and the only permanent

---

square kilometers: António Rodrigues Neves, *Memoria da expedição a Cassange commandado pelo Major Graduado Francisco de Salles Ferreira em 1850* (Lisbon: Imprensa Silviana, 1854), pp. 35–36; Capello and Ivens, *From Benguella*, 1:321; David Livingstone, *Missionary Travels and Researches in South Africa* (London: J. Murray, 1857), pp. 360–70. The several officially recognized marketplaces ringing the Portuguese territory inland from Luanda (or *feiras* in government parlance) belonged to the Atlantic economy rather than to African states, with the exceptions of those at Holo, Jinga, Mbwila/Mbwela in the *ndembu* region, and Mbondo, in addition to Kasanje. For discussion of their history and significance, see Chapters 17–18 following.

African residents of the market center.[2] Occasionally a few foreigners stayed
on as long-term occupants and added small gardens of their own and pens
for livestock. While such provision grounds may have supported some of
the captors in the market center and a few of their captives, the itinerant
majority of traders remained dependent on the surrounding African economy for food, water, and other supplies necessary to prepare a caravan to
depart or to stock ships for the ocean crossing. Kings often prohibited
agriculture or stock-keeping within the marketplaces and deliberately restricted the immigrant traders to their confines to add to their dependence
for foodstuffs, permitting sales of supplies to them only at the highest
prices, and sometimes not at all.[3] The implied threat of starvation hit most
heavily at the already malnourished slaves awaiting dispatch, though indirectly also at the slavers who owned them.

Ordinary African producers sensed the foreignness of the commercial
centers as clearly as Europeans recognized the African environment as alien
to them. They were reluctant to initiate exchanges of slaves and commonly
offered only wax, ivory, or other commodities on their own. As producers
in a use-value economy, they expected consumers to come to them rather
than having to take what surpluses they had out in search of potential
buyers. The distrust that rural folk north of the Zaire River had for the
trading towns of the Loango Coast, which they later remembered as
sirenlike snares, typified the general view of the market centers as strange
and even dangerous places. Their wariness derived only in part from the
near-universal peasant aversion to outsiders. It also expressed the distinctions that they—and perhaps people in political economies based on use-
values elsewhere as well—perceived between their own ways of exchange
and the capitalist basis of commerce in the market centers. Experienced
eighteenth-century traders in the Luanda hinterland cited the same rural
fears of being duped in warning colonial officials that planned government
feiras (regulated market centers) in and around Angola would prevent
Africans with goods or slaves from bringing them in to sell.[4]

Villagers especially avoided the city of Luanda, easily the greatest
concentration of Portuguese commercial investment in western central

2. Martin, *External Trade,* pp. 94–95, 102. The term for these brokers along the
Loango Coast, *mafouk,* apparently derived from the term used during the 1620s in Angola,
nfuka, meaning "a debt or loan": Heintze, *Fontes,* p. 118. Designation of these officials as
"the great borrower" thus directly expressed their functions in channeling credit from the
Atlantic into the African economies.
3. E.g., Graça, "Viagem feita de Loanda," p. 141, for Lunda. Vasconcelos *bando,* 10
Nov. 1759, AHU, Angola cx. 28, made clear the importance of maintaining plantations
under the control of the traders in the marketplace.
4. De Mello, 12 Aug. 1805, AHU, Angola cx. 55; Ferreira, *memória,* 26 June 1762,
AHU, Angola cx. 29; also the *memória,* enclosed in João Alvares de Mello (*ouvidor geral*),
7 Dec. 1798, AHU, Angola cx. 46. On the distrust of rural people north of the Zaire for
the towns, see Janzen, *Lemba,* p. xiii.

Africa, and flatly refused to come to the city to trade. African traders seem to have brought slaves there themselves only once, under highly exceptional pressures at the end of the eighteenth century, and on that occasion they behaved in naive ways that demonstrated how far out of their element they felt in the commercial environment of the town. Groups of Kongo appeared then to sell captives either because the slaves were reportedly unacceptable to agents of their usual customers at home, the British ship captains at the mouths of the Loje and other rivers north of Luanda, or because British buyers failed to appear there.[5] They may have revealed their inexperience in trade and the real hazards lurking in the towns for rustics from the countryside, since they bought all varieties of otherwise unsalable refuse, including dead cats and dogs that unscrupulous Portuguese merchants hauled in from off the streets to take advantage of them.

On the other hand, this story of Kongo willingness to buy carrion from the city's alleyways came in the midst of the devastating drought of 1784–95. The desperation with which they bought anything vaguely edible could also suggest starvation at home as the proximate cause behind the unusual appearance at Luanda of inexperienced traders, though ones accustomed to receiving goods from the bays to the north on their own terms in the African political economy. In addition, war in Europe may have temporarily removed French and British buyers at this time. The urgency of the Kongo quest to relieve themselves of captives in exchange for any item of even trifling value, rather than retain them for domestic employment, probably indicates that the traders could not have fed their slaves at home or have maintained them alive much longer in the city, thus confirming the extremity of the circumstances—drought and virtually nonexistent opportunity costs of selling dying slaves—behind the uncharacteristic Kongo trek down to the unfamiliar economic environment of the city.

In broad terms, the eighteenth century saw the investment of an unprecedented amount of European capital in the western central African commercial sector, with the timing of investment varying from north to south but with remarkably similar implications for economic growth and politics everywhere, beyond the universal atmosphere of alienness that it conveyed. The ivory, camwood, and other forest products delivered to the beaches of the Loango Coast in the seventeenth century had probably arrived largely on the accounts of African producers and traders working through the Zaire basic commercial system and its western outliers. The

5. "Informação breve sobre o terreno, de que se compoem o Reino de Angola, nomes das Cidades, Villas, Districtos, e Prezidios, Governo Civil e Militar, etc.," n.d. (probably briefing and instructions provided for Gov. de Mello, ca. 1797), AHU, Angola cx. 42; de Mello, 24 April 1798, AHU, Angola cx. 46.

addition of slaves to that trade after 1670 drew its impetus more from trade goods supplied on "trust" to prospective African trading partners by the British, Dutch, and other Europeans. European participants in the trade there implicitly referred to several forms of the credit that backed much of their business by the eighteenth century. Ship captains ordinarily offered advance "gifts" to African market officials, who were usually also the major traders in the local market, before they received permission to begin trading on a cash basis with lesser competitors, minor suppliers who handed slaves over to European factors and ship captains immediately in payment for goods they received.[6] The "gifts" initiating bulk transactions introduced European financing to the major traders' operations that subsequent outright purchases of small lots of slaves did not contain.

At other times Europeans advanced goods on explicit credit terms to big African brokers who kept no slaves near the beach but who borrowed the imports and took them to the interior to acquire captives from other owners left to hold them in readiness there.[7] Foreign loans of this sort often required the African borrower to put up formal collateral in the person of a hostage, usually a kinsperson, left with his European creditor.[8] European merchants recognized the personal bonds that "trust" of this sort created, if not also the economic benefits it conferred on its recipient, and manipulated credit as part of their trading strategies.[9] Late-eighteenth-century Portuguese clearly recognized and envied the advantages that British and French traders gained from their superior ability to send goods far into the interior from the coast north of Luanda with African agents and then await later deliveries of slaves.[10] The widespread depiction of

6. In general, Martin, *External Trade,* esp. pp. 93–103. Precisely this distinction was evident on the Gold Coast, where a corps of large traders dealt directly with ships direct from Europe and a host of smaller merchants sold to the resident factor of the English Company of Merchants in the 1770s: Metcalf, "Gold, Assortments, and the Trade Ounce," pp. 29–31.

7. Gaulme, "Document sur le Ngoyo," pp. 361 ff., describes advances necessary to trade at Cabinda, 1780s; an American testifying as to the trade of the 1820s reported that the Portuguese then buying slaves north of the Zaire both furnished the "money" with which Africans procured slaves and bought from stocks of captives already on hand. Phyllis Martin generously provided references to a Dutch ship in the 1770s (Middleburg Commercial Co. 406, ship's logbook [name not recorded], 22 July 1770) and to two French vessels (*L'Africaine* at Cabinda 1784 and the *Usbek* out of Nantes at Cabinda on 23 Aug. 1783, Archives Coloniales, Paris, B4.467 and C6 no. 24) reporting significant commitments of goods on trust. Hilton, *Kingdom of Kongo,* pp. 113, 116, 164, 166, refers to Portuguese and Dutch capital supplanting Kongo wealth in the first half of the seventeenth century and to substantial unrecovered indebtedness in Kongo as of 1649.

8. Martin, *External Trade,* pp. 100–105 passim, 114, for the incidents mentioned (though without emphasis on the credit aspects of the transactions described). Ship captains sometimes accepted sons of aristocratic African families as wards whom they took back to Brazil (or Europe?) for education: Karasch, *Slave Life in Rio,* p. 217. Also see Carlos Serrano, *Os senhores da terra e os homens do mar* (São Paulo: FLHC/USP, 1983), pp. 131–32.

9. Gaulme, "Document sur le Ngoyo," pp. 359, 361.

10. Corrêa, *História de Angola,* 2:178, 180.

these loans in the African idiom of "gifts" (or sometimes translated into European terms as "bribes") offered to superiors and the acceptance of humans pledged as pawns against them neatly captured the simultaneously capitalist and humanistic, European and African, aspects of transactions across the boundary of the two distinct economic systems. Other practices in the mediatory market centers must have carried similarly incompatible but cognate dual meanings of the same order.

Despite the concentration of traders in these central marketplaces and their single-minded devotion to exchange, they need not have created a "market" in the economic sense of a system with supply-and-demand-determined prices for transactions between anonymous and autonomous buyers and sellers. To argue from the persistence of administratively determined prices everywhere in these interior trading centers, commercialized markets functioned only in the ambivalent sense typical of the western central African transport sector. Though traders from Luanda evidently bought and sold imported goods and slaves for export among themselves according to the fully "market" norms of the Atlantic economy, in public and at varying prices expressed in the Portuguese currency of account (*réis*), the same traders negotiated affairs with their African customers and suppliers in the privacy of compounds and at the fixed exchange ratios typical of the African political economy. Among the foreign merchants, capitalist customs prevailed, but the habits of a political economy of use-values structured interactions with the Africans.

Commercially, the market centers facilitated the assorting function crucial to the African notion of exchange for use. They assembled in a single location traders offering the whole range of imports mandatory in every "bundle" given for a slave but available only from different parts of the coast. Traders with connections to only one or two of these sources could then fill out assortments, meeting the requirements of their customers by trading among themselves. Ships from Britain, France, and Holland each sent parts of the full selection of imports through shoreside markets on the Loango Coast. These emporia, in turn, supplied partially assorted bundles to other markets in places like Kasanje, eastern Kongo, or Jinga, where caravans and representatives of trade diaspora also bought goods of Portuguese or Brazilian origin from supply points to the south. The durable commercial center at Malebo Pool attracted imports landed all the way from the Kwanza to Cape Lopes, and the big *ndembu* marketplace near the main pass across the mountain spine of southern Kongo lay similarly at a crossroads of trade routes that, in its case, reached the sea along 500 kilometers of coastline from Luanda to Loango. Bihe lay at the juncture of trails coming east from Benguela and southeast from outposts of the Luanda network along the middle Kwanza River. The fact that traders could buy slaves only by offering complete selections of imports accounted for both the multiple trade routes linking each interior market to the coast and the impossibility of confining trade in any one center to merchants from a single port.

The investment of foreign funds in African slaving spread imported goods through the transportation and distribution sector of the trade as new commodity currencies. Special-purpose monetary tokens of local origin, copper rings and crosses, *nzimbu* shells from the bay at Luanda, iron hoes in the central highlands, and the small squares of raffia cloth used in the Zaire basin regional trade and related political systems had smoothed flows of goods along regional trade routes in western central Africa before imports began to arrive from the Atlantic. These African commodity currencies generally remained in circulation even after the Atlantic trade began, but they tended to diminish in significance as the financing of the trade became more European. At the beginning of the eighteenth century, textiles of European and Asian provenance had replaced squares of raffia cloth, at least in the international trade circuits, and the imports reduced the circulation of hoes as currencies in the central highlands a century later.[11] Copper coinage introduced in much smaller quantities through Luanda disappeared into African hoards in the interior of the colony to supplement crosses and rings smelted from local ores. Brass basins, which African traders presumably added to the copper circulating from ancient mines along both banks of the lower Zaire, became major imports along the Loango Coast.[12] Shells resembling the Luanda *nzimbu* began pouring into Kongo from Brazil, the Indian Ocean, and Benguela.[13] The Portu-

11. See the history and explanation of the change in "Instrucções que fez a base do Alvara referido e decreto junto," 5 Aug. 1769, AHU, cód. 408, no. 215. Cf. Owen, *Narrative of Voyages*, 2:296, for the marginality of the raffia cloths by 1824. For the highlands, Heywood, "Production, Trade, and Power," pp. 74–75.

Lovejoy, *Transformations in Slavery*, pp. 103–5, rightly emphasizes the vast significance of the currencies and commodity currencies imported to monetize the commercial sectors of African economies generally during the era of slave exporting but underestimates the importance of textiles in central Africa and overestimates the cost to the African merchants. Campbell, "Monetary and Financial Crisis," details the dependence of early-nineteenth-century Madagascar on imported silver. Jan Hogendorn and Marion Johnson, *The Shell Money of the Slave Trade* (New York: Cambridge University Press, 1986), have the most detailed study of an imported currency (the Indian Ocean cowrie). Also see Philip D. Curtin, "Africa and the Wider Monetary World, 1250–1850," in John Richards, ed., *Precious Metals in the Later Medieval and Early Modern Worlds* (Durham, N.C.: Carolina Academic Press, 1982), pp. 231–68.

12. E.g., de Mello, 11 Oct. 1797, AHU, Angola cx. 44; Francisco Xavier de Souza Cabral, 1 Sept. 1823, AHTC, livro no. 1, fols. 12–13.

13. References to imported *nzimbu* shells in Taunay, *Subsídios*, pp. 161–64; Corrêa, *História de Angola*, 1:135–37. For allusions to the Benguela sources, Domingos Dias da Silva (contract holder) to Jozé Lopes Bandeira and Florentino João de Carvalho (Luanda administrators), 8 Jan. 1767, AHU, Angola cx. 31, and Bowdich, *Account of the Discoveries*, p. 30, paraphrasing report of José Gregorio Mendes (1785). British traders north of Luanda also introduced competing shells, probably from the Indian Ocean: de Mello, 24 April 1798, AHU, Angola cx. 44. See Carlos Couto, *O zimbo na historiografia angolana* (Luanda: Instituto de Investigação Científica de Angola, 1973), esp. p. 38.

guese introduced sea salt from Benguela and other coastal sources under their control to undermine the bars of rock salt still quarried by independent Africans in Kisama and circulated through the marketplaces east of Luanda.[14]

The dividing line between the foreign and domestic currency zones could be quite distinct. As of the late 1750s, one of the two adjacent *ndembu* markets, Mbwila, looked east into the Kwango valley and conducted its trade (at least nominally) in terms of the old African currency unit, while British and French goods then flooding in through Loango had brought its west-facing neighbor, Mbwela, within the Atlantic currency system, with prices at its market set in terms of imports (and/or their Portuguese currency equivalents).[15] The two incumbent *ndembu* lords of the era were in continual conflict with one another as they fought for supremacy in the trade across the economic watershed, just as Kasanje and Malundo dueled over the same divide further south.

The actual imported currencies hoarded and in circulation, as opposed to the habit of using these commodities as abstract standards of value to express equivalencies between goods of local origin,[16] represented working capital that African traders borrowed from the Atlantic economy. From the African point of view, these stocks of goods were debts owed to the world economy in "hard" currency—that is, in people. The European suppliers of the goods, by providing the main sources of credit, effectively owned the monetary basis of the trade and tried to manipulate it in their own interests whenever they could. One Luanda governor praised the control that Portuguese merchants had gained over commerce in the interior owing to the African merchants' dependence on imported textiles and the tendency of the cheap textiles and other flimsy items provided as currencies to deteriorate with use, thus necessitating continued purchases simply to maintain the money supply.[17] Salt, which dissolved in the humidity of the African rains, possessed this advantage to an extreme degree.

The competing groups of foreigners in the Portuguese colony, local Luso-Africans, Lisbon merchants and their Luanda agents, and the government, each endeavored to establish commodities they alone could furnish as the currencies of the trade—copper coinage for the government,

14. Amidst much documentation, José António Gonçalves de Mello, *João Fernandes Vieira: Mestre de Campo do terço de infantaria do Pernambuco* (Recife: Universidade do Recife, 1956), pp. 196–97; Avellar, 20 May 1731 and 28 May 1732, AHU, Angola maço 18–A and cx. 21. See Chapter 8 below.

15. Vasconcelos *bando*, 10 Nov. 1759, AHU, Angola cx. 28.

16. E.g., by the end of the eighteenth century, the *folhinha*, originally an imported piece of printed Indian cotton, and the *beirame*, also an imported textile, had nominal equivalents in several other forms, though, significantly, all of them imported: de Mello, 21 Oct. 1801, AHU, Angola cx. 50.

17. De Mello, 11 Oct. 1797, AHU, Angola cx. 44.

coastal salt for the Luso-Africans, imported shells for the Brazilians, and Asian textiles and Indian Ocean cowries and beads for Lisbon importers— each at the expense of the Africans who had owned the equivalent earlier currency: various smelters and importers of copper crosses and bracelets, lords of the Kisama salt mines, Kongo kings who had circulated shells from Luanda Bay, and eastern Kongo traders selling raffia cloths from the forest margins. Substitution of the foreign imports doubtless forced the dispossessed African trading groups to resort to selling slaves to make up their losses.

Since the monetary control that imported currencies gave to the Europeans was limited by the extent to which physical imports served as currencies and wealth, African traders could have created substantial amounts of equivalent commercial capital from purely local sources by, for example, declaring goats, chickens, or any other domestic item interchangeable with given qualities of cloth for internal obligations. The relatively established traders inland from the Loango Coast seem to have adopted such equivalencies, while still carefully distinguishing the physical goods from the corresponding abstractions as "wet" rather than "dry," perhaps because such "soft" African substitutes circulated at discounts in relation to their imported "hard" equivalents from the Atlantic.[18] In parts of the Angolan *conquista,* African residents could pay small livestock as taxes that the colonial government levied in *réis,* the imperial Portuguese currency of account, but only when Portuguese monetary policies failed to establish their own competing imported media of payment.[19] At Luanda, which lay firmly within the Atlantic economy, trade textiles that served as "hard" currencies in the interior became "soft" and could be exchanged for the next "harder" range of Portuguese imperial currencies of account (bills of exchange) only at substantial discounts.[20]

Quarantine of the often aggressive foreign traders and their crews of unruly slave guards and bearers within the market settlements helped to insulate the surrounding neighborhoods from the unsettling influence of the foreign trade. The African kings who benefited from the trade, with the instructive exception of sixteenth-century Kongo, usually also located their courts far enough from their market to shield the domestic politics of their realms from the disruptive intrigues of the commercial community. They habitually appointed ministers of trade to administer the foreigners'

18. Also see Janzen, *Lemba,* pp. 31–35, for the distinction "wet" versus "dry" east of Loango.

19. "Convenção dos dizimos," 1796, AHU, Angola cx. 42.

20. Heintze, "Angolan Vassal Tributes," pp. 62–63, notes the resulting double pricing system as early as 1626 at Luanda. For later evidence, Câmara, 7 May 1732, AHU, Angola cx. 19; Meneses, 3 March 1737, AHU, Angola cx. 19; Corrêa, *História de Angola* (as cited in Taunay, *Subsídios,* pp. 164–65).

affairs in the markets, like the *mafouks* and *mambouks* of the Loango Coast.[21] The almost explosive power of the imports made keeping their stocks of trade goods within the market confines even more vital to the political interests of the African merchant princes who sponsored them. By restricting goods and the conduct of commerce to the marketplace, the kings could better—though seldom very efficiently in practice—regulate the circulation of imports, especially guns, channel opportunities to sell slaves to their political allies and subordinates, assess taxes and fees in the form of gifts and bribes before granting permission to trade, and generally manipulate the availability of commercial credit in ways that supported their own power.

The principal danger for the trading kings was that the officers they appointed as market administrators would enrich themselves so much that they became powerful in their own rights, as happened along the Loango Coast and at Kasanje, as well as elsewhere.[22] Such appointments often seem to have recognized major traders already prominent in the import/export trade, and the European credit available to them through the marketplaces in fact usually enabled them to overwhelm the kings in the end. Credit offered advantages both in distributing goods through the interior and in supplying slaves to financial backers at the coast. In the distribution phase it allowed market officials, or even upstarts without large followings of dependents of their own, to increase the scale of their trading at rates faster than the taxes available to kings, trading profits alone, or the returns from investments in dependents would otherwise have supported.

These European-backed brokers characteristically often became the most dynamic and powerful elements of the African supply system. They rose from positions ancillary to the established power structure to positions as legitimate political authorities in their own rights in stages closely analogous to the advance of the contemporary bourgeoisie in eighteenth-century France, though they held their wealth in retinues rather than revenues. Merchants and brokers first bought titles of nobility from the aristocratic older regimes. The most successful invested their profits in dependents and carved out positions of de facto power in their own rights within the old political systems. Their heirs eventually controlled a large

---

21. For the Loango coast, Martin, *External Trade,* pp. 97 ff.; Souza Magalhães, 16 March 1780, AHU, Angola cx. 37, has similar officials in the Kongo principalities south of the Zaire estuary; for Kasanje, interview with Apolo de Matos, 6 Oct. 1969, and the *requerimento* and documents in de Mello, 30 May 1801, AHU, Angola cx. 51. In the central highlands, the analogous position was termed a *sekulu:* Santos, "Perspectiva do comércio sertanejo," p. 83.

22. One may also apply the point to the later prominence of the *sekulu* among the Ovimbundu and to the Chokwe licensed as traders by the Lunda slaving aristocracy by the 1870s or so; see Gervase Clarence-Smith, "The Farmer-Herders of Southern Angola and Northern Namibia, 1840s to 1920s," in Franz-Wilhelm Heimer, ed., *The Formation of Angolan Society* (forthcoming); Miller, "Cokwe Trade and Conquest," esp. p. 198.

enough proportion of the population to redefine political authority on the basis of commercial wealth and slave followers rather than on magico-ritual technique, agriculture, and tribute. The final product was a thoroughly bourgeois African polity constructed out of European credit and trading profits invested in human entourages.

States and mercantile federations based very extensively on imported goods, commodity currencies, and debt eroded the power of kings of the older order at Loango, Kakongo, and Ngoyo in the course of the eighteenth century. *Mafouks* or *mambouks* appointed at first to manage trade on the beaches on behalf of the monarchy gradually applied their growing wealth to take over the levers of political power in the realm for themselves. The royalty, which had begun by insulating itself from the commercial sphere, found itself compelled to remain distanced from the new sources of power, ironically forbidden "by [its own] custom" from viewing the ocean and the ships from which came the imports behind nominal subordinates' wealth, and sometimes prevented even from dressing in the Asian and European cloths that symbolized the new wealth, for the sake of "tradition."[23]

In the east a parallel decline in the power of sixteenth-century political authorities among the Tio of the plateau above Malebo Pool and the rise of new commercial lords followed consolidation of foreign-financed Loango Coast commerce.[24] By the late seventeenth century, Kongo nobles of the Christian ancien régime still claimed a royal throne, but a new gentry of slaving lords grown wealthy from the trade exercised real power south of the Zaire.[25] Similarly, in Kasanje by the nineteenth century two "kings" ruled, one more and more ceremonially within the palace compound and the other externally over the kingdom's market and the sources of its commercial wealth.[26] The same pattern prevailed on the central highlands, where bourgeois *sekulu* village leaders gradually supplanted trading kings, and doubtless also in less well-documented regions elsewhere. Certainly, the old land-owning Chokwe chiefs yielded to a new class of traders in the nineteenth century.

On the slave supply side, European credit brought the crucial advantage of allowing its recipients to avoid owning the captives longer than

23. The political transition from kings to commercial interests along the Loango Coast appears in Martin, *External Trade;* is stressed in Janzen, *Lemba,* esp. pp. 46–47, 54–55; and appears to form the central thesis of Carlos Serrano, "O poder político no Reino Ngoyo: um estudo sociológico," summarized in *Africa* (São Paulo) 4 (1981): 129–30 (dissertação de mestrado, Departamento de Ciências Sociais, Faculdade de Filosofia, Letras e Ciências Humanas, Universidade de São Paulo).
24. Vansina, *Tio Kingdom,* pp. 451–57 ff., as stressed in Janzen, *Lemba,* pp. 58–61.
25. Broadhead, "Beyond Decline."
26. Interview with Apolo de Matos, 6 Oct. 1969; José de Oliveira Ferreira Diniz, *Populações indígenas de Angola* (Coimbra: Imprensa da Universidade, 1918), pp. 117–18; interviews with Sousa Kalunga, 11 and 30 Sept. 1969.

absolutely necessary. Credit thus offered wealthy merchants relief from the mortality risk of owning living slaves, a commercial equivalent of the security of the old kings' holdings of abstract "respect" in the African political economy, as compared to the inevitable fragility of the power that lineage leaders could build out of followings of descendants who might happen to die. Not holding captives assumed considerable significance in a business where new slaves acquired from remote sources for resale to the Europeans, however valuable, were also among the most vulnerable to disease and therefore among the most risky of a wealthy African's dependents. Even captives who did not bear wounds from warfare and raids could arrive in time of drought as half-starved cast-offs from famished populations, exhausted from forced marches to the west, and vulnerable to contagious diseases in the towns and compounds along the slaving trails.[27] The healthy remainder were the strongest and most likely to have fled, or to have been retained by producers nearer the source of the trade. Whatever the reason for the frailty of trade slaves as an investment, it made little sense to build up large numbers of such people also because they were expensive to guard and to feed.

A credit-worthy broker could avoid stocking crowds of suffering captives by borrowing goods to buy up dependents held by others and then delivering those persons immediately to his European creditor before mortality among his prisoners had reduced his gains. He could discharge his obligations with the weakest slaves he could induce a buyer to accept and retain his profits in the form of the healthier individuals and as debt alliances with local suppliers owing him other captives in the future. Such strategies probably contributed to the universal wariness among European traders about the physical condition of the slaves offered to them. Other African sellers who held slaves on their own accounts and then sold them for cash had to bear all the costs of flight, deaths, and maintenance that brokers endowed with European credit could minimize. By giving big suppliers of slaves time to find strangers to sell, credit also protected traders from having to deliver people belonging to their own communities and

27. De Mello, 12 Aug. 1805, AHU, Angola cx. 55, for African fears of the illnesses contracted in the trading centers. In general, Alden and Miller, "Unwanted Cargoes," for smallpox. It is tempting to speculate on the epidemiological and physiological bases for the therapeutic idiom of the Lemba commercial cult north of the Zaire, as per Janzen, *Lemba*.

Metcalf, "Gold, Assortments and the Ounce Trade," p. 27, notes that on the Gold Coast in the 1770s, Fante (African) sellers did not barracoon their slaves, while European merchants did. This contrast, of course, also reflected the difference between an African economy, in which traders tended not to invest in commercial inventories, and the European capitalist economy, in which merchants did. On the Loango Coast, leading Cabinda trading families made the transition to a fully commercial operation—trading on their own accounts with stockpiles of wood to sell to European ship captains, sending canoes that carried commodities they owned, and even financing purchases by the Spanish and Portuguese—only after 1850: Martin, "Family Strategies," pp. 81, 83.

thus permitted them to evade the ethical and moral difficulties of giving up "one's own" to the foreigners. Demographically, economically, and ideologically, credit lurked near the core of the complex forces that fueled the transport and distribution sectors of western central Africa's eighteenth-century political economy. Though the trade was nowhere conducted exclusively on "trust," the European ability to advance goods often gave crucial advantages to its recipients in the highly competitive environment of western central African slaving. Commercial capital provided the initial impetus behind changes that then gained momentum from the force of deep-running currents in the African political systems.

If the marketplaces channeled and controlled the merchant credit that underwrote the rise of new African trading regimes, containment failed to insulate the merchant states fully from the fundamental incompatibility between the African and European uses of material wealth. Africans treated the imported goods as largesse distributed among clients and subjects, or invested them in permanent relationships of marriage and in other sorts of alliance to create lines of loyalty and human dependence. One avoided canceling obligations of this sort. Though European traders also deliberately used goods to establish analogous links with their debtors in the African manner and might personally appreciate the social disruptions of foreclosing on such loans, they had themselves usually borrowed the imports they loaned and had thereby exposed themselves to pressures inherent in the capitalist world economy that could force them to call in these debts. Their own suppliers, fully enmeshed in the capitalist economies of Europe and Asia and ignorant of the patronage overtones of credit in Africa,[28] owed cash interest charges to merchant bankers on funds they had invested in the inventories of goods that traders spread throughout the African interior, and the bankers insisted on prompt conversion of these debts to slaves worth currency or specie in America. Downswings in the business cycle of the Atlantic world could thus periodically force Angolan traders to collect on their investments in African associates in order to meet liquidity crises in Europe. Such collections threatened to collapse the entire African structure built on multiplying loans through chains of borrowers,

---

28. Both situations were more pronounced in the eighteenth century than in the seventeenth; for lingering overtones of patronage in an early Luanda merchant's accounts, see Miller, "Capitalism and Slaving." Early evidence from Kongo repeatedly demonstrates the clear distinction that kings there observed between the complementing economies of people (on the African side) and of goods (from the Atlantic). See D. Alvaro, *mani* Kongo, 7 June 1526, in Brásio, *Monumenta missionaria africana*, 1:468–71, begging for support from Portugal in the form of people (priests, teachers) but no further merchandise (with the exception of wine and bread for the Holy Sacrament); also see Emilia Viotti da Costa, "The Portuguese-African Slave Trade: A Lesson in Colonialism," *Latin American Perspectives* 12, 1 (no. 44) (1985): 41–61. Thornton, *Kingdom of Kongo*, p. 25, cites Cavazzi, *Descrição histórica*, on the distinction observed in the mid-seventeenth century between holding slaves and possessing European imports, which he expressed as one between "leisure" and "wealth."

with overtones of reneging on implicit commitments to their trading partners.

In concrete terms, the disjuncture between notions of debt in the two political economies made the commercial centers of the African coast and interior where those economies met into battlegrounds in which European capitalist merchants and their agents sought to attract customers by offering goods on credit and at the same time alienated them by expecting quick repayment in slaves. African lords heavily committed to their subjects accepted the credit precisely to delay yielding up the dependents they could assemble with the goods and accordingly resisted payment.

If European lenders used commercial credit as a prime competitive method, African borrowers fought back by extending their aggressive use of the morbidity and mortality of their slaves, their corresponding main asset, from holding the slaves in the market centers hostage to shortages of provisions to holding slave buyers hostage against payment on their loans. Traders without tight affinal and other ties to suppliers in the interior knew that they could write off debts outstanding at the time they left for the coast. They were prevented from abandoning these debts, or from accepting reduced profits, by the fact that the only way they could pay for goods they had already accepted on "trust" from the coast was by returning with a complete coffle.[29] Hence, they waited for debtors to come up with the slaves they owed. They also postponed departures to amass efficient-sized coffles, *libambos*, or "chains" of captives numbering up to one hundred or more. By delaying, they thus inevitably built up the numbers of people confined to the market center, taxed the resources of food available to it, increased the risks of epidemic in the crowded conditions they created, and endangered their investments in the slaves they had assembled to await departure.[30]

A trader owning forty or fifty dying slaves penned up in a marketplace with an epidemic beginning to spread was in a weak position to quibble over the cost of the thirty or forty more he needed to depart. He could afford to buy the rest of his coffle at premium prices, paying as much for the remainder as he expected to lose from deaths among the slaves he already possessed if he delayed further. The nearer he came to completing his purchases, the more slaves he owned whose lives depended on the speed with which he could obtain the last few, and the more he was willing to pay to get on his way. African sellers exploited the trader's vulnerability at this point with "malicious canniness," as one Angolan governor lamented

---

29. Santos, "Perspectiva do comércio sertanejo," p. 112, for formalities and details of clearing up the debts.

30. Cf. Santos, "Perspectiva do comércio sertanejo," p. 95, for emphasis on the need for speed at a later date.

on behalf of the helpless buyers.[31] Because of the crowd of traders in the market center, all simultaneously trying to buy slaves under these trying conditions, one or two had reached this exposed position at nearly all times and therefore bid up the general price level that all had to pay, even to begin assembling their chains of captives, by acceding to the demands of the African lord.[32] African sellers generally kept their slaves in smaller lots dispersed outside the marketplace until the moment of sale and thereby gained a decided advantage from their much reduced exposure to losses from illness and mortality in this grim, credit-fueled maneuvering with the slaves' lives.

Transport and Marketing Alternatives

The institutions through which traders transmitted credit and moved slaves differed in form according to the demographic density of the areas on which they drew and according to the proximity of customers and sources of slaves to the nodal market centers. In the immediate vicinity of the commercial centers, itinerant peddlers, known to the Portuguese as *pombeiros*, took modest quantities of goods on consignment and hawked those goods on a cash basis in surrounding villages and local markets (or *pumbos*) for whatever slaves they might buy. Distributing goods out from enclaves of foreign investment in this manner gave alien importers contact with consumers through local men who spoke their language, who knew something of local tastes and needs, and who might also have had personal contacts of kinship or affinity in the regions in which they worked. In structural terms, it presented goods directly to producers in the African manner of effecting exchange. Selling through such agents had been accordingly the first method of distribution to arise in the sixteenth-century Kongo. At that time *pombeiros* had functioned on a grand scale, linking the distribution center at São Salvador to the great Mpumbu market at Malebo Pool, and the generic term for these African consignees had derived from the name of their principal destination at that time.[33]

31. Vasconcelos *bando*, 10 Nov. 1759, AHU, Angola cx. 28.
32. João de Alvellos Leiria (governor, Benguela), 24 Aug. 1814, AHU, Angola cx. 62, for the Benguela hinterland; Corrêa, *História de Angola*, 2:21–22, describes the psychology from the point of view of the traders in the marketplaces. A trader anticipating a modest 5% loss on 40 slaves and needing 40 more to cover his investment could afford to pay premiums averaging 5% for the remainder. With 60 slaves in hand, the same trader would be willing to pay a 15% premium for the 20 remaining. With 70 slaves in hand, his break-even point rose to a premium of 35%, and it increased at an accelerating rate for the last 10 to a theoretical maximum of 395% for the final one.
33. Willy Bal, "Portugais *pombeiro*, commerçant ambulant du 'sertão,' " *Annali dell'Istituto Universitario Orientalis* (Naples) 7 (1965): 123–61.

By the eighteenth century, the *pombeiros* still retained the same function of taking the Europeans' goods out to African producers who had commodities and slaves to sell, but the enlarged area in which imports circulated and the greater prominence of foreign capital had reduced these peddlers' significance relative to broader-scale externally financed organizations covering greatly lengthened trade routes. The image of the *pombeiro* became that of a trader's slave, or hanger-on, probably a local person of lowly status whom traders commissioned to hawk small quantities of goods in the immediate vicinity of a trading station.[34] African kings tried to limit this means of trading out from their market centers, since it could give the immigrant traders dangerous access to potential suppliers in the villages whom the kings preferred to contact directly themselves. Small-scale peddlers of this sort hovered on the fringes of trade at Luanda and were especially prominent at the Portuguese-dominated market centers along the Kwanza, where no powerful African lords restricted their roamings. Slaves there came from a great number of small sources, most of them close to the main markets and none of them individually worth serving through permanent trading stations.

On a larger scale, the economics of transporting vulnerable slaves favored moving them from points of purchase to embarkation points as rapidly as possible, in coffles of only a few. The ever-present specter of deaths among the captives provided the strongest motive for sending off a continuous series of small lots, but the danger of revolts or escapes from larger groups also gave good reasons for limiting the numbers in each party. Nevertheless, in most of the central marketplaces traders bulked large parties of slaves and dispatched them in good-sized caravans, even at the considerable costs that this practice enabled African kings to extract from them in higher prices as they hastened to depart. The reasons for this apparently costly strategy, adopted in spite of still other delays and costs arising from large-scale operations on the westward journey itself, lay partly in the geography of transport and partly in the foreign finance that backed most caravans employed in the eighteenth-century trade in slaves.

In the eighteenth-century trade, the term *caravan* (*conduta* in Portuguese, *kibuka* in southern Kongo, and *libambo* in the Luanda hinterland)

---

34. Compare the earlier more respectful sense given the term in Luanda at the beginning of the eighteenth century (Câmara, 5 May 1732, AHU, Angola cx. 19) with its much more modest connotations by the 1780s and 1790s: "Extinção do prezidio das Pedras," n.d. (ca. 1777), AHU, Angola cx. 37; memorial, AHU, Sala 12, no. 825; de Mello, 21 Oct. 1801, AHU, Angola cx. 50; Jean-Baptiste Douville, *Voyage au Congo et dans l'intérieur de l'Afrique équinoxiale—fait dans les années 1828, 1829 et 1830* (Paris: J. Renouard, 1832), 1:62, note; Vellut, "Africa central do oeste," p. 115. Venâncio, "Economia de Luanda," pp. 166–67, correctly notes the distinction between *pumbeiros* and the agents of Luanda merchants by the later eighteenth century.

meant a relatively large, centrally owned corps of head bearers and guards who carried goods or drove slaves in groups of substantial size between distant major market centers, usually between ports on the coast and the trading settlements of the interior. These caravans were intermediate in size and range between the small-scale local operations of the *pombeiros*, who might be accompanied by five or eight bearers at the most, and the gigantic, years-long, and wide-ranging 1,000-bearer caravans that nineteenth-century Ovimbundu, Imbangala, and other African traders mounted on their own accounts in the era of wax, ivory, and rubber trading.[35] Twenty to one hundred slaves would not have been an uncommon range of sizes for commercial expeditions in the eighteenth century.[36]

Their modest scale, of course, reflected efficiencies to be attained in the greater speed that accompanied limited size, but centralized ownership of the goods, and sometimes also of the bearers, tended to limit them to the amount of financial resources that a single trader could muster, or that backers at ports like Luanda would risk in the hands of a single agent. In contrast, those huge later caravans were financed as joint ventures by many different African producers and sellers and conveyed export commodities much less perishable than slaves. Dozens of individual African entrepreneurs then joined forces for protection against marauders more than to unify the financial structure of the venture. The centrally owned caravans of the eighteenth-century slave trade were more heavily capitalized, more dependent on financing advanced from abroad, and hence more tightly controlled by the coastal merchants' agents. The only exception noted was the Kongo-initiated trade to Luanda in the 1790s, which, uncharacteristically, came at the initiative of the African sellers of the slaves, who arrived with extraordinarily large totals of 200–1,000 slaves at a time.[37]

On the inbound leg of a journey the owner of the goods, or his designated agent, rode pretentiously at the head of the party in a covered litter or hammock (a *tipoia*, for the Portuguese) borne by two or four men. Sometimes he had himself transported well ahead of the main party to negotiate its terms of passage through the toll stations that frequently blocked the trails, or to arrange canoes through the ferrymen who con-

---

35. Miller, "Cokwe Trade and Conquest"; Clarence-Smith, "Farmer-Herders of Southern Angola"; Vansina, *Tio Kingdom*, pp. 251, 260–62; Martin, *External Trade*, pp. 118–22; and esp. Santos, "Perspectiva do comércio sertanejo," pp. 86 ff. Among primary sources, Livingstone, *Missionary Travels*, pp. 374, 457; Capello and Ivens, *From Benguella*, 1:17–18, 144, 192; Graça, "Viagem feita de Loanda," p. 108; Matos, *Compêndio histórico*, p. 330; interview with Ngangu a Kungu, 1969; Henrique Augusto Dias de Carvalho, *Ethnographia e história tradicional dos povos da Lunda* (Lisbon: Imprensa Nacional, 1890), pp. 186, 192, 193, 700.

36. Gov. Almeida e Vasconcelos, 27 Aug. 1791, AHA, cód. 84, fols. 254–54v; *requerimento* and documents in de Mello, 30 May 1801 and 12 Aug. 1805, AHU, Angola cx. 51 and cx. 55.

37. "Informacão breve," n.d. (ca. 1797), AHU, Angola cx. 42.

trolled the river crossings, or to begin business discussions at the caravan's destination.[38] The main body of the caravan advanced very slowly and inefficiently, often broken into several sections, each small enough to camp in the clearings that dotted the sides of footpaths through the bush. They marched in a single file of men with carefully packed bales on their heads, or slung from bamboo poles positioned on their shoulders. The packets were wrapped to protect their contents from dampness, dust, theft, or rough handling, balanced for ease in carrying, and often equipped with grips made of sticks to facilitate hoisting or lowering to the ground.

Each section moved for perhaps three and one-half to four hours each day, on the half or one-third of the days on the trail that they managed to go forward at all. The remainder of the time was consumed in repacking loads and preparing food. Protracted negotiations with ferrymen at river crossings, local gentry who set up toll stations, and rumors of highwaymen lurking ahead stopped them cold for days on end. They seldom covered more than 10 kilometers in a day's march and ordinarily progressed less than 150 kilometers in a month. At such stately rates of progress, Kasanje was four months from Luanda, and the Lunda capital lay four to five months more beyond the Kwango.[39] The Zambezi headwaters were even farther from the central-plateau caravan bases in Bihe.

Bearers ordinarily supported bundles, casks, and boxes of 25–30 kilograms each. The heaviest loads, including the caravan leader himself in his covered litter, were suspended from long poles to distribute the weight in tolerable portions among two or four men. Large tusks of ivory, which could weigh 100 kilograms or more, presented special problems of this sort on the westward trek, but bulky imports—the huge pipes of wines, crates of firearms, or bales of textiles—were repacked in smaller parcels in the coastal centers for the march to the interior.[40]

---

38. De Mello, 12 Aug. 1805, AHU, Angola cx. 55; Matos, *Compêndio histórico,* pp. 330, 336; Livingstone, *Missionary Travels,* p. 374. Cf. Sousa Coutinho *portaria* of 7 Dec. 1770 (enclosed in letter of 10 Jan. 1771, AHU, Angola cx. 33) allotting 4 bearers to military officers dispatched to the interior, obviously for the hammock; 6 to *capitães-mores* (i.e., an additional 75 kilos of baggage); and only a single bearer to ordinary soldiers, who clearly had to walk on foot.

39. Manoel Correia Leitão (cf. Dias, ed., "Viagem a Cassange") required 6 months to reach Kasanje with a party of 150 men in 1755–56: *patente* from Gov. da Cunha, 11 Dec. 1755, AHU, Angola cx. 26. Reports of ideal or planned travel times generally ran much more. Standard was 6 leagues, or ca. 40 kilometers per day, but such progress applied to individual travelers, African professional message-bearers, or small parties: Wilson, "Kongo Kingdom," p. 90; "Convenção dos dizimos," 1796, AHU, Angola cx. 42. A lone professional could cover 100–120 kilometers per day: Carvalho, *Ethnographia e história tradicional,* p. 193. Heywood, "Production, Trade, and Power," cites Magyar as giving a high estimate of up to 19 kilometers per day, with loads of up to 45 kilograms.

40. The powder went to the interior in *barris* (sing. *barril*) of two *arrobas* (30 kg.): Câmara, 22 Feb. 1780, AHU, Angola cx. 38; Almeida e Vasconcelos, 23 Jan. 1796, AHU, Angola cx. 44; cf. Christóvão Avelino Dias (governor, Angola), 14 May 1824, to Jaga

Ideally, caravan organizers added as few provisions as possible to these loads, to maximize the ratio of paying cargo to porters. It is not clear that the European-run expeditions of the eighteenth century included the logistical support, women and youths carrying food and other supplies, typical of African armies and of the African trading groups of the later commodity trade. The party therefore stopped whenever possible in villages to purchase its food and other supplies. Some of these places became minor commercial centers in their own right, surrounded by plantations of cassava and other crops grown for sale to the passing caravans. In practice, since the caravans were often employed to traverse the vast uninhabited zones between major market centers in the drier savannas, bearers had to sling small knapsacks of dried meat and manioc meal on their backs, beneath the cargo they balanced on their heads.

Theft by bearers raised the caravan operator's costs in spite of determined efforts to secure the repacked bundles of goods from pilferage. These losses in part expressed the inherent divergence of interest between the wealthy owner of the caravan's goods and the slaves and hired bearers carrying them. The porters proceeded reluctantly and cautiously as they advanced into unknown terrain, wearing protective charms and watching carefully for omens that might foretell dangers lurking along the trail—a log fallen across the line of march, or certain species of antelope bounding across the path in front of the party. The bearers' fears for their personal safety in alien territory merged with their efforts to resist the pressures of their caravan's owner and could erupt into wholesale desertion by the entire group.[41]

If the caravan was thus a laborious and slow form of transportation for goods, the tribulations of prodding undependable guards and reluctant bearers became major costs when compounded further by the infirmities and recalcitrance of the slaves on the outbound leg of the journey, to the direct detriment of the captives and the indirect loss of their owner. Twenty

---

Calandula, AHA, cód. 95, fols. 93v–94. The ivory sent to Luanda was carried mostly by the bound slaves because the price offered by Portuguese authorities did not repay the costs of hired or purchased transport: draft *regimento* (for Gov. Câmara), n.d. (ca. 1779); also *provisão*, 26 May 1780, AHTC, livro no. 1, fols. 233–34; Moçâmedes *apontamentos*, n.d. (ca. 1784), AHU, Angola maço 2–A; João Victo da Silva *relatório*, n.d. (ca. 1792), AHU, Angola cx. 42; Matos, *Compêndio histórico*, pp. 330–31; Tams, *Visit to the Portuguese Possessions*, 1:138; Capello and Ivens, *From Benguella*, 1:17–18; Carvalho, *Ethnographia e história tradicional*, p. 192.

41. Details compiled from Dias, ed. (Leitão), "Viagem a Cassange," pp. 13–14; "Convenção dos dízimos," AHU, Angola cx. 42; Graça, "Viagem feita de Loanda," p. 108; Livingstone, *Missionary Travels*, p. 457; also see Santos, "Perspectiva do comércio sertanejo," and Heywood, "Production, Trade, and Power," pp. 121 ff. Capello and Ivens, *From Benguella*, 1:144, put the average food consumption of a bearer at about 2–2.5 liters of manioc meal (plus dried meat or fish) per day; this amount translates into a standard ration of 1 kilogram of carbohydrate per day (at 1 pound to the liter), or one food bearer for each 4–5 porters assuming restocking every 6 days.

to one hundred frightened and angry captives, each ready to flee at the slightest opportunity and all prepared to harm or slay captors who blocked efforts to regain their liberty, presented real dangers. The drivers accordingly shackled the slaves together in *libambos* ("chains") of about thirty, separated into groups of males, females, and children when the size of the party merited subdivision. A ring around the right wrist of each individual bound her or him to the main chain and inhibited use of the right hand to break the fetters. Individuals who resisted or fell found themselves dragged along the ground by the remainder of the group.

These fetters did not relieve the caravan guards' fears of their captives, who, they believed, might carry herbs or other magical methods of breaking their chains, even without use of the bound right hand. A second chain around the neck further restrained rebellious slaves. The guards sometimes attempted to destroy their prisoners' will to resist by keeping the entire group awake for days on end, seating them each night around a large fire, and kicking any who managed to doze off back to wakefulness. Fatigue would eventually push the tormented captives to a stupified state that would make them easier to manage and less to be feared. The slaves carried their own small sacks of provisions, usually badly preserved meat and spoiled manioc meal, never in quantities sufficient to sustain health through the extreme exertions of the march. They received water to drink only when the caravan came across pools or streams, which could expose them to prolonged thirst when small streams ceased to flow toward the end of the dry season.[42] United by these brutal circumstances, the slaves always shared among themselves what they had to eat and drink, no matter how little. Still, deaths and the physical deterioration of survivors significantly reduced the value of the captives on their way to the coast. Such losses, while damaging to the owner of the slaves and dangerous also to the merchant backing his caravan, had less impact on the fortunes of the hired drivers or slaves in immediate charge of the party, and they regularly disregarded the efforts of their owners or employers to ameliorate the conditions under which the slaves marched.

Owners of trade goods most commonly sent them to the interior in caravans of this sort where they had to traverse extensive uninhabited or commercially unproductive areas in order to reach distant sources of large quantities of slaves. Peddlers could distribute small quantities of goods more efficiently through the proximate vicinity of market centers in densely populated areas, and repeated negotiations for low numbers of slaves in many small trading sites delayed a caravan's progress to the point of en-

---

42. Mendes (Carreira ed.), "Discurso academico ao programma," pp. 422–26; Johann Baptist von Spix and C.F.P. von Martius, *Viagem pelo Brasil, 1817–1820,* trans. Lúcia Furquim Lahmeyer (São Paulo: Editôra da Universidade de São Paulo, 1976), 2:154, note V. Also see Martin, *External Trade,* p. 119, for other methods of imprisonment on the Loango Coast.

dangering the lives of the slaves it already held. These larger expeditions repaid the required heavy investment only where goods and slaves could be handled in bulk, and particularly in wilderness regions where bandits lurked, or in war zones, or wherever disorders placed a premium on the defensive strength to be gained from numbers. Extensive uninhabited and uncultivated spaces also required the self-sufficiency attainable through large and complex organizations that could carry much of their own food and supplies, if need be.

The conditions favoring the use of caravans held most strongly in the sandy regions east of the Kwango and the Kwanza. Lunda, 500 kilometers distant from Kasanje across the Kasai or from the central plateau, the equally remote headwaters of the upper Zambezi, or some of the other rivers in the remote southeast all offered slaves in the requisite quantities. All of them lay beyond the scantily populated Ngangela woodlands, and some required traders to traverse broad expanses so barren that travelers termed them the "hungry country."

Caravans appear to have been the principal mode of maintaining contact from the beginning of commerce across these dry savannas. At first, Lunda warlords seem to have mounted these expeditions on their own accounts and to have supported them by posting relays of related Lunda chiefs in charge of provisioning stations in the fertile river valleys east of the Kasai.[43] Later, Imbangala caravans also moved out eastward during one dry season, spent the rains negotiating at the Lunda court, and returned some fourteen months later at the end of the following dry season.[44] Less explicit descriptions of the eighteenth-century trade across the Kwanza from the outpost of foreign-backed Luanda trade on the eastern edge of the central highlands at Bihe seem similarly predicated on long-distance caravans of this same sort.[45]

Comparable distances and the need to pass through similarly unproductive commercial terrain made caravans a common form of transportation also for merchants hoping to move goods from Luanda to sources of slaves at marketplaces in the Angolan interior where foreign capital played a major role in supporting the trade.[46] Traders seem to have relied on caravans especially to get through the wooded and bandit-infested plateau separating Kasanje from Ambaca. Near Luanda, too, the nominal peace of the military *conquista* protected its inhabitants from broad-scale enslavement, whatever other hardships it imposed, and thus limited direct slave-buying in the regions, however populous, through which the caravans passed.

43. Vellut, "Notes sur la Lunda"; Hoover, "Seduction of Ruwej."
44. Annexo no. 10 to de Mello, 30 May 1801, AHU, Angola cx. 51.
45. Bontinck, "Voyage des pombeiros."
46. See Chapter 16 below. Also Dias, ed. (Leitão), "Viagem a Cassange," p. 12; Sandoval, "Noticia do sertão do Balundo," p. 520.

East of Benguela, traders resident in the highlands also seem to have used caravans to send slaves off through the perilous empty territories between populations long retreated into defensible mountaintop refuges and down through the barren steppes leading to the coast.[47] These caravans moved out not at the initiative of coastal merchants but rather at that of the settlers, who aggregated parties of slaves and accompanied them down to the coast to sell for goods and supplies, looking very much the rude country bumpkins even in the rough frontier atmosphere of the small port town when they appeared.[48] Though the financing of the Benguela trade involved less foreign capital than that of Luanda, the organizers in both instances employed caravans because they sold few goods and took few slaves in the areas through which they moved.

Commercial caravans of this sort also frequently followed military expeditions according to patterns that evolved from early evacuations of captives from battles between African armies to later direct stimulation of the wars producing slaves for themselves. In the seventeenth century, Portuguese caravans had accompanied marauding armies into the violence of the frontier zone near Luanda that then dominated slaving, waiting in the rear to exchange textiles and wines for people brought in to them from the field of battle.[49] The caravans at that time provided services vital to converting military campaigns to slaving forays because armies on the march had little time to support the people whom they captured, particularly since soldiers often seized mainly women and children unused to the rigors of military life.[50] Commanders found it hard enough to keep their own men fed, particularly when the conflict involved the destruction of enemy fields and grain supplies, as it often did,[51] without undertaking

47. Miller, "Central and Southern Angola." Details of the Benguela routes to the interior appear in the "Derrota de Benguella para o sertão," in Felner, Angola, 2:13–27; for similar descriptions and a critique, see F. Bontinck, "Derrota de Benguella para o sertão: critique d'authenticité," Bulletin de l'Académie royale des sciences d'outre-mer (Brussels) 3 (1977): 279–300. Only Luanda-based merchants despoiled this region by outright slaving, over the strenuous opposition of the Benguela traders and their settler suppliers; cf. the circumstances surrounding the extended slave raid of António José da Costa in 1785, described in Corrêa, História de Angola, 2:128, 133–35, and Chapter 17 below.

48. António da Silva Lisboa (juiz de fóra, Benguela), 17/18 July 1791, AHU, Angola cx. 41. For a description of the end of the trade that seems to imply that the interior traders controlled transport at Benguela, see Joaquim Aurelio de Oliveira (governor, Benguela), 1 Dec. 1829, in Delgado, Famosa e histórica Benguela, pp. 481–82.

49. Cadornega, História geral.

50. See the low values of the slaves supplied as the royal fifth from military campaigns in 1739, 1744, 1745: Miller, "Slave Prices," Table III; Manoel Soares Vega, 18 Sept. 1744, AHU, Angola cx. 23.

51. E.g., Vasconcelos, 10 Jan. 1761, AHU, Angola maço 11; Sousa Coutinho portaria, 7 Dec. 1770, AHU, Angola cx. 33; Matos, Compêndio histórico, p. 247. Corrêa, História de Angola, 2:15, lists four reasons for Africans' willingness to sell their captives for merchandise of any sort at all in the wake of a battle. The victors wished to avoid the problems of caring for prisoners and of guarding them, feared rebellion, and wanted to avoid the expense of feeding them.

the additional obligation of feeding large numbers of helpless captives or guarding those less incapacitated. Caravans could remove them quickly. A caravan harvesting slaves in such circumstances functioned as a special case of the general rule: a link between (temporary) concentrations of large numbers of slaves and remote sources of European goods, with the caravan's inherent mobility giving it the added advantage of staying in touch with shifting sites of engagements in a prolonged campaign or with the changing locations of confrontations from one year to the next.

By the eighteenth century, African political institutions specialized in conducting most of the warfare associated with slaving, while the European-financed caravans of that period limited themselves to the more purely commercial ties between central markets, into which flowed the captives seized in battle between African armies, and the coast. Caravans occasionally still removed captives promptly from scenes of the infrequent Portuguese military campaigns in the interior, and the Lunda of that time presumably employed caravans to evacuate their war prisoners toward the west.[52] Once in a while a planned commercial expedition degenerated into outright military raiding on its own, but in doing so it clearly transgressed the primarily trading strategies for which its merchant backers were prepared.[53] These exceptions served mainly to confirm the fact that foreign capital backed most of the caravans that traversed the western central African bush in the eighteenth century and that their aims were commercial ones. By the later nineteenth century, commercialization of the African political economy had progressed to the point that trade blended again with warfare in large African-organized and heavily armed caravans that became little more than mobile military camps, alternatively trading with their commercial partners and raiding on their behalf, and eventually making war on their own accounts when the occasion suited them.[54] The African mercantile gentry of the nineteenth century deployed its superior weaponry to impose its power through small, mobile caravan-based empires throughout the savannas.

Elsewhere, mostly in the more densely and continuously inhabited regions nearer the equator, where sources of slaves were not so widely separated in distant population centers, networks of permanently settled specialized merchants, or trading diaspora, tended to predominate in the transportation and distribution sector of the slave trade. These diaspora thrived where debt and judicial condemnation replaced large-scale violence as the preferred means of enslavement. These methods produced contin-

52. Vasconcelos, 12 June 1762, AHU, Angola cx. 29, for the war against the "Hungos"; also Tavares expedition against the *ndembu*, de Mello, "Angola no começo do século," p. 554; Corrêa, *História de Angola*, 2: esp. 61.

53. Again, the example of António José da Costa; see note 47 above.

54. The Chokwe are the best-known examples (see Miller, "Cokwe Trade and Conquest," pp. 184–94), but the phenomenon was general: e.g., Birmingham, *Central Africa to 1870*, pp. 108–55.

uous exchanges of slaves in small quantities that favored permanent residence over the occasional contact of passing caravans suited more to carrying off sporadically large numbers of captives generated by war. The slaving diaspora also appear commonly to have grown in the north as extensions of existing African-financed regional commodity trading systems there, while foreign-owned caravans and other alien methods of transporting imports and slaves predominated in the south, where fewer established African competitors had been present to exclude outside capital from longer-distance transport and communication. In general, the geographical distribution of settled diaspora traders complemented that of the caravans that elsewhere traversed the empty spaces between concentrated sources of slaves. The resident traders had fewer military capabilities and less mobility than caravans.

Although the detailed organization of eighteenth-century institutions of this type is not directly documented in western central Africa, their presence is clearly indicated in general terms. A good deal is known about the nineteenth-century organization of trade in the hinterland of the southern Loango Coast and among the Bobangi of the Zaire River. By analogy with well-known West African examples, the significance of the type of economic institutions their eighteenth-century predecessors developed for the slave trade may be inferred with considerable confidence.

Trading diaspora typically moved goods and slaves through networks of dispersed villages. They expanded by settling relatives and clients throughout the areas across which they intended to convey goods. They maintained the cohesion of the system through these personal ties and tended to marry mostly among themselves, though they also established analogously personal connections with their suppliers and customers by selective marriages with prominent local families.[55] The institution of "blood brotherhood," common later though not directly reported from the eighteenth century, may have provided another means of linking these strangers as trading partners with their hosts through an idiom of fictive kinship: merchants and their customers each drew blood from their wrist and mixed it with that of their opposite number, swearing obligations patterned on those of close kinsmen to translate the commercial buying-selling relationship into its African cognate, "sharing." As later Europeans observed, when they followed these precedents in linking into the mid-nineteenth-century African-financed commodity trades, kinship, residence, and marriages provided virtually the only means of doing business in Africa without

55. In general, Curtin, *Cross-Cultural Trade,* esp. chap. 3, though with differing analytical emphases, and the "landlord-stranger" relationship reported from many areas in West Africa. Heywood, "Production, Trade, and Power," p. 130, on marriages.

the sort of diplomatic representation at political capitals that caravans often established.[56]

The trading diaspora lay discernibly on the African side of the membrane separating the partially commercialized political economies of the interior from the more fully capitalist economy of the Atlantic. The contrast appeared in geographical terms in their locations mostly inland from the most advanced market outposts of the Atlantic trade. Thus the diaspora extended closer to the Loango Coast, where the market centers were on the beaches, than they did farther to the south. In economic terms, the same distinction appeared in the traders' tendency to invest profits in the African form of people, the inhabitants of the villages of their diaspora, rather than to build up wealth in inventories of goods or credits in the Atlantic economy. Economically the diaspora were African also in that they seem to have consolidated largely on the basis of locally generated trading profits rather than from external financing, although foreign credit probably supported the original expansions of some diaspora into new areas. While they were African, too, in the chain-link relays through which they moved commodities and captives from village to village, direct lines of credit and dependence extending through them from the coast to the most remote sources of slaves in the interior added long-distance contacts more characteristic of the Atlantic trade.

Since pure diaspora traders usually lacked the coercive powers of large caravans or kings to seize people by force,[57] the first importers to borrow European capital would have invested their goods through existing commercial institutions to redirect commodities from the regional trade system toward the coast. The intimate relationships between goods and people in the African political economy would explain how a successful initial trading contact could create a small, but growing, community of wives, clients, and slaves around the trader's compound. These people could become numerous enough that the trader at their head could send trusted sons or slaves out from his own village to settle among his steadiest customers, where opportunities to repeat the segmentation and expansion would recur, gradually forming the widespread network of a mature diaspora. Their subsequent addition of slaves to this sort of trade, without substantial investment in credit, must have depended on their ability to offer imports to suppliers already holding temporary surpluses of slaves

---

56. Ladislaus Magyar (1840s–1850s), as quoted in Vellut, "Relations internationales," p. 102.

57. The gangs of thugs that accompanied the well-known Aro traders inland from the Niger Delta represent an evolved and militarized diaspora specialized in forcible extraction of slaves; cf. David Northrup, *Trade without Rulers: Pre-Colonial Economic Development in South-Eastern Nigeria* (Oxford: Clarendon Press, 1978).

or on the backing of local political authorities willing to use force on their behalf. They thus flourished, as did Vili diaspora traders from Loango, in areas like Kongo, where local political authorities had already become dependent on slaving. The dates of the Vili arrival in Kongo, and in the Mbundu lands farther south in the first half of the seventeenth century, coincided with turns toward slave exporting in both areas.

In western central Africa, culturally defined diaspora tended to appear mostly outside the boundaries of the recognized ethnolinguistic communities that arose from local ecological distinctiveness and that maintained productive relations by marriage relationships among neighboring villages in which the diaspora traders had no need to participate. In foreign lands, the people of the diaspora expressed the economic and other differences between themselves and the villagers among whom they lived in a strongly ethnic idiom of identity derived from their home base, maintaining themselves as a kind of "closed," quasi-autonomous community even while rapidly assimilating slaves, wives, and clients to it. The Bobangi River traders, who scattered a long chain of waterside villages up and down the central Zaire among local communities defined by segments of the river's banks and adjacent inland ridges, offered one western central African example of an ethnically defined trading diaspora of this type. The *mubire* traders, or Vili from the Loango kingdom, among the Kongo and Mbundu, apparently lived in similarly self-contained and ethnically distinct villages, at least south of the lower Zaire.[58]

The physical and cultural isolation of these ethnically alien merchant communities, with whom the African political economy still coexisted intact, paralleled the separateness of the central markets in regions. Their ethnic distinctiveness resembled the separation usually expressed in religious terms in savanna West Africa, where traders were often foreign Muslims descended from immigrants who had come south from the desert-side regions in direct touch with sources of commercial capital in North Africa, "strangers" living among animist holders of the land, commercial intruders amidst an agricultural political economy of use-values. The con-

---

58. As characterized in Thornton, *Kingdom of Kongo*, p. 26, and elsewhere. Martin, *External Trade*, pp. 69–70, 119–20, has them as "itinerant traders and workers" and working through caravans, though this portrait is apparently based mostly on evidence from the late nineteenth century. Francisco Barboza Mourais, 2 Sept. 1721, AHU, Angola cx. 16, referred to the established settlements of Vili near Angola and described Portuguese efforts to drive them out by burning their dwellings; in the same tone, see Henrique de Figueiredo (e Alarcão) (governor, Angola), 12 Dec. 1721, AHU, Angola cx. 16; Antonio de Albuquerque Coelho de Carvalho (governor, Angola), 13 June 1722, AHU, Angola cx. 26, adds that the Vili had lived in southern Kongo for an extremely long time and were intermarried there with the *ndembu* nobility. David Birmingham, "The Coffee Barons of Cazengo," *Journal of African History* 19, no. 4 (1983): 530, has other Vili settled along the Bengo and Zenza rivers, and farther south, still in the mid-nineteenth century. No doubt, others conducted goods and slaves in caravans nearer the market centers of the Loango Coast.

tinuing financial dependence of the emigrants in the diaspora on their ancestral home gave economic substance to the ties of kinship and affinity that kept them in close touch with their commercial base, and helped to preserve the cultural unity of their scattered settlements.

Ambitious underlings in the outlying settlements would have tried to escape such dependency on their elders at home and to break free also of their landlord hosts by taking their profits in slave retainers. The extreme result of this practice appeared in the "houses" composed almost entirely of slaves whom Bobangi traders employed in their commercial activities along the Zaire River, almost residential "firms" rather than "communities."[59] Building slave personnel of this sort would have established an arms-length relationship with local residents, one not dependent on close contacts through marriage and affinity, suited to the ambivalent and contradictory implications of dealing with them for people.

Within the old ethnic communities, agents of the Atlantic trade intermarried more widely with their customers as their commerce intensified and as exchanges generalized beyond the bounds of communal enclaves like those of the Vili or Bobangi. They thus appeared more "open" sociologically to the people they linked to the regional and international trades than did "closed" diaspora in alien territories. Such diffuse commercial contacts within a community achieved no less distinctiveness and coherence than the diaspora, but their members expressed their separate identity in images relating to individuals rather than to groups. Their trading networks had in fact taken commercialization still another step beyond African communalism and toward the individualism of the Atlantic economy.

In the only western central African example of such an "open" trading network at all well studied, northern Kongo traders inland from Cabinda and Ngoyo joined together as individuals in an association called *lemba* north of the lower Zaire River. They gave it the form of a therapeutic cult of adepts perceived to be afflicted with the goods and wealth flowing from the Atlantic economy, that is, an association of sufferers who distributed goods and assembled slaves for shipment back to the coast. It originated in the early, mostly local trade in copper and dispatched fewer people into alien regions than the Vili/*mubire* diaspora from Loango. Rather, *lemba* formalized the commercial ties that intensified as imports percolated through local networks of kinship and alliance within the broadly defined ethnic community of northern Kongo. The expression of these commercial relations centered in part on marriages, a quite logical extension of existing notions involving exchange within the set of intermarrying groups. But the ideology of the *lemba* cult also emphasized the anomaly of its members'

59. Harms, *River of Wealth, River of Sorrow*.

commitment to material wealth rather than to transactions in humans, a violation of the norm particularly jarring because the traders also remained participants in the political economy of sharing. In the eyes of village people, the cult members' association with merchant capitalism amounted to a social disease.[60]

Lemba inland from Cabinda was the local social equivalent of the moral decline and physical sickness that threatened villagers who ventured into commercial centers at Luanda and in its hinterland. It also paralleled the similar malaise that the Bobangi perceived as witchcraft and sterility, but could not cure, deriving from their wholesale commitment to commerce along the interior basin of the Zaire.[61] The rituals and offices of the *lemba* cult featured prestations of material wealth that novitiates offered to rich and powerful high priests, who then redistributed their material gleanings to their own kin and affines in a kind of tax paid to the use-value sector by those engaged in the commercial trade. *Lemba* thus recycled the profits of commerce among a wider circle of kin and kept relations between the traders and the local communities "open" in a way that the "closed" diaspora of foreign traders did not in the alien areas they penetrated. Yet its marginalization of the traders as anomalous "sick" persons simultaneously still insulated Kongo farmers from the capitalist currents flowing from the Atlantic in the same way that ethnic foreignness made enclaves of the closed diaspora settlements abroad. Elsewhere the caravans and markets, in which European capital had even greater importance, achieved a still more extreme separation of the same order between the distinct political economies inextricably joined through western central African slaving.

Compared to the centralized caravans and to the merchants cooped up in central markets characteristic of the trade run on European credit, the decentralized trading diaspora drew several advantages from the greater survival rates among the people they moved through marriage/exchange alliances with farmers and transport along the chain-link structure of resident villages. Each settlement in the diaspora functioned as an interim bulking station where the traders could support captives acquired from the settlement's immediate area while they waited to forward them toward the coast. The resulting lots of slaves were generally smaller and kept dispersed outside the main marketplaces until the moment of their sale. They consequently sustained lower losses to illness or mortality.[62] Their

60. Janzen, *Lemba*. One must wonder whether Janzen's brilliant reconstruction applies to the interior before the late nineteenth century, while accepting his documentation of the cult's earlier presence in the neighborhood of the highly commercialized marketplaces on the coast.

61. Harms, *River of Wealth, River of Sorrow*.

62. Interview with Ngandu a Kungu, 1969, for an explicit reference to this strategy at Kasanje; Martin, *External Trade*, p. 77, reports it at Kakongo (Cabinda) in 1687.

own fields, or the farmers among whom they lived, could feed these relatively modest numbers of captives until traders sent them on, once again in small lots, to the next community along the way to the coast. A village could even put its captives temporarily to work in its own fields to support themselves. As the slaves finally approached the sea, where they might have to wait weeks or months for the arrival of European buyers and the brokers from the shoreside markets, they could once again be fed from local agriculture.[63]

This gradual drift of slaves through the links in a chain of diaspora villages, in short stages compared to the long forced marches of the caravans, supplemented the superior nutrition available to them along the way, and the lesser degree of violence involved in the entire process enabled diaspora traders to deliver slaves at the coast in less battered physical condition than others who arrived in caravans. Where riverain transport underwrote the regional commodity trading systems at the base of slave-trading diasporas, use of canoes further lessened the exhaustion of slaves allowed to ride rather than being forced to walk for months on end. The slaves' fears of the water in that case replaced the physically debilitating forms of intimidation and control practiced by the caravans.[64] All of these factors lowered the mortality costs of trading diaspora transportation systems. Ship captains consequently could expect lower death rates at sea among captives they acquired from sources linked to trading diaspora in western central Africa, mostly from the Zaire estuary and the Loango Coast to the north.[65]

Politics and Economics: Blurred Boundaries

Just as militarized caravans sometimes acquired statelike qualities, it is easy to overdraw the distinctions between the caravan trade, the trading dias-

63. Corrêa, *História de Angola,* 2:85, 208–9, has the point for both the Kongo embarkation points and for Cabinda. The situation at Cabinda may have changed by 1815 with loss of local control over the trade; by that time Portuguese traders went directly up the Zaire in a form of trading that approximated, on a smaller scale, the caravans employed earlier farther south. Perhaps as a consequence, there was no food to be had at Cabinda. See Spix and Martius, *Viagem pelo Brasil,* 2:153–54, note V, and cf. Owen, *Narrative of Voyages,* 2:291 ff. Martin, "Family Strategies," pp. 66, 68, has detailed descriptions of the water, wood, and other resources of the vicinity of the bay there. Richard Sheridan, *Doctors and Slaves: A Medical and Demographic History of Slavery in the British West Indies, 1680–1834* (New York: Cambridge University Press, 1985), p. 106, cites various authorities on the same tendency to distribute slaves out among villages until they could be boarded on ships.

64. Harms, *River of Wealth, River of Sorrow,* p. 38.

65. See mortality statistics in Joseph C. Miller, "Legal Portuguese Slaving from Angola: Some Preliminary Indications of Volume and Direction, 1760–1830," *Revue française d'histoire d'outre-mer* 62, 1–2 (nos. 226–27) (1975): 135–76; also Klein, *Middle Passage,* pp. 56, 84–85 (see "Congo" category).

pora, and the "open" networks of commerce, since caravans might be said to have moved among a "diaspora" of central markets, and the slaves passing through the diaspora marched in groups resembling small caravans.[66] Nonetheless, caravans and diaspora had generally distinct geographical distributions, and the diaspora seem to have delivered slaves in substantially better physical shape than the caravans. The diaspora also depended less on financing from the Atlantic.

Further, only the finest of distinctions set off "economic" organizations of the commercial sector, like the trading diaspora, from the more "political" institutions that structured parallel flows of material wealth through the use-value political economies.[67] Some "states" and "empires" functioned so prominently as distributors of goods and producers of captives that they differed in economic function—however much their ideologies may have contrasted—only very subtly from cults like *lemba* within their own ethnic context or from trading diaspora beyond the political community.[68] The contrast in this case would appear to be between the kings' investments of their goods in respect and loyalty and the diaspora traders' investments in people themselves, dependents acquired by exchange rather than through reproduction. The immigrant traders of a diaspora and their local customers also settled up their exchanges of goods and people, thus making the diaspora appear an "economic" institution among equals in European terms, while states created hierarchy with the outstanding debts left from the "largesse" with which they dispensed "tribute" they received, even when these exchanges clearly articulated the domestic and Atlantic economies no less than did the "trade" of diaspora or caravans. The nineteenth-century Lunda *mwaant yaav*, for example, sent out mostly imported goods and took in mostly domestic produce and people, but Lunda is usually viewed as a political rather than an economic institution.[69]

The *lemba* cult acquired a "sociological" aura because it allowed individuals, rather than groups, to establish commercial links transcending boundaries between their natal communities but did so without removing them from their other social relationships. *Lemba* also took on a limited "political" coloration in its ability to structure contacts between members of otherwise unrelated local groups. In other parts of Africa analogous "secret societies" of titled and often masked officials allowed wealthy and

66. E.g., the double aspect of the Vili, as participants in both the Atlantic and the African economies; see note 58 above.
67. As Janzen, *Lemba*, p. 6 et passim, has emphasized.
68. See Anne Wilson's description of the Luba "empire" as a commercial network in "Long-Distance Trade and the Luba Lomami Empire," *Journal of African History* 13, no. 4 (1972): 575–89.
69. Vellut, "Relations internationales," pp. 82–84.

influential men to cooperate even more formally in governing closely settled groups of dependents having few other institutionalized means of interacting.[70] Explicitly heterogeneous, compact settlements of the sort that elsewhere fostered secret societies seldom grew up in western central Africa, perhaps because landholding lineages and patrons seem to have defined most residential communities as at least nominally homogeneous groupings under their centralized authority.

The organization of trade, and in particular the exchange of imports for slaves, beyond the localized scale of neighboring communities in western central Africa tended to generate institutions with a more explicitly "political" coloration, in which trade was represented as "tribute." Although the centralization of power often depended on merchant princes' distributing imported capital goods they obtained through central markets, when it was not imposed outright by warlords, these looked like governments rather than businesses. These monarchs issued subordinate titles of nobility to the men who also acted as their commercial agents, and it is a good bet that the titles awarded from major kings reflected economic indebtedness in addition to their well-known political aspects. The more geographically compact of these institutions, like Kasanje and, earlier, Kongo, thus produced hierarchical trading associations with a territorial dimension. The proximity of the central lords and patrons to their subordinates and their wealth in followers gave them considerable power to intervene by force in local affairs, to extract tribute, to enforce justice, or to claim people to satisfy debts. Trade produced plutocracies that were recognizably also states.

In politically organized trading federations dispersed over wider areas, the commercial agents acted with so much day-to-day autonomy from their nominal superiors that historians have described these federations as "empires" rather than "states." Among the Lunda, local lords on the Kwango, others on the headwaters of the Zambezi, and still others scattered elsewhere sent tribute outside the commercial sphere to the *mwaant yaav* on the Kalanyi no more than occasionally. The regional lords intermarried and exchanged women and goods so intensively with local populations that the "empire" functioned as a politicized trading diaspora on all but the ideological level.[71]

The principal distinction between the "politics" of these "empires" and the "economics" of the "trading diasporas" and caravans lay in the forms in which they held wealth. Goods, often imported, backed the trading diaspora, and to that extent they were intermediate in structure

70. For the general theoretical statement, see Robin Horton, "Stateless Societies in the History of West Africa," in J.F.A. Ajayi and Michael Crowder, eds., *History of West Africa,* 2d ed. (New York: Columbia University Press, 1971), 1:72–113.
71. Vellut, "Relations internationales" and "Notes sur la Lunda."

between the material and financial wealth of the Atlantic economy, with which they traded, and the African political economy in which they worked. People—the slaves seized by military means, and nobles obligated by loans and gifts of material wealth—underwrote the integration of the African "political" systems and supported their expansive phases. Integrated states thus expressed the priority that indigenous African institutions accorded to holding people and loyalties—hence their political tone—while traders committed to the exchange element in the African political economy retreated into the isolation of small commercial enclaves and eventually disintegrated into materialist individualism that their neighbors, and sometimes they themselves, could describe only as sick.

7

A History of Competition, Comparative Advantage, and Credit

The African Commercial and Transport Sector in the Eighteenth Century

The theoretical distinctions between the various forms of transportation and market distribution, subtle as they appear when described abstractly in terms derived from Western ideologies, blurred still further in practice. Eighteenth-century kings, caravan leaders, and diaspora traders all clustered around the same central markets and combined their respective styles to transport goods and slaves across western central Africa. In general, they constructed overlapping trade routes linking the multiple sources of trade goods and capital at the coast with the relatively limited set of population nuclei that constituted the region's consumer markets for imports and its sources of slaves for export.

Over the long term, the main slaving trails tended to fan out from each of these population centers toward the west. The greatest of these centers was, of course, the belt of dense habitation between 6° and 8° south latitude. In the eighteenth century paths also radiated down from the populous central highlands and, though later and more marginally, west from the pockets of people living on the wetter margins of the Kalahari. Where the diagonally oriented, lengthy outer edges of each fan partially parallelled the coast, the routes tended to lose slaves to buyers who diverted them off on shorter trails leading directly down the river valleys to the west.

In the shorter run, from year to year or decade to decade, the principal markets for goods and the sources of slaves changed as drought and the political and economic transformations of the slaving frontier, with its temporary depopulation and warfare and its residue of commercialized slaving, shifted the relative availability of people from region to region. The Kwango, Kwanza, and other river valleys near the coast remained steady sources of slaves because they retained so many captives from the coffles passing through from the east before releasing them, or their descendants, into the Atlantic trade. The comings and goings of the European suppliers of goods along different portions of the coast also drew the slaves toward one set of trade routes or another in each fan at particular times.

Complexity and change on this detailed scale resolved itself on a more abstract level into stable geographical and structural distinctions between three main slave transporting systems. In a high-profit northern trading sector, African diaspora traders drew on the relatively populous and accessible regions east of Kongo and exposed their captives to only moderate risks of mortality during the westward trek to Loango. In a central system, Portuguese-financed caravans of slaves had to endure much higher losses, and expenses, on their way down to Luanda. Finally, a southern dry-zone complex of routes with its main outlet at Benguela grew with the low costs of war captives from the highlands up to about the 1770s and then thrived for the remainder of the century on the disruptions of drought. The importers working through the middle network at Luanda competed with Loango traders for the dense populations of the forest fringes at a severe disadvantage in transport expenses, and they also absorbed high purchase costs relative to the inexpensive slaves taken from wars in the south. In addition, on the Atlantic side of their operations they had to buy and sell within a Portuguese mercantilist system anchored at Luanda and stacked heavily against them. As a result they tried to overcome their considerable handicaps by offering goods on ruinously liberal terms of credit. These economic distinctions among the three principal western central African commercial networks explain much of the eighteenth-century histories of the African transporters of slaves for the southern Atlantic trade, as well as part of the successes and failures of their respective European suppliers of goods and credit.

Geography and History of the Trade Routes

Each African importing region maintained trading connections with as many different sources of imports as it could. These coastal sources of goods fell into three general groups corresponding to the three transport networks in the interior, one along the northern coasts, another centered on Luanda, and still another around Benguela. The latter two focused on the Portuguese towns, but both also featured lesser peripheral outlets used mostly for smuggling—Catumbela north of Benguela, the mouths of the Kikombo and Kuvo between Luanda and Benguela, the Dande and Musulu north of Luanda, and so on. The paths leading to these ports crisscrossed one another as they meandered westward, and slavedrivers and owners came upon numerous forks that offered them a series of choices among the alternative outlets. As a result slaves from any given source, particularly the areas farthest in the interior, might ultimately reach the coast anywhere from beaches north of the Zaire all the way south to Benguela. The African slave-sellers, acting as buyers of goods, enjoyed the opportunity to play rival importers from each of these regions against one another to reduce the prices they paid for goods available at more than one point, principally the textiles. While the need for proper assorting gave each European national supplier certain unique strengths, the options also open to the African transporters of slaves, including the Luso-Africans of Angola, made the coastal ports highly competitive with one another. These options available to the Africans pressured European sellers of goods to offer advantageous prices or terms and, in the longer run, must also have tended (though always imperfectly) to equalize the delivered prices of goods in the interior and of slaves at the coast.

From all indications, the broad band of woodland and gallery forest running from the middle and lower Kwango east across the lower courses of the Kasai affluents and north of Lunda was the single major source of the slaves delivered to the Angolan coast during the eighteenth century. Traders sent most slaves from the Kwilu region between the Kwango and Chikapa directly west toward the middle Kwango valley. There agents of the principal valley kingdoms, principally the Yaka, divided them into lots headed either southwest toward Luanda or northwest in the direction of the Loango Coast.[1] Those who continued directly west from the Kwango passed through commercial networks developed by the northeastern Kongo, known as Zombo, and on westward through the Kongo province of Nsundi, where resident traders of the Vili diaspora picked some up and took them on northwest to Loango.

Others headed southwest out of Yaka to the major market in the rugged *ndembu* (Dembos) region at Kisoza. Soso traders of the south-eastern Kongo drove most of the Kwilu slaves who converged on this market by the 1700s.[2] Kisoza owed its preeminence throughout the century in part to its position at the bottleneck of passes crossing the central Kongo mountains in that area. To the west these passes opened into the valleys of the Dande, Bengo, and Onzo rivers, the main communication routes running down toward the sea. The Kisoza marketplace remained under the effective authority of the *ndembu* lord Mbwila, whose heavily fortified redoubt gave him command of the complex of trails leading up through the mountain passes from the Kwango valley.[3] His *ndembu* rival,

1. Vansina, *Children of Woot,* pp. 186–95.

2. Janzen, *Lemba,* pp. 61–70, for the Nsundi side; Hilton, "Political and Social Change," MS pp. 18–19, 25. De Mello, 21 Oct. 1801, AHU, Angola cx. 50, notes the Yaka-Soso connection with specific reference to copper.

3. Meneses, 30 Jan. 1734, AHU, Angola cx. 20; Vasconcelos, 6 May 1760 and 22 April 1762, AHU, Angola cx. 28 and 29, and *bando,* 10 Nov. 1759, AHU, Angola cx. 28; Almeida e Vasconcelos, 7 July 1794, AHU, Angola maço 11.

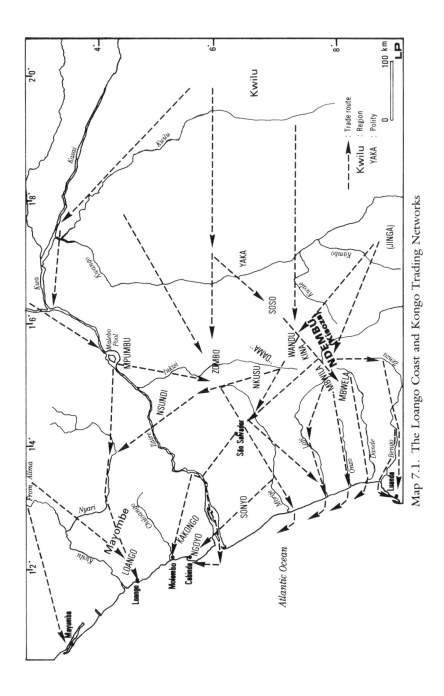

Map 7.1. The Loango Coast and Kongo Trading Networks

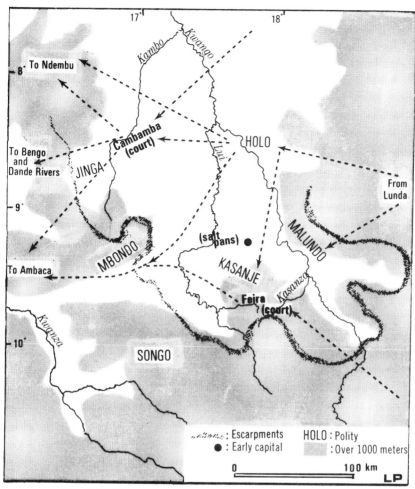

Map 7.2. The Middle Kwango Valley, Eighteenth Century

the lord Mbwela, commanded the western approaches to the same market.[4] An alternative route to the coast from this *ndembu* market center led northwest through the Kongo provinces of Wandu, Kina, and Bembe toward the semi-autonomous principality of Sonyo on the south bank of the lower Zaire. Western Kongo chiefs could divert captives from the trail to Sonyo toward closer embarkation points at the mouths of the Loje and

4. Other *ndembu* authorities and a powerful "Lilunda" held other plateaux and mountains in the vicinity, but none seems to have exercised as continuously a long-lasting influence over the trade as Mbwila and Mbwela; see Map 7.1. On the Mbwila-Mbwela opposition, see esp. Vasconcelos *bando,* 10 Nov. 1759, and letter of 22 April 1762, AHU, Angola cx. 28 and 29. For the Kina trade route, Sousa Coutinho, 30 July 1771, AHU, Angola cx. 33. For the location of other *ndembu* lords, Moçâmedes, 20 Sept. 1791, AHU, Angola maço 11.

Mbrije rivers.[5] Slaves who continued on to the Zaire estuary crossed to the Kakongo and Ngoyo ports of Molembo and Cabinda. A third series of paths down to the sea from this *ndembu* crossroads descended the upper Zenza (Bengo) toward the Portuguese port of Luanda.

Slaves from the Kwilu also descended toward more southerly Kwango valley marketplaces in the kingdoms of Jinga, Kasanje, and Holo. Jinga and Kasanje evidently competed for many of the same trans-Kwango sources of slaves for most of the century, drawing some southwestwards out of the nearby parts of the Kwilu but relying heavily also on the Lunda-dominated regions farther to the east. These last arrived through the intermediation of Lunda outposts founded among the Yaka and among the Shinje on the eastern bank of the river.

Holo, a small, independent lordship of the west bank just to the north of Kasanje, became the pivotal authority sitting astride the trade routes leading from the east to Jinga. The volume of Holo's trade waxed with the consolidation of Lunda slave raiding during the 1730s, 1740s, and 1750s, partly at Jinga's expense, but also ultimately to the detriment of Kasanje. The sketchy history of this market suggests that late-seventeenth-century Kasanje kings had stationed subordinates in Holo, on the northern edge of their domain, in about the 1680s when they moved their capitals to the southern end of the valley. Authorities in Holo loyal to Kasanje could divert slaves then beginning to arrive through Lunda outposts across the river away from Jinga and south toward the main Kasanje market. The lords of Holo seem to have taken advantage of their isolation and their strategic position in the disputed borderlands between the two main kingdoms in the valley, Jinga and Kasanje, to attempt to make independent contact with the Portuguese in the 1730s. During the next decade or so, the Holo rulers developed a significant connection of their own with Portuguese traders working out of Angola, but by the 1760s they redirected their trade northwest to take advantage of the better terms offered from the Kongo and Loango coasts through Mbwila and Mbwela.[6] The Portuguese tried to attract the Holo trade back to Luanda in the 1790s, probably to move into the opening in that area left by the disappearance of French goods sent through the *ndembu* marketplace during the Napoleonic wars in Europe, but little seems to have come of this initiative.[7]

The major trading state of Jinga divided its multiple contacts to the

5. Detailed reports on the Kongo coast by Souza Magalhães, 16 March 1780, AHU, Angola cx. 37; 18 March 1773, AHU, Angola cx. 36.

6. Vasconcelos, 7 Jan. 1750, AHU, Angola cx. 28; Dias, ed. (Leitão), "Viagem a Cassange," p. 29. The initial contact had come in the 1730s: *certidão* (Antonio da Fonseca Coutinho, 25 Sept. 1739), AHU, Angola cx. 21, and copy of letter from Francisco Xavier (*capitão-mor*, Ambaca), 5 July 1739, AHU, Angola cx. 21; Magalhães, 16 Aug. 1739, AHU, Angola cx. 21.

7. Da Cunha, 23 March 1755, AHU, Angola cx. 26; Sousa Coutinho's treaty of July 1765, published in *Annaes do Conselho Ultramarino* (parte não oficial) 1 (1858): 523–24,

west from a marketplace known as Kambamba among Portuguese at Luanda, British and French interlopers just to its north, and the *ndembu* Mwbila and the Loango Coast beyond. During the 1730s and 1740s, Jinga obtained most of its slaves from the northeast through the Yaka and through the Kikongo-speaking Soso and Ndamba, thus evading the road-block temporarily erected by Holo directly to the east.[8] The dominating presence of Kasanje to the southeast of Jinga seems to have blocked its access to markets approached through the southerly parts of the Kwango valley, but it acquired other captives from that quarter through a corridor extending from the center of the kingdom on the Kambo River up onto the highland wildernesses west of Kasanje, east of Ambaca, and on to the islands of Kindonga in the middle Kwanza. From there Jinga agents could contact sources of slaves south of the river and perhaps even in the central highlands, and they were even reported to have remained in touch with the rock-salt mines of Kisama, far to the southwest beyond the intervening Portuguese-conquered areas.[9] Jinga's warriors took frequent opportunity to harass the Luanda caravans moving back and forth through this corridor between the Portuguese *conquista* and its two Kwango valley rivals, Holo and Kasanje.[10]

Smaller *ndembu* lords on the ridges overlooking the upper Bengo and Dande handled the bulk of Jinga's trade to the west. These slaves went mostly to British and French ships trading at Musulu and other parts of the coast just north of Luanda. Jinga's outlets through Mbwila became particularly significant during the 1780s, when its rulers may have gained direct access to the east through Holo, financed in part by the infusions of French trade goods coming from those parts of the coast in that de-cade.[11] The sudden ending of French trading early in the 1790s accordingly left Jinga without its major sources of imported goods. In the first decades of the nineteenth century, its kings became much more amenable to con-tacts with the Portuguese at Luanda.[12] They probably continued to send

---

in which the Holo lord agreed to exclude Vili from his domains and to permit a settlement of traders from Luanda; Vasconcelos, 17 Nov. 1790, AHU, cód. 1627, fols. 23–24v; idem, 12 April 1791, AHA, cód. 84, fols. 177–78v; Vellut, "Relations internationales," pp. 87–88, 90, 118; *Arquivos de Angola* 2, nos. 13–15 (1936): 580.

8. "Termo de recebimento da embaixada . . . ," 25 Oct. 1744, AHU, Angola cx. 23. Ndamba/"Dama" appears on the map entitled "Angola and Neighboring Regions in Ap-proximately 1700" in John K. Thornton, "The Kingdom of the Kongo in the Era of the Civil Wars, 1641–1718" (Ph.D. diss., University of California, Los Angeles, 1979).

9. "Termo do que se determinou na Junta . . . ," 13 April 1744, AHU, Angola cx. 23.

10. E.g., da Cunha, 22 Jan. 1756, AHU, Angola cx. 27, and frequent references later in the century.

11. Peçanha, 27 June 1785, AHU, Angola cx. 40; also *instruções,* 1 June 1793, AHA, cód. 313, fols. 185–91v.

12. Letters to the *rei* Ginga, 23 Oct. 1806 and 19 Feb. 1807, AHA, cód. 240; de Brito, enclosed in D. António de Saldanha da Gama (governor, Angola), 14 April 1809, AHU, Angola cx. 58.

slaves toward Musulu and other areas north of Luanda, but their weakness eventually allowed governors at Luanda to establish a fortified Portuguese position overlooking these paths in the former western marches of the Jinga state at Duque de Bragança on the upper Lukala in 1838. Jinga never emerged as an important contributor to the commodity commerce of the later nineteenth century, probably because its location just south of the dense population band of the forest-savanna mosaic, however advantageous in the slaving era, left it cut off from the forest sources of ivory, wood, and dyestuffs controlled by Kongo and the Kasanje-dominated woodland exports of wax and rubber, as well as ivory.

Kasanje, at the apex of its economic and political power during the second half of the eighteenth century, was the main terminus for the southerly Lunda outpost in the Kwango valley among the Shinje under Malundo.[13] It also received slaves from the northeast, from the Pende and other parts of the Kwilu region.[14] The kings in Kasanje, tied directly in the east to the Lunda *mwaant yaav*, whom they treated as distant relatives, were linked more closely than any other Kwango valley trading state to Lisbon merchants at Luanda through the famous government market, or *feira*, near their capital. Of all the slave-brokering potentates in the Kwango valley, those of Kasanje alone sent most of their captives directly into Portuguese territory and held honorary military patents from the governors of the colony. For most of the century colonial officials selectively represented Kasanje as the major source of slaves reaching Luanda, as indeed it was for the minority of traders based in Portugal. So important to imperial planners in Lisbon did the Kasanje kings become, in fact, that their high repute in the colony's correspondence with the home government eclipsed other sources of slaves around the *conquista* important to other merchants not so intimately tied to the metropole.

Toward the end of the eighteenth century, the royal monopoly over trade in Kasanje began to break down. With it went both the kingdom's close connection to Luanda and the unity of the state. Provincial Kasanje nobles used Portuguese trade goods obtained on credit to send out the independent caravans direct to Lunda that bypassed the old connection through the royal court to Malundo and the Shinje. Others made contact with imports coming through the *ndembu* Mbwila and diverted their slaves away from Luanda to the northwest.[15] Still others probably developed production of local tobacco and salt entirely outside the court's import-based trade and sold them for slaves throughout the salt-short territories

13. Dias, ed. (Leitão), "Viagem a Cassange"; also Vellut, "Relations internationales."
14. Dias, ed. (Leitão), "Viagem a Cassange"; Birmingham, *Trade and Conflict in Angola*, p. 149.
15. *Annexo* no. 10, to the *requerimento* enclosed in de Mello, 30 May 1801, AHU, Angola cx. 51.

east of the Kwango.[16] The monarchy lost its ability to regulate trade, both for itself and in favor of its Portuguese commercial partners, and the Luanda merchants withdrew from the government marketplace in the valley for several years between 1804 and 1827.[17]

Later Kasanje kings, overwhelmed by growing competition from their own nobles, some of whom were in alliance with independent merchants from Luanda and others of whom were drifting off to trade with the northern coasts through Holo and Jinga, returned to seek closer relations with the Portuguese government in the mid-nineteenth century. But it was too late, since by then the Dande, the Loje, and other northern ports reached through Mbwila had become major outlets for slaves from the Kasanje area. The political authority of the old kings accordingly declined through the 1830s and 1840s. Portuguese military intervention against the kings finally cleared the way for the prospering provincial nobles to take the lead in developing the wax and ivory exports that largely replaced slaving in succeeding decades and left Kasanje itself more a federation of regional principalities than a centralized kingdom.[18]

The growing importance of the Lunda as producers of slaves through-out the eighteenth century gave rise to trade routes that spread out from the Kalanyi affluent of the upper Sankuru toward the entire length of the Kwango valley, from the river's headwaters on the flanks of the central plateau north to where the river emptied into the Kasai.[19] The first Lunda traders to make contact with Portuguese goods available in the Kwango valley, probably in the middle third of the seventeenth century, seem to have added these goods as a sideline to an older trade in salt from Kasanje's excellent saline springs along the Lui. That trade conformed to the tendency evident elsewhere for African buyers of foreign imports to pay for them with commodities rather than with slaves for as long as they could, since the Lunda at that time offered palm cloths from the edges of the great equatorial forest. They also offered copper from Katanga.[20]

This original Lunda commodity trade shifted to slaves during the first half of the eighteenth century, during the years in which militaristic *mwaant yaav* thrust their power outward from the banks of the Kalanyi. Royal

16. Interview with Alexandre Vaz and Ngonga a Mbande, 23 Sept. 1969.
17. Noronha to Director da Feira de Cassange (Francisco Honorato da Costa), 7 Jan. 1805, AHA, cód. 90, fols. 229v–30; Vellut, "Royaume de Cassange"; Castelobranco to *regente* de Ambaca, 17 Oct. 1827, AHA, cód. 96, fols. 136v–37v. Also see Chapter 17 below.
18. Joseph C. Miller, "Slaves, Slavers, and Social Change in Nineteenth-Century Kasanje," in Franz-Wilhelm Heimer, ed., *Social Change in Angola* (Munich: Weltforum Verlag, 1973), pp. 9–29.
19. Birmingham, *Trade and Conflict in Angola*, pp. 148–49. Vellut, "Notes sur le Lunda," is excellent and detailed, particularly for ca. 1770s–1850.
20. Cadornega, *História geral*, 3:215–21; Birmingham, *Trade and Conflict in Angola*, pp. 127–28.

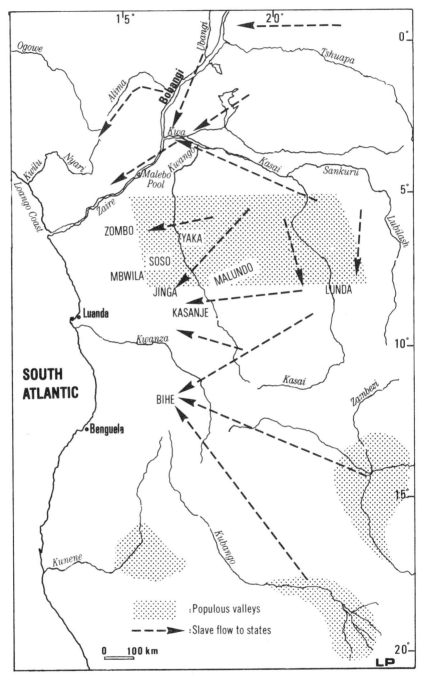

Map 7.3. Slave Sources in the Far Interior

Lunda caravans presumably conducted the captives from these wars of expansion; and leaders of the expeditions, at the same time commercial agents of the Lunda rulers, settled the advanced Lunda staging posts in the river valleys west of the Kasai to handle the slaves moving westward as far as the east bank of the Kwango River. By the 1750s, one of the westernmost Lunda chiefs, Malundo among the Shinje, had grown powerful enough on the basis of this trade to pose a serious military threat to Kasanje, the major power on the west bank of the river.[21] In the late eighteenth century, both Kasanje and the central Lunda court made efforts to bypass this troublesome go-between, with Kasanje nobles sending their own Portuguese-financed expeditions east to the Kalanyi and the Lunda countering with a royal embassy and caravan direct to Luanda in 1807–8.

Sometime before the 1750s the Lunda developed a parallel northerly route to the lower portions of the Kwango, where they sold slaves to southeastern Kongo and to immigrant Vili buyers of slaves west of the river. This route also supported an outlying Lunda-style polity like Malundo on the east bank of the Kwango, this one centered on the court of Mwene Puto Kasongo among the Yaka people of the valley.[22] A still more northerly route running by canoe down the Kasai may have sent other Lunda slaves into the trade networks of the lower Zaire, from where they could eventually have emerged at the coast anywhere from Loango to the Loje.[23]

Kasanje's introduction of borrowed goods at the heart of the Lunda empire reoriented Lunda slave exports from north to south as the eighteenth century progressed. Earlier northern Lunda initiatives toward the Yaka and Lunda consolidation of political outposts along the middle and lower Kwango, even as Malundo began to block the central court's contacts at Kasanje, had represented the strategy of the eighteenth-century Lunda military aristocracy for selling enslaved captives seized in royal raids on the dense populations of the forest fringes. But surely even that area reached the limits of its capacity to yield population after three generations of losses, and the Lunda warrior party must have welcomed commercial initiatives from traders from the west to supplement the old sources of slaves after about the 1770s.

21. In general, Vellut, "Notes sur le Lunda," esp. pp. 94–95, 100–102.

22. Dias, ed. (Leitão), "Viagem a Cassange," p. 25; Vellut, "Notes sur le Lunda," pp. 95–97. On Yaka history, there is only M. Plancquaert, *Les Yaka: essai d'histoire*, 2d ed. (Brussels: Musée Royale de l'Afrique Centrale, 1971), but see Vansina, *Kingdoms of the Savanna*, pp. 203–7.

23. The reference comes from F. J. Maria de Lacerda e Almeida, *Travessia da Africa* (Lisbon: Agência Geral das Colónias, 1936); cf. Birmingham, *Trade and Conflict in Angola*, pp. 136–37, but the point is disputed. Also see Hoover, "Seduction of Ruwej," pp. 337–38, and Vellut, "Notes sur le Lunda," pp. 92, 163.

The southern side of the fan of Lunda trade routes carried the foreign capital that the Portuguese and others began to push toward Lunda, probably starting with a build-up of credit through Kasanje in the 1740s. These credits, which would then have provoked the great hostility of Malundo in the 1750s and 1760s, eliminated this Shinje representative of Lunda militarism as a significant commercial factor by the 1770s, after which little more is heard of the state. The financial vectors of the main Lunda trade route to the west had reversed at least by the early 1790s, when Kasanje-backed caravans took the initiative from the old royal shipments of war prisoners in trading to central Lunda.[24] At the same time, other traders bearing Luanda imports began to contact Lunda chiefs between the upper Kasai and Kwango through the Songo areas south and west of Kasanje.[25] Still other foreign traders from the central highlands, even farther to the south, particularly a mixture of Angolan Luso-Africans and Ovimbundu from the Bihe kingdom, may also have begun to probe the southern flanks of the main Lunda route to Kasanje as they projected commercialized trade eastward in the late 1770s. The goods arriving from all these sources began Lunda's conversion from slave exporting through raiding to goods importing through trade and debt.

To the extent that all these initiatives from the west succeeded in opening foreign-financed southerly trails to central Lunda, they must have begun to weaken the trading ties that bound the old western Lunda intermediaries back to the imperial court on the Kalanyi. Such threats, together with the erosion of the old royal ownership of the trade through Kasanje, would explain the apparent eagerness with which the *mwaant yaav* and his courtiers responded to Portuguese invitations to send a Lunda royal caravan directly to the Portuguese in Luanda shortly after 1800.[26] This Lunda expedition amounted to a reassertion of royal financial authority over the southerly branches of the trade. The effort evidently led to precisely the opposite result, merely putting the Lunda court in direct touch with foreign sources of funds, because merchants from Angola settled on the Kalanyi soon after 1810 and supported the lengthy reign of the *mwaant yaav* Nawej II from about 1820 into the 1850s on Portuguese, not Lunda, credit. Royal caravans from Lunda may have continued to reach Kasanje from time to time in those later decades, since a Portuguese military commander met an emissary from the Lunda court there in 1851,[27] but these yielded gradually to the large Imbangala and

24. Contemporaneous evidence in the documents enclosed in de Mello, 30 March 1801, AHU, Angola cx. 51; Carvalho, *Ethnographia e história tradicional*, p. 529. Cf. Vellut, "Notes sur le Lunda," pp. 92, 163.

25. Vellut, "Notes sur le Lunda," pp. 94–96, 102 ff.

26. Saldanha da Gama, 18 Jan. 1808, AHU, Angola cx. 58; Torres, *Memórias*, pp. 300–301; Vellut, "Notes sur le Lunda," pp. 110–15.

27. Vellut, "Notes sur le Lunda," p. 118.

Ovimbundu trading expeditions from the Kwango valley and central highland areas much closer to the coast that carried the vast majority of the ivory, wax, and eventually rubber that supplemented slaves after 1830 in the export trade of western central Africa.

As Lunda slaving along the forest fringes approached the capacity of the population there to bear losses in the later eighteenth century, the rivers of the central Zaire basin became more significant sources of slaves for the ports north of Luanda. Those regions had grown accustomed to imported textiles, coastal shells, marine salt, and other commodities in the seventeenth century by exporting raffia cloths, along with some slaves, through Loango and Kongo to the Portuguese *conquista,* where local Portuguese used them to buy slaves.[28] Then the Asian and European textiles that gradually took over the trading economy inland from Luanda at the beginning of the eighteenth century eliminated much of the market for these established exports from the fringes of the forest.[29] Traders and producers in the forest sought alternative means of paying for imports at Malebo Pool by developing ivory exports after 1790, but in the meanwhile they came to rely more heavily on slaves.

The sources of the captives delivered to Loango extended first up the Kasai toward Lunda and then later up the main channel of the Zaire River to the confluence of the Ubangi.[30] Some of the slaves brought in from upriver were forwarded by land from the transfer point for the river trade at the Pool along a southwesterly route through the central Kongo provinces of Wandu and Nkusu to reach European buyers along the lower Zaire. Some may have continued on to Mbwila, but most of these equatorial slaves would have gone directly west from Malebo Pool to the ports of the Loango Coast, principally to Loango itself. Slaves from the upper parts of the Zaire were also taken directly west up the Alima River, across the plateau, and sold to Mayombe, who in turn resold them to the brokers at the coast.[31] All of these became important components of the renewed slave trade of that part of the coast in the 1810s and 1820s.

Central highland traders, while busy developing sources of slaves from the southwestern Lunda empire after the 1750s, also opened trails leading to the entire set of population nodes along the margins of the Kalahari during the last decades of the eighteenth century. The fall of the warlords of the central highlands in the 1770s restructured trade there from African-initiated warring to foreign-financed commerce. The Portuguese military expeditions that destroyed the old regimes on the western part of the

28. Wilson, "Kongo Kingdom," pp. 61, 120, 126–29; Harms, *River of Wealth, River of Sorrow,* p. 63, for the main areas of production in the nineteenth century.
29. For the earlier effect on Kongo, Wilson, "Kongo Kingdom," p. 205.
30. Harms, *River of Wealth, River of Sorrow,* pp. 26–39.
31. Martin, *External Trade,* p. 122; Furtado, 13 Aug. 1783, AHU, Angola cx. 40.

plateau opened the eastern province of Bihe and the interior beyond the Kubango. Agents of the Portuguese traders settled on the crest of the plateau and had penetrated the sandy Ngangela country beyond the upper Kubango in the 1760s, though at that time they had returned from its sparsely populated woodlands mostly with wax. Contact, however, had driven the opening wedge of commodity exports into the political econ- omies of these woodlands and had predisposed powerful men there toward further trading, even on the basis of selling slaves. With better financing through Luanda, and with the boom in French purchases of slaves near Benguela in the 1780s, the most intrepid of them made contact with Domingos's village, the Luvale, and the Lozi (Luyi) of the upper Zambezi valley before 1790.[32] They probably also began to trade with the people living along the lower Kubango. With drought after 1785, all these south- eastern regions increased in importance as sources of slaves moving up into the highlands and remained significant well into the nineteenth century.

This Luanda trade through Bihe to the far southeast extended a much older involvement in slaving the northern slopes of the central highlands by Angolan Portuguese settled around colonial outposts along the middle Kwanza. Around the turn of the eighteenth century, from about 1680 to the 1720s, most slaves taken captive in African wars and Portuguese raids around that edge of the plateau had gone northwest to Luanda through Pungo Andongo, Massangano, or Cambambe. Only captives from the mountains along the plateau's western rim went to Benguela, at the ini- tiative, mostly military, of other Portuguese settled there. When Benguela- linked settlers overspread the plateau surface itself in the 1720s and 1730s, establishing the main outlet for the captives seized in the wars of that era directly west between the Katumbela and Kuporolo rivers to the smaller southern Portuguese port, Luanda lost its position in the portions of the highlands nearer the coast. British and French buyers also diverted a con- siderable number of slaves from the northern and western sides of the plateau down the Kuvo after the 1750s, though it happened that Domin- gos's captors sold him to a Brazilian ship when they followed that route to the coast at Novo Redondo. Luanda's policies toward the highlands in the 1760s and 1770s were aimed largely at recovering slaving territories lost to these competitors, both Brazilian and foreign.

The reports of Luanda officials to Lisbon, preoccupied with the Ka- sanje trade, do not make entirely clear how slaves from south of the Kwanza may have continued to reach traders sending slaves out through Luanda,

32. Alvares de Mello, 7 Dec. 1798, AHU, Angola cx. 46; Lacerda, "Noticia da cidade de Benguella"; "Derrota de Benguella para o sertão," in Felner, *Angola*, 2:13–27; Alexandre da Silva Teixeira and José da Silva Costa, "Relação da viagem que fiz desta cidade de Benguella para as terras de Lovar no anno de mil setecentos noventa e quatro," *Arquivos de Angola* 1, no. 4 (1935), doc. X (also in Felner, *Angola*, 1:236–27); Miller, "Central and Southern Angola."

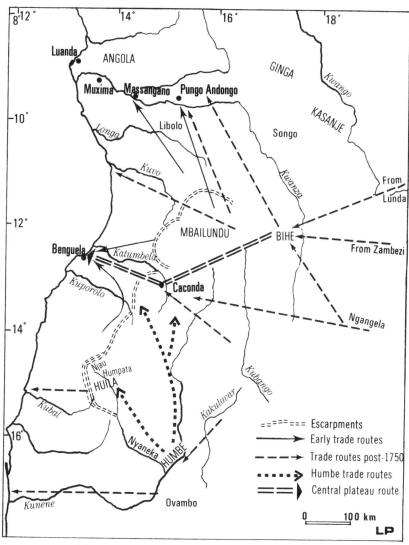

Map 7.4. Trade Routes of the Central Highlands

mostly settlers in Pungo Andongo, but they leave the impression that their *pombeiro* agents regularly scoured the valleys of the rivers flowing down from its northeastern side, behind the western areas sending slaves to Benguela. Some of these traders took advantage of Benguela as an alternative outlet for captives they bought with goods from Luanda, where they sold them on the cash basis prevailing there and thus gained for themselves revenues owed in fact to their backers at the colonial capital.[33] With Lisbon's abandonment of Kasanje after 1804 this trans-Kwanza trade became a major source of slaves for Luanda in the 1810s and probably in the 1820s.

Traders from Benguela managed only indirect contact with the agropastoral Nkhumbi and Ovambo populations of the lower Kunene and Kakulovar floodplains in the eighteenth century. Since the cattle-owning Humbe elite of this area had no urgent need of foreign credits to enlist clients among their subjects, for a long time they alternated between selling livestock and hides in the higher elevations, sometimes founding colonies of settlers in the process up the Kunene to the north, and intermittently raiding the highland populations for slaves. By sending ivory out through their own trading diaspora, they acquired limited quantities of imports but sold only a few slaves, probably individuals taken from existing sources in their own societies and economies. By the 1780s, a militaristic phase of expansion, certainly seeking relief from spreading drought, led the Humbe to move out directly west for the first time, down the Kunene toward the sea. The slaves they took, probably in part seized by raiding parties sent up toward the populous crest of the main plateau and also taken from the agro-pastoral people of the interior floodplains of the Kakulovar and the Kunene, they offered to French ships calling there. Only the adoption of more modern firearms after the middle of the nineteenth century, to steal cattle from their rivals or to protect their own herds from rustlers, finally forced these lords to intensify the demands that they made on their own clients and subjects for labor and slaves.[34]

The Portuguese made similarly few inroads before 1830 against the Nyaneka, clustered for self-defense against Humbe raiders under the kings of Huila around the mountainous Humpata Plateau at the southern tip of the western rim of the highlands. By the 1790s, however, the guardian of the western approach to Humpata, originally a minor noble, Njau, broke away from his Huila overlords to raid the upper steppes and to add

33. Miller, "Central and Southern Angola"; cf. Birmingham, *Trade and Conflict in Angola*, pp. 140–41.
34. Mesquita, 20 July 1781, AHU, Angola cx. 38; Souza Magalhães, 24 Feb. 1785, AHU, Angola maço 13 (D.O.); Pilarte da Silva, n.d. (1770), AHU, Angola maço 13 (D.O.) (in Felner, *Angola*, 1:177–86); Moçâmedes *parecer*, 24 Feb. 1796, AHU, Angola maço 6; Valente, 8 Feb. 1791, AHU, Angola cx. 41. Cf. the "Ruegas/Regas/Ruengas" mentioned in Matos, *Compêndio histórico*, p. 323.

the captives he took to the expanded numbers of slaves sent down the Kubal River to French ships active along the coast just below.[35] The considerable distances over which foreign traders had to range on this southern and southeastern fringe of the commercial slave networks, the inability of the small and dispersed populations along the desert edge to supply large numbers of slaves in the long run, and the defensive strength of the mobile cattle lords of the margins of the Kalahari gave a certain amount of protection to the agro-pastoral populations there from commercialized, if not militaristic, slaving. The hides and livestock available locally to pay for imports, along with wax and ivory, supplemented by slave raids mounted against more populous neighbors, thus made it possible for the cattle-raising regions of the lower Kunene to maintain the phase of commodity exporting typical of initial contact, their own power, and a degree of isolation from the Atlantic trade rather longer than areas without livestock usually managed.

The lengthening trails that opened new slave catchment areas in the far interior as the century progressed did not eliminate older sources nearer the coast. These near zones added slaves to the caravans as they passed through on their way westward, mostly through foreclosures on debts among populations subject to local merchant princes. "Yombe" slaves delivered to the ports of the Loango Coast must have included residents of the Mayombe Mountains and the valley of the Kwilu-Niari River just to the east, areas within the sphere of *lemba,* as well as slaves from farther inland resold by Yombe traders. The merchants of the Kwango valley, from the Zombo and Soso in eastern Kongo south through Jinga and Kasanje, surely provided subjects in much the same way through their own markets and caravans. The court at Kasanje, beyond its role as broker in the trade to Lunda, gained fame as the judicial center where a great and terrible *ndua* poison oracle condemned defendants to slavery and exile. Plaintiffs came from Kongo, from elsewhere in the Kwango valley, and even from the Portuguese-ruled highlands to the west to bring suits against neighbors and debtors. The reputation of the Kasanje *ndua* oracle surely derived as much from the force with which Kasanje kings could seize defendants declared guilty and hand them over to their accusers as slaves as from the justice of its verdicts.[36] The new owners of the condemned found ready buyers for them in the Kasanje market near the king's court.

35. Miller, "Central and Southern Angola."
36. See Chapter 4 above. But Kasanje was not unique in its development of this means of legitimating enslavement. Cf. Corrêa, *História de Angola,* 2:19, on the "law of *kitushi*" (*quituxi* in Portuguese, an offense for which the penalty was loss of civil status, or enslavement) and its systematic extension to the most contrived and trivial offenses among the *ndembu* after formalization of Portuguese commercial relations with that area in 1759. Similarly also the *mukanu* and *milonga,* later among the highly commercialized Ovimbundu and Chokwe: Heywood, "Production, Trade, and Power," pp. 80–85; Miller, "Cokwe Trade and Conquest," pp. 193–94.

The principal area near the coast to resort to outright wars as supplementary sources of slaves was the central Kongo region, where conflict among declining Kongo nobles, who fought one another regularly to capture the remnant sixteenth- and seventeenth-century Catholic cult, augmented the chains of captives coming from farther east. "Beyond decline," as one historian has described the Kongo in this era,[37] the aristocracy vainly defended an ancien régime in the highlands made anachronistic by the commercial power of lowland Zombo and Soso traders and by western Kongo merchant princes in command of the bays where British and French ships, and canoes and launches from the Loango Coast, put in to tap the trade routes moving slaves northwest through Sonyo to Kakongo and Ngoyo.[38] Vili trading communities resident in Kongo also evacuated slaves from these wars to Loango through the lower Zaire River province of Nsundi.[39]

A single captive woman or youth might thus experience the full range of trading institutions, diaspora, itinerant *pombeiros,* central markets, and caravans in an agonizing progress toward the coast that lasted months if not years. Prisoners seized in Lunda raids in the southern fringe of the forest, for example, covered the first few hundred kilometers in royal caravans evacuating them toward the Kwango. By the 1760s and 1770s, caravan leaders or Lunda political/commercial agents in the west might sell off a few of their prisoners to petty traders from Bihe whom they encountered roaming the woodlands east of the Kwango in search of wax. Sooner or later, most of these captives would have entered one of the central markets along the frontier between the African and Atlantic economies, perhaps by canoes paddled down the Kasai to Malebo Pool, but more likely by walking into some part of the wooded valley of the Kwango. There the merchant elite of the region, settled as Yaka, as Shinje under Malundo, as Imbangala under the kings of Kasanje, in Holo or Jinga, or as eastern Kongo under the Soso or Zombo would retain some as slaves, their profits from the trade. Some of their companions would find themselves drawn gradually through the Vili trading diaspora toward the Loango Coast, while still others would end up plodding relentlessly in caravans headed toward Luanda.

The western central African commercial and transport sector was thus an integrated circulatory system of many linked segments, in which the central markets functioned as hearts pumping trade goods out through arterial caravan routes and through the capillaries of trading diaspora and *pombeiro* peddlers. Through the corresponding veins of trade they received

37. Broadhead, "Beyond Decline."
38. Souza Magalhães, 18 March 1773 and 16 March 1780, AHU, Angola cx. 36 and 37.
39. Hilton, "Political and Social Change."

back the slaves who nourished much of the African body politic west of the slaving frontier. Some of these slaves the African merchant princes bled intermittently toward the coast, as if to purge the political and social organism of the fever provoked by commercial contact with the world economy. In some areas, traders underwent cures to relieve the individual afflictions that commercial success brought and to restore them to the communities from which they had fallen away.

Though traders rushed most slaves along these paths as fast as they could, no doubt some of the people taken by commercial and judicial methods near the coast had arrived in the areas of their proximate seizure years earlier. All along the way, traders, masters, and patrons continued to select the individual captives whom they regarded as most adaptable or promising, probably mostly the children and youths, and particularly females, and retain them as new dependent members of their own communities. Even more of the slaves originating in the western areas would have been locally born descendants of parents originally brought there as slaves. The eastern and western sources of slaves, acquired by violence or by debt, from either side of the slaving frontier, thus merged over time in practice, as individuals were kidnapped, sold, resold, and captured again in the course of repeatedly disrupted lifetimes. The "ethnic" origins of slaves reaching the coast might therefore mean very little, less even than the complex and changing communal identities themselves. Incidents of capture outnumbered the persons taken, perhaps by a significant amount, and vastly exceeded the numbers of those sent out of Africa.

The multiple and interlocking sources of exported labor in western central Africa also meant that the slaves' final ports of embarkation gave only the roughest indication of their origins. Ships moored at Ngoyo or Cabinda drew not only from the Zaire estuary and Malebo Pool but also from the inland routes to Mbwila and the middle Kwango valley, or even from the series of smaller Kongo ports located as far south as the Dande and Bengo rivers. Similarly, the *mubire,* or Vili, dispatched southeast from Loango drew slaves from the middle Kwango by the 1660s, then from Lunda farther to the east, and finally also from Bobangi sources up the Zaire toward the northern savannas by the 1790s. Slaves from Lunda could have reached the sea anywhere from Loango all the way south to Benguela. Captives sold at Jinga or Kasanje might have ended their treks along several different networks leading to Luanda, to the mouth of the Dande, or to Cabinda, Molembo, or Loango. Those from the upper tributaries of the Zaire might have turned west up the Alima toward Loango, or continued downriver to Malebo Pool and from there proceeded as far south as Luanda. People from the central highlands boarded ships from the mouth of the Kunene to at least as far north as Luanda. Even slaves from isolated Humbe in the far south could have first seen the sea anywhere from the mouth of the Kunene north to Benguela. The sequence of multiple sales attending transfers of slaves between their place of seizure and the coast could divert the flow in almost any direction within a full quadrant from southwest to northwest, in an exact mirror image of the equally complex fan of trade routes distributing selections of imported goods widely throughout the interior.

Growing Export Volumes

In the short run, the alternative routings allowed African transporters to respond sensitively and quickly to advantages offered at one point relative to others over long stretches of the coast. Traders thus flexibly directed slaves to particular ports in response to changing European demand, prices, and credit. The aggregate number of slaves boarded at each one reflected these diversions from one route to another more than they represented changing conditions in the source regions of the African interior. In one striking reorientation of the trade from the central highlands, Brazilians buying at Benguela prevented Luanda merchants from expanding their seventeenth-century sources south of the Kwanza onto the main surface of the plateau. The British, French, and other competitors along the northern and the southern coasts, with lower prices for goods as well as superior capital resources to drive the longer-term expansion of the trade inland, made enormous inroads on Luanda's slave-producing hinterland in the Kwango valley until about 1810. Metropolitan Portuguese concentrated at Luanda tried to protect these diminished markets by selling their own higher-priced goods on less restrictive credit terms but fell steadily behind nonetheless. After 1810, Luanda continued to lose even more ground, as Portuguese traders based in Brazil moved into the long-coveted positions on the coasts north of the Dande vacated by the French and British.

The trade routes serving the government port at Benguela grew steadily as sources of slaves throughout the eighteenth century, as the collage of regions in its African hinterland expanded to include the farming populations of the central highlands and the pockets of people east beyond the Kubango. Beginning with perhaps 1,000–2,000 captives officially embarked annually before 1730, the peak came in the 1780s and 1790s, when as many as 7,000–8,000 slaves boarded ships headed for Brazil each year during the great drought of 1785–94.[40] The volume of slave exports there dropped after 1800 or 1810, eventually to levels in the range of one-third to one-half of the maximum attained during the early 1790s.[41] Benguela's decline may have resulted in part from temporary depopulation

40. Figures to 1800 presented in Klein, *Middle Passage,* pp. 255–56.
41. Miller, "Legal Portuguese Slaving," pp. 166–67, for continuation of the series.

in the southern highlands after what must have been enormous mortality from starvation, warfare, and smallpox epidemics at the conclusion of the drought.[42] Continuing conflicts among the stricken Africans between 1810 and 1820 also blocked the bottleneck of trade routes between the sources of the Katumbela and Kuporolo rivers, where all the slaves from the southern slaving sources funneled down toward Benguela. These wars disrupted supply lines just at the time when slave buyers were, for unrelated reasons, redirecting their shipping to Luanda and ports north. As credit replaced warfare as the source of most slaves, Benguela, up to then not an entry point for European capital in any quantity, lost its trade. It revived as an illegal outlet for slaves only later in the 1830s and 1840s, then for ivory and wax, and still later also for wild rubber generated from African sources in the highlands and supported by a new cycle of population expansion based on importations of slaves there from the east.[43]

To the relatively firm numbers of slaves moving toward Benguela through the central highlands in the eighteenth century must be added a less certain number of others delivered along the same routes to British and French ships anchored near the mouths of the Kuvo, the Kuporolo, the Kubal, and the Kunene, as well as just beyond the sight of government officials along outlying beaches near Benguela itself. Several British vessels may have bought slaves south of the Kwanza each year in the 1750s and 1760s, taking on perhaps 1,000 captives per annum. The French, who reentered the Atlantic slave trade in force after the Seven Years' War ended in 1763, took over this trade during the 1770s and 1780s and expanded it to perhaps 3,000–5,000 from Benguela alone in their peak years of smuggling there before 1792. By the time the Napoleonic wars in Europe finally forced the French to withdraw after 1791, the British had concentrated their western central African slave-buying well to the north, along the Loango Coast. The disappearance of the French left subsequent trading south of the Kwanza almost entirely to the Brazilians, and eventually to the Portuguese.[44] At a rough guess French and British ship captains together probably boarded slaves on the order of 1,000 or so each year along all the coast south of Luanda in the 1750s and increased their purchases (briefly) to as many as 10,000 annually by 1790–92.[45]

42. See Chapter 17 below.
43. Clarence-Smith, "Farmer-Herders of Southern Angola"; Childs, *Umbundu Kinship and Character*, pp. 199–209.
44. For the general history of French slaving, Stein, *French Slave Trade*, esp. pp. 35–47; also Rawley, *Transatlantic Slave Trade*, chaps. 5 and 6.
45. E.g., 18 French slaves at Benguela alone in the months from June to December 1791: Francisco Paim da Câmara Ornellas, 30 March 1792, AHU, Angola cx. 42. At 350 slaves per ship, contraband loadings at that rate would total 10,800 slaves in a year. See other figures in Ornellas, 23 Jan. 1793 and 20 Jan. 1795, both AHU, Angola cx. 42, and also the Benguela *mappa*, AHU, Angola cx. 45. The figures are not inconsistent with Stein, *French Slave Trade*, p. 211.

Exports from the northern parts of the coast similarly rose steadily through the eighteenth century to a peak in the 1780s, before dropping sharply back in the early 1790s. There, however, volume rose again in the late years of that decade, faltered between 1800 and 1809, and then resumed its long-term climb through the 1820s. The overall scale of this increase was moderately greater than that at Benguela, from annual exports of a few thousand at the start to 15,000 or so per annum towards the end. On the European side, the long-term growth reflected the increased interest of the British and French in "Angola" slaves, whom they could buy less expensively than others available in West Africa. The decline of the 1790s followed French withdrawal from the trade, and the fluctuations after 1800 reflected instability in the British trade as it drew to a close in 1808. Portuguese buyers supported the generally rising trend of the two decades ending in 1830 as they moved after 1809 into the place left vacant by the British.[46]

Official exports of slaves from Luanda remained nearly steady in the general range of 8,000–10,000 slaves per year through the eighteenth century before beginning to rise shortly after 1800. They stagnated as buyers moved off to the north after 1809, increased again between 1817 and 1822 as Lisbon attempted to reenter a trade it had virtually abandoned in the preceding decade, and declined slightly in the later 1820s until the end of the legal trade with Brazilian independence from Portuguese rule. The slaves counted through customs at Luanda in fact entered the city not only by land but also in canoes and small coastal craft from the Bengo, the Kwanza, and as far south as the Kuvo, at least at some periods after the foundation of Novo Redondo on the Kikombo in 1769 and again after the French disappeared in 1792.[47] Some of these outlying ports also

46. The basic export series for the Loango coast comes from Martin, *External Trade*, pp. 56, 65–68 passim, 74, 124, 139, 141. Other estimates from Portuguese sources include Francisco de Tavora, 12 Aug. 1670, AHU, cód. 17, fol. 25v; doc. 12, Dec. 1720, AHU, Angola cx. 16 (for these two last I am indebted to John K. Thornton); Lourenço de Freitas de Noronha, 28 March 1735, AHU, Angola cx. 20; Câmara, draft *regimento*, n.d. (ca. 1770), AHU, Angola maço 3 (D.O.); Souza Magalhães, 18 March 1773, AHU, Angola cx. 36; Furtado, 5 Nov. 1783, AHU, Angola cx. 38; "Extinção do prezidio das Pedras," n.d. (ca. 1785), AHU, Angola cx. 37. Also see Gaulme, "Document sur le Ngoyo," p. 374.

47. In addition to the well-known figures in Klein, *Middle Passage*, pp. 254–55, and Miller, "Legal Portuguese Slaving," pp. 166–67, compare Wilson, "Kongo Kingdom," p. 208, and Mauro, "L'Atlantique portugais," pp. 51–52, for the 1650s; copy of proposal (5 Oct. 1662) for tax to subsidize royal dowry, in *petição* from the Senado da Câmara (Luanda), 30 Dec. 1744, AHU, Angola cx. 23 (cf. Charles R. Boxer, *Portuguese Society in the Tropics* [Madison: University of Wisconsin Press, 1965], pp. 114, 195); doc. 10, Oct. 1670, AHU, Angola cx. 7; doc. 24, May 1671, AHU, Angola cx. 8 (for these two references, I am grateful to Franz Binder); Cadornega, *História geral*, 3:31; Carl A. Hanson, *Economy and Society in Baroque Portugal, 1668–1703* (Minneapolis: University of Minnesota Press, 1981), p. 233; also see Birmingham, *Trade and Conflict in Angola*, pp. 137, 141, 154–55. The reported figures for the 1710s and 1720s may be too low by the amount of smuggling accomplished by governors and their associates. Benguela slaves before 1730 were dispatched through Luanda.

contributed slaves to the French and British at periods when they were generally active in Angola.

The relatively stable volume of Luanda's exports before about 1800 concealed substantial changes in its catchment areas in the interior. The early-eighteenth-century trade, established on the basis of military conquests along the Kwanza, eroded in favor of commercially based methods as the slaving frontier retreated. Luanda's main sources became the Kwango valley, usually Kasanje, and the areas southwest of it along either bank of the upper Kwanza. Vili diverted significant numbers of slaves from the eastern termini of this network in the Kwango valley after the 1750s. French and British competition at the Kuvo from 1760 to 1790 attracted slaves from the northern slopes of the central highlands who would formerly have been sent down to Portuguese outposts like Pungo Andongo overlooking the Kwanza. Lunda thus assumed a growing importance for Luanda by default, but its remote eastern location also made slaves from there easy to divert to parts of the coast well outside Luanda's control, from Benguela to Loango. Luanda's early-nineteenth-century increases probably came in large part from recapturing sources in the central highlands back from Benguela, from maturation of the direct commercial connection to Lunda begun in the later decades of the eighteenth century, and possibly also from encroachment on the western Kongo sources of slaves along the coast north of the city.

Conversely, merchants at Luanda diverted a modest proportion of the slaves they acquired to outports where they could avoid surveillance in the capital town by creditors and government tax collectors. A minor portion of Benguela slaves, perhaps 5 percent or so, as well as some of the captives sold to British ships lying off the Bengo and Dande in the 1760s–1790s and a larger fraction of the slaves loaded at Ambriz (the mouth of the Loje) after 1810 came directly from trails meant to funnel slaves to Luanda. Though these slaves were "smuggled" from the point of view of the crown's officers in Angola and were often lost to Portuguese buyers, nearly all of them numbered among the captives reaching the Caribbean aboard British and French ships. The "contraband" captives lamented in the Portuguese sources were therefore also among the thousands counted as bought by foreigners working outlying parts of the Angolan coast and did not increase export totals estimated on that basis.[48]

In the earlier part of the eighteenth century, the overall totals of slaves exported from the entire Angolan coastline, from the mouth of the Kunene north to Loango, probably ran in the vicinity of 12,000–15,000 persons each year. Exports were then concentrated mostly at Luanda and came from the immediate vicinity of the *conquista,* particularly the populous Kwango and Kwanza river valleys and the plateaux above their banks. In

48. See Chapters 16 and 17 below.

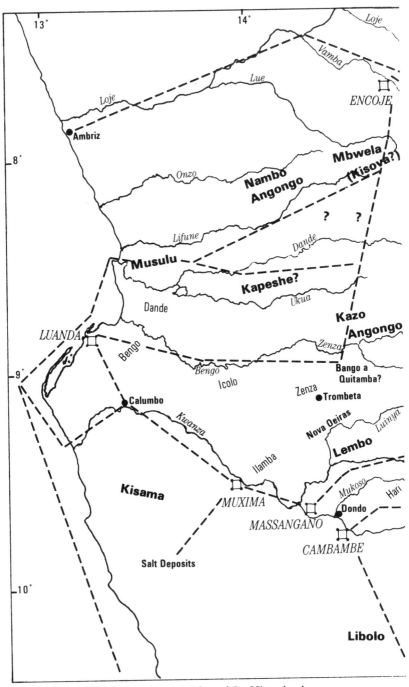

Map 7.5. Luanda and Its Hinterland

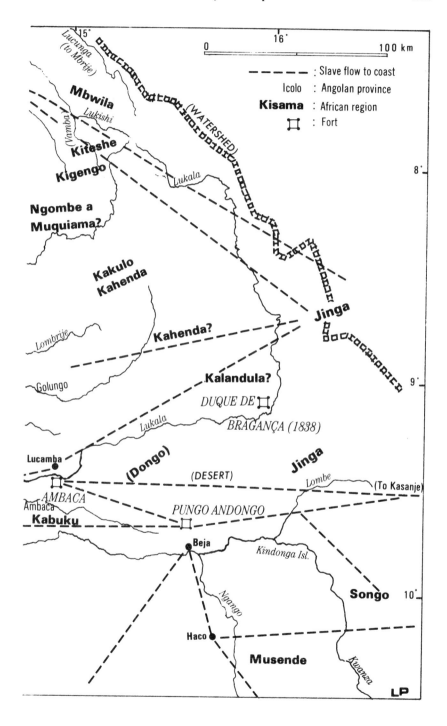

succeeding years, the band of dense population farther east between the latitudes of 6° and 8° south and the central highlands generated greater and greater numbers of slaves through warfare to supplement the people seized against commercial default nearer the coast. The Benguela and Loango outlets for these slaves, together with Luanda, reached their combined maximum in the drought decades of the 1780s and 1790s, altogether totaling as many as 40,000 slaves per year. The complete trade then declined slightly but remained in the range of 30,000–35,000 annually for some time thereafter, though drawing from an enlarged area that by 1830 encompassed much of the western forest, adjacent savannas to the north, and the entire southern savanna to the Zambezi and the Kalahari Desert.

The highest losses to western central African populations thus coincided with the period of greatest ecological distress at the very end of the eighteenth century. The expansion of the Atlantic zone by the early nineteenth century relieved the pressures in given locales of the high numbers of slaves exported during the last decades of the legal trade, as it did also during the illegal trade that followed, by spreading slaving more widely. The true rate of population loss—that is, the proportion taken from the changing areas afflicted at any one time—may well have remained relatively constant over the entire course of the trade, with a tendency to increase temporarily with drought and just before and as the slaving frontier made its eastward lurches.

Though the transportation networks that arose to link the retreating slaving frontier with the coast also moved captives from region to region within western central Africa in significant numbers, one may no more than speculate on the additional quantities involved. Probably, slaving resettled more people around the Lunda court, in the Kwango valley, around the warlords of the central highlands, from province to province in Kongo, or within the Portuguese *conquista* than were exported abroad each year. Forty thousand such persons, equal to the maximum numbers sold off in any given year at the coast, would have amounted to less than 0.5 percent of the 10 million assumed inhabitants of the region at the time, or 12 percent over an individual's estimated lifetime of thirty years. Reports of population structures in nineteenth-century Africa leave an impression that slaves constituted much larger proportions of those left behind. Slaves remaining as the caravans departed with their erstwhile companions sometimes found themselves also sent on toward the coast later, but in the interim they had contributed labor, perhaps children, and political support to the slavers, merchant princes, and other Africans who became wealthy and powerful from their presence. Adding those retained to the others exported would double-count the portion enduring both experiences and would correspondingly overstate the estimated numbers of captives seized originally. Something of the general directions of these

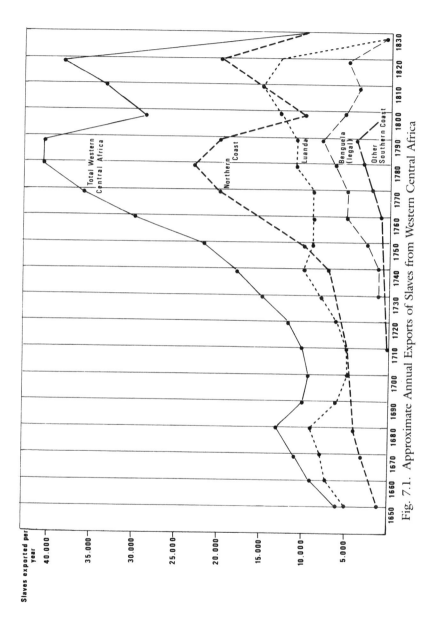

Fig. 7.1. Approximate Annual Exports of Slaves from Western Central Africa

population movements within western central Africa may be inferred from the advances of the slaving frontier, on the assumption that the violence of its passage temporarily drove out populations in the areas where it flared and that its survivors clustered around the warlords who took in refugees and under the mercantile princes who rebuilt the demographic resources of the lands where the turmoil had subsided.

The Economics of the Moving Slaving Frontier

The inland advances of the slaving frontier dominated the economics and history of the eighteenth-century trading sector because those movements increased the size of the areas that African traders had to cover faster than the merchants could accumulate profits to support the new trade structures needed to cover them. Though traders made momentous gains—as their numerous followings of slaves, caravans, diaspora, and trading currencies all demonstrated—sometimes with revolutionary force, the expanded zone of commercialized slaving kept them continually short of the working capital they needed to stay in touch with their sources of slaves. The hesitations in the advance of the slaving frontier, beyond the political inertia of the old regimes, derived in part from the enormous costs of moving it inland. Further, the shift in the African kings' and lords' methods of generating slaves, away from war and violence to debt-based seizures, added to the strains on their capital resources also. Merely harvesting captives taken in the wars that marked passage of the slaving frontier required relatively little commercial investment, beyond the bare-bones infrastructure necessary to position caravans in the trains of armies in the field and to march the slaves off to the west. On the other hand, generating captives through seizures for debt demanded costly prior extensions of credit in trade goods to merchant princes and no less expensive investments in the judicial and police institutions of the states that coerced repayment from indebted subjects. Merchants' costs increased further still because, as distances grew between the coast and the captive-producing regions, they held the slaves for greater periods of time, with attendant higher risks of morbidity and mortality.

Theoretically, the retreat of the slaving frontier might have bestowed profitably strategic advantages on the merchants. The lengthening slaving trails left them sole and specialized occupants of the critical transport and communication links between buyers and sellers unknown to one another beyond rumors of savagery and cannibalism and separated physically on the opposite ends of the trade routes. But in fact the multiple distribution networks and rival groups of traders made the transport and financing sector a highly competitive one and limited the overall profits to be made in it. The traders' gains, however substantial by the standards of the African political economy, and not insignificant by capitalist measures either, seem to have fallen below the level necessary for fully self-financed growth. Most merchants active in the interior thus remained, or became, no less dependent on sources of credit at the coast than were the slave-producing merchant kings.

Changes in the geographical patterns of trade provide trace elements that indicate the African traders' increased reliance on foreign sources of credit. Along the coasts north of Luanda, the primary commercial centers shifted westward when the African-financed commodity trade of the sixteenth century yielded to the more capital-dependent slaving of the eighteenth century. Descriptions of early exchanges of copper, ivory, elephant bristles, and dyewoods show that the Atlantic and the regional African economies then met at established centers of African commercial strength located well into the interior. The concentration of Kongo trade at the court of the kings at São Salvador contrasted with the marginality of its sixteenth-century seaport at Mpinda on the south bank of the Zaire, for example. São Salvador's centrality demonstrated the considerable extent to which the modestly financed Portuguese commerce of that era depended on the economic resources of the Kongo monarchy's extensive tribute system and its regional commercial network.[49] Similarly, the first inland extensions of the export trade of that era depended on tapping other sources of African working capital, particularly the wealth concentrated at the great Mpumbu market at Malebo Pool and later along the lower Kwango in Okango.[50]

Only much later, in the seventeenth century, when better-capitalized Dutch and English buyers began to provide foreign financial underpinnings for the mature trade in slaves, did the locus of the economic interface pull back to the west. From São Salvador it moved first to Sonyo in the hinterland of the old Kongo port at Mpinda. Finally, at the end of the century it settled on the coast itself, north of the river at Cabinda and Molembo. The burden of transporting slaves and goods shifted then also from the interior traders, who had once added the Atlantic trade as a sideline to their commerce in commodities, to agents of capitalist-financed buyers at the coast who were more interested in acquiring people than in buying goods.

Changes in the geography of the African commercial networks between Loango and the lower Zaire thus seem to have reflected the addition of foreign capital and to have fuelled the rise of systematic slavers distinguishable from the several trading groups active in the region in earlier

49. John K. Thornton, "Early Kongo-Portuguese Relations: A New Interpretation," *History in Africa* 8 (1981): 183–204, makes the analogous argument in noneconomic terms.
50. Wilson, "Kingdom of Kongo," pp. 51 ff.

periods. In time this initial distinction between the slavers and the others became blurred. The slavers invested part of the profits they accumulated from selling people in expanding the regional commodity trade, buying up the commerce in copper, shells, salt, and foodstuffs exchanged in the interior. It is thus at least arguable that the slaving sector of this complex commercial political economy originated in loans of European trade goods to its less reputable members, on terms specifying repayment in captives. Continuing foreign financial support provided the expansiveness that allowed slavers to remain in direct touch with retreating sources of slaves in the far interior, without having to share the profits of this trade with local intermediaries, each providing funds for a small part of the large network of local links necessary to the operation of an African-financed trade. The long-distance diaspora thus excluded their smaller competitors, at least in part, because of the credit they obtained from the Atlantic economy.

A parallel relocation of the central market in the upper middle Kwango valley at about the same time in the seventeenth century marked submersion of the preexisting locally financed exchange of salt for Lunda raffia cloth and iron implements from the surrounding highlands beneath the wave of slaving. Slaving in this case began when European capital financed the 400-kilometer relay east from Luanda to the valley floor in the 1650s. The ancient regional trade had centered on the northerly salt pans of the lower Lui, but in 1680 the kings of the mature slave-brokering state of Kasanje moved their capitals to the southerly parts of the upper valley, near the new marketplace through which they channeled slaves from Lunda military campaigns to traders from Angola.

The events of the following decades in Kasanje revealed the growing amount of European capital underlying slaving there, as well as pointing to corresponding changes in the geography of the trade routes. In the early eighteenth century, the Lunda had largely owned the slaves up to their point of sale in the Kasanje marketplace, supported by the low cost of captives taken in their wars east of the Kwango rather than by the African commercial resources that had backed the early commodities trade at Loango. The foreign credits invested in the Kwango valley grew in the 1730s and 1740s. Though no further move of the marketplace followed, other telltale signs appeared. The trade goods that became available at that time underwrote the long reign of the Kasanje king Ngunza a Kambamba in the 1750s. Modern local historians, imbued with the commercial ethic of more recent times, remembered him as the first of the state's rulers to have passed the material wealth of his office on to his personal heirs and as one of the most powerful rulers in the entire history of the realm.[51] The

---

51. For Ngunza a Kambamba, see Joseph C. Miller, "Kings, Lists, and History in Kasanje," *History in Africa* 6 (1979): 51–96. A parallel oral tradition from the Ngoyo state

goods available to Kasanje on this new basis also threatened the formerly active role of Malundo, the westernmost agent of the Lunda trading system living on the opposite bank of the Kwango, and provoked the great and violent conflict that raged back and forth across the river at that time between the front-line agents of the two opposing sources of wealth.[52]

Still later, after goods borrowed from Portuguese traders had enabled Kasanje nobles to become active buyers of slaves east of the Kwango in the 1780s, the main lines of contention shifted to struggles between Kasanje and the Portuguese. Portuguese traders began to bypass the Kasanje royal market entirely and to dispatch caravans of their own east to the main trans-Kwango sources of Kasanje's slaves among the Lunda.[53] Disputes between these traders and the kings produced a formal commercial treaty early in the 1790s to clarify the African kingdom's novel position as broker for imported goods rather than agent for Lunda sellers of slaves.[54] The failure of this agreement later led to Portuguese severance of economic relations with Kasanje and then to armed invasion from Angola and finally to dissolution of the state. Foreign loans had culminated in foreign intervention.

When this last extension of European investment in the commerce of Luanda's remote hinterland pushed outposts of foreign capital beyond the Kwango to the Lunda *mwaant yaav*'s courts near the Kalanyi, the same sequence of a strong, long-ruling king followed by political fragmentation once again marked the conversion. By the 1810s and 1820s, the substantial community of Portuguese-Angolan traders gathered in central Lunda had invested reportedly significant sums in slaving through the Lunda ruler Nawej II, a king grown both domestically powerful and externally dependent on foreign capital. The importance of European credit in allowing the emperor to stabilize the Lunda political and commercial systems under his personal control was evident in his well-known recalcitrance in paying off the large sums he owed.[55] Like Kasanje after Ngunza a Kambamba,

---

near Cabinda also noted this change: a lord subordinate to the Kakongo king was remembered as having married the mulatto daughter of a wealthy Portuguese and as having used the wealth and credit he obtained from his father-in-law to make himself independent as king in Ngoyo and able to stand aloof from the essentially military conflicts of the neighboring African states. This tradition, recorded in the 1740s, thus stresses the role of credit and the contrast between older politics based on war and new power based on European wealth: Abbé Prévost, *Histoire génerale des voyages* (La Haye: Chez Pierre de Hondt, 1748), 6:300 (as quoted in Serrano, *Senhores da terra,* p. 41).

52. Dias, ed. (Leitão), "Viagem a Cassange," pp. 19, 21, 23.

53. For details, see Chapter 17 below.

54. The relevant published documents appear in *Arquivos de Angola,* vols. 1 and 2 (1936), and have been used by Vellut, "Royaume de Cassange." The key unpublished sources are the *requerimento* from Francisco Honorato da Costa and other documents included in de Mello, 30 May 1801, AHU, Angola cx. 51.

55. Vellut, "Notes sur le Lunda," pp. 132–33 ff., and idem, "Africa central do oeste," p. 99.

Lunda edged toward civil wars when Nawej died in 1853. The conflict broke into the open in the 1880s. Profits the provincial parties in the empire made from their independent trades in wax, ivory, slaves, and goods enabled them to bring down the Lunda central authority in much less time than the parallel process had taken earlier in Kasanje. But they had the larger and more lucrative commodity trade of the nineteenth century to work with, compared to late-eighteenth-century Kasanje nobles in the Kwango valley.

On the central plateau and on its eastern and southern flanks, trading centers and patterns of politics comparable to those marking conversion of the merchants in the Luanda hinterland and along the Loango Coast to foreign capital appeared only belatedly and in weak forms, since European financing spread there before the 1770s only in greatly reduced amounts. In these regions, the scattered settlers of Portuguese origin who had run the early trade had usually been renegades with few connections to the capitalist merchants of Lisbon. They paid very little for captives taken in the wars that regularly wracked the central plateau. These inexpensive slaves more than adequately absorbed the modest resources of the Brazilian buyers, who at that time dropped off most of the goods circulating in the highlands at Benguela, the main embarkation point for slaves from these parts of the plateau, and who mostly settled their accounts on the spot. The African financing of trade at Benguela's beaches and in the tumbledown settlement behind them thus no more resembled the much greater metropolitan capital invested through Luanda than the plateau settlers' palisaded mud-and-wattle compounds looked like the elegant two-storied townhouses at Luanda where foreign merchants loaned European goods to Kasanje and other central markets in its hinterland.

Before the 1770s, these settlers' trading stations, rather than concentrating in the seaport like the establishments of the merchants of Luanda, had tended to spread outward toward the sources of slaves in remote parts of the highlands in imitation of the scattered diaspora of African trading communities that conducted the seventeenth-century trade along both banks of the lower Zaire River through Loango and Kongo. Though the highland traders were often of European rather than local background, and although they dealt in war captives from the plateau rather than the commodity produce of the equatorial latitudes, their trade's financing by local residents matched that of the riverain trading networks. As if to confirm the economically African character of this commercial system, the colonial governors condemned it in virulent terms usually reserved for "heathen" adversaries when they tried to replace the settlers' self-financed trade with Lisbon goods in the 1760s.[56]

56. See Chapter 16 following.

When the old warrior kings of the highlands went down to military defeat in the 1770s, trade goods and credit soon followed from Luanda and from the eastern portions of the Angolan *conquista*. The old settlers of the highlands countered by channeling into their own trade substantial quantities of French goods smuggled through Benguela, and perhaps also British goods that Brazilians brought there illegally from Rio de Janeiro. All these imports helped to consolidate the new commercial polities and to build the market at Bihe on the highlands' eastern slope. From those outposts of commercial capital, trading contacts then spread out by the end of the eighteenth century as far as the headwaters of the Zambezi.[57] The last of the African-financed trades of the commercial and transport sector south of the forest had yielded to foreign capital.

Though the commercial sector provided the goods and credit that helped to expand the slaving frontier, the low cost of captives seized in the warfare there itself also defrayed the merchants' rising costs of remaining in touch with distant sources of slaves. The value of human life cheapened on the collapse of old regimes, during raids of hunger-stricken marauders, and when self-sale of refugees into captivity in return for food exposed individuals to resale to the transportation and distribution sector. Failed harvests, or fields laid waste by armies, made it impossible for would-be African buyers of these refugees to retain them as dependents, since they could not feed them as they would have preferred. When the odds of survival for these refugees and captives fell at home, captives, masters, and even kin then put them on the market at low prices that even financially strapped merchants could afford.

Given the high start-up costs of slaving in most areas outside the forest and its rivers, where few earlier commercial contacts reached out across open savanna woodlands, the reduced entry costs of slaving during periods of political and ecological crisis were probably decisive in propelling merchants inland. Marketers and transporters from the west were able to generate the necessary massive initial investments of working capital from higher profits made from reselling people purchased in such a buyers' market. Coastal prices for captives taken under such circumstances apparently dipped less than the costs of acquiring them, leaving widened trading margins available to consolidate commercial institutions in new areas of the interior. Certainly, slave exports at the coast tended to increase as the frontier lurched inland with droughts in the 1610s, and 1670s, the 1710s–20s, and the 1780s–90s, even if the people sent to the Americas at those times suffered, often fatally, from malnutrition and frequently also from smallpox. The principal offsetting cost to the transporters at those times therefore came in sharp rises in mortality among their prisoners. The

57. For details, Miller, "Central and Southern Angola."

economics of the transport and commercial sector thus depended ultimately on high mortality rates among populations on the slaving frontier.
But because increased deaths among the slaves they marched westward
also tended to cap the gains they could make from selling weak and dying
captives, slave mortality in the end also reinforced the merchants' dependence on credit from abroad.

Rising slave prices in the Atlantic economy helped as well to finance
the expansion of the slaving zone. The influence of prices appeared in a
rough correlation between the movements of the frontier and general
increases in prices in the interior markets and also, though to a lesser
extent, with the prices of slaves sold at the coast.[58] The African "prices"
at issue in these events had relatively little to do with the European
currency costs of the goods Lisbon merchants sold in Angola but rather
involved relatively independent physical exchange ratios received by the
Africans. When slaves stopped coming from the existing position of the
slaving frontier, Africans demanded greater quantities of goods for the
captives they offered. Depending on local circumstances, the strains might
arise from pure demographic shortages of people, from the kings' growing costs of dispatching warriors farther and farther afield, from larger
and more liberal loans offered to upstart borrowers by merchants, or
from the reluctance of all these acquirers of dependents to part with
captives in flush times of plentiful rains and an inflationary economy.
These pressures building on prices from the African side could accumulate for some time before rising values of slaves in Brazil allowed
buyers to afford them and finally translated them into actual increases in
western central Africa.

Prices for slaves at Luanda doubled in the 1610s, even as the slaving
frontier spread into southern Kongo, the Kwango valley, and up the hills
south of the Kwanza.[59] By 1711, after the wars heralding another major
advance of the slaving frontier during the 1680s, they rose another 50
percent or more on the strength of new demand for labor from gold
miners in Brazil.[60] By the 1720s and 1730s, despite famine and sickness
in the interior, slave prices had stabilized at the higher levels, both at the
coast and in Luanda's hinterland, and systematic slaving spread east of the

58. Miller, "Slave Prices."
59. André Velho da Fonseca, 28 Feb. 1612, in Alfredo de Albuquerque Felner, *Angola:
apontamentos sôbre a ocupação e início do estabelecimento dos portugueses no Congo, Angola e
Benguela (extraídos de documentos históricos)* (Coimbra: Imprensa da Universidade, 1933), p.
429; also Brásio, *Monumenta missionaria africana*, 6:64–70.
60. Taunay, *Subsídios*, pp. 140–41; Boxer, *Portuguese Society in the Tropics*, p. 226. Torres,
Memórias, p. 398, notes the pressure on prices and an early attempt to set ceilings at Kasanje
in 1688–91.

Kwango.[61] A further price revolution reportedly doubled the cost of slaves again at both Kasanje and Loango in the 1750s, this time clearly owing to British and French demand and to rising purchase and delivery costs in the then-stable slave-catchment zone of western central Africa.[62] Still another increase indicative of strain on the mid-century position of the slaving frontier reached the coast at Loango in 1774–77[63] and was reported at Kasanje in the 1780s.[64] Traders were thus positioned to take advantage of the opportunity that appeared for another low-cost expansion to the east at the end of that decade, when drought expanded the slave trade to its full nineteenth-century geographical extent.[65]

The increased prices Africans demanded for their slaves tended to provoke movements of the slaving frontier also by forcing European buyers to avoid the rising costs. To attract scarce and expensive captives, the Europeans distributed credit more widely, both into regions where they had not previously penetrated and also into the hands of potential local suppliers outside established channels. They thus found themselves constrained to advance trade goods to regional nobles in centralized states and to leaders of trading diaspora communities who would organize new sources of slaves. In the process, they moved into regions beyond what was then the frontier, transforming established political systems and beginning the skimming of unwanted outcasts that would later drift into violence as a further movement of the slaving zone. In the Angola hinterland, Portuguese agents themselves settled farther and farther east for these reasons, inland from Luanda in the seventeenth century, up the central highlands early in the eighteenth century, and by the 1790s beyond the Kwango to Lunda.

Conclusion: From Commerce to Production

Viewing the stages in which African traders invested European commercial credit in their own political economies in a longer temporal perspective, the slaving frontier oscillated between periods of expanding slaving, when

61. (Luanda) Senado da Câmara, 24 Jan. 1728, AHU, Angola cx. 18; Meneses, 3 March 1737, AHU, Angola cx. 19; Dr. Joseph Miranda de Vasconcelos, 20 Feb. 1740, AHU, Angola cx. 22.

62. For Loango, Bean, *British Trans-Atlantic Slave Trade*, pp. 151–52; Martin, *External Trade*, p. 113. For Luanda and hinterland, Vasconcelos, *bando* of 10 Nov. 1759, AHU, Angola cx. 28; also letters of 12 Jan. 1759 and 6 May 1760, AHU, Angola cx. 28.

63. Martin, *External Trade*, p. 114; Debien, "Traite nantaise vue par un Nantais," p. 209.

64. "Directorio para o Capitão Chagas."

65. Also see Vellut, "Relations internationales," p. 87.

drought spawned violence and warfare, and contrasting times of African mercantile regime consolidation on the basis of foreign investment within the existing slaving zones. The periods of war and violence financed expansions of the transportation and distribution networks into more remote slaving zones by lowering the cost of the captives and refugees they created and forcing sales of them as an expedient means of avoiding the likelihood of death if they were kept. Lowered acquisiton costs allowed trading profits that traders invested in working capital. The periods of consolidation were times in which long-term increases in the New World demand for slaves supported rising prices for captives in Africa and larger commitments of commercial capital.

Other shifts in the terms of trade favorable to the Africans, the addition of firearms after the 1670s and 1680s, or lowered costs of the goods delivered to African buyers early in the nineteenth century occasionally supplemented these demand pressures in enabling African transporters to afford significant investment in the transportation and production sectors of the African political economies, usually in the form of goods taken on foreign credit. In the long term the northern parts of western central Africa relied more on commercialized methods of slaving, mostly because of the smaller scale and relative rarity of ecological crises there. The tendency to resort to warfare in the south surely derived from the greater frequency and extent of drought and of demographic collapse in the dry plains leading off to the Kasai and down to the Kalahari. The irregularity of the multiple factors that interacted to move western central Africa's slaving frontier meant that its advances followed far less than perfectly regular patterns in time and space.

Finally, the several distinct institutions of transportation and distribution linking the slaving frontier to the coast also formed a rough sequence correlated with its movements and phases. In a given region, African state-controlled military expeditions and royal caravans usually hacked open routes from established markets to remote new sources of slaves in the first violent phases of organized slaving. Commercial caravans marked the expansive phases of merchant princes and regional nobles in the succeeding generation. Trading diaspora arose still later to draw slaves from within a consolidated "Atlantic zone" where commerce had supplemented the more "political" or "social" relations common on the inland side of the slaving frontier. Peddlers of the *pombeiro* type worked the immediate vicinities of marketplaces and diaspora settlements to the western side of the divide. This steady trend toward commercial methods of distributing goods through the interior and of transporting slaves back to the coast contributed to the general inflation of goods against people, the political transformations, and the geographical movements that steadily drew more western central Africans into a political economy based on debt to the world economy.

The retreat of the slaving frontier away from the coast and conversion to relatively peaceful methods of generating slaves through seizures for debt effectively absorbed all the profits that traders earned from the Atlantic trade in slaves. In human terms, traders distributed goods for wives, slaves, and clients, whom they settled to farm their village domains or whom they employed as bearers, armed as guards, or engaged as agents circulating more goods among their neighbors. In the language of Western economics, traders invested the gains they accumulated in people in market organization and in transportation, just as merchant princes guiding production of dependents and potential captives invested their profits in the reproductive capacity of African women. The creation of trading diaspora, no less than of principalities or long-distance caravans, represented substantial development, and one logical by the human standards of wealth in the African political economy. These institutions were all substantially geared to furthering relations with the world economy, and to the extent that they were in debt to the world economy or dependent for their prosperity on the continued dealings with it, they were constrained from applying their assets to other purposes.

The traders of western central Africa's commercial and transport sector, like the politicians, followed a nonindustrialized trajectory to prominence parallel to the contemporaneous rise of merchants as capitalism developed in Western Europe. They began as casual traders, facilitating transfers of surplus products between producers and consumers acting primarily in terms of use values, or evacuating the tribute surpluses of agricultural states. They invested their profits from these occasional ventures in slaves and other dependents, gradually building full-time and specialized retinues of followers engaged in a discernibly distinct nascent commercial sector. Other portions of their gains they held in trade goods and commodity currencies. To the extent that they loaned these out to encourage clients to produce more slaves for exchange, they were creating an African analog of European merchants' early underwriting of dependent cottagers' industrial production. Even lacking evidence for or against such investment in Africa prior to contact with the world economy (though one suspects direct stimulation of production was minor), there is little doubt that African traders in the seventeenth and eighteenth centuries put significant amounts of imports into processes productive of slaves owned by others: war, debt, and fertile women.

Again like their counterparts in Europe, the most successful of the African merchant investors—eighteenth-century princes and kings extracting slaves from the lineages and other small communities they ruled—

went on to become producers of slaves for themselves from the offspring of their personal retinues of captives. Contemporary analogs were to be found in the New World, where Dutch, French, and British commercial interests held miners and planters in debt and gradually assumed direct ownership of those American forms of production, or in England, where merchants and merchant-bankers invested in early British factory production. Western central African merchants, once again like their opposite numbers in Britain, moved directly into production for themselves only later in the nineteenth century, though—unlike Europeans and Americans—they still used goods to acquire slaves to exploit wax, ivory, and rubber rather than buying technology with currency credits or paying out cash in wages. In the process, the African entrepreneurs brought all of the region under their only partially monetized and nontechnological version of worldwide commercial capitalism, no less than had merchants and industrialists assumed control of Europe.

The human costs of this transformation—the unfortunates sent off to pay Europeans for the goods imported—contradictorily put local political systems and population bases under stresses that constantly forced the trade's participants to spread their goods more widely toward the east, in geometrically increasing quantities that exceeded the arithmetic gains they earned from exchanges. As elsewhere in the history of capitalism, simply protecting what they had gained thus meant growth, and growth called for further borrowing from European sources beyond profits generated internally. The African transporters therefore remained dependent on European credit to stay in business. Low-cost captives from the expanded slaving frontier and generally improving terms of trade with the Atlantic economy relieved some of these strains during the century before 1830, but by entrenching powerful beneficiaries of this temporary relief, they also sharpened the potential for conflict if imports should later become more expensive relative to Africans' abilities to pay for them, or if slavers should run out of new populations to exploit. Transporters and producers would then find themselves responsible for expensive commercial institutions which they could preserve only by depleting the natural wealth of the habitat they occupied and which would then grow dangerously fragile when ecological degradation deprived them of room for continued growth by exploitation.

8

Casualties of Merchant Capital

The Luso-Africans in Angola

Nominally "Portuguese" Luso-Africans living in and around Angola in the eighteenth century transported many of the slaves destined for Luanda, Benguela, and parts of the coast adjacent to these two seaports.[1] Their investments in land and in slaves gave them a tenable position, though usually well short of a commanding one, in the trade of the interior and also lent them important similarities to other African transporters in western central Africa's commercial economy. Though heterogeneous, their commitment to the colony's interior also made them collectively quite distinguishable from other "Portuguese" in Angola, immigrant traders from Portugal or Brazil temporarily resident at Luanda but more thoroughly a part of the Atlantic world than they.

Still, compared to the other African transporters, branches of the Luso-African community had a substantial stake in the Portuguese empire for most of the eighteenth century. They retained ownership of slaves they delivered to the coast on through the middle passage and up to the point of the slaves' sale in Brazil. Consequently they suffered losses both from the rising costs of bringing captives down to the sea and also from the high mortality risk of holding slaves as they moved on across the ocean to America. Though Luso-Africans sometimes made trading gains from selling slaves in Brazil during the earlier part of the century, profits from this source declined as time went on. Toward the end of the eighteenth century, the Luso-Africans gave up their ownership of the slaves at sea and, during the last years of legal slaving and the ensuing period of the illegal trade, concentrated their resources on the internal African trading networks. Through consolidating their own commercial investments in this way they survived as a group, but only within the confines of the African economy. On the larger scale of the southern Atlantic as a whole, they became casualties of the increased commercialization of the trade.

1. This chapter inevitably introduces points bearing on Portuguese and Brazilian activities in Angola that cannot be documented until the succeeding chapters focus on them.

Luso-African Community and Identity

The Angolan Luso-Africans, or creoles,[2] are best known in the historical literature for their cultural syncretism and mixed race—dark-skinned colonials of Angolan birth with a veneer of Portuguese Catholicism, dress, and language overlaid on local non-Catholic religious beliefs, a preference for speaking Kimbundu within the home, and other habits derived from their African antecedents. The Luso-Africans' mixed culture was generally a focus of official denigration in the early eighteenth century, and their cognate racial blend replaced culture as the nineteenth-century idiom of metropolitan contempt. The group possessed a no less hybrid economic position in the colony's trade. Because they retained ownership of the slaves aboard ships making for Brazil and sold them there for currency, not goods, they combined characteristically African dealings in slaves and trade goods in the interior with a European-like stake in the monetized economy of the Portuguese empire. As a special case of the general class of African traders who brokered exchanges between the African and European worlds, the Angolan Luso-Africans bore many similarities to Euro-African (and Asian-African) holders of Crown estates in Mozambique's Zambezi valley and also to Cape Verdean traders and Portuguese *lançados* married into African merchant families of the mainland Upper Guinea Coast.[3] But unlike these other Euro-Africans, who became fully African-

2. I have adopted the designation "Luso-African" for this complex group, fully aware of the differing terms ("Eur-Africans," "creoles," "Afro-Portuguese," "black Portuguese," and just "Portuguese") that other authors have used to describe the same people, though usually with emphasis on only one or two of their multiple aspects. Without asserting exclusive validity for the phrase I have chosen, "Luso-African" may be defended by pointing to its emphasis on the essentially African character of the group in political, economic, and structural terms, with a specifically Lusophone veneer that distinguished it from similar African groups who also adopted aspects of European culture at the Loango Coast and elsewhere in eighteenth-century Africa. Jill Dias, "A sociedade colonial de Angola e o liberalismo português, c. 1820–1850," in *O liberalismo na península Ibérica na primeira metade do século XIX* (Lisbon: Sá da Costa, 1982), 1:267–86, has an excellent understanding of the group in the nineteenth century; also see her "Uma questão de identidade: respostas intelectuais às transformações económicas no seio da elite crioula da Angola portuguesa entre 1870 e 1930," *Revista internacional de estudos africanos* 1 (1983): 61–94. Vellut, "Notes sur le Lunda," develops numerous related points, some in greater detail than is possible here, in connection with his notion of a Luso-African frontier. José Carlos Venâncio, "Espaço e dinâmica populacional em Luanda no século XVIII," and "Economia de Luanda," designates the group also as "Luso-African" (*Luso-africanos*). For other aspects of the history of the Luso-Africans in the eighteenth century, see Joseph C. Miller and John K. Thornton, "The Chronicle as Source, History, and Historiography: The 'Catálogo dos Governadores de Angola,'" *Paideuma* 33 (1987): 359–89.

3. For Mozambique, see Allen F. Isaacman, *Mozambique: The Africanization of a European Institution: The Zambezi Prazos, 1750–1902* (Madison: University of Wisconsin Press, 1972). The phenomenon is broadly familiar in the literature on Upper Guinea, and it bears further comparison with the Asian/Muslim-African variant on the Swahili coast of East Africa. Carreira, "Companhias pombalinas de navegação," pp. 39 et passim, describes the Cape Verdean traders in appropriate terms.

ized in economic terms, the Luso-Africans of Angola also sold slaves abroad, like the British and French slavers who bought captive labor elsewhere along the African coast to sell for themselves in America.

Since the term *Luso-African* in Angola properly describes not just race or culture but also an economically specialized group of eighteenth-century slave transporters and shippers, it includes immigrants from Europe who cast their lots with locally born Angolans. These new Luso-Africans, probably a significant proportion of all who came to Luanda or Benguela from Europe and Brazil, at least temporarily abandoned residence at the coast, ending their association with other traders who retained business ties to Europe to embrace life in the colony's interior. Living in the backlands almost always meant buying and transporting slaves, and so these immigrants quickly merged into the community of Luso-African slaveowners and landholders established there, at least in relation to the economic structure of the empire as a whole.

Many, though far from all, Luso-Africans descended from old families of joint African and European parentage that had formed in and around Luanda during the seventeenth century. Portuguese soldiers and military officers sent down to defend Lisbon's western central African *conquista,* supplemented also by Dutch merchants and soldiers who held the city briefly during the 1640s, had married African women and sired Euro-African children who grew up in the colony and later, as adults, had become prominent among the "Portuguese" conquerors in the areas east of Luanda.[4]

While these older, thoroughly *mestiço* families formed the original core of the group, later-arriving immigrant males—many of them criminals or political exiles (*degradados*) from Portugal, but sometimes also Brazilian or metropolitan merchants fallen on hard times and seeking to recoup their fortunes in Africa—continued to fill out the eighteenth-century Luso-African community in the interior. At the other end of the tunnel, some of the wealthiest and most successful Luso-Africans of the interior moved back to Luanda. A few even transferred their accumulated assets out of Angola and sailed on to other parts of the empire, usually Brazil.[5] New

4. Fragmentary evidence for the moment, awaiting further research in progress by Beatrix Heintze and Jill R. Dias. An example is Luis Lopes de Sequeira, the dominant commander of Portuguese forces from the battle of Ambuila (1665) until his death fighting against Matamba in 1681, who came from this sort of background; Cadornega, *História geral,* 3:470 (index), identifies him as a "natural de Luanda," and the "Extinção do prezidio das Pedras," n.d. (ca. 1777), AHU, Angola cx. 37, described him as *pardo* (mixed blood). For references to his military career, see Birmingham, *Trade and Conflict in Angola,* pp. 122, 125–26, 130. Governor João Fernandes Vieira (1658–61) complained of his inability to pursue military campaigns in the colony without the support of the Massangano Luso-Africans: Mello, *João Fernandes Vieira,* pp. 176–77, 357; see also Cadornega, *História geral,* 2:141–54; Torres, *Memórias,* pp. 216–21; or Corrêa, *História de Angola,* 1:313–20.

5. A famous example is Rodrigo da Costa Almeida, who founded an important Bahian family with Angolan wealth in 1713: Rae Jean Flory, "Bahian Society in the Mid-Colonial

men, arrived more recently from Portugal or Brazil, could move into the places these departing patriarchs had abandoned by hiring themselves out as trading agents, marrying creole women, using their wife's family's trading connections among the Africans to prosper in the slave trade, and fathering more children of mixed racial and cultural background who would grow up to make careers as minor functionaries in the colonial government, as local priests, as lower-ranking officers of Angola's military, or, like their fathers, as clerks or traders of modest means. On the inland, African, side of the racial, social, and economic divide straddled by these extended Luso-African families, other members of the group married nieces of their African business partners, exchanged daughters as wives with them, and apprenticed children on both sides to train as future representatives to the other.[6]

The culture these mixed marriages created appeared clearly African to shocked government officials just out from metropolitan Portugal, but it was no less strongly Portuguese from the point of view of most Africans. In the interior the worn shoes and tattered trousers Luso-African men prided themselves on wearing were sufficient symbols of their foreignness. In fact, the essence of the Luso-Africans' resiliency as a group was precisely the ambiguity and flexibility they derived from the ability of individuals to move through the community, along the entire range of its personal and cultural continuum between the African and the European worlds of the southern Atlantic. Locally born bilingual Portuguese-Mbundu stalwarts, immigrant peddlers who managed to marry into creole families, raw *degradados* heading for the interior to look for slaves, and big colonial traders aiming to retire to Brazil were all Luso-Africans and shared much more in their common ownership of slaves and land in the colony than in their varied conventions of personal behavior, their skin colors, or their ancestries.

Period: The Sugar Planters, Tobacco Growers, Merchants, and Artisans of Salvador and the Recôncavo, 1680–1725" (Ph.D. diss., University of Texas, 1978), p. 132.

6. These marriages of commercial convenience were surely much more extensive than yet documented; for Ambaca in the 1750s, da Cunha, 9 June 1757, AHU, Angola cx. 27; for Huila in the 1830s and 1840s, Clarence-Smith, "Capitalist Penetration," p. 165; Tams, *Visit to the Portuguese Possessions,* 1:116, for Moçâmedes in 1841. See also the well-known story of A. F. da Silva Porto, the celebrated native of Porto in Portugal who settled as a trader in nineteenth-century Angola and married a daughter of the king of Bihe on the central plateau. Maria Emília Madeira Santos has just published a new critical edition of the Silva Porto diary, *Viagens e apontamentos de um portuense em África* (Coimbra: Biblioteca Geral da Universidade de Coimbra, 1986). In general, Thornton, "Early Kongo-Portuguese Relations"; Dias, "Sociedade colonial," p. 270; Santos, "Perspectivas do comércio sertanejo," pp. 74–75; another nineteenth-century traveler, Magyar, as quoted in Vellut, "Relations internationales," p. 102. The famous king of Kasanje, Mbumba, who fought the Portuguese in the 1840s and 1850s, had been educated in a Luso-African household in Angola; I am indebted to Jill Dias for this revealing detail.

The Luso-Africans also had nothing approaching unity on the level of politics within the colony despite their shared commitment to the Angolan slave economy, a corresponding collective hostility to pressures from Lisbon, and their stereotyped uniformity in the minds of metropolitan detractors opposed to them on economic and political grounds.[7] Strong loyalties to extended familial factions had probably already developed by the early eighteenth century, at least. Names like Machado, Correia Leitão, Matozo de Andrade, Vandunem, and Ornellas reappeared over and again in local affairs down through the decades.[8] The competing Luso-African camps represented by these established surnames each sought to control government offices for their own members, to attract the favor of the governors, to hold land, and to consolidate ties with African sources of slaves at the expense of the others.

These clan loyalties coalesced also into unstable regional groupings centered on towns and districts in the colony, though politics at this level appear even more dimly in the extant documentation than family rivalries. The Luanda Luso-Africans were the most clearly defined of these factions, but similar groups formed along the lower Bengo, Kwanza, and Lukala rivers, later at Benguela, and around such military posts in the interior of the colony as Caconda, Ambaca, and Pungo Andongo.[9] Short-term political and commercial alliances also formed from time to time. Each sort of grouping—by descent and affinity, by region, or ephemerally for reasons of expediency—crosscut the others. The resulting web of alliances and feuds lent a kaleidoscopic unpredictability and impenetrability to the colony's internal politics in the eyes of outsiders. Complexity also offered protection against outsiders, since it typically baffled governors and left them unable to manipulate local divisions to their personal advantage to any significant extent.

The Luso-African community's resident core, the stable nucleus that forged its distinctive cultural synthesis and probably led its resistance to meddling from Portugal, consisted of the daughters and younger sons born in Angola. Immigrant males affiliated themselves to this native-born heart mostly by marriage and often provided its main ties to the slave trade and to the African and imperial economies to which slaving led on either side. Some remained in Angola for their lifetimes and became community leaders, but others, probably as many as could manage, eventually joined

---

7. This perceived uniformity is reflected in the documents and hence also in most literature on them; Dias, "Sociedade colonial," is moving usefully toward recognizing the complexity and diversity of the group.

8. An admittedly impressionistic judgment at the moment; an important study awaits anyone willing to reconstruct family history from papers in the AHU. But cf. Dias's emphasis on the point for the early nineteenth century in "Sociedade colonial," pp. 272 et passim.

9. "Extinção do prezidio das Pedras," n.d. (ca. 1777), AHU, Angola cx. 37.

the few who returned to Brazil or to Portugal with fortunes made in slaving.

The typical career pattern of such an immigrant would find him arriving in the African colony in disgrace or in distress, probably as a criminal *degradado* or as a debtor. Since few Portuguese, or even Brazilians, went to Angola voluntarily, new arrivals burned with ambition to escape from the moment they set foot on shore. Their desperation typically drove them first to retreat alone to the interior, usually, if they left from Luanda, taking with them as many trade goods as they could borrow from some merchant sponsor in the city. Those condemned to exile in Benguela, if they survived its much more mortiferous disease environment, started off up the trails with even less. In both cases they attempted to reconstruct their shattered financial fortunes by wheeling and dealing in slaves. If they possessed the toughness, canniness, and even unscrupulousness and luck required to succeed in the rough frontier environment of the interior, they might acquire trading connections among the Africans, usually confirmed by taking kinswomen of their customers as wives, slaves of their own, and an inventory of trade goods beyond what they owed. With these they could occupy land, or at least gain permission to reside in the domain of an allied African trader, and begin to send caravans of slaves off toward the coast on their own accounts. By that point such a successful trader would have become a large and favored customer of his merchant suppliers and backers at Luanda, or Benguela, and perhaps even a *capitão-mor* ("captain-major"), or military commander, appointed by the Angolan governors to command an important district in the colony's interior.

The minority who managed to survive the diseases that struck down most newcomers to the tropics then set out on the road back toward the coast and to respectability. They would have put themselves in a strong position to buy into one of the merchant firms headquartered at the coast as a formal partner, not only continuing to ship slaves they owned off to Brazil but also stocking trade goods and extending a portion of those goods on credit to more recently arrived traders in the same straitened circumstances that they had themselves just overcome. If prices stayed high in Brazil, and if they managed to avoid high losses to mortality among the slaves they shipped, sales of their captives might build up Brazilian credits and investments sufficient to support eventual resettlement there as members of the American colonial gentry.

This archetypal career cycle of the successful Angola trader represented only the faintest hope for *degradados* and failed merchants first stepping ashore in Angola. Most died within months after getting off the ship. Some survived for years but failed to climb the commercial and financial ladder up out of debt and ownership of slaves to selling goods and eventually dealing in credit and imperial currencies from Luanda or Brazil.

Others survived and prospered but chose not to retire abroad. This minority consolidated its gains in Africa as patriarchs of new Luso-African families making their way into the colonial establishment, surrounded by their African and creole women, buying land in Ambaca or along the lower Bengo, plating local altars and tombstones with silver, and scheming to place their sons and nephews in crucial positions in the military forces and civilian administration of the colony. Though immigrant Portuguese fathers who remained in Angola might set the tone of Luso-African public life, they remained affines of its local core of sons and daughters. The financial successes of the minority who escaped from Angola did not so much blur the boundaries between the distinct creole community of Angola and the traders oriented toward Lisbon or Brazil as they linked it independently to the wider, usually hostile, commercial world of the empire.

From Luanda into the Interior

Luso-African settlement expanded in the eighteenth century from its old center at Luanda toward the outer edges of the zone of Atlantic-influenced slaving, in step with the eastward movement of all western central African trading communities. At the beginning of the 1700s, the Angolan Luso-Africans had hardly existed outside the colonial capital and the lower valleys of the adjacent rivers, but there they exerted formidable influence over the trade in slaves. These Luanda branches of old Luso-African families owned or operated slave-worked agricultural properties of modest size along the fertile banks of the lower Bengo and Dande rivers, as well as along the Lukala and Kwanza rivers at Massangano. These privileges dated from the days of the colony's first proprietor late in the sixteenth century and the associates to whom he awarded title to African lands and labor.[10] Their ownership of these estates gave them leverage over provisioning the city of Luanda with foodstuffs, both for local consumption and for slave ships preparing there for departure. The younger sons of these same families had all but taken control, too, of the local clergy, and they staffed much of the colonial army below its topmost ranks by the

10. Boxer, *Portuguese Society in the Tropics*, p. 112. The correspondence from the Luanda council clearly represented Luso-African interests in the 1720s but Luso-African influence there gradually disappeared in the 1730s and 1740s: letters of 24 Jan. 1728 and 17 April 1728, AHU, Angola cx. 18; 7 May 1732, AHU, Angola cx. 19; 30 Dec. 1744, AHU, Angola cx. 23. See also the studies of this period by Beatrix Heintze, notably "Die portugiesische Besiedlungs- und Wirtschaftspolitik in Angola, 1570–1607," *Aufsätze zur portugiesischen Kulturgeschichte* 17 (1981–82): 200–219. Venâncio, "Espaço e dinâmica populacional," *Revista de história econômica e social* 14 (1984): 69, concedes control of the Câmara in the 1770s to the immigrant merchants, though without drawing as sharp a distinction between creole and immigrant groups as I do here.

beginning of the eighteenth century.[11] Heads of prominent Luso-African families led the civilian militia as well, at least until the late 1820s. Their first institutional centers had included the town's municipal council, its *Senado da Câmara*.

Within the larger confines of the seventeenth-century colony between the lower Bengo and Kwanza rivers, these families had prospered later through a continuing close working alliance with governors of that era, mostly Brazilians who came to the colony with the intent of engrossing its trade in slaves for themselves and who encouraged the military captains (*capitães-mores*) of the districts and forts in the interior to serve as their agents.[12] Luso-African families seem gradually to have taken these positions into their own hands as the governors lost influence after 1720. By the 1730s they had also built up alliances with the low-level African authorities of the colony under their command. They behaved like the heirs of the old African warrior aristocracies that they were, with retinues of slaves and client mercenaries of their own and landholdings from whose populations they drew some of the captives they sent down through town branches of their clans in Luanda for shipment to Brazil. The Luso-Africans as a whole had thus achieved a prominent position in slave exporting from Angola, based on military raids on the frontiers, on supervision of the transportation system bringing slaves to Luanda, on control over critical provisioning sectors of the town's economy, and on staffing the ecclesiastical and government bureaucracies charged to baptize, inspect, and tax the slaves. They appear, finally, to have owned the majority of slaves reaching the coast and to have shipped them to Brazil on their own accounts, using the immigrant merchants of Luanda only as forwarding agents.

The origins of Luso-Africans' ownership of the slaves dated back to the early years of the conquest, presumably because the wars from which most slaves came at that time put the captives in the hands of the creole commanders who led the campaigns. The high prices for slaves in the thriving seventeenth-century sugar captaincies of Brazil, and other opportunities for trading profits in Spanish territories, gave them every reason to try to sell the slaves they took on their own accounts, sharing only as

11. Dias, "Sociedade colonial," pp. 271, 277, brings out the sensitivity of military appointments around 1800 and later. A *provisão* of 2 Oct. 1664, published in Brásio, *Monumenta missionaria africana*, 12:502–3, probably formed the legal basis for the Luso-Africans' monopoly of middle- and lower-level offices in the colony, a privilege conceded at a time of other measures favorable to the Luso-Africans, probably designed to counter the Brazilian influence otherwise dominant in that decade. Miller and Thornton, "Chronicle," detail a struggle over appointments to the colonial regiment in the 1770s and 1780s. Dias, "Sociedade colonial," p. 271, cites a 1799 confirmation of these privileges but emphasizes their erosion after 1822.

12. The *provisão* of 2 Oct. 1664 virtually prescribed this alliance, by placing the colony's governors in charge of Luso-African nominations to the administrative appointments reserved to them.

many of them as necessary with the governors. Astronomical prices for slaves sold to southern Brazil's booming gold mines early in the eighteenth century could only have confirmed the Luso-Africans' determination to retain possession of slaves they sent abroad, though they conceded a portion of their gains in this prosperous period to their suppliers in higher payments for goods equivalent to a slave.

The tendency of the Luso-Africans to own the slaves derived in part also, of course, from general limitations of merchant investment in production everywhere in Europe's overseas commerce before the nineteenth century. Producers of commodities of any sort—sugar, tobacco, and so on—controlled their products through transportation and marketing to their point of sale in Europe. In this case, Angolan slavers owned the slaves until they were sold in America. To metropolitan merchants active at Luanda, however, efficiency may also have meant avoiding so risky an investment as the ownership of sick and dying slaves tossing on the waves of the remote southern Atlantic.

Of course, Luso-African possession of the slaves departing Luanda also left the Angolan creole community to bear the financial risks for the slaves' lives, under conditions that worked strongly against them by the mid-1700s. As the eighteenth century proceeded, they found themselves confronting not just increased operating costs in Africa but also low prices in Brazil. They paid more for imports from Portugal, and they depended to a growing extent on imported credit for buying slaves rather than relying on raids mounted from their local resources in slave warriors or alliances with African suppliers. High morbidity and mortality among the slaves they sent across the ocean could become critical determinants of their fortunes abroad under these circumstances.

Whatever the disadvantages, the typical Luso-African providers of slaves at Luanda had little choice in the terms on which they bought. The vast majority continued to originate as debtors on the immigrant male fringe of the Luso-African community, able to acquire their initial working capital in imported trade goods only through borrowing. The land, commodity currencies, and other assets that more established merchants had accumulated in the colony were valuable only in Luanda and its hinterland and not acceptable tender for imports. They therefore took the goods they bought on credit, even if they were wealthy in local terms. The richest Luso-African traders held account balances in Brazil or Portugal in *réis*, but though theoretically able to buy imports for themselves, they still would have preferred to protect assets they had managed to send abroad by investing them there and continuing to use credit for the working capital they kept in imports in Africa. Even prosperous Luso-Africans thus had many reasons to remain as deeply in debt as their creditors would allow and to pay for goods they received in Angola only later with currencies earned from selling their slaves in Brazil.

Under the pressure of their general indebtedness Luso-Africans sought to restore solvency by creating a low-cost trading area for themselves in and around the interior of the *conquista*. These domains were relatively safe from merchants representing wealthy Lisbon firms and from officials posted out to the colony from Europe, who seldom dared to travel in the interior for fear of the diseases that felled most immigrants who ventured out of Luanda.[13] Newcomers lacked the immunities to tropical diseases that Luso-Africans had acquired painfully through "seasoning" or possessed by virtue of growing up locally. Even the agricultural river bottoms within a day's journey or two of the city lay beyond the effective reach of expatriate creditors and government officials. Only one governor, for example, traveled to these nearby regions in the course of the entire eighteenth century, and not a single one dared to visit the Lukala or the higher elevations inland. Benguela, though located on the coast, was equally inaccessible in practice, a notorious sink of disease for Portuguese from the metropole. The town received only the briefest of nervous visits from arriving high functionaries as they hastened north down the coast to the comparative safety of Luanda. A Luso-African who left the city could therefore consider himself well beyond the reach of royal justice unless he managed to provoke the dispatch of an armed government patrol, manned by locals, on his trail.

Such patrols occasionally did set out in the course of the eighteenth century, but the ambitious and daring among the convicts exiled to Angola usually escaped the difficulties they encountered on the imperial side of their business by settling in the far interior of the colony, or in the surrounding backlands, the *sertões* in the parlance of the time. These fugitives, as subject as any other European to the fevers of the lowlands, increased their chances of survival by seeking the elevated parts of the central highlands east of Benguela. Convicts who escaped to the highlands were sent to Benguela or Pungo Andongo, often settled as local traders, intermediaries between the Africans among whom they lived and the less marginal merchants of the Atlantic economy they had fled. When officials at Luanda tried to bring these renegades under control, the convicts simply withdrew their slaves and households to more remote *sertões*, beyond the limited grasp of the government *presídios*, without further regard for importunings from the colonial capital.[14]

Luso-Africans of every sort had shown these tendencies to flee toward the interior from the earliest days of the colony, though at first moving

---

13. *Parecer,* Conselho Ultramarino (Lisbon), 7 May 1755, AHU, Angola cx. 26; Vasconcelos, 3 Jan. 1759, AHU, Angola cx. 28; Silva *memória,* 25 June 1762, AHU, Angola cx. 29, among many.
14. Stories of renegades fleeing to the interior abound; e.g., Meneses, 20 Dec. 1734, AHU, Angola cx. 20 (regarding Cahumba, a slave of a Luanda Luso-African); Mesquita, 20 July 1781, AHU, Angola cx. 38.

out only into the immediate environs of Luanda. The first visible concentration of Luso-African strength outside the port town had grown up at Massangano, recognized by the Crown since 1676–77, with its own municipal council, or *Senado da Câmara*.[15] Massangano lay at the juncture of the Lukala and Kwanza rivers, an unhealthy location for outsiders but conveniently near the dense African populations farming the lower valleys of these rivers. The town's location at the juncture of two major arteries of trade also made it a commercial center when eastern and southeastern sources of slaves opened up with the advance of the slaving frontier in the mid-seventeenth century. The Luso-Africans there, in addition to buying slaves through markets facing south across the lower Kwanza at Muxima and at Massangano itself, traded up the Lukala through a *feira* at Lembo in the lower valley of the river. Lembo surely served as the *entrepôt* where Luso-Africans from Massangano took over distribution of bars of Kisama rock salt, which African traders had formerly circulated as currency in the African economies around the upper Lukala valley, and then converted the salt trade to furthering new sources of slaves in Ambaca and beyond.[16]

Beyond trading, these early Luso-African residents of the interior thrived on sheer military domination of African populations within their reach. Some of them forced tributes in slaves from the farming communities around their own compounds, while others made careers out of leading government military expeditions into more remote areas on what amounted to extended private slave raids. All competed for formal appointments as *capitães-mores* of the districts where they lived. Luso-African patriarchs still maintained private militias of slaves within the small area of Luso-African settlement between the Kwanza and the Dande at the end of the seventeenth century. Though they employed these mercenaries according to the exigencies of local politics or in support of occasional "legitimate" wars authorized by officials in Luanda, slaving by outright violence had begun to subside as the location of the slaving frontier grew more remote.

Though these semiautonomous early-eighteenth-century Luso-Africans contributed to the slave trade largely through violence they had already begun to employ the goods and credit typical of later mercantile slaving.[17]

15. Boxer, *Portuguese Society in the Tropics,* pp. 139–40; among other evidence of disputes between governors in Luanda and an apparently independent community of Luso-African *"moradores"* in Massangano (ca. 1658), Mello, *João Fernandes Vieira,* pp. 176–77, 182–83, 185 ff.; Torres, *Memórias,* pp. 216–21.

16. Oeyras *parecer,* 20 Nov. 1760, AHU, Angola cx. 28; draft *regimento,* 22 June 1779, AHU, Angola maço 3 (D.O.); Castelobranco, 16 May 1828, AHU, Angola cx. 72.

17. E.g., the connections evident in Coelho Guerreiro's books: see Miller, "Capitalism and Slaving." Also Virginia Rau, introduction to *O "Livro de Razão" de António Coelho Guerreiro* (Lisbon: DIAMANG, 1956). The indebtedness of the local residents was extreme as early as the 1620s and caused financial crises for borrowers and lenders alike then and

In the early sixteenth century, the agents of metropolitan merchants at Luanda had sometimes sent goods out with slave *pombeiro* traders who followed Luso-African armies through distant parts of the interior, but these agents had done business largely as conduits for slaves that Luso-Africans, or other African sellers, sent down to the coast. They tended to wait for slaves to come down to the city or to send goods out in advance only to sites very near the town.[18] Colonial governors from Brazil had made their way into the trade after 1650 by reaching out past these passive commercial strategies. By nominating the heads of powerful families resident in the districts of the colony's interior as the commanders of the government *presídios* and supplying them with goods to trade, these governors had become the dominant exporters of slaves to Brazil in the second half of the seventeenth century.

The governors encouraged their Luso-African favorites to employ the powers they exercised as government officers for private commercial advantage.[19] The Luso-Africans obtained textiles and other European goods as loans from governors and forced the African headmen of their military districts to accept these goods as debts collectable in slaves, on the demand of the captain-major. This debt-peonage arrangement, particularly when backed by the captain's armed force, generated captives with the same profitable efficacy that parallel injections of credit, also supported by coercion, achieved in the overlord-retainer relationships of the African states to the east. The profits that Luso-African families derived from their simultaneously military and commercial ties to the governors allowed some of them to convert their official royal patents into unofficial personal fiefdoms comprising whole regions in the interior.

The *capitães-mores* as a group, and the creole clans behind them, thus entrenched themselves as important suppliers of slaves from the central portions of the *conquista*. When Lisbon excluded the governors from trading openly in the 1720s and 1730s,[20] the Luso-Africans lost their main sources of trade goods and held the colony's interior throughout the second

---

again in the 1650s: Heintze, *Fontes*, pp. 223, 232, 267; Hilton, *Kingdom of Kongo*, pp. 166–67. Nonetheless, at the time warfare and extortion usually enabled them to cover what they owed.

18. Senado da Câmara (Luanda), 24 Jan. 1728, AHU, Angola cx. 18; Avellar, 20 May 1731, AHU, Angola maço 18–A.

19. As acknowledged by the Crown's firm prohibitions of the practice in the governors' charters of 1666 and 1676, published in *Boletim do Conselho Ultramarino* (legislação antiga), pp. 295–307, 311–29, and elsewhere; also *parecer* of the Conselho Ultramarino (Lisbon), 7 June 1703, AHU, Angola cx. 14; Pereira da Costa, 28 Jan. 1726, AHU, Angola cx. 17. Couto, *Capitães-mores*, cites most of the relevant documentation.

20. *Alvará* of 29 Aug. 1720 (of applicability throughout the empire, not just to Angola), in *Boletim do Conselho Ultramarino* (legislação antiga), pp. 403–4. Much of the language merely repeated that of the ineffective provision in the 1676 *regimento* specifying duties and powers of the Angola governors.

half of the eighteenth century as virtually autonomous military chieftains. Later governors tried unsuccessfully to reduce the captains to responsive executors of Crown policy. Though they occasionally managed to put men loyal to the metropole in command of the colony's *presídios*, they usually found themselves compelled to depend on representatives of the Luso-African families and seldom exerted more than the most tenuous influence over the actions of these hinterland commanders.

Lisbon merchants replaced the governors as the principal sources of trade goods in Angola from the 1720s onward. They at once reduced Luso-African influence in Luanda itself and, by converting slaving near the city to a more commercial style of trade, compelled weaker branches of the creole families to relocate their violent slaving operations farther into the interior, closer to the distant position of the mid-eighteenth-century slaving frontier.

One wing of this Luso-African withdrawal led east of Luanda past the early center at Massangano and up into the adjoining plateau districts of Ambaca and Pungo Andongo (or Pedras) between the middle Kwanza and Lukala rivers. Construction of a bridge over the lower Lukala in the late 1720s consolidated this movement. The project eliminated a lengthy detour around the lower river and greatly shortened the road up to the old seventeenth-century military outpost at Ambaca.[21] Though governors must have intended the bridge to facilitate the Lisbon merchants' access to eastern marketplaces like Kasanje, the Luso-Africans, probably including newcomers attracted by the relative healthfulness of the highlands around Ambaca, took advantage of the new road to begin to settle in the region. They took up agriculture on a modest scale, mobilized labor for trading expeditions they sent on to the east, and intermarried with the African nobility of the neighboring Jinga state, where they apparently bought many of their slaves.

At an unknown time, but probably not long afterwards, other Luso-Africans moved even farther east to establish a similar commercial presence around the government garrison at Pungo Andongo. From that base they traded south across the Kwanza into Hako and Libolo, as well as in the Songo regions immediately to the southeast.[22] The slaves they bought in those parts they sent out mostly down trails leading to Massangano. The general drift of these Luso-Africans' trade southward beyond the Kwanza eventually carried them on up the river valleys on the north slope of the highlands to open the northeastern plateau to Luanda slaving. Bihe's early-nineteenth-century community of resident Luso-African families, which

21. Caetano de Albuquerque, 21 May 1729, AHU, Angola cx. 18.
22. "Umba, Malemba, Ma[u]ssende, Haco," in "Extinção do prezidio das Pedras," n.d. (ca. 1777), AHU, Angola cx. 37.

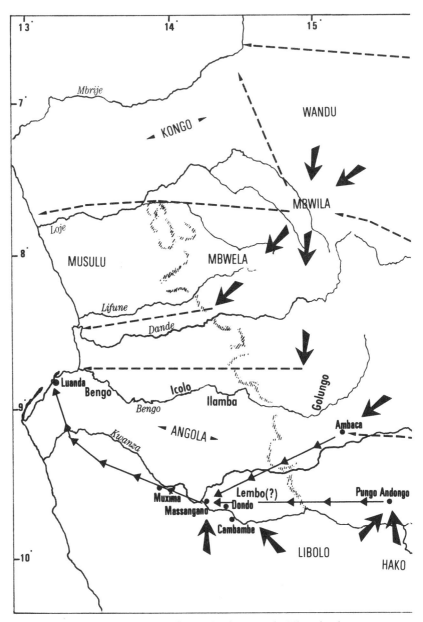

Map 8.1. Luso-Africans in the Luanda Hinterland

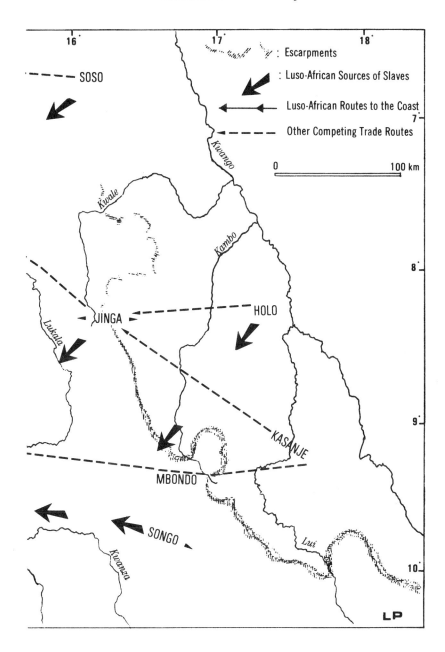

originated mostly in Ambaca and Pungo Andongo, descended from those pioneers.[23]

These eastward shifts in the bases of Luso-African trading caused the old Massangano marketplace to decline.[24] Massangano itself, beyond its function as a staging point where traders transferred loads sent up the lower Kwanza from canoes to the heads of porters bound for Pungo Andongo or Ambaca, consolidated its primary trading contacts on the southern bank of the Kwanza directly opposite. By the 1770s, branches of Massango trading firms had developed the trade across the river further through a trading fair just up the Kwanza in the neighboring district of Cambambe.[25] A second, competing *feira* on the north bank at Dondo, inexplicably close by, gives the impression of serving not the local Luso-Africans but rather the Kwanza trade of metropolitan interests from Luanda.[26]

Another branch of the Luso-African retreat east of Luanda, though less clearly dated, extended the seventeenth-century agricultural area of the lower Bengo (or Zenza) valley upriver to Golungo. Golungo became the jumping-off place for further trade to southern Kongo and an alternative route to Ambaca. Traders of this group had settled as far north as the lands of the *ndembu* Mbwela as early as the 1730s and remained there into the 1760s.[27] They sent food to Luanda and traded through Mbwela and Mbwila to the Kongo of Wandu and to the Soso, bringing their slaves down the Bengo, Dande, and Lifune rivers.

Other Luso-Africans settled in the early eighteenth century at Benguela, though the details of their movement there lie mostly lost in the obscurity of their illiteracy and the town's insalubrious reputation among Portuguese immigrant officials, generally the only people in the colony at all committed to recording their impressions in writing.[28] Early events at Benguela remain unclear also precisely because Luso-Africans went there with every intention of concealing the purposes of their flight from the government in Luanda. Joined at Benguela by all sorts of Portuguese fugitives from the Crown's justice, they converted the colony's southern

23. Vellut, "Notes sur le Lunda," pp. 125–27, citing Graça, "Viagem feita de Loanda," pp. 399–400.

24. Adriano de Faria e Mello, 15 Dec. 1732, AHU, Angola cx. 20.

25. Vasconcelos, 22 May 1760, AHU, Angola cx. 28, which contains a list of the residents at Massangano, including 30 of local birth and 4 immigrant Portuguese, excluding 5 military officers; also Vasconcelos, 8 Oct. 1760, AHU, Angola maço 11.

26. Birmingham, *Trade and Conflict in Angola*, p. 140, dates Lisbon's interest in promoting trade to the northern slopes of the central plateau from the Kwanza somewhat earlier, to at least 1729.

27. Meneses, 15 Dec. 1735, AHU, Angola cx. 20; Matos, *Compêndio histórico*, p. 318.

28. Good collections of the available documentation are in Felner, *Angola;* Delgado, *Famosa e histórica Benguela;* Delgado, *Ao Sul do Cuanza;* and Delgado, *Reino.* I have presented the narrative in greater detail in "Central and Southern Angola."

port from a provisioning station for ships inbound from Brazil into a base for independent sales of slaves, a bastion of Luso-African opposition to the governors and metropolitan merchants in control at the colony's capital by the 1730s.

The first Luso-African families from Luanda at Benguela probably established small trading houses there by the middle of the seventeenth century. They bought the occasional slaves that military men roaming uplands between the Katumbela and Kuporolo sent down from as far away as the edge of the high plateau.[29] Most of these captives they shipped out on vessels heading down the coast to Luanda, where associates dispatched them to Brazil.

In the 1710s or 1720s, about the same time that Luso-Africans began moving inland east of Luanda, those at Benguela increased the volume of their trade and began to send slaves directly to Rio de Janeiro.[30] Their apparent avoidance of Luanda thus coincided with tightening Lisbon control over the colony's capital town in those decades. The governors, who were losing their contacts with Luso-African collaborators in the Luanda backlands as enforcement of the prohibitions against their slaving took effect after 1720, had to adopt more circumspect methods of continuing to trade. They therefore transferred their personal dealings to the less closely supervised harbor at Benguela, working with Luso-African associates there and dispatching their slaves straight to the mining areas served through Rio, rather than risking detection by attempting to slip them by metropolitan inspectors at Luanda.[31]

Debtors, criminals, gypsies, and political exiles from the metropole supported this increase in Benguela slaving by carrying the southern frontier of Luso-African slaving east onto the plateau surface itself in the 1720s.[32] The lessened intensity of tropical diseases in the high elevations enabled enough of these men to survive that they and their children by local women became primary sources of the slaves sent down through Benguela in the 1730s and 1740s. At first they raided on their own, but they soon became traders buying captives from the African lords who carried on the wars in the highlands in the 1750s and 1760s. Though they had also bought some of these first slaves with goods taken on credit from governors and even merchants based in Luanda, opportunities to

29. *Representação* from the Senado da Câmara (Luanda), 17 April 1728, AHU, Angola cx. 17.

30. *Requerimento* of Marsal Domingues, n.d. (but before 16 March 1735), AHU, Angola cx. 20.

31. Implied in Caetano de Albuquerque, 21 May 1729, AHU, Angola cx. 18. The lack of officials at Benguela is noted in a minute to a *requerimento* of Antonio de Almeida e Souza, n.d. (late 1720s?), AHU, Angola cx. 16.

32. Miller, "Central and Southern Angola," and Chapter 7 above for the dates and geography.

sell their captives in Benguela to Brazilian ships leaving directly for Rio, the low cost of war captives, and the high slave prices then available in the gold fields allowed them to accumulate substantial profits, which they invested in transforming their slaving from military raiding to commerce conducted largely on their own accounts.

Working capital stolen in this fashion from the merchants of Luanda added momentum to the expansiveness of slaving on the high plateau in the 1730s and 1740s and helped to consolidate its independence from slave trading centered at the colony's capital.[33] Luso-Africans at Benguela and on the central highlands thus organized the southern wing of Angolan slaving around the exchange of slaves for trade goods on the coast, much more like British and French slaving at Loango than like the Portuguese credit employed at Luanda.

Beyond Benguela town a string of Luso-African settlements approached the high plateau along the valleys of rivers flowing down from its western edge, mainly the Katumbela. On the upper steppes, still below the crest, a number of families had compounds in the nearby and relatively populous lands of Kilenges, a good agricultural area growing provisions for the trade and a commercial gateway to Huila. Others settled east on the high plateau itself, mostly near the main trail that followed the southwest-northeast watershed to avoid having to ford the numerous rivers flowing perpendicular to it on either side. By the 1760s, this axis of Luso-African settlement and commerce extended diagonally northeast from Kilenges, past a relocated government fort at Caconda (Nova), and on toward Bihe.[34] Probably several hundred descendants of the thousands of Portuguese who had fled there over the years were still alive, busy collecting slaves from neighboring African warlords and starting them off down to the coast.[35]

33. Role of Luanda merchants in the 1730s: Meneses, 22 Dec. 1734, AHU, Angola cx. 20; Avellar, 7 July 1731, AHU, Angola maço 18–A, for five ships arriving at Luanda with Benguela slaves. The rising number of slaves dispatched directly at Benguela is evident in the official figures presented in Klein, *Middle Passage*, Table A.3, pp. 255–56.

34. The situation in the highlands at that time is known mostly through the plans of Governor Sousa Coutinho: "Relação das provincias que comprehendem os Certoens de Benguela e Caconda," n.d. (ca. 1768), AHU, Angola cx. 31; "Bando que ordena as Feiras nos certoens de Benguela, e Caconda," 23 Sept. 1768, AHU, Angola cx. 31; letter of 18 Dec. 1769, AHU, Angola cx. 32 (published in *Arquivos de Angola* 1, no. 1 [1933]: n.p., and in Felner, *Angola*, 1:163–69); *memória*, n.d. (ca. 1772), AHU, Angola cx. 31.

35. Gladwyn M. Childs, "The Kingdom of Wambu (Huambo): A Tentative Chronology," *Journal of African History* 5, no. 3 (1964): 374–76, cites a 1799 report of the Benguela governor identifying only 78 "whites" in the interior, surely only a subset of the entire dark-skinned Luso-African population resident there. Cf. Delgado, *Ao sul do Cuanza*, 1:619–21, specifying 205 *moradores* (local residents) in Mbailundu, of whom only 15% of the 107 identified by race were "white"; also discussion in Vellut, "Notes sur le Lunda," pp. 97–98. Sousa Coutinho's plans for creating compact settlements of the highland Luso-African population envisaged at least 20 such parishes, each surely of at least 20–30 Catholics. In addition to the above, see the Pinheiro Furtado map (1790) published in Cadornega, *História geral*, vol. 3, following p. 422.

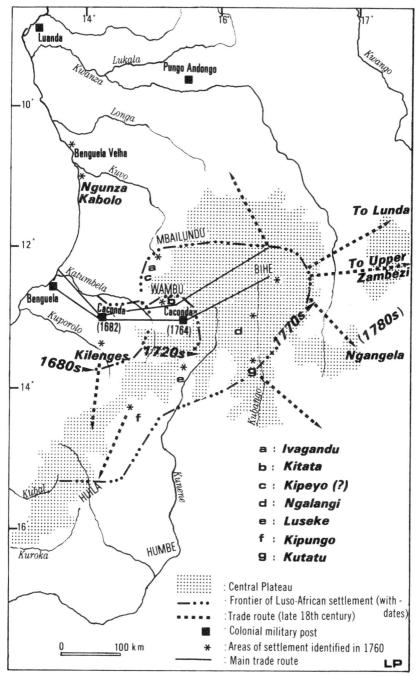

Map 8.2. Luso-Africans in the Central Highlands

From this main trail later trade routes and settlements radiated south toward Huila and southeast beyond the upper Kunene toward the upper Zambezi, the lower Kubango, and Lunda.

The geography of Luso-African residence and slaving had thus broken down into several separate regional centers by mid-century, with those in higher elevations in the interior of the colony linked to affiliated families at Luanda or Benguela. The trade of the northern wing, based on settlements along the lower Bengo and Zenza, reached out toward the *ndembu* and southern Kongo. In the center Ambaca's Luso-Africans looked northeast to the Kwango valley, mostly the African kingdom of Jinga. Massangano and the lower Lukala valley traded south across the Kwanza to the northwestern slopes of the central highlands, while settlers in Pungo Andongo worked the upper Kwanza and its affluents flowing off the plateau's northeastern flank. All these sent their caravans of slaves toward Luanda. Benguela drained captives from other Luso-Africans settled in Kilenges and on the main surface of the central plateau and also, by the 1770s, from caravans they sent far to the southeast. Of course, the commercial spheres of each overlapped in practice, and as the slaving zones expanded further several of them could merge in new centers, as slavers from Ambaca, Pungo Andongo, and probably older settlements on the high plateau as well had converged at still another nucleus at Bihe by the early nineteenth century. The only major eighteenth-century source of slaves that Luso-Africans did not control was the route directly east from Ambaca to the Kwango valley and Kasanje, favored by the Luanda agents of merchants from Lisbon.

Colonial-Metropolitan Conflict

Conflict grew throughout the eighteenth century between the militaristic creoles and the immigrant traders working Luanda's immediate hinterland with metropolitan capital. Since merchants on both sides of this contest routed their slaving to the Kwango valley through Ambaca, the district became a major battleground between the two factions. Reports of struggles there between old Luso-African settlers, trying to buy slaves without independent access to the Atlantic economy, and newer traders bearing the Lisbon goods that began to flood the colony after 1730 reveal how military slavers defended their position in the trade as fighting faded and as metropolitan capital infused areas that African merchant princes were reconstructing for commercialized slaving.

As soon as the late-seventeenth-century slaving frontier had retreated, *capitães-mores* east of Luanda had supplemented outright violence with tactics characteristic of commercial slaving. Later, when Lisbon had removed the governors from their positions as major suppliers of imports in the 1720s, the Luso-Africans who did not retreat to Benguela or to the east had such sway over commerce in the colony's interior that Lisbon merchants at Luanda found themselves virtually compelled to offer these settlers goods on credit in order to trade at all. The Luso-African captains used these goods to coerce slaves from inhabitants of their jurisdictions by means of debt. They also invested the goods in the advanced eastern trading contacts they created in the eighteenth century.[36] No doubt, such investments helped to extend the Luso-African trading diaspora that led from Massangano to Ambaca and Pungo Andongo and, eventually, to Bihe and beyond. However, these *capitães-mores* meant to allow the new metropolitan merchants into their domains only on their own terms, to protect their profits before about 1760 and to limit their losses thereafter.

Lacking commercial capital of their own, the Luso-Africans protected themselves primarily by asserting exclusive claim to the African labor in the districts they controlled. Most of the African inhabitants of the colony lived under the immediate authority of African headmen (*sobas*). Whether these Africans were kin, clients, or slaves in relation to these village communities, the Portuguese considered them "free" vassals and subjects of the Crown, as distinct from the "slaves" of the Luso-Africans. They treated these subjects as liable for corvée labor, mostly as porters for the caravans carrying goods belonging to metropolitan traders inland. Impressment for this purpose increased as the slaving frontier receded and increased the distances over which someone had to carry imports destined for faraway marketplaces, and it placed enormous strains on the available population in the colony. The quantities of merchandise to be transported multiplied even faster as trading replaced raiding and as goods prices for slaves rose.

The resulting depletion of "free" caravan porters hit particularly hard at Luanda merchants trying to arrange deliveries to remote marketplaces like Kasanje. They depended heavily on conscripting villagers, since they hesitated to divert working capital into inefficiently large holdings of slaves of their own. Too many slaves fled or died, and those who remained cost too much to maintain during periods of idleness between journeys to make investment in them worthwhile. But the merchants could not draft villagers without the collaboration of the *capitães-mores*. Furious storms of controversy thus blew up between the Luso-Africans and the Luanda merchants over the issue of distributing forced laborers among the competing trading groups.

Governors and immigrant merchants at Luanda fought back against the Luso-Africans' *de facto* monopoly of the nonslave labor force of the

---

36. "Informação breve sobre o terreno de que se compoem o Reino de Angola . . . ," n.d. (ca. 1790s), AHU, Angola cx. 42.

colony's interior. They represented their attack on the creoles to Lisbon as a pious concern to protect vulnerable African subjects of the Crown from the depredations of ruthless and uncivilized *capitães-mores*. But they failed to add that the restrictions they advocated on the Luso-Africans' impressment of African labor would have exposed the same villagers to recruitment by equivalent means, or worse, into the service of the town merchants.

The captains of Ambaca came under particularly heavy criticism of this sort, since they commanded the most populous area under nominal Portuguese control[37] and wielded a heavy influence over the main trail to the Kwango valley. Without their cooperation neither bundles of cloth nor casks of cane brandy, or *gerebita*, would reach Luanda's favored slave markets there. Merchants organized transport from Luanda in stages that also made Ambaca a focal point of these conflicts. They first loaded their goods on the heads of town slaves or on the backs of vassals recruited from the African quarters of the town. They sometimes saved labor by sending their goods up the Kwanza by canoe, but there they had to risk losing the cargo on the dangerous bar blocking the river's mouth, run the gamut of Kisama raiders lurking on the left bank of the lower river, and still transship the goods through uncooperative Luso-African traders in control of the African labor around Massangano. In either event, slaves from Luanda or other porters impressed at Massangano generally ascended the Lukala River valley only as far as Ambaca before returning to the lowland near the coast. The next stage in the relay, the long journey from Ambaca to Kasanje, depended on acquiring new men through the Ambaca captain-major.

The large volume of this Luanda trade severely strained an Ambaca African population already dependent for decades on replenishing its able-bodied males through imports of slave youths.[38] Demands for bearers came on top of all the other tasks that the Luso-Africans settled in the district already assigned to the villagers around their compounds. They customarily demanded food, women, field labor, and other services from everyone within their reach. The captains stepped in as local brokers and provided caravan porters only to their friends or to associates willing to pay dearly for their cooperation. For such favorites they would send an order out to the African headmen of their jurisdiction, calling on them to send specified numbers of their men to the caravans' assembly point. They would punish any who failed to comply by imprisoning them in stocks, or with whippings, fines, torture wheels, or assassination.[39] Meanwhile, goods belong-

37. E.g., da Cunha, 4 March 1756, AHU, Angola cx. 26; also series of *mappas estatísticos* for Ambaca and other districts covering 1797–1832 (with gaps), AHU, Angola cxs. 52 ff.
38. See Chapter 5 above; also Thornton, "Slave Trade in Angola."
39. Couto, *Capitães-mores;* Corrêa, *História de Angola*, 2:168; "Informação breve," n.d. (ca. 1790s), AHU, Angola cx. 42; Ferreira, *memória*, 26 June 1762, AHU, Angola cx. 29;

ing to less favored traders would remain waiting for transport in crudely constructed straw-roofed sheds bunched around the residence of the *capitão-mor,* where they would quickly deteriorate in the dust and rains. Thefts, perhaps tolerated by the captain, reduced what remained far below the point where their owners had the slightest chance of recovering their investment.[40] Pungo Andongo became a second focus of such complaints at times, as Luanda merchants evidently resorted to it as an alternative route to Kasanje through Dondo.

The *capitães-mores* typically used their control over the labor markets of the interior to finance their own preeminence as slave traders. They straightforwardly commandeered the choicest trade goods as bribes from Luanda merchants desperate for their collaboration. They simply kept for themselves other goods that colonial law required caravan backers to deposit with the government as a guarantee of day wages for the bearers they recruited.[41] The captains could either send the prime goods they collected in this manner off to trading sites with the porters they kept for themselves, or they could sell at high prices what they had collected back to the traders requiring these items to complete the assortments needed to buy any slaves at all.[42]

As authorities in charge of the vast array of bureaucratic technicalities on which the Portuguese empire turned, the Luso-African captains could also favor supportive merchants from the city by selectively pressing lawsuits that these merchants had to route through the captains to collect debts from customers and agents resident in the interior. The importance of commercial credit in and around the Angolan *conquista* made the cooperation of the Luso-African district commanders in enforcing such claims absolutely vital to creditors trapped in Luanda by their fear of the diseases of the interior.

When caravans of slaves returned through their domains from the interior, these Luso-African bosses found further opportunities to make or break the owners of the captives, or their backers at Luanda. They could decide which coffles would receive the provisions and other facilities absolutely necessary to make prompt progress on toward the coast.[43] They expected generous bribes to relax such impediments, since speed was cru-

---

"Memorial sobre os males," 1823, IHGB, lata 28, doc. 21; Castelbranco, 16 May 1828, AHU, Angola cx. 72.

40. Silva *memória,* 25 June 1762, AHU, Angola cx. 29; Corrêa, *História de Angola,* 1:37; "Informação breve," n.d. (ca. 1790s), AHU, Angola cx. 42; Godinho, 23 Oct. 1804, AHU, Angola cx. 55; "Memorial sobre os males," 1823, IHGB, lata 28, doc. 21.

41. Oeyras, *parecer,* 20 Nov. 1760, AHU, Angola cx. 28.

42. Junta do Comercio (Luanda), copy of *termo,* 3 July 1762, AHU, Angola cx. 38 (published in *Arquivos de Angola* 2, no. 9 [1936]: 163–64).

43. "Informação breve," n.d. (ca. 1790s), AHU, Angola cx. 42. There is ample circumstantial detail in the *requerimento* of Manuel de Faria Marinho, n.d. (minuted 28 April 1798), AHU, Angola cx. 46.

cial to reduce deaths en route and to bring the slaves to the port at opportune moments, when ships about to leave the harbor were willing to pay premium prices for the last captives necessary to complete their cargoes and carry them safely to Brazil.

Although colonial decrees repeatedly forbade the Luso-African captains from profiting personally from the commerce of merchants whom they were theoretically appointed to protect,[44] they remained largely invulnerable to prosecution in practice, except for infrequent occasions on which Luanda officials exerted themselves to limit growing Luso-African power in the interior.[45] At the end of the eighteenth century the captain-majors still held absolute power over the conduct of trade in Angola.[46] Even far-reaching administrative reforms in 1811 and again in the 1830s made only partial inroads on the powerful position these captains and their relatives held in the slave trade. At the termination of the legal slave trade in 1830, one governor expressed the forlorn hope that, even if the end of slave exports clouded the future of the colony as a whole, a faint silver lining gleamed in the possibility that it might at last also deprive the *capitães-mores* of their principal sources of revenues and bring them under the control of authorities at Luanda.[47]

Labor Shortages

Chronic shortages of African backs and heads, which placed all the demographic high cards in the hands of these Luso-Africans, enabled them to maintain their dominance in the colony in spite of government decrees. Forced loans to villagers and seizure of defaulted African debtors as captives removed able-bodied inhabitants of districts subject to the abuses of the *capitães-mores* as fast as imports of new slaves from the east replaced them. Impressment of the free laborers drove off many of the men remaining.[48] African farmers used their cherished mobility to escape oppressive demands of their Luso-African overlords as well as to survive failed harvests in times

44. E.g., decrees of 9 Aug. 1720 and 19 Nov. 1761, and the principal *regimento* governing their conduct, 24 Feb. 1765; Couto, *Capitães-mores*, pp. 69, 96, 117 ff., 323–29 et passim.

45. E.g., for the 1740s, *requerimento* and *certidões* of João Pereira da Cunha and Bartholomeo Duarte de Sequeira (a descendant of Luis Lopes de Sequeira in Pungo Andongo in the late seventeenth century?), AHU, Angola cx. 23; also reforms attempted by Sousa Coutinho, as discussed in Chapter 16 below.

46. José António Valente, "Estado atual da Conquista d'Angola, e seu comercio . . . ," 1 Feb. 1792, AHU, Angola cx. 42; "Memorial sobre os males," IHGB, lata 28, doc. 21.

47. Barão de Santa Comba Dão (governor, Angola), 11 Oct. 1830, AHU, Angola cx. 74.

48. "Informação breve," n.d. (ca. 1790s), AHU, Angola cx. 42; de Mello, "Angola no começo do século," p. 551; Godinho, 23 Oct. 1804, AHU, Angola cx. 55.

of drought. They simply fled to nearby territories ruled by African kings, who were only too happy to receive them in return for tribute and client-age. Even the slaves brought in to replace such losses were difficult to retain. They regularly fled into local maroon colonies and into parts of Kisama, Jinga, Kongo, and Kasanje. Low mid-century prices for slaves in Brazil may have deepened the labor shortages further by forcing Luso-Africans to cover trading losses by selling off slaves employed in their operations and by relying more on impressing local labor instead.

All these pressures contributed to a general shortage of male labor throughout the colony, reported in government correspondence as "de-population." The deficit, which became another focus of the Luso-Africans' conflicts with Luanda, spread along with creole settlement in the interior and with expansion of the Atlantic trading zone. It appeared in the vicinity of Luanda in the 1730s[49] and extended out along the lower Kwanza and Bengo by the 1750s.[50] Losses seriously afflicted even formerly "populous" Ambaca by the 1780s.[51] By 1800, widespread shortages of bearers east of Luanda had become critical enough to place severe constraints even on the relatively non-labor-intensive trade in slaves, who did not require trans-port, since they walked themselves to the coast, and who sometimes carried the ivory and wax also sent there. The lack of transport boded ill, as government economic planners frequently complained early in the nine-teenth century, for the commerce in wax, ivory, and other commodities that they expected to replace captives when slaving ended. Commodity exports would create an unfulfillable demand for porters to carry these goods to Luanda.[52]

The manpower shortage did not attain the same degree of severity in the central highlands above Benguela, where Lisbon traders sent fewer goods on their own. The government viewed the Luso-African captains there as "pernicious and dangerous" in the 1760s at a time when officials were planning to send metropolitan goods to the area in large quantities, but by the time this effort had failed in the 1790s Luso-African traders in the highlands contracted freely with African lords for the labor of the subjects.[53] Consequently, these captains never attained the power that their counterparts in Ambaca and other centers east of Luanda were able to

---

49. Senado da Câmara (Luanda), 7 May 1732, AHU, Angola cx. 19.
50. Da Cunha, 1 March 1756, AHU, Angola cx. 26; *regimento* to Manoel Correa Leitão, 23 Jan. 1757, AHU, Angola cx. 27; da Cunha, 9 June 1757, AHU, Angola cx. 27.
51. Almeida e Vasconcelos to Manoel da Fonseca Coutinho, 17 Nov. 1790, AHU, cód. 1627; see also Taunay, *Subsídios,* p. 13. Labor shortages may have appeared even earlier (late 1750s) in Ambaca; e.g., Dias, ed. (Leitão), "Viagem a Cassange," p. 13.
52. Noronha, 1 Jan. 1804, AHU, Angola cx. 54; Godinho, 23 Oct. 1804, AHU, Angola cx. 55; and much subsequent documentation.
53. Sousa Coutinho, "Memoria" on Benguela, n.d. (ca. 1772), AHU, Angola cx. 31; de Mello, "Angola no começo do século," pp. 550–51.

build out of labor scarcities there. The contrast showed the extent to which the *capitães-mores,* though vilified by their metropolitan critics, could not have perpetrated their abuses so successfully without the persistent efforts of their detractors to enter the trade of the interior themselves.

Control of slave labor also lay close to the heart of Luso-African power everywhere in the colony.[54] Near Luanda the Luso-Africans tended to own slaves rather than to attempt to conscript hands from the nominally free African population. Several factors contributed to their preference for slaves. Luso-African merchants retained trade slaves too ill to embark, or women and children arriving from the war zones of the interior but of lesser value in Brazil, at very little cost in hard currencies to themselves. Most they sent to plantations they owned along the lower Bengo, where the slaves lived primarily from their own resources and grew the food that supplied the town of Luanda. In addition, the Luso-Africans had few other sources of labor by the eighteenth century. Most of the Africans living in and around Luanda had arrived there as captives. There were few unattached Africans to conscript, and laborers working for day wages took their pay in textiles that merchant importers could supply at much lower cost than the Luso-Africans. The stronger presence of the government in districts accessible from the city also allowed officials to draft free African subjects of the Crown for their own purposes rather than leaving them for Luso-Africans to exploit privately. Slavery under these circumstances became a way for Luso-Africans to protect personal followings, even members of their own families, from government military call-ups, since the law forbade governors from placing arms in the hands of slaves.[55] As a result, officials contemplating public works in and around the capital frequently had to impress labor from as far away as Golungo. Using Golungo as their source, of course, avoided the shortages of able-bodied males around Ambaca and competed mostly with Luso-Africans trading north to Kongo rather than with Lisbon merchants sending goods to Kasanje.

Luso-African residents of the seaport and in the plantation areas along the lower Bengo had held strikingly large numbers of slaves during the prosperous years of the early seventeenth century.[56] Dionisio da Piacenza, a Capuchin missionary in Luanda, reported slaves by the hundreds in the

54. De Mello, 25 Aug. 1801, AHU, Angola cx. 51. Venâncio, "Economia de Luanda," pp. 93–108, 113, 115, 141 et passim, stresses the reliance on slaves in the local economy, though not always distinguishing Luso-African settlers clearly from government and other masters.

55. João Victo da Silva, *memoria,* n.d. (ca. 1792), AHU, Angola cx. 42.

56. Cadornega, *História geral,* 1:210, 235–36, stresses the number of slaves taken by the Portuguese when they abandoned the city to the Dutch in 1641. The Dutch may have captured many more, since they delivered *ladino* slaves with Portuguese names to several American markets at that period; see, e.g., Timothy H. Breen and Stephen Innes, *"Myne Owne Ground": Race and Freedom on Virginia's Eastern Shore, 1640–1676* (New York: Oxford University Press, 1980), for Virginia.

hands of the city's residents as of 1667–68, with the wealthiest of the owners possessing 2,000–3,000 of them.[57] These slaves, mostly just in from the interior and often not healthy enough to ship to Brazil, worked the plantations along the Bengo that provided most of the city's food. Other skilled and experienced slaves, so-called *ladinos,* staffed the large Luso-African households of the city, often serving in the trades as masons, carpenters, smiths, and sailors, and even working as cashiers in the commercial houses.[58] Beyond these domestic slaves, Luso-African merchants also employed the famed slave *pombeiro* traders who conducted most of the early commercial operations between the city and its hinterland. In the first half of the eighteenth century, the free residents of Luanda felt dominated by their slaves, who populated the sprawling straw-roofed slums around the town, congregated in uncontrollable crowds around the city's main well at Mayanga, prowled its alleyways by night brandishing lethal Flemish knives at passersby, and at least once were reported to have threatened revolt.[59]

By the latter part of the eighteenth century, the number of Luanda slaves had declined noticeably. All sectors of the population still owned slaves in the 1760s, including the Catholic church and the religious orders,[60] but the city's enumerated population included only about twice as many slaves as free subjects of any complexion. The hundreds and thousands of captives reported in Luso-African retinues a century earlier had shrunk by 1773 to none larger than thirty.[61] Even allowing for massive concealment of slave holdings from government census takers and slaves kept on the Bengo estates, the earlier great crowds of slaves seem to have dwindled with the Angolan creoles' movement out of the city and with the hard times encountered by those who remained. An echo of the reduced Luso-African holdings of slave labor may appear also in the peripheral role left to slave *pombeiros* in the later trade of the interior. Free agents of the Lisbon merchants by then preeminent in Luanda (known as *funantes,*

57. Taunay, *Subsídios,* p. 135; also see *avizo* of 27 April 1697, AHU, Angola cx. 16, protecting *ladino* slaves in Luanda. De Mello, 25 Aug. 1801, AHU, Angola cx. 50, referred to the decree as still in force early in the nineteenth century.

58. Magalhães, 28 May 1739, AHU, Angola cx. 22; Vasconcelos, 14 May 1760, AHU, Angola cx. 28; de Mello, 29 Aug. 1801, AHU, Angola cx. 50, and idem, "Angola no começo do século," p. 564.

59. Report of the Capuchin Giacinto da Bologna, 1747, according to Taunay, *Subsídios,* p. 143; cf. Teobaldo Filesi and I. Villapadierna, *La "Missio Antiqua" dei Cappuccini nel Congo (1645–1835)* (Rome: Istituto Storico dei Cappuccini, 1978), p. 175, who ascribe this report to Bernardino Ignazio da Asti, after 1757. Also de Mello, 25 Aug. 1801, AHU, Angola cx. 50; José de Oliveira Barboza (governor, Angola), 4 May 1813 and 2 Oct. 1813, AHU, Angola cx. 61.

60. The Jesuits had held 350 slaves at their Luanda *colégio* alone at the time of their expulsion: Vasconcelos, 17 Jan. 1761, AHU, Angola cx. 28; Venâncio, "Economia de Luanda," pp. 98–99.

61. Mappa de Loanda (1773), in Lencastre, 31 March 1773, AHU, Angola cx. 36.

aviados, and by other terms) worked the main trade routes up to Ambaca and the government *feiras,* while *pombeiros* of that era mainly collected slaves in marginal trading sites around Luso-African settlements in the hinterland.

The skilled slaves present in earlier decades had fallen first into the hands of the Jesuits, as families protected the estates of their deceased patriarchs from tax assessors and from creditors by donating the estates to the order. Expulsion of the Jesuits from the Portuguese empire in 1759 had caused these holdings to be sold and dispersed.[62] By the end of the eighteenth century, slave masters in Luanda had been reduced to using their slave women as prostitutes, partly as favors to friends and business associates, but also, it was alleged, to increase the quantity and value of labor they could control under the prevailing manpower shortage, through the mulatto slave children they expected to result.[63] Slaves formed a higher proportion of the late-eighteenth-century population at Benguela, where Luso-Africans had maintained their old styles of prosperity more successfully than at Luanda.[64]

Abuses of slaves noted at Luanda may constitute additional evidence of the general decline of Luso-African owners and their skilled slaves from the prosperity of the seventeenth and early eighteenth centuries. It may reasonably be assumed that the same hard times that drove some Luso-Africans away from Luanda compelled those who remained to liquidate valuable holdings in *ladinos,* either selling them directly to merchant creditors in Luanda or shipping them to Brazil for sale.[65] The mounting threat that hard times posed to the city's slave community might well have motivated the only attempted slave revolt known in the history of Luanda. The unrest came in the 1740s, just at the critical moment of social upheaval as the Luso-Africans adjusted to the commercialized slaving that Lisbon had undertaken in the 1730s.

Slaves, though important also to the Luso-Africans of the interior, had less value there. Closer to protection from neighboring African kings and not so far removed from their own homelands, the slaves tended to flee.[66] As a result, the Luso-Africans turned to coercing the nominally free

---

62. Vasconcelos, 14 May 1760, AHU, Angola cx. 28.

63. E.g., accounts covering transportation of obviously skilled and cultured slaves from Luanda to Brazil and Portugal, in the books of Proença e Silva, 1759, BNL, cód. 617, fols. 115 ff.

64. They represented 75% of the total population, according to Mappa das pessoas livres e escravos, Benguela, 15 June 1796, AHU, Angola cx. 43.

65. Nostalgic recollection of "the good old days" is evident already in the early 1760s, in de Lima, *memorial,* 10 June 1762, AHU, Angola cx. 29. High costs and shortages of skilled labor were reported widely by 1800, e.g., de Mello, *apontamentos,* 2 Dec. 1795, AHU, Angola maço 3 (D.O.); also merchants' petition, 20 Jan. 1803, Felix Correa de Araujo (*juiz de fora, e alfandega, e ouvidor geral interino*), 9 March 1803, AHU, Angola cx. 54.

66. The documentation on relations with nearly every neighboring African power refers constantly to disputes over escaped slaves, and the Luso-Africans regularly used accusations

Africans living in villages under their domination, merely supplementing corvée labor with use of slaves.[67] Masters tended to concentrate their limited investments in captive labor in the skilled categories, trading agents, artisans, and the trained warriors of the private militias that the most powerful creole settlers maintained. Like the immigrant merchants, they thus employed slaves principally in occupations where year-round service would repay the fixed costs of maintaining them. For intermittent and short-term construction projects or transporting goods for the slave trade, they impressed men from villages they reserved for their exclusive use,[68] detained trade slaves from passing coffles for temporary work, and applied their influence with the *capitães-mores* to call up detachments of government troops when they needed to pursue freemen who hid from their heavy-handed recruiting tactics in caves and other inaccessible locations.[69] By employing this forcibly conscripted, nominally "free-wage" labor, they focused their conflict with the metropole on the issue of caravan porters and helped to depopulate the lands they ruled.

Eighteenth-Century Changes in the Methods of Luso-African Slaving

Luso-Africans converted from militarism to commerce as they distributed goods through the Portuguese *conquista* and beyond its fringes, occasion-ally fought, and forwarded slaves back to the west in the course of the eighteenth century. Geographical dispersal lowered the prices they paid for slaves, and caravans they sent into remote eastern areas helped to ignite the violence of the slaving frontier there, but diminishing reliance on military methods of slaving elsewhere raised overall acquisition costs of slaves in the long run. At the same time, the expanded range their caravans had to cover forced them to invest more and more in transport and con-fronted them with the same long-term shortage of working capital that

---

of harboring fugitives as pretexts to attack; each center of Luso-African settlement lost slaves to a different African protector, e.g., Luanda to the lower Lukala, the lower Kwanza to Kisama, the Bengo plantations to Musulu and southern Kongo, and Ambaca and Pungo Andongo to Jinga. Manuel Vieira de Albuquerque e Tovar (governor, Angola), 23 Jan. 1821, AHU, Angola cx. 67, reported 251 fugitives absent from Luanda at that time, or about 5%–10% of the city's reported slave population.

67. Slaves in the interior: Sousa Coutinho, "Ordem que o capitão mor de Benguela deve entregar . . . ," 20 Nov. 1768, AHU, Angola cx. 31; Oliveira Barboza, 24 Oct. 1811, AHU, Angola cx. 60; Motta Feo e Torres, 7 Aug. 1816, AHU, Angola cx. 64. Mbailundu was reported to have 13 whites, 26 *pardos,* 32 free blacks with 180 of their own people, 363 other followers, and 689 slaves (or 9.7 slaves per free person).

68. Parecer dos negociantes da praça de Luanda, n.d. (ca. 1821–23), paras. 9, 10, AHU, Sala 12, diversos no. 825.

69. Dias, ed. (Leitão), "Viagem a Cassange," p. 13.

all western central African merchants suffered as the commercial sector expanded. Transport costs, even by mid-century, already equaled the prime cost of goods moved between Luanda and points of sale in the interior.[70] Mortality on the lengthened return trip alone added another 40 percent to their costs, with escapes causing further losses on top of that.[71] Though the Luso-Africans' movement off into the *sertões* also located them far beyond the reach of judicial and even police control exercised from Luanda, the economic pressures they suffered from having to sell through Lisbon merchants there added to the constraints, forcing them to seek cheaper sources of imports, to reduce their costs of acquiring slaves, and to scrimp on the expenses of delivering both goods and captives.

The Luso-Africans' increased reliance on goods for trading increased the financial pressure because it entailed substituting imported merchandise, with payments owed in currency in Brazil, for commodities of local origin. Before the 1720s and 1730s, Luso-African traders had been able to limit their *réis* debts by filling out the basic assortments paid for slaves with significant quantities of goods acquired locally—dried fish from the seas near Luanda, salt from Kisama, raffia cloths from Kongo, and so on, all purchased outside the *réis* currency zone—to imports they bought from abroad. Firearms and powder became essential components of the *banzo* between 1730 and 1760, and imported Asian textiles all but replaced woven palm squares as trade currencies in many parts of the interior at about the same time.

Luso-Africans also lost control over the trade in Kisama salt to the Jinga region east of Luanda. At least two episodes of this story stand out in the history of the contested district of Ambaca. From the early seventeenth century, governors and merchants had brought salt from Luso-Africans at Benguela up to Luanda, where they used it for curing the fish they fed to the slaves of the city, distributed it to the interior of the colony, and stocked it on slave ships ready to depart for Brazil. But the Massangano Luso-Africans had used their strong position astride the old rock salt route from Kisama to its main markets on the Ambaca plateau to control distribution of the local mineral there.[72] Kisama salt continued to circulate as a commodity currency even in slaving sectors of the district's economy into the 1740s, supplemented by smaller quantities of an inferior substitute that other Luso-Africans seem to have produced from salt pans located in Pungo Andongo. The importance of the trade made salt a convenient

70. E.g., "Mostrão se nesta pauta os preços . . . ," n.d., AHU, Angola cx. 21; cf. Couto, *Capitães-mores,* p. 227, n. 76, dating the document to the 1730s.

71. Relação sobre escravatura, n.d. (ca. 1760s?), AHU, Angola maço 10 (D.O.); Miller, "Mortality in the Atlantic Slave Trade," pp. 413–14.

72. Suggested by Avellar, 20 Feb. 1731, AHU, maço 18–A; Venâncio, "Economia de Luanda," pp. 71–73, 121–24, 145, 154.

target in the metropolitan effort to limit the Luso-Africans' influence over the interior of the colony.

In the 1750s one *capitão-mor* in Ambaca, a certain Apolonario Francisco, apparently backed from Luanda, reduced the remaining circulation of salt and imposed himself over older Luso-African families from Massangano at about the time that Luso-Africans had settled on the plateau in the late 1740s. He seized their salt trade by declaring it the exclusive legal tender for the government's ecclesiastical tax (the *dizimo*, or tithe). He also permitted his tax collectors to employ strong-arm methods against Africans liable for the impost and thus quickly drained his jurisdiction of its Kisama salt. He then substituted a requirement that Africans would pay future taxes only in imported textiles, supplies of which he presumably controlled himself. He reportedly made the transition at equivalency rates between salt and textiles that increased his personal *réis* profits by approximately 50 percent.[73] Francisco's replacement of the salt commodity currency with imported cloth formed one incident in the general substitution of European goods for African commodities in the eighteenth-century Angolan currency systems.

A further episode in the same struggle surfaced later. In the 1760s, metropolitan efforts to take control of the colonial economy had transferred monopoly rights over the Benguela marine salt pans to contractors favored by Lisbon.[74] By that time, salt had returned to use in Ambaca, at least as the medium of petty exchanges, even though textiles had replaced it as the currency of the import-export trade, once more indicating the underlying resiliency of the Luso-African economy in the interior against initiatives taken from the coast. The activist governor in office at Luanda on this later occasion attempted to regulate the remaining circulation of salt as a currency rather than trying again to eliminate it. He placed political allies in charge of its distribution.[75] Since the government had proved unable to substitute its own currency, he issued an edict reestablishing blocks of Kisama salt as the legal means of paying taxes in Ambaca, but with a contract designating unnamed favorites in Massangano, presumably affiliates of Lisbon merchants, as its sole suppliers.[76] The appointed contractors would sell authorized salt to Africans, and the Africans would then pay their salt blocks to tax collectors, and the tax collectors would then turn the revenues over to the *capitães-mores*. The captains had to use

---

73. Da Cunha, 4 March 1756, AHU, Angola maço 18 (D.O.).

74. Tenente General Joseph Correa Leitão to Avellar, 28 May 1732, AHU, Angola cx. 19; Oeyras, *parecer,* 20 Nov. 1760, AHU, Angola cx. 28; Vasconcelos, 18 April 1762, AHU, Angola cx. 29; Sousa Coutinho, 26 Jan. 1765, AHU, Angola cx. 30.

75. Part of a larger program to secure government control over Angola's substantial local trade in salt; see Chapter 16 below. Also cf. the Massangano fish contract of about the same time, AHU, Angola cx. 36.

76. *Portaria,* 9 May 1769, AHU, Angola cx. 32.

these salt receipts to pay salaries and other allowances to soldiers and other employees of the government, as they had always done.[77] The soldiers would buy food from African farmers with the salt, thus returning the blocks to general circulation and another round of paying taxes. The government would then control the district's principal currency. Only if official expenses payable in salt exceeded the supplies of the currency that the tax collectors had on hand could the *capitães-mores* purchase blocks from private residents and traders, seemingly the Luso-Africans against whom the scheme was directed.

The continuing sensitivity of the salt currency in the struggles between metropolitan officials and the colony's Luso-African settlers reappeared one last time in 1782–83. A *junta* of Luso-Africans had seized control of the colony's government in 1782, after the death of Governor Lencastre, and were using their temporary power to restore the sagging fortunes of their kin when an expedition sent from Lisbon to replace them reached Luanda and began preparations for a military expedition intended to prevent the French and British from trading at Cabinda. The local *junta* subverted the metropolitan military initiative by dispatching the colonial forces, commanded by their relatives, off in the opposite direction to seize the rock salt mines in Kisama.[78]

The viselike grip of the growing need for *réis* currency credits to pay for imports and unfavorable movements of Brazilian prices for slaves in the middle of the eighteenth century forced the Luso-Africans to supplement their incomes with bribes they could derive from colonial government appointments they held[79] and by liquidating their holdings in slaves. More important, concealment in inaccessible corners of the interior not only allowed them to avoid paying debts they owed in the city but also enabled them to smuggle slaves along the alternate trails leading to foreigners who paid much higher prices for them, and in the goods equivalent of "cash," along other parts of the coast. They never abandoned Luanda entirely, since merchants there provided credit to beginning traders without assets of their own. Luanda also offered necessary components of the *banzos* available only from Brazilians and Portuguese—notably *gerebita* cane brandy and the weak gunpowder that did not split the barrels of the cheap muskets the foreigners sold.

Luso-Africans frequently resorted to this form of embezzlement, which the unpaid lenders of trade goods in Luanda termed a *reviro*, throughout the period from about 1730 to 1810. Beginners most in need of borrowed

---

77. Implicit in da Cunha, 3 March 1756, AHU, Angola maço 18 (D.O.).

78. Miller and Thornton, "Chronicle."

79. A tendency evident since earlier in the eighteenth century: Magalhães, 29 April 1738, AHU, Angola cx. 22. See also Dias, "Sociedade colonial," pp. 270–72; Venâncio, "Espaço e dinâmica populacional em Luanda," tables.

working capital would start out with goods obtained from importers at Luanda and then head off in classic style toward the low slave prices of the remote backlands. Rather than sending slaves they bought with Luanda goods back to creditors in Luanda, they would divert their best captives to other African transporters bringing cheaper British and French goods to the same marketplaces. The technique was an adaptation of the fraud that settlers in the central highlands had developed in the early years of trading there, when they had sent slaves they bought with goods from Luanda directly to Brazil and had sold them there on their own accounts. In effect, they used capital borrowed at Luanda to finance a profitable trade with foreign suppliers of the firearms often prohibited at Portuguese-controlled ports, of British woolens at good prices, or of Asian cottons delivered in quantity by the French. To retain the toleration, if not the support, of their original backers in Luanda, they would send inferior slaves down as partial payment on the debts they owed at the colonial capital, at least when trading profits permitted. If successful, such smuggling would make them wealthy enough to repay what they owed at Luanda long before their creditors caught up with them. If not, as was commonly the case, they fled farther into the backlands.

Luanda traders had little choice but to play along with these *reviros,* even while railing against the "gypsies, Jews, and depraved and Africanized heathen" who victimized them in that way. They could either wait and hope, or they could write off the debt. The defaulting borrowers made many plausible excuses for their delinquency, often arguing that returns on goods already loaned depended on further credit for fresh merchandise to complete the assortment necessary to buy any slaves at all. For the Luso-Africans, *reviros* represented one way out of the impossible economic constraints that Portugal placed on Angolan subjects selling slaves within the empire.

The Golungo Luso-Africans on the northern edges of the *conquista* had ample opportunity to engage in such smuggling at Mwbila and Mbwela, as well as at Jinga in the Kwango valley, where foreign goods arrived in plenty through the *ndembu* market at Kisova from the 1740s and 1750s. They may have shifted their commerce back to Luanda during the 1760s, at least for a few years, after the Portuguese government constructed a fortress in the area at Encoje in 1759 to staunch the flow of foreign goods through the region.[80] In the 1760s the Lisbon government also briefly allowed traders to buy Asian textiles direct from ships calling at Luanda on their return from the Indian Ocean.[81] More important, the Seven Years' War in Europe distracted the British and French from slaving along An-

---

80. Birmingham, *Trade and Conflict in Angola,* pp. 150 ff., on Encoje.
81. For documentation, see Chapter 16 below.

golan coasts between 1756 and 1763, thus cutting off the supply of foreign goods at its source.[82] But Encoje totally failed to block foreign goods when the northern Europeans returned in force at the end of the war and when the India ships avoided calling regularly at Luanda. The Luso-Africans then resumed their *reviros,* and their contraband dealings with foreigners grew through the 1770s to become a major problem for Lisbon for the duration of the legal trade.

Benguela, the only major Luso-African center remaining near the coast after the 1750s, became the focal point of another illicit branch of Luso-African trade beginning in the 1760s, particularly with the French. France lost its supplies of slaves from Senegal to the British in the European peace settlement of 1763 and therefore looked to Angolan coasts to replace them. Simultaneously slipping prices at Rio de Janeiro, Benguela's only significant Brazilian market, invited Luso-African traders there to find other more profitable buyers for their captives. The growth of sugar planting in French Saint Domingue over the next three decades sustained French demand for western central African labor and completed the recipe for rampant smuggling at Benguela. Government officials there, often of Luso-African extraction or affiliation until the 1790s, permitted the French to land goods openly in the city. At times, even the Pungo Andongo Luso-Africans working the north sides of the central plateau may have obtained Asian cottons from French ships at Benguela, or at ports like the Kikombo nearer the Kwanza. This illegal trade consolidated the direct slaves-goods exchanges prevailing at Benguela, without elaborate credit arrangements like those in use at Luanda. Luso-African smuggling at Benguela declined only after 1790, when the Napoleonic wars in Europe forced the French to withdraw entirely from Atlantic slaving.

Even Luso-Africans living immediately east of Luanda bought goods from French and British ships, sometimes directly through the harbor of the city itself. Foreign ships, though technically forbidden to enter Luanda Bay, could gain government permission to anchor under pretexts of distress, equipment failure, or urgent need for food or water. Others put into the mouths of the Bengo or Dande just to the north, where canoes carrying slaves of the Luso-Africans downriver from Golungo passed on their way down to Portuguese creditors in the capital. Luso-Africans employed other small craft in a coastal trade to embarkation points even farther north and sent slaves already in the city in these craft down to waiting British and French ships. They brought foreign goods back right through the Luanda port. Luso-Africans bringing British merchandise along these routes from the north met colleagues with French goods from the Kikombo and from Benguela in the Kwango valley, thus ringing the small sphere just east of

---

82. Curtin, *Atlantic Slave Trade,* pp. 176–77.

Luanda in which Lisbon's goods circulated unchallenged with a broad arch of smuggled foreign goods.

Though the Luso-Africans escaped difficult times in the middle third of the eighteenth century through these gaps in the shell of mercantilist trade protectionism, their resort to selling slaves for cash to the foreigners and their growing investments in the trading networks of the interior left them committed exclusively to the colonial economy by the 1780s, just as widening trading margins between Angola and Brazil might otherwise have revived their fortunes within the empire. Costs of acquiring slaves must have dropped everywhere during the great drought of 1785–94, and the direct contacts which Luso-Africans and their agents opened with Lunda and along the upper Zambezi between 1790 and 1810 must have put them in touch with new sources of plentiful and inexpensive slaves as well. Prices in Brazil revived at the end of the century, and at the same time a mid-century administrative assault that Lisbon had launched in Angola lost its momentum. The way must have seemed open for a return to selling slaves in Brazil for *réis* credits that comfortably exceeded the cost of goods bought in Angola.

In fact events abroad had restructured financing of the maritime segment of the southern Atlantic slave trade to cut the Luso-Africans out of this promising scenario. The Portuguese, formerly the main sources of the credit that financed these Brazilian sales, nearly dropped out of the trade. The Brazilians, backed by British suppliers of smuggled woolens and cottons, expanded their direct goods-for-slaves trade north from Benguela to become the major buyers at Luanda as well. French slavers disappeared after 1792, and the British were gone by 1808, allowing Rio to extend the Brazilian style of buying slaves outright on the coast north to Loango. The North Americans and Spaniards, who became the main interlopers after 1810, occasionally paid in specie but mainly paid with goods, in Africa, for the labor they bought. Non-Angolans thus captured for themselves the gains to be made from selling slaves for Brazilian *cruzados*, Portuguese *réis*, and Spanish *patacas* in the prosperous early-nineteenth-century economies of the Americas.

The Luso-Africans therefore took their not insignificant share of the prosperity of these last years of legal slaving mostly in the form of imports and slaves. These assets they employed in the far-flung trading systems they built up to deliver near-record numbers of slaves from the most distant parts of the central African interior during those years. Luso-Africans regained some of the influence their grandparents had lost in Luanda, but their transatlantic ties weakened. The inflow of newcomers marrying into the old families dwindled as itinerant ship's factors and sales agents (*comissários volantes*) replaced resident traders as buyers of slaves. The slave-buyers' racist contempt for the dark complexions of the Luso-Africans after 1800 or so cut the affinal ties that had once integrated them into the wider southern Atlantic world. The Luso-Africans of the interior consolidated semi-independent and self-financed commercial systems centered on Ambaca and Bihe, where the preceding generation had retreated to escape pressures earlier in the century. Luso-African slaving at Benguela declined, leaving the Ovimbundu in the central highlands to take the initiative in organizing the wax and ivory trades that replaced exports of slaves by the 1830s.

In effect, the Luso-Africans had shifted their wealth back up the supply "pipeline" toward the sources of the slaves they sold, retreating from the European merchant capital flowing through Lisbon, Rio, and Havana that replaced the Luso-Africans' ownership of Brazil-bound slaves. The strong position the Luso-Africans salvaged within the colony, of course, allowed them to prosper from the nineteenth-century commodity trade in wax, ivory, and later rubber, and to create the colorful creole culture for which Luanda became known then.[83] However, their concentration on slaves, caravans, marital alliances with African powers, and land in Angola left them without the foothold in the Atlantic currency zone that their ancestors a century earlier had possessed and isolated them in a stronger sense than ever before. A century of successful defense against Lisbon merchant capitalism built on their advantages in the interior of the colony had produced a victory that their children might find they wished their parents had never won.

Conclusion: The Economics of the Conquista and the Ironies of Success

The Luso-Africans' lingering nineteenth-century commitments to the slave trade, the land, the church, and the military of the Angolan interior left them disabled premodern anachronisms. While the world, including even parts of the Portuguese empire, moved toward industrialization and the *conquista* evolved toward civil administrative status under close metropolitan control, the Luso-Africans clung to their ancestors' productive agricultural lands near Luanda, still worked them with slaves, supported local parishes dating from the seventeenth century, and sought military honors. They managed to preserve these older ways not because of their inherent viability in the modern world but because they alone could survive

---

83. Anne Stamm, "La société créole à Saint-Paul de Loanda dans les années 1836–1848," *Revue française d'histoire d'outre-mer* 59, 4 (no. 217) (1977): 578–610. Dias, "Sociedade colonial," qualifies the notion of a creole "golden age" in Luanda at that time and details losses suffered from about the 1820s onward.

the tropical diseases that still decimated the few Portuguese who came to the colony with more modern notions and with funds from the metropole.

The late "feudal"[84] style of the Luso-Africans allowed them to withdraw from the outside world at the same time as they drew strength from it. The lack of water-borne and animal-drawn transport in the regions between the forests and the deserts that the Luso-Africans occupied made transport expensive relative to comparable costs sustained by African competitors to the north and south. They compensated by resorting to low-cost labor-impressment policies. In the early days they had relied on slaves captured near Luanda. Later, when vastly increased operations and burdensome debts to merchants from Portugal had deepened the disadvantages under which they traded, they saved on labor costs by impressing "free" villagers from areas they dominated militarily. The *conquista* thus became a cheap labor reserve for the Luso-Africans as commercialization proceeded. Within it, *capitães-mores* pressured local inhabitants to the point of depopulating entire regions in their search for heads and backs to carry goods at costs they could afford.

Though internal exploitation helped Luso-Africans send imports at reduced cost to competitive marketplaces in Kongo, the Kwango valley, and the central highlands, the Portuguese *conquista* served them so well partly because they could also draw on the resources of the Atlantic economy. Backed by their military power, they pressed imported goods at high prices on unwilling African customers and extracted slaves in return. In the end, the villagers of the *conquista* paid the bill in forced labor. And to the villagers' sufferings must be added further losses in lives and health by slaves the Luso-Africans could not afford to maintain adequately as they marched their captives toward the coast.

Metropolitan merchants reaped the currency profits that Luso-Africans squeezed from the Africans under their authority in Angola. The economic weaknesses of the eighteenth-century Portuguese domestic economy, passed on out to the empire by heavy taxes and mercantilist monopolies, thus ultimately lay behind the violence and oppressive tactics for which Lisbon officials condemned the Luso-African colonials. The Portuguese empire clearly put Luso-Africans who were within the reach of governors at Luanda at a disadvantage compared to other African transporters in the surrounding regions. Ovimbundu, the Vili, Jinga, Kasanje, and the eastern Kongo, among others, worked longer trails and brought slaves from the same marketplaces as the Luso-Africans while making profits sufficient to

84. António da Silva Rego, *O Ultramar português no século XVIII* (Lisbon: Agência Geral do Ultramar, 1967), advances the notion of a "Luso-African feudalism" to describe related aspects of this phenomenon, though not on the political-diplomatic level on which Beatrix Heintze dismisses the notion, in "Luso-African Feudalism in Angola?" pp. 111–31. The discussion here takes up the economic and social aspects of the concept.

support far-flung trade diasporas, mercantile states, and elites wealthy in European textiles and in followings of slaves. Ordinary villagers seem to have found life under independent African rule enough superior to Luso-African domination in Angola that slaves and nonslaves alike sought refuge outside the *conquista*.

Behind these persistent structural features of eighteenth-century Angolan colonialism, Luso-African economic fortunes also underwent vast changes before 1830, ranging from the successes and failures of individuals to profound alterations in the context within which all traded. New traders arrived and died. Some survived to follow the characteristic career cycle of retreat to the interior, scrambling for commercial success there and eventual return to the coast. The few who prospered sometimes founded prominent Luso-African families, whose members intermarried with other local clans to alter the balance among the obscure factions that divided the community as a whole.

The Luso-Africans as a group gradually converted from autonomous military methods of procuring slaves to commercial dependency on borrowed goods. They first obtained imports by collaborating with colonial governors in the seventeenth century, but after 1730 most of them gradually defected to the credit that merchant capitalists from Lisbon offered. In terms of the Luso-Africans' position within the African political economy, they had transformed themselves, along with the African warlords, from militarists competing to capture slaves beyond the periphery of European commercial capitalism to advance agents carrying merchant credit to the very heart of the continent. Later generations accumulated assets of their own as they enlarged the region within which they traded, but they substituted marital alliances and commercial debt for fighting, except for conflicts that continued to break out between rival African and Luso-African merchant princes.

While the Luso-Africans never escaped from the disadvantages they suffered as borrowers with respect to the world commercial system of which they became a part, the reasons for their losses in the Atlantic economy evolved through time. Each of their failures ironically succeeded from entirely appropriate moves which one generation of Luso-Africans made to protect itself in the short run but which turned in the course of time into liabilities for their children. Low prices for slaves in late-seventeenth-century Brazil reduced trading margins and encouraged Brazilian and Portuguese merchants to leave the slaves in Luso-African hands through the middle passage. The risks inherent in owning slaves at a time of high mortality among the war captives and drought victims who were often shipped early in the eighteenth century allowed this ownership pattern to persist through the Brazilian gold boom of the first third of the eighteenth century, though the high trading profits of that time also enabled Luso-Africans to defend themselves, at least in part, from the first Lisbon merchants using credit to bypass Luso-African slaving networks in the interior dating back to the seventeenth century. But their ownership of slaves on the middle passage turned into an unmitigated liability when Brazilian prices dropped in the 1750s and 1760s. The Luso-Africans then salvaged some of their fortunes by selling slaves to foreigners for commodity currencies, thus preserving expanded networks of trade routes and markets in the interior for themselves but also giving up the access to world currencies that they had once earned by controlling sales of their slaves in the Americas. They thus withdrew from the Atlantic economy at precisely the moment when *réis* credits become crucial to keeping up with advancing modern technology.

Finally, their inability to keep up with escalating European commercial investment at the end of the eighteenth century removed them from the Atlantic economy just when Brazilian slave prices turned back upwards in the 1780s and 1790s. At the same time, the Luso-Africans found their working capital stretched to its limit in the backlands, their operating costs increasing, and themselves in need of further funding from abroad just to maintain contact with increasingly remote sources of the slaves they offered for sale. They thus satisfied rising American demand for slaves only at the cost of abandoning the transatlantic trading gains during the legal trade's last decade or two to buyers and creditors from Brazil.

The final burst of legal slave exports thus brought the Luso-Africans generous credit, improved prices, and increased volume but few assets of much value outside the colony. Successful Luso-African traders then built a glittering but hollow colonial prosperity out of their slaves, marriages, and luxury imports in the final years of slaving, but the autonomous creole culture they created from these materials also isolated them from the sources of credit in Brazil, Portugal, and Britain. The pride these later generations developed in their distinctive "African" ways of living by the nineteenth century may have provided some solace for the fact that they faced the end of the slave trade as parochial anachronisms, supported and encouraged by the same expanding industrial capitalism in the Atlantic economy that was also excluding them as dark-skinned Africans despised in an era of European racism, exploiters of forced labor offensive to liberal freedoms, and seemingly incorrigible slavers virtually created by the age of emancipation.

9

The White Man's Grave

Expatriate Merchants in Luanda

Eighteenth-century Luanda became a city of refuse, up from the very ground on which it sat. The loose sand of its lower parish, the center of the slave trade, had eroded from the Ovimbundu and the Mbundu highlands hundreds of kilometers to the east, drifted as silt down the Kwanza, and built up as the shallow bar that blocked the river's mouth. The Benguela current then swirled the excess north into the long island forming Luanda Bay and the mainland shores where the commercial part of the town squatted. Behind blocks of warehouses lining the waterfront, a line of steep, sandy banks rose toward the more solid upper city on the rocky headland where the city's principal fortress hulked and toward the ridge that supported the governor's palace, the edifices of the ecclesiastical establishment, and the residences of the stable Luso-African sector of the city's populace.

Below these elevated symbols of permanence and stability, the slave trade was all transience and flux. Many of the merchants came and went with hardly more volition of their own than the sand that glided with the currents through the roadstead in the bay or the slaves, leached from their home communities by drought, debt, and war and brought to the town for the sole purpose of leaving it again aboard ships bound for Brazil. The traders often entered as desperate men, driven to Angola to recoup their fortunes after failure elsewhere, sometimes from America and other times from Portugal. They settled temporarily in the commercial quarter of the lower city; then within weeks or months the majority was carried off to the European graveyard on the town's edge, making room for yet another wave of new arrivals. The pervasiveness of death, and the consequently perpetual renewal of the corps of ambitious novices in Luanda's commercial district set the tumultuous style of business in a city that truly merited the sobriquet of the "white man's grave."

A few expatriates survived the fevers and enjoyed sufficient success handling goods and services in the town to leave for Brazil after a few years. Many more survivors found that fortune again eluded them at Luanda and headed instead for the backlands to trade for slaves or, still unable to succeed even there, to cast their lot with the Africans. Only a Luso-African minority and their slaves accepted Luanda as their home. To nearly everyone else it was a place where every variety of flotsam and jetsam from three continents washed up on the shore, including not only people but also merchandise, spoiled wines, bad rum, flimsy textiles, faulty guns, and other goods unsalable elsewhere in the world but sent to Angola for dumping on African markets. The stench of decay and death was everywhere. Only the fortunate left alive. The Africans departed below decks to the Americas, however unwillingly, so that some Europeans could afford to follow them later, above board and in the comfort to which they aspired.

During the eighteenth century, Luanda lost its flavor as an African city where passing ship captains and supercargoes loaded captives belonging to Luso-African slavers, agents of the clans dominant in the colony's interior. It became a more heterogeneous entrepôt, with an influential community of immigrant traders who supervised the European commercial capital that swelled the arteries of trade and slavery inland. At first these Portuguese came to Angola mostly as factors for Lisbon merchant houses primarily to sell textiles, Portuguese foods and crafts, and northern European manufactures. Though in the course of the eighteenth century they represented different and even opposed interests in Lisbon—merchants fronting for British capital, tax farmers chartered by the Portuguese Crown, national traders with connections in Asia, and others—they all functioned similarly at Luanda in relation to the Luso-Africans and the trade in slaves. Their direct line back to the center of the Portuguese imperial economy meant that they aimed to accumulate profits in forms valuable there: specie, the Brazilian *cruzado* gold coin or the Spanish silver *pataca,* or a currency of account like *réis* (the Portuguese "crown," or *real* in the singular) readily convertible to silver and gold. They had few uses for large numbers of slaves in their own business operations and no particular expertise in their management. Excessive ownership of human capital they in fact avoided as an undesirably risky form of investment. They therefore seldom themselves bought or sold the captive Africans passing through the city, except for a few individuals, often trained servants, acquired from time to time for specialized purposes.

Lisbon's agents in Luanda made their profits instead from high margins claimed on the goods they imported and sold to Luso-Africans for distribution through the interior. Secondarily they also charged fees for servicing the ships anchored in the harbor, took commissions for handling the slaves Luso-Africans sent to Brazil, and manipulated credit extended to associates and competitors less well capitalized than themselves. With hollow pride, they distinguished themselves from the uncultivated and dusky colonists who actually owned slaves, whom they despised as businessmen of a less reputable class, even while they maintained the stinking slave pens of the lower city and suburbs filled with captives awaiting embarkation or death.

Though reverses might force some to join the Luso-Africans who were buying slaves in the interior, those who managed to remain part of the expatriate group in Luanda had a strong position as lenders from the Atlantic economy rather than borrowers in Africa, as owners of merchandise and of debt rather than of slaves. Their efforts to change the organization of business at Luanda from a slave trade, where Brazilian buyers and Luso-African sellers competed for gain by selling labor in Brazil, to a conduit through which metropolitan merchants pushed trade goods and credit into Africa animated much of the political and economic history of the city between 1730 and 1830, just as it drove the struggles between the Luso-Africans of the interior and the importers' agents in Luanda. The rapaciousness with which they nonetheless attempted to make their killing and flee the city lent little charm to the short, nasty, and brutish existence that awaited most people, European and African alike, in western central Africa's largest slaving port.

Failure and Success

From the point of view of merchants in Portugal or Brazil, Luanda lay both at the end of a long road leading to failure and at the beginning of the shortcut back to success. It was a place to make money fast and then decamp for pleasanter and less perilous surroundings. In either case, life there was an unpleasant experience that some had to endure temporarily, a commercial purgatory to which past follies condemned them, in the hope of making it also the gateway to an Eldorado for the ambitious and aggressive few who might lay the foundations of a more respectable career elsewhere. As one Portuguese critic of the narrow and self-interested behavior of most merchants in Luanda observed:

> We (here in Luanda) live in a country most unsuited to our nature. We are disturbed by the threat to life brought by continual and devastating diseases, and we become wanton with our sights set on the Fatherland, to which we do not expect to return as poor as we left it. The absence of more gratifying pleasures turns us to the love of money, which we still cannot acquire in quantities sufficient for the great expenses that we must here sustain, especially with the European imports on which we depend, and particularly with the drugs and physics of which we are in daily need. If this sole object of our desires did not quiet our spirits, we would be men worth nothing. Indolence would possess us, and misery would overwhelm

our lives, because our wages and salaries come to only a small part of what it costs us to live.[1]

Accordingly, few immigrant Portuguese came to Luanda under anything but conditions amounting to duress. Many who later became prominent businessmen in the city first arrived in the fetters of exiled criminals. Others landed as merchants intending to recoup business reverses elsewhere. Some must have chosen to come to Luanda because they knew that its free-wheeling atmosphere would reward unscrupulous styles of conducting commerce that they had perfected in more constraining environments.

The careers of some of eighteenth-century Luanda's best-known merchants epitomized this cycle of failure and success. To take only one example, Francisco Honorato da Costa—the famous director of the slave market in Kasanje at the end of the century and the trader responsible for sending two slaves through Lunda to Mozambique in the first recorded transcontinental journey under European sponsorship—first set foot in Angola in 1777 as a junior factor for the Lisbon-based, government-chartered Companhia Geral de Pernambuco e Paraíba (Pernambuco Company).[2] He supervised the conclusion of the Pernambuco Company's unsuccessful ventures into Luanda, allegedly contributing to its failure by converting company assets to personal gain in the process, and then moved east to Kasanje in 1794 to restore the sagging fortunes of a private partnership he had formed locally with António José da Costa, one of Angola's most notorious plunderers of the 1780s and 1790s.

In Kasanje, Honorato da Costa failed again. He became director of the government marketplace in the Kwango valley, but his direction of the trading fair concluded with its withdrawal from the valley and its repositioning on the eastern margins of the Portuguese *conquista* in Pungo Andongo. He had to abandon that site also in 1815 under attack from the armies of the Mbailundu kingdom, which was assaulting Portuguese positions from Benguela to Ambaca at that time. He derived his later repute primarily from the achievement of two of his slave *pombeiros* in finding their way across the continent to Mozambique through the African commercial trails of the remote interior—a deed for which he could claim little personal credit. Though Honorato da Costa otherwise earned few returns for his backers in Luanda and Lisbon and died owing substantial sums to his original employers, the Pernambuco Company, in Angola he was lionized with military honors and spent his last years secure in possession of land and slaves in the backlands of Luanda.[3]

1. João Victo da Silva, report, n.d. (ca. 1792), AHU, Angola cx. 42.
2. See F. Bontinck, "Voyage des pombeiros," for the most recent commentary and full bibliography on the *pombeiros.*
3. Records of the Companhia Geral de Pernambuco e Paraíba, livro 125 (Copiador de Angola), letters of 3 Sept. 1777, 30 June 1783, 3 April 1784, 21 July 1786, and 15 May

In the manner typical of "failures" by metropolitan standards, Francisco Honorato da Costa had prospered in the commerce of Angola.[4] His career followed the pattern standard for immigrants beset by frustrated efforts to get rich quick in Luanda. Pressed by his creditors in the city and threatened there with prosecution under metropolitan law, he reestablished himself in the backlands, where his unorthodox ways of conducting his affairs could not be hindered by Portuguese judicial proceedings. There his methods evidently produced more bountiful fruit than they had in the more conventional environment of the city. Earlier in the century, merchants who had defaulted on royal contracts elsewhere in the empire provided other examples of the same pattern: they sometimes went to Angola to buy slaves, with whom they hoped to make profits sufficient to restore their credit with the Crown.[5]

In another earlier instance of this repeated tale of European rags to Angolan riches, Francisco Roque Souto, hailed in some circles for opening the trail to Holo in the Kwango valley in the 1730s and eventually a *capitão-mor* in Pungo Andongo, came to Luanda as captain of a ship. He suffered business reverses in the town and left immediately for the backlands, first to Kisama, where he gained the affections of a wife of the lord of the region. He then began buying slaves in areas farther east, evidently avoiding trails frequented by representatives of merchants from Luanda, no doubt because he owed them money. He thus found his way to Holo, a very peripheral market at the time. He eluded his creditors whenever he returned to the city by taking refuge in churches and soon accumulated profits sufficient to repay what he owed. Then he went on to become an influential trader in his own right, living among the Luso-Africans of Pungo Andongo.[6]

1789, in AHMF; *procuração* (Francisco Honorato da Costa), enclosed in de Mello, 30 May 1801, AHU, Angola cx. 51; Almeida e Vasconcelos, order of 27 June 1794, AHA, cód. 273, fol. 139; Almeida e Vasconcelos to Joaquim Jozé da Silva, 6 Dec. 1794, AHA, cód. 87, fols. 229–32; *certidão*, of a *provisão* of the Junta da Real Fazenda, 1 May 1789, AHU, Angola cx. 41; *Capitão-mor* of Pungo Andongo to Oliveira Barboza, 24 May 1815, AHA, cód. 3058, fols. 69–70; *requerimento* from Joaquim Correia Pinto, n.d. (ca. 1812), AHU, Angola cx. 61; *consulta* of the Junta da Liquidação das Companhias Pombalinas, 13 Aug. 1829, AHU, Angola maço 12–B. For correctives to some modern historiography, which has greatly magnified Honorato da Costa's stature, see Vellut, "Notes sur le Lunda," pp. 99–110, and Bontinck, "Voyage des pombeiros."

4. See also the career of Bernardo Nunes Portella, who came to Luanda under the pressures of debt in Lisbon, married into the Luso-African establishment, and attempted to steal the assets of both his local wife and her family in Angola and of his correspondents in Portugal: numerous documents enclosed in Almeida e Vasconcelos, 11 Feb. 1795, AHU, Angola cx. 44; *requerimento* of Anna Luiza de Araujo, n.d. (after 1791), AHU, Angola maço 5.

5. *Requerimento* of Antonio Marques Gomes, n.d. (ca. 1735), AHU, Angola cx. 20.

6. Magalhães, 24 Sept. 1739, AHU, Angola cx. 21; *requerimento* of Capitão-Mor Francisco Roque Souto, n.d. (ca. 1745), AHU, Angola cx. 23; Magalhães, 17 July 1744,

Traders willing to take the risks implied by ownership of slaves, which more conventional merchants wryly likened to a game of chance rather than a business,[7] and hardy and lucky enough to survive to undertake the hazards of the backlands, could reap considerable rewards. Stories circulated of convicts who arrived condemned to penal labor and left Luanda with hundreds of thousands of *cruzados* to their names.[8] To be sure, such tales thrived because they expressed a hope rather than a reality for most, but they also contained an element of truth. Certainly, reputable merchants also came to Angola and remained in Luanda pursuing respectable and uneventfully prosperous careers wholesaling imports,[9] but the legendary immigrant merchants characteristically found success in buying and owning slaves, if only after business setbacks forced them out of selling goods.[10] Still, if the most flourishing of the immigrants retired to affluence and dignity in Brazil, the majority undoubtedly died penniless in Angola, victims of the diseases that slaughtered newcomers, assassinated by competitors they provoked in the marketplaces of the interior, murdered by bandits along the trails, or executed by African lords whom they offended in their heedless quests for slaves.

Marriages of Convenience

Although the immigrant traders kept Luanda oriented out toward the Atlantic, the city also remained a center of the Luso-African community, to judge from the disgust of metropolitan-oriented governors at the lingering African tone of social and domestic life there in the later eighteenth century. One may reconstruct something of the colonial splendor in which

---

AHU, Angola cx. 23, which shows Roque Souto last as *capitão-mor* at Caconda in the central highlands.

7. A *jogo de parar*, i.e., a lottery or a roulette wheel: e.g., Sebastião Xavier Botelho, *Escravatura: benefícios qũe podem provir ás nossas possessões d'Africa da prohibição daquelle tráfico* . . . (Lisbon: Typographia de José B. Morando, 1840), pp. 22–23.

8. Moçâmedes, 25 May 1787, AHU, Angola maço 4–B (cont.); Oliveira Barboza, 15 July 1811, AHU, Angola cx. 59. The implicit standard of wealth was roughly the value of a modest-sized ship's cargo of slaves.

9. Or if daring, only discreetly so. One example is Capt. João Xavier Proença e Sylva, whose correspondence is in BNL, Coleção Pombalina, cód. 617; his activities are mentioned in Klein, *Middle Passage*, pp. 38–40. The *requerimento* of José Severino de Sousa, n.d. (ca. 1819–20?), AHU, Angola maço 1–A, shows him to have been of similar respectability. Slightly earlier, António Coelho Guerreiro also conducted business without substantial dealings in slaves; see Rau, *"Livro de Razão,"* and Miller, "Capitalism and Slaving."

10. *Requerimento* of Domingos Dias da Silva (holder of the slave duty contract for Angola), with José Alz. Bandeira e Cia, n.d. (ca. 1772), AHU, Angola cx. 36, containing an "Instrução em q mostra a formalidade do Commercio do Reino de Angola, e Benguella . . . ," 7 Jan. 1772, re: Manoel José Esteves; also José Vieira de Araujo, who owed a debt in Pernambuco.

traders lived in Luanda at the peaks of their careers. These Luso-African families set the pace particularly in the earlier years of the eighteenth century, when they still clung to their historic base in the city. But Luso-Africans no longer controlled its external commerce from the 1740s onward. By mid-century the urban and ecclesiastical geography of the town accordingly reflected its division into two contrasting parts, one immigrant, bourgeois, and commercial, and the other Luso-African, genteel, landed, religious, and native. Demographic and economic differences between the town's original two Catholic parishes, that of Nossa Senhora dos Remédios (Our Lady of Mercies) and the other that of the diocese, or Sé, captured something of this contrast.[11] Geographically the Remédios parish lay in the lower town near the port, and it contained the commercial district with its large merchant houses and related service enterprises. Immigrant Portuguese and Brazilians dominated life in that quarter of the city, running most of the greatest trading houses and accounting for more than two-thirds of the substantial traders residing there in 1760.[12]

The Luso-Africans set the tone for the upper town, the Sé parish, laid out above the lower commercial district on the ridge that ran back from the headland occupied by the city's principal fortress. This upper city contained the governor's palace and other government offices in addition to the cathedral, the bishop's residence, and—until 1759—the Jesuit college. But its family heads and householders were principally military men of Luso-African background and local people living from their investments in land and slaves. A few retired Portuguese and immigrant professionals in the arts, letters, and sciences also lived there—physicians, the town's only lawyer, scribes, and so on—all secluded from the hustle and bustle of the business district below. The upper city was decidedly quieter in tone, more settled, and much more Angolan than the cosmopolitan lower parish.[13] And just as the two parishes together formed the town, the relationships between the two communities residing in each, Luso-African and expatriate, jointly linked the separate economies of Africa and the Atlantic through the complementing trades in goods and slaves in which each engaged.

The key relationship in Luanda, as in the interior, was the commercial marriage, always between a male European trader and a Luso-African woman, a sister or a daughter of the slaving families in the interior. When

11. Cf. Ilídio do Amaral, *Luanda (estudo de geografia urbana)* (Lisbon: Junta de Investigações do Ultramar, 1968); idem, "Descrição da Luanda oitocentista, vista através de uma planta do ano de 1755," *Garcia de Orta* 9, no. 3 (1961): 409–20; Venâncio, "Espaço e dinâmica populacional em Luanda," pp. 67–89; Corrêa, *História de Angola*.
12. List of Luanda residents (*moradores*), in Vasconcelos, 22 May 1760, AHU, Angola cx. 28.
13. Venâncio, in "Espaço e dinâmica populacional em Luanda" and "Economia de Luanda," adds a great amount of useful detail in support of the basic distinction.

the immigrant traders died, as they frequently did, these marital linkages with creole families left wealthy Luso-African widows, most of whom lived in eighteenth-century Luanda's upper town.[14] The high death rates and transience of the immigrant Portuguese left these women classed officially as spinsters or widows in the eyes of royal administrators, who counted by standards derived from sacraments of the Portuguese Catholic church. In practice, such females would have entered into a series of informal, presumably intimate liaisons with European merchants, military officers, and royal officials whom the records acknowledged only as men *casados na terra* ("married by local custom"). Creole trading families would give a female relative in marriage to the Portuguese merchant through whom they bought their imported trade goods and through whom they sent their slaves to Brazil. The marriage formalized and added stability to a commercial relationship between two parties otherwise strangers, in a way not uncommon anywhere in the Portuguese empire of the time.[15] It also provided an alternative source of working capital to impecunious beginning immigrant traders, one not necessarily repayable in the *réis*-credits they hoped would one day allow them to escape from Luanda.

The advantages of this relationship for the immigrant husbands clearly included business contacts, since they derived sexual services, and perhaps also affection in some cases, from the large numbers of female slaves they

14. For a direct reference to these wealthy widows, Sousa Coutinho, 15 March 1770, AHU, Angola cx. 32. For references to marriages by immigrant males, Pereira da Costa, 8 June 1725, AHU, Angola cx. 16; ANTT, Ministério do Reino, maço 499, census figures on "casado na terra" ("locally married," implying a union not blessed by the Catholic church), the case of Fernando Martins do Amaral, 1740s; case of José da Costa Faria, in Almeida e Vasconcelos, 15 March 1799, AHU, Angola cx. 28. There are dozens of other traces of this pattern in the records. For later women of the same sort in Luanda, Mário António Fernandes de Oliveira, *Alguns aspectos da administração de Angola em época de reformas (1834–1851)* (Lisbon: Universidade Nova de Lisboa, 1981), pp. 16, 36 ff.; Dias, "Questão de identidade," p. 65.

15. George Brooks, "The *Signares* of Saint-Louis and Gorée: Women Entrepreneurs in Eighteenth-Century Senegal," in Nancy J. Hafkin and Edna G. Bay, eds., *Women in Africa: Studies In Social and Economic Change* (Stanford: Stanford University Press, 1976), pp. 19–44. For Portuguese Upper Guinea, see Brooks, "A Nhara of the Guinea-Bissau Region: Mãe Aurélia Correa," in Robertson and Klein, *Women and Slavery in Africa,* pp. 295–317. Compare the parallel marriage pattern in Bahia, though with the males surviving longer and with the assets involved concentrated on land rather than slaves and trade goods: Flory, "Bahian Society," pp. 96, 101, 107, 109–12, 229–31; Catherine Lugar, "The Merchant Community of Salvador, Bahia, 1780–1830" (Ph.D. diss., State University of New York, Stony Brook, 1980), pp. 235 et passim. The term in Angola was *sinhá*, equivalent to *nhara*, the word that Portuguese employed on the Upper Guinea Coast: Delgado, *Reino*, p. 375. Both derived from Portuguese *senhora*, or "lady."

Gwyn R. Campbell, "The Role of the London Missionary Society in the Rise of the Merina Empire, 1810–1861" (Ph.D. diss., University College, Swansea, 1985), p. 79, describes exactly the same marital arrangements prevailing in nineteenth-century Madagascar. He specifies further that small traders needing links into a local firm to establish a foothold would enter into such marriages, while wealthier traders could afford to hire professional traders (i.e., the sons of such women).

kept as concubines.[16] Portuguese males also sometimes abused their marriages into the local Luso-African community by using them to establish legal pretexts for seizure of the assets that their wives brought into the marriage.[17] In at least two recorded instances Luso-African widows fought back through the royal courts to prevent Lisbon business associates and creditors of their deceased immigrant husbands from raiding estates they had been left.[18] Given the widespread metropolitan credit extended through Luso-African families and the wealth these women personally accumulated, Lisbon business interests probably tried to seize the widow's property to replace debts they could not otherwise collect from the interior, though perceiving the situation as one in which colonial relatives failed to repay sums they had borrowed from the deceased husband, brother-in-law, and trader.

These wealthy female partners—conjugal and commercial—were often key personages on the European flank of the core Luso-African group as a whole. The 1773 census of the town noted sixteen "white" and five *mulatta* (i.e., racially mixed) women owning up to seventeen slaves each in the Luso-African Sé parish. The racial distinctions carefully recorded in this census certainly reflected wealth and local prestige more than the physical features of these women, since almost no European "white" women of any sort, and none at all of means, ventured out to Angola at that time.[19] The women designated "white" in the census were therefore probably the influential daughters of Luso-African families evident in other sources, whose wealth lightened their social and legal complexions no less than in Brazil, where, as is well known, "money whitened." In the Sé parish these twenty-one wealthy women owned nearly seven out of every ten slaves listed in the enumeration (93 slaves, or 68.3%), even though these mistresses numbered less than a third (32.3%) of the population in the economically privileged categories of "white" and "mixed." Their ownership of these slaves in their own names adds to the impression that they had acted, in their roles as wives, as business intermediaries between their local kinsmen and the immigrant Portuguese commercial and official communities.

16. E.g., Vasconcelos, 22 May 1760, AHU, Angola cx. 28; de Mello, 25 Aug. 1801, AHU, Angola cx. 50.

17. De Mello, 25 Aug. 1801, AHU, Angola cx. 50.

18. De Mello, 21 Oct. 1801, AHU, Angola cx. 50; also see the *requerimento* of Maria da Conceição Simões, n.d. (but ca. 1767), AHU, Angola maço 1.

19. Sousa Coutinho comments to this effect: 26 Nov. 1772, AHU, Angola cx. 36. For the women sent as *degradados,* see Amaral, *Luanda,* p. 49. The census is the "Mapa de todos os moradores, e habitantes deste reino de Angola . . . tirado no fim do anno de 1778 . . . ," enclosed in Lencastre, 26 June 1779, AHU, Angola cx. 37. For similar "whitening" of wealthy *signares* in Senegambia, see Brooks, "*Signares* of St. Louis and Gorée."

Even more of these slave-owning women had lived in the lower city in 1773, presumably residing with merchant spouses in houses that contained active business establishments. The forty-eight of them in the Remédios parish were more or less evenly divided between the "white" and *parda* ("mixed") racial categories of the census. Reflecting the commercial district's more metropolitan population, including much larger numbers of transient males and the big immigrant merchants' holdings of commercially employed slaves, they accounted for a smaller proportion of the people listed in their respective racial groups (14.8%) and owned fewer of the slaves (20.8%) than in the upper town, though still disproportionately large percentages. Nonetheless, their affluence as a group stands out clearly in the 1773 census, since every female honored by a listing in the roll of town residents owned slaves, while only half (48.7%) of the "white" males and hardly more than a quarter (25.3%) of the "mulatto" males possessed them. The female slave owners held an average of 3.7 slaves per woman, while the men of the Remédios parish had 5.8 slaves per owner (or 2.4 slaves per person, for all males).

These Luso-African businesswomen may be presumed to have maintained a discreet prominence in the public life of the city's commercial district. They generally remained secluded in the upper level of the imposing two-story dwellings they shared with their merchant spouses and ventured into the streets only in elegant closed litters (*tipoias,* or palenquins), surrounded by numerous and elaborately liveried entourages of the slaves recorded in the census, veiled and wrapped in expensive fabrics, to attend religious services in the churches.[20] Presumably those who retired from the commercial world when their last husband died moved up on the hill to live among their Luso-African kin as dowagers in the Sé parish. Their larger holdings of slaves reflected their long and successful careers.

The documents leave the impression that such women became more influential in the course of the eighteenth century. Their increasing stature surely reflected not only their personal abilities as entrepreneurs but also the withdrawal of the Luso-African menfolk into the interior and the increased opportunities for commercial marriages derived from expanded use of the credit that their husbands and male kinsmen employed in the Angolan slave trade from the 1730s onwards. Local women emerged from seclusion in the 1740s to become major owners of slaves in the 1760s. By the 1770s, they were taking assertive positions before the imperial courts, and a few established themselves in landownership and stock raising by

20. *Parecer* of the Conselho Ultramarino (Lisbon), 12 May 1741, AHU, Angola cx. 22; Peçanha, 20 March 1784, AHU, Angola cx. 39; Corrêa, *História de Angola,* 1:52; Castelobranco, 26 Aug. 1829, AHU, Angola cx. 73. Cf. Amaral, *Luanda,* pp. 47–48.

1812.[21] At least one such woman became a commercial power in her own
right in the colony's interior by the middle of the nineteenth century.[22]
As Luso-African traders in Luanda and its hinterland became dependent
on loans from immigrant merchants, these traders would have offered their
sisters, nieces, and daughters to consolidate their business relationships
with the European bearers of the new wealth, and some of these women
prospered accordingly.

On the other end of the series of exchanges of women and credits,
Luso-African traders in the interior also offered the goods they borrowed
to noble African families in the states where they traded, taking women
from them as wives in return. Typically for the interface of the Atlantic
and African political economies, the set of commercial practices created
coastward flows of people moving in the direction opposite to the incoming current of goods and credit. In this case, aristocratic African and Luso-
African clans gave women as wives as well as supplying dependent males
as slaves. As the Luso-African financial structure shifted toward their expanded trade networks in the interior, and as resident male traders tended
to evacuate Luanda in the late eighteenth century, leaving the trade in the
hands of itinerant ship's factors, an economic space opened on the mainland that allowed more of these women to replace the departed men as
recognized traders in their own rights. Commercialization of the slave
trade eroded the immigrant male shell of the Luso-African community to
expose the Angolan-born women at its heart.

The wealthy Luso-African minority in Luanda affected an aristocratic
style of living, putting a highly visible portion of their profits into luxury
imports—fine silks, velvets, and other costly textiles, as well as silver fur-
nishings for their houses, for the churches of the town, and for ornate
decorations on their tombstones.[23] Nothing could have expressed the Luso-
Africans' fundamental orientation to the African political economy more

21. Though the marriage pattern dated from early in the seventeenth century in Angola,
at the very least; according to Cadornega, *História geral*, 3:382–83, "Here where the child
is colored, and the grandchild almost black, and the great-grandchild completely so." Delgado,
Reino, pp. 79–80, and Boxer, *Portuguese Society in the Tropics*, p. 128, refer to these marriages.
For cattle and land in the early nineteenth century, Oliveira Barboza, 15 Feb. 1812, AHU,
Angola cx. 61.

22. I.e., Dona Ana Joaquina dos Santos e Silva: see Dias, preface to Fernandes de
Oliveira, *Alguns aspectos*, p. 16. Also Tams, *Visit to the Portuguese Possessions*, 1:116; Fernandes
de Oliveira, *Alguns aspectos*, pp. 36 ff.

23. E.g., Magalhães, 29 April 1738, AHU, Angola cx. 22, for complaints about ostentatious fabrics and silver that he regarded as tasteless and pretentious, though already beyond
the means of the Luso-Africans to afford at that time. A *parecer* of the Conselho Ultramarino
(Lisbon), 12 May 1741, AHU, Angola cx. 22, mentions a mausoleum lined with silver by
the son of the Matthozo (de Andrade?) family, almost certainly one of the early and wealthy
Luso-African lineages of the town. For houses, Dionisio da Piacenza (1667–68), quoted in
Taunay, *Subsídios*, p. 135. De Mello, 11 Oct. 1797, AHU, Angola cx. 44, refers to hoards
of worked silver, evidently from melted-down coins.

clearly than this sacrifice of the monetary metal of the Atlantic economy
to their Angolan ancestors. Still more, they invested in the large slave
retinues that visitors to the city noted in the late seventeenth and early
eighteenth centuries. If individual ambition and affectation encouraged
ostentatious expenditures, the dependence of the trade on credit extended
only in the form of imported goods and the difficulty of transferring assets
out of Angola also intensified Luso-African displays of consumer luxury
in Luanda. Luso-Africans generally found it easier to arrange deliveries of
material indulgences in Angola than to accumulate more substantial forms
of wealth of their own in Brazil. Their evident treatment of goods as
wealth reflected their roots in African trading economies based on commodity currencies and slaves.

Aside from frenetically conspicuous consumption, the Luso-Africans
also invested in colonial real estate. Large multistoried townhouses known
as *sobrados* became virtual symbols of local aristocratic pretensions at Luanda.
Some Luso-Africans lived with their families on the second stories of the
sobrados in the upper part of the city, where large balconied windows
opened on the sea and brought a measure of comfort and, it was fondly
but vainly assumed, also of health from onshore daytime breezes that
lessened the oppressiveness of the humidity. The *sobrados* in the lower
commercial district of the town housed merchants, mostly immigrants but
surely also a few established local traders. The ground floors of these
structures contained storehouses for goods and the business chambers
where proprietors met with ship captains, merchant associates, government
functionaries, and cronies to supervise distribution of the merchandise
they stocked. These public rooms opened onto the hot sandy street in
front and perhaps onto a slave pen on the side or in the back. Gradually
in the course of the eighteenth century, immigrant merchants from Lisbon
or Brazil displaced the Luso-Africans from these quarters in the lower
town, retaining only the sisters of the Luso-Africans as wives and perhaps
their younger bilingual nephews as junior clerks in charge of dealings with
the street—procuring day-to-day services, managing the trade slaves, supervising trained *ladino* slaves who rolled casks and toted bales, and negotiating directly with Kimbundu- and Kikongo-speaking customers and
agents who took the merchandise into the interior and brought captives
back down to the city.

Conduct of Business in Luanda: The "School for Thieves"

Immigrant traders in Luanda before the 1770s essentially sold Asian cloths
and the manufactures of northern Europe belonging to trading houses in
Portugal to Luso-Africans, who carried them on to the markets of the

Angolan interior.[24] They were factors, *commissários,* who took goods on consignment from owners in the metropole and earned commissions on the value of the merchandise and slaves they handled or who simply worked for an annual salary. In addition, expatriate traders in Luanda found it useful to develop contacts with the Brazilian merchants and ship captains who supplied Angolan ports with casks of the *gerebita* cane brandy vital to the trade and, from time to time, also with construction timber, marine supplies, and other necessities of American origin.[25] Early in the eighteenth century, these Brazilian products arrived in substantial part in the charge of captains and supercargoes empowered to sell them on the spot, for immediate payment in slaves or other assets on hand.[26] By the 1770s and after, Brazilian merchants and planters seem to have replaced their itinerant agents with resident factors in Luanda, and some of these Brazilians became rich and prominent enough to take over the Lisbon traders' leadership role among Luanda's immigrant merchants.

Locally, the immigrant traders, whatever their external connections, also had to establish working relationships with the Luso-African traders of the interior, including hard-up characters of all sorts ranging from convicts to sailors who had jumped ship, soldiers who had defected from the colonial army, and former competitors on their way to the interior to recover from a run of adverse luck in the city. A secondary urban distribution network in Luanda also put them in touch with the city's legions of tavern keepers and other petty retail traders, also probably on credit. The imports the Luanda factors thus merchandised indicated their position at the juncture of distinct mercantile structures based on three continents, Europe, America, and Africa.

The Luso-African merchants at Luanda performed the important commercial function of assorting the exact qualities of textiles, the precise colors and sizes of beads, and the proper proportions of Asian textiles, Flemish knives, salt, and Brazilian *gerebita* that would enable them to buy slaves efficiently in the various trading sites of the interior. Since at Luanda, as elsewhere along the coast, no single importer was likely to provide the entire range of items that had become essential components of the *banzos* actually exchanged for slaves in the eighteenth century, Luso-African traders had to buy from many sources. From some Lisbon agents they obtained goods from northern Europe—German linens, English woolens, and knives—while

24. The characterization of Luanda as a "school for thieves" was that of Governor Sousa Coutinho, 28 Nov. 1764, AHU, Angola cx. 30.
25. On imports, Miller, "Imports at Luanda," esp. app. 1. Also for wood, Francisco Miguel Ayres, 30 April 1759, AHU, Angola maço 3 (D.O.), and Venâncio, "Economia de Luanda," pp. 139–41.
26. See correspondence of the Pernambuco Company, AHMF, livro 126, passim; also Dias da Silva "Instrução," n.d. (ca. 1772), AHU, Angola cx. 36.

other Portuguese traders offered mainly cotton textiles from Portuguese India. Neither of these was likely to provide rum, and perhaps also sugar, from Brazil, without which no one could expect to buy top-quality slaves. Brazilian ships, in turn, could not land fashionable European or Asian wares at prices competitive with ships direct from Portugal. Both American and European suppliers lacked the items of African origin that also comprised vital portions of every *banzo* sent to the interior—salt from Benguela or from the Kakwako salt flats near the town, raffia cloth from Kongo or the Loango Coast, and dried and salted fish from the seas near Luanda.

For these last purposes Luso-African traders therefore committed some of their wealth to working capital in the local service and supply operations necessary to support their principal function of assembling assortments of goods and bringing slaves back from the interior. One important sector of this commerce was the coastal canoe trade that linked the city with other bays and river mouths both south and north of the city. Slaves came from these outlying points, often in substantial numbers. A significant branch of this trade made the passage from Luanda Bay up to the Kwanza, worked its way across the dangerous bar at the mouth of the river with the aid of African pilots who lived on the shore there, and continued on to the forts and trading settlements along the lower river as far upstream as Massangano or Dondo. Another connected the city to food plantations along the lower Bengo and to other sources of slaves from the upper reaches of the river.

For the most successful of the Luso-Africans trading in the lower town, the death of some immigrant partner in a Luanda firm importing goods from Europe, a misfortune common enough, would enable him to take over as proprietor of an import-export business tied solidly into the imperial side of the economy. The former despised exile then became a prominent and respected trader in direct touch with backers in Lisbon and perhaps a confidant to the governor, no longer buying goods with credit from others and selling slaves of his own but increasingly supplying other slavers with goods on his account and dispatching human cargoes to Brazil for them. The greater the success, as a rule, the greater the trader's remove from direct ownership of slaves. Further gains led to partnerships with exporting firms in Brazil, relocation to one American seaport or another, and from there conceivably even to retirement in Lisbon or to a landed property somewhere in Portugal.

The expatriate factors sent the outbound slaves off through a network of commercial correspondents focused on Brazil rather than Portugal. They received slaves from the Luso-Africans and backwoodsmen, or from agents whom slavers in the interior sent to Luanda to deliver chains of captives. The Lisbon agents supervised the slaves from their arrival in the city until embarkation of the survivors on ships waiting in the harbor.²⁷ Maintenance of the slaves brought these agents into uneasy contact with the local and coastal traders of the city and its environs, mostly Luso-Africans. In addition to their slaving, they provisioned the ships and barracoons with salt from Benguela; fish from the seas beyond the bay; flour, beans, and other victuals from the plantations along the Bengo and Kwanza banks; and drinking water from the lower Bengo necessary to support the slaves during the middle passage.

Meanwhile traders carefully cultivated the Brazilian captains in command of most of the ships in the harbor to drum up business as ship chandlers. They simultaneously made arrangements for the thousand-and-one minor goods and services required to prepare other vessels sent by their employers in Europe for setting out to sea. Finally, they maintained relationships with the merchants in Bahia, Pernambuco, and Rio de Janeiro, to whose further care they entrusted the slaves in Brazil and through whose agency they would attempt to collect payment for services they had provided in Angola and to obtain the Brazilian goods they needed more cheaply than they could buy them in Angola.

Immigrant traders settled the obligations that Luso-Africans incurred in Angola through their correspondents on the opposite shore of the Atlantic in a series of financial transactions that took several months, if not years, to complete. The process began when a Luso-African associate handling affairs in Luanda for relatives in the interior first bought British woolens, Portuguese leggings and hats, or Indian cotton prints from an agent in charge of a large Lisbon merchant's, or merchant banker's, affairs in the city. These goods, and whatever else the Luso-African required to create assortments of wares needed to bargain for slaves in remote interior marketplaces, he normally bought on credit terms that specified repayment not directly in slaves in Luanda but instead in specie or Portuguese currencies of account. Because coins of the realm never circulated in Angola in amounts adequate to support the trade in slaves,²⁸ and since the colony by and large lacked precious metals of its own, the Angolan slaver had to obligate himself legally to pay in the stipulated form somewhere else.

Under the circumstances, that obligation meant giving payment in personal notes, bills of exchange, or *letras* as they were termed, that con-

27. The accounts of Coelho Guerreiro (1684–92) were archetypal in this respect, as in many others: Miller, "Capitalism and Slaving," esp. pp. 21–23, 24 ff.

28. Taunay, *Subsídios*, p. 135 (citing Dionisio da Piacenza, 1668). Also repeated discussion surrounding the contractual obligation of tax farmers to supply coin and commodity currencies before 1769: e.g., *requerimento* of Manoel Monteyro da Rocha (contractor), n.d. (before 27 Aug. 1733), AHU, Angola maço 19–A. Correspondence in AHTC, livro no. 1 de registo, for the 1770s and later, e.g., Cabral, 1 Sept. 1823, fols. 12–13; de Mello, 11 Oct. 1797, AHU, Angola cx. 44; Castelobranco, 24 Sept. 1824, AHU, Angola cx. 70; Santa Comba Dão, 11 Oct. 1830, AHU, Angola cx. 74; as well as much else.

veyed an appraised valuation of slaves a Luso-African owner planned to ship in the Portuguese imperial unit of account, the *real*. That amount, if not too many slaves died at sea, would be raised by selling the surviving captives in Brazil for currency or coin, with the note ordering the specified sum paid over to the creditor from the proceeds. The appraisal value of individual slaves was based on a standard set for the prime adult male *peça* slave (or "piece") delivered at Luanda. This conventional valuation, though usually reported as the "price" of slaves at Luanda, was not so much a price that varied with short-term scarcity or plenty of either goods or slaves as it was a relatively stable exchange rate between the *réis* and *cruzado* currencies of the Atlantic economy and the corresponding core currency units in the political economies of Africa, slaves. It functioned exactly like the "bundles," "ounces," "bars," and other more or less fixed abstract equivalencies of the same order employed in slaving outside the Portuguese currency zone. It differed from them only in its phrasing in European currency units rather than in the commodity currencies circulating in the African economies.

This *réis-peça* conversion ratio could also be likened to an appraisal used within a European economy to establish the mortgage value of property given as security but having no direct relationship to the market price at which an owner might manage to sell the assets pledged. In effect, Luso-Africans at Luanda "mortgaged" the *réis* value of slaves they would sell in the future in Brazil against textiles they needed in Luanda to buy captives in the African interior. The Lisbon merchant in this sale was thus acting both as seller of goods from the Atlantic economy and as lender of funds in the African economy. The imports functioned as currencies for the Luso-African and enabled him to acquire the slaves he had pledged as security for the loan that supported his purchases.

In a hypothetically typical transaction, the Luso-African at Luanda would buy imports priced in imperial currencies on the understanding that he would pay in bills of exchange, the *letras*, backed by future slaves to be appraised in *réis* in relation to the *peça* standard prevailing at the time of their delivery. He would take the first step toward realizing the *réis* or *cruzados* to pay off his debt by sending his newly bought goods to some marketplace in the interior, having them exchanged there for slaves, and having the slaves brought down to him at Luanda. At that point, his supplier assessed the slaves he presented and accepted his *letra* representing the appraised values of the lot, whether children, aged males, women, or standard *peças,* according to the established conversion ratio. The merchant who had supplied the goods did not take ownership of the slaves themselves but, rather, left them in the name of the Luso-African.

Since the Lisbon importers also controlled much of the shipping space available to send the slaves to Brazil, particularly earlier in the eighteenth century,[29] they were in strong positions to provide safe passage for the slave assets backing the bills of exchange they thus accepted. They might require that the Luso-African allow them to house and feed his slaves in Luanda, attend to the myriad formalities of embarkation, and eventually arrange for their shipment to a Brazilian port of their own choosing, aboard a ship commanded by a captain whom they knew and trusted and with whom they probably also had long-established business connections. Handling and sale of the slaves in Brazil they would consign to relatives or affines in Rio, Bahia, or Pernambuco, who would arrange to receive, care for, and sell the Luso-African's human property. They would also forward the Luso-African's bill of exchange under the care of the same captain who carried the slaves to the Brazilian consignee. Upon the Brazilian merchant's disposal of the slaves, he would first credit the proceeds, in *réis* or specie, to an account he held for the Luso-African. He would conclude the whole series of steps by transferring the value of the bill of exchange to another account he held for the Lisbon merchant, the original owner of the goods sent to Luanda, whose agent in Brazil presented the *letra* for collection.[30] The Luso-African owners, of course, paid fees for all the services that merchants in Luanda and Brazil provided for handling and selling their slaves.

Each party to the transaction derived different advantages from this particular form of settlement. If gains were to be had from selling the surviving slaves in Brazil, they accrued to the Luso-African, but he also bore the equally uncertain risks of mortality. It is also easy to sense the potential losses abroad awaiting Luso-Africans under these arrangements. The ability of a Luso-African debtor to raise the currency value of the *letra* he had given depended absolutely on his slaves' safely traversing thousands of kilometers of ocean toward American markets of which he had little current information. Also, although Angolan slavers paid for the maintenance of the slaves' lives and health, Luso-Africans had little real influence over the circumstances under which captives proceeded toward their eventual owners in Brazil.

The Lisbon merchant, on the other hand, had managed to sell his goods in the remote and cash-short Angolan market for a guaranteed return in *réis,* or gold or silver, in Brazil. The *letra* conveyed a legal first claim against proceeds from the sale of the Luso-African's surviving slaves. The Lisbon merchant had further safeguarded that claim by putting his own

29. See Chapter 15 below. The basic decree regulating the trade (30 March 1684) prohibited Luanda merchants from dispatching more than 400 slaves per year in ships of their own, the capacity of approximately two small (or one average-sized) vessels, out of an annual total of twenty to forty ships leaving the port. Luso-Africans never mounted substantial numbers of ventures of their own.

30. Based on detailed analysis of the accounts of António Coelho Guerreiro, in Miller, "Capitalism and Slaving," and on other aspects of the trade detailed in chapters following.

agents in Brazil in charge of collecting its returns. Most important, he had substituted an absolute value in Brazil for the highly uncertain proceeds that might result from trying to sell the malnourished, badly-cared-for, and sick human beings crowded into aging and filthy vessels at Luanda.

It is easy to imagine how immigrant lenders offering plentiful goods on these easy terms would have driven Luso-African merchants in Luanda out of managing the embarkation of slaves for their relatives in the interior and forced them to specialize only in dispatching imported goods toward the interior. The commercial houses in Luanda's lower town would have divided into two distinct sectors as the eighteenth century progressed, a declining Luso-African one oriented toward selling goods in the interior and receiving slaves in return, and a growing Lisbon-based complement handling the shipping of the slaves to Brazil and owning their value in currencies, though seldom the captives themselves nor the risks of holding them. The resulting separation of slave maintenance from ownership—with the Lisbon expediters protected from slave mortalities by their *letra* claims, payable in *réis* and assessable against all the assets of the creole shipper and collectable through the imperial courts—added considerable room for lethal disregard of the welfare of the human merchandise to all the other hazards the Luso-Africans faced.

If Brazilian prices were high, the sale of their slaves would earn the Luso-Africans revenues sufficient to cover the *réis* value of the goods they had purchased, as well as the commissions, handling fees, taxes, and other costs they paid. And with some good luck, with honest and reliable service from the Brazilian merchants they paid to represent their interests abroad, and with low mortalities among their slaves, they could pay off their debts and still build up the credit balances in Brazil they sought or import luxuries to Luanda. But such favorable combinations of circumstances rarely prevailed in the southern Atlantic from the 1720s on through the 1780s. The ailing and malnourished remnants of slave shipments that reached Brazil in those years often did not equal the value of the bills of exchange that Luso-Africans had committed themselves to cover. Even wealthy Angolan slavers caught in this position had to sell slaves for less than they owed, sustained losses, became bad credit risks, and found themselves squeezed to obtain continued supplies of the trade goods on which their African business depended. They could realize a limited amount of capital to support further imports by drawing down whatever credit balances they had accumulated in Brazil. However, eventually they would have to liquidate their African assets also, mostly by selling off the skilled slaves they had employed in their commercial operations, and retreat farther into the interior. Others who tried to collect on the standing indebtedness that supported their trading connections with African suppliers severed relationships of vital importance to their business and generally drifted back toward the impoverished dependence on Lisbon credit that supported the majority of beginners in the trade.

Insofar as Luanda traders left a record of their multiple commercial relationships, they seem to have cemented them by dealing by preference with people with whom they shared some enduring bond beyond the ephemeral contacts of the marketplace, a pattern typical of both the seventeenth- and eighteenth-century Portuguese empire and the African political economies with which they dealt.[31] Within the Atlantic economy, traders who came voluntarily to Luanda often represented brothers, uncles, and cousins in Lisbon or Brazil.[32] Once in Angola they associated themselves with the African trading sphere by marrying the women of the established creole trading families of Luanda and the interior, hiring the sons of Luso-African families, and forming partnerships with already established merchants of good local connections. If they survived to return to Brazil, they left their Angolan affairs in the charge of these relatives and associates, probably their wives, but perhaps also their sons, who were nephews of the Luso-Africans as well.[33] The merchants of Luanda, as governor after governor complained, were hopelessly divided into hostile factions, undoubtedly expressions of the networks of kin and affines to which they clung to reduce, however slightly, the risks of doing business with strangers separated from them by racial stereotyping, unreliable communications, thousands of kilometers of ocean, or leagues of African forest and savanna they dared not personally enter.

Every successful merchant carefully nurtured the favor of the officials of the colonial government. The Crown's officers in Angola administered a welter of complex and often contradictory regulations that they might invoke at any time against a trader unwise enough to cross the purposes of a governor, chief judge (*ouvidor*), secretary, or customs superintendent. Though governors were formally prohibited from engaging personally in trade, they continued to wield an enormous influence over commerce through their power to authorize the departure of ships, to enforce taxes, and in many other ways. With the slaves dying daily as they awaited

---

31. For merchants elsewhere in the southern Atlantic Portuguese empire, see David Grant Smith, "The Mercantile Class of Portugal and Brazil in the Seventeenth Century: A Socioeconomic Study of the Merchants of Lisbon and Bahia, 1620–1690" (Ph.D. diss., University of Texas, 1975); Flory, "Bahian Society"; Lugar, "Merchant Community"; Luis Lisanti, ed., *Negócios coloniais (uma correspondência comercial do século XVIII)*, 5 vols. (São Paulo: Visão Editorial, 1973); Dauril Alden, "Vicissitudes of Trade in the Portuguese Atlantic Empire during the First Half of the Eighteenth Century: A Review Article," *Americas* 32, no. 2 (1975): 282–91.

32. Lisanti, *Negócios coloniais*. The correspondence of Proença e Sylva (cf. note 9 above) also features references to relatives with whom he traded; also see José Vieira de Araujo, in the Dias da Silva "Instrução," n.d. (ca. 1772), AHU, Angola cx. 36; Saldanha da Gama, 2 Dec. 1807, AHU, Angola cx. 51; Oliveira Barboza, 4 Dec. 1813, AHU, Angola cx. 61.

33. Alexandre José Botelho de Vasconcelos (governor, Benguela), 27 July 1796, AHU, Angola cx. 49; Oliveira Barboza, 15 July 1811, AHU, Angola cx. 49.

permission to board, every minor delay became a possible source of major loss. Many governors probably accepted silent partnerships in the ventures of traders whom they allowed to succeed.[34]

Any of a multitude of minor Luso-African functionaries, jealously and zealously guarding their own perquisites in the name of the king's due, might also impose disastrous delays on the slaves' progress toward the ships. The endless bureaucratic formalities that encumbered the conduct of trade, essential to creditors because they gave contracts a status enforceable in a court of law, each required the assent of a different sinecure-holder who usually knew the decrees defining his function just well enough to discover improper procedures on any occasion on which he might choose to delay or obstruct a transaction.[35] Best of all, traders who could claim key offices and appointments for themselves could use them to hinder the affairs of their competitors. Merchants were well advised to say no ill of anyone and to treat all others with perfect respect, since even the humblest competitor of today could become tomorrow's officeholder, or at least be related to someone who was.

Since the merchants of Luanda were generally there in part because they had proven their incompetence by eighteenth-century mercantile standards, at a time when modern methods of accountancy were only just spreading widely through the empire,[36] bookkeeping in Angola was still more a creative art than a science. Many traders were illiterate, and others kept only the most rudimentary of records. Failing to keep books must also have been an effective method of avoiding taxes, obstructing creditors looking for assets to seize, evading responsibility for losses merchants caused their principals, and skirting the morass of government regulation.[37] Their dealings with the traders of the interior almost never involved them

34. The governor always remained the key "friend in high places"; for the early years of the century, see Pinheiro to Pretto, 28 March 1725, in Lisanti, *Negócios coloniais*, 5:77. The "Instrução" of Dias da Silva, n.d. (ca. 1772), AHU, Angola cx. 36, was explicitly insistent on this point. The governors' involvement in and power over commerce did not disappear despite repeated royal decrees devised after 1720 to remove them from competition with private merchants. In general, see Lencastre, 27 July 1775, AHU, Angola, cx. 36. Vellut, "Relations internationales," p. 86, n. 14, notes that Governor Moçâmedes (1784–90) returned wealthy from Angola in spite of his repeated complaints about the "decadence of trade" there, and in "Notes sur le Lunda," p. 100, Vellut hints that Francisco Honorato da Costa had the financial backing of Governor Almeida e Vasconcelos (1790–97).

35. *Provisão*, 5 Sept. 1770, AHU, Angola cx. 32. References to merchants holding offices are in Oliveira Barboza, 15 July 1811, AHU, Angola cx. 59; da Cunha, 6 April 1754, AHU, Angola maço 18 (D.O.).

36. On accounting in general, Dauril Alden, *Royal Government in Colonial Brazil* (Berkeley and Los Angeles: University of California Press, 1968), pp. 288–94. The trend culminated in the compendious José da Silva Lisboa, *Princípios de direito mercantil e leis de marinha* (Lisbon: Regia Officina Typografia, 1798), and subsequent editions. See, for example, Tratado IV, on *letras de cambio* (bills of exchange). Forthcoming work by William Donovan, of the Johns Hopkins University, may shed further light on the history of Portuguese accounting: personal communication, Dec. 29, 1986.

37. See strategies and accounts attributed to Bernardo Nunes Portela and the general allegations of ignorance in de Mello, 21 Oct. 1801, AHU, Angola cx. 50. See also Sousa

with associates who could read or write, and so most found little profit
in paying scribes to record that side of their business in any detail.[38] Precise
awareness of the profitability of their operations was nonexistent, at least
in modern terms of a percentage return on funds invested. Merchants
calculated instead according to rules of thumb, fond expectations, experience, and how hard their creditors were pressing them.

Since so many died and so many others owed so much, unfounded
optimism often prevailed. Merchants exaggerated their prosperity, counting as "profits" the returns they expected from vast quantities of goods
given out at high nominal prices but on terms of credit that simply piled
up uncollectable debts. One such rule held, for example, that they should
double the prices of the Lisbon goods they sold and should take 60 to
70 percent (roughly two-thirds?) above prime cost for wares they brought
in from Brazil.[39] These illiquid "profits" would dissolve into ruin whenever
their own creditors demanded payment. Most traders' marginal awareness
of the true effects of these practices and the unlikelihood that anyone
would hold them accountable for what they did gave them no reason to
change these habits, and their reliance on rules of thumb believed tried
and true, even if tested only in more controlled commercial environments,
made them wary of adopting changes with results that they had no confidence of predicting.[40]

Making sales at those prices left factors holding nothing more than
the oral pledge of a criminal-turned-backwoods-trader to return with a
specified number of slaves. The loan was expressed in terms of *banzos,* each
banzo theoretically the equivalent of one slave owed, but it was carried on
the merchants' rudimentary books in terms of *réis* values assigned to goods
in Luanda that had no more than hypothetical status in an economy where
imperial currency did not circulate.[41] In the first two-thirds of the eighteenth century, these nominal *réis* prices merely stated a currency value of

---

Coutinho, 3 June 1770, AHU, Angola cx. 32, for confirmation that virtually no one kept
books.
    38. Noronha, 1 Jan. 1804, AHU, Angola cx. 54.
    39. Sousa Coutinho, 17 June 1774, cited in Vellut, "Royaume de Cassange," p. 133,
gave the markup as 100% from Lisbon. A "Calculo dos Effeitos que annualmente sahem de
Loanda e Benguela e da importancia da Fazenda que annualmente deve entrar nos ditos
dous Portos," ca. 1770, AHU, Angola cx. 32, shows 80%; the *parecer* of the Junta do
Comércio (Lisbon), 19 Aug. 1782, ANTT, Junta do Comércio, maço 62, macete 122, says
that the "return" was at least 60%–70% above prime cost; Almeida e Vasconcelos, 23 Jan.
1796, AHU, Angola cx. 44 makes the markup at least 50%. De Mello, 12 Aug. 1798, AHU,
Angola cx. 45, and 22 Dec. 1799, AHU, Angola maço 9, put the figure as 50%, presumably
expressing the percentage from the Luanda perspective, that is, in terms of the sales price
rather than cost.
    40. De Mello, 21 Dec. 1801, AHU, Angola cx. 50; "Requerimento dos commerciantes
de Loanda," 25 Jan. 1804, AHU, Angola maço 1.
    41. At least *réis* values appear by the early nineteenth century: Noronha, 1 Jan. 1804,
AHU, Angola cx. 54.

the goods that merchants thought it safe to lend Luso-Africans in antic-ipation of eventual settlement by selling a slave in Brazil. But the high turnover of merchants at Luanda meant that generations of newcomers repeatedly had to rediscover for themselves what one beleaguered new-comer to the city lamented: "Here the facility with which promises are given is equalled or exceeded by that with which they are broken."[42] Debtors were seldom as accountable in Angola for what they owed as they were in Portugal.

While profits claimed from sales of this sort were confined to the realm of the potential, backwoodsmen disappeared with the goods into the interior, traded for slaves, requested additional goods from the city to complete their assortments, and eventually dispatched whatever slaves they could acquire back to the coast. Those sent honestly to the creditor in Luanda, and surviving the long march, the merchant might then send to Brazil for sale and only then conclude with repayment there of the debt contracted long before in Luanda. But the verbal nature of most of these agreements left creditors' claims with dubious standing before the law,[43] and the claims regularly became impossible to enforce on slave owners hopelessly indebted after periods of low slave prices in Brazil, hidden in the interior, shielded by cooperative *capitães-mores,* or busily engaged in surreptitious deliveries of slaves to Brazilians for rum in Luanda or to British and French outside the city for greater quantities of other goods. It took years, even decades beyond the normal delays to wind up trans-actions predicated on so much credit. Meanwhile, most of a merchant's assets remained frozen in bad debts in the African interior, totally un-realizable as specie.

Yet credit sales were still the only way newcomers could break into the tight networks of established expatriates and their Luso-African affines in Luanda. The high proportion of impoverished recent arrivals in the unstable business district of the town, its "white man's grave," kept up the collective pressure to extend such loans. Even better-connected traders had to follow suit or lose out to more aggressive competitors. These practices produced a typical balance sheet for an immigrant merchant at Luanda, which, if any had cared to draw up an honest one, would have accurately reflected his primary function as a seller of goods by showing assets mostly in an inventory of imported merchandise for sale, and his secondary func-tion as financier of the trade in the form of large debts in the interior.[44]

42. Unsigned copy of letter no. 33 of 2 Nov. 1821, to Francisco de Paula da Silva, ANRJ, cód. 1142.

43. Noronha, 1 Jan. 1804, AHU, Angola cx. 54; also *requerimento* of Boaventura José de Mello, n.d. (ca. 1807), AHU, Angola maço 10 (D.O.).

44. See the *requerimento* of Maria de Conceição Simões, petitioning for a five-year stay of bankruptcy proceedings against the large and "successful" house of her husband, Coronel Thomé da Silva Coutinho (n.d., but minuted 24 Dec. 1767), AHU, Angola maço 1, which

Profits in the form of negotiable currency instruments or specie remained far in the future, if ever, even though the optimistic accounting conventions at Luanda tended to regard these chickens as hatched from the moment the egg was fertilized.

The commission system by which factors nominally earned their livings also encouraged anticipatory accounting. Merchants selling goods on behalf of Lisbon or Brazilian correspondents claimed their principal authorized revenues in commissions calculated on the value of merchandise they advanced. Beyond the invitation inherent in this compensation structure to defend the high prices charged, they collected the bulk of these commissions, 8 percent out of a total of 13 percent (usually in the form of goods from the shipments handled), at the time of making the initial sale. The lesser proportion, 5 percent more, was due at the time of repayment of the loan, half of that upon collection in Brazil, with the other half upon remission of the funds received to the owner of the goods in Portugal.[45] Luanda agents received less for the other services they performed. They earned 6 percent on the value of provisions they bought for captains of ships in the harbor.[46] From the Luso-Africans, or other owners of slaves, they also earned 6 percent on the value of captives they sent to Brazil, whether those captives lived or died.[47] The higher percentages paid for selling goods encouraged the Luanda factors to pursue quick nominal sales through liberal grants of credit, especially since the goods went into the interior mostly at the risk of sponsors in Portugal unable to keep tabs on their factors' excesses.

The traders' tendency to overextend themselves lay at the heart of the basic strategem of commercial competition at Luanda. Rivals used the courts to force indebted competitors into bankruptcy by securing orders for prompt collection on credit arranged under the highly informal terms prevailing in the colony. By pressing claims against a small competitor who found himself momentarily illiquid as a result of overdue loans in the backlands, a large merchant could induce a judge to award the assets

---

put 64.2% of the assets as inventory but wrote off bad debts in the backlands estimated at twice the remaining physical assets of the estate. A later estate inventory, of José Joaquim da Silva Braga, ANRJ, cód. 388, pac. 2, who died in Luanda in 1809, shows both the larger holdings of slaves typical of the early nineteenth century (33.3% of the assets) but also the outstanding debts characteristic of the trade throughout its history (46.0%). Silva Braga held only 2.2% of his wealth in specie and had 18.5% of it in inventory and personal effects.

45. Assuming that the Pernambuco Company followed procedures standard among Lisbon merchants shipping to Africa; anonymous letter of 23 Jan. 1767, AHMF, livro 125. Cf. the *proposta* of the Lisbon merchants in ANTT, Ministério do Reino, maço 499, which allotted commissions of 3% on receipt of the goods in Angola, 3% on their sale, and 3% on collection of the debt.

46. Saldanha da Gama, 22 Sept. 1808, AHU, Angola cx. 58.

47. "Relação sobre a escravatura," n.d. (but after 1758), AHU, Angola maço 10 (D.O.).

of the delinquent trader, including his own outstanding loans, to his large rival. The well-heeled and well-connected plaintiff could then collect on them at his leisure, perhaps assisted by government troops. He could also take advantage of the legal hold he had gained over the debtor to force goods on him at high prices and/or to buy his slaves at preferentially low rates.[48] This foreclosure tactic generated cash in a commercial version of the same debt peonage and violent seizures that African merchant princes imposed on their subjects in the interior to create slaves.

Seizures for debt were nonetheless a risky procedure. Most debtors took care to obtain credit from as many different sources as possible. They thus created opportunities to put off one creditor in order to compensate another who applied pressure, and they invited counterclaims on the assets to be distributed following foreclosure. The initiator of bankruptcy proceedings would then find himself forced to share the spoils with others and would risk losing a significant percentage of what he was owed if all proceeded at once. Creditors also had to accept the probability that bankruptcy litigation would consume five or six years or more in the courts. During that period the debtor could continue to operate secretly with the capital he had borrowed from others.[49] Moreover, debtors under threat of a bankruptcy suit seldom experienced significant difficulty in secreting their returns out of the colony as they realized them, thus rendering them forever inaccessible to their creditors.[50]

Overly enthusiastic prosecutions of debtors thus either encouraged smuggling and illegal sales to competing creditors (*reviros*) or collapsed the whole credit structure of the trade. Such limitations made deliberate abuse of debt an attractive proposition to Luso-African borrowers, particularly at times of inflating slave values in Brazil, when they could borrow goods at prices current in one year and pay for them by selling slaves at higher prices several years later. As a result Luso-African indebtedness persisted throughout the century at levels high enough to finance significant portions of the interior trade. The debt caused annoying, though not always ruinous losses to Lisbon and become a focus of the continuing dispute over trade and politics in the colony.

On the other hand, the mortiferous surroundings in which heavily indebted immigrants tried to sell trade goods in Angola afforded frustrated creditors ample opportunity for outright plunder. Merchants in Luanda appear to have hovered like vultures over the newcomers they sent off to the interior with goods, counting on their vulnerability to the fevers and

48. See the *requerimentos* of Boaventura José de Mello, n.d. (ca. 1807), AHU, Angola maço 10 (D.O.), and of Maria da Conceição Simões, n.d. (ca. 1767), AHU, Angola maço 1.
49. Lencastre, 27 July 1775, AHU, Angola cx. 36.
50. *Consulta* of the Junta da Liquidação das Companhias Pombalinas, 13 Aug. 1829, AHU, Angola maço 12–B.

dysenteries that afflicted Europeans there. Since probate law authorized collection of all outstanding debts at the settlement of an estate, immigrant debtors who died in the backlands left golden opportunities to raid their assets. The expectation was that if a Luanda creditor could act quickly enough when a trader died, he could move in through his information sources and connections among the *capitães-mores,* directors of the government *feiras,* or other traders he had sent to the same marketplace as the deceased debtor, to sequester whatever slaves the trader might have bought for all his backers before his death and claim them all in full satisfaction of what he was owed, leaving the deceased trader's other creditors, not so quick or so well connected, to lament the loss of what they had loaned.[51]

These lugubrious strategies made the ability of the *capitães-mores* to press debt claims in the interior selectively the critical issue it became in Luanda. They also sometimes provoked open looting of the possessions of deceased inland traders to beat the game. Probate judges (*juizes de defuntos e auzentes,* or the *juiz dos orfãos*) in Luanda and Benguela became powerful figures owing to their legal authority over the disposal of assets in the estates of the numerous Europeans who died within their jurisdictions.[52] Disputes between the local heirs of Portuguese immigrants who died in Luanda and Benguela, presumably their Luso-African wives and their kinsmen, and opposing claimants in Lisbon broke out when judges awarded legacies to heirs in Luanda.[53] In so ruling, these judges distorted the purpose of a long series of metropolitan decrees promulgated to funnel estates safely back from overseas to business associates, and perhaps also legally married spouses and relatives, in Lisbon.[54]

Effective rates of interest on the ubiquitous credit behind slaving in Angola must have varied enormously according to the availability of imported goods, the reputation of the borrower, his access to bond by an established guarantor, the term of the loan, or whether or not the agreement carried a specified term at all. Charges for interest were rarely explicit but were usually phrased instead as higher nominal sales prices for the

51. Silva, *memória,* 25 June 1762, AHU, Angola cx. 29; "Regimento dos escrivães das feiras," 16 Sept. 1764, AHU, Angola maço 12–B (published in Couto, *Capitães-mores,* pp. 318–22, and in Maria Tereza Amado Neves, *D. Francisco Inocêncio de Sousa Coutinho: aspecto moral da sua acção em Angola* [Lisbon: Sociedade Nacional de Tipografia, 1938], pp. 52–55); *memorial* from Luanda merchants, cap. 19, n.d. (ca. 1821–23), AHU, Sala 12, no. 815.
52. Saldanha da Gama, 2 Dec. 1807, AHU, Angola cx. 57.
53. E.g., Lencastre, 27 July 1775, AHU, Angola cx. 36.
54. *Memória* on the *Juizo de defuntos e auzentes,* n.d. (after 1766), AHU, Angola maço 3 (D.O.). Lencastre, 27 July 1775, AHU, Angola cx. 36, cites the Pombaline legislation of 1768–70 that reformed procedures to facilitate the return of assets from overseas to the metropole.

goods borrowed.[55] Allegations that importers at Luanda demanded astronomical prices certainly indicate that local commercial loan rates were high by eighteenth-century standards. The substantial risks to lenders in Angola enhance the probability. On the other hand, borrowers commonly reduced the effective cost of credit simply by failing to repay a portion of what they owed. The 100 percent markup taken by merchants could have concealed implicit interest rates in the vicinity of 30 percent (at compound rates) for loans averaging two years and four months in duration, 50 percent for loans of a year and a half, and 70 percent for twelve months, less all other delivery costs and profits.[56] It is impossible to estimate the exact level of the offsetting bad debts accurately, though the range of 25 percent might not be excessive.

The complexity of the operations that each merchant carried on within his establishment in Luanda's lower city opened the door to almost unlimited opportunities for unauthorized personal gain through commingling the assets entrusted to him by distant correspondents, each with their own goods and funds. Even established Luanda commission agents had typically assembled only a modest personal working capital, which they might have held in almost any form—goods, slaves, debts owed to them, real estate, or personal property. But their warehouses contained large quantities of the imported goods that they distributed for principals in Lisbon and Brazil. Also in their control might be other goods assigned to multiple short-term partnerships that they formed with other local merchants, on their own or on behalf of their principals. They also had captives belonging to inland Luso-African slavers awaiting ships in Luanda.

By quietly borrowing from inattentive creditors to pay another who was demanding a transfer of funds collected but not yet forwarded, thus mixing theoretically immiscible assets they should have kept in carefully separated accounts, merchants could divert substantial sums of money to

---

55. Silva, *memória*, 25 June 1762, AHU, Angola cx. 29. The legal rate of interest in Portugal and its dominions was 6.25% until 1757, and it was then lowered to 5% to stimulate investment and capital formation; see Stuart B. Schwartz, *Sugar Plantations in the Formation of Brazilian Society* (New York: Cambridge University Press, 1985), pp. 205–6. Venâncio, "Economia de Luanda," pp. 98–99, notes that the Jesuits in Luanda (before 1759) lent funds at 5% interest, though perhaps not for commercial purposes.

One may thus distinguish commercial credit extended from Lisbon (from all indications vastly greater than any other source), credit available from local religious establishments in the colonies (preeminently the Jesuits in Angola, but many different orders in Brazil), and credit in trade goods and other assets held in the African economies. See Chapter 16 for other, much less secure commercial notes and paper constituting credit in the Luanda economy; also the discussion of *livranças*, following pages.

56. Salvador, *Magnatas do tráfico negreiro*, pp. 88–89, citing Ambrósio Fernandes Brandão's story of a merchant able to buy slaves with cash who then immediately resold the slaves for delayed payments at a nominal price increase of 85%. De Mello, 31 Jan. 1801, AHU, Angola cx. 51, specified the premium as 40% or more in the 1790s.

their own use. Though deliberate fraud surely explains much of this practice, newcomers need not have begun so calculatedly. Luanda factors needed to buy rum to fill out a well-assorted stock from Brazilians who demanded payment in "cash," for example, and so many an agent must have diverted slaves pledged to the accounts of remote backers in Lisbon to acquire *gerebita* from Brazil. They could rationalize the "loan" as protecting their Lisbon backers' assets which they had already loaned to the interior and as readily repayable from the gains it promised to return if future slaves lived to cover it. These loyal, if inexperienced, efforts to advance their employers' interests turned into failure when the slaves died.

In extreme cases, factors representing reputable and even royally chartered merchants from Lisbon used the good names of their principals to issue personal notes, known as *livranças,* backed by nothing more substantial than the prestige of their association with creditworthy patrons.[57] A favored variant of this strategy purloined assets of the Luso-African women whom many immigrant merchants married "in the local manner" (*no estilo da terra*). Since few of these women knew how to read or write, their husbands could induce them to authorize legal documents transferring the joint property of the conjugal unit to the husband alone, or persuade them to free female slaves belonging to the wife whom the husband had taken as mistresses, thereby manumitting also their own children born through the relationship.[58] No doubt, a good many of the influential merchants of Luanda, men who at the peaks of their careers employed substantial capital of their own in slaving and other related lines of business, got their starts as eager, if not overly principled or at least naive, young commission agents working with the wealth of others and borrowing through the informal, but well-worn channels that unwilling lenders condemned as theft.

The commerce of the immigrant merchants at Luanda was therefore typical of the eighteenth century in its diversity, if not also in its dishonesty. They sold at retail to the residents of the city and to its tavern- and shop-keepers, who also ran notorious fencing operations for stolen and smuggled goods. They also brought supplies for ships from Luso-African estate owners and solicited information from anyone likely to have advance knowledge of a profitable opportunity. Even the trading houses most specialized in the importation and sale of European and Asian textiles from Lisbon had to acquire Brazilian cane brandies to complete the assortments financed for traders heading for the backlands. Firms with sufficient capital behind them dealt liberally in credit, as a means of engaging people without goods to

---

57. Dias da Silva "Instrução," n.d. (ca. 1772), AHU, Angola cx. 36. And see also the almost uniform experience of the Pernambuco Company with their administrators in Angola: Angola and Benguela *copiadores*, AHMF.

58. De Mello, 25 Aug. 1801, AHU, Angola cx. 50.

assume the high risks of taking their wares to the slave markets of the back-lands. They made ephemeral, *ad hoc* arrangements with one another and lent goods back and forth to accomplish specific short-term goals. On other occasions they set up formal partnerships that endured for years, cemented where possible by bonds of kinship and affinity. These immigrant Portuguese tended to represent the Lisbon owners of trade goods and debt, who, high as were the risks of lending in the interior, preferred those hazards to the still higher losses associated with owning slaves. Factors bought for themselves only individual slaves whose skills or physical attractiveness made them unusually good investments, of use around their townhouses in Luanda, or when high prices in Brazil reduced the risks of owning captives in larger quantities. But as a rule, they merely managed the mass of slaves for Luso-African allies and affines and kept their employers' assets in the more secure forms of debt, textiles, and bills of exchange.

Capital versus the "Climate": Conclusions

Luanda, a Luso-African city of slaves and slaveowners in 1720, had by the later eighteenth-century become a town divided into deeply opposed communities of immigrant Portuguese merchants in the lower city and old but less and less affluent Angolan families in the upper town. Relationships between the two communities were simultaneously as intimate and hostile as the marriages that linked the individuals representing them. The merchants of the lower city typically avoided ownership of slaves and therefore depended on the Luso-Africans for means to collect the human returns on the goods they came to Africa to sell. To this end they formed partnerships with members of the Angolan families, married their women, and attempted to steal their slaves and assets. They hired some of them as employees, bribed those who held petty positions of official power, and entrusted large sums in trade goods to others whom they sent as traders to the marketplaces of the interior. When they had to, they paid off *capitães-mores* whose favor they needed to protect the investments they thus committed to the interior. The Luso-Africans had less need of the outsiders in Luanda's lower town than the newcomers had of them, since they never relinquished their access to French and British ships that cruised along adjacent coasts, only too eager to assist the Angolans in undercutting the Lisbon-based merchants' pretensions to a monopoly of imports in the *conquista*. The durability of the Luso-Africans, secure atop the sandstone ridge of their upper city, contrasted strikingly with the fleeting passage of the slaves and immigrant traders through the commercial town below.

The changes that occurred in the city between 1730 and 1770, a period of ascendancy for commission agents representing contractors, companies, and big ships coming directly from Lisbon, pushed the Luso-Africans and their methods of conducting the slave trade out of the city but not out of existence. The assorting system and bargains made in terms of *banzos* disappeared in favor of metropolitan-style prices in *réis* and even wholesale dealings with traders from the interior, who assorted the goods for slaves later in the marketplaces there. Power ceased to be a function of how many slaves one owned and the extent to which one could control supplies of food to the city and came to hinge instead on the ability to distribute imports on credit and on how reliably one could cover a bill of exchange payable on Lisbon. Slaving governors ceased to ally themselves with Luso-African slavers and instead became champions of Lisbon interests, mercantilists rather than military commanders, though always careful to seek out collaborators among the local Angolan families.

The immigrant merchants of the town also attempted to extend their control to the interior, where the Luso-Africans survived, battered but still fighting. Their measures usually left the old African ways of doing business intact but subjected them to closer government supervision. They licensed traders leaving for the backlands, restricted the arbitrary powers of *capitães-mores,* confined traders to *feiras* that were supervised by directors the Luanda merchants themselves appointed, and put food stocks for the slave ships under direct government authority. All these steps represented efforts to extend Luanda's control over the produce, human and vegetable alike, of interior regions where the people immigrant to the city dared not venture in person. But their vulnerability to the diseases of the interior left them ignorant of conditions there and in the end doomed all their efforts to failure.

The single advantage held by the immigrants was their capital, which a succession of them deployed in vastly increasing amounts through *livranças,* trade goods, high-priced loans, and legal proceedings to bankrupt competitors. Successful merchant importers in Luanda, as elsewhere in the Portuguese empire, turned themselves into merchant bankers as quickly as they could. In control of the colony's commodity currencies, of *livranças* in the city, of trade goods in the interior, and of credit, they were able to force the Luso-Africans into owning the slaves, the least profitable aspect of commerce in Angola, during a long mid-century period of falling or stagnant prices in Brazil. Their loans of trade goods also financed much of the expanded commerce that kept trade in the interior in nominally Portuguese hands as the moving slaving frontier lengthened routes leading to the east. Loans made through men like Francisco Honorato da Costa in Kasanje, particularly when not repaid, enabled African merchant princes in the Kwango valley and elsewhere to extend slaving diasporas into the very heart of central Africa by 1800. Without the funds that they left invested in the interior, which creditors perceived as losses but which subsidized the Luso-Africans, it is doubtful that Portuguese importers could have remained competitive against the British and French or that the slave trade to Brazil would have grown as it did throughout the eighteenth century.

Although the merchants of Lisbon, beset by their inability to collect sums their factors at Luanda entrusted to slaving associates in the interior and unable to compete with foreigners trading along nearby coasts, fundamentally commercialized the institutions of slaving in eighteenth-century Angola, they benefited little in the longer run. They all but abandoned Luanda late in the period, leaving the field to Brazilians, indirectly to the British behind them, and to the Luso-Africans. The Luso-Africans, having lost money for several decades on the slaves they sent to Brazil and having been driven out of their historic center in Luanda, remained as unintended recipients of subsidies given in the form of debts that many undertook but never meant to repay. African slavers benefited from higher prices as the flood of trade goods inflated the value of captives against imports. Lisbon capital increased the volume of slaving and added to the miseries of impressed African laborers and nobles forced to take loans of textiles within the *conquista,* but Portuguese resources were far too feeble to displace either the African economies beyond Luanda itself or their European competitors on the coasts.

A final irony of the success with which Lisbon merchants displaced the Luso-Africans from Luanda with Portuguese currencies and credit was that no one from Portugal possessed the skills or market knowledge necessary to trade anywhere else on the African coast, where business was done on the basis of bundles of goods and involved face-to-face dealings with wily Africans accustomed to trading on their own terms. Thus Lisbon rarely tried to trade at Benguela, where the Luso-Africans remained in command and business was done in terms of *banzos.* Late-eighteenth-century attempts to reoccupy the Loango Coast region (known to the Portuguese as Cabinda) foundered on the sheer incompetence of the captains sent there to trade. The irony was all the greater because Lisbon exporters apparently remained so oblivious to their inability to sell goods without the collaboration of the Luso-Africans that in the 1780s they considered abandonment of the interior of the colony that sustained their entire strategy. Or did they realize that the goods their factors loaned drew trade toward Luanda much more effectively than political and military control could ever have achieved?

10

Floating Tombs

The Maritime Trade of the Brazilians

If Luanda was a school for thieves, its port was the examination room where eager colonial students exhibited skills they had learned in Angola by evading self-serving legal and moral standards proclaimed by the metropole. Imperial law in Angola applied most fully in Luanda's harbor, and so its all-enveloping taxes and commercial regulations, nobly phrased in terms of the welfare of the slaves, were the questions to which owners, merchants, and shippers each responded to protect their personal fortunes. In this context, among Luso-African slavers and their allies in the local bureaucracy, factors representing Lisbon merchants, and ship captains from Brazil, the victors usually gained by sacrificing the lives of the slaves they claimed to defend.

The captains of this separate Brazilian shipping sector brought the ships—the *tumbeiros* as they were called, or "floating tombs"[1]—into the harbor to await cargoes of slaves. They sometimes joined the Luso-Africans in owning a few of the captives they carried, and at other times they sided with the metropolitan factors as importers of goods, but they mostly acted in terms of their own quite distinct economic specialization in maritime transport. As the catch phrase referring to their vessels implied, slave mortality reached its highest point as the captives boarded their vessels. Fear of financial losses owing to slave deaths thus supplemented close government supervision of the harbor in provoking the regulators of the trade and the captives' owners, financiers, and handlers all to struggle feverishly at this stage of the slaves' journey, each attempting to pass the looming mortality risk on to someone else by hastening, or by obstructing, the captives' progress toward sale in Brazil.

1. My free translation of the slang term, based on the Portuguese word *tumba*, cognate to English *tomb* and connoting "coffin bearer" or "coffin" in Portuguese. For origins of the term, see Salvador, *Magnatas do tráfico negreiro*, p. 91. Hanson, *Economy and Society in Baroque Portugal*, p. 231, translates it as "undertakers." Robert Conrad, *World of Sorrow: The African Slave Trade to Brazil* (Baton Rouge: Louisiana State University Press, 1986), pp. 3–4, n. 3, renders the word "bear to the tomb," notes that it applied also to the Africans who brought slaves down to the coast, and offers an alternative Portuguese phrase for the ships, *túmolos flutuantes,* literally "floating tombs."

In this highly charged economic and political arena, every protective regulation carried overtones favoring one group or another. The competitors could not have failed to seize on these and exploit them. Government decrees promulgated to protect slaves from exploitation became avenues of personal enrichment for the officials entrusted with the administration of those decrees. The formalities of collecting customs duties on departing slaves were a battleground where the body count pitched governors, whose budget depended almost solely on these revenues, against merchants, for whom every tariff evaded was a profit earned. The ships' order of precedence in departure, set by law to speed the flow of slaves through the port, gave officials a club that they wielded to delay vessels belonging to their opponents.

The Brazilian officers and crews of the ships, along with everyone else, defended themselves with contempt for such legal niceties. They bribed, misrepresented their intended destinations, negotiated with stowaways, falsified the contents of the boxes and bales they unloaded, and concealed a portion of the slaves that they took on board from government inspectors. Their struggles also reflected deeper-running disadvantages that these hard-bitten seafarers, on whom all the others depended to deliver the slaves alive in Brazil, faced in the Portuguese southern Atlantic empire. The Brazilians had to contend not only with the sheer physical dangers of living for one to two months alone on the high seas with hundreds of sick, hostile, and sullen prisoners, who usually outnumbered them by factors of ten or more to one, but also with severe economic constraints that rendered their business of carrying slaves from Angola a venture of marginal profitability at best and therefore, as a rule, one severely undercapitalized and subject to constant pressures on costs. As in all other segments of the trade, those least able to resist, the slaves, paid in suffering and death the expenses that shippers managed to avoid.

Brazilian soldiers hauling into the Luanda port suffered first by being excluded from a much more remunerative trade back to Portugal, reserved by decree to metropolitan merchants, and second from a generalized shortage of capital in the colonial Brazilian economy. It was precisely the Brazilians' lack of capital that left the Luso-Africans of Angola to own the slaves moving through the maritime segment of the trade, at least until the last decade or two of the eighteenth century.

Capital also defined the differing degrees of direct interest held by Brazilian slavers and Lisbon shippers in the welfare of the slaves whom both carried, or the risk of mortality each assumed in their voyages. On one extreme of the continuum, wealthy Lisbon merchants sometimes owned the slave cargoes on ships they operated, purchased with the trade goods they sent out to Angola. In that case, the shipper's profits depended principally on the number of slaves that he was able to deliver alive in Brazil and sell there.[2] On the opposite end of the same continuum were the ship operators typical of Brazil, whose lesser means came from consortia of partners usually able to invest only in the outbound portion of the voyage. Some contributed European goods transshipped through Brazil that they thought they could sell in Angola, others had American produce to offer, still others owned the vessel, and a few invested liquid funds in a share of the venture. The Brazilian shippers often brought the ship back with slaves belonging to merchants in Luanda, thus contributing even less to the return voyage. Since the ship operators in this case merely transported slaves for other owners, their profits depended on the efficiency with which they minimized expenses on the voyage, even if fewer slaves survived.

Two crucial decrees issued in 1758 regulated the trade explicitly in terms of the distinction in wealth embodied in these two extreme cases. They awarded priority in departure from Luanda to ships leaving *de efeitos próprios*, or carrying their own slaves for sale, over those departing *fretado* (or *de bando*), or common carriers of slaves belonging to others for freight charges. Certainly, not all ships fit either ideal type in practice. Most combined aspects of both, as optimal risk-averting strategies encouraged captains to balance revenues from carrying charges against prospective gains from buying and selling slaves. But the law placed all ships not fully *efeitos próprios* in the lower priority category of *fretado*. As a result, every Brazilian venture not well enough capitalized to fill its hold entirely with slaves of its own ownership waited behind the minority of Lisbon ships that bought the slaves they carried. The favored Lisbon ships made prompt departures with their slaves in relatively good condition. The remainder, including most of the Brazilians, had much less control over the crucial timing of their departure, which affected the health and mortality of their slaves, and hence the prices they might obtain in Brazil.[3] That left the Brazilian majority of shippers to recover a margin of profit from the freight

2. Allusions to the sensitivity of profits to slave mortality in the documentation are frequent and uniform. For a particularly explicit rationalization of the calculus, see de Mello, "Angola no começo do século," p. 559, n. 1, specifying that the Rio ships of the 1790s calculated costs and prices according to a break-even point set at 10% mortality. Their estimate was convincingly close to actual reported mortality at the time, during a period of unusually high losses to smallpox, and a plausible margin above good years, with losses in the 3%–5% range; cf. the figures in Miller, "Legal Portuguese Slaving." Coughtry, *Notorious Triangle*, p. 145, also concluded that slave mortality was central for the Rhode Island trade. Also quite explicit were the letters from the Senado da Câmara (Luanda) to Governor Albuquerque, 24 Jan. 1728, AHU, Angola cx. 18, at a time when mortality (owing to malnutrition and severe smallpox epidemics) had reached the point of damaging both Lisbon and Luso-African interests; and Alvellos Leiria, 7 March 1814, AHU, Angola cx. 62. For the Bahia trade from Mina, but also in general, José da Silva Lisboa letter, 18 Oct. 1781, published in the *Annaes da Biblioteca nacional do Rio de Janeiro* 32 (1910): 504–5. See also Chapter 19 below.

3. The model of the economics of a slaving voyage in Raymond L. Cohn and Richard A. Jensen, "The Determinants of Slave Mortality Rates on the Middle Passage," *Explorations in Economic History* 19, no. 3 (1982): 269–82, has very little relevance to the typical venture in the southern Atlantic, and little also to the exceptional voyages under unified ownership; for the factors limiting control for the latter, see Chapter 11 following.

fees they charged and—critically—from savings they could scrape up out of their costs of slave maintenance.

The big Lisbon ships ultimately financed the slaves that the Brazilians carried. They arrived at Luanda laden with textiles and manufactures worth more than the cargoes they could carry over to Brazil, and so they filled their holds completely with captives they owned, thus qualifying *efeitos próprios*, while still leaving debts and slaves to follow aboard the ships of the Brazilians, *fretado*. The Brazilians, whose *gerebitas* were not worth enough to fill the decks of even their smaller vessels with slaves,[4] found themselves with space available to carry the captives that Luso-Africans sent under *letra* bills of exchange to pay off debts owed to Lisbon.

Lisbon's heavy introductions of trade goods at times in the eighteenth century left Luanda filled with slaves just in from the backlands but without ships on hand to carry them away. The urgency of moving the excess captives through the port and on to Brazil produced a tendency to overload the ships on hand with slaves. Tight-packing,[5] facilitated, if not caused, by merchant capital, thus became another enduring dispute between Brazilian shippers and the government, this time with the Luso-African owners of the slaves on the side of an imperial policy formulated in line with official metropolitan sympathies for the slaves. Shippers who also owned the slaves they transported could afford to carry fewer of them under superior conditions and still earn profits from selling them at higher prices. Brazilian ships carrying slaves purely for the freight charges they could earn found their interests better served by cramming as many bodies as possible into the space they had available, to the likely detriment of the captives. Most of their ventures included slaves carried on both types of accounts, so that the interested parties—officers and crew, exporters from Brazil or Portugal, Angolan owners of slaves—could turn up on either side of the issue as it applied to a particular voyage.

All shippers, whatever their interest in their human cargoes, shared an additional concern with speed beyond the vulnerability of the slaves' lives to delays. They aimed to minimize the total elapsed time between their departures from Brazil or Lisbon and the ship's return and sale of its contents. A number of costs varied directly with time, like the salaries of officers and crew or the interest paid on funds borrowed to support the venture.[6] The emphasis on speed applied only in a limited way to

4. Vellut, "Royaume de Cassange," p. 131, presents figures for 1770 showing the value of *gerebita* imports at about 28% of all exports, or 41.7% of the value of slaves. Other data on *gerebita* for 1699 and the 1780s through the 1820s conform to this ratio.

5. The key Portuguese technical term for the rated capacity of a ship to carry slaves was *arqueação*, and sometimes *lotação*. Klein, *Middle Passage*, pp. 29, 35, specifies the meaning correctly, although it has not always been correctly defined in the secondary literature.

6. See the economic model of (a Bahian) voyage in the anonymous "Discurso preliminar, histórico, introductivo, com natureza de descripção económico da comarca e cidade da Bahia . . . ," *Anais da Biblioteca nacional do Rio de Janeiro* 27 (1905): 338.

progress at sea, since captains were then mostly at the mercy of the elements and since most vessels spent much more time in port than under way. Speed derived more from the alacrity with which they could offload their incoming cargoes, clear port formalities, engage an outgoing cargo, always of slaves in the case of Angola, and get under way. Disastrous delays could beset a ship at sea, but these were exceptional and far beyond the control of the ship operators in any case. On the other hand, delays in port were routine, often caused by rivals, at least at Luanda, and had the appearance of being partially subject to the wills of captains. Where slaves were also involved, mortality became a constant preoccupation, and it could be cut most efficiently by reducing the period during which an owner exposed himself to a risk he could hardly control otherwise. General strategies for decreasing the time required for a complete venture, and thereby increasing returns, once again turned attention to the port at Luanda. The economics of slaving voyages in the southern Atlantic, reduced to their most abstract terms, hinged on the swiftness of the turnaround in Angola, and all these pressures therefore converged on the hectic rough-and-tumble of the colony's port.

Winds and Currents

Highly stable winds and currents promoted the Brazilians' prominence in the slave trade of the southern Atlantic. Brazilian and Portuguese vessels alike sailed in a counterclockwise circle around a vast mid-Atlantic zone of high pressure centered between 15° and 20° south latitude (Map 10.1). The prevailing winds off this giant anticyclone blew down the Brazilian coast from the equatorial latitudes, past the northeastern captaincies of Pernambuco and Bahia and on beyond Rio de Janeiro toward the Spanish colonies of the Rio de la Plata. Off Rio the winds curved eastward as the prevailing northwesterlies of the higher southern latitudes. On the African side of the southern Atlantic, they swung back to the north as the southwesterly airflow that pulled the Antarctic waters of the massive Benguela current along all the Angolan coast as far as the mouth of the Zaire River. There, the fresh, muddy waters of the Zaire finally broke up the oceanic flow before it could reach the Loango Coast and deflected it into a westward-drifting low-latitude current. This northern side of the south Atlantic high pressure system consisted of easterly winds that blew back toward Brazil and dissipated to the north in the doldrums of the equator. The precise positions of the high-latitude westerlies and the low-latitude easterlies varied with the season of the year, advancing equatorward with the sun during the southern winter and drifting back to higher latitudes with the southern summer.

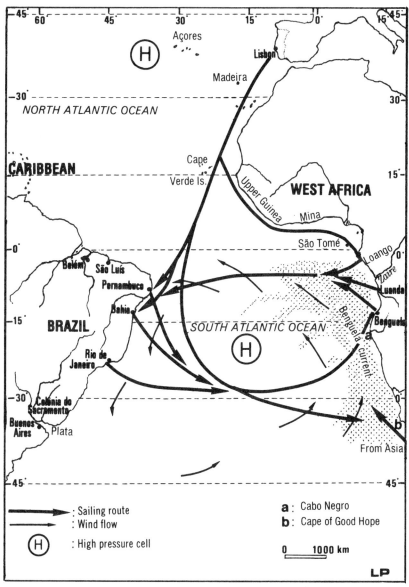

Map 10.1. Southern Atlantic Sailing Routes

Ships wishing to reach Angola from Portugal nearly always made use of the circuitous but reasonably steady winds of this anticyclonic system. They set out on the northeasterly air currents down along the western coast of Africa, passed the Portuguese islands of Madeira and the Cape Verdes, perhaps stopping to take on wines or crew members, crossed the doldrums in mid-ocean, and finally picked up the winds blowing down the coast of Brazil. They could continue southwest to call at Pernambuco, Bahia, or Rio de Janeiro, if necessary, but most turned out into the open ocean in the vicinity of 4°–5° south, well north of the American mainland.[7] Few Lisbon ships, therefore, stopped in Brazil to pick up goods for Angola.

Once ships set out on the transoceanic course leading to every part of western central and southern Africa, as well as India, they headed well to the south of east, for ships making for the Indian Ocean to clear the Cape of Good Hope (at nearly 35° south), and for vessels aiming for Angola to leave adequate margin for error in the southerly winds of the eastern Atlantic that could carry them helplessly north of Luanda if they miscalculated. So strongly did these eastern Atlantic currents and winds drive ships northward toward the equator that failure to attain sufficiently high latitudes by mid-ocean doomed Indiamen to abandon hope of making the Cape and forced them to turn back a thousand kilometers or more down the Angolan coast.[8] Ships from Brazil sailed directly out from their home ports to pick up the same route.

Though ships intending to go to Angola had no port of call south of Benguela, which lay just above 12° south, and although the majority were making for still lower latitudes—Luanda in 9° or the Loango/Cabinda region and the Zaire estuary between 5° and 6° south—all nonetheless aimed for at least 26° south (and sometimes 29° or 30°) before turning east.[9] They hoped to sight the African coast near Cabo Negro (16° south, modern Porto Alexandre). From there they simply turned north and ran down to their destinations with the prevailing winds and currents, normally calling briefly for provisions at Benguela, sometimes to pick up salt, and sometimes also to smuggle. Those planning to go on to the Zaire or to Cabinda put in also at Luanda.

The unvarying northward movement of ships down the Angolan coast put Luanda very near for vessels leaving Benguela, normally three or four

7. De Mello, 17 June 1799, AHU, Angola cx. 47.

8. See the example of the Dutch East Indiaman *Bechvliet,* headed for the Indian Ocean but forced in at Luanda in a state of extreme distress on 22 Jan. 1772: Sousa Coutinho, 8 Feb. 1772, AHU, Angola maço 9–A.

9. De Mello, 17 June 1799, AHU, Angola cx. 47; Saldanha da Gama, 12 Aug. 1806, AHU, Angola maço 10 (D.O.); Corrêa, *História de Angola,* 1:19. Heintze, *Fontes,* p. 213, notes that 29° to 30° south was normal in the early seventeenth century, so that maritime techniques may have improved slightly between then and the late eighteenth century, permitting a less circuitous route.

days' easy sailing, but left Benguela an extremely long and difficult passage upwind from Luanda. Sailing to Benguela from Luanda was so difficult, in fact, that it was said to be accomplished only *a força de braços*, by sheer force of human arms, that is, by oared vessels.[10] From Luanda, captains found it easier to reach Benguela by sailing north, then west toward Brazil, and back along the customary easterly course than to fight their way directly south. In fact, one or two small schooners beat laboriously up and down the coast, but the dominant south-to-north sailing pattern contributed greatly to the freedom from Luanda's interference that Luso-Africans and others enjoyed at Benguela.

For the same reasons, the barren coasts south of Benguela could not be reached directly from either of the two principal Portuguese ports. Because they remained permanently beyond the control of the government garrisons downwind, they became havens for foreign slave buyers, particularly French slavers from the Indian Ocean on their way north down the coast laden with Asian textiles.[11] Also because of the winds Portuguese officials at Luanda directed their concern about the foreigners active all along Angolan shores principally to accessible coasts downwind to their north.

The passage from European Portugal to Brazil normally lasted up to forty days to Rio de Janeiro, less if a ship made port in Pernambuco or Bahia.[12] The Brazilian vessels joining the parade of Lisbon ships making for Angola across the southern Atlantic required anywhere from forty to sixty days, depending on the season, the strength of the winds, and the position of the southern Atlantic high-pressure zone.[13] These sailing routes and times changed little in the eighteenth century, and Brazilians continued

10. João Victo da Silva, n.d. (ca. 1792), AHU, Angola cx. 42.

11. Oeyras, *parecer,* 20 Nov. 1760, AHU, Angola cx. 28. On the remoteness of the southern coasts from Luanda's point of view, see the report on the matter in Moçâmedes, 18 Jan. 1786, AHU, Angola maço 4–B (cont.).

12. On the passage to Rio, AHMAE, Correspondence Consulaire (C.C.), Rio de Janeiro, France (1825–26), Comte de Gestes to Ministre, 28 Feb. 1825, fols. 22–37v.

Making port in Pernambuco or Bahia, meant a rather longer return voyage direct from Brazil to Portugal (80–110 days average for a small sample in 1795): Klein, *Middle Passage,* p. 41, n. 24. Corcino Medeiros dos Santos, *Relações comerciais do Rio de Janeiro com Lisboa (1763–1808)* (Rio de Janeiro: Tempo Brasileiro, 1980), p. 115, mentions a mean Rio-to-Lisbon time of around 60 days in a highly variable sample for the late eighteenth century. Lugar, "Merchant Community," p. 86, has times out to Bahia declining from a mean of 39 days in 1790 to only 28 days in 1820–21, with the return passage to Lisbon dropping from 75 to 39 days over the same period.

13. E.g., for passage times, Lencastre, 29 Nov. 1772, AHU, Angola cx. 33; Moçâmedes, 30 Sept. 1784, AHU, Angola maço 4–B; Saldanha da Gama, 10 Jan. 1807, AHU, Angola cx. 57; José Maria Vieira (*capitão de Mar e guerra,* commandant of the *fragata Venus*), 8 Feb. 1821, AHU, Angola cx. 67. Cf. the "Mappa dos navios mercantes entradas no porto de Loanda durante o ano de 1848," showing 11 ships from Rio reaching Luanda in an average of 47.1 days, with individual voyages ranging from 31 to 72 days: AHU, Angola maço 15.

to follow them well into the nineteenth. A few Lisbon ships began to cut the corner from West Africa direct to Angola in the 1790s along a shorter route long since frequented by the British and French, for whom "Angola" was an extension of their more common lower Guinea journeys to the region north of the Zaire, rather than a prolongation of a passage to Brazil and then to more southerly parts of the coast. They turned east well above the equator and coasted along West Africa before veering southeast to leave São Tomé to the south on their way to Loango. Ships from Lisbon adopted this route as their basic course to Angola after Brazilian independence in 1821 chilled the reception accorded Portuguese vessels in the ports of the new empire. It reduced total passage times from the former 90 to 120 days (to Benguela, and more to Luanda or Loango) to 70 days or less.[14]

These southern Atlantic trade winds blew more or less steadily throughout the year and so imposed few seasonal obstacles to passages from either east or west. Ships carrying slaves west along the northern flank of the system seldom risked delays unless they strayed well to the right of their usual course, unlike slavers of other nations heading from West Africa to the Caribbean, which always crossed the hazardous zone of unreliable winds along the equator. In fact, the reliability of navigation in the southern Atlantic, particularly from Angola to Brazil, the relatively direct routes available, and the low risk of delays that might reduce the survival rates of slaves aboard the *tumbeiros* contributed to the closeness of the link between African markets for Brazilian *gerebita* and the Brazilian markets for African labor.

Only a limited seasonality influenced sailings across the southern Atlantic. When the high pressure system moved north in the southern winter, heavy Antarctic storms from the higher southern latitudes moved down into the zone traversed by Angola-bound ships. These hazards, most severe in June, led merchants to avoid eastward crossings from May through July, if possible.[15] Weather affected the westward transport of slaves less strongly, though departures from Luanda dropped noticeably from May to June. Avoidance of these months may have reflected captains' wariness of undependable winds and squalls along the westward course in those months.[16] However, this slight seasonal variability in sailings from Angola

14. De Mello, 17 June 1799 and 12 Nov. 1798, AHU, Angola cxs. 47 and 45. Cf. the *parecer* of Manoel da Cruz, 20 March 1824, ANTT, Junta do Comércio, maço 62, macete 122, counting only 60 days from Lisbon to Luanda. Gaulme, "Document sur le Ngoyo," p. 352, describes this route from the French perspective. In 1848 the 14 ships reaching Luanda directly from Portugal averaged 72.4 days, although they fell into two distinct groups, one evidently detouring through Brazil (averaging 102.3 days) and the other coming direct (averaging 64.2 days).

15. Moçâmedes, 30 Sept. 1784, AHU, Angola maço 4–B.

16. John Luccock, *Notes on Rio de Janeiro and the Southern Parts of Brazil (1808–1818)* (London: S. Leigh, 1820), Table II, p. 615, shows longer passage times for the April–June

to Brazil resulted more from the rhythm of trade in the ports of Africa. Difficult rainy-season travel from the interior to the coast between January and April retarded the arrival of slaves in Luanda and Benguela in those months and hence the departure of ships waiting to take them on as cargo.[17] The delays became evident in the reduced departures of ships during the following two months, May and June. Seasonal shortages of food in Luanda had less effect on the timing of departures.[18]

The only strong seasonal influence on Angolan slaving limited the number of ships taking slaves to the far northern regions of Brazil beyond Pernambuco, mainly Maranhão and Pará.[19] Brazil's northeastern coast came under the influence of steady easterly winds that made it difficult to return from there to the main ports of central and southern Brazil. Imperial restrictions did not permit this voyage before the 1750s, but even after

---

quarter than for any other time of the year for ships reaching Rio from (all of?) "West Africa." Cf. Klein, *Middle Passage,* p. 34, Table 2.5 (for 1795–1810) and p. 57, Table 3.3 (for 1825–30), which show differing seasonal peaks of arrivals at Rio de Janeiro. These tables do not illuminate the arguments developed in this chapter, as they are constructed in terms of the less relevant seasons in Brazil and do not distinguish ships of entirely different sailing patterns from eastern and western Africa. For the earlier period, 1795–1810, Angolan ships dominate, with slaves reaching Luanda in the African dry season and allowing more ships to depart from about July or August onwards. In the later period, 1825–30, ships from Mozambique, strongly influenced by severe winter weather off the coasts of southeastern Africa, became much more numerous and advanced the aggregate seasonal peak in Rio arrivals to November through January.

17. AHMF, livro 125, letter of 25 Feb. 1763.

18. Manioc meal entered the city regularly throughout the year, barring interruptions by engrossers. Bean supplies rose with the beginning of the rains in October and peaked from January through March. Introduction of a *terreiro público* (public grain market) in 1764 muted these variations still further. Reports in Sousa Coutinho, 28 May 1770, AHU, Angola cx. 32, for 1768 and 1769; *terreiro público* reports for 1771, AHU, Angola cx. 33, and for 1776–78, AHU, Angola cx. 37. Spix and Martius, *Viagem pelo Brasil,* 2:143, mention two varieties of beans in Angola, a rainy-season one planted in March and harvested in June, and a dry-season bean planted in June and harvested in September; the latter was more important at Luanda, to judge from the receipts of the public granary.

Klein, *Middle Passage,* pp. 33–35, 56–57, extends to the Angolan trade his general hypothesis that slavers timed their annual deliveries of new labor to coincide with American planters' peak demands for hands during the harvest period, with qualifications, esp. pp. 239–40. But the tightly controlled departures from Luanda and Benguela; the diverse employments of slaves in mining, ranching, various crops, and urban labor in Brazil; and the long harvest season for Brazilian sugar would seem to place the main seasonal constraints on the African rather than the American side for all Brazilian captaincies from Pernambuco south.

19. Vasconcelos, 2 May 1762, AHU, Angola cx. 29, refers to the special risks of the Maranhão Coast, especially (but with unhelpful vagueness) "fora da monção" ("outside the monsoon," or unseasonably).

For Pará and Maranhão there is a case to be made for strongly seasonal American markets, as there is also for the monocultural labor systems of the Caribbean and the compressed harvest seasons of temperate North America. The chartered company ships servicing Pará and Maranhão were privileged to leave Angola *efeitos próprios* and hence were free to time departures in terms of their markets in northern Brazil, again more like the British and French ships carrying slaves to the Caribbean than like the *bando* ships on the Bahian and Rio runs in the southern Atlantic, which had very little ability to influence their schedules.

that date most ships taking slaves destined for the far northeastern captaincies went to Pernambuco on the regular Brazil run and left their cargoes
there to continue on via the coastal trade network. Slavers intending to
return to the southern Atlantic circuit seldom attempted to go to Pará or
Maranhão. The Maranhão Company ships chartered to sail directly in the
1760s made no apparent adjustment to the seasonal sailing conditions in
the timing of their departures from Luanda. Rather, they generally avoided
buying slaves in Angola, in part because of the navigational difficulties at
their destination. Few independent slavers attempted to take slaves to Pará
or Maranhão from Luanda later in the century.

The slight but persistent seasonal pulse in the movement of slaves
through Luanda and Benguela was the result of a combination of maritime
conditions in two oceans with travel difficulties on the land. Portuguese
India ships and the French smugglers of the Compagnie des Indes fed
their Asian textiles into this pattern. They arrived in Angola from beyond
the Cape almost exclusively between April and June, thus allowing merchants at the coast to ready inventories of fresh trade cloth for the expected
increase in traders arriving with slaves from the backlands as the dry season
became established from May onwards. *Gerebita* and other trade goods
arriving through Brazil tended to become more plentiful during the rains
as well, as ships from the north and west took advantage of the relatively
calm southern Atlantic summer to reach Benguela and Luanda between
October and May. Departures with slaves then picked up in July and
August. The numbers of ships lying at anchor in Luanda's harbor would
thus have tended to rise during the first half of the calendar year and then
to drop toward the year's end. Deliveries of goods during the slow slaving
months of the rainy season built up inventories of trade goods and food
supplies in time to facilitate departures of slaves during the following dry
season. The marginal ebb and flow in Angolan slaving thus delayed the
ships in the harbor but hastened the movement of the slaves on to Brazil.
The dominant effect of the steady winds and currents in the southern
Atlantic on slaving was toward the same end. It enabled merchants to
distribute ship departures relatively evenly throughout the year and thus
to achieve the speedy embarkations fundamental to limiting the risks of
mortality among their slaves.

The Economics of the Brazilian Slaving Venture

The ships that carried the slaves belonged mostly to modest merchants of
three ports in Brazil—Rio de Janeiro, Pernambuco, and Bahia. These men
were often general traders early in the eighteenth century, using vessels
they could contribute to ventures of the most diverse sorts beside slaving.

Larger, specialized import-export merchants with connections in Lisbon usually had their sights fixed on the trade with Portugal, not Angola. Merchants from Portugal with ships in Brazil probably seldom committed ships to Angolan slaving except under duress or by selling worn-out hulks to colonial shippers who then refitted them for the Africa trade. Virtually none of the oceangoing ships engaged in the transport of slaves belonged to the Luso-African owners of the slaves in Luanda and Benguela before the 1820s, and even after that date Angola-based slavers amounted to only a small fraction of the entire fleet.[20] In the course of the century, certain Bahian merchants developed a specialized trade in slaves to the West African Mina Coast, and others at Rio became similarly committed to slaving from Angola. Slaving ventures at Pernambuco remained only an occasional diversion from other commercial sectors.

Shipowners in Brazil, though largely excluded from the trade to Portugal, had several alternatives more important than the Brazil-Angola-Brazil circuit of goods and slaves. Only thirty to forty ships from all ports in Brazil went to Luanda and Benguela at any given time, a small number relative to the overall movement of shipping in these ports. An active coastwise trade (*cabotagem*) linked each major city there to its outports, and a lively interregional commerce moved goods among the major captaincies from Rio Grande do Sul to Pernambuco and beyond, in addition to a largely illicit trade that reached south from Rio de Janeiro to the Spanish colonies of the Plata estuary.[21] Shippers in Brazil could thus select the most profitable marine ventures from among numerous possibilities at any given time and would elect to carry slaves mostly when the returns were attractive.

The economics of ventures to Angola differed according to whether they originated in Brazil or Portugal. General merchants in Brazil constructed voyages to Angola out of diverse interests, none of whom had much capital or leverage in the African market—planters or local distillers with third-rate cane brandy to dispose of and importers with European goods unsalable in Brazil. Shipowners tended to send their ships to Africa

20. Avellar, 28 May 1723, AHU, Angola cx. 21; Meneses, 12 June 1734, AHU, Angola cx. 21; *requerimento* of Anselmo de Fonseca Coutinho, n.d. (ca. 1799), AHU, Angola cx. 47. Botelho de Vasconcelos, 3 Jan. 1799, AHU, Angola cx. 47, remarked that not a single Benguela merchant, where slavers were exceptionally large by Luanda standards, could raise the 80.000$000 (200,000 *cruzados*) necessary for a venture from Africa to Brazil to Portugal and back. With the exception of river canoes and launches used for provisioning the city, Luso-Africans operated only one or two small schooners back and forth between Luanda and Benguela and, occasionally, out and back to São Tomé.

21. In addition to Lugar, "Merchant Community," see Rudolph William Bauss, "Rio de Janeiro; The Rise of Late Colonial Brazil's Dominant Emporium, 1770–1808" (Ph.D. diss., Tulane University, 1977), and especially Larissa V. Brown, "Internal Commerce in a Colonial Economy: Rio de Janeiro and Its Hinterland, 1790–1822" (Ph.D. diss., University of Virginia, 1985).

when they had no better employment for them. Unless the Brazilians could make trading profits from buying and selling the slaves, they found little inherent attraction in fetching slaves from Angola. But ownership raised further problems. Finding the necessary financial resources for trade other than to Europe was a persistent limitation in Brazil's undercapitalized colonial economy. Breaking into the closed circle of Luso-African slaving at Luanda was another, since Luso-Africans owned the slaves available there, or had pledged them to sell for specie and currency in Brazil. Brazilians, who had only *gerebita* or second-quality goods of other sorts to offer, found it difficult to buy prime-quality slaves for themselves. Gains for such merchants, including the growing core of slavers at Rio specialized in the African trade, therefore depended heavily on freight charges they collected for transporting the human property of the Luso-Africans.

Slaving on this basis offered few attractions to pure shippers for long periods in the eighteenth century. The regulatory structure of the trade derived from the seventeenth century, when influential Pernambuco and Bahian merchants had made enough profit from their dominant position in European sugar markets to bring slaves to their labor-short sugar sector even at prices that did not cover costs of transport. Though Brazilians later continued to own most of the ships bringing slaves from Angola, Portuguese merchants sending goods out to Africa took over the favored position in a regulatory environment stacked very much against slave transporters. Vessels coming out from Lisbon were frequently larger ones drawn off the pool of general European maritime shipping primarily to return profits from the outward voyage, through economies of scale in the transportation of bulk textiles, wines, and manufactures, and particularly through the generous trading margins they took when they sold these commodities in Luanda and Benguela. They could carry away the Luso-Africans' slaves at an operating loss and still return profits from collections on the Luso-Africans' bills of exchange in Brazil.

Something of the contrast between the two was evident in the differing sizes of the vessels taking slaves on at Luanda. One Lisbon ship, belonging to the metropolitan contractor of the slave export duties, rated at 800 slaves at Benguela in 1729, compared to the 200- to 300-slave vessels from Brazil then common in the trade.[22] The great size of the Lisbon ships was again clear thirty years later. The capacities of vessels sent out by the Pernambuco and Maranhão (Companhia Geral de Grão Pará e Maranhão) companies during the first years of their operations in Angola tended to run 50 to 80 percent larger than ordinary slavers based in Brazil (see Table 10.1). All Pernambuco- and Pará/Maranhão-bound ships leaving Luanda were company ships, as required by law, and though

---

22. Albuquerque, 20 Dec. 1729, AHU, Angola cx. 18. Bahian slavers were also reported "generally small" in 1699: Taunay, *Subsídios*, pp. 249–50.

Table 10.1. Mean Rated Slave Capacity of Vessels Bound from Luanda for the Ports of Brazil, 1762–1775

Year[a]	Destination			
	Rio	Bahia	Pernambuco	Maranhão/Pará
1762	371.1	414.3	473.8	585.0
1763	345.1	299.4	517.8	
1764	386.2	478.0	530.8	714.4
1765	384.5	387.0	440.1	537.0
1766	356.0	358.0	396.0	...
1767	370.8	257.2	441.5	...
1769	338.1	303.2	377.0	...
1770	317.7	293.6	418.8	...
1771	355.5	333.7	426.0	...
1772	364.2	374.0	395.0	...
1774	395.0	363.4	374.0	...
1775	430.0	382.1	422.0	...

SOURCES: The data in this table derive from annual summaries of the ships clearing the Luanda port with slaves, all found in the Angola series of the AHU. For 1762, the report is enclosed in Vasconcelos, 11 Feb. 1763, cx. 29; for 1763, Vasconcelos, 30 March 1764, cx. 30; for 1764, Sousa Coutinho, 27 Feb. 1765, cx. 30; for 1765, "Mappa dos navios, que destro Porto, e do Prezidio de Benguela sahirão para os do Brazil com carge de escravos conforme suas arquiaçoens . . . ," cx. 31; for 1766, "Mapa do rendimento das embarcaçoens . . . no anno de 1766," cx. 31; for 1767, maço 18 (D.O.); for 1769, cx. 32; for 1770, Sousa Coutinho, 3 Jan. 1771, cx. 33; for 1771, "Conta do Rendimento dos Direitos dos Escravos . . . ," 28 Jan. 1772, cx. 33; for 1772, cx. 36; for 1775, cx. 36; for 1776, cx. 36. The series ends thereafter with reforms in the administration of the slave duties from Angola.

Note: Figures in italic are for slaves boarded rather than rated capacity—generally near or at capacity for Rio and Bahia ships, but lower for the big company ships from Pernambuco and Maranhão/Pará.

[a] There are no records extant for 1768 and 1773.

often based in Brazil, represented a Lisbon effort to ship large quantities of merchandise out to Angola, particularly as they entered the market at Luanda. Over the twelve years between 1762 and 1775 for which records are extant, Rio and Bahia ships leaving Luanda averaged 354.3 slaves capacity, while those from Lisbon destined for Pernambuco and Maranhão/Pará were nearly a full third larger, averaging a capacity of 462.3 slaves. The companies sent out the largest ships during the first few years of their operations in Angola but tended to replace these huge vessels in later years with smaller craft more suitable for carrying slaves when they began to withdraw trading "profits" they had accumulated in debts spread through the interior.[23]

23. During the first four years of the 1762–75 period, company ships averaged 520.0 slaves each, or almost half again as many (46.8%) as the long-term average of the Brazilian ships over the entire period. The companies' large vessels achieved a load factor of only

Company reliance on huge ships is all the clearer because they delivered slaves to markets smaller than those at Rio and Bahia and thus risked depressing prices for their cargoes by arriving with large numbers of captives. They apparently did not even intend to take on full complements of slaves during the earlier period of their activity in Angola, when they were mostly trying to flood the Luanda market with metropolitan textiles. Rather, they loaded only as many captives as they could conveniently manage in order to satisfy planters needing labor in Brazil and then left below their capacity. They even obtained special license from the Crown to leave Luanda less than fully loaded, a privilege not available to ordinary slaving vessels from Brazil, who could not depart until they had filled the last place on their slave decks.[24] The great size of these ships was evident also in the thorough resentment they provoked from their smaller Brazilian competitors at Luanda. Brazilians complained that the Portuguese ships overloaded the Luanda market with imports, causing the prices of the goods in traders' inventories to drop and blocking the flow of slaves through the port until they could fill their huge holds with captives.[25]

Since Lisbon merchants concentrated profits in the goods-transporting and -selling phases of the slave trade, they thereby limited gains that others might seek from engaging in its transport phase. All-but-guaranteed high prices for goods sold in Angola, backed by legally privileged seizures of the assets of debtors and by payments in specie in Brazil, established a strong position for the well-capitalized sellers of goods from Asia and Europe. By combining profitable sales of goods with shipping slaves for Luso-Africans, Lisbon contractors, chartered companies, and other merchants could afford to transport captives under a pricing structure that did not fully cover the costs incurred in that phase of their ventures. This policy left Brazilians—whose business was mostly to carry slaves, without owning them or selling trade goods profitably in Angola—operating at a severe disadvantage.

Eighteenth-century Brazilian shippers therefore found advantage in slaving voyages mostly by selling low-cost American commodities in Africa, thus absorbing operating losses from the transport of slaves. After sugar prices declined in the eighteenth century, Bahian slavers found a margin of profit only from selling low-production-cost third-grade tobacco on the Mina Coast in West Africa and thus continued to supply slaves at

---

86.5% during the 1762–65 period, compared to the 100.0% load factor required by law of the Brazilian common carriers, which in fact ran 98% to 99% in all but the most exceptional years.

24. See the petition of Lisbon merchants requesting such a privilege, n.d. (ca. 1760s), ANTT, Ministério do Reino, maço 499. Para. 4 refers to the exemption granted to the Pará Company.

25. E.g., Corrêa, *História de Angola*, 1:48–55.

prices planters could afford. But the only commodity that could subsidize southern Brazilian sugar planters, the main customers for Luanda and Benguela slaves after about 1750, was selling *gerebita* cane brandy, a virtually costless by-product of their main business of producing sugar for shipment to Portugal. The cheap cane brandy served as ballast on the outbound voyage, and the *pipas* in which it was shipped could be reused economically as containers for the water that slaves drank on the return. Bahian tobacco found no significant market in Angola, where the *conquista* and particularly the middle Kwango valley were tobacco-exporting regions for areas nearer the forest fringe. Shipping in the Angola slave trade therefore became heavily dependent on participation by the planting sector of the Rio economy.

Freight Charges

The key regulation by which Lisbon favored metropolitan merchants selling European and Asian goods in the southern Atlantic set slave transport charges (*fretes*) well below levels likely to return a profit in themselves.[26] These limits on freight charges for slaves also lowered the delivered cost of African labor to American planter-consumers. In another sense they protected the Luso-African owners of the slaves in Angola from rate bidding wars that otherwise would have surely forced up freight rates whenever shipping shortages forced them to pay premiums just to get their sick and dying slaves moving through the ports and on to America. Everyone gained in the short run, except for the Brazilians dependent on covering operating costs from charges for carrying slaves. Over the longer run, of course, fixed low rates helped to create occasional shortages of shipping in Angola that raised mortality among slaves left waiting on shore. In no other branch of the Atlantic slave trade did freight rates assume the same significance, since everywhere else, including the West African trade to Bahia, investors owned the slaves on their ships.[27]

Since the middle of the seventeenth century, freight rates from Angola to Brazil had been set at 4$000 per slave (*peça*).[28] The records make no

26. Regulated rates for shipping charges were general in the economic and legal structure of an empire designed to favor Lisbon merchants: Lugar, "Merchant Community," p. 274. For other eighteenth-century decrees respecting *fretes* between Brazil and Portugal, see Joaquim Ignacio de Freitas, ed., *Collecção chronologica de leis extravagantes* (Coimbra: Real Imprensa da Universidade, 1819), 3:535–37, 4:21–22. For freights in general, Humberto Leitão and José Vicente Lopes, *Dicionário da linguagem de marinha antiga e atual* (Lisbon: Centro de Estudos Ultramarinos, 1963), p. 215; also Silva Lisboa, *Princípios de directo mercantil*, pp. 653–64.

27. For general comments, Bean, *British Trans-Atlantic Slave Trade*, pp. 175–77.

28. BAL, 50–V–37, no. 135, fols. 390–91v. Rates from Angola to Bahia early in the century had been 2$400: Mattoso, *Etre esclave au Brésil*, pp. 77, 81.

mention of reduced rates for children at that time, and so children were then probably carried at the full adult rate. The fundamental regulation of the eighteenth-century slave trade in the southern Atlantic was a law (*alvará*) of 18 March 1684 which, among other provisions, raised rates from Luanda to 5$000 per slave, partially to compensate slave transporters for reductions imposed by the same law on the number of slaves that their vessels could legally board.[29] Since this restriction, although phrased as protective of slaves' lives, reduced the freight charges that shippers could earn, it worked selectively against the Brazilians.

The 1684 law constituted the first step in a century-long effort by metropolitan sellers of goods to seize control of the Angolan trade away from slavers on the spot in western Africa, then mainly the governors at Luanda, their Brazilian associates, and the Luso-Africans. These political tensions showed through the superficial philanthropical tone of the law in sections that vested control over measurement of the vessels—the pivotal step in limiting the number of slaves a ship could carry and hence the total freight charges it could collect—outside Angola. No remeasurement in Angola could raise a capacity rating (*arqueação*) made elsewhere, and no measurement obtained under the new system could increase the total freight charges received under the arrangements already in force.[30] Lisbon, not authorities in any of the colonies, had responsibility for prosecuting violators.[31] Thus, the negative import of the law for slave carriers was clear.

The law reduced carrying charges to shippers below profitable levels at the same time that a new rank of pure transporters, only dimly visible in the historical record, came on the scene in Angola. The rising demand for slaves during the Minas Gerais gold boom drew slaves to remote mining areas where buyers had fewer direct connections with shippers at the coast than the planter gentry of northeastern Brazil had had with the seventeenth-century Bahia and Pernambuco ships dominant at Luanda until then. The high prices available on the mines supported the growth of specialized slave carriers at Rio, probably originally small coastal shippers in Brazil who merely transported slaves belonging to governors, Luso-Africans, and others, often to the voluble dismay of the sugar growers cut out of the trade. Some of these carriers may have come from Pernambuco and Bahia, but they would have abandoned their association with the colonies' planter establishment. Others surely sailed to Angola for the first time from Rio

29. This key legislation governing slaving at sea is published in *Arquivos de Angola* 2, no. 11 (1936): 313–19; also in Freitas, *Collecção chronologica de leis extravagantes*, 2:136–45; *Anais da Biblioteca nacional do Rio de Janeiro* 28 (1906): 206–11; and José Justino de Andrade e Silva, *Collecção chronologica da legislação portugueza* (Lisbon: Imprensa Nacional, 1859), pp. 8–11.

30. Arts. 5 and 13, in *Arquivos de Angola* 2, no. 11 (1936): 314–15, 316–17.

31. Arts. 21, 22, 24, ibid., pp. 319–20.

de Janeiro. This southern Brazilian port, though nearest the mines, had until then been a town without the merchant wealth and African connections of the two larger cities of northeastern Brazil.

These new operators in the slave-transporting business behaved as though they were less well-capitalized than their predecessors and more dependent on revenues from charges for carrying slaves. From the high prices that slaveowners could receive for slaves sold in Rio and Minas Gerais they siphoned off a share of the gain in the form of illegal increased fees and charges for ocean transport. Shipping space at Luanda had grown short as the restrictions of the 1684 law had driven Brazilians into other maritime routes in the last decades of the seventeenth century, including the Mina slave trade at Bahia. By the 1690s, shippers still were scrupulously observing the letter of the law by charging no more than 5$000 for space to ship a slave, but shortages of shipping had become great enough that they were able to add a surcharge in the still legal form of selling the right to claim that space. This surcharge (termed a *venda de praça*, or "sale of a space") grew valuable enough by 1700 that the slaveowning local merchants in Luanda, who exercised power as an interim governing junta for two or three years from 1703 to 1705 after the death of Governor Bernadino de Tavora de Souza Tavares (in office 1701–3), adopted an ordinance monopolizing the right to buy these shipping spaces for themselves. A later governor revoked the merchants' ordinance and went on to gain the usual standing of officials of his rank as one of the largest slavers in the colony.[32]

Further reforms in 1720 excluded the governors from slaving, but since the top colonial officers controlled a significant portion of the Brazilian shipping coming to the port up to that time, removal of their vessels from the trade also exacerbated the shortage of ships.[33] At that point, demand from the gold fields in southern Brazil was at its peak, and the price of buying rights to embark a slave at the fixed charge for freight rose also, to 15$000 and 20$000 per slave, three to four times the legal rate of 5$000.[34] When the local party, behind an interim governor, *mestre de*

32. Noronha, 21 March 1716, confirmed by *carta regia* of 29 April 1718, AHU, Angola cx. 16.

33. Barboza Mourais, 14 March 1722, AHU, Angola cx. 16; Coelho de Carvalho, 28 June 1724, AHU, Angola cx. 16.

34. Bean, *British Trans-Atlantic Slave Trade*, pp. 175–77, put nominal freight charges for the longer British passage from Africa to markets in the Caribbean trade stable at £4–£6 during peacetime throughout the eighteenth century; at 3$555 to the pound sterling, the *réis* equivalent would have been 14$220 to 21$330, thus very close to what Rio shippers were able to charge. Palmer, *Human Cargoes*, p. 22, notes that the South Seas Company paid freight charges to other shippers of its own slaves (including the Royal Africa Company) at £6–£6.5 per slave in 1715 (or 21$330 to 23$108) and £8–£10 all the way to Spanish ports on the mainland (28$440 to 35$550) by 1730. The Royal Africa Company charge of £5 (17$775) to Barbados in 1715 rose to £7 (24$885) by 1719. In 1797 freight for

campo José Carvalho da Costa (1725–26), took power again, an open battle ensued between Luso-African merchants and other government officials scrambling to garner revenues from the surcharge on places on the ships for themselves.[35] The confusing charges and countercharges that survive from this phase of the battle over the reorganization of trade in the 1720s leave the impression that both shippers and government officers sold the places. The new governor attempted to lessen the shipping shortage and resolve the dispute by raising freight charges from 5$000 to 7$000 on his own authority and prohibiting sales of *praças* ("places"). He failed to resolve the dispute, owing to the inadequacy of the proposed increase and the consequent further reduction in the supply of shipping caused by inability to collect the surcharge.[36] The Luso-African slaveowners attacked the practice in the name of their captives, implying that shippers sold spaces in excess of the number permitted by the decree of 18 March 1684. They probably did, but the allegation was surely yet another instance of invoking the humanitarian rhetoric of the law in support of the very greed it was proclaimed to hinder.

The dispute also involved a further obscure charge of 2$000 per slave, known as the *preferência*. The Crown apparently introduced this wrinkle in the seventeenth century as yet another means of favoring Lisbon merchants over the Brazilians then dominant in carrying slaves for Luso-African owners. Captains waiting to sail with slaves carried for freight charges, or *de bando*, could jump the queue of ships and thus rush their slaves to markets in the New World ahead of competitors by paying the charge to the Lisbon merchant in charge of the royal contract for slave export duties in Angola.[37] The *preferência* seems to have functioned as a premium paid to this contractor by his Brazilian competitors in lieu of higher freight charges applicable to all, and shippers evidently passed the 2$000 they paid on to owners whose slaves they carried. The contractor was obligated in return to distribute a portion of his revenues from this source to the missions of the colony, to its hospital, and as rations for the troops, up to a limit of 1,800 *preferências* (out of the 7,000–10,000 slaves then shipped annually from Luanda and Benguela), or 36,000$000 per

---

slaves on the much shorter, unregulated Mina-Bahia run were cited as 10$000: Pierre Verger, *Flux et reflux de la traite des nègres entre le golfe de Bénin et Bahia de Todos os Santos du XVIIe au XIXe siècle* (Paris: Mouton, 1968), p. 33.

35. Memorial from the Senado da Câmara (Luanda), 20 July 1724, AHU, Angola cx. 16; *bando,* 24 May 1725, and accompanying documentation, AHU, Angola cx. 16; Pereira da Costa, 8 June 1725, AHU, Angola cx. 16.

36. Coelho de Carvalho, 28 June 1724, AHU, Angola cx. 16.

37. See Francisco e Manoel Gomes Lisboa, 26 June 1715, AHU, Angola cx. 15; also *representação* from the Senado da Câmara (Luanda), enclosed with *bando* of 24 May 1725, AHU, Angola cx. 16.

year. By the 1750s, ships collected the charge on all slaves as a matter of course and paid it to the contractor, simply in order to maintain their places in the order of departure, as owners complained, or, as the contractor replied, as a badly needed supplement to the scandalously low freight rates they were able to charge.[38] The government abolished this complex arrangement by incorporating the 2$000 in the revised tax schedule of the slave export duty reform of 1758 (discussed below).

Selling the spaces aboard the slave ships at the inflated prices that prevailed in the 1720s attracted new Brazilian shipping to Angola, but in the longer run it depressed the trade by drawing down the credit on which it functioned. Undercapitalized small ship owners, who came for profits from carrying slaves alone, brought only small incoming cargoes. They could not meet the specialized requirement of the Angolan trade that arriving ships bring trade goods to support purchases of slaves in the interior, at least when drought and warfare did not account for most of the people reaching the coast as slaves. Slaveowners at Luanda could afford to pay what shippers demanded in the 1720s, when increased mining had temporarily raised slave prices to peaks that easily covered freights, high surcharges, and profits as well.[39] But sending slaves out without bringing goods in allowed the Luanda Luso-Africans to liquidate their businesses prosperously by selling slaves for the gold abundant in Brazil and to retire to America without maintaining commercial investments in the interior with goods from Bahia or Lisbon.[40]

When the Crown confirmed the order of the interim governor, *mestre do campo* Carvalho da Costa, to cease the sale of shipping space,[41] shippers evaded the intent of the proclamation by selling their ships to consortia of slaveowners in Angola at prices offering returns equivalent to what the owners of the vessels might otherwise have realized from selling the space aboard them. No doubt such contrived sales contained repurchase agreements that allowed the original owners to buy their ships back at prearranged prices in Brazil. The Crown, in accordance with established policy against encouraging Brazilian shippers or any other colonial interests to accumulate significant wealth, concurred in ending the Brazilians' sales of access to space on Angolan slavers. But two years later, in 1727, it com-

---

38. See the *carta regia* of 8 May 1693 granting revenues from 700 *preferências* to the missions of the colony, AHU, Angola cx. 24; Miranda de Vasconcelos, 20 Aug. 1739, AHU, Angola cx. 21; *alvará*, 25 Jan. 1758, *Arquivos de Angola* 2, no. 14 (1936): 537; *apontamentos* issued to Governor Moçâmedes, n.d. (ca. 1784), AHU, Angola maço 2–A; de Mello, 14 Aug. 1802, AHU, Angola cx. 52. At times, probably including the 1720s, there was a secondary trading market in these rights.

39. For prices, Miller, "Slave Prices."

40. Carvalho da Costa *bando*, 24 May 1725, AHU, Angola cx. 16.

41. *Parecer* of the Conselho Ultramarino (Lisbon), 6 June 1725, and *carta regia*, 22 Nov. 1725, both AHU, Angola cx. 16.

promised by raising the officially allowed freight charges for slaves carried under the contract to 8$000.[42] But even at this increased level, allowed charges remained uneconomically low for shippers and discriminatory against the Brazilians. This nominally increased *frete* charge included the 2$000 *preferência*, which went to the contractor (above the revenues conceded to local charities in Luanda) rather than to shippers. The contractor thus kept the full 8$000 freight charge for slaves he sent out on his own ships and received an additional 2$000 fee for slaves sent on the ships of anyone else—in practice the Brazilians, who netted only 6$000.[43]

The later history of taxation of the southern Atlantic trade continued to favor Lisbon merchants doing business in Angola, though no longer the metropolitan investors behind the contractor. The decree of 25 January 1758 included the 2$000 *preferência* in a new consolidated single export duty of 8$700. The contract holders, against whom the 1758 decree was subtly but carefully framed, had previously collected the charge without having to account for it in the bids they submitted to the Crown; the change made them responsible for paying the Crown a share of the 25 percent that it contributed to their actual revenues. This reallocation also had the effect of applying the fee to all ships, even those sailing *efeitos próprios* with slaves of their own, previously exempt, which would include those of the contractor. The contractor would henceforth have to make higher payments to the Crown that would cancel out the subsidies received from other shippers in the form of the *preferência*. By the late eighteenth century, a new rule based on the doctrine of *efeitos próprios* had replaced the *preferências* as the means of assuring precedence to Lisbon-based ships, and no one any longer had a clear idea about how the old system had functioned.[44]

Freight rates remained at the 6$000 ceiling set in 1727 for the three main Brazilian slaving ports for the remainder of the century, but like the *preferência*, they had yielded in practice, if not in theory, to economic changes and no longer functioned as a means of disabling Brazilian slavers in the port at Luanda.[45] The Pombaline Companies opened direct trade

42. With the letting of the 1730–38 contract on 10 Nov. 1727; see the "relação dos contratos" (1674–1765) in AHU, Angola cx. 31, for the date. For confirmation, see the *requerimento* of (contractor) Manoel Monteiro da Rocha, 12 Sept. 1732, AHU, Angola cx. 19; *requerimento* (illegible petitioner), 24 Oct. 1739, AHU, Angola cx. 21; *requerimento* of Jacinto Dias Braga (contractor), 29 Oct. 1742, AHU, Angola cx. 22; *condição* 5 of the slave contract for 1742–48, AHU, Angola cx. 23.

43. For this discrimination in the 1720s, *representação* of the Senado da Câmara (Luanda), with the *bando* of 24 May 1725, AHU, Angola cx. 16. The contractors themselves, sailing *efeitos próprios*, did not pay the *preferência*.

44. *Apontamentos* (given to Gov. Moçâmedes), n.d. (ca. 1784), AHU, Angola maço 2–A; de Mello, 14 Aug. 1802, AHU, Angola cx. 52.

45. By way of comparison, it may be noted that the passenger fare from Rio de Janeiro to Lisbon was 8$000 in 1821: *requerimento* of Manoel d'Abreu de Mello, n.d. (ca. 1821)

to the distant northern Brazilian captaincies of Maranhão and Pará in the 1760s with higher charges of 12$000 and 16$000 authorized on these monopoly routes.[46] The Napoleonic wars in Europe broke regular contact between Lisbon and Luanda in the 1790s, and the imperial government, relocated in Rio, suspended regulated freight rates to allow charges to the main Brazilian ports to rise to 12$800 (i.e., one Brazilian *dobra*) for adults and to 9$000 for slave youths, apparently profitable levels about double the legal maximum.[47] With the Lisbon merchants resident at Rio and in the process of taking over its slave trade at that time, the belated increase benefited home merchants as much as the Brazilians.

During an 1811 shortage of shipping at Luanda, caused by the movement of Rio-based slavers to Cabindan beaches, Luso-African merchants offered to pay 15$000 per slave to attract ships to relieve pressure on barracoons overcrowded with dying slaves they could not evacuate to Brazil.[48] The only recorded application of the old 1758 restriction to 6$000 was by the governor Oliveira Barboza, who invoked it to gain cheap passage for his personal slaves at the lower, legal rate when he ended his term in Angola and returned to Brazil in 1816.[49] The century ended profitably for shippers, including the Brazilians, in another sense as well. Since they received these freight charges only on slaves reaching Brazil alive, high death rates earlier in the century had lowered the amounts they collected even below the legal ceiling.[50] Declining mortality rates after 1800 allowed them to collect on a larger surviving percentage of the slaves embarked.

AHU, Angola maço 7. Freight charges are cited in Corrêa, *História de Angola,* 1:48; Mattoso, *Etre esclave au Brésil,* p. 81; de Mello, 7 and 12 March 1799, AHU, Angola cx. 46; Correa da Silva, 9 March 1803, enclosing merchants' petition of 20 Jan. 1803, AHU, Angola cx. 54; Oliveira Barboza, 8 April 1811, AHU, Angola cx. 59; Motta Feo e Torres, 8 Aug. 1816, AHU, Angola cx. 64. António Carreira, *Notas sobre o tráfico português de escravos* (Lisbon: Universidade Nova de Lisboa, 1978), p. 56, seems imprecise on the history of freight rates in the southern Atlantic.

46. "Relação sobre escravatura," n.d. (ca. 1760s), AHU, Angola maço 10 (D.O.); Carreira, "Companhias pombalinas de navegação," p. 63; Manuel Nunes Dias, *A Companhia Geral do Grão Pará e Maranhão (1755–1778)* (São Paulo: Universidade de São Paulo, 1971), p. 381; Rebelo, *Relações,* p. 89.

47. De Mello, 12 March 1799, AHU, Angola cx. 46.

48. Oliveira Barboza, 8 April 1811, AHU, Angola cx. 59, confirming that the 6$000 ceiling was still technically in effect.

49. Motta Feo e Torres, 8 Aug. 1816, AHU, Angola cx. 64.

50. *Fretes* were paid by means of the same bills of exchange that merchants used to pay for the imports they bought. The *armador,* or ship handler, in Luanda undertook to discharge the slave owner's obligation for freight with such a bill, payable only upon the safe arrival of the slave in Brazil. The record is consistent throughout the eighteenth century that freight charges were not paid on slaves dying at sea (Taunay, *Subsídios,* p. 232, to the contrary): "Relação sobre escravatura," n.d. (ca. 1760s), AHU, Angola maço 10 (D.O.); Corrêa, *História de Angola,* 1:48; de Mello, 12 March and 8 Nov. 1799, AHU, Angola cx. 46.

Tight-Packing

With the defeats that Brazilian shippers suffered in their search for adequate returns from transporting slaves to the gold fields of Minas Gerais, they developed alternative strategies. Sales of *praça* surcharges evaded the imperial ceiling on freight rates only briefly, and Brazilians surely found sales and repurchases of their vessels a cumbersome means of covering their costs of sailing the Angola circuit. Intensified government surveillance at Luanda sharply limited opportunities of this sort in the 1730s, and in the 1740s dissipation of the mining boom removed the high prices underpinning these strategies. The shippers were unable to purchase slaves when, also in the 1730s and 1740s, the contractor introduced growing quantities of trade goods and bought up the supply of Angolan bills of exchange secured by the slaves whom the Luso-Africans sent for sale in Brazil. Brazilian shippers therefore invented legal pretexts for loading slaves beyond the limits established by the law of 18 March 1684, in part to collect the extra regulation freight rates that each paid and in part to capture a share of the trading profit for themselves.[51] The protective decree of 1684 had explicitly acknowledged the direct connection of load factors to revenues from slave transporting when it compensated its reduction in slave cargoes with a rise in freight rates from 4$000 to 5$000, citing overcrowding as the primary abuse that justified its issuance.

In the Portuguese trade, efforts to cram as many slaves as possible between decks were discussed in terms of the ships' *arqueações* (singular, *arqueação*)—that is, the legally authorized carrying capacities assigned to slavers through procedures specified by the fundamental law of 18 March 1684.[52] The *arqueação* was generally a technical measure of the interior volume of any vessel, whether a cask or a ship, but in the context of the slave trade it meant specifically the area of deck space available for lodging slaves. As usual, the various parties interested in the slave trade had conflicting interests in how many slaves a given ship might carry, since tight-packing, as the Brazilians practiced it, traded losses to Luso-African owners of the slaves who died or sickened from insufficient food, water, and care

---

51. Pereira da Costa, 19 Feb. 1728, AHU, Angola cx. 17. I also considered this subject in Miller, "Overcrowded and Undernourished."

52. Art. 6, in *Arquivos de Angola* 2, no. 11 (1936): 315. The first known regulations of the slave trade from São Tomé to Mina (1519) did not address the issue in those terms. Limitations on the Angola-Brazil trade, though defined in other ways, were much older, dating to the 1607 *regimento* given to the Spanish-appointed governor, D. Manoel Pereira Forjaz, according to José Gonçalves Salvador, *Os Cristãos-novos e o comércio no Atlântico Meridional (com enfoque nas capitanias do sul 1530–1680)* (São Paulo: Livraria Pioneira Editora, 1978), p. 332. Restoration of Angola to Portuguese control after the Dutch occupation in 1648 brought a new *provisão*, which was reiterated by a further *provisão* of 23 Sept. 1664: Taunay, *Subsídios*, p. 99.

aboard an overloaded ship against the *réis* that freight haulers earned from the remainder who survived and from buying and squeezing still other unauthorized slaves into their already crowded deck on their personal accounts.

As long as Lisbon merchants owned so few slaves aboard the *tumbeiros*, tight-packing did little to damage metropolitan interests. In fact, crowding coincided neatly with Lisbon's basic mid-century strategy of selling as many goods as possible and claiming returns in bills of exchange without much responsibility for subsequent financial and human costs in slave mortality. Lisbon factors had no objection to putting more slaves aboard the vessels available in Angola, the more quickly to convert their bills to cash, whether the slaves lived or died. Their uneconomically low freight rates also encouraged tight-packing by creating shipping shortages. That the humanitarian provisions of 1684 were enforced only irregularly, and probably selectively, was therefore owing only in part to the cleverness with which shippers manipulated the language of the law and to the selfish connivance of bribed government officials in Luanda. In addition, colonial government revenues were almost totally dependent on slave export duties, and they rose when officials allowed more than the proper quotas of slaves to depart.

Conflict over the practice of tight-packing thus formed part of the battle in the first two-thirds of the century at Luanda between Lisbon factors, who were there to sell goods and allied on this issue with the Brazilian shippers, and Luso-Africans, who owned the slaves. It was the tax contractors who supervised embarkations and condoned the crowding because only large numbers of slaves leaving Angola could pay for their sales of huge quantities of Asian textiles. The slaves' fates at sea mattered less, since their owners paid export duties to the contract holder on slaves leaving Angola, before embarkation, rather than on those who reached Brazil alive.[53] However, when the chartered companies came on the scene, they were often owners of slaves and joined the Luso-Africans in urging reduced load factors. By the last decades of the 1700s, the alliance had shifted. A small group of liberal reformers in the metropole opposed the Brazilians' tendency to overload their ships, only in part because they could thus hinder colonial shippers who had all but taken slave transport in the southern Atlantic away from metropolitan merchants. When Lisbon merchants, relocated after 1808 in Rio de Janeiro, themselves became owners of slaves, the Crown finally turned seriously to limiting this ancient abuse.[54]

53. See the *requerimento* of Francisco Gomes Lisboa, 23 Jan. 1723, AHU, Angola cx. 16, for a reflection of this situation.
54. For a remarkably clear statement of the opposing interests, see de Mello, 12 March 1799, AHU, Angola cx. 46.

The shifting trade-offs implicit in the division of opportunities among the varying interests in the slaves aboard the typical Brazilian slaver worked out to favor a limited degree of tight-packing, disregarding the lives of the individual slaves who fell victim to these strategies. Slaves did not succumb in economically significant numbers to cramped conditions alone.[55] They were more sensitive to the adequacy with which captains provisioned their ships with food, and especially with water.[56] Given the relatively reliable winds of the southern Atlantic, the shortness of the usual passage, and the theoretical availability of emergency provisioning stops at São Tomé or, for ships bound for Rio, along the northeastern Brazilian coast, losses from such shortages were by no means a certainty for captains who took on more slaves than the law, if not some less restrictive rule of thumb, permitted. In practice, on voyages that made the ocean crossing within the time foreseen, slave mortality increased only moderately as a direct result of taking more slaves.[57]

The economics of the voyage predisposed captains to take chances with a ship loaded beyond the legal limits. Packing more slaves into the paying cargo increased freight revenues for Brazilian ship operators, though only up to a point, since they forfeited charges on slaves who died on the way to Brazil. In the simplest hypothetical case, an average eighteenth-century ship carried 400 slaves, all for other owners, and could expect losses of from 3 to 5 percent on the way to Brazil. These were deaths beyond the shippers' ability to control, even with heroic efforts on behalf of the slaves.[58] The extent of tight-packing probably seldom ran much more than 10 percent above the legal rated capacity of a ship, or 40 slaves in this hypothetical instance.[59] On the extreme assumption that tight-packing at this level doubled the rate of mortality among the entire cargo, at the prevailing freight charges a ship overloaded to that degree could

55. Cf. David Eltis, "Free and Coerced Transatlantic Migrations: Some Comparisons," *American Historical Review* 88, no. 2 (1983): 251–80. Data in Stein, *French Slave Trade*, p. 20, allow a crude estimate of the elasticity of mortality in relation to tight-packing (*assuming* that the ships in his two samples had similar routings, voyage durations, internal designs, provisioning, and so on): private French traders carrying 2.0 slaves/ton experienced 16% mortality, while company ships carrying only 1.1 slaves/ton lowered mortality to 13%, an elasticity of 0.28 (23.1% decrease in mortality from an 81.8% reduction in density).

56. Discussed further below. See Klein, *Middle Passage*, pp. 201–2, for the point in general.

57. Klein, *Middle Passage*, pp. 65–67, 194–96, 199–200, 229, 234; Miller, "Mortality in the Atlantic Slave Trade," and idem, "Overcrowded and Undernourished."

58. See the evidence and logic developed in Miller, "Legal Portuguese Slaving," pp. 135–76, and idem, "Mortality in the Atlantic Slave Trade."

59. The most clearly documented instance of the extent of tight-packing involved 25 additional slaves on a vessel rated to carry 475 slaves. The captain, when apprehended, cited other examples of illegal boardings in excess of rated capacities involving only 15, 25, and 30 slaves. *Requerimento* of Guilherme Jozé Ferreira, in Correa de Araujo to de Mello, 15 March 1799, AHU, Angola cx. 49. Further evidence in Miller, "Overcrowded and Undernourished."

expect incremental losses of from 12 to 20 slaves. It would thus lose between 96$000 and 120$000 in freights on the slaves who died from the strategy.[60] However, tight-packing brought an additional 20 to 28 slaves across alive, and these, if carried for others, would have earned at least 120$000, and perhaps 148$000, in freight charges. The level of tight-packing apparently accepted under normal circumstances thus appears to have fallen comfortably below the break-even point that slavers were likely to have assumed. Higher freight rates after 1810 reduced the incentive to tight-pack, both by making the financial attractiveness of the voyage less dependent on doing so and by raising the opportunity cost of losing charges on slaves who died.

Tight-packers developed other techniques of carrying extra slaves that compensated for the possible loss of freight charges with trading gains accruing to the venture and its officers. The strained finances of the typical Brazilian slaving voyage and the limited value of the *gerebita* it carried meant that ships seldom had the means to leave Luanda other than *de bando*, carrying mostly slaves owned by Luso-Africans, only part of whom secured bills of exchange the operators of the venture took as proceeds of their inbound cargo.[61] The shoestring on which the backers of these voyages operated also meant that they tended to pay the officers and crews of the slaving ships not in cash wages but with authorization to sell a small portion of the inbound cargo for slaves for themselves. These slaves traveled above the deck, free of charges for freight, and beyond the rated capacity of the ship, which officials generously interpreted to apply only to paying captives. Whatever modest number of slaves the venture could acquire for itself made the middle passage in the same privileged conditions. They ate and drank provisions which were calculated according to the ship's rated capacity, and which barely sufficed for the slaves of the *arqueação* at that, and often preempted space meant for facilities for the main cargo of captives below decks. The resulting hardships fell selectively on the human property of the Luso-Africans rather than on slaves belonging to the ship and its officers. If mortality struck down the slaves of the officers or crew, they merely substituted living individuals owned by others for the personal slaves they lost and reported the stolen captives as having died en route.

---

60. At the legal freight rate of 6$000; the loss could be 153$000 to 256$000 at times when the premium rate of 12$800 could be charged.

61. E.g., the 1727 voyage of the *Santo António, Santa Anna e Almas* to Bahia: the ship owned 26.6% of the 462 slaves aboard, the captain owned another 10 slaves, and 88 "residents of Luanda" owned the remaining 329 (or 3.7 slaves per owner). Klein, *Middle Passage*, pp. 38 ff. There is, e.g., also an unidentified list of slaves by owners, n.d. (ca. 1741?), AHU, Angola cx. 22: the captain and principal of the venture owned 38.6% (or 249 slaves), the first mate 12.0%, and 23 others the remainder. See, in general, Verger, *Flux et reflux*, p. 109.

Generally declining mortality rates worked out to favor moderate tight-packing still in the early nineteenth century, even though shippers owned greater proportions of the slaves by that time. Even under the extreme assumption that the slaves were entirely the property of the vessel's backers, attributing an incremental loss of 5 percent of the 440 slaves packed aboard a hypothetical 400-slave ship would cost owners 2,400$000 in revenues forfeited on the 24 additional individuals who died. But even with total losses to mortality at 10 percent—the 5 percent increment plus the 5 percent expectable under any circumstances—the ship would still arrive with 396 slaves alive rather than the 380 who would have survived if the ship had sailed at the legal limit. The advantage was sixteen slaves, or 1,600$000 in revenues, offset by the costs of buying the extra 40, also about 1,600$000, for a venture exactly at the break-even point.[62] The attractiveness of overcrowding was, of course, sensitive to the assumptions slavers actually made about their costs and mortality rates, but the returns from tight-packing at this level were sufficient to justify the rules of thumb evidently in effect. Even under the extremely incomplete data available on the actual mortality function of tight-packing, these break-even points defined limits sufficiently broader than slavers were likely to have perceived so that few besides the most idealistic liberals in the eighteenth-century southern Atlantic—or the chartered Pombaline companies, who faced special circumstances—would have seen moderate overloading as anything but money in their pockets.[63]

All of these calculations aside, even the owners of slaves who were most pessimistic about the fatal consequences of tight-packing occasionally faced circumstances in which overloading a ship would save more of their property than it would harm. In practice, the decision to crowd one's slaves aboard a ship depended on comparing the death rates expected from tight-packing at sea to the fates of slaves temporarily left behind at Luanda or Benguela. The shortages of shipping recurrent under the low freight rates and unreliable arrivals of ships from Lisbon could hold up departures for slaves on the coast, so that fewer deaths might result amidst less than optimal conditions on a speedy middle passage than from continued delays

---

62. All assuming the 100$000 dockside price for new slaves current at Rio at the end of the eighteenth century and a generous total cost to board a slave at Luanda (less markups on goods sold): see Miller, "Slave Prices," Fig. 3.2.

63. An early-nineteenth-century Bahian caustically referred to the *arqueação* as nothing more than "an invention for extracting money": cited in Lopes, *Escravatura*, p. 179. My discussion here is intended to approximate the notion of "rationality" in contemporaneous terms rather than to rely on abstract imputations of perfect knowledge of the costs and risks involved to the slavers. Nonetheless, the hypothetical calculations presented confirm that the limited sort of tight-packing in which slavers engaged was in fact also profitable in the aggregate, the level of experience approximating a fully informed individual decision-maker.

in the port.[64] Such circumstances arose during food shortages in Luanda, especially frequent before 1764, when Angolan droughts often forced slave ships to sacrifice paying inbound cargo to bring provisions for their cargoes from Brazil. The shippers' ability to feed slaves on board could save many who would otherwise have died of starvation in the city.[65] In less dramatic terms of slave maintenance costs, feeding captives imported food aboard the ships could become less costly than provisioning them from the expensive and insufficient supplies in the city.

The decree of 1684 established the legal pretexts under which captains conducted their tight-packing strategies, in collusion with government officials in Luanda who usually assisted in stretching a veil of legality over their contraventions of the law. According to the 1684 regulation, officials were to measure the area available for carrying slaves on ships on the basis of a fundamental distinction between the hold (*porão*) and the decks (*cubertas*). The holds (*porões*) were reserved for cargo, particularly provisions for the slaves, and only the decks, either a space built above the hold and below the main deck or the enclosed cabins and bunks, were defined as suitable for human occupation, whether for officers, crew, passengers, or slaves. Another article of the 1684 law required food and water in quantities that assumed hold capacity sufficient for the slaves boarded. Therein lay a loophole that slavers could exploit by counting space intended for cargo as decks measured as suitable for slaves.

Nothing specified the headroom to be provided in the areas measured, and the law explicitly confirmed that capacity ratings were to be based on deck area rather than volume. However, it was accepted that space was important for slave comfort, if not safety, since the air in crowded deck areas became notoriously fetid and stale in the tropics. The law took indirect account of this through a provision which allowed greater numbers of slaves in ventilated upper deck areas, as opposed to unventilated lower regions of the ship. Spaces open to the air could take five slaves per *tonelada*, the unit of measurement specified by the law of 1684, specifically children (*moleques*) and women believed to be weaker than adult males. Covered decks with gratings in their ceiling or portholes (at an unspecified fre-

---

64. De Mello, 12 March 1799, AHU, Angola cx. 46, acknowledged (and supported) the rationality of this type of calculation. Also see the case of the *Livramento* in Benguela: Alvellos Leiria, 18 Nov. 1814, AHU, Angola cx. 62.

65. One may note the effect on the economics of the typical slaving voyage of the need to fill cargo space needed for the low-value (and therefore high-bulk) *gerebita* with beans, flour, and water for the slaves; it left such ships even more dependent on freight charges for their revenues. Accordingly, slavers were understandably reluctant to bring foodstuffs to Angola beyond those absolutely necessary for the slaves they carried, and the residents of the city sometimes went hungry as a result, conceivably suffering even more from malnutrition than the slaves fortunate enough to be sent off on the slave ships.

quency) could carry fewer, seven adults per two *toneladas*, and areas lacking any sort of opening the fewest, only five adult slaves per two *toneladas*.[66] Infants, defined as children too small to walk, were not counted at all, or, rather, were considered as part of the mothers who carried them.

This legal framework placed a clear premium on designing ships to maximize the proportion of deck area available for carrying slaves relative to the hold volume reserved for supplies and ship's equipment. By reducing the height of the decks to a minimum, carpenters could squeeze in an extra deck and virtually double the rated capacity of the ship without increasing at all the volume of space available to the slaves. It also paid to distribute portholes down as near the waterline as was structurally feasible, even though waves might prevent them from being opened for days on end. Nominal portholes and hatches, opened for purposes of measuring the *arqueação* while the ship lay at anchor in the calm waters of a protected harbor, were sometimes battened tight as soon as she put to sea.[67]

The law's influence on ship design thus fell on altering the interior spaces of the ship; on technical interpretations of what constituted a "child," since *moleques* could be carried at densities up to twice those for adults; and on even finer distinctions among the several different categories of slaves carried—some belonging to the crew, others owned by the officers, still others accompanying passengers, and the majority of the cargo boarded as freight—since the law of 1684 was invitingly silent on which of them were to be counted toward filling the rated capacity and which of them were not.

One favorite method of altering the numbers of slaves in the *arqueação* of a given vessel was to change the standard by which one measured its capacity. Measurement was an inexact science at best in a time when the same nominal unit could vary by 50 percent and more between Lisbon and Porto, the two major seaports of metropolitan Portugal. Physical standards in Angola varied as a matter of course by the quantity-bargaining logic prevalent there, and authorities responsible for rating the ships often came from Luso-African families of local background. Just as they altered weights and measures as a means of changing prices of goods exchanged, so officials in Luanda could produce *toneladas* that differed sharply from those in the ports of Brazil or Lisbon without violating practices accepted locally.

Local assessors apparently tended to reduce *arqueações* on behalf of the Luso-African owners of the slaves, simply by lengthening the standard used to measure the space. In some cases, the official unit of length, the

66. Art. 6, in *Arquivos de Angola* 2, no. 11 (1936): 315. The exact size of the *tonelada* was a matter of negotiation, as described below.

67. Art. 11 in the 1684 *regimento*, ibid., p. 316. On portholes battened down see Lopes, *Escravatura*, p. 175.

rumo, was simply refined to include more *dedos*, on the rationalization that the original *tonelada*, defined in 1694 according to the length and height of the cask then in use (24–25 *almudes*, a *pipa*, or 435.5 liters), had subsequently increased with the switch to the larger wine *pipa* (roughly 28–32 *almudes*, or 535 liters) that came into later use.[68] In Luanda the technique of varying measures also depended on taking them with a flexible cord, knotted to mark the width and length construed to represent one *tonelada*. An official intent on reducing the number of slaves a ship could carry determined its dimensions with the cord stretched taut.[69] In at least one instance, the measurer pulled so hard to lengthen the cord that he snapped it.

Under these circumstances one would have expected standards to shift in directions that favored the most powerful interests in each port, and the drift indeed seems to have run with the changing balance of power at Luanda. Already by the 1730s representatives of the contractors, who favored liberal measurements to get more slaves aboard the ships, and the Luso-African slaveowners, who favored stricter measurements and fewer slaves, argued over where the slave ships should be measured. Lisbon ships, which all belonged to the contractors themselves, arrived at Luanda with capacities already rated in the metropole, and the contractor defended the legality of loading slaves according to these presumably more liberal limits. Officials in Luanda asserted their right to determine new, lower capacities there, and the contractor at times complained to the Crown of low capacity ratings given in Angola, surely by Luso-African owners of the slaves his ships carried.[70] These pressures ran in quite the opposite direction from those anticipated by the decree of 1684, which had specified the problem as higher ratings expectable in Angola. Its first five clauses designated the authorities responsible for measuring *arqueações* in Lisbon, Porto, other metropolitan ports, Brazil, and Angola, and in fact authorized officials in Angola to reduce, but never to raise, capacities determined elsewhere. It implicitly assumed that governors with an interest in tight-packing would determine ratings in Angola, as was the greater danger at that time, not the Luso-African owners of the slaves, who had substantial influence in Luanda in the 1730s.

---

68. The number of *dedos* (fingers) in the *rumo* (rhumb?) is discussed in the *requerimento* of Manoel Monteiro da Rocha (contractor), 14 March 1731, AHU, Angola maço 18–A.

69. Albuquerque, 21 July 1730, AHU, Angola maço 18–A; Monteiro da Rocha *requerimento*, 14 March 1731, AHU, Angola maço 18–A; *parecer* of the Conselho Ultramarino, 7 March 1731, AHU, Angola maço 18–A; also see Vasconcelos, 4 Feb. 1759, AHU, Angola cx. 28.

70. Albuquerque, 21 July 1730, AHU, Angola maço 18–A. For other evidence on disputes over the *arqueações*, see *requerimento* of Marsal Domingues, n.d. (but before 16 March 1735), AHU, Angola cx. 20; *requerimento* of José Glz. Lamas, n.d. (but before 13 Jan. 1737), AHU, Angola cx. 21; Barboza Mourais, 14 March 1722, AHU, Angola cx. 16.

By the 1740s, the contractor had established firm control over port procedures at Luanda and was petitioning the Crown to legalize remeasurements of ship capacities. He directed his concern at ratings done in Brazil, presumably at the instigation of the shippers there whom he was in the process of driving out of the trade.[71] The shippers' strategy in this case was to rate the contractors' ships low and their own ships high. The freight-dependent Brazilian slavers thus tried to use the *arqueação* provisions of the 1684 law against the contractor in the 1730s just after they had failed in the 1720s to gain higher freight rates and other fees for carrying slaves for themselves. Brazilians in competition with the contractor nonetheless made a practice of obtaining a first *arqueação* in Brazil before they left and then cruising down the Angolan coast, obtaining larger capacity ratings wherever local officials would cooperate, in Benguela, or Luanda.[72]

Given the flexibility with which the law was interpreted, disputes also swirled around the identity of the official at Luanda authorized to render the crucial measurement. Ship captains had originally been allowed to make their own capacity measurements,[73] with the predictable consequence of overstating capacities and authorizing much larger cargoes of slaves. Responsibility in Angola formally fell to the *provedor* (inspector) of the Royal Treasury, a theoretically reliable Lisbon appointee, but in practice local delegates of the opposing shippers and slaveowners concurred in nominating compromise candidates with a sense for how many slaves a ship could safely carry and still bring its owners an acceptable return on their investment. Such pliable standards no doubt varied with the politics and economics of the trade, with the measures shrinking to provide growing capacities for the same ships when costs rose or when quantities of slaves in the port exceeded the capacity of the ships present to remove them. *Arqueações* should thus have risen in the eighteenth century to reflect the cost squeeze on shippers caught between inflating costs and stable freight rates. The evidence is that the *tonelada* in fact decreased in size throughout the period.[74]

Another opportunity to influence the capacity rating given a ship lay in employing fictional conversion factors to turn measured widths and lengths into the area-*toneladas* on which the *arqueação* rested. As late as

71. *Requerimento* of Jacinto Dias Braga (contractor), n.d. (ca. 1745), AHU, Angola cx. 23.

72. Inferred from practices noted in Carvalho da Costa, 8 June 1725, AHU, Angola cx. 16; Magalhães, Nov. 1744, AHU, Angola cx. 23; and Lencastre, 3 Feb. 1773, AHU, Angola cx. 36. Concealment of slaves loaded and dispatched in remote Benguela was an important part of the strategy and was probably connected to the eventual concentration of southern Brazilian trading there.

73. *Parecer* of the Conselho Ultramarino (Lisbon), 7 March 1731, AHU, Angola maço 18–A.

74. Miller, "Overcrowded and Undernourished."

the 1750s, the official in charge of ratings based them on a book of fictional tables accepted as representing area-equivalents of the dimensions reported to him. Whether marginally literate Luanda assessors lacked arithmetical skills to make the conversions according to true multiplication tables or deliberately falsified capacities on behalf of the contractor, these semi-mystical numerological charts produced official, and arguably legal, *arqueações* substantially in excess of the true products.[75] Failing that, the scribe (*escrivão*) in charge of registering the assessors' verdict could simply be bribed to record a figure greater than that obtained through measurement.[76] The spread of better training in elementary geometry as the eighteenth century proceeded and increasingly insistent directives from the Crown gradually eliminated tight-packing through these technical manipulations of the measures.[77]

Standardization simply forced shippers determined to pack slaves tightly to refine another widely practiced method of creating nominal space for slaves without violating the letter of the law. The deception in this case turned on the question of which spaces among the multiple chambers inside a ship should count toward its *arqueação*. Misrepresentations grew from an old practice of loading baggage of the sailors and passengers (and probably such other freight as was available from Angola) in spaces measured as "empty" and available for slaves:[78] deck areas normally used for storing equipment that could be cleared for purposes of inspection, bunks and hammock space reserved for the crew at sea but not occupied while they were at liberty in the port, quarters for the officers and for passengers and their baggage, and even bunkers reserved by the law of 1684 for food supplies and water that, temporarily emptied, could be construed as slave decks. Altars from the chapel, stoves from the galley, sails, cordage, cables, tables, chairs, and any kind of movable fittings went ashore before the measurement, only to be reloaded and stowed in spaces assigned in the interim to slaves.[79]

An alternative version of this technique falsified the rigging classification of the ship. The slavers calling at Benguela and Luanda fell into a variety of technical categories—*curvetas, galeras, escunas, sumacas, bergan-*

75. Vasconcelos, 4 Feb. 1759, AHU, Angola cx. 28.
76. Magalhães, 6 Nov. 1744, AHU, Angola cx. 23.
77. On Crown directives see Lencastre, 3 Feb. 1773, AHU, Angola cx. 36. "Instruções" given to Gov. Lencastre, n.d. (ca. 1772), AHU, Angola maço 11, admitted that Lisbon had no idea how measurements were actually taken. Detailed formal instructions for making the *arqueação* measurements seem to have been issued only in 1810: Lopes, *Escravatura*, p. 181; Miller, "Overcrowded and Undernourished."
78. Pereira da Costa, 9 March 1723, AHU, Angola cx. 16; Magalhães, 9 Nov. 1745, AHU, Angola cx. 23.
79. Corrêa, *História de Angola*, 1:56; *Consulta* of the Conselho Ultramarino (Lisbon), 16 June 1796, and letter from Moçâmedes 24 Feb. 1796, AHU, Angola maço 6; de Mello, 12 March 1799, AHU, Angola cx. 46.

tins, and several others—distinguished partly by the number of masts they carried and the number and types of sails flown but also partly by the disposition of their internal spaces. Redesignation from one category to another could convert spaces treated as storage bunkers in one type of ship into cabins or slave decks in another ship class.[80] Alterations of the actual spaces aboard the ships and of their legal designation became prominent evasive techniques as falsifications of other measures grew more difficult.

Tight-packers relied on these techniques all the more because government officials eliminated another ancient method based on a loophole in the definition of which slaves counted in the "cargoes" limited by the seventeenth-century decree. Originally, only adults (*cabeças*) on whom full export duties were paid counted toward the slaves in the ship's designated capacity. This convention excluded a moderate number of enslaved individuals embarked in a wide range of other categories.[81] No duty was paid on slaves the colonial government sent to Brazil on its own account, usually captives obtained as parts of the royal share (one-fifth of the total, or the *quinto*) of booty seized in just wars;[82] these were simply added to the load after the ship had been filled to its legal capacity of tax-revenue-producing slaves. Captains also purchased as many slaves as they could, declared them members of the crew, and carried them, too, above and beyond their ship's authorized limit.[83] Passengers, especially departing government officials, left with entourages of slaves whom they declared as personal servants, but these "servants" certainly included captives destined for sale in Brazil, neither subject to duties nor counting toward the allotment of space that they would in fact occupy.

Perhaps the greatest abuse of the early eighteenth century was the misclassification of adult slaves as "children," or *crias.* The 1684 law, albeit somewhat vaguely, permitted ships to carry children above decks at slave-*tonelada* ratios twice those for the slaves kept below decks.[84] It made much clearer, however, that *crias de peito,* or infants in arms, were not to

---

80. Preliminary reconstructions of the histories of individual ships in the trade show not-infrequent reclassifications of the same ship from one category to another; Gov. de Mello, 13 March 1799, AHU, Angola cx. 46, made a clear reference to the changes. See also Lopes, *Escravatura,* pp. 182–83, for a detailed calculation of the differences made by this practice.
    81. E.g., the "Lista dos navios" for 1724, AHU, Angola cx. 16, in which untaxed slaves amounted to approximately 2% of the taxed slaves.
    82. Implicit in Magalhães, 9 Nov. 1745, AHU, Angola cx. 23.
    83. Pereira da Costa, 9 March 1723, AHU, Angola cx. 16; Avellar, 25 May 1730, AHU, Angola maço 18–A; Ferreira *requerimento,* n.d. (ca. 1762), AHU, Angola cx. 49. See also the consistency of registry of slave "crew members" aboard ships reaching Rio in 1795–1811, ANRJ, cód. 242; also Delgado, *Famosa e histórica Benguela,* doc. 4, pp. 447–49. The relevant regulation was cap. 1, para. 2, of the 1799 Luanda customs *regimento;* see *Arquivos de Angola* 2, no. 12 (1936): 406.
    84. Art. 6, in *Arquivos de Angola* 2, no. 11 (1936): 315.

be counted at all against the ships' rated capacity.[85] Already by the 1720s, tight-packers construed this partial exemption for children as license to board unlimited numbers of slaves of any sort beyond the ship's *arqueação*, even crowded into space already assigned for occupancy by adults.[86] This subterfuge misrepresented the excess slaves in the official documentation of the trade as *crias de pé*, or children "on foot," a contradiction in terms, since *crias* were by definition infants unable to stand by themselves. Young adult slaves, properly considered *moleques* or *molecas* (5–7 *palmos* in height), were boarded as *crias* (below 4 *palmos* in height, that is roughly 3 feet, or 22 centimeters) for purposes of filling the *arqueação*.[87] In some cases the distortion extended to taking youths or children on board and registering them as *crias* on the eve of the departure, then debarking them under cover of darkness and putting full adults in their already cramped places.[88]

This form of tight-packing produced especially large numbers of overgrown "infants": 5 to 15 percent of the adults boarded legally in the 1730s and 1740s, when slavers were under pressure from both the contractor and slaveowners (see Table 10.2).[89] The decree of 11 January 1758 outlawed tight-packing by this means, though with greater attention paid to the duties it cost the government on untaxed "children" than to the comfort or safety of the slaves.[90] However, this method of compensating for limited revenues from legal freight charges continued on at reduced levels under an informal compromise with the colonial government into the 1760s. Slaveowners consented to be taxed at half rates for "*crias*" that they would otherwise have attempted to embark as duty-free infants accompanying their mothers.[91] This arrangement, in line with other aggressive moves by Lisbon in that decade, transferred the costs to the slaveowners from freights they paid to shippers to taxes given to the government. The fictions surrounding the stature of the slaves seem to have been abandoned thereafter, though there is a hint that late-eighteenth-century assessors informally authorized higher capacity ratings for the "youths" of diminishing stature shipped as "adult" slaves, as the trade depleted reserves of fully grown

85. Formal reaffirmation of this exemption appeared in the law of 11 Jan. 1758: *Arquivos de Angola* 11, no. 14 (1936): 531–36.

86. Memorial, Senado da Câmara (Luanda), 20 July 1724, AHU, Angola cx. 16.

87. Pereira da Costa, 9 March 1723, AHU, Angola cx. 16; idem, 19 Feb. 1728, AHU, Angola cx. 17; Albuquerque, 1729, AHU, Angola cx. 18; Avellar, 25 May 1730, AHU, Angola maço 18–A; Magalhães, 9 Nov. 1745, AHU, Angola cx. 23.

88. Magalhães, 9 Nov. 1745, AHU, Angola cx. 23; Dias da Silva instructions to Bandeira and Carvalho, 8 Jan. 1767, AHU, Angola cx. 31.

89. See the figures in Klein, *Middle Passage,* Table 2.6, p. 36. Vasconcelos, 11 Feb. 1763, AHU, Angola cx. 29, seems to imply a figure around 5%.

90. Vasconcelos, 11 Feb. 1763, AHU, Angola cx. 29.

91. Sousa Coutinho, 27 Feb. 1765, AHU, Angola cx. 30. Klein, *Middle Passage,* Table 2.6, p. 36, notes the appearance of this new category in the tax records.

Table 10.2. Children, by Tax Category, Shipped from Luanda, 1726–1769

Year	Taxed children	Half-taxed children (*crias de pé*)	Untaxed children at breast (*crias de peito*)	Total children	Total slaves
1726	. . .	. . .	119	. . .	8,440
1727	. . .	. . .	94	. . .	7,633
1728	. . .	. . .	114	. . .	8,532
1731	. . .	. . .	93	. . .	5,808
1734	. . .	. . .	. . .	1,396	10,109
1738	. . .	. . .	. . .	1,187	8,810
1740	. . .	311	98	409	8,484
1741	. . .	736	154	890	9,158
1742	. . .	249	135	384	10,591
1744	. . .	426	166	592	8,848
1747	. . .	1,422	99	1,541	9,869
1748	. . .	894	101	995	11,810
1749	. . .	782	99	881	9,776
1758	. . .	. . .	. . .	139	9,938
1762	45	22	80	147	8,415
1763	31	17	61	109	7,634
1764	54	18	76	148	7,648
1765	16	62	200	278	10,672
1766	72	14	97	183	9,420
1767	13	8	69	90	9,318
1769	. . .	36	46	82	5,733

SOURCE: Reproduced from Klein, *Middle Passage,* Table 2.6, p. 36.

males in Africa, than they would have done for larger individuals.[92] While the law of 1684 certainly centered disputes over tight-packing on the meaning of *cria*, discussions over issues of the size and age of the slaves in the end gained plausibility from the younger and smaller people that slavers extracted from Africa as the trade wore on.

Smuggling

The obvious possible method of tight-packing, outright smuggling, prob-ably did not happen frequently. Slavers outward bound from Luanda, loaded to the gunwales with slaves as they were when they passed the tip of the island forming Luanda Bay, could easily and unobtrusively have paused along the coasts just north of the town to take on slaves diverted down the Bengo or the Dande and held in reserve for them as they passed

92. Lopes, *Escravatura,* p. 186.

down the coast along the usual course to Brazil. Entirely unregulated boardings of this sort could conceivably have produced the grossly over-loaded vessels that the trade's most avid detractors sometimes later depicted arriving in America. But the economics of the eighteenth-century trade ran strongly against this tactic. Smuggling of this sort presumed that slavers had conserved enough of their scarce financial resources while still at Luanda to buy significant quantities of additional slaves outright as they moved on down the coast to the north. The bill-of-exchange system, which could have allowed Brazilian tight-packers to take on slaves belonging to owners in Africa without investing their own capital, left too many trails and involved too many parties in Brazil to have supported an illegal trade of this sort. Even more important, the northern coasts were then the trading preserve of the British, and sometimes the French, who offered higher prices and superior merchandise to any Portuguese subject ambi-tious enough to offer his slaves for sale there. As soon as these conditions disappeared early in the nineteenth century, the northern coasts did become a significant source of slaves diverted to Brazilians, though in the context of the legalities of the early-nineteenth-century trade rather than of sur-reptitious tight-packing.[93] Earlier, Brazilians simply could not have met the foreign competition there.

As for smuggling through the port at Luanda, the fact that slavers resorted to elaborate legal subterfuges to tight-pack to escape the economic pressures under which they labored throughout the century suggests that officials generally established a record of most of the slaves embarked there, however creatively.[94] Some ships, to be sure, paused at the mouth of the Dande as they headed north from Luanda to pick up slaves sent there rather than through Luanda, but the few recorded instances of this tactic followed the establishment of a new customs house over strident objections of traders more concerned to sneak prohibited imports into the colony than to evade taxes on slaves leaving it.[95] Most smuggling of slaves through the town's port took place when officers and crew of the ships concealed a few personal servants in inaccessible compartments of the ship known only to them. They bribed the guard posted by the Royal Treasury, de-clared a portion of the captives they owned and then boarded a larger

---

93. Miller, "Overcrowded and Undernourished."

94. Notwithstanding the prevailing opinion to the contrary in most of the secondary literature: e.g., Taunay, *Subsídios,* p. 250, and Carreira, *Notas,* p. 17, where the conventional estimate of smuggled slaves in the vicinity of 50% of legally reported exports is repeated. This 50% figure, which pervades the literature, turns out upon close inspection to be based either on early estimates (e.g., Abreu e Brito [1592], in Brásio, *Monumenta missionaria africana,* 4:536–45) that do not apply to the later trade or refer to other kinds of "smuggling" than the loading of slaves at Luanda or Benguela in excess of those declared to customs authorities there.

95. De Mello, 12 Aug. 1801, AHU, Angola cx. 50.

number, counted carelessly by a guard whose eyes saw coins promised more clearly than the slaves passing before him.[96] Otherwise, inspection procedures at Luanda were gradually tightened throughout the century to the point that risks exceeded the possible gain.[97] On the whole, therefore, Brazilian slavers found marginal tight-packing more effective than smuggling as a response to the constraints of low capitalization and regulated freight rates under which they sailed.

The number of slaves boarded in excess of the ships' capacity ratings, and also the inflation of *arqueações* earlier in the century by inaccurate measuring techniques, probably declined over time. The quantities depended at least as much on demand in Brazil, on shortages of shipping, and on the lack of alternative outlets for slaves to French and British buyers along the coasts near Luanda as on pressure from Lisbon or on the vigilance of officials in Luanda, who influenced the methods rather than the amounts. The controversies over sales of *praças* aboard the ships, misclassification of adults and youths as "children," adaptable measuring procedures, and the like were concentrated in the 1720s, 1730s, and 1740s, when high demand for slaves in the gold fields of Minas Gerais exceeded the opportunities for Brazilians to gain from legitimate ways of carrying slaves. During that period, the percentage of slaves tight-packed under all those pretexts might have come to a fifth or so above the standards envisaged under the decree of 1684, although exceptionally cleverly run ships might have managed a bit more.[98]

Tighter administrative controls and declining American demand in the 1750s and 1760s would have reduced the excess toward the 5 to 15 percent that captains could achieve by any single method.[99] By the 1770s and 1780s, merchants in Luanda and Benguela had so many other more profitable opportunities to smuggle their slaves via the French and English that few incentives remained to crowd captives onto the Brazilian ships in the ports. After 1810 growing pressures from British abolitionists, renewed government controls imposed on the slaves' behalf, and an influx of new shipping capacity kept the resurgent Brazilian demand of the 1810s and 1820s from reviving the worst times of tight-packing of the 1720s and before. By that time, the trade was also shifting toward owner-operated slaving ventures, whose captains had less need to compensate for low freight rates with tight-packed cargoes and more interest in the survival of their property. The repeated metamorphoses of tight-packing in the

96. Instructions, AHU, Angola cx. 31.
97. E.g., the elaborate procedures specified in the customs *regimento*, Part III, *Arquivos de Angola* 2, no. 12 (1936): 405–22.
98. Estimates in Albuquerque, 12 March 1729, AHU, Angola cx. 18; Pereira da Costa, 9 March 1723, AHU, Angola cx. 16; Albuquerque, 21 July 1730, AHU, Angola maço 18–A.
99. Gov. Vasconcelos was unable to detect more than marginal violations of the law, 11 Feb. 1763, AHU, Angola cx. 29. Cf. Lencastre, 3 Feb. 1773, AHU, Angola cx. 36.

southern Atlantic as its context changed through the eighteenth century thus also marked its declining significance.

Nonetheless, pressures on the Brazilians did not relent. They remained so sensitive to the number of slaves they could load that when the decree of 1813 finally lowered boarding limits to those that had been in effect in the British trade before 1808, both Luanda and Benguela experienced sharp declines in arrivals of ships.[100] The shippers who refused to observe the new law were probably Brazilians, once again discriminated against by yet another law promulgated to protect the slaves. Their antiquated vessels were unable to compete with the British fleet, constructed to perform under these restrictions, redeployed to Brazil after the ending of the British trade, and mostly in the hands of merchants relocated there from the metropole.[101]

Provisioning Costs

Closely related to tight-packing as a strategy for bringing in a profitable slaving voyage was the shippers' effort to load absolute minima of the cheapest possible provisions for the slaves. Cost in itself was far from the major consideration, since the slavers collected set *per diem* charges for feeding the slaves on board their ships. But the growing disparity between fixed freight revenues and rising operating costs led the shippers to try to recoup their losses from the maintenance charge, thus placing pressure on food supplies. The persistence and urgency with which officials complained about inadequate provisions through three hundred years of Angolan slaving confirm the fact that reducing the slaves' diet was an ancient and tenacious method of cutting expenses on the middle passage.[102]

The law of 1684 emphasized the absolute need for sufficient supplies of food and water aboard the ships that carried the slaves, reiterating a principle long-standing in the regulatory history of the Portuguese slave trade.[103] The 1684 law required undefined quantities of food, stated vaguely

100. José Soares da Sylva Pereira (royal treasury inspector, Benguela), 18 Nov. 1814, enclosing merchant petition, AHU, Angola cx. 62; Alvellos Leiria, 18 Nov. 1814, AHU, Angola cx. 62; idem, 22 Feb. 1815, AHU, Angola cx. 63. See also the case of the nominally Brazilian ship *Dido* in Lopes, *Escravatura*, p. 182.

101. David Eltis, "The British Trans-Atlantic Slave Trade after 1807," *Maritime History* 4, no. 1 (1974): 1–11, and idem, "The British Contribution to the Nineteenth-Century Trans-Atlantic Slave Trade," *Economic History Review* 32, no. 2 (1979): 211–27; also David M. Williams, "Abolition and the Re-deployment of the Slave Fleet, 1807–11," *Journal of Transport History* 2, no. 2 (1973): 175–91.

102. Instructions to Gov. Oliveira Barboza, 28 Feb. 1810, AHU, cód. 551, fol. 44, and extracted in Rebelo, *Relações*, pp. 342–44. These instructions are apparently related to the documents referred to (without specification) in Lopes, *Escravatura*, pp. 18 ff.

103. Prominent in the earliest references to slaving and present in the 1519 decree regulating the São Tomé to Mina trade: "Regimento do negoceo e trato que foy pᵃ a Ilha de Sam Tomé sôbre os escravos," 8 Feb. 1519, in Lopes, *Escravatura*, p. 186. See also

as adequate for three meals per day on voyages of standard lengths on each of the three routes from Angola to Brazil, counted from the day on which the ships raised their sails: thirty-five days to Pernambuco, forty days to Bahia, and fifty to Rio.[104] Water was to be provided in more explicitly specified quantities of one *canada* (about 1.4 liters) per day.

Critics of the trade and owners of slaves consistently identified insufficiencies and poor quality of foodstuffs aboard the ships as major contributors to slave mortality and, by implication, one area in which transporters saved costs.[105] It was the sensitivity of profits to outlays for provisions, for one indicator of the importance of the food factor, that made the Luanda grain market (the *terreiro público*, founded in 1764) one of the most politically sensitive institutions of the city. Luso-African provisioners fully appreciated the urgency of food supplies and repeatedly turned ships' needs for beans and manioc flour to their advantage in the period before the Luanda public granary. Regulation of the order of departure became as important for determining which ship could buy food when prices rose during famines as for which captain would load slaves.[106] In times of shortage slaving vessels brought manioc flour and beans from Brazil in order to be safe.[107]

---

regimento given to Simão da Silva (1512) in Brásio, *Monumenta missionaria africana*, 1:239–40; letter to *feitor* and *oficais* of São Tomé, 12 Dec. 1530, ibid., pp. 551–52. Abdoulaye Bathily, "La traite atlantique des esclaves et ses effets économiques et sociaux en Afrique: le cas du Galam, royaume de l'hinterland sénégambien au dix-huitième siècle," *Journal of African History* 27, no. 2 (1986): 276–77, detects the same sensitivity to food among French slavers in Senegambia.

104. Arts. 7 and 8, in *Arquivos de Angola* 2, no. 11 (1936): 315. One may accept these sailing times as reflecting actual conditions in the seventeenth century, although subsequent technical improvements seem to have reduced the Luanda-to-Rio passage to 30–35 days by the early nineteenth century. Alternatively, one may impute artifically lengthened requirements for Pernambuco to the influence of merchants in Bahia, then important in the trade, who were concerned to protect their position as middlemen in the trade from the Rio-based interlopers who subsequently, in fact, became dominant at Luanda.

105. Pereira da Costa, 9 March 1723, AHU, Angola cx. 16; memorial from the Luanda mechants, 20 July 1724, AHU, Angola cx. 15; Pereira da Costa, 19 Feb. 1728, AHU, Angola cx. 17; Magalhães, 9 Nov. 1745, AHU, Angola cx. 23; *carta regia* of 25 Jan. 1758, AHU, Angola maço 7 (expressing crown concern); Vasconcelos, 11 Feb. 1763, AHU, Angola cx. 29; Corrêa, *História de Angola*, 1:46–47; Almeida e Vasconcelos, 2 Oct. 1794, AHU, Angola maço 6; de Mello, 12 March 1799, AHU, Angola cx. 46; Lopes, *Escravatura*, p. 186 (for 1810); Oliveira Barboza, 1 May 1811, AHU, Angola cx. 59; and especially Hélio Vianna, "Um humanitário alvará de 1813, sôbre o tráfico de africanos em navios portuguêses," *Revista do Instituto histórico e geográfico brasileiro* 256 (1962): 79–88.

106. Corrêa, *História de Angola*, 1:46–47. Venâncio, "Economia de Luanda," pp. 73–74, implies that regulated prices for food were also a means for the government to reduce expenditures on provisions for its troops in Luanda. Corrêa, *História de Angola*, 2:168, has an acute direct observer's statement on the politics of food.

107. Avellar, 7 July 1731, AHU, Angola maço 18–A; Meneses, 26 April 1735 and 9 July 1736, AHU, Angola cx. 20; Magalhães, 28 May 1739, AHU, Angola cx. 22; *requer-*

But expense was only part of the significance of provisions to the slave ships, since it amounted to a small fraction of the total costs of the voyage and since captains collected a standard allowance for provisions for the slaves.[108] Taking manioc and bean prices in the vicinity of $600 per *exeque* early in the century and rising to 1$200 toward 1800 in times of normally adequate supply (though capable of rising to 6$000 to 8$000 in periods of scarcity) and with water at 1$000 per *pipa* early in the century but declining to $500 or less in later decades,[109] and using quantities specified by law, it should have cost slavers about $700 to 1$500 per person for the basic components of the slaves' diet.[110] Other victuals might have added an additional $500, to make the total cost of provisions 1$200 per slave early in the century and 2$000 by 1800 or so.[111] The total cost of 1$200 worked out to $30 or so per day early in the century, half of

imento of Jacinto Dias Braga, n.d. (ca. 4 April 1741), AHU, Angola cx. 22; Magalhães, 3 July 1746, AHU, Angola cx. 23; da Cunha, 6 March 1755, AHU, Angola cx. 27; Sousa Coutinho, 18 July 1766, AHU, Angola cx. 31; Peçanha, 18 June 1783, AHU, Angola cx. 40; Joseph Antonio Ferreira Dias *requerimento*, enclosed in Moçâmedes, 28 April 1789, AHU, Angola cx. 41; Moçâmedes to governor of Bahia, 3 Nov. 1790, ANRJ, II, 33–32.29; Motta Feo e Torres, 18 Jan. and 22 Nov. 1817, AHU, Angola cx. 64; Marçal Pedro da Cunha Maldona do Ataide (*capitão de mar e guerra*), 25 Sept. 1824, AHU, Angola maço 4–A. Nearly all these reports coincide with reported droughts and famines in Angola; cf. Miller, "Significance of Drought, Disease, and Famine," appendix.

108. Above and beyond the allowed freight charge, an arrangement that virtually invited skimping on actual expenses and could become a means to profit; e.g., Salvador, *Cristãos-novos*, p. 333 (1685); Meneses, 3 March 1737, AHU, Angola cx. 19; the customs *regimento* of 1799, parte III, cap. 3, para. 3, *Arquivos de Angola* 2, no. 12 (1936): 411.

109. Detailed records of food prices at Luanda will be presented in another study now in preparation; see especially the records of the *terreiro público* in AHU, Angola cxs. 30–37. Prices on water varied according to quantities purchased, who supplied it and from what source, the degree of monopoly, and enforcement of municipal price ceilings; for available data, see Magalhães, 29 Dec. 1742, AHU, Angola cx. 23; *auto de dezobediencia* (Jozé Gonçalo da Câmara), 3 April 1782, AHU, Angola maço 2; Oliveira Barboza, 4 May 1813, AHU, Angola cx. 61; Motta Feo e Torres, 6 Oct. 1818, AHU, Angola cx. 65.

110. The standards specified in da Cunha, 21 Dec. 1753, AHU, Angola cx. 25, were 1 *canada* of water per day per slave, and flour at ½ to 1 *exeque*. Cf. the *alvará* of 1813 in Vianna, "Humanitário alvará."

111. Cf. Corrêa, *História de Angola*, 1:48, for a confirming estimate of 2$000 to 2$400 in the 1780s. Merchants in the 1820s assumed that they could make money by charging slave owners $100 per day for provisions for the slaves they carried, or 3$000 to 3$500 for the usual voyage: ANRJ, cód. 1142. A late-seventeenth-century estimate of these costs requested 4$000 from the Crown for the much longer voyage to the West Indies. A proposal ca. 1770 for a company to carry slaves to the distant ports of northern Brazil allowed 7$200, which was probably inflated, since the costs were in fact only about 20% higher (thus equivalent to 6$000 on the run to the main Brazilian ports): proposal in AHU, Angola maço 10 (D.O.), and for the incremental cost estimate, see *termo* of Manoel de Souza Guimarães (of the *Pensamento*, a *sumaca*), in Almeida e Vasconcelos, 2 Oct. 1794, AHU, Angola cx. 43. Klein, *Middle Passage*, p. 200, and Stein, *French Slave Trade*, p. 139, both put the cost of provisions at about 5% of the total costs of the outfit; the former judges that percentage no financial restraint, while the latter conveys the perception of sensitivity apparent in the Portuguese trade.

the $60 that shore merchants received for feeding slaves; and 2$000 absorbed not much more than half the $100 daily food allowance that was standard later on. Those margins amounted to a useful supplement of 25 percent above the 6$000 to 8$000 that the law allowed shippers to charge for freight, though famine prices in Africa could triple or quadruple food costs and may have raised provisioning expenses near the fees charged in the longer run. Additional costs came from the loss of incoming cargo space in having to bring food from Brazil. Greater yet was the cost of having to spend cash for provisions, unless the venture included a planter with excess flour or beans on hand, since the strategy of most voyages rested on disbursing as little currency as possible.[112]

For ships carrying slaves on their own accounts, food costs became a much smaller proportion of the entire investment, while the opportunity costs of not sustaining their human property throughout the voyage mounted. A ship of 300 slaves would have required an outlay of about 600$000 for food at normal Luanda prices, 2 to 3 percent of the total, or the value of about six slaves at late-eighteenth-century prices in Brazil.

Much more important than the direct expense in supplies was the loss in space available for slaves from every cubic meter allocated to provisions. Under the prevailing reliance on tight-packing, food and water sacrificed freights and trading profits.[113] Slaving vessels in the southern Atlantic never sailed with unused space. Sails, cordage, equipment, and paying cargo, whether slaves or baggage, could not be eliminated in order to make room for the extra slaves that tight-packers boarded. On the other hand, captains gained no revenue from carrying extra food, and so they could reduce provisions for the slaves to an absolute minimum and cover the risk of leaving their cargoes without food and water from the extra slaves they boarded. Skimping on provisions therefore became not only a major way of saving money but also a basic technique of tight-packing.

In part, captains simply refused to purchase rations up to the minima set by the law of 1684, especially in times of famine prices at Luanda before 1764, or at almost any period in Benguela.[114] Those who brought food supplies from Brazil in times of scarcity in Angola hoarded them for the exclusive use of their own slaves and refused to sell them to merchants on shore trying to feed themselves and their captives. This hoarding strategy probably produced the intended effect of inducing owners of slaves

112. Patrick Villiers, *Traite des Noirs et navires négriers au XVIIIe siècle* (Grenoble: Editions des 4 Seigneurs, 1982), p. 105 et passim.
113. The Luanda Luso-Africans stated the point: memorial, 20 July 1724, AHU, Angola cx. 16. See also *carta regia* of 20 Jan. 1714, *Anais da Biblioteca nacional do Rio de Janeiro* 28 (1906): 213.
114. E.g., da Cunha, 6 March 1755, AHU, Angola cx. 27. Benguela was an importer of provisions from Luanda, in the Luso-African network of exchanges of local products, in this case manioc meal sent south for the salt that figured in the colonial economy: Venâncio, "Economia de Luanda," p. 144.

starving in the city to sell them at bargain prices to shippers who could at least feed them and partially restore them to health on their way to Brazil.

The major pretext covering failure to purchase sufficient supplies was a strict interpretation placed on the clause in the law of 1684 which required ships to load food only for the slaves of their rated capacity. Since tight-packing techniques added slaves of the officers and crew beyond the *arqueação* and boarded others as "children" above the rated capacity, this loophole sometimes allowed captains to depart with provisions a full third short of standards.[115] Officials in Luanda occasionally cracked down on captains preparing to sail without necessary food and water, requiring them to show receipts for purchases adequate for the slaves they actually intended to board before advancing their ships to the head of the order of departure. Officials also inspected the provisions aboard ships making ready to leave and then sealed the holds to prevent subsequent off-loading to make room for more slaves. At times slavers had to place adequate supplies under bond in a government warehouse on shore in order to qualify for permission to depart.[116]

The government-appointed guardians of slave welfare probably had only limited success in regulating the quality of the food purchased and stored. On at least one occasion spoiled flour from Lisbon found buyers at low prices in Luanda, most likely merchants preparing a slave ship for departure.[117] The impure water of Luanda was ordinarily poured into the casks that had held *gerebita* on the incoming voyage, to save the cost of building fresh barrels and the space necessary to bring them from Brazil. The old ones were rarely cured properly, so that the unfiltered river water put in them for the slaves, fairly aboil with organisms after days and weeks of storage at elevated tropical temperatures, added the stench of its own putrifaction to the foul aroma of stale cheap rum.[118]

Other Operating Costs

The Brazilian ships coming to Angola further reduced their operating costs by trimming the cash wages paid to officers and crew, offering them

115. Pereira da Costa, 9 March 1723, AHU, Angola cx. 16; Luanda merchants' memorial, 20 July 1724, AHU, Angola cx. 16; Pereira da Costa, 19 Feb. 1728, AHU, Angola cx. 17; Magalhães, 19 Nov. 1745, AHU, Angola cx. 23; Vasconcelos, 11 Feb. 1763, AHU, Angola cx. 29; Ferreira Dias *requerimento* in Moçâmedes, 28 April 1789, AHU, Angola cx. 41; Oliveira Barboza, 1 May 1811, AHU, Angola cx. 59.
116. Miller, "Overcrowded and Undernourished."
117. Almeida e Vasconcelos, 11 Feb. 1795, AHU, Angola cx. 44.
118. Pereira da Costa, 18 Feb. 1728, AHU, Angola cx. 17; Vasconcelos, 21 June 1760, AHU, Angola cx. 28; idem, 2 May 1762, AHU, Angola cx. 29; de Mello, 12 March 1799, AHU, Angola cx. 46.

instead the opportunity to trade for slaves on their own accounts.[119] Beyond contributing to the tight-packing that afflicted the slaves, indirect remuneration in this form—not really a form of incentive payment, since it encouraged no efficiencies on behalf of the voyage itself—was consistent with the low capitalization of these ventures. In some instances, at least, backers of the venture multiplied its ill effects by lending goods for sailors to trade for slaves in Angola, to be repaid with interest from the proceeds of their sale in Brazil. At least as often, no doubt, they resorted to straightforward impressment of down-and-out men in taverns and along the wharves.[120]

These loans were a particularly efficient way to save costs because of the relatively large crews carried on ships bringing slaves to Brazil, like those engaged in other segments of Atlantic slaving.[121] By the 1820s, ships of Portuguese registration reaching Pernambuco, of which about 15 to 20 percent were slavers, were carrying nearly one crewman for every four to seven tons (or 10–18 slaves) of capacity. Foreign merchantmen engaged in other trades were sailing twelve to twenty tons of capacity for every member of the crew, or three to four times as much.[122] Slavers heading out of Lisbon for Angola at the same period averaged one crewman for a low 7.4 tons (or 15 slaves) of capacity.[123] From Rio, slightly earlier, slavers would have carried about ten slaves for each member of the crew.[124] Given these high crew costs, quite unproductive on the way out to Africa but absolutely necessitated by the need to manage a dangerous slave cargo on the return, it made sense to pay low nominal wages but to allow crew to trade as best they could and to provide free carrying space in the form of tight-packing. No wonder that the officers and crew at times diverted food supplies required by law for slaves in the *arqueação* to the exclusive use of their own unregistered property. Or that they also falsified death records, recording others' slaves carried for freight as deceased in place of the captives of their own who died.[125]

119. Pereira da Costa, 19 Feb. 1728, AHU, Angola cx. 17; Lencastre, 27 July 1775, AHU, Angola cx. 36. The Lisbon ships, at least those of the Pombaline Companies, paid in cash: Julgação da equipage da curveta N. S.ra da Livrança de Cacheu pa Maram, 11 Mar. 1774, 140, no. 35, BAPP (with thanks to Dauril Alden). For payments from the ship's cargo in the French trade, Stein, *French Slave Trade,* pp. 69–70, 89–90.

120. Brown, "Internal Commerce," p. 194.

121. E.g., Klein, *Middle Passage,* pp. 164–68; Coughtry, *Notorious Triangle,* p. 152.

122. AHMAE, C.C., Pernambouc, no. 1.

123. ANTT, Junta do Comércio, maço 62, macete 123.

124. Corcino Medeiros dos Santos, "Relações de Angola com o Rio de Janeiro (1736–1808)," *Estudos históricos* (Marília) 12 (1973): 172.

125. Domingos Dias da Silva (contractor) *requerimento,* 7 Jan. 1772, AHU, Angola cx. 36; *certidão* of 23 Sept. 1816, AHU, Angola cx. 64. Cf. the same tactic employed aboard Royal Africa Company ships: Palmer, *Human Cargoes,* p. 94, n. 1. English consuls in Brazil believed that the practice continued into the 1820s: David Eltis, "The Transatlantic Slave Trade, 1821–1843" (Ph.D. diss., University of Rochester, 1978), p. 86.

Port Regulations

With the utter frustration of the slaving captains' efforts to raise their freight charges and the contradictory effects and limited gains to be made from tight-packing, it is not surprising that Brazilian shippers expanded the field of battle to include regulation of the order in which ships carrying slaves left the harbor at Luanda. Nearly everyone agreed that slave mortality made the principal difference between a successful voyage and a losing one. Yet nearly everyone also conceded fatalistically, at least before the very end of the eighteenth century, that human intervention could do little to influence God's will, as expressed in what they saw as the slaves' inherent propensity to die, in droughts, in epidemics, and in other hazards of the voyage at sea.[126] As some Portuguese are still fond of remarking, if partly only as a figure of speech, "Se Deus quiser . . . ," God willing!

Under pressure to avoid the costs of slave deaths, but convinced of the inevitability of the risk, owners of slaves found that the logical method of reducing losses was to pass the dying slaves on to someone else as quickly as possible.[127] Slave mortality damaged everyone in the port, from the import merchants who also handled the dispatch of slaves, to the Lisbon firms who bought slaves, to the captains of the ships who transported them.[128] Though the Luso-African owners of the slaves suffered most directly, shippers collected freight charges only on slaves whom they delivered alive in Brazil, and—though to a lesser extent—captains responsible for notoriously slow and lethal passages lost repute. As a result, speed in moving the slaves on through the port to sale in Brazil became the focal point of competition at Luanda. "The great heat of the climate there and the waters of that coast destroy more [slaves] in two months than those of Brazil do in a year," one mid-eighteenth-century analyst of the problem lamented, blaming these environmental factors for great losses in morbidity and mortality to owners of slaves delayed in Angola. A foreign visitor to Luanda concurred in the 1840s: "The detention of the negroes on the coast, in consequence of the market being overstocked, or of the nonarrival of the slavers which are to transport them to another shore, is a melancholy and notorious cause of mortality among them."[129]

126. E.g., the attitude expressed by Corrêa, *História de Angola,* 1:173n.

127. Magalhães, 26 April 1742, AHU, Angola cx. 22. Venâncio, "Economia de Luanda," p. 151, alludes in passing to this vital point.

128. The internal correspondence of the Maranhão Company, which offers almost unique glimpses of the day-to-day concerns of the merchants at Luanda, contains clear examples of the company's land-based administrators desperately passing smallpox-infested slaves on to a captain of a company ship, overloading the vessel in the process, and blaming losses on the "known" propensity of Kongo slaves to die in excessive numbers: Carreira, "Companhias pombalinas de navegação," pp. 350–51. The ship was the *Nossa Senhora da Conceição,* which reached Pará on 8 July 1759.

129. "Exposição das rezoens . . . ," n.d.(ca. 1750s), ANTT, Ministério do Reino, maço 499; Tams, *Visit to the Portuguese Possessions,* 1:282–83. But allusions to the urgency of speed

From early in the seventeenth century, port regulations at Luanda were designed to reduce the mortality risk of holding slaves by getting them aboard Brazil-bound ships and on their way with as little delay as possible. Since ten to twenty ships usually lay anchored at Luanda at any given time, with smaller, though still significant, numbers waiting off the beach at Benguela, they threatened to congest the provisioning and administrative services of the town and thus to retard preparations for leaving if all competed simultaneously to take on slaves and depart. Beyond the risks of slave mortality, the high costs of feeding slaves kept waiting in shoreside barracoons added to the urgency of establishing an orderly priority for the ships in line to load and leave. Finally, government officials (or the contractors) found it easier to detect smuggling when they had to watch no more than a single ship in the process of boarding at any given time.

For all these reasons, the fundamental law of 28 March 1684 had authorized port authorities (in practice, the governor) to restrict loading to only a few ships at any one time.[130] It was evidently already the practice in the seventeenth century to order departures of ships for each of the three legal destinations in Brazil according to the sequence in which they had entered the port.[131] Thus three freighted ships, the ones longest in the port, would normally have been taking on the Luso-Africans' slaves simultaneously and continuously in Luanda, one ship each for Rio de Janeiro, Bahia, and Pernambuco. More recent arrivals would have remained in a queue behind them in various preliminary stages of preparation, repairing equipment, disposing of imports they had brought for sale, establishing contacts with merchants anticipating deliveries of slaves from the interior weeks or months hence, sending their crew off to engage in trading of their own, and so on. When each vessel's turn to board came

were much older: Meneses, 9 July 1736, AHU, Angola cx. 20; AHMF, Benguela *copiador*, letters of 4 July 1777, fol. 1, and 14 March 1781, fols. 40–45 (cf. Carreira, "Companhias pombalinas de navegação," p. 67); Corrêa, *História de Angola*, 1:49 (referring to the 1780s); Moçâmedes, 28 April 1789, AHU, Angola cx. 41; *requerimento* of Anselmo da Fonseca Coutinho, n.d. (ca. April 1794), AHU, Angola cx. 47; Alvellos Leiria, 1 March 1814, AHU, Angola cx. 62; Albuquerque e Tovar, 29 Oct. 1819, AHU, Angola cx. 65. The earliest explicit reference to the point was 1548 at the Kongo kingdom's port of Mpinda: "Inquirição," 12 Nov. 1548, in Brásio, *Monumenta missionaria africana*, 2:197–206.

130. Arts. 12 and 14, in *Arquivos de Angola* 2, no. 11 (1936): 316, 317. Rebelo, *Relações*, pp. 196–202, discusses the *efeitos próprios* rule, though he does not bring out its significance in the context developed here. Similar procedures were in effect throughout the empire and elsewhere: e.g., Coughtry, *Notorious Triangle*, p. 134.

131. I have not located the origin of the practice, but the seventeenth-century *preferência* system (see the text at notes 37–38 above) and other early decrees granting priority in order of departure to ships bringing horses to the Angolan colonial armed forces from Brazil (see the governor's *regimento*, 12 Feb. 1676, *Arquivos de Angola* 1, no. 5 [1936]: n.p.) depended on its existence.

around, the governor issued a public proclamation announcing the fact to merchants with slaves. A written *bando* (a proclamation) granted the ship permission to take on slaves for a specified number of days before a stated date scheduled for its departure. If the ship completed its full complement of slaves within the allotted time, it left, with numerous legal formalities culminating in formal dispatch from the governor, and the ship behind it in line for that port in Brazil moved up the ladder of priority into the loading position. These arrangements promised to allow slaves entering Luanda to advance rapidly through the slave yards and onto a ship very likely to make sail within only a few days for a destination of the merchant's or owner's choice.

The system functioned much less smoothly in practice than in theory. Governors wielded their authority over issuance of the proclamations on behalf of captains whom they favored, or of ships carrying slaves in which they held a personal financial interest. Subordinate officials in charge of certifying the preparedness of a ship to depart invoked obscure technicalities in the regulations to obtain bribes and favors from captains whom they thus held prisoner to bureaucratic delaying tactics. Captains facing a lengthy wait behind a large ship declared for their intended port in Brazil but likely to take weeks to fill its *arqueação* declared false destinations and thereby bypassed competitors stuck in a slow-moving queue.[132]

Tactics to take advantage of the order of ship departures were important weapons in the commercial armories of the Angola slavers too. The inalterable order of departure allowed Luso-African merchants to demand concessions as a ship neared its posted departure date, since other regulations forbade dispatch with less than the complete *arqueação*. A captain with a ship 80 percent filled with dying slaves could afford to be very flexible in making arrangements for the remaining 20 percent, in order to save the majority from the deaths and morbidity threatened by delay. Such losses could become devastating to ships buying slaves on their own accounts. One Antonio Ramalho was caught with an uncompleted cargo of slaves who were dying faster than he could replace them by claiming returns on goods he had loaned off into the interior—for two years![133] The high prices such a captain would pay attracted slaves that would otherwise have gone to other ports and thereby slowed the progress of ships loading for those destinations as well. Merchants could destroy a competitor by buying up the supply of slaves entering the city just at the moment when he had nearly completed his cargo, thus delaying him and imposing losses through mortality and the high prices he would have

132. *Aviso*, 31 July 1727, AHU, Angola cx. 27.
133. E.g., AHMF, Benguela *copiador*, letter of 4 July 1777, fol. 1; ANTT, Ministério do Reino, maço 499.

to pay for the remaining slaves he required.[134] This rule—though, like others, proclaimed to save slave lives—became a means by which ruthless traders sacrificed them, lengthening the delays its framers intended it to avoid. Priorities in the order of departure were retained despite the abuses because they were an efficient way of regulating a trade in property as perishable as slaves.

These regulations, though generally intended to weight the conduct of the trade in favor of large Lisbon merchants, evolved with the rise and fall of metropolitan participation in Angolan slaving. During the ascendancy of the contractors before the 1750s, a crucial clause in their contracts with the Crown accorded them absolute precedence over all other ships loading slaves in Luanda.[135] The Pombaline companies subsequently enjoyed similarly explicit preference in the order of departure. The contractors, or their successors as Lisbon's favorites, could thus bring a ship into the harbor at any time, offload and sell imports at prices undercutting small shipments brought from Lisbon or Brazil on the accounts of local merchants, take on the entire supply of slaves available in the port, and leave ahead of Brazilian ships already months in line for the same port.

The law encouraged metropolitan merchants to raise their prices, or reduce the credit terms they offered, on cargoes that were huge by Angolan standards and then to depart quickly with as many slaves as they cared to acquire. Their ability to speed slaves on their way to America offset their high charges with gains from lowered maintenance and mortality costs to the owners of the slaves they carried. Their priority may indeed have reduced deaths among the captives they carried, or at least compensated for the mortality their larger size caused, but it also allowed the Lisbon ships to beat their Brazilian competitors to American markets short of slave labor and thus to raise prices for their imports again by the amount that slaveowners hoped to gain from advantageous sales in Brazil. It was a subtle but powerful privilege, one of the many conferred on the Crown's designated favorites in Angola at the expense of smaller, usually colonial, competitors.

The free trade decree of 1758 extended identical concessions to other favored Lisbon merchants by means of the distinction between ships arriving under the *bando* system—that is, hiring their space out to local merchants paying freight charges on goods ordered or slaves sent—and large ventures coming with goods carried on their own accounts, or *efeitos*

---

134. E.g., the cases of the *Livramento* and the *Mato Grosso* at Benguela in 1813: Alvellos Leiria, 7 March and 24 May 1814, AHU, Angola cx. 62.

135. "Exposição das rezoens . . . ," n.d. (ca. 1750s), ANTT, Ministério do Reino, maço 499. Antonio de Campos Rego (*provedor*), 10 July 1753, AHU, Angola cx. 25, also alleges the considerable advantage that the contractors gained from this clause.

próprios.[136] Although the decree did not thus distinguish Lisbon ships explicitly from vessels from Brazil, the superior size and capitalization of metropolitan ships made it unlikely that many non-Lisbon vessels would obtain priority under this law.[137] At periods when Lisbon merchants intended to break into the Luso-African monopoly on slave-selling in Brazil, priority in departure gave them a wedge with which to crack open the tight local networks prevalent in Luanda, and it accorded them an added edge over Brazilian shippers.

The spuriously technical distinction between ships sailing freighted and those owning the slaves they carried (or owning the rights to them) was in fact applied to favor the overlarge ships of the two Lisbon chartered companies sent to Angola on the heels of the law's issuance. Though the financial organization of most ships leaving Luanda is not known in detail, data on load factors in the early 1760s provide a useful proxy, since ships in a hurry that met the legal standard could leave before filling their *arqueação.* A few Rio- and Bahia-bound ships evidently qualified at first, leaving with part cargoes in 1762 and dropping the overall percentages of capacity filled for those two ports to 91.1 percent and 79.8 percent.[138] The distinction applied more narrowly to company ships alone by 1763, when the Rio and Bahia ships belonging to Brazilians sailed with 97.8 percent of their allotted spaces filled, while company ships making for Pernambuco carried only 86.4 percent of their capacity. The corresponding figures for 1764 were 98.1 percent for Rio and Bahia, against 82.6 percent for Pernambuco and Pará. For 1765, they were 97.9 percent for Rio and Bahia and 89.0 percent for the Company ships. In all four years, not a single company vessel left Luanda with its full rated quota of slaves.[139]

Later refinements of the distinction reflected techniques that Brazilians and Luso-Africans in Luanda developed to circumvent the law. Cer-

---

136. *Alvará* of 11 Jan. 1758, *Arquivos de Angola* 2, no. 14 (1936): 531. The law quite explicitly applied to the ship's status upon entering Luanda rather than to arrangements that might be made in the port to affect its status at the time of departure: Homem e Magalhães, 16 Nov. 1785, AHU, Angola maço 13 (D.O.); *parecer* of Miguel Riveira Gomes in the *consulta* of the Junta do Commercio (Rio), 12 Sept. 1820, AHU, Angola maço 3.

137. This intention of the law was acknowledged explicitly in a clarification of the decree of 1758: *consulta* of the Conselho Ultramarino (Lisbon) on the decree of 11 Jan. 1758, 12 Sept. 1758, AHU, Angola maço 3; Homem e Magalhães, 16 Nov. 1785, AHU, Angola maço 13 (D.O.).

138. One must also take into account that 1762 was a year in which Brazilian slave prices were low and the market there generally flooded with fresh slave labor, as well as a bad year for sickness at Luanda. Both these factors would have made Luso-Africans reluctant to bring slaves down to Luanda for boarding, and the delays could have been accordingly devastating to Brazilian ships in the port.

139. See the records of ship departures for 1762–63 in Vasconcelos, 11 Feb. 1763, AHU, Angola cx. 29; idem, 30 March 1764, AHU, Angola cx. 30; Sousa Coutinho, 27 Feb. 1765, AHU, Angola cx. 30; "Mappa dos navios . . . ," AHU, Angola cx. 31.

tainly with creole officeholders in mind, the decree enjoined colonial officials from hindering the timely departure of such ships under any technical pretext whatsoever. It specified further that ships sailing under an association of charterers or even a single charterer—who could only have been Luso-African owners at Luanda—had to line up in the queue of ships waiting for their *bando*. These latter would continue to leave according to the first-in-first-out system already in effect, with priority given only to the larger of two ships that might have entered the port simultaneously. It distinguished between ships sailing *de bando* and those going *efeitos próprios* according to ownership of the inbound cargo rather than by ownership of the slaves aboard as they left, thus leaving Lisbon merchants free to own as few slaves as they chose without sacrificing precedence. The decree acknowledged the urgency of speed by prohibiting the contractor from delaying such ships on the pretext that they had not boarded their full complements of slaves. This clause extended to all Lisbon ships another advantage enjoyed for decades by the contractors alone.

Luanda and Brazilian merchants persistently conspired to avoid these restrictions on their ability to get ahead in the highly regulated order of departure from Angolan ports. One tactic depended on the ambiguity of the law's phrasing of the distinction between ships entering *efeitos próprios* and those departing thus.[140] Merchants locally would form secret partnerships behind the nominal ownership of a single representative, who would then attempt to board slaves belonging to the entire group as a single lot, take fictitious title to a Brazilian vessel, and request its immediate dispatch under the priority intended for metropolitan ships under similarly unified ownership. After the mid-1760s Lisbon merchants failed to provide shipping adequate to remove the slaves arriving at Luanda, and a drop in demand in Brazil kept American slavers away. Shortages of shipping ensued, which left governors caught between the law's favoritism toward metropolitan traders and their need to raise government revenues by increasing slave exports. If the lives of the slaves and the interests of Luso-African slaveowners commanded their sympathies as well, they did not emphasize them in their communications to Lisbon. In technical compliance with the prevailing distinction, Governor Sousa Coutinho (1764–72) therefore recognized these local combinations of merchants desperate to move their fragile human property on toward Brazil as *efeitos próprios*.

He thus set a precedent that allegedly became subject to abuse under Governor Lencastre (1772–79) and was protested by the Pernambuco Company in the last declining days of its operations in Angola. The com-

---

140. Though clarified by subsequent royal *aviso*, 27 April 1776, and implemented by *bando* of Gov. José Gonçalo da Câmara, 5 July 1780, both referred to in Homem e Magalhães, 16 Nov. 1785, AHU, Angola maço 13 (D.O.).

pany petitioned for enforcement of the original restricted interpretation of the decree against such a Bahian consortium in 1775,[141] at a time when its Lisbon directors were already failing to send enough ships to carry the slaves needed in Brazil and were also taking captives owned by the Luso-Africans as freight. Governor Lencastre had ruled in favor of the Bahians, and surely the Luso-African owners of the slaves as well, but the colonial chief justice (*ouvidor*) challenged the governor's ruling on behalf of superiors in Lisbon and in response to the complaint of the Pernambuco Company. The justice alleged that Lencastre had used the distinction as a device to protect people he favored.[142]

The political utility of the decree was less at issue than the identity of those whom the governor chose to protect. However, the dispute probably surfaced because of the quiet increase in Brazilian initiative in the Angolan slave trade toward the end of the eighteenth century. In this case, the hidden substance of the conflict may have involved Asian textiles smuggled through Bahia to Angola after failure of a Lisbon effort to cut off persistent Brazilian violations of mercantilist restrictions on intercolonial commerce in the southern Atlantic during the 1760s.

Colonial societies formed to qualify as *efeitos próprios* seem still to have been prevalent in the early 1780s, at a time when Lisbon was steadily losing ground to the Brazilians in southern Atlantic slaving. The Crown had terminated the contract system in 1769, and the chartered companies had concluded their operations in failure. Other Lisbon merchants had not filled the gap they left in supplying goods and carrying slaves. Brazilians, backed in part by contraband imports of British goods at Rio and elsewhere, moved in, buying more and more slaves for themselves at both Benguela and Luanda. They collaborated to gain priority under the terms of the 1758 decree by forming wholly owned ventures, but so many of them adopted this tactic that they hindered the efficiency with which slaves moved through the port. Often as many as four or six ships declaring themselves *efeitos próprios* competed with one another to take on slaves simultaneously, while the additional three ships officially *de bando* for Rio, Bahia, and Pernambuco also sought to complete their *arqueações*. The resulting delays prejudiced all concerned, owing to the high losses in slave deaths that they occasioned aboard the partly loaded ships, all unable to depart.[143] Delays in the movement of slaves through the port because of

141. Lencastre, 27 July 1775, AHU, Angola cx. 36.
142. Joaquim Manoel Garcia de Castro Barboza (*ouvidor*), 1 Aug. 1781, AHU, Angola cx. 38.
143. Moçâmedes, 16 Dec. 1784, AHU, Angola cx. 40; *consulta* (Moçâmedes), AHU, Angola maço 6; *bandos* of Jan. 1781 and 1 Nov. 1784, and royal order of 23 March 1784 confirming local measures, all referred to in Homem e Magalhães, 16 Nov. 1785, AHU, Angola maço 13 (D.O.).

multiple *efeitos próprios* ships had apparently not held the same urgency for Lisbon during the days of the monopoly companies, when governors had left ships free to come and go as they pleased, without worrying about the harm they caused the slaves and their owners.[144] However, the slaves' plight had more appeal in Lisbon when Brazilians caused the problem. Concern about Brazil's near-dominant position in Angola during the late 1780s led to another, more sustained attempt to enforce the law under Governor Moçâmedes (1784–90).

In another subterfuge designed to evade the decree of 1758, Brazilian captains sailed into Luanda, assessed the number of ships ahead of them declared for each Brazilian port, and falsely declared for the destination presenting the least competition at the moment. Luso-Africans would have eagerly joined in this gambit because it allowed them to get slaves quickly on the way to Brazilian markets others waited to reach, if not also to sell them for cash in a town of their choice while defrauding metropolitan creditors holding bills of exchange payable in some other port where the ship had no intention of calling. The general restriction of slave entries in Brazil to only Rio de Janeiro, Bahia, and Pernambuco limited opportunities to gain from this strategy, but captains could also petition for special license to sail to smaller captaincies like Espírito Santo, conveniently just north of Rio; Santos or Santa Catarina, both gateways to Rio's São Paulo hinterland; or the Portuguese smuggling outpost of Colônia (do Sacramento) on the north bank of the Plata estuary across from Spanish Buenos Aires. They could thus obtain absolute priority for a port for which no other ship had declared, *efeitos próprios* or not.[145] Shipping to Colônia even offered a chance to sell their slaves directly for Spanish silver.

When Brazilian shippers began to appear with great quantities of smuggled British goods in the last decade of the century, official vigilance had to evolve to catch up with the new pretexts that attended prosperity. In a tactic apparently used at the center of the Brazilians' smuggling at Benguela, ships would arrive with so many goods that they could not take all the slaves they bought back on their own vessels, arguably *efeitos próprios* under the terms of the decree of 1758. They would load as many slaves as they could, deliver them to Brazil, return to Benguela, and again claim the *efeitos próprios* status earned by their previous entry on the grounds that they were embarking only the further proceeds of the original cargo

144. See the *bando* of Sousa Coutinho, 5 Aug. 1772, allowing ships *efeitos próprios* to establish their own order of departure (and surely affording the relevant precedent for the Luso-Africans of the next decade). A similar policy had informally been in effect earlier, according to instructions given to the Luanda administrators of the contract by Domingos Dias da Silva, cap. 27, 8 Jan. 1767, AHU, Angola cx. 3l.

145. Campos Rego, 10 July 1753, AHU, Angola cx. 25; *aviso*, 31 July 1757, AHU, Angola cx. 27; "Exposição das rezoens . . . ," n.d. (ca. 1750s), ANTT, Ministério do Reino, maço 499 (esp. para. 4).

of qualified imports. However, the urgency of moving slaves speedily through the port had usually led their Benguela agents to forward those slaves earlier, as they had reached the city, as freight on other ships, and so the returning venture would carry slaves actually belonging to other merchants of the town.[146] Such legalisms helped legitimate soaring levels of exports from Benguela in these years.

At Luanda, where smaller and less wealthy Brazilian ventures still tended to congregate, at least one legally astute captain resurrected ancient priorities accorded to ships bringing horses or criminals sentenced to penal transportation to justify sailing as if *efeitos próprios*.[147] There was no pretext too faint to invoke to overcome the delays that the law imposed in dispatching slaves through the ports. And these maneuvers seem to have been effective. By the late 1780s, a knowledgeable observer perceived no practical distinction between ships sailing *de bando* and those going *efeitos próprios*.[148]

Growing prosperity brought higher slave prices to Brazil after 1810, and priorities at the court, relocated at Rio after the Napoleonic invasion of Portugal forced its flight to Brazil in 1807–8, apparently shifted to encouraging imports of labor by anyone available to do the job. The flexibility of the law in Portugal's southern Atlantic empire was again demonstrated in these changed circumstances. The Portuguese merchants reentered the Angolan slave trade in force from their new base in Brazil, assuming that the distinction between *efeitos próprios* and ships sailing *de bando* would apply exclusively in their favor as before.[149] But Luanda slaveowners, and presumably those of Benguela as well, were feeling the pinch of Rio's intensified purchases of slaves in Angola.[150] They attempted to recover something of their ownership position in the trade by once again availing themselves of the privilege accorded to ships sailing *efeitos próprios*. Though no single Angolan slaver possessed the capital to mount an entire venture alone, several of them tried to combine according to the practices established during the 1770s and 1780s, forming associations to qualify outgoing ships filled with their slaves as wholly owned, whatever the vessel's status had been upon its arrival in the port. The Portuguese merchants in Brazil objected to this challenge from the Angolan slave exporters, very much in the vein of the Pernambuco Company's complaints of 1775. They even alleged darkly that foreign capital might have been

146. Homem e Magalhães, 16 Nov. 1785, AHU, Angola maço 13 (D.O.).
147. *Requerimento* of Balthasar dos Reis (1784), discussed in Santos, "Relações de Angola com o Rio de Janeiro," pp. 13–14.
148. Corrêa, *História de Angola*, 1:46, 47.
149. Recall also the favoritism toward Brazilian-based shippers allowed at this time through toleration of premium freight charges.
150. E.g., the cases of the *Mato Grosso* and the *Livramento* in Benguela in 1813: Alvellos Leiria, 18 Nov. 1814, AHU, Angola cx. 62.

backing the otherwise inexplicable prosperity of the Luandans.[151] Government authorities in Rio backed the merchants of Luanda in the name of freedom of trade, citing the 1758 decree and its ideological principles but thus reversing the political impact of a legal instrument that before had always favored fully owned ventures of metropolitan merchants over chartered vessels from the colonies.

Maritime Technology

An emphasis on speed echoes through the vague evidence available on the technical characteristics of the ships employed in Angolan slaving, usually within limits set by the modest capital Brazilian merchants had to invest in them.[152] In general, shippers advanced during the eighteenth century from early diversions of unspecialized vessels designed either for the long-distance open ocean routes of the Portuguese empire or for the coastal and riverain trade of Brazil toward employing more specialized types of slaving craft later, as some Brazilian merchants grew committed to the trade and eventually consolidated their hold over it by the 1780s.

As they did so, they faced trade-offs between speed and freight-carrying efficiency familiar to ship operators in any sort of trade, though of intensified import in the southern Atlantic owing to the perishability of the human cargoes their ships carried.[153] The slaves below decks also created

151. Spanish and U.S. smugglers come to mind as candidates for the role: *consulta* of the Junta do Comércio (Lisbon), 12 Sept. 1820, AHU, Angola maço 3, with attached documentation.

152. Despite a modest amount of research on Brazilian ship-building—virtually the only colonial industrial sector allowed to flourish within imperial restrictions on the Brazilian economy, owing to the excellent tropical hardwoods available there—virtually nothing is known about the relevant aspects of ship construction, design, and operation in any part of the Portuguese slave trade. For Brazil, see José Roberto do Amaral Lapa, *Bahia e a carreira da India* (São Paulo: Companhia Editora Nacional, 1968); Eulália Maria Lahmeyer Lobo, "O comércio atlântico e a comunidade de mercadores no Rio de Janeiro e em Charleston no século XVIII," *Revista de história* (São Paulo), no. 101 (1975): 84 ff.; Bauss, "Rio de Janeiro," pp. 108–9; "Discurso preliminar . . . ," p. 332; Spix and Martius, *Viagem pelo Brasil,* 2:145, n. I; José Ribeiro Júnior *Colonização e monopólio no nordeste brasileiro: A Companhia Geral de Pernambuco e Paraíba (1759–1780)* (São Paulo: HUCITEC, 1976), pp. 49, 51, 118.

153. For the Portuguese trade, Salvador, *Magnatas do tráfico negreiro,* pp. 93–96. Otherwise: Gary M. Walton, "Obstacles to Technical Diffusion in Colonial Shipping, 1675–1775," *Explorations in Economic History* 8, no. 2 (1970–71): 123–40; idem, "Trade Routes, Ownership Proportions, and American Colonial Shipping Characteristics," in *Les routes de l'Atlantique,* Travaux, 9th Colloque international d'histoire maritime, Seville, 1967 (Seville, 1968), pp. 471–502; idem, "Sources of Productivity Change in American Colonial Shipping, 1675–1775," *Economic History Review* 20, no. 1 (1967): 67–78; Richard B. Sheridan, "The Commercial and Financial Organization of the British Slave Trade, 1750–1807," *Economic History Review* 11, no. 2 (1958): 249–63; Frédéric C. Lane, "Progrès technologiques et productivité dans les transports maritimes de la fin du Moyen Âge au début des temps

contradictory economic constraints between the venturers' need to acquire vessels cheaply and to sail them at low costs in wages, and the large complements of officers and crew that slaving required.

The preferred slavers were of a middling size, though small by the standards of Brazil's European trade: large enough to carry slaves efficiently but small enough to provision and load at Luanda or Benguela without slowing the movement of slaves through the port and without oversupplying Brazilian markets for new labor. The ships should also be fast sailors at sea, and therefore relatively trim in their lines, though also sufficiently rounded (and thereby slowed) that they could carry rum casks and slaves and water rations for them in sufficient quantity. Broad-beamed ships suitable for bulky cargo were probably more highly valued by Lisbon merchants concerned with delivering goods to Angola than by the more highly specialized slavers from Brazil. Maneuverability and decks appropriate for carrying large artillery became important advantages when pirates and privateers threatened the areas through which the slavers sailed, as they frequently did from the 1740s through the 1760s and again in the 1790s, but not many Brazilian ships would sacrifice the room that armaments required.[154]

To judge from the individual histories of the ships calling at Luanda and Benguela and from other indications, most vessels in the trade were of American construction, based in Brazilian ports, and ordinarily employed in general colonial commerce but diverted from time to time to Angolan ventures.[155] A smaller number of Brazilian ships made up to four or five consecutive trips to pick up slaves in Africa, and their five to eight-year histories in the trade may have represented the normal life expectancy for hulls subject to tropical seaworms and to the stresses of carrying tight-packed slaves. Only a few made a dozen or more slaving voyages to Angola, and one wonders at the decrepit condition in which some must have survived the rigors of so many crossings. Altogether, the minority of relatively specialized ships making repeated calls at Luanda or Benguela carried more slaves than did the greater number of occasional slavers, at least by the latter half of the century. The experienced Africa merchants and captains behind them presumably would have operated more efficiently

modernes," *Revue historique,* 98ᵉ année, 51, no. 510 (1974): 277–302; Douglas C. North, "Sources of Productivity Change in Ocean Shipping, 1600–1850," *Journal of Political Economy* 76, no. 5 (1968): 953–70.

154. On French privateers, Verger, *Flux et reflux,* pp. 227–28, 240–41. Various documentation in the Angolan *caixas* of the AHU for the Angola coast.

155. Ship's histories are reconstructed in unpublished data processing analysis of shipping records; cf. Joseph C. Miller, "The Portuguese Slave Trade in the Southern Atlantic, 1780–1830" (seminar paper, Institute of Commonwealth Studies, University of London, 1974), and "Sources and Knowledge of the Slave Trade in the Southern Atlantic" (unpublished paper, Western Branch of the American Historical Association, La Jolla, 1976).

than the opportunists who occasionally attempted a single slaving venture, and they would have forced their novice competitors to resort to tight-packing and other methods of reducing expenses that worked hardships mostly on the slaves.

The technical characteristics of the vessels committed to slaving in the southern Atlantic reflected the general evolution of maritime technology in Brazil as well as the special demands of the African voyage. Indications of the types of ships employed as slavers come primarily from registries of arrivals and departures in all colonial ports according to ship designations defined by rigging and by other ill-understood characteristics of their construction.[156] Given the broad importance of size in the economics of the trade, the men who sailed the ships obviously planned in terms of a broad distinction between the several smaller types of craft— *pataxos, charruinhas, paquetes, balandras, sumacas, briques,* and miniature early-eighteenth-century versions of *bergantins* and *curvetas*—and the much larger *fragatas, galeras, navios,* and *naus* in those years. In general, they employed the smaller types in lower-volume short-range commerce, mostly in Brazilian coastal waters, and sent the larger ones out on the longer hauls from Europe to America, Africa, and Asia, and back.

The early decades of the eighteenth century saw a variety of types of Brazilian shipping at Angolan ports, distinctively the small two-masted *pataxos* and *sumacas* developed for the coasting trade overseas.[157] They contrasted sharply with the larger open-ocean shipping from Lisbon. By the 1740s and 1750s, the Brazilian *curveta* (sometimes spelled *corveta*), a middle-sized merchant ship with the capability of carrying as many as twenty-four to thirty artillery pieces, made its appearance as a specific adaptation to the requirements of slaving in the southern Atlantic: large enough to cover routes of moderate length, with adequate speed, and having the capability to defend itself during the mid-century wars without the support of convoys or accompanying warships, which were almost never employed in slaving owing to the need for keeping the slave ships moving and for spacing out their arrivals. The *curveta* distributed its sails over three masts.[158] Both the *curvetas* and the Lisbon ships of mid-century

156. See the relevant subject headings ("Marinha mercante," "Marinha de Guerra," etc.) in Joel Serrão, ed., *Dicionário de história de Portugal* (Lisbon: Iniciativas Editoriais, 1963–71), 4 vols; also Leitão and Lopes, *Dicionário da linguagem de marinha,* and António Marques Esparteiro, *Dicionário ilustrado de Marinha* (Lisbon: Clássica Editora, 1962); Lisanti, *Negócios coloniais,* glossary, 1:li–lxx. Brown, "Internal Commerce," pp. 189–216, has a useful discussion of shipping at Rio late in the eighteenth century and early in the nineteenth.

157. In addition to sources cited above, Flory, "Bahian Society," p. 246; "Discurso preliminar," p. 302.

158. Mattoso, *Etre esclave au Brésil,* p. 53, adds that the *curvetas* were known for their maneuverability, also a defensive strength. Lugar, "Merchant Community," p. 127, n. 1, indirectly supports the point by stressing their speed.

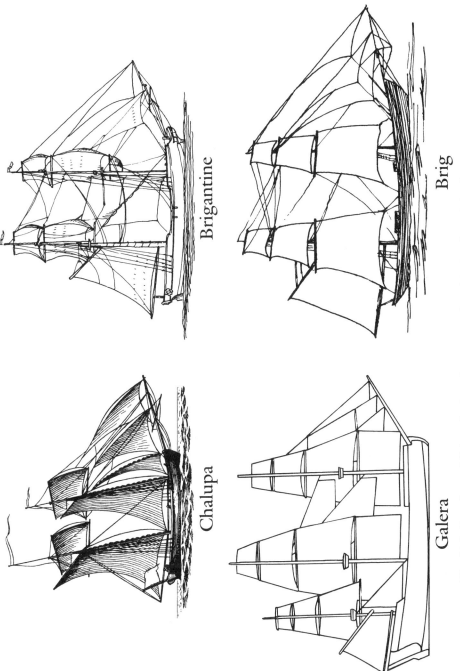

Brigantine

Brig

Chalupa

Galera

Fig. 10.1. Drawings of Ships of Selected Types Employed in Southern Atlantic Slaving

tended toward medium size—roughly some 120–160 tons with a capacity for 300–400 slaves—at a time when the ships of the annual convoys linking Brazil to Portugal were growing beyond 500 tons up to 1,000 tons and more, four to six times as large.[159] By the 1760s, a trend away from dual-purpose military-merchant designs and toward purely commercial vessels added a new, larger type of Brazilian *sumaca*, probably of the sort developed especially for the Bahia-Mina slave trade, to the *curveta* as the workhorses of the Angolan slaving fleet.[160] By the end of the century, a general abandonment of military features and a growing emphasis on purely commercial aspects of ship design, speed, carrying capacity, and operating efficiency led to the growing prominence of two- and three-masted *bergantins, galeras*, and, by the early nineteenth century, also *briques*.[161] These larger open-ocean designs in the trade were always supplemented by lesser coastal types—*escunas, chalupas, hiates,* and the like—as Brazilians appropriated them for slaving ventures when opportunities arose. One imagines that slaves suffered most of all in the completely inadequate conditions that such diminuitive craft could offer for five to eight weeks at sea.

One constant feature of ship design for the Angolan slave trade was a tendency toward an optimal middle size, defined by the need to balance speed in loading and turnaround time against efficiency of operation. Early on, ships clustered in a range between 300 and 400 slaves. Later the optimum grew, but only to between 350 and 450 slaves. Though the overall tendency was to approach a single optimal, though growing, size, Lisbon ships always remained larger than those from Brazil, owing in part to greater distances they had to travel to reach Angola, but also to the greater wealth backing metropolitan ventures. The bigger ships from Europe or from the Brazil-Portugal run were too large not to cause delays in loading slaves at Luanda, and they were even more disruptive at the smaller port at Benguela. The huge quantities of goods that they disgorged

159. For the specific comparison, Corcino Medeiros dos Santos, "O comércio do porto do Rio de Janeiro com o de Lisboa de 1763 a 1808" (Ph.D. diss., Marília, 1973), p. 152. The middling size of the *curveta* at Bahia is also clear in Jozé Antonio Caldas, "Notícia geral de toda esta capitania da Bahia desde o seu descobrimento até o prezente anno de 1759," *Revista do Instituto geografico e histórico da Bahia* 57 (1931): 303, who has *sumacas* carrying 1,500–2,500 rolls of tobacco, *curvetas* carrying 2,500–4,000, and large *navios* carrying 4,000–6,000.

160. Nunes Dias, *Companhia Geral,* pp. 246–60, presents cost figures for the ships owned by the Pernambuco Company, which included a number of vessels in Brazilian waters as well as those engaged in its transoceanic trade; it valued its four *sumacas* almost as highly as its *curvetas*.

161. Lugar, "Merchant Community," p. 68, Table 2.1, shows locations of the commercial fleet claiming Bahia as home port in 1775 that confirm their differentiation of type by specific routes available to Brazilians. Of the 10 large *galeras* and *navios*, 7 were in Portugal, 2 in Bahia, and 2 in Rio. Of the 37 *curvetas*, 20 were in Africa, 12 in Bahia, only 3 in Portugal, and 1 elsewhere in Brazil. Of the *sumacas* (and similar small coasting craft), 33 out of 40 were in and around Bahia, 4 in Africa, and 3 elsewhere in Brazil, with none at all in Portugal.

depressed prices for the imports they delivered, and the delays involved in filling them to capacity caused rising numbers of deaths among captives, as the chartered companies learned in the 1760s and 1770s. Smaller ships, in the 200- to 300-slave range, and occasionally less, must have been more dangerous and difficult to maneuver in the open ocean—particularly as overloaded as they were with tight-packed slaves—and therefore doubly hard on the captives they carried below decks.

Other than size and speed, the relative efficiency with which ships could be manned surely also influenced these changes in slave ship design, given the large size of the crews and the pervasive emphasis on minimizing operating costs. Ships of all types tended to employ a relatively constant complement of four or five officers (captain, first and second mates, quartermaster; sometimes a supercargo; always a chaplain, as required by law; occasionally tradesmen like tailors/sailmasters, carpenters, and coopers). The number of crewmen varied over a wide range, anywhere from fifteen to forty, and occasionally up to fifty or more. Cash was the scarce component in assembling most Brazilian (and for that matter, also Portuguese) ventures, since the shippers' strategy at base was to dispose of goods and equipment on hand, or borrowed, in order to acquire specie. The largest cash outlay of a voyage was potentially in the salaries paid to officers and members of the crew. Hence, the relationship between the number of slaves carried and the number of crew would go far to determine the success of the voyage. By the 1820s, individual ships varied enormously in this respect, from as few as nine slaves carried per crewman on smaller ships to thirty or more on some big vessels. In general, therefore, greater slaves-crew efficiencies on larger vessels probably raised the size of the ships employed beyond the optimum that would have derived solely from their loading and mortality cost functions.[162]

But the loading and mortality costs were significant enough that investors could probably achieve maximum efficiency by first taking ships near the optimal size and then choosing a crew-efficient rigging type and hull design. Presumably, the arrangement of the sails influenced the number of men necessary to maneuver the ship, while still leaving crew available to guard and care for the slaves. Among ships leaving Lisbon in the 1810s and 1820s, the popular new mid-sized *bergantins* ranked at the top in this respect, able to carry about 19.3 slaves for each member of the crew. The *galera* of the same period, also a rather large ship, could carry slaves with about equal crew-efficiency (19.4 slaves per crew member) but was gen-

---

162. Among various glimpses: *despacho* in Magalhães, 6 Nov. 1744, AHU, Angola cx. 23; Julgação, 14 Jan. 1774, BAPP, 140, no. 353; Almeida e Vasconcelos, 2 Oct. 1794, AHU, Angola cx. 43; documentation on the *São João Deligente,* 25 Feb. 1799, AHU, Angola cx. 46; Delgado, *Famosa e histórica Benguela,* pp. 447–49 (for 1799); Oliveira Barboza, 24 Mar. 1812, AHU, Angola cx. 61.

erally oversized for Angola, averaging 644.6 slaves capacity versus the *bergantim*'s average of 446.6 in the 1820s. The *navio*, a huge ocean-going ship (capacities averaging 765.7 even on the African run and probably larger elsewhere), was the most crew-efficient of all but far too bulky to load slaves safely in Angola. Smaller vessels, less suited to the long Europe-Africa voyage, also required 25 percent more crew per slave carried (15.2 for the *brique*, of an average 367.8 slaves capacity; 14.4 for the *brique-escuna*, of 245.8 slaves capacity).[163] Brazilians accordingly seem to have employed ships of these last two types with greater frequency in this period than did metropolitan merchants. Their use of these smaller ships, despite their higher crew costs, may have reflected savings in slave mortality owing to their moderate size and superior speed, or they could represent one more instance of the disadvantages that limited capital placed on Brazilian shippers.

Specialization of ship design culminated in the nineteenth century, as the volume of slaving rose and as the commercial organization of southern Atlantic trade generally became much more refined than it had been in the eighteenth century. The proportions of each type of rigging employed in the 1820s reflected a tendency to balance the opposing constraints of voyage distance and crew efficiency (implying larger ships) against slave loading and mortality in Angola (implying a middle size, but much smaller than general ocean shipping). The mid-sized and crew-efficient *bergantins* appeared more than twice as frequently (47.6%) as the next most preferred style, the crew-efficient long-distance, but large, *galera* (21.4%). Use of the *galera*, despite the inefficiency of its great size, may have indicated the importance of wage costs, but under the law of 1684 it also carried fewer slaves in the low slaves per ton areas below deck than other types and may therefore have permitted tighter packing per unit of nominal rated capacity.[164] The excessively large though most crew-efficient *navio* represented a weak 7.1 percent of the trade, in part because it was a metropolitan rather than a colonial vessel and because of the marginal position of Lisbon merchants in the Angolan trade. The smallish and labor-costly Brazilian *briques* and *brique-escunas* each had about 9.5 percent of the voyages.[165] Proliferating new designs in the late eighteenth and early nineteenth centuries probably improved the efficiency of slaving in the southern Atlantic,

163. Figures for ships in Lisbon preparing to leave for Angola, 1818–28: ANTT, Junta do Comércio, maço 62, macete 123. The sample size is 43 ships. See the comparable French estimate for slavers reaching Pernambuco at the same time, in the text at note 122 above. Henry A. Gemery and Jan S. Hogendorn, "Technological Change, Slavery, and the Slave Trade," in Clive Dewey and A. G. Hopkins, eds., *The Imperial Impact: Studies in the Economic History of Africa and India* (London: Athlone Press, 1978), p. 255, have British ships carrying 35 slaves per man by 1766.

164. Lopes, *Escravatura*, pp. 182–83.

165. ANTT, Junta do Comércio, maço 62, macete 123.

reducing costs over the long term and rendering the voyage less hazardous, if not more comfortable, for the slaves.

The technicalities of measuring carrying capacities also increased the popularity of some types of ships. In the *sumaca*, for example, the officers' cabins and bunks for the crew were located above the main deck rather than below it. Under the highly legalistic, if also generous, interpretations of the decree of 1684 prevailing in Angola, these main-deck spaces therefore added authorized capacity at the higher rates applicable to ventilated and above-decks spaces rather than at the lower below-decks rates for the same chambers in other types of vessel—regardless, of course, of whether slaves would actually occupy these areas during the middle passage.[166]

The same distinction between spaces above and below the main deck reappeared in a study performed to estimate the differential effects of new British-inspired tight-packing limitations proposed in 1810. It showed that two *bergantins* would have carried 76–87 percent of their slaves in the areas below the main deck designed for them under the old rule, whereas allocations of space to other purposes in the two less specialized but similar-sized *curvetas* still in use left only 69–75 percent of the slave-carrying capacity there. The huge *galera* measured on that occasion was a general-purpose merchantman with space for officers and passengers and had the lowest proportion of all of its capacity below decks, only about 57 percent.[167] Though the popular, specialized *bergantins* offered less above-decks space available for packing slaves at greater densities under Portuguese measuring methods, they carried more captives per ton of overall capacity: 7.1 and 7.2 slaves per measured ton overall, as opposed to 6.8 and 6.3 for the two *curvetas* and 6.4 for the *galera*. The British methods of measurement proposed to replace the Portuguese methods in 1810 would have applied a single slaves-per-ton rate to all parts of the ship and would have discouraged the Portuguese habit of packing slaves in above-decks spaces actually intended for other purposes. The specialized slavers would have lost significantly less capacity than the other types.

Once again, the economics of regulation worked to favor the Portuguese merchants, who were buying the specially designed British ships in the wake of British abolition in 1808, at the expense of the general Brazilian merchantmen. After the British excluded their own subjects from slaving in 1808, a number of Liverpool guineamen formerly engaged in transporting slaves to the West Indies were sold off to Portuguese merchants in Brazil.[168] These specially constructed vessels also introduced copper-sheathed hulls to the Portuguese slave trade in the southern At-

---

166. De Mello, 12 March 1799, AHU, Angola cx. 46.
167. See the table in Lopes, *Escravatura*, pp. 182–83.
168. Williams, "Abolition and the Re-deployment of the Slave Fleet"; Eltis, "British Trans-Atlantic Slave Trade after 1807."

lantic, bringing a technical innovation known to the French and British competitors of the Portuguese for at least three decades. Copper sheathing extended the life of wooden hulls in tropical water by protecting them from shipworms and increased the ships' speed by reducing drag from barnacles and other clinging marine life common in warm seas.[169] In the hands of the Portuguese resident in Brazil, these ships put the Brazilian fleet at a severe disadvantage in carrying slaves and helped to exclude Brazilians from African buying areas that the metropolitan merchants favored.

The economics of southern Atlantic slaving changed again in the last decade or two of the legal trade, as the combined functions of carrying goods to Africa and returning with slaves to Brazil were separated more and more. Specialized merchant ships began to deliver goods to factors in Africa, who stocked them for sale to slaving captains for cash. The slavers then used the goods to buy the slaves they intended to take to America, returning to Africa later in ballast.[170] These refinements, which applied particularly to western central African ports other than Luanda and Benguela, reduced delays in getting slaves on their way, allowed Portuguese and Brazilian merchants to do business smoothly with Spanish and North American slavers, and protected the merchant wing of the trade from growing British pressures against slaving. The British and associated Portuguese merchants in Brazil became the dominant parties involved in the selling of goods, while the Brazilians found themselves pushed off into buying, transporting, and selling slaves. The separation of function became complete with illegalization of the trade after 1830, with the formerly colonial Brazilians still marginal to the changed structure of southern Atlantic shipping in the nineteenth century.

Conclusion

The maritime segment of the southern Atlantic slave trade thus witnessed the emergence of a distinct slave-carrying sector of the Brazilian shipping industry in the course of the eighteenth century. At Angola, more than on the West African coast north of the equator, though not so different from slaving at Mozambique, the ships that carried the slaves came mostly

---

169. De Mello, 17 June 1799, AHU, Angola cx. 47; Botelho de Vasconcelos, 1 July 1799, in Delgado, *Famosa e histórica Benguela*, doc. 4, pp. 447, 448. On copper sheathing generally, Tom Glasgow, Jr., "Sixteenth-Century English Seamen Meet a New Enemy—the Shipworm," *American Neptune* 27, no. 3 (1967): 177–84; Gemery and Hogendorn, "Technological Change," pp. 255–56.

170. Susan Herlin Broadhead, "Trade and Politics on the Congo Coast: 1770–1870" (Ph.D. diss., Boston University, 1971), p. 184.

from Rio de Janeiro. They delivered a lower proportion of the imports than did the Lisbon ships with whom they competed, though they brought essential rum and minor quantities of other American commodities. They first appeared as suppliers of slaves to the gold fields of Minas Gerais, then survived mid-century pressures from Lisbon by transporting slaves to smugglers servicing the Spanish colonies along and above the Plata estuary, and then by delivering to merchants who supplied Rio de Janeiro's urban market and its growing sugar industry at the end of the century. Unlike the slavers of Bahia, and secondarily also those of Pernambuco, the Rio slavers had fewer direct links to the planter establishment of the American colony. They were therefore distinctively dependent on transportation charges for whatever profits they might glean from their role in the trade.

Like the Luso-Africans, the Rio ship operators found themselves caught between costs that rose beyond their control and revenues that they could not increase. The key constraints were fixed freight charges and the costs and space allocations for provisions necessary to preserve slave lives. These prevented slavers from cramming more captives aboard their ships than they could ordinarily carry safely. These limits also put the Brazilians at a disadvantage relative to metropolitan merchants, whose more heavily capitalized and more complex ventures more than covered the expense of carrying slaves to Brazil with trading profits on goods sold in Angola. Brazilians carried only the bulky but low-value *gerebita* on the outbound leg of their voyage and so had to recoup their losses by tight-packing the slaves they carried on the return.

The Brazilians obtained some compensating advantage from their greater specialization in slaving, which enabled them to develop mid-sized *curvetas* during the second third of the eighteenth century, large enough to make the transatlantic crossings between South America and Angola and to carry slaves without excessively fatal hardship, but still sufficiently small that they could load slaves and get underway in the African ports without damaging delays. Metropolitan competitors, more diverse in their operations and more remote from the African sources of slaves, tended to employ bigger and less efficient slavers, *galeras* and *navios*, although the early-nineteenth-century *bergantim*, which evidently gave Lisbon the capacity to sail long distances with ships of moderate size, gradually reduced the modest technological advantage gained earlier by the Brazilians. The *bergantim* also improved the crew efficiency of Portuguese slavers, although the overall performance of the Lisbon fleet never approached that obtained decades earlier in the British West Indian trade.

Decreed constraints on carrying capacities and on freight rates, while not wholly enforced in practice, increased overall costs of slave transportation on the ocean in the long run. Tight-packing, short rations, smuggling, and all the other subterfuges that Brazilians devised to evade the law may have raised the long-term profitability of slaving to the modest level available otherwise in Brazil, but the subterfuges themselves were expensive costs of doing business illegally that Brazilian slavers passed along through a variety of channels to others, mostly in the form of increased morbidity and mortality among the slaves carried. But these losses also hit the Luso-African owners of the captives, who found their investments in human labor reduced or eliminated through death and debility. To the extent that slavers also raised freight rates for Brazilian goods sold in Angola or increased their trading profits on such goods to compensate, they added to the costs that Luso-African transporters had to recover from their operations in the interior of the colony. Deliveries of sick and dying slaves to Brazilian buyers passed maintenance and re-placement costs on to planters and miners, who, often unable to transfer such costs to European consumers, recovered them in turn by skimping on slave maintenance costs, to the detriment of slave longevity and health in the New World.

The multiple ownership of the slaves aboard nearly every vessel, itself a product of slaveowner strategies intended to minimize risk by spreading assets over numerous ships and simultaneously hasten every slave to Brazil on the first available vessel, ironically also placed the ship-operators' op-timal load factors above those that might have minimized slave mortality. Slaveowners and defenders of the slaves intuitively placed safe levels of slave packing at about one-third to one-half below those the Brazilians actually practiced.[171] Captains fatalistically estimated that extra mainte-nance costs would exceed the freight charges protected by saving slave lives. Their ability to substitute living slaves belonging to others for captives of their own who died safeguarded trading profits for the ship owners and officers on the minority of the cargo that they owned, usually carried in excess of legal limits. The same technique limited freights lost on others' slaves who died as a result of their tight-packing. Multiple ownership also offered captains opportunities to feed slaves they personally owned by depriving the others. All these opportunities for fraud placed their personal level of optimal profitability well above what they could in fact achieve with bribery and misrepresentation. Ship operators agreed with the owners that they could carry a third more people than they admitted to loading, perhaps 50 percent above the legal limit, though with only secondary regard for the welfare of all the slaves on board their ships. The shippers' figure probably represented the absolute physical capacity of the ships to hold people, which would have been their most profitable position under the productivity function of their voyages.

So long as the Portuguese empire remained sealed to outside investors, the modest capitalization of the Brazilians also forced them to squeeze

---

171. Miller, "Overcrowded and Undernourished."

operating costs rather than covering their expenses with trading profits on goods or slaves sold. Their potential backers in Brazil were generally indebted to Lisbon merchants, without funds to spare for a trade as risky as slaving, and Lisbon had no desire to invest in slaving ventures mounted from Brazil that would have competed with their own business directly from Portugal to Angola. The Brazilians made unsuccessful efforts to buy up slaves on the Angolan market in the 1710s and 1720s, the height of the Brazilian gold rush that supported the earliest phases of their development. They then instead had to develop all the subterfuges and legal fictions that Lisbon subsequently condemned. Unacknowledged amidst Lisbon's anguished objections were the contributions that metropolitan loans and debt strategies made to tight-packing through the support they provided for higher volumes of slave exports. The holders of the tax-farming contract intensified these pressures in the 1730s and 1740s. The Pombaline chartered companies took over the task in the 1750s and 1760s. The whole while, governors in Angola collaborated with underlying policies that raised the revenues they received from export duties collected on the slaves.

The financial isolation of slave transporting in the southern Atlantic began to break down at the end of the eighteenth century, shifting toward the British, or Lisbon, model of slaves owned by the backers of the shipping ventures. British capital, channeled through colonial merchants engaged in smuggling their woolens and cottons to Africa, enabled supercargoes aboard Rio slavers in the 1770s and 1780s to buy more and more bills of exchange, or slaves, for themselves at Angolan ports. This trend began quietly at Benguela and spread to Luanda only in the 1780s and 1790s, when Lisbon virtually withdrew from direct participation in Angolan slaving. With transplantation of Lisbon's British-backed merchants from Portugal to Rio, it became the dominant model of slave transporting all up and down the coast after 1810, from Benguela north to the Zaire River and Cabinda. With the backing of the British, these Portuguese merchants in Rio at first displaced the Brazilians from slaving and then drifted toward specialized deliveries of trade goods, thus terminating the Brazilians' brief period of prosperously integrated selling of goods and buying of slaves. Brazilian merchants and shippers without similar backing found themselves confined to the riskiest slave-carrying peripheries of the last years of the legal trade.

The legal and administrative history of the maritime trade consisted mainly of Lisbon's only partially successful efforts to enforce decrees already on the books that favored metropolitan merchants and to devise responses to the Brazilians' evasions of the law. The Crown worked principally through its delegated officials in Luanda, but much less at Benguela, where the home government was far weaker. It gradually reduced the extent of tight-packing and smuggling at Luanda, although legal and administrative restrictions in themselves may have had less effect in this regard than relaxed freight charges and the upturn in slave prices in Brazil that late-century traders were able to capture for themselves. Meanwhile, Brazilian shippers congregated at Benguela. Throughout all the maneuvering by governors, Lisbon merchants, and ship operators, slaves continued to die aboard the ships in numbers that forced even the transporters to resist the otherwise inexorable pressures to tight-pack. The deepest irony arose from the fact that some slaves had to die in order to reduce the afflictions of others. And some of those who survived might have viewed their lives in Brazil as fates worse than the death at sea that had released many of their fellows from suffering.

11

Voyage of No Return

The Experience of Enslavement:
Flight, Disease, and Death

The horrors of enslavement in western central Africa would surely elude all who escaped that ordeal even if the slaves had left a personal record of what they suffered. Only one person enslaved and sent through Angola to Brazil is known to have left even a brief recorded impression of the march to the coast, the transfer there to a sailing vessel, the oppressively crowded conditions of the middle passage, and sale and settlement in the cities and mines and estates of Brazil.[1] The slavers, with rare exceptions, touched only peripherally on the experience of their slaves in what they wrote, principally as the captives managed to reach their captors across the gulf of callous disinterest through flight, revolt, sickness, and death. Government regulations prescribed elaborate formalities, with minimal amenities, through which slaves were supposed to pass in Luanda and Benguela, and complaints of official venality and negligence described something of the rather more tortuous paths that most actually followed.

The conflicting allegations that merchants, governors, ship operators, and slaveowners levied against one another as they competed for space aboard the ships provide other indirect glimpses of the hardships that slaves endured in the port and at sea. Proprietary concern with why the slaves died elicited inquiries and treatises, but eighteenth-century physiology and epidemiology offered only the vaguest clues as to why slaves in fact died, leaving slavers with money invested in the lives of their captives to express little more than helpless alarm in times of unusually high death rates. No one then knew exactly how many slaves sickened and died as they passed through the commercial channels that carried them to the New World, but everyone realized that the number was high and calculated the advantage they might gain from the fact. Through these fogged windows opening on what the slaves may have seen and felt the modern reader

---

1. See Chapter 1 above. For accounts of slaves from West Africa, Philip D. Curtin, ed., *Africa Remembered: Narratives by West Africans from the Era of the Slave Trade* (Madison: University of Wisconsin Press, 1967). Also see Robert Edgar Conrad, *Children of God's Fire: A Documentary History of Black Slavery in Brazil* (Princeton: Princeton University Press, 1983), pp. 23–28 et passim, for other direct accounts of enslavement in Brazil.

can perceive the shape, if not the details, of the experience of enslavement, in which virtually the sole initiatives available to the captive Africans were escape, attack, or death.

Initial Capture and Sale

The morbidity and mortality that so concerned the owners of the slaves began with enslavement and rose during the slaves' movement to the market centers of the interior. The general patterns of these processes, restated in terms of their implications for sickness and death, permit an informed guess at what the captives suffered then.[2]

The background hunger and epidemics that sometimes forced patrons to give up clients and compelled parents to part with children set a tone of physical weakness and vulnerability behind slaving in the interior.[3] Where warfare and violence stimulated the initial capture, the victims would have begun their odysseys in exhausted, shaken, and perhaps wounded physical condition. Though the buyers preferred strong adult males, the people actually captured in warfare, even in pitched battles between formal armies, included disproportionately high numbers of less fit women and children, since the men could take flight and leave the less mobile retinue of young and female dependents to the pursuers. People sold for food, the last resort in time of famine, also started out physically ill-prepared for the rigors of the journey to come. In the commercialized areas, lords, creditors, and patrons, employing less dramatic methods to seize and sell the dependents who paid for imports or covered their debts, would have selected the least promising among their followings—young boys, older women, the sick, the indebted, the troublesome, and the lame. Populations raided consistently by stronger neighbors, harassed and driven from their homes and fields, and refugee populations hiding on infertile mountaintops could not have been as well-nourished as stronger groups who yielded fewer of their members to the slave trade.

The mixture of people swept off by thousands of isolated decisions and haphazard actions separated into two distinguishable drifts of people. One was a slow, favored one composed principally of the stronger and healthier women and younger children that dissipated into the communities of western central Africa, to remain there as wives and slaves for months or years, or perhaps for life. The debilitated residue became the faster-flowing and sharply defined main channel of people destined for immediate sale and export, victims of drought and raids at the source,

2. Chapters 4–7 above.
3. Miller, "Significance of Drought, Disease and Famine," and Alden and Miller, "Unwanted Cargoes."

joined by small feeder streams of older youths ejected from local communities along its banks as it flowed westward, along with a few women
and older folk, and a variety of outcasts and criminals.

The flow he _ed for the Atlantic coast thus carried weakened individuals relatively vulnerable to disease and death, even by the low health
standards of their time. These slaves were not necessarily constitutionally
weaker than those left behind or kept but, rather, individuals taken at
defenseless and enfeebled moments in their lives. Their temporarily reduced ability to withstand the stresses of enslavement, dislocation, and
forced travel could not have failed to produce higher incidences of sickness
and death among them than among the population of western central
Africa as a whole, even without adding the physical traumas of violent
seizure or the psychological shocks of nonviolent enslavement.

Although the mortality experienced at this stage in the trade is virtually
undocumented, death rates characteristic of stable, resident populations
in the modern tropics establish a floor above which the possible fatalities
associated with enslavement may be speculatively estimated. Taking no
account of eighteenth-century mortality from droughts and warfare, the
demographic structure of populations assumed to have been present in
western central Africa[4] would have experienced a long-term overall death
rate of around 48 per 1,000 per year. Infant mortality at a level of 25 per
1,000 per year would have accounted for most of those deaths, leaving an
age-specific death rate among the children and young adults most at risk
to slaving well below 5 per 1,000 per year.

Overall loss rates in raids or wars approached 50 percent among the
segment of the population under assault for the short periods of time
involved, though figures as high as 90 percent and as low as 10 percent
were also reported for violent raiding elsewhere.[5] Incremental death rates
associated with enslavement through seizures for debt, through condemnations as criminals, and through other commercialized means would have
been negligible. Balancing the peaceful methods of enslavement against
the increasingly marginal role of large-scale violence, these highly various
losses might have averaged 10 percent for all the people enslaved. Converting losses at that level to annual mortality rates by assuming a two-
month season for violent slaving would produce yearly deaths in wars and
raids of some 90 per 1,000 or more than fifteen times those among the

4. Coale and Demeny "east" model, level 4, with a birth rate of 7.5/1,000, from
Thornton, "Demography and History," p. 517.

5. Hogendorn, "Slave Acquisition and Delivery," p. 486, cites Nachtigal's statement
that Bornu raiders lost 3–4 people to death *and escapes* for every one that they brought back
alive from remote raiding grounds in the central Sudan to the towns and markets on the
desert edge. Cordell, *Dar al-Kuti*, pp. 109–10, summarizes scattered indications of deaths
at the origins of enslavement as 10%–60% in initial violent assaults, followed by 40%–67%
of the remainder on the march to the capital.

same age cohort not caught up in the net.[6] At a ratio of two slaves from the Atlantic zone for every slave coming from the slaving frontier, the overall death rates attributable to the processes of enslavement would have been perhaps 30 per 1,000 per year. Higher death rates owing to famine and warfare would have blended indistinguishably into those associated with slaving, each of the three simultaneously both causes and consequences of the others, leading to the occasionally higher mortality estimates of outsiders who did not take explicit account of the multiple factors contributing to the tragedies they observed.

Movement to the Coast

These slaves advanced from the hands of their captors, sometimes with periods of rest and partial recuperation in villages along the way, into the market centers where African sellers met European and Luso-African slave-buyers in the interior. People raised in small, dispersed settlements would have encountered the much more volatile disease environments among populations concentrated along the trails, at the staging posts, and finally in the marketplaces themselves. Those from more densely inhabited areas, and even captives who had lived along the roads, encountered new disease environments as they moved into terrain unlike that of their native lands and came into direct contact with foreigners. They would have suffered accordingly from pathogens against which they had no immunities.

The slaves' diets also deteriorated. Whatever plantains, sorghum, or millet they might have eaten at home, supplemented by a healthy variety of game, other crops, and wild plants, as they moved westward they depended increasingly on manioc—the dietary staple that was cheapest to grow, easiest to transport, and most resistant to spoilage—prepared poorly in one form or another.[7] Fresh fruits and vegetables and meat virtually disappeared from their diet. Much of what they were given rotted or became vermin-infested. They were unlikely to have received foods of any sort in quantities sufficient to sustain them, particularly in their weakened conditions, and with vicious circularity they grew too weak to carry what little they were

6. Patrick Manning, "The Impact of Slave Trade Exports on the Population of the Western Coast of Africa, 1700–1850" (Paper presented to the Colloque International sur la Traite des Noirs, Nantes, 1985), p. 18, uses a similarly arbitrary procedure to arrive at a figure of 15%, implicitly for a population subject to more violent processes of enslavement than was the case in western central Africa.

7. Mendes (Capela ed.), *Memória a respeito dos escravos*, p. 46. Venâncio, "Economia de Luanda," p. 115, describes the dried tuber being grated into sacks and then ground, or stomped on by slaves. The resulting flour was darker than the Brazilian product and more bitter, but Portuguese confidently believed that it was more nutritious and was preferred by the Africans. The grinding mill employed in Brazil was not used in Angola. Also Vansina, *Tio Kingdom*, p. 149, for the Zaire River trade, and Harms, *River of Wealth, River of Sorrow*, pp. 52–58.

given as they moved. Those who stumbled from weakness were driven onward to keep the remainder moving, all bound together. They drank from
inadequate water supplies along the way, sometimes streams, but often not,
owing to the tendency of the trails to follow the elevated ridges along the
watersheds and the caravan drivers' preference for travel in the dry months.
Pools dug out at stopping places were often contaminated from the concentrations of slave caravans that built up around them.[8]

Under such conditions, the slaves developed both dietary imbalances
and sheer nutritional insufficiencies. Scurvy, so common among slaves who
lived to cross the southern Atlantic that it was known as the *mal de Loanda*
(or "Luanda sickness"), was the primary recognized form of undernour-
ishment.[9] The symptoms appeared on slave ships at sea long before they
could have developed from shortages of rations on board except among
slaves already debilitated by weeks or months of a diet restricted to low
vitamin, low acetic acid starches like manioc. With innocent destructiveness
some physicians prescribed more manioc as an anti-escorbutic. The slaves
who died along the path must have suffered malnutrition to a degree
approaching sheer starvation. Racialist Portuguese theories of tropical
medicine at the time misdiagnosed the condition, holding that blacks
needed to eat less than whites, since they could thrive for days at a time
on nothing more than a few millet heads and a kola nut.[10]

8. Mendes (Capela ed.), *Memória a respeito dos escravos*, pp. 43–47.
9. It was also recognized that fresh fruits and vegetables mitigated the condition; the
problem arose when slavers misguidedly supplied slaves only with the cheaper manioc. Use
of the term *mal de Loanda* dates at least to early in the seventeenth century and extended
throughout the Portuguese- and Spanish-speaking Atlantic world. See Alexo de Abreu,
Tratado de las siete enfermedades (Lisbon: Pedro Craesbeeck, 1623), who identified the condition as *mal de Loanda* already by 1594–1602; cf. Waldemar Jorge Gomes Teixeira, "Subsídios para a história da medicina portuguesa em Angola," *Boletim do Instituto de Angola* 30–
32 (1968): 9; Francisco Guerra, "Aleixo de Abreu (1568–1630), Author of the Earliest
Book on Tropical Medicine," *Journal of Tropical Medicine and Hygiene* 71, no. 3 (1968): esp.
63–64. Cf. Johannes Postma, "Mortality in the Dutch Slave Trade, 1675–1795," in Gemery
and Hogendorn, *Uncommon Market*, p. 252, who found scurvy common, and Stein, *French
Slave Trade*, p. 100, but note also Klein, *Middle Passage*, pp. 201–2, who restricts its
appearance (in the French trade only?) to the end of unexpectedly long voyages that forced
slaves (and crew) to go on short rations. For contemporary documentation of the condition,
António Brásio, "O inimigo dos antigos colonos e missionários de Africa," *Portugal em Africa*
1 (1944): 215–29; Cadornega, *História geral*, 1:21; Mendes (Capela ed.), *Memória a respeito
dos escravos*, p. 63. See also Robert J. Ferry, "Encomienda, African Slavery, and Agriculture
in Seventeenth-Century Caracas," *Hispanic American Historical Review* 61, no. 4 (1981): 628,
n. 46, for Venezuela; David L. Chandler, "Health Conditions in the Slave Trade of Colonial
New Granada," in Robert B. Toplin, ed., *Slavery and Race Relations in Latin America* (Westport, Conn.: Greenwood Press, 1974), p. 59, for Cartagena; Elena F. S. Scheuss de Studer,
La trata de negros en el Río de la Plata durante el siglo xviii (Buenos Aires: Universidad de
Buenos Aires, 1958), p. 117; and much other contemporary evidence. There is some suggestion also that the name *mal de Loanda* arose from the sufferings that sailors on the India
ships inbound to Portugal experienced as they neared the Angola coast.
10. Azeredo, *Ensaios sobre algumas enfermidades*, pp. 59–60. Cosme (Pina ed.), "Tractado," p. 263, felt it necessary to admonish slavers that Africans were not chameleons, which
were believed to survive from breathing air and eating flies alone.

The alterations in diet and the amoeba in contaminated water supplies must also have caused the early spread of dysenteries and other intestinal disorders, the infamous "flux" that the British lamented among the slaves they carried across the Atlantic, known as *câmaras* among the Portuguese.[11] Infected excreta left everywhere about water sources, in camp sites, and in the slave pens of the marketplaces assured that few individuals escaped debilitating and dehydrating epidemics of bloody bacillary dysenteries.[12]

Exposure to the dry-season chill in the high elevations and to damp nights spent sitting in open pathside camps, utter lack of clothing and shelter, and increasingly weakened constitutions all contributed to the appearance of respiratory ailments vaguely described as *constipações*. As slaves neared the marketplaces and the main routes running from them down to the coast, they grew weaker and more susceptible to parasites and other diseases that swept in epidemic form through the coffles. The slave trade must have been a veritable incubator for typhus, typhoid, and other fevers or *carneiradas*,[13] particularly smallpox, and other diseases that broke out in times of drought and famine from their usual confinement in the streams of slaves into the general rural population.[14] The normal concentration of these diseases along the commercial routes may have contributed to the impression of overwhelming deadliness that Portuguese held of most of the central African interior, since every European who ventured there necessarily walked within these reservoirs of slave-borne infection on the pathways leading to the interior.

The inferable lethal consequences of malnutrition, disease, and other hardships along the path were death rates that rose at an increasing tempo as slaves flowed into the central channels of the slave trade, perhaps to catastrophic levels in the range of 400–600 per 1,000 per annum by the time slaves reached the coast. One experienced Luanda merchant reported that slavers toward the second half of the eighteenth century expected to lose about 40 percent of their captives to flight and death between the time they purchased them in the interior and the time they put them

11. Azeredo, *Ensaios sobre algumas enfermidades*, pp. 95–124; also Brásio, "Inimigo dos antigos colonos," as reprinted in idem, *História e missiologia: inéditos e esparsos* (Luanda: Instituto de Investigação Científica de Angola, 1973), pp. 741–42.

12. On epidemic dysentery in Angola, Owen, *Narrative of Voyages*, 2:281; José Joaquim Moreira, "Memoria sobre as molestias endémicas da costa occidental d'Africa," *Jornal da Sociedade das sciências médicas de Lisboa* 15, no. 1 (1842): 140; Azeredo, *Ensaios sobre algumas enfermidades*, p. 93. Also see Mendes (Capela ed.), *Memória a respeito dos escravos*, pp. 56–57, unaccountably mislabeling it *mal de Loanda*.

13. This is not the place to attempt to differentiate the various fevers that may have contributed to the general notion that contemporaries had of *carneiradas*; see, e.g., Mendes (Capela ed.), *Memória a respeito dos escravos*, pp. 55–56; Moreira, "Memoria sobre as molestias," pp. 128–39; Azeredo, *Ensaios sobre algumas enfermidades*, pp. 1–92. The term *carneiradas* surely came from *carneiro*, "burial urn."

14. Observers almost uniformly focused on smallpox as the preeminent epidemic disease at Luanda and Benguela: Alden and Miller, "Unwanted Cargoes."

aboard the ships in Luanda.[15] If the westward march averaged about six months from the central highlands or the Kwango valley,[16] where most agents of the town merchants bought slaves at that time, and deaths in the seaport ran about 15 percent,[17] that estimate would mean 25 percent of the slaves died en route to the coast.[18] Such a figure would imply a mean death rate between time of purchase and time of arrival in the towns of 500 per 1,000 per year.[19] In practice, lower death rates at the outset of the trek would have risen at an increasing rate to peak somewhere above that level at the coast, but averaging out to that overall percentage loss. A certain proportion of the losses would have been attributable to flight and to theft, leaving a bit less than the reported total owing to mortality.

Flight from the slave coffles heading toward the coast, though impossible to estimate precisely in terms of frequency, was not uncommon. Despite the nutritional and epidemiological odds against the slaves, some individuals somehow found the strength to flee their captors.[20] Slaves fled from the marketplaces of the interior, taking refuge among the very people who had just sold them to the Europeans.[21] As they neared the coast, they found willing, though often calculatingly self-interested, asylum among the independent Africans living on either side of Luanda, south of the Kwanza in Kisama, and north of the Dande among the southern Kongo of Musulu.[22] Some fugitives established maroon colonies of their own

15. Raymundo Jalamá, quoted in Mendes (Capela ed.), *Memória a respeito dos escravos,* p. 48.

16. Mendes, *Memória a respeito dos escravos,* p. 45, but also see the fuller version of the manuscript in Carreira, "Companhias pombalinas de navegação," p. 424.

17. See the text below at note 87.

18. João Marinho dos Santos, "Angola na governação dos Felipes: uma perspectiva económica e social," *Revista de história económica e social* 3 (1979): 68, has an estimate of 50% for slaves coming down the Kwanza route during the 1610s.

19. One may compare this estimate against the conventional ratio of 100% markup on goods prices between Luanda and marketplaces at about that distance in the interior. Restated in terms of slaves, it would cover costs of 50%, a figure sufficiently above estimated losses of 25% to mortality to absorb maintenance, bad debts, and other expenses of an equal amount.

20. The accounts of the Maranhão Company from time to time noted flight by slaves after company agents had taken possession of them in the city of Luanda itself: 2 (of 547, or 0.4%) in 1758, 9 (of 514, 1.8%) in 1762, and 12 (of 6,085, or 0.2%) in all: Carreira, "Companhias pombalinas de navegação," pp. 366–77. A new edition of Carreira, *As companhias pombalinas de Grão-Pará e Maranhão e Pernambuco e Paraíba* (Lisbon: Presença, 1983), not available at the time of writing, has increased these and other figures for death and flight among company slaves. The "Relação sobre escravatura," n.d. (ca. 1760s), AHU, Angola maço 10 (D.O.), also included an unquantified allowance for flight in its estimate of the costs of slaving in Angola.

21. For Mbwila, Meneses, 30 Jan. 1734, AHU, Angola cx. 20; for Kasanje, Dias, ed. (Leitão), "Viagem a Cassange," pp. 16–17.

22. Where they were joined by slaves fleeing the city, the estates along the Bengo, and the military posts in the interior. For Kisama generally, see Heintze, "Historical Notes"; in particular, Meneses, 20 Dec. 1734, AHU, Angola cx. 20; *requerimento* (from Luanda residents?), n.d. (but minuted 27 Oct. 1747), AHU, Angola cx. 24; "Capitullaçoes que fez Sova Dom Bento Catala Casalla . . . ," Oct. 1745, AHU, Angola cx. 23; Corrêa, *História de*

within Portuguese territory, and there are hints that a major colony of renegades existed throughout the century virtually on the outskirts of Luanda. Some of these colonies had extensive fields and fortifications, including up to forty houses and populations of about 200 people, and lived by raiding Portuguese slave-run plantations in the river valleys.[23]

The nearness of Kisama made it the favored destination for Luanda slaves seeking protection from independent Africans, and the willingness of chiefs there to welcome fugitives underlay the persistent enmity between the Portuguese and the Africans living south of the river. Kisama was in effect an enormous fugitive slave colony, or *quilombo*, as these were known in both Brazil and Angola. Kisama's role as a haven for fugitives probably declined at the end of the eighteenth century, since nineteenth-century references to the region no longer picked up the ancient refrain of hostility.[24]

The fugitives generally hid out beyond rivers, in deep forests, and on inaccessible mountaintops, but individuals also found refuge in the churches of the town and on missionary-run estates in the vicinity, all of them ecclesiastical property exempt from intrusions by the civilian authorities.[25] Slaves who fled the Portuguese after years of experience in Luanda found a particular welcome among the lords of Kisama, who used them as spies who could return undetected to the city, dressed like its other African residents, and report back on Portuguese military capacities and intentions. Other groups of fugitive slaves constantly assaulted the roads leading eastward from Luanda, particularly in the 1740s, 1750s, and 1760s to judge from the incidence of official government concern, mostly stealing trade goods from the caravans.[26] The organization and tactics of these refugee

---

Angola, 2:8 (for 1749–53), but cf. Torres, *Memórias,* p. 255; Vasconcelos, 12 June 1762, AHU, Angola cx. 29; Sousa Coutinho, 18 Oct. 1769, AHU, Angola cx. 32; Valente, "Estado Actual da Conquista d'Angola . . . ," 1 Feb. 1792, AHU, Angola cx. 42. For Musulu, north of the Dande, the *representação* of the Senado da Câmara (Luanda), 17 Aug. 1790, AHU, Angola cx. 41 (and published—though misdated as 18 Aug. 1790—in *Arquivos de Angola* 4 [1938]: 159). Portuguese demands for the return of fugitive slaves ran through all formal treaties reached with African authorities: e.g., Sousa Coutinho, 10 Jan. 1771, enclosing "Capitulos do Juramento que prometeu guardar o Duque de Hoando . . . ," 11 Jan. 1666, and *carta circular,* 3 Oct. 1770, AHU, Angola cx. 33; *termo de vassalagem* (Sova Manoel de Noronha Xote Muxima Quita Gombe), n.d. (ca. 1740s), AHU, Angola cx. 23; "Termo do que se determinou na Junta q se fez sobre se castigar a Raynha Ginga," 13 April 1744, and *regimento* given to Capitão-mor Francisco Roque Souto, AHU, Angola cx. 23; Santa Comba Dão, 14 Dec. 1830, AHU, Angola cx. 73.
    23. E.g., the José Gregorio Mendes report (1785) translated in Bowdich, *Discoveries of the Portuguese,* p. 30; *bando* of 6 April 1765 detailing conditions in the wilderness of BemBem adjacent to Luanda, AHU, Angola cx. 30; Noronha, 8 Nov. 1803, AHU, Angola cx. 54.
    24. Castelobranco, 24 Sept. 1824, AHU, Angola cx. 70; idem, 19 Oct. 1825, cx. 69.
    25. Magalhães, 28 Dec. 1746, AHU, Angola cx. 24; letter from Padre José de Santa Cecilia, 7 May 1747, AHU, Angola cx. 24.
    26. See the Oeyras *parecer,* 20 Nov. 1760, AHU, Angola cx. 28.

communities seem to have differed hardly at all from maroon colonies elsewhere in Africa, Brazil, the Caribbean, and mainland North America.[27]

The Barracoons of Luanda and Benguela

The slave population entering Luanda was heavily weighted toward younger males by the eighteenth century, reflecting the strain on western central African populations by that time and the widespread resort to debt as means of creating slaves. Older men (*barbados*) also passed through Luanda in significant numbers. Predominant among the women were young females, with a scattering of prime (nubile) women, mothers with infants, and girls, precisely the category of slave that African lords must have been least willing to give up and therefore a further indication of demographic and commercial pressures then bearing on the slave supply zones.

The ideal slave *peça*, or prime adult male, was in short supply, no longer available from the areas of commercialized slaving, and relatively few of the women taken in wars made it through the African transporters to arrive at the coast. The proportion of able-bodied adult males reaching the coast had declined to only one-eighth to one-sixth of the individuals offered for sale in the 1780s and 1790s.[28] Scattered detailed breakdowns of prices received for mixed lots of captives show only a few individuals in the highest-priced, presumably *peça* category; none at all appeared in some groups changing hands in 1774 and 1799, and 10 percent (or perhaps 20 percent) showed up in others in the mid-1780s.[29] An appar-

27. Richard Price, ed., *Maroon Societies: Rebel Slave Communities in the Americas* (New York: Anchor Press, 1973). For Angola later in the nineteenth century, Clarence-Smith, *Slaves, Peasants, and Capitalists*, pp. 82–88, comments on "social bandits." Cf. also Robert Ross, *Cape of Torments: Slavery and Resistance in South Africa* (London: Routledge and Kegan Paul, 1983), esp. pp. 54–72, and Gwyn Campbell, "Madagascar and the Slave Trade, 1810–1895," *Journal of African History* 22, no. 2 (1981): 224–25. There was only a very subtle distinction between these refugee colonies and the early phases of the African "states" around the borders of Angola that got their start from defending refugees from wars and from slaving and continued to welcome escaped slaves well into their maturity. Even the most established African polities rested heavily on slave retainers at the central courts.
28. Silva Lisboa letter, 18 Oct. 1781, *Annaes da Biblioteca nacional do Rio de Janeiro* 32 (1910); *consulta* of the Junta do Comércio (Lisbon), 19 Aug. 1782, ANTT, Junta do Comércio, maço 62 and maço 122. Mendes (Capela ed.), *Memória a respeito dos escravos*, p. 49, refers to youths and women as "the best part" of the slaves reaching Brazil. For further discussion, see Miller, "Slave Prices." David Eltis, "Fluctuations in the Age and Sex Ratios of Slaves in the Nineteenth-Century Transatlantic Slave Traffic," *Slavery and Abolition* 7, no. 3 (1986): 259, 262, has assembled impressive quantitative documentation of the youth of the slaves leaving Angola and Loango in the early nineteenth century. Conrad, *World of Sorrow*, pp. 87–88, has 200 children under 12 in a cargo of 430 slaves in 1833 and indicates even greater preference for carrying them after 1835.
29. *Processo* of Belchior Clemente Domingos Martins, n.d. (ca. 1774), AHU, Angola cx. 36; *auto*, 4 Oct. 1784, ANRJ, cx. 388, pac. 2; *auto*, Domingos de Araujo e Azevedo and João da Silva Guimarães, 1 March 1799, AHU, Angola cx. 48.

ently prime shipment in 1809 still contained only one-third *peças*. A lot
of 100 slave couples purchased for the Crown in 1819, and therefore
presumably the very best to be found in Luanda, managed only just over
half of the males in the top price category. This purchase indicated the
absolute maximum proportion of prime slaves who could be assembled at
that time. The usual coffle contained far fewer.

The terms employed to describe the slaves also reflected the decline
in age and strength of the individuals being delivered by then. *Moleque,*
a word that had referred to nearly adult youths a century or more before,
became the general form of reference to ordinary slaves, but augmentative
derivations, *molecão* or *molecote,* appeared to cover the mature young men
left out as the original term was applied to the boys who constituted the
majority of the captives.

Older people and small children appeared in relatively low numbers,
and their absence probably reflected the high death rates along the trail
that worked selectively against weaker individuals for months before the
coffles reached the cities. These numbers also reflected Portuguese reluctance to buy the very old and the very young. In particular, slavers in
Luanda avoided sending off young children, who, for all their usefulness
for avoiding taxes and for tight-packing, were bad risks for shipment, since
they were widely regarded as unlikely to survive the middle passage.[30] In
addition, infants imported to Brazil brought low prices. Their continued
high death rates, their low productivity compared to new adult slaves, and
the competition from American-born slave infants, who would grow up
knowing Portuguese and were surely less costly to raise within the household or estate than paying out the cash necessary to buy new children
from Angola, all made them bad investments. The *moleque* majority of the
slaves shipped, on the other hand, who by this time included older children
from eight to fifteen years of age,[31] were regarded as trainable, capable of
learning Portuguese, and less likely to flee or to die from shock and depression.[32] The Portuguese reluctance to buy younger African children complemented the African desire to retain them and raise them for sale as
young adults, with the result that few of them actually arrived at Luanda
or Benguela for shipment or sale.

30. Letter to Felix José da Costa of 4 July 1777, AHMF, Pernambuco Co., Benguela
copiador, published in Carreira, "Companhias pombalinas de navegação," pp. 67–68, 393–
94; also letter of 18 Sept. 1765 to de Lemos and Souza Portella, AHMF, Pernambuco Co.,
Angola *copiador;* António Guedes Quinhões (governor, Benguela), 29 Dec. 1821, AHU,
Angola cx. 67. Cf. David Northrup, "African Mortality in the Suppression of the Slave Trade:
The Case of the Bight of Benin," *Journal of Interdisciplinary History* 9, no. 1 (1978): 47–64.
31. Luccock, *Notes on Rio de Janeiro,* p. 590, described the arriving slaves during the
1810–20 decade as ranging in age from 7 to 30 years but "on the average, certainly not
more than from twelve to fifteen." See also Conrad, *Children of God's Fire,* pp. 29, 33;
Santos,"Relações entre o Rio de Janeiro e Angola," pp. 58–59; Karasch, *Slave Life,* pp. 31–
34 ff., esp. illus. p. 37, for children in Rio.
32. Taunay, *Subsídios,* p. 119.

The survivors plodding into the port cities therefore were mostly male youths capable of significant recuperation within a short period of time, if given proper food and rest, despite the hardships they had endured on the paths and their weakened physical condition. They approached the towns escorted, or herded, in groups of twenty, thirty, or one hundred.[33] Others arrived in coasting schooners, canoes, and other small craft that came down to Benguela from the Katumbela River and Lobito Bay or into Luanda from bays and river mouths as remote as Novo Redondo. Drivers approaching the towns by land would have encountered a series of buyers eager to divert their slaves from their intended destinations in the pens of their merchant-creditors. Some slaves found themselves once again on the march, headed toward northern ports where they would be sold for French and British trade goods. Others entered the warren of illicit channels that led through the back streets of the town.[34] They waited hidden outside the town, then slipped into the city by night, furtively concealed in the straw houses of the African suburbs or in back rooms of the small taverns all over the city. There they changed hands again, perhaps several times, as they went from smuggler to tavern-keeper to specialist brokers of small lots and defective slaves (*adelos*). Eventually some sailor, a ship's chaplain, or a minor official of the city intent on dispatching a dutyless slave or two as the product of petty dealings in the city's thriving underworld would board them by one subterfuge or another on a ship in the harbor.

All the slaves trembled in terror at meeting the white cannibals of the cities, the first Europeans whom many of the slaves would have seen. They feared the whites' intention of converting Africans' brains into cheese or rendering the fat of African bodies into cooking oil, as well as burning their bones into gunpowder.[35] They clearly regarded the towns as places of certain death, as indeed they became for many, if not for the reasons slaves feared.

Slaves purchased by ships' supercargoes, or by factors representing Brazilian buyers without resident correspondents in Luanda or Benguela, might be taken directly on board the ships in the harbor and kept there to await the arrival of captives belonging to other buyers and eventual departure.[36] Presumably, ship operators who bought slaves for themselves found that they could maintain captives for less aboard their vessels than

---

33. Though slightly later in time, the description given by Tams, *Visit to the Portuguese Possessions*, 1:258–63, rings true for earlier periods.

34. "Very few are unsold by the time they arrive; and, hence, the petty dealer in the town can only procure the few slaves whom those commissioners have missed": ibid., p. 258.

35. Cosme (Pina ed.), "Tractado," p. 264.

36. Implicit in Correa da Silva, 9 March 1803, and the enclosed merchants' petition, 20 Jan. 1803, AHU, Angola cx. 54; also Ornellas, 19 Jan. 1794, AHU, Angola cx. 43, for Benguela.

they would have had to pay for food and shelter provided by merchants on the land.[37] In theory, one other alternative to embarkation was open. Individuals who believed they had been enslaved unjustly could claim their freedom by appearing before the governor of the colony, but few of the disoriented and exhausted slaves from the coffles entering the town could have known or availed themselves of these token gestures toward the legal niceties of slaving as envisioned in Lisbon.[38]

The great majority of the slaves went directly to the slave pens of the city's large expatriate merchants. These barracoons—known as *quintais* (singular *quintal*), a word also applied to farmyards for keeping animals— were usually barren enclosures located immediately behind the large two-story residences in the lower town, but traders also constructed them around the edges of the city and on the beach.[39] Large numbers of slaves accumulated within these pens, living for days and weeks surrounded by walls too high for a person to scale, squatting helplessly, naked, on the dirt and entirely exposed to the skies except for a few adjoining cells where they could be locked at night. They lived in a "wormy morass" (*ascaroz-issimo charco*) and slept in their own excrement, without even a bonfire for warmth.[40] One observer described "two hundred, sometimes three and four hundred slaves in each *quintal,* and there they stayed, ate, slept, and satisfied every human necessity, and from there they infected the houses and the city with the most putrid miasmas; and because dried fish is their usual and preferred food, it was on the walls of these *quintais* and on the roofs of the straw dwellings that such preparation was done, with manifest damage to the public health."[41] To the smell of rotting fish were added the foul odors of the slaves' dysenteries and the putrid fragrance of the bodies of those who died. The stench emanating from these squalid prisons overpowered visitors to the town.[42]

At Benguela the slave pens were about 17 meters square, with walls 3 meters or more in height, and they sometimes contained as many as

37. Corrêa, *História de Angola,* 1:49.

38. E.g., da Cunha, 29 Oct. 1753, AHU, Angola cx. 25; Corrêa, *História de Angola,* 2:116. The 1799 *regimento* for the Luanda customs house included provision for a final certification of the legitimate slave status of the captives embarked. It was surely intended to identify free residents of the city kidnapped and sold illegally as slaves: *Arquivos de Angola* 2, no. 12 (1936): 415–17 (parte III, cap. 5). See Cosme (Pina ed.), "Tractado," pp. 263, 264, for the reality.

39. Corrêa, *História de Angola,* 1:80; Venâncio, "Espaço e dinâmica populacional em Luanda," pp. 73–75.

40. Mendes (Capela ed.), *Memória a respecto dos escravos,* p. 47; Cosme (Pina ed.), "Tractado," pp. 261, 265.

41. Manuel da Costa Lobo Cardoso, *Subsídios para a história de Luanda* (Luanda: Edição do Museu de Angola, 1954), p. 50, attributed to the early seventeenth century but clearly belonging to a much later period.

42. The emphasis on the stench recurs: e.g., Azeredo, *Ensaios sobre algumas enfermidades,* p. 50; Cosme (Pina ed.), "Tractado," p. 261.

150 to 200 slaves, intermixed with pigs and goats also kept in them.[43] That left about two square meters per individual, or barely enough to lie down and to move about a bit. In some instances, at least, the walls had openings cut in them, through which guards outside could thrust musket barrels to fire on slaves within who grew unruly.[44]

The merchants' casual disrespect for the mortal remains of the thousands of slaves dying in and around the city created a grisly hazard to public health. Few aspects of the trade expressed the valuelessness of dead slaves more clearly than the merchants' habit of dumping the bodies in a heap in a small cemetery adjacent to the Nazareth chapel near Luanda's commercial district, or depositing them in shallow graves in numbers far greater than the ground could cover decently.[45] They preferred to leave them for the hyenas (*lobos*) to pick over during the night rather than pay the fees the vicar of the chapel charged for proper burials. The poor cleric was left to try to support his place of worship by accepting far more remains of the wealthy for interment than his crypt could hold.[46] The sharp distinctions of wealth among the living at Luanda thus carried through to the disposal of the dead.

At Benguela, widely regarded as even more mortiferous than Luanda, traders simply threw out the bodies of the slaves on the beach along with sewage until the very end of the eighteenth century. They then laid out a special cemetery for slaves dying on the ships and for other unbaptized Africans, but the new policy seems merely to have led to the corpses being partially burnt and left there for scavenging birds and animals. Even later in the nineteenth century, the "great number of cadavers" buried each year was covered with only a few inches of earth, again excepting the rich, for the hyenas to dig up and eat what they liked, and then strew the residue about.[47]

Few captains or slavers from Brazil would have taken particular notice of the stench of death that accordingly hung heavily over Luanda and Benguela. At Rio, slave traders heaped up "a 'mountain' of earth and decomposing naked corpses" awaiting burial once each week or so. Heavy rains would leave the bodies partially exposed, and when gravediggers could not keep up

43. Tams, *Visit to the Portuguese Possessions*, 1:95–96.
44. Owen, *Narrative of Voyages*, 2:275.
45. Corrêa, *História de Angola*, 2:168; Azeredo, *Ensaios sobre algumas enfermidades*, pp. 50–51.
46. Castelobranco, 24 Sept. 1824, AHU, Angola cx. 70. Church authorities everywhere in Portuguese territories were under orders after 1801 to cease burying bodies in crypts and to open proper cemeteries: Ernesto d'Esaguy, *Notulas para a história da medicina de Angola (Documentos)* (Lisbon: Editorial Império, 1952), p. 2.
47. Delgado, *Famosa e histórica Benguela*, pp. 20–21, 42–43, 66–67; Castelobranco, 24 Sept. 1824, AHU, Angola cx. 70; Moreira, "Memoria sobre as molestias," p. 124n. See Tams, *Visit to the Portuguese Possessions*, 1:157 ff., for a particularly explicit description of the gory scene.

with the growth of the accumulated "mountain of semi-decomposed ca-davers," they simply burned them. The odor was "insupportable."[48]

Merchants in Angola showed virtually no concern for sanitation in the slave quarters. Only when epidemics spread uncontrollably through the barracoons early in the eighteenth century did the Luanda municipal council, then controlled by Luso-African slaveowners threatened with losses from the alarming slave mortality, impose public health measures on the Lisbon factors managing their property. No further official acknowledgment of the horrors of life in the barracoons appeared during Lisbon's mid-century domination of the colonial and municipal governments, until supporters of the miasmic theory of tropical fevers toward the end of the century began to find ample cause for alarm in the smell of decomposing flesh that permeated the African ports.[49]

It was the separation of slave overseeing and maintenance, ordinarily the responsibility of Lisbon factors, from Luso-African ownership of the slaves, already an underlying cause of deaths among slaves on the way from the interior, that continued to produce deaths in the coastal cities. Angolans resident in remote districts often had to send their captives off under the care of agents of the town merchants, the *sertanejos* to whom the traders in Luanda had loaned goods, whose main interest in the Luso-African's coffle was to steal from it. In town, many slave barracoons, spread around the edges of the city as they were, received little direct supervision from the merchants that slaveowners employed as agents, who resided in the center of the commercial district. Even where town factors resided adjacent to their slave pens, their main interest remained in selling goods and collecting debts. They assigned direct responsibility for handling the slaves to their own slaves and to local employees who whipped and beat them without cease. They saved thus on slave supervision costs up to the point of causing so many deaths that their debtors would be unable to pay for trade goods they had sent to them on credit. But the merchants' ability to seize their assets through bankruptcy proceedings lessened even that limited concern.[50]

The slaveowners paid the merchants who maintained their human property a fee for provisions (*sustentos*) they were to supply on a daily basis. At 60 *réis* per day throughout the eighteenth century, the charge was not far from the rate paid unskilled day laborers in the city in 1770,[51]

---

48. Karasch, *Slave Life,* esp. chap. 4 and pp. 38–39.

49. Boxer, *Portuguese Society in the Tropics,* p. 158, for local alarms during the smallpox epidemic of 1717–20. Cosme (Pina ed.), "Tractado," has the most explicit analysis of terms of the miasmic theory.

50. Lencastre, 27 July 1775, AHU, Angola cx. 36, for general emphasis on the town merchants' neglect of the slaves under their care; Cosme (Pina ed.), "Tractado," p. 263, for brutality and the economics.

51. Lisanti, *Negócios coloniais,* 3:723–25 (1744); *portaria* of 23 May 1770, AHU, Angola cx. 33. Klein, *Middle Passage,* p. 39, n. 22, has 60 *réis*/diem also at Rio at this period.

and hence reasonable enough in theory. Despite numerous diversions of these funds from the mouths of the slaves into the pockets of the merchants, these charges seem to have been high enough to fund profiteering and still support the slaves in the towns better than the starvation levels of nutrition they had endured on the march to the coast, at least until the early nineteenth century. The politics of feeding slaves presumably followed the pattern clear in other aspects of the trade: a generous level fixed to favor Lisbon factors early in the century that remained unchanged into the years after 1800 when the slave ownership and maintenance roles reversed. By the last two decades of the trade, Luso-Africans in Luanda were caring for the slaves of Portuguese traders based in Brazil, and the Crown then began to allege that the shore merchants in Angola simply kept revenues they received for *sustentos* as profit rather than expending them to buy decent provisions.[52] The *sustentos* charge rose to $100 per diem in the wake of the reforms of the 1810–13 period.[53]

What the slaves received for the charges their owners paid consisted mainly of *farinha* (flour), or *farinha* and beans. The exact composition of these "mealies" is obscured by the generic vagueness of the term *farinha* that all observers used to describe the starchy base of the diet, distinguished clearly only from the *feijões*, or beans, or indeterminate varieties but probably the Old World horsebean (*Vicia faba*, locally *maindona*) that constituted the other half of what they ate. These beans were otherwise used to feed pigs, but they provided essential protein to the slaves.[54]

Along with the beans came small amounts of animal protein in the form of the small, rank-smelling fish, *savelha* (a kind of small shad known locally as *pungo*), which, laid out to dry on the walls and straw roofs of the barracoons without salting, contributed richly to the effluvia of the lower town. *Savelha* were plentiful in the ocean waters near Luanda but

---

The rate was higher in Bahia: $100 in 1669 and 1714, $120 in 1751, and $140 in 1802 (Schwartz, *Sugar Plantations*, pp. 321, 327).

52. Instruction to Gov. Oliveira Barboza, 28 Feb. 1810, AHU, cód. 551, published in Rebelo, *Relações*, pp. 342–44.

53. ANRJ, Sec. Jud., no. 8919, cx. 1118, gal. A, Inventario de Maximo Felix dos Santos (fallecido); *requerimento* of José de Mello and Joaquim José Ferreira Campos, n.d. (but 1816), AHU, Angola cx. 64; Motta Feo e Torres, 11 Sept. 1816, AHU, Angola cx. 64; ANRJ, cód. 1142, passim. Later still in the nineteenth century the charge at Rio had risen to $160/day: Karasch, *Slave Life*, p. 48. See also the 1796 *regimento* of the Benguela governors in Carlos Couto, "Regimento do governo subalterno de Benguela," *Studia* 45 (1981): 290.

54. On beans generally, Luis da Camara Cascudo, *História da alimentação no Brasil* (São Paulo: Companhia Editora Nacional, 1967–68), 1:163, 223, and 2:95–108. There were apparently several species of Angolan beans, at least some of them native to Africa and unfamiliar to European Portuguese: P.e Ruela Pombo, "Angola—medicina indígena," *Diogo Cão* 4–5 (Lisbon, 1935): 105–12; Spix and Martius, *Viagem pelo Brasil*, 2:143; Lopes de Lima, *Ensaios sôbre a statistica*, 3, pt. 1:14. Tams, *Visit to the Portuguese Possessions*, 1:147 and 2:102, says that the term *farinha* properly applied to bean flour by the 1840s.

unsalable in the town market to permanent residents of the city, even for its enslaved majority, since the fish was believed positively injurious to health. Its inherent unpalatability was enhanced by the failure to dry or to preserve it adequately, hence its rotting stink amidst the other rank odors of the slave pens.[55] Nonetheless, the starving slaves accepted these fish as better than what they had been able to eat on the path.

Generic *farinha* was almost certainly the American import, manioc or cassava (more properly *mandioca, farinha de pau, farinha de guerra*).[56] The term *milho* also described the "mealies" of the slaves' diet. Though generally connoting maize, or Indian corn, it could have consisted of sorghum (more precisely *sorgo*) or millet (*massambala* in the local Portuguese, but also *massa*, or *massango*),[57] both grains native to western central Africa and basic to the diets of people, free and slave, elsewhere in the city. On the other hand, American maize had become common throughout the region by the eighteenth century, though several sources of the period regarded it as fit only for livestock feed.[58] It is less likely that the slaves ate what everyone else despised as fit only for animals than that the term *milho* carried a colloquial connotation of "feed" for chickens or cattle. The language otherwise employed to describe the slaves as they passed through the city was liberally studded with terms similarly derived from livestock handling: the infants were *crias*, "young" animals; the adults were "head," *cabeças*; they lived in *quintais*, sometimes literally amidst the swine kept also in these "yards"; and the principal eighteenth-century compilation of commercial law and practice bluntly headed its chapter regarding insurance for cargoes at sea as "Marine Insurance for Slaves and Beasts."[59]

Whatever the origins of the *farinha*, it reached the slaves as a dry meal that, mixed with water, became the stiff starchy porridge that probably formed 90 percent or more of their diet from the moment of their arrival

55. Azeredo, *Ensaios sobre algumas enfermidades,* p. 50; Corrêa, *História de Angola,* 1:134; Castelobranco, 24 Sept. 1824, AHU, Angola cx. 70; Mendes (Capela ed.), *Memória a respeito dos escravos,* p. 47; Tams, *Visit to the Portuguese Possessions,* 1:101–8.

56. For locally grown manioc, see the records of the Luanda *terreiro público;* also Mendes (Capela ed.), *Memória a respeito dos escravos,* p. 47; Azeredo, *Ensaios sobre algumas enfermidades,* p. 59. Venâncio, "Economia de Luanda," pp. 73–74, 222–23 et passim, has the best discussion of the sources of the city's basic food supplies.

57. Cascudo, *História da alimentação,* 1:183; Ruela Pombo, "Angola—medicina indígena," pp. 107, 108–9; Lacerda, "Noticia da cidade de Benguella," pp. 486–87; Azeredo, *Ensaios sobre algumas enfermidades,* p. 59; António de Saldanha da Gama, *Memoria sobre as colonias de Portugal situadas no costa occidental d'Africa* . . . (Paris: Tipographia de Casimir, 1839), p. 73.

58. Miscellaneous inventories of provisions supplied to naval vessels and East Indiamen at Luanda show the meal as supplied specifically for chicken feed; Tams, *Visit to the Portuguese Possessions,* 1:150, observed that maize "grows wild in many places, but it is generally used only as food for the cattle. Sometimes, though very rarely, the negroes make it into bread." (See also ibid., 2:101.) For similar attitudes toward maize as animal feed in Rio (ca. 1810), see Brown, "Internal Commerce," p. 113.

59. Silva Lisboa, *Princípios de direito mercantil,* p. 60.

in the city.[60] Gourds and squashes may sometimes have supplemented this monotonous and vitamin-deficient fare, especially when the basic starches were scarce.[61] No doubt the *farinha* varied with seasonal availability and with the necessity of relying on manioc meal brought aboard the slave ships from Brazil to replace provisions locally unavailable in Luanda. Rice, one of the important foods supplied to slaves along many parts of the West African coast, did not figure significantly in the rations given to the captives penned in the barracoons of Benguela and Luanda.[62] The yams and plantains common in moister latitudes were never mentioned. In the shoreside towns, for the first time in their long journeys, slaves received plentiful rations of salt, almost nonexistent along the trails of the interior.

Water at Luanda and Benguela was neither good nor plentiful, and the slaves certainly drank the least and the worst available. One of the great advantages that ports north of the Zaire mouth enjoyed over the two Portuguese towns was their ample supply of fresh water.[63] At Luanda, the town's official and commercial elite normally enjoyed clean and clear rain-water collected and stored in cisterns maintained on the roofs of the principal government buildings, at least by the second half of the eighteenth century.[64] The only local source of water for less exalted ranks of the city's population was the old well at Mayanga, some distance from the slave pens of the commercial quarter.[65] The Senado da Câmara held formal responsibility for maintaining this well, but its privileged members drank from the government's cistern and tended to spend municipal funds on religious festivals rather than on providing potable or palatable water to

60. Azeredo, *Ensaios sobre algumas enfermidades*, p. 59, on methods of preparation.
61. Carreira, "Companhias pombalinas de navegação," p. 68 (instructions to Felix José da Costa, 1777, at Benguela).
62. Though rice is mentioned as among foods eaten by African residents of the colony: Azeredo, *Ensaios sobre algumas enfermidades*, p. 59; Ruela Pombo, "Angola—medicina indígena," pp. 108–9. Dias, ed. (Leitão), "Viagem a Cassange," p. 18, said that the Portuguese had experimented with the crop in Kasanje before the 1750s.
63. E.g., Gaulme, "Document sur le Ngoyo," p. 359; Martin, "Family Strategies," pp. 66–68.
64. Cisterns were first mentioned by Vasconcelos, 7 June 1761, AHU, Angola cx. 28; were improved by Sousa Coutinho (1764–72), Corrêa, *História de Angola*, 2:33; were expanded by Moçâmedes (1784–90), Corrêa, *História de Angola*, 2:117, 118; and thereafter were taken for granted: Azeredo, *Ensaios sobre algumas enfermidades*, p. 41; Oliveira Barboza, 4 May 1813, AHU, Angola cx. 61; Motta Feo e Torres, 6 Oct. 1818, AHU, Angola cx. 65; *requerimento* of João Paulo Cordeiro and Joaquim Gomes Alves, 19 June 1825, AHU, Angola maço 6 (D.O.); Douville, *Voyage au Congo*, 1:46–49; Moreira, "Memoria sobre as molestias," pp. 124–27. Venâncio, "Economia de Luanda," p. 76, also notes the social stratification expressed in water sources in Luanda.
65. The well was cited as the only water available in the city by Albuquerque, 21 May 1728, AHU, Angola cx. 18; mentioned further in Magalhães, 3 Jan. 1743, AHU, Angola cx. 23; Senado da Câmara (Luanda), 16 May 1774, AHU, Angola cx. 23; rebuilt by Sousa Coutinho, Corrêa, *História de Angola*, 2:117, 118; Azeredo, *Ensaios sobre algumas enfermidades*, pp. 38–39; expanded in 1794 to two pits: Venâncio, "Economia de Luanda," p. 76; Oliveira Barboza, 4 May 1813, AHU, Angola cx. 61.

the city's humble inhabitants, particularly after the municipal chamber became the preserve of the expatriate merchants.[66] They also had every interest in promoting sales of the cane brandy and wines that they imported.

The crush of the slaves around the Mayanga well, all trying to draw the brackish water for their masters' households, grew so great that they frequently spent most of the day waiting for the depleted pool at its bottom to refill.[67] The crowd sometimes pressed so close to the edge that slaves slipped down its crumbling sixty-foot sides.[68] Legendary stories circulated about miraculously fresh water said to have once bubbled up through the sands of the island facing Luanda Bay, but by the mid-1700s no one could find anything there but salty seepage from the surrounding ocean.[69] When failed rains left the cisterns that normally watered the elite dry, however, the government took the shortage seriously, even considering digging a 50-kilometer canal from the Kwanza to supply the city by means of water barges from the river.[70] In Benguela, domestic slaves carried or rolled barrels of water several kilometers from the mouth of the Katumbela River north of the town to merchants' homes, but the poorer people and slaves drank the saline seepage into shallow pits dug in the sand.[71]

Supplies of water for the slave yards at Luanda had to be developed commercially, quite beyond the free, if inadequate, municipal sources reserved for residents of the town. This business, as with other aspects of provisioning the town, fell to the Luso-Africans, who seem to have developed a thriving trade in bringing river water by canoe from the lower Bengo to sell to town merchants and to ship captains readying for departure. This opportunity seems to have arisen after a royal decree in 1693 prohibited further use of the brackish water from the island,[72] but water

66. A reluctance evident at least earlier in the eighteenth century: Magalhães, 3 Jan. 1743, AHU, Angola cx. 23; Senado da Câmara (Luanda), 16 May 1774, AHU, Angola cx. 23; Moçâmedes, 8 Oct. 1784, AHU, Angola cx. 40. The colonial government, not the municipality, financed most of the improvements toward the end of the eighteenth century, but the Câmara resumed responsibility sometime after 1800: Oliveira Barboza, 4 May 1813, AHU, Angola cx. 61.

67. Oliveira Barboza, 4 May 1813, AHU, Angola cx. 61.

68. Corrêa, *História de Angola*, 2:118; Oliveira Barboza, 4 May 1813, AHU, Angola cx. 61.

69. E.g., Azeredo, *Ensaios sobre algumas enfermidades,* pp. 39–40; also da Cunha, 29 Oct. 1753, AHU, Angola cx. 25; Oliveira Barboza, 5 May 1813, AHU, Angola cx. 61. Even contemporary documentation from ca. 1622 leaves it unclear whether the stories were fact or fantasy: Heintze, *Fontes,* pp. 163–64.

70. Interest in a canal occurred mostly in the 1750s and 1760s: Avellar, 7 July 1731, AHU, Angola maço 18–A; da Cunha, 29 Oct. 1753, AHU, Angola cx. 25; Vasconcelos, 6 July 1762, AHU, Angola cx. 29; João Victo da Silva, n.d. (but ca. 1792), AHU, Angola cx. 42; Oliveira Barboza, 4 May 1813, AHU, Angola cx. 61.

71. Delgado, *Famosa e histórica Benguela,* pp. 58, 90; Matos, *Compêndio histórico,* p. 322; Douville, *Voyage au Congo,* 1:9–11; Tams, *Visit to the Portuguese Possessions,* 1:101.

72. A governor who gained notoriety as an abusive slave trader had sent at least one shipload of slaves to Brazil with insufficient supplies of this salty water, and the incident had

became a contentious political issue only in the 1750s and 1760s—once again, as the gulf between local residents and foreign merchants opened wide.[73] Merchants and ship captains may occasionally have tried to break this monopoly, but the local suppliers boycotted any outsider who intruded on one of their most effective methods of combating the financial power of the Portuguese factors and Brazilian shippers, delaying dehydrated slaves and threatening their lives.[74] The sensitivity of the issue graphically underlined how important water was to the conduct of the trade in slaves, even the foul, garbage-laden, silty, and smelly fluid given to the slaves to drink.[75]

Ordinary townspeople paid the high prices demanded, filtered the river water through porous stones that removed visible particles but not its odor, mixed it with sharp Brazilian *gerebita,* and chewed bitter kola nuts to make the water taste sweeter.[76] Only the swarm of tavern-keepers lurking in every alley of the town would have smiled as they quenched their customers' unslaked thirst with cheap rum and bad wines. Slaves in the guinea yards accepted what little water dripped down to them through the rigid hierarchy of drink in the parched towns as superior to the excruciating thirst of the walk to the coast.

The Luanda prices of these provisions varied enormously with drought, good rains, temporary monopolies, and the post-1760s creation of a publicly regulated market. The normal cost of manioc meal rose from around $400 per *exeque* (of 4 *cazonguelos,* or *alqueires*) before 1710 to $600 in the 1730s, to 1$000 in the 1760s, 1$600 in the 1790s, and 3$200 in the 1810s.[77] At $400 per *exeque,* assuming that slaves were in fact fed what custom regarded as adequate when food was available, merchants could buy a slave's cereal ration for only about 3.3 *réis* per day early in the

---

become part of the indictment against him: Rau, *"Livro de Razão",* p. 48. The decrees were *provisões* of 6 April 1693 and 15 Dec. 1694: da Cunha, 3 Dec. 1754, AHU, Angola maço 11 (D.O.).

73. Mentioned first in Vasconcelos, 7 June 1761, AHU, Angola cx. 28, at the end of a period of growing concern over the issue in government circles; also Vasconcelos, 6 July 1762, AHU, Angola cx. 29; Senado da Câmara (Luanda), *auto de dezobediencia,* 3 April 1782, AHU, Angola maço 2; Corrêa, *História de Angola,* 1:144–45; Azeredo, *Ensaios sobre algumas enfermidades,* pp. 37–38; Oliveira Barboza, 4 May 1813, AHU, Angola cx. 61; Owen, *Narrative of Voyages,* 2:281; Douville, *Voyage au Congo,* 1:46–49.

74. See esp. Owen, *Narrative of Voyages,* 2:236, for a classic boycott of a British vessel regarded as hostile to local slaving interests and the tensions evident between colonial officials and those of the town. The Luso-African suppliers were also protected by the ability of their shallow-draft canoes to negotiate the dangerous bar at the river's mouth.

75. Cosme (Pina ed.), "Tractado," pp. 265–66. Almost no source mentioned the Bengo water without condemning its foulness, except, inexplicably, Owen, *Narrative of Voyages,* 2:281.

76. Azeredo, *Ensaios sobre algumas enfermidades,* pp. 37–38, 46; Oliveira Barboza, 4 May 1813, AHU, Angola cx. 61; Tams, *Visit to the Portuguese Possessions,* 1:101; Moreira, "Memoria sobre as molestias," pp. 124–27.

77. Forthcoming study of the Luanda food market.

eighteenth century, a tiny fraction of the 60 *réis* they received in *sustentos*. Even at famine prices, ranging from 2$000 to 3$000 at that time, the cost of mealies did not rise above 17–25 *réis* daily. Expenditures on palm oil, salt, dried fish, vinegar, *gerebita*, and tobacco (the last supplied as an anti-escorbutic as well as to raise the spirits of slaves widely regarded as addicted to the weed) would not have added more than another 5–10 *réis* per day. In good times, therefore, merchants would have spent 10 *réis*, or about 15 percent of the *sustentos* charge, to feed slaves according to prevailing standards, and famine would have raised their costs not more than 25–35 *réis*.[78]

By the 1790s, the basic cereal ration would have cost around 15 *réis* in good years, but the great drought of those years created absolute shortages at any price that forced imports of inadequate stocks of Brazilian meal. Presumably Brazilians began to feed the slaves they were buying from their own supplies at about this period. By the 1810s, when the complaints of profiteering became common, the daily allotment of manioc meal would have cost more than 25 *réis* even in good years and about 50 *réis* in not-infrequent famine years. Total costs of feeding slaves had thus risen to or beyond the established $60 *sustento* fee. Making allowance for the marginal expenses of clothing and for losses on slaves who died, it seems likely that Luanda merchants were in fact no longer covering their costs. Even the increase to $100 allowed in the fees after 1813 would not have gone far in the environment of tighter enforcement of government regulations. The ample revenues that slave handlers from Lisbon had once earned from the slaves' Angolan owners, justified as always by pious bows in the direction of the slaves' welfare, evaporated just as the *sustentos* fell to Angolan traders early in the nineteenth century. The colonial merchants thus joined the Brazilian shippers caught in the familiar vicious circle of being unable to buy provisions to keep the slaves alive because the slaves died from the inadequacy of the supplies bought.

The slaves' wait in the barracoons, filthy and unhealthful as it was, leaves the impression of food and water adequate to begin the long process of recuperation from the greater hardships of enslavement and the westward trail. Daily visits to the bay to bathe afforded some slaves an opportunity for limited personal hygiene even amidst the squalor of the slave pens, though they received little that would require cash expenditures by their managers: no clothing, and food barely adequate to sustain them until they would be sold or handed on to the care of the ships' captains waiting to transport them to Brazil.[79] Living conditions for slaves at Benguela would have been worse, owing to the greater shortages of food and

78. Cosme (Pina ed.), "Tractado," p. 261, put the figures at "ao muito hum vintem, ou meia macuta," i.e., 20–25 *réis*.

79. Mendes (Capela ed.), *Memória a respeito dos escravos*, pp. 47–48.

water there than in Luanda.[80] But in both ports the sheer opportunity for rest after the rigors of the march from the interior and the availability of salt, iodine, and protein from fish probably allowed the strongest of the young male slaves to recover some of the strength drained from them on their way to the coast.[81] The most penurious merchant could have honestly prided himself on restoring the captives he received toward health, in conformity with his responsibilities to their owners. There may even have been some modest substance to merchants' exaggerated claims that they were doing so.[82]

The critical effects of nutritional deprivation on the path and in the barracoons on maritime morbidity and mortality seem confirmed by the contrast between higher recorded deaths aboard ships from Luanda and Benguela than aboard those from Cabinda and other parts of the Loango Coast. The inadequate food and polluted water available along the dry coast of Angola strictly limited the ability of merchants to restore captives awaiting embarkation in the Portuguese ports, but the methods of slave trading north of the Zaire, where African slavers kept captives awaiting transport in well-watered villages in the interior, made it much easier for them to recuperate before embarkation. Even acknowledging that captains at Cabinda could have falsified their records of deaths at sea, owing to the total absence of government inspection of boarding in the bays north of Luanda,[83] the area around Cabinda was known for its extensive plantations

80. In the early 1840s, Tams, *Visit to the Portuguese Possessions*, 1:101–8, noted that the water in Benguela came only from small pits dug in the slave yards that would have been thoroughly polluted from the human and animal wastes deposited around them. Cosme (Pina ed.), "Tractado," p. 265, proposed that merchants lessen the sanitation problem by walking slaves daily for them to take care of personal necessities—as one would walk a dog? He also advocated chamber pots in the *quintais* that the slaves themselves would empty on the beaches during their exercise periods.

81. Owen comments on the status of the slaves arriving from the interior as "mere skeleton[s]," with flesh worn through to the bone by fetters and ulcerated wounds filled with flies that laid eggs in the "gangrenous cavities": *Narrative of Voyages*, 2:234. See, more generally, Mendes (Capela ed.), *Memória a respeito dos escravos*, pp. 43–47 et passim, and Cosme (Pina ed.), "Tractado." The point was not unremarked in Mozambique, where slavers paid more for captives originating near the coast than for others from remote parts of the interior, owing to the superior physical condition and lesser exhaustion of the former: Scheuss de Studer, *Trata de negros*, p. 324. Dr. Johan Peter A. Schotte, *A Treatise on the Synochus Atrabiliosa, A Contagious Fever Which Raged in Senegal in the Year 1778* (London: M. Scott, 1782), pp. 89–91, indicates the greater debility of slaves reaching Senegambia from far inland.

82. An assertion common in the secondary literature: Mattoso, *Etre esclave au Brésil*, p. 45; Charles R. Boxer, *Salvador de Sá and the Struggle for Brazil and Angola* (London: University of London Press, 1952), pp. 230–31. There was only a limited contradiction between this notion and the objective conditions reported from the barracoons.

83. For discussion of this administrative problem in terms of taxes, Corrêa, *História de Angola*, 2:85; Almeida e Vasconcelos, 2 Oct. 1794, AHU, Angola cx. 43; Motta Feo e Torres, 18 Jan. 1817, AHU, Angola cx. 64; Manoel d'Abreu de Mello e Alvim (governor, Benguela), 21 Jan. 1817, AHU, Angola cx. 64.

of manioc and peanuts. Food in those moister equatorial latitudes was obviously seldom scarce, whatever difficulty individual ships might sometimes have experienced in buying some of it for their own use.[84] The slavers themselves attributed the lower death rates they reported from Cabinda to the fact that slaves there were held for some while in this fertile zone after they arrived from the interior. They contrasted the positive effects of the delay on the physical condition of the people they bought with what they saw as the damage done to slaves penned in the guinea yards of Benguela and Luanda.[85]

The resultant mortality among slaves held at Luanda, and probably generally in other ports along the coast south of the Zaire, may have run as high as 40 percent during the 1760s, good years of relatively plentiful rains interrupted by only one short famine.[86] At about the same time Maranhão Company factors at Luanda reported about 11 percent of the slaves they bought either as dying in Luanda or remaining in the town, too ill to board the ships. Individual company cargoes experienced mortality on shore between 20 and 45 percent, however. A budget prepared to estimate general costs of slaving in Angola used 10 to 15 percent as the range of losses that owners should expect among slaves awaiting embarkation.[87] Another indication of mortality at this stage of the slaves' journey may come from an undefined category of slaves "consumed" in annual revenue reports from Benguela during occasional years between 1808 and 1819. Though it is unclear whether the term *consumption* referred to individuals retained for local service or euphemistically acknowledged deaths in the town's barracoons, the figures rose suggestively in rhythm with one of the several droughts to afflict the region in that decade.[88] The

84. Corrêa, *História de Angola*, 2:85; Owen, *Narrative of Voyages*, 2:292.

85. Cosme (Pina ed.), "Tractado," was emphatic on the accumulated ill effects of prior treatment, esp. pp. 262–63; see also Spix and Martius, *Viagem pelo Brasil*, 2:154, note V. Bathily, "Traite atlantique," pp. 276–77, notes ships in Senegambia delaying departure until their slaves had regained enough strength to withstand the ocean crossing.

86. Mendes (Capela ed.), *Memória a respeito dos escravos*, p. 48. The estimate may have been exaggerated, since it was based on a reported 10,000–12,000 slaves entering the city each year, of which only 6,000–7,000 finally embarked for Brazil. Taxed exports for the decade in fact total somewhat more, about 8,150 per year, and some of the difference between the reported numbers of entering slaves and those leaving legally through the port could also have been accounted for by smuggling and by individuals kept as part of the slave population of Luanda.

87. Carreira, "Companhias pombalinas de navegação," pp. 366–77 (but also see revised [1983] edition for substantially increased loss estimates); "Relação sobre escravatura," n.d. (ca. 1760s), AHU, Angola maço 10 (D.O.). Carreira, *Notas sobre o tráfico português de escravos* (2d ed. rev.), p. 42, refers to Maranhão Company records showing 8.6% losses in Upper Guinea after purchase and before embarkation (1756–78); his figure of 0.5% for the Pernambuco Company (p. 69) is far too low, as it seems to compare very incomplete indications of deaths among slaves awaiting embarkation with comprehensive totals of slaves shipped. Debien, "Journal de traite de la *Licorne*," p. 99, shows losses of 2% and nearly 20% at this stage for two French ships on the Mozambique coast, the latter having delayed too long trying to complete its cargo.

88. AHU, Angola cxs. 57, 59, etc.

slaves "consumed" accounted for only about 5 percent of taxed departures at that time.

Allowing conservatively for the lack of concordance among these sources, a general estimate on the order of 10 to 15 percent ought not to be far out of line for mid- to late-eighteenth-century mortality among the slaves held at Angolan ports. It is probable, though undocumented, that rates had been higher in the past and declined through the 1700s, except in periods of drought and famine. The damages wrought by famine in the town, too, were lessened after the 1760s by the operation of the *terreiro público* public granary.

Though owners and handlers expected constantly to move the slaves onto the ships at any time, the slaves in fact remained in the barracoons for weeks, sometimes for months, awaiting embarkation. Even under the best organization, when slaves arrived in the city just in time to meet the turn of a ship leaving for their intended destination, they would have met delay. Freighted ships were authorized to load *de bando* for at least thirty days, and slaves moving through the slave pens at a constant rate over that month's preparation for departure would have remained in the city for an average of two weeks. Ships departing *efeitos próprios* would have required slaves to linger for much longer periods of time. An assumed best-performance stay of one month in Luanda or Benguela might not err by much from actual experience. Since conditions rarely, if ever, approached these optimal circumstances, one must assume that the true delays were somewhat longer. On the other hand, the longer the delay, the more time slaves had to recover from the trail with rest and feeding in the barracoons. The trade-off between the restorative and debilitating influences of delay on total losses to mortality during this period lessens the sensitivity of the estimating procedure to the time assumed.

The annualized mortality rate for the slaves' stay on the coast, based on these assumptions, would have averaged twice the mean for the preceding months on the trails of the interior,[89] mostly as an extension of the highest rates attained toward the end of their march to the sea into their first few days or weeks in the city. Slaves from higher elevations in the interior would have succumbed to unfamiliar diseases endemic along the coast soon after their arrival. Death rates probably declined perceptibly thereafter, and many slaves boarded the ships in physical condition marginally stronger than the near-delirium in which they had stumbled into the city.

89. Representative—and conservative—estimates intended no more than to suggest the range of possibilities would divide 12% losses by the portion of a year spent in the slave pens by the average slave: e.g., one month in the barracoons would produce a preposterous annual rate of 1,440/1,000, two months a rate of about 720/1,000. Losses at rates twice those of the interior trails (ca. 500/1,000/annum) would make the estimate of time spent in the town barracoons, on these assumptions, about six weeks, all equally plausible inferences from the general patterns evident in the historical records.

Embarkation Procedures

When the day of the slaves' departure finally dawned, they and their owners and managers set out along yet another tortuous course leading from the slave pens through the long chain of government officials charged with enforcing the maze of rules intended to protect the slaves' bodies and souls and the revenues of the king, though in fact often to the enhancement of none of these. The procedures had been relatively simple earlier in the eighteenth century, but later efforts to curtail tight-packing and smuggling and to improve supplies of food and water aboard the slave ships gradually lengthened the gantlet through which they passed.

In broad terms, all embarking slaves had to be certified as Christian, which implied instruction in the Catholic faith followed by baptism,[90] certified as to their taxable status (adult *cabeça,* child, or infant), and then formally dispatched in conformity with loading limits on the ships and counted to document the contractor's or government's claims to export duties from their owners. Two underlying conflicts came to a head in the course of these formalities. The first concerned the amounts of the fees, duties, and other charges owners owed on each slave. The other, and probably the more vital of the two, focused on the speed with which the slaves could be processed. Since owners desired to avoid every possible expense on slaves, particularly weakened and dying ones who might bring no return on further investments, they delayed religious instruction, baptism, and payment of taxes until the last possible moment.[91] The missions, the church, and the government, on the other hand, wished to save as many souls and to collect as many fees and duties as they could, and they therefore attempted to advance the processing of the slaves as early as possible in their stay in the city. The difference in revenues was potentially significant, equal in theory to deaths that reduced taxable bodies and redeemable souls entering the city by as much as 40 percent before the survivors left it. The counterpoint to this rhythm of rush and delay was generated by petty officials who, paid only the most derisory of official salaries, stalled deliberately to collect bribes from owners desperate to get their slaves on board the ships before they died.

Slaves on their way to the port, dressed in loincloths (*tangas*) or crude camisoles made, as often as not, of burlap wrappings recovered from the bundles and bales of imported goods,[92] were initially assembled before cus-

90. By the terms of a *carta regia* of 5 March 1697, reconfirmed by a *provisão* of the Conselho Ultramarino issued on 24 April 1719: Carreira, *Notas sobre o tráfico português,* p. 57.

91. "Bando para todos os Escravos que embarcão levarem carimbo que demonstre se vão baptisados, e o mais que contem," 15 Jan. 1792, AHU, cód. 1634, fols. 6v–8.

92. AHMF, Benguela, letter of 4 July 1777, fol. 1, published in Carreira, "Companhias pombalinas de navegação," p. 68. These *tangas* were to be replaced with better ones just

toms officials competent to mark their progress. Holders of the official position of catechist for slaves (*catequizador dos negros/dos escravos,* and other
variant titles), normally clerics, were responsible for their religious instruction. None could be processed through the customs house without a *bilhete*
(chit or pass) certifying their knowledge of the Catholic faith and their baptism. The catechists gradually acquired other responsibilities in the course
of the eighteenth century, including defense of the minimal rights conceded
to the unfortunate individuals brought as captives to Luanda. In particular,
these priests acted as official interpreters between the captives and officials
of the colony, directed by increasingly enlightened governments in Lisbon
to free slaves captured unjustly in the interior upon their arrival in Luanda.
The catechists were eventually recognized officially as *enqueredores das cou-
zas de liberdades,* or *catequizadores das liberdades,* and may in fact have represented occasional cases of unjust capture to the governors, some of whom
claimed regularly to free the victims of such misfortunes.

The official government catechist, usually a local appointed to the
position as a sinecure, did not personally supervise instruction and baptism
of each of the 8,000–10,000 slaves passing through the city each year,[93]
but rather, employed slaves who spoke Kimbundu, the *lingua franca* of
the town, and taught the written Kimbundu catechism in use by the end
of the eighteenth century.[94] How much of this instruction the thousands
of captives from Kikongo, Ruund, Ovimbundu, and other distant African
language areas might have understood is an open question. The government salary of the *catequizador,* originally 40$000 per year, or hardly more
than the price of a single prime slave at the time, was raised to 60$000
in 1748, about the time that prime slave prices rose to a similar level.[95]

---

before arrival in Brazil. Mendes (Capela ed.), *Memória a respeito dos escravos,* pp. 47–48,
emphasizes the reluctance of the merchants to spend money to clothe the slaves, whom he
describes as "almost naked."

93. One may discount the picturesque but legendary story of the stone bishop's chair
set on the Luanda quay, e.g., Taunay, *Subsídios,* p. 77. For the facts, see *provisão* of appointment
for Manoel Roiz Barros, 28 Sept. 1715, AHU, Angola maço 3 (D.O.); Meneses, 30 May
1734, AHU, Angola cx. 20; *parecer* of the Conselho Ultramarino, 21 Aug. 1748, AHU,
Angola cx. 24; Lavradio, 2 Feb. 1750, AHU, Angola cx. 25; *provisão,* Padre António Rodrigues da Costa, 20 Jan. 1770; Manuel Dantas Lima (*vigário geral*), 27 Sept. 1799, published
in "Angola no fim do século XVIII: Documentos," *Boletim da Sociedade de geografia de Lisboa*
6, no. 5 (1886): 298; *bando* of 15 Jan. 1792, AHU, cód. 1634, fols. 6v–8; de Mello, 3 Feb.
1800, in "Angola no fim do século," pp. 287–88.

94. Dantas Lima, in "Angola no fim do século," p. 298. See the published Kimbundu
linguistic studies by Padre Bernardo Maria de Cannecattim, *Diccionario da lingua bunda ou
angolense, explicada na lingua portugueza e latina* (Lisbon: Impressão Regia, 1804), and
*Collecção de observações grammaticaes sobre a lingua Bunda ou Angolense e Diccionario da lingua
Congueza* (Lisbon: Impressão Regia, 1805). Also for linguistic difficulties of communicating
with the slaves, and the contribution of malcomprehension to racial stereotypes and brutality,
see Cosme (Pina ed.), "Tractado," p. 263.

95. *Parecer* of the Conselho Ultramarino, 21 Aug. 1748, AHU, Angola cx. 24.

On behalf of the bishopric and his parish or order, and for his personal benefit, he collected a variety of other fees from the owners of the slaves, probably varying through time and sometimes of dubious official status, beyond whatever additional emoluments he might claim in return for prompt execution of his duties. Something of the extent of these fees— evidently collected on many, though not all, of the slaves passing through Luanda—may be judged from the fact that the end of the legal slave trade and the concomitant termination of these revenues threw the Luanda bishopric into a financial crisis.[96]

Though publication of a late-eighteenth-century Kimbundu cate- chism indicated at least a minimal seriousness of purpose, ecclesiastics' protests of sincerity, thoroughness, and care showed mostly their obvious pecuniary interest in observing at least the formalities.[97] The instruction given most slaves and the baptism itself were in fact little more than caricatures. Cynical and careless priests fulfilled their duties by last-minute sprinklings from a hog trough filled with holy water rigged hastily aboard ships ready to leave. Such callousness obviously stemmed from the owners' desires not to waste the cost of saving souls that death would release before government certification or retard the movement of dying slaves from their pens to the ships and on to Brazil.[98]

The principal memory that most slaves retained of their encounter with imperial bureaucracy was probably the repeated applications of hot irons to their chests and upper arms. The Portuguese branded slaves as evidence of ownership,[99] exactly as they branded cattle or horses, and also to certify various aspects of the captives' legal status, like customs inspectors burning marks on bales of goods as they dispatched them through the customs shed. To judge from the tatooing ubiquitous on many of the people taken as slaves,[100] such marking not only inflicted pain but also in a profound sense humiliated and disfigured people who expressed their status by designs on their skins. The brands applied in Angola seared their new identities as capitalist property into their very flesh.

All parties with an interest in the slave, through ownership or through rights to fees levied on his or her passage through Luanda, registered their

96. Santa Comba Dão, 11 Oct. 1830, AHU, Angola cx. 74.

97. Paulino Ribeyro, 28 Nov. 1732, AHU, Angola cx. 19, gave some idea of the pecuniary interest in the proceedings, referring to a pastoral letter issued in Luanda preventing the churches of the interior from teaching or baptizing adult slaves redeemed from their heathenness. He pointed to the souls lost through the deaths of unbaptized captives in the interior as well as to the neglect of the official *catequizadores* in Luanda.

98. Albuquerque e Tovar, 9 Feb. 1821, AHU, Angola cx. 67. See also the supple- mentary *carta regia* of 29 April 1719, acknowledging deficiencies in Angola and establishing backup baptismal procedures in Pernambuco.

99. E.g., the insistence on branding by a Brazilian merchant contemplating buying slaves at Luanda in 1712–25: Lisanti, *Negócios coloniais*, 4:423, 5:46.

100. Tams, *Visit to the Portuguese Possessions*, 1:128 ff., 133.

claims by the application of hot metal to the slaves. The first Luso-Africans to own the slaves applied their personal brands to the captives' arms upon purchase, to identify and to certify their possession of specific individuals as they continued on their way under the supervision of subsequent agents and shippers. Early in the eighteenth century, contractors added a further mark of fiscal identity to slaves whose owners had paid export duties on them. At least since the late seventeenth century, the government appointed an official slave brander, the *marcador dos escravos,* charged with burning the royal arms onto the right breast of slaves, signifying their vassalage to the Crown.[101] Efforts to enforce the provisions for baptism led to addition of a cross brand overlaying the royal mark.[102] The only slaves excepted from enduring the brands of baptism, ownership, and export duty nec-essary to clear customs were mulattoes born and raised in the town of Luanda and taken with their masters (and fathers?) when they retired to Brazil.

Reform regulations of 1813 replaced scarred flesh with a metal brace-let or collar bearing these marks. Further reform in 1818 restored brand-ing, though only with "irons" made of silver.[103] Evidently bracelets and collars had proved insufficient to deter captains from substituting healthy slaves they carried for others for the captives of their own who died at sea.[104] Branding, however cruel to the slaves, was effective in controlling frauds that played on the slaves' mortality. This last attempt to dress the medieval custom in modern garb revealed a callous toleration of pain, so long as it was inflicted by the monetary metal of the southern Atlantic economy.

To the Ships

The slaves finally boarded the ships attended by the full panoply of Por-tuguese imperial bureaucratic ritual, performed at a customs house located,

101. Though a very late *certidão* of 23 Sept. 1816, AHU, Angola cx. 64, specified the left breast.

102. Carreira, *Notas sobre o tráfico português,* pp. 59–60; *requerimento* of Coronel Fran-cisco Lobo Barreto, n.d. (ca. 1740), AHU, Angola cx. 22; *requerimento* of Antonio de Faria de Mello, n.d. (ca. 1744), AHU, Angola maço 5; *provisão,* 9 Nov. 1785, AHTC, "Registo das provisões e cartas régias expedidas para Angola . . . ," livro 2, fols. 49–50; Oliveira Barboza, 14 Nov. 1814, AHA, cód. 92, fol. 48; *certidão,* 23 Sept. 1816, AHU, Angola cx. 64. The first *regimento* for the *marcador* dated from 1519 in São Tomé and the fee schedule for the eighteenth century from 24 Nov. 1707. The 1799 *regimento* for the Luanda customs house merely presumed the existence of the arrangements in effect: *Arquivos de Angola* 2, no. 12 (1936): 415–17 (cap. 5.).

103. *Regimento* (1799), parte III, cap. 5, in *Arquivos de Angola* 2, no. 12 (1936): 415–17; Vianna, "Humanitário alvará," p. 82; Rebelo, *Relações,* p. 75.

104. This was precisely the period in which complaints about this practice surfaced in the documentation.

not on the mainland in the lower city, but on the island forming the outer shore of Luanda Bay.[105] Large ships could not anchor close to the mainland owing to the tendency of the current to throw up sandbars in the landward part of the bay and the consequent shallowness of the water there. No doubt isolating the last stages of clearing a ship from the port on the island also helped reduce smuggling and limit the slaves' opportunities for escape. The slaves were taken to the island in small boats belonging to the merchants in charge of them and herded into the slave pen of the customs shed to await official ministrations. A properly prepared ship would have had its carrying capacity certified already, would have purchased provisions for its slaves and had them inspected for both quantity and quality, and, if leaving *de bando* with slaves belonging to merchants in the city other than its owners, would have received authorization to begin arranging its cargo with public proclamation of the fact throughout the city.

On the appointed day, government officials (the *ouvidor,* or chief judge, in his capacity as treasury inspector; his scribe; and the treasurer of the government coffers in charge of receiving the taxes owed) would go to the island and take their places at a ceremonial table. Obsequiously fawning merchants, dependent on official lenience with respect to tax assessments of their slaves, and perhaps also involved with them in plans to tight-pack under one pretext or another, would complete the procession. The slaves would then be marched past the customs board, have their brands checked for payment of duties and for baptism, and be counted and recounted until the number ready to board exactly matched the ship's legal capacity. Confusion usually overwhelmed official efforts to conduct these ceremonies on an orderly basis, with the various owners of the slaves each pressing their special individual claims. The crowd of 400 or more slaves, uncertain about the meaning of the formalities surrounding them, shuffled awkwardly in their chains and fearfully eyed the water and the huge ship lying at anchor just offshore.

Aboard the ship guards stood alert to prevent illegal loadings of untaxed slaves, especially in excess of the *arqueação.* The final boarding procedures began with a thorough search of the empty ship by an inspector accompanied by a dozen or so men. The thoroughness of this inspection, or the cooperation the inspectors extended to the ship operators, probably determined how many slaves the ship's officers and crew were able to smuggle beyond the registered capacity. If the ship already housed slaves brought for the venture itself, the inspectors forced them, together with slaves belonging to the ship's complement (and boarded without prior

---

105. For further details on the history of customs regulation at Luanda, see Miller, "Imports at Luanda," esp. pp. 172–89; Avellar, 23 Feb. 1732, AHU, Angola cx. 19; *consulta* of the Junta do Comércio (Lisbon), 19 Aug. 1782, ANTT, Junta do Comércio, maço 62, macete 122.

formal inspection), into small boats, where they could be kept from fleeing during the proceedings. It was a perilous time for slaves unused to the water, and also for the masters, as slaves sometimes fell into the sea and drowned during the transfer.[106]

Each slaveowner, or his agent, declared the number and identities of the slaves he presented for boarding and gave formal custody of them to the officers of the ship before the witnessing representatives of the government. Captains customarily absented themselves from this proceeding, since the law made them responsible for violations of their ship's capacity limits, and they could lessen their legal culpability in case of later detection of tight-packing by claiming that they had not personally witnessed the boarding and therefore could not be prosecuted for violations that others might have committed. The merchants' declarations of the slaves boarded were assembled as the ship's manifest and became the basis on which duties were charged. The government scribe issued each owner and agent a receipt for the duties paid, and this document became the formal authorization to drive the stated number of slaves over the gunwale past the inspector and his attendants. A certified copy of the entire manifest was then drawn up for delivery aboard the ship to Brazilian authorities responsible for verifying the slaves' arrival in America.

One final aspect of the abundant documentation prescribed for boarding underlined the centrality of the deaths that government and owners all knew would continue to befall the slaves at sea. Slave ships in the southern Atlantic had long been required to keep "death books," *livros dos mortos,* in which captains certified the losses that each owner incurred as his slaves died on the middle passage.[107] The records of the trade refer seldom enough to these death books to confirm the impression of extreme neglect created by scattered allusions to the laxity with which officials enforced these regulations.[108] Discussion of the issue took place primarily in the oblique form characteristic of all vital issues in the politics of the empire, over a related requirement that each ship carry a chaplain responsible for administering the sacrament of extreme unction to Catholics dying aboard.[109] In that capacity the chaplain had to countersign and verify the captain's record of baptized slaves entered in the *livro dos mortos.* Understandably under such

106. Correa da Silva, 9 March 1803, including merchants' petition of 20 Jan. 1803, AHU, Angola cx. 54.

107. From the original slave trade *regimento* of 1519, in Lopes, *Escravatura,* p. 42; the relevant article of the 1684 *regimento* governing the trade in the eighteenth century, which supplemented that of 1519 in this regard, would have been no. 20 (*Arquivos de Angola* 2, no. 11 [1936]: 317), which ordered officials in Brazil to reconcile the arriving cargo (i.e., the survivors) with the ship's embarkation papers.

108. Avellar, 25 May 1730, AHU, Angola maço 18–A; *requerimento* of Domingos Dias da Silva, n.d. (ca. 1772), AHU, Angola cx. 36.

109. Art. 11 in the 1684 *regimento,* in *Arquivos de Angola* 2, no. 11 (1936): 316.

circumstances, captains neglected to hire chaplains, mainly under the pretext—probably also a true circumstance—that ecclesiastical authorities in Brazil and Angola could find no clergy willing to undertake unpleasant and dangerous chores beneath the decks of the slave ships.[110]

With growing secularization of the imperial administration in the second half of the eighteenth century and greater metropolitan ownership of the slaves, Lisbon finally took a greater interest in these death records and assigned responsibility for keeping them to the new customs service it established in the 1780s. Surgeons supplemented chaplains aboard the slave ships. Customs judges in Brazil would countersign the captains' declarations of deaths during the crossing when the ships arrived, and the definitive procedures established at Luanda in 1799 provided that departing ships present a full quarto volume of twenty blank pages for recording slave losses by date of death ("insofar as it could be determined"!) and by the brand of their owners.[111] Even these seemingly thorough measures failed to contain captains' skills at juggling their records, and the continuing controversies over branding and fraud testified to the anticipation with which all parties interested in the slaves awaited the certainty of deaths aboard the *tumbeiros*.

Life and Death at Sea

When the slaves had been twice counted, the ship's provisions inspected again, and all necessary papers signed and registered,[112] the captain raised his sails and rode southwesterly onshore winds that rose every afternoon northeast toward the mouth of the bay. A small government pilot boat accompanied the ship some ways out to sea to prevent its stopping to pick up smuggled slaves as it approached the mainland shore at the bay's narrow mouth. The methods regularly employed to tight-pack and to avoid carrying adequate provisions took place off the stage on which captains, crews, and government officials played out their ritualized departure.[113]

The scene aboard the departing ship would have featured fear on all

110. Magalhães, 28 July 1739, AHU, Angola cx. 21; Campos Rego, 17 Sept. 1753, AHU, Angola cx. 26; "Ordem para as Embarcaçoens trazerem capellaens e não sahirem sem elles . . . ," 25 Jan. 1791, AHU, cód. 1634, fol. 10; *regimento* for the Luanda customs house (1799), parte III, cap. 1, para. 8, in *Arquivos de Angola* 2, no. 12 (1936): 408.

111. Peçanha, 27 June 1785, AHU, Angola cx. 40; Almeida e Vasconcelos, 2 Oct. 1794, AHU, Angola cx. 43; de Mello, 12 March 1799, AHU, Angola cx. 46; *Arquivos de Angola* 2, no. 12 (1936): 408 (1799 *regimento*; see above); Saldanha da Gama, 2 Dec. 1807, AHU, Angola cx. 57; *certidão* of 23 Sept. 1816, AHU, Angola cx. 64.

112. For details, and other procedures regarding payment of duties and fiscal responsibilities, see the full *regimento*, parte III, in *Arquivos de Angola* 2, no. 12 (1936): 405–22, and a partial summary in Rebelo, *Relações*, pp. 90–92.

113. Avellar, 23 Feb. 1732, AHU, Angola cx. 19; Domingos Dias da Silva, instructions to contract administrators, esp. arts. 28–30 and 37–38, 8 Jan. 1767, AHU, Angola cx. 31;

sides, amidst enormous clutter. Rigging and equipment, temporarily removed for purposes of maximizing the rated capacity of the ship to carry slaves, was piled up and stowed in every corner. The personal baggage of the officers, seamen, and passengers occupied any remaining space. The twenty or twenty-five men of the crew, though momentarily preoccupied with getting the ship squared away for the voyage, shared a deep dread of the 400 to 500 slaves crammed below and squeezed into all available cabin space above deck. They feared the first few days at sea as the most dangerous, when they faced partially recuperated captives driven to desperation by the certain death they anticipated in their totally unfamiliar surroundings. As a result, the crew kept the human cargo locked tightly below, to the point of risking suffocating them in the humid and airless spaces there.[114] The youth, diminuitive stature, and inexperience of most of the slaves must have given the crew some consolation, but they took elaborate precautions nonetheless.[115]

They used the whip as one means of enforcing discipline.[116] No slave was ever released from his (or her) arm irons within sight of land, a period of several days on the voyage from Angola to Brazil while the ships followed the coast north to catch the westward turn in the current off the mouth of the Zaire. The slaves played on their captors' fears of their own deaths at this stage of the voyage, feigning illnesses that would release them from their fetters for treatment in the ship's infirmary, set up by law in the forecastle. A core of organizers could gather above deck by this means to plot an uprising, but captains customarily hired as nurses and surgeons African healers who could understand the slaves' languages and, no doubt, also act as spies.[117] These Africans, as well as the slave members

---

Guilherme José Ferreira *requerimento,* enclosed in *parecer* of the Conselho Ultramarino (Lisbon), 20 March 1800, AHU, Angola cx. 49; *consulta* of the Junta do Comércio (Lisbon), 19 Aug. 1782, ANTT, Junta do Comércio, maço 62, macete 122; de Mello, 22 Oct. 1799, AHU, Angola maço 9; Peçanha, 27 June 1785, AHU, Angola cx. 40; also Mendes (Capela ed.), *Memória a respeito dos escravos,* pp. 73–76, who alleges that these regulations were regularly ignored.

114. Lopes, *Escravatura,* p. 175; Mendes (Capela ed.), *Memória a respeito dos escravos,* pp. 48–49. This precaution, while being condemned by some observers toward the end of the eighteenth century, was widely justified by medical theories of the time that held that blacks thrived under the heat of the tropics, contrary to whites, for whom the tropical sun was thought extraordinarily fatal; hence, the greater danger was the chill that slaves below decks might catch from excessive ventilation. See, e.g., de Mello, 12 March 1799, AHU, Angola cx. 46; Mendes (Capela ed.), *Memória a respeito dos escravos,* p. 35; Scheuss de Studer, *Trata de negroes,* pp. 311–32. Recognition of the need for adequate air prevailed in the revised regulations issued in 1813: Vianna, "Humanitário alvará," p. 86.

115. See Jean Boudriot, "Etude sur le navire négrier" (Paper presented to the Colloque International sur la Traite des Noirs, Nantes, 1985), for comparable fears among the French; cf. Villiers, *Traite des Noirs,* p. 84.

116. Corrêa, *História de Angola,* 1:173n.

117. AHMF, Benguela *copiador,* letter and instructions of 4 July 1777; Cosme (Pina ed.), "Tractado," pp. 264–65, for other recommendations for use of bilingual slaves on shore.

of nearly every crew, also tried to counter the captives' absolute certainty—seemingly confirmed by everything they witnessed—that the whites meant to eat them.

Against all these odds the slaves occasionally succeeded in mounting revolts. No details are available on how any specific slave rebellion began aboard a ship leaving Angola, but it would have taken only a few desperate slaves bound by faulty locks and allowed on deck for exercise, joined by confederates pretending to be sick in the infirmary, and perhaps assisted by disgruntled slave members of the crew,[118] to overpower the four or five officers of the ship and the dozen or so European members of its crew.

The ruthlessness of slaves who managed to seize control varied according to their faith in their own abilities to get the vessel safely to shore. Enough cargoes included slaves who had been resident for years in Luanda, and perhaps even skilled Cabindans with maritime experience, that the rebels sometimes mustered the competence to kill all whites on board and run the ship aground north of Luanda. Most spared a few Europeans to beach the ship for them. In one reported revolt the slaves did not slay their captors but, rather, put them in longboats and left them to make their own way back to shore; inexplicable magnanimity, as well as considerable nautical skill, must be assumed in these cases.

Captains and crews sometimes were able to defend themselves for a few hours but then escaped to the longboats and made for shore. Thorough pillaging of the ships' stores and equipment accompanied these revolts, as the slaves helped themselves to the food they craved and seized apparel, adornment, and equipment of which they had been deprived. The slaves who managed to reach dry land safely did not often preserve their liberty for long. They landed on unfamiliar parts of the coast and so fell back into the hands of African slave exporters, who controlled nearly the entire coast from the Dande to Loango. Enslaved again, they were resold to the French or the British. Shipboard rebellions, while infrequent and usually ultimately futile, broke out often enough that Portuguese sailors cast a wary eye on their cargoes and kept the locks and hatches of the slave deck closed until the ships were well out to sea.[119]

118. This occurred in at least one instance, the revolt aboard the galera *Feliz Eugenia* on 15 April 1812: Vasconcelos e Souza, 17 April 1812, AHU, Angola cx. 60.
119. The text discussion is developed from the circumstances reported in the cases of the slaves of the curveta *Nossa Senhoa de Agoa de Lupe e Bom Jesuz dos Navegantes* on 20 Jan. 1763, Manoel da Costa Pinheiro, *representação*, n.d. (but referred to in Sousa Coutinho, 4 Aug. 1764), AHU, Angola cx. 30; (see also Venâncio, "Economia de Luanda," p. 284n); the slaves of the galera *Espera Dinheiro* in 1796, Almeida e Vasconcelos, 4 Oct. 1796, AHU, Angola cx. 44, and *requerimento* of José Antonio Pereira, 1804, ANTT, Junta do Comércio, maço 12, macete 122; reports of the slaves aboard the British ship *Lightning* (owners, Farlton and Rigg, Liverpool), in de Mello, 17 June 1799, AHU, Angola cx. 47; the slaves and crew of the galera *Feliz Eugenia* on 15 April 1812, Vasconcelos e Souza, 17 April 1812, AHU, Angola cx. 60; the slaves of the *Aguia do Douro* on 27 Jan. 1813, in Oliveira Barboza, 17

The slaves' impressions of their first days and hours in the hold would have certainly centered on the oppressiveness of the hot, humid, close atmosphere below decks. Some ships, particularly earlier in the century, had brought salt from Benguela to Luanda just previous to taking on slaves, and the residue caused an overwhelming, lingering dampness—not to mention what salt residue could do to open wounds and sores.[120] The theme of corrupted air ran through official Portuguese regulations concerning slave safety, but more as an expression of the miasmic disease theories that informed Portuguese medical opinion at the time than as direct perceptions of the insufficiency of oxygen in the crowded spaces below decks.[121] Secure in their racialist faith that Africans, unlike Europeans, preferred the heat that built up between decks, they refused to enlarge the portholes for fear that the chill of fresh air would add to the respiratory ailments of the Africans. While in port, captains sometimes rigged a sail to draw the breeze down through the hatch leading to the slave deck, but it could not have been very effective owing to the absence of exhaust ports for the humid air within. It was difficult to ventilate a hold adequately without sacrificing seaworthiness and security.

The infamous stink of the slave ships would have begun to build up also at this time.[122] A large portion of the lot suffering from dysenteries helplessly fouled their pallets, and frightened slaves, trapped in the dark, close quarters below decks, reacted to the incomprehensible rolling of a ship at sea with the retching that afflicts many landlubbers.[123] Perspiration and the odors of unwashed bodies added to the effluence until the stench in itself became a factor contributing to the misery below decks. Portuguese efforts at hygiene consisted mostly of mopping up the mess, scrubbing down all parts of the ship at least every other day. But the movement and temporary freeing of dangerous slaves involved in thorough cleansing could not have encouraged many crews to follow these procedures too closely. Bathing on the ships appears to have been a late innovation in the

Feb. 1813, AHU, Angola cx. 61; also the *portaria* of 16 Feb. 1817, with respect to the same slaves, by then safely on shore and sheltered in the lands of Ambriz and Sonyo; the unidentified galera in the Zaire River, in a *declaração* of Antonio Vicente, ca. 4 Sept. 1819, AHU, Angola cx. 65; and the slaves of the galera *São Pedro Aguia*, on 19 Aug. 1819, in Albuquerque e Tovar, 17 Sept. 1819, AHU, Angola cx. 65.

120. Magalhães, 26 April 1742, AHU, Angola cx. 22; also 24 Dec. 1742, AHU, Angola cx. 23. Later on, some slavers also carried Benguela sulfur in their holds, destined for the powder factory in Rio de Janeiro, and early-nineteenth-century increases in mortality were blamed on it: Mello e Alvim to Motta Feo e Torres, 27 Jan. 1819, AHU, Angola cx. 66.

121. E.g., the ambivalence in Mendes (Capela ed.), *Memória a respeito dos escravos,* pp. 35, 48–49.

122. José da Costa Pereira, 20 March 1759, BNL, cód. 617.

123. Correa da Silva, 9 March 1803, enclosing merchants' petition of 20 Jan. 1803, AHU, Angola cx. 54.

Portuguese trade. Prior to then, the risk of disorder and the danger that despairing slaves brought topside to wash would hurl themselves into the sea outweighed the benefits attributed to personal cleanliness.[124]

The Portuguese attempted persistently but vainly to clear the air below decks, if partly for their own comfort, also to keep the slaves alive. Fumigation, which temporarily covered up the stink embedded in the very bulkheads of the decks, was a favored technique. Crews used vinegar, and sometimes mixed it with gunpowder, dried the mixture into cakes, and burned the cakes to combine the pungent odor of sulphur with the sharp smell of the vinegar.[125] They also favored hot tar at some periods.[126] Captains prepared their ships for easier cleansing by whitewashing the walls and the platforms for the slaves, thus leaving the decks with the additional strong odor of lime.[127] All in all, such potions could only have thickened the African organic stench with the suffocating fumes of eighteenth-century European chemistry.

The slaves were segregated by sexes aboard the larger Portuguese ships, with the women placed in the cabins with small children and infants at the breast. There they were believed to survive better than on the slave deck, but they were also accessible for sexual abuse without requiring the crew to offend their senses or to risk assault by the males by venturing below.[128] Whatever the conditions in the women's cabins, which were probably less dark, fetid, and cramped than those for the men, the male majority of the cargo lay side by side on rough planked bunks barely large enough to allow them to remain supine or perhaps to raise themselves on one arm from time to time.[129] On the Spanish ship *La Panchiata,* active during the late 1820s, the men on the slave deck sat upright in rows in a space so low that none could stand, legs spread and knees raised so that each occupied the space between the limbs of the man behind. A long chain ran through rings on their arms and was attached firmly to fastenings to the side of the vessel. The chain could presumably be pulled through the rings to release a gang of men for feeding or exercise on deck, but at all other times it bound them together in their sufferings. As one horrified

124. Vianna, "Humanitário alvará," pp. 86–87 (1813); Spix and Martius, *Viagem pelo Brazil,* 2:153; Mendes, "Discurso academico ao programma," in Carreira, "Companhias pombalinas de navegação," pp. 451–52, or the Capela ed., *Memória a respeito dos escravos,* p. 75. This unconcern makes a strong contrast with the French emphasis on personal hygiene, as represented in Stein, *French Slave Trade,* p. 102.

125. Cf. the French pouring vinegar over hot stones to fumigate with the resulting acrid steam: Labat, cited in Taunay, *Subsídios,* p. 127.

126. *Portaria,* 23 May 1770, AHU, Angola cx. 33.

127. De Mello, 12 March 1799, AHU, Angola cx. 46.

128. Taunay, *Subsídios,* p. 208; Mendes (Capela ed.), *Memória a respeito dos escravos,* p. 49.

129. Slaves tight-packed above decks and in the cabin areas of the ship sometimes had to huddle beneath the hammocks on which the crew slept: de Mello, 12 March 1799, AHU, Angola cx. 46. See also Botelho, *Escravatura,* p. 27.

British observer of conditions below decks remarked, "Should any of these unfortunate creatures be attacked with seasickness, and dysentery, their situation may be more easily imagined than described."[130] The inevitability of both these conditions was well-attested. Ubiquitous fears of Portuguese cannibalism grew in the darkness.[131] The constant movement of the ship, particularly in rough weather, produced a slow clanging and rattling as the slaves' chains swayed back and forth, and their illnesses and terrors produced a crescendo of moans and whimpers that filled the air with mournful sound as well as noxious smells.[132]

Nutrition: Bom Para Pretos

The only breaks in the monotonous oppressiveness of existence on the slave deck came two or three times a day, when the crew brought small lots of ten or so slaves on deck for feeding. However, not all slaves enjoyed even this modest relief, since the clutter on the deck of many ships left no room for feeding above board. Beyond the danger of revolt, bringing the captives into the open risked having them fling themselves into the sea.[133] Their diet was simple: manioc meal, supplemented by beans, boiled—or sometimes only heated—into a mush served from large copper kettles or from animal troughs, no doubt rehabilitated from having been used to feed livestock on the voyage to Angola, and the same ones from which chaplains had sprinkled holy water as the ship weighed anchor.[134] Metal cauldrons steaming on the deck struck many slaves as prepared to boil the slaves rather than to cook their food, and owners urged that ships avoid using these pots to prepare the slaves' rations. The mush, never supplied in plentiful quantities, frequently contained rotted or wormy meal brought from Brazil and stored too long and carelessly while the ship had waited

130. Nicolls to Hay, Woolwich, 14 Dec. 1830, PRO, CO82/3.
131. Brugevin journal off the Mozambique coast, in Debien, "Journal de traite de la *Licorne*," pp. 105–6, or Villiers, *Traite des Noirs*, p. 87.
132. Botelho, *Escravatura*, pp. 21–22.
133. The impression left by the descriptions of the Portuguese trade is that the slaves came up on deck much less often than in the French trade: e.g., Taunay, *Subsídios*, p. 126; Mendes, "Discurso academico ao programma," in Carreira, "Companhias pombalinas de navegação," p. 451.
134. In the North American trade, it was the huge kettles that confirmed the slaves' fears of being eaten by white cannibals on board the ships: Coughtry, *Notorious Triangle*, p. 147. Cf. Mattoso, *Etre esclave au Brésil*, p. 58, for a revolt (presumably aboard a slaver from Mozambique) inspired by fears of cannibalism. In the Portuguese trade these kettles were not properly cleaned after use, and the green corrosion that formed was believed to poison food prepared in them: Conrad, *Children of God's Fire*, pp. 93–94; de Mello, 3 March 1799, AHU, Angola cx. 46; *portaria*, 23 May 1779, AHU, Angola cx. 33. The kettles were prohibited by the *alvará* of 1813 but reinstated, if tin-plated, by the further *alvará* of 1818: Vianna, "Humanitário alvará," p. 84; Rebelo, *Relações*, p. 75.

its turn in Luanda harbor, or purchased at bargain prices in Angola.[135] The euphemism used for spoiled or adulterated foods in the Rio marketplace, and probably also in Luanda, was "bom para pretos"—good (only) for blacks.[136]

The slaves' primary source of protein was beans.[137] Small quantities of dried fish from Luanda, which rotted and became less and less palatable as the voyage lengthened, added animal protein.[138] To this captains concerned with the survival of their slaves added condiments, particularly hot pepper (*jindungo*), to which most slaves were highly partial, perhaps palm oil, vinegar, and salt, a cup or two of lukewarm and putrid water, probably smelling and tasting of the *gerebita* that had preceded it in its storage casks, and perhaps a swallow of *gerebita* itself. Red wine, if not too expensive for slavers, was avoided because it alarmed the captives, who suspected that the Portuguese had made it from the blood of their predecessors. Some captains employed the strong Brazilian rum to keep their slave cargoes quieted, but others found it a problem for the drunkenness that it caused. Toward the end of the eighteenth century, the practice spread of adding vinegar to the diet, either as a mouthwash or as a medicine mixed with sugar, to treat scurvy.[139]

Some captains made efforts to provide food of a sort to which the slaves had been accustomed at home, with ships outbound from Benguela

135. E.g., Moçâmedes, 28 April 1789, AHU, Angola cx. 41.

136. ANRJ, códs. 368 and 1091.

137. Kenneth F. Kiple, "Historical Dimensions of Disease in the Plantation Economies" (Paper presented to the Ontario Cooperative Program in Latin Caribbean Studies, Windsor, Ont., 1980), p. 8, and Coughtry, *Notorious Triangle*, p. 148, also stress the nutritional importance of vegetable protein in beans.

138. Mendes (Capela ed.), *Memória a respeito dos escravos*, p. 50; Corrêa, *História de Angola*, 1:153; Vianna, "Humanitário alvará," p. 84. The *portaria* of 23 May 1770, AHU, Angola cx. 33, specified one *motete* (an unknown local measure, probably of volume, i.e., a basket?) of fish per slave per voyage (regardless of distance), half made up of the usual small fry, which spoiled within two weeks, and half of larger and better-preserved fish (*corvina*) to be given the slaves on the later portions of the passage. Some ships, probably those from southern Brazil in particular, brought dried beef for the slaves, but their jerky was often improperly prepared and grew rancid: *regimento* (Gov. da Câmara), 1779, AHU, Angola maço 3 (D.O.); Commissioners Campbell and Raffell to Canning, Sierra Leone, 31 Mar. 1827, PRO, FO84/65, fols. 39–42. In some cases, meat was reserved as a remedy for slaves who became ill: Carreira, "Companhias pombalinas de navegação," p. 68. The owners of the royal monopoly on whaling recommended whale meat salvaged from fisheries off the Angolan and Brazilian southern coasts: *requerimento* of Domingos Lopes Loureiro, n.d. (but minuted 10 Sept. 1766), AHU, Angola maço 4–A.

139. Cosme (Pina ed.), "Tractado," p. 266; *portaria*, 23 May 1770, AHU, Angola cx. 33; de Mello, 12 March 1799, AHU, Angola cx. 46. These recommendations assumed the availability of vinegar in Luanda, where it in fact sometimes ran short; cf. the consistently significant quantities of vinegar imported at Luanda from 1785 to 1823: Miller, "Imports at Luanda." The recommended quantity of vinegar was about 5 cc per day, estimated from the stated 1½ *pipas* (or about 750 liters) for larger ships (carrying 500 slaves or more?) and 1 *pipa* for smaller ships (i.e., in the 300- to 400-slave range?) on a 40-day passage, i.e., 1,125 liters/600 slaves/40 days, or 750 liters/350 slaves/40 days.

early in the century resisting the required call at Luanda on the grounds that such a stop necessitated acquiring additional food supplies at the northern port, of a sort different from those to which Benguela slaves were used.[140] Leaving aside the shippers' obvious self-interest in protesting a stop that also involved paying export duties at Luanda, the change of diet could bring death to numbers of slaves, presumably as a result of diarrheas and dehydration induced by the change in diet.[141] Reformers also urged attention to providing familiar foods and recommended that the slave women be employed to prepare food according to the culinary techniques of their homelands for the slaves kept in the Luanda slave pens and that slaves on board the ships be given foods which appealed to them.[142] More often than not, however, the compulsion to limit cash outlays for provisions overcame abstract appreciation of the value of tasty rations in adequate quantity, and the slaves subsisted on manioc mush and beans.[143] The shippers' preference for manioc derived in large part from its superior storage qualities.

Prescribed quantities of mealies seem to have been marginally adequate for the slaves, or at least standard in comparison to rations given unskilled labor elsewhere in Angola and Brazil at the time. While the decree of 1684 did not specify exact amounts, by the end of the eighteenth century, experience had established 3 *cazongueis* (or *cazonguelos,* singular *cazonguel*) of manioc meal per slave for the (official) forty- to fifty-day voyage to Rio and 2 *cazongueis* per slave for the shorter (i.e., thirty-day) crossings to Pernambuco and Bahia.[144] These were to be supplemented by an additional *cazonguel* of beans for each slave on either route,[145] thus making 3 *cazongueis* of food per month the rough standard to be met, or a total of 1/10 *cazonguel* per day. The Luanda *cazonguel* equalled 1 *alqueire,* a widely used measure of dry capacity in the Portuguese empire, but one

140. Especially by the Pernambuco Company, which itself owned the slaves it carried: AHMF, Angola *copiador,* 25 Feb. 1763; AHMF, Benguela *copiador,* 4 July 1777, fol. 1.

141. *Requerimento,* Manoel da Silva, n.d. (early 1730s?), AHU, Angola cx. 20; Almeida e Vasconcelos, 3 March 1794, AHU, Angola cx. 43, specifying that the change in diet involved a shift from *milho* (cornmeal?) to the manioc that prevailed at Luanda.

142. Cosme (Pina ed.), "Tractado," p. 266; cf. Brugevin, in Debien, "Journal de traite de la *Licorne,*" pp. 105–6; Villiers, *Traite des Noirs,* p. 87.

143. Mendes (Capela ed.), *Memória a respeito dos escravos,* p. 72, though with reference to the shore barracoons rather than the ships at sea; de Mello, 12 Mar. 1799, AHU, Angola cx. 43.

144. The same 2-*alqueire* ration (of rice) was allotted on the *Nossa Senhora da Oliveira,* which carried 400 slaves from Cacheu to Pará in 1774: "Despezas que nos Felipe Damazio de Aguiar e Francisco José Gomes fizemos com a curveta N. S.ª da Oliveira," Cacheu, 24 Jan. 1774, BAPP, 140, no. 38. I am grateful to Dauril Alden for making this information available to me.

145. Corrêa, *História de Angola,* 1:56. For the Bahia rations see the "Discurso preliminar," pp. 139, 141, in [Manuel] Pinto de Aguiar, intro., *Aspectos da economia colonial* (Salvador: Livraria Progresso Editora, 1957)—either 1 or 2 *alqueires* per slave per voyage of about 25 days. The ration would appear roughly similar.

that varied widely from place to place. It is uncertain whether the *cazonguel* used aboard the slave ships was that of Lisbon, approximately 8.4 liters, or that of Brazil, generally cited as 14 liters but sometimes specified more precisely as 13.8 liters.[146] If the Angolan *cazonguel* equalled the larger Brazilian *alqueire*, the slaves' 3 *cazongueis* would have amounted to just under 1 liter (0.92, almost exactly 1 dry quart) of basic cereals each day, plus less than 1/2 liter of beans (or 1 dry pint). If the *alqueire* of Lisbon was the measure in use, the slaves would have received about 60 percent as much, or a total of 0.83 liters (about 1 1/2 pints).

Eighteenth-century Angolan estimates of the basic starch requirements of a working adult male afford an easy comparison to the provisioning of the trade, as they were also stated in terms of *cazongueis* per month, presumably the same measure as that applied in the slave trade. An adult male laborer in the mid-eighteenth century was estimated to require 1/2 *exeque* of manioc flour per month, or 2 *cazongueis,* and that reference should probably be taken to indicate the amount of food actually given to workers: a third less than what was prescribed for slaves on board the *tumbeiros*. However, a careful review of the conditions under which impressed Africans labored in the colony in the late 1760s produced a government order specifying a full *exeque* of manioc flour (or its equivalent in beans or other carbohydrate) as due (and necessary?) each month.[147] This doubling of the apparent standard prevailing in Angola to 4 *cazongueis*, a third more than prescribed on the slaving ships, may be taken as an intended improvement on the existing ration. Workers employed in the digging of a proposed canal from the Kwanza River to Luanda in 1816 were actually allotted 1/10 *cazonguel* of manioc flour per day, precisely the same ration as prescribed on the ships, plus 1/40 *cazonguel* of beans, as well as salt, palm oil, rum, and tobacco.

The government provided smaller amounts of food for slaves employed in mining and other industrial enterprises in Angola. Early in the nineteenth century, in the Mundombe sulfur mines south of Benguela, a gang of thirty-three workers and bearers received ony 24.15 *cazongueis* of beans and 49 *cazongueis* of manioc flour, plus tobacco and *gerebita*, for thirty days' work—that is, 0.07 *alqueires* per worker per day (as well as 7 cc *gerebita*), or 30 percent below the tenth of an *alqueire* standard in other

---

146. Conversion built up from Peçanha, 18 June 1783, AHU, Angola cx. 40; Rau, "*Livro de Razão,*" p. 48; and dictionary entries, including *Grande Enciclopédia portuguesa e brasileira* (Lisbon: Editorial Enciclopédia, 1950–), 2:137. James Lang, *Portuguese Brazil: The King's Plantation* (New York: Academic Press, 1979), p. 130, gives the *alqueire* as 1.6 pecks, or 14.08 liters, and Brown, "Internal Commerce," p. 74, confirms for Pernambuco, ca. 1810.

147. Da Cunha, 21 Dec. 1753, AHU, Angola cx. 25; the proclaimed increase in provisions was Sousa Coutinho's *portaria* of 7 Dec. 1770, in *Arquivos de Angola* 2, no. 1 (1933): n.p.

kinds of work. Gangs of thirty slaves working in gold mines along the Lombige River had received far less in the 1760s: 3 *sacos* of *farinha* and 1/3 *saco* of beans each month. The *saco* was equivalent to an *exeque*, thus 4 *alqueires* to the *saco*, or 13.33 *alqueires* per month for the gang, or a miniscule 0.015 *alqueires* for each slave each day, only 15 percent of the usual 1/10 *alqueire*, plus negligible rations of beans. The anomalously low figure for provisions probably arises because the mineworkers would have belonged to slave households *(cazaes)* settled around the mining site, at least in the northerly and relatively fertile Lombige area, if not in the sterile sands south of Benguela at Mundombe, with the women of the pairs responsible for supplying a substantial portion of the family diet from their own fields; the government ration would have been a supplement, no more.[148]

Taking the Brazilian *alqueire* as equal to about 57 pounds (25.8 kg) of cassava flour and beans at 72 pounds (32.73 kg) to the same volume,[149] the legally required ration for the slaves at sea worked out to an ample 2.81 kilograms of manioc and beans per day. Using the smaller Lisbon *alqueire*, the ration would have amounted to a still-adequate 1.71 kilograms daily. In either case, the ration by weight compared favorably with the diet supplied to Portuguese soldiers dispatched from Luanda for Bahia in 1822 at the time of the Brazilian declaration of independence. They received only 1.31 kilos per day: 1 *arratel* (0.46 kg) of sea biscuit and 0.35 liters of beans (0.025 *alqueire*, 0.85 kg) per day, plus 0.47 liters of wine, 5 cubic centimeters of vinegar, 2.5 cubic centimeters of cooking oil, and a rotation of salt beef (1 *arratel*), pork (3/4 *arratel*), or salt cod (1/2 *arratel*), plus occasional rice, bacon, manioc meal, butter, and fresh chicken.[150] What the soldiers gained over the slaves' rations was variety. The 100 pairs of choice slaves sent to the king of Portugal in 1819, then residing in Rio, were supported more generously with 240 *alqueires* of manioc meal (1.13 *alqueires* per slave for the voyage, or 29.2 kg, almost a full kilo per day),

148. Memória sobre o encanamento do Rio Coanza, 1816, AHU, Angola cx. 64; Rebelo, *Relações*, pp. 171–73, for Mundombe; figures reported in Venâncio, "Economia de Luanda," p. 125, for the Lombige mines. For a labor system involving slave households considered in relation to another mineral industry in the colony—the iron foundry at Nova Oeiras in the lower Lukala valley—see Sousa Coutinho, *portaria*, 7 Dec. 1770, in *Arquivos de Angola* 1, no. 2 (1770): n.p.

149. Precisely 2.81 kilograms. See Pennell to Bidwell, 14 Aug. 1826, PRO, FO13/29, fols. 169–83, for a Brazilian *alqueire* in terms of British grain measures: 56 ¾ Eng. lbs. flour, 57 ¾ Eng. lbs. corn, 72 Eng. lbs. rice, 72 Eng. lbs. beans. Obviously, the uncertainty of the exact size of the *alqueires* referred to in other documentation limits the precision of estimates derived from them.

150. AHTC, "Registo das provisões e cartas régias expedidas para Angola," 2 Aug. 1822, fols. 89 ff. Also compare the rations on the India voyage in the sixteenth and seventeenth centuries, which consisted of sea biscuit, salt cod, beans, salted meat, rice, and wine: José Rodrigues de Abreu, *Luz de cirurgiões embarcadissos* (Lisbon: Antonio Pedrozo Galvam, 1711), pp. 34–35.

92 *alqueires* of *milho* (corn?) (0.44 *alqueires* per slave, 15.4 kg, or about 1/2 kilo per day), 128 *alqueires* of beans (0.60 per slave, also 15.5 kg, and similarly about 1/2 kilo per day), plus prepared manioc flour slightly greater in value than the beans or corn (but unspecified in terms of quantity), fish, palm oil, three unidentified *"bolos da terra"* apiece (prepared manioc loaves?), citrus fruits, salt, pepper, tobacco, and brandy.[151] They would appear to have received nearly 3 kilos of basic foodstuffs each day, if the Brazilian *alqueire* applied (or 1 2/3 kilos using that of Lisbon), approximately the same as set by law for ordinary trade slaves.

Generally throughout the premodern world, working adult males received daily rations of only about a kilogram of cereals, although the figures ranged upward to about the level prescribed for slaves at sea on the southern Atlantic.[152] Whatever the vitamin deficiencies of the manioc given the slaves, the beans supplied protein; and, in theory at least, small quantities of dried fish, rum, vinegar, hot red peppers, squash and such other vegetables as could be preserved at sea, and salt beef or pork filled out a diet that was sufficiently nourishing to keep the slaves alive within foreseen voyage times and was a continued improvement over what they had eaten before reaching Luanda. The comparison becomes less unfavorable still when the reduced nutritional needs of the small, inactive, and in some proportion female population aboard the slave ships are contrasted with those of the adult male laborers receiving similar allowances on land. Not even in comparison with the favored royal slaves did the prescribed rations for captives crossing the southern Atlantic suffer. Of course, as with so many other high-sounding regulations in the Portuguese trade, principles seldom reflected practice.

Nutritional problems for the slaves on the middle passage arose from the *abuso antiquissimo* of the trade—captains' unwillingness, and frequently their inability, to supply first-quality, adequately prepared food or to allot the space required to stock the quantities prescribed.[153] The difficulties were insurmountable. Brazilian slavers lacked the cash to buy American produce that could have found any other market. The months and months spent waiting at Luanda and Benguela virtually guaranteed that whatever provisions they had brought with them would spoil before they could feed them to the slaves. Vermin-infested and putrid meal surely occasioned

151. Account enclosed in Motta Feo e Torres, 3 Sept. 1819, AHU, Angola cx. 66.
152. See Appendix A.
153. For the prescribed standards, see all decrees and official recommendations concerning the trade, cited above; Mendes (Capela ed.), *Memória a respeito dos escravos,* pp. 50, 74; Pereira da Costa, 9 March 1723, AHU, Angola cx. 16; memorial from Luanda merchants, 20 July 1724, AHU, Angola cx. 16; Taunay, *Subsídios,* pp. 200–201 (for the 1730s); Corrêa, *História de Angola,* 1:56–57; "Informação breve," n.d. (but ca. 1790s), AHU, Angola cx. 42; instruction to Gov. Oliveira Barboza, 28 Feb. 1810, AHU, cód. 551, published in Rebelo, *Relações,* pp. 342–44; etc.

renewed waves of dysentery. Food shortages arose from Luso-African boycotts as well as from drought. Stocks of provisions imported from Brazil kept prices paid to Luanda producers too low to improve local supplies to the city market. And captains sacrificed storage space for food to carrying capacity for slaves whenever possible.[154] A delayed landfall in Brazil would reduce rations adequate for the expected voyage below a level that could support the restoration of slave health and would expose weakened slaves to mounting risks of disease.

Under these unyielding constraints, elaborate government procedures to guarantee adequate food supplies only increased the opportunities for graft and bribery by captains unable as well as unwilling to comply. The certifying procedures in effect at Luanda by the 1780s, in the best replicated style of the Portuguese bureaucracy, required the head of the official grain market (the *juiz do terreiro público*) to verify that captains had purchased provisions adequate for their measured tonnage, detached a sergeant *(sargento)* from the colonial garrison to accompany the sacks of meal to the waterside, and had the harbormaster *(patrão mor)* confirm them as having gone aboard the ship. Of these arrangements one acutely cynical observer remarked: "In view of this excellent arrangement, unrelenting before impiety, who could fail to assume that the obligations of charity would be unfailingly observed? However, experience has shown me that their senses of responsibility are corrupted by their ambition. The *patrão mor* and the *sargento* never fail to certify the list of required provisions, but because they are (in fact) lacking, and the water too, the slaves suffer whenever the voyage does not end within the short period hoped for."[155] The starvation that plagued slaves at the end of delayed crossings must have resulted from background malnutrition in Africa, compounded by the economics of a trade that obligated shippers to cut every possible operating cost and to increase revenues by forcing slaves into their already overloaded vessels beyond the *arqueação* that determined the quantities of food they carried.

The dimension of ship provisioning most crucial to slave lives and health was, by this and nearly all other accounts, not food but water. Slaves often entered Luanda dehydrated, surely so in times of drought, but also in the best of seasons after passing through the dry coastal lowlands as they neared the sea. The shortages of clean water available to slaves in the towns evaporated in comparison to those aboard the ships on their way to America.

Water, because of its bulk and the otherwise valuable space that storing the large casks took from carrying slaves, had always been in short supply

154. Miller, "Overcrowded and Undernourished."
155. Corrêa, *História de Angola*, 1:56–57.

aboard the slavers.[156] The shortages were worsened by the inadequacies of Luanda's and Benguela's water supply systems. They were exacerbated further still by the loss of body fluids slaves experienced once confined on the ships. The high temperatures of the hold induced profuse sweating,[157] and seasickness and dysenteries accelerated dehydration. If such reductions in body fluid levels did not bring death by themselves, Portuguese medicine could complete the job. Medical theories of the time frequently identified these effluents as symptoms of excessive liquid in the slaves' systems, prescribed limited water intake and recommended enemas and vomiting as treatments![158] The slaves complained of burning thirst, and survivors remembered shortages of water as the principal hardship of the middle passage.[159] The despair and lethargy that overtook many led them to refuse all food and water. Some Europeans interpreted the slaves' suicidal urges to hurl themselves into the sea as a desperate quest for water, even the undrinkable salt water of the ocean.[160]

The sensitivity of slave mortality to water supplies, and hence the impact of sufficient water on the profitability of the voyage, was no mystery to very many connected with the slave trade in the southern Atlantic.[161] Regulations governing the slave trade focused on the quantities of water necessary to deliver slaves safely to the New World and on the need to store water in clean casks that would preserve its potability until the end

156. E.g., the first recorded instruction regarding the slave trade in the southern Atlantic, which specified minimum standards for water but not for food, a *regimento* given to Simão da Silva, 1512, in Brásio, *Monumenta missionaria africana*, 1:239–40. Also Salvador, *Magnatas do tráfico negreiro*, pp. 100–101 (for pre-1684 regulations concerning water at Angola).

157. Magalhães, 9 Nov. 1745, AHU, Angola cx. 23, referred to "a quentura das cobertas," "the heat of the slave decks."

158. E.g., George Reid Andrews, *The Afro-Argentines of Buenos Aires, 1800–1900* (Madison: University of Wisconsin Press, 1980), p. 26, citing Ricardo Rodríguez Molas quoting a British surgeon in the 1740s. Cosme (Pina ed.), "Tractado," p. 267, with his exceptionally accurate perception of the circumstances, opposed these practices.

159. Baquaqua, cited in Conrad, *Children of God's Fire*, p. 27 (1840s).

160. Conrad, *Children of God's Fire*, p. 34.

161. Especially to those sailing the lengthy and often delayed passage from Mozambique around the Cape of Good Hope to Buenos Aires and Brazil, where provisioning stops were absolutely necessary and miscalculations meant disastrously high losses among the slaves. There was, e.g., the case of the *El Joaquín*, reaching Buenos Aires in 179 days with only 60 of 376 slaves alive: Scheuss de Studer, *Trata de negros*, pp. 309–10. British antislavery policies at the Cape of Good Hope after about 1812 forced some Mozambique ships to pass without filling up their water supplies, with predictable losses among the slaves and a certain alarm among other British officials in Brazil: George McCall Theal, *Records of the Cape Colony from February 1793* (London: Printed for the Government of the Cape Colony, 1897–1903), 1:129, 181–82, 458–59 (with thanks to Mary Rayner for supplying this reference). The Mozambique slavers then took to calling for provisions at Benguela, São Tomé, and Príncipe: Benguela shipping reports, e.g., AHU, Angola cx. 70; Lopes, *Escravatura*, p. 182. But insufficient water supplies persisted: Conrad, *Children of God's Fire*, pp. 37–39 (a slave's recollection); Botelho, *Escravatura*, p. 27 (observations of a critic of the trade).

of the voyage.[162] The Brazilian vessels that carried most of the slaves arrived in Angola with their holds so filled with huge *pipas* of *gerebita* that they could not bring fresh water casks (*toneis*, generally twice the size of the *pipa*) to fill for the slaves' use on the return voyage, and there was little chance of finding room for clean, empty casks aboard the jammed incoming merchantmen from Lisbon. The cost of water containers could also be prohibitive under the economic constraints of slaving in the southern Atlantic.[163] The Brazilian captains therefore simply refilled the emptied rum casks with water at Luanda or Benguela, a practice which imparted the rotten smell of the *gerebita* to the water, allegedly caused the death of thousands of slaves, and brought the issue to the attention of the government. Captains also had to refill emptied water *pipas* with seawater as they emptied them on the westward voyage to maintain the stability of the ships, to the detriment of both the rum and the fresh water that they would later hold again.

Lisbon merchants and Brazilian shippers each tried to use the issue of water supplies to drive the other out of business at Luanda, just as they cynically employed every other cause they could present in the name of the slaves to lure the Crown to support their private interest.[164] If, for example, as some Lisbon merchants insisted, Brazilians had been required to bring clean water casks with them, the substantial Angolan market for imported alcohol would have been left entirely to the wines of the metropole. Nominally in the interest of the slaves' welfare, governors at Luanda appointed an official to inspect all water casks aboard departing slavers to ascertain that they had been properly cured. At least after 1744 this *cheirador das pipas*, or *cheirâdor das agoadas*, ("sniffer" of the casks, or of the water supplies) was nominated by the owners of the slaves as represented in the Luanda Senado da Câmara, whose financial interests in the slaves' lives he represented, but toward the end of the eighteenth century the colonial government took the position over directly and ex-

162. A royal order of 23 Sept. 1664 set a flat figure for water supplies regardless of voyage length: Silva, *Collecção chronologica,* supplementary volume (1640–83), p. 271, and cited in Salvador, *Magnatas do tráfico negreiro,* pp. 100–101, 103. For other regulations on water supply, see arts. 7 and 8 of the 1684 *regimento,* in *Arquivos de Angola* 2, no. 11 (1936): 315; *parecer* of Francisco da Costa Barboza e Moura (Lisbon), 4 Aug. 1744, AHU, Angola cx. 23; de Mello, 12 July 1799, AHU, Angola cx. 40; Vianna, "Humanitário alvará," pp. 84–85. For quality, order of 9 April 1693, a *provisão* of 15 Dec. 1694, and a further order of 25 Oct. 1744, all mentioned in da Cunha, 3 Dec. 1754, AHU, Angola maço 11 (D.O.). Cf. Palmer, *Human Cargoes,* p. 57, n. 25, for the Royal African Company's concern about the same problem.

163. Villiers, *Traite des Noirs,* p. 105.

164. For the controversy, copy (17 March 1742) of appointment papers for Vicente Ferreira, AHU, Angola cx. 23; Magalhães, 29 Dec. 1742, AHU, Angola cx. 23; Barboza e Moura *parecer,* 4 Aug. 1744, AHU, Angola cx. 23; da Cunha, 3 Dec. 1754, AHU, Angola maço 11 (D.O.).

panded its authority to include overseeing the quality of both foodstuffs and water. Ships had to carry water only in proper *toneis,* and if it was necessary to use *gerebita pipas,* the water stored in the old rum casks had to be consumed before that in the *toneis.*[165] The old and badly cured rum casks probably in fact hastened spoilage only marginally beyond the putrifaction of organic matter introduced by filling containers of any sort with the filthy water that slavers bought in Benguela and Luanda. Whether or not supplies lasted to the end of the voyage, the fluid that remained in the casks after two or three months in the heat of the tropics grew noxious beyond toleration, and only the extreme thirst of the slaves (and crew) could have driven them to continue to consume it.

Amounts of water—set by law and inspected for quality and quantity at Luanda and, at least by the late eighteenth century, also at Benguela—were established on the basis of the registered *arqueação* and normal crossing times that left little allowance for delays at sea. When ships carried slaves in excess of their legal allotment, captains were courting disaster at the slightest lengthening of their passage. The ration set by the *regimento* of 1684 was 1 *canada* (about 1.375 liters, or 2.6 American pints) per day, with voyages to Pernambuco, Bahia, and Rio de Janeiro realistically defined as thirty-five, forty, and fifty days, respectively.[166] The 1684 law effectively halved the allotment established in 1664 of 25 *pipas* per 100 *peça* slaves, doubtless as a concession to the shippers, on whom many other of its provisions·weighed heavily.[167] Since the *pipa* contained 300 *canadas,* ships should have carried only 11.7 *pipas* (3,500 *canadas*) for 100 slaves for the passage to Pernambuco, 13.3 *pipas* (4,000 *canadas*) to Bahia, and 16.7 *pipas* (5,000 *canadas*) to Rio. A *parecer* of 1744 recommended 20 *pipas* per 100 slaves to Pernambuco, 25 to Bahia, and 30 to Rio, thus endorsing the old standard of about double the amount then required by law.[168] The Pernambuco Company instructed its agents at Benguela to provide double

165. Confirmed by de Mello, "Angola no fim do século," p. 288; this move was part of the generally growing involvement of the Crown in regulating the details of the trade, dating roughly from the *portaria* of 23 May 1770 (art. 2), AHU, Angola cx. 33. The Pernambuco Company directors also showed concern about the issue: letter of 25 Feb. 1763, AHMF, Pernambuco Co., Angola *copiador;* letter of 4 July 1777, AHMF, Benguela *copiador.*

166. Mattoso, *Etre esclave au Brésil,* p. 47, and T. Bentley Duncan, *Atlantic Islands: Madeira, the Azores and the Cape Verdes in Seventeenth-Century Commerce and Navigation* (Chicago: University of Chicago Press, 1972), pp. 230–32, appear to use the modern Brazilian *canada* of 2.77 liters. I have made conversions based the Portuguese *canada* of 1.4 liters; see Adrien Balbi, *Essai statistique sur le royaume de Portugal et d'Algarve* (Paris: Rey et Gravier, 1822), p. 473; Grant, *History of Brazil,* p. 169; and the Memória sobre o encanamento do Rio Coanza, 1816, AHU, Angola cx. 64. Shippers would have had every incentive to interpret the law according to the smaller standard of the metropole, where, indeed, the laws were phrased.

167. *Consulta* of the Conselho Ultramarino, 12 Aug. 1664, AHU, Angola cx. 6; see Mauro, "L'Atlantique portugais," p. 37; Salvador, *Magnatas do tráfico negreiro,* p. 101.

168. AHU, Angola cx. 23.

the legally required supply of water, and the reform *alvará* of 1813 finally brought the required water ration back to a full 2 *canadas* per day, with at least half reserved for drinking and the remainder presumably allotted to cooking purposes.[169]

How far the required supplies might actually have gone depended on the extent of tight-packing, the weight and health of the slaves, weather conditions and the degree of heat below decks, how much rainwater crews might have been able to collect and save for drinking during the voyage, the requirements of the crew, the tightness of the casks, and too many other unknown variables to judge the effect too closely. The standard was not always met, despite awareness of the problems on all sides,[170] largely because the ships simply had holds too small to carry the prescribed rations. Ships carrying 300 to 400 slaves would have had to find room for 35 to 65 *pipas,* each occupying about 4 cubic meters, or a total of from 140 to 200 cubic meters. Taking the measured capacity ton used in the southern Atlantic at 3–4 cubic meters, and averaging the 1684 load factors of five slaves per 2 tons in unventilated decks and seven slaves per 2 tons in ventilated ones, ships carried provisions about equal in volume to the space allocated to the slaves. Tight-packing at 20 percent and a ten-day delay at sea would reduce the required daily ration by a third.

One may also compare this standard with the water carried in other parts of the trade. Eighteenth-century Liverpool slavers carried more than 2 liters per slave per day.[171] By the 1840s, British expert opinion recommended a full gallon per day, or more than three times the *canada* set for slaves of the Portuguese.[172] French slavers prescribed 3 liters of water daily, buttressed by medical opinion of the time that urged a full 2 liters (half again the *canada*) under tropical conditions, or about the standard that critics in Brazil and Angola prescribed in the southern Atlantic, but may have actually distributed only about 3/4 liter per day, slightly more than half the Portuguese allotment.[173] Some reports put the "standard" (Brit-

---

169. Thirty-five *pipas* per 100 slaves: letter of 4 July 1777, AHMF, Pernambuco Co., Benguela *copiador;* Vianna, "Humanitário alvará," cond. 7, pp. 84–85.

170. Mendes (Capela ed.), *Memória a respeito dos escravos,* pp. 49–50, and many other sources cited in footnotes above. However, shortages probably did not approach those endured during the unregulated illegal trade of the 1840s, when a teacup every two or three days was judged sufficient to sustain life: Conrad, *Children of God's Fire,* p. 33.

171. David Richardson, "The Costs of Survival: The Treatment of Slaves in the Middle Passage and the Profitability of the Eighteenth-Century British Slave Trade" (Paper presented to the Colloque International sur la Traite des Noirs, Nantes, 1985).

172. Conrad, *Children of God's Fire,* p. 33.

173. Boudriot, "Etude sur le navire négrier"; Villiers, *Traite des Noirs,* p. 98. The very cautious—and successful—Captain Brugevin of the *Licorne* provided 4.2 liters per day for a 60-day passage from Capetown to Saint Domingue: Villiers, p. 154. For the typical ration, Pierre Pluchon, *La route des esclaves: négriers et bois d'ébène au XVIIIe siècle* (Paris: Hachette, 1980), pp. 206–7. Stein, *French Slave Trade,* p. 95, specifies only that French slavers provisioning at São Tomé took on one barrel of unspecified dimensions per "passenger." Villiers, p. 45, gives the French *barrique* as 228 liters, and such a ration for a 75-day crossing (Stein's

ish?) ration at about a pint per day, or 40 percent of the Portuguese *canada*.[174]

Whatever the theoretical water ration, the pattern of the mortality statistics makes the amounts actually carried appear barely adequate for voyages falling within the range of expected passage times. For normal voyages, the bacteria in the water hurt the slaves most, through the dysenteries and fevers that they caused. But for delayed crossings, or for missed attempts to make port to reprovision along the way, shortages of water became critical and deadly.[175] Fortunately these delayed landings were the exception rather than the rule, though they were by no means uncommon.

Deficiency Diseases

Failure to stock prescribed food supplies, the marginal quantity and miserable quality of the water most ships carried, and the deprived nutritional status of many slaves before they ever climbed below deck combined to produce the terminal lethargy that the Portuguese knew as *banzo*. Described as a sort of "delirium," a loss of heart, a giving up the will to live,[176] and familiar also to the English as "fixed melancholy,"[177] it was unanimously feared but ascribed variously to homesickness, despair at the circumstances in which slaves found themselves, and mental trauma at their loss of liberty.[178] Without denying the impact of psychological shock,

---

assumption) would have allowed 2.2 *canadas* (3.04 liters), or about twice the Portuguese rate, but only half again that, or less, for the 113-day trip (less sailing time to São Tomé and stopover there?) that was average for Nantes ships making from the Gold Coast/Slave Coast to Saint Domingue, reported in Klein, *Middle Passage,* p. 192. Gaulme, "Document sur le Ngoyo," p. 356, put the São Tomé stopover at about a month.

174. Mannix and Cowley, *Black Cargoes,* p. 114.

175. Klein, *Middle Passage,* p. 200 et passim; Chandler, *Health and Slavery,* p. 44; Miller, "Mortality in the Atlantic Slave Trade." And the Portuguese records are filled with reports of the disasters attending such circumstances: Mauro, "L'Atlantique portugais," pp. 37–38; Taunay, *Subsídios,* p. 125; Pereira da Costa, 9 March 1723, AHU, Angola cx. 16; Vasconcelos, 11 Feb. 1763, AHU, Angola cx. 29; Corrêa, *História de Angola,* 1:56–57; de Mello, 12 March 1799, AHU, Angola cx. 46; Spix and Martius, *Viagem pelo Brasil,* 2:153. See Villiers, *Traite des Noirs,* p. 154, for a missed call at St. Helena.

176. Taunay, *Subsídios,* p. 250; Lopes, *Escravatura,* p. 177; Avellar, 25 May 1730, AHU, Angola maço 18–A; Mendes (Capela ed.), *Memória a respeito dos escravos,* p. 62; Corrêa, *História de Angola,* 1:173; Spix and Martius, *Viagem pelo Brasil,* 2:153, note V.

177. Chandler, *Health and Slavery,* pp. 34–37.

178. The psychological explanation has been much favored by twentieth-century lay commentators: Brásio, "Inimigo dos antigos colonos," in *História e missiologia,* pp. 747–48; Lycurgo de Castro Santos Filho, *História geral da medicina brasileira* (São Paulo: HUCITEC, 1977), 2:39. Tropical medicine specialists more enamored of parasites than of existential angst have also tried to identify it with sleeping sickness: Lycurgo de Castro Santos Filho, *Pequena história da medicina brasileira* (São Paulo: Universidade de São Paulo, 1966), pp. 100, 137.

the despondency, and the overwhelming terror of enslavement and embarkation by deathly white cannibals, it is likely that the *banzo* in fact represented the primary symptom of the slaves' underlying state of malnourishment. One of the fullest descriptions of the same condition aboard French slavers linked it to dirt-eating, a recognized sign of nutritional deficiencies and likewise associated with languor and loss of appetite.[179] It was also observed that this overwhelming "discouragement" seemed to be contagious, so that if some of the slaves gave up and died, so also would the remainder.[180] Given the intermittent outright starvation owing to western central African droughts and the crude eighteenth-century understanding of malnutrition in starkly unanalytical terms of "starvation,"[181] advanced malnutrition overtaking an entire cargo of slaves could well have acquired the appearance of "epidemic" contagion.[182]

Other complaints prevalent among the slaves, particularly the swellings known as *hidropsias*—"dropsy" or edema—were also symptomatic of extreme states of malnutrition, particularly thiamin (vitamin B^1) deficiencies, and similarly connected with dirt-eating.[183] The prevalence of these deficiency diseases, together with the notorious prominence of scurvy, would seem to seal the case identifying food shortages on the mainland as the principal predisposing factor behind the deaths of slaves at sea. Most striking to bewildered slavers was the obstinate refusal of slaves suffering from the *banzo* to eat. This last defiant act, for many of the victims of the trade, incorporated all the complex factors that combined to cause mortality in the slave decks. It was at once a passive protest against their helplessness, a final symptom of their nutritional deprivation, and a par-

179. Cosme (Pina ed.), "Tractado," p. 266, accurately identified malnutrition and dehydration. For the French slavers, Labat, cited in Brásio, "Inimigo dos antigos colonos," in *História e missiologia*, pp. 747–48; cf. Kiple, "Historical Dimensions," pp. 10–11, and elsewhere.

180. Lopes, *Escravatura*, p. 177.

181. E.g., the attempt to interpret unmistakable signs of malnutrition as "aftereffects" of fevers as late as the 1840s, in Moreira, "Memoria sobre as molestias," p. 139, though acknowledging that the symptoms also seemed aggravated by "bad diet." Likewise Azeredo, *Ensaios sobre as enfermidades*, pp. 24–25; José Maria Bomtempo, *Compendio de medicina pratica* (Rio de Janeiro: Regia Officina Typografica, 1815), pp. 201–3. The *Gazeta de Lisboa* of 10 Aug. 1719 reported the loss of the majority of a cargo of slaves reaching Rio from Angola from *banzo*, during a period of severe drought and epidemic: Almeida, *Notícias históricas*, 1:30 (with thanks to Dauril Alden).

182. Brazilian health authorities sometimes treated it as an "epidemic" and accordingly quarantined ships arriving with slaves suffering from it: e.g., Manoel Lopes de Almeida, ed., *Notícias históricas de Portugal e Brasil* (Coimbra: n.p., 1961), 1:30. The date of the arrival of the Angola vessel in question was 1719, precisely at the end of a severe western central African drought and in the midst of a genuine epidemic of smallpox.

183. A connection made in the 1780s by Mendes, "Discurso academico ao programma," in Carreira, "Companhias pombalinas de navegação," p. 442, if tragically interpreted as a consequence of drinking too much water. See also Robert Dirks, "Social Responses during Severe Food Shortages and Famine," p. 24; idem, "Slaves' Holiday," *Natural History* 84, no. 10 (1975): 58.

alyzed dread that their cannibal masters fed them only to fatten them up for the slaughter.[184]

Survival was thus precarious and conditions miserable under the best of circumstances at sea, but bad weather brought unrelenting misery. One slaver of the 1820s was struck twice by lightening in twenty-seven successive days of squalls at sea, each bolt killing two slaves. On the second occasion, the main mast fell away, useless. The vessel, which had left the African coast (Cameroon) hastily and was consequently ill-prepared for such emergencies, made slow headway from that point on. Sickness broke out among the officers and crew, and the slaves refused to eat the manioc meal and salt beef brought from Brazil, allegedly being accustomed to rice and yams. They finally agreed to consume the manioc flour dry and uncooked, but the change in diet brought dysentery on top of scurvy. The crush below decks was so great that no room remained to separate the well from the sick. Of the 440 slaves aboard at the outset of the voyage, 178 (40.5%) died in sixty-one days.[185] Ships delayed en route put their slaves on half rations, often less than half the way across the ocean, and made for the first Brazilian port where they might find suppliers willing to sell them even rotten, insect-infested flour at high prices.[186]

One Brazilian critic's description of conditions on the Mozambique run can be taken to apply generally:

> Suddenly the weather closes in, and the seas rise so high and so strongly that the ships must obey the waves, sailing at the mercy of the winds without true course or control. It is then that the din from the slaves, bound to one another, becomes horrible. The clanking of the irons, the moans, the weeping, the cries, the waves breaking over one side of the ship and then the other, the shouting of the sailors, the whistling of the winds, and the continuous roar of the waves. The tempo of the storm increases, and with it the danger. A portion of the food provisions is heaved overboard, and also other objects, to save the cargo and the crew. Many slaves break legs and arms; others die of suffocation. One ship or another will break apart from the fury of the storm, and sink. Another drifts on, dismasted, its rigging ruined by the will of the ocean, unable to heed the helm, on the verge of capsizing.[187]

Catastrophes like these, storms and delays en route, were not typical enough to force slavers to change their methods of conducting the trade, but they

---

184. A fear reported aboard a ship reaching Buenos Aires from Mozambique in 1804: Andrews, *Afro-Argentines of Buenos Aires*, p. 26.

185. Campbell and Raffell to Canning, Sierra Leone, 31 March 1827, PRO, FO84/65, fols. 39–42.

186. Corrêa, *História de Angola*, 1:52.

187. Botelho, *Escravatura*, pp. 21–22.

occurred with sufficient frequency that they caused the deaths of thousands of slaves in the century, perhaps 5 percent overall, or nearly 1,000 per year in the higher-volume years after 1770.

Adding the sheer accidents, as well as beatings and whippings to enforce discipline, to water withheld as "medical treatment" to slaves losing fluids through every orifice and pore in their bodies, aggravated further by purgatives, bleedings given to slaves already too weakened by malnutrition to move, and other conditions contributing to slave mortality leaves one wondering how so many could survive the middle passage, not to mention how even a few marshaled the courage, against all odds, to revolt and to seize ships at sea to return alive to the mainland. It could have expressed only life-and-death desperation at that stage of the voyage. Other slaves broke away from their captors during their brief interludes above decks to leap suicidally into the sea.[188] Death by drowning, they must have hoped, would take them back to ancestors at home, where the ocean, they rightly believed, was the abode of the dead.[189]

Morbidity and Mortality at Sea

The complex causes of seaborne morbidity and mortality produced overall levels of sickness and death that rose and fell slightly with the season but varied much more from year to year with drought and disease conditions in Africa. A middle range of variation depended on general levels of demand for slaves. In the long run, over the course of the entire eighteenth century, fundamental improvements in the technology and organization of slaving contributed to a declining secular trend in deaths among the slaves.

Deaths in the worst years at the beginning of the century attained truly catastrophic levels, probably averaging in excess of half of all the slaves shipped. By the 1820s, similarly elevated losses on the Angolan run hit mostly the isolated ships that arrived after extreme delays at sea. Average deaths had fallen well below 10 percent on a yearly basis by then, and the slaves on most vessels suffered mortality in the range of 3 to 5 percent. Time-specific mortality rates declined slightly less rapidly, since part of the improvement apparent in terms of percentage losses resulted from the shorter times that slaves remained on board the ships by the 1820s compared to their predecessors a century before. Even if the same number of slaves had continued to die each day, the percentage of those perishing

188. Mendes, "Discurso academico ao programma," in Carreira, "Companhias pombalinas de navegação," p. 451.
189. Cf. Piersen, "White Cannibals," pp. 150–51, 153.

would have gone down, perhaps as much as 30 percent, because of shorter times spent at sea.

At the base of the multiple factors contributing to death rates aboard the *tumbeiros* was the quiet constant, the chronically small rations of food and water that the captains supplied. Though often buried beneath more arresting proximate causes of death as various as epidemics, unfavorable weather, and tight-packing, inadequate provisions seldom contributed actively to fatalities by themselves but often allowed lingering injuries to the slaves prior to boarding—the inherent strains of kidnapping or seizure, travel under premodern conditions, near-starvation, exposure to unfamiliar lowland and coastal disease environments, extremely unsanitary living conditions in Luanda's barracoons, unaccustomed foods, and fear of whites—to take their lethal tolls.[190] Provisioning became critical only in the modest number of instances where sheer incompetence, accidents, or adverse weather prevented the timely arrival of a ship at its destination or at some reprovisioning point along the way. Though outright brutality had its place among the unvarying causes of background mortality, it was not a major one. Tight-packing *per se,* within the limited range over which Portuguese and Brazilians practiced it, made only indirect contributions to slave mortality, and then principally through the pressures that it put on space for provisions.

To estimate the stable percentage of deaths attributable to these relatively fixed conditions, one may turn to the minimum levels of mortality common aboard Angolan ships reaching Brazilian ports between 1795 and 1830, roughly 2 to 3 percent.[191] Assuming an average voyage of about thirty-five days, percentage losses of that magnitude would equal annual mortality rates of 208.6 to 312.9 per 1,000 per year. As a long-term stable rate it would be directly comparable to the unknown (but expectable) death rates for populations of young adults aged ten to twenty-five in the central African interior. These, according to standard demographic tables, would have lain somewhere between 15 per 1,000 per annum and 30 per 1,000 per annum for a stable population, and the tenfold magnitude of the increase is sufficient to indicate the inherent deadliness of capture and transport, even without attempting to document the assumptions underlying the estimate more precisely. The increase was probably somewhat less in actuality, since the inhabitants of the slaves' homelands were in fact considerably displaced by drought and slaving in the eighteenth and nine-

---

190. Cosme (Pina ed.), "Tractado," pp. 262–68, focused on treatment prior to boarding as the primary contributor to deaths at sea.

191. Klein, *Middle Passage*, pp. 56, 77, 231, 233; further analysis of additional data in Miller, "Legal Portuguese Slaving," pp. 156–60. These "background" mortality levels may have been 5%–10% earlier in the century.

teenth centuries, and so even those who were not enslaved would have endured death rates higher than a model stable population.

A painful variety of ordinarily nonlethal disorders became deadly among malnourished slaves and so contributed to this background mortality on the ships. Not all these complaints were unfamiliar in the villages from which the slaves had come, but the close physical contact into which enslavement threw them and their unhygienic surroundings spread these disorders widely through the decks of the ships. Yaws (or *boubas* to the Portuguese), a nonvenereal form of syphilis, a highly contagious skin ulceration in its most visible aspect, thrived in the warm and moist conditions of the slave decks, and it was one of the most common afflictions reported among the slaves.[192] Other noisome skin conditions, most specifically scabies, were generally lumped indistinctly together as *sarna*.[193] Intestinal parasites *(lombrigas)* of several sorts—including roundworm, hookworms, tapeworms, and threadworms, all debilitating and potentially fatal under conditions of extreme malnourishment—complicated the struggles of the slaves to survive on what they were fed. Combined with dysenteries and other diarrheas, intestinal worms gave rise to one of the most spectacularly repulsive of the afflictions evident to the slavers, the

192. Mendes (Capela ed.), *Memória a respeito dos escravos*, p. 63; Bomtempo, *Compendios*, pp. 200–201. Yaws was a rural form of the same, or a very similar, treponematosis that caused syphilis in urban populations. Syphilis (*morbo galico, lues, sarnas galicas, gôta galica*, etc.) is mentioned in early sources for Angola and by Mendes for the eighteenth century, although its ravages may by then also have been subsumed under the heterogeneous rubric of *sarnas* (see below), or in its manifestations in the nervous system under seizures (epilepsies). See also Matos, *Compêndio histórico*, pp. 334–35; Francisco Guerra, "Medicine in Dutch Brazil, 1624–1654," in E. van den Boogaart, H. R. Hoetink, and J. P. Whitehead, eds., *Johan Maurits van Nassau-Siegen, 1604–1679; A Humanist Prince in Europe and Brazil: Essays on the Occasion of the Tercentenary of his Death* (The Hague: Johan Maurits van Nassau Stichting, 1979), p. 487. Also, for the following discussion: Henry Harold Scott, *A History of Tropical Medicine* (London: E. Arnold, 1939), 2 vols., esp. "The Slave Trade and Disease," 2:982–1010; R. Hoeppli, *Parasitic Diseases in Africa and the Western Hemisphere: Early Documentation and Transmission by the Slave Trade* (Basel: Verlag für Recht und Gesellschaft AF, 1969); Octavio de Freitas, *Doenças africanas no Brasil* (São Paulo: Editora Nacional, 1935); Santos Filho, *História geral da medicina* (and other publications); E. R. Stitt, "Our Disease Inheritance from Slavery," *United States Naval Medical Bulletin* 26, no. 4 (1928): 801–17; especially Kiple and King, *Another Dimension to the African Diaspora*, and other general studies. For yaws among slaves on Jamaican plantations, Michael Craton, "Death, Disease, and Medicine on Jamaican Slave Plantations: The Example of Worthy Park, 1767–1838," *Histoire Sociale/Social History* 9, no. 18 (1976): 248. Mendes (Capela ed.), *Memória a respeito dos escravos*, pp. 55–56, listed maladies discussed in this section as the foremost killers.

193. Mendes (Capela ed.), *Memória a respeito dos escravos*, p. 62; Bomtempo, *Compendios*, pp. 73–75. And, tragically, these skin conditions were blamed for the slaves' known insatiable desire for vinegar, citrus fruits, and other forms of the vitamin C they lacked, which were therefore denied them as pathogenic: Mendes (Capela ed.), p. 64. These conditions were also believed to be a reaction to quinine, and thus a case was mobilized against its use in treating (malarial) fevers: Azeredo, *Ensaios sobre algumas enfermidades*, pp. 22, 84–85.

mal do bicho (also *bicho de cu* or *de culo,* and *maculo*), in which prolonged suffering from these afflictions terminated in gangrenous rectal and anal prolapse.[194] Contemporary descriptions of these maladies, and others,[195] uniformly specified symptoms of advanced malnutrition, even if the slaves' simultaneous suffering from most, or all, of them together made it impossible for physicians of the time to distinguish nutritional deficiencies from the fevers and fluxes also present. The slavers thus continued in the ignorance, racism, and fatalism that permitted slaves to die from what even an enlightened turn-of-the-century governor termed "molestia natural que na mão dos homens não esteja prevenir, nem remediar"—natural afflictions beyond the reach of man to prevent or cure.[196]

Seasonal variation in mortality evident in detailed records of Angolan ships reaching Rio de Janeiro between 1795 and 1811 attained a noticeable peak between April and August.[197] Arrivals in those months would have corresponded to departures from Luanda and Benguela during the latter part of the rainy season and the beginning of the following dry season, when the fevers known collectively as *carneiradas* raged most destructively.[198] These higher mortality levels also corresponded to the season

194. Mendes (Capela ed.), *Memória a respeito dos escravos,* pp. 56–57, who gives only a vague description of it as *mal de Luanda* (which he, alone, distinguished from scurvy); José Maria Bomtempo, *Trabalhos medicos oferecidos a Magestade do Senhor D. Pedro I, Imperador do Brasil* (Rio de Janeiro: Typographia Nacional, [1825]), pp. 50–51; Joseph François Xavier Sigaud, *Du climat et des maladies du Brésil: ou statistique médicale de cet empire* (Paris: Fortin, Masson et Cie, 1844), pp. 131–32. The offensiveness of the condition has led to much puzzling and to diverse opinions in the modern medical literature; best is Dr. Jaime Walter, "A propósito de uma doença de Angola de há mais de três séculos: doença do bicho ou maculo," *Boletim clínico e estatístico do Hospital do ultramar* 7 (1957), pp. 47–68, who linked it to malnutrition; see also Brásio, "Inimigo dos antigos colonos," in *História e missiologia,* pp. 745–47; Henry R. Carter, *Yellow Fever: An Epidemiological and Historical Study of its Place of Origin* (Baltimore: Williams and Wilkins, 1931), pp. 224–28; Eustaquio Duarte, "Introdução histórica," pp. 440–59, in Simão Pinheiro Morão, João Ferreyra da Rosa, and Miguel Dias Pimenta, *Morão, Rosa, e Pimenta: Notícia dos três primeiros livros em vernáculo sôbre a medicina no Brasil* (Pernambuco: Arquivo Público Estadual, 1956). The affliction was also known under the name *mal do bicho* to the Spanish and the British: Chandler, *Health and Slavery,* pp. 41, 103; Eltis, "Free and Coerced Migration," p. 276.
195. Mendes' list also included colds and coughs (*constipações*) that the slaves remedied with heat; blackouts (*opilações*); other sorts of skin parasites (which he blamed for fevers and chills, i.e., malaria); and undifferentiated swellings. A modern list would distinguish the causes and symptoms differently but not add much to the roll of afflictions.
196. De Mello, 12 March 1799, AHU, Angola cx. 46. Cosme (Pina ed.), "Tractado," p. 264, comments on the generality of this fatalism.
197. The rising mortality from February through June noted by Klein, *Middle Passage,* p. 57, is partially an illusion created by the concentration of Mozambique ships reaching Rio in those months. Since vessels from Mozambique were en route several times as long as the Angola ships, their percentage losses were correspondingly higher and were raised even further by the malnutrition and insufficient water common on that run. The following conclusions are derived from independent port-specific analysis of the same data.
198. Corrêa, *História de Angola,* 1:80; Mendes (Capela ed.), *Memória a respeito dos escravos,* pp. 55–56, for emphasis on the primacy of the fevers as a source of slave suffering; esp. Azeredo, *Ensaios sobre algumas enfermidades,* pp. 1–92 et passim.

with the greatest variability in passage times from Benguela, and hence the greatest risk of delays long enough to occasion critical shortages of water and food.[199] It was a time of year that slavers seemed to avoid throughout the eighteenth century, perhaps to reduce their losses to mortality, if not also the season in which slowed rainy-season movement of slaves through the ports in Angola forced many to miss their intended departure dates. The lowest mortality rates were concentrated on ships leaving Luanda and Benguela at the end of the dry season, from September through about December, when coastal fevers would have been least severe.

Deaths among slaves varied much more widely from year to year than they did seasonally, owing largely to failed rains, population movements within Africa as responses to drought, and the epidemics that also seemed to break out after periods of dryness.[200] Even at the end of the eighteenth century, mortality during the worst epidemic years averaged 15 to 20 percent, approximately three to five times the levels of death experienced in intervening healthful intervals.[201] Principal among the epidemic maladies that afflicted the slaves was smallpox, which spread widely in Africa, especially along the slaving trails, and which seem to have been carried aboard the ships mostly during periods of drought.[202] The Portuguese, who had no very clear notion of contagious infection, also saw other famine- and drought-connected conditions as "epidemic"—particularly scurvy, but also the *banzo* delirium and despair of terminal malnutrition.

Droughts befell eighteenth-century Angolans principally from about 1715 to 1726, with brief intervals of better rains, and from 1785 to 1794, with virtually no relief. Lesser droughts marked nearly every decade except the 1770s, and so no prolonged respite from extreme hunger and epidemic disease broke the tempo of elevated mortality at sea.[203] Waves of slave fatalities recorded for the 1810s and 1820s showed the aftereffects of the great drought of 1785–94 as well as of periods of aridity that recurred in the middle of both of the later decades; but greater attention paid to provisioning the ships after 1813, spreading inoculation against smallpox, and, after about 1819, Jennerian vaccine significantly reduced the annual variation in mortality owing to drought and its associated ills. The persistently lower levels of deaths reported from the Loango Coast, beyond

199. Though not from Luanda. It was a time of year when passages tended to be slightly shorter, which reemphasizes the importance of variability rather than absolute duration of the voyage in contributing to slave mortality.

200. See Miller, "Legal Portuguese Slaving," pp. 156–60, for the port-specific annual figures.

201. Albuquerque, 16 Feb. 1728, AHU, Angola cx. 17, repeated in *parecer* of the Conselho Ultramarino, 16 May 1729, AHU, Angola cx. 18, had estimated losses of three-fourths of all the slaves shipped during the great drought of the early part of the century.

202. See Alden and Miller, "Unwanted Cargoes," for detailed discussion and documentation.

203. Miller, "Significance of Drought, Disease, and Famine."

sheer falsification of the death books and also the better food available to slaves awaiting embarkation there, were surely also a happy result of more regular rains that lessened year-to-year variation in mortality aboard ships sailing from equatorial latitudes.

Mortality among slaves making the Atlantic crossing varied more with African weather conditions, annually and seasonally, than with medium-term changes in American demand for slaves, but deaths at sea rose also when intensified labor requirements in Brazil increased sharply the numbers of slaves embarked over a three- to five-year span. Detailed statistics suggesting such a tendency come from uncharacteristic increases in mortality at the ports north of Luanda in the mid-1810s, and again in the late 1820s. Portuguese slavers moved down to Cabinda from Angola and Benguela in force after 1811 owing to the opening of these ports to slavers from Brazil after British withdrawal from slaving, and deaths rose among the slaves.[204] The same combination of growing volume and rising deaths recurred in the late 1820s at Ambriz and also, again, at Cabinda as slavers scrambled to anticipate the termination of legal slaving.

Higher deaths at sea in periods of rising volume derived from the strain that higher prices and stronger demand placed on African delivery systems. Slaving captains at Cabinda in 1817 found the Africans unable to supply provisions in the quantities they required, and they even sent back up the coast to undernourished Luanda for food.[205] The Portuguese and Brazilians would buy any living, breathing individual at such times,[206] regardless of his or her condition, and heedless, too, of their own ability to carry increased numbers of slaves with safety. Africans would have matched such short-term opportunism and greed by drawing down the reservoir of previously unsalable individuals accessible through established supply systems. Older, younger, less healthy, and more vulnerable people of all sorts would have been started off down the slave trails in these times, and they would have strained the capacity of the existing logistical networks to feed and care for them.

204. Motta Feo e Torres, 18 Jan. 1817, and Mello e Alvim, 27 Jan. 1817, both AHU, Angola cx. 64.

205. Miller, "Legal Portuguese Slaving," pp. 158, 169; see also Chapters 14 and 18 below. It was also a period of considerable drought further south (cf. Miller, "Significance of Drought, Disease, and Famine," esp. pp. 56–57), but shortages at Cabinda are more likely to have been a product of the strain that the growing volume of the trade put on food-supply systems keyed to lower volumes of trade, and possibly also depleted of agricultural laborers sold off into the export slave trade. No similar reservations mitigate the force of the evidence for the late 1820s.

206. As alleged by British consular officials with specific reference to the Mozambique trade, but surely applicable to slaving from Angola; see officials in Rio to Castlereagh, 15 Feb. 1813, in Theal, *Records of the Cape Colony,* 9:181–82: "The Portuguese slave merchants are at present so eager to carry on this trade, in consequence of the increased profit with which it is now attended . . . that they are determined to run all risques."

High prices offered African suppliers would also have supported raids into new areas that, if continued long enough, could turn into a full-scale advance of the slaving frontier zone. The slaves who reached the coast at these times had endured the hardships of war, flight, concealment in the wilderness, and capture. They would have been more susceptible to the hardships of the ocean voyage and would thus have died in greater numbers at sea. Of the four types of variation in mortality—background mortality, gradually declining over the century; seasonal increases and decreases; annual responses to climate; and medium-term changes in volume—the medium-term increases during periods of growing volume are documented only for the 1810s. Another such wave should have appeared in the undocumented early eighteenth century at Luanda, and references to it may indeed occur as the brutalities reported during the intrusion of metropolitan slavers in the 1730s. Their efforts to supply slaves to the Minas gold fields increased trade by about 50 percent. Benguela's dramatic surge in volume late in the century looks more like castoffs and captives created by drought, and hence high mortality there in the late 1790s would illustrate the ravages of malnutrition and smallpox more than demand-stimulated deaths at sea.

Behind all these shorter-term irregularities, mortality in the southern Atlantic followed non-Portuguese branches of slaving in dropping persistently through the entire century.[207] Two mutually contradictory African factors contributed to the downward drift in mortality from Luanda and Benguela, both connected with the movement of the slaving frontier. On the one hand, slaves had to walk farther and farther to the coast as the trade's catchment zone increased in size; and the privations of the trek, malnutrition and the dramatic changes in altitude, food, and disease environments increased the vulnerability of slaves from far inland. On the other hand, the zone of violence decreased in relation to the area well within the slaving frontier, where more highly capitalized and less damaging methods of seizure sent greater numbers of slaves from nearer the coast, who would have reached the sea in better physical condition than the diminishing proportion taken by violence. On balance, slaves boarded the ships in better shape to survive the rigors of the middle passage as the century progressed.

Growing commercial capital committed to maritime slaving from Portugal and Brazil also decreased mortality at sea because it gave the shippers financial responsibility for the slaves' lives. Large metropolitan merchants who bought slaves in Angola after the 1750s and carried them across the ocean in their own ships were the first to decry the brutal and lethal treatment accorded

---

207. E.g., Klein, *Middle Passage,* p. 229, who speaks of the "uniform drop in mortality figures in the period from 1700 to 1830."

slaves by Luanda commission agents and Brazilian shippers with no personal financial stake in the slaves' survival.[208] As slavers based in Brazil joined in the trend toward owning the slaves they carried at the end of the eighteenth century, further pressure arose to apply modern medicine for the benefit of the slavers, even if always propounded in the name of the slaves.[209]

By the time that the Crown imposed British standards of medical care, provisioning, and tight-packing on the slavers in 1813, the consolidated ownership of the entire venture—goods, ships, and slaves all together—very much resembled that of the French and British for the entire preceding century.[210] The entire train of government measures proclaimed after about 1770 certainly reflected the glow of Enlightened humanism in Portugal, but the greater direct interest of metropolitan Portuguese and of well-connected Brazilians in the lives of the slaves backed its application to the trade. The persistently higher losses aboard the ships bringing slaves from Mozambique in the early nineteenth century were partly the result of Brazilian operators being driven out of the less risky Angola trade and off to the remote shores of southeastern Africa, where the British textiles carried by Portuguese shippers still could not compete with cottons delivered direct from India before 1830 and where Rio traders smuggling Spanish and Brazilian bullion remained the core of the trade.[211]

Humanitarianism, administrative sophistication, and technological change thus percolated through the Portuguese empire from northwestern Europe after about 1780 in a series of small increments to reduce mortality aboard southern Atlantic slavers. The Luanda public grain market eased provisioning after about 1765. A governor's order introduced new standards of hygiene after 1770, and the colonial government thereafter took over responsibility for inspections formerly left to locals. Improved customs procedures throughout the empire after 1785 made it more and more difficult for slavers to evade legal restrictions on loading and carrying

208. Cf. the precautions ordered by the Pernambuco Company, cited in notes 30, 142, 165, and 169 above. A major source behind Mendes' conviction that greater expenditures on slave welfare would increase returns was Raymundo Jalamá, Pernambuco Co. administrator at Luanda; (Mendes was oblivious to the impossibility of undercapitalized Brazilians' affording such expenses). See also the horrified emphasis on the same theme in the "Tractado" of Francisco Damião Cosme (Pina ed.), also an associate of the metropolitan interests affiliated with the companies and with Gov. Sousa Coutinho, whose *portaria* of 1770 initiated the turn toward closer government regulation of the slavers' treatment of their slaves.

209. Culminating in the *alvará* of 1813 (Vianna, "Humanitário alvará"), shortly after Portuguese merchant houses associated with the royal court gained a stake in the matter through their reestablishment in Rio de Janeiro.

210. The concern for slave welfare among the British and the French was noticeably more intense than in the Portuguese trade long before the 1810s; e.g., see Stein, *French Slave Trade*, pp. 95–107, where the emphasis on sanitation, recreation, and nutrition was strikingly greater than that aboard the ships leaving Luanda and Benguela at the same time.

211. See the distinct regional specializations even among the largest Rio traders, 1825–30, in Klein, *Middle Passage*, p. 82; the point requires a great deal of additional research. Cf. Chapter 14 following.

the required provisions for the slaves. Lisbon tightened its authority at Benguela in many ways from the 1790s on. After 1810, increased freight charges for shippers and higher fees allowed to commission agents in Africa for the slaves' *sustentos* eased the economic pressures that were behind the worst abuses. By the early nineteenth century, these new initiatives extended even into the field of public health. Trained physicians began to influence policy with regard to the trade in Africa and Brazil, and surgeons backed up chaplains on the ships.[212]

Actual applications of new medical technology known to be effective against tropical diseases also came along, though more slowly. The Portuguese understood, in a confused way, the value of quinine against "fevers" and took the bitter medicine themselves, but they did not administer it to slaves, whose fevers were believed to arise from causes congenital to their race.[213] The value of fresh fruits and vegetables in combating scurvy was also appreciated in some circles, but fresh produce was extremely difficult to supply to slaves at sea, and in any case fruits and vegetables were administered not as prophylactics but only as remedies, after vitamin deficiencies had manifested themselves in gross form. Their use was nonetheless spreading by the 1790s.[214] Inoculation against smallpox, used on

212. James Goodyear, "The Slave Trade, Public Health, and Yellow Fever: The Image of Africa in Brazil" (Paper presented to the annual meeting of the American Historical Association, Washington, D.C., 1982); Santos Filho, *História geral da medicina;* Leonidio Ribeiro, *Medicina no Brasil* (Rio de Janeiro: Imprensa Nacional, 1940). Though the efficacy of early nineteenth-century medicine and hygiene should not be overestimated, government regulations stressed the presence of trained surgeons on the slavers, rejection of diseased slaves at the time of boarding, isolation of slaves who became ill at sea, and quarantine of those who were sick upon arrival at Brazil.

213. Derived from a hot-cold distinction in physiologies, with whites injured by heat upon which Africans thrived. E.g., Azeredo, *Ensaios sobre algumas enfermidades.* Quinine was a highly controversial remedy for "fevers" until well into the nineteenth century; it was administered in the form of powdered chinchona bark and as a patent medicine, *agoa da Inglaterra* (the "English water"), an infusion of the bitter powder in wine. In addition to Azeredo, who was a great supporter of quinine (as a tonic, administered in the remissions between periods of high malarial fever), see Bomtempo, "Memoria sobre algumas enfermidades . . . ," in *Trabalhos medicos,* against its overuse in Angola, and Moreira, "Memoria sobre as molestias," pp. 128–39, who favored bleeding over quinine. On the *agoa da Inglaterra,* see Augusto d'Esaguy, *Breve notícia sobre a escola medica de Luanda* (Lisbon, 1951), *separata* from *Imprensa médica* (Lisbon); Luis de Pina, "Notas para a história médica nacional ultramarina: a água de Inglaterra em Angola," *Jornal do médico* 1 (1940): 5–6.

214. But also proscribed as part of a general avoidance of substances regarded as "acid" (and therefore "hot"). Conditions were much better in the India trade: José Alves de Lima (captain of the fragata *Nossa Senhora Senha de França,* in Rio), 7 July 1770, AHU, Angola cx. 32; Joaquim José Monteiro Torres (captain of the nau *Medusa,* in Benguela). For Angolan slavers, see AHMF, Benguela *copiador,* letter of 4 July 1777, fol. 1; Azeredo, *Ensaios sobre algumas enfermidades,* pp. 45–46, where the emphasis on the value of fresh fruits and vegetables was much more on prescription than application. Fruits and vegetables were conspicuously absent from the recommendations on food contained in government measures. Confused notions still prevailed among the slavers, who attributed scurvy to humidity, chill air, inaction, excessive salt in the diet, and so on: Matos, *Compêndio histórico,* pp. 334–35; Bomtempo, *Compendios,* pp. 201–3. Treatment was limited to relief of these "causes" and to useless administrations of quinine, tobacco, etc.

some French and British slavers after outbreaks of the disease to stop its spread rather than as a preventative, came late and only sporadically to the Portuguese trade, and then mostly in Mozambique rather than Angola. Jennerian vaccination, when it finally reached Angola in the 1820s, had a much greater impact on reducing mortality rates.[215] The post-1811 shift in slaving from the arid southern areas around Benguela toward the better-watered coasts north of Luanda generally improved the nutritional status of the slaves and thus quite fortuitously contributed at least as much as any other single medical factor to the generally low losses recorded by the end of the 1820s.

Behind all of these slight lessenings of the slaves' burdens lay increased prices for labor in Brazil during the American colony's post-1770s agricultural "renaissance." Shippers carried more goods to Africa to buy slaves at higher costs, thus making it impossible to buy as many slaves per unit of cargo- and water-carrying hold space as earlier in the century. Higher profit margins enabled both shippers and slave buyers better to afford the luxury of saving their slaves' lives. The appearance of the specialized *bergantim* as the main type of slaving vessel in the period from 1800 to 1830 may also have had salutary effects, by providing more nearly adequate hold space for provisions without sacrificing speed. The introduction of copper-sheathed hulls after abolition of the British trade in 1808 would have marginally lowered average sailing times.[216] In all, total slave mortality at sea dropped irregularly from something like 25 to 30 percent early in the eighteenth century to 10 to 15 percent by the end of the eighteenth century and finally to 5 to 10 percent by the 1820s.[217]

Even the relatively low average losses during the final years of the legal trade, restated on an annual basis, amounted to mortality rates above 500 per 1,000 per year during the five weeks or so that slaves spent at sea. It was a figure anywhere from fifteen to thirty times the expectable mortality rate among a stable population of similarly aged individuals in

---

215. Alden and Miller, "Unwanted Cargoes."

216. Though the abandonment of the short crossing from the Mina Coast and the turn to the long Mozambique route around the Cape of Good Hope lengthened the average voyage of slavers from other parts of Africa and hence raised overall losses among the total range of slavers reaching Brazil.

217. The indications are scattered and of problematic significance. Seventeenth-century allowances for mortality on Spanish *asiento* contracts were in the range of 30%. The Maranhão Company experienced nearly 20% losses on the rather longer route to northern Brazil in the 1760s and 1770s, and a proposal for a chartered company in the 1770s estimated about 15% losses at sea. During the epidemics at the end of the eighteenth century, the casual estimate was about 25%, but the reported deaths by 1795–1810 on the Rio crossing were 8%–10% overall. By 1825–30, losses from Cabinda were about 3% and those from Luanda and Benguela about 7%. In addition to Miller, "Legal Portuguese Slaving," and Klein, *Middle Passage,* see Carreira, "Companhias pombalinas de navegação," pp. 303, 311, 366, 374 et passim, João Victo da Silva, n.d. (ca. 1792), AHU, Angola cx. 42; Correa de Araujo, 12 April 1801, AHU, Angola cx. 51.

Africa. And those who survived were described as crippled, covered with mange, losing their hair, emaciated in frame, suffering from fevers and dysenteries, often barely alive. On the European side, though slaving remained a notoriously risky investment, prices had risen high enough and mortality had dropped low enough in the Angolan trade that southern Atlantic slaving attracted competitors from Brazil and backers from Portugal and England who, fifty years before, would not have contemplated owning dying people in such large numbers.

Conclusion: Mortality in Comparison

Mortality along the path, in the barracoons, and during the middle passage thus rose above even that experienced during frequent times of drought, warfare, famine, and epidemics characteristic of the disrupted parts of the southwestern central African mainland, though for some of the people from these troubled regions capture and removal changed the nature of the risks as much as it raised them. Compared to the stability of rural life in well-watered valleys ruled by political regimes large enough and powerful enough to protect their subjects from such violence, the experience of enslavement radically lowered life expectancies.

The whole of the multiple causes behind slave mortality was greater than the sum of the individual factors contributing to it. Shortages of water on the ships would have been less lethal without the dysenteries that arose from bad food at sea or the woeful sanitary conditions in shore barracoons. Droughts in Africa would, in all likelihood, have been less destructive had it not been for resettlement of refugee and slave populations that attended slaving violence and trade-based political regimes. Brazilian ship operators would not have had to cut rations of water and food if metropolitan pressures working through the Portuguese imperial system had not reduced their freight revenues below the point where they could afford to carry slaves safely. Well-intended medical intervention inadvertently prescribed remedies—beyond extensive bleedings that further weakened starving slaves, and highly toxic mercury-, arsenic-, and opium-based concoctions—that did nothing to cure the condition for which they were prescribed and surely killed many patients unfortunate enough to attract the ministrations of physicians. Deaths at each stage of the journey resulted from accumulated prior hardships that the parties then in charge of the slaves could not have influenced, even if they had possessed the technical and financial means to do so.[218]

218. Recent work on other parts of the slave trade has included a similar emphasis on pre-embarkation influences on slave mortality at sea: see Eltis, "Free and Coerced Migrations," pp. 275 ff.; Chandler, *Health and Slavery*, p. 262.

A rising and then falling curve of slave mortality emerges from this complex combination of factors contributing to death rates among slaves on their way to Brazil. While not ascertainable in exact detail, it must have possessed the general shape produced as Figure 11.1. A background mortality of 15–30 per 1,000 per annum would have jumped sporadically to 90 per 1,000 in the process of enslavement. Death rates then rose quickly into the range of 300–500 per 1,000, lower in the well-watered north than in the dry south, as the slaves started to move west. Peaking above 500 per 1,000 as the slaves reached the barracoons from Luanda south, though significantly less along the Loango Coast, mortality then leveled off and may even have begun to decline on the middle passage. In good years, deaths could be significantly less, though in time of drought and epidemics slaves died in numbers even above these average levels.

Once the slaves landed in Brazil, dealers there could expect to see another 4 to 10 percent of the slaves perish in the weeks before sale, depending on their condition upon arrival.[219] For slaves destined to continue on to other markets in the interior before final sale, the journey could last months longer, and perhaps 10 to 15 percent of those who started that last trek would succumb along the way.[220] Even after masters had settled the survivors on plantations and elsewhere in Brazil, the elevated death rates associated with "seasoning" continued to claim slaves in numbers above losses expectable in a stable population. At a rough guess, the annual mortality rates typical of settlement in America began as high in the Brazilian merchants' slave pens as they had been at sea, dropped to an average of around 200 per 1,000 per annum in the first year of "seasoning," to 125 per 1,000 per annum in the second year, below 100 per 1,000 per annum in the third, and leveled out at 30 per 1,000 per annum by the fifth year to produce the ten- to fifteen-year life expectancy often assumed for the Brazilian slave population as a whole.[221] Common esti-

219. See Appendix B.
220. Taunay, *Subsídios,* pp. 278–79, summarizes the records of a slave dealer taking Rio slaves out into the surrounding plantation areas from 1818 to 1830 which shows losses of 12 out of 55 (21.8%) and 25 out of 228 (11.0%) over an unspecified period of time. On the long boat ride and walk from Buenos Aires to Potosí in 1731, 70 of 408 died in one party, or 17.2%, and in another that same year 41 of 285 died in 68 days, for a loss of 14.4% at a rate (773/1,000/annum)—about twice the rate in the slave pens of the ports: Palmer, *Human Cargoes,* p. 71; Scheuss de Studer, *Trata de negros,* p. 223. From Cartagena to the interior of Gran Colombia losses ran as much as 20% over unknown periods of time: Chandler, *Health and Slavery,* p. 263.
221. Mircea Buescu, *300 anos de inflação* (Rio de Janeiro: APEC, 1973), p. 110 et passim; also Conrad, *World of Sorrow,* p. 17. Karasch, *Slave Life,* p. 98, Table 4.5, calculated deaths among a highly selected group of new arrivals in Rio in the 1840s. She found 8.5% dying in the first year, 7.2% (but 7.9% of the survivors) in the second, and 4.8% (or 5.7% of the survivors) in the third, for a total of 20.5% in three years. The year-specific mortality rates of 85/1,000, 79/1,000, and 57/1,000 average 73.7/1,000/annum. According to Conrad, *World of Sorrow,* p. 17, an 1843 British report put losses in the Brazilian interior at similar levels: 8% in the first year and 6% in the second.

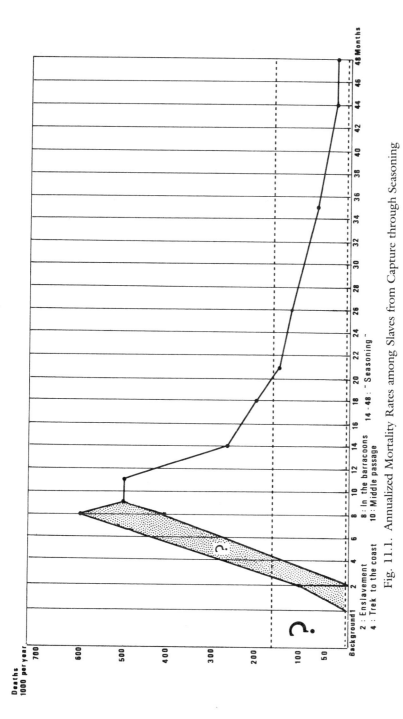

Fig. 11.1. Annualized Mortality Rates among Slaves from Capture through Seasoning

mates of slave mortality in Brazil and the Caribbean center on about 3 percent per year in the long run, up to twice the level that a stable African population of comparably young adults might have suffered, but surely not much greater, if at all, than would have prevailed among a population including the growing proportions of infants and the elderly that actually prevailed on the western side of the Atlantic.[222]

Summarizing the losses late in the history of the trade as a generously estimated 10 percent fatalities in the process of capture, 25 percent of the remainder lost on the way to the coast, 10 to 15 percent in the port towns, another 10 percent at sea, and perhaps 5 percent during the process of sale in Brazil, the total would compound to deaths in excess of half the people originally captured in Africa. The first year of "seasoning" in America would have claimed about 15 percent more. Of 100 people seized in Africa, 75 would have reached the marketplaces in the interior; 85 percent of them, or about 64 of the original 100, would have arrived at the coast; after losses of 11 percent in the barracoons, 57 or so would have boarded the ships; of those 57, 51 would have stepped onto Brazilian soil, and 48 or 49 would have lived to behold their first master in the New World.

Mortality in the range usually assumed would conform to the commonly cited estimates of seasoning losses in the vicinity of one-half to one-third of all arrivals in the first 4–5 years. For similar estimates in the Caribbean, see Jean Fouchard, "The Slave Trade and the Peopling of Santo Domingo, 1764–1793," in UNESCO, *The African Slave Trade from the Fifteenth to the Nineteenth Century* (Paris: UNESCO, 1979), p. 271; Bean, *Trans-Atlantic Slave Trade*, p. 221; Chandler, *Health and Slavery*, pp. 137 ff.; Craton, *Sinews of Empire*, p. 194. Kenneth F. Kiple, *The Caribbean Slave: A Biological History* (New York: Cambridge University Press, 1984), pp. 64–65 ff., treats the seasoning period in the Caribbean as three years and summarizes haphazard data there as indicating that about a fourth of the slaves died in that period. Death rates were higher on mines and plantations and lower in cities, owing to the tendency to concentrate acculturated, "seasoned," and creole slaves in urban areas.

222. Sigaud, *Discurso sobre a statistica*, p. 13, and *Du climat et des maladies*, p. 138, discussing the 1820s in and around Rio de Janeiro, estimated about 20% mortality per year for all blacks, free and slave, and cited official figures running in the vicinity of 3% for the adjacent highland regions of Minas Gerais and São Paulo. Bahians figured they needed replacements at about 3% annum to maintain a stable slave population of 200,000 late in the eighteenth century: Aguiar, intro., "Discurso preliminar," p. 143. The crude mortality rate in Pernambuco from 1774 until well into the nineteenth century (for a population not defined) was 3.3%, and slaves in Maranhão in 1798 had died at 2.7% per annum: Stuart B. Schwartz, "Indian Labor and New World Plantations: European Demands and Indian Responses in Northeastern Brazil," *American Historical Review* 83, no. 1 (1978): 67. The 3% figure for slaves was general throughout the Americas by the late eighteenth century: Curtin, in Curtin, Feierman, Thompson, and Vansina, *African History*, p. 220. Seventeenth-century mortality had been perhaps twice as high; Mattoso, *Etre esclave au Brésil*, p. 61, cites a 6.3% replacement rate on Brazilian plantations before 1640; cf. Antonil's famous estimate of 7% replacement rate in sugar areas, ca. 1700, as cited, e.g., in Taunay, *Subsídios*, p. 173. Kenneth F. Kiple, *Blacks in Colonial Cuba, 1774–1899* (Gainesville: University Presses of Florida, 1976), p. 53, has the same figure for nineteenth-century Cuban sugar plantations, then at an early stage of development comparable to those of Brazil in the seventeenth century; for other parts of the island Kiple cites the standard 3% mortality.

The full "seasoning" period of 3–4 years would leave only 28 or 30 of the original 100 alive and working. A total "wastage" factor of about two-thirds may thus be estimated for the late-eighteenth-century Angolan trade, higher earlier in the trade, probably a bit lower by the 1820s, with slaves from the wetter equatorial latitudes always showing a lower mortality rate than those from Luanda and Benguela.[223] As such, even at that late date it was a number amply large to rivet the fatalistic attention of the slavers in the Angolan trade and the merchants supporting them, to force all involved to stress speed, and to prompt the wealthy and powerful to organize its financial structures so as to avoid, where they could, the risks and costs resulting from mortality they could not control. It was literally, and sadly, true that "if few die the profit is certain, but if many are lost so also is their owner."[224]

Allocating mortality to the separate owners of the slaves, African producers using commercial techniques could expect something much less than the 10 percent overall losses attributed to capture. Indeed, many of the deaths associated with enslavement and concentration of the slaves in the markets they turned back on the captives' relatives and patrons in the lineages. Warrior kings could expect many more. Capitalism required higher investments of goods, but it lowered the risk of mortality among the slave returns.

The Vili and other traders who ran the northern trade diasporas channeling slaves down to the Kongo and Loango coasts kept the slaves in their pipelines dispersed and relatively well fed, and so their losses would have been significantly lower—perhaps by half to two-thirds—than those estimated for the slaving trails feeding Luanda. The Ovimbundu traders who worked the sandy plains east of the Kunene after the middle of the eighteenth century would have had even higher costs attributable to slave mortality. But the southern transporters owned the slaves for only the leg of the journey from the Zambezi and Kasai headwaters to the central Angolan plateau, rather than from the interior to the coast as in the case of the Vili.

The Luso-Africans of Angola assumed the remainder of the risk from the Kwango to the sea, which they hoped to cover with trading profits from selling their slaves in Brazil. But this strategy meant also that they

223. For the less-well-documented early years of the eighteenth century, fatalities within Africa would have remained much the same. Higher mortality at sea and in Brazil at that time would have brought the overall losses to approximately 70%, only marginally greater than the later figure. Improvements in maritime transport and care of slaves in the New World affected only the 55%–60% of the persons originally enslaved who reached the ships, and thus had a relatively small impact on the overall efficiency of the trade, however much those improvements might have increased the profit margins of the traders and masters who owned the survivors.

224. Silva Lisboa, cited in Salvador, *Magnatas do tráfico negreiro*, p. 104.

owned the captives the longest, and during the most lethal segments of the trajectory—on the trail, in the barracoons, and at sea. The Luso-Africans who assumed ownership at the markets of Libolo, Kasanje, and southern Kongo therefore sustained the greatest losses from slave mortality, the 25 percent on the path to Luanda, the 10 to 15 percent in the coastal port, the 10 percent on the late-eighteenth-century middle passage, and the last 4 to 5 percent before the slaves were sold in Brazil: a compounded total of 35 percent on the average, and easily twice that when epidemics hit.

Lisbon merchants who bought slaves in Luanda, and the Luso-Africans who sold the slaves to Brazilians at Benguela, by a similar series of estimates, would have sustained 20 percent or so in losses (arbitrarily assigning half of the deaths in the barracoons to them). Brazilians who bought slaves at Benguela, and after the 1770s also at Luanda, had to absorb the 20 percent remaining before selling their captives in America. Slaveowners in Brazil would have sustained mortality costs averaging 7 percent or so per year, but they would have enjoyed compensating returns from the slaves' labor for as long as they lived. The Luso-Africans and Brazilian traders had no similar recompense but instead experienced slave mortality as a cost of buying and selling, concentrated in a short few weeks or months that translated to a rate of loss ten to twenty times that of Brazilian masters. The grand financiers of the trade, the exporters of goods in Lisbon, experienced the Brazilian traders' 20 percent mortality costs only when they dared to take title to the slaves themselves. They did so only rarely during the mortiferous first half of the eighteenth century but were able to accept more as deaths at sea and in the American slave pens dropped below 10 percent early in the nineteenth century.

Within Africa mortality increased most among people of fertile or well-watered regions seized through the indebtedness engendered by the Atlantic trade. They suffered indignities, terror, and deprivations unlikely to have affected them under other circumstances, and their short-term odds of survival fell to a fraction, as little as a tenth to a twentieth, of what they might have expected at home. The commercialized zone may have generated slaves at lower mortality cost than did wars of the slaving frontier and the disruptions of drought, but the relative damage to the enslaved was hardly less. However limited a demographic impact slaving might have had on aggregate African populations, and whatever power neighbors and enemies of the enslaved might have gained from the imports they received, captives treading paths toward the west were indeed following the way of death that legend held to lie beneath the sea.

Part 3

Brazil
The Last Stop

12

Trading on the Fringes

The Rise of Brazilian Interests in the Southern Atlantic Trade to the 1770s

Brazilians needed the African slave trade to obtain the black laborers on whom virtually every significant sector of their export economy depended, as historians have often observed. But Brazilian planters and miners, and also residents of the coastal towns who employed slaves, need not, after all, have engaged in slaving for themselves to acquire the workers who planted their cane, dug out their gold, or picked their cotton. Slave trading itself had the additional, and crucial, functions for Brazil of offering planters an outlet for produce unsalable in European markets and replenishing slave labor forces without increasing their already burdensome currency obligations to creditors in Portugal. For merchants in the colony slaving also afforded direct access to northern European and Asian goods otherwise available through Lisbon only at much higher prices and provided an arena in which they could build maritime commercial networks of their own, not so remunerative as the colony's principal trade back to Portugal, but at least partially outside the constraints of an imperial system that otherwise channeled profits into the hands of competing merchants from the metropole.

The sort of people who sought the limited advantages to be found in the African trade merit designation as "Brazilians" already in the eighteenth century, in contrast to the indistinctly broader concept of "Portuguese" that virtually all residents of the colony would have insisted on using to describe themselves at the time. Like the Luso-Africans of Angola, they professed utter loyalty to the Portuguese Crown in Lisbon, and in a narrowly legal sense all were indeed equally Portuguese subjects. Yet in Luanda, Luso-Africans found themselves repeatedly on the opposite side of economic issues from factors representing Lisbon merchant houses, and their protestations of common fealty to the king no more than structured the language in which they argued their deep divisions over the trade before the court.

Analogously divergent interests in the slave trade emerged also on the American side of the Atlantic, essentially according to whether individuals, families, regions, or economic sectors found themselves positioned on the debtor or the creditor side of the colony's financial divide. Though mere residence in Brazil might influence economic and political sympathies, if never one's public loyalty to the king, it did so only to a limited degree. Wealthy commission agents representing Lisbon merchant houses in Brazil, providing credit, and foreclosing on debts owed by Brazilian sugar planters enjoyed preferred positions in the colonial system and sided accordingly with the metropole regardless of the fact that they lived in Bahia or Rio. Other merchants in the same towns, who struggled to live off the interregional coastal trade in provisions and could not break into importing British woolens through Lisbon, had far more American interests and, incipiently, loyalties. To put the contrast between those who shared in the benefits of Portugal's mercantile empire and those who paid its bills in terms of the slave trade, Brazilians who sent slaving ventures out to Angola and distributed new Africans from the three ports of legal slave entry to neighboring captaincies seldom dined at the same table with commission agents handling the import-export trade with Lisbon.

This real, if shadowy, distinction between "Brazilian" debtors and Portuguese creditors was not always much clearer in terms of economic function. The commercial representatives of Lisbon creditors frequently found themselves drawn toward the sugar-planting sector, often at first through marriage to a sugar baron's daughter, later by management of her family estate, and eventually through full legal title to the plantation and—frequently—responsibility for its debts. Owners of large, efficient, and unencumbered estates, few as they were, could invest in slaving ventures to acquire slaves without committing currency reserves, while other planters mired deeply in debt might be forced to buy slaves from their Lisbon creditors at high prices that only increased their obligations to the metropole. The ability of the entire sugar industry to afford its labor costs declined during much of the eighteenth century and then rose later, so that time, too, made a difference in who sat on which side of the colony's financial fence and who might therefore belong among metropolitan creditors or among the colonial "Brazilian" debtors.

If the identities of the debtors thus changed, individually and collectively, there were nearly always discernible groups of people somewhere in Brazil who found the trade in slaves a useful way to recoup, or to gain, fortunes that the Portuguese imperial system otherwise denied them. It was these slavers, the difficulties under which they labored, and their distinctive strategies of buying slaves who constituted the "Brazilian" interest in the Angolan trade. Rival residents of Brazil, mostly immigrant merchants from Portugal but also government officials posted out to the colony and producers more closely oriented to interests based in the mother country, receive due attention in the following chapter as colonial associates of the "Portuguese" interest in the trade.[1]

Brazil: Lodestone of the Eighteenth-Century Empire

By the eighteenth century, Portugal's far-flung sixteenth-century commerce with Asia, Africa, and the Americas had effectively shrunk to the collection of Brazilian captaincies strung out along the Atlantic shore of South America.[2] With its Asian trade all but lost to the British, Dutch, and French and with trade in Africa severely limited by the same foreign competitors, Brazil gained an almost magnetic attraction as a profitable market for Lisbon merchants and their foreign bankers, much more so than African slaving.

The captaincies of Brazil reached from an often disputed southern boundary with Spanish territory somewhere near the Plata estuary to the mouth of the Amazon at the equator. They offered varied economic potential from the metropolitan perspective. Prime grazing lands in the far south supported cattle herds that cowboys—free and slave—culled for hides, tallow, and dried and salted beef. The mountains north and west of Rio de Janeiro—in Minas Gerais and Goiás—proved rich in gold and

1. In Schwartz's felicitous phrase, "the welfare of crown, colony, empire, and society was often used as a banner to drape class motives": *Sugar Plantations,* p. 208.

This chapter does not systematically cite the general authorities on the colonial history of Brazil that support its broad interpretive thrust. Though specialists will immediately recognize how most of my specific conclusions, based largely on Angolan data, match the broader interpretations of many imaginative Brazilianists, I have focused on the commercial and maritime aspects of their story that the entirely appropriate orientation of the national historiography toward Portuguese-Brazilian relations and issues of Brazilian nationalism allows them to bypass without explicit comment. If themes prominent in the Angolan perspective nuance my general summary of eighteenth-century developments in Brazil, I hope the experts will sometimes find these insights at least as stimulating as they may also find them sometimes heterodox.

2. Readers interested in overviews of colonial Brazil less focused on its trade in slaves have two recent and excellent surveys: Lang, *Portuguese Brazil,* and the chapters on Brazil in James Lockhart and Stuart B. Schwartz, *Early Latin America: A History of Colonial Spanish America and Brazil* (New York: Cambridge University Press, 1983). Also see the chapters in the *Cambridge History of Latin America,* ed. Leslie Bethell (Cambridge: Cambridge University Press, 1984), esp. Stuart B. Schwartz, "Colonial Brazil, c. 1580–c. 1750: Plantations and Peripheries," 2:422–99; A.J.R. Russell–Wood, "Colonial Brazil: The Gold Cycle, c. 1690–1750," 2:547–600; and Dauril Alden, "Late Colonial Brazil, 1750–1807: Demographic, Economic, and Political Aspects," 2: 601–60. In many ways, one still cannot do better than to begin with Charles R. Boxer's *The Portuguese Seaborne Empire, 1415–1825* (New York: Knopf, 1969) and *The Golden Age of Brazil, 1695–1750* (Berkeley and Los Angeles: University of California Press, 1962). Schwartz, *Sugar Plantations,* sets a new standard for the single captaincy of Bahia.

Map 12.1. Brazil

diamonds, and the moist coastal plain from Rio all the way north past
Pernambuco held pockets of rich clayey soils well suited to sugar cane. In
the dry backlands of the northeastern captaincies—Espírito Santo, Bahia,
and Pernambuco—still other herds of cattle roamed. The tropical forests
of the far northern territories of Pará, Maranhão, and Ceará behind the
coast running west to the mouth of the Amazon yielded hardwoods, spices,
and dyestuffs also of considerable value to the metropole. These northerly

regions, along with Pernambuco, Paraíba, Rio Grande do Norte, and Piauí, also proved eminently suited to cotton. The labor employed in the export sectors of nearly all these regions came predominantly from the African trade in slaves, especially in periods of growth.

This variety of potential exports was what kept Brazil as a whole continually at the forefront of Portuguese imperial strategies through the profound changes in world economic conditions during the course of the eighteenth and early nineteenth centuries. The old sugar sector, concentrated in Pernambuco, Bahia, and Rio, led the Brazilian economy in the first half of the seventeenth century, but it suffered through a long decline after 1660, broken only when wars in the North Atlantic and slave revolt in France's prime Caribbean sugar island, Saint Domingue, temporarily drove European sugar prices high enough to revitalize Brazil's inefficient cane plantations at the end of the eighteenth century. Gold, first discovered in significant quantities in Minas Gerais in the 1695, took over as the almost bewitching lure for merchants in Portugal through the 1750s, with mining eventually extending to Goiás, Bahia, and other captaincies before production declined in the second half of the century. Tobacco, centered mostly in Pernambuco and Bahia, helped to sustain the lagging sugar regions through most of the eighteenth century and took up some of the slack that spread through the Brazilian economy with the decline of mining in the 1750s and 1760s, for want of a new boom commodity to replace sugar and gold as the exports that paid for the food, clothing, and equipment that Brazilian masters, slaves, and free farmers bought from Portugal.

Cotton came on the scene as Brazil's next commodity savior with the development of industrialized textile production in Britain and disruption of its North American sources by warfare in the Atlantic at the end of the century. Supported also by higher prices for Brazil's other produce and by the beginnings of what would become a nineteenth-century boom in coffee grown mostly in Rio, Minas Gerais, and São Paulo, Brazil resumed its historic role as milch cow to merchants in Portugal in the 1780s. Cotton, supported more and more by coffee and eventually supplanted by it, led the way on through the first three decades of the nineteenth century.

More than anywhere else in the Americas, except for the highly specialized sugar colonies of the Caribbean, economic growth in each of these cases depended on continuous supplies of fresh slave labor from Africa. European Portugal was a small nation with few sons and daughters to send abroad to open these vast American territories. Most Portuguese who went to Brazil resisted manual labor and would, in any case, have been unlikely to work as efficiently under tropical conditions as could slaves imported from Africa. The Indians native to Brazil, though briefly enslaved in the sixteenth century and later pressed into forced labor systems in the northern captaincies, were too few, too hard to control, and too vulnerable to European diseases to supply the labor power needed to support the high growth rates characteristic of the Brazilian export booms. Reproduction among the slaves did not keep up with the demand for hands, owing to high mortality, more males than females in the slave population, and the masters' habit of manumitting females and their Brazilian-born children. Heavy indebtedness among the masters, to be discussed in detail in what follows, also hindered the emergence of a self-reproducing slave labor force. Brazil's economy thus remained largely dependent on inputs of new slaves rather than on locally bred slave workers.

Though at most times slaves entered Brazil legally through only three ports—Salvador in Bahia, Recife in Pernambuco, and the port of Rio de Janeiro on Guanabara Bay—at some periods slavers could also deliver cargoes direct to Santos, the main port south of Rio servicing the São Paulo plateau; to the outpost at Colônia do Sacramento, on the north shore of the Plata estuary; and to the northern towns of Belém (do Pará) and São Luís (do Maranhão). Ships landed slaves direct from Africa in other captaincies only very occasionally. The complex financing of the eighteenth-century trade rendered captains dependent on collecting bills of exchange through merchants established in the legal ports. Few investors in the other smaller coastal towns of Brazil had the means to mount illegal slaving ventures for themselves. Only minor taxes and fees burdened official entries of slaves into Brazil, and so no financial incentive drove shippers to evade the law. As a result, smuggling on the Brazilian side never attained significant levels before illegalization of the trade in 1830, except for occasional efforts to avoid medical quarantines, shipwrecks, and other unusual circumstances. Otherwise, favored importers in Bahia, Pernambuco, and Rio enjoyed a monopoly and sent captive labor on to the smaller outports via the thriving coastal trade. Discussion of the overall structure of Brazilian slaving proceeds coherently in terms of the authorized ports alone.

Brazil's successive cycles of import-dependent economic growth dragged the slave trade as a whole from a focus on the sugar captaincies of Pernambuco and Bahia in the late sixteenth and seventeenth centuries to a concentration at Rio de Janeiro, the principal port serving the booming mining camps in Minas Gerais, in the early eighteenth century. Later in the 1700s, the geographical distribution of imports took on more balanced proportions with the spread of prosperity throughout the colony. Slavers delivered captives to Rio, the emerging commercial entrepôt of the entire colony; to Bahia to toil on sugar plantations and in tobacco fields; and to Pernambuco and the northern captaincies to clear forests and plant cotton bushes. Each new boom drove slave prices to new heights,[3]

---

3. Miller, "Slave Prices."

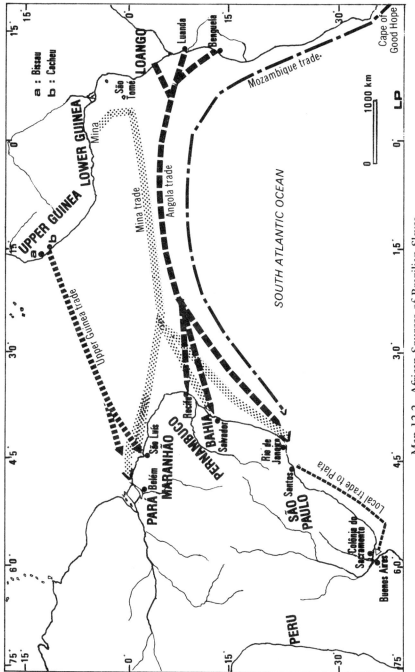

Map 12.2. African Sources of Brazilian Slaves

451

with each emergent export center of the colonial economy draining half-acculturated slaves from the less prosperous captaincies in an intracolonial trade of sometimes major proportions and attracting the bulk of the raw new labor direct from Africa.

Angola, mostly Luanda, had become Brazil's principal source of slaves in the seventeenth century. A smaller trade from a string of Portuguese trading posts along the rivers of Upper Guinea in West Africa also supported the northeastern areas. Toward the 1680s and 1690s, when an unusually severe period of drought and epidemics in western central Africa strained supplies of slaves from Angola, Bahia and Pernambuco opened a new trade to the so-called Mina Coast—the portion of Lower Guinea to the east of the Volta River, known to the British as the Slave Coast, and centered in the area of the modern nation of Bénin.[4] Bahians consolidated their slaving in West Africa during the subsequent gold rush in Minas Gerais and continued to draw most of the captives destined for northeastern Brazil from there until the second or third decade of the nineteenth century.

The late-eighteenth-century rise in demand for new slave labor all over Brazil brought southern Angola, or Benguela, on line as a yet another major supplier. Slaving spread on around the Cape of Good Hope early in the nineteenth century to draw captives also from Portuguese-influenced parts of eastern Africa from Mozambique Island south past Quelimane and the mouth of the Zambezi to Inhambane.[5] When the French and British abandoned their prime slaving territories along the Loango Coast and in the mouth of the Zaire River in the 1790s and 1800s, these regions north of Luanda joined the regular sources of new slaves for the cotton and coffee estates of Brazil. Only the Mina trade, outlawed by international treaties after 1815, declined under threat of seizure by Britain's antislavery West African Squadron. The geographical extent of the African trade, from a pan-Brazilian point of view, grew to its maximum in the 1810s and 1820s, just as the trade passed into the obscurity of outlawry in 1830.

The Marginality of Slaving

From both the Brazilian and Portuguese points of view, legal slaving never assumed much importance relative to the much larger volumes of commerce moving between the American colonies and the metropole. Nor, for that matter, did the African trade amount to much in relation to vibrant

---

4. Of which little can yet be added to the classic study by Verger, *Flux et reflux*.

5. For the statistics, see Klein, *Middle Passage*, pp. 56, 77–78, and Miller, "Sources and Knowledge," appendix, and for a summary of the Mozambique background to the trade, Vail and White, *Capitalism and Colonialism*, chap. 1.

intracolonial transfers of manioc, hides, salt, sugar, and dried meat along the Brazilian coast.[6] The exact proportion of African shipping at Recife in Pernambuco is not known, but the two or three modest-sized Angolan slavers that reached the town each year throughout the first half of the eighteenth century could not have amounted to much more than a tenth of the larger ships bound to and from Europe. A much larger number of small coastal craft brought slaves into Pernambuco from Bahia. Pernambuco also conducted its own independent trade to the Mina and Upper Guinea coasts of West Africa before the late 1750s, though not on a large scale. The chartered Pernambuco Company briefly raised the volume of African shipping at Recife in the 1760s and 1770s to perhaps six or eight ships in active years, but this trade would have declined again by the 1780s. Ten or fifteen slavers headed for Recife each year at the end of the eighteenth century, but agricultural expansion and diversification in the captaincy probably produced corresponding growth in other sorts of shipping that kept the slave trade, even at its height after 1810, to a minor percentage of the total maritime commerce of the port, at least by the measures of volume and freight rates that counted to the shipping industry.[7]

The significance of slaves by value—the aspect of the trade of more direct interest to merchants—was somewhat higher, owing to the greater value of slaves relative to bulk agricultural commodities, but still marginal. Taking a rough average price for white sugar during the period (2$000/ *arroba*, which was 32 lbs. or about 14.5 kg)[8] and estimating Pernambuco exports at about 500,000 *arrobas* per annum,[9] the value of sugar exports alone (1.000.000$000)—not counting tobacco, hides, and cotton—was nearly double the estimated worth of the slaves entering the port (4,000 slaves at ca. 150$000 each = 600.000$000).[10] A rough guess would put

6. In fact, surprisingly lower than the much larger bill paid for expensive illegally imported slaves after 1830, which Luis-Felipe de Alencastro and Robert W. Slenes place as high as 34% of exports between 1841 and 1849: see Alencastro, "La traite nègriére et l'unité nationale brésilienne," *Revue française d'histoire d'outre-mer* 66, 3–4 (nos. 244–45) (1979): 395–419, and Slenes, "Comment" on Amilcar Martins Filho and Roberto B. Martins, "Slavery in a Nonexport Economy: Nineteenth-Century Minas Gerais Revisited," *Hispanic American Historical Review* 63, no. 3 (1983): 571.

7. Carreira, "Companhias pombalinas de navegação," gives annual volumes at Pernambuco in terms of slaves but not directly in terms of ships; see pp. 378–83 for figures offering a good estimate. Ribeiro Júnior, *Colonização e monopólio*, is not at all helpful on this point. For the period after 1810, the estimate is derived from slave import figures in Maurício Goulart, *Escravidão africana no Brasil: das origins á extinção do tráfico* (São Paulo: Livraria Martins, 1949), p. 269.

8. Harold B. Johnson, Jr., "A Preliminary Inquiry into Money, Prices, and Wages in Rio de Janeiro, 1763–1823," in Dauril Alden, ed., *Colonial Roots of Modern Brazil* (Berkeley and Los Angeles: University of California Press, 1973), pp. 274–75; Buescu, *300 anos de inflação*, p. 133; José Jobson de Andrade Arruda, *O Brasil no comércio colonial* (São Paulo: Editora Atica, 1980), Tabela 5.

9. Alden, "Late Colonial Brazil," Table 6.

10. Goulart, *Escravidão africana*, p. 269.

the usual value of Pernambuco's Africa trade at no more than 10 percent of its total maritime commerce, including slaves in transit to the northern captaincies.[11]

At Bahia the overall significance of slaving remained at approximately the same low level as at Pernambuco, and not surprisingly so, given the similar economies of the two sugar captaincies. Angola accounted for far less of the trade at Bahia than the dominant imports from Mina, probably seldom more than 10 to 20 percent. As of the late 1750s, only 8 of 121 mostly medium-sized specialized Bahian merchants (6.6%) claimed Angola as their primary area of operation, compared to 22 (18.2%) trading to Mina and 43 engaged in commerce with Portugal.[12] But the Angola traders probably handled an even smaller percentage of the city's commerce by value or volume than their numbers would suggest, owing to the disproportionately large share of trade held by the general traders engaged with Lisbon. The significance of Africa generally, and of Angola in particular, was greater when viewed in terms of the home fleet of Bahia vessels. In 1775, Bahians owned eighty-eight ships capable of undertaking ocean voyages. Forty-one of those were outside their home port at the moment of enumeration and thus positioned to indicate the distribution of local Bahian ventures at that time. Of the forty-one ships in foreign ports, no less than twenty-four (or 58.5%) were in Africa, and more than half of those (thirteen, 54.1%) were at Luanda or Benguela.[13]

In the early 1780s twenty or so slavers arrived annually at Bahia with perhaps 8,000–10,000 slaves. Of them, a small and decreasing proportion—often only three or four ships per year—came from Angola. Altogether the slavers amounted to half the number of the much more capacious ships going to and from Europe and no more than a tiny fraction of the forty or so small coasting craft that cleared the port each day.[14] The proportion of slavers shrank still more after 1810 at Bahia, as slaving remained in the vicinity of twenty to thirty ships each year, while daily movements of ships through the port rose to 300 or so between 1798 and 1810 and

11. Using Rio prices in Buescu, *300 anos de inflação*, p. 133; quantities from Alden, "Late Colonial Brazil," Table 8; and projecting roughly into the early nineteenth century, Pernambuco's total export trade would have run in the range of 4.000.000$000 to 8.000.000$000 per year.

12. Caldas, "Notícia geral," pp. 317–33. Schwartz, *Sugar Plantations*, p. 344, shows Angolan slaves at 57.7% for the years 1731–33.

13. Lugar, "Merchant Community," p. 60, Table 2.1. The much longer turnaround of ships in the Luanda port more than outweighed the larger size of Angola vessels to reduce the number of slaves they delivered each year at Bahia, compared to the smaller ships on the shorter and briefer ventures to Mina. Schwartz, *Sugar Plantations*, p. 344, has the proportion of Angolan slaves for 1792–1807 as 46.2%, with none at all from Angola in 1808 and small percentages—10% or less—for 1809–10.

14. Silva Lisboa letter, 18 Oct. 1781, *Anais da Biblioteca nacional do Rio de Janeiro* 32 (1910): 504.

to higher numbers after that.[15] Official trade balances from Bahia for 1798–1810 leave the impression that the value of the slave trade approximated only 5 to 6 percent of Bahian exports and accounted for 18 to 20 percent of imports.[16] Yet the significance of this small trade for certain sectors of the Bahian economy—the tobacco growers in particular—was rather larger, and the locally based shipping industry found it absolutely vital.

Rio de Janeiro, late colonial Brazil's largest port, was also the Brazilian city where slaving held the least prominent position in the overall commercial structure. But, paradoxically, slaving there was probably most important to local merchants by the end of the eighteenth century. One must assume that imports of labor for Minas Gerais must have made slaving more significant to Rio-based traders before 1750 or 1760 than it became later,[17] since a metropolitan-dominated transit trade in slaves, foodstuffs, and equipment to Minas Gerais occupied a more prominent position in the movement of the port in the first half of the century than local imports and exports based on the urban economy of the city and sugar from its immediate hinterland.[18] Ships committed to the Angolan trade might have exceeded a quarter to a third of the total moving through the port of Rio during the years of the gold rush. Between twenty and forty Rio vessels reached Lisbon in the years of heaviest trade in the great annual fleets, to which shipping between Brazil and Portugal was restricted before 1763, while ten, mostly smaller, Rio vessels were appearing at Luanda to take on slaves.[19] However, as the local Rio economy grew and diversified after 1760 and as the relative volume of the labor moving through the city toward Minas declined,[20] slaves became less important in the overall commercial balance.

By the time the viceregal bureaucracy moved to Rio from Bahia in 1769, the prominent Carioca merchants were mostly factors of Lisbon houses not directly engaged in slaving. The larger *comerciantes,* probably

15. Lugar, "Merchant Community," pp. 76, 78, 85, Tables 2.4, 2.5, 2.8; Luccock, *Notes on Rio de Janeiro,* p. 628, Table V; Spix and Martius, *Viagem pelo Brasil,* 2:133.

16. Lugar, "Merchant Community," p. 106, Table 2.18, making a rough allowance for wax, ivory, gold, and other commodities reaching Bahia from Africa, aside from slaves. For 1797, see Verger, *Flux et reflux,* p. 55, no. 3.

17. Documentation for Rio before the 1760s is very sparse. One therefore eagerly anticipates the results of the research in the Pinheiro papers (cf. Lisanti, *Negócios coloniais*) of William Donovan of the Johns Hopkins University. The hypotheses inferred here regarding the commercial history of Rio in the early eighteenth century will surely receive much-needed discussion in Donovan's work.

18. Brown, "Internal Commerce," chap. 1 for background.

19. Virgílio B. Noya Pinto, *O ouro brasileiro e o comércio anglo-português, uma contribuição aos estudos da economia atlântica no século XVIII* (São Paulo: Nacional, 1979), pp. 137–84.

20. The estimates of later Minas imports from Rio in Martins Filho and Martins, "Slavery in a Nonexport Economy," p. 543, Table III, probably overstate the volume of continuing imports after mid-century, owing to the authors' neglect of local slave reproduction.

agents of the Lisbon firms, had 98 establishments of a total of some 2,093 enumerated in 1779. Only 34 establishments (or 1.6% of the total) specialized in the sale of slaves,[21] although a good many other general merchants handled the complex arrangements necessary to get slaves from Africa into the hands of these (retail?) specialists. If Rio took 8,000 slaves in an average year at about that time, an average specialist would have handled fewer than 250 slaves per year, or hardly more than one for each working day. The typical large *comerciante* would have processed papers attending the sale of only one or two slaves per week.

By 1791, only 16 of the 625 vessels entering the Rio port (or 2.6%) came from Africa, although they represented more than a quarter (28.6%) of the 56 transatlantic clearances. Figures for scattered years later in that decade occasionally ran higher (46.5% of ocean crossings in 1793, 35.8% in 1796, 27.8% in 1798), but they were relatively small.[22] Rio's exports to Angola and Benguela totaled only 5.3% of all exports by value in 1796, heavily concentrated in sugar and *gerebita*, hides, and foodstuffs.[23] Rio's export tonnage to Europe exploded after 1809, so that even the increased African cargoes pouring into Rio between 1813 and 1817 amounted only to approximately 4 percent of the shipping space on Portuguese vessels alone, which in turn paled in comparison to the trade carried in British bottoms. In 1816, ships arriving from Africa numbered slightly more than half the national vessels inbound from Europe, less than a fifth of the foreign vessels calling at Rio, and about the same number as the coasting craft from the Plata.[24] By 1822–23, 114 out of 506 (or 22.5%) of the Portuguese transoceanic ship movements at Rio were heading to or from Africa, with an increasing proportion of those going to Mozambique rather than Angola. Counting foreign ships, the proportion of Africa ships dropped to 114 of 1,739, or 6.6 percent.[25]

By no measure did slaving occupy a prominent place in the commerce of any of Brazil's three main slaving ports. The big general traders supplying Portuguese produce to Brazil concentrated on olive oil, wine, dried codfish, sausages, preserves, and other national and regional specialties prized by the commercially consuming urban public, mostly of metropolitan background or, during the height of the gold rush, immigrants in

21. Lobo, "Comércio atlântico," p. 80.
22. Ibid., pp. 72, 74, 84–85. Lobo's figures do not seem entirely consistent. Cf. her source for 1763, in the *Revista do Instituto Histórico e Geográfico Brasileiro* 66 (1883): 197–204. See also Anne W. Pardo, "A Comparative Study of the Portuguese Colonies of Angola and Brazil and their Interdependence from 1648 to 1825" (Ph.D. diss., Boston University, 1977), p. 106; and Bauss, "Rio de Janeiro," pp. 106–7, for 1798–1801.
23. *Revista do Instituto Histórico e Geográfico Brasileiro* 66 (1883): 197–204.
24. Luccock, *Notes on Rio de Janeiro,* pp. 605–28, Tables I–V; cf. Lugar, "Merchant Community," p. 85, Table 2.8.
25. AHMAE, C.C., Rio de Janeiro, 2 (1821–24), fols. 95, 105, 118, 143–44, 161, 171.

the gold fields of Minas Gerais. Even more important was the trade in textiles from Europe, in large part cheap woolens and linens, and in cottons from Asia for the slaves and poorer free people of the captaincies. Some of these fabrics arrived from Portuguese manufactures, but British merchants working through intermediaries in Lisbon financed the bulk of the piece goods trade and naturally sent woolens from the mills of England. Simplifying Brazil's import-export trade enormously, 80 to 90 percent or more of the total consisted in consumer goods and agricultural and mining equipment brought from Europe and in payments sent out in the form of sugar, gold, cotton, tobacco, and coffee. The slave trade was an extremely minor appendage, risky and not especially profitable, for merchants with capital and alternatives.

Exclusive focus on the sequence of colonial export booms slights the perspective of the Brazilian slavers, since it emphasizes the story of the well-placed merchants in Lisbon intending to cash in selectively on Brazilian bonanzas. A partially autonomous colonial economy also operated in Brazil, just as in Angola, and other captaincies continued to import slaves even in times of stagnant exports. It was in these backwaters, from the point of view of the metropole, that the Brazilians found their niche. Brazilian slaving thus assumed the configuration of a prosperous core and a fringe of marginal slave importing areas, where depressed prices for the primary exports made slaves sold against *réis* or crop liens expensive relative to the currency credits, earned only in Europe, available to pay for them.

Slavers preparing to leave Luanda could head for whichever Brazilian port promised the highest *réis* prices to cover currency debts owed from Luanda for imported trade goods. Well-capitalized Lisbon merchants active at Luanda directed their Brazilian strategies toward buying the American colony's leading export, with the supplying of labor from Africa to the favored captaincy of only secondary concern. Selling slaves in the less prosperous peripheral captaincies of the colony was of less than tertiary interest. Lisbon's preoccupation with buying sugar, gold, tobacco, cotton, or coffee nearly always left Brazilians in one captaincy or another, sometimes at Rio and at other times in Bahia, to find African supplies of slaves on their own. Few Lisbon merchants would have chosen Rio in the seventeenth century, for example, when it was still a minor sugar producer whose manioc farmers could hardly meet the high prices that wealthy Bahian and Pernambucan planters could afford to pay for slaves. Cariocas, the people of Rio, in fact relied mostly on local Indians to work their modest enterprises at that time, but prominent landowners also developed their own branch of slaving to Angola. When Rio came to depend on African slaves for its much-expanded labor needs after 1700, other local Rio interests defended this trade stoutly against the big Lisbon factors for the next hundred years. Similarly, as the Bahians loudly complained, the gold rush in Minas Gerais drove prices for slaves so high throughout the remainder of Brazil after about 1710 that the stagnant northeastern sugar industry had to sell excess slaves off to the mines to realize cash and to develop new and cheaper African sources of labor of their own on the Mina Coast, in part to sell for gold in the Rio market (for Minas Gerais) and in part for their own needs.

No similar group of autonomous merchants interested in the slave trade seems to have formed in Pernambuco, even during its century of hard times before 1780. The landed gentry of the captaincy had so successfully dominated late-seventeenth-century military slaving at Luanda through their control of the colonial governor's office that they found themselves on the sidelines when the Angolan wars of conquest flickered out after 1680. When Lisbon reined in self-aggrandizing military governors after about 1720, Pernambuco lost out completely to metropolitan bureaucrats at Luanda who were more and more attentive to the interests of commercial houses in Lisbon. Bahian traders took up the slack in delivering slaves to Pernambuco during the following decades, and Lisbon merchants, always better established at Recife than in other Brazilian ports, seem to have limited the opportunities available to colonial slavers for the remainder of the illegal trade. The northern captaincies, Maranhão and Pará, were too remote, undeveloped, and dependent for local merchants there ever to have contemplated significant independent slaving of their own.

Brazilian ports were not otherwise major bases for metropolitan traders selling goods at Luanda in the eighteenth century, and merchants from Portugal seldom showed their faces at Mina and Benguela. Rio factors for Lisbon principals might reexport wares brought in from Portugal to support African slaving, but mostly on occasions when they needed to dispose of stocks intended for sale in America that they could not get rid of in any other way, and Lisbon ships carrying goods direct to southwestern Africa might call at Brazilian ports as they made the wide westward swing on their usual outbound course. But it is not clear that Portuguese merchants often sent goods on the Brazil fleet to agents in Rio for forwarding to Angola aboard Brazilian vessels engaged in the independent southern Atlantic shuttle trade out of American ports. All of these transshipments through Brazil formed parts of the central metropolitan sector of the trade, quite distinct from the Brazilians' position on its margins.[26]

If wealth, commercial capital, distinguished Lisbon's primary commercial relations with Brazil, poverty and undercapitalization structured the American slavers' much smaller, though grisly, trade with Mina, Luanda,

---

26. Lang, *Portuguese Brazil*, p. 144, and other authorities assume that Lisbon goods destined for Angola passed through merchants in Brazil, but the exact mechanisms of their forwarding to Africa await systematic investigation.

and Benguela. This "Brazilian" interest in African slaving arose in general among planters, merchants (including the shipowners and captains who actually carried the captives), and other colonial debtors forced into slaving in order to survive financially.

Angola in the Brazilian Economy at the Beginning of the Eighteenth Century

By the turn of the eighteenth century, Angolan slaving had entered the throes of a sharp transition away from its late-seventeenth-century orientation toward Bahian and Pernambucan sugar plantations and toward the prominence that Rio de Janeiro would maintain thereafter, first as gateway to the gold and diamonds of Minas Gerais.[27] Rio also served as the principal base for officially tolerated smuggling to the Spanish possessions around the River Plate, became an urban and sugar-growing market in its own right, and finally served the coffee estates in its own hinterland and in neighboring São Paulo.

The preceding fifty years, since Angola's restoration to nominal Portuguese sovereignty after Dutch occupation during the 1640s, had seen a series of Pernambuco-oriented Angolan governors replace the Crown's earlier evangelical policies with local militarism in the wars of conquest that established the eighteenth-century boundaries of the African colony.[28] Authoritarian governors hostile to Lisbon commercial interests and the Luso-Africans had then taken over ownership of most of the slaves sent off to Brazil.[29] The depressed sugar prices of the later seventeenth century encouraged metropolitan merchants, at that time transshipping through

27. See the measures taken to exclude Rio slavers at Luanda in 1656, 1668, and 1674: Taunay, *Subsídios*, pp. 98–99; also *carta regia* of 6 Nov. 1679, *Anais da Biblioteca nacional do Rio de Janeiro* 28 (1906): 211.

28. Mello, *João Fernandes Vieira*, esp. chaps. 6, 7. Vieira was governor in Angola from 1658 to 1661 and retired back to Pernambuco an extremely wealthy man. Also, e.g., the introduction in Rau, *"Livro de Razão."*

29. The seventeenth-century position of Angola in the imperial system has hardly been investigated. During the years of Spanish overrule (1580–1640) Lisbon merchants had bought slaves because they could sell them for silver at authorized ports of entry to Spain's American mainland colonies. Portuguese colonials from Brazil had then secured their foothold in Africa, selling slaves through Rio into the Plata and providing labor for their sugar plantations in the northeast. The Dutch capture of Pernambuco (and Bahia briefly) and then Luanda (1641–48) left the planters and merchants of Rio as the prime candidates to seize the Angolan slave trade for themselves in 1648, in the process of restoring the colony to Portugal. On the Rio position see Sidney M. Greenfield, "Entrepreneurship and Dynasty Building in the Portuguese Empire in the Seventeenth Century: The Career of Salvador Correia de Sá e Benevides," in Sidney M. Greenfield, Arnold Strickon, and Robert T. Aubey, eds., *Entrepreneurs in Cultural Context* (Albuquerque: University of New Mexico Press, 1979), pp. 21–63; Salvador, *Cristãos-novos*, pp. 343, 351; Salvador, *Magnatas do tráfico negreiro*, pp. 141–50.

Bahia and selling in Angola mainly under the privileges of the tax contracts of that era, to keep their investments in the trade goods that they lent at high prices and to remit profits from those sales in the form of secure financial instruments, mostly letters of exchange, rather than trying to sell slaves to impoverished planters in Brazil.[30]

Lisbon's retreat to the high ground of textiles and finance left ownership of the slaves to the Angolans and the Brazilians at precisely the moment in 1695 when the discovery of gold in the hills north of Rio de Janeiro resurrected the Brazilian markets for African labor. The eighteenth century therefore opened with a succession of measures taken in Lisbon to reassert direct royal authority over southern Atlantic slaving on behalf of Portuguese merchants, who lacked significant commercial contacts at Guanabara Bay and were unable to intrude on the revived Luanda–Rio axis that was in control of trade from Angola to the mines. The larger Lisbon merchants attempted to cash in directly on the wealth of Minas by supplying the mining camps with Portuguese foodstuffs and manufactures of northern European provenience, without involving themselves in the African trade.[31] Established metropolitan traders to Africa found themselves confined to the old sugar markets in Pernambuco and secondarily Bahia.[32] They therefore secured royal decrees to channel the new trade in slaves to Rio through the old, now fading, centers of Portugal's American commerce. One such restriction continued earlier limitations on the number of slaves that traders could ship directly to Rio each year.[33] The 1,200 slaves allowed to the Rio traders probably amounted to no more than a fifth to a sixth of the total number of captives leaving Luanda at that time and to only a tiny fraction of Minas Gerais's voracious appetite for African miners. The remainder, it was assumed, would proceed through Pernambuco (allotted only a modest 1,300 slaves) and Bahia in the hands of established metropolitan interests, to be reshipped down the Brazilian coast to Rio or sent from the northeast directly overland to the mines.[34]

Greed for a share of the lucrative Minas trade drove a wedge between the Rio shippers and the Angolans of Luanda. Brazilians wanted to buy slaves in Angola to resell for gold in Brazil, thus keeping the specie profits expected from the transaction for themselves. The Luso-Africans were accustomed to retaining ownership of the slaves during the ocean passage

---

30. Miller, "Capitalism and Slaving."

31. E.g., Pinheiro, in Lisanti, *Negócios coloniais;* cf. Alden, "Vicissitudes of Trade."

32. *Certidão,* Joseph da Roza, 16 Sept. 1715, AHU, Angola cx. 16, testifies to the control that the governors of that time exerted over the trade to Rio; there are anguished confirmations in Lisanti, *Negócios coloniais,* 5:77, 79–80, 91 (for 1725).

33. *Carta regia* of 28 Sept. 1703; the restriction was abolished in 1715.

34. Generally on this well-known dispute, Taunay, *Subsídios,* pp. 179–87; see also letter from the Luanda Senado da Câmara, 20 Sept. 1711, published in Boxer, *Portuguese Society in the Tropics,* pp. 193–94.

and expected to continue selling their slaves for gold through commission agents in Brazil. Having absorbed the losses entailed in this arrangement during the 1680s and 1690s, they could not have relished having to give up the opportunities it presented when the times turned dramatically better after 1700. The dispute over the sale of *praças,* or shipping space on Brazil-bound vessels, that flared during the 1720s surely drew its force from causes of this order.

One can surmise that the leaders of the Brazilian initiative at this stage must have been small Rio traders and mariners who raised part of their capital for the voyage from better-established local merchants, acquired a ship, and went to Angola without sufficient trade goods to buy slaves on the spot. But since they were in control of scarce shipping space, the Brazilians were in positions to demand *praça* surcharges for carrying slaves owned by the Angolans, though they would have preferred to board slaves that the merchants resident at Luanda would sell for their promise to pay later from the proceeds of selling the slaves in Brazil. The same secured bills of exchange, or *letras,* that currency-poor Luso-Africans used to pay for imports would have permitted sales of slaves to Brazilians without funds, though in this case the slaveowners would have accepted the notes as financiers of the trade rather than giving them in return for imports financed by Lisbon. The low capitalization of these Brazilians and their reliance on risk funds advanced by investors at Rio unwilling to assume the risks of the trade in slaves directly established the patterns of Luso-African slave ownership and Brazilian marginality that prevailed throughout much of the remainder of the eighteenth century.[35]

Bahia's trade in Angolan slaves tended to divide into two distinct streams as demand for labor rose in the gold mines of Minas Gerais in the 1700s and 1710s. The old trade in slaves to replenish the work forces of local sugar and tobacco plantations near the seaport capital of Salvador diminished in a time of soft sugar prices in Europe and quickening inflation in the cost of the goods the colonials imported from Lisbon. A flourishing new transit trade in slaves destined for the thriving goldfields attracted the metropolitan merchants still trading through Bahia in the time-honored seventeenth-century style. Sold for specie in Minas Gerais, such slaves could richly repay even the expensive transportation of European goods to Africa via Brazil. By the 1720s, Bahia-based Portuguese traders seemed to be yielding their old preeminence to competitors positioned in Rio. Having vainly protested to Lisbon about the rising costs of the labor they required to replace slaves of their own who died, Bahian planters turned to lower-cost methods of acquiring the hands they needed from the West African Mina Coast.

---

35. See the *bando* on *praças,* 24 May 1725, and supporting documentation, AHU, Angola cx. 16; also Boxer, *Portuguese Society in the Tropics,* p. 195.

The Mina Coast slave trade resembled Rio's trade to Angola in the modesty of its capital requirements and in the low cost of the goods the Bahians sold in Africa. Salvador merchants in possession of almost any small ocean-going vessel could combine with tobacco growers to mount a venture on the relatively direct and short route to the Mina Coast. These exports of tobacco to Africa neatly evaded royal monopolies on shipments of the weed to Europe that had been granted to Lisbon-based, or well-connected local, merchants. It also took advantage of a third picking of strong Brazilian leaf regarded in Lisbon as of "the worst variety," after the superior primary and secondary growths had been sent to Europe. But the West African market developed a strong preference for this harsh tobacco, when cured with molasses in the distinctive Bahian manner.

Bahians consolidated this trade in sweetened tobacco for slaves in the opening decade of the gold boom. Its significant economic feature was the profitable use it made of virtually costless by-products of sugar and tobacco industries otherwise oriented primarily toward Europe. It also drew on locally built ships and apparently relied on Bahian risk capital for the miscellaneous other products sent out to exchange for slaves. Given the African smokers' partiality toward the Bahian leaf, it became a small gold mine in itself for American growers and merchants—sometimes literally so, since Bahians sold it also to the Dutch on the Gold Coast for African gold, while providing slaves for the plantations of the sugar captaincy at virtually no cost at all in *réis*. This Mina trade left Bahia, secondarily Pernambuco, and to a lesser extent also Pará and Maranhão, less dependent on labor from Angola in the eighteenth century than it had been in the seventeenth and confirmed a century-long decline in the presence of Bahian slavers at Luanda.

Pernambuco's participation in the Angolan slave trade reached its nadir in the opening decades of the eighteenth century. The need to restock its plantation labor force after the ending of Dutch occupation in 1654, a resumption of sugar exports, and Lisbon's desire to wrest control over Angola from its Rio-based restorers had all combined to make Pernambuco a major consumer of Angolan labor in the latter third of the seventeenth century. But the late-century decline in sugar and the concentration of the renewed commercial activity focused on Minas Gerais in Bahia and Rio, both nearer the gold fields than the northerly port of Recife, left Pernambuco a weak third in the competition for Angolan slaves in the 1720s and 1730s. Tobacco growers in Pernambuco, like the merchants of Bahia, attempted to carve out a share of the West African market, but they never developed their Mina trade as successfully as the Bahians.[36] The weakness of the local commitment to slaving left the captaincy vulnerable to traders

36. Carreira, *Notas sobre o tráfico português*, 2d ed., p. 47.

from other Brazilian seaports, and Pernambuco bought many of its slaves in the middle decades of the eighteenth century from the merchants in Bahia. Pernambuco was therefore also available later in the 1750s to Lisbon interests looking for a way to participate in the African slave trade for themselves.

Angolan Slaving in the Economy of Rio during the Gold Boom

The gold and diamond fields of Minas Gerais and Goiás fueled the engine driving early-eighteenth-century slaving. Estimated gold production rose swiftly from negligibility in the 1690s to over 15,000 kilograms annually in the early 1750s,[37] making Brazil the major contributor to the world's supplies of the precious metal in those decades. Lisbon merchants, favored by mercantilistic decrees issued by the Crown, gained control over most of Brazil's production of mineral wealth and spent it to pay for goods from abroad, very largely in Britain, which they then had to resell in the limited overseas markets open to them in competition with British, French, and Dutch traders, each also favored by similar imperial boundaries throughout the world. The four merchant nations also contended for legal access to Spain's American possessions and their valuable bars of silver.

The strengths of the foreigners, with Bahian competition added along the Lower Guinea Coast, left only Brazil and western central Africa as markets for the English woolens, Indian cottons, French linens, Dutch and North German metalwares, and other foreign manufactures that filled Lisbon warehouses in return for the bullion Portugal shipped abroad. The minimal amenities provided for slaves on the mines, a sugar sector slipping deeper and deeper into debt to Europe, and a significant subsistence component in the provisioning of the American labor force turned attention to Angola as an alternative route to the bullion-based prosperity in Minas Gerais. The Angolan slave trade thus received a second boost from the discovery of precious metals in Brazil: not only did Brazilians from Rio seek labor for the mines, but merchants from Portugal financed the purchase of those slaves with massive imports of Asian and European trade goods through Luanda.[38]

The combination allowed imports of Angolan slaves through Rio to grow steadily through the 1740s and to remain at high levels until the end of the 1750s.[39] To the economy of the Rio port this trade contributed

37. Utilizing the summary estimates in Pinto, *Ouro brasileiro*, pp. 114–15.
38. See next chapter for details.
39. Edmundo Correia Lopes, *Escravatura (subsídios para a sua história)* (Lisbon: Agência Geral das Colónias, 1944), pp. 134–35; cf. Martins Filho and Martins, "Slave Labor in a Nonexport Economy," p. 543, Table III. Evidence that these were Angola slaves rather than Mina ones, as most assume, is in, e.g., Lockhart and Schwartz, *Early Latin America*, p. 372.

support for a modest local merchant marine. The Angola fleet, small as it was in relation to European shipping to and from Lisbon, probably constituted a rather larger proportion of the Rio-owned and operated merchantmen that otherwise engaged only in regional shipments of salt, in ventures along the southern coast leading to the Spanish territories above the Plata estuary, and in southern Atlantic whaling.[40] Particularly in the first twenty years of the gold boom, from roughly 1700 to 1720, the shortage of shipping space from Luanda directly to Rio and the consequent ability of Rio ship operators to impose surcharges on Angolans avid to get their slaves to the mines must have generated significant shipping profits for those engaged in the trade. Sales of *praças* at Luanda at up to 12$000 and 15$000 above the nominal freight charge of 5$000 or 6$000 per slave meant that a medium-sized Rio vessel carrying 300 slaves could generate as much as 6.000$000 or more in transportation charges, almost half the Luanda value of the cargo it carried for the Luso-Africans of Angola.

While surcharges of these proportions disappeared in the face of determined government and Luso-African opposition in the 1730s, slaving in Angola must have made a significant contribution to the consolidation of an autonomous Rio shipping industry in a maritime sector otherwise dominated by ships from Portugal. In the 1740s, at the very peak of the demand for slaves in Minas Gerais, Rio merchants even proposed to break the Bahians' monopoly over the Mina trade by organizing a chartered company of their own, under royal protection, to venture there.[41] Though this attempt failed, the Rio fleet had become so dominant in Angolan slaving by the 1760s that it alarmed metropolitan shipping interests in Portugal. It even began to experiment with ventures of its own direct to the Indian Ocean (probably Mozambique rather than all the way to India itself) to acquire the Asian textiles that figured so importantly in buying slaves in Angola.[42]

For sugar growers around Guanabara Bay, the Angolan trade offered a market for specialized cane brandies, the *gerebita* basic to the *banzo* assortments in Africa. Returns from sales of these rums, in slaves, allowed planters to circumvent the soft European market for raw sugar and the favored position in the imperial liquor trade accorded Portuguese wines and grape-based *aguardentes* and brandies. Douro valley vintners enjoyed the protection of treaties and carefully cultivated British tastes for the

---

40. Lobo, "Comércio atlântico," pp. 63, 84; Alden, *Royal Government,* p. 44.

41. Taunay, *Subsídios,* p. 253. See also the earlier efforts of the Rio merchants to acquire the tobacco crucial to the Mina trade at Pernambuco, always the weak spot in Brazilian slaving interests: *carta regia,* 19 Dec. 1724, published in *Anais da Biblioteca nacional do Rio de Janeiro* 28 (1906): 202–3.

42. *Parecer* of the Conselho Ultramarino, n.d. (ca. 1760), AHU, Angola maço 11. See Hoppe, *África oriental portuguesa,* pp. 166 ff., 266, for the Mozambique side.

sweet and mellow wines of northern Portugal, but other Portuguese grape growers looked to Brazil (and to Angola) as an important market for their fine *aguardentes* and cheaper wines. On the other hand, active metropolitan opposition and discriminatory duties discouraged the sale of coarse Brazilian cane brandies in Europe.[43] But slavers could offload *gerebitas* at Luanda at prices less than a third of the competing Portuguese *aguardentes*.[44] This advantage provoked royal prohibitions against their importation in 1679 and 1690 in two of several discriminatory measures directed against Rio cane growers in these decades, masked by invocations of the harm done by "Demon Rum" to the African subjects of the king. Fortunately for the Brazilians, Lisbon's administrative reach exceeded its grasp by nearly as much as the piety of the metropolitan producers of *aguardente* concealed their jealousy, and the trade never paused. Slaving depended too heavily on including Brazilian *gerebita* in every purchase, and so the last ban against the shipment of brandies and rums to Angola was lifted in 1695, just in time to sustain Rio's position in the boom in slaves for Minas.

In Angola sellers of *gerebita* found almost unlimited markets in Luanda's ubiquitous grog shops and in the slave markets of the interior.[45] African hemp, fermented palm sap, and millet beers lacked the strength and sharpness of the highly distilled Brazilian cane brandies which were up to 90 percent alcohol, or 180 proof, but usually cut to around 50 to 60 percent for sale.[46] The giant *pipas* (or hogsheads of four barrels, or 500 bottles) each yielded a tax of 1$600 to the coffers of the perpetually underfinanced Luanda town council,[47] with the revenue devoted to such local projects as repairs to sandy streets washed out by heavy rains and (later) the only

---

43. Salvador, *Cristãos-novos*, p. 351 et passim; *carta regia* of 17 Nov. 1692, mentioned in Delgado, *Reino*, p. 397; Luis da Camara Cascudo, *Prelúdio da cachaça: etnografia, história e sociologia da aguardente no Brasil* (Rio de Janeiro: Instituto do Açúcar e do Alcool, 1968), pp. 26–27; Boxer, *Portuguese Society in the Tropics*, pp. 122–24.

44. E.g., the accounts of Coelho Guerreiro, which show 2$268 as prime cost for a *pipa* of Brazilian *aguardente* versus 7$000 for the equivalent volume of Portuguese brandy in 1689: Rau, "*Livro de Razão*," fol. 100. By official customs evaluations in 1794, which may or may not have reflected prime or Luanda costs, Portuguese *aguardente do Reino* was worth 95$000/*pipa* while Brazilian cane brandies were 46$000/*pipa*: IHGB, lata 77, no. 1 ("Balanço da importação e exportação deste Reino de Angola . . . "); cf. Cascudo, *Prelúdio da cachaça*, pp. 22–24.

45. As early as 1620: Cascudo, *Prelúdio da cachaça*, p. 26; see also remarks by Rau, "*Livro de Razão*," p. 48, for the late seventeenth century. Also Miller, "Imports at Luanda," p. 39, Table I, for later in the eighteenth century. According to at least one report, Africans preferred *gerebita* to wines and European spirits because of its sharp flavor: anonymous *memória*, enclosed in de Mello, 7 Dec. 1798, AHU, Angola cx. 46.

46. Spix and Martius, *Viagem pelo Brasil*, 2:155, n. VI, for the early nineteenth century.

47. *Carta regia* of 4 Sept. 1696 (cited in Peçanha, 27 June 1785, AHU, Angola cx. 40), and retained throughout the eighteenth century. See códs. 17 (1736–50 and 1751–70) and 27 (Jan. 1774–6 July 1774 and 24 Jan. 1781–9 Nov. 1816) in AHCML.

school in the city.[48] Broken down into *frasqueiras* ($\frac{1}{16}$ *pipa*) most of the brandy went to the interior on the heads of bearers, an irreplaceable lubricant of every exchange for slaves throughout the century.[49]

Imports of *gerebita* at Luanda, though not all from Rio, remained roughly steady throughout the eighteenth century at around 2,000 *pipas* per year, except for a temporary decline in the 1780s, or around one barrel (125 bottles, 4 *frasqueiras*) for every slave shipped.[50] Aside from *gerebita's* obvious value as an intoxicant, these consistently large imports also became an essential component of the rations given slaves and conscripted laborers in Angola, were offered as gestures of hospitality by the African gentry, provided quick calories to people who were often short of nourishment, and even sustained life, if barely and badly, in times of failed harvests and among the poorer inhabitants of the seaports.

In and around Rio, *gerebita* production, much of it for Angola, supported a hundred to two hundred small stills, sometimes on the large plantations that produced the raw sugar and at other times in small-scale independent operations situated in sheds off the byways of the city. The *gerebita* itself was distilled from the "wash," or foam skimmed off the second boiling of the cane juice as it was reduced toward a thick syrup that would in turn be drained to leave the crystalline *muscovado* (brown) sugar shipped in chests to Lisbon. The molasses drained from the finished sugar could also be converted into rum. The wash or the molasses could simply be allowed to ferment into *garapa azeda*, which was given to the slaves of the plantation, or it could be boiled, usually with relatively simple equipment, to the higher proofs that qualified as *gerebita* (or, later, in Brazil, *cachaça*).

Gerebita was cheap "home brew" that the common man drank in Brazil, and it was Rio's principal export to Angola.[51] By the end of the gold boom, Rio had a reported 320 great sugar mills (*engenhos*) processing

48. *Provisão* of 7 April 1701, AHU, Angola cx. 18; on the origins of the Pombaline *subsídio literário* collected on imported spirits, Francisco José Calazans Falcon, *A época pombalina: política econômica e monarquia ilustrada* (São Paulo: Atica, 1982), p. 461. Also Alden, *Royal Government,* pp. 304–5, for similar excise taxes on luxuries in general.

49. Peçanha, 27 June 1785, AHU, Angola cx. 40; Moçâmedes, 15 Oct. 1786, AHU, Angola cx. 40; de Mello, 24 April 1798, AHU, Angola cx. 46; anonymous *memória*, n.d. (ca. 1810), AHU, Angola cx. 60; Saldanha da Gama, *Memoria sobre as colonias de Portugal,* p. 39.

50. Peçanha, 27 June 1785, AHU, Angola cx. 40, for the 1780s; Santos, "Relações de Angola com o Rio de Janeiro," p. 9, for 1803–8; *parecer* (Manuel da Cruz), 20 March 1824, ANTT, Junta do Comércio, maço 62, macete 122; Câmara, 22 May 1781, AHU, Angola maço 17 (D.O.); esp. de Mello, 22 July 1798, AHU, Angola cx. 46; "Cartas de receita e despeza que o Senado da Camara . . . teve . . . 1791 athé . . . 1801," AHU, Angola cx. 53; Junta da Real Fazenda, 3 March 1804, AHU, Angola cx. 56; idem (later dates) in cx. 58. Also see customs house reports cited in Miller, "Imports at Luanda."

51. Cascudo, *Prelúdio da cachaça,* pp. 12, 16–17, 24–25. Schwartz, *Sugar Plantations,* pp. 121, 162–63, 214, also stresses the importance of *cachaça* sales to the profitability of sugar mills in Bahia.

cane into *muscovado* and its wash into rums, and another 176 *engenhocas* (smaller "contraptions") specialized only in distilling the wash into *gerebita*. The 320 sugar mills employed some 11,735 slaves in the late 1760s, and the 176 *engenhocas* had a work force approximately 15 percent as large, or 1,752 slaves. Each *engenhoca* turned out something over a full hogshead of highly distilled rum each year (1.35 *pipas/engenho*), and the total commercial production of the province amounted to 2,477 hogsheads.[52] Of that amount, about half found its way to Luanda, and probably almost as much went to Benguela by the 1780s, so that Angola constituted the primary market for Rio *gerebita* exports at times during the eighteenth century.[53] By the end of the century, Rio was producing half again as much *gerebita*,[54] of which less than a third went to markets in Europe and North America. Nearly two-thirds ended up in Angola,[55] no doubt to the great relief of local moralists, who decried the power of so much alcohol, if allowed to remain in Brazil, to ruin slave discipline. Cane brandies were also Pernambuco's and Bahia's most important export to Angola.[56] Africa, however, presented limitless opportunities for the middle strata of the Rio economy engaged in the production of *gerebita*.[57]

From 1785 to the 1820s *gerebita* was, in terms of value, more than two-thirds of all Brazilian imports passing through the Luanda customs house, about six times greater than all other comestibles taken together, which made up the next most significant category of American imports, and almost 15 percent of the total value of imports entering Luanda.[58] At a time of serious competition from British interlopers in all other commodities, it was praised even by official sources in Angola as one area in which "Portuguese" subjects enjoyed unchallenged superiority.[59] From the Brazilian point of view, it was about the size of the trade in slaves.[60]

Rio agriculture also sold smaller quantities of manioc flour, rice, beans, and sugar in Angola. To these local products, merchants in Rio added

52. *Relatório* of the Marques de Lavradio, ANRJ, cód. 71, as reported in Santos, "Comércio do porto do Rio," p. 39. Unknown, from these figures, is the additional quantity consumed on the plantations, in the city of Rio, and perhaps transported to Minas Gerais and other non-sugar-growing adjacent inland regions.

53. Vellut, "Royaume de Cassange," pp. 133–34; Peçanha, 27 June 1785, AHU, Angola cx. 40, for Luanda imports at a later period.

54. Estimated at 3,500–3,600 *pipas* per annum: Lobo, "Comércio atlântico," p. 73.

55. Santos, "Comércio do porto do Rio," pp. 198, Tabela 5; Rebelo, *Relações*, p. 9; *Revista do Instituto Histórico e Geográfico Brasileiro* 66 (1883): 197–204.

56. *Anais da Biblioteca nacional do Rio de Janeiro* 28 (1906): 482 (Pernambuco, ca. 1747); AHMF, letter of 12 Jan. 1774 (Pernambuco); Caldas, "Notícia geral," p. 229 (Bahia, 1750s).

57. José Feliciano da Rocha Gameiro, 28 April 1778, quoted in Taunay, *Subsídios*, p. 254.

58. Miller, "Imports at Luanda," Table I et passim.

59. Anonymous *memória*, n.d. (ca. 1790s), in Alvares de Mello, 7 Dec. 1798, AHU, Angola cx. 46; de Mello, 24 April 1798 and 22 Aug. 1798, AHU, Angola cx. 46.

60. Brown, "Internal Commerce," p. 296, estimates the value of *aguardente* produced in the Campos das Goitacás near Rio in 1816 as 5% of the value of sugar.

hides and leather products, like shoe soles and chairs, and dried meats from the captaincies to the south, particularly as the century progressed. They also shipped the famous cheeses of Minas Gerais.[61] Brazilian timber and roofing tiles, furniture, and naval stores also appeared in minor quantities.[62]

On the African side of the trade, it was primarily these Rio traders who developed Benguela as a significant slaving port after the 1720s.[63] They opened that remote trading site in ways that reinforced the autonomous tendencies of the southern Brazilian slaving industry. Benguela's location on a dry coastal plain and its vulnerability to droughts left the town relatively dependent on the foodstuffs Brazil could provide, since it lacked the complex and politically sensitive Luso-African provisioning network serving Luanda.[64] Since the maritime route from Rio to Luanda and the Loango Coast (though not necessarily from Bahia or Pernambuco) passed Benguela, and since ships always put in along that section of the coast for water after the long transatlantic crossing, it was a natural spot for Rio traders to stop to trade in Angola. It was also of difficult access from Luanda, owing to the southwesterly onshore breezes and the strong north-flowing current along the coast. Benguela's easy accessibility from Rio and its remoteness from the center of colonial government authority at Luanda made it the ideal refuge for Brazilians trying to buy slaves without suffering the disadvantages imposed on them in places subject to closer Portuguese imperial control. As a result, 80 to 90 percent and more of the slaving at Benguela went to Rio, and probably nearly all of that in Brazilian-backed ventures.

61. For the import values at Luanda late in the century, Miller, "Imports at Luanda." From the Brazilian side: Cascudo, *Prelúdio da cachaça*, p. 26 (1620s); Rau, *"Livro de Razão,"* p. 48 (1680s–90s); Pardo, "Comparative Study," pp. 105–6; Lobo, "Comércio atlântico," p. 73, citing *Revista do Instituto Histórico e Geográfico Brasileiro*, no. 266 (1965): 213; Santos, "Relações de Angola com o Rio de Janeiro," p. 9. Also *parecer*, n.d. (ca. 1760s), AHU, Angola maço 11 (D.O.).

62. See also Corrêa, *História de Angola*, 1:46; Luccock, *Notes on Rio de Janeiro*, pp. 589–90, 615.

63. Representação does vereadores da Câmara Municipal de Luanda, 17 April 1728, AHU, Angola cx. 17.

64. E.g., Moçâmedes, 15 Oct. 1786, AHU, Angola cx. 40; idem, 28 April 1789, AHU, Angola cx. 41; Oliveira Barboza, 24 Oct. 1811, AHU, Angola cx. 60; Almeida e Vasconcelos, 3 March 1794, AHU, Angola cx. 43. There are other indications of provisions brought in to Benguela from the adjacent river valleys, but these were also under pressure as labor-recruiting areas. Some food for the settlement came from the distant highlands, particularly after Brazilian slaving dropped off in the nineteenth century: Fernando Joseph da Cunha Pereira, 16 March 1748, AHU, Angola cx. 26; Torres, *Memórias*, pp. 364–65; Delgado, *Reino*, pp. 38–85; Delgado, *Famosa e histórica Benguela*, pp. 69, 443, 451 et passim; Spix and Martius, *Viagem pelo Brasil*, 2:151, n. V. Venâncio, "Economia de Luanda," p. 144, notes that manioc from Luanda was the main staple supplied to Benguela in the Luso-African trade in salt and other commodities from the small southern port. The lower Katumbela River valley and the coast immediately north of the town became provisioning areas only early in the nineteenth century.

The low capitalization of the Brazilian slavers also matched up well with the direct sales of slaves that prevailed at Benguela. The use of bills of exchange made the organization of slaving at Luanda unlike slaving anywhere else on the African coast, but trading at Benguela was much more similar to arrangements along the Loango Coast or in West Africa. Rio merchants at Benguela, seldom impeded by large Lisbon ships attempting to engross the trade with goods offered on generous terms of credit, could command the trade by selling cane brandies for slaves they acquired on the spot from the rather less well-heeled traders of the town.

Most of the suppliers of slaves at Benguela were Portuguese who had arrived in chains, as criminals condemned to penal transportation overseas, and who had settled in remote portions of the interior. Since they were less committed than traders in Luanda to trying to build up wealth in Brazil, they would sell slaves outright, even in times of high American prices, and the Brazilians consequently preferred Benguela as a place where they could keep the trading profits of slaving for themselves. Rio traders gained royal permission to dispatch slaves directly from Benguela to Brazil in 1730, rather than sending them all through the contractors' inspectors at Luanda, and they were effectively left on their own after that, despite the contractors' subsequent futile efforts to supervise the trade in Benguela.[65] By the 1780s, three or four big merchants, doubtless Brazilians, had established themselves as commission agents for everyone doing business in the town.[66] They collaborated with French smugglers of Asian textiles and other goods to remain the dominant buyers of Benguela slaves until the end of the legal trade.

At Luanda, given the strong position of the Luso-Africans, the disadvantages heaped on shippers, and the formidable competition from Lisbon merchants, Rio slavers had to resort to illegal tactics to make money from slaving. At first, in their primary role as carriers who owned few slaves, they concentrated on tight-packing. They also engaged in marginal smuggling, but the cards were stacked against this promising evasion. In yet another example of the subtle favoritism toward metropolitan traders inherent in Lisbon's regulation of the trade, the most constraining aspect of the small import duties levied on Brazilian spirits may have been not the very modest amounts paid in excise (*subsídios*) taxes to the Luanda Senado da Câmara but rather the unmentioned consequence of having to present their ships' manifests to the town councilors: it forced all *gerebita*

---

65. *Requerimentos* of José de Torres (contractor) and others, n.d. (1735–39), AHU, Angola cxs. 20, 21; Eduardo de Castro e Almeida, *Inventario dos documentos relativos ao Brasil existentes no Archivo de Marinha e Ultramar de Lisboa* (Rio de Janeiro: Biblioteca Nacional, 1936), vol. 7, docs. 7:335, 8:63–64, 8:714–15, 11:610–11, 11:935–36, 12:357–58, 12:369, 12:557–58, 12:804–5, 13:205–6; Taunay, *Subsídios*, p. 201; and other sources.
66. Corrêa, *História de Angola*, 1:39, 2:158.

imports into the regular commercial channels of the city. Thus, few casks could have slipped past the Lisbon factors to buy slaves directly from Luso-African caravans bringing captives down from the interior, in the strategy known as *reviro*. Rather, the Brazilians had to content themselves with payment in bills drawn on metropolitan merchants in Rio and to carry slaves belonging to others. The final irony lay in the benefit the excise taxes on *gerebita* originally gave to the Luso-Africans in the otherwise poor Luanda Senado da Câmara, thus enlisting the Brazilians' potential creole allies in the *reviro* strategy to hold the net spread to trap them.

Commercial Strategies

In general terms, Rio planters and merchants "dumped" goods in Angola. *Gerebita,* the backbone of the business, was an otherwise useless by-product of the sugar planters' principal business of sending crystalline sugars to Europe. Insofar as specialized *gerebita* producers maintained their own stills, they were only small operators located in the back streets of the city. Brazilian products of other sorts also found their way to Angola, but not in significant quantities. Though Luanda customs records do not indicate how many European and Asian goods brought originally from Lisbon to Rio or other ports in Brazil were transshipped on to Africa through local Brazilian commercial houses, the scattered available evidence suggests that they usually consisted of little more than inferior and ruined merchandise unsalable in Brazil.[67] If Brazilian ships carried large quantities of these reexports, they handled them only as freight for wealthy metropolitan competitors.

   The financial organization of Brazilian-based slaving turned on marshaling illiquid physical assets on hand, supplemented with as much venture capital as necessary to fill out a viable expedition. Owners of a ship and planters contributing agricultural products for sale in Africa usually formed its core, but import merchants with goods to dump in Africa and speculators willing to advance cash or credits for the remaining components of the voyage also involved themselves from time to time. They, together with a captain and officers willing to work for consignments of trade goods rather than cash wages, would form a partnership (*sociedade*) limited to a single voyage, with the expected returns to be distributed in shares agreed in advance as reflecting the contributions of each investor.[68]

67. E.g., the Pinheiro correspondence in Lisanti, *Negócios coloniais,* 2:68, 94, 126, 385. Cf. Susan Migden Socolow, *The Merchants of Buenos Aires, 1778–1810: Family and Commerce* (London: Cambridge University Press, 1978), p. 55, for similar practices in Argentina.

68. Cf. the earlier style of commercial partnership developed in Portugal, also under conditions of undercapitalization and illiquidity no longer typical in British and Dutch

For the Brazilian slavers in general, but in particular at Rio, where the tendencies toward autonomy were greatest, these partnerships included mostly local interests. Because of the high risks of slaving, Brazilian merchants no less than slavers in Luanda tended to spread small commitments over a great number of separate ventures rather than to assume a major responsibility for a single voyage. The *sociedades* also made it possible for investors in the Benguela trade to move quickly to take advantage of temporary shortages of slaves in Brazil or price dips in Angola.

Clearance records of ships appearing at Luanda and Benguela suggest that most of the individuals involved in slaving entered it on just this sort of occasional basis.[69] On the other hand, a few ships and captains plied the southern Atlantic on a regular basis, each of them usually managing about one round trip a year, for as many as eight or ten or even fifteen journeys. Such long-term participants in the trade must have been backed by specialized producers of *gerebita* for the African trade or by Portuguese reexporting to Africa, probably had vessels specially modified to carry slaves, and employed captains experienced in managing human cargoes.

Since the maritime transporters were oriented more toward the export of Brazilian agricultural produce than toward the marketing of slaves in Brazil, they must have handed their captives over to a separate class of town merchants, contracted by the slaves' owners in Angola, once they returned to the ports of America. Alternatively, their partnerships might have included local merchant associates eager to make contacts with the Luanda owners of the captives. These land-based associates housed the slaves and displayed them for sale to their final purchasers. Given the variety of arrangements possible, some general merchant bankers may have provided both goods and funds for the slaving venture and then participated in the final disposition of the return cargo of slaves, but such comprehensive participation involved too much capital investment and risk to have typified their role in the trade.

The commercial relations of these Brazilian ventures with the merchants of Luanda ranged from casual contacts of ship captains with local suppliers of water or wood to long-term contractual arrangements of wide-ranging scale and responsibility.[70] The minority of Brazilian merchants committed to slaving on a regular basis might send nephews or sons to

---

commerce (and finance) in the eighteenth century: Lockhart and Schwartz, *Early Latin America*, p. 16. Combinations of real assets were apparently more common in the French trade: Stein, *French Slave Trade*, pp. 64 ff. et passim. Also see Eltis, "The Transatlantic Slave Trade," pp. 117–26 ff., for the early nineteenth century.

69. Miller, "Portuguese Slave Trade."

70. The Pinheiro correspondence in Lisanti, *Negócios coloniais*, may once again be read with profit on this point. See also Miller, "Capitalism and Slaving," for the role of several Brazilian-based merchants in a metropolitan trader's business in the 1680s and 1690s.

establish themselves as resident factors, receiving and selling cargoes sent from Brazil to Africa and lining up the owners of slaves in Angola to fill the shipping space available on the return voyage. Brazilian factors with knowledge of local conditions and good Luso-African contacts might attempt also to buy selected slaves for shipment on the accounts of their Brazilian principals. Though warning of the impending arrival of a venture backed by their employers in Rio enabled them to dispose efficiently of incoming cargoes, the tight regulation of ship departures from Luanda made it futile for them to prepare outbound slaves or provisions very far in advance of the highly uncertain departure time eventually assigned to the captain.

Otherwise, given the limited advantages to be gained from maintaining permanent representation on the spot in Luanda and the no more than occasional investment in slaveownership by most Brazilians, the majority of small, occasional ventures worked through the *comissários* of Luanda, the big merchants with metropolitan connections (but some of local background), who added the Brazilians' *gerebitas* to their own imports from the metropole to make up *banzos* for the interior and who expedited slave exports for owners from the colony's interior and in the city in return for commissions on the value of the goods and slaves they handled. If several associates in a Brazilian venture consigned their wares to different Luanda *comissários*, the captain could make up his return cargo of slaves more quickly by dealing with more than one of these self-styled colonial gentlemen and spread the risks of the voyage over a greater number of owners of the slaves.

Rio merchants employed specie to buy slaves primarily during the first years of the Minas gold rush early in the eighteenth century, when disgruntled Bahians complained that Carioca slavers were cutting them out of the Luanda market by offering gold on the spot.[71] But the imperial net soon channeled the available American bullion toward Portugal, and by 1739 the Angolan treasury inspector reported that the Crown had never allowed gold to circulate in Luanda for fear that the Brazilians' needs for slaves would divert most of the production of Brazil's mines to the African colony.[72] The sumptuary decrees of the 1740s further discouraged consumption of gold in the empire by making it illegal to display gold, or silver, trim on clothing.[73] Insofar as Rio traders invested the Spanish silver they managed to accumulate in commerce, they sent it directly to

71. D. Rodrigo da Costa, 26 June 1703, cited in Carreira, "Companhias pombalinas de navegação," p. 25.
72. Vasconcelos, 6 July 1739, AHU, Angola cx. 21.
73. *Alvará*, 5 Oct. 1742, published in *Boletim do Conselho Ultramarino* (legislação antiga), pp. 413–14. Venâncio, "Economia de Luanda," pp. 18–19, gives background to this legislation.

Mozambique, where silver was necessary to buy Asian textiles, or slaves later in the nineteenth century, when Brazilians and others paid the Mozambican creole traders—the counterparts of the Luanda Luso-Africans—in Spanish coin. The Mozambique traders then forwarded the American silver to India in payment for the cotton goods they used to acquire captives in the interior.[74]

Only at the end of the eighteenth century did Brazilians once again begin bringing gold to Angola to exchange for slaves, but only in small quantities. The Brazilians in question were probably traders from the northern cotton-growing captaincies, which at about that time became net importers of gold from British merchants eager to acquire Brazilian fiber for the textile mills of the English midlands.[75] Even then, the specie in the hands of the wealthiest Luanda merchants represented the value of no more than about a thousand slaves, or less than 10 percent of annual slave exports at Luanda.[76] If unrecorded Brazilian specie went from Brazil to Angola, it wound up in the hands of British and French smugglers willing to sell their trade goods for gold rather than slaves, not in the hands of the Luso-Africans of Angola; but the British had other, more efficient access routes to southern Brazil that made this roundabout search for American precious metals in Africa an unlikely one. The general lack of gold flowing to western central Africa distinguished the Brazilians' Angola trade sharply from the Bahians' early sales of American bullion for slaves on the Mina Coast and their later use of tobacco to buy gold dust mined in its African hinterland.[77]

74. Carreira, *Tráfico português de escravos,* pp. 25–26.

75. Rudy Bauss, "General Observations of Bullion Movements in the Portuguese Empire, 1785–1815" (Unpublished paper, ca. 1978), p. 3.

76. De Mello, 11 Oct. 1797, AHU, Angola cx. 44, referring also to former times when gold had been extremely rare in Angola. See the efforts at transcontinental exploration in the 1750s and 1760s, directed in part at establishing a more efficient route of access to the gold sources of the Shona Plateau (Rios de Sena in Portuguese parlance of the time) through Angola: R. Avila de Azevedo, "Princípios de uma economia de fixação em Africa (século XVIII)," *Actas do V Colóquio internacional de estudos luso-brasileiros* (Coimbra, 1963), 1:121–31, and Venâncio, "Economia de Luanda," pp. 124–26. Cf. also the fruitless efforts made to discover gold in Angola in the 1750s as Brazilian production began declining: da Cunha, 1 April 1754, 16 March 1755, 26 Jan. 1756, and 10 March 1756, all in AHU, Angola cx. 26. The false hopes died hard: Vasconcelos, 5 April 1762, AHU, Angola cx. 29; José Pinheiro de Morais Fronteira, 30 Aug. 1782, AHU, Angola cx. 38. By the middle of the nineteenth century, local rumor had converted the illusions of the 1750s into actual samples of Angolan gold sent to Lisbon in 1754, 1758, and 1759 and had reversed the government's explicit encouragement to prospecting to alleged orders from the marquis of Pombal to the Angolan governors of the time to cease the search so as not to diminish the flow of slaves from Angola to Brazil: Francisco de Salles Ferreira, *Minas em Angola: memória histórica* (Lisbon: n.p., 1896), as cited in Hoppe, *Africa oriental portuguesa,* p. 303. The contemporary documentation bears no trace of such policies, but this lack more clearly reflects Angolan creole preoccupations of the late nineteenth century than the facts of the 1750s.

77. The evident source of the misimpression widespread in recent literature that significant amounts of gold went also to Angola: e.g., Taunay, *Subsídios,* p. 162.

Settling Up

The scarce information on methods of selling Angolan slaves in Brazil comes almost exclusively from the records of the atypical, large, vertically integrated chartered companies of the Pombaline era rather than from ordinary Brazilian shippers dealing through multipurpose merchants in Rio, Pernambuco, or Bahia. Large companies putting whole lots of slaves up for sale—and presumably also any Brazilian shipper with a substantial interest in the cargo he landed—used an auction system in which the sellers opened the sale by allowing prospective buyers to make their selection at the standard, almost fixed, price for the theoretically "prime" slave—usually a derivative of the old *peça*, or "piece," of the seventeenth century. Depending on general market conditions, purchasers would then select as many slaves as they were willing to buy at the proclaimed price.[78] This was the *primeira escolha,* or "first selection." A *segunda escolha,* or "second selection" round of buying, then took place at a slightly lower set price, and so on through a succession of price reductions until the young, the infirm, and otherwise undesirable captives were sold to whatever buyers might find a use for them.[79] Specialists in handling the least promising of the new slaves, many of them near death, usually took the last of the lot off the hands of the importers, perhaps in hopes of restoring these unfortunates to health. The other buyers, while not identified in the surviving records, surely ranged from planters buying laborers for their cane fields to dealers intending to march coffles of slaves off to the mines and farms of the remote interior. Selling methods generally reflected the slaveowners' underlying concern with haste, extended from the Luanda port, across the southern Atlantic, to the moment of final sale in America. The longer it took to dispose of the slaves, the greater were their losses to mortality.

    The auction method clearly revealed an underlying tendency for slavers to deliver labor in excess of market demand in Brazil, at least during the depressed 1760s and 1770s, when the Pombaline companies were active. The procedure reversed the usual method of auctioneering in a sellers' market, where buyers bid up the price of scarce commodities. Instead it turned the sale into a buyers' auction that left the initiative with the purchasers of the slaves. This concession to Brazilian purchasers may also have reflected the slaveowners' uneasiness at holding sick and dying slaves for longer than absolutely necessary once they finally delivered them to Brazil. With the resumption of strong demand for slaves during Brazil's

---

    78. E.g., Carreira, "Companhias pombalinas de navegação," pp. 61 ff.; Karasch, *Slave Life,* pp. 35–36, 46–49 ff., has good details on auctions in Rio after 1810.

    79. For examples of the resulting distribution of prices actually received, see Joseph C. Miller, "Quantities and Currencies: Bargaining for Slaves on the Fringes of the World Capitalist Economy" (forthcoming).

agricultural renaissance of the 1780s–1790s, a new breed of Rio buyers sold their slaves in predetermined lots of mixed quality slaves, thus taking advantage of what had become a sellers' market with rising prices to dispose of the bad along with the good.[80] Grouping slaves in lots in this fashion may also reflect the prominence of specialized slave retailers at Rio, who bought slaves in large numbers from importers bringing slaves into the city's Valongo market to resell them to final purchasers in sometimes remote parts of the interior.[81] Planters and other final owners in the less commercialized markets in the sugar captaincies earlier in the century may have bought individual slaves as needed directly from the importers.

Some multifunction merchants may have handled sufficiently large numbers of slaves to hold their own public *escolha* without undue risk of deaths, as the agents of the Pombaline companies did, but most probably hastened to dispose of the small lots of five, ten, or fifteen slaves as they received them from individual correspondents in Angola. The threat of mortality hung heavy over their decision to sell the slaves as quickly as possible. They had their choice of putting them on the block in a public market for individual slaves or resorting to other more specialized dealers in captive African labor.[82] General merchants performed these services for the Angolan owners of the labor as *comissários,* or commission agents, arranging for food and clothing for the slaves; providing or renting accommodations in damp, dirt-floored warehouses near the waterfront; hiring medical assistance for those in need of it; negotiating with the host of government officers empowered to collect fees, make inspections, and threaten delays in making the slaves available for sale; and, finally, taking a percentage of the final sales price as their fee for services rendered.[83] They charged all the expenses of debarkation and maintenance back to the owners of the slaves and then credited the remaining proceeds of the sale to accounts they held for the Angolans. Slaveowners in need of quicker returns than the *comissários* might provide could turn to specialists (*consignatários*) who would lend a (discounted?) value on their slaves at once and then sell them to recover the loan, like pawnbrokers.[84]

It was at that point that the Angolan sellers, who had originally sent the slaves off to Brazil to cover bills of exchange written in Luanda, were finally in a position to order satisfaction of the Lisbon merchants' claims against them. The owner of their note had sent it to Brazil for collection through a merchant banker of his own choice, not likely to have been the

---

80. De Mello, "Angola no começo do século," p. 559, n. 1.
81. E.g., merchants of the type described by Taunay, *Subsídios,* pp. 278–84.
82. Cf. Mattoso, *Etre esclave au Brésil,* pp. 82–83.
83. See the breakdown of costs for services rendered in any of the available accounts from the eighteenth century.
84. Karasch, *Slave Life,* pp. 47 ff.

same merchant as the agent handling the sale of the slaves for the Angolan owner. At the term specified on the face of the note, the creditor's representative presented his bill for payment. The Angolan's representative then drew specie, *réis,* Brazilian gold *cruzados,* or some other form of currency valuable in Portugal from the account containing the proceeds from the slaves. If the slaves had generated net proceeds more than sufficient to cover the bill, the Angolan had funds remaining in Brazil for investment in any way that he chose, including purchase there of trade goods to build up a slaving business conducted on his own account in Africa.

Most slaveowners in this fortunate position preferred to remit their hard-won assets to Portugal, of course, rather than reinvesting them in the risky business of owning slaves. Nor would many have chanced ordering remittance of the proceeds to Angola in specie. If deaths, sickness, delays, deceptions, or disasters had reduced the Angolan slaveowner's returns beneath what he owed, he could only try to embark more slaves to generate additional funds sufficient to cover his bill. Excessive delays or repeated misfortunes at worst brought the threat of bankruptcy proceedings initiated by his creditors.[85] At best, an Angolan slaver fallen in arrears on payments owed in Brazil could expect growing difficulties in obtaining more goods on credit from the Lisbon suppliers whom he owed, thus threatening his ability to maintain the assortments necessary in slave markets in the African interior. Poor assortments would slow the rate of returns on the borrowed goods he already had invested there and expose his remaining assets to seizure by other creditors. It was a position that virtually compelled him to try to restore his fortunes by resorting to *reviros* or by buying assortments from the foreigners waiting all along the coast beyond Luanda Bay.

Angolan sellers realized revenues that ran significantly less than the nominal sale prices of their slaves and the delivered costs of slave labor to Brazilian buyers[86] and far below the nominal "price" of prime slaves in the *primeira escolha* (Table 12.1). The costs of maintaining slaves on their arrival, freight and other transportation charges paid in Brazil rather than in Angola, commissions paid to agents handling the slaves in the port towns, and the difference between the theoretically standard healthy adult male and the usual run of ailing youths and malnourished females actually offered for sale narrowed the owners' margins dramatically. Net returns

85. Jeronimo Caetano de Barros Araujo de Beça (*juiz de fora interino,* Benguela), 1796, AHU, Angola cx. 43, is clear on the mechanisms of these hazards.
86. One indication of the margin is a remark by the governor of Pernambuco in 1778 that the cost of a slave to a final purchaser was 100$000 at a time when the Pernambuco Company was realizing about 78$000 per slave: Ribeiro Júnior, *Colonização e monopólio,* p. 131.

of 75 percent on the nominal price of a prime slave seem good, with some bad voyages falling below 50 percent and a few fortunate ones rising well into the 80 percent range. These revenues had to cover all the other costs of boarding slaves in Angola, as well as duties of around 10 to 30 percent over prime costs owed the Angolan government and paid in bills good in Brazil[87] and freight charges also paid in *letras* against the proceeds of Brazilian sales, together usually about 15$000, or 10 to 25 percent of prices in Brazil. The apparent generous spreads between nominal prices in Luanda and in Brazil eroded to the point where net profits might not cover the Angolan's outstanding *letras*, depending always on how many slaves survived the ocean crossing.

Some very rough estimates of the range of *réis* profits available to owners of slaves may be hazarded from the price data available on the southern Atlantic slave trade at various times in the eighteenth century.[88] While the Minas gold boom raised Brazilian prices for Angolan slaves in the 1730s and 1740s, but after the Rio traders had ceased to levy excess charges for *praças*, the *letra* value in bills of exchange covering prime slaves was rising from 40$000 to 50$000.[89] Records of Rio slave sales prices do not exist for this period, but nominal *primeira escolha* prices at Bahia at the time rose as high as 200$000, and slave sales prices in Minas were reported at 400$000, which, at a plausible further coast-to-interior markup of a round 100 percent, would have given Rio prices of the same order. Adding an estimated 25 percent of the Angola value for loading charges f.o.b. Luanda, 15$000 for freight and duties, 20 percent of all costs f.o.b. Brazil for mortality, and 20 percent more for selling costs (and mortality) in Brazil, a merchant carried a total cost of 102$600 on the average at the time his slave finally sold. With slaves averaging 75 percent of the nominal "price" in both Luanda and Rio, he would have had returns of 150$000 per slave to cover charges of 72$000. To make money, he had to experience losses to mortality of about 50 percent or less.

That is, at the period of greatest margins between Angolan *réis* costs of the goods necessary to buy a slave and Brazilian *réis* prices for African labor, a shipper would have been able to cover the bills of exchange he owed in Brazil from the proceeds of the surviving slaves even with losses

87. Carreira, "Companhias pombalinas de navegação," pp. 373–78, for the 1750s–70s. Coelho Guerreiro in the 1680s and 1690s had been able to charge more than 30% of the value of the slaves he handled for Luso-African owners: Miller, "Capitalism and Slaving," esp. Table 3.

88. All based on prices presented and discussed in Miller, "Slave Prices."

89. Note that these prices refer only to the currency gains and losses on the maritime segment of the trade between Angola and Brazil. They reveal nothing about trading conditions in the Angolan goods economy, in which slave holdings could be accumulated (or depleted), depending on slave prices in the interior and rising delivery costs as the slaving frontier receded, and eventually sold off for *réis* in Brazil by successful merchants.

Table 12.1. Some Accounts of Returns Realized on Slave Sales in Brazil

No. of slaves shipped (source)[a]	Nominal prices (adult male)	No. of slaves surviving to be sold	% sold at full price	Av. price	% of nominal price	Deaths, escapes	Av. price, net of deaths and escapes	% net returns to nominal price
10 (1)	28$000	7	70.0	28$000	100	3	19$600	70.0
7 (2)	90$000	4	14.0	68$900	76.5	3	39$371	43.7
221[b] (3)	80$000	221	48.0	66$407	83.0	...	...	...
550[b] (4)	100$000	526	64.4	88$584	88.6	2 (?)	88$248 (?)	88.2 (?)
221 (5)	80$000	186	57.0	68$860	86.1	35	57$955	72.4
120[b] (6)	120$000	117	45.0	88$795	74.0	3 (?)	86$575 (?)	72.1
220[b] (7)	80$000	220	64.5	73$204	91.5			
131[b] (8)	80$000	131	49.6	68$370	85.5			88.4
200[b] (9)	80$000	121	60.5	70$723	88.4	0	70$723	70.9
512 (10)	c. 80$000	...	...	...	...	...	56$713	47.0
503	c. 80$000	...	...	...	...	...	37$600	75.3
456	84$000	...	...	...	...	...	64$127	88.3
551	c. 85$000	...	...	...	...	...	75$083	

457	c. 85$000	...	...	...	46$228	54.4
467	c. 85$000	...	...	...	69$979	82.3
446	c. 85$000	...	...	...	57$684	67.9
470	90$000	...	...	...	52$257	59.2
14[b] (11)	130$000 (?)	4	0	75$077	57.7	1	69$714	53.6

[a] Locations, dates, and sources of prices are as follows:

(1) Bahia, 1612: Mattoso, *Etre esclave au Brésil*, pp. 77–78; Mauro, "L'Atlantique portugais," pp. 39–40.

(2) Rio, 1762: from the Proença e Sylva accounts, BNL, Colecção pombalina, as cited in Mattoso, *Etre esclave au Brésil*, p. 78.

(3) Pará, 1774, Maranhão Company slaves from Bissau: Carreira, "Companhias pombalinas de navegação," pp. 378–79.

(4) Pará, 1774, Maranhão Company slaves: Carreira, "Companhias pombalinas de navegação," p. 369.

(5) Pará, 1774, Maranhão Company slaves: Carreira, "Companhias pombalinas de navegação," pp. 378–79; Nunes Dias, *Companhia geral*, p. 391.

(6) Maranhão, 1774, Maranhão Company slaves: Nunes Dias, *Companhia geral*, pp. 393–94.

(7) Pará, 1774, Maranhão Company slaves: Nunes Dias, *Companhia geral*, p. 396–97.

(8) Pará, 1774, Maranhão Company slaves: Nunes Dias, *Companhia geral*, p. 398.

(9) Pará, 1775, Maranhão Company slaves: Carreira, "Companhias pombalinas de navegação," pp. 380–81; Nunes Dias, *Companhia geral*, p. 400.

(10) Miscellaneous Maranhão Company slaves, 1758–77: Carreira, "Companhias pombalinas de navegação," pp. 373–78.

(11) Bahia, 1795: Mattoso, *Etre esclave au Brésil*, pp. 79–81.

[b] Number of slaves landed alive in Brazil (i.e., less than the number shipped from Africa by an unknown number of deaths at sea) and therefore not directly comparable to figures in this column for slaves shipped.

479

of half of the slaves embarked at Luanda. But in this best of all eras of the Angolan slave trade, epidemics occasionally produced deaths of that magnitude among the slaves.[90] Though gains were by no means assured, the avidity with which Lisbon contractors and other metropolitan merchants fought to gain a stake in slave ownership at that period seems justified. Assuming that the *letra* cost of individuals of less than prime quality in Angola declined in proportion to the lower sales prices they also realized in Brazil, the slave seller's likelihood of gain diminished whenever the actual ages, sex, health, and skills of the slaves he shipped departed from the *peça* ideal, since duties, maintenance fees, freights, and other charges were fixed regardless of the quality of the person on whom they were paid. This cost structure also surely contributed to the reluctance of slavers to ship small children, whose low value in Brazil would not have covered the costs of delivering them.[91]

For Brazilian investors, the profits of a slaving venture depended entirely on the character of their participation in it. Some might gain handsomely while others lost, depending on the partnership arrangements in effect. The members of a formal *sociedade* all shared in the net benefits and costs of the entire venture. But if a shipper took both outbound cargo and inbound slaves solely as freight, then his gains depended on the fixed freight rates in effect and whatever tight-packing he managed to accomplish. The imperial ceiling on Angola-to-Brazil freights probably discouraged shippers from undertaking this type of voyage, except when they could sell places for premium rates in Luanda or when they might smuggle slaves of their own beyond the authorized capacity of their vessel to carry slaves for others, thus supplementing transportation revenues with trading profits. Shippers must have relied considerably on these illegal methods, since the margin between slave prices in Luanda and Brazil shrank in the 1760s, and reports then reached Lisbon about shortages of shipping at the colonial capital. It was then also that Brazilians from Rio turned in force to picking up slaves at less carefully supervised Benguela. Otherwise they had to squeeze as many slaves as possible into their crowded vessels and economize at every turn on the services and provisions they were supposed to offer in return for the transportation fees they received.

Investors in trade goods to be sold in Angola gained or lost depending on the *réis* prices they could obtain in Luanda, and these prices depended

90. Complaints of losses to owners during the wave of smallpox epidemics of the 1720s, when shippers were still paying high charges for *praças* aboard the slavers, placed damaging mortality losses at sea around 50%.

91. Youths worth half the *peça* price in both Luanda and Rio (the full prices being 20$000 and 100$000)—assuming slightly elevated mortality at 25%, and taking other costs as in the example above—would have returned 80$000 to cover 49$500. Small children costing 10$000 in Africa and selling for 50$000 in Brazil, with mortality somewhat higher still at 35%, would have brought only 40$000, not enough to compensate for expenses of 40$200.

on the momentary demand for the specific items they had to offer. Irregularities in supplies and the rigidities in African demand, by all accounts, temporarily drove prices for selected items very high, but the same conditions also rendered other unwanted goods virtually unsalable. Few in Brazil invested much in slaves before the 1790s, owing to the difficulty of acquiring them at times of high prices in America and the disadvantages of owning them at a time of low prices and high mortality. Speculators who loaned funds at interest to venturers to buy goods for sale in Angola had an even more remote connection with the supply and demand of raw labor, since they held notes collectable from funds to be deposited in the form of bills of exchange at the conclusion of the voyage. Only if disasters so wrecked a series of voyages that large numbers of Angolan slavers drew down their American accounts to the point of being unable to cover the bills they had given might such an investor find the value of his note threatened. Significant epidemics, as in the 1720s, and prolonged periods of low prices, which prevailed during the 1760s and 1770s, were the only evident disasters capable of threatening financiers thus indirectly involved in slaving.

In the longer term, the golden decades of the Angolan slave trade and the headlong rush of Portuguese, Brazilians, and Angolans to garner a share of the precious metal by sending slaves to the pits and placers of the auriferous zones left the trade overextended in relation to the reduced demand that followed the decline of mining in the later 1750s. High prices for slaves had financed the increases in transportation and maintenance expenditures in Africa that propelled the slaving frontier inland from the Kwango valley east of Luanda and the highlands above Benguela to the Kasai and Lunda regions in the north and over the entire Ovimbundu highlands in the south between 1700 and 1750. African aristocracies consolidated themselves out of their cut of the profits to be made from sending labor off to the mines of America. The Luanda creoles fended off efforts by Brazilian and metropolitan competitors to buy slaves in Africa and made their private arrangements with Brazilian buyers at remote Benguela.

The Angolan slave trade of 1760 was a much higher cost industry than its predecessor had been in 1680, with the costs temporarily covered by the high specie value of the slaves sold at Rio de Janeiro. The doubling of the loan values of goods given against slaves in this period, from 22$000 to 40$000 or 50$000, attracted the attention of Lisbon merchants unable to find markets elsewhere that might absorb the quantities of foreign goods they bought with Brazilian gold. And so the volume of the trade rose, spreading dependence on it through western central Africa even as depletion of the gold and diamond deposits foretold the coming of a difficult period of consolidation and retrenchment when the bubble would burst in the late 1750s.

13

Toward the Center

Brazilian Investment in the Southern Atlantic Trade, ca. 1780–1810

The robust demand for slaves in Minas Gerais slackened in the 1750s, and prices throughout Brazil collapsed in the 1760s.[1] With growing diversification in the Minas provincial economy and slowed need for agricultural imports to feed masses of raw slaves there, the Brazilian slavers' strategy changed subtly from satisfying unmet demand for labor on the mines to covering losses in their trade with the metropole by selling Brazilian produce in Africa. The attractiveness of African slaves shifted from their value as assets convertible into gold to laborers who could be acquired without expending the scarce specie remaining in the colony and who might also be sold for silver in the Spanish colonies to the south. In Rio, these cheaper slaves contributed to growth in sugar and other commodity exports and supported economic diversification as the viceregal capital was moved there from Bahia in 1769. It also sustained a thriving illegal (but condoned) trade in slaves to the Plata estuary.

In Bahia, local merchants turned definitively to West African "Mina" slaves, whom they could buy almost exclusively with local tobacco. Pernambuco, where no strong local slaving interest had developed, and the long-neglected captaincies of the far north, Pará and Maranhão (for most purposes dependent on Pernambuco), became the targets of metropolitan merchants intent upon utilizing the slave trade for purposes of their own in Portugal. All of these motives, though predicated on the colony's underlying need for labor, turned Brazilians toward African slaving also as a means to other ends. The entire set of objectives kept the overall level of slave exports from Angola near or above the peaks of the 1740s and 1750s, though at reduced price levels that in less visible ways compelled the Brazilians to find other sources of profit in it.

---

1. Sousa Coutinho, 15 March 1770, AHU, Angola cx. 32, treats low Brazilian prices as an existing condition. See Miller, "Slave Prices."

The Rio Trade for Plata Silver

Given the Brazilians' limited access to *réis* credits—low prices for sugar in Lisbon, monopolies on prime grade tobacco, prohibitions against Brazilian brandies that might compete with the wines of northern Portugal, and diminished Minas gold—every planter or trader sought other sources of specie in the decades after 1760. Only in that way could Brazilians afford inflation-driven increases in the prices of Portuguese imports, on which all depended for the necessities of colonial life.[2] The trade in African slaves became a vital link in the chain of strategies by which Brazilians drew gold and silver into their own hands for a full generation in the middle third of the eighteenth century. Although only less noble forms of the wealth they gained ever reached Angola, Spanish silver sent out to Asia through Lisbon was a vital means of paying for the cotton textiles that generated slaves in Africa.[3]

Bahians partially converted their slaving at Mina to a source of gold dust after mid-century by ceasing to sell gold from Minas Gerais in Lower Guinea for British, French, and Dutch wares[4] and using their tobacco instead to buy it from European and African sellers on the "Gold Coast."[5] The merchants of Rio supplemented their search for bullion from nearby Minas by resurrecting their historic smuggling to the north bank of the Río de la Prata, or the Banda Oriental, through the Colônia do Sacramento, provocatively situated directly across the estuary from the main Spanish port at Buenos Aires. Lisbon's implicit support for this contraband search for silver expressed itself in intensification of disputes over the area with Spain that had simmered since the early seventeenth century.[6] Behind the aggressive policies of the metropole, Brazilians sold slaves and American produce, sugar, rum, and tobacco, in return for Argentine dried beef and hides, but most of all for silver bars from Potosí.[7]

Rio de Janeiro's return to active selling of slaves for silver through the Plata after 1760 in fact revived a connection of ancient standing be-

---

2. Buescu, *300 Anos de inflação,* pp. 78 ff. et passim.

3. The Crown allowed Spanish shippers that could pay for slaves with specie to buy directly in Angola in 1676, but governors and tax contract holders surely cornered all of the modest quantities of silver that might have entered the colony by this route: Hanson, *Economy and Society,* p. 249. Cf. the silver in the accounts of Coelho Guerreiro ten years later; Miller, "Capitalism and Slaving."

4. Verger, *Flux et reflux,* pp. 30–31, 47, 69, 95 (n. 61), 131; Flory, "Bahian Society," p. 250 et passim; Lourenço de Freitas de Noronha, 28 March 1735, AHU, Angola cx. 20; *Anais da Biblioteca nacional do Rio de Janeiro* 28 (1906): 202. See the description for 1702 in Ferrez, "Diário anônimo," p. 20.

5. Lugar, "Merchant Community," p. 43.

6. Esp. Alden, *Royal Government.*

7. Salvador, *Magnatas do tráfico negreiro,* pp. 51, 141–50, is best on the early smuggling trade to the Plata; also Socolow, *Merchants of Buenos Aires,* p. 59.

tween the Angolan trade and the mining camps in the Andes. The sixteenth-century origins of slaving from Luanda had been rooted in buying *asiento* slaves to sell legally for Spanish silver, both through the Caribbean (Cartagena de las Indias) and through the Plata, particularly during the period of Spanish domination, from 1580 to 1640.[8] Rio slavers had taken over delivery of Angolan slaves to the remote southern Spanish territories, though illegally, after these slavers restored Luanda to Portuguese authority in 1648[9] and before gold exports from Minas Gerais temporarily diverted the flow of captives through Rio into the Portuguese colonial domain. Spanish miners in Alto Perú and collaborating merchants at Buenos Aires meant to evade Madrid's policy of channeling all slaves for Potosí circuitously and expensively through Porto Bello and Cartagena in the Caribbean.

Angola's geographical proximity to the Plata, directly across the southern Atlantic, made Luanda and Benguela natural sources for the labor sent up to the silver mines along the direct route on the rivers flowing into the Plata. Increasingly in the eighteenth century diversifying production of hides and tallow for export, woolens for local consumption and in the mines, and wines and *aguardente* nearer the Atlantic also supported brisk sales of slaves in the markets of the Plata. Though French and British owners of the *asiento* monopolies on supplying slaves excluded Brazilians and Portuguese from Buenos Aires until 1740, they failed to meet the region's demand for slave labor.[10] Behind the authority to introduce slaves, the northern European licensees preferred to sell contraband manufactures, a less risky form of trade. Because their ships arrived partially filled with goods, they consistently carried fewer slaves than their contracts required.

The Brazilians, particularly Rio merchants, who intruded on the British *asiento* (1711–39) met this unsatisfied demand by bringing slaves through the Portuguese settlement at Colônia do Sacramento, mainly from Benguela and Mozambique.[11] Their motivation for trading along the Plata at a time of plentiful gold from Minas Gerais could only have been their exclusion from trading at Luanda and Rio by metropolitan merchants who were supplying the machinery, food, and other imports needed on the mines. Termination of the British *asiento* in 1739 opened even greater

---

8. Mauro, "L'Atlantique portugais," pp. 45–46; Salvador, *Cristãos-Novos*, p. 365; Hanson, *Economy and Society*, p. 208; in general, Lockhart and Schwartz, *Early Latin America*, p. 250; Lopes, *Escravatura*, pp. 89–91; Taunay, *Subsídios*, p. 239. Also BAL, 50-V-37 (proposal), fols. 390–91v.

9. Salvador, *Magnatas do tráfico negreiro*, pp. 141–50.

10. Diégo Luis Molinari, *La trata de negros: datos para su estudio en el Río de la Plata*, 2d ed. (Buenos Aires: Universidad de Buenos Aires, 1944); Scheuss de Studer, *Trata de negros*; Palmer, *Human Cargoes*.

11. E.g., Palmer, *Human Cargoes*, pp. 71, 85–86; Scheuss de Studer, *Trata de negros*, pp. 225–26; *requerimento* of José Gonçalves Lamas, n.d. (before 13 Jan. 1737), AHU, Angola cx. 21.

opportunities for Brazilians to supply slaves to the Plata in the 1740s. A treaty prohibited Angolan slave ships from sailing direct to Colônia in 1747,[12] but traders simply ignored it for the term of the Angolan governor Conde de Lavradio (1749–53).

Further legal restrictions were not long in coming from Lisbon. In the wake of a global settlement of Spanish and Portuguese differences in 1750,[13] a royal decree (*alvará*) of 14 October 1751 excluded all Brazilian traders from the Spanish colonies,[14] but it evidently merely diverted some of the direct contraband from Angola to a nominally legal indirect commerce through Rio to the Colônia do Sacramento in the 1750s. With a new Angolan governor more responsive to Lisbon's directives in office (Dom António Alvares da Cunha, 1753–58), Angolan slavers still making for the Plata simply declared their destination as "Santos," the Brazilian port just southwest of Rio serving São Paulo, and probably continued on to the south as they pleased.[15] Spain also attempted to meet its American colonies' needs for slaves itself during that period, awarding a series of small, limited-term licenses to private Spanish citizens, usually backed by British mercantile capital. Some of these Spaniards sought their slaves along outlying portions of the Angolan coast.[16]

The decline in the Minas Gerais market renewed the Rio slavers' interest in the illegal Platine trade in the 1760s. Bougainville, a French traveler visiting Rio in 1766, estimated that thirty or so small coasting vessels were then engaged in delivering slaves to the Plata in exchange for hides and silver,[17] no doubt operating under the shelter of the prohibition of direct trade from Angola. For the entire period 1742–1806, Rio accounted for over 70 percent of the slaves of known origin arriving from Brazil at Buenos Aires, and other ports to the south of Rio (Santos, Santa Catarina) sent another 16 percent or more.[18] Given southern Brazil's heavy

12. Taunay, *Subsídios*, p. 202.

13. The Treaty of Madrid; see Alden, *Royal Government*, pp. 88–89.

14. Ribeiro Júnior, *Colonização e monopólio*, p. 128, though anticipated by a Spanish-Portuguese treaty of 7 Jan. 1747; Taunay, *Subsídios*, p. 202.

15. The Luanda clearance records noted ships dispatched to "Colônia" or Santos (taken as a proxy destination south of Rio standing for Colônia), beginning in 1748 (one ship) and continuing in 1749 (four), 1752 (one), 1753 (one), 1756 (two), and 1757 (four).

16. E.g., at Loango; cf. Vasconcelos, 20 June 1760, AHU, Angola maço 3, seeking 8,000 slaves in five years. Molinari, *Trata de negros*, p. 62, indicates that none of these licenses specified deliveries to Buenos Aires, thus leaving the Plata open still to the southern Brazilians.

17. Kenneth R. Maxwell, *Conflicts and Conspiracies: Portugal and Brazil, 1750–1808* (New York: Cambridge University Press, 1973), pp. 8–9. Sousa Coutinho, 15 March 1770, AHU, Angola cx. 32, seemed to note that smuggling of slaves through Colônia directly from Angola had ceased in the 1750s, presumably leaving the way open to the Rio fleet noted in the 1760s. But Enrique M. Barba, "Sobre el contrabando de la Colônia del Sacramento (siglo XVIII)," *Investigaciones y ensayos* (Buenos Aires) 28 (1980): 69–70, put the legal demand for slaves at only about 600 (contemporary estimate).

18. Scheuss de Studer, *Trata de negros*, p. 324, Cuadro XVI.

dependence on slaves imported from Angola at this period, most of the captives taken to the Plata must be assumed to have come from Luanda or Benguela.

Slaving to the Plata apparently continued on into the 1770s, though perhaps disrupted by persistent Portuguese-Spanish hostilities along the coast south of Rio and proceeding temporarily under even deeper cover than before.[19] Angola's most astute eighteenth-century governor, Sousa Coutinho, remarked on the essential value of that part of the slave trade to Portugal's bullionist policy as other specie supplies dwindled in the 1760s and 1770s: slaves efficiently converted goods cheap in terms of silver, especially the Asian cottons sold in Africa, into laborers who brought high currency prices in the fields and silver mines of America.[20]

The Spanish-Portuguese peace settlement of 1777 apparently opened the floodgates to satisfy pent-up demand for contraband slaves through the Spanish stronghold on the Banda Oriental, Montevideo.[21] The stimulus that the opening of trade gave to Angolan exports is probably evident in the jump in exports of slaves at Benguela, from the depressed figure of 3,959 in 1777, the year of most intensive Spanish-Portuguese conflict in the "debatable lands" along the Plata, to 5,499 slaves in 1778 and an all-time high of 7,065 in 1779. The figures at Luanda, where Rio smugglers were presumably less prominent than at Benguela, showed a lesser dip in 1777 and then moved back into the range of normal levels in the years following.[22] Treating half of the increase as equivalent to the normal levels of trade to the Spanish territories would put its volume at 20 percent or more of Benguela exports.

Further Spanish efforts to establish independent national supplies of African labor for Buenos Aires and the Plata also followed the peace settlement of 1777, but the Spaniards once again failed to displace the Brazilians. The 1778 treaty of Amistad, Garantía, y Comercio awarded

19. Alden, *Royal Government*, p. 118, notes the Rio fleet trading through Colônia during the 1770s but deemphasizes the significance of silver in the trade, on the basis of evidence of silver shortages at the Rio mint during the decade, Spanish blockades around Colônia, and a Portuguese prohibition (10 Oct. 1770) against dispatching slaves from Rio to the Plata. Official complaints of this sort, however, may have testified only to the success of the colonials in avoiding metropolitan intervention in a trade that they utilized specifically to thwart the control of institutions like the Rio mint. It was also a period in which Brazilians attempted ventures into the Indian Ocean that must have consumed silver. They also managed somehow to support an active trade with returning Portuguese Asia ships that called illegally at Brazilian ports. Scheuss de Studer, *Trata de Negros*, pp. 260–61, 323–24, stresses the extent of "Portuguese" (i.e., Brazilian?) smuggling of slaves throughout the period down to 1778, as well as Spain's authorization of its own subjects to buy slaves in Rio; also see Sergio R. Villalobos, *Comercio y contrabando en el Rio de la Plata y Chile, 1700–1811* (Buenos Aires: Editorial de la Universidad de Buenos Aires, 1965), pp. 20–21.

20. Sousa Coutinho, 8 July 1770, AHU, Angola cx. 32.

21. Rocha Gameiro, in Taunay, *Subsídios*, p. 254.

22. These were not years in which African droughts might have affected deliveries of slaves to either of these two ports.

Spain African bases on the Atlantic islands of Anno Bon and Fernando Po, from which it could support Spanish slaving ventures. It also gave Spaniards permission to provision their shipping at the Portuguese islands of São Tomé and Príncipe in the Gulf of Guinea. It also included Portuguese recognition of Spanish rights to buy slaves along coasts adjacent to areas the Portuguese claimed in western central Africa. In practice, these concessions became reduced to rights in the Loango area, since Anno Bon and Fernando Po fought off the Spanish attempts at establishing sovereignty.[23] The terms of the treaty also gave Spanish merchants permission to buy slaves in Rio de Janeiro themselves, on the order of 1,500 or so per year. They did so only briefly before the Brazilian viceroy Dom Luís de Vasconcelos e Sousa barred them from the Brazilian capital on the grounds of shortages of labor in Rio de Janeiro.[24] In view of the generally depressed labor market of Brazil in the 1780s, and even allowing for the first signs of recovery with disruption of North American shipments of rice and cotton to England after the outbreak of the American War for Independence, it is still probable that Viceroy Vasconcelos e Sousa also had his eye on the competition that such direct Spanish purchases would work against his own countrymen's smuggling to the south. With the Spanish excluded from Brazil after 1780, with their subsequent loss of Fernando Po and Anno Bon, and with labor demands in the Plata rising even more with the economic upswing that followed liberal Bourbon reforms introduced in 1779, the stage was set for even more active Rio-based smuggling from Angola to the Plata in the 1780s and 1790s.[25]

In the preceding two decades Spanish markets had, by all accounts, played a crucial role in sustaining southern Brazil's slavers, even giving them a limited financial initiative in a trade otherwise financed by merchants from Lisbon. Argentine hides and the silver of Potosí yielded sufficient riches that they could carry goods to Africa on their own accounts, primarily local *gerebita* sold at Benguela. The concentration of these independent Rio merchants there began Benguela's late-century rise toward volumes equal to those at Luanda, reinforced its isolation from Lisbon's direct control, and left Luanda itself relatively open to metropolitan initiatives similarly motivated by the decline in bullion production in Brazil.

The Bahia and Pernambuco Trade at Luanda

Pernambuco's commercial weakness forced its traders to seek slaves where the strong and autonomous slavers of Bahia and Rio de Janeiro left open-

---

23. Scheuss de Studer, *Trata de negros,* p. 248.
24. Ibid., pp. 264–66.
25. Rudy Bauss, "Rio Grande do Sul in the Portuguese Empire: The Formative Years, 1777–1808," *Americas* 39, no. 4 (1983): 531, dates the late-century upsurge to this period.

ings for them. Bahia had excluded Pernambuco from the Mina Coast trade, Brazil's only alternative mid-eighteenth-century source of African labor, with Mozambique slaving only intermittent and insignificant at that time.[26] Since Recife could not compete at Rio-dominated Benguela, it looked to Luanda in particular for its slaves. There the Pernambuco trade generally varied inversely with the competition from its Bahian rivals. Pernambuco's share of Luanda slaves, low at the beginning of the century, rose as Bahia gradually excluded the slavers of Recife from its quasi-private slaving preserve at Mina through the 1750s. In the 1760s and 1770s, the chartered Lisbon companies added to their woes.

Local planter and commercial interests at Bahia developed their Mina trade against a competing Lisbon interest that was unable to sell goods in West Africa in competition with the British and French and that therefore continued the old seventeenth-century pattern of bringing slaves to Bahia from Angola.[27] The "Bahian" presence at Luanda thus reflected the fortunes of this Lisbon minority. So successful were the local Bahians by the 1720s that they rose to positions of prominence in the institutions of Salvador and were bringing 5,000 to 6,000 slaves yearly to Bahia from Mina at a time when imports to Bahia from Angola were running only 3,000 to 4,000.[28] Their successes at Mina deprived the Lisbon merchants of their sales of Angolan slaves. In 1735 the Luanda governor decried the export duties lost to the Angola government and called for prohibitions against the Bahians frequenting the Mina Coast.[29] Erosion of the Lisbon merchants' former strength at Bahia also reduced the deliveries of slaves that they had routed through Salvador to Rio at the peak of the gold boom and thus helped to open the markets of southern Brazil to the Rio slavers then building their own trade at Benguela.[30] By a directive of 25 May 1731, Lisbon had in fact closed the Mina trade, but the Bahian merchants, who did not depend on capital from Lisbon sources and who enjoyed the tacit support of a viceroy eager to retain tax revenues generated by their trade, ignored the order and intensified their slaving from Lower Guinea.[31]

26. Bahians did not like Mozambique slaves and regarded the voyage as too long for their small ships: Verger, *Flux et reflux,* p. 109 (doc. of 9 Aug. 1756); "Discurso preliminar," p. 145. They also had to face Lisbon's fears that Brazilian ventures into the Indian Ocean would become means of smuggling Indian cottons directly to America rather than through Portugal as the merchants of the metropole preferred: Jacob Pedro Arauss *(contratador do consulado da Casa da India), recopilação* and *alvará* of 12 Dec. 1772, AHU, India maço 120. I am grateful to Dauril Alden for calling my attention to this useful compilation of decrees respecting the India trade in the 1760s.

27. Flory, "Bahian Society," p. 218 et passim.

28. Ibid., p. 268; Verger, *Flux et reflux,* p. 141, on slaves from Mina. But cf. ibid., pp. 94–95, for estimates roughly double for Angola imports. On the politics of the Câmara, see Schwartz, *Sugar Plantations,* p. 277.

29. Freitas de Noronha, 28 March 1735, AHU, Angola cx. 20.

30. *Requerimento,* Manoel da Silva, n.d. (but ca. 1730s), AHU, Angola cx. 20.

31. Verger, *Flux et reflux,* pp. 66 ff., 94–95.

The proportion of ships from Bahia seeking slaves at Luanda thus declined sharply as its Mina trade thrived through the 1730s and 1740s. It reached its nadir in the 1750s, at the time that a tight local monopoly at Bahia exercised its greatest influence over the Mina trade, which then ran at a steady 3,500 slaves per year to Salvador alone, with others going on to Pernambuco and ports to the north.[32] Many fewer slaves departed Angola for Bahia at that period, by all indications.[33] Only with abolition of the local Bahians' monopoly in 1756 were Salvador's Lisbon merchants, and doubtless other traders as well, again able to sell slaves from Angola successfully. Bahia's percentage of Luanda exports accordingly rose slightly in the 1760s and 1770s.[34]

Pernambuco's direct trade from Angola rose as the Bahians withdrew through the 1750s and then fell again when they returned. Part of the apparent inverse relationship between Pernambuco and Bahia slaving at Luanda resulted from the Lisbon-based traders' habit of forwarding slave cargoes sent to Bahia but not disposed of profitably there to satisfy demand in the northern Brazilian port. Pernambuco's traders had mounted efforts to crack the Bahian monopoly on the Mina Coast in the 1720s, but they seem never to have generated much more than half the Bahians' volume there.[35] Lisbon had attempted to preserve a role for the Pernambucans in the settlement that had conceded the local Bahia traders' monopoly in 1743, doubtless with its own stake in the Pernambuco trade in mind. Pernambuco's marginal tobacco growers continued to find their main, though modest, market in Mina, where they apparently obtained slaves for transshipment to Minas Gerais.[36] Most Pernambuco imports of slaves after 1760 came from Angola, under the terms of a monopoly conceded to the Pernambuco Company.

32. APB, OR/54/no. 83, with thanks to Dauril Alden for this reference; the figures were also apparently used by Verger, *Flux et reflux*, p. 61. Also Verger, pp. 50, 100–108, 664.

33. APB, OR/49/fols. 41v–44v, give the 1727–48 total slave imports at Bahia as 5,022 per annum, which, given the 3,500 annually from Mina (see text above), leaves 1,500 or so from Angola. The average of 2,213 Angola/Luanda exports to Bahia recorded for 9 of those 22 years probably included some slaves sent on to Pernambuco and the other captaincies to the north, as mortality would not by then have reduced slave cargoes by 33%. Contemporary estimates sometimes ran higher: Carreira, "Companhias pombalinas de navegação," p. 75, has annual figures of 10,000–12,000 from Mina and 6,000–7,000 from Angola between 1727 and 1737; the "Discurso preliminar," p. 342, puts the total from all sources between 1754 and 1775 at 10,000 per year. Also see Alden, "Late Colonial Brazil," pp. 10–11, Table 5. By 1781, around 20 small vessels (ca. 250 slaves each?) would have been delivering 5,000 slaves per year from Mina, and 8–10 larger ones (ca. 350 slaves?) would have brought another 2,800–3,500 slaves from Angola: Taunay, *Subsídios*, p. 103, citing Silva Lisboa. Cf. Schwartz, *Sugar Plantations*, p. 344.

34. See the recollection of this shift in "Discurso preliminar," pp. 345–46.

35. Verger, *Flux et reflux*, p. 36, for 1727–40.

36. Alden, "Late Colonial Brazil," p. 12, implies average annual imports for the 1750s at Pernambuco of 2,187 slaves, with more than 60% being sent on to Rio and eventual sale to Minas Gerais. Presumably those sent on were Mina slaves, as Rio would seem to have had more direct sources for the Angolan slaves reaching the mines.

As an African market for local produce—in addition to tobacco, also sugar and *gerebita,* various hides and oxtails, and nets or hammocks—the local merchants regarded Mina as their main objective. Angola took a much larger percentage of the European and Asian goods transshipped from Europe, as well as the same *gerebitas* and foodstuffs, footwear, roofing tiles, and flour grinding mills.[37] But Pernambuco remained dependent to a much larger extent than Bahia on Angolan slaves and dependent on Bahia for its labor from Mina, particularly after the 1760s.[38] As only a secondary market for the slavers of Bahia and with higher prices for slaves than Salvador, it presented an attractive opportunity for Lisbon monopolists working through Angola.

Though Brazilian prices for slaves had slipped disastrously by the 1760s and 1770s, importers of trade goods at Luanda not only maintained but even raised the *réis* values of the *letras* covering goods they loaned against future sales of slaves in Brazil. With *letra* costs around 60$000 owed for each slave shipped and something less 100$000 available at Rio, Bahia, or Pernambuco to cover that prime cost and all delivery expenses, margins had dropped well below the level of profitability. Taking the same percentage estimates of costs as had prevailed before 1760 (in effect allowing for inflation equal to the rise in *letra* values charged against slaves)[39] and lowering the estimate of mortality losses to 15 percent, the all-in costs of prime slaves put up for sale in Rio would have been 125$000, or more than 25 percent above the revenues likely to be available to cover them. Ordinary slaves sold at still greater losses. The *réis* terms of trade had swung so strongly against Luso-African sellers of slaves that their resort to cheaper goods available by smuggling with the French and British, their retreat to the interior, and the other evasive strategies of the distressed mainland traders in this period seem at least justified by the economics working against them. Any mortality at all among the slaves would have been fatal (though in a figurative sense) to the slaves' owners, as they repeatedly asserted. The Pombal Company records, which show few gains from buying and selling slaves in this period even under the privileges of the companies' monopolies, confirm the broadly disastrous position of slave owners inferred from these estimates.[40]

37. *Anais da Biblioteca nacional do Rio de Janeiro* 28 (1906): 482, with specific reference to patterns of trade in 1747.

38. Taunay, *Subsídios,* p. 225, paraphrasing Corrêa, *História de Angola.* By the 1760s less than 8% of the 2,123 slaves entering Pernambuco continued on to the declining mining regions; Alden, "Late Colonial Brazil," p. 12.

39. See the text of Chapter 12, above, following n. 89, for percentage estimates.

40. Carreira, "Companhias pombalinas de navegação"; Carreira, *Notas sobre o tráfico português,* pp. 47, 49, however, rationalized that the companies deliberately limited accounting profits in the slaving phases of their integrated operations in order to stimulate production in Brazil. The "Relação sobre escravatura," n.d. (ca. 1760s), AHU, Angola maço 10 (D.O.), estimated a break-even delivery cost of 159$000 to northern Brazil.

The slave trade as a whole was obviously operating near or below its break-even point after 1760, and so the 25 percent difference between the cost of landing Angola slaves shipped legally and the 100$000 available in Brazil to cover them may represent the value of Luso-African defaults on their *letra* debts at that time, less liquidation of their assets to pay their debts. The Luso-Africans' *reviros* would have achieved savings from taxes avoided (about 10%) and from reduced costs of the goods obtained from the French and British, less the added costs of paying "cash" to the foreigners rather than charging back some of the Luanda cost of borrowed goods in eventual bankruptcy and flight (the two together amounting to the other 15%).[41]

Brazilian Advances into the Angolan Slave Trade after 1780

From the Plata to the Amazon, South American agriculture and ranching took on new life beginning about 1780, and the better times in Brazil created demands for African labor that allowed the autonomous Rio de Janeiro slavers to advance further from passive transporters to active owners of the Angolan cargoes they carried. They also acquired the backing of British merchants selling goods illegally in Brazil, thus beginning a long-term shift from Lisbon to Britain as the direct source of the textiles and other manufactures sold for slaves, laying the base both for the domination of post-1810 Brazilian commerce by British finance and for the illegal trade of 1830s and 1840s. Also in the 1790s, Spaniards from the Plata regions moved up to Rio to escape civil conflicts. With them they brought liquid capital that added fuel to the independent growth of slaving at Brazil's viceregal capital.[42] The Brazilians added a novel nineteenth-century veneer, based on providing labor to produce industrial raw materials, especially cottons from Brazil, over the eighteenth-century bullionist and mercantilist core of Angolan slaving.

The Brazilians found the field in Africa wide open, in part because

41. Extending the chain of inferences even further, one might guess that Luso-Africans were buying goods from the British for something over half the price of equivalent goods available at Luanda (i.e., the advantage that Luanda officials attributed to foreign competition), or at savings of about 30$000. Suppose then that successful smugglers dealt about equally in contraband imports and in legal goods bought from Luanda factors of Lisbon merchants. They thus reduced the average costs of a slave by the 15$000 needed to support the trade. Losses to defaulted debtors working entirely within the legal trade would have amounted to about the same 15$000 for every slave, or 25% of the value of the goods loaned against them. The calculation clearly portrays the hard choice that mercantilist restraints forced upon Lisbon merchants: sales lost to the foreigners or returns lost to bad debts. Figures in this range, while not directly verifiable, seem plausible and consistent with the general picture of the trade reconstructed in nonquantified terms.

42. Santos, "Comércio do porto do Rio de Janeiro," p. 5.

Lisbon merchants effectively withdrew from the Angola trade after the
death of the king Dom José in 1777 and dismissal of his chief minister,
the Marquis of Pombal. Nor could Luanda's Luso-Africans, weakened by
decades of reduced prices for slaves in Brazil and by the hostility of the
Pombal regime, offer serious resistance as the Brazilians moved in to take
advantage of rising prices in America by buying slaves in Angola. The
main competition that the newly expansive Brazilians faced along the
shores of southwestern Africa in the years from 1780 until 1809 came
from foreigners, French as well as British, who matched the Brazilians'
willingness to buy slaves on the spot, collaborating freely and even openly
with Angolan creoles eager to play them off against buyers from Portuguese America, and from growing numbers of Spaniards venturing out
under the stimulus of Bourbon reforms that emanated out over the southern Atlantic from Madrid.

The agricultural renaissance in South America drew its vitality from
growing northern European capacity to process tropical raw materials,
combined with interrupted supplies of those commodities from the Caribbean and North American colonies directly controlled by Britain and
France. European sugar prices also rose for the first time in more than a
century, particularly after the Saint Domingue slave revolt effectively removed France's largest producer from the market early in the 1790s.
Bahia's stagnant economy began to revive moderately during the preceding
two decades of Pombaline stimulation but picked up speed and roughly
doubled its exports of sugar between the late 1770s and 1809.[43] Pernambuco sugar followed a similar upward course. The two northeastern captaincies found the slave labor necessary to support such growth in part by
continuing their imports of Mina slaves and in part by keeping those slaves
for local agriculture rather than sending a portion on to Minas Gerais. As
a result, the overall numbers of slaves entering Brazil through Salvador
and Recife increased relatively little compared to the preceding years, and
the Bahian and Pernambuco presence at Luanda slipped again. Pernambuco dropped particularly after the Pernambuco Company wound down
its operations in the late 1770s.

Of greater significance for Angolan slaving was the even more rapid
growth of sugar production in southern Brazil from its historically modest
levels and its orientation toward the production of *gerebita* for Angola to
buoyant exports of *muscovado* sugar to Portugal. By 1800 the volume of
sugar leaving Rio de Janeiro in good years tripled or quadrupled that of
the 1770s. The dynamism of the southern sugar industry also propelled
cane cultivation into the adjoining interior captaincy of São Paulo, where
it became the major export crop until the very end of Brazilian slave

43. All production figures from Alden, "Late Colonial Brazil."

importing, although eclipsed in most studies of the era by the later fame of the nineteenth-century coffee of the region.[44] Angola thus acquired renewed significance as a supplier of labor, as well as a market for the by-products of Brazilian agriculture, and Brazilian slavers consequently sought to gain ownership of the labor as well as of the *aguardente*.

A brand new cotton sector emerged in Brazil's northern and northeastern captaincies when prices soared as war between Britain and its former North American colonies disrupted that country's main supply lines for raw fiber just as its textile industry matured. Cotton thus provided an even more important stimulus than sugar to the demand for new slaves from Pernambuco north and west to Maranhão. Maranhão's cotton exports had begun rising before 1780 under favorable Pombaline economic policies, but on only a modest scale that the increases of the 1790s dwarfed, both there and in Pernambuco.[45]

Expansion in other exports throughout the colony—tobacco (Bahia), rice (mainly Maranhão but also secondarily Pará), wheat (the far south), coffee (Rio de Janeiro before 1809, with São Paulo becoming important later), and hides (Rio Grande do Sul)—added to the need for African labor to work Brazilian agriculture. Corresponding dynamism in coastal and interior provisioning trades for the thriving seaport towns and the plantations completed the portrait of a Brazilian economy more in need of new Angolan slave labor from the tropical north to the far south than it had ever been before.[46]

The diversifying economy of the Spanish domains served through the Plata also grew as a market for the slavers of Rio de Janeiro at the end of the eighteenth century. A hide industry on the southern pampas, under ranchers eager to evade the high costs of slaves available through Spanish merchants resident in Buenos Aires, particularly slaves provided by the royally chartered traders bringing labor direct from Africa; the inability of Buenos Aires merchants to crack African slave markets on their own; and wartime interruptions of Spanish efforts to supply slaves to the Platine colonies created high prices that Rio merchants hastened to capture for themselves.[47] Such illegal trade received implicit intermittent encouragement from top Portuguese officials in Rio still eager in the 1780s to replace lost Brazilian gold output with imports of Spanish silver.[48]

During the 1790s, the Napoleonic wars in Europe disrupted the flow of European trade goods sent on to Angola for slaves, particularly from

44. Ibid., esp. p. 628, and Table 6, pp. 630–31. Also Brown, "Internal Commerce."

45. Alden, "Late Colonial Brazil," pp. 635–39, Table 8.

46. See also Bauss, "Rio de Janeiro"; Brown, "Internal Commerce."

47. Socolow, *Merchants of Buenos Aires*, pp. 67, 124–25; Scheuss de Studer, *Trata de negros*, pp. 279–81, on the apparent lone Spanish merchant able to supply slaves on his own with any success; Bauss, "Rio de Janeiro," pp. 194–95.

48. Bauss, "Rio de Janeiro," p. 196.

Britain. The shortages forced the Rio traders to divert a modest portion of the gold and silver ordinarily sent on to Lisbon or London into the African trade to pay for slaves.[49] Spanish traders also became briefly active along Angolan coasts in the period, adding to a flow of specie that paradoxically threatened to ruin slaving. Since the gold and silver did not circulate in the African interior, they instead accumulated as profits in the hands of slave exporters in Luanda and Benguela, liquidated out of slaving businesses run on textiles rather than on coin.

In effect, specie reduced the working capital on which the entire African credit structure depended and depressed the volume of the trade. By 1796 and 1797, after a delay created by the plentiful supplies of slaves available during the drought of the preceding decade and by the ability of exporters to draw on the previous credit they had extended to African suppliers in goods, the volume of slaving leaving both Luanda and Benguela declined by 30 percent and more.

At Benguela in the 1780s, local officials apparently tapped the specie in the hands of Rio traders by personally demanding a portion of the export duties in coin.[50] One can imagine easily enough how the transaction worked by analogy to twentieth-century techniques employed to capture wages paid in gold by South African mines to workers from the adjoining Portuguese territory of Mozambique. With Brazilians buying the slaves outright on the African coast, creole sellers had no means with which to pay the export taxes owed. The Benguela official in charge of dispatching slaves would have offered to pay the duties others owed on their slaves with his personal bills of exchange, which he would write only against repayment by the slave shippers in specie. Thus he personally collected bullion at Benguela, and the government received *letras* that he paid later from whatever less valuable forms of asset he held in Brazil—most likely *letras* of sugar exporters that he received for slaves he sold there. In essence, he would have managed to sell his own slaves for silver in Benguela, greatly streamlining the complicated series of transactions otherwise required to obtain bullion in America.

Further liberalization of Spanish commercial policy in 1791 gave foreigners, including Brazilians, permission to sell slaves into Spanish possessions through Montevideo, while reserving most other imports to Spanish merchants. Judging from the strong impression that the slave trade to Spanish colonies made on Angolan governors of the 1790s—who regarded

49. For reports of gold, Almeida e Vasconcelos, 7 Feb. 1795, 21 Oct. 1795, and 23 Jan. 1796, AHU, Angola cx. 44; Botelho de Vasconcelos, 27 July 1796, AHU, Angola cx. 44; de Mello, 11 Oct. 1797, AHU, Angola cx. 44. Also João Victo da Silva, n.d. (ca. 1792), AHU, Angola cx. 42.

50. See the Joseph António Ferreira Diniz memo in Moçâmedes, 28 April 1789, AHU, Angola cx. 41. Similar official skimming of bullion was at the center of the Brazilian trade to Mozambique in the 1810s: Carreira, *Tráfico português de escravos,* pp. 25–26.

a "good part" of the 6,000 to 7,000 slaves that Luanda sent to Rio each
year (and perhaps an equal number from Benguela?) as continuing on to
the Plata[51]—2,500 to 3,500 slaves annually would not seem an excessive
estimate for the peak years of the 1790s, or around 25 percent of Rio's
total imports of slaves.[52] To some extent, at least, these transfers of slaves
to the Spaniards relieved a tendency toward oversupply and weak prices
that had developed in southern Brazil as Rio-based capital tapped the
increased number of slaves offered in Angola during the drought of the
1780s and 1790s.[53]

Official permission to introduce slaves at Montevideo also provided
Brazilians with the opportunity to smuggle other goods to the Plata, very
much as the British and French had done a century before. The list of
products resembled those the Brazilians had formerly sent to Angola:
sugar, *aguardente,* timber, rice, tiles, and so on, with the addition of Angolan wax.[54] The Brazilians were offering a wider range of goods in Angola
at that time and began to face difficulties in taking their returns entirely
in slaves. Restrictions on tight-packing may also have forced them to
recover lost freight revenues by stowing wax in unused corners of the
holds of their ships. At the end of the century they began to make more
substantial purchases of African beeswax, mostly for Brazilian and Spanish
consumption, since it found little acceptance in Portuguese markets dominated by the favored competing wax of the Algarve, southern Portugal.

Rio slave exporting to the Plata became an important part of a flourishing trade to the south by the early nineteenth century. Spaniards sent
coasting launches and fishing boats up to outports south of the city to
buy slaves with livestock, salt, and hides, but the trade conducted on
Portuguese initiative must have involved silver, since government officials
regarded it as "extremely advantageous." An 1808 estimate placed the
number of slaves sent south over the preceding two decades at 60,000,
or about 3,000 annually. It was a large enough proportion of the total
that officials at the southernmost transshipment point, Porto Alegre in
Rio Grande do Sul, blamed Montevideo for doubling local prices for slaves.
Slaves accounted for 29 percent of the value of the trade from Rio to
Santos, also on the way south, in 1816.[55]

If Luanda's strong trading ties with Rio in the 1780s and 1790s

51. De Mello, 12 March 1799, published in *Arquivos de Angola* 2, no. 14 (1936): 593–
602.

52. Cf. Bauss's estimate of Brazilian slave shipments to the Plata in "Rio Grande do
Sul," pp. 532–33.

53. Moçâmedes, 28 March 1787, AHU, Angola cx. 40; João Victo da Silva, n.d.
(ca. 1792), AHU, Angola cx. 42.

54. Scheuss de Studer, *Trata de negros,* pp. 296–97; Corrêa, *História de Angola,* 1:174n,
on the lack of adequate markets in Brazil. On wax generally, Vellut, "Diversification de
l'économie de cueillete."

55. Brown, "Internal Commerce," pp. 205–7, 363, 364.

suggest generally growing Brazilian influence in Angola at the end of the century, the Brazilian buyers of slaves concentrated much of their activity at Benguela and drove Benguela's legal exports of slaves to their all-time peaks. The searing drought of 1785–94 brought captive refugees onto the African market, and simultaneously peaking French deliveries of Asian textiles enabled Benguela merchants to assort them with *gerebitas* to double the volume of slaves leaving the Brazilians' southern Angolan hideout between 1780 and 1793–95. The Rio merchants had always sold their goods directly for slaves at Benguela, unlike the Lisbon merchants' use of bills of exchange at Luanda, and so they did not have to overcome as strong an Angolan position in ownership of the slaves. The high profits that Rio slavers earned from selling Benguela slaves for high prices in Brazil must have generated some of the working capital that allowed them to expand their operations north to Luanda.

The Battle over British Goods

The Brazilians found additional financing principally from British sources, whose influence spread around Rio long in advance of the formal opening of Brazilian ports to merchants from Britain in 1809.[56] British and French traders, attracted by booming prosperity, became notoriously active along Brazilian coasts by the 1780s.[57] The British in particular sought direct access to the Brazilian market, because cottons were replacing woolens as the principal British textile export but were excluded from Portugal to protect nascent domestic Portuguese manufacturers and Lisbon's ancient cotton trade with Asia. British merchantmen outbound for Cape Horn and the Pacific with woolens and cottons made the island of Santa Catarina, southwest of Rio, a favorite stopping point, which added to the ostensible attractions of the trade south to the Plata.[58] Portuguese customs reforms introduced in 1784 were directed in large part against such British con-

---

56. E.g., *requerimento* of John Truecross (ca. 1807), AHU, Angola cx. 58, for details of arrangements he had made with a Brazilian merchant in Bahia. Also Saldanha da Gama, 22 Sept. 1808, AHU, Angola cx. 58.

57. Maxwell, *Conflicts and Conspiracies*, p. 77. See also Fernando A. Novais, *Portugal e Brasil na crise do antigo sistema colonial (1777–1808)* (São Paulo: HUCITEC, 1979), pp. 176 ff., esp. 185–87, and various emphases on the same point in Rudy Bauss, "A Preliminary Examination of the British Role in the Destruction of the Lusitanian and Indian Cotton Manufacturers and the Cessation of Trade between the Luso-Brazilian Empire and India: 1780–1830" (Unpublished paper, ca. 1979).

58. See *parecer* of Joaquim José da Rocha, in Junta do Comercio, Agricultura, Fabricas e Navegação do Reino e Dominios Ultramarinos (Rio de Janeiro), *consulta* (sobre o alvará de 11 Jan. 1758) of 12 Sept. 1820, AHU, Angola maço 3, for admission of foreign backing behind earlier slave sales to the Plata. Also Santos, "Comércio do porto do Rio de Janeiro," p. 116.

traband, and not least at Luanda.[59] Part of the Brazilian motivation for relocating at less closely regulated Benguela would have been to bring illegal foreign cottons from Rio after French sources of Asian textiles dried up at the southern Angolan port in 1792 or 1793.

After 1791 British ships acquired formal rights to put in to Brazilian ports in time of distress, and captains shamelessly used the pretext to supply the main Brazilian ports with British goods. Already in 1792 a visiting English lord found Rio's shops "full of Manchester manufactures, and other English goods even to English prints"—not all of them imported legally through Lisbon.[60] At Rio, almost under the nose of the Portuguese viceroy, no less than 152 English merchant ships sought "succor" between 1791 and 1800, well over one every month for the entire decade, and at rates approaching two per month in some years.[61] They would certainly have dealt mainly with the local Rio traders more than with factors representing Lisbon merchants, and the Brazilians must have sent some proportion of the smuggled wares they took on to Angola in their autonomous trade in slaves.

The illegal British goods were a matter of particular delicacy in Angola. Southern Brazil required these goods to keep new slaves flowing in to support its agricultural prosperity, and that prosperity in turn sustained Portugal. On the other hand, Lisbon merchants lost African sales to the Brazilians bringing the slaves. By the late 1790s, imports of contraband textiles at Luanda, though never mentioned explicitly in official correspondence because of their contradictory implications, compelled the governor finally to implement the customs procedures outlined in 1784. Inspections of goods entering Luanda provoked enormous opposition among the slavers dependent on such imports to continue their businesses.[62] The Rio traders, once again using Benguela as their main route of illegal access to Angolan slaves, introduced British goods from Rio through the lax administration at the southern port and then sent them on down the coast to Luanda to pass the much more rigorous customs inspections there as internal "Benguela" goods, already entered into the Portuguese commercial sphere even though they might lack the Lisbon tax stamps that technically certified their legality.[63] The governor and the traders disputed this vital economic issue in official documents entirely in terms of inconsequential fees and other legal and technical side issues associated with it.

59. Santos, "Comércio do porto do Rio de Janeiro," p. 159.

60. Lang, *Portuguese Brazil*, p. 189.

61. ANRJ, cód. 76, lists 12–20 British ships, as compared to 30–40 Lisbon ships annually at the same period.

62. Esp. the emphasis on local merchants' resistance in de Mello, 12 Aug. 1801, AHU, Angola cx. 50. For the whole story, Miller, "Imports at Luanda."

63. De Mello, 12 Aug. 1801, AHU, Angola cx. 50.

This illegal British trade undercut merchants of Portuguese origin resident in Brazil the most and confirmed the prominence of the independent Rio commercial stratum in Angolan slaving. Thus, well before 1809 the British had a firm foothold in Rio commercial circles, were tied in to the creole trade networks at Luanda and Benguela, and were providing many of the goods with which the Brazilians bought slaves outright in Angola.[64]

The clear-sighted Angolan governor of the 1780s, the Barão de Moçâmedes (1784–90), realistically accepted the Brazilians as the major sources of financial strength in the slave trade of that time, even though he had been sent out by Lisbon to bring the colony back under closer metropolitan control. One of his initial dispatches, written in 1784, soon after he arrived in the colony, obliquely alluded to the growing Brazilian influence in terms of the standing dispute over the order in which ships loaded their fragile slave cargoes and made sail for Brazil. The precedence given vessels of greater capitalization and consequent ability to buy slaves on the spot in Luanda (*efeitos próprios*) in the decree of 1758 he straightforwardly presented as meaning ships from Portugal. Metropolitan privileges were being violated, he reported, evidently by local friends of the Brazilians during the two-year interim government since the death of the previous royally appointed governor in 1782. Although defending the Lisbon ships by alleging the falsity of the Brazilians' claims to *efeitos próprios* standing, he proposed a compromise that implicitly acknowledged their importance to the trade. He reinterpreted the 1758 decree, highly obsolete under the altered financial structure of Angolan slaving, to mean that no two Lisbon ships could ever depart in sequence, thus allowing at least one Brazilian captain to be boarding at all times.[65] He thus offered a significant concession in the revered Portuguese style of honoring the letter of the law while altering its application to accommodate changing circumstances. In this case, with Brazilian capital at the base of slaving, the established favoritism to Lisbon wealth threatened to bring desperately needed sources of labor for southern Brazil to a halt.

By 1786, Moçâmedes was writing more directly about the advantage that the Brazilians brought to the trade, though still bowing carefully toward Lisbon's sensitivity to the growing American competition. He noted specifically that the Brazilians were bringing in trade goods (*fazendas*) as well as the customary *gerebita*, underselling equivalent goods from Lisbon, and winning the business of the Angolan sellers of slaves.[66]

It is likely, though difficult to perceive in the elaborate avoidance of

64. Cf. Lugar, "Merchant Community," pp. 12–13, 74–75; José Jobson de Andrade Arruda, "O Brasil no comércio colonial (1796–1808): contribuição ao estudo quantitativo da economia colonial" (Ph.D. diss., Universidade de São Paulo, 1972), pp. 288, 296–98.

65. Moçâmedes, 16 Dec. 1784, AHU, Angola cx. 40.

66. Moçâmedes, 15 Oct. 1786, AHU, Angola cx. 40.

the real issue in the official documentation, that a significant group of new immigrants entered the Luanda merchant community at this time, not factors from Lisbon but rather traders from Rio de Janeiro. These men came as commission agents of merchants in southern Brazil in charge of the huge quantities of British trade goods that helped to advance Angolan slaving to record levels in the 1780s and 1790s. Their wealth allowed them to make inflationary loans of goods that stole a leaf from the book written by the well-heeled merchants of Lisbon on previous occasions in the 1720s and 1730s and in the 1760s.[67] From their investments flowed a whole range of commercial problems stressed in the 1790s by governors less realistic than Moçâmedes and much less sympathetic to the Brazilians.[68] Governors attempted to bring the trade in the interior under closer government control by reforming regulated marketplaces (the *feiras*) and by inspecting all goods that traders sent out from Luanda, both policies resurrected from measures that Governor Sousa Coutinho had taken to rein in Luso-Africans who were smuggling to the French and British during the 1760s. The conflict thus added commercial turmoil to the drought and warfare that also disturbed the decade.

The traders of the interior, as usual, were depicted as the villains. These accusations were as familiar as the measures taken to render them more responsive to Portuguese, rather than Brazilian, credit and capital. The trading agents were described as financially irresponsible, which meant in practice that they were accepting Lisbon goods on credit, buying slaves with them, and selling the slaves for cash to Brazilians offering American *gerebita,* British textiles, and specie. The classic *reviro* thus still thrived.

Governor Moçâmedes initiated the campaign against Brazilians bearing British imports at Luanda in 1785 by creating a local board of trade (the Junta do Comércio), composed of favored Lisbon merchants and empowered to authorize all dispatches of goods into the interior.[69] In 1789 the Junta recalled all traders then in the interior with goods taken from the city, by way of clearing the ground for their replacement by new men of its own choosing.[70] Reforms of the administration of the *feiras* followed, generally to strengthen the powers of new "directors" appointed by the Luanda *junta* over the unreliable *escrivães* (scribes) formerly nominated by Luso-African merchants and their men based in the interior.[71]

---

67. Also see Corrêa, *História de Angola,* 1:57, for an implied reference to financing coming from Brazil during his era (ca. 1780s).

68. Again, e.g., de Mello, 12 Aug. 1801, AHU, Angola cx. 50.

69. The documentation for this sequence of regulations is too extensive to cite here in detail. For a resumé of some of it, see Couto, *Capitães-mores,* pp. 209–11. Much has been published in the *Arquivos de Angola,* esp. vol. 2, nos. 9 and 14 (1936). The key archival sources are in the Arquivo Histórico de Angola, esp. códs. 85–91 and 2693.

70. Discussed in Chapter 17 below.

71. See the published correspondence on the key *feira* at Kasanje in *Arquivos de Angola,* vol. 2; also Chapter 17 below.

The Junta produced ordinances in 1793 that strictly controlled the "legitimate" agents sent to the interior and even provided military escorts to make certain that slaves sent down to the coast reached the merchants who had financed their purchase.[72]

By the term of Governor Dom Miguel António de Mello (1795–1800), tensions so deeply divided government officials and Lisbon merchants opposing the illegal Brazilian trade from its Angolan supporters that traders at Luanda took the unprecedented step of filing a formal complaint against the Crown's representative appointed to carry out these policies. The governor had evicted some of the worst offenders among the merchants from Luanda and had driven others to depart voluntarily for Brazil.[73] Lisbon merchants joined the fight against the Brazilian trade by sending their own ships laden with Asian goods to Luanda,[74] but the Angolans continued to take these goods on credit and then disappear with them into the interior.

Together, these factors—the infusion of Brazilian capital, the flight of the local traders from tightened government regulation, and the cheap slaves available during the drought—produced the eastward movement of the slaving frontier at the end of the eighteenth century. For the first time credit from the Atlantic reached through Kwango valley kingdoms like Kasanje and penetrated the heart of the Lunda empire, where also for the first time, European-financed traders began to buy slaves at the Lunda *musumba,* the imperial capital, for themselves.

It was from this perspective that the chronicler of the colony's history, Elias Alexandre da Silva Corrêa, wrote his celebrated description of Angola at the end of the eighteenth century. Corrêa was a south Brazilian, and his attribution of the commercial problems in Portugal's African colony to its metropolitan creditors betrays his sympathies with his American countrymen. He described the respectable established *comissário* merchants of Luanda as selling imported goods (the ones they bought from Brazilian ships) on credit to traders who took them on to the interior and as handling the slaves coming back on the basis of commissions. That is, they took no ownership of the slaves, but rather merely expedited their sale to buyers on ships from Brazil in Luanda harbor.[75] The villains of his economic scenario were not these debtors, but rather the big Lisbon ships that unloaded trade goods in quantities greater than the local markets could

---

72. *Bando* and Crown endorsement in AHU, Angola maço 4-A.
73. Among a good deal of correspondence surrounding this dispute, de Mello letters in AHU, Angola cx. 46, and his response to charges in 3 Jan. 1801, AHU, Angola cx. 51, and 26 Feb. 1802, AHU, Angola cx. 52. Also the report by Godinho, 19 Oct. 1804, AHU, Angola cx. 55, and de Mello's reply of 12 July 1805, AHU, Angola cx. 55.
74. See following chapter.
75. Corrêa, *História de Angola,* 1:32.

handle and who sold them directly off the ship through their own super-cargoes to anyone who would buy. At such times, the established merchants survived only through their monopoly of the Brazilian staples of the trade—sugar, *gerebita,* food, leathers, and timber.[76] He discreetly made no mention of the British goods to which all other evidence points.[77]

The interruption of contact with Europe during the postrevolutionary wars between France and Britain seems to have consolidated the Brazilian merchants' position in Angola, bypassing the Portuguese goods importers and the Angolan sellers of slaves in Brazil. The wars knocked the French out of the trade, and the Angolan creoles, unable to smuggle independently to obtain goods they needed, became dependent on the Brazilians.[78] Shipping was disrupted from about 1793 to 1797 at Benguela,[79] and traders experienced a serious shortage of the Indian-type *fazendas de negro,* cheap cottons (mostly British imitations by then), on which the purchase of slaves depended. Some Brazilian merchants even took advantage of the absence of Portugal's foreign competitors from Cabinda and bought slaves north of the Zaire mouth for the first time in years.[80] Enough Brazilians went there that they created a shortage of shipping at Luanda.[81] When hostilities ceased in Europe, a new wave of Brazilian traders appeared on the scene to buy slaves directly for goods and—almost unprecedented in Angola—even for cash.[82] Their timing betrayed the probable involvement of the British and the Spanish as financial backers of these ventures, as only one Lisbon ship landed with foreign goods at Luanda, presumably of British-Asian origin sent through a free port created in Lisbon to restore the role in the transit trade in cotton textiles to Brazil and Africa that the metropole had lost.[83]

By the end of the century, Brazilians virtually controlled Angolan slaving and had even gained support within the government hierarchy from the *ouvidor geral,* or chief judge, Félix Correa de Araujo. When Governor de Mello tried to protect the faltering Lisbon merchants in

76. Ibid., 1:51–52, 56–57.
77. But for *reviros,* see ibid., 1:31.
78. Almeida e Vasconcelos, 7 Feb. 1795 and 21 Sept. 1795, AHU, Angola cx. 44; Almeida e Vasconcelos to Joaquim Jozé da Silva (*capitão-mor,* Ambaca), 7 Feb. 1796, AHU, Ofícios para Angola, cód. 89, fols. 19–21; also 7 Feb. 1797, fols. 253v–55; end of shortages noted ibid., 1 March 1797, fols. 264v–65.
79. Botelho de Vasconcelos, 28 Feb. 1797, AHU, Angola cx. 49.
80. Almeida e Vasconcelos to Luiz Pinto de Souza, 4 Oct. 1796, AHU, cód. 1633, fols. 163v–64; de Mello, 12 Nov. 1798, AHU, Angola cx. 45.
81. Almeida e Vasconcelos, 29 Jan. 1797, AHU, Angola cx. 45.
82. De Mello, 11 Oct. 1797 and 12 Aug. 1798, AHU, Angola cx. 44 and 45.
83. De Mello, 12 Nov. 1798, AHU, Angola cx. 45. See also Rudy Bauss, "A Legacy of British Free Trade Policies: The End of the Trade and Commerce between India and the Portuguese Empire, 1780–1830" (Unpublished paper, ca. 1981), and idem, "A Preliminary Examination," for the "free port" at Goa and the routing of British Asian textiles through it to Lisbon.

Luanda, the *ouvidor* attempted to seize control of the regulatory process
and began authorizing traders and goods to enter the interior on his own
authority. He also forwarded to Lisbon the merchant's allegations that
Governor de Mello had limited commerce and thus reduced the king's
slave export duties by placing artificial restrictions on the freedom of trade.
When de Mello had forced three or four of Luanda's largest traders to
return to Brazil, they had taken with them significant amounts of capital,
perhaps the equivalent of 2,000 slaves, or 10 to 15 percent of the colony's
annual exports.[84]

The Brazilian Fringe

Brazil's far northern captaincies of Pará and Maranháo became more important markets for Angolan slaves at the end of the century as their exports
of cotton and other tropical products increased. Owing to the lack of an
established Brazilian merchant marine there capable of mounting the lengthy
voyage all the way down to Angola, the far north was the only part of
the trade in which Brazilians did not dominate. The new demands of the
northern captaincies for labor, though still filled for the most part by slaves
from Upper Guinea, became apparent at Luanda in the early 1790s, principally in the hands of merchants from Portugal. The northern Brazilians
had cotton, of interest to Portugal, but lacked currency or commodities
in demand by slavers from other parts of Brazil. Southern Brazilians headed
for Pará complained that they could obtain payment there for slaves only
in agricultural produce, and even then only after significant delays.[85] Ships
would have had to arrive at the time of the harvest to obtain payment,
and produce equal in value to a single shipload of slaves required no less
than three vessels to carry away.

The voyage was thus a difficult and unprofitable one for any but
merchants from Portugal, particularly given the alternative of selling the
same slaves in nearby central and southern Brazil. The Portuguese were
only too glad to take the profits they received for slaves in agricultural
commodities, which in practice meant cotton that they could sell in Lisbon
to the British for gold. So attractive was this business that early in the
nineteenth century, merchants, probably from Lisbon and doubtless backed
by British buyers of Maranháo cotton, proposed a company that would
have delivered some 3,000 slaves to Pará alone each year for an entire

84. E.g., de Mello, 31 Jan. 1801, AHU, Angola cx. 52; Félix Correa de Araujo, 12
April 1801, AHU, Angola cx. 51. The Godinho exoneration of 19 Oct. 1804, AHU, Angola
cx. 55, on this as on other points was a clear whitewash.
    85. Moçâmedes, 26 March 1787, AHU, Angola cx. 40; Botelho de Vasconcelos, 3
March 1799, AHU, Angola cx. 47.

decade.[86] The Crown gave special encouragement to Lisbon's Pará trade at Luanda through higher freight rates and by exempting it after 1794 from the 8$700 duty paid on slaves the Brazilians shipped to all other ports. It attracted frequent merchants in the 1790s.[87] Its true extent may have been even greater than that revealed in official export figures that show only Luanda and Benguela slaves sent directly to Pará and Maranhão, as in many ways it remained an extension of the old metropolitan-dominated commercial system centered on Pernambuco. Some of the slaves nominally dispatched to Recife must have gone on from that port in smaller craft to buyers in the far north.

Northern Brazil's proximity to the even higher prices for slaves in the British, Spanish, and other non-Portuguese islands of the Caribbean worried Luanda officials responsible for preventing ships from sailing to ports outside the relatively tightly regulated nexus of the trade to Brazil south of Pernambuco. Slaves nominally sent to Pernambuco and Pará may therefore also have occasionally found their way entirely past northeastern Brazil and on to foreign buyers in the West Indies.

As a result of these attractions in the equatorial latitudes, reported Luanda exports of slaves to Maranhão and Pará rose after 1800 into the range of 3,000 to 4,000 slaves each year. The ten or more ships leaving annually often formed a major component of Luanda's total trade and surely constituted the only route on which non-Brazilian slavers held any significant position. In any case, to the extent that cotton led Brazil's late-eighteenth-century revival of trade with Europe and to the degree that gold sent from Britain to pay for Brazilian fibers turned into the decade's main source of specie, Lisbon's merchants had once again managed to position themselves at the center of the Brazilian economy as it was viewed from Portugal, with substantial government influence exerted in their favor from Lisbon as well as at Luanda. The Brazilians, however advantageous they found slave prices in the sugar captaincies of the south and in the Plata, still sold slaves partly on the fringes of the colonial economy. In terms of slaving, however, the fringe—the complex and increasingly autonomous economy of central and southern Brazil—had grown larger than the center.

At Luanda, Governor de Mello, even while defending his application of Lisbon's Angolan commercial policies, acknowledged that the tensions there stemmed from the greed and high costs of goods from merchants in the metropole. The Luanda traders, with no choice but to deal with Lisbon rather than with the Brazilians (he avoided putting this distinction

86. Rebelo, *Relações*, pp. 88–89.
87. Almeida e Vasconcelos, 20 Jan. 1794 and 2 Oct. 1794, AHU, Angola cx. 43; ANTT, Junta do Comércio, maço 62, macete 123 (*alvará* of 19 Oct. 1798); cf. Lopes, *Escravatura*, p. 96.

in such invidious terms), were broke and had no capital of their own. The goods they obtained from Lisbon they had to accept on terms that had run in the vicinity of 40 percent interest during the recent years of warfare in Europe.[88] It was these Luso-Africans, desperate for a way out of the dilemma created by his policies, not the well-capitalized traders from Brazil against whom he had primarily directed them, whom he blamed for the charges brought against him. This distinction between the wealthy Brazilians and their Luso-African allies at Luanda and Benguela, and the poorer merchants of Angola, was to structure the politics surrounding the tumultuous decade that followed, as the Portuguese court moved to Rio de Janeiro, the British entered the Portuguese imperial trade directly, and Brazil proclaimed its independence in 1822, with obvious implications for the slave trade in an African colony that had become Brazil's dependency in all but name.

88. De Mello, 31 Jan. 1801, AHU, Angola cx. 52; cf. de Mello, "Angola no começo do século," p. 550.

14

Back to Trading on the Fringes

Liberalism, Abolition, and the British in Brazil in the Nineteenth Century

Napoleon's invasion of Portugal late in 1807 pushed the Brazilians back out to the fringes of southern Atlantic slaving, reversing the centripetal trend of the last thirty years. Formerly illicit British exports of textiles to Angola through Brazil became legal, channeled through emigrant Lisbon merchants resettled in Rio as agents for British importers. In Africa, relocation of Britain's entry point into the Portuguese empire from Lisbon to Brazil sent factors of the displaced metropolitan merchants to Luanda in force, ready to take over the main flow of Angolan slaves to southern Brazil for themselves. The Brazilians, deprived of British capital, abandoned the strong position at Luanda they had built up in the preceding three decades and dispersed to seek slaves at more remote points along the African coasts.

The Anglo-Portuguese merchants from Lisbon, resettled at Rio, owned the maritime trade to Angola, goods and slaves alike, increasing the relative poverty of the Luso-Africans of Luanda and leaving them unable to send slaves to Brazil on their own accounts except through unofficial channels that circumvented the strengthened customs house at Luanda or evaded other government methods of protecting the agents of the metropolitan merchants relocated at Rio. The Benguela Luso-Africans fell on hard times as the Brazilians, long the main financial support for their trade, sought other sources of slaves and let the volume of their southern Angolan trade fall. In adjusting to these changes, the Luanda creoles were unwittingly setting up the covert commercial institutions that would support illegal trading after 1830, while the erstwhile African suppliers of slaves to Benguela, driven by the necessity of finding alternative exports, were primed to turn to the wax, ivory, and eventually rubber that supported the import-export trade of the central highlands after 1830.

The Arrival of the British

Napoleon had demanded that the Portuguese government abandon its support of Britain, its "oldest ally," and expel from Lisbon the British factors on whom the city's merchants depended for most of their trade with the empire, particularly Brazil. The government turned to Britain for help in this extremity and found it in the form of a Royal Navy flotilla that in 1807 evacuated the Portuguese royal family, the court, and thousands of its supporters, including many merchants connected with the so-called "British factory" in Lisbon, just as French armies approached the city. The exiles sailed off to take up a fourteen-year residence in Rio de Janeiro, the leading city of the overseas empire. Arriving there early in 1808, the royal government immediately opened Brazilian ports to British merchants, thus recognizing the de facto presence of British goods and making an initial payment on its debt to its foreign saviors. Continental Portugal fell temporarily into the hands of the invading French and afterwards came under the military authority of the reconquering British general Beresford.[1] From the perspective of some Brazilian traders, Rio fell under an economic equivalent of the British military occupation of the metropole.

At the same time, the British undertook to abolish all maritime trading in slaves from West Africa, thereby committing themselves to hindering slaving by northern Brazilians. The British-Portuguese treaty agreements that embodied this part of the abolition campaign selectively restricted slaving only north of the equator but left it open south of the line, at least temporarily.[2] This distinction, though the treaties were phrased in blandly geographical terms, clearly favored Rio de Janeiro and permitted the British merchants centered there to preserve their sales of goods to Portuguese slavers heading directly across the southern Atlantic to Angola. But the Bahian slavers, as independent of British imports as they were of Lisbon merchants, were utterly confined to the Mina trade prohibited by these same agreements and had to elude the antislaving squadron of British warships positioned off the shores of western Africa. The ports and captaincies of the far north, always heavily dependent on the now-prohibited trade to Cacheu and Bissau, despite considerable contraband slaving from Upper Guinea,[3] developed the Angolan connection that had grown since the brief entry of the Maranhão Company at Luanda in the 1760s. Pernambuco, with no particular commitment to Mina slaves, whom it had previously had to buy through Bahia, had received Angolan slaves through Lisbon merchants less closely connected to the British in the 1790s and

1. From a general summary in A. H. de Oliveira Marques, *History of Portugal* (New York: Columbia University Press, 1972), 1:427–30. For further implications in Portugal, see Chapter 18, following.

2. In general, see Leslie Bethell, *The Abolition of the Brazilian Slave Trade: Britain, Brazil, and the Slave Trade Question, 1807–1869* (Cambridge: Cambridge University Press, 1970).

3. Carreira, *Notas sobre o tráfico português*, 2d ed., p. 43.

1800s and was thus positioned to become Brazil's main nineteenth-century conduit for metropolitan Portugal's remaining investment in slaving from Luanda and Benguela.

By 1809, years of smuggling British goods through Rio de Janeiro had accustomed southern Brazilian slavers to owning many of the goods they sold to Luso-Africans in Angola, often through their own *comissário* factors, but the opening of Brazil to British imports excluded them from this active role in the trade. The British, accorded the protection of Portuguese commercial law, could thereafter risk extending credit directly to factors of their choosing in Portugal's American colony, mostly the Rio merchants of Lisbon origins, whom they supplied with trade goods in quantities vastly beyond Brazil's ability to consume.[4] Though the British may have intended primarily to extend their influence over the much larger Brazilian market, some of the excess goods indirectly financed the entry of these Anglo-Portuguese merchants into Angolan slaving, in line with the traders' long-standing tendency to dump surplus merchandise in Brazil on the African market. When local Rio slavers thus lost their British sources of capital, they had to fall back on selling the old American staples in Africa. At Luanda their agents began to yield to a new wave of *comissários* bringing British goods from the favored Portuguese merchants in Rio.

The southern Brazilians simultaneously lost some of the financial support they had formerly derived from selling slaves in the Plata estuary for silver. After a last burst of Spanish importing after 1804, Britain occupied Buenos Aires militarily in 1806, and British traders took control of nearly all trade there. British occupation also led to abolition of legal slave imports through the Plata in 1812. Despite some continuing smuggling, the bulk of Spanish slaving then shifted to a very differently financed sort of trade to Havana or to Spanish ports on the Pacific coast.[5] Rio traders had to find other markets and methods of profiting from slaving.

These Brazilian slavers moved out to the fringes of the Portuguese trading sphere, some to slaving areas at Loango and in the lower Zaire

4. Alan K. Manchester, *British Preëminence in Brazil: Its Rise and Decline: A Study in European Expansion* (Chapel Hill: University of North Carolina Press, 1933), though oriented principally toward the diplomatic level of the issues, is still basic for this period and is filled with hints at the discrimination against Brazilians around the court of the prince regent D. João. For explicit emphasis on the economic point, Olga Pantaleão, "Aspectos do comércio dos domínios portuguêses no período de 1808 a 1821," *Revista de história* (São Paulo), no. 41 (1960): 99–100; Sandro Sideri, *Trade and Power: Informal Colonialism in Anglo-Portuguese Relations* (Rotterdam: Rotterdam University Press, 1970), p. 126; also see Eltis, "Transatlantic Slave Trade," pp. 127–28. Luccock, *Notes on Rio de Janeiro*, p. 580, gives a charmingly complacent and condescending description of how the Brazilians were "learning" at that time to be in debt to the British.

5. Gervase Clarence-Smith, "The Portuguese Contribution to the Cuban Slave and Coolie Trades in the Nineteenth Century," *Slavery and Abolition* 5, no. 1 (1984): 25–33; Molinari, *Trata de negros*, pp. 97 ff.; Andrews, *Afro-Argentines of Buenos Aires*, pp. 56–57; Verger, *Flux et reflux*, p. 293; Eltis, "Transatlantic Slave Trade," pp. 116–17.

that the British had abandoned with Parliament's abolition of slave buying in 1808, and others to southeastern Africa. As they drew these outlying sources into the Portuguese trade, the long-standing prominence of Luanda and Benguela in supplying labor to southern Brazil began to fade. With the Brazilians active along the Loango Coast, and with the arrival there too of Spaniards and North Americans seeking slaves for the Cuban trade but driven south of the equator by the British West Africa squadron, the creole traders of Luanda renovated their old habits of smuggling to survive economically as the legal trade drew to a close.

The British at the Brazilian end of the trade assumed the remote position characteristic of European capital invested in southern Atlantic slaving, tending to finance the ownership of goods and leaving possession of the slaves to others.[6] Some of the Liverpool slavers active in the last days of direct British participation in the trade sold their vessels, rendered useless by the prohibition against British subjects' engaging in slaving, to Portuguese and Brazilian merchants.[7] Such sales provided the nucleus of a new fleet of ships specifically designed for slaving that their favored Portuguese associates could use in competition with the established Brazilian slavers. Their Manchester initiations of the Indian cotton goods available through Lisbon constituted the major British financial contribution to Rio firms formed to carry out slaving voyages, thus taking the places of the Lisbon factors who had once supplied working capital for ventures from Pernambuco and of the Brazilian planters and merchants who had underwritten the Rio trade with *gerebitas* and smuggled British goods.

British capital made it possible for the larger merchants to remove themselves even more from the slaving phase of an African venture in the post-1810 era. Cash credits advanced to Brazilian buyers of slaves, mainly planters, enabled them to deploy other assets of their own, released by these loans, to buy British goods that they contributed to slaving voyages of this sort. The less direct forms of British participation tended to predominate after abolition of the legal trade in 1830 and the more direct ones earlier.[8] The British commercial capital behind the healthy growth after 1810 in Angolan slave imports to Brazil thus consolidated a final step in the steady advance into Portuguese slaving that dated from the first indirect shipments of English woolens for the Luanda market through Lisbon in the 1600s, had grown with direct smuggling through the Luso-

6. Luccock, *Notes on Rio de Janeiro*, p. 590.

7. Eltis, "British Trans-Atlantic Slave Trade after 1807," pp. 1–11. See also Carreira, *Notas sobre o tráfico português*, p. 182, on the British origins of the *Dido*; also Rebelo, *Relações*, p. 69, on the *Urbano*.

8. Eltis, "Transatlantic Slave Trade," pp. 132–34; also Eltis, "British Contribution," pp. 214–15.

Africans and the African trade diaspora along the Loango Coast in the early eighteenth century, had expanded next by selling cottons through Rio slavers in the 1780s and 1790s, and finally surfaced in backing Anglo-Portuguese slavers after 1810.

The Brazilian Role

The overwhelming British dominance in Brazilian commerce after 1810 pressured local mercantile interests at both Rio and at Bahia to remain in slaving, even as it marginalized their position in the trade. British ships quickly became the primary carriers of Brazilian produce back to European markets, excluding the Brazilians from a route in which they had won a modest share since abolition of the old fleet system in 1765. Many Portuguese, too, found themselves left with empty ships available for trading to Africa and Asia.

Rio traders probably redeployed some of their vessels in the growing slave trade from Mozambique, since the 1809 decree admitting the British to Brazil specifically excluded them from trading in the Portuguese territories in southeastern Africa.[9] The Mozambique trade, centered on the Brazilian end almost entirely at Rio, increased from a few hundred slaves in the 1790s to an average of 10,000 per year, more than a fourth of the southern Brazil's total imports by the late 1820s.[10] The volume and lethality of slaving from Mozambican ports rose together, in the classic coupling of high African mortality with underfinanced American slavers unable to afford the food and water necessary to bring their captives through alive. Though differing climatic conditions in southeastern and western central Africa complicate comparisons of mortality on the Atlantic and Indian Ocean routes, ships reaching Rio from Mozambique tended to show more of the disastrously high death rates characteristic of delayed arrivals of inadequately supplied and overcrowded ships than the better-capitalized nineteenth-century traders from Angola.[11] British observers of Mozambique slavers putting in for provisions at Cape Town noted the excessive numbers of captives aboard them and the insufficient food and water they carried for their cargoes, though they recognized the shortage of the Brazilians' financial means only obliquely, attributing such conditions to the "greed" of Portuguese slavers generally.[12]

The local Rio contribution to these late Angolan voyages remained

---

9. Pantaleão, "Aspectos," p. 92.

10. See statistics published in Klein, *Middle Passage*, pp. 76–77. Also Miller, "Sources and Knowledge," for annual figures. Also Vail and White, *Capitalism and Colonialism*, chap. 1.

11. E.g., Klein, *Middle Passage*, pp. 84–85; Miller, "Sources and Knowledge."

12. Theal, *Records of the Cape Colony,* 1:129, 181–82, 458–59.

very much as it had always been: American produce, tobacco, *gerebita,* and foodstuffs.[13] Brazilian merchants might own the hull and fittings, and local planters and farmers contributed supplies for the voyage and provisions for the cargo of slaves on the return, thus reducing the expenditure of borrowed trade goods or currency in Africa for purchases of foodstuffs.[14] After 1809, Rio de Janeiro's trade to the Indian Ocean expanded beyond slaving to include a variety of imports, mostly Indian cottons. Brazilian gold, Spanish silver, and beads imported through Portugal formed the core of the outbound cargoes. Brazilians reexported some of the Asian textiles to Angola as part of their contribution to the outfit of their voyages, competing directly with the product of Manchester looms.

Merchants at Bahia had similarly few alternatives to continued slaving. Their dependence on selling tobacco on the Mina Coast for slaves forced them to violate Portugal's 1815 treaty with Great Britain that prohibited slaving north of the equator, effectively protecting West African markets for British goods from Brazilian competition. Some of the Bahian traders withdrew into landownership and finance, thus probably helping to support the modest investments in new technology that began to spread through Bahian sugar planting in the nineteenth century, but also maintaining local demand for African slaves.[15] Others attempted to compete against Rio merchants in the legal trading areas north of the mouth of the Zaire, where their tobacco found better markets than in the regions nearer Luanda that grew their own leaf. Farther south they found themselves involved in virtually open warfare with Britain's favored Rio associates and subject to seizure by British cruisers, as two Bahian ships discovered to their great loss in 1811.[16] Thus the irony of London's well-publicized campaign against Bahians caught buying slaves in competition with British ships seeking palm oil and other "legitimate" African exports off the West African coast: British support for the southern Brazilian slave trade after 1809, backed by an almost immediate show of force at Cabinda in 1811, prevented Bahians from operating commercially in the areas left legally open to them south of the line, and so they had to risk playing hide-and-seek with naval patrols off the Lower Guinea Coast to obtain the labor supplies on which the captaincy depended.[17]

13. For a small tobacco merchant at Rio in 1813, see ANRJ, Sec. Jud. no. 8919, cx. 1118, gav. A, Inventário de Maximo Felis dos Santos (fallecido). Thanks to Larissa Brown for this reference; cf. her "Internal Commerce," p. 537.

14. Spix and Martius, *Viagem pelo Brasil,* 2:153; Luccock, *Notes on Rio de Janeiro,* pp. 589–90.

15. Lugar, "Merchant Community," pp. iv, 317–18; F. W. Orde-Morton, "Growth and Innovation: The Bahian Sugar Industry, 1790–1860," *Canadian Journal of Latin American Studies* 5, no. 10 (1980): 37–54.

16. Oliveira Barboza, 8 April 1811, AHU, Angola cx. 59, and 22 Nov. 1811, AHU, Angola cx. 60; Bethell, *Abolition of the Brazilian Slave Trade.*

17. See Lugar, "Merchant Community," pp. 82–83, for a view of the same point from a slightly different angle.

If the Bahians suffered more than the southern Brazilians from restrictions on Atlantic slaving north of the equator, the Portuguese Crown made other concessions to the British over abolition of the slave trade that fell heavily on the local Rio traders, further buttressing the commercial advantage of the British-backed metropolitan merchants. The Crown attempted to ward off growing British pressure to end the trade in 1810 by sanitizing its conduct with modern hygiene, better and more plentiful provisions for the slaves, and application of the pre-1808 British limits on the numbers of slaves that a ship could carry for each of its registered tons. Since the Anglo-Portuguese merchants owned the slaves they carried, they had a direct interest in protecting the lives of their property with the most modern methods known. But the Rio slavers, who had been driven back into depending on freight charges and low operating costs for their profits more than had Anglo-Portuguese ventures—who had valuable British goods to sell in Africa and who cashed in on high Brazilian prices for slaves[18]—felt the added costs of the resulting "humanitarian decree" of 1813 more profoundly than their competitors.[19]

Seemingly minor improvements offered on behalf of the slaves, like the prohibition against slavers refilling *gerebita* casks with drinking water for their captives, selectively hit the Brazilians, who carried most of the cane brandies sent to Angola. Since responsibility for administering these new measures fell primarily on relatively dependable royal officials at Luanda, the decree helped to drive Brazilians determined to evade them off to other parts of the coast.[20] At Benguela, where the Brazilians were chafing under renewed Crown attempts to bring their quasi "free" port under closer government regulation, the decree provoked immediate heavy protests that forced its suspension.[21] The British later seized on subsequent violations of these same tight-packing regulations as a major instrument of their public propaganda against Brazilian slaving, once again especially at Bahia.[22] As frequently in the history of the trade, the costs of measures proclaimed on behalf of the slaves fell on the Crown's closest merchant associates less heavily than on its colonial subjects.

Given the organizational complexity of nineteenth-century slaving and the variety of Rio de Janeiro merchants involved in one way or another in the trade, "slave traders" formed no single unified or homogeneous group.[23] Some general merchants had interests in the "African trade" only

18. E.g., Santos in note 13 above.
19. For discussion of the *alvará*, Vianna, "Humanitário alvará."
20. For reports of earlier effective implementation of regulations at Luanda see Oliveira Barboza, 1 May 1811, AHU, Angola cx. 59, and discussion in Rebelo, *Relações*, p. 74, 342–44. The background to this decree dates to 1808 in Portugal: Alencastro, "Traite négrière et l'unité nationale," pp. 399–400.
21. Alvellos Leiria, 22 Feb. 1815, AHU, Angola cx. 62.
22. For a survey, Bethell, *Abolition of the Brazilian Slave Trade*.
23. The commercial correspondence in ANRJ, cód. 1142, amply reveals the multiplicity

as shippers of goods they needed to sell in Angola, and they could do so without ever owning slaves themselves by taking their returns from Angola in the familiar *letras*, or bills of exchange.[24] These might act as agents for the British, as agents of other Brazilians who imported cotton goods from India, or as specialists in the agricultural produce of the southern interior or adjacent captaincies. Each competed with the others for shipping space on vessels outbound for Africa.

Most of them probably traded to Angola only for special purposes, as part of a much larger and more general business.[25] Importers of cotton goods saw Luanda as a minor part of a worldwide commerce that also included contracts in Britain and distribution networks in Minas Gerais. Provisioners involved in the intracolonial trade ranging up and down the Brazilian coast from the Plata to Pernambuco supplied the city of Rio as well as slave ships heading for Benguela. The British factors participated in Angolan slaving as part of their general import business centered on Brazil but used Africa as an outlet for goods they could not sell in America. On the slave-importing side, other merchants acted primarily as Rio de Janeiro consignees of the captives shipped by others, mostly Anglo-Portuguese selling goods in Africa but probably also some Angolan owners at Luanda and Benguela. Still others borrowed funds or goods in order to acquire slaves in Africa, whom they owned during the middle passage and then sold in America.[26] It would have been this last group, aided by the abundance of British capital, that grew in prominence in the 1810s and 1820s.[27] Still others drew advantage from the thriving trade in African labor by renting out warehouses at Rio in which newly arrived slaves were detained while awaiting sale, supplying the consignees and owners with food for them and in acting in dozens of other supportive roles. Warehousing, in particular, became lucrative as the flood of British goods absorbed all available storage facilities and left the slavers to search for lodgings for their captives.[28]

---

of interests involved in the business of one trade, among several, aboard a ship at Luanda in 1821; see also Brown, "Internal Commerce," pp. 523 ff., et passim.

24. Brown, "Internal Commerce," p. 540, for an example from this period.

25. As early as 1814, for example, João Rodrigues Pereira de Almeida, an influential general merchant; see the circumstances in ANRJ, cód. 323, Registo da correspondência da polícia, officio expedido ao Min⁰ de Est⁰ dos Neg⁰ˢ do Brazil, 1 July 1814; ANRJ, cód. 325, vol. 1, fols. 189–89v, Registo do officio expedido ao Juiz da Alfandega do Rio Corᵉ (Jozé Feliciano Frz Pinrᵒ), 6 Sept. 1814. These references were supplied by Larissa Brown.

26. See the *representação* in BNRJ, II–34, 26, 19, which distinguished (in 1811) parties interested in the slave trade as *proprietários* (owners, or proprietors, presumably of ships, goods, or slaves), *consignatários* (those handling goods or slaves owned by others on consignment), and *armadores* (backers, financiers); Brown, "Internal Commerce," for the terminology.

27. For the dominance of British goods at Luanda in 1821, to the detriment of Portuguese and Asian ones, see ANRJ, cód. 1142, esp. letter no. 23, 25 Aug. 1821.

28. Brown, "Internal Commerce," pp. 372–73 ff., for the problem as importers of wheat from Rio Grande do Sul experienced it in 1810–12.

After 1810 prices for new slaves rose toward 150$000 to 200$000 in Brazil, while the actual *réis* prices paid for slaves in Luanda hovered in the 70$000 to 80$000 range, with Benguela values not dissimilar.[29] The modesty of the increases on the Angolan side reflected the lower price of the British goods used by then to buy the slaves and the competition from lower-cost slaves from points north of Luanda and in southeastern Africa. Under the set of expenses assumed for estimates of profits in earlier periods,[30] though with mortality reduced to 10 percent and freight charges increased to 13$000, the total investment borne by the Anglo-Portuguese and Brazilian traders, who were by then the major owners of slaves crossing the southern Atlantic, would have run between 143$000 and 163$000 (rounded) f.o.b. Rio, and the break-even mortality levels would have run between the 5 to 10 percent actually recorded before about 1820 and 25 to 30 percent. With the low and relatively consistent maritime mortality of the 1820s, few ventures would have suffered losses from owning and transporting slaves. To the extent that Brazilians trading in the north toward the mouth of the Zaire escaped government taxation, avoided the commissions charged at Luanda and Benguela by factors, and paid lower prime costs for slaves, they reduced the risks further still, particularly in view of the exceptionally high survival rates of slaves from those parts of the coast. The eagerness of Brazil-based metropolitan traders to gain ownership of the slaves in those decades thus seems to find ample confirmation in even this crude guess at the profitability inherent in the price structure of the era.

By the late 1820s, these high slave prices had allowed some merchants to specialize to a greater degree in slaving than many earlier traders had managed. With profits accumulating from buying and selling slaves, and excluded from similarly advantageous investment in other forms of commerce by the British presence, some Rio merchants evidently ploughed their gains back into more slaving. Mortality risks had fallen with application of the "humanitarian decree" of 1813 and again with the introduction of smallpox vaccinations early in the 1820s, and it became correspondingly less hazardous to undertake an entire venture on one's own account. Merchants apparently took on entire cargoes of 300 or 400 slaves as consignees, reflecting the fact that they were by then working for large investors in Rio rather than for the numerous Angolan slaveowners who had once shipped small lots to a variety of merchant receivers in Rio. This emergence of a distinct class of slave-importing merchants made sense, of course, because of the knowledge and facilities necessary to handle living commodities like slaves successfully and because of the contacts necessary to forward lots of them on through other specialists to markets in the

---

29. Miller, "Slave Prices."
30. Chapters 12 and 13, above.

interior and in ports up and down the coast that had formed with growing diversity in the Brazilian economy.[31] By the late 1820s, the most active 6 percent of 428 known consignees (out of 436 total) of slaves reaching Rio took 33.2 percent of the shipments.[32] A similar concentration of activity obtained in terms of shipping, with a few ships devoted exclusively to making regular Africa runs and a great many more vessels appearing only occasionally when venturers took advantage of opportune circumstances to attempt a crossing to Angola.[33]

Marginalization of the Brazilian shippers and the emergence of large, specialized consignee merchants weakened the old slaving interests in Luanda and Benguela linked to Rio. The new, better-financed British-backed Portuguese merchants mounted their own ventures to Africa and bought slaves for themselves. They had no need to rely on the elaborate bills of exchange that traders based in Lisbon had once used to link the slaving ports on both sides of the southern Atlantic. Since this officially favored faction concentrated their trading under the protection of the royal governors at Luanda, the Brazilians withdrew from there in 1810. Their departure cost the African colony its largest and most wealthy traders,[34] who may safely be assumed to have included agents of the Rio smugglers of British goods who had prospered in the years before meaningful customs inspections and the opening of Brazil to foreign traders.

The years 1810 and 1811 also saw the Brazilians abandon Luanda en masse for the haunts that the British had abandoned in the mouth of the Zaire River and along the Loango Coast.[35] Reports from 1809 to 1811 on ship movements through the port at Luanda refer to the departure of vessel after vessel for "Cabinda" and other ports to the north, and a shortage of shipping persisted at the colony's capital through the decade.[36] The northern opening created for the Brazilians also left Benguela with a serious lack of ships to carry off its slaves, especially when the anti–tight-packing decree of 1813 exacerbated the situation by forcing the withdrawal of shippers no longer able to carry slaves profitably.[37] This shift toward

31. E.g., the interior distribution network visible in the records of the Rio slave traders of the 1820s, cited in Taunay, *Subsídios*, pp. 280, 284. For the structure of this internal trade, see Brown, "Internal Commerce," pp. 385–92.

32. Klein, *Middle Passage*, p. 94.

33. In the period before 1810, ships that were visibly specialized in the trade to Angola over many years (4.3%) had accounted for 23.9% of the voyages recorded: Miller, unpublished analysis of shipping data. See Miller, "Portuguese Slave Trade," and "Legal Portuguese Slaving." The figures for shipping are not comparable to those on the Rio consignees.

34. Oliveira Barboza, 15 July 1811, AHU, Angola cx. 60.

35. E.g., the Pereira de Almeida venture (1814), cited in note 25.

36. Oliveira Barboza, 8 April 1811, AHU, Angola cx. 59; Oliveira Barboza, 22 Nov. 1811, AHU, Angola cx. 60; Oliveira Barboza to Alvellos Leiria, 26 Oct. 1814, enclosed in Pereira, 18 Nov. 1814, AHU, Angola cx. 62; Albuquerque e Tovar, 16 Sept. 1819, AHU, Angola cx. 66.

37. And particularly also when smallpox heightened the urgency of getting the slaves on their way to Brazil—e.g., for 1813–16, Alvellos Leiria, 7 March 1814, AHU, Angola

equatorial sources of slaves became the distinguishing feature of Rio's post-1810 trade, to the slight consternation of royal officials. They rationalized their unease by wondering about London's attitude toward such trading, in view of Britain's capture of Bahian ships along that same coast in 1811, but—perhaps more to the point—they must also have had in view the harm that competition from the "Cabinda" trade might do to slaving by the Crown's favored few at Luanda.[38] The percentage of Luanda slaves among Rio's imports dropped steadily, and Brazilians who had formerly stopped at Luanda for provisions on their way down the coast toward the Zaire began to stock up instead at Benguela. There they presumably avoided delays imposed by the governors at the colonial capital and certainly stimulated a minor agricultural boom in the lower valley of the Katumbela River just north of the port.[39]

Anglo-Portuguese Restrictions in Angola

The Crown apparently moved against the Luso-Africans at Luanda almost immediately after consolidating its dependence on the British at Rio. Merchants at Luanda after 1810—by that time surely representatives of Anglo-Portuguese houses in Brazil—petitioned the queen to enforce restrictions on credit and goods sent to the interior that the Luanda Junta do Comércio had proposed in 1793.[40] The key provision in these restrictions limited the amount of credit that a Luanda merchant could advance to a single agent sent into the interior to 4.800$000, or about the goods price of eighty to one hundred slaves, that is, the value of a single *libambo,* or coffle of slaves. Compared to the 40.000$000 to 60.000$000 of indebtedness taken on by traders up to that time,[41] this limitation virtually eliminated the Luso-African strategy of living in the interior off credit obtained at the coast and also made it more difficult for them to fund *reviros.* In response to predictable protests that restricting credit to this extent would render trading impossible, owing to traders' inability to

---

cx. 62; Alvellos Leiria, 22 Feb. and 7 April 1815, AHU, Angola cx. 63; Jozé Joaquim Marques de Graça, 30 March 1816, AHU, Angola cx. 63.

38. Oliveira Barboza, 26 Oct. 1814, in Pereira, 18 Nov. 1814, AHU, Angola cx. 62; Rebelo, *Relações,* doc. 37, pp. 372–73.

39. Spix and Martius, *Viagem pelo Brasil,* 2:153, note V; Delgado, *Famosa e histórica Benguela,* pp. 63, 119. See also the concentration of Brazilians at Benguela in 1820: Dias, "Sociedade colonial," p. 169.

40. Oliveira Barboza, 16 Dec. 1810, AHU, Angola cx. 66; *carta regia,* in "Negócios de Angola," fols. 12–13, IHGB (also in AHU, Angola cx. 58); merchants' petition in AHU, Angola maço 4-A. For the Crown concession to the request (with errors), Rebelo, *Relações,* pp. 208 ff.

41. João Victo da Silva, n.d. (ca. 1792), AHU, Angola cx. 42; Almeida e Vasconcelos, 24 Aug. 1792, AHU, Angola cx. 42; Almeida e Vasconcelos, 11 Feb. 1795, AHU, Angola cx. 44.

assort goods they had already assembled in the interior, the government authorized additional loans, but only to the value of two or three slaves. The new rules also proposed armed government escorts for all goods and slaves and confined their movements to specified routes to make certain that both reached their intended destinations. The rules also drastically increased penalties assessable against agents in Angola who failed to pay debts as contracted. These measures finally implemented a policy considered by Lisbon for most of the preceding decade,[42] in effect pulling Portuguese assets out of the interior and draining the Luso-Africans' working capital. At Benguela, Rio simply extended no further commercial credit to slaving, refused to support a punitive expedition into the interior that the local Luso-Africans requested to recover the money they could not pay to Brazil from their own African debtors, and let the trade collapse.[43]

The Luanda representatives of the Anglo-Portuguese merchants, again convened in the colony's local Junta do Comércio, also resurrected another tactic of earlier government-protected creditors in Angola. Like both the old contractors of the slave export duties and the Pombaline companies, they requested privileged creditor status in recovering debts owed in the colony. Implementation of the strategy on this occasion centered on the position of *provedor* (inspector) of the estates of persons deceased. Like most middle-level positions in the colonial government, the *provedoria* may be assumed to have continued under the control of the Luso-Africans,[44] who would have used the position then, as they had used it for generations, to frustrate metropolitan creditors' efforts to recover funds lent out to Luso-Africans and others who died in Angola. The requested priority in claims on estates would circumvent the jurisdiction of the unreliable local *provedor*.

The Crown conceded these critical privileges in 1815,[45] in addition to confirming the pass controls on movements of goods and slaves in the interior and all the other restrictions stipulated in the government-sponsored request of 1793. In the name of freedom of trade the Luanda Junta do Comércio, and indirectly also its British tutors in liberal free-

42. E.g., de Mello, 11 Jan. and 24 April 1798, AHU, Angola cx. 44; de Mello, 3 and 31 Jan. 1801, AHU, Angola cx. 52; Correa de Araujo, 12 April 1801, AHU, Angola cx. 51; Godinho report, 23 Oct. 1804, AHU, Angola cx. 55.

43. Merchants' *requerimento* (Benguela), AHU, Angola maço 15.

44. For the unreliability of local government officials from the point of view of the Crown's governors at Luanda, see Oliveira Barboza, 15 July 1811, AHU, Angola cx. 59; Albuquerque e Tovar, 5 Nov. 1819, AHU, Angola cx. 66. Cf. Mello e Castro remark quoted in preface, 7 Aug. 1791, in Mário António Fernandes de Oliveira, *Angolana* (*Documentação sobre Angola* (Luanda: Instituto de Investigação Científica de Angola, 1968), 1:31; in general Birmingham, *Trade and Conflict in Angola*, p. 159, citing Corrêa, *História de Angola*, 1:27–57.

45. Rebelo, *Relações,* p. 155.

doms, received greater autonomy from supervision by the governor in the form of permanent and continuous constitution rather than meeting only at the call of the colony's chief officer. The government protected its fiscal interests by authorizing the *ouvidor* (Crown magistrate), who also headed the customs service, to summon in formal session the merchants who, as owners of the slaves sent from Luanda to Brazil, paid the export duties that provided the government's chief source of revenues.[46] Thus positioned to foreclose on colonial debtors,[47] with government escorts provided for their trade goods and slaves, armed with criminal penalties against debtors who had no assets to seize, and assembled in a public conspiracy to limit the credit on which traders in the interior depended, the Crown and its Anglo-Portuguese protégés in Rio gathered their forces anew to employ commercial wealth against Luso-Africans in Angola and the Brazilians through whom they sent their slaves to America. The familiar aura of failure glowed nonetheless behind the optimistic energy of these oft-tried reforms.

Luso-African Smuggling

At the same time, Spaniards and North Americans sailing under Spanish colors, all seeking labor for Cuba, attracted other Luso-African sellers of slaves away from aggressive Portuguese buyers in Luanda.[48] Some Brazilians surely joined in this profitable trade to the Caribbean, and a portion of the slaves formally dispatched for "Pernambuco" at this period must have continued right on downwind to Havana.[49] Benguela, the historic center for Brazilian contraband in Angola, became a favored location for such subterfuges, but the Spaniards and North Americans also frequented all other parts of the coast, particularly after 1815, when increasingly effective British antislaving patrols off West Africa forced many of them south of the equator. Some of the Spaniards boldly put in at Luanda harbor itself, alleging lack of provisions or claiming leaks or other mishaps in accordance with the smuggler's time-honored pretense of distress at sea. More novel was their payment for slaves in specie. Occasionally they became daring enough to attack Portuguese or Brazilian slavers on the coasts to the north of Luanda. But for the most part, they simply slipped into

46. Ibid., p. 158.
47. For reports of actual foreclosures, or pressures placed on debtors, see Oliveira Barboza, 21 July 1811, AHU, Angola cx. 60; also Rebelo, *Relações*, pp. 211–12, 368–69, 373–74.
48. Spix and Martius, *Viagem pelo Brasil*, 2:141; for the Plata, Andrews, *Afro-Argentines of Buenos Aires*, pp. 56–57, 68–70, 74–75.
49. Journal of (British) consul Lindemann at Bahia for 1811–15, cited in Verger, *Flux et reflux*, p. 293.

the old British anchorages at Musulu just north of Luanda, at Ambriz near the mouth of the river Mbrije, and at the Loje.[50]

The Spaniards, as a source of coin and hard currency, posed a direct threat to the effort of the British-backed Anglo-Portuguese in Rio to run the trade through Luanda on the old basis of trade goods. The Rio government countered with decrees requiring payment of the slave duties in Angola, and in coin, rather than allowing payment in Brazil by means of the conventional bills of exchange.[51] Despite such attempts to tap the wealth of the Luso-Africans in Luanda, contraband trade with Spaniards and North Americans in these last years of legal slaving surely contributed to some of the nineteenth-century creole trading fortunes in Angola.[52]

Other Luso-Africans must have begun to accumulate wealth of their own in the interior in this period by leaving Luanda to poorer newcomers, merchants and peddlers dependent on the imported commercial capital of the Anglo-Portuguese, and consolidating an independent, highly unofficial network of trade routes serving Brazilians, Spaniards, and North Americans on the beaches north of Luanda, at Musulu, at Ambriz, and to the Zaire and beyond. The river mouths were established outlets for the old trade routes running diagonally northwest from Jinga and Kasanje in the middle Kwango valley through Mbwila and Mbwela to Kongo and the coast. Incapacitation of the French and the withdrawal of the British after 1807 had left those coasts largely abandoned, and the 1810 Anglo-Portuguese Treaty of Friendship and Alliance had prohibited the British from interfering with Portuguese and Brazilian slaving there.

The Luso-Africans of the 1810s simply smuggled directly from their bases in the interior of the colony to the unregulated coast north of Luanda Bay where eager Brazilian and foreign buyers congregated. Luanda's position in the coastwise trade nearly reversed itself, declining from a center

50. Alvellos Leiria, 25 Jan. 1815, AHU, Angola cx. 63; Motta Feo e Torres, 1 Aug. 1816, AHU, Angola cx. 65; Motta Feo e Torres, 14 Jan. 1817, 15 May 1817, 14 Sept. 1817, and 5 Oct. 1818, AHU, Angola cx. 65; *requerimento* of Manoel da Cruz e Socio, n.d. (ca. 1818), AHU, Angola maço 19; Motta Feo e Torres, 24 March and 28 July 1819, AHU, Angola cx. 66; Albuquerque e Tovar, 25 Oct. and 6 Nov. 1819, and 5 May, 21 June, 28 June, 16 Aug., 30 Aug., and 30 Sept. 1820, all AHU, Angola cx. 66; Albuquerque e Tovar, 23 Jan. 1821, AHU, Angola cx. 67; E. D. Macarthy Moreira, "O caso das presas espanholas," *Revista do Instituto de filosofia e ciências humanas da Universidade Federal do Rio Grande do Sul* (1974), pp. 185–205. Eltis, "Transatlantic Slave Trade," pp. 124, 126, dates these developments much too late, to the 1830s.

51. E.g., *portaria* of 27 April 1810 and *provisão* (Conde de Aguiar) of 30 Sept. 1813, fols. 20–20v, AHU, Angola cx. 58; Albuquerque e Tovar, 6 Nov. 1819, enclosing merchants' petition, AHU, Angola cx. 66. This provision appears to have been made effective at Benguela only belatedly, in 1821, as with so many other government measures taken against Luso-Africans in Angola: Delgado, *Famosa e histórica Benguela*, p. 77; Quinhões, 29 Dec. 1821, AHU, Angola cx. 67.

52. For whom, see in general Dias, "Sociedade colonial," pp. 267–86, and Fernandes de Oliveira, *Alguns aspectos*, chap. 1.

into which slaves flowed from small outlying ports from the Kikombo (Novo Redondo since 1769) to the Dande, to a subsidiary outport servicing untaxed major slave-trading stations at Ambriz, near the mouth of the Loje, in the lower Zaire, and even at Cabinda itself.[53]

Ambriz, a port that had long vented slaves coming from the Kwango and other areas that the government at Luanda vainly considered its protected hinterland, got its start as an acknowledged Luso-African outlet in 1813. A number of merchants left Luanda then to take deliveries of slaves there and to forward them to Brazil without paying the export duties levied in Luanda. Equally important as a motivation behind this move must have been other restrictions added to the Luso-Africans at Luanda after 1810, since they received other slaves at Luanda, presumably paid taxes on them there, and still put them aboard small coasting vessels for transfer to transoceanic ships waiting at Ambriz.[54] The "humanitarian decree" of that year is an obvious possibility. The Crown ordered its governor in Angola not to permit such evasions,[55] but one large Luanda trader, Manuel José de Sousa Lopes, remained at Ambriz and became the monopoly broker on trade conducted there until 1819. He also served as consul general for foreigners who came there to buy slaves.

Sousa Lopes not only sent slaves out to Brazil without paying duties owed in Luanda, but he also used the silver that he obtained from selling captives to Spanish and North American slavers heading for Havana to buy up slaves destined for Luanda that had been financed with the less desirable trade goods on which the Portuguese-Brazilian trade worked. His strategy was identical to that of the Kongo trading chiefs who had preceded him in that location and provided yet another example of the attractions of liquidity in the credit-bound economy of the colony. From the point of view of Luanda factors trying to collect on trade goods sent into the hinterland on credit, Sousa Lopes's diversions of their slave returns merely continued the ancient and dishonorable custom of the *reviro*.[56]

The economic and geographical distinction between the trade in Luanda and that to the north of the city roughly matched the contrast between the better-financed factors selling goods for the Rio Anglo-Portuguese and the modest Brazilian slavers. The latter tended to avoid Luanda and the financial pressures placed on them by the renewed flow of British and Spanish merchant capital into the trade. The lethal consequences of the financial pressure thus placed on the Brazilians may perhaps

53. Oliveira Barboza, 2 Oct. 1813 and 21 Jan. 1815, AHU, Angola cx. 63; Albuquerque e Tovar, 6 Nov. 1819, AHU, Angola cx. 66; Castelobranco, 16 May 1828, AHU, Angola cx. 72.

54. Oliveira Barboza, 2 Oct. 1813, AHU, Angola cx. 61.

55. Oliveira Barboza, 21 Jan. 1815, AHU, Angola cx. 63.

56. Albuquerque e Tovar, 6 Nov. 1819, AHU, Angola cx. 66.

be sensed in the decrepit condition of the *Mato Grosso,* an old, slow-moving tub sent repeatedly to carry off slaves owned by Luso-Africans and Brazilians during this period and notorious for high mortality among the captives it carried, according to a complaint filed at Benguela in 1814.[57]

The sketchy data available for this period might theoretically tolerate a reversal of the roles assigned to the Anglo-Portuguese and the Brazilians who respectively traded at Luanda and elsewhere along Angolan shores after 1810, but it is an unlikely possibility. Alternatively, lesser traders of both the Anglo-Portuguese and local American categories might have centered their operations on Luanda, and secondarily Benguela, sending small quantities, ships freighted with goods on consignment, and old-fashioned *comissários volantes* to take advantage of developed Portuguese commercial institutions and shore-based agents in the towns, while the more independent Anglo-Portuguese and the emerging specialized large Brazilian slavers capable of mounting entire ventures in the historic style of the British and French might have returned straight to the sites of the foreigners' old trade of this type at Loango and in the Zaire mouth. However, general precedent rules against these possibilities, since Portuguese merchant capitalists had always shielded themselves behind the government's regulatory powers at Luanda, and the continuity in their tactics in regulating the trade inland from Luanda at this period would suggest a corresponding continuity in the geography of the trade and in the identities of the protagonists.

Complaints from the Luanda Luso-Africans and their smuggling all centered on the classic strategy of trying to avoid the damage that Anglo-Portuguese capital and government favoritism did to their precarious position in the export trade. The departure in 1810 of the big Brazilian factors, with whom the Luso-Africans had been linked since the 1790s, left the colonials with a much restricted role in the trade. No longer supported by European capital, no longer owners of the slaves all the way to Brazil, as they had been during the depressed American markets of the 1760s and 1770s, they had become sellers at the slaves' point of embarkation in Luanda at the very time that prices in Brazil rose above the level required to cover even the high slave mortality at sea in the 1790s and 1800s. After 1810, with the introduction of smallpox vaccinations at sea imminent, they found themselves even more excluded at Luanda from what had become the most lucrative segment of the trade. The Anglo-Portuguese factors sitting as the Luanda Junta do Comércio had stated as much when they justified their requests for priority in debt collection and for other privileges against the Luso-Africans by citing the risks they were assuming as owners of the slaves shipped to Brazil.[58]

57. Alvellos Leiria, 7 March 1814, AHU, Angola cx. 62. The ship turned up several times between at least 1806 and 1816: Miller, unpublished analysis of shipping data.

58. Merchants' petition, 1809, AHU, Angola maço 4-A.

As during the preceding boom in Angolan slaving a century earlier, a few Luanda Luso-Africans attempted to win back a position in the maritime trade for themselves by collectively buying vessels on which they could ship slaves of their own to capture the high prices available in Brazil.[59] Though they largely failed to send home-owned ventures to Brazil,[60] at least two Angolan merchants had managed to acquire a ship by the end of the 1810s under circumstances that brought a hostile response from their rivals in Brazil, in the form of an attempt to deny them the old privilege of priority in departure granted ships owning the slaves they carried, *de efeitos próprios*.

In the 1820 test case that brought the Angolans' initiatives to the attention of the Crown, two Luanda merchants, António João de Menezes and Joaquim Teixeira de Macedo, pointedly identified in the suit against them as natives of the African colony (and thus almost surely dark-skinned Luso-Africans), had bought a *bergantim* and had managed to gain permission to sail with *efeitos próprios* priority. The factors of the Anglo-Portuguese merchants challenged the authorization, and the Crown consulted their principals in Rio as to the proper application of the decree of 11 January 1758 to the case. The Anglo-Portuguese defended their own sales of goods in Luanda by alluding darkly to the possibility that Menezes and Macedo had acquired the assets needed to buy the ship by smuggling slaves to the Spaniards and warned that profits from such foreign financing could lead to "monopolies" based in Angola that would restrict the existing Rio monopoly that they characterized as "freedom of trade."[61] Some implied that the foreigners might even be lending funds to the Angolans as a means of buying indirectly into the Portuguese slave trade and thus excluding the domestic Portuguese capital invested in the industry.[62] The Crown ruled in favor of the Luanda merchants, reasoning its decision in terms of "freedom of trade," though for reasons difficult to reconcile with the political interests participating in the decision.[63] Perhaps

59. Governor Oliveira Barboza had established a precedent by allowing Luanda residents to band together as *efeitos próprios* shippers in 1811 in order to evacuate accumulating inventories of slaves in the port during a smallpox epidemic: Oliveira Barboza, 8 April 1811, AHU, Angola cx. 59.

60. See Eltis, "Transatlantic Slave Trade," figures on p. 142, to the effect that no more than 2 of the 117 Brazil-bound vessels captured by the British West Africa Squadron had evidence of Luanda ownership. The Conde de Linhares (Portuguese minister for war and foreign affairs) ominously requested an inventory of colonial-owned vessels in 1811: AHU, Angola maço 15-A. Botelho de Vasconcelos, 3 Jan. 1799, AHU, Angola cx. 47, had set the investment necessary for the optimal Angola–Pará–Lisbon–Angola voyage at 80.000$000, a huge sum by colonial standards, equivalent to 1,231 slaves at the current price of 65$000.

61. See the *parecer*, especially, of José Ignacio Vaz Vieira, *consulta* of 12 Sept. 1820, AHU, Angola maço 3.

62. *Parecer* of da Rocha, *consulta* of 12 Sept. 1820, AHU, Angola maço 3 (still active in 1825–30; see Klein, *Middle Passage*, p. 82). Also Rebelo, *Relações*, pp. 197–202, 391–92.

63. *Consulta*, 12 Sept. 1820, AHU, Angola maço 3.

ideological consistency prevailed for once, but it is more likely that the Crown valued the specie in which the Spaniards paid.

The stresses of increased volume on the slave delivery system at Cabinda grew evident by about 1816 or 1817, as Brazilian ships taking on slaves north of the Zaire began sending down to Luanda and even to Benguela for food.[64] In the same year, a British frigate was nosing into ports along the lower Zaire looking for slavers who had drifted there in search of better access to slaves.[65] By 1819, competition had driven up prices, slowed the rate of purchases and loading, and allowed African sellers to begin imposing "customs" equivalent to the export duties levied by the Portuguese government at Luanda.[66] Tensions had risen to the point of open hostility between frustrated slaving captains and assertive African sellers of slaves.[67] The Luanda governor of the time found himself constrained to counsel captains heading down the coast to exercise restraint to protect the trade at Cabinda, even against his own interests in promoting deliveries of slaves through Luanda.[68]

Brazilian slaving north of Luanda thus turned tactics the British had used against the Portuguese in the eighteenth century back against British-financed Portuguese merchants in Rio. Like their predecessors, the Brazilians intercepted slaves financed with Luanda goods on their way down to the city where they were owed and drew them off to the northern ports. Given the nearness to the coast of the routes leading up from the Kwango valley to Cabinda, it was inevitable that Brazilians and Luso-Africans would move to Ambriz, where they could attract caravans as well as intercept slaves coming down toward Luanda from the northeast, São Salvador, Zombo, and beyond.

When competition intensified in the late 1810s at Cabinda, Brazilians buying slaves there started moving south up the lines of supply to the Zaire River and eventually, by the 1820s, to the Kongo court itself in order to buy slaves who might otherwise have reached competitors elsewhere. Slavers from Brazil would hit the African coast in the south, as they had always done, provision for the slave cargo at Benguela with food from Katumbela, carry on down to Cabinda Bay, and send small river canoes up the lower Zaire with their trade goods. They avoided Sonyo,

---

64. Motta Feo e Torres, 18 Jan. 1817, AHU, Angola cx. 64; Mello e Alvim, 27 Jan. 1817, AHU, Angola cx. 64.

65. Motta Feo e Torres, 3 March 1817, AHU, Angola cx. 64. Also António Gomes Fogaça, 28 Feb. 1819, in Motta Feo e Torres, 24 Mar. 1819, AHU, Angola cx. 66. The frigate was no doubt the *Congo*, under the command of Captain J. K. Tuckey. See Tuckey's *Narrative of an Expedition to Explore the River Zaire* . . . (London: John Murray, 1818).

66. "Nota a bem do melhoramento do Commercio do resgate de Escravos que os Portuguezes fazem em Cabinda," in Motta Feo e Torres, 24 March 1819, AHU, Angola cx. 66.

67. Mambuco to Motta Feo e Torres, 16 Dec. 1818, AHU, Angola cx. 66.

68. Motta Feo e Torres to Fogaça, 19 Dec. 1819, AHU, Angola cx. 66.

which had acquired a bad reputation in the Cabinda trade by this time, in favor of small upriver ports from which they would then enter the Kongo lands on the south bank, sometimes going all the way to the Kongo capital to buy slaves in small lots of eight, ten, or twenty.[69] Meanwhile, the Spaniards and other non-Brazilians buying slaves with specie dealt with Luso-Africans at the mouth of the Loje and at Benguela. This outport trade thus reconstituted older patterns with new actors and reduced Luanda's role to a supporting one well before the termination of legal slaving in 1830. From all indications Luanda carried on mostly as a provisioning stop from 1831 on.[70]

It may be that earlier distinctions between the Luso-Africans of Golungo and others in Ambaca fed into this separation of the Luanda trade into profitable contraband to the north and unprofitable legal sales to Anglo-Portuguese buyers at Luanda. Differences between the two groups may have widened in these years, as traders in Golungo with access to the foreigners grew large and wealthy from smuggling, while those of Ambaca, dependent on Luanda, became smaller-scale peddlers of Luanda goods taken toward the interior on credit. Small Ambaca traders were thus available to take up the wax and ivory trade of the 1830s at a time when their counterparts in Golungo remained committed to slaving, for illegal exports through the 1840s and for employment on coffee estates in Angola thereafter.

Within the Luanda hinterland, the successes of the Luso-Africans to the north of a line running roughly up the Bengo and then east and southeast on the near side of Jinga and Kasanje left government-sponsored traders based in the city to develop their own slaving mostly to the southeast in the 1810s, along the Kwanza and through Songo territory toward the sand country beyond the Kwango. A minor aspect of this reorientation of Luanda's slaving hinterland to the southeast was the highly publicized maturation of initiatives taken during the preceding decade to establish contact with the Lunda by circumventing Kasanje to the south.[71] A more substantial element in the strategy was the attempt beginning in 1807–8 to isolate Kasanje by relocating the Luanda-sponsored market there in Songo lands some hundred kilometers nearer the coast.[72] Opportunity beckoned across the Kwanza because elimination of the French south of

---

69. Spix and Martius, *Viagem pelo Brasil*, 2:154, note V.

70. Santa Comba Dão, 2 Aug. 1831, AHU, Angola maço 22 and cx. 72; also Mary C. Karasch, "The Brazilian Slavers and the Illegal Slave Trade, 1836–1851" (M.A. thesis, University of Wisconsin–Madison, 1967); Eltis, "Transatlantic Slave Trade"; Conrad, *World of Sorrow*.

71. E.g., Torres, *Memórias*, pp. 299–302, and much subsequent publicity and study. See F. Bontinck, "Voyage des pombeiros," or Vellut, "Notes sur le Lunda," pp. 110–15.

72. Vellut, "Notes sur le Lunda," pp. 108–9, and much correspondence in the AHA, cód. 91 ff., 240.

Luanda in the 1790s had left the northern slopes of the Ovimbundu
highlands with no source of textiles other than Luanda once the Brazilian
trade at Benguela also collapsed.

In the critical period around 1821 to 1823, when Brazil was in the
process of declaring its independence from Portugal, and Angola temporarily lacked the steadying hand of a royal governor, representatives of
the Anglo-Portuguese merchants at Luanda submitted a formal plan to
organize government marketplaces to the southeast at Dondo, Beja, and
Haco, all looking south beyond the Kwanza.[73] Directors and secretaries
of these *feiras,* appointed by the merchants themselves and reporting exclusively back to them, would supervise all traders taking goods to the
interior. Shipments of goods to Jinga—where, it can safely be assumed,
credit would support only Luso-African *reviros* connected with the ports
north of Luanda—would be absolutely prohibited. The merchants would
instead establish a new market at the mouth of the Kuvo, a site just north
of Novo Redondo formerly much frequented by the French. To limit
competition from the Luso-Africans settled on the Ovimbundu plateau
itself, on whom Governor Sousa Coutinho had tried to impose severe
restraints a half century earlier, they proposed to prohibit government
assignments of bearers to any trader from the highland states of Bihe or
Mbailundu. The merchants would further appoint an inspector (*examina-
dor*) to verify the rightful owners of all slaves sent down from the interior
and would control the issuance of government passes to every trader
departing with goods from the city. Finally, the directors of the markets
would exercise the crucial responsibility of collecting and forwarding the
assets of traders who died in the interior to the rightful creditors. The
aggressive, southward-looking commercial strategies of the Anglo-
Portuguese factors, who would have all but run Luanda by the early 1820s,
must have derived from frustration at their inability to penetrate the Luso-
African strongholds in the more populous and commercially wealthier
areas to the north.

Brazilian traders from Bahia and Pernambuco found themselves subject to all the disadvantages placed on their Rio compatriots by the firm
Anglo-Portuguese grip on the administrative apparatus at Luanda in the
decade after 1810. Bahians for the most part simply steered clear of the
port, given their strength in West African slaving and the warm reception
accorded their tobaccos at Cabinda. Nothing is known about the sources
of the textiles that the Bahians must also have sold there, though they
could have used currency generated by cotton and sugar sales in Europe
to bring goods from Britain through Lisbon. The near invisibility of the
Bahians in the Luanda sources of this period suggests their insignificance
there.

73. Merchants' petition in no. 825, Sala 12, AHU.

Pernambuco merchants, on the other hand, had a thriving market for labor to work in the captaincy's surging cotton sector after 1810 and no sources of slaves in West Africa. Even more than the Bahians they had built up gold balances from selling raw cotton to the British, and some of this cash they must have spent on Angolan slaves, if outside Luanda in some part. The attractiveness of Pernambuco is surely visible in the destinations chosen by the Brazilian traders who fled Luanda in 1810: they headed straight for Recife.[74] During the decade after 1810, British specie spent for cotton in Pernambuco flowed into the coffers of slave traders at Luanda, and Rio's share of the slaves leaving Luanda dropped accordingly, in spite of the Rio merchants' strong hand in official regulation of the trade there.[75] Among the Pernambucan buyers active at Luanda, factors representing Portuguese merchants who had remained behind in Lisbon after the departure of the court and its commercial entourage for Rio de Janeiro in 1807 were probably prominent. These metropolitan traders bought Pernambuco cotton for sale in Britain, and from the metropole they channeled gunpowder and various other products of Portuguese domestic manufacture to Africa through the only Brazilian port not effectively controlled either by British merchants, as was Rio, or by local interests, as was Bahia.[76] Local Pernambuco merchants, insofar as they moved into slaving in this decade and were not disrupted by revolt in 1817, probably followed other Brazilians in trading in the mouth of the Zaire and elsewhere north of Luanda.[77]

And not without reason, since the Pernambucans came under the full range of harassing techniques available at Luanda to the colony's favored Rio traders. The barrage once again trained old laws nominally decreed to protect the slaves, the peace and tranquility of the colony, and other apparently benign and nonpartisan causes selectively on commercial competitors of the faction in power. Pernambuco ships, and only those from Recife, were repeatedly charged with failing to carry the chaplains required by laws that long antedated the modern emphasis on hygiene and provisions in the *alvará* of 1813.[78] The 1813 decree itself was also employed against them for bringing insufficient provisions to feed their slaves. These charges may have contained some truth, since the Pernambuco ships alone continued to carry captives belonging to the Luanda Luso-Africans. They

74. Oliveira Barboza, 15 July 1811, AHU, Angola cx. 60.

75. See the remarkably revealing analysis of this period in Pernambuco in Luccock, *Notes on Rio de Janeiro*, p. 555. Rio's share of the Luanda trade often ran 50%–70% over the preceding decades and was near the top of that range in 1810, but fell toward 20%–30% over the remainder of the trade: Miller, "Legal Portuguese Slaving," p. 151.

76. See the import figures in Miller, "Imports at Luanda." AHU, Angola cxs. 42–43, contain repeated indications of Lisbon ships coming through Recife to Luanda.

77. E.g., the voyage described in Spix and Martius, *Viagem pelo Brasil*, 2:153–54.

78. Oliveira Barboza, 4 Oct. 1813, AHU, Angola cx. 61, basing his authority on an "Ordem para as embarcaçoens trazerem capellaens . . . ," 25 Jan. 1791, AHU, cód. 1634, fol. 10. Cf. Rebelo, *Relações*, p. 206.

were also alleged to smuggle gunpowder into the colony in defiance of long-standing prohibitions that few Portuguese importers had even taken seriously.[79] Lacking the British trade goods of their Rio rivals, they had little else with which to compete at Luanda, except, of course, the specie that they preferred to spend in the ports to the north. Finally, when Pernambuco authorities seized non-Pernambuco ships in Recife during the revolt of 1817, Angola officials made counterseizures of Pernambuco ships in Luanda.[80]

Independence in Brazil

The liberal revolution of 1820 in Portugal drew the king João VI back to Lisbon in 1821 to take the throne of a new constitutional monarchy dominated by the same metropolitan commercial bourgeoisie that had long viewed Brazil as the principal source of colonial wealth nurturing the mother country.[81] The prospect of renewed neomercantilist pressures from Portugal provoked the Brazilians, and some Anglo-Portuguese merchants remaining in Rio, to back the prince regent Pedro, who had remained behind in the American colony, in proclaiming Brazilian independence from Lisbon in 1822. For slavers in Angola these events in the political sphere translated into contradictory prospects: on the one hand, they saw an opportunity to escape the burden of debt placed on them under the old imperial system by joining Brazil, but they also sensed a growing possibility of an end to the entire Angolan slave trade to Brazil, since Brazilian independence would remove them from the toleration accorded intra-imperial slaving in recent treaties with the British. The specter of an end to slave imports drove prices of slaves in Brazil to heights not attained since the gold boom a full century earlier, so that merchants of all sorts entered the slave trade in the late 1820s to capture the final profits available from it. All of these last-minute developments occurred within the framework of steadily increasing British efforts to abolish slaving anywhere in the Atlantic.

Brazilian independence thus first of all raised the issue of whether Luanda and Benguela would remain Portuguese, as they had always been governed, or would shift their political allegiance to the Brazilians, who

79. Euzebio Queiroz Coutinho da Silva (*ouvidor geral*), 27 Dec. 1814, AHU, Angola cx. 62, on the authority of a *carta regia* of 7 Jan. 1812, AHU, Angola cx. 58. For more on the case, Oliveira Barboza, 24 Jan. and 28 Nov. 1815, AHU, Angola cx. 63. The governor had tried to shield a close associate from prosecution under this law.

80. Motta Feo e Torres, 18 Nov. 1817, AHU, Angola cx. 64.

81. Valentim Alexandre, "O liberalismo português e as colonias de Africa, 1820–1839," *Análise social* 16, nos. 61–62 (1980): 319–40.

had for almost as long backed much of the colonial economy outside the limited authority of Lisbon's governors and Crown magistrates.[82] The events of 1822–23 were extremely confused, especially at Luanda. The new constitutional arrangements in Lisbon produced a temporary lapse in metropolitan authority in Angola, as the last royally appointed officials left the colony in 1822, several months before the first governor named by the Liberal constitutional assembly in Lisbon (the Cortes) arrived in 1823. Merchant factions of both Angolan towns took advantage of the interim to air their differences over where the colony's future affiliation should lie. At Benguela, the town's long-standing orientation toward Rio de Janeiro turned the tide temporarily toward Brazil for as long as the locals remained in control, under the leadership of one of the largest merchants, António Lopes Anjo. But none of the prospective Benguela rebels appears to have had the courage to resist a series of moderate restraints extended from Luanda in 1823 and 1824, owing probably to the deep factionalism that rent its trading community. Benguela finally turned definitively Portuguese after a compromise allowed the ringleaders of the dissenting faction to return to their native Brazil.[83]

At Luanda, a party of traders deeply in debt to the Portuguese government, presumably for imperial duties on slaves shipped, tried to escape what they owed by swinging the larger of the two Angolan ports toward Brazil.[84] The Luanda rebels may also have been associated with the resident factors of the big Anglo-Portuguese slavers in Rio, who used the same moment to claim direct and tight control over the trade of the interior.[85] Opposition to affiliation with independent Brazil would have arisen from among smaller traders, who saw a break with their sources of goods as an opportunity to rid themselves of commercial debts owed there. It is not clear how a Brazilian decree of 11 December 1822, which declared assets of Brazilians not loyal to the independent government subject to seizure, might have affected the lines drawn over the issue.[86] Nor can one see at all clearly which side of the dispute the Luso-Africans engaged in diverting slaves to the northern ports might have taken, since the trade regulations proposed by the Brazilian merchant *junta* seemed to threaten their own debtors more than the relatively autonomous Luso-African trading network on the northern flank of the colony.

82. The sources employed in nearly all studies of the 1820s in Angola (AHU, Angola cxs. 67–74), including this one, have recently been revealed to represent only a small portion of the records in fact available. So far we have only a single work—Dias, "Sociedade colonial,"—that draws on the bulk of the records stored in a second series of AHU caixas apparently numbered from the 130s into the 160s.

83. Rebelo, *Relações,* pp. 235–61.

84. Dias, "Sociedade colonial," pp. 272–73.

85. See the text at note 73 and following, above.

86. Rebelo, *Relações,* pp. 285–91.

The arrival of the new Portuguese governor, Christovão Avelino Dias, in May 1823 accompanied by a detachment of troops from Lisbon was sufficient to restore Luanda definitively to the Portuguese sphere. Dias imposed immediate counterdecrees of seizures of Brazilian property in Luanda (2 June 1823) and Benguela (6 June 1823). The threatened Brazilian group then tried to subvert the new governor's only real strength, the expeditionary forces he had brought with him, and provoked a mutiny that Dias suppressed harshly.[87] Lisbon then called a halt to the spreading economic war of confiscation, possibly owing to the loss that Dias's measures would cause to Anglo-Portuguese houses in Brazil that held assets in Angola but possibly also to keep the slave trade moving and the export duties levied on it flowing into the depleted colonial government coffers. Whatever his reasons, Dias commandeered several ships viewed as Brazilian and had them sent to Lisbon.[88] Lisbon strongly reprimanded its own governor for endangering the slave trade and forced a compromise under which the government accepted bonds posted against property deemed liable to seizure as Brazilian as satisfying the terms of the decrees.[89]

Luanda thus remained Portuguese under terms that placed the continuation of slaving, whether by Brazilian subjects or by Portuguese citizens, above matters of political allegiance.[90] The volume of slaves shipped from Luanda to Rio dropped back in 1822 and 1823, doubtless reflecting the uncertainties of those two years, but the losses were more than made up by increased exports at less troubled Benguela, Cabinda, and Ambriz. Lisbon had thus secured the metropolitan slavers' historic anchor on the Angolan coast at Luanda but saw the tax revenues it sought there slipping away to Brazilians calling at other ports it did not control.

In 1826, Brazil gained British recognition of its independence in a treaty that also imposed the terms under which the new South American nation would cease to import slaves.[91] Slave prices and the volume of imports both rose in anticipation of cessation, despite continuing hopes in some quarters that further negotiations might delay the end. A British-Brazilian agreement reached in 1827 finally stipulated that the trade would end in 1830, as it indeed did after only minor further refinements in the

87. Ibid., pp. 226–31.

88. *Requerimento* of Francisco Jozé Gomes Guimarães, n.d. (ca. 1823), AHU, Angola maço 1–A; Avelino Dias, 7 May 1823 and 11 April 1824, AHU, Angola cx. 68; Castelobranco, 27 July 1824, AHU, Angola cx. 68.

89. Rebelo, *Relações,* pp. 283–91.

90. An *alvará* of 6 Dec. 1824 had met the urgent problem of establishing formal Luso-Brazilian commercial relations in advance of the final resolution by treaty in 1825 of the political status of Portugal and Brazil with regard to each other: Pardo, "Comparative Study," p. 185.

91. Manchester, *British Preëminence in Brazil,* esp. chap. 8; Bethell, *Abolition of the Brazilian Slave Trade.*

interpretation of the accord. So fervent was the resulting Brazilian rush to bring slaves in before the deadline that for the first time in history slave buyers in Brazil went into debt to Angolan sellers, taking slaves in Angola on the promise of future shipments of trade goods to pay for them.[92] To meet the high demand, the Luso-Africans had to have sold off a portion of their accumulated holdings of slaves employed in other sectors of the economy of Luanda and its hinterland, thus in effect liquidating their slaving operations and reducing local labor supplies at precisely the moment when metropolitan policy was turning in the direction of putting the colony's slaves to work in Africa. Depletion of colonial labor supplies in turn could not have helped but sharpen the conflicts of the 1830s in Angola between government proponents of commercial alternatives to continued, by then illegal slaving and the Luso-Africans, who put the trade goods they would have been receiving from Brazil by then back to work in the old slaving channels.

Although Luanda's exports between 1826 and 1830 are known only in part, owing to the absence of local figures and to a corresponding lack of import data from anywhere in Brazil north of Bahia, Rio statistics make it clear that the city continued to lose ground relative to ports to its north, except, apparently, for the last-minute, Luso-African sell-off through Luanda in 1830.[93] Another wave of merchants departed the city that year, this time heading to Portugal as well as to Brazil, where they apparently intended to retire on the funds they could withdraw from slaving while high prices for slaves in Brazil allowed them to convert their assets to forms valuable abroad.[94] A temporary drop in the volume of slaving at Luanda in 1827 may have owed something to their departure. The remaining Luso-Africans had an open field for illegal slaving in the years that followed.

Brazilian slavers who bothered to put in to Luanda at all after 1826 did so mostly to reprovision on their way down the coast to ports where they were not subject to export duties.[95] Lisbon contemplated declaring Ambriz, one of the favored Brazilian slaving stations from 1824 to 1828, a Portuguese port in order to tax the slaves being boarded there. But the British—who had designs on "legitimate" commodities from the same part of the coast and regarded the latitude of 8°, just south of Ambriz, as the northern limit of Portuguese territory (from which slaves might legally be shipped)—apparently intimidated the Portuguese from making such a

92. Santa Comba Dão, 11 Oct. 1830, AHU, Angola cx. 74.
93. Miller, "Legal Portuguese Slaving," pp. 169–70.
94. *Requerimentos* of António Lopes Anjo, n.d., AHU, Angola maço 7; Francisco de Paula Graça and Henrique Martins Pereira, n.d., AHU, Angola maço 6; Castelobranco, 27 April 1826, AHU, Angola cx. 70.
95. Castelobranco, 31 March and 16 May 1828, AHU, Angola cx. 72.

move.[96] Contributing also to British interest in Ambriz was the beginning of the nineteenth-century boom in African ivory, which Luso-Africans and others avoided selling in Luanda at the low monopoly price still imposed there in the 1820s and instead delivered to outports to the north.

On the whole, Rio probably strengthened its dominant position in the Angola trade overall as legal slaving drew to a close in the 1820s, thus positioning itself to lead the illegal slave trading that would arise later in the 1830s. Pernambuco, disturbed by further political revolt and a blockade of shipping headed for Recife in 1817, probably declined as a factor in southern Atlantic slaving. Bahia may have continued to take some Luanda slaves in the legal trade's last years but preferred to continue its evasion of British cruisers patrolling the waters off West Africa and to direct its central African ventures to Cabinda.

Continuities: Trading on the Fringes

Brazilians found a series of places on the peripheries of Angolan slaving throughout its long history, adapting again and again to the evolution of the European economies that Brazil's colonial exports served but only once moving toward the core of the trade at Luanda. As Lisbon developed southern Atlantic slaving to Spanish American territories through the Caribbean and the vibrant sugar regions of northeastern Brazil in the sixteenth century, the distinctively Brazilian current in the trade got its start at Rio to smuggle slaves to Spaniards through the Plata. When Brazil's boom in sugar faded after 1660, Pernambucan planters worked through militaristic governors in Angola to raid for slaves, which they could still afford at low wartime costs, from the frontier margins of the colony. With the southward shift of metropolitan attention to Minas Gerais gold from about 1700 and the Lisbon merchants' reentry into slaving in force through Luanda, Bahians developed their own autonomous slave trade on the Mina coast of West Africa, entirely beyond the limits of Portuguese authority. In Angola administrative reforms eliminated Pernambuco militarists at Luanda in the 1720s, and slavers from Rio then moved south to establish themselves at Benguela. Both Rio and Bahian buyers sold marginal by-products of American agriculture to meet a metropolitan competition possessed of both superior wealth and government protection. These Brazilians were Portuguese counterparts of the British "interlopers" who shredded the monopoly of the wealthy Royal African Company in West Africa, and they

---

96. Castelobranco, 27 July 1824, 23 Feb. 1825, and 13 July 1825, AHU, Angola cxs. 68, 70, and 69.

operated with strategies resembling those of the North American colonials who sold Rhode Island rum for slaves in Lower Guinea.[97]

Slavers at Rio recovered from the general decline in Brazilian demand for labor during the 1760s and 1770s by selling a significant portion of the slaves they bought in that era to Spanish sources of silver in the estuary of the Plata, outside the Portuguese imperial sphere. When industrial production rose in late-eighteenth-century Britain, and British merchants sought both raw materials and markets for the products of its mills and factories in America's Portuguese territories, the Rio merchants added smuggled British imports to the goods they sold in Africa. So successful were these new exploitations of peripheries in America and Africa that Rio buyers penetrated even the imperial center at Luanda by the 1790s.

When the Portuguese court moved from Lisbon to Rio and converted this thriving British contraband trade to legal imports handled by immigrant metropolitan merchants allied to the Crown in 1810, the Brazilians once again retreated to the fringes of the empire. At Luanda, Rio traders yielded to the superior force of early-nineteenth-century British capitalism, channeled through Anglo-Portuguese merchants settled in Rio, and sought slaves instead in Mozambique, in the ports north of Luanda, and, still, at Benguela. Bahia struggled to slip past British antislaving patrols at its customary sources of slaves on the Mina Coast. Pernambuco, after 1720, and the far northern captaincies of Pará and Maranhão never developed local slave-trading interests comparable to the flexible and sometimes prosperous slavers at Bahia and Rio, and so they generally remained subject to merchants from Portugal. But the Rio traders in particular had survived and generated sufficient commercial capital of their own in the last high-priced days of legal slaving to underwrite the illegal trade of the 1830s and 1840s. They thus still operated exactly where Brazilian slavers had always found their niche, on the fringes of the main commercial circuits of the southern Atlantic, though defined by the mid–nineteenth century as pirates violating the international treaty agreements typical of industrial capitalism rather than as smugglers defying the constraints of empire in the earlier age of mercantilism.

97. Coughtry, *Notorious Triangle*. See also Susan Westbury, "Analyzing a Regional Slave Trade: The West Indies and Virginia, 1698–1775," *Slavery and Abolition* 7, no. 3 (1986): 241–56, for a precisely analogously structured trade run by local Virginia merchants from the Norfolk-Hampton-Portsmouth area in competition with large British slavers selling in the rivers of the Old Dominion. Westbury attempts to deemphasize the role of credit in leaving the Virginia merchants outside the main axis of commerce in slaves for tobacco destined to Britain but implicitly acknowledges the same importance that I attribute to metropolitan wealth here (her p. 254).

Part 4

Portugal
Merchants of Death

15

The Slave Duty Contracts in the Southern Atlantic, before 1760

Toward the persistent end of accumulating the noble metals in the mercantilistic style characteristic of eighteenth-century Portugal, Lisbon merchants shipped substantial quantities of less exalted trade goods to American and African colonies and were more than willing to offer them on the easy credit terms that underlay slaving in Angola. Metropolitan credit was equally significant on the Brazilian end of the slave trade, where funds extended through Lisbon firmed the city's grip on sugars, metals, and cotton that might otherwise have escaped to wealthier foreign buyers until British investors moved in directly after 1810.[1] Wealth and prosperity, to the Portuguese royal family, its noble courtiers and ecclesiastical supporters, and to most merchants in Lisbon, meant primarily specie: the golden treasure of Minas Gerais in the first half of the century, Spanish silver diverted from the Plata through Rio de Janeiro before the Minas gold boom and again after 1760, and finally the positive international trade balances that brought British remittances in gold for northern Brazilian cotton from the 1790s on into the early nineteenth century. If Africa acted as "Black Mother" to Brazil, maternal land of the slave miners, domestic servants, and cane-cutters laboring in Portuguese America, it was Brazil—not Angola—that served as the mother lode of Portugal's imperial revenues and as cruel stepmother to the country's deepening domestic economic crisis in the eighteenth century.[2] Slaving provided no more than a secondary means to that end, and a risky one that was best avoided.

1. The theme of mercantile credit, "a staple of the literature on colonial Brazil," though apparently difficult to document and not systematically developed in the secondary literature on periods prior to the British investment of the nineteenth century, emerges from scattered indications throughout the materials I have consulted on Brazilian history and is fully consistent with the general structure of the empire as it appears from my more detailed research on Angola. For Rio, see Brown, "Internal Commerce," pp. 170, 291–93, 331, 459, 544 ff., for the quote above and commentary. Schwartz, *Sugar Plantations,* emphasizes the importance of credit, esp. pp. 204 ff., and also pp. 195, 198. He also brings out the vital shortage of cash or currency credits in Lisbon that underlay the economics of Brazilian sales of local products—rum, tobacco, etc.—for slaves in Africa.

2. I offer no detailed references for the general outline of the Portuguese empire that follows, relying on the plausibility of events at Luanda documented in following sections

The Entrepôt Empire: The Politics and Economics of Portuguese Mercantilism

The relative ease of acquiring bullion in Brazil, directly through its ports or indirectly from selling Brazilian produce and spending the returns abroad, in Asia as well as Europe, distracted Lisbon's merchants away from investing their commercial revenues in domestic agriculture and industry. The glittering but superficial "prosperity" achieved by this metropolitan entrepôt strategy left Portugal less and less able to meet its own needs for manufactures of most sorts, and even for basic foods, as the eighteenth century progressed. Instead, Portugal imported necessities and luxuries alike from Britain, northern Europe, and France and paid for them mostly with American specie, supplemented only by Port wines and a few other semiprocessed commodities of domestic origin. A central consequence of this dependence for the history of Lisbon's involvement in southern Atlantic slaving was that Portugal came to rely on British woolen mills for the goods it sent out to Africa and Brazil, and on British bankers for the credit that nurtured trade with its own empire. Portugal's principal sources of imperial wealth in Brazil thus tended to become little more than a foreign-owned exchange of British woolens, and later also cottons, for American gold, silver, and agricultural commodities, taxed by the Portuguese Crown for its own benefit and brokered by a wealthy but unproductive Portuguese community of British factors, resident in Lisbon until 1807 and transplanted thereafter to Rio.

Lisbon merchants lacking contacts in Britain thus found themselves displaced by British goods and funds from the lucrative Brazil trade in the first half of the eighteenth century. They looked instead to Angola as one of the few markets in the world sufficiently protected where they could sell the expensive domestic products of inferior quality that they had to offer or the Asian textiles that they still brought in from the remaining western Indian outposts of Portugal's sixteenth-century Asian commercial

---

and interpreted in terms of it to confirm its accuracy. I have, of course, drawn on the few older studies of the eighteenth-century empire: Boxer's *Golden Age of Brazil, Portuguese Society in the Tropics,* and *The Portuguese Seaborne Empire;* and Oliveira Marques's *History of Portugal.* Two recent surveys of Brazilian and Luso-Brazilian history have largely confirmed my interpretation: Lang, *Portuguese Brazil,* and the Brazil chapters in Lockhart and Schwartz, *Early Latin America.* In addition, there is the entire set of recent monographs on aspects of Brazil and Portugal in the eighteenth century (more or less in chronological order): Hanson, *Economy and Society;* Pinto, *Ouro brasileiro;* Falcon, *Epoca pombalina;* Novais, *Portugal e Brasil;* Maxwell, *Conflicts and Conspiracies;* Santos, *Relações comerciais;* Arruda, *Brasil no comércio colonial;* and Valentim Alexandre, *Origins do colonialismo português moderno* (Lisbon: Sá da Costa, 1979). On the British connection, see Manchester, *British Preëminence in Brazil;* H.E.S. Fisher, *The Portugal Trade: A Study of Anglo-Portuguese Commerce, 1700–1770* (London: Methuen, 1971); Sideri, *Trade and Power.*

empire. Angola thus became a commercial refuge and dumping ground on a global scale for Portuguese merchants and products not competitive in the world market.

The Lisbon merchants thus forced off into the Angola market seldom viewed African trading as an end in itself. Rather, they treated Luanda as a back door through which they might tap some of the American specie or Brazilian agricultural commodities salable for bullion or merchandise credits in Europe. American miners and planters required labor, and Europe (if not Portugal itself) was broadly prepared to finance their purchases of slaves. Further, the Brazilian labor market lay entirely open to merchants from Lisbon, since the dominance of the British in the direct Brazilian goods and commodities trade removed any need for them to intrude also on Portugal's South American preserve by offering slaves. The Bristol, Liverpool, or London traders who specialized in slaving, beyond being legally excluded from Portuguese territories, found themselves fully occupied in delivering African labor for higher prices to their own, more efficient sugar colonies in the Caribbean or in supplying French and other West Indian islands able for many years to pay more for slaves than depressed Brazilian export sectors could afford. Only when these Caribbean markets closed after 1807 did British manufacturers support the Portuguese trade in slaves to Brazil, indirectly.

Selling goods in Angola offered a highly problematic alternative route to American wealth for these marginal Lisbon traders precisely because it required investing in slaves as the commercial bridge across the Atlantic. Ownership of the slaves threatened to impose the high mortality risks of the trade on merchants unwilling to bear them. It also forced Lisbon traders to challenge entrenched Luso-Africans on their own ground in Angola and to work through the Brazilian sailors usually in control of the maritime portions of the trade. Offsetting these obstacles, Lisbon merchants trying to dispose of stocks in Angola usually had the advantage of close connections to the Crown and the backing of ministries responsible for governing the colonies. Metropolitan traders consequently took consistent advantage of the influence they could bring to bear in these high places. They also had more capital with which to work than the colonials, whatever their weakness in relation to banks and merchants in Britain, and they employed this wealth also in every way they could. Finally, they lessened the slave risk—even eliminated it when prices squeezed trading profits—by limiting their investment in slaves to indirect forms, through the bills of exchange basic to southern Atlantic slaving. In that way Lisbon merchants remained primarily sellers of merchandise in Africa, claiming their credits in Brazil as specie, in bills, or in commodities redeemable in Lisbon, and leaving the elevated slave mortality of the trade and of slavery itself in Brazil to the colonials. These deaths in turn generated needs for replacement labor, thus maintaining the demand for slaves in America and the momentum of the entire circuitous system Lisbon had devised of cashing in, at reduced risk, on forced sales of shoddy goods in Africa.

Commercial credit lent the strategy its coercive quality from the point of view of ambitious but persistently undercapitalized Angolan slave sellers and Brazilian slave buyers. Credit in the southern Atlantic meant not only the trade goods that Lisbon sent to Angola but also the indebtedness fostered in Brazil by the ultimate backers of the slave trade, the British-supported merchants of Lisbon and their agents in American port cities, who provided supplies and equipment from Europe on delayed terms of payments and accepted slave property as collateral for such loans. Indebted Brazilian sugar planters, though protected from foreclosure by imperial decrees, had little choice but to continue buying new slaves to keep encumbered estates running, even unprofitably, if their returns barely sufficed to stave off metropolitan creditors. In Angola commercial credit gave Portuguese merchants the only advantage they enjoyed against British and French competition, since it supported an entire group of slavers there—exiles, deserters, criminals, and other aspirant members of the Luso-Africans—who could not have assembled the working capital necessary to offer slaves elsewhere for cash.

Though pervasive colonial indebtedness and Angola's principal significance to Portugal as an indirect route to American wealth remained remarkably constant down to the end of the eighteenth century, a succession of different Lisbon merchants fought one another over the right to represent European merchant capital in Luanda as Portugal itself moved through distinct stages of mercantilism associated with its drift from autocracy to parliamentary monarchy in the course of the eighteenth century. The ways in which each merchant faction manipulated its government connections also evolved with the accompanying administrative reforms at home and overseas. And the objectives these merchants sought in Brazil shifted from silver to sugar, to gold, back to silver, and finally to cotton and sugar again before Britain's direct entry into Portugal's colonial American market finally forced Lisbon traders over to Africa as an end in itself by the 1830s. Though metropolitan merchants colluded in Angola to maintain high prices for the goods they sold there, and though they also united formally from time to time in official colonial advisory boards, they also competed furiously among themselves as new groups replaced older ones at Luanda. Out of these struggles emerged the detailed history of Lisbon's presence in Angolan slaving.

In broad terms, the collisions between Lisbon factions at Luanda tended to oppose "Europeanist" traders, who specialized in northern European manufactures largely on the strength of British finance, against national merchants who drew more extensively (if not entirely) on Portuguese capital and traded mostly within the empire and around the Mediterranean. Their contrasting commercial strategies partly reflected distinctions between newer and more mercantilist brokers handling British goods sent to Brazil and older trading interests with connections to the nobility and the Crown who had fallen on increasingly hard times in the seventeenth century as the Asian empire declined and as domestic production faltered. For both, Africa, the third leg of the tricontinental Portuguese imperial system, helped to stabilize the rest of the structure—for the national merchants by absorbing domestic exports and a portion of the cheaper Asian cottons, and for the Europeanist group by furnishing the slaves who produced most of the mineral and agricultural wealth that paid for the British goods they sent out to Brazil.

The two Lisbon factions accordingly viewed Angola differently, the Asia merchants as a market for goods and the European factors as a source of slaves. The division reappeared in the returns from Brazil, since by the eighteenth century the gold went mostly to Britain, while Brazilian sugar found its main markets in Mediterranean kingdoms lacking Caribbean plantations of their own. Spanish silver, channeled to Lisbon through Brazil, went principally to Portuguese India, where it purchased the Asian cottons that figured so prominently in the African trade and, later, paid off commercial loans from Indian textile producers. Cotton, on the other hand, went to Britain. The basic distinction, translated into Continental politics, paralleled that between pro-British and pro-French parties at the court.

Though opposed on all these levels, the conflicting sectors of the Portuguese bourgeoisie also depended on each other, as even this sketchy outline of commodity, goods, and specie flows through the empire implies. Brazil traders sold their sugars through merchants specialized in the Mediterranean, and the Asia traders disposed of most of their cottons and silks in America. The larger general trading houses surely spread their risks over ventures in all fields of commerce, participating in both underlying patterns of imperial commerce and in Portugal's intra-European trade besides; but in peripheral and specialized corners of the empire like Angola the two tendencies separated in revealing ways.

A further and, at least in Angola, crucial dimension of the distinction was between the greater wealth of Portuguese merchants reexporting British woolens to Brazil, with the backing of the wealthiest and fastest-growing financial system in the world by the eighteenth century, and the lesser wealth of domestic merchants with no remotely comparable resources. Though wealthy by local standards, these national traders tended to survive with the aid of government monopolies and contracts that allowed them to generate working capital through privileges and exemptions, protected markets, and negotiated prices reminiscent of the earlier era from which they descended, usually in return for stipulated payments to the royal treasury. Without the financial strength to compete economically with the newer merchants, they took refuge in administered trade and in peripheral branches of imperial commerce, including the slave trade, on the basis of relatively short-term investments. For them, the eighteenth century was a period of defense against liberal currents of "free trade," and by 1800 they had gone down to defeat on nearly every significant front.

The relatively limited assets of these Africa traders, made all the less adequate by the necessity of paying for Asian textiles in cash, silver, and of meeting regular contract payments to the Crown also in currency, pressured them to take their returns as rapidly and efficiently as possible. Once again, the bill of exchange served them well. *Letras* allowed an almost immediate return on goods offloaded in Africa, long before the slaves acquired with the actual merchandise distributed in the interior appeared even at Luanda itself. Discounting these notes in Brazil, again in advance of the arrival of the slaves, further hastened realization in Portugal of the returns from their investment in Africa and maintained the accelerated rates of turnover at which they aimed. When Angolan debtors defaulted, they fell back on the privileges of their charters and contracts or sued through friendly royal courts. As a last resort, and as an implicit admission of failure, on both sides of the Atlantic they married into the families of the colonials who owed them money.

Overseas lending and legal proceedings against debtors were, of course, ideal strategies attainable in practice only by a narrow band of established Lisbon merchant houses within what must have been a broad spectrum of metropolitan merchants of varying capabilities who had many different individual reasons for involving themselves in Angolan slaving. The extant documentation seldom suggests the idiosyncratic strategies behind individual voyages[3] or the heterodox purposes of the less conventional traders, who kept few records and who mounted ventures out to Luanda largely to save their financial skins. But the basic approaches to slaving that emerge from this chapter adequately account for its structure, since the less established merchants who entered the trade only from time to time from Lisbon were, by definition, marginal. The hazards of the Angolan trade meant that anyone in Lisbon contemplating slaving on a basis of less than solid political and financial respectability, of either of the two major styles of Portuguese imperial trade, would have appeared in the Luanda reports that castigated gunrunners, smugglers who bought slaves from Luso-

---

3. With the exception, of course, of the copious correspondence of Pinheiro in Lisanti, *Negócios coloniais*. Analysis of the papers of the Pombaline companies in terms of these commercial strategies would surely allow further understanding of the trade in the terms proposed here. See Miller, "Capitalism and Slaving," for inferences on strategies in the 1680s and 1690s.

Africans through *reviros,* and other outlaws who disturbed the established merchants' vision of orderly commerce.

The Interests and Capabilities of the Portuguese State in Angola

The Portuguese Crown itself had only a limited direct financial interest in Angolan slaving, beyond the important diplomatic value of its African colony in an age of territorial expansion in Europe. It levied export duties on the slaves leaving the colony, collecting these revenues indirectly through a tax-farming contract until 1769 and directly through its own fiscal institutions thereafter. In addition, it claimed monopoly rights to purchase ivory passing through Luanda, also let by contract to the tax farmers until 1769. The returns from these contracts, as well as the ivory after 1706, accumulated in the royal treasury in Portugal. Resale of the tusks on the European market, though at high mark-ups, amounted to very little, owing to the unwillingness of African ivory producers to deliver tusks to Luanda at the low administered price set by the Crown and long left unaltered, no doubt precisely because financial planners at the court regarded ivory as a revenue source of marginal significance before the 1830s.

The slave duties went directly or indirectly into the colonial coffers and not back to Portugal. Angola's budget consisted mostly of salaries for the governor and other officials. It also provided quite inadequate maintenance of the regular colonial military forces, various coastal fortifications, the troops of the line, and a small cavalry squadron stationed mainly in Luanda, with a few detachments of foot soldiers posted at the *presídios* along the lower Kwanza and inland from Luanda. They were too few, too ill-equipped, and too poorly trained to be of much service in the Crown's primary European concerns—utterly incapable, for example, of preventing British and French smuggling along Angolan shores. Portugal was generally reluctant in any case to authorize serious anti-contraband measures that might affront its financial and diplomatic guarantors in Europe, even when they openly transgressed on its claimed national trading sphere in Africa. Official Lisbon restraint in this instance illustrated the marginality of the Crown's direct stake in Angola. Portuguese possessions in western central Africa were in fact defended mainly in the interior, and even then only intermittently in the eighteenth century, and by African levies commanded by Luso-African officers of the colonial civilian militia. But because the governor, the colonial judiciary, and the regular troops were Lisbon's only means of keeping local slave traders in line and bringing debtors to heel, the slave export duty, though spent only on the local scene, assumed a certain indirect significance to the Crown in Portugal, on behalf of the Lisbon merchants trading there whose investments the king's ministers often defended.

The governor-general of the colony represented the Crown in Angola, undependably in earlier years but more and more responsively as the decades passed. In the seventeenth century Lisbon's appointees followed mostly their private commercial interest, because they were usually the biggest merchants in residence, and hence Brazilians. The Crown thereafter gradually separated its own chief colonial officer from the merchants, but it continued to accord official standing to Lisbon merchants in other ways. Early in the eighteenth century, it allowed holders of the tax-farming contract on the slave export duties considerable influence over Angolan slaving. The government of the Marquis of Pombal passed the succession to the chartered commercial companies selling slaves in Pernambuco, Paraíba, Maranhão, and Pará from the 1750s into the 1770s. Then and later in the 1700s, governors charged the Lisbon factors resident in Luanda with supervision of commerce in the interior of the colony as an official advisory board, the Junta do Comércio, reporting to the governor. Lisbon thus continuously favored the mercantile presence in Luanda, though in forms that varied through the century and left the traders less and less influential in colonial officialdom as governors yielded to contractors, contractors to companies, and companies to local advisers. At the same time, as "free traders" their unofficial economic influence grew.

Concomitant with the decline in direct merchant participation in colonial governance, Lisbon steadily increased its independent administrative capabilities over the years. The Crown had little control over its governors of the 1650s, but it then began to issue charters for the office (*regimentos*) that set standards of conduct to which it could hold its appointees.[4] Also, in line with generally tightened administrative controls implemented throughout the empire, it dispatched separate Crown magistrates (the *ouvidores gerais*) and various fiscal inspectors (*provedores*) to assume some of the powers formerly assigned to the governorship. The resulting jurisdictional conflicts among these multiplying officials hedged the autonomy of them all and gave the Crown a method of checking the personal ambitions of its delegates overseas, but strategies of this sort also tended to paralyze central government initiatives as officials played out their rivalries in the legalistic idioms of Portuguese imperial administration and frustrated measures that Lisbon attempted to promulgate through any one of the multitude of channels it had created. The disputes sometimes

---

4. See the *regimentos* of 1666, esp. caps. 17 and 18, and of 1676, esp. caps. 18–20, and 40, which clearly spell out the practices of the time, by way of prohibiting them. Published in *Boletim do Conselho Ultramarino* (legislação antiga), pp. 295–307, 311–29; also in *Arquivos de Angola*, ser. 1, no. 5 (1936), n.p. (doc. 2), and in *Arquivo das colónias* 3, no. 14 (1918): 60–73; ibid., no. 15, pp. 124–36; ibid., no. 16, pp. 188–92.

also reflected divisions among the commercial factions contending at Luanda, though only dimly through the haze of the official personalities and lawyers also involved.

Nonetheless, Lisbon gradually increased its direct power. An administrative reform decreed in 1720 forbade future holders of the governorship, or of any other high-ranking military post, to pursue private business interests in the colony. Richly symbolic of the shift then under way from administered trade to "free" trade, from politics to economics, this step also cut sharply against colonial slavers wedded to military methods of slaving. As the Luso-Africans in the Luanda Senado de Câmara complained, the decree as phrased also excluded from slaving the residents of the colony, who all held some sort of royal commission, usually in the colonial militia.[5] They circumspectly described the law as "inapplicable" as written; unenforcible this secondary effect of the decree may have been, but it was probably not also unintended.

The reform was indeed largely ineffective at first, but it prepared the way for a series of stronger appointees to the colony's top administrative post, with firm backing from Lisbon, who held office under the Pombal regime, beginning in the 1750s and culminated in the memorable firmness with which Francisco Inocêncio de Sousa Coutinho exercised the powers of his position from 1764 to 1772. Formal termination of the slave duty contract in 1769 eliminated one form in which Lisbon merchants had continued to interfere with governors' prerogatives, and the failure of the Pombaline companies during the following decade left the governors relatively free to act without fear of merchants undercutting them at the royal court.[6] For the slave traders, growing government autonomy meant better record-keeping and greater pressures on the Brazilians and Angolans active in Luanda, but for metropolitans only a shift from merchants openly pursuing private gain in the name of the king to government influence exerted in subtle forms on behalf of Lisbon traders.

This alliance between the Crown and the metropolitan merchants survived the changing times largely because Lisbon and its Luanda governors shared every interest in moving as many duty-paying captives as they could through the port. Large numbers of slaves attracted higher bids from prospective bidders on the tax contract up to the 1760s and returned greater revenues directly to the colonial treasury thereafter. High export volumes also found consistent favor with the merchants of Lisbon, who saw only advantages in selling increased quantities of textiles at high prices in Angola. The policy ignored Luso-African owners of the slaves, who found themselves less in favor of increased volume when slave exports

5. *Parecer* of the Conselho Ultramarino (Lisbon), 10 Dec. 1722, AHU, Angola cx. 16.
6. Late-eighteenth-century governors arrived with increasingly explicit and detailed instructions drafted by the colonial ministry in Lisbon.

exceeded demand in Brazil and thus reduced the prices they could obtain for captives they were forced to sell there, or when the Lisbon merchants attempted to increase exports on their own, bypassing local slavers. In general, despite the weakness of the state's inherent devotion to Angolan slaving, the king, his ministers in Portugal, and royal governors in Luanda did all they could to defend both imports, for their utility to merchants in the metropole, and slaving, for its fiscal benefits in the colony, regardless of the consequences for local Angolans.

Slaves, Silver, and Sugar in the Seventeenth Century

Since late in the sixteenth century Lisbon merchants had viewed Angola as a prime source of the slaves that gave them entrée to the silver of Spain's territories in the New World, and also to Brazilian sugars, for a while seemingly also worth almost their weight in specie. Governors sent out from Lisbon early in the seventeenth century were also the principal merchants active in the colony, and other metropolitan commercial interests obtained licenses (the *asientos*) from Madrid during the Dual Monarchy, from 1580 to 1640, to supply the Spanish Indies with African labor. One may surmise that the small quantities of goods then paid for slave casualties of the wars, disease, and starvation behind the export trade of that era meant that Portuguese merchants then made few fortunes solely on sending merchandise to Angola, to enable others to buy and ship slaves in the manner common later in the eighteenth century. Rather, gains came from owning the slaves and selling them in labor-hungry American markets for silver and sugar. If patterns visible later had already formed, Lisbon concentrated on acquiring Spanish silver and left the task of supplying labor to Brazilian sugar plantations to the first generations of Luso-Africans and to the planters of Pernambuco and Bahia.[7]

Lisbon's use of commercial capital to work its way into Angolan slaving probably arose from its exclusion from these early networks following Portugal's separation from Spain in 1640. It then lost access through the *asiento* to Spain's American territories. Dutch seizure of Luanda from 1641 to 1648 further weakened the metropole's tenuous hold on the African end of the slave trade. The Angolan restoration of 1648, accomplished by Brazilians from Rio de Janeiro, turned the slave trade of the

7. A Spanish inspector's report of 1591 already confirmed that the slaves leaving Luanda belonged to "many owners": Salvador, *Magnatas do tráfico negreiro*, p. 102, citing Abreu e Brito. The multiple owners, otherwise unidentified, could have been metropolitan sublicensees *(avençadores)* of the *asiento* holders *(armadores)*, or they could have been Brazilian and Angolan (and São Tomé) settlers. The former was more likely for ships bound for Spanish territories, and the latter for ships heading for Brazil. Also see Heintze, *Fontes*, p. 232.

1650s over to the American colonists and their Luso-African allies. Merchants from Portugal found themselves largely on the sidelines during the subsequent half century of strong Brazilian influence in the affairs of Angola, as the tendency of Brazilian *gerebitas* to replace Portuguese wines and *aguardentes* at that time neatly symbolized. Continuing emphasis on militaristic methods of acquiring captives and on development of a thriving trade in local raffia palm textiles and in salt further lessened the dependence of Angolan slaving on goods sent all the way out from Portugal. These intercolonial and intracolonial exchanges threatened Lisbon's position in its own nominal dependencies. Even a large proportion of the European and Asian goods reaching Angola arrived under the auspices of Brazilian governors, not metropolitan merchants.

Lisbon merchants banded together behind privileges embedded in the slave duty contracts of the second half of the seventeenth century to reenter the Angolan trade, though no longer to own slaves. The Portuguese kings seem to have resisted letting the slave duty contracts of the time directly to Brazilian or Angolan interests, but the favored Lisbon merchants who bought the duties were careful to establish close associations with the governors and Luso-Africans and sometimes helped to finance the personal commercial operations of the top colonial officers. Not many successful Lisbon traders would have wanted to expose themselves to the risks of owning slaves as Brazilian prices declined in the 1660s and 1670s. Those who sought ways to reenter slaving, virtually abandoned in the southern Atlantic to Brazilians in the late seventeenth century, directed their efforts rather to Cacheu in Upper Guinea under royal charters awarded to "companies" formed then for that purpose.

In Angola, Lisbon investors secured the right to sell goods as one of the terms of their tax farming contracts, apparently in the 1660s. Issues familiar later in the eighteenth century quickly loomed: there were complaints that the contractors were overloading ships with the slaves produced by excessive loans of goods into the African economy, and the loans created debts that African customers were unable to pay off for many years.[8] Metropolitan capital had begun to supplement Angolan and Brazilian militarism as a significant source of slaves.

Simultaneously the Crown moved to dispossess the Brazilian governors of their Angolan fiefdom and thus open the way for metropolitan merchants to enlarge the beachhead they had established. The restrictive *regimentos* of 1666 and 1676 formed parts of that effort, though without great immediate effect owing to the continuing prevalence of wars around the *conquista* and the great wars and epidemics among the Africans during the 1680s. The Crown's campaign against the colonials matured in the

8. Salvador, *Magnatas do tráfico negreiro*, pp. 56–57.

empirewide effort to curb the governor's independence expressed in the decree of 1720. In it the Crown not only reiterated earlier prohibitions against the participation of high-ranking military officers in commerce of any sort but also raised gubernatorial and other salaries high enough that it could attract candidates of its own who would enforce royal dictates. In excluding the governors from slaving at Luanda (though without by any means eliminating them), the Crown cleared the way by a single stroke of the quill for merchants from Lisbon to enter the southern Atlantic slave trade in force before 1730, under the established privileges of the contract for the slave export duties.

The Lure of Minas Gold

Realization that the Minas Gerais gold strikes of the 1690s promised enormous wealth to any who could cash in on the produce of the mines provided ample motivation. The poor flocked in classic gold-rush style directly to the placers of Minas Gerais, while wealthy Lisbon merchants siphoned the flow of gold directly by sending British woolens, domestic foodstuffs, and implements and other supplies out to the miners and their slaves in Brazil. Luso-Africans and governors, merchants, and planters from northeastern Brazil holding firm positions in Luanda sought to gain their cut of the bonanza by supplying slaves to the mining zones through Rio de Janeiro. Money prices for merchandise sold in Angola doubled, and the quantities of imports needed to buy a slave tripled.[9] The obscure jockeying for position evident in Angola between about 1700 and the 1720s seems to suggest that this vastly expanded African market attracted a cohort of metropolitan traders who initially tried to sell goods in Luanda through their established commercial contacts in northeastern Brazil.

If the potential sixfold increase in *réis* returns for goods delivered to Angola, enhanced by the promise of eventual payment in Brazil in pure gold rather than in sugar, provided Lisbon's merchants with the will to confront colonial governors and their henchmen from the start of the century, it took three decades for them to bring adequate means to bear on the project. Governors, the *capitães-mores* in charge of the colonial military government, and favored sectors of the Luso-African community distributed Brazilian goods, *gerebita,* and European imports reshipped through Pernambuco and Bahia through the interior and extorted slaves by means of various forms of force applied to the African inhabitants of the colony. Governors and Luso-Africans would have owned most of the

9. Taunay, *Subsídios,* pp. 140–41; Boxer, *Portuguese Society in the Tropics,* p. 226. Also Miller, "Slave Prices."

captives sent out at first to Rio.[10] The agents of Lisbon's commercial wealth sought to pry their way into this quasi monopoly by economic means, sending their own imports directly to the interior in well-financed abundance that the colonial militarists could not match. They operated independently of the Luso-African families resident there and dispatched their goods under the care of the famous slave *pombeiros*. Luso-African factions in Luanda, prominent in the town's Senado da Câmara and competitors of the governor in trying to ship slaves to Brazil, seem to have supported these Lisbon representatives. Lisbon offered goods to Africans with slaves to sell at three times the former rate but partially covered the costs of these increases by doubling the *réis* prices of wares they sold to competing Luso-African and Brazilian buyers. Doubled *réis* prices also increased the values of *letras* that they could claim from Luso-Africans who insisted on shipping slaves on their own accounts. Lisbon also expected this strategy to attract African sellers to Luanda itself, thus moving transactions from the terrain of the Africans and Luso-Africans in the interior of the colony to the home turf of the Lisbon factors in Luanda.

Metropolitan merchant capital was demonstrating its power in ways that set precedents for the entire century, but Lisbon's financial strength at that time, and for this peripheral skirmish in the larger battle for Brazilian gold, was evidently insufficient to carry the day by itself. The Lisbon traders also maneuvered on the legal front starting in 1703 to replace militarism with capitalism in Angolan slaving. In Lisbon, the Overseas Council (Conselho Ultramarino) of royal advisers on colonial policy resurrected a neglected old petition from the Luanda municipal council and on its basis proposed an outright prohibition against Angolan governors engaging in any sort of commerce.[11]

Though the council's recommendation did not result in a royal decree on that occasion, in Luanda the Lisbon merchants acted more directly. In that same year Governor Bernadino de Tavora (1701–3) died.[12] The Luanda Senado da Câmara assumed formal authority in the colony during the interim before his successor could arrive to take office, and its Luso-African members seized this opportunity to attack both the governors' trading and plundering system in the interior and their external connections to Rio and Minas Gerais, where they apparently enjoyed direct ties that the Luso-Africans' Bahia and Pernambuco contacts could not duplicate. Citing the Crown's ancient commitment to protect its African subjects from the

10. There is a very clear description of this system in Roza Coutinho *certidão*, 16 Sept. 1715, AHU, Angola cx. 16. Boxer, *Portuguese Society in the Tropics*, pp. 209 ff., identifies this critic of gubernatorial abuses as a former *escrivão* of the Luanda town council.

11. Couto, *Capitães-mores,* p. 80.

12. Tavora had arrived in Angola as an elderly man already in his eighties: Corrêa, *História de Angola,* 1:33.

depredations of unscrupulous Portuguese, though not naming the governors and their military allies, they begged that the king exclude them from trading through the *capitães-mores* in the interior.[13] The Crown, if unwilling to challenge the governors' business dealings in general terms, had fewer reservations about striking down the specific bases of the Angolan system and so ordered in 1704. The merchants in the Luanda council, acting under their temporary jurisdiction over colonial officers in the interior, then recalled all the military captains to the city and proposed to replace them with civilian scribes of their own choosing. This maneuver, if it had been successful, would have put the interior districts in the charge of clerks, useful in documenting debts owed there to the merchants of the council but incapable of mounting military raids harmful to the commercial strategies of Lisbon.[14] The Luso-Africans of Luanda were evidently bidding through the town council's official access to the Crown to ship slaves under *letras* given to Lisbon suppliers of trade goods.

Carrying the oblique challenge to the northeastern Brazilian governors on to the imperial level, where the Luanda Senado de Câmara could not legislate, the Crown restricted the number of slaves that Angolan shippers could embark directly to Rio de Janeiro, the route in which the governors enjoyed their strongest position, to only 1,200 per year. The allotted number amounted to something less than a fourth to a sixth of the slaves then going to Minas through the southern Brazilian port.[15] The Luanda Senado da Câmara consolidated this gain by reserving authority to award the scarce spaces available on Rio-bound ships to itself—that is, ensuring that slaves belonging to Lisbon merchants, or Angolans shipping slaves under *letras* owing to them, would crowd out those of the governors and their allies. Once the next governor (Dom Lourenço de Almada, 1705–9) took office, the merchants received further protection from Lisbon in the form of a 1706 decree that appointed the *ouvidor geral,* the colony's chief royal magistrate, as president of the council, thus placing him to protect its members from overbearing governors.[16] These moves spread Lisbon's regulatory net over the Brazilian governors' external contacts as well as their interior connections.

The governors, though challenged by growing Lisbon control of the Luanda council, managed a strong comeback in the following decade,

---

13. Couto, *Capitães-mores,* p. 198.
14. Ibid., pp. 53, 74–76.
15. Boxer, *Portuguese Society in the Tropics,* pp. 193 ff. The proposal clearly favored Bahia, since it also limited slaves shipped to Pernambuco and Paraíba to 1,300 per year. On the imperial level, it was also a concession protecting Bahian planters from the competition and high prices for slaves coming from Minas and Rio.
16. Delgado, *Reino,* p. 397; *carta regia* of 14 March 1706. Cf. Boxer, *Portuguese Society in the Tropics,* p. 113. For parallel (and slightly earlier) changes in Bahia, see Schwartz, *Sugar Plantations,* p. 277.

based on Lisbon's 1709 confirmation of the governors' abstract right to engage in private business. Faced with empirewide financial exigencies, the Crown was resolved to attract ambitious and capable men into colonial service at minimal expense to the royal treasury. With that support, the Angolan merchant-governors of the 1710s ranked among the wealthiest, most arbitrary, and most powerful in Angola's history. Governor Dom João Manuel de Noronha (1713–17) arbitrarily suspended this provision confirming the Luanda council's right to distribute coveted spaces on Rio-bound ships.[17]

The governors also benefited from divisions among the Lisbon merchants over strategy in response to the growth of Bahia's independent slave trade from the Mina Coast to Rio de Janeiro. Lisbon's agents at Luanda had begun by routing slaves to the mines through their established connections in Bahia, as the 1703 limitation on sending captives direct from Angola to Rio had implicitly provided. But this strategy quickly failed, as the Bahians' West African captives and surplus slaves they sold off from their ailing sugar economy acquired a favored position in the labor market in Minas Gerais and began to undercut Lisbon's reexport trade through their port to Angola. The Luanda councilmen felt sufficiently threatened by 1711 that they evidently decided to ship directly to Rio, producing a petition to the Crown protesting the same limitation on direct Angola shipping to Rio that they had supported only eight years before.[18] No doubt they had hoped that council authority over space on the Rio vessels would protect them from the governors and their local allies, but the disunity in the merchants' ranks could only have worked to the governors' favor.

Lisbon attempted to circumvent the governors at Luanda also by developing an independent trade in slaves along the Loango Coast, then just beginning to emerge as a major supplier of captives to all the European commercial nations involved in the Atlantic trade. Though ships approaching Loango from the north via the direct route along the West African coast kept well beyond the reach of the Angola governors, Lisbon ships passing first through Brazil and then coming down the Angolan coast from the south often had to put in at the colonial capital to repair and reprovision. Governors imposed a mass of legal technicalities and pretexts that could delay the progress of those vessels for months.[19] The price of release would surely have included loading the governor's slaves at cut rates that forced these Lisbon-backed shippers to tight-pack captives they later bought for themselves north of the Zaire. The governors then

---

17. *Provisão* of 21 March 1716, in *Arquivos de Angola* 3, nos. 16–18 (1937): 21–22.
18. Boxer, *Portuguese Society in the Tropics,* pp. 193–94.
19. E.g., Francisco Manuel Gomes, Lisbon, 26 June 1715, AHU, Angola cx. 16.

reported these violations of the tight-packing decree to Lisbon.[20] Brazilian captains reaching Loango also ran into stiff competition from the Dutch, the British, and the French active there. But Lisbon's interest in developing Loango Coast slaving ports as an alternative to Luanda for metropolitan traders, and probably also as a supplementary labor source for Minas Gerais, remained high enough to prompt a military expedition sent out from Europe in 1723 to expel a British garrison from a fort the British had recently constructed on a promontory overlooking Cabinda Bay.[21] This Loango strategy also failed when it aroused the opposition of Britain.

When the 1720 imperial reform finally turned the tide back against the governors, the struggle over buying the slaves sent to Rio changed from a mercantile alliance against the military system of the seventeenth century to the competition among different factions of traders of the sort that would typify eighteenth-century mercantilism. The Bahians had already developed their own distinct approach to the Rio slave trade in West Africa, and the merchants in Luanda also began to fall out among themselves in the 1720s.

The first to make their move were the Luso-Africans, obviously threatened directly by decrees which their Lisbon opponents interpreted to remove the entire colonial establishment from trading. All of them held some sort of military commission, in the militia if not as *capitão-mor*,[22] and they took advantage of the next interim between Lisbon-appointed governors in 1725–26 to put one of their own military men, the *mestre de campo* José Carvalho da Costa, in temporary charge of the colonial administration. This unprecedented departure from the usual custom of lodging interim power in the Luanda Senado da Câmara[23] gave da Costa the authority to unleash the full military power of the local slavers against the *pombeiro* slave agents of the Lisbon merchants, at allegedly serious cost to the merchants' business.[24] The Luso-African militarists, deprived of powerful governors to protect them abroad, were apparently taking advantage of their strong position within the colony to keep the Lisbon merchants on the defensive. The intricate interplay of political and economic strategies, transformed with each partial victory but never resolved, thus continued.[25]

20. E.g., Coelho de Carvalho, 13 June 1722, AHU, Angola cx. 26, an allegation against Miguel Lopes da Silva at Loango for loading 800 slaves on a ship rated at only 460 capacity.

21. Martin, *Loango Coast,* pp. 80–83.

22. *Parecer* of the Conselho Ultramarino, 10 Dec. 1722, AHU, Angola cx. 16.

23. Cf. Corrêa's puzzlement at this anomaly, *Historia de Angola,* 1:357. The king had placed his own *juiz de fora* (royal judge) in charge of the Senado da Câmara in 1722, thus making it clearly an agency of the central power: Boxer, *Portuguese Society in the Tropics,* p. 113.

24. Pereira da Costa, 18 Sept. 1725, AHU, Angola cx. 16.

25. Pereira da Costa, 28 Jan. 1726, AHU, Angola cx. 17.

The opposing lineups may have changed one last time in the wake of da Costa's demonstration that Lisbon's agents at Luanda might have won the battle against domineering governors at the imperial level but still had to face formidable local slavers in the colony's interior. The sensible metropolitan strategy in this situation would have been to take over the governors' old position as sponsor of cooperative factions among the Luso-Africans, as some had done in the previous decades. A group of this sort allied to the dispossessed families of the interior might have been the perpetrators of an abortive attempt to seize the colonial government after the death of Governor Paulo Caetano de Albuquerque (1726–32) in 1732.[26] Albuquerque had presided over the real turning point in the transition from old-style military slaving to the new era of mercantile capitalism, which came ten years after the decrees of 1720, and the Luso-Africans' failed *coup d'état* might well have represented their last desperate overt challenge to the new order. But the next stage in the consolidation of Lisbon's position in Angolan slaving came not through the Bahia-linked merchants of the 1700s and 1710s but rather through resurgent Lisbon interests working through the tax contracts. These interests were better capitalized and willing to deploy greater inventories of goods to fight their way into the Angolan interior behind governors more and more obedient to policies set in Lisbon in their favor.[27]

The Slave-Duty Contractors

When the zone of slaving frontier violence moved far off toward the east between the 1680s and the 1730s, and as British and French slavers at Loango put a cost squeeze on the Luso-African commercial network, trading through Luanda grew dependent on even the modest capital resources available from Lisbon in that early phase of Portuguese mercantilism.[28] The African conflicts arising from drought and from the sixteenth-century commercial revolution near the coast had enabled the Angolan governors of the late seventeenth century to harvest slaves by military methods from the captives and refugees of the time. But by the 1660s and 1670s the collapse of the old African military regimes near Angola was already making trade goods a more efficient method of buying slaves from nascent merchant princes than expensive and hard-to-control raiding

26. See Caldas, "Notícia geral," p. 174, for the story of José Correa Leitão and "alguns paizanos" ("certain peasants," taken to mean local interests).
27. The enormous losses to slave mortality reported in the 1710s and 1720s may well have hastened the transition, by ruining many of the old slave-owning Luso-Africans; see Miller, "Significance of Drought, Disease, and Famine."
28. See Hanson, *Economy and Society*, pp. 208, 232–33, for the origins of domestic Portuguese investments in the empire.

parties sent off into remote parts of the interior. It also became more costly to bring injured and exhausted survivors of distant wars safely all the way to the sea than to pay more for less fragile human merchandise nearer the coast. It was no small irony that significant quantities of trade muskets became available to Africans late in the seventeenth century just as their military applications began to diminish in the relatively peaceful, commercially oriented space taking shape near the coast. The governors' warlike style was similarly becoming an inefficient anachronism, as Lisbon merchants collaborated with them from the 1680s through the 1710s, and it ended when Lisbon developed its distinctive mercantilistic style of supporting Angolan slaving in the 1720s and 1730s to the point of dispensing entirely with government-sponsored raiding in the conduct of the trade.

Imperial interests that were tied to the Asian trade and were at least partially distinct from the Europeanist merchants who specialized in brokering the much larger Brazilian trade in British woolens probably consolidated Lisbon's mercantilist role in Angolan slaving.[29] These Lisbon merchants squeezed financial gain from slaving by extending technical privileges granted to protect their claims to the duties in the tax farming contract to cover the private commercial credit they spread through the colonial economy. The obliqueness of this strategy resembled that of the better-known advantage that European merchants, including several generations of Portuguese, had taken of the old Spanish *asiento,* which they valued as much for the rights it conferred to smuggle goods into Spain's American colonies as for the slaves it formally authorized them to sell there.[30] The risks of slave ownership were high enough that *asientistas* often avoided direct responsibility for the lives of the cargoes they arranged, licensing the slaving phase of their operations to others, even where captives could be sold for silver.

The Portuguese tax contracts bore no further resemblance to the *asientos* sold by Spain.[31] The Angolan contracts granted only rights to duties levied in specified Portuguese ports of embarkation in Africa. Awarded

29. Detailed research into the standing of the contract holders in Lisbon, named below in Table 15.1, must await another occasion.

30. Cf. Molinari, *Trata de negros,* pp. 51, 58–59 et passim; and Mauro, "L'Atlantique portugais," p. 26. António Carreira, "Tratos e resgates dos Portugueses nos Rios de Guiné e Ilhas de Cabo Verde nos começos do século XVIII," *Revista de história económica e social* 2 (1978): 97–98, accurately identifies the point of these early contracts but in other work (e.g., *Notas sobre o tráfico português,* 2d ed., pp. 41–42) does not recognize the extent to which circumstances had changed by the eighteenth century. Heintze, "Ende des unabhängigen Staates Ndongo," pp. 205, 207, has the point very clearly for the early seventeenth century. For other discussion of the early Portuguese contracts, see Salvador, *Magnatas do tráfico negreiro,* pp. 15–58 et passim.

31. The following discussion is based on the contracts preserved in the AHU Angola series for 1724–27 (cx. 23), for 1754–59 (maço 13; also published in *Arquivos de Angola* 2, no. 13 [1936]: 497–528), for 1760–65 (maço 13), and for 1766–71 (maço 1), and on substantial additional documentation that awaits full exposition in a separate detailed study.

to Lisbon merchants selling goods there, these contracts positioned them on the spot with authority to oversee trading in such a way as to collect appropriate sums from whoever shipped slaves and then to pass an agreed portion of the revenues (the bid price of the contract) on to the royal treasury, in quarterly or annual payments in a form and at levels stipulated in the contract itself. While slave ownership had constituted the core of the *asiento* contract for supplying labor to Spanish America, the Portuguese tax contract contained no similar requirement that its holders buy and own slaves for themselves, or authorize anyone else to do so. Unlike Portugal, Spain had no African colonies and assessed no export duties, and holders of the Spanish *asientos* did not collect taxes but, rather, paid them to Spain's imperial administration in American ports.

The key advantage of the Portuguese contract lay in allowing Lisbon merchants to introduce the huge quantities of goods for which they were notorious in Angola and then to avail themselves of a seemingly innocuous clause extending the "privileges of the Royal Treasury" (the Fazenda Real) to its holders. These unspecified royal privileges principally included priority in legal claims against "the effects of insolvent debtors" to the contract.[32] This privilege protected the Crown by effectively guaranteeing the contractor's ability to meet his own obligations to the royal treasury, and strictly speaking, these special powers may have covered only debts owed for duties that the contractor collected in the name of the king. However, the same clause, if interpreted to apply equally to the private claims of the contractor acting as merchant, became a potent weapon against customers and competitors. An ambitious contract-holder had only to lend sufficient quantities of trade goods to other merchants and to slave traders in the colony, secure the collaboration of appropriate judicial officers, and then invoke his "privileges of the Royal Treasury" to step in front of all other creditors to foreclose on personal debts. Capital resources adequate to create such claims were the *sine qua non* of the strategy. Angolan slaving was small enough by Lisbon standards that even midsized merchants of the sort attracted to bid on the contract had sufficient wealth, and royal favor gave them enough influence over colonial officials until about the 1750s, that the contract privileges conferred considerable power over the slave trade for more than a generation in the first half of the eighteenth century.

Holders of the contract made secondary profits from the monopoly right it conveyed to buy ivory in Angola. Although the trading margin on African ivory sold in Lisbon was indisputably high,[33] the profit to be made from the small volume of tusks available at Luanda never approached

---

32. As phrased much later by Luccock, *Notes on Rio de Janeiro*, p. 581.
33. Cf. Roza Coutinho *certidão*, 16 Sept. 1715, AHU, Angola cx. 16. Also see Miller, "Capitalism and Slaving," pp. 41–44, 51.

the gains to be secured from techniques based on importing and selling large quantities of trade goods, and it probably declined as the eighteenth century progressed.

Nor did revenues from the duties collected—the Crown's principal interest in the contract and therefore the aspect always featured in official correspondence concerning the issue—constitute a significant advantage to the merchants holding the contract. The royal slave-export duties, technically several different taxes, some of them contracted separately, totaled about 8$700 per slave from the 1720s onward. The administrative costs, though unknown, must have been significant. Although some earlier contract holders had gone out to Luanda to administer their affairs personally,[34] by the 1730s the Lisbon merchants who bought the colony's slave-export duties remained at home in Portugal, near the royal court where they could inundate the king's ministers with petitions pleading their own interpretations of the ancillary rights and privileges on which they made their gains. They sent factors out to Angola to act as local administrators for their affairs, always stationing them in Luanda and sometimes also at Benguela. In the ports of Brazil, where the contract holders had frequent occasion to convert the bills of exchange usually accepted in satisfaction of the duties payable in Angola, they also had to hire other representatives. All of these overseas agents were expensive. The owners of the contracts also sustained other expenses for solicitors in Lisbon, bribes paid to officials in the colonies, defaulted notes, and other costs of remitting proceeds toward Portugal.

An approximate comparison of the prices paid for the contract and the duties available to cover payments owed to the royal treasury suggests how little the tax revenues mattered compared to the private commercial advantages that possession of the contract bestowed. The early contract bids varied more closely with opportunities for the contractor to trade on his own account than they did with the rising demand for slaves in Brazil after 1710. The prices for the contracts negotiated in 1711 and 1717 dropped, obviously in reaction to the 1709 confirmation of the governors' ability to trade on their own accounts and thus to hinder the personal operations of Lisbon merchants behind the contract. The Angolan advisers to one contract-holder had urged no renewal bid at all unless the rampaging colonial governors of that era were brought under control.[35] Though it is difficult to estimate the exact increase in slaves taxed during the 1710s,

---

34. And much earlier in the seventeenth century, traders resident in Angola itself had received the right to bid on the contract; for the confused circumstances that followed from this authority, see Rau, "*Livro de Razão*," pp. 54–55, and Salvador, *Magnatas do tráfico negreiro*, pp. 56–57. A copy of the *parecer* of the Conselho Ultramarino recommending the privilege (12 Oct. 1665, confirming an earlier *carta regia* of 13 Oct. 1660) is in AHU, cód. 234, fol. 8.

35. Roza Coutinho *certidão*, 16 Sept. 1715, AHU, Angola cx. 16.

Table 15.1. Summary of Slave Duty Contracts, 1674–1769

Date of award	Beginning of contract period	Contract holder	Contract price[a]

I. Contracts for the "direitos velhos do Reino de Angola, Congo, Loango, e Benguela" (4$000 per slave)

Date of award	Beginning of contract period	Contract holder	Contract price[a]
21 June 1674	1 April 1675	Diogo de Affonseca Henriques	18.100$000/yr. for 6 yrs.
23 Dec. 1679	1 July 1691	Diogo de Affonseca Henriques	23.600$000/yr. for 6 yrs.
25 March 1693	1 July 1693	Antonio Buzia	24.600$000
28 July 1704	1 July 1705	Rodrigo da Costa de Almeida	25.500$000
20 March 1711	"dia em que seus procuradores tomassem posse em Angola" (early 1712?)	Manuel Diaz Felgueira	44,000 *cruzados* (17.600$000)
3 March 1717	5 Jan. 1718	Francisco Gomes Lisboa	44,000 *cruzados* (17.600$000)
18 Feb. 1723	5 Jan. 1724	Vasco Lourenço Vellozo	58,000 *cruzados* (23.200$000)
10 Nov. 1727	5 Jan. 1730	João Barboza de Almeida	60,000 *cruzados* (24.000$000)
13 May 1733	5 Jan. 1736	João da Costa Lima	66,000 *cruzados* (26.400$000)
28 March 1740	1 Jan. 1742	Jacintho Diaz Braga	73,000 *cruzados* and 10$000 (29.210$000)
10 Dec. 1745	1 Jan. 1748	Manuel Ferreira Marques	73,500 *cruzados* (29.400$000)
8 Oct. 1751	1 Jan. 1754	Manuel Barboza Torres	31.395$849

(Thereafter combined with *direitos novos*; see sec. III of this table)

II. Contracts for the "Direitos novos dos escravos do dito Reino de Angola e suas Conquistas, e novo Imposto . . ."

Date of award	Beginning of contract period	Contract holder	Contract price[a]
18 March 1723	"dia em que findasse antecedente rematação" (5 Jan. 1724)	Vasco Lourenço Vellozo	56,000 *cruzados*[b] (22.400$000)
10 Nov. 1727	(same as the *direitos velhos*)	João Barboza de Almeida	71,000 *cruzados* (28.400$000)

Continued on following page

Table 15.1.—*continued*

Date of award	Beginning of contract period	Contract holder	Contract price[a]
13 May 1733	5 Jan. 1736	João da Costa Lima	81,000 *cruzados* (32.400$000)
28 March 1740	(not specified; presumably 1 Jan. 1742)	Jacintho Diaz Braga	120,000 *cruzados* (48.000$000)
10 Dec. 1745	1 Jan. 1748	Manoel Ferreira Marques	120,500 *cruzados* (48.200$000)
8 Oct. 1751	5 Jan. 1754	Manuel Barboza Torres	56.364$151[c]

(Thereafter combined with *direitos velhos;* see sec. III of this table)

III. *Contract for "Todos os direitos velhos, novos, novo imposto, e preferencia q pagao os Escravos reduzidos todos os ditos direitos a 8$700 por cabeça, maxo ou femea, e assim mais o direito de 4º e vintena do Marfim"*

Date of award	Beginning of contract period	Contract holder	Contract price[a]
6 March 1758	5 Jan. 1760	Estevão Jozé de Almeida	87.800$000, plus other payments totaling 3.480$000 and 2 *arrobas* of wax (64 lbs., approx.)
12 Jan. 1765	5 Jan. 1766	Domingos Dias da Silva	88.300$000, plus similar extras

SOURCE: Relação de todos os Contractos respectivos ao Reino de Angola, q na Secretaria do Conº Ultramarino consta haverem-se rematado pelo mesmo Conº, com declaração do tempo em q foraó rematados, das pessoas a quem, e dos seus preços livres para a Fazenda Real, AHU, Angola cx. 31.

[a] As specified, with *réis* values added in parentheses.

[b] Contemporaneous documentation gave slightly different figures for several of these earlier contracts; cf. Miranda de Vasconcelos, 20 Aug. 1739, AHU, Angola cx. 21; Memoria do rendimento do Contrato de Angola desde o anno de 1722 té 12 de Janeiro de 1752, AHU, Angola maço 5; and so on.

[c] Specified as for "direitos novos e novo imposto."

owing to incomplete returns of annual exports, estimating from average exports for 1712–14, slave volume rose 23.5 percent from the 1712–17 contract period to the following one (1718–23). For the next contract period (1724–29), the average of exports from 1724–28 would give a further increase in volume of 18.2 percent. The contract for 1718, while the governors ruled supreme in Angola, brought no price increase at all over its predecessor, but after only nominal removal of the governors from

Table 15.2. Calculation of Estimated Margins on Slave Duty Contracts

Contract period	Total value of contracts (in réis)[a]	Estimated duties collected[b]	Margin of estimated duties over contract price[c]
1724–29	45.600$000	65.143$860[d]	42.8%
1730–35	52.400$000	72.558$000[e]	38.5%
1736–41	58.800$000	68.501$190	16.5%
1742–47	77.210$000	92.624$550	20.0%
1748–53	77.600$000	86.641$560	11.6%
1754–59	87.760$000	86.282$250	− 1.7%
1760–65	91.280$000	107.550$840	17.8%
1766–69	91.700$000	79.448$000	−13.4%

[a] Totals from secs. I, II, and III, Table 15.1.

[b] Taken from numbers of slaves reported as taxed by contractor and certified by Angolan treasury officials, except as estimated per notes *d* and *e*.

[c] Estimated from middle columns, this table.

[d] Data missing for 1729; estimated from mean exports, 1724–28.

[e] Data missing for 1730 and 1732–33; estimated from mean exports, 1731 and 1734–35.

further private business dealings in 1720, the bid price for the same share of the slave duties awarded in 1723 jumped by almost a third (by 31.2%).[36]

Thereafter, as table 15.2 indicates, the contract price rose more rapidly than the volume of slaves taxed, with the estimated revenues from duties dropping from 42.8 percent above the bid price for the 1724–29 contract to levels that, calculated on the same basis, produced losses in the 1750s and 1760s.[37] Even the relatively ample margins of the 1720s and 1730s, once the expenses of collecting the duties and remitting the proceeds to Lisbon had been covered, would hardly have sufficed in themselves to attract investors. The high prices that bidder after bidder was willing to offer must therefore have included premiums for the private commercial advantages that the contract also conveyed, and the declining margin of tax revenues relative to bid prices indicates that these probably increased over the years as contractors and their administrators gained control over the colony's export economy and as they grew wealthier and thus better prepared to prosper from credit extended under the "privileges of the Royal Treasury."

36. I.e., the *direitos velhos* only. Slave exports for 1712–23 from Klein, *Middle Passage*, p. 254, Table A.2.

37. The anomalously high duties collected in the 1760–65 contract period may have been a windfall from improved supervision of the trade at Benguela and from the increase in volume stimulated by competition between the contractor and the Pernambuco Company, both added on to a serious famine year with high exports in 1765.

Since the amounts collected were not overwhelmingly profitable, the Lisbon owners of the contract concentrated on technicalities involving the means of making the payments owed the Crown. The usual formula allowed a contractor to gain modestly from claiming credit for a portion of his obligation locally in Angola, in trade cloth meant for the uniforms of the colonial troops and in flour for their rations, which were greatly overvalued in terms of *réis* or *cruzados*. Contractors bought goods inexpensively in Europe but charged them off at high Angolan prices for both food and fabric. Beyond what the contract holder could pay in "soft" colonial cloth currencies and local provisions, he could also use the colonial copper currency he received in duties to pay amounts that he might owe to the Angolan treasury. The Crown intended this clause to keep the colony's official medium of exchange in circulation locally, since the treasury would pay out whatever coin it received from the contract holders in salaries and other local expenses. The advantage for the contractor in this arrangement came from the opportunity it provided to keep other items of value that he received in satisfaction of the duties owed by slave shippers—ivory, *letras,* silver when available—and send them back to Portugal as his own profit. He would have paid much of what he owed to the Crown in commodities and currencies of no value outside Angola. The general difficulty of remitting funds from Africa back to the metropole, given the insecurity of owning the colony's principal export, slaves, meant that contract holders gained considerably from this clause's implicit permission to hoard goods and financial instruments worth hard currency for themselves.

Since the copper coins circulating in Angola never amounted to more than a tiny fraction of the currency required to support the colony's commercial activity, the contractors remitted most of the duties they collected in the usual bills of exchange, in this case special bills termed "export duty bills" (*letras dos direitos*). These bills clearly carried the priority of the "privileges of the Royal Treasury," and they accordingly had a high standing in southern Atlantic markets for such commercial paper, barely a step short of bearing the imprimatur of the monarchy itself. In the risky context of southern Atlantic maritime trade, the claim they conferred to the first 15 to 25 percent of the proceeds of slaves sold in Brazil[38] represented the closest thing available to a sure bet. Everyone sought to get their hands on these notes, but they became increasingly scarce as slave prices rose in the first half of the eighteenth century relative to duties, which remained stable. The advantage for the contractor, who received these bills in the first instance and thus enjoyed a certain control over their disposition, lay in presenting these bills himself in Brazil for the *réis* credits and, later, for

38. Based on Luanda prices as calculated in Miller, "Slave Prices."

the coin in which he was required to make the great bulk of his own annual deposits to royal treasury officials in Brazil or Lisbon.[39] The colonial government was then left to draw on the balances eventually created from sale of the slaves who secured the notes for its own expenditures in America and Europe. When gold and other superior forms of assets grew scarce in Brazil during the depression of the 1760s, the contractors kept the duty bills to secure their own profits and attempted to pay the treasury bonds there in plentiful but less valuable *letras de risco* that they took in exchange for most of the goods they sold in Angola.[40]

The Luanda administrators of the tax contract gained an enormous influence over the colonial economy during the 1730s and 1740s. Even their narrow legal responsibilities for the affairs of the contract itself—supervising departing ships, watching for slaves smuggled without payment of the required tax, and so on—allowed the Lisbon tax farmers to obstruct the progress of captains and shippers who failed to cooperate with their schemes. But the contract holders also, even primarily, employed their Angolan agents as commercial representatives, distributing both trade goods and paper notes in quantities that gave the contractors far greater power still, given adequate capital resources from Europe. In practice they often operated well beyond the effective control of the government in Lisbon, in a political vacuum created by the fascination of the principal metropolitan merchants with Brazil and filled by the protective influence they cultivated at the court. So long as the burden of the contractors' manipulations fell mostly on Brazilians and Luso-Africans, no compelling political reasons turned the king's ministers against their Luanda factors. They accordingly became the dominant importers and financiers of slaving at Luanda. The administrators of the contract at Luanda often extended this influence even beyond these tolerated limits, since they found considerable opportunity for private aggrandizement by mixing the legal powers of the contract and the dealings of their sponsors in Europe with personal ventures in full accord with the loose business practices of the times.[41]

Complaints against the heavily capitalized strategies of the contractors or their agents surfaced in the pivotal decades between 1710 and 1730.

39. Note that the contract terms began to specify payment in gold *cruzados* as Minas Gerais developed after 1700. Cf. Flory, "Bahian Society," p. 254, for emphasis on the requirement of payment in specie usually found in the Brazilian contracts of the eighteenth century. One function of the contracts, from the point of view of the royal exchequer, was thus to convert taxes collected in kind or in notes to Brazilian gold.

40. Sousa Coutinho, 5 Feb. 1770, AHU, Angola cx. 32, makes clear this and other strategies of the late contract holders.

41. For an extensive and revealing set of instructions from a Lisbon contract holder to his Luanda factors in the 1760s, see Domingos Dias da Silva to Jozé Lopes Bandeira and Florentino João de Carvalho, 8 Jan. 1767, AHU, Angola cx. 31.

In arguments piously phrased in terms of the established royal obligation to protect Angola's African inhabitants from unscrupulous Europeans, outraged slavers in Luanda accused the contractors of hiring any vagabond at large in the colony, criminals, sailors, military deserters, and gypsies, to take goods out into the backlands, where they abused and extorted from the African subjects of the king.[42] No doubt the contractors did all this, but so did the *pombeiro* slave agents of the Bahia-linked merchants in the Luanda council or of the governors and their *capitães-mores,* all of whom in actuality found themselves outspent by the new entrants in the game.

One initial tactic of these newcomers in the interior—referred to only obliquely as "overseas traders" (*homens do mar em fora*) out of concern not to make overly direct allegations against the king's declared favorites— was to intercept caravans of slaves on their way down to owners among the established trading interests at Luanda.[43] Given the contract agents' lack of connections in the local slaving networks, this shortcut, really a version of what later critics termed the *reviros* practiced by Luso-Africans, made sense. It also shortened the turnover of the trade goods that contractors sent to the interior and thus maximized the effectiveness of their modest working capital, more ample than that of their competitors but by no means yet plentiful by international standards. They used the capital they could invest in the trade instead to bid the coffles of slaves away from other creditors by paying generous prices. They were accordingly accused of raising the goods prices of slaves at Luanda by 50 to 100 percent, thus threatening to drive out of business other traders lacking the merchandise to meet their competition.[44] They also resorted to bullying rural populations around Luanda for labor and supplies for their caravans, no doubt in part because they lacked contacts among the African authorities and Luso-African settlers who controlled the market in bearers and in provisions. They may have found their only local allies among the dissident Luso-Africans up the Kwanza at Massangano, who were great rivals of the creole traders of Luanda and who may have used credit from the contractors to set up their new trading center some ways up the Lukala at "Lembo," on the route to sources of slaves on the northeastern flanks of the colony.[45]

Though the contractors appear to have continued their strategy of flooding the interior with trade goods throughout the 1730s and 1740s, they attained only partial successes by these means. They hastened conversion of the trade currency of the interior from local textiles to imported

---

42. Roza Coutinho *certidão,* 16 Sept. 1715, AHU, Angola cx. 16.
43. Complaint of the Luanda Senado da Câmara to Gov. Albuquerque, 7 May 1732, AHU, Angola cx. 19.
44. Faria e Mello, 15 Dec. 1732, AHU, Angola cx. 20.
45. Cf. Avellar, 20 Feb. 1731, AHU, Angola maço 18-A.

Asian cloth.[46] But the contractors continued to provoke howls of protest. Their dusky colonial competitors—increasingly only the Luanda Luso-Africans as the Brazilian governors and the Bahia traders faded from the scene—effectively invoked seventeenth-century legal barriers against whites entering the backlands against them, always in disingenuous terms of protecting the Africans of the interior.[47] Gradually their overweening power and arrogance, which Lisbon's governors could not contain, swung colonial officials against them also. Governor Rodrigo Cezar de Meneses (1733–38) rounded up the most notorious disturbers of the peace then at large in the interior and brought them back to Luanda. By the 1750s the contractors were on the defensive in the interior and reduced to petitioning the Crown in Lisbon, where they could expect greater favor than in the colony, to revoke the decrees employed in Africa against them.[48]

On the whole, the contractors' trade goods, distributed on credit to *ad hoc* agents who peddled them through the interior, had their most significant inflationary effects not in the backlands, which remained the preserve of the Luso-Africans, but in the price revolution they provoked in the city. The Luso-Africans may have objected less to what the contractors were doing than to their initial efforts to exclude them from the strategy, and the contractors' period of overwhelming influence in Angola, and the governors' hostility to them, may have rested on alliances they established with factions of the colonial traders.

Defeated in the interior, the contractors seem then to have tried to consolidate their advantage in and near Luanda by manipulating the town's market in notes and bills for remitting *réis* profits abroad. Their financial manipulations depended on issuing copious quantities, at the outset of the six-year term of each contract, of a type of unsecured commercial note known as a *livrança*.[49] Though the exact technique remains obscured behind the emotional terms in which opponents complained to the Crown about the contractors' *livranças*, a speculative interpretation would fit them into the known structure of the economy as follows. In the hierarchy of commercial paper generally circulating in Luanda, the *livranças* ranked at the very bottom, since nothing more than the issuer's good faith and credit backed them—qualities by no means abundant at Luanda—and since they bore no date by which the obligation they represented had to be dis-

46. But Asian textiles were apparently already being used in the 1680s, according to the accounts of Coelho Guerreiro: Miller, "Capitalism and Slaving," pp. 31–40; Salvador, *Magnatas do tráfico negreiro,* pp. 56–57.

47. Meneses, 3 March 1737, AHU, Angola cx. 19; Senado da Câmara (Luanda), 30 Dec. 1744, AHU, Angola cx. 23; da Cunha, 18 Dec. 1753, AHU, Angola cx. 25.

48. *Requerimento* of Manoel Barboza e Torres, n.d. (ca. 1751–54), AHU, Angola cx. 19.

49. Cf. Socolow, *Merchants of Buenos Aires,* pp. 152–54, for the same instrument (*libranza* in Spanish) in Argentina.

charged.⁵⁰ In effect, these notes were little more than personal IOUs, and small quantities of them usually circulated on an informal basis among the traders resident in the city and doing business with one another on a daily basis. As such, they partially filled the credit and currency vacuum created by the constant drain on all assets of greater value out to Brazil and Portugal to pay off the indebtedness of the colonial economy. Traders could meet small obligations in Luanda with *livranças* without spending scarce *réis* credits or coin. Outside the sphere of these local transactions, in which they served well enough as chits, the notes had no value, and they played no role whatsoever in the sensitive market for slave-backed *letras* or duty bills of exchange suitable for remitting funds to Brazil or Portugal.

Most private merchants would have quickly encountered limits on the quantity of *livranças* that they could offer to their associates without arousing suspicions of insolvency and thus choking off returns from continued issuance of such certificates. The administrators of the contract, on the other hand, could legitimately extend the technique a bit further, owing to the prestige they enjoyed as local favorites of the king and as well-heeled representatives of big Lisbon capital. But some of them took advantage of this standing to flood the market with excessive amounts of their *livranças,* with or without the encouragement of the contract-holders themselves in Lisbon. The exact shares of responsibility for such abuses were, of course, disputed in the official correspondence generated from complaints against the practice. The Lisbon contractors blamed everything on their Luanda factors, and the local administrators claimed to have acted on instructions from their principals in Portugal. But at the instigation of one party to the contract or another, the administrators repeatedly issued large quantities of *livranças* at the outset of the contract term and then maneuvered to buy up other bills of superior quality as they prepared to depart from the colony six years later, leaving their *livranças* as worthless paper in the hands of the merchants of the Luanda *praça*. In effect, they exchanged unredeemed personal promises to pay at an unspecified future

50. *Livranças* turn up in small amounts in the accounts of Coelho Guerreiro in the 1680s: Miller, "Capitalism and Slaving," p. 40. Exact texts of the notes are available from the 1730s and 1760s and vary hardly at all: "Val esta livransa quatrocentos vinte e nove mil e sincoenta reis que pagarei de letra ao mostrador todas vezes q mos pedir q procede de outra tanta quantia q me fes merce emprestar José Machado Pinto Administrador dos Contratos Reais pertencente ao mesmo contracto. Loanda, 29 de outubro de 1738" (Miranda de Vasconcelos [provedor da Fazenda Real], 6 July 1739, AHU, Angola cx. 21). For other comments on this difficult problem, see Carlos Couto, "O pacto colonial e a interferência brasileira no domínio das relações econômicas entre Angola e o Reino no séc. XVIII," *Estudos históricos* (Marília) 10 (1971), p. 26n; Rau, *"Livro de razão,"* fols. 16, 24v. Quasi currencies or scrip of this sort were not unknown elsewhere in Portugal and the empire at the time, owing to the continual flight of coin out of the realm; see Ribeiro Júnior, *Colonização e monopólio,* pp. 28, 97 (n. 121), 185.

date against secured bills of stated term drawn in *réis* on the cities of Brazil. Once again Gresham's Law stood confirmed: bad money always drives out the good.

Although the precise means that successive teams of administrators repeatedly used to perpetrate frauds of this sort are not clear, the "privileges of the Royal Treasury" that stood behind the contract played a crucial role. The language of the *livranças* invoked the prestige of the contract, even though the notes in fact represented nothing more than the personal worth of the local administrators.[51] The practice was, first of all, a salient example of the administrators' habit of promoting their private affairs on the high repute of the Crown and its contractual representative in Angola.

Why the scheme took in the buyers of the *livranças* is not so clear. The general shortage of capital must have made even this extremely soft form of credit acceptable, particularly among the novice traders always showing up in Luanda. Given the broad influence of the contractors over the local economy, the administrators may also have been able to press *livranças* on even unwilling suppliers through outright intimidation or other threats of economic pressure. In economic terms the *livranças* may have carried the connotation of buying future favors from the representatives of the contract, or even of a more concrete investment in the returns to be expected from a wealthy and powerful mercantile enterprise, distinguished more in name than in function from the stock shares issued by modern corporations. To the extent that the aura of a prudent investment in each contract administration prevailed, buyers of the *livranças* might have reasonably expected to redeem them for full value as each administration liquidated its affairs in Angola. They would have found themselves left with worthless paper only in the case of commercial failure that left the administrators without assets to pay off the contracts' debts. Supporting this generous interpretation of the *livranças* is the fact that they seem to have become a serious problem only when the margin of duty revenues over the contract's payment to the Crown declined, and as the contractors began to lose influence in Angola in the 1750s.[52]

In the meanwhile, administrators had employed *livranças* to buy up the good Brazilian bills of exchange available upon their arrival at Luanda and to replace them with their own notes as a medium of exchange circulating in the city. To the extent that they accomplished this strategy, they in effect became an unofficial local bank of emission and owner of the commercial currency of the city. But the restricted circulation of the

51. The notes sometimes carried a representation of the royal arms as well; see *alvará* of 5 Aug. 1769, AHTC, livro 1, fols. 29–31.

52. They had been used much earlier, though not without complaint: Miranda de Vasconcelos, 6 July 1739, AHU, Angola cx. 21; *requerimento* of Estevão Martins Torres, 5 Oct. 1745, AHU, Angola cx. 23; Campos Rego, 10 July 1753, AHU, Angola cx. 25. These sources also indicate a number of elements of the *livrança* scheme.

notes removed *letra* claims to slaves without replacing them with goods useful to the traders of the interior. In this way administrators multiplied the amount of personal credit they put into the town economy and diverted slaves valuable in Brazil away from their competitors but drained the interior of the imported merchandise that supported further deliveries of slaves, effectively collapsing the capital structure of slaving other than what they supported with their own imports. By the time the administrators left at the end of their six-year term, business slowed by the amount of notes left in the hands of Luanda houses unable either to spend the *livranças* for slaves from the backlands or to remit them as profits to Brazil.

The *livranças* thus created shortages of trade goods that also brought the whole commercial market of Luanda under the thumbs of the contract administrators. By floating what amounted to a private currency, of no value except as presented back to its issuers, they made certain that merchants without goods to sell would turn to them as suppliers. They even gained customers for the goods they could not otherwise sell. Desperate competitors, unable to assort stocks already committed to the interior, had the option of redeeming their *livranças* for unwanted merchandise from the administrators' warehouses, even at high prices, or simply burning the notes. The contractors' profits from such coerced exchanges, particularly useful because they permitted the liquidation of stocks left over as the contractors prepared to leave the colony at the end of the contract term, would have been remitted long before to Brazil. The availability of this strategy would have invited contract administrators to dump merchandise on the Angolan market that was even more worthless than the run-of-the-mill inferior goods underlying the general strategy of Portugal's African trade. Administrators thus parlayed the capital and the prestige behind the contract through the *livranças* into near monopolies over both sales of goods in Luanda and remittances of profits to Brazil.

The contractors also seem to have dominated the import of Asian textiles in the colony, and they would have used their monopoly over these essential components of the *banzos* similarly to bring under their control all the other merchants in Luanda needing cottons to complete assortments headed for the backlands. With the financial capital the contract holders commanded, they could reinflate local credit with these goods. Protected against defaults by those "privileges of the Royal Treasury" that they could enforce through the local courts, they could seize their debtors' assets and exclude rival claims to them. They worked similarly through the office of *defuntos e auzentes* to secure the wealth of deceased debtors, except for clergy, who frequently borrowed and traded but claimed exemption from all injunctions of worldly governments.[53] The commercial successes of the

---

53. E.g., *parecer* of the Conselho Ultramarino, 26 Sept. 1754, AHU, Angola cx. 19.

colonial clergy in Angola, and also the predilection of the Luso-Africans for the priesthood, perhaps stemmed in part from the immunity that ecclesiastical status conferred on debtors.

The contractors' great wealth also enabled them to dispatch enough vessels to dominate the transport capacity available to carry slaves from Angola to Brazil during the shipping shortage of the 1720s and 1730s. They began by excluding Rio traders from Benguela, where the Brazilians had tended to congregate to escape the harassment they could expect from the Pernambuco governors and the Bahian merchants dominant at Luanda.[54] The contract administrators, once established at Benguela, took slaves directly to Rio without sending them north to Luanda for formal dispatch as the regulations of the contract required other traders to do.[55] They also distorted the order in which ships loaded and then left the port so as to favor the vessels of the Lisbon backers of the contract.[56] The large quantities of goods that they had introduced in the 1720s, no doubt deployed effectively through the use of *livranças* and other techniques already described, won them a near monopoly on shipping space leaving the city.[57] They then secured a new condition in the contract negotiated in 1727 (to take effect in 1730) that entitled them to raise the freight rates they could charge by a third, from 6$000 to 8$000—that is, to an amount nearly equal to the duties they collected and up to a quarter of the value of a prime male slave at the time. When shippers refused to send their slaves at the higher rates, interpreting the new contract condition as only an enabling clause without authorization for implementation, the contractors petitioned the king to enforce it as a *requerimento*.[58] Brazilian shippers were largely excluded from benefiting from the increased freight revenues.

The struggles between duty collectors from Lisbon and slaveowners in the colony also focused on the contract's provisions regarding the export taxes themselves. One conflict arose from the legal ambiguities that surfaced from the gradual abandonment of the *peça*, or prime adult male slave, as the standard unit for taxing the trade and its replacement by the more inclusive category of *cabeça*, or slave "head" of any sort, as fewer of the individuals shipped met the standard of the full *peça*. Owners of these lesser slaves apparently argued the full 7$000 in duties levied in the 1730s applied only to prime adult males and that they should pay proportionately

54. Albuquerque, 20 Dec. 1729, AHU, Angola cx. 18. Cf. the spread of the Benguela slave catchment area into the high plateau at that time: Miller, "Central and Southern Angola."
55. Lourenço de Freitas de Noronha, 28 March 1735, AHU, Angola cx. 20; *requerimento* of Jacinto Dias Braga, 15 June 1742, AHU, Angola cx. 22.
56. Magalhães, 26 April 1742, AHU, Angola cx. 22.
57. Albuquerque, 28 June 1724, AHU, Angola cx. 16.
58. Condition 5 of the contract for 1730: *requerimento* of Manoel Monteiro da Rocha, 12 Sept. 1732, AHU, Angola cx. 19; *requerimento* of Jacinto Dias Braga, 29 Oct. 1742, AHU, Angola cx. 22.

reduced rates on the smaller and younger captives they were actually boarding. Proration of the duties in this fashion would have significantly diminished the amount of the duties that contractors collected.

The contractor's Luanda administrators responded to this interpretation of the contract in an elegant application of the hallowed principle
of preserving the letter of the law to produce entirely novel effects. They
acknowledged the proration of duties charged, but they calculated the
adjustment on the price rather than on the physical characteristics of the
slave, based on the standard 22$000 lien-value for a *peça* that had prevailed
through much of the seventeenth century. But by the date of the dispute,
the Minas gold boom and the contractors' own inflationary policies in
Angola had driven the prime slave price upwards to between 30$000 and
50$000. Thus, even a small boy brought the old *peça* price of 22$000 by
the 1740s, and the contract administrators could collect the equivalent of
full duties on him under their price-based interpretation of the law. The
divergent standards sometimes exposed unwary Brazilian ship captains to
significant losses. They would accept *letras* from owners of the slaves to
cover duties assessed at the smaller value—22$000 discounted for the
youth and diminuitive stature of the boys actually embarked—but then
encounter agents of the contract in Brazil claiming greater amounts based
on the slaves' higher current values.[59] The contractors' interpretation,
whether the merchants of Luanda paid the costs or whether they tricked
unsuspecting Brazilian ship captains into assuming them, protected the
contractors from the declining quality of slaves to which their own credit-
based overproduction of slaves contributed.[60]

In a parallel exercise in creative legalism, the contractors joined other
shippers from Brazil in applying the 1684 restrictions on crowding aboard
the slave vessels only to the diminishing minority of fully taxed adult males.
The agents of the contract holders and Luanda government officials, perhaps at first also to alleviate the shortages in shipping at the time, had
gradually relaxed the provision allowing shippers to exempt infants at the
breast from duties and to count them as occupying part of their mothers'
allotted space on the ship. But the older children thus allowed on board
beyond the ship's rated capacity as untaxed *crias* cost the contract the full
duties that the administrators were otherwise conniving to apply to the
youthful majority of slaves. The contractors therefore had it both ways by

59. *Portaria,* 18 Feb. 1740, AHU, Angola cx. 22; Miranda de Vasconcelos, 15 Dec.
1740, AHU, Angola cx. 22; *requerimento* of Jacinto Dias Braga, 29 Oct. 1740, AHU, Angola
cx. 22; Manoel Monteiro da Rocha, 15 Dec. 1740, AHU, Angola cx. 22. The dispute was
quite old; see Rau, *"Livro de razão,"* pp. 54–55 (for the 1680s–90s), and Carvalho da Costa,
8 June 1725, AHU, Angola cx. 16.
60. Revenue reforms of the 1750s eventually clarified the point by consolidating the
several separate duties then in effect into a single tax of 8$700 payable on each *cabeça: alvará*
of 25 Jan. 1758, published in *Arquivos de Angola* 2, no. 14 (1936): 537–40.

qualifying such "children" boarded in excess of the ship's rated capacity as *crias de pé* (walking children, to distinguish them from the untaxed infants carried at the breast), or more to the point, as *crias de todo o direito* (children paying full duties).[61] On the other hand, government officers also colluded with the contract administrators to assess small children belonging to other traders as full *peças* thus increasing the returns to the contract, in exchange for gaining allotments of scarce shipping space from the administrators for their personal remittances of slaves.[62]

Contract administrators also connived with local officials in all the other techniques of tight-packing at Luanda. They enlarged ship capacity ratings designed to protect the slaves to permit vessels to carry away the slave proceeds of the debt they created in Angola and increase the flow of duties into the coffers of the contract. With local clerks and inspectors securely in their pockets, they could obtain ample measurements, at least until owners and buyers of slaves in Brazil retaliated by remeasuring the ships in the American ports and obtaining lower capacity ratings. It was the contractors who petitioned the Crown to recognize only the Angolan standards, citing a condition to that effect written into the contract, but the king's Overseas Council neatly rendered this concession meaningless by interpreting the contract-holder's right to obtain measurements in Luanda to cover only ratings that did not exceed those made elsewhere.[63] The decree of 1684, as the administrators of the contract interpreted it with the support of government officials bribed in these and doubtless many other fashions, became more a source of revenues for the tax farmers than the shield protecting the slaves that its rhetoric proclaimed it to be. As a pawn in the political contest between opposing economic factions in Angola it shared the fate of laws nominally protecting Africans by restricting European entry into the interior.

The Limits of the Contractors' Coercion

The contract holders thus threw the considerable weight of their capital resources into Angolan slaving through pressure applied mostly to the financial market in Luanda itself and to the shipping in its port. But some of their tactics ran up against the local strengths of the Luso-Africans, and others foundered on royal decrees prohibiting practices that crowded the

61. Magalhães, 9 Nov. 1734, AHU, Angola cx. 23. For the resulting exports of *crias de pé* officially reported between 1734 and 1769, see Klein, *Middle Passage,* p. 254, Table A.2, and Table 2.6, p. 36.

62. Carvalho da Costa, 8 June 1725, AHU, Angola cx. 16.

63. *Requerimento* of Jacinto Dias Braga, n.d. (ca. 1745), AHU, Angola cx. 23; *parecer* of the Conselho Ultramarino, 19 Oct. 1745, AHU, Angola cx. 23.

slaves too drastically into the holds of the ships or threatened to delay the departures of captives accumulating in the barracoons of their competitors. They did somewhat better with the _livranças_ and with assessments of slaves that protected the currency revenues from sales of trade goods in Africa that they could collect in Brazil. The practical politics of the contract thus left its main advantages precisely where its legal privileges positioned it: in the _réis_ and bullion sphere of a multilevel southern Atlantic economy. Gains the Luso-Africans and Africans might accumulate in the form of trade goods or slaves within Angola remained relatively secure from invasion by the contractors.

In that position, the contract holders threatened no one powerful in Lisbon until serious competitors for the advantageous access to American wealth the contract conferred appeared in Portugal in the 1750s. These challengers in the metropole, working behind the Marquis of Pombal, then forced the contract-holders into a defensive posture they would maintain until formal abolition of the tax-farming arrangement in 1769. In Angola the tide turned with the arrival of Governor D. António Alvares da Cunha (1753–58), the first of a new breed of appointees determined to remodel Angolan slaving according to the principles of "freedom of trade" then becoming fashionable in Portugal. The old-style administered trade on which the contractors thrived had finally seen its day, even in the southern Atlantic. Alvares da Cunha at once called attention to the abuses perpetrated by the holder of the 1754–59 contract, Manoel Barboza Torres. He jailed Torres' local administrators and wrote stinging indictments of their practices back to the Overseas Council in Lisbon.[64] The contractors, also attuned to the new liberal philosophical currents of the times, modernized the old seventeenth-century debate over entry of whites into the hinterland by demanding access there for themselves in the name of "free trade." Alvares da Cunha picked up the tune, condemning in the same liberal language the restrictions on free trade that the contract administrators had achieved through their effective monopolization of imports. Looking back too, he added to the case against the contractors by pointing to ways in which they had also failed to meet their financial commitments to the Crown. In fact, the _livranças_ had become so numerous and burdensome to the local economy that the administrators were attempting to make even their deposits to the Royal Treasury in this worthless paper.[65] He also moved forcefully against the commercial agents of

64. First critical report from Campos Rego, 10 July 1753, AHU, Angola cx. 25; da Cunha, 2 Dec. 1754, AHU, Angola maço 18 (D.O.) and cx. 26; _parecer_ of the Conselho Ultramarino, 17 Dec. 1755, AHU, Angola maço 6.

65. Da Cunha, 2 Dec. 1754, AHU, Angola cx. 26; idem, 16 March 1757, AHU, Angola cx. 27; _requerimento_, with draft proposal for 1760 contract, n.d. (ca. 1758), AHU, Angola maço 13.

the contract in the interior and disingenuously took credit for increasing the volume of slaves reaching the city in 1756–58 by having eliminated the contractors' monopoly. In fact, of course, drought had then spread warfare through large parts of the interior, forcing Africans to sell off starving dependents regardless of the free-trade policies pronounced in Luanda. But the future of the contract was from then on in jeopardy.

16

"Freedom of Trade" in the Pombal Era, 1755–1772

From the early 1750s until about 1770, new Lisbon merchants as-sociated with the forceful Portuguese prime minister, the Marquis of Pombal, wrested the advantage in Angolan slaving from the older imperial circles behind the holders of the export duty contract. The Pombal group's challenge to the contractors in the western central African colony was only peripheral to a much grander domestic program of enlightened economic and political reform, but Luanda was an attractive target because Angola represented a relatively accessible spot in an empire otherwise dominated by foreign capital—British in Brazil and Asian in the Indian Ocean. The contract holders had clearly become anachronisms, and ownership of slaves was not a priority of the Anglo-Portuguese factory. Angola seemed to present a modest market for the infant national industries at the heart of the Pombal program for modernizing Portugal.

Both sides brought all the financial and political armaments they could muster against each other at Luanda. In the end, the new mer-chants, trading under the umbrella of Pombal's laws and supported by his appointees in high positions in the colonial government, won out over the tax farmers in an early gust from the gathering storm of lib-eralism that would later overwhelm the *ancien régime* in Lisbon. They succeeded in abolishing the contract by 1769, but they then found themselves facing two much more formidable sets of foes on the scene in western central Africa: the Luso-Africans in the colony itself and the British and French, who had stepped up slaving along adjacent coasts after the end of the Seven Years' War in 1763. The domestic financial resources available in mid-eighteenth-century Portugal proved insufficient to dislodge the colonial slavers or to resist the waxing commercial strength of the northern Europeans. With metropolitan Portugal's economic frailty demonstrated in Angola, Lisbon interests turned away almost entirely from the slave trade in the 1770s and 1780s to try instead to ride the renewed wave of prosperity then passing through Brazilian agriculture to power in Portugal.

The Struggle of the Titans

Economic crisis at home in Portugal, informed by the same liberal philosophical doctrines that Governor Alvares da Cunha had first invoked against the contract holders in Angola in 1753, lay behind these remote events in the southern Atlantic. Portugal's lagging domestic productivity and the decline of gold production in Brazil turned the attention of metropolitan planners toward Angola. In the background of both of these seemingly insoluble problems always loomed the growing wealth of the British and their dominance in Portugal and in the Brazil trade. As prime minister, Sebastião José de Carvalho e Mello, then count of Oeyras, identified one element of the solution in mobilizing domestic Portuguese capital to compete with British commerce and industry. In Portugal, the strategy implied a certain amount of direct confrontation with the British, through limitations on imports of their textiles and other items to create protected domestic markets for national industrial development. Abroad, he would employ the resources mobilized to explore new Brazilian commodity exports that would replace the lost revenues from gold. In the American colony, Lisbon began more circumspectly, avoiding the main centers of Britain's trade to its own empire and sharing the new initiatives with powerful colonial interests established in Brazil.

Africa entered this picture only secondarily. Increased agricultural production in Brazil meant more enslaved Africans, of course. Angola, as usual, seemed to represent a back door into Brazil that circumvented the main line of British-backed commerce direct from Lisbon. Luanda, more than any other part of the African coast, also promised a relatively protected colonial market for the output of the new factories planned for Portugal. But to succeed at Luanda, Lisbon merchants had to break the hold of the contractors and their Asian cottons and British woolens.

British liberal principles of free trade guided Pombal's entire program, and these ideas readily justified condemnation of the monopolistic abuses that the contractors had created behind the privileges they received from the Crown. Pombal's representatives in Angola thus espoused this liberal rhetoric as they launched their assault on the colony's slave trade. The imperial weakness of the Portuguese, and the modest amounts of capital they could actually throw into the fray, forced them to abandon the practice even as they introduced the principle, though they clung inconsistently to the ideology long after realities forced them back into relying on refurbished versions of the old protectionism.

Lisbon in the 1750s faced opponents in Angola and an economy much changed from the time of the preceding metropolitan effort led by the contract holders. Brazilian militarists were no longer factors, and governors had gradually become Lisbon appointees loyally responsive to directives from the Crown, particularly after a new ministry headed by a secretary for the colonies replaced the old Overseas Council in 1736. Forty years earlier, most slaves had come from military districts occupied by Luso-Africans and Portuguese and near enough to the coast that caravans working out from Luanda or Massangano could bring in captives directly. But the contract holders' subsequent commercialization of the trade had expanded the area within the slaving frontier so that by the 1750s slaves arrived through relays of African and Luso-African caravan networks reaching out through the Kwango valley to Lunda and up the central plateau to beyond the upper Kunene. The expanded geography and complexity of trade gave the Luso-Africans stronger control over the backlands than they had had before, if lessened influence in Luanda itself. The enlarged slave catchment zone also allowed African traders from the Loango Coast, and others in the central highlands, to divert captives off toward outlying bays and beaches where British and French slavers waited to tap a system originally designed to attract labor to Luanda.[1]

A subtle change in attitude toward the dark-skinned colonial participants in the trade also began to creep into Lisbon's policy regarding slaving in the 1750s and 1760s. The Africans, formerly accepted as well-intended traders eager to come down to sell slaves at Portuguese outposts and in need only of protection from rapacious Europeans, began to be seen as savage barbarians who attacked free Portuguese merchants seeking an honest living from trade in the interior and who were incapable of organizing for themselves the lengthy journeys required to keep remote sources of captives in reliable contact with the coast. These racist attitudes extended increasingly to the Luso-Africans as well.

The problems of commercial restructuring, annoying but explained away as the dishonesty of individual contractors in the 1740s and early 1750s, were revealed in an entirely new light with the appointment of Carvalho e Mello as first minister to the king D. José I in 1755. As Carvalho e Mello's authority grew in Lisbon, as count of Oeyras after 1759 and then as marquis of Pombal in 1770, and as the count's own brother assumed control over the new Ministry for the Colonies in 1762, the free-trade doctrines of his government were applied to open trade in Angola to the merchant associates of his government in Lisbon.[2] Capital was to provide their means of entry, and its designated bearers were to be private merchants sending out large quantities of trade goods from Lisbon, mainly operating through the two trading companies chartered to develop the agriculture of northeastern and northern Brazil, Pernambuco, Paraíba, Pará, and Maranhão.

1. The Bastos Viana *aviso* of 31 July 1737, AHU, Angola cx. 27, tacitly but clearly recognized all these factors.
2. For a summary of these events, see Alden, *Royal Government*, pp. 8–9.

Beyond that solid foundation in the commercial strength of metropolitan merchants, liberal theory required only that Lisbon traders acquire the freedom to trade throughout the Angolan hinterland and that the colonial government find some indirect means to cut off the slaves going from Portuguese territory to the British and French all along the Angolan coasts, without directly confronting the superior naval power of these rivals. Distraction of both northern European nations by the outbreak of the Seven Years' War in 1756 offered an opportunity to exclude them during a moment of weakness. Lisbon began to implement sanguine policies formulated along these lines in the latter half of the 1750s but then turned gradually to more direct measures against the contractor and the Luso-Africans as Lisbon learned how much the ability to trade freely depended also on intervention in the politics of the colony.

The Maranhão and Pernambuco Companies

Pombal's coterie of Lisbon merchants exploited Angolan slaving primarily by using their consolidated commercial power, favored by legal privilege, to buy slaves whom they sold in monopoly Brazilian markets through the two chartered companies. Shareholders profited from the monopoly companies mostly from manipulating their internal accounts, from selling Portuguese and northern European manufactures in Africa, and from distributing American agricultural commodities through Lisbon. Hence, they could afford to own slaves whom less vertically integrated competitors in the southern Atlantic could not. By buying the slaves outright at Luanda they also avoided the complications of dealing in the contractors' market for bills of exchange and other commercial paper in the colony.[3] Though both chartered Pombaline companies owned slaves, the ultimate benefits to their shareholders depended on slaving hardly more than did the strategies of any other Lisbon merchant active in Angola. The chartered company structure simply represented a technical advance over the bills of exchange in furthering Lisbon's consistent strategy of deflecting unavoidable losses from slave mortality through financial instruments. Also like other Lisbon merchants selling goods in Angola, company directors meant to displace everyone else concerned through the sheer bulk of the companies' transactions.[4]

3. It is probably significant that the companies switched to carrying slaves on the accounts of other owners in the 1770s, in part, no doubt, because of their own lack of capital to continue buying slaves for themselves, but surely in part also because the contractor had then been removed from the scene, as is discussed later in this chapter.
4. Existing studies on the Pombaline companies concentrate on aspects of their complicated operations quite removed from the way they fit into the trade in Angola; the following discussion merely sketches out elements illustrating general Lisbon strategies from

The Maranhão Company (Companhia Geral do Grão Pará e Maranhão, or CGGPM) obtained royal confirmation of its statutes in 1755 and exercised a limited influence in the Angolan market for slaves for about ten years, from 1756 to 1765.[5] The company's exemption from the 8$700 export duties levied on all its Angolan competitors laid down the challenge to the contract holders and gave it an initial 15 percent advantage over the cost at which others had to embark slaves at Luanda.[6] It could also dispatch its ships at any time its local administrators determined, without waiting for a turn in the long queue of vessels waiting to take on slave cargoes, or even without filling its rated capacity, as the contractors were authorized to require all other ships to do.

Despite these considerable advantages, the Maranhão Company never exercised a major influence over slaving at Angola. It possessed an outright monopoly over slave-buying at Portugal's Upper Guinea Coast trading stations, Bissau and Cacheu, much closer to its markets along Brazil's far northern coast, and it could extract other financial advantages from buying there rather than at Luanda, where it had to compete with the contractors, with an active Rio-based merchant marine, and eventually with its sister Pernambuco Company (the Companhia Geral de Pernambuco e Paraíba, or CGPP). As a result the Maranhão Company generally dispatched no more than a single ship each year and boarded hardly more than 8,000 slaves from both Luanda and Benguela during its entire quarter-century of activity there from 1756 to 1782, or something under 4 percent of the total volume for those years. The company's only significant short-term impact came between 1762 and 1764, when it loaded some 3,300 slaves, or over 14 percent of the total, during a period when Angolan prices for slaves dipped because of drought and while favorable Pombaline policies of several sorts were falling heavily on the colony.[7]

The potential of the big company ships to disrupt the smooth flow of others' slaves through the Luanda port nonetheless became evident in that short time. The Maranhão Company vessels were often much larger, in the 500–800 slave range, than the 300–400-slave ships of the Brazilians. One or two Lisbon behemoths of that size in the port with priority boarding rights could so drain the Luanda market of slaves ready for

---

the fuller study waiting to be developed. For background to the interpretation offered here, see Carreira, "Companhias pombalinas de navegação"; Nunes Dias, *Companhia Geral*; and Ribeiro Júnior, *Colonização e monopólio*.

    5. For the confirmation diploma, see "Alvará, em que se confirmão os Capitulos e Condições da Companhia do Grão Para (6 June 1755)," in *Collecção chronologica de leis extravagantes*, 3:435–65; also Carreira, "Companhias pombalinas de navegação," docs. E–G, pp. 128–62.

    6. Miller, "Slave Prices."

    7. See Carreira, "Companhias pombalinas de navegação," p. 77, for the statistical summary.

embarkation that Brazilian ships trying to make up a complete cargo at the same time could not acquire enough captives to fill their holds. Though ships normally left at 100 percent (and more) of their rated capacities, in 1762 a Maranhão Company ship took on 450 slaves of its capacity of 510, forcing the next vessel in line, an unusually large Rio ship, to carry only 428 slaves of its rated capacity of 558. A small Bahia ship followed in relatively good condition (227 aboard out of 237 capacity), but then a huge Maranhão Company load of 700 slaves (aboard a ship rated for 800) weighed anchor in mid-May. The next three ships to depart, one for Rio and two for Bahia, together carried less than 72 percent of their capacity, and the first ship able to make up its full cargo did not clear Luanda until mid-October.[8] Two other Maranhão Company ships and one under Pernambuco Company colors left also in that obviously congested period.

Partially filled slave decks cost the companies much less than they did Brazilians dependent on freight charges, of course, since the companies owned the slaves they carried and gained from the lowered slave mortality obtained by carrying more provisions and giving better care to fewer slaves, from the modest trading gains they earned on selling slaves in protected markets, and from other commercial aspects of operations that extended all the way from accounting profits taken on goods sold in Angola to the value of the Brazilian commodities in which they realized their final returns in Lisbon. The delays the big company ships caused in the port at Luanda also raised mortality costs for owners forced to hold slaves in the barracoons until other vessels could carry them to Brazil. Many of them must have decided to dispose of their human property to company agents at low prices rather than wait to try to send their slaves to Brazil themselves.

The Pernambuco Company, prevented from trading on the Upper Guinea Coast by the Maranhão Company monopoly and quite powerless along the Mina Coast against Bahians, Dutch, British, and French, concentrated its slave-buying at Luanda after receiving its charter in 1759.[9] During its quarter-century of activity in Angola from 1761 to 1786, it boarded over 41,000 slaves at Luanda, and another 1,500 or more at Benguela during intermittent explorations there in the latter 1770s. From 1761 to 1783 it was probably the major single buyer of slaves at Luanda, consistently taking more than 2,000 slaves in most years during the 1760s and often more than 1,000 each year in the 1770s and early 1780s.[10] The Pernambuco Company in its heyday thus accounted for perhaps as much

8. See the annual report of slave exports for 1762, in Vasconcelos, 11 Feb. 1763, AHU, Angola cx. 29.

9. "Alvará, em que se confirma e estabelece a Instituição da Companhia Geral de Pernambuco e Paraíba (30 Aug. 1759)," in *Collecção chronologica de leis extravagantes,* 3:261–94; Carreira, "Companhias pombalinas de navegação," doc. H, pp. 163–88.

10. Carreira, "Companhias pombalinas de navegação," p. 311, for summary statistics.

as a quarter of the slaves moving through Luanda. It may have posed a more direct threat to Brazilian shippers from Rio than to the contractor, since it based its operations in Pernambuco and tended to buy its slaves with Brazilian *gerebita* and tobaccos more than did the Maranhão Company or other Lisbon merchants. Its emphasis on selling domestic and northern European manufactures hit the contractor's strengths in Asian textiles only obliquely but competed directly with alternative sources of northern European goods as reexports from Brazil.[11]

At Luanda the Pernambuco Company, like the Maranhão Company early in the 1760s, conducted its affairs through pairs of administrators stationed there as factors, very much as did the contractors.[12] These included the later-famous Francisco Honorato da Costa,[13] whose down-and-up career neatly recapitulated the company's local commercial losses, in spite of its dominance in terms of the volume of slaves it bought. Da Costa—who arrived at Luanda in 1777, late in the company's history in Angola—and his partners and predecessors competed in the Luanda market with the same techniques that big Lisbon firms customarily adopted to beat the local competition: widespread credit in trade goods offered to almost anyone willing to take them off to the interior in search of slaves. The parent chartered company in Lisbon charged its shipments to the accounts of its Luanda administrators at profitable markups of from 30 to 70 percent.[14] The local administrators, responsible from then on for the value of the goods they had received, cleared their account with Lisbon by embarking slaves for the company to sell in its protected Pernambuco market.

Credit figured prominently in the company factors' selling strategies, in part because of the substantial capital behind the chartered parent company in Lisbon but also because they had no other means of penetrating the tight linkages among contractors, Brazilians, and Luso-Africans and others long established in the trade of the interior. But ample credit did not guarantee prompt returns. The Luanda administrators received consignments of goods from Portugal only infrequently, lacked essential components (especially Asian textiles) of the necessary full assortment, and often found themselves with stocks of unsalable merchandise that shareholders in Lisbon, investing in kind and simultaneously clearing their personal domestic stocks of worthless goods, dumped on the company. Credit also enabled the company's Angola factors to hire beginners and down-at-the-heel failures as their trading agents in the interior. The pre-

---

11. Ribeiro Júnior, *Colonização e monopólio*, pp. 125, 205–6 et passim, is the best source on the commercial strategies of the company.

12. See the Angola and Benguela *copiadores* in the company files housed in the AHMF. For the Maranhão factors in 1761, Nunes Dias, *Companhia Geral*, p. 241.

13. See Chapters 9 and 17.

14. Nunes Dias, *Companhia Geral*, p. 431, offers this figure for the Maranhão Company in Africa generally, and other merchants charged even more.

dictable result was that the companies ended up holding enormous amounts of unrecoverable debt. When da Costa eventually moved his personal commercial operations to Kasanje in 1794, he went to the Kwango to recover the substantial funds that he had sunk there while acting as Luanda agent for the Pernambuco Company.

In this fashion the company financed expansion of the commercialized trading zone within Angola's slaving frontier and saddled its administrators in Luanda and its creditors in Portugal with the bad debts while preserving assets of value to line the pockets of insiders in Lisbon. The slave-owning aspects of its strategy inconvenienced the Brazilians and Luso-Africans trying to ship captives on their own accounts in competition with it, but they could escape the pressure by moving their trade to Benguela, where exports grew rapidly at that time and where the company sent its own ships only belatedly and infrequently. The slaves left languishing in the barracoons of Luanda paid the greater prices, since they could only wait for their ship to load, or die.

The limited successes that the companies enjoyed in Angola stemmed at least as much from legal and administrative reforms that Pombal's government imposed on the colony as they did from commercial strength, and certainly much more from favorable regulations than from the trading skills of their local agents. In 1761, for example, the Maranhão Company, though apparently not its generally less favored Pernambuco counterpart, received the priority in executing debt claims that made overseas trading in the established style of selling goods profitable for Lisbon.[15] At Luanda, the doctrines of "freedom of trade" produced a crucial *alvará* on 11 January 1758 that proclaimed utterly free entry into the backlands for anyone sending goods into the colony.[16] Its designated but unnamed targets, "certain specific individuals who have succeeded in monopolizing (trade) to their private advantage," could have meant no one other than the contractor.[17] With free access to the hinterland thus established, the chartered companies were positioned to send off their own agents, circumventing the power of the contractor in Luanda's financial market, confronting the Luso-Africans directly in the backlands, and attracting slaves away from trade routes serving the British and French.

15. Carreira, "Companhias pombalinas de navegação," pp. 371–72.

16. Published in *Arquivos de Angola* 2, no. 14 (1936): 531–35, and several other places. A slightly earlier *provisão*, of 30 March 1756, had asserted the general principle of all ports in Africa being open: Taunay, *Subsídios*, p. 142.

17. A series of reports from Angola and studies by government advisers in Lisbon had steadily developed the case against the contractor from Governor da Cunha's lead in 1753–54: *aviso* of Bastos Viana, Lisbon, 31 July 1757, AHU, Angola cx. 27; Oeyras *parecer*, 20 Nov. 1760, AHU, Angola cx. 28; "Exposição das rezoens . . . ," ANTT, Ministério do Reino, maço 499; "Assento sobre o commercio de Angola," Belem, 3 Jan. 1758, AHU, Angola cx. 27; and so on.

The 1758 decree went on to forbid any colonial official from hindering Lisbon's favored strategy, a proviso standard in royal fiats but in this case also a clear warning to the Luso-African *capitães-mores*. It also confirmed the priority to depart from the port enjoyed by ships arriving *efeitos próprios*, with the advantages of lowered mortality risks obviously intended for the companies, or any other ventures sent out under Lisbon auspices, and the deleterious effects observed in 1762 for all others. For the contractors, the decree confirmed only their right to collect the slave-export duties, thus threatening to gut future contracts of the commercial advantages that alone had made Angolan tax farming profitable. It also moved against some of the financial manipulations that contractors ordinarily promoted, by specifying that ship captains were to pay duties owed to the contractor only through government treasury boards established in Brazil as part of the broader Pombal reform program, thus forcing the contractors to loosen their hold on the *letras* issued in Luanda. A supplementary decree, the *alvará* of 25 January 1758, may have partially compensated the contractor for his commercial losses by simplifying the complicated set of duties then in force and thereby authorizing collection of the full amount originally assessed on a *peça* on all slaves of whatever quality.[18] At the same time, it made these revenues more accessible to the royal treasury whenever Pombal might decide to claim them directly for the Crown.

Those in Luanda whom Pombaline "freedom of trade" threatened to restrain at first delayed implementation of the new principle. Governor Antonio de Vasconcelos (1758–64), faced with the prudently tacit hostility of these ostensibly loyal subjects who were in fact deeply opposed to their sovereign's policy,[19] reported that none of the city's merchants—and least of all the administrators of the contract, he added pointedly—had mentioned the decrees to him despite his distribution of numerous copies of them throughout the town. One could presumably not be held responsible for regulations of which one had no knowledge. The governor could not ignore their discreet invitation to pretend that nothing had changed, however, and so he admonished Lisbon that too literal an application of the law would release a Pandora's box of "Jews, gypsies, and criminals" from the jail into the interior, where they would surely abuse the Africans. More to the point, he added that in the unregulated commerce of the distant interior, where all the slaves in Angola originated, freedom to trade also constituted license to defraud creditors.

18. The *alvará* is, among other places, in *Arquivos de Angola* 2, no. 14 (1936): 537–40. All of these reforms fit squarely within the framework of much broader policies developed to tighten the fiscal system of the empire and bring the trade to all Portuguese colonies back under the control of metropolitan merchants. The specific decrees and their effects in Angola may therefore suggest the generality of the impact of Pombal's mercantilism elsewhere as well.

19. Pombal was even then taking forceful steps in Portugal against members of the nobility accused of conspiracy against the king, and so expressions of disloyalty were to be avoided at any cost.

Having indicated the implications of Lisbon's new trade freedom for commerce to the slaving frontier in its new remote location, Vasconcelos offered a compromise to meet the new regulation's practical objectives without quite opening the floodgate by too broad an interpretation of philosophical principles alien to the administered trading systems of the interior. The governor therefore introduced a pass system under which all traders departing for the interior with goods taken on credit would register their debts with the government. He hastened to reassure Lisbon that such licenses did not in practice restrict trade in any way, since he granted them freely to all who requested them.[20] Perhaps Lisbon was to trust him to favor the trustworthy emissaries of company traders but to deny passes to disreputable characters of the sort that the contractor was alleged to employ. In the end, Governor Vasconcelos's early warnings proved prophetic both of the restrictive flavor of subsequent "freedom of trade" in Angola and of the resiliency of the Luso-Africans' hold on the conduct of trade in the interior.

The Asian Trade

The Lisbon government soon escalated its campaign against the contractors by short-circuiting the advantage they held from supplying most of the Asian textiles on which Angolan slaving depended. Like many other planks in the legislative scaffolding that supported the new Lisbon traders at Luanda, this reform of the Asia trade developed from application of broader policies formulated to deal with problems of imperial scope. In this case, Lisbon's general fiscal crisis motivated the government to seek out every *real* of duties and taxes that it could collect, and ministers accordingly grew concerned over the habit of the Goa and Macao ships of calling for "repairs and provisions" at Brazilian ports as they returned from the Indian Ocean and then using the occasion to sell reportedly vast quantities of cottons and silks there from stocks legally destined for Portugal. Such smuggling contravened firm mercantilist rules requiring routing these goods out to Brazil only after they had first gone all the way around to Lisbon, where metropolitan merchants took their cut and where the government levied its duties on them. If Asia merchants associated with the Angola slave duty contract engaged in this contraband, they would have earned the deep-seated hostility of the Pombal government evident in Luanda.

Accordingly, a decree of 7 May 1761 extended the absolute freedom to trade granted to Angola in 1758 to ships returning from Macao and Goa. In particular, this freedom broke whatever former restraints the con-

20. Vasconcelos, 3 and 4 Jan. 1759 and 22 May 1760, AHU, Angola cx. 28; the letter of 3 Jan. 1759 is published in *Arquivos de Angola* 1, no. 5 (1936): n.p.

tractor had imposed by routing Asia goods in his own ships through Brazil or Lisbon and thus enabled local Pernambuco Company agents to obtain the cottons they desperately needed to buy slaves in Luanda. The company's Angola operations suffered particularly from its directors' inability to acquire Asian goods in Lisbon, probably as a consequence of the enmity of the old-line merchants associated with the contract there toward the chartered intruders. The 1761 decree further favored the company by restricting the inbound Asia ships to Luanda, where its administrators were in place and where governors could look after its affairs, thus denying the privilege to Brazilians and Luso-Africans then busy at Benguela.[21]

The Asia traders evidently still did not cooperate with the clear thrust of Lisbon's policy favoring the company merchants. A further decree (17 November 1761) upgraded the permission granted six months earlier to a requirement that all inbound Asia ships stop at Luanda. It protected the Crown's financial interest by imposing a 10 percent duty on goods the ships might sell there in lieu of payments the contractors would otherwise have made in the Casa da India in Lisbon.[22] The customs house nominally established to collect these duties at Luanda in fact once again favored the Pernambuco Company, since the company's charter gave it priority in obtaining customs dispatches. This privilege should have constituted a substantial advantage for company administrators, who were thus able to get critical cottons into the interior ahead of their competitors, perhaps—with the cooperation of the proper officials—weeks and months in advance.[23] Luso-African merchants with commercial connections only in Brazil would experience further difficulties in purchasing India goods directly off these ships in Luanda, since they lacked convenient means of paying for them in Lisbon. The metropolitan sellers of Indian textiles had little use for slave-backed bills of exchange drawn on Brazil, where they were expressly forbidden to call on their way on toward Europe.[24] Angolan slavers would meanwhile shoulder the substantial costs of repairing and reprovisioning huge vessels after months at sea through charges for these services to be made against the slave-duty revenues they paid.[25]

21. For this emphasis applied similarly in Mozambique, see Hoppe, *Africa oriental portuguesa,* pp. 166 ff., 283–84.

22. *Alvará* in AHU, Angola maço 17. See also the policy study in the Oeyras *parecer* of 20 Nov. 1760, AHU, Angola cx. 28.

23. Vasconcelos, 3 April 1762, AHU, Angola cx. 29; *provisão* of 6 Sept. 1766, AHU, Angola cx. 31; Ribeiro Júnior, *Colonização e monopólio,* p. 91. See also Corrêa, *História de Angola,* 2:31.

24. "Apontamentos do que occorre a respeito da Carta do Governador de Angola de 23 de Junho de 1771, em que trate do que passou com as Naus q por alli vierão da India naquelle anno," n.d. (ca. 1771), AHU, Angola cx. 33.

25. Vasconcelos, 3 April 1762, AHU, Angola cx. 29. Even Sousa Coutinho, that most loyal of the governors of the era, complained of the expense in view of the many other uses he envisioned for the funds: 20 Aug. 1766, AHU, Angola cx. 31.

Direct sales of India goods in Angola, however much they undercut the contractors in Luanda and Lisbon, produced only mixed results. The annual India ships continued to pass through Bahia in spite of the 1761 requirement that they stop in Angola. They finally stopped at Luanda in 1766 and 1767, but thereafter they simply ignored the requirement.[26] Local Luanda interests managed to acquire textiles on their own on the occasions when the India ships called there, sometimes literally selling the family silver to raise payment for them, and some merchants even succeeded in illegally reexporting them to Brazil. The government then, by an *aviso* of the overseas ministry, suspended freedom of the Asian trade in 1770, certainly more than coincidentally in the year after it had abolished the contract itself.

The previous control over imports of India goods by the contractors seems to explain why the Asia ships returned to Angola almost immediately afterward, this time evidently with cargoes planned for smuggling to Brazil. Two enormous India ships showed up at the port in 1771, armed with copies of decrees liberalizing restraints on other branches of direct trade among the colonies,[27] and managed to gain permission to sell goods destined for the Africa trade but not to deal in categories of goods normally sold in Brazil.[28] The Lisbon government then revoked the privilege of direct trade among the colonies with a full royal decree of 19 June 1772, citing its ruinous effects on the Pernambuco Company's ability to obtain Asian goods in Lisbon to assort with its shipments of European wares.[29] The defunct contractors had conspicuously not received similarly sympathetic attention to wounds inflicted by nearly a decade of Lisbon's reforms in the Asia trade.

Assault on the Luso-Africans

With the Pernambuco and Maranhão Companies in place at Luanda, abstract freedom of trade proclaimed, and Lisbon's main competition, the contractors, coming under indirect pressure exerted through adjusting the old restrictions on the Asian trade, governors set out to limit the new

26. Sousa Coutinho, 3 June 1770, AHU, Angola cx. 32. A further *aviso* in 1765 had ordered the viceroy in India to enforce the 1761 decrees, but the Overseas Ministry relaxed the prohibition in 1767 by giving the Asia ships of that year permission to call at Bahia or Rio on condition that they sold nothing.

27. The decrees of 10 Sept. 1765 and 27 June 1769 abolishing the old, highly restrictive fleet system between Brazil and Portugal and otherwise liberalizing trade between Brazil and Mozambique.

28. "Apontamentos do que occorre . . . com as Naus . . . ," AHU, Angola cx. 33.

29. *Alvará* of 19 June 1772, AHU, Angola maço 4-A and maço 11; see also Arauss, *requerimento*, AHU, India maço 120.

trade franchise to metropolitan hands by placing severe restrictions on Luso-Africans and any other debtors taking the goods then flooding the backlands. As Governor Vasconcelos had predicted, free trade called for safeguards to protect the debts that credit would create. It also required steps to contain the rise in slave prices that such inflationary tactics might occasion. Measures followed concentrating all slaving in a set of regulated marketplaces, called *feiras,* positioned where the main African supply routes for slaves entered colonial territory. The *feiras* might also cut down on the diversion of slaves from these points to the French and British, but their main objectives converged on securing remittances at Luanda for the trade goods that Lisbon distributed through the Angolan hinterland.

The government directed its attention at what were basically Luso-African trading settlements, more or less temporary, informal agglomerations of straw huts, storage sheds, and fields where traders lived among their African wives and slaves. Some of the women represented African families trading with their husbands, but most of them certainly tended the fields. Male slaves performed skilled tasks connected with the trade—storing and packing goods, guarding warehouses against theft and sabotage, supervising the slaves being readied for dispatch to the coast, preparing chains, drying meat and cassava, and assembling other supplies necessary for the trip.[30] One such Luso-African trading settlement had existed in the Mbwela area at Kisoza for some time before the 1750s.[31] Those in Kasanje and in Jinga, Holo, and at Kalandula on the trail to Jinga survived from the seventeenth century but had become satellites of the Luso-African community in Ambaca.[32] On the south side of the Kwanza, similar settlements in Libolo sent slaves down to Dondo, and others in the valley of the Ngango River fed a market at Beja near the Luso-African center in Pungo Andongo.[33] These also tapped slaves coming from the Luso-Africans settled in less centralized patterns all over the central highlands.

Although old Luso-African families and newcomers from the city tended to congregate in these settlements, trading tended to spread constantly into the surrounding villages. Unsuccessful traders and new arrivals tried to establish contacts, and even to settle, in remote locations where they could buy slaves more cheaply than they could obtain them in the settlements. Sometimes they intercepted slaves belonging to merchants in the centers. Disorders were the order of the day. Fires were extremely

---

30. De Mello, 7 Dec. 1798, with enclosed memorial on trade, AHU, Angola cx. 46.
31. Vasconcelos *bando,* 10 Nov. 1759, AHU, Angola cx. 28.
32. "Termo de recebimento da embaxada . . . ," 25 Oct. 1744, AHU, Angola cx. 23.
33. Da Cunha, 23 March 1755, AHU, Angola maço 18 (D.O.); "Angola no fim do século," pp. 288–89 (de Mello); de Mello, 21 Oct. 1801, AHU, Angola cx. 50; Sandoval, "Noticia do sertão do Balundo," p. 219.

common in the settlements, and disastrous when gunpowder was among the trade goods kept in straw storage sheds. The members of different factions within the Luso-African communities regarded each other with suspicion, though together they also did all they could to hinder the commerce of the intruders sent directly from Luanda. The numerous convicts among these did little to soften the rough-and-tumble frontier quality of life there.[34] Aggressive and ruthless characters, usually down on their luck and deeply in debt, confined in alien and dangerous surroundings, they coveted their wealthier competitors' successes. The losers tended to band together to ruin those who were doing better, leading to the formation of factions, to frequent violation of contracts, and to great commercial disorder.[35]

Opportunities for subversion arose constantly, because the traders resident in these settlements constantly borrowed and bought goods back and forth to balance their individual stocks. Slavers with the majority of a coffle ready to send to the coast would pay premium prices for goods they lacked to acquire the few captives they needed to complete their business. The network of debts produced a rush to claim the assets of traders who died, whether those assets were trade goods or slaves on hand, with each competitor presenting himself as a major creditor of the estate to gain control of the choicest wares and prime slaves for himself. The skilled slaves of a deceased trader usually took their master's death as their own opportunity to escape and disappeared into the surrounding bush almost before the body had cooled.[36] Traders who lived alone in the compounds scattered over the central highlands often left nothing more for heirs and creditors in Lisbon or at the coast to recover than a decapitated head atop a pole at the entrance to their compound.[37]

The Pombaline emphasis on freely sending goods to the interior on credit necessitated a renewed government effort to order these wild and woolly centers. Governor Vasconcelos (1758–64) introduced exactly this policy within months of the decrees of 1758, establishing two regulated *feiras* in 1759, one near the government military post set astride the forested mountain passes of the Ndembu territory at Encoje to block slave routes leading from the middle Kwango valley to the French and British buying slaves everywhere north of Luanda.[38] He extended the tactic to

<hr/>

34. De Lima, *memória*, 10 June 1762, AHU, Angola cx. 29; Ferreira, *memória*, 26 June 1762, AHU, Angola cx. 29.

35. Ferreira, *memória*, 26 June 1762, AHU, Angola cx. 29; *requerimento* and attached documents in de Mello, 30 May 1801, AHU, Angola cx. 51.

36. Ferreira, *memória*, 26 June 1762, AHU, Angola cx. 29.

37. Sousa Coutinho, "Ordem que o capitão mor de Benguela deve entregar . . . ," 20 Nov. 1768, AHU, Angola cx. 31.

38. Vasconcelos, *bando* of 10 Nov. 1759, AHU, Angola cx. 28; cf. Couto, *Capitães-mores*, p. 207.

the trading centers along the Kwanza and Lukala rivers in 1762, setting up official *feiras* at Beja, near Pungo Andongo, and Lucamba, in Ambaca, both of them at crossroads of the Luso-African networks in the highlands east of Luanda.[39] When Governor Sousa Coutinho replaced Vasconcelos in 1764, he turned almost immediately to further consolidation of the *feira* system by pulling a trading settlement at Ndala Jinga, probably somewhere in Mbondo on the Luso-Africans' trail to Jinga and/or Holo, back to Lukamba near Ambaca and by pushing the system out to the Kwango valley itself in the major slaving kingdom of Kasanje.[40] With that, Sousa Coutinho in effect ringed the Luso-Africans' old Massangano-Lembo-Dondo core on the lower Kwanza with government officials positioned to protect agents of the Luanda merchants by intercepting slaves headed for Luanda before they could fall into the hands of their colonial competitors. The government had thereby extended a legal version of the contractors' strategy, a half century earlier and much nearer the coast, of using trade goods to expand the commercialized slaving zones beyond the reach of the Luso-Africans and then intercepting deliveries of slaves to their old centers near the coast.

The mere establishment of government *feiras* created nothing more than a propitious environment for other methods of wresting slaving away from the Luso-Africans. Pombal's Lisbon allies intended to interfere also with the colonial slavers' Brazilian suppliers of *gerebita* and their sources of Asian cottons through the contractor. The companies' stocks of northern European goods did not include enough of these indispensable components of the *banzo* bundle of goods. Their northern European goods also suffered in Angola from the high prices with which metropolitan taxes and company monopoly-pricing strategies burdened merchandise that was virtually identical to goods that the British and French offered directly from the original suppliers in their own countries at much lower prices. Vasconcelos thus found himself under orders from superiors in Lisbon to restrict exchanges of trade goods among traders in the interior that would enable proper assorting of their inventories. Rather, they should make up all *banzos* in Luanda, where close government supervision would presumably exclude, or reduce, contributions from anywhere in the world but Lisbon.[41] The traders of Luanda protested so violently against this plan,[42]

---

39. Vasconcelos, 7 July 1762, AHU, Angola cx. 29, published in *Arquivos de Angola* 2, no. 9 (1936): 167–68. Earlier in the year Vasconcelos had reorganized the Encoje *feira* to bring it under closer control from the nearby government military post: idem, 22 April 1762, AHU, Angola cx. 29.

40. Sousa Coutinho, 12 June 1764 and 9 May 1765, AHU, Angola cx. 30, published in *Arquivos de Angola* 1, no. 1 (1936): n.p.

41. *Carta regia,* 14 Nov. 1761, in *Arquivos de Angola* 2, no. 9 (1936): 157–59; also Vasconcelos *bando* of 7 July 1762, ibid., pp. 165–66.

42. See the three memorials of June 1762 (Ferreira, de Lima, Silva) in AHU, Angola cx. 29.

and it was so obviously impractical under the necessity of meeting changing African demand in the backlands, that even Governor Sousa Coutinho, normally the arch-executor of Pombaline policies in Angola, was writing within a year of his arrival to suggest obliquely that he had devised alternative means of preventing traders from exchanging goods with one another in the interior that would render it unnecessary to pack all *banzos* in the city.[43]

The pains taken to favor Lisbon goods also meant putting pressure on the long-standing Luso-African trade in salt that circulated as currency in the Luanda hinterland and formed another integral ingredient in the trade *banzo*. Sousa Coutinho was the activist governor who attempted to interdict salt entering Angola from the rock salt mines in Kisama, directly up the Kwanza from Kisama through Luso-African traders in Massangano and then to Lembo and Ambaca, in competition with Benguela marine salt coming through Luanda town.[44] Lisbon officials had suggested earlier in the 1730s that the colonial government put this commerce in the hands of Lisbon-favored contractors,[45] and skirmishes in the continuing struggle had taken place in the 1750s over whether Africans in Ambaca should pay their local taxes in salt blocks or in Lisbon's cottons and woolens.[46] With Pombal's thorough application of general imperial policies to Angola came a project to let a monopoly contract for the Benguela salt, and a royal order to that effect was issued on 13 November 1761.[47]

The Angola salt contract extended to the African colony a method of raising revenues long established elsewhere in the empire, and Sousa Coutinho later attempted to raise its value to prospective bidders with semi-industrial projects—beef curing, processing of local leather into shoe soles, and so on—that would increase the quantities of salt consumed locally beyond those expended in the slave trade.[48] The government and its contractors experienced some difficulty in buying up the inventories of salt built up by residents in Luanda, presumably Luso-Africans intent on evading the monopoly established at the point of import into the city, and were unable to dispossess them of competing salt pans near Luanda at Kakwako and the mouth of the Bengo.[49] In the end, even Sousa Coutinho seems to have been unable to block circulation of salt through Luso-African channels, since he ended up promoting its circulation in the interior,

43. Sousa Coutinho, 9 May 1765, AHU, Angola cx. 30.
44. Avellar, 20 May 1731, AHU, Angola maço 18-A; also idem, 28 May 1732, AHU, Angola cx. 21.
45. Meneses, 12 June 1734, AHU, Angola cx. 21.
46. Da Cunha, 4 March 1756, AHU, Angola maço 18 (D.O.). See Chapter 8 above.
47. See the Oeyras *parecer* of 20 Nov. 1760, paras. 13–25, AHU, Angola cx. 28.
48. Referred to in Vasconcelos, 18 April 1762, AHU, Angola cx. 29.
49. Sousa Coutinho, 20 Aug. 1768, AHU, Angola cx. 31. The contract for colonial salt was reportedly an effective arrangement: Sousa Coutinho, 26 Nov. 1772, AHU, Angola cx. 36.

though under government auspices, by having local posts pay it out in salaries for troops and for workers in other semi-industrial projects underway.[50]

Beyond inhibiting the flow of local trade goods and commodity currencies not favored by Lisbon's narrowing conception of free trade, Sousa Coutinho formed a colonial board of trade (the Junta do Comércio), composed of the Luanda agents of the Lisbon traders, to advise him on managing the *feiras* and on other issues vital to Lisbon's definition of healthy commerce in Angola.[51] This board of trade replaced the Luanda Senado da Câmara, which was no longer responsive to the priorities of the Luso-Africans and which Sousa Coutinho intended to exclude from influence over the trade because it was a carryover from an earlier era of local autonomy that the Pombal regime disfavored anywhere in the empire.[52] The board's membership included local representatives of the royal contract as well as the administrators of the two chartered companies and other "principal traders" active at Luanda. Sousa Coutinho's proclamation identified the "good businessmen"—the importers and creditors of the local slave traders—as those whom the trade board would defend against "intrigues, envy, disparagements (*detrações*), and bad faith" that were ruining commerce from Lisbon's point of view. He pointedly made clear his intention of assisting creditors in the collection of whatever debts they were owed. Every merchant could rest assured of the "security of assets invested in the interior," with the governor's personal devotion to them and with the advice and support of merchants committed to the same cause against "second-rate traders" who ruined trade by not paying what they owed. Sousa Coutinho thus welcomed the interests of metropolitan capital directly into the halls of government in Luanda, as he turned also to other restrictions on those who did not deserve the freedom of trade he had come to Angola to defend.

The Lisbon merchants assembled in the Junta then assumed direct control over conduct of trade in the government *feiras* in the interior by appointing the clerks, or *escrivães das feiras* (market scribes, secretaries, or administrators), empowered to exercise complete authority over business done in the interior. These *escrivães* were to enforce fixed prices set by the merchants in Luanda and to exclude non-Lisbon goods from the *banzos* traded for slaves in the marketplaces. The merchants also attempted to fix exchange rates in the interior, agreeing on the quantities of their goods

50. Sousa Coutinho, 26 Jan. 1765, AHU, Angola cx. 30.

51. *Portaria,* 9 May 1769, AHU, Angola cx. 32.

52. This board of trade replaced a distinctly different Luanda Junta Commercial created in 1761 by Governor Vasconcelos, consisting entirely of Lisbon-appointed officials of the colonial government; see Couto, *Capitães-mores,* pp. 206–7. Sousa Coutinho's *ordem* of 18 June 1764 creating the board is published in *Arquivos de Angola* 2, no. 9 (1936): 169–71.

equivalent to the various African currencies actually employed in transactions in the *feiras*. Traders were to take goods out from Luanda only under cover of *guias*—in effect, bills of lading identifying the merchandise, its owner, and its destination—which they had to present to the marketplace *escrivão* upon arrival in his jurisdiction, thus allowing him to verify that the contents of bundles matched the list of items that Luanda merchants had authorized their agents to carry. The Junta-appointed market administrators received explicit precedence over the Luso-Africans, specified as the *capitães-mores* of the military districts in which the *feiras* were located, in regulating all commercial disputes and particularly in sequestering assets of deceased traders to protect the interests of their creditors in Luanda.[53]

Once Sousa Coutinho had created the regulatory institutions necessary to administer free trade in the Angolan interior in the interest of metropolitan capital, he turned directly against the Luso-Africans, identified in increasingly open racist terms as "those who would claim association with whites on the basis of the cheap shoes that they wear."[54] Wealth in imperial currencies, here symbolized by emphasis on European footwear as the hallmark of civilization, and skin color were jointly replacing prominence in the colonial economy of slaves and marital alliances as standards of respectability in Pombal's mercantilist Angola.

Metropolitan hostility to Luso-Africans had focused as early as the late 1730s on the allegedly high markups that stereotyped barefoot African peddlers, living off the natural bounty of the lands where they traded at virtually no expense, took on goods they obtained in Luanda and resold in the interior.[55] With such assumptions, it was difficult to perceive the rising operating costs that traders faced as the slaving frontier moved off toward the east. The Pombal government picked up the old allegations of unjustified high margins taken in the interior, ignored the fact that the same report had specified the metropolitan merchants' Lisbon-to-Luanda add-on as more than 25 percent higher than that of the Luso-Africans, implicated the Jesuits (whose low repute among Lisbon reformers of that

---

53. The strategy reflected, once again, broader policies, including the creation of a new Junta do Comércio in Lisbon to replace the old merchant guild of the city. For the comparable institution in Bahia, see Lugar, "Merchant Community," pp. 50–51. In Angola the Senado da Câmara lost more of its once-substantial powers in 1770, when a new law defined the order of devolution of the governor's powers in case of his death or disability first to the bishop, then to the Crown justice (*ouvidor geral*), and then to the ranking military officer, all presumably metropolitan appointees and not part of the local creole establishment. The Senado da Câmara had stood first in line earlier in the century, when it still represented Lisbon merchants. See Pardo, "Comparative Study," p. 55; also Chapter 15 above.

54. *Regimento* of 16 Sept. 1764, AHU, Angola maço 12-B, published in Neves, *D. Francisco Inocencio de Sousa Coutinho*, pp. 52–55, and in Couto, *Capitães-mores*, pp. 318–22. For other proclamations of the same tenor, see Chapter 8, above.

55. Magalhães, 29 April 1738, AHU, Angola cx. 21.

era could contaminate anyone with whom the order could be associated), and exaggerated the extent of the reported difference to blame the traders of the interior for the uncompetitively high prices at which Lisbon's reexports reached areas in the interior also served directly by the British and French.[56]

This racist hostility toward the Luso-Africans was used to justify fixed prices in protected *feiras* administered by the Luanda Junta do Comércio and its resident clerks and to deflect attention from the high margins at which Lisbon merchants sold goods at Luanda, quite rightly at the expense of uncivilized colonials in the interior. The Luso-Africans defended themselves only very unclearly, owing to their perception of what Lisbon saw as "markups" instead in terms of mediating between the separate textile-based and other African currency zones of the interior and the *réis* zone of the southern Atlantic. According to them, the doubled price in *réis de fazenda* at which traders exchanged goods in remote marketplaces in the interior simply equaled the Luanda prices in different currencies, *réis de letras* mostly, used there. They took no trading gains, by their own definition, and were acting as international currency dealers, not slave traders.

It then remained, in theory, at least, to deprive the Luso-African *capitães-mores* of the considerable influence they still exerted over the new institutions of trade that Luanda had positioned in their districts. For years, the colonial military commanders had come under severe criticism from Lisbon for their effective control of the porters needed in the trade to the exclusion of Lisbon's agents, and especially since 1761.[57] Sousa Coutinho broadened restrictions on the district commanders already in place to cover all aspects of their official behavior in a new *regimento* promulgated on 24 February 1765.[58] The key sixth article of this charter expressly and comprehensively forbade *capitães-mores* to involve themselves personally in commerce or to interfere with the freedom of private subjects to trade. The governor of the colony assumed full authority over appointments to this formerly powerful position, with future further weakening of the office clearly foretold in the preference to be given to nominees promoted from the ranks of the regular troops, where few wealthy Luso-African colonels in the civilian militia were to be found.

All these steps intended to bring the trade of the interior into line with Lisbon's expensive ways of selling goods in Africa failed, of course. Pombal's expanded credit and all the proclamations involving *feiras, escrivães, banzos,* and the like merely supported the Luso-Africans' accustomed

56. Oeyras *parecer* of 20 Nov. 1760, AHU, Angola cx. 28.
57. Cf. Chapter 8; Vasconcelos, 14 Nov. 1761, in *Arquivos de Angola* 2 (1936): 157–59, also Couto, *Capitães-mores,* pp. 230 ff.
58. "Regimento dos capitães-mores," 24 Feb. 1765, in Neves, *D. Francisco Inocencio de Sousa Coutinho,* pp. 37–52, and in Couto, *Capitães-mores,* pp. 323–38.

sales of slaves bought with Lisbon goods to foreigners or enabled them to ship captives on Brazilian vessels on their own accounts. These *reviros*, which nearly every new law specifically aimed to eliminate, supported the thriving illegal Luso-African trade from the Kwango valley northwest to the British, the Libolo trade up to the central highlands that found its outlet at the mouths of the Kuvo and other rivers south of Luanda, and perhaps even the southerly trade from Huila and Njau on the Humpata plateau down to Cabo Negro and the bay that later became the town of Moçamedes. Sousa Coutinho's methods of containing the Luso-Africans by regulating their trade in the interior, as consolidated from Vasconcelos's earlier initiatives in 1759–62, thus produced only limited gains from Lisbon's point of view.

Sousa Coutinho therefore resorted to draconian resettlement policies near the end of his term that implicitly admitted the defeat of his earlier attempts. At first he proposed to settle the central highlands with reliable immigrants from metropolitan Portugal, in an effort that anticipated modern Portuguese efforts to populate their African colonies with dependent colonists.[59] He also established a government military post on the coast at Novo Redondo, near one of the sites where the British and French were accustomed to taking on slaves from the central highlands.[60] In the end, with these initiatives also bearing little fruit, he ordered the forcible apprehension of all debtors at large in the backlands, condemned them for the most part in racial terms, and recalled all whites and authorized traders to assemble within two weeks in the *feiras*. This proclamation amounted to total regimentation of trade and settlement in the interior. Everyone involved with trade in the interior was henceforth to reside permanently under the authority of a civilian headman to be named by the government's new generation of responsible *capitães-mores*, and no one was to travel anywhere outside of the authorized settlements without a pass from the appropriate official. The proclamation merely stated in more comprehensive and less rhetorical terms the principles governing Sousa Coutinho's better-known plans for establishing docile immigrants from Europe in the central highlands in similarly controlled settlements and, also like the highland settlement scheme, was a prototype for villagization policies that twentieth-century colonial rulers adopted against Africans in Angola.

---

59. "Bando que ordena as Feiras nos certoens de Benguela, e Caconda," 23 Sept. 1768, AHU, Angola cx. 31; also "Ordem que o capitão mor de Benguela deve entregar . . . ," 20 Nov. 1768, AHU, Angola cx. 31; and the initial report on implementation of these orders, 18 Oct. 1769, AHU, Angola cx. 32. See also Delgado, *Reino*, pp. 294–306; *Arquivos de Angola* 1, no. 1 (1933): n.p.; Felner, *Angola*, pp. 163–69.

60. Miscellaneous correspondence in AHU, Angola cx. 32; Delgado, *Reino*, pp. 307–17; Corrêa, *História de Angola*, 2:36–37.

These authoritarian plans, some of which subsequently earned Pombal's most active representative in Angola an only partially deserved reputation as a liberal reformer,[61] revealed how far the defense of Lisbon's assets in Africa had drawn the government away from the free-trade principles under which it had begun, only a decade earlier, to reform Angola's trade in slaves.[62] With years of frustrating experience in administering mercantilism in the backlands, the governor even hinted heretically at abandoning the interior in favor of securing the coasts, given the high cost of regulating the colonial population by his high standards.[63] Within a few months, Sousa Coutinho, burdened by his failures, wearied by the effort, and weakened by his vulnerability to African diseases, would be begging his sovereign for permission to return to Europe, where he would enjoy an illustrious career as minister to the court of Spain, a position worthy of his considerable energy and talents.

The End of the Slave Duty Contract

Before Sousa Coutinho would finally leave Angola in 1772 he had to oversee the last discouraging task of implementing Lisbon's final effort in the long campaign to protect its favored merchants at Luanda: outright cancellation of the contract on the slave export duties. Pombal referred again to the principle of freedom of trade to justify its termination, without remarking on the irony of the rationale from the point of view of the Luso-Africans. The holder of the contract let for 1766–71, Domingos Dias da Silva, under obvious pressure from the reforms in the Asian trade and the regimentation of slaving in the interior, had fought back with every means at his command. As the India ships of 1766 and 1767 stopped at Luanda, as required, at the start of the term of Dias da Silva's contract, his administrators responded by filling the city with *livranças*. The contract holders in Lisbon—the nominal owner and the consortium of backers behind him—disclaimed responsibility for the tactic, alternatively blaming the administrators of the previous contract for the flood of worthless paper and denying any connection with allegedly independent issuance of these notes by the traders they had innocently hired to represent them in Angola.[64] When government officials in Luanda then tightened their super-

61. E.g., Ralph Delgado, "O governo de Sousa Coutinho em Angola," *Studia* 6 (1960): 19–56; 7 (1961): 49–86; 10 (1962): 7–48.

62. The *bando*, nominally directed at criminals, was dated 26 Oct. 1769 and was forwarded by Sousa Coutinho on 4 Dec. 1769, AHU, Angola cx. 32. See also the similarly harsh terms of another proclamation directed at Africans absent from their home territories, 2 Nov. 1769, enclosed in same.

63. Sousa Coutinho, 15 March 1770, AHU, Angola cx. 32.

64. *Requerimento* of Domingos Dias da Silva and Jozé Alvares Bandeira, n.d. (ca. 1767), AHU, Angola maço 13; also *requerimento* of Domingos Dias da Silva, n.d., AHU, Angola cx. 36.

vision of the operations of the contract, the contractors in Lisbon transferred their attention to less closely watched Benguela, continuing their accustomed practices of engrossing the trade by accepting only ivory in satisfaction of slave duties and leaving Benguela filled with "less valuable forms of assets," presumably *livranças*.[65] At Benguela, where bills of exchange owed to competitors did not circulate as they did at Luanda, ivory must have constituted the only asset transferrable to Brazil that the contractors could monopolize. Also, when tensions rose during the drought of 1765–67, Sousa Coutinho complained that the Luanda administrators of the contract were refusing to heed his pleas to stock ships they had sent over from Brazil with adequate food to sustain the slaves on the return journey. As a result of their "laxity," slaves were dying in Angola and at sea, and the survivors were selling poorly in Brazil.[66] The administrators of the contract even had the effrontery to resist making their required payments to the Angola treasury in good bills of exchange drawn on Brazil, doubtless attempting to pay in *livranças* instead; and when constrained to agree to yield up bona fide bills, they still delayed or used the pretext of loss to evade presenting them to government treasurers in Brazil.[67]

But caution was advisable in moving too directly against the contractor, since the Pernambuco Company and other Lisbon merchants had outstanding loans in trade goods made to the same Angolan debtors who owed the contract for duties on the slaves they shipped, or were in debt to the administrators for goods they had borrowed. The administrators of the contract could invoke their executive privilege in judicial proceedings against insolvent debtors at any time and thus claim assets owed to others. The low slave prices of the 1760s in Brazil had placed Angolan slavers in generally precarious financial condition, and under these circumstances the contractors could simply liquidate and leave the competing, but subordinated, claims of the company all but worthless.[68] The pigeons that the 1758 free trade decrees had released into the colony's interior were coming home to roost. Overextended loans permitted the contractor to hold the Luso-Africans of Angola hostage against further assault from his enemies in Lisbon, perhaps not entirely against the will of the hostages at a moment when the downturn in slave prices had exposed them also to jeopardy from Sousa Coutinho and the companies. Meanwhile, the contractor was using tried-and-true financial manipulations to substitute his own *livranças* for Luso-African slaves owed the wealthy merchants favored by Pombal.

---

65. *Parecer* of the Conselho Ultramarino, n.d. (ca. 1769), AHU, Angola maço 17 (D.O.).

66. Sousa Coutinho, 28 May and 18 Aug. 1766, AHU, Angola cx. 31.

67. Sousa Coutinho, 28 May 1766, AHU, Angola cx. 31; cf. Manuel Pinto da Cunha e Souza, 23 Oct. 1767, AHU, Angola cx. 15.

68. Sousa Coutinho, 20 Aug. 1768, AHU, Angola cx. 31, explains the entire affair in these terms.

By 1769 the situation had gone beyond the tolerance of the government. Pernambuco Company initiatives clearly lay behind the final decision to abolish the contract, as its directors were not satisfied at all with the Angolan end of their operations. The company's Luanda administrators had virtually greeted Sousa Coutinho upon his arrival in Angola with sharp complaints against the financial manipulations of the contract holders of 1760–65.[69] The proceedings that finally eliminated these abuses coincided with a renewed Pernambuco Company complaint directly to the court in Lisbon, supported by a letter from Sousa Coutinho confirming the company's allegations.[70] Before this formal complaint from Luanda could have reached Lisbon, the Crown issued a decree annulling the contract as of the end of 1769, two years before the end of an agreement scheduled to run through 1771.[71]

The cancellation rested on the grounds that the holders of the contract had consistently perverted its intended purposes of collecting slave export duties to monopolize the trade in imports, in flagrant violation of the principles of free trade declared in 1758. True enough, with respect to purposes both stated and unstated. The decree went on to review the techniques based on the *livranças* and on liberal credit in trade goods that the contractors had used to abuse their privileges in Angola. It fixed the blame squarely on the Lisbon owners of the contract, absolved their administration in Luanda of guilt, and transferred collection of future slave duties directly to the royal treasury.[72]

The contractors' substantial ownership of the credit extended in the Angolan economy, together with the precariousness of the colony's debt structure in the 1760s, the delays and difficulties of setting up local sources of credit and currency to replace those supplied by the contract, and the failure of the Pernambuco and Maranhão companies to fulfill their expected promise in this last regard, had all delayed direct action on this front long after the Crown had reduced the power of other elements of the old regime in Portugal, as early as 1758–59 with wide-ranging investigations of nobles accused of conspiracy against the king and expulsion of the Jesuits from the entire empire. Lisbon had reformed other aspects of its fiscal administration in 1761. That it was still necessary, even in 1769–70, to manage with great care the transition to a slave trade in Angola financed without the contractor testifies eloquently to the enormous power of these old interests over the economy of the imperial periphery.

69. Sousa Coutinho, 4 Aug. 1764, AHU, Angola cx. 30.

70. Sousa Coutinho, 17 July 1769, AHU, Angola cx. 32; also see "Introdução previa ou demonstração da Ruina, em que ainda se acha o Reino de Angola . . ." (incomplete fragment), July 1769, AHU, Angola cx. 32.

71. *Alvará* of 5 Aug. 1769, accompanied by private instructions, AHU, Angola maço 2-A; AHTC, "Livro no. 1 de registo das provisões e cartas régias expedidas para Angola . . . ," fols. 28–29.

72. Sousa Coutinho, 17 May 1770, AHU, Angola maço 13.

The *alvará* implementing the decree of abolition therefore condemned the *livranças* as counterfeit currency but also protected the Angolan economy by requiring the contractors to make good on all obligations outstanding in that form. It ordered them to redeem within two weeks all such notes presented to them, after which time the government would no longer recognize the *livranças* as legal tender. Redemption on such short notice could, of course, exhaust the liquid assets of the contractors and expose them to default and their assets to seizure by the government under the terms of the *alvará*. The government was thus turning the tables on the last of a line of contractors who had long employed the very same technique to bankrupt their customers and competitors. In any event, the contractors stood to lose substantial sums as the *livranças'* value inflated in anticipation of the deadline, in addition to conceding their legal privileges and prospects for further gains from trading in Angola. Many of the payments ordered would have gone directly to the Pernambuco Company, evidently a major holder of the notes, while those made to Luso-African owners of *livranças* would presumably end up also in the hands of the company administrators as creditors of the indebted slavers of the interior. The company's remaining debts would then be pressed safely, without losses to the prior claims of the defunct contract, and it may have been much more than coincidental that Sousa Coutinho's strongly worded orders calling all traders in the interior to reside in closely supervised towns and *feiras* followed these arrangements by only two months. There they would have been accessible to company legal proceedings.

The intended victims of Lisbon's power play responded predictably, in view of their established strategies. The contract holders in Lisbon filed a lengthy petition in defense of their conduct and laid all the abuses at the door of the holders of the preceding contract, who, they alleged, had issued most of the *livranças* then in circulation and had forced their own administrators to back those notes out of fear of ruining the export trade (and, of course, also the king's own revenues) by disavowing the economy's main source of credit. No one reading these charges would have missed the implied criticism of royal instructions that had just commanded the damaging step they themselves had loyally, and now at great personal cost, refrained from taking. Further, the administrators had issued the *livranças* entirely on their own initiative and against the express orders of their employers in Lisbon. Finally, the king's own governor in the colony, Sousa Coutinho himself, had contributed to the excess of *livranças* by hesitating to withdraw the credit that propped up slave exports that would otherwise have declined as the Brazilian economy slumped with low commodity prices and declining gold production. They thus neatly summarized the effect of Lisbon's indirect financial role in Angolan slaving, promoting sales of goods without responsibility for either the associated costs in slave mortality or the oversupply of labor in Brazil.

Pushing self-exculpation to an extreme that must have struck free traders in Lisbon as wholly implausible, the contract-holders claimed further that it had been only their own complaints about their predecessors that had finally forced a reluctant (and presumably complicit) colonial governor to report the abuses that finally led the Crown to terminate the contract system. Sousa Coutinho, they alleged (and they might have added Pombal's first appointment as governor, Vasconcelos, as well), had continued the universally condemned seventeenth-century practices of the Brazilian governors, allying with favored merchant importers and pushing goods into the interior through the *capitães-mores*. And they were right enough, if one chose to look at the companies and the new nomination procedures for commanders of the colonial districts.

These uncomprehending practitioners of older forms of commerce, perhaps with the insight of those who understood little of the rhetoric of modern capitalism, sensed the extent to which their liberal adversaries conducted "free trade" through government-chartered companies and carefully selected military captains in charge of tightly controlled government markets in the interior. Like the little boy who saw the king's new clothes for what they really were, or weren't, the contractors argued with plausible sincerity that these liberal arrangements precisely duplicated the very practices that Sousa Coutinho and Pombal had proclaimed freedom of trade to oppose.

It required the passion of these beleaguered nonbelievers to penetrate the ideological veils of "freedom of trade" in Angolan slaving in a representation to the king, but few among the Luso-Africans, who also traded by other standards, would have been deceived either. The petitioner, in fact, associated himself with the traders in Angola, noting that he was a businessman experienced there from 1750 to 1764. He used this fact to distance himself even more from the condemned financial maneuvers of other "interested parties" in Lisbon, whom he served only as a front man. There was undoubtedly truth in this allegation, too. The petition then concluded much more threateningly by hinting at the substantive legal issue involved, laying out the basis on which the contractors could apply the executive privilege conceded in the cancelled contract to seize the assets of their own administrators and of all other debtors in Luanda as they followed the Crown's orders in redeeming the *livranças*.[73] According to Sousa Coutinho, they proceeded to do just that,[74] thus realizing what had all along been the worst fears of the government.

The contractors thus retreated, firing back over their shoulders a final volley of the financial barrage that had made the contract so valuable from

---

73. *Requerimento* of Domingos Dias da Silva, n.d. (ca. 1772?), AHU, Angola cx. 36.
74. Sousa Coutinho, 3 June 1770, AHU, Angola cx. 32.

the start. Its opportunities for creating debt in Angola by making credit sales of goods at high prices, for manipulating the colonial markets in means of payment for the goods, and for seizing the most valuable assets of defaulters who became casualties of their generosity—*letras* whenever possible, and not slaves—gave the contract-holders the specie and other wealth remittable to Portugal and left their competitors and customers with inventories of unwanted goods, bad debts, worthless *livranças,* and dying slaves that circulated on the debtor side of the southern Atlantic economy.

The debtors of the colony, consulted formally under the near-emergency circumstances of 1770, attempted to appropriate the transition to give themselves some breathing room. They emphasized the threat to slaving and the Crown's revenues occasioned by Pombal's order to call in the debts of the contract, combined with the inability of the Pernambuco Company to replace the capital withdrawn. They carefully explained the dependence of the interior trade on credit and stressed the slowness with which any supplier in Luanda could expect to collect returns on the goods he thus risked. They assured the government that they would eventually pay all that they owed both the company and the contract. Citing the intimate knowledge of these and other local conditions required to administer the affair without damage to the common interests of all, they offered to assess their own creditworthiness and to propose a timetable according to which all would loyally pay.[75]

This artfully crafted proposal remedied bankruptcy by self-administration of the bankrupt. It also revealed the debtors' preference for the none-too-gentle methods of monopolist contractors over the relentless pressures they had experienced under Pombal's policies of free trade. Since they in effect asked for suspension of the contractors' executive privilege and thus for removal of the keystone of the contractor's strength in Angola, they might reasonably have expected a tolerant reception of what amounted to an alternative method of rendering the contract bankrupt, though to the advantage of the colonists rather than Lisbon. In the end, a compromise allowed the contract administrators two years to pay off the *livranças* for which they were responsible.[76]

The Luso-Africans fell back on other tricks tried and true to ease the adjustment in the years that followed cancellation of the contract. One unidentified faction attempted almost immediately to convert its control over the slaving trails inland from Luanda to engross the supply of slaves

---

75. In Sousa Coutinho, 3 June 1770, AHU, Angola cx. 32, copy of Assento de Junta sobre os executivos, and Termo que se fiz na prezença do Doutor Ouvidor Geral sobre os executivos, 10 March 1770.

76. AHTC, letter to Sousa Coutinho, 21 July 1770, livro no. 1, fols. 79–81; also Sousa Coutinho, 3 Jan. 1771, AHU, Angola cx. 33.

headed toward the city and thus force up the prices they could demand from company administrators desperate to load ships and recover on their own debts.[77] Where they obtained the assets is unclear, though growing Pernambuco Company shipments of slaves and credit in the interior might have attracted attention. Upon Sousa Coutinho's departure from the colony in 1772, and before his successor could gain control, the Luso-Africans celebrated what they must have seen as release from bondage by launching their military campaign against Mbailundu and other slave suppliers on the central plateau in 1773. This war—which turned into three years of unrestrained slave raiding throughout the highlands, with government munitions and authorization to impress Africans as warriors in the name of official conscription—must have produced hundreds of captives at little or no cost in further borrowings of trade goods. Sale of these slaves would have discharged a significant proportion of the Luso-Africans' indebtedness to the company and to others.[78] Continued resort to *reviros* and to smuggling with the British and French later in the 1770s, all in open defiance of the elaborate prohibitions that Sousa Coutinho had left on the colony's law books,[79] must also have helped traders to restore their creditworthiness in the aftermath of the contract's elimination.

The government utterly failed to provide other forms of credit that would adequately replace the *livranças* retired by the contractors. The colonial treasury, through its local board (Junta da Fazenda), created as part of the empirewide fiscal reforms of 1761,[80] took over collection of the slave export duties, which gave it the assets necessary to float bills of its own in place of the contract administrators' *livranças,* with backing no less theoretical than the condemned private notes. Lisbon seems to have intended that the Pernambuco Company supply some of the needed funds, but it was in fact unable to do so.[81] The Treasury in Lisbon managed to send a modest amount of coin, and the local government issued notes payable at specified terms from deposits that it held (from slave duties paid there) in the fiscal "Inspection Boards" established to handle transfers of government funds in Brazil.[82] But none of these measures sufficed, and as the Pernambuco Company gradually withdrew its investment in An-

77. *Bando* of Sousa Coutinho, 18 Oct. 1771, AHU, Angola cx. 33.

78. Sousa Coutinho had understood very well the purposes and functions of the war when it was first proposed: Sousa Coutinho to José Vieira d'Araujo, 12 Oct. 1769; Delgado, *Reino,* pp. 341–42; Felner, *Angola,* 1:170–72; Corrêa, *História de Angola,* 2:48–67, for the war and its abuses.

79. Câmara, 24 April 1780, AHU, Angola cx. 38.

80. Alden, *Royal Government,* pp. 279–311.

81. AHTC, letter to Sousa Coutinho, 22 Aug. 1770, livro no. 1, fols. 81–83; cf. Sousa Coutinho, 3 June 1770, AHU, Angola cx. 32, and enclosed Assento.

82. Conde de Oeyras to Sousa Coutinho, 21 Aug. 1770, AHU, Angola cx. 32; AHTC, *provizão* of 30 April 1772, livro no. 1, fols. 115–22.

golan slaving as it closed down its operations over the following decade, Lisbon lost control of the financing of the trade to the Brazilians. They were only too eager to use their growing connections with the British, their smuggling to the Spaniards, and their profits from a reviving agricultural sector to extend their transport of slaves to owning the people they carried.

Conclusion

The Pombal era, for all its failures in Angola, consolidated several broader trends in southern Atlantic slaving marginal to the decades that preceded it but central to those that followed. By limiting British influence in Portugal, particularly imports of the Manchester cottons then starting to replace Indian textiles in the African trade, the Portuguese ended up encouraging smuggling directly to Brazil rather than continued utilization of the Lisbon factors through whom British merchants had earlier sold woolens throughout the empire. British smuggling through Brazil accordingly became an important factor in Angola's slave trade for the governments that followed Pombal's at the end of the eighteenth century. By using the Pombaline companies to focus the metropolitan slaving initiative on Pernambuco and the northern captaincies, Lisbon left the Bahians free to develop their own slaving from Mina and allowed traders from Rio to become major factors in Angola. By eliminating the tenacious grip of the contractors over the paper currency of the Luanda economy and forcing Angolan slavers to liquidate parts of their trading operations, they left the Luso-Africans to smuggle more and more actively with the French around Benguela and with the British north of Luanda, not to mention to welcome new initiatives from Brazil. Portuguese credit, offered too late and in insufficient amounts to stem the tide pulling Angolan slaving out of Lisbon's hands, had the contradictory effect of speeding along the new capitalist currents that were drawing the southern Atlantic economy into British and Brazilian channels. Portuguese merchant capitalism under Pombal had made Angolan slaving at once more capitalist and less Portuguese.

17

The Dry Well, 1772–1810

Lisbon merchants, hampered by Portugal's growing economic weakness relative to Britain and by its dependence on its own colony of Brazil once the American agricultural economy began to revive in the 1770s and 1780s, could not match the resources that the Brazilians and foreigners invested by then in Angolan slaving.[1] They largely withdrew from Angola at the end of the century, and the Portuguese government pursued essentially negative and reactive policies intended primarily to protect its own tax revenues, secondarily to hinder British and French competition that diverted slaves from the Luanda customs house, thirdly to support the supply of labor to Brazil, and lastly, in Angola at most lay the groundwork for some future renewal of private commercial initiatives. These last would in fact never materialize, at least not with regard to slaving. In the meanwhile, Lisbon sharply reduced the financial and political commitment to the interior that had so challenged Sousa Coutinho and settled for policing the port towns and the coast.

Government Consolidation at the Coast, 1772–1810

Lisbon's overseas policy focused rather narrowly on Brazil at the end of the century, particularly after a political conspiracy in Minas Gerais discovered in 1788–89 drew shocked attention to the discontent then surfacing among the debtors in Portugal's wealthiest colony. In Angola, only confused and even contradictory failed initiatives characterized the period between Sousa Coutinho's departure in 1772 and the opening of Brazil to British trade in 1810. The goods supporting trade in the interior belonged mostly to Brazilian and Luso-African interests, not Portuguese, and Lisbon clearly had mixed feelings about defending them. To the limited extent that Lisbon's moves in southern Atlantic slaving cohered into a

---

1. The most comprehensive summary of the statistics on Brazil's economy is Alden, "Late Colonial Brazil."

consistent thrust during this period, merchants reduced their role to that of buying slaves at Luanda for Maranhão, and probably also Pernambuco, while the government took advantage of fortuitous openings that presented themselves to attempt to expand its influence outward along the coast from Luanda.

The increasing remoteness of the sources of western central African slaves by that time framed the metropolitan merchants' tendency to withdraw their investments from the interior. The greater distances sharply raised the cost of credits in trade goods for the creditors no less than for the Luso-Africans, and the colonial government had no way to implement the grandiose administrative plans that Pombal and Sousa Coutinho had laid to protect the Lisbon importers' returns. These policies had in fact been self-defeating, since the credit sunk into the backlands in the 1750s and 1760s helped to propel the slaving frontier off toward the headwaters of the Zambezi and beyond the middle Kasai by the beginning of the nineteenth century. Supervision of trade through *feiras* and regimented settlements had proved failures even in the vicinity of Luanda by the late 1760s, and it made no sense at all to pursue similar plans at still further removes from the coast, in lands barely known to Europe.[2]

At the same time, conflict among the hard-pressed Africans during the ten years of severe drought in Africa from 1785 to 1794 generated war captives, and famine necessitated selling dependents who could not be fed at home, thus reducing the urgency of using commercial credit to stimulate sources of slaves. It therefore became possible for Lisbon to contemplate abandoning the colony's interior to its de facto Luso-African masters, in theory at least, if only officials could restrict the Luso-Africans' opportunities to buy goods from the French at Benguela and from the British and the French along the coasts north of Luanda. Otherwise, the government could hope to control deliveries of slaves indirectly through tightened administrative procedures at the colonial capital. Merchants from Lisbon would limit the credit they made available in the interior, sell their manufactures outright at the coast, take the risk of owning the slaves they acquired in return, and hope that trading gains from rising slave and commodity prices in Brazil would eventually yield a profit for the entire venture in Portugal.

Lisbon's generally lessened interest in Angola also allowed government policy to drift in the direction of consolidation. In the 1770s, at the end of Pombal's long tenure as chief minister, attention at the court turned

---

2. Nevertheless, government, as opposed to commercial, efforts at exploration continued to preoccupy officials in Lisbon and Luanda, in large part owing to their hope that Angola might provide a convenient route of access to the gold mines of southern Africa, which might help to make up for the decline in gold production in Brazil: Azevedo, "Princípios de uma economia de fixação," pp. 123–27.

toward fostering industrial development at home and toward Brazil. With the removal of Pombal from office in 1778 and the failure of the Pernambuco and Maranhão companies by 1782, Pombal's successors put all their energies into projects to secure some of the gains to be made from selling Brazilian sugar and cotton in Europe. Thus, the big Lisbon merchants, engaged primarily in selling American agricultural produce and supplying Brazil with European manufactures, had no strong objection to Rio slavers' reexporting their merchandise to buy slaves for themselves in Africa to power the Brazilian agricultural boom. The merchants' principal concern lay in preventing contraband British goods, also widely available in Brazil, from taking the place of their own merchandise.

The same higher Brazilian commodity prices that attracted the major Lisbon merchants directly to Brazil also supported an upturn in the value of slaves that encouraged lesser Lisbon investors to try their luck in Angola, risking ownership of slaves carried on the middle passage to penetrate soft spots in the colonial economy.[3] This group complained passionately about the prominence of the Brazilians in slaving but could not dislodge them. The group probably included domestic Portuguese industrial interests, who saw Luanda as a relatively promising market for their domestic linens, silks, woolens, and cotton textiles, as well as for hats, wearing apparel, and other products of national origin. The British goods reshipped to Brazil through Lisbon and smuggled in through Rio de Janeiro, aside from reinforcing the Brazilians' competitive edge in slaving, also limited the potential of the preferred American market for the uncompetitive manufacturers of the metropole. Direct slave trading also acquired a positive attraction during this period, as slaves could be sold in Maranhão and Pernambuco for the bullion then flowing from Portugal and Britain into the northern Brazilian cotton captaincies. Wealthy planters there were positioned financially to spend a portion of their specie for the slave labor they needed to increase the acreage they planted in cotton, and neither the British nor a strong competing community of Brazilian merchants barred entry.

Lisbon was thus left with a highly specialized trade in Angolan slaves bought through Luanda for delivery to Maranhão and Pernambuco, where payment could be expected in gold. Angola thus remained as it had frequently been before: a dumping ground for inferior wares and a back door through which the weaker commercial interests of the metropole sought American riches that otherwise eluded their grasp. On the whole, relatively few Lisbon merchants bothered to chance the circuitous and difficult route to Brazil through Angolan slaving. The 1780s and 1790s

---

3. One can sense the changeover in the prices reported from Luanda, where the old *letra* values, relatively stable and expressed in terms of the standard prime male, yielded in the 1770s and 1780s to market prices for individual slaves: Miller, "Slave Prices."

therefore became the years in which southern Brazilians, with indirect backing from British and Anglo-Portuguese merchants, virtually overwhelmed the Luanda and Benguela portions of Angolan slaving not already dominated directly by northern Europeans.

The British and French bought slaves everywhere else. They had turned to western central Africa with new determination after 1763, and they traded constantly during the next forty years whenever their recurrent naval conflicts did not prevent their ships from reaching the southern Atlantic. They were in part fleeing rising costs of slaves from West Africa, and the British in particular found their aging sugar plantations in the West Indies unable to bear the increased charges for labor that continued buying in West Africa would have implied by the 1780s. Delivery expense also increased for Britain after 1788, in the wake of parliamentary restrictions on the carrying capacity of British slavers, and slavers therefore sought lower costs of acquiring labor in central Africa to compensate for reduced margins on the middle passage. The French were exploiting every possible source of captive labor between 1783 and 1791 to satisfy exploding demands for slaves on their sugar plantations on Saint Domingue. The extent to which Lisbon funds ended up supporting these French and British slavers through *reviros* also tempted Lisbon to reduce its commitment to the interior during the 1770s, while trying to block the Luso-Africans' opportunities to divert the slave proceeds of loans to the foreigners by securing the coasts. Reduced credit would inhibit the Luso-Africans' ability to engage in this sort of contraband.

Lisbon's limited strategy in Angola after the early 1770s made good sense, finally, in view of the fact that the interested sectors of the domestic economy possessed nothing near the capital resources that they needed to compete with the great wealth of the British and French, not to mention the resources available in Brazil from sugar, cotton, and the British. Better in this situation to allow the Angola backlands to take care of themselves, to occupy outlying coasts when the British and French momentarily withdrew during their internecine conflicts, restrict the entry of illicit British cottons from Brazil at Luanda and Benguela, and count on the colonial courts to foreclose against Angolan slavers who persisted in engaging in the debt-based trade of an earlier era. Angolan slaves they would temporarily allow the southern Brazilians to buy for themselves, so long as the Brazilians sold only colonial products or goods supplied them by Lisbon merchants, and did so on terms that did not prevent Lisbon from conducting its own small competing trade to the northern ports in Brazil. With respect to supplies of slaves at Luanda, the Africans could apparently be counted on to deliver the required numbers on their own initiative, particularly if encouraged indirectly and inexpensively in ways that did not involve major investments of scarce domestic capital in colonial administration.

The trend toward outright metropolitan purchases of slaves, coupled with Brazilian inclinations in the same direction, derived from several factors beyond the trading profits augured by high prices in Brazil. For one thing, the reliable rains of the 1770s must have reduced slave mortality at sea, and stricter government requirements for water, food, and sanitation aboard the slavers, proclaimed in 1770,[4] expressed at least Sousa Coutinho's interest in reducing the major risk involved in slave ownership. In addition, the government eliminated the old opportunities for private speculation in the bills of exchange used to avoid owning slaves when it took charge of the colonial currency after 1770. The unrecoverable loans of the Pernambuco Company must have made all too plain the disadvantages of excessive credit when not protected by legal privileges to claims on debtors' assets and by chances for financial manipulation.

By 1779, instructions issued to the governor-designate about to leave Portugal to take up his post in Angola clearly expressed Lisbon's interest in ceasing entirely the long-established emphasis on lending goods to the traders of the interior.[5] The governor, José Gonçalo da Câmara (1779–82), was also to explore constraints contained in the "free trade" decree of 14 November 1761 to recover debts then outstanding in the backlands, surely with understood emphasis on the slaves owed to the Pernambuco Company. Though Câmara, like many of his predecessors, found it impossible to recover the value of trade goods long since dispersed or to contain the Luso-Africans' methods of avoiding metropolitan pressure, a new Lisbon preference for buying slaves in Luanda on a cash basis (though with goods) was becoming clear.

But not without risks. Lisbon's withdrawal of funds from the commercial economy of the interior in the 1770s threatened to reduce the volume of slaves it produced, and all the more so during that decade of unusually reliable rains. If so, an implicit two-pronged strategy constructed to maintain the level of slave exports and government revenues at low cost, both in commercial investments and administrative costs, would explain the limited image of the 1770s available from the scant records of the period: the government concentrated its own energies on expelling foreigners from their main areas of buying slaves at the coast, while allowing the Luso-Africans to resort to military methods that they had used long before to capture slaves in the interior without relying on commercial capital.

Fending off the foreign traders at the coast continued policies that Sousa Coutinho had initiated in the 1760s. He had placed a garrison at the mouth of the Kikombo River, where slaves from the central highlands,

---

4. Chapter 11, above.
5. Draft *regimento*, 22 June 1779, AHU, Angola maço 3 (D.O.).

mostly originating at Mbailundu, were reaching the sea. The French had been the most frequent buyers there since resuming large-scale slaving following the end of the Seven Years' War in 1763.[6] He had followed up this establishment of what became Novo Redondo by occupying the nearby mouth of the Kuvo in 1771 also, evidently to block an alternative outlet for the same trade route from the interior through which slaves continued to leak out to the French.[7] He had also authorized the first government expedition intended to reconnoiter the barren far southern coasts, particularly the mouth of the Kunene, the bay at Cabo Negro (modern Porto Alexandre), and the Angra do Negro at the mouth of the Kubal River (modern Moçâmedes, or Namibe), where the French bought slaves from Humbe, Huila, and Njau.[8] Sousa Coutinho's reforms of the Benguela administration formed the best-known aspect of the broad attention he had paid to southern Angola.

French ships seem to have called along these remote shores on their return from the Indian Ocean, where they had gone to buy Mozambique slaves for the sugar plantations of the Mascarenes Islands. For the return journey to the Atlantic, they must have carried the Asian cottons available everywhere along their Indian Ocean itinerary for sale in southern Angola, where the standard course from the Cape to the North Atlantic carried them close to the shore. Riding the currents and winds along the coast, they stopped also at Benguela and as far north as the Kuvo and the Kikombo for Angolan slaves that they could sell for further gains in the Caribbean on their way back to France.[9] Their Asian goods would have filled the Angolan demand for goods formerly supplied by the contractors until their elimination in 1769 and since 1772 available only through Portugal. While some French vessels directly out from Europe may also have participated in the southern Angolan trade, they would have had few goods to offer the African buyers on terms superior to the Brazilians there, other than glass beads and miscellaneous products of French industry. The circuitous outbound course from Europe through the western Atlantic made southern Angola excessively remote compared to the much more

6. Delgado, *Reino*, pp. 307–17. The French had long been active at the mouth of the Kikombo: Antonio de Albuquerque, 23 Jan. 1724, AHU, Angola cx. 16. Also see Corrêa, *História de Angola*, 2:36–37.

7. Delgado, *Reino*, pp. 330–34.

8. Ibid., pp. 329–30; Felner, *Angola*, 1:177–86; *Arquivos de Angola* 1, no. 2 (n.d.): doc. xviii.

9. Sousa Coutinho, 26 Nov. 1772, AHU, Angola cx. 36. Cf. the description of the Indian Ocean end of this trade in Stein, *French Slave Trade*, pp. 119–26. Its Angolan variant, or coda, seems relatively unknown to historians. Nigel Worden, *Slavery in Dutch South Africa* (Cambridge: Cambridge University Press, 1985), p. 43, notes that the French slavers sold part of the cargoes of slaves they had acquired in Mozambique at the Cape of Good Hope on their return. They may well have replenished the slaves sold, and also replaced those lost to mortality, as they passed Angola.

accessible coasts of Loango.[10] Some ships from the Indian Ocean may have begun buying slaves at the Kunene, then stopped at every port on down the coast, and concluded their purchasing at Loango.

Accommodating the Luso-Africans

The next governor, D. António de Lencastre (1772–79), arrived in Luanda with instructions to further Sousa Coutinho's efforts to expand Portuguese authority along the coast, particularly to the north of Luanda. Amidst audacious proposals to station a frigate to patrol the bays where foreigners traded, he settled for a more judicious beginning by dispatching a small launch merely to report on the situation north of Luanda as far as Loango.[11]

Simultaneously Lencastre abandoned his predecessor's measures to bring the Luso-Africans of the colony under the control of the government, apparently on the assumption that closer control over their outlets for selling slaves north of Luanda would force them back into Lisbon's fold, whatever happened in the backlands. This reorientation of government strategy took place against the advice contained in memorials that Sousa Coutinho had left to orient his successor and over repeated objections that Sousa Coutinho submitted to the court in Lisbon after his return to Portugal,[12] in part because it limited colonial economic policy to slave-trading, as opposed to Sousa Coutinho's much broader—and expensive–stress on agricultural and industrial development in the colony.[13] The return to using Angola primarily as a source of slaves for Brazil, without significant metropolitan investment of either commercial or industrial capital, conformed to the priority the late Pombal regime gave to manufacturing at home in Portugal, and secondarily in Brazil, and to the extension of those development policies under the governments that followed Pombal's fall in 1778.

Lencastre thus seems to have arrived predisposed to cooperate with the rude *capitães-mores,* the Luso-African clans, and the local allies whom Sousa Coutinho had so despised.[14] His personal willingness to collaborate

10. Seemingly implied in Sousa Coutinho, 26 Nov. 1772, AHU, Angola cx. 36; specified in draft *regimento* (Câmara), 22 June 1779, AHU, Angola maço 3 (D.O.).

11. Souza Magalhães, 18 March 1773, AHU, Angola cx. 36; Lencastre, 22 Sept. 1774, AHU, Angola cx. 36.

12. "Memorias do Reino de Angola," *Arquivos de Angola* 4, no. 49 (1939): 172–209; Felner, *Angola,* 1:188–209. Also see AHU, Angola cxs. 31, 36.

13. António Brásio, "Descripção dos governos dos Ill.^{mos} e Ex.^{mos} Snr.^{es} António de Vasconcellos, e D. Francisco Innocencio de Souza Coutinho," *Studia* 41–42 (1979): 210, 214, stresses Lencastre's hostility to the centerpiece of Sousa Coutinho's efforts to diversify the Angolan economy—the iron foundry at Nova Oeiras in the lower Lukala valley.

14. Though not necessarily those in artisan categories, as Sousa Coutinho attempted to train local youths in the badly needed skills in his industrial program when European workmen who had been brought down to do the job all died: Brásio, "Descripção," p. 222.

with the Luso-Africans must have come in part from his own primary experience as a military officer prior to coming out to Angola, but he must also have been concerned to establish his own authority as governor in a context still dominated by Sousa Coutinho's strong impact on the colony, the instructions Sousa Coutinho bequeathed for its governance, and the allies he must have left in place for their execution.[15] Against those considerable odds Lencastre would have had little choice but to cultivate his own allies among his predecessor's Luso-African enemies, even at the risk of confronting their tendency, once endowed with the military patents and supplied with the government munitions he had to offer, to convert official missions to the interior into private raiding for slaves. On the other hand, Lencastre could tolerate Luso-African perversions of short-term government policies of military restraint so long as his colonial allies' wars served the longer-term goal of channeling the slaves they captured through Luanda, rather than diverting their human booty to foreigners anchored in outlying bays, all without the continued cost of bad debts in the backlands.

Lencastre's first lesson in the entanglements of Angolan politics came soon after his initial endorsement of local proposals for military action. In 1773 he supported the local Novo Redondo commander's aggressive methods of punishing Africans who were selling slaves to the French near there.[16] No doubt Lencastre could present his decision as following the established policy of controlling the coast without giving direct affront to the powerful French. He did not, however, make the distinction Sousa Coutinho had observed between cutting off slaves offered to the foreigners at the coast and involving the government in Luso-Africans' pleas for war to avenge insults, provoked or not, to Portuguese prestige in the interior. The initial raid thus escalated into full-scale war lasting three years.

Sousa Coutinho had earlier specifically rejected nearly identical petitions from the Benguela Luso-Africans for military action against Mbailundu sellers of slaves to the French at Novo Redondo.[17] Lencastre, evidently not anticipating the intensity of the long-standing battle between the Luso-Africans of Pungo Andongo and other regions east of Luanda and others from Benguela over the slave-supply regions on the northern slopes of the central plateau, authorized both factions to proceed under arms toward Mbailundu in the name of the king. The resulting disorderly campaigns of 1773–75 were marred by internecine feuding among the competing leaders of the various companies composing the army.[18] The war hardly

---

15. For the tone of the time, see Corrêa, *História de Angola*, 2:44 ff.

16. The versions of what happened differ—often an indication of the political sensitivity of the events reported; compare Corrêa, *História de Angola*, 2:36, 46, and Torres, *Memórias*, p. 267.

17. Sousa Coutinho to José Vieira d'Araujo, 12 Oct. 1769, in Felner, *Angola*, 1:170–72, doc. 5.

18. Corrêa, *História de Angola*, 2:48–68.

raised the number of slaves available for taxation at Benguela and Luanda, perhaps again demonstrating the inefficiency of raiding as a source of slaves from the government's point of view, though probably also confirming its effectiveness as a substitute for drought and borrowed trade goods to Luso-Africans lacking both in the 1770s.

Doubtless with these painful lessons in mind, Lencastre shifted his tactics over to the administrative terrain of his predecessor. He reversed the political impact of at least two key institutions that Sousa Coutinho had employed to favor Lisbon traders at the expense of the Luso-Africans. Pombal's reservation of priority in the order of ship departures for metropolitan shippers, in terms of *efeitos próprios,* Lencastre expanded to include local slaveowners by interpreting the criterion of ownership to apply to slaves on the departing ships as well as to trade goods on vessels entering the port. This revisionary broadening of the decree of 1758 allowed merchants in Luanda and Benguela to combine their slaves under temporary *sociedades,* or partnerships, that met Lencastre's loose standards for priority in dispatches from the port.[19] Favoritism toward the Luso-Africans in this case set back mainly the Brazilians, momentarily the only competing buyers of slaves at Luanda, while Brazilian prices had not yet risen high enough to attract Lisbon merchants as direct purchasers. The modification would not have hurt the failing Pernambuco Company, which was then shifting toward carrying slaves for others and would have lost the priority accorded it on the out-of-date assumption that it would always own the cargoes on its ships. Lencastre's expansion of Lisbon's former favoritism toward traders from the metropole thus promised to attract Luso-African slave sellers to Luanda at little cost to Lisbon commerce, though without repeal of legislation that might later prove useful again in its original sense.

At the same time Lencastre took Sousa Coutinho's regulated marketplaces away from the agents of Lisbon capital appointed as clerks to use the *feiras* to collect slaves that indebted Luso-Africans owed them. These *feiras* had been prime battlegrounds in the offensive of the previous administration, since they were the frontier areas where the latest generation of Lisbon merchants had invested much of their trade goods and were also the sources of the slaves whom the Luso-Africans of Ambaca and Pungo Andongo diverted to foreigners both south and north of Luanda. In the name of curbing "excesses" attributed to the *escrivães*—surely the very draconian practices that these clerks had been appointed to apply to safe-

---

19. Lencastre, 27 July 1775, AHU, Angola cx. 36; Castro Barboza, 1 Aug. 1781, AHU, Angola cx. 38; Homem e Magalhães, 16 Nov. 1786, AHU, Angola maço 13 (D.O.). Corrêa, *História de Angola,* 1:46–47, observed conditions not long afterwards in Luanda, perhaps from the inexpert perspective of a professional military man, and perceived no significant distinction in practice between the two categories of ships, *de bando* and *efeitos próprios.*

guard the "integrity of commerce," but reinterpreted from the Luso-African point of view as "abuses"—Lencastre issued new regulations returning the conduct of business in the far eastern and southeastern slave markets at Beja, Haco, and Kasanje to the traders.[20]

In combination, Lencastre's two measures clearly signaled that the Luso-Africans could afford to abandon their dealings with the foreigners and expect to trade on an equal basis with merchants representing Lisbon through the institutions of the colonial government in the valleys of the Kwango, the Kwanza, and the Ngango rivers, where the three *feiras* in question were situated, and at Luanda. Lencastre also reported scathingly back to Lisbon on the harsh commercial practices that Pernambuco Company administrators employed to wind up their business by collecting on the debts they had sunk in the interior.[21] Through these reforms Lencastre in effect finally freed "free trade" in the interior, and the volume of slaves passing through Luanda dropped for two years in succession in 1776 and 1777. The loss came entirely at the expense of the Pernambuco Company.[22]

The Angolan Market

Lencastre's successor, José Gonçalo da Câmara, introduced Angola to the implications of the emphasis of the post-Pombal government in Lisbon on domestic economic development. The government's renewed search for overseas markets in the colonies—though for domestic manufactures rather than for reexported foreign goods—sent Câmara off to Angola with elaborate instructions intended to heal the injury to Portuguese commerce that Brazilian control of the trade in slaves inflicted and to repair the damage to Lisbon's interests done by foreign goods' circulating within the empire.[23]

Lisbon's general effort to sell domestic manufactures in the colonies appeared in Angola most clearly in directives virtually ordering governors to allow gunpowder to pass into the backlands in quantities that the governors responsible for peace and security within the colony found highly unsettling. Lencastre, about the time that he reformed trade in the interior in favor of the Luso-Africans, had prohibited imports of powder and had virtually confiscated stores of it from private homes in Luanda.[24]

20. "Regimento dos escrivães das feiras de Cassange, Haco e Beja," 29 July 1775, AHU, Angola cx. 51, published in Couto, *Capitães-mores*, pp. 373–76.

21. Lencastre, 27 July 1775, AHU, Angola cx. 36.

22. Miller, "Legal Portuguese Slaving," p. 164, Table 1; Carreira, "Companhias pombalinas de navegação," p. 77.

23. Draft *regimento*, 22 June 1779, AHU, Angola maço 3 (D.O.).

24. *Bando* of 18 March 1776, AHU, Angola cx. 37. The issue had a long history, with governors generally against imports of powder but Sousa Coutinho strongly in favor.

Restrictions of this sort clearly protected the Luso-Africans from armed African assault in the interior, but they also deprived Lisbon of a market for one of the few products of Portuguese industry competitive in the African market. The Lisbon-appointed Crown justice (*ouvidor*) accordingly refused to prosecute smugglers under the terms of Lencastre's prohibition.

Câmara's 1779 instructions made clear the interest of the government in promoting sales of Portuguese gunpowder in Angola and urged a compromise level of imports that would partially satisfy both sides in the dispute.[25] Apparently Câmara was unable to work out an agreement with local traders that was acceptable to Lisbon arms dealers, and so the secretary of state for the colonies in Lisbon, Martinho de Mello e Castro—basing his argument on metropolitan rationalizations that African "savages" used muskets only for hunting and still made war exclusively with bows, arrows, spears, and hatchets—made it clear that he expected his governor to lift existing restrictions on sales of powder in the backlands.[26] Pressures like these smacked loudly of Lisbon's unwillingness to take responsibility for the interior of its colony, or for its inhabitants.

Câmara made greater progress in pursuing the second prong of Lisbon's dual policy, the extension of Portuguese authority out along the coasts beyond Luanda Bay itself. With the French and British temporarily distracted by their own wars after 1778, the governor expected to take advantage of the momentary drop in their slaving along the coasts north of Luanda to erect a fortified Portuguese stronghold at Cabinda on the Loango Coast.[27] The plan not only foresaw a fortification that could repel the foreigners when they might attempt to return but also sought to impose export duties on the slaves from Luanda's hinterland that were leaving Africa along that portion of the shore.[28] French and British withdrawal also created an opportunity for the Portuguese to smuggle slaves into the two northern European powers' sugar-producing islands in the Caribbean. The entire enterprise promised profits to Lisbon rather than to the Luso-Africans or the Brazilians, since it would block the foreign goods on which the Angolans depended, compete with Brazilian shippers, and supply slaves

25. Draft *regimento,* 22 June 1779, paras. 58–60, AHU, Angola maço 3 (D.O.).

26. Martinho de Mello e Castro (minister for the colonies) to Governor da Câmara, 8 Aug. 1782, AHU, Angola cx. 38. Cf. the *requerimento* from Manoel da Silva Ribeiro, n.d. (ca. 1778 or later), AHU, Angola maço 17 (D.O.). Other correspondence on the issue: Lencastre, 9 Oct. 1779, AHU, Angola cx. 37; Câmara, 22 Feb. 1780, AHU, Angola cx. 38. Lisbon's promotion of powder in the backlands continued on through the instructions given to Câmara's successor, Moçâmedes, in 1784: *apontamentos* (minuted by Mello e Castro, 23 March 1784), AHU, Angola maço 2-A.

27. Câmara, 20 Dec. 1779, AHU, Angola cx. 37; idem, 23 Feb. 1780, AHU, Angola cx. 38; Corrêa, *História de Angola,* 2:85.

28. *Provisão,* 18 Feb. 1784, AHTC, livro no. 1, fols. 293–95.

to foreign cane growers at the expense of Bahia and Rio de Janeiro sugar.[29] Câmara might well have anticipated opposition from the Luso-Africans and Brazilians then prominent in slaving at Luanda.

Implementation of this renewal of Lisbon's Loango strategy began with a second reconnoitering expedition sent north from Luanda in 1780 and continued with the dispatch of government troops to fortify and occupy a position at Cabinda in 1782.[30] Câmara died in the latter year, and Lisbon then sustained another lesson about the Luso-Africans' ability to thwart metropolitan initiatives not closely supervised by strong governors. The interim government that replaced him was a triumvirate that held office from 1782 to 1784 under the 1770 decree redefining the succession of powers to exclude the Luanda municipal council from twisting policies in the interest of the Luso-Africans. It included a prominent *coronel* of the Angolan militia, João Monteiro de Moraes; a king's justice hostile to the deceased governor; and the bishop. These three attempted to consolidate Luso-African control of the colony's government but had to yield to a corps of military officers fresh from Lisbon late in 1782.[31] That left the initiative to Portuguese who were sympathetic to metropolitan traders eager to expand their markets at the expense of Luso-African smugglers. In a hurry to get the planned expedition on its way to Cabinda before the French and British might return,[32] with peace negotiations proceeding at Paris in 1783, they assembled the expeditionary force and sent it off that same year. However, the Luso-Africans in Luanda fell back on their control of the food supplies to the city and refused to support the expedition with provisions[33] and diverted the personal followings they had collected as military reinforcements for the Cabinda garrison into a large unauthorized raid intended to recover slaves they owned who had fled to the maroon colony in Kisama.[34] Tried and true Luso-African techniques, based on their local control of land and labor, food and slaves, thus once again subverted Lisbon's efforts on behalf of metropolitan merchants.

The Peace of Paris enabled the French to return to Angolan coasts in 1783. The Luso-African betrayal had weakened the expeditionary force

29. It is unclear who in Lisbon might have promoted such a scheme, or rather, how parties so little committed to the Brazil trade could have obtained a hearing at high levels of the government.

30. Souza Magalhães, 16 March 1780, AHU, Angola cx. 37.

31. Cf. Chapter 16, note 53, above, on the decree of 12 Dec. 1770; Corrêa, *História de Angola,* 2:77; Peçanha, 6 Oct. 1783, AHU, Angola cx. 39. For more on the background to these events, see Miller and Thornton, "Chronicle as Source, History, and Hagiography."

32. Souza Magalhães, 8 Oct. 1784, AHU, Angola cx. 39.

33. Peçanha, 18 June 1783, AHU, Angola cx. 40; Souza Magalhães, 8 Oct. 1784, AHU, Angola cx. 39.

34. Corrêa, *História de Angola,* 2:93–96.

at Cabinda sufficiently that diseases and an alliance between the returning French and the African authorities at the bay wrecked Lisbon's plans.[35] In Luanda, the Luso-Africans opened the bay to foreign ships, piously (if unconvincingly) swearing that they intended to engage in no contraband trade with them.[36] Although the charge that the Angola Luso-Africans had diverted provisions to the Kisama raid might have been made falsely by the humiliated commanders of the debacle at Cabinda in order to cover their own incompetence or private designs, the Luso-Africans, emboldened by their recent successes in the war against Mbailundu and left to their own devices by the absence of most of the colony's paid government troops in Cabinda, could have only intended the Kisama expedition as subversion.

In the south, Câmara had to apply Lisbon's policy of occupying the coast not only against the French but also against the firm position at Benguela of the Brazilians, who had been linked since the victories of 1775 in the Mbailundu war in an alliance of unclear proportions with the Luso-Africans firmly in control of the slaving sources on the highlands. A Benguela *capitão* appointed directly from Portugal had arrived with the new Luanda governor to bring metropolitan authority, until then virtually absent at the southern Angolan port, to bear on Brazilians who introduced British goods smuggled through Rio de Janeiro and on local traders who dealt openly with the French.[37] This *capitão*, a certain Pimentel de Castro e Mesquita, made no impression on the entrenched local interests and seemed to express the hopelessness of his mission when he warned that the planned exclusion of foreigners from northern coasts would merely displace them to his own jurisdiction in the south.[38] As a remedy, he urged Lisbon to provide men and materiel to take military control of favored French trading spots in the vicinity of Cabo Negro, far to the south, as well.

The Moçâmedes Interlude

Though Lisbon heeded this advice, metropolitan objectives in Angola grew ambivalent and even contradictory in 1784 with restoration of metropolitan authority at Luanda through the arrival of the next governor, the energetic but enigmatic baron of Moçâmedes (1784–90). On the one hand, shipments of slaves for Brazilian agriculture could not be delayed

35. Ibid., pp. 79–92, 96–109.

36. *Governo interino*, 8 July 1784, AHU, Angola cx. 40; Mesquita, 16 and 25 Aug. 1783, AHU, Angola cx. 39.

37. Although Sousa Coutinho had raised the administrative status of the post from a *presídio* with a *capitão-mor* to a *capitania subalterna* (subordinate captaincy) with a *juiz de fora*; Delgado, *Reino*, pp. 334–36.

38. Mesquita, 27 Jan. 1783, in Felner, *Angola*, 1:211.

without dampening the export growth rapidly picking up steam in Brazil. On the other hand, Lisbon's Brazil faction had no real interest in undertaking the commercial investment in Africa needed to provide labor in America. That left Moçâmedes to reconcile the Luso-Africans and Brazilians (who were thus left to run the main branch of the trade) with competing initiatives coming apparently from a separate faction of Lisbon merchants who identified Angola as a promising market for the Indian cottons that returned briefly to the forefront of imperial policies at about that time. Moçâmedes, who had served as governor of the Brazilian captaincy of Goiás, seems to have found his way out of the dilemma by putting Luso-Africans, whom no committed partisan of Lisbon could possibly have trusted after the experiences of the previous ten years, safely in charge of measures he took in response to directives from Portugal. He seemed, in short, to pursue both policies at once—as contradictory signals from Lisbon all but forced him to do.[39]

The renewed Asian initiative originated as a side effect of Lisbon's efforts to counter growing British competition in the world market for India-style cottons. Portugal's own trade in Indian textiles must have faltered with Pombal's blow at the contractors in 1769, in the midst of general favoritism toward domestic cottons and reexports of northern European woolens and linens for Brazil. Pombal's successors attempted to revive the Asian textile business and to support domestic shipping by opening Portugal's western Indian port of Goa in 1783 to duty-free transport of textiles woven in surrounding producing areas that had fallen under British imperial control. They expected that the British East India Company would send its cottons through Goa to Lisbon for distribution in Europe, to Brazil, and doubtless also back to Angola.[40] The stratagem increased the number of Portuguese ships bringing Indian textiles around the Cape of Good Hope toward Lisbon, but it could not prevent them from stopping off at Benguela to resume the old practice of smuggling Asian textiles directly to eager creole buyers.[41] While Lisbon could hardly have failed to foresee the opportunity and might have viewed such contraband with mixed feelings at worst, since it seems to have reduced the activity of the French at Benguela for a few years between 1784 and 1787, Moçâmedes reported it with alarm. The competition these cottons also

39. The implication is that Moçâmedes may have favored the Brazilians then taking control of Angolan slaving. He was alleged to have returned to Lisbon a wealthy man after his six years in Angola: Vellut, "Relations internationales," p. 86, n. 14.

40. Bauss, "Legacy of British Free Trade Policies." Cf. the Francisco Henrique Hubens *memória* on assortments of India goods for trading in Angola, n.d. (ca. 1780s), AHU, Angola cx. 39.

41. Moçâmedes, 11 March 1784, and the anonymous *apontamentos*, n.d. (ca. 1784), AHU, Angola maço 2-A; Moçâmedes, 15 Oct. 1786, and 12 July 1787, AHU, Angola cx. 40; Junta da Fazenda do Reyno de Angola to Real Erario, 1791 *declaração*, AHU, Angola maço 5.

offered to the British goods of the Brazilians might account for some of his concern.

For the southern coast, Moçâmedes brought instructions to follow up on the suggestion of the new Benguela *capitão* to occupy Cabo Negro.[42] A recurrence of Moçâmedes's seeming ambivalence may help to explain the failure of the strategy he adopted to implement these orders, although the confused reports of what followed easily tolerate additional, and even alternative, explanations. The expedition to Cabo Negro, as Moçâmedes finally designed it, had two components, one sent south from Benguela by land and the other by sea, together ostensibly intended to deny the French further opportunities to buy slaves along that section of the coast. António José Valente, a reliable military officer from Lisbon, commanded the small vessel that set off upwind to reach the region by sea. But Moçâmedes appointed a local veteran of the wars that the Luso-Africans had conducted against Mbailundu in the 1770s, a certain António José da Costa evidently established in the trade of the Luanda area, to command an army sent off through the hinterland of Benguela toward Huila, Njau, and the Kunene, the interior sources of the slaves the French were buying, and then on to link up with Valente at the Kunene's mouth. He charged a three-man *junta* (commission) with overall responsibility for the mission. The triumvirate included Costa and a Lisbon majority of two, Valente and the famed Portuguese naturalist Joaquim José da Silva, who had arrived at Luanda with Moçâmedes.[43] The Lisbon pair could presumably outvote the local man, Costa, if the commission had to face choices with differing implications for Lisbon and any of its colonial opponents. Moçâmedes based the expedition at Benguela, perhaps expecting local support from Lisbon's chosen captain there, but also exposing it to intrigues from both the Brazilians and the Luso-Africans in influential unofficial positions.

In the event, none of these formal controls in the least deterred Costa from turning the expedition to his private advantage. He marched his forces up the hills inland from Benguela, settled down in Kilenges, the staging area where slavers coming off the high plateau prepared for the final trek down to the coast, and loosed the army he commanded on the government's behalf in a two-year private slave raid. In effect Costa renewed the Luanda Luso-African assault of the 1770s on sources of captives otherwise controlled by *sertanejos* of the highlands and by Brazilians at Benguela. Both these Benguela factions opposed Costa as an intruder representing Luanda interests, if not also those of Lisbon.[44] The Benguela

42. *Apontamentos,* n.d. (ca. 1784), AHU, Angola maço 2-A; Felner, *Angola,* 1:211.

43. William Joel Simon, "Scientific Expeditions in the Portuguese Overseas Territories, 1783–1808: The Role of Lisbon in the Intellectual-Scientific Community of the Late Eighteenth Century" (Ph.D. diss., City University of New York, 1974), pp. 161–213.

44. Moçâmedes, 11 Nov. 1785 and 18 Jan. 1786, AHU, Angola maço 4-B cont.;

capitão, evidently typical of early weak appointees in this position, was no greater help. He had welcomed the French as his personal allies against the local Benguela Luso-Africans and their Brazilian associates and had become the primary smuggler of slaves to them.[45]

Valente, although encountering predictable hostility in Benguela, fought his way against contrary winds and currents at sea to achieve a certain ephemeral success in occupying the mouth of the Kunene.[46] Later, upon his return to Lisbon, he puzzled discreetly in his report to the government over the project's failure, blaming Costa's depredations in the interior for a decline in ships leaving Benguela with slaves from twenty in 1784 to only fourteen and twelve in 1785 and 1786, respectively.[47] How, he wondered, could Governor Moçâmedes have rewarded so unworthy a man as Costa with subsequent appointments as *sargento mor,* by placing him in effective charge of the government troops in the colony and making him commander of the Luanda fortress of São Francisco do Penedo after Costa had subverted the government's purposes in the south of the colony? He complained of Costa's arrogation of his command, emphasized the harm he caused the Luso-Africans of the highlands, but gave no stress to his diversion of slaves from Brazilian shippers in favor of those from Lisbon. The colonial secretary in Lisbon must have considered these complaints well-founded, since he later brought charges against Moçâmedes in connection with actions that seemed to favor the Brazilians and Luso-Africans of Luanda at least as much as they hindered the French.

Moçâmedes' actions on another front reinforced this appearance of collusion with Brazilian and Luanda Luso-African interests, for he implemented the empirewide customs reform of 1784 only very reluctantly at Luanda. In 1782, the Treasury Board in Lisbon had undertaken to tighten controls against uninspected entries of British and other foreign goods throughout the empire while the principal smugglers were occupied with war against the French. Moçâmedes had brought to Luanda the royal order (the *carta regia* of 16 February 1784) creating a customs house with authority to open and inspect all goods entering the colony.[48] The Crown expressly denied any intention, for the present at least, of adding import

merchants' *requerimento,* Benguela, n.d. (ca. 1785?), AHU, Angola cx. 41; Valente, 8 Feb. 1791, AHU, Angola cx. 41 (published in Felner, *Angola,* 1:233–35); Mello e Castro, extract from instructions to Governor Almeida e Vasconcelos, Aug. 1791, Angola, maço 4-B cont.; Corrêa, *História de Angola,* 2:133, 135.

45. Moçâmedes, 24 Feb. 1796 (*parecer* on a *consulta* of the Conselho Ultramarino, 16 June 1796), AHU, Angola maço 6.

46. Felner, *Angola,* 1:229–35.

47. Ibid., p. 235n. Also see allegations of Moçâmedes's unresponsiveness to pleas from Benguela in Homem e Magalhães, 18 Aug. 1786, AHU, Angola maço 4-B cont.

48. *Carta regia,* 16 Feb. 1784, AHU, Angola cx. 54. See the more complete discussion of the Luanda customs house in Miller, "Imports at Luanda."

duties to the high prices slavers in Angola already paid for goods from Europe. Lisbon clearly meant to detect and confiscate wares of British origin smuggled through Brazil and then sent on to Angola rather than to handicap legitimate Lisbon goods with duties that would raise their prices further above those of the cheap competing merchandise the British offered on the coasts just north of Luanda. The royal order closed with explicit permission for gunpowder and firearms to enter the backlands of the colony, a prudent addendum on behalf of Lisbon merchants hoping to sell muskets and powder in competition with the British munitions industry.[49]

This move against the established contraband trade of the Luso-Africans and their Brazilian suppliers opened a struggle over inspection of imports at Luanda that continued throughout the following half-century. The royal order of 1784, though inserting the thin end of the wedge by creating a mechanism that could potentially collect duties in the future, reminded the residents of the colony of the existing decree that forbade establishment of any new duties on imports and reassured them that the new customs formalities were intended for statistical purposes only.[50] Documentation of their contraband was, of course, precisely what Luanda's smugglers feared.

Moçâmedes showed a sympathetic appreciation of the local point of view. He immediately warned Lisbon of "inconveniences" in the new order, not questioning the principles involved but rather emphasizing the hardships their implementation would impose on harried merchants whom it would require to stand long hours in the hot tropical sun waiting to see their goods dispatched. The procedures would also surely cause them losses by allowing the "thieving niggers" to steal the contents of bundles opened for inspection in the customs shed. The governor came closer to acknowledging the real issues behind the creation of the customs house by pointing out that a wave of Lisbon vessels, like the one that had showed up at Luanda in 1783 in vain anticipation of trading for slaves at Cabinda under the guns of the fortification erected there, would drive the Brazilians away from Luanda.[51] Moçâmedes then allowed local employees to run the new institution with such inefficiency that they managed to keep no records at all for an entire decade, or at least none that his successors could use to identify specific shipments or their owners.[52]

49. *Consulta* of the Junta do Comércio, 19 Aug. 1782, ANTT, Junta do Comércio, maço 62, macete 122; also preceding report from Câmara, 22 May 1781, AHU, Angola maço 17 (D.O.).

50. Moçâmedes, 23 Dec. 1784, AHU, Angola cx. 39.

51. Moçâmedes, 25 June 1785, AHU, Angola maço 13 (D.O.). Cf. Corrêa's deep resentment of the big Lisbon ships, dating from just this period: *História de Angola*, 1:48 ff.

52. De Mello, 30 May 1801, AHU, Angola cx. 51.

To the north, Moçâmedes began by taking firmer steps to protect Lisbon interests. Overt moves against British shipping there ran the risk of offending Portugal's most dangerous ally, and so Moçâmedes attempted to intercept slaves moving through the interior in the old Kongo kingdom toward Ngoyo from the middle Kwango. Greeted by an embassy from the ordained king of Kongo, customary at the arrival of new governors in Luanda, he took the opportunity to respond with a joint religious-commercial mission to both Kongo and Sonyo, its coastal rival south of the Zaire, in 1784–85.[53] The mission failed from Lisbon's point of view because the appointed ambassadors occupied themselves primarily in private trading, a miscarriage not without precedent in previous Lisbon moves that had been thwarted by Luso-Africans who were given the job because they alone had the knowledge of the interior to undertake such tasks. Given the prospect of customs inspections at Luanda, Luso-Africans must have regarded this expedition as a serious threat to their access to the British through Kongo and elsewhere.

Moçâmedes must have caused similar alarms among the Luso-Africans by simultaneously attempting to stop the flow of foreign goods and slaves up and down the Bengo through Musulu, just north of Luanda. He sent a friendly embassy to the "Marquis of Mossul," the potentate of the southern Kongo province of Musulu, who had waxed powerful from the influx of British and French goods destined for the Golungo, Icollo, and Dande districts just northeast of Luanda.[54] When Musulu rebuffed this overture, Moçâmedes then appointed his old henchman—the same António José da Costa, just back from his notorious misadventures in Kilenges—to lead a full-scale government military expedition across the Dande into Musulu in 1788.[55] Costa left Luanda over the nearly open opposition of the merchants in the city, but the Luso-Africans need not have worried, since Costa conducted himself true to his usual calculatedly self-interested form. In a year of deepening drought and famine, he privately stocked supplies of food from all around the vicinity of Luanda, delayed the advance of his army until his men had consumed all the rations provided by the government, and then sold off his hoarded stocks at famine prices.[56] Costa finally converted his personal opportunity into disaster for the colonial

53. Moçâmedes, 26 March 1787, AHU, Angola cx. 40; Corrêa, *História de Angola*, 2:145, 147. Sousa Coutinho had earlier made overtures toward Kongo authorities at Ambriz and Zaire: Sousa Coutinho, 28 Jan. 1771, AHU, Angola cx. 33; also Lencastre, 24 Sept. 1774, AHU, Angola cx. 36. Câmara brought explicit instructions to pursue these initiatives: draft *regimento*, 22 June 1779, AHU, Angola maço 3 (D.O.); see also the dreams of the *ouvidor*, Peçanha, 18 June 1783, AHU, Angola cx. 40; 6 Oct. 1783, AHU, Angola cx. 39; etc.

54. *Bando* (copy), 6 Feb. 1785, AHU, Angola cx. 52; Moçâmedes, 25 June 1785, AHU, Angola cx. 40.

55. Corrêa, *História de Angola*, 2:141–44.

56. Matos, *Compêndio histórico*, p. 304.

government by leading his army into a rout at the hands of the Musulu army.[57] Foreign goods continued to flow into the Luanda hinterland through Musulu, and Angola's relations with the marquis worsened until intensifying drought drove the starving residents of the province to descend in massive waves on the Luso-African plantations along the Dande in 1789 and 1790.[58]

Meanwhile French slavers swarmed all along Angolan coasts between about 1788 and 1791, from Cabo Negro to Cabinda. The British concentrated their slaving along the Loango Coast to the north of the Zaire and sent small boats south to trade at the mouths of the Mbrije and Loje rivers, perhaps because their countrymen had ample access to Luanda and Benguela through smuggling via Brazil. Even though the French traded all the way south to the mouth of the Kunene, they worked the Loango Coast also, having expelled the Portuguese from the fort at Cabinda in 1784. The entire Kongo was reportedly filled with French goods by the later 1780s, and Africans carrying French merchandise received blame for fomenting an attack by local residents in 1789 against a Portuguese government caravan carrying supplies to the government garrison at Encoje.[59] In view of the drought then reaching disastrous proportions, the Africans around Encoje may have been well primed to respond to such instigation. The French goods in Kongo followed the established trade routes up to the *ndembu* highlands and went on east through Jinga and Holo to compete beyond the Kwango with merchandise Luanda sent there through Kasanje.

To the south, the French found no difficulty in buying slaves through the government officials posted to Benguela to stop them. Their ships simply put in to Benguela Bay under the usual pretexts of seeking water and supplies and then unloaded their goods directly onto the beaches near the town when night fell.[60] The *capitão* acted as their agent, or, when wealthy *sertanejo* traders from the highlands came down to the coast to sell slaves directly to the French, taxed them (in both senses of the word) unofficially in slaves for the privilege of evading laws he was appointed to enforce.[61] Such obstacles, and the occasional official loyal to Lisbon (especially after elevation of the position to a full governorship with appointments made directly from Lisbon in 1791), merely displaced French

57. Corrêa, *História de Angola*, 2:143.

58. Which, of course, converted the Luanda Senado da Câmara to militant advocates of war against Musulu: *representação*, 17 Aug. 1790, AHU, Angola cx. 41; cf. Moçâmedes, 20 Sept. 1791, AHU, Angola maço 11, and de Mello, "Angola no começo do século," p. 555.

59. "Instrucçoens relativas a execução do Plano da Campanha . . . sendo Commandante . . . Paulo Martins Pinheiro de Lacerda," 1 June 1793, AHA, cód. 313, fols. 185–91v.

60. Delgado, *Famosa e histórica Benguela*, pp. 19–21.

61. Botelho de Vasconcelos, "Descrição," n.d. (ca. 1796), AHU, Angola maço 3 (D.O.); on the wealth of the settlers in the interior, Corrêa, *História de Angola*, 2:133.

trading off to the nearby mouth of the Katumbela River and to the bay of Lobito, both not far north of the town.[62] The mouth of the Katumbela was especially convenient, since the main trail from the interior ran down the river's valley to reach the coast at its mouth before turning south to the town. It was during this period that French smuggling at Benguela peaked, in 1789–91, with purchases of as many as 2,000 slaves per year, or around 20 percent of the total, to judge from the amount by which the town's legal exports rose with suspension of French trading in 1793.[63] The French appeared again also at Novo Redondo. One particularly brazen Nantes ship sent a Portuguese ashore there to announce that it had come to pick up slaves being held for forwarding on to owners in Luanda.[64]

The effectiveness of the French smugglers by about 1789 seems finally to have spurred Governor Moçâmedes, perhaps chastened by the unsatisfactory outcomes of the military expeditions he had entrusted to Costa, to make another stab at occupying the coast north of Luanda in 1790. His project this time was to fortify positions overlooking the mouths of the Lifune and Loje rivers, the ocean termini of the main trade routes through Musulu and southern Kongo. Occupation of the Lifune would position the Portuguese on Musulu's north flank and facilitate reprisals for its people's invasion of the valley of the Dande. The foreign goods entering southern Kongo at the Loje surely competed with Luanda's trading system, since they went directly east to the Soso, the Yaka, and on through the Pende to Mai Munene, in regions on the northern edge of Luanda's trans-Kwango trading sphere. The idea was to extend the line of colonial coastguard stations already existing at the mouths of the Kikombo, Kwanza, Bengo, and Dande rivers slightly to the north, position the new forts quietly out of sight from the sea, and thus block the slaves coming from the interior without exciting objections from the British, also trading there. These local posts fell within the province of the governor to create and to staff, without specific authorization from Lisbon. Moreover, the strategy left completely unobstructed the mouth of the Mbrije River, favored by the British from the Loango Coast and the outlet for an increasingly important trade route leading through the eastern Kongo,

62. Delgado, *Ao Sul do Cuanza,* p. 164; Beça, 30 Sept. 1796, AHU, Angola cx. 43.

63. Miller, "Legal Portuguese Slaving," p. 166, Table 3. The same estimating method produces a similar figure for the period just before the North American war interrupted French slaving in 1778; see Câmara, 20 Dec. 1779, AHU, Angola cx. 37, for the drop-off at Benguela. Cf. Fouchard, "Slave Trade," annexe, and idem, *Les marrons de la liberté* (Paris: Editions de l'Ecole, 1972), pp. 197–227, for annual figures (1764–93) on legal arrivals in Saint Domingue of ships trading in "Angole."

64. Almeida e Vasconcelos, 5 Nov. 1791, AHU, Angola cx. 41. Other details on the French are in Almeida e Vasconcelos, 31 Dec. 1791, ANTT, Ministério do Reino, maço 499; de Mello, 12 Dec. 1801, AHU, Angola cx. 50; de Mello, "Angola no começo do século," p. 522; João Victo da Silva, n.d. (ca. 1792?), AHU, Angola cx. 42.

or Zombo, to the Yaka in the southeast and to the Tio and the entire interior basin of the Zaire in the northeast.[65] The Crown refused to support what it seemed to regard as Moçâmedes's unauthorized initiatives at the Lifune and the Loje, presumably for fear of offending its powerful British protector. Lisbon ordered Moçâmedes's successor, Governor Almeida e Vasconcelos (1790–97), to remove the fortifications at the end of 1791, and he did so early in 1792.[66] The forts had been quite successful in deflecting the flow of slaves through Mbwila and Mbwela off to Luanda, but they had not disrupted the more distant Soso routes east through the Yaka.[67]

The Delicacy of Withdrawing Credit from the Interior

Moçâmedes's unauthorized fortification of the Lifune and the Loje coincided with other measures to withdraw the credit still outstanding in the interior of the colony, finally implementing the pullback first broached in the 1779 instructions issued to Moçâmedes's predecessor. The exact thrust of Lisbon's policies does not appear clearly in the records of the confused period in Angola after about 1790, when French and British goods were flooding into the backlands, Portuguese gunpowder was sparking off the conflicts building among the Africans as drought intensified, and merchants from Brazil were dominating the trade through Luanda behind what appears to have amounted to the tacit collusion of Governor Moçâmedes. For Lisbon the problems of the period seem to have centered on the big *feira* at Kasanje, where the minority of metropolitan merchants had concentrated their investments in the interior since the time of the Pernambuco Company. They had developed this remote market in order to bypass trading centers at Ambaca and Pungo Andongo that the Luso-Africans had comfortably in hand as outlets for goods from Brazil and as bases for smuggling slaves down the Kwanza and out through Musulu and ports to the north to British and French.[68] In this context, around 1789, Lisbon merchants, probably seeking access to Maranhão and Pará cotton, seem to have decided to attempt again to break into the Angola

65. For the trade routes, see Hilton, "Political and Social Change," and Peçanha, 27 June 1785, AHU, Angola cx. 40. For the fortifications, Moçâmedes, 20 Sept. 1791, AHU, Angola maço 11; Almeida e Vasconcelos, 31 Dec. 1791, ANTT, Ministério do Reino maço 499; Almeida e Vasconcelos, 30 March 1791, AHU, Angola cx. 42.

66. Godinho, 23 Oct. 1804, AHU, Angola cx. 55.

67. Almeida e Vasconcelos, 30 March 1791, AHU, Angola cx. 42.

68. Peçanha, 27 June 1785, AHU, Angola cx. 40, clearly emphasizes the Kwango valley as the center of Lisbon's interest in the interior. For the control of the Luso-Africans in the nearer presidios, Moçâmedes to *capitães-mores* of Massangano, Muxima, and Cambambe, 15 May 1787, AHA, cód. 82, fol. 43.

market, at first by selling goods through Kasanje and then, finding conditions throughout the interior far too unsettled for profitable trading, to resurrect the suggestions of Sousa Coutinho and others to limit slaving to cash buying at the coast.[69] A policy drift in these directions, at the very least, would explain the flurry of commercial reforms that Moçâmedes and the two governors who succeeded him introduced in Angola and also the strenuous opposition that they provoked from the Luanda agents of Brazil-based slave-buyers.

Several local circumstances led Moçâmedes to commence overtures to the Kasanje king on behalf of the Lisbon merchants trading at the *feira* there. French goods penetrating Lisbon's favored market through neighboring Jinga caused some alarm. Immediate concern arose over the demands of the Kasanje king that Portuguese traders pay higher prices for slaves they bought there, no doubt because he could sell all the captives he wanted to agents of the French for more than Lisbon was willing to offer. In addition, the regulations limiting trading to the marketplace itself, in force since 1761, had fallen into neglect, owing to Luanda's inability to control the *escrivão* in charge of supervising the trade.[70] One may safely read this oblique phrasing as an allusion to the usual situation: traders were buying French goods and selling slaves to their African agents in secluded *pumbos* outside the *feira,* and the market administrator, as the largest trader in the vicinity, was foremost among the smugglers.

Moçâmedes, reflecting the Luanda merchants' wariness of the expenses and risks of trying to safeguard assets positioned at so great a distance into the interior,[71] attempted to enlist the cooperation of the Kasanje king himself in a pact that obligated the king to work closely with a new "director" of the *feira,* appointed by the governor rather than by the merchants, to keep traders within the marketplace, halt the rise in prices, and encourage Africans owing slaves to the Portuguese to reduce the amount of their indebtedness.[72] Among the several implications of this complex package of measures, two stand out: the government's assertion of direct authority over trade and the scepticism expressed over the value

69. At a guess, the unsatisfied creditors of the defunct Pernambuco Company would have been involved, but the research necessary to document this hypothesis remains unfinished; for the moment, letters of 15 May 1789 and 23 Oct. 1789, Angola *copiador* of the Pernambuco Company, AHMF.

70. E.g., Fonseca Coutinho, 17 Nov. 1790, AHU, cód. 1627, fols. 23–24v. The regulations finally issued by Almeida e Vasconcelos appear to have been formulated by Moçâmedes; see Moçâmedes to Coutinho, 4 May 1790 (fragment), AHA, cód. 83, fols. 32v–34v. For other aspects of this period, see Vellut, "Royaume de Cassange."

71. Moçâmedes to Coutinho, ca. Feb. 1790 (fragment), AHA, cód. 83, fols. 9–9v.

72. Moçâmedes to Jaga Cassangi, 26 July 1789, *Arquivos de Angola* 2, no. 14 (1936): 567–70; Couto, *Capitães-mores,* p. 222. See the "Termo de Fidelidade e Vassalagem . . . ," *Arquivos de Angola* 2, no. 11 (1936): 341 ff. For circumstantial detail, enclosures in de Mello, 30 May 1801, AHU, Angola cx. 51.

of investing large amounts of trade goods at extremely high risk in remote portions of the backlands. Given the likelihood that the merchant creditors whom these policies would undermine were mainly Brazilian, Moçâmedes seems finally, at the end of his years in Angola in office, to have acted unambiguously on Lisbon's behalf. His previous erratic execution of steps taken nominally at Lisbon's direction had surely jeopardized his career by that late point in his term.

The same turn against the Brazilians and the Luso-Africans may also be inferred from a proclamation of 1789 that recalled all traders in the interior with borrowed goods back to Luanda. The government would then issue new licenses to a select few, and only these would be allowed to return to the backlands. Moçâmedes's brother and successor as governor, Almeida e Vasconcelos, bared the teeth in this provision by ordering at least one *capitão-mor* to arrest anyone trading without the new authorization and to send them back to Luanda for trial and punishment.[73] Moçâmedes reinforced the effort with instructions that the bundles (*banzos*) to be exchanged for slaves by these properly legitimated traders, within the confines of the designated *feiras,* be made up before leaving Luanda.[74] Lisbon thus dredged up failed regulatory tactics of the 1760s nearly thirty years later, when not only the local trading families but also Brazilian buyers of their slaves dwarfed the metropolitan presence in Angola.

Almeida e Vasconcelos pursued the futile struggle to enforce the low fixed prices for slaves that Moçâmedes had proposed to protect Lisbon traders at Kasanje. He appointed several directors at the Kasanje marketplace, nominated by the merchants, but they accomplished little.[75] Among the priorities assigned to these men was hastening returns of slaves from the interior by reducing the size of the coffle in which they were sent down to the city. The governor also convened the merchants of the city in a reconstituted Junta do Comércio, again resurrecting an institution from the days of the illustrious Sousa Coutinho but by the 1790s evidently including Brazilian slavers and allied Luso-Africans more than the merchants of Lisbon favored in the 1760s.

These merchants submitted a formal proposal for regulating commerce in the interior that captured the uneasiness of the compromise between the governor, who was evidently mostly concerned to limit credit sent to the interior, and the Brazilians, who had taken over the generous

73. Couto, *Capitães-mores,* p. 210.
74. These instructions are referred to in the merchants' petition of 5 March 1793, included in *carta regia,* 30 Jan. 1810, AHU, Angola maço 4-A.
75. For the extensive documentation on the difficulties of regulating the *feira* at Kasanje, see AHA, códs. 83–86 and 273, and selected documents published in *Arquivos de Angola* 1, no. 5 (1936): n.p. On speeding up the remittances of slaves: Almeida e Vasconcelos to Paulo Jozé de Loureiro (director, *feira de Cassange*), 27 July 1791, AHA, cód. 84, fols. 254–54v.

strategies that had failed the metropole. The governor would interview traders seeking legitimation to take trade goods to the interior, but the merchants would certify them, and for the relatively lengthy period of six years. Shorter periods, the merchants argued, would have compromised their agents' ability to remain on the scene in the backlands to recover long-term commercial loans of trade goods. Of course, the agreed term of six years set certified traders beyond the reach of governors, who were likely to remain in the colony for no more than two three-year terms. The merchants would accept the government's proposed restriction of trading only in the *feiras,* but the government would recognize such marketplaces at the old Luso-African centers of Ambaca (Lucamba) and Pungo Andongo (Haco), and also at a site north of Kasanje (Holo) that amounted to conceding an alternative route from Ambaca through the area filled with French goods to the trans-Kwango region that Luanda reached through Kasanje.

This careful compromise, which essentially preserved the rigid rules promulgated in 1790 but applied them in ways that vitiated their effect, continued on through the entire set of twenty-one provisions that the merchants offered. Lisbon retracted its intention of making up *banzos* in Luanda but received priority in sending traders to Kasanje. Prices, again except for Kasanje, would be freed to rise above what Lisbon would have preferred, to levels the Brazilians could pay. Almost half the clauses attempted to limit *reviros,* a matter of great concern in Luanda at that time for reasons obvious to Lisbon merchants worried about the French.

Lisbon's concern to change the basis of trade from sending goods on trust deep into the interior to buying slaves outright at the coast also helps to explain the sensitivity to *reviros* embodied in this document, which the Brazilians also shared, though for different reasons. Traders showing up from Portugal to acquire slaves on their own accounts for shipment to Maranhão would have had perfect opportunities to buy captives owed to Brazilians who persisted in dealing with credit within the colony. The roles had thus partially reversed since the 1760s, with Lisbon traders now seeking toleration of a Brazilian practice they had earlier written elaborate laws to prohibit. But the trade-off on this count also revealed the concessions made to Lisbon, since metropolitan merchants convicted of promoting a *reviro* would pay fines of hardly more than the value of a single slave, while Luso-Africans implicated in the illicit exchange faced two months in jail for the first offense, four months for the second, and three years on the chain gang for the third.[76] No governor could expose Lisbon merchants to risk of serious punishment in Portugal's own colony.

76. *Termo* of the (Luanda) Junta do Comércio, 5 March 1793, included with *carta regia,* 30 Jan. 1810, AHU, Angola maço 4-A. A similar tension between local and metro-

On the other hand, the largest Brazilian traders in the city also owed significant sums to the colonial treasury, no doubt in risk bills in which they had paid duties owed on slaves they had shipped.[77] The Crown, caught between its desire to promote metropolitan trade and its need for these revenues, failed to endorse these arrangements until 1810. By then, the metropolitan traders' relocation to Rio de Janeiro had placed them in the dominant position occupied twenty years earlier by their colonial rivals and had removed the conflicts hidden behind the original set of compromises. Neither side was satisfied with its qualified gains up to that time, and merchants in both Portugal and Angola later charged that governors had implemented the agreement unevenly (which was probably precisely the point) and had resisted the rules on grounds that Portuguese subjects had no obligation to abide by regulations that had never received the endorsement of the king.[78]

The Northern Coasts

With Portugal's sensitivity to her British allies in Europe frustrating Moçâmedes's attempt to occupy coastal positions north of Luanda, Almeida e Vasconcelos renewed the attempt to block the interior trails channeling slaves to those rivers and bays. At the same time that Almeida e Vasconcelos was working out his awkward agreement with the merchants of Luanda, he gathered the entire military force of the colony and sent it off during the dry season of 1793, under the command of a reliable officer, Paulo Martins Pinheiro de Lacerda, to discipline the southern Kongo who were distributing foreign merchandise east of Musulu. Portuguese caravans in the area had again come under attack, and Almeida e Vasconcelos blamed the assaults on the French without taking note of the drought then just reaching its climax. The army advanced to the northeast of Luanda, first to the *ndembu* region and then continuing to Encoje to spend the failed rainy season of 1793–94. Battle plans had specified that the army would continue on a grand sweep down the trade routes to Holo and Jinga in the Kwango valley before swinging back through the suspect Luso-African areas of Pungo Andongo and Ambaca.[79] However, African opponents, driven to uncharacteristic desperation by the

---

politan traders pervades the documentation on the Kasanje market (see note 75 above). See also AHA, cód. D-20-3 (and copy, cód. 3259), for this *junta*.

77. E.g., Almeida e Vasconcelos to Pedro Beltrão (*tenente regente*, Ambaca), 15 May 1794, AHA, cód. 87, fols. 74–74v; idem to Fonceca Coutinho, 27 July 1791, AHA, cód. 84, fols. 254v–55.

78. Rodrigo de Sousa Coutinho to de Mello, 17 Nov. 1799, in *Arquivos de Angola* 2, no. 14 (1936): 603–5; de Mello, 3 Jan. 1801, AHU, Angola cx. 51.

79. "Instrucçoens," AHA, cód. 313, fols. 185–91v.

famine abroad in the land, prevented the Portuguese army from advancing beyond Encoje. With smallpox spreading through the troops, Pinheiro de Lacerda led a straggling remnant of his force, starving and reduced in numbers, back to Luanda in June 1794 to celebrate a hollow triumph.[80] The damage this campaign may have done to commerce through southern Kongo, as distinct from the disruptions of the drought, famine, and epidemics in the following years, is uncertain.

Much more effective in reducing foreign competition north of Luanda, without a doubt, was the great European war of the end of the eighteenth century, which knocked the French permanently out of slaving in Angola and momentarily distracted the British. Earlier wars between these two powers had seemed to leave Loango open to the Portuguese,[81] and the outbreak of hostilities in 1793 provided still another opportunity for Lisbon merchants uncomfortable with their weak position at Luanda to buy Angolan slaves north of the Zaire. Their objectives were mixed. Most probably intended to sell slaves in Pará and Maranhão, where they were to enjoy exemption from the duties applicable to slaves from Luanda and Benguela, but some, at least, contemplated sailing right on past those northern Brazilian captaincies to smuggle slaves to French islands in the Caribbean that were left without labor by the disruptions of the war.[82] Whatever destination these merchants contemplated, the cash basis on which Africans north of Luanda sold slaves at the coast fit in with Lisbon's plans to reduce its own commercial investment in the African interior, and if possible, that of Brazil as well.

A fleet of Lisbon ships accordingly made for Cabinda in 1794 and 1795. The captains and factors of the fleet, accustomed to the relatively conventional style of trading with Europeans at Luanda, found quite baffling the elaborate negotiations and palavers that African sellers imposed on slavers at Cabinda, and they failed to acquire slaves in quantities sufficient to justify the venture.[83] Some of the unsuccessful captains then

80. See the official diary of this expedition, reproduced in Corrêa, *História de Angola*, 2:179–232; also Almeida e Vasconcelos, 31 July 1794, AHU, Angola cx. 43.

81. E.g., Moçâmedes, 12 June 1784, AHU, Angola cx. 40, for the American War of Independence.

82. Almeida e Vasconcelos, 24 Aug. 1793, AHU, Angola cx. 42; idem, 23 April 1795, 12 May 1795, and 14 July 1795, all AHU, Angola cx. 44; de Mello, 24 April 1798, AHU, Angola cx. 46; Saldanha da Gama, 17 Aug. 1807, AHU, Angola cx. 59. This West Indian strategy did not include Saint Domingue, then in revolt and under British influence. Lisbon ships renewed the West Indian strategy at least in 1805 and 1807, and the Bahians may have joined in after 1809: *requerimento* of João Oliveira Dias, n.d. (ca. 1807), AHU, Angola cx. 57; anonymous note of Sept. 1805, AHU, Angola cx. 56; Verger, *Flux et reflux*, p. 293. For the continuation of Portuguese smuggling to the West Indies in the changed circumstances after 1807, see Clarence-Smith, "Portuguese Contribution," pp. 25 ff.

83. Almeida e Vasconcelos, 2 Oct. 1794, AHU, Angola cx. 43; idem, 25 Jan. 1795 and 4 May 1796, AHU, Angola cx. 44; *carta regia*, 4 Aug. 1795, AHU, Angola maço 11 (D.O.); *requerimento* of José António Pereira, n.d. (ca. 1806), AHU, Angola cx. 56.

returned to Luanda and Benguela to complete their cargoes, delivered their slaves to Salvador, and attempted to transfer their exemption from duties in the north to intrude on the Brazilian trade at Bahia by offering their captives there at corresponding discounts. This abortive adventure highlighted the marginality of Lisbon merchants in the Angolan slave trade by the 1790s. They were reduced to the equivalent of smuggling on the fringes of their own empire.

Renewed Pullback to Luanda

Lisbon's conservative policy of reducing metropolitan investment in the Luanda hinterland approached its apogee under the following governor, D. Miguel António de Mello (1797–1802). De Mello represented a new secretary of state for the colonies who was preoccupied with reform of the Portuguese administration in Brazil and who was unwilling, apparently, to devote scarce resources to the hopeless situation in Angola.[84] Governor de Mello argued that Africans with slaves to sell could be induced to bring them to Portuguese merchants in Luanda. He later cited Luanda's existing trade with the central Kongo as exemplifying the sort of business that he would prefer to generalize throughout the colony. He interpreted the arrival of Kongo traders with caravans of slaves at Luanda at the height of the drought, and the profligacy with which they had spent the proceeds of their sales, despite the fact that Portugal had had no military or administrative presence in Kongo since the seventeenth century, as justifying a general abandonment of the colony's *presídios* along the Kwanza. The fort at Encoje, he admitted, had never seriously impeded the traffic in slaves from the Kwango valley to foreigners at the Loje and Mbrije. He acknowledged that his proposals amounted to writing off the trade goods that some merchants had invested in the backlands, but he discounted the significance of admitting these losses by pointing out that most debtors there had been hopelessly in default for years. He also questioned the justice of the creditors' claims in any case, alluding to immorally high interest charges, in the vicinity of 40 percent, that they added to the price of goods they lent.[85] The possibility of the government's reducing its commitment to the interior evoked an impassioned argument from the Luso-Africans of Pungo Andongo in defense of the value of their lands to Portugal, though one that went without formal response in the extant records.[86] One can imagine also the opposition in Luanda to the prospect

84. Maxwell, *Conflicts and Conspiracies,* pp. 204 ff.

85. De Mello, 24 April 1798, AHU, Angola cx. 46; idem, 11 Jan. 1798, AHU, Angola cx. 44; idem, 3 Jan. 1801, AHU, Angola cx. 51; idem, 31 Jan. 1801, AHU, Angola cx. 52.

86. "Extinção do Prezidio das Pedras," n.d., AHU, Angola cx. 37. The document is dated to ca. 1777 by the AHU staff and in some ways appears to date from the early 1780s.

of losing the government officers, *capitães-mores, escrivães,* and occasional military patrols sent out to clear the trails of bandits besetting the slave caravans, on whom merchants depended for the security of the credit that supported their trade.

De Mello also implemented the 1793 accord with Luanda's merchants in the interfering spirit intended by Lisbon. He drove out four of the largest merchants active in the colony, presumably those with major commitments of goods in the backlands. All of them retired to Brazil, and their choice of destination surely revealed the identity of de Mello's real targets.[87] In forcing the colonial slavers to leave, de Mello was persisting in a tactic that his predecessor, Almeida e Vasconcelos, had begun some years before by prosecuting another prominent Luanda slaver on behalf of a Lisbon creditor, Miguel Rodrigues Collaço, in a classic application of the imperial judicial system to harass wealthy debtors in the colonies.[88] Encouraging large merchants to liquidate and bankrupting defaulting debtors were recognized means of collapsing the credit structure of the colony's interior trade.

At Kasanje, de Mello likewise continued his predecessor's initiatives in reducing debts outstanding at Lisbon's major marketplace in the interior, then probably amounting to substantially more than a thousand slaves.[89] Governors Moçâmedes and Almeida e Vasconcelos had both vacillated between terminating government protection of traders at the Kasanje *feira,* thus recognizing the worthlessness of the "debts" claimed there, and seeking to protect them by cultivating the Kasanje king. Whatever the government's preference for abandoning the amounts owed—mostly to Brazilians and Luso-Africans rather than to merchants from Lisbon by this time—the Luanda factors of the creditors resisted having to acknowledge that goods carried on their books as loans in fact represented nothing more than bad debts. Abandonment of the Kasanje *feira* thus meant personal ruin to them.

Almeida e Vasconcelos had in fact come within an eyelash of withdrawing government recognition of the Kasanje *feira* in 1793.[90] In the

---

However, I am provisionally treating it as reflecting (also?) reactions to policies of the sort articulated after about 1798 by de Mello.

87. De Mello, 26 Feb. 1802, AHU, Angola cx. 52.

88. Portella *processo,* AHU, Angola maço 5; Almeida e Vasconcelos, 11 Feb. 1795, AHU, Angola cx. 44.

89. A rough estimate derived from the account of remittances and debts of António José da Costa, enclosed in de Mello, 30 May 1801, AHU, Angola cx. 51. See below for further details on these circumstances.

90. E.g., Moçâmedes to Couttinho, 30 Jan. 1790, AHA, cód. 83, fols. 1–1v; Almeida e Vasconcelos to Coutinho, 4 Feb. 1791 (1792?), AHA, cód. 85, fols. 120–21; idem to Francisco das Chagas Veiga (director, Cassange *feira*), 24 June 1793, AHA, cód. 86, fols. 194–94v; idem to Francisco Antonio Pitta (*capitão commissário da conquista*), 25 Sept. 1793, AHA, cód. 86, fols. 229v–31.

next year, however, he authorized a final try at recovering debts left by one of the most important traders in Kasanje, none other than that utterly consistent nemesis of Lisbon's plans in Angola, António José da Costa. Costa had died at Kasanje in 1793 or 1794, and so Almeida e Vasconcelos dispatched the former Pernambuco Company administrator, Francisco Honorato da Costa, to represent Lisbon's interests at Kasanje as director of the *feira* there. Honorato da Costa was beholden to the governor because he was himself under suit for debts that he had run up while representing the company in Luanda.[91] If Honorato da Costa could recover enough of the slaves owed to Lisbon, it may be inferred, the government would free itself to pursue its longer-term strategy of general pullback from expensive and useless positions in the far interior. In return, Honorato da Costa might expect continued delays in pressing the charges against him.

The obliqueness of the governors' correspondence concerning affairs at Kasanje prior to de Mello surely conceals the delicacy of the issue amidst these conflicting pressures. Governors were charged with recovering amounts owing to Lisbon merchants, but their ability to do so depended on the cooperation of the Luso-Africans and Brazilians who provided the bulk of the finance then committed to trade in the interior, since the governor's Portuguese protégés could not expect to receive slaves in payment on outstanding debts without allowing loans of new goods to assort with the old. Withdrawal from the *feira* would undercut these needed shipments. The governors also feared that word of impending abandonment would prompt the Kasanje king, on whose support the whole credit system depended, to declare null and void his subjects' debts to Brazilians and Portuguese alike. Thus the inconsistency of orders to withdraw from the Kasanje marketplace in line with Lisbon's wishes, followed by renewed permission to send still more goods out to Kasanje under government protection at the insistence of Luanda merchants who feared for their own assets invested there. And finally, thus also the inaction of Almeida e Vasconcelos's last three years, while Lisbon merchants sought to realize whatever they could of their claims at Kasanje under Honorato da Costa's direction.

When de Mello arrived at Luanda in 1798, he immediately moved to cut further losses at Kasanje and to tighten the screws on the colonial slave traders. Interruption of supplies of Asian textiles during the war years of 1795 and 1796 had temporarily slowed Honorato da Costa's returns,

---

91. *Ordem* (to) Tenente Coronel Francisco Honorato da Costa, 27 June 1794, AHA, cód. 273, fol. 139; numerous letters in AHA, cód. 87 et seq. I have not determined whether the two Costas were brothers (or cousins, or otherwise related). For Honorato da Costa's highly unsatisfactory record as Pernambuco Company administrator, see Angola *copiador*, letters of 30 June 1783, 3 April 1784, 21 July 1786, 15 May 1789, 23 March 1791, and others, AHMF.

but he seems to have made adequate progress in reducing debts in that part of the hinterland for several years, not only to his own creditors and to those of Antonio José da Costa, but also slaves owed by others to merchants in Luanda.[92] De Mello at first greeted Honorato da Costa warmly and supportively as director of the *feira*, but the limits of this calculated endorsement appeared soon. Once the expected benefits of Honorato da Costa's recovery expedition would have been in hand, de Mello proposed that traders carrying goods from Luanda should not proceed beyond the government outpost at Ambaca, about a third of the way to Kasanje. Instructions followed to send further remittances from Kasanje under government escort to Ambaca. Soon de Mello was ordering Honorato da Costa to remain on duty as Kasanje marketplace director over the latter's objections.[93] The noose was being tightened ever so gradually, still so as not to threaten the remaining uncollected slaves, but in 1801 the trapdoor finally snapped open. One of Honorato da Costa's creditors in Lisbon obtained a royal order foreclosing on his long-overdue obligations, and de Mello brusquely ordered him to pay up at once or expect enforcement of the same.[94] It was an order entirely consistent with the general Lisbon policy toward cautious abandonment of the credit-based commerce of the interior.

At about the same time, Lisbon grew extremely interested in establishing transcontinental communication between its western African colony in Angola and its east African possessions along the Zambezi River. Its reasons centered on inducing the African merchants to invest the commercial capital that merchants with goods off east of the Kwango could not collect in transporting slaves to the west themselves. Correspondence concerning efforts to learn more about the remote eastern frontiers of slaving made clear that the Portuguese expected the Lunda, then in the full thrust of their own imperial consolidation and generating plenty of captives in their wars of expansion, to send their own caravans directly to Portuguese buyers waiting in Luanda, just like Kongo trading at Luanda on their own accounts whom de Mello praised as models of the sort of trading partners Lisbon desired in Angola. Interest in contracting Lunda also rose from hopes that in the longer run the trade in copper reported

92. Details of Honorato da Costa's first five years at Kasanje in the *requerimento* and documents enclosed in de Mello, 30 May 1801, AHU, Angola cx. 51. For the lack of trade goods, Almeida e Vasconcelos to Joaquim Jozé da Silva (*capitão-mor* and *regente*, Ambaca), 19 July 1795, AHA, cód. 88, fols. 125–28; idem to idem, 20 Dec. 1796, AHA, cód. 89, fols. 226–27.
93. See the following, all in AHA, cód. 90: de Mello to *capitão-mor*, Ambaca, 24 Jan. 1798, fols. 23v–24v; idem to idem, 28 Feb. 1798, fols. 29–30; de Mello to Honorato da Costa, 8 Sept. 1798, fols. 59–59v; idem to idem, 16 Sept. 1799, fols. 85–85v; idem to Vicente Roiz Rialho (*capitão-mor*, Ambaca), 28 May 1800, fol. 110v; idem to Honorato da Costa, 28 May 1800, fols. 110v–11.
94. De Mello to Honorato da Costa, 28 March 1801, AHA, cód. 90, fol. 129.

from the far interior of the continent might supplement slaves as Angola's main export. As part of a broad effort in the 1790s to explore the trans-Kwango to these ends, de Mello asked Honorato da Costa, still director of the *feira* in Kasanje, to make official contact with Lunda through personal contacts that he had developed with them through his trade.[95] Against this background developed the mission of Honorato da Costa's two slave *pombeiros,* who subsequently gained fame as the first agents of the Portuguese known to have made the transcontinental journey from Angola to the middle Zambezi and back.[96]

Lisbon also began to make progress in the last five or six years of the eighteenth century against the Brazilian and Luso-African slavers entrenched at Benguela. A new Benguela governor, Alexandre José Botelho de Vasconcelos, took office under a full *regimento* in 1796, with the principal protagonists of the old order in disarray.[97] The French had disappeared from the scene. Botelho de Vasconcelos's predecessor, another close collaborator with foreign smugglers, had been condemned by the Conselho Ultramarino, the highest colonial tribunal in the empire, and sent back to imprisonment in Lisbon.[98] The resulting interruption in supplies of the contraband goods on which Benguela slaving depended had discouraged traders dependent on the old ways of doing business, and they had abandoned the town, returning home, once again, to Brazil.[99] With an effective royal governor firmly and loyally in charge, Benguela also lost its importance to the Brazilians as a means of avoiding imperial authority stronger elsewhere. Lisbon had no real capability to fill the void. Slave exports from Benguela then began the long, slow decline from peaks attained in the early 1790s that they would follow for the remainder of the legal trade. By 1810 or so, when the Portuguese merchants relocated in Rio de Janeiro further reduced the capacity of the Brazilians to buy slaves at Benguela, the merchants there complained to the Crown of the declining volume of their trade, specifically noting their inability to obtain trade goods on credit from Brazil.[100]

95. De Mello to Honorato da Costa, 17 Oct. 1801, AHA, cód. 90, fols. 135v–36; de Mello to Visconde de Anadia, 23 March 1802, AHU, Angola cx. 53. I cannot resolve the inconsistency of the simultaneous threat to foreclose and this request for assistance to the government's project, except to suppose that the latter became a condition of forbearance on the former. In fact, as is shown below, Honorato da Costa succeeded in sending his slave agents to Lunda, remained active in the colony, and never paid off the debts claimed against him. Also on the Lunda initiative see Noronha, 22 Oct. 1803, AHA, cód. 90, fols. 180v–82v; Godinho, 23 Oct. 1803, AHU, Angola cx. 55.

96. Bontinck, "Voyage des pombeiros."

97. AHU, Angola maço 6; also see Delgado, *Famosa e histórica Benguela,* pp. 441–43, and Couto, "Regimento."

98. Almeida e Vasconcelos, 28 July 1796 and 4 Oct. 1796, AHU, Angola maço 9.

99. Botelho de Vasconcelos, 27 July 1796, AHU, Angola cx. 49.

100. *Requerimento* dos negociantes da praça de Benguela, n.d. (ca. 1810–12), AHU, Angola maço 15. See also the foreclosures ordered in 1813 and 1815: Rebelo, *Relações,* pp. 211–12.

If Governor Almeida e Vasconcelos's first steps toward closer government regulation of credit and trade in the interior had encountered tactful resistance from the merchants of Luanda, and if the Luso-Africans had dared to protest formally against withdrawing government posts from Ambaca and Pungo Andongo early in the 1790s, at the end of the century Brazilian and local Angolan resentment boiled over into overt resistance to Lisbon's refusal to support credit-based slaving to which the metropole contributed very little and from which it gained less. Matters came to a head over the final element in Lisbon's strategy: implementation of the customs inspections ordered from the Court but evaded fifteen years earlier by Moçâmedes. The Crown issued the formal Luanda customs house *regimento* on 21 October 1799, to take effect 1 January 1800. The responsibility for enforcing it, as with other metropolitan restraints, fell to Governor de Mello.[101] Although de Mello had anticipated objections to any serious effort at stopping the rampant smuggling,[102] he turned with zeal to checking all imports for evidence of legal entry through Portugal and to searching for statutory justification to seize contraband goods when they were detected.[103]

Unidentified detractors then fought back through the courts by petitioning the Crown to impeach its governor. Brazilian allies of the merchants de Mello had expelled to Brazil provide obvious candidates for the authors of this thinly disguised rebellion. They won a limited concession delaying implementation of critical provisions in the customs charter for a year, though the concession applied only to importers wealthy enough to post bonds covering any possible liability for bringing in unauthorized goods in the meanwhile. De Mello made another crucial concession in exempting Brazilian *gerebitas* destined for the interior—that is, for the slave trade rather than for consumption in Luanda—from the import duty Brazilians had paid since the seventeenth century.

He nonetheless found himself the object of a complicated formal complaint claiming that he could not properly execute an order given to a predecessor (meaning Governor Moçâmedes in 1784) and asserting that the terms of the original *carta regia,* which forbade additional duties on imports, restricted him from imposing any charges at all, even the minor fees specified in the customs *regimento* for inspection and dispatch of the goods coming into the colony. The complainants further objected to de Mello's intention of raising these fees, which they must have quite rightly feared would increase the cost of bribing officials of the customs shed to admit their contraband goods. They added numerous other allegations against what they viewed as de Mello's misconduct in other spheres, mostly

101. The *regimento* is published in *Arquivos de Angola* 2, no. 12 (1936): 357–447. For a more extended discussion of the following points, see Miller, "Imports at Luanda."
102. De Mello, 22 Oct. 1799, AHU, Angola maço 9.
103. De Mello, 12 Aug. 1801, AHU, Angola cx. 50.

to the effect that he had tightened up against their smuggling operations and was cutting their ties to their correspondents in Brazil.[104] Lisbon, perhaps seeing an opportunity to discredit anyone audacious enough to register a formal protest, agreed to investigate the conduct of its governor in Angola. The eventual report thoroughly exonerated de Mello and went on to reiterate clearly the guiding philosophy of reducing metropolitan commitments in the interior and policing the coast more closely, from Luanda Bay itself outwards to Benguela and the ports to the north.[105]

Further Plans for African-Financed Trade

With the distractions of war in Europe increasing at home, Lisbon had little time to devote to the Angolan slave trade in the first decade of the nineteenth century. The next governor, D. Fernando António Soares Noronha (1802–6), managed to submit the first of the elaborate customs reports required under the 1801 *regimento,* summarizing goods imported at both Luanda and Benguela. At Kasanje, he collaborated with Honorato da Costa in 1804 to renew plans to withdraw the government marketplace from the Kwango valley to a highland site at Mucari, some two hundred kilometers closer to Luanda, though not without continued vacillation to assuage the fears of merchants who stood to lose the goods and slaves that such a move would force them to abandon there. At the end of that year, Honorato da Costa abruptly pulled back to Mucari without explicit authority from the governor, and one may guess that he welcomed the opportunity to crawl out from under his own debts that the governor's impending permission seemed to promise. The merchants then forced Noronha to appoint a new director at a restored *feira* in the Kwango valley itself, though Noronha stuck to Lisbon's priorities by urging the Kasanje king, in the letter agreeing to reestablishment of the *feira* in his territory, to send his own caravans west to Ambaca to pick up trade goods that would be held for him there.[106] The eastern trade finally proceeded on the basis of two marketplaces that neatly expressed the division of interests in

104. Correa de Araujo, 12 April 1801, AHU, Angola cx. 51; Correa da Silva, 9 March 1803, AHU, Angola cx. 54. De Mello's defense is in his letter of 3 Jan. 1801, AHU, Angola cx. 52.

105. Godinho, 23 Oct. 1804, AHU, Angola cx. 55. De Mello returned to Portugal to an illustrious career in government finance, as secretary of state for finances and as president of the Royal Treasury Board: Torres, *Memórias,* pp. 296–97. At that time he completely revised his position on the wisdom of confining trade to Luanda: de Mello, 12 July 1805, AHU, Angola cx. 55.

106. Noronha to the director of the Feira de Cassange, 23 Nov. 1804, AHA, cód. 90, fols. 226–26v; idem to idem, 7 Jan. 1805, AHA, cód. 90, fols. 229v–30; Noronha to Jaga Cassange, 13 July 1805, AHA, cód. 240, fols. 36–37v.

the colony's interior, Honorato da Costa's semiofficial establishment at Mucari and the merchants' old settlement in Kasanje.

It was from Mucari that Honorato da Costa set in motion the expedition of the *pombeiros* that finally brought Lisbon and Luanda into direct contact with the Lunda. Although the private merchants opposed the idea to protect their debts in Kasanje, which the king would surely renounce at the slightest threat to his own position as borrower and broker, Noronha renewed de Mello's instructions to Honorato da Costa to do all he could to bring Africans from beyond the Kwango to Luanda to trade on their own accounts. From the tone of Noronha's instructions, the fact that the Lunda brought their own slaves into Kasanje, rather than waiting for caravans bearing goods from the Kwango to enter their own territories, was a very attractive feature of their trade, and one entirely consistent with Lisbon's policy of limiting investments in the remote interior.[107] The issue revolved not only around whether direct Lunda contact with the Portuguese at Luanda would reduce prices for slaves but also around which party to the transactions would finance the trade: Kasanje and the Brazilians stood for further credit extended through Kwango valley brokers, while Lisbon proposed to await African-financed initiatives from the slaving frontier. Honorato da Costa then dispatched his two *pombeiros* to Lunda, probably early in 1805, clearly to invite wealthy nobles at the Lunda court to send their own shipments of slaves directly to the coast.

When the Lunda fulfilled these Lisbon hopes by dispatching a caravan to the west in the dry season of 1807, the broad metropolitan goal of buying slaves at the coast must have seemed within reach. Word of the impending Lunda caravan reached Luanda during an interim government in 1806–7, and the new governor, António de Saldanha da Gama (1807–10), immediately upon his arrival mobilized all the troops available in the colony for an all-out assault against Kasanje and the two neighboring Kwango valley slave-trading markets in Holo and Jinga.[108] The governor's

107. Noronha to Honorato da Costa, 22 Oct. 1803, AHA, cód. 90, fols. 180–82v. For strategy, especially see Saldanha da Gama to the director at Cassange, 7 Aug. 1807, AHA, cód. 91, fols. 72v–73v.

108. Noronha had previously, in 1805, made clear the objection of the Portuguese to Kasanje's obstruction of the trade beyond the Kwango: Noronha to Jaga Cassangy, 2 Aug. 1805, AHA, cód. 240, fols. 37v–38. He also informed the king of his intention of making direct contact with the Lunda and threatened to send troops to overcome possible Kasanje objections. For the government military expeditions sent to the interior, Saldanha da Gama to *regente de Ambaca*, 20 June 1807, AHA, cód. 91, fols. 62v–63v; idem to Jaga de Cassange, 25 June 1807, AHA, cód. 240, fols. 51–51v; other relevant correspondence in AHA, cód. 91. The general plan of battle is in Saldanha da Gama to Tenente coronel (Euzebio Catéla de Lemos), 21 Aug. 1807, published in *Arquivos de Angola* 4, nos. 37–40 (1938): 43–45, 47–48, 63.

intention, to judge from his actions during the latter half of 1807, was to knock out the main African powers that could be expected to bar the Lunda from getting through to open direct communication with the Portuguese. As the Lunda emissaries finally entered Luanda amidst great pomp and celebration late in 1807, the threatened kings of the African states in the Kwango valley dispatched ambassadors to ascertain the possible significance of an event with potentially momentous commercial consequences, beyond the well-known precedent it set for later European exploration in central Africa aimed at quite different objectives.[109]

The Portuguese attempt to lure the Lunda into bringing their slaves to Luanda was clearly premature and had no chance against the much greater wealth that the Brazilians and Luso-Africans were even then using to convert Lunda slaving from autonomous warfare to debt and dependency, and nothing more came of the project during the ensuing long reign of Nawej II on the Kalanyi. Governor Saldanha da Gama's military thrust also dissipated for want of adequate African support troops from the Luso-African–controlled backlands of Pungo Andongo, desertions among those actually mustered in, a suspicious fire that broke out among the army's stores, changes in command, and, finally, the onset of the 1807–8 wet season.[110] But in the end, the *coup de grâce* to the governor's planned conquest of the Kwango valley came from objections raised once again by merchants in Luanda when word reached them that the French had invaded Lisbon. Saldanha da Gama then pulled the regular government troops back from the interior to protect the colonial capital against the French attack that was expected to follow there.[111] He also, finally, withdrew government recognition of the Kasanje *feira* at the end of 1808.[112] The conservative Lisbon policy of the preceding twenty years, predicated as it was on opposing Brazilian domination of the slave trade at minimal cost to the metropole, became irrelevant with the subsequent retreat of the Lisbon court and merchants to the very center of Brazilian slaving to Angola at Rio de Janeiro.

109. The correspondence on the Lunda embassy to Luanda begins with Saldanha da Gama to Honorato da Costa, 15 May 1807, AHA, cód. 91, fols. 57–57v, and continues on to fols. 61v–62, 79v–80, 80–80v. A letter of 30 Dec. 1807 to the *regente de Ambaca*, AHA, cód. 91, fol. 89, notes the impending departure of the Lunda emissaries from Luanda.
110. Saldanha da Gama to Tenente Leiria, 2 Sept. 1807, AHA, cód. 91, fol. 77; also see fols. 15v–16, 17v–18, 22v, 24, 27v, etc.; and *Arquivos de Angola* 4, nos. 37–40 (1938): 67, 73–74, 79–80, 87, 105–6.
111. Saldanha da Gama to the director of the Feira de Cassange, 23 Jan. 1808, AHA, cód. 91, fols. 87v; idem to the director of the Feira de Mucari, 25 May 1808, AHA, cód. 91, fols. 95v–96.
112. Saldanha da Gama to the director of the Feira de Cassange, 11 Aug. 1808, AHA, cód. 91, fol. 99v, and following correspondence.

A Balance

The net effect of Lisbon's moves in Angola after about 1770 had been to strengthen administrative institutions at the coast while proceeding toward liquidating its losing commercial investments in the interior. Shortages of metropolitan capital for Angolan slaving underlay the strategy, which had begun with abortive resort to Luso-African military adventures, moved on through coastal forts to fend off foreign traders, and eventually settled on an ambivalent and halting effort to extract what could be saved of the trade goods invested at the Kasanje marketplace in the Kwango valley. The Brazilians and their Luso-African allies, much more capable than the Portuguese of sustaining mercantilist strategies at this late date, often with direct or indirect support from the British, offered little assistance with Lisbon's plans. Contradictory pulses from the metropole designed to salvage the remaining debts of the Pernambuco Company further complicated the plans. In the end, governors were reduced to the extraordinary expedient of seeking African financing of their trade, from Kongo, at the Loango Coast, and even from Lunda. Nothing could have expressed more clearly the poverty of the resources Portugal had to invest in Angolan slaving by 1800 than this low-budget neomercantilist reversion to an anachronistic strategy that Portuguese contractors and free traders, not to mention wealthy Dutch, French, and British competitors, and lately even the Brazilians, had rendered forever obsolete a century before. Lisbon had failed to beat back the capitalist investment then solidly entrenched in western central African slaving, but British finance admitted through Brazil after 1808 would allow the metropolitan merchants transplanted at Rio to ride more modern methods of slaving back to prominence at Luanda for the last two decades of the legal trade.

18

Lisbon's Lost Colony, 1810–1830

Lisbon, after thirty years of very restricted trading in Angola, had lost most of the southern Atlantic slave trade to the Brazilians, and departure of the metropolitan slaving interest to join them in Rio in 1807 freed the merchants who remained behind in Portugal to contemplate other aspects of the African colony's economic potential. Within Angola, even in the city of Luanda itself, the slaving trade had fallen into the hands of Brazilians and Luso-Africans to the extent that local smugglers could prompt a high-level review of the conduct of the governor who finally dared to implement customs reforms promulgated no less than fifteen years previously. Portuguese manufactures, with the exception of gunpowder, competed weakly against reexports of Asian textiles, and these in turn were suffering ever greater setbacks from the Manchester imitations illegally available through Brazil.

In the last two decades of the legal trade, the old contests over who should benefit from Angolan slaving—among eighteenth-century mercantilists within Portugal and between the metropole and its colonies on the imperial scale—gradually sank beneath a tide of new issues that had been rising in the background since Pombal's domestic policies in the 1770s had introduced the possibility of industrialization in Portugal. Pombal and his immediate successors had viewed Angola primarily as an appendage of Brazil, as a source of slaves for American agriculture, though also secondarily as a market for Portuguese domestic manufacture. It was funds that were lacking. Sousa Coutinho's plans for diversification of the colonial economy could not compete with the Brazilian resources committed to commerce.

But liberal ideas of economic development at home in Portugal had advanced far enough by about 1800 that a new vision of Angola began to spread, not just as a protected market for domestic manufactured goods but also as a source of cheap raw materials for the industries in the metropole. So long as Lisbon continued to broker Britain's trade with Portuguese Brazil, American cotton, and hence slaves, would prevail, with only a minority of marginal Lisbon merchants interested in slaving per se and occasionally using it to probe the weak spots in the commercial structure of Brazil. But the nineteenth century, industrialism, and liberalism all reached Portugal in the decisive decade beginning in 1807. The only ingredient of economic reform still missing was capital to implement the plans formulated.

Portugal's political and economic climate moved on from the slaving of the earlier era at that moment. When the principal suppliers of goods for the old-style African trade moved to Brazil during these years, Lisbon all but lost any direct voice in Angola's politics. Liberals assumed political power in Portugal in 1820, and Brazil separated itself politically from Portugal in 1821–22, leaving the direct commitment to slaving lodged even more separately on the American side thereafter, though with residual ties back to Portugal that prevented Lisbon from formulating a clear liberal policy with respect to Angola for the rest of the 1820s. Even after legal slaving ended in 1830, the constitutional monarchy in Lisbon required several more years before it began actively to promote its African colonies' role in a reformed post-slave-exporting nineteenth-century empire.

French and British Occupation

The French invaded Portugal at the end of 1807, provoking the flight of the Portuguese court to Rio de Janeiro. The big Lisbon merchants most closely connected to the Crown and to the British moved with the monarchy to the center of the existing Brazilian-British slave trade in southern Brazil. The consequent transfer of their African reexport trade to Brazil put these Portuguese firmly in control of the main channels of trade to Luanda and blurred the former relatively clear-cut distinctions between "Brazilian" and "Portuguese" merchants engaged in southern Atlantic slaving. The combinations reached far beyond the financial resources and commercial skills that became blended into a single Luso-Brazilian slave trade at Luanda—based mostly at Rio but with variant syntheses also at Pernambuco—to deliberate muddying of what was "Portuguese" and what was "Brazilian" to obscure national identities in an age when Anglo-Portuguese treaties put both parties in need of the funds, flags, and factors of the other in order to circumvent the legalities of British abolitionism.[1] What had formerly been a "Lisbon" interest in Angolan slaving thus became the principal "Brazilian" trade after 1810 or so, with the most significant distinction between the two being the tendency of local Brazilian

1. I am grateful to Gervase Clarence-Smith for having allowed me to see draft versions of the chapters on this period from his recently published work *The Third Portuguese Empire, 1825–1975: A Study in Economic Imperialism* (Manchester: Manchester University Press, 1985).

slavers not tied into the Anglo-Portuguese establishment at Rio to avoid the centers of imperial authority at Benguela and Luanda between 1810 and 1822.[2] Portuguese who were committed to the real economic alternative, industrialization, remained in Lisbon, and it is these metropolitan merchants and would-be industrialists who form the focus of this chapter.

These Lisbon merchants' direct involvement with Angolan slaving virtually ceased after 1807. When the royal court departed for Rio, the French invaded Portugal, and the crown opened Brazil to British commerce and capital.[3] British forces drove the French army back out of Portugal between 1808 and 1814 but stayed on to rule Portugal under military law until 1820. Lisbon merchants remained almost entirely on the sidelines of the slave trade until the end of the Napoleonic Wars in Europe in 1815, but they then reappeared weakly at Luanda, selling British reexports and products of domestic fabrication—still emphasizing gunpowder, mostly shipped through Pernambuco. These exports competed with the British goods sent through Rio de Janeiro in an Angolan slave trade expanded to the coasts north of Luanda, to the lower Zaire, and to Loango by Britain's withdrawal from slaving under its own flag.

The weakness of the Pernambucans among Brazilian participants in Angolan slaving made them natural allies of metropolitan merchants equally peripheral to the main flow of the trade. Some of the Pernambuco-centered trade which Lisbon contributed in the later 1810s may have included reshipments of slaves on to Maranhão.[4] To the limited extent that Lisbon joined at all before about 1823, its exports also went to Benguela and to the estuary of the Zaire aboard Pernambuco slavers. On the American side Lisbon had thus resumed its limited prewar deliveries of slaves to northern Brazil, but along the African shores it had added these outports, where purchases of slaves depended less on capital supplied through Brazil, to the old anchor of its direct trade at Luanda.

The Ambiguities of Independence in Brazil

When Brazil declared itself independent of Portugal in 1822, the altered diplomatic context threatened to convert the Rio-based trade to Angola from an internal Portuguese commerce, permitted by the terms of Anglo-Portuguese treaties then in force, to a foreign slave trade that the treaties

---

2. See Chapter 14 above.
3. As later recalled: *memória,* José Anacleto Gonçalves, 24 March 1824, ANTT, Junta do Comércio, maço 62, macete 122.
4. See patterns of imports at Luanda, discussed in Miller, "Imports at Luanda"; also Glacyra Lazzari Leite, "Pernambuco dentro do império português: o setor de exportação—final do século XVIII e início do século XIX," *Anais de história* 9 (1977): 52–53.

not only prohibited but also exposed to British seizure. Portuguese subjects could no longer buy slaves in Angola for shipment to Brazil, at least not directly in their own names. The end of legal trading had also heaved into sight for the Brazilians not long after, subject only to negotiations between the government in Rio and the British over means and timing. It was apparent also that slave prices would jump upward in Brazil in the late 1820s and that merchants there would engage in a last-minute race to supply American plantations with slave labor before the British permanently cut off supplies, or at the very least, increased the costs of continued importing by forcing the trade to operate illegally.

Lisbon merchants could have entertained no hope of joining to any meaningful degree in the anticipated boom, but some still dreamed of supplying slaves through legal subterfuges involving nominal Brazilian ownership of the slaves and of the vessels employed to transport them. More forward-looking circles focused on the altered status of the imports to colonial Angola from independent Brazil that underlay nearly all Angolan slaving. With political separation these had ceased to be goods circulating duty-free within the Portuguese empire and had become foreign merchandise subject to tariffs upon entry at Luanda and Benguela. The customs reforms of 1784 and 1800 once again offered a possible basis for excluding the Brazilians and the British. Beyond the revenues that high taxes on such imports might generate to support the colonial government, in the anticipated absence of the slave-export duties that had always sustained the regime, a wall of tariff protection might also create markets in Angola for products of the embryonic Portuguese domestic manufacturing sector. Lisbon's peripheral role in the last seven or eight years of Angolan slaving derived largely from plans developed along these lines to create a protected African market for metropolitan exports.[5]

From the point of view of Lisbon and Angola conversion of the Brazilian slave trade to foreign commerce probably reduced the metropole's indirect involvement with slaving the most at Luanda, since traders would have sought the slaves they hoped to send to northern Brazil at African ports other than the most regulated place on the coast. Customs records cover exports for the period between 1822 and 1825 there alone, and Luanda shipments of slaves to Pernambuco, Maranhão, and Pará then dropped well below levels they had attained during the resurgence of

---

5. Clarence-Smith, *Third Portuguese Empire*. For the Portuguese background also see Alexandre, *Origens do colonialismo português*. For Angola, Rebelo, *Relações*; Fernandes de Oliveira, *Alguns aspectos*; Dias, "Sociedade colonial." Dr. Dias has apparently located extensive documentation not integrated into the main series of Angola *caixas* in the AHU used by others who have studied the period, including myself. The arguments that follow here must accordingly be regarded as no more than provisional, pending publication of the results of Dr. Dias's research.

Portuguese dealings through Pernambuco slavers during the last years of internal slaving, between about 1815 and 1819.[6] No data show the extent to which Lisbon may have returned to routing its goods through Pernambuco after treaties of 1825 definitively recognized Brazilian independence, but the strategy would have retained little allure in view of the uncertain duty status of Portuguese goods from Brazil, since shipments from Lisbon paid duties there and possibly became subject to taxation again when offloaded in Luanda.

A commerce direct from Lisbon to Luanda made greater economic sense for Portuguese merchants after 1822. Following a year or two of hesitation while Portugal reestablished its political control in Angola through new governors sent out in 1823 and 1824, Lisbon began to organize for the dispatch of ships laden with metropolitan products straight for Angola. Since metropolitan merchants could not have expected these ventures to return to Europe with slaves, and their public talk of alternative Angolan exports could not have amounted to more than just that, they surely expected to supply traders from Brazil with goods to support their slaving.

Trading directly to Angola might have enabled merchants in Lisbon to deliver domestic products more cheaply than other Portuguese might send goods through Brazil, but these merchants also sought administrative privilege, surely against the superior British goods also available through Rio. They began with a forlorn hope of resurrecting the old strategy of forming trading companies protected by government charters, again featuring the familiar concession of privileged claims to assets of defaulting colonial debtors that metropolitan investors from the contractors onwards had enjoyed.[7] But effective use of such privileges depended on having more wealth to invest than merchants interested in Africa in 1823 or 1824 could probably muster, and outright monopolies in any case could no longer command the support of even the moderately liberal government in power in Lisbon.

However, equivalent favors of a more modern tone were forthcoming in the form of tariff concessions. A decree of 8 December 1824 halved the existing duties on all goods leaving Portugal for Angola.[8] Direct imports to Portugal from Angola—that is, anything that Angola would ship other than slaves—would likewise pay half the former rate, with taxes on

---

6. Miller, "Legal Portuguese Slaving," pp. 171–72, Table 3. Pernambuco was also briefly blockaded in this period, owing to a revolt there in 1817.

7. *Requerimento* of João Paulo Cordeiro and Joaquim Gomes Alves, n.d. (ca. 1823), AHU, Angola maço 19; *requerimentos* of João Paulo Cordeiro, 19 July 1826, AHU, Angola maço 6 (D.O.) and 11 July 1825, AHU, Angola maço 1-A; *carta regia*, 16 May 1825, AHU, Angola maço 22; Rebelo, *Relações*, p. 442.

8. Cited in *requerimento* of José António de Almeida, n.d. (ca. 1825), AHU, Angola maço 18. Also *requerimentos* of captains making departures, esp. AHU, Angola maço 20.

minerals (sulfur, saltpeter, iron, copper) halved again, and dyestuffs and gums useful in domestic textile manufacturing exempt from any duty at all. Perhaps infant munitions factories and textile mills in Portugal could grow from the cheap raw materials thus obtained.

With that encouragement, Lisbon merchants claimed to have sent no fewer than twenty ships to Angola in 1824–25.[9] Perhaps the formally still unresolved technical status of Portugal's relationship with Brazil at that date, not settled by treaty until 29 August 1825,[10] with commercial arrangements not finalized until late 1827, encouraged them to make haste while they could hide behind the ambiguities of supporting slaving between two former colonies not yet recognized as foreign entities. These Lisbon ventures may have acquired some slaves, but caution seems to have led them also to take payment in Spanish coin, which was circulating in Angola from the influx of Cuban slavers working Luanda and adjacent coasts in those years, and to buy wax.[11]

Once Portugal (and also Britain, it should not be forgotten) had acknowledged Brazilian independence, Lisbon's merchants had to restructure their trade with Angola from its base. Since the 1825 treaty not only rendered slaving by Portuguese subjects illegal but also committed the Brazilians to negotiating a further agreement to end their own trade in slaves, the two principal Portuguese merchants in Luanda—Francisco de Paula Graça and Henrique Martins Pereira—both left the colony.[12] In Lisbon, merchants petitioned the Crown to exclude Brazilian ships from Luanda as those of a foreign power.[13] They detailed the commercial obstacles standing in the way of direct trade with Angola—listing the gunpowder, domestic ironwares, linens, woolens, and domestic cottons, as well as hats, notions, and wines that they could expect to sell—but pointed out that they paid export duties totaling 12 to 15 percent in Lisbon and had to face Brazilian goods not only coming at lower tax rates but also sold at losses in Angola, owing to the profits to be made on selling slave remittances in Brazil. Clearly, merchants in Lisbon did not expect to take great profit from partnerships they might have to form with Brazilian citizens in order to provide a legal veneer of Brazilian ownership for their vessels and the slaves they would carry. The illegality of Portuguese par-

9. Merchants' petition of 14 Dec. 1825, AHU, Angola maço 18; Rebelo, *Relações,* p. 425.

10. And ratified, thus taking effect, on 15 Nov. 1825: Manchester, *British Preëminence in Brazil,* p. 202, n. 58.

11. Castelobranco, 6 June 1825, AHU, Angola cx. 69.

12. *Requerimentos* of Francisco de Paula Graça, n.d. (ca. 1826) and Henrique Martins Pereira, n.d. (ca. 1826), AHU, Angola maço 6; also *requerimento* of Antonio Lopes Anjo (Benguela), n.d. (ca. 1825), AHU, Angola maço 7; Castelobranco, 27 April 1826, AHU, Angola cx. 70.

13. Merchants' petition, 14 Dec. 1825, AHU, Angola maço 18; Rebelo, *Relações,* pp. 421–25.

ticipation in slaving after 1825 forced Lisbon's merchants, unwillingly by this late date, back in the very position their predecessors had sought before 1750: they sold goods in Angola but left ownership of the slaves to others. Sale-and-buy-back partnerships with Brazilians trading at Luanda, which transferred ownership of Portuguese sailing vessels to legal slavers, along with bills of exchange taken from Luso-Africans and Brazilians who bought their goods but owned the slaves, would have allowed them to gain only a limited position in the last, highly profitable years of Angolan slaving.[14]

New Markets and Neomercantilists

How limited Lisbon's position may have become may be estimated only roughly. Its exports in 1824 ran at about 65.000$000, increased fourfold to around 250.000$000 between 1825 and 1828, and then dropped back to 140.000$000 as the end of the slave trade neared in 1829.[15] Trade in this range would have accounted for around 15 percent of the value of goods entering Luanda in the 1820s, assuming equal valuations in both Portugal and Angola, or more if goods entered the colony at the higher prices usually prevailing there.[16] The significance of Lisbon's direct trade to Angola diminishes even more in relation to the total trade in slaves, since Luanda declined in importance relative to other ports supplying slaves to Brazilians in the 1820s. Nonetheless, a detectable increase in metropolitan efforts, if a small one in comparison to Brazilian trading, seems to have occurred at Luanda in the latter half of the 1820s.

With Portuguese gunpowder apparently an accepted part of the trade,[17] the effort to increase metropolitan exports to Angola in the 1820s fell largely on the wines and brandies of northern Portugal. Vintners sensed an opportunity to supplement Brazilian *gerebitas* and Cuban rums, the

---

14. Resort to such subterfuges may have become common only after 1827, when British naval patrols began actively to intercept ships of Portuguese registry as they approached Brazilian ports. Castelobranco, 31 March 1828 and 27 Sept. 1828, AHU, Angola cx. 72; instructions to Governor Santa Comba Dão, 4 Jan. 1830; Rebelo, *Relações,* pp. 262–63, 298–99, 442.

15. "Comercio do Reino de Portugal com as Praças da Africa," ANTT, Junta do Comércio, maço 62, macete 122. Direct imports from Angola ran at only 10%–20% of the value of exports. Cf. Lugar, "Merchant Community," pp. 87–89, for evidence of increased Portuguese activity to both Africa and Bahia in 1827.

16. Estimated from import values at Luanda in preceding years: Miller, "Imports at Luanda."

17. Rebelo, *Relações,* pp. 155–62 ff., discusses the laws restricting imports of gunpowder at Angola to the product of the new factory at Rio de Janeiro after 1811. It is clear from the import data that Portuguese powder continued to arrive as contraband through Pernambuco, however.

latter brought in recently by Spanish American slavers, in satisfying African thirsts for alcohol already conditioned by more than two centuries of selling slaves for booze.[18] A decree of 4 June 1825 positioned metropolitan wine merchants favorably by reducing duties on the fine brandies (*aguardentes*) and wines they sent directly to the African colonies. The clarification of Portugal's commercial relationship with its former colony in late 1825 began with a halving of duties applicable to Portuguese spirits sent out to established Brazilian markets. At the same time, merchants requested further tariff concessions on behalf of metropolitan wines and begged for total exclusion of cheap Brazilian spirits from Angola.[19] Without the competition from *gerebita*, they hoped to develop Angolan markets beyond the town's consumption of costly metropolitan brandies to include the much larger market in the backlands for inexpensive wines and rum.

The limits of Portugal's ability to favor its own merchants or, for that matter, even to tax the main flow of imports from Brazil became readily apparent as the doubts surrounding the exact status of foreign spirits entering Angola were resolved in 1826. An interpretation issued within a month after ratification of the treaty separating Brazil from Portugal maintained the principle of prohibiting foreign alcohol from Portuguese territories, including Angola, but it temporarily suspended the prohibition as it applied to Brazilian spirits, "until further order to the contrary." The government dared not go further, for fear of driving the Brazilians away from what trade they still conducted through Luanda to untaxed sources of slaves at Ambriz, in the lower Zaire, and elsewhere along the coast outside Luanda. Without the duties collected on the Brazilians' slaves, the colonial government's budget would collapse. Lisbon's solicitude for merchants of Portuguese nationality who remained in Brazil as slavers long after formal separation of the two nations but maintained close ties with affiliates in the former metropole also protected the key elements of Brazilian slaving.[20] After 1826, authorities in Lisbon proposed a creative compromise interpretation of legislation then on the books: a decree of 1818 had established high duties on all "fine" foreign spirits, then meaning mostly French brandies entering Brazil in competition with metropolitan *aguardentes*. As reapplied later to Angola, the decree excluded a shipment of Cuban rum arriving aboard a Brazilian ship but did not extend to the cheap *gerebitas* of Brazil.[21] The ruling thus protected the limited market for the better products of metropolitan viticulture but did not threaten the Brazilian cane brandies at the basis of slaving.

18. Research remains to be done on the early wine trade to Africa; for later periods, see José Capela, *O vinho para o preto* (Porto: Afrontamento, 1973).

19. Almeida *Requerimento*, n.d. (ca. 1825), AHU, Angola maço 18.

20. Clarence-Smith, *Third Portuguese Empire*, chap. 2.

21. Rebelo, *Relações*, pp. 273, 280–81.

Abandonment of efforts to levy import duties on "foreign" Brazilian spirits was only part of the larger problem of luring slavers to Luanda after 1825, when Brazilians could readily acquire untaxed slaves north of the city, sometimes from the very same Luso-Africans who also supplied slaves in the colonial port.[22] About the only attraction that Luanda offered to the Brazilians was the food and water that they could take on there to sustain the slaves they would buy farther on down the coast. At about the time that the Luso-Africans, as Portuguese subjects, had had their own vessels detained by British anti-slave trade patrols lying in wait off the ports of Brazil, the Luso-African provisioners of Luanda seem to have withheld supplies in what must have been retaliation for what they saw as unfair competition from Brazilian slavers, still legal in the eyes of the British and allowed to pass unimpeded.[23] It was one more redirection of the same tactic that local suppliers had employed in years past against Lisbon merchants and others whom they had come to regard as intruders.

The Angola governors of the 1820s hesitated to take overt measures to occupy the ports at Ambriz, Cabinda, and other places the foreigners frequented north of the city in order to tax trade there for fear of British opposition and Brazilian resistance. They lacked the means to do so in any event. In the end, one governor recommended fomenting rivalries among the African lords of those northern ports. He expected that rumors of warfare on the shore would make the security of Luanda Bay, even if imports were taxed there, preferable to the risks of trade with warlike savages elsewhere. He even proposed inviting the British antislaving patrols, then confined to waters north of the equator, south as far as Ambriz in order to drive the Brazilians back under the shelter of the Portuguese customs house in Luanda.[24] Such schemes came to nothing, and Brazilians continued to avoid Luanda after 1825 much as they had done between 1810 and 1821.

Toward Abolition

The storm clouds of abolition, gathering since 1811, finally broke over the southern Atlantic late in 1826. On 23 November of that year the Brazilians agreed to a treaty fixing the end of the legal trade three years hence. Though the deadline was subsequently extended to allow ships departing Brazil before that date to return with slaves, with an absolute cut-off date of 30 March 1830 for ships leaving Africa, the end was clearly

22. Castelobranco, 27 July 1824, AHU, Angola cx. 68; Rebelo, *Relações,* pp. 294–95.
23. Rebelo, *Relações,* pp. 299–301.
24. Castelobranco, 23 Feb. 1824, AHU, Angola cx. 70.

in view.[25] The remaining months of the legal trade brought pandemonium as slavers ran for financial cover.

The volume of slaving rose to new heights all along the coast, with a significant rise even at Luanda. Meanwhile, the government in Angola contemplated its utter inability to pay its own employees, including the colonial army, when exports would cease after 1830. "Pirates" attacked Brazilians at Cabinda, doubtless in search of slaves to sell in Cuba. Merchants with assets invested through Luanda tried to collect their debts for transfer out of the colony in the form of slaves, thus drawing down the working capital available, even in the form of captive labor, for economic reconstruction in Angola after the trade would end.[26]

In the interior of both Luanda and Benguela disquiet spread as African suppliers tried to foresee how they would survive without the imports that they had bought for so long with slaves. The governor sent out to oversee the transition arrived from Portugal with a detachment of 150 troops to try to contain the unrest.[27] Lisbon requested local Angolan merchants to reinvest their assets in agriculture, presumably meaning that they should attempt to employ the slaves they held in Angola rather than selling them off to Brazil. African customers, the government further proposed, should earn the currency necessary to continue buying Portuguese imports by offering their labor as headbearers, *carregadores,* who would carry agricultural and other produce down to the coast.[28] At the very least, the final departure of the Brazilian slavers would leave the field open to Lisbon, even at the modest levels of investment that these forlorn proposals revealed the metropole prepared to afford.

Lisbon's other plans for stimulating commodity production departed similarly from the premise that Portugal could commit only limited means to Angola in the 1820s, and hardly any of them went beyond projects proposed by generations of governors going back to Sousa Coutinho and before. Attention therefore focused on beeswax and ivory, the two main extractive products already reaching Luanda from non-slave-producing areas in the interior, and for the very reasons that Africans engaged in these extractive enterprises: scarce Portuguese goods might increase exports of both without significant investment in productive capacity, land, slaves, buildings, or machinery. Insofar as planners in Lisbon seriously contemplated investment, they resurrected old mercantilist transportation schemes like the canal linking Luanda to the navigable lower reaches of

25. And 30 June 1830 for clearing customs in Brazil.
26. Dias, "Sociedade colonial," p. 274.
27. Castelobranco, 22 Sept. 1828, AHU, Angola cx. 72; idem, 10 and 13 Feb. 1829, AHU, Angola cx. 73; Santa Comba Dão, 10 June and 21 Sept. 1829, AHU, Angola cx. 73; Joaquim Aurelio de Oliveira (governor, Benguela), 1 Dec. 1829, AHU, Angola cx. 73; Delgado, *Famosa e histórica Benguela,* pp. 481–82; Douville, *Voyage au Congo,* 1:8.
28. Santa Comba Dão, 10 June 1830, AHU, Angola cx. 73.

the Kwanza River—an idea mooted since the seventeenth century. Otherwise, few dared to dream far beyond modifying the plans envisaged in the 1790s, replacing African deliveries of slaves to the coast, with the delivery, by Africans, of ivory and wax from the vast regions then enclosed within the slaving frontier.

Beeswax had continued to hold its minor position in Angola's early-nineteenth-century export ledger, usually at about one-tenth the value of slaves at Luanda and probably somewhat more than that at Benguela by the 1820s.[29] The high cost of Angolan wax—usually $200 to $300 per *libra* (pound) for yellow and $300 to $400 for more highly refined white—made it too expensive to sell widely on world markets, but traders found a limited market for it in Brazil for votive candles. Merchants also occasionally found Angolan wax an economical means of remitting proceeds from their sales of goods in forms less risky than slaves.[30] Once Lisbon merchants found themselves unable to carry slaves legally after 1825, they turned to beeswax as the next best means of taking gains from goods sold at Luanda. The new demand raised prices, and with customs valuations set artificially low as a means of negating the effect of the export duties, exports of Angolan beeswax began to rise.

Wax had come mainly from the efforts of small part-time producers before 1825, often from Africans living around the government posts, from south of the Kwanza through Pungo Andongo and from the uninhabited woodlands between Ambaca and Kasanje.[31] Specialized collection then spread into the wooded regions where bees proliferated east of the Kwango. These new eastern wax-gathering regions allowed the community of Luso-African petty traders around Ambaca to develop a modest prosperity independent of the old slave-trading aristocracies during the 1830s and 1840s, and some of them would have been predecessors of the "Ambaquistas" famed in the middle of the nineteenth century for their wide-ranging small-scale trades throughout central Africa. A parallel evolution of wax trading would have begun among African commoners in the Benguela highlands, partially distinct from the slave trade of the aristocracy there.[32]

29. Miller, "Imports at Luanda," p. 241, Table VI.9. Comparable data for Benguela may be found in AHU, Angola cxs. 43, 45–50, 53, 55–60, 62–64, 66, and 72. Also see Rebelo, *Relações*, Quadro 13.

30. Various Pernambuco Company instructions to administrators in Angola, AHMF; Moçâmedes *parecer* (on a *consulta* of the Conselho Ultramarino, 16 June 1796), AHU, Angola maço 6.

31. Castelobranco, 6 June 1825, AHU, Angola cx. 69; Santa Comba Dão, 14 Dec. 1830 (cf. the enclosed customs schedule for 1830, which used prices from the 1760s), AHU, Angola cx. 74; Saldanha da Gama, *Memoria sobre as colonias,* p. 79; Vellut, "Diversification de l'économie de cueillette," pp. 13, 14. Also "Reflexão anonima sobre o comercio de Angola," n.d. (ca. 1780s?), AHU, Sala 12 diversos, cx. 1; I am grateful to Jill Dias for this reference.

32. Miller, "Central and Southern Angola"; Clarence-Smith, "Farmer-Herders of Southern Angola"; also Heywood, "Production, Trade, and Power."

In the 1820s ivory exports still remained the monopoly of the Royal Treasury. The low prices that the treasury paid continued to inhibit shipments of tusks out through Luanda.[33] Since the treasury's monopoly extended only to export of the tusks, ivory circulated in Luanda and elsewhere in the colony as the equivalent of a treasury note, a special-purpose currency useful for paying the duties owed on exported slaves in Angola rather than having to expend coin or currency there or to draw bills of exchange on Brazil.[34] Deliveries of ivory to Luanda had declined in the 1770s as rising world ivory prices had caused the French and the British to buy increasing quantities elsewhere from Luso-African smugglers. The treasury had unsuccessfully attempted to attract ivory back to Luanda in 1790 by offering slightly higher prices.[35] Deliveries had then increased noticeably in the mid-1790s, especially during the years when the wars in Europe disrupted foreign competition, but smuggling had resumed as soon as the foreigners returned.[36] The governor at Benguela had attempted to attract ivory by inventing a new "prime" category that the treasury would buy at a price higher than that authorized for the existing official grades, but he had run into Lisbon's refusal to alter the existing structure of low prices.[37] As a result, ivory dispatched through the Royal Treasury at Luanda seldom had amounted to more than 1 percent of the value of slaves, or about 10 percent of the value of beeswax.[38]

With Brazil independent and Portugal's redoubled interest in exports other than slaves from Angola, liberal opinion in Portugal began to solidify against the treasury's ancient ivory monopoly. The contraband markets for Angolan ivory had driven the price at which it circulated within the colony well above what the treasury was authorized to offer for it. Brazilian ship captains smuggled tusks right through the port at Luanda in the containers of provisions they bought there for slaves they intended to load at ports on down the coast to the north. One merchant even requested a private secondary monopoly to buy all "the ivory the treasury could not afford" at Luanda, thereby suggesting that the government left the price low because it lacked the funds to buy the greater quantities that a more

33. The number of tusks delivered to Luanda declined from 1,371 in 1771 to only 721 in 1813: figures in AHU, Angola cxs. 33, 36, 62.

34. E.g., Maranhão Company instructions in Carreira, "Companhias pombalinas de navegação," p. 65; Benguela *regimento,* in Delgado, *Famosa e histórica Benguela,* pp. 441, 442.

35. The formulation of the decision to increase prices is found in Registo das provisões e cartas régias expedidas para Angola, 27 June 1788, AHTC, livro no. 1, fol. 88; ibid., 8 July 1790, fols. 122–23; *bando* (Almeida e Vasconcelos), 19 Jan. 1791, AHA, cód. 314, fols. 1v–2.

36. Miller, "Imports at Luanda," p. 241, Table VI.9; also Delgado, *Reino,* p. 386; Santos, "Relações de Angola com o Rio de Janeiro," p. 10; de Mello, "Angola no começo do século," pp. 559n, 560n; Godinho, 23 Oct. 1804, AHU, Angola cx. 55; Spix and Martius, *Viagem pelo Brasil,* 2:154, note V; Saldanha da Gama, *Memoria sobre as colonias de Portugal,* pp. 86–91.

37. Letter of 13 March 1792, AHTC, livro no. 1, fol. 156.

38. Miller, "Imports at Luanda," p. 241, Table VI.9.

generous offer might have attracted. Lisbon, apparently unwilling to share even wealth it could not itself claim, rejected this petition. Most of the ivory that fell into the hands of the Luso-Africans went through Ambriz to foreigners rather than into the treasury's storehouses at Luanda.[39]

The prospect of the end of legal slaving made the already difficult situation nearly impossible from the point of view of treasury officials seeking ivory. These losses loomed all the larger, since the treasury would need profits from reselling ivory in Portugal to replace the export duties it would lose when slaves became illegal. Without claims from the slave export duty, payable in ivory, they expected no longer to receive any tusks at all. Costs of bringing the ivory to Luanda would rise owing to loss of the indirect subsidy it enjoyed in the form of free transport on the backs of slaves being driven down to the city. No one with ivory in the interior could afford to pay the labor that future deliveries of tusks to the coast at Luanda would require.[40] In fact, merchants in Luanda petitioned for permission to sell ivory directly to private buyers from Europe at open-market prices only in 1834, four years after termination of the legal trade, when revived illegal slaving through ports north of Luanda again made transportation of tusks to the coast economical. Lisbon merchants must have supported this request, since ivory would give them a commodity of increasing value in Europe that they could ship straight back to Lisbon without having to risk the forbidden trade in slaves to Brazil, whether directly, or indirectly via bills secured by slaves. The government then finally freed the ivory trade from the treasury's monopoly and touched off the beginning of the ivory boom that became the prominent feature of Angola's mid-nineteenth-century legal export trade.[41]

Ivory and beeswax, particularly in combination with unacknowledged and illicit continued slaving, admirably filled the main requirement Lisbon imposed on plans for economic reconstruction after slaving in Angola: minimal commitment of capital. Both products came entirely from African producers, who, with adequate export price incentives, would invest their own time and dependent labor. Further, ivory was susceptible to technological development merely through increasing the existing trade in gunpowder and muskets. Higher prices at Portuguese ports would increase shipments there immediately and substantially by diverting tusks away from the existing supply systems already serving foreigners, thus necessitating virtually no investment in new commercial institutions. The Luso-Africans and Africans would manage production quite well without financial support from Lisbon, leaving metropolitan merchants with their preferred

39. AHTC, livro no. 1, 17 Jan. 1827, fols. 116–17; *bando* (Oliveira), 13 Jan. 1828, AHU, Angola cx. 71.

40. Santa Comba Dão, 14 Dec. 1830, AHU, Angola cx. 73.

41. Delgado, *Famosa e histórica Benguela*, pp. 111–12.

role of buyer at the coast and obligating the government only for facilitating transport from the interior.

Other proposed forms of economic diversification languished if they depended on more substantial investments of metropolitan capital. Since 1808 government interdictions no longer prevented private entrepreneurs from establishing enterprises of any sort in the colonies,[42] but Portuguese investors of the 1820s lacked the capital to take advantage of the opening. Proposals abounded, mostly intended to develop Angola as a replacement for the tropical commodities that Lisbon had lost to Britain's domination of the Brazilian economy. Sugar, cotton, and tobacco, the established boom crops in the lost American colony, accordingly attracted the most attention, mostly as available in the wild or from African peasant producers. Others stressed the Africans' potential as collectors of valuable gums and resins, sylvan coffee, dyewoods, fish, spices, and other products from the colony's woods and waters. Traders contemplated buying cattle from African herdsmen at Benguela, potentially another Rio Grande do Sul in the eyes of the planners.[43] A limited awareness of the risks of capitalized agriculture in an area of highly unpredictable rainfall crept into planning for exports in the aftermath of slaving, but most schemes rested blindly on myths justifying the low-investment strategies within the capabilities of Portugal: tropical natural abundance and African peasants needing coercion, but not economic incentives or resources, to produce. All of these plans consequently remained sterile dreams until commodity prices rose and systematic investment in the most promising of these agricultural sectors began later in the century.

For the moment, metropolitan attention focused primarily on transportation. Complaints of labor shortages inland from Luanda had grown steadily in the 1780s and 1790s, perhaps contributing to the government's reluctance to continue supervising the colony's interior in those decades.[44] The drought of the same period, which forced many Africans away from their usual places of residence to forage in the woodlands, must have contributed to the crisis by removing labor from the reach of Portuguese recruiters. Further, the growing distances over which traders had to transport goods by the end of the century must also have exceeded the capacity of the porterage relay system devised when the slaving frontier had been

42. *Alvará* of 12 April 1808, AHU, Angola cx. 58.

43. Delgado, *Famosa e histórica Benguela*, pp. 83, 90, 97, 100–101 et passim; Saldanha da Gama, *Memoria sobre as colonias de Portugal*; Albuquerque e Tovar, 16 Sept. 1819, 13 Nov. 1819, 4 Feb. 1820, 17 Aug. 1820, 28 Sept. 1820, all AHU, Angola cx. 65; Godinho, 23 Oct. 1804, AHU, Angola cx. 55; de Mello, 12 July 1805, AHU, Angola cx. 55; Manoel José Maria da Costa e Silva (*secretaria de estado*), memorial of 22 Dec. 1823, IHGB, Docs. negócios de Angola, fols. 45–53.

44. E.g., Moçâmedes *apontamentos*, AHU, Angola maço 2-A; "Informação breve," AHU, Angola cx. 42; Saldanha da Gama, *Memoria sobre as colonias de Portugal*, pp. 74–78.

much nearer the coast. What labor there was often remained inaccessible to Lisbon merchants and their agents in Luanda, since the *capitães-mores* continued to use their near-absolute authority over the Africans of their districts to favor themselves and their associates, particularly in the old Luso-African strongholds of Pungo Andongo and Ambaca.[45] The shortage of backs and hands became all the more critical after 1810 as Lisbon merchants and the colonial government began considering where they could find headbearers required for the commodity exports that might follow slaving.

The severity of the labor shortage emerged clearly from a petition that merchants in Luanda drafted during the interim government of 1821–23. Their primary concern focused on finding porters to carry their goods to the interior. The residents of Ambaca, in particular, they alleged, were hoarding entire villages of Africans as private labor reserves and declaring them ineligible for assignment to merchants from the city as *carregadores*. The Luanda merchants proposed to take direct charge of allocating African labor, removing the *capitães-mores* from any role in the recruitment process, and to restrict allocated labor to the transport of goods. Certain people, they alleged, had been requesting Africans as "bearers" but employing them for long periods as ordinary fieldhands and as construction labor. Even priests were to be strictly limited in the claims they could make on African time.[46] The interim government in Luanda responded to these pleas by removing the *capitães-mores* from their role in labor recruitment and limiting the number of Africans who could be taken from any single jurisdiction.[47]

But the problem of head porterage, too, remained unresolved in 1830 as the legal slave trade ended, and Lisbon looked for other means to take control of the colony's African labor. Battles over labor supplies would continue on between metropolitan investors and Luso-African slaveholders through much of the nineteenth century. In the meanwhile, Africans from the central plateau and from the Kwango valley, with ample reserves of slaves and other dependents built up during the last years of illegal slaving in the 1840s, emerged as the main carriers in the wax and ivory caravans that began to arrive in growing numbers from the east. When these illicit slave exports finally ended after 1850, a surplus of labor built up in the interior and fueled the African-financed commodity export booms of the last half of the century.

45. Godinho, 23 Oct. 1804, AHU, Angola cx. 55; Albuquerque e Tovar, 6 Nov. 1819, AHU, Angola cx. 66.
46. Memorial, AHU, Sala 12 diversos, no. 825.
47. Avelino Dias, 8 Nov. 1823, AHA, cód. 95, fols. 32v–33; Castelobranco, 29 Oct. 1824, AHA, cód. 95, fols. 118v–19; Manoel Patricio Correa de Castro memorial (1823), IHGB, lata 28, doc. 21, fols. 15v–16.

Government officials also thought more broadly about transport policy in terms that bypassed the immediate struggle over impressed African labor. Early in the nineteenth century, planners in Lisbon had urged formation of herds of mules and horses near Luanda.[48] Oxen came into use on a limited basis along the overburdened corridor east of Ambaca, an area particularly short of human transport and also one relatively healthy for livestock. In 1813–17 the government again took up the old idea of building a canal to link the port at Luanda to the navigable reaches of the Kwanza, but the project failed once again.[49] The next governor, Albuquerque e Tovar, perceived the futility of so grandiose a construction project and instead substituted modest measures to improve existing canoe transportation from the Bengo and the Kwanza into the city.[50] At both Benguela and Luanda governors built piers suited for loading bulky agricultural goods onto ships, to replace the small boats in which slavers had always rowed their captives out to *tumbeiros* anchored some distance from the shore.[51] Implicit was the recognition that ivory, wax, and coffee would not respond to the invitation to escape or revolt that a ship moored close alongshore offered to slaves.

The End

Legal slaving finally ended in 1830, as yet another African drought devastated the initial agricultural experiments undertaken to prepare for the long-anticipated new era of commodity exports.[52] The Luso-Africans, very much in charge during the sellers' market of the trade's last months of virtually unlimited Brazilian demand, had taken advantage of the panic buying of slaves to deplete their own holdings of labor, shipping captives faster than Brazil could pay for them. Another group of traders left Luanda, presumably with their profits safely transferred out of the colony in the last surge of slaves shipped. Angola thus found itself depleted of the human resources—its slaves and other African peasant producers and porters—

48. Rebelo, *Relações,* pp. 133–40.

49. Oliveira Barboza, 4 April 1813, AHU, Angola cx. 61; idem, 28 May 1814, AHU, Angola cx. 62; idem, 26 Jan. 1815 and 6 March 1816, AHU, Angola cx. 63; "Memoria sobre o encanamento do Rio Coanza" (1816), AHU, Angola cx. 64; Motta Feo e Torres, 12 Aug. 1816 and 2 March 1817, AHU, Angola cx. 64; idem, 6 Oct. 1818, AHU, Angola cx. 65; idem, 19 July 1819, AHU, Angola cx. 66.

50. Albuquerque e Tovar, 13 Sept. 1819, AHU, Angola cx. 65; idem, 18 Sept. 1820, AHU, Angola cx. 67.

51. Albuquerque e Tovar, 24 March 1820, AHU, Angola cx. 66; idem, 26 June 1820, AHU, Angola cx. 67; Delgado, *Famosa e histórica Benguela,* pp. 90, 97, 102.

52. Santa Comba Dão, 14 Dec. 1830, AHU, Angola cx. 73; among earlier warnings on drought, see de Mello, 12 July 1805, AHU, Angola cx. 55; Manoel da Cruz memorial, 20 March 1824, ANTT, Junta do Comércio, maço 62, macete 122.

on which the planned new sorts of commerce might be built. Owing to the exhausted supplies of labor in Angola, slaving at the ports to the north dropped sharply for two or three years, and only occasional Brazilian ships and Spaniards and Americans buying for Cuba braved British patrols at sea to take on the slaves offered.[53] Traders who remained at Luanda rode out the first years of the 1830s by collecting on amounts owed them from the last burst of exports in 1829 and 1830.[54] The northern drift of slaving established in the last years of the legal trade thus continued, though at temporarily reduced levels, and became the root from which illegal trading would spring up again after about 1834.

At Luanda, government preparations for the new era arrived with Governor Baron of Santa Comba Dão in 1829. The instructions he brought with him finally implemented the customs duties on imports, foreseen as early as 1784 but finally made utterly necessary by the ending of the government's revenues from slaves leaving the colony. Portuguese goods coming in from Lisbon would pay no tariffs at all, while goods of any sort arriving from Brazil would pay the 15 percent stipulated by the treaties and agreements of 1825–27. Foreign imports of any other origin would be subject to a duty of 24 percent. Exports, already shifting toward beeswax, would pay 2 percent only. Talk about freeing the trade in ivory was already going around. There was even a wholly impractical proposal, never implemented, to establish a new tax on slaves *imported* into Angolan territory from the African lands to the east.[55]

The old notions died hard. Everyone assumed at the very least that slavery, still legal within the colony, would form the basis for whatever form of economic development might ensue. However liberal the anti-slavery pronouncements of government ministers in Lisbon, realists in Angola knew better. The colonials must also have assumed that an export slave trade would soon revive in illicit forms, and so their proposal to tax imports also subtly promised to restore the established fiscal foundation of the government on slave trading, by taxing the movement of labor at the point where Portugal still retained the right to conduct slaving, within its own dominions. The proposal also represented business as usual in imposing the tax on colonial slavers and leaving metropolitan exporters unburdened by the high costs of owning other human beings.

Conclusion

Commercial capital had become the key to Angolan slaving as the trade shifted from its militaristic variant, associated with warlike Brazilian gov-

---

53. Santa Comba Dão, 3 July 1831, AHU, Angola cx. 74.
54. Santa Comba Dão, 11 Oct. 1830, AHU, Angola cx. 74.
55. Santa Comba Dão, 11 Oct. 1830, AHU, Angola cx. 73.

ernors' raiding and trading in the late seventeenth century amidst the chaos
of an accessible slaving frontier near Angola's Atlantic coast, to the mercantilistic form that predominated by the early nineteenth century, with
commercial credit supporting less violent methods of slaving over a large
area of western central Africa and Luso-African and African transporters
sharing the role of financier with European slavers based in Brazil.

As capital had become determinative, Lisbon's modestly wealthy merchants had lost out. On the scale of the entire southern Atlantic trading
nexus, Portuguese merchants had devoted most of the eighteenth century
to unsuccessful efforts at using their limited financial strength in Angola
to maintain a position for themselves on the margins of their own empire.
In so doing they helped to expand and commercialize the trade, to their
own advantage over local slavers in the short run, but to the advantage
of foreigners with greater mercantile strengths in the long run.

Meanwhile Britain became the world's greatest commercial power. In
the small corner of that great transformation involving Angola and Brazil,
Britain's Industrial Revolution meant that American raw materials, principally cotton, replaced gold as the main sources of wealth to be derived
from Portugal's empire. British merchants accordingly advanced steadily
toward financial control of the Brazilian agricultural economy. The British
moved in indirectly through Lisbon's community of Anglo-Portuguese
merchants, then more directly through independent smuggling to Brazil
and finally through fully legal imports, exports, and investment after 1810.
As British capital helped finance increases in Brazilian production, it also
flowed into the Angolan slave trade through Brazilian and Portuguese
commercial houses in Rio de Janeiro and overwhelmed the increasingly
modest assets that Portuguese merchants were willing to subject to the
high risks of owning slaves.

Only when the French drove the Portuguese court and the majority
of Lisbon merchants to Rio de Janeiro did the commercial elite finally,
after 1810, attain the control they had long sought over Angola's wealth
in slaves. They did so, of course, in significant part as agents of the British.
But at that late date, with abolition already an accomplished fact in other
sectors of the Atlantic slave trade, they had won little more than a risky
anachronism, able at last to own the slaves they carried but only because
British bankers and industrialists preferred safer investments, with longer
futures, in commodities, manufactures, and productive capacity. Legal and
diplomatic hazards had become more significant than the mortality costs
of owning slaves, and so the British remained safely in the background
while allowing Rio Portuguese to use their wealth to move in on commercial terrain once consigned to Brazilians and Luso-Africans.

Merchants of metropolitan origins and connections finally made significant profits from trading in slaves after 1810, but mostly in return for
lending their names, their vessels, and the Portuguese flag to wealthy

foreigners, more as Brazilians than as Portuguese, and as appendages of British dominance in Brazil rather than as masters in their own empire. By 1830, Portuguese slavers in Brazil found themselves poised to reap large profits from the illicit trade that would follow but also found themselves declared pirates, foreigners in their own former colony, and outlaws forced to buy and sell slaves beyond the shell of imperial protection they had long used to maintain the series of limited contributions they had made to earlier slaving in Angola. If any looked beyond the profits of the morrow, they might well have asked themselves to what extent the trade they had gained retained the value of what their predecessors had so long sought.

Ownership of slaves made economic sense for these Brazilian-Portuguese slavers because they had finally gained objectives that made the trade the profitable one that Lisbon had sought for more than a century. Brazilian prices for slaves had risen high enough to cover the mortality costs of owning people on the middle passage, thanks to the British demand for Brazilian commodities. It may be assumed that the low-priced British manufactured goods with which nineteenth-century slavers bought captives in Africa also reduced their real costs of buying Angolan labor beyond what they had to pay to support expanded slaving networks in Angola. The risk of owning slaves itself also dropped with the spread of British inoculation and vaccination against smallpox and with the introduction of other modern medical and hygienic techniques inspired by abolitionist pressures from Britain. The drift of Portuguese slaving toward wetter regions nearer the equator and the increased speed with which slavers boarded their cargoes and departed everywhere to escape detection by British cruisers at sea also reduced deaths among their captives. It was more than a little ironic that slavers from Portugal benefited from these efficiencies, mostly of British origin, only under London's threat of illegalization and extinction and after having spent the preceding hundred years using imperial law to foist the risks of slave ownership that were unavoidable in that earlier age onto their colonial subjects.

With improved profits from Angolan slaving accruing to Portuguese in Brazil for all these reasons, the liberal interests left behind in metropolitan Portugal in the 1810s and 1820s inherited the peripheral position that Lisbon never quite overcame with respect to the economy of its western central African colony. They had no means to alter the colony's near-total commitment to slaving between 1815 and the mid-1830s and therefore had to content themselves with minor adjustments to tariffs and with laying plans for future commerce in wax, or ivory, or some other tropical commodity that might replace the Brazilian raw materials they had lost to the British.

Legacies of slaving lingered on well after 1830. Former slavers in western central Africa put dependents they could not sell to work collecting and processing wax, hunting elephants, or tapping the latex sap from creepers and bushes in the second half of the nineteenth century. The last Brazil-based burst of Angolan slaving belatedly enabled the metropole to incorporate Angola in the reformed Portuguese empire that early-nineteenth-century reformers in Lisbon envisaged. As Gervase Clarence-Smith has plausibly argued, Portuguese commercial wealth gained there from the last forty years of southern Atlantic slave-trading from 1810 to 1850 helped to finance the modest industrial revolution that led to modern Portuguese colonialism after 1860. With exports of slaves largely banished after 1850, the liberal reformers of Lisbon finally set their industrial and financial capital to work employing quasi slaves in Africa rather than in Brazil.

Part 5

Conclusion

19

The Economics of Mortality

Angolan captives followed a way of death on their long and perilous journeys to Brazil in multiple senses far more immediate than the metaphorical "social death" that awaited them as dishonored slaves in America,[1] the vague and hellish Kongo "land of the dead"[2] across an ocean that the Portuguese might well have likened to the River Styx of their own Western mythology.

For the Portuguese and Brazilians who invested in, operated, and supervised Angolan slaving, slaves were "a commodity that died with such ease"[3] that the Europeans organized the early-eighteenth-century trade around avoiding ownership of the perishable human merchandise. Only with reduced slave mortality toward the end of the eighteenth century, and with the first glimmerings of enlightened confidence, modern medical and sanitary technology, and prosperity, did Brazilians and then the Portuguese take on the risks of death attendant on owning southern Atlantic slaves that they had formerly assigned to others.

The assumption of slave ownership by wealthier parties to the trade after the 1770s sustained a higher generalization that few in positions to determine the nature of their participation in colonial trade and development chose to own its riskiest element—the slaves from Angola. As the Atlantic world moved from mercantilism toward the industrial age, Brazilians who had left the slaves to die on the hands of the Luso-Africans in the late seventeenth century began to buy into slaving, with British backing, using profits from the late-eighteenth-century recovery in Amer-

---

1. Patterson, *Slavery and Social Death.*
2. Or, as a famous Brazilian aphorism noted in imagery that unknowingly, and therefore probably significantly, mirrored the fatalistic perspective of the Kongo, colonial Portuguese America was "hell for blacks" (if also purgatory for whites and paradise for mulattoes). Mary Karasch picks up the strong stench of death hovering over early-nineteenth-century Rio de Janeiro in her sensitive and intimate reconstruction, *Slave Life.* See also Mattoso, *Etre esclave au Brésil,* pp. 170–71: "The Brazilian black lived with an intense preoccupation with dying properly."
3. "Um género que com tanta facilidade perece": Governor Almeida e Vasconcelos, 12 March 1792, as cited in Carreira, *Notas sobre o tráfico português,* p. 17.

ican agriculture that they could not put into productive use in economically stagnant Portugal. The Portuguese of the metropole, who earlier had avoided buying slaves, gradually extended their ownership position in the trade by the early nineteenth century, but only because British financial strength both supported their slaving indirectly and left them no better alternative elsewhere in their own empire. The British, easily wealthy enough to call the tune in the American territories of Spain and Portugal by 1810, abolished their own trade in slaves even as they continued as organizers and financiers behind late Portuguese-, Spanish-, and Anglo-American slaving in the Atlantic, with the dying slaves safely consigned to others.

Witnesses to the Facts

Those left to own the slaves frequently expressed accurately morbid preoccupations in their analyses of the trade, often in detailed commercial advice far more explicit than the habitual designation of the slave ships themselves as floating "coffins" (*tumbeiros*). One Bahian, commenting on the trade's economics of mortality, explained that "if only a few die in the middle passage, one's profit is certain; if many perish, the investor is lost, as he is then required to pay for the exorbitant risk that he took upon himself" in borrowing funds for his voyage.[4] A draft budget for a proposed slaving company remarked, "The only attractive feature of this trade is the vain hope of experiencing the rare fortune of fewer deaths in the transport of the slaves, both on the land and on the sea"; the proposal matter-of-factly included cost estimates of 12 percent for deaths prior to embarkation in Africa and another 15 percent for mortality at sea, along with expenses for trade goods, duties, and other ordinary categories of costs.[5] As if defining the commodity, one correspondent cautioned a buyer of slaves in Luanda that "the slave (*moleque*) is a thing that may die" at any time.[6] A century earlier, another correspondent in Rio had written advising investment in a slaving venture "which, if it should be undertaken, may God deliver us from deaths among the slaves so that the profit may be assured."[7]

4. Silva Lisboa, 18 Oct. 1781, in *Annaes da Biblioteca nacional do Rio de Janeiro*, pp. 504–5 (also cited in Taunay, *Subsídios*, p. 219). The very high mortality characteristic of the sixteenth century had impressed the point on the earliest Portuguese involved in the trade. Merchants in the Cape Verde Islands wrote to the king in 1512: "Slaves are a very risky commodity, and many of them die": Elbl, "Portuguese Trade," p. 488. A sixteenth-century description of Portuguese interests in western central Africa specified that most slaves came from the Luanda area, as most captives available from Kongo came from up the Zaire River ("Anzicos," or Tio) "and many of them die": Heintze, *Fontes*, p. 197.

5. "Relação sobre escravatura," n.d. (ca. 1760s), AHU, Angola maço 10 (D.O.). Cf. paraphrase in Rebelo, *Relações*, p. 89.

6. Anonymous letter of 1 March 1824, ANRJ, cód. 1142.

7. Muzzi, 4 May 1723, in Lisanti, *Negócios coloniais*, 2:357.

The same writer had already urged his principal in Lisbon to give the captain of the ship employed to carry the slaves a personal interest in the project so that he would treat the slaves better, thus reducing deaths, "as it is there that the greatest gain is to be made."[8]

One mid-eighteenth-century proposal for reforms in the trade explained the multiple costs of slave deaths when competition between ships loading in Luanda held up departures from the port. If the waiting slaves sickened and died, the Royal Treasury lost the duties that would not be paid on the dead. If ships arrived too close, one after the other, in Brazil, owners of the slaves raced to sell their captives as quickly as possible "to avoid the expense of maintaining them and to free themselves of the risk of their dying." One vessel, belonging to a certain António Ramalho, had reached Luanda in 1750 and two years later was still attempting to make up the full cargo that the contractors required him to take, because the slaves he had taken on were dying faster than he could load replacements. He had thrown out more than 500 worthless corpses on the shore, trying to fill a hold that probably could have carried no more than 300 or 350 survivors.[9]

The holders of the contract for Angolan slave duties instructed their Luanda administrators thoroughly in the trade's economics of mortality. The administrators were to avoid buying slaves for the contract, so as not to take on themselves the risk of the slaves dying en route to Brazil. Moreover, "the profitability of the Contract consists in the speed with which ships leave the port, so that there should not be mortality among the slaves on the shore, as the Contract will thus lose the duties on them." They were also to avoid allowing two large ships to buy slaves for delivery to the same port in Brazil at the same time, as the competition would delay them both, and then slaves "brought over one side [of the ship] die [and are thrown overboard] over the other."[10] Pernambuco Company directors made the same point to their Angola delegates, though with the strategy adjusted to the economics of having to own the dying slaves: they should simply rid themselves of captives found to be sick or at risk of perishing.[11] An acute observer described the dilemma from the point of view of Brazilian ships buying slaves at Luanda at the end of the eighteenth century: "None ought to buy slaves before his turn [in the order of departure] so as not to expose his capital to the insubstantiality of human flesh."[12] When slave prices dropped in Brazil, the directors of the company in Lisbon advised their Luanda administrators to buy wax, even at prices that promised no trading profit, since wax sustained fewer losses through "damage."[13]

8. Muzzi, 15 Oct. 1721, ibid., p. 228; see also Lisanti's introduction, ibid., 1:di.
9. "Exposição das rezoens . . . ," n.d. (ca. 1753?), ANTT, Ministério do Reino, maço 499.
10. "Instrução," 8 Jan. 1767 (Domingos Dias da Silva), AHU, Angola cx. 31.
11. Carreira, "Companhias pombalinas de navegação," p. 353.
12. Corrêa, *História de Angola*, 1:49.
13. AHMF, Angola *copiador*, letter of 4 July 1769.

Governor Sousa Coutinho, too, noted the economics of slave mortality from the point of view of government officials trying to organize a regular supply of the Asian cottons on which trading depended: "This business is not of the kind that may be kept in storehouses until trade goods might arrive, nor does it tolerate uncertainties that might increase those inherent in the nature of the merchandise itself."[14] That, he implied, explained the necessity of advancing goods on credit to suppliers of slaves, so as to expedite later movements of captive Africans through the ports and on to Brazil. Better risk postponed returns on goods invested in the interior, or even bad debts, than delays and deaths in the barracoons. Or, more generally, as observer after observer stressed, the principal risks and costs of slaving followed from the fact that so many of the slaves died.[15] To refer to this central human fact of the trade, traders and government officials customarily employed the euphemism *o risco dos escravos,* "the slave risk" or "the risk of the slaves" (dying).[16] With that oblique phrasing it was easier to look beyond the distracting human losses and focus clearly on the economic cost that mattered.

To judge from the accounting logic evident in the business records of the trade, the slave risk need not even have been high in absolute terms to have commanded the slavers' attention, since it was the most variable of the expense categories of which they took note. Goods delivered for the slaves or the value of the notes received for them, commissions and costs of refitting and preparing a ship for a voyage, provisions for the slaves, and other taxes and fees all varied much less from venture to venture than did mortality among the slaves. In general, too, the closely related discounts for slave morbidity in the prices that Brazilians would pay for sick slaves varied more than did the nominal "market" prices prevailing for abstractly healthy slaves.[17] Nor did it matter that slave mortality declined over the history of the trade, since other elements of risk dropped also over time, perhaps more so, and slave deaths remained relatively the greatest of the hazards faced. With profit margins shaved close by competition, by the inefficiencies of the Portuguese economy, and by the strains that the metropole imposed on its colonies, this least predictable of the cost components of a slaving venture appropriately assumed the greatest prominence in the eyes of slavers.

14. Sousa Coutinho, 8 July 1770, AHU, Angola cx. 32.
15. E.g., Meneses, 3 March 1737, AHU, Angola cx. 19; Moçâmedes, 25 June 1785, AHU, Angola maço 13 (D.O.); Corrêa, *História de Angola,* 1:46–47; Botelho, *Escravatura,* p. 21.
16. Among other explicit references to *o risco dos escravos,* Moçâmedes, 16 Oct. 1786, enclosing letter from Rafael Jozé de Souza Correa e Mello (*juiz de fora,* Benguela), 16 Sept. 1786, AHU, Angola cx. 40.
17. E.g., the Pombaline Company records in Carreira, "Companhias pombalinas de navegação"; also Miller, "Quantities and Currencies."

Though the point may have applied with special force to the Portuguese, mortality losses also struck observers of other sectors of the Atlantic slave trade, especially earlier in the eighteenth century.[18] Slave deaths had an immediate economic impact, beyond other costs of maintenance or the issues of morality also involved.[19] As is well known—notoriously so in the case of the infamous *Zong,* when the ship's officers threw slaves into the sea to claim insurance coverage on them—slavers could not insure human cargoes against "common mortality" in any part of the trade.[20] The losses thus fell directly on whomever owned the slave.

To minimize such losses, it was common lore that, far beyond the isolated instance of the *Zong,* slavers simply disposed of the sick or the slow or any other sort of disabled captive whose handicap threatened to spoil the value of others. Since everyone knew that delays in the ports of embarkation would bring on epidemics among slaves penned up in cramped barracoons for long periods of time, it became the practice to kill the first slaves to show symptoms of diseases feared to be contagious. Slavers simply could not release infected slaves alive, for fear of spreading contagion even more widely and to avoid loosing freedmen capable of inciting revolts. Instead, they murdered a few in order to save the costs of mortality among the remainder.[21]

Whenever possible, of course, slaveowners avoided this last resort. At Luanda in 1811, when the opening of Cabinda to Brazilian slavers had reduced the number of vessels taking on slaves belonging to Luso-Africans there, and as epidemic smallpox raged among the population of slaves building up in the town, eight merchants petitioned the government to be allowed to load their captives on a vessel destined for the ports north of the city but anchored briefly in Luanda Bay to take on provisions. These desperate owners were in effect asking the government to authorize their private seizure of property of the ship's owners. They offered to pay 15$000 in freight charges for every slave who reached Rio de Janeiro alive, two and one half times the official rate and almost 10 percent above the unofficial going price for *fretes* at the time. Citing their inability to sustain the maintenance and mortality costs they would otherwise have

18. A French observer on the Bahian trade at Mina wrote: "These seamen navigate along the coasts of Guinea. . . . As long as there is not a high death rate on the ships, this trade is profitable": Verger, *Flux et reflux,* p. 91, n. 31 (as translated on p. 70 of the English edition).

19. The costs of maintenance are emphasized, e.g., in Curtin, *Economic Change,* pp. 168, 170–71, and see Palmer, *Human Cargoes,* p. 157, on morality issues. To be sure, the economic concerns of the traders were entirely analogous to the moral doubts of the humanists.

20. E.g., for the North American trade, Coughtry, *Notorious Triangle,* pp. 98–99. For the Portuguese trade, Silva Lisboa, *Princípios de direito mercantil,* cap. XXIV, pp. 60–61. Phillips, *Slavery from Roman Times,* p. 101, notes the apparent sources of this insurance rule in Renaissance Venice.

21. Taunay, *Subsídios,* pp. 119–20.

had to bear, the merchants further guaranteed to fill the ship's capacity of 746 slaves.[22] Not long afterward, the merchants had so many slaves dying in their barracoons that they hailed a ship passing Luanda on its way on down the coast with a cannon shot across its bow.[23]

Politics of Mortality

Given the conflicts that divided the collaborators in the trade, the economics of slave deaths became a political economy of mortality as well. The struggle to avoid losses to the *risco dos escravos* became a battle to transfer the unavoidable to others, with the greatest costs ultimately passed on to the utterly powerless slaves. The question that influenced the organization and history of Angolan slaving became not "who died" but rather "whose would die." Governor de Mello explained in 1799, not long after he had reached Luanda and begun to perceive the ethical and political complexities of southern Atlantic slaving: "The British come to buy slaves . . . and . . . attend in the precautions they take [exclusively] to the advantage [utility] of those who take them on; but in Angola it is also necessary to consider those who remain" on the shore. "What remedy could there possibly be . . . that might reconcile the just interests and profits of the owner of the ship with those of Her Majesty's Royal Treasury, and with the general commercial interests of all subjects of the Crown, without exposing the wretched slave who is transported to Brazil to die of misery?"[24]

The issue of "whose slaves died" was resolved by placing most of the burden on the participants least able to influence the rules of the deadly game in which the slaves were the pawns. The lineages in Africa, the Luso-Africans and other African trading groups, and the planters of Brazil— each of them politically weak and economically in debt to the European capitalists who supplied the credit that supported the entire trade—ended up possessing the human merchandise at the times when the slaves were most likely to succumb. The powerful interests on both ends of the long series of transactions—lords and kings in the African interior and merchants and imperial authorities in Lisbon, with the British frequently standing safely well behind their associates in Portugal—controlled the most abstract and hence the least perishable forms of assets. From the point of view of these mercantilists, commerce in the southern Atlantic was an exchange of trade goods, commodities, and debt, not of human

22. Oliveira Barboza, 8 April 1811, AHU, Angola cx. 59.
23. Oliveira Barboza, 22 Dec. 1811, AHU, Angola cx. 60.
24. De Mello, 12 March 1799, AHU, Angola cx. 46, published in *Arquivos de Angola* 2, no. 14 (1936): 597.

beings at all, with slaves entering the picture only to allow others to settle accounts. African merchant princes exchanged imported rarities for loyalties, not loyalists, while merchants in Europe shipped out woolens and gunpowder to obtain sugar, or cotton, or—in the best of all possible transactions—specie.

The trade as a whole, from the Bank of England to the banks of the Zambezi, flowed on two distinct, though interacting, levels, one consisting of relatively durable goods and credit outward from Europe into the center of Africa with final remittances of profit ideally in specie, and the other of fragile and perishable slaves from Africa across the southern Atlantic to Brazil. At least until the beginning of the nineteenth century, fatalistic acceptance of the fact that the slaves died set up conflicts between the parties who had their investment in each current over avoiding the slave risk. Participants strong in either political economy sought to avoid slave-ownership entirely, at least at times when slaves died faster than profits on the survivors would cover; in operational terms, European merchants tried to sell out of slaves and control the flow of goods and specie, while in Africa kings sought debts and loyalties. But since so few completed this preferred transaction, most participants fought among themselves within the flow of slaves, with each owner of human property trying to minimize his exposure to the inevitable losses, mainly by reducing the length of time that he assumed the slave risk. The Luso-Africans, who held both goods and slaves, tried, but seldom managed, to shift from one flow to the other as the circumstances dictated.

Detailed tactics that played on the slave risk appeared at every point in the trade, and tensions predictably crescendoed toward continuous conflict at times and places where slave mortality reached its most destructive heights: between the marketplaces in the African interior and the time of the slaves' final sale in Brazil. The advantage went consistently to the holders of goods or other nonhuman assets, since they could usually impose delays on owners of slaves and could afford to wait, while the slave-owners had only the choice of holding out, thus sustaining ruinous losses, or of submitting at once, saving the costs of slave deaths but accepting subordination. Submission meant survival, while losses meant economic or political obscurity no less humiliating to ambitious speculators than the "social death" of the slaves: forfeiture of one's following and hence of one's standing on the African side, or bankruptcy and economic failure on the side of the Atlantic economy. Buyers of slaves could hold sellers at bay, and owners of slaves inevitably exposed themselves to extortion by others who did not own the flesh-and-blood "commodity that died with such ease."

To recall only the prominent manifestations of the ubiquitous conflict between suppliers of goods and credit and the owners of slaves underlying

the history of Angolan slaving, metropolitan merchants distanced themselves from all financial responsibility for slave lives by selling goods for
bills of exchange, until slave prices in Brazil rose high enough early in the
nineteenth century to compensate for a declining slave risk. Though Lisbon
stimulated the entire trade by supplying the credit that brought slaves forth
from Africa and supported the indebted Brazilians who bought them,
metropolitan merchants took payment for their trade goods largely in
American commodities, other bills of exchange, or in gold and silver, and
seldom in slaves.

The first exceptions to the pattern of avoiding slave ownership on the
European side were the Pombaline companies, which began buying Angolan slaves in the 1750s. These exceptions in fact proved the rule, since
their monopoly privileges in Brazil covered the slave risk with higher prices
than competitive markets would have then provided, both for selling slaves
and in buying northern Brazilian produce for resale in Europe. The companies probably nonetheless accepted trading losses on the slaving phases
of their operations. On the African side, merchant princes in charge of
marketplaces where Europeans bought slaves likewise tended to restrict
themselves to brokering direct trade between subordinates left to own the
slaves—clients, lineages and nobles from their own realms—and foreign
traders, African and European, in the *feiras*. Accumulating large inventories
of slaves in unsanitary compounds to wait for buyers to arrive made no
sense. In some part owing to this reluctance of the kings to inventory
slaves, as Governor Sousa Coutinho once implied, the trade came to depend on Europeans' paying in advance, supplying the credit or "trust"
everywhere behind the slaving, and to feature the lengthy delays in deliveries of slaves that it did.[25]

Africans produced slaves on their own accounts, but usually only when
catastrophes, warfare, or droughts temporarily reduced the costs of acquiring captives enough to cover the risks of holding them. This limited
African initiative, while always important on the fringes of the system,
burned itself out in given areas within a relatively short period of time.[26]
The mortality costs associated with it were too high to sustain for long:
deaths during the fighting, abandonment of fields and consequent famine,
losses among refugees driven away from the areas of endemic conflict,
epidemics and malnutrition among captives held in the military camps,
and so on. The limited zones of conflict where Africans assembled trade

25. Sousa Coutinho, 8 July 1770, AHU, Angola cx. 32. Compare the conclusion of
Serge Daget, "A Vieux-Calabar, en 1825: l'éxpedition du *Charles* (ou de l'*Eugène*) comme
élément du modèle de la traite négrière illégal," in *Etudes africaines offerts à Henri Brunschwig*
(Paris: Editions de l'Ecole des Hautes Etudes en Sciences Sociales, 1982), p. 124, who
discerned the same practice by Duke Ephraim in Old Calabar in the nineteenth century.

26. Cadornega, *História geral,* 1:143–44.

slaves in advance of commercial stimulation from the Atlantic paradoxically recurred again and again in the first phases of local conversion to the Atlantic political economy of trade goods and merchant princes, and thus these zones retreated steadily away from the coast. The forced extortions of people that occurred west of the slaving frontier—through kidnappings, state raids on villages fallen out of political favor, depredations by large armed caravans, bandit assaults, and other violent forms of slaving—all derived in one way or another from prior commercial relations that often involved credit from the coast, or at least included opportunities to pass slaves taken by such means on to buyers ready to pay in trade goods without delay. No producer of slaves would have accepted Lisbon's late-eighteenth-century scheme to shift the financing of slave mortality along trade routes in the interior from European merchants to African suppliers without extracting major price concessions in return. As these were not forthcoming under the straitened circumstances of Portuguese trade at that time, only Kongo sellers came to Luanda to dispose quickly of slaves too inferior and too subject to death to sell to the British.

The economics of mortality that lay at the commercial heart of slaving from the African producers' point of view thus contributed to its ultimate dependence on European capital—Portuguese trade goods in the first instance but often backed by British finance. Other general features of the southern Atlantic trade derived from the invulnerability that bills of exchange conferred on the Lisbon financiers behind it all. Merchants in Portugal had no immediate reason to lower high nominal prices they charged for goods they offered for sale at Luanda, or to reduce the quantities of goods they shipped, so long as they, or their backers, could afford the credit necessary to underwrite inefficient novice peddlers in the interior and endure slow returns from debtors and the other costs of slaving on "trust" at Luanda. One result of Lisbon's heavy reliance on expensive credit was its inability to compete in terms of price with the British and French, who sold goods much more cheaply everywhere outside Lisbon's haven at Luanda, and sometimes there as well. The Portuguese so lacked the ability to engage in price bargaining, for example, that they utterly failed to trade successfully by those means at Cabinda in 1794–95, even with the foreign competition totally absent.

Without having to face the penalties in lowered prices for overselling the African market, Lisbon constantly tended to pump more trade goods into Angola than the existing institutions of the hinterland could absorb. Among the many consequences of this tendency were constant inflation in the goods-for-people political economies of the African states, consequent civil wars that formed the slaving frontier, and the expansion of the commercial economy that drove its conflicts farther and farther inland. Among the further consequences, too, were debt on the African side and a tendency to satisfy overextended Portuguese creditors in slaves of lower quality than less fully committed suppliers would have been willing to accept. The mere children common in the trade by the late eighteenth century bore the consequences of Lisbon's financial insulation from the human suffering of the trade.

The young, often diseased, and worn-out captives who arrived from the remote interior in turn contributed to the distinctively high mortality and low prices associated with Brazilian slavery. The low quality of the slaves supplied and their tendency to appear in numbers in excess of real demand, especially during the 1760s and 1770s, kept Brazilian prices for slaves relatively low. But these same characteristics also kept mortality high among the slaves in America, necessitating replacements at accelerated rates that animated Lisbon's sales in Africa by creating markets for new slaves from Angola. A merchant made the point as early as 1589, explaining that Portugal had needed to restore Kongo in 1568–72 because Africans died in such large numbers in Spain's Indies that slavers would never lack a market for them.[27] Capitalistic traders later took the utility of slave deaths for granted and played deliberately, if implicitly, on that component of built-in obsolescence in the economics of mortality in Brazil, using indebtedness to force Brazilians to buy more and weaker slaves just to forestall bankruptcy. The same commercial credit that supported the African economy also enabled the Brazilian planters to buy slaves they could not have otherwise afforded. Thus slave mortality blended again with merchant credit to sustain Lisbon's African sales and returns from Brazil.

Though those who held the slaves, as debtors, might seem to have had no reason to remain in this credit-based slave trade, they in fact stayed because slaving, bad as it was, was an optimal response for people trying to make the best of the none-too-good circumstances in which they found themselves. A Luso-African confronting low prices for slaves in Brazil would not refuse to ship more there, even at a loss, since he was usually hastening captives for whom he had already paid on their way to sale in America before they died, and he might postpone bankruptcy if even a portion of the revenues they brought went to pay his creditors. The point was survival, not profit. A Brazilian planter had no alternative but to go on buying more slaves, even the diseased children usually offered to him, if they could help to bring in a harvest that he could use to pay other debts outstanding on the land, equipment, animals, or other components of a plantation complex he hoped to avoid having to sell as a whole. Slaves,

---

27. Duarte Lopes, *relatório,* 14 Dec. 1589, in Brásio, *Monumenta missionaria africana,* 4:515. Schwartz, *Sugar Plantations,* p. 456 et passim, regards slaves as relatively cheap in Brazil. He also quotes Bahians on the economics of mortality: "The work is great and many die" (p. 364), and "[slaves were] the most precious and riskiest property in Brazil" (p. 421). Also, in general, pp. 204 ff.

unlike provisions or personal effects, constituted collateral for loans, and so planters spent cash on hand for daily necessities and accumulated debt for the mortgaged slaves they needed to keep their estates working. With similarly easy financing available in no other form, and merchants owning slaves just landed in Brazil eager to sell dying property on whatever extended credit terms might be necessary, slave mortality again contributed to the well-known indebtedness to Portuguese merchants of Brazil's slave plantation sector. Detailed data would surely show that the high implicit interest rates that slaveowners paid throughout the entire southern Atlantic economy covered the slave risk component on the loans they held.

Of course, in the longer run Lisbon paid the costs of using credit to maintain monopoly prices and volume in other ways, all of them also prominent general features of Angolan slaving. On the African side of the Atlantic, Luso-Africans smuggling to foreigners, with the associated *reviros,* reduced the volume of what Lisbon could sell and further delayed, or even eliminated, its returns. The high nominal prices at which Lisbon sold trade goods at Luanda in fact would have fallen significantly if discounted for eventual losses to debtors who absconded into the remote interior. By drawing too heavily on western central Africa's political and demographic resources, Lisbon merchants let themselves in for indirectly financing expensive transportation systems linking the coast to the far interior and for underwriting also the coercive and therefore expensive African merchant princes who started many, if not most, of the slaves on their way to the west. By indirectly promoting high turnover in Brazil's slave population, they lowered the efficiency of Brazilian agriculture, owing to the constant high proportion of sick, untrained, and angry new slaves in the work force. The elevated mortality costs of "seasoning" new arrivals added further to the inefficiency. But just as colonial debts to the metropole forced Luso-Africans and Brazilians to maximize short-run gains at long-term cost, Portugal's own debt to the British encouraged Lisbon merchants to resort to strategies keyed on immediate returns, and on that level they could generate adequate profits. If, in the end, they also replaced the immediate risks of slave mortality with the eventual probability of a stagnant economy in Brazil, bad debts, contraband, and failed customers in America and Africa, that, too, made sense in the high-interest-rate environment that their credit helped to create.[28]

Luso-Africans could seldom influence rules set by the African producers from whom they bought or by the merchants and politicians of the Portuguese imperial system in which they sold. They therefore played the economics of slave mortality by shifting their holdings back and forth

28. The economic "efficiency" of the system is at issue, though it would be possible to show why and how the arrangements in effect optimized returns to the collectivity, if not to individual economic sectors.

between trade goods and captives, since they usually held both, and by outright violation of rules that they did not set against smuggling, stealing, and reneging on debts. The clearest reported instance of converting assets from slaves to goods comes from an early-seventeenth-century military campaign in the Luanda hinterland, where a trader holding a large inventory of captives taken in the wars of the 1620s noticed smallpox beginning to spread among his people. With some foresight, for which he was later celebrated among the slavers, he immediately sold off his slaves, even at low prices, for the trade goods of his competitors, with the result that the others lost their investment in sick captives during the ensuing epidemic and the canny trader went on later to sell his goods for more slaves after the survival crisis had passed.[29]

The superior durability of the trade goods meant that Luso-Africans converted from slaves to imports when they could. In the eighteenth century, exploitive *capitães-mores* accepted bribes only in trade goods of the best sort, unless the trader was willing to guarantee slaves paid instead against dying.[30] They limited their slave retinues to non-seasonal occupational categories—military guards, domestic servants, commercial agents, skilled craftsmen, hands for year-round river-bottom agriculture, and the like—using them less often for seasonal or occasional tasks like hoeing upland fields or, above all, for head porterage. For such intermittent work they preferred to impress "free" Africans rather than assume the risks of holding slaves. Only the general shortage of labor in and around Angola, the exemption of slaves from government conscription, the utter unavailability of labor in any other form in the lineage environment of the African areas, and low prices for slaves abroad forced Luso-Africans to keep people they would rather have exchanged for more secure forms of asset. And they sold off even these reserves in 1828–30, when prices rose in Brazil.

In the broadest sense, high background mortality in Africa conditioned kings, patrons, and elders to part with dependents in the first place. Drought, famine, and impending death provided the most compelling, arguably compassionate, reasons for selling children, but trade goods brought opportunities to substitute enduring abstract claims to loyalty for mortal followers that underlay a more cynical part of the trade. The elevated infant mortality of a premodern tropical population placed a premium on reproducing lineages and other communities by acquiring youths and adults as slaves rather than by bearing children. Sales of some to European slavers in return for trade goods bought the wealth to acquire and retain others in the future. The celebrated Portuguese trader of the 1620s would have understood the logic.

---

29. Cadornega, *História geral*, 1:143–44.
30. Silva, *memória*, 25 June 1762, AHU, Angola cx. 29.

Once slaves began moving toward the coast, competition centered on passing mortality risks on down the chain of credit, to buyers unable to refuse slaves because of their own indebtedness. Since adequate food became critical to the malnourished slaves' survival on the trails, in the ports, and on the middle passage, provisioners of the marketplaces and ships extracted advantage from the owners of the slaves whenever they could. African kings choked off supplies to feed slaves awaiting dispatch from the *feiras* when they wished to discipline European traders there, or when they wanted to raise prices for the slaves they sold. Luso-Africans with agricultural estates in and around Luanda repeatedly withheld food and water from competitors, or from the entire city. Although monopolists in the interior of Angola sometimes also bought captives from the coffles on their way down to Luanda and held them off the market to force up the price of slaves in the city, they did so only at the cost of mortality from hunger and disease in the camps where they detained them.[31] Intercepting slaves in this manner worked well only near the coast and when the buyer had a ship waiting to take them on.

Officials who had the ability to retard the onward movement of slaves through the pipeline could virtually guarantee themselves bribes to facilitate the slaves' passage, up to the losses from mortality that delays threatened to cause slaveowners. From all appearances, the owners paid dearly, and the slaves more so. The African kings who hindered the departure of traders with big inventories of slaves took their cut in the high prices charged for the last slaves sold to traders hurrying to complete their coffles. *Capitães-mores* regularly extorted by slowing caravans of slaves on their way toward Luanda. The elaborate procedures that structured the loading and departure of the slaves in Luanda's port, though imposed nominally on the slaves' behalf, gave officials there no end of opportunities to cause delays and suffering. Lisbon assured metropolitan ships of priority in departures more to lessen mortality, to judge from the tenor of the arguments that swirled endlessly about the issue, than to enable them to reach Brazilian markets before their competition.[32] However, since the economics of mortality made the endless formalities, paperwork, baptisms, certifications, and fees of the imperial bureaucracy a financial burden for

31. Moçâmedes to *capitães-mores* of Massangano, Muxima, and Cambambe, 15 May 1787, AHA, cód. 82, fol. 43.
32. The point about deaths mounting while ships lay at anchor is well known for the West African trade: Mannix and Cowley, *Black Cargoes*, p. 90; also Gemery and Hogendorn, "Technological Change," p. 257. Heintze, *Fontes*, p. 232 (and p. 305, n. 283), describes the origin of the rule of ship departure by time in the port as explicitly in reaction to the deaths among slaves held up on shore awaiting a full cargo. For general comments from Luanda, da Cunha, 5 Feb. 1755, AHU, Angola cx. 26; Campos Rego, 10 July 1753, AHU, Angola cx. 25; *aviso*, 3 July 1757, AHU, Angola cx. 27; Moçâmedes, 28 April 1789, AHU, Angola cx. 41; Joaquim Doutel de Almeida (governor, Benguela), 12 May 1810, AHU, Angola cx. 59—all in addition to sources cited in Chapter 11.

owners as well as a threat to the slaves, minor officials who impeded the boarding process to excess could expect censure.[33]

Probate judges received bribes for settling the estates of deceased traders to refrain from imposing legal technicalities that could bleed those estates of assets held in dying slaves.[34] The captain of one notoriously slow and inefficient ship found himself boycotted at Benguela in 1814 by slave-owners unwilling to entrust their captives to his incompetence. The captain retaliated by refusing to give up his place in the departure queue until he had obtained a full cargo. Shippers on the shore, with slaves dying daily and unable to send them off on vessels blocked behind the half-loaded vessel, tried every trick they knew to bypass the obstacle, finally forming a partnership to buy another vessel thus qualified as *efeitos próprios* and eligible to make sail immediately. They also requested suspension of the capacity limits on another *efeitos próprios* ship about to get under way, and they probably also sold slaves to Spaniards along nearby parts of the coast, while the governor, primarily concerned to reduce mortality, looked the other way. The desperation of the slaveowners was exacerbated in this case, far from untypically, by drought, shortages of provisions in the barracoons, and an epidemic of smallpox.[35] Even governors sometimes had no alternative but to tolerate evasions of their own rules when enforcement meant delays and death.

Permutations of the concessions wrung from needs for haste to beat the specter of death seemingly had no end, where money was involved. One Pernambuco ship introduced contraband gunpowder at Benguela but managed to avoid condemnation by taking enough slaves on board to secure not only immunity from prosecution but also immediate departure in the interest of preserving the wealth invested in slaves when smallpox appeared on board.[36] With slaves held hostage, owners would reward criminality. One Angola governor, pursuing economic diversification as the end of the trade loomed in 1819, bought slaves to begin his program of public works. When superiors in Brazil objected, apparently wondering why he had substituted expensive purchases of labor for the impressment procedures the government usually favored, he responded that he was in fact saving the lives of the poor slaves he had taken into the government service. An oversupply of captives threatened delays in boarding that would otherwise have condemned slaves left in shoreside barracoons and on board ships in the port to death.[37]

33. E.g., the allegations against Manuel do Porto Barboza (inspector of slaves) in Rau, "*Livro de Razão*," pp. 54–55.

34. *Requerimento* of Maria da Conceição Simões, 24 Dec. 1767, AHU, Angola maço 1.

35. *Requerimentos* of José da Costa Moniz and José Miguel Pereira, n.d. (ca. 1814), enclosed in Alvellos Leiria, 7 March 1814, AHU, Angola cx. 62.

36. Marques de Graça, 10 June 1816, AHU, Angola cx. 63.

37. Albuquerque e Tovar, 29 Oct. 1819, AHU, Angola cx. 65.

Manipulation of the economics of mortality continued on the high seas. Captains substituted slaves they carried for others for captives of their own who died during the voyage. The Portuguese tried protecting vessels and cargoes during the mid-seventeenth-century wars with the Dutch by delaying departures until all could cross together in convoy, but they experienced so many losses among the slaves that they afterwards preferred to risk seizure by pirates and enemies rather than suffer certain slave mortality.[38] Even the slaves found their own vulnerability to death a potential weapon in their fight for survival, since they sometimes played on their captors' fears of their sickening and dying, feigning illness to secure release from their chains below decks, and, once brought topside, used their freedom to attack the crew.[39] When smallpox epidemics broke out on ships in the seventeenth century, captains had cut their losses by changing course, hastening to the nearest port, and thus disposing of their cargoes as quickly as possible.[40]

Continuing deaths among the slaves who finally arrived in Brazil created still further conflicts between owners holding depreciating assets and buyers unwilling to assume the risk. Such confrontations arose most dramatically when epidemics elevated mortality among the slaves. The arrival of a ship bearing smallpox more than once inspired Brazilian public health authorities, representing the prospective buyers, to quarantine the vessel until the disease had died down. Local merchants, representing owners who wanted to sell their dying slaves as rapidly as possible, objected vociferously.[41] One unscrupulous official allegedly invoked his power to quarantine arriving ships, even though no epidemic was present, just as gold-rush fever spread at Rio de Janeiro. He held up the release of the slaves aboard arriving ships until owners paid the best slaves they owned to him in bribes and sold him the remainder of the cargo at low prices. He no doubt turned a handsome profit by reselling in the strong sellers' market of the time.[42] Whether the accused officer was in fact so clever, or whether owners fabricated the charges to sell infected slaves to miners desperate for labor, the tactic in either case depended on economics of mortality basic to the trade. Everywhere in the slave markets of the New World sellers sought to streamline port procedures and made arrangements to dispose of their slaves to local merchants as quickly as possible in order to lessen the cost of sickness and death among the slaves.[43] New World

---

38. Taunay, *Subsídios*, p. 100.

39. AHMF, Benguela *copiador* (no. 216), 4 July 1777, fols. 1 ff., published in Carreira, "Companhias pombalinas de navegação," pp. 393–94.

40. Taunay, *Subsídios*, p. 99.

41. James Goodyear, "A Preliminary Epidemiology of the Bahian Slave Trade, 1780–1810" (unpublished paper, 1981), pp. 2–3.

42. Taunay, *Subsídios*, pp. 177–78.

43. Chandler, "Health and Slavery," pp. 57, 65; Bean, *British Trans-Atlantic Slave Trade*, p. 63; Bathily, "Traite atlantique," pp. 276–77.

masters of the slaves paid whatever such tactics saved in the subsequent mortality costs of "seasoning." This ubiquitous emphasis on speed in transferring slaves on to their final owners clearly shows that the purpose was to save money, not lives.

The producers and transporters of the slaves sought to limit their losses to mortality by reducing the scale of their operations. Kidnapping and small-scale raids produced slaves more efficiently than massive warfare. Large lots of slaves, aside from the danger of revolt they presented, burdened local provisioning systems and harbored the risk of epidemic diseases. Creditors expecting slaves in Luanda wanted smaller, more frequent shipments to save slave lives, though debtors in the backlands tried to minimize operating costs by sending slaves in larger coffles. Owners boarding slaves at Luanda tried to spread their risks by sending small groups on several vessels. Modest-sized ships carrying 300 to 400 slaves gradually replaced huge vessels on the middle passage. The complex commercial and financial organization of Brazilian slaving ventures, with numerous owners typically holding small shares in a number of different ships engaged in the trade,[44] derived from the same desire to reduce the hazards of owning slaves. The shortage of capital in colonial Brazil, compared to the much greater wealth of merchants in Britain and France, and the inability of Brazilian slavers to cushion the risks of slaving with simultaneous investments in other branches of trade, as European merchants did, forced Brazilian slavers to minimize the consequences of slave mortality in these ways. Big slavers could survive catastrophes that small slavers could not,[45] but big operators thrived on the operating level of the trade only toward the last days of the trade.[46] Before then, ordinary Brazilians took elaborate precautions to disperse their holdings of human property. Scattered business records demonstrate that the biggest capital of all steered well away from direct ownership of slaves, and every known aspect of the trade supports the hypothesis.

Other prominent aspects of the trade, especially in and around Luanda, derived from the same economics of mortality, extended from deaths among the slaves to comprehend also the high rates at which European

44. Silva Lisboa, 18 Oct. 1781, in *Annaes da Biblioteca nacional do Rio de Janeiro,* pp. 504–5; see also Taunay, *Subsídios,* p. 219. Also as emphasized in the Lavradio description of mid-eighteenth-century merchants in Rio, *Revista trimestral de historia e geographia* 16 (1843): 453, and subsequently republished in various places, including António de Sousa Pedroso Carnaxide, *O Brasil na administração pombalina (economia e política externa)* (São Paulo: Companhia Editora Nacional, 1940).

45. Corrêa, *História de Angola,* 1:174n.

46. E.g., the concentration of Rio merchants handling incoming slavers in the 1820s: see Klein, *Middle Passage,* p. 82, Table 4.5. These data on consignment did not imply slave ownership under the complex business organization of the southern Atlantic trade. Cf. the wide distribution of assets handled by one factor buying slaves in Luanda, 1821–23, in ANRJ, cód. 1142.

newcomers to Africa also died. Fraud and theft generally pervade relationships where parties believe that their opposite numbers will not detect deceit or will not survive long enough to retaliate.[47] Angola's remoteness from creditors in Lisbon and the lethal disease environment of its tropical coastlands must have jointly contributed to the Luso-Africans' consistent disregard of metropolitan rules. Immigrant agents of Lisbon capitalists on more than one occasion cited the mortiferous "climate" everywhere outside the city as the reason why they trusted unreliable traders of local birth to distribute valuable goods through the interior.[48] Traders from Lisbon virtually abandoned Benguela to Luso-Africans and Brazilians largely because of its reputation as a "white man's grave." The Luso-Africans held the colony's backlands in significant part because no European sent there to dislodge them could survive long enough to do the job. Traders survived crushing burdens of debt by plundering the estates of competitors who died in remote marketplaces before creditors and heirs could recover them.[49] So many other features of southern Atlantic slaving derived from its economics of mortality that it becomes superfluous to continue recapitulating virtually its entire history in terms of the deaths it caused, or the deaths that caused it.

The Land of the Dead

The keepers of western central African village lore thus had their point when they grimly judged Mwene Puto's a land of the dead. In a profound philosophical sense, financiers in distant Portugal, the planters, merchants, and ship captains of Brazil, importers at Luanda, and the African merchants of the trade diasporas had committed themselves to materialistic values that African specialists in the fertility of the land and in the fecundity of their daughters and nieces rightly viewed as fatal to the communities and political economies they knew in the days before slaving. The fundamental difference between these philosophies was whether wealth resided in people or in money. Whereas Africans attributed ultimate value to claims on human life, the world capitalist economy increasingly in the eighteenth century freed individuals to pursue private material gain without formal regard for the lives and welfare of others. As Africans expressed it, men

47. Charles D. Laughlin, Jr., and Ivan A. Brady, "Introduction: Diaphasis and Change in Human Populations," in Laughlin and Brady, eds., *Extinction and Survival in Human Populations* (New York: Columbia University Press, 1978), citing R. L. Trivers, "The Evolution of Reciprocal Altruism," *Quarterly Review of Biology* 46 (1971): 48.

48. E.g., Representação dos vereadores da Câmara Municipal de Loanda, 17 April 1728, AHU, Angola cx. 17; Silva, *memória*, 25 June 1762, AHU, Angola cx. 29.

49. Among many references, Noronha to the *presídios* of Ambaca, Pedras, Massangano, Muchima, and the District of Golungo, 4 Oct. 1805, AHA, cód. 91, fol. 24.

who bought and sold people merely in order to hold goods had gone "dead" in their hearts.

The African ethic, even applied to trade goods without reference to slaves, stressed the value of mutual (if hierarchical) ties among people, not the isolation of individuals (however theoretically equal in social rank and political rights) turned forever inward on their material possessions. That ethic did not change, even after three centuries of intense trade. In nineteenth-century Kongo, prosperous traders still felt morally bound to disperse their wealth in goods, thus furthering the spread of credit available to underlings to join the growing trade.[50] With values that so actively facilitated the diffusion of the wealth imported from Europe, it is no wonder that commercial capital assumed the importance that it did in the history of the slave trade. East of the Loango Coast, individual success made traders "ill" in social terms, and healers developed communal "cures" that dispersed disruptive concentrations of material wealth and slaves, again spreading the contagion of the Atlantic economy in the process. The old values survived at least in part because a few wealthy men, slavers and kings, accepted the reputations for witchcraft that their prosperity brought them. The have-nots could console themselves with their rectitude.[51] Material wealth supplemented land and followers as a means of exerting power among Tio chiefs east of Loango, but remained only a minor element of the idiom of politics there; and the Bobangi of the Zaire River, the most devoted traders and slavers of all, among whom almost no one had the moral security of poverty, grew guiltily preoccupied with fears of the witchcraft they sensed behind their collective commercial success.[52]

The Angolan slave trade linked the two conceptually opposed and spatially separated but complementary forms of political economy, those in Africa and the one from beyond the Atlantic, by transferring surpluses of the ultimately valued products from each into the territories of the other. Northern Europe's prized capacity for material production exceeded its home market's ability to consume, while in western central Africa, the products of British, French, and German industry remained rare in comparison to people. Conversely, women farming the sandier soils, particularly in areas of precarious rainfall, bore children at rates that exceeded the long-term capacity of western central African agriculture to feed. Meanwhile, people became scarce around the Atlantic economy with the opening of vast new lands in America, gradually emptied of their native American

50. Broadhead, "Beyond Decline," pp. 639–41; idem, "Trade and Politics," pp. 22–23. Cf. Dias, "Questão de identidade," p. 64, on the shift east of Luanda in the nineteenth century from dispersal of property to father-son inheritance; cf. also the same conversion recalled in oral traditions from Kasanje, probably datable there to about the 1750s.

51. Janzen, *Lemba*, pp. 6, 58–61, et passim.

52. Harms, *River of Wealth, River of Sorrow*.

residents. Contact between Europe and Africa, in part catalyzed by an-cilliary contacts with Asia, quite predictably resulted in balancing rushes of goods and people toward the complementing vacuums, in the southern parts of the Atlantic through the eighteenth-century Angolan slave trade.

In the most abstract sense, the eighteenth-century structure of this way of death derived from spatial, functional, and political-economic spe-cializations necessary to link remote, diametrically contrasting sources of people and goods in conveniently graduated steps. It was a period when merchants from very different economic systems worked out institutions and mechanisms of exchange that transformed early, unintegrated en-counters, sometimes violent, into regular interactions allowing participants from both sides to engage their opposite numbers without abandoning the places that each held in their own equally vital political economies. One may envisage the resulting series of political-economic sectors, or clusters of these institutions, as a double-ranked continuum of forms of wealth, running from people to bank notes, and inversely. Lineage elders and patrons on the African end maximized control over people and human reproductive capacities, female fertility supported by good rains and rich land. Bankers in Lisbon and London plotted to amass specie, gold and silver, or financial instruments secured by deposits of bullion. To the lineage authorities of Africa, bullion and banknotes meant very little. Correspond-ingly, human lives had grown conveniently remote from the Lisbon *praça* and the city of London. Each side sought what was most productive in their own economic environment: vulnerable and fragile human life in the African forests and savannas, but in Europe glittering metals and new technologies turning out immense quantities of manufactures. Currencies gave indirect control over persons freed by individualism in Europe, while obligations to patrons and lords gave direct expression to community and hierarchy in Africa.

The relative primacies accorded people and capital along the com-plementing flows of the slaves and credit between northern Europe, through Portugal, Brazil, and Angola, and the heart of western central Africa de-fined a set of distinct political economies based on varying combinations of these two conceptual and commercial poles. Each such specialized sector of the Angolan slave trade had its own distinctive commitment to one or another of the several kinds of wealth lying along the continuum com-prising the whole.

African elders and landowners managed technologies for the physical reproduction of people, as the ideology of the theoretical lineage system emphasized. Insofar as material goods entered calculations, they were sec-ondary gains from their primary emphasis on followers, objects made for use within a community of dependents. This ideology survived in many parts of eighteenth-century central Africa, even though widespread regional exchange systems in most areas had allowed leaders of primary communities to build or expand their retinues by acquisition, adding material tokens to their transactions in women and clients, as well as by reproduction. African monarchs and warlords had taken a further step toward greater reliance on goods. Kings converted privileged rights over trade in material goods beyond the local scale of exchanges among neighbors—at first in products of local origin but later from increasingly remote sources—into means of surrounding themselves with the followers, slaves, clients, and subjects, who gave men power in an economy of manual technology. Although the kings, like the lineages, attributed ultimate value to people, and although in practice their power depended similarly on the size of their human entourages, they could not directly reproduce members of their own political communities. They also lacked the direct authority over land and fertility that gave lineage authorities an upper hand in a pure political economy of interlineage marriage alliances. The kings thus depended on commodities, though principally still to acquire people from the lineages around them. The intellectual priority accorded to people remained, if more faintly, as older generations of lords heading lineage federations yielded to kings who based their power on regional trade, and still, too, as the last heirs of this *ancien régime* of regional monarchs increased their control over their subjects by redistributing imports gained by selling captives to the Europeans.

By attempting to perfect the old system, the importing kings destroyed it. The resulting violence and civil wars of the slaving frontier marked their fall and central Africa's passage to a fundamentally different political and economic regime that accorded primacy to material goods and slaves, both as commodities. The new rulers, merchant princes, continued to deal in both goods and people, just as had the last of the old kings, but they tended to stockpile textiles rather than loyalties, to rule by force rather than by participation, using their control over people to accumulate imports, slaves, and debt rather than to cement negotiated relationships with the lineages of their realms. They claimed slaves, not wives, from important local families and thus cast themselves loose from their predecessors' moorings in their subjects' lands and women. Slave-worked royal plantations supplied food to their courts, and representatives of these kings loaned goods in outlying villages to lay the basis of future claims from them in satisfaction of the debt, no longer leaving these obligations outstanding and accepting occasional provisions or tribute in recognition of them. Production rested on the coerced labor of slaves rather than on relatives and wives' cooperating to work the land. The kings used people to get more goods, not goods to obtain further claims on people. Though they remained solidly within the African political economy, their reliance on goods as the motor now driving the political mechanism had also committed them irrevocably to the economy of the Atlantic.

The specialized merchants inland from Luanda and Benguela, whether African or "Portuguese," further narrowed their interests in people to holding slaves, and they used the slaves more exclusively even than the kings to acquire other goods. Residents of the trading diaspora settlements and commercial marketplaces supplied goods, of which they had plenty, to the kings in return for the slaves accessible to the kings, and they sold the slaves to the Atlantic economy for its material bounty. Thus the growing commercial sector at the juncture between African producers of labor and European (and Asian) manufacturers of goods formed a fourth distinct segment of the political economic continuum, in which goods had become exclusively means to acquire people, not loyalties. The value of their captives, now very nearly "slaves" in the conventional Western sense, no longer resided in the captives' ability to produce but rather in their value in exchange for imported goods. The commercialized slavery of captives chained in westward-moving caravans thus lost the residual humaneness of enslavement of village or even court dependents retained for their personal contribution to the elegance of a noble's compound or to the prestige of a village patron. If Africans acquired goods mostly in order to control people and their labor, traders obtained people with the primary goal of exchanging them for goods. Their commercial networks, whether organized as trading diaspora or as labor impressment systems like the Angola *conquista,* retained a small number of the captives they acquired and restored them to productive economic "life" as headbearers, field laborers, and other contributing members of the commercial communities. The rest, except for the ivory they carried, became dead wood in terms of production. If African lords used goods to retain people, of whom they traded some, the traders, though still sufficiently within the African political economy through which they traveled to use their goods to acquire people, participated also in the Atlantic economy enough to sell most and retain only a few.

In the coastal towns of Portuguese Angola, and aboard the English and French ships anchored in bays elsewhere along the coast, the slaves passed the great divide into an economic world in which their living ability to produce lost even the residual value it had kept along the trails of the interior. The merchants of the oceanic segment of the continuum were rich in goods but in the end sought not people but rather currencies or commodities—sugar, cotton, rice, coffee—readily convertible into currency credits in the Atlantic economy. They were willing to hold slaves only reluctantly, if forced by circumstances to do so or if compensated for the high risks of slaveownership by high sales prices in the New World, but they thought ultimately in terms of returns in commodities and currencies. The slaves, for them, had "died" that much more in relation to the values ultimately sought. In the portion of the trade operated by Brazilian shippers during most of the eighteenth century, captains and crews took still another step into the commercial economy, holding few goods of any sort, and functioned entirely on the basis of currencies, supplying transportation services for freight charges and other payments in *réis*, buying ships and supplies, and paying crews in the same abstract forms of wealth. The shippers occupied a fully modern sector of abstract currencies and credits, owning slaves only temporarily to make up for shortages of those preferred forms of capital, though with variations. Merchant importers at Luanda primarily held goods and a very few slaves, the Brazilian shippers dealt mostly in currency and only secondarily in slaves, and the integrated British and French trading and transporting ventures—as well as the Pombaline chartered companies—owned goods and bought slaves to obtain currency credits. The Portuguese sector of the Atlantic slave trade differed from its foreign counterparts early in the century by the extent to which it separated the holders of goods and currencies from the owners of the slaves. Some Luso-Africans sold slaves abroad to obtain goods for reinvestment in the interior of Angola, but most had their sights set squarely on currency credits to support retirement in the monetized economy of Brazil.

Brazilian planters, miners, and merchants, though even more enmeshed in the exchange economy of the Portuguese empire, occupied a segment of the Africa-to-Europe continuum paradoxically defined by its use of unpaid labor to produce commodities to be sold for the cash on which it depended. The planters and miners organized the growing productive fringe of a mercantilistic imperial economy, a production sector steadily expanding in the aggregate—despite occasional temporary stagnation of individual commodity exports or declines in yields of specific minerals—at rates beyond what the limited merchant capital available in Portugal could support on a fully monetized basis. The consequent shortages of capital in the colony grew acute at a phase in the growth of the Atlantic economy when specie and currency reserves were fully absorbed in commercial networks recently expanded to a near-global scale, in shifting to support of labor through wages at home in Portugal, and in buying new technologies then multiplying European productive capacity, as well as in remedying the deficiencies of the domestic Portuguese economy by importing. There was little specie to finance the growth of production of the New World agricultural commodities and bullion that contributed to this transformation, or, later, raw materials for the maturing European industrial plant, on a similarly monetized basis. Merchants therefore relied on credit to sustain economic expansion in America, thereby placing Brazil (and Africa, too, as a source of labor) in the position of chronic indebtedness that it occupied within the larger Atlantic economy. The productive sectors of the Brazilian economy thus became slave-worked plantations and mines, using African labor obtainable without substantial commitments of specie and tending toward a chronic cash-deficit position with regard to Portugal.

Slavery in Brazil, in the context of the continuum of political-economic sectors linking Europe to Africa through the southern Atlantic, was essentially a labor system that arose out of the massive imports of new people who were necessary to create rapid growth in commodity and mineral production and who could be fed and housed (though seldom clothed) without further expenditures of scarce currency. It thrived because it conserved cash for investors in Portuguese America's rapidly growing, and therefore underfinanced, commodity-producing sector of the southern Atlantic economy. Growing sectors of the Brazilian economy thus valued their slaves primarily, and almost exclusively at times and places of intense expansion, for the gold they could pan or the sugar they could process or the cotton they could pick. The slaves caught in this position suffered and died accordingly. Only where growth stagnated did a more humane ethos of manumission and patriarchal concern begin to emerge and, occasionally, actually mitigate the hardships of the slaves' lives.

The economic strategies of the Brazilians who delivered labor from Africa to America similarly reflected the colonial economy's full integration into the currency economy of the Atlantic, indeed its very creation as a part of it—unlike the African economies that possessed entirely autonomous components long antedating and still vital within their relatively recent and very partial integration into Atlantic exchanges—together with its structural shortage of the funds necessary to perform the functions that it contributed to the prosperity of the whole on which it depended. American slavers earlier in the century, though working entirely in terms of currencies and exchange, bought African labor to the extent that they could sell by-products of the Brazilian commodity sector that had little or no cash value. They financed their voyages to Africa in significant part with contributions in kind, or with credit, but not with specie. They were characteristically otherwise unable to invest significantly in slave cargoes worth credit in export commodities or currency itself. They thus intruded on slave ownership at that period mostly by surreptitious means, by tight-packing and other techniques devised to enlarge their share of the cash returns from a slaving voyage. The extreme shortages of currency typical of earlier times diminished later in the century with greater prosperity in the colony and with greater investment from both Portugal and Britain, but they tended to persist even then on the Brazilian peripheries of the early-nineteenth-century quest for slaves. The captives the Brazilians carried for others thus had little value to them beyond fees lost for failing to deliver their human cargoes alive.

The Brazilian political economy thus restored no economic vitality to the slaves. It resembled the African economies that had substituted slaves for wives, clients, and kin in its reliance on acquired labor; but the greater extent to which its slaves worked to pay off their owners' cash debts, joined by cultural and other factors, significantly attenuated recognition of the slaves' humanity in the New World.

The slaves, by the time they finally settled in Brazil, thus labored in a commercial political-economic context far less humane than that of their African origins. Though African and American masters alike sometimes found themselves forced to sell off slaves they would rather have retained in order to relieve external indebtedness, Africans where slaving had not yet broken into violence conceded dependents mostly during ecological collapse or under the pressure of political demands. Within the slaving frontier they also gave up dependents to relieve indebtedness under pressures more analogous to those under which Brazilian planters often bent. Brazilians, who acquired their slaves by purchase and often on credit, had to produce commodities for further exchange simply to pay for the slaves themselves rather than valuing them for their descendants and for material objects they might make for use. Exchange in Brazil occurred on the opposite structural leg of the entire southern Atlantic economy from Africa, no longer focusing on slaves at all, but rather using them as social and political ciphers in planters' primary dealings in commodities and currencies. Brazilians deliberately traded for slaves only exceptionally, when they found themselves excluded from the European sources of cash that they preferred.

The merchants of Portugal stood even farther from the slaves. Lisbon supplied goods to Africa and bought commodities and coins that slaves produced in America. They invested their gains only very secondarily, if with growing discomfort at their failure to do so, in further production of goods, having removed themselves from the risks of slaveownership but not having yet found a replacement for the slaves' productivity. Their anxiety may bear comparison to the distress of the similarly mercantilistic Bobangi of the Zaire at their abandonment of reproduction, the African equivalent to industrial power in late-eighteenth-century Europe. Instead, Lisbon almost exclusively sought specie, the monetized form of wealth accorded greatest value in the world economy at the beginning of the eighteenth century.

Portugal thus occupied the currency end of the slave-trading continuum directly opposed to the human basis of wealth in Africa. Lisbon's greatest strength lay precisely in this financial sphere, in her merchants' ability to extend the credit supporting the goods and slaves flowing through all other segments of the trade based on specie, bullion, and commercial paper. In buying goods with currencies and credit, investors thought of amassing coin and bullion. They avoided trading on the uncertain worth of mortal flesh whenever possible, substituting bills of exchange or liens of nominally fixed values and of greater security. Human beings hardly entered into their calculations at all, except as tokens in preferred exchanges of other orders. Portuguese merchant capitalism's ability to convert people into cold metal thus constituted the Midas touch that rendered southern Atlantic slaving the Africans' way of death.

Most removed of all from the human realities of Portugal's southern Atlantic slave trade were British manufacturers and financiers. Already in the eighteenth century they had moved Britain well along its way toward the industrial capitalism that would replace the mercantilistic styles of trade still prevalent in the Portuguese empire. To do so, Britain had siphoned off much of the gold that Portuguese slaving yielded, among other sources of specie, amplified many times over through innovations in banking and insurance, to underwrite the expansion of finance and credit that supported the enormous investments in wage labor, technology, equipment, plant, materials, and all the other components of what had become an industrial "revolution" by the time legal slave trading ended. The silver that Portuguese-delivered slaves extracted from Spanish America went mostly to India, which put the bullion back into people—through personal ornamentation in India and the expanded hand-weaving industry that supplied the cotton textiles supporting much eighteenth-century slaving in Africa. But, of course, Indian cloth merchants and weavers lost out in the end to British capital and to power-driven looms in Manchester, as if to confirm the deadening overtones of commercial slaving, American slavery, and modern capitalism as they appeared from Africa.

One could not invent a more graphic statement of this deepest meaning of Portuguese slave trading in the mercantilist sectors of the southern Atlantic trade than Governor Almeida e Vasconcelos's characterization of Angolan slaves as "a commodity that died with such ease." He employed the phrase in a larger, oblique rationalization to superiors in Lisbon inviting them to tolerate the forbidden activity of Spanish slavers, just then beginning to use bullion to buy slaves in quantity along the Angolan coast. So highly desirable an exchange, he admitted, might be technically opposed to the orders of Her Majesty the Queen, but he could ignore the taint of fraud surrounding exchanges of "a commodity that died with such ease" for "silver that many centuries would not consume."[53] He thus made clear the preference of all Portuguese involved in the trade since the seventeenth century, who had consistently used slaves to wrest Spanish silver from Mexico and Potosí, then gold from Minas Gerais, coin from the Plata again after 1760, and by the end of the eighteenth century gold through raw cotton sold to Britain and silver by tolerating Spanish smugglers in

---

53. Almeida e Vasconcelos, 12 March 1792, as cited in Carreira, *Notas sobre o tráfico português*, p. 17.

Africa itself. Lisbon's primary interest even in the Angolan interior focused directly on African mines by the late 1700s.

Metaphorically turning slaves into gold and silver thus remained the underlying constant of the metropole's interest in the trade, from Portugal's first deliveries of slaves to the Mina Coast just after 1500 to their nineteenth-century shipments to Cuba.[54] But this alchemy worked only through a lengthy chain of intermediate reactions, characteristic of mercantile capitalism generally, left to the other participants in the trade. African farming communities sacrificed young males for food, females, protection, and, increasingly, a share of imports from Europe. Kings of the African *ancien régime* turned goods into power, and merchant princes converted them into slaves. Traders in the African diasporas made the slaves over into more goods, while merchants from the Atlantic put their goods into commodities or currency credits, which the Portuguese at Luanda claimed directly in Africa but which other Europeans transferred via the slaves themselves to the West Indies. The New World masters of the slaves finally completed the transformation by turning the slaves' labor, and the slaves themselves, too, through working them to death, into commodities, currency credits, silver, and gold. Europe—which banked these proceeds and left only deteriorating residues of worn fabric, rusting muskets, alcoholism, and dying slaves in Africa—presided like a wizard over it all, adding its capital as credit, as the catalyst that kept the entire chain of reactions going. Africans, when they observed that the Europeans turned the body parts of their countrymen into gunpowder, wine, and oil, had compressed these economic mechanisms into metaphors of magic, but they had not distorted their meaning.

Merchant Capital

The metaphors of an earlier age—life, death, and money—translate finally into those of capital, the theme that emerges gradually from contemporaries' visions of the trade. These views of the victims and participants in southern Atlantic slaving nuance current theories about this central image of contemporary social science and may help to explain mercantilist Europe's structural relationships with the rest of the world. Without undertaking the additional book necessary to review systematically the implications of Angolan slaving for the vast literature in this field, the series of distinguishable sectors of the trade, each linked to the others by credit emanating from merchants in Europe, points toward some concluding comments

---

54. Walter Rodney, "Gold and Slaves on the Gold Coast," *Transactions of the Historical Society of Ghana* 10 (1969): 13–28; Clarence-Smith, "Portuguese Contribution."

about how the expanding eighteenth-century world economy articulated with the political economies of western central Africa.[55]

It is clear that these sectors—though all clearly formed, functionally specialized, and geographically localized segments of a single larger system—had the local political autonomy, ideological coherence, internal currencies, and economic strategies to constitute political economies on their own terms.[56] The first point, then, is that the eighteenth-century world system makes sense only in terms of mediatory borrowers who wielded the enormous power conveyed by goods and slaves that Europe sold on credit.[57]

Yet capital in itself accomplished little, contrary to anthropomorphic phrasings popular in some theoretically oriented literature, and it surely did not "penetrate" Africa directly from Europe in any sense. It did allow many hands along the line to restructure local social relations by creating debt, always in ways quite specific to the sectors in which local intermediaries each sought distinctive goals. Though the chains of indebtedness bound people and regions together for the first time, they also liberated. Human values counted, in short.

The capital resources of Europe were too modest relative to the vast scale of the global integration under way in the eighteenth century to have achieved their momentous effects other than multiplied through social and political tensions in the noncapitalist segments of the chain. Capital, though not European currencies, nonetheless excited resonances far beyond the

55. Hence I make no effort to elaborate footnotes to my readings in these areas, beyond two or three key recent contributions to the debate. Nor is it possible to explore the contrasts between the heavily use-value oriented economies of western central Africa, at least at the outset of intensified contact with the Atlantic, and the much more commercialized economies in West Africa, already in contact with the commercial economy of the Sahara and North Africa for centuries before the arrival of the first Europeans along the coast.

56. Schwartz, "Colonial Brazil," has made this remark with respect to the options available for understanding the subject of his title: whether colonial Brazil was an autonomous "colonial slave mode of production" or a dependent branch of a world capitalist "mode of production" depends in part at least on the scale on which the viewer chooses to analyze it. See the concluding section of this chapter for further comments on the ways in which both levels interacted.

57. The implicit reference point here is, of course, Immanuel Wallerstein, *The Modern World System* (New York: Academic Press, 1974–80), whose two volumes thus far published (of a projected four volumes) extend in detail only to 1750. For some of the voluminous commentary and criticism surrounding this seminal work, see John R. Hall, "World-System Holism and Colonial Brazilian Agriculture: A Critical Analysis," *Latin American Research Review* 19, no. 2 (1984): 43–69. Readers may also sense my sympathy with the sort of localist reservations raised by Sidney Mintz, "The So-Called World System: Local Initiative and Local Response," *Dialectical Anthropology* 2 (1977): 253–70; Wolf, *Europe and the People without History*, has a comprehensive statement along lines that I find salutary. Eighteenth-century Africa could be said to have lain beyond Wallerstein's "periphery" only in the strictly technical sense that Europe had not yet engaged its African labor in direct relations of production. Others' (and my) definition of *mercantilism* or *merchant capitalism* centers on capital, which was clearly present (see below).

still narrow sphere in parts of northwestern Europe where wages were then beginning to appear as an important component of the social relations of production. Indeed, the exchanges of goods for slaves for gold that underlay the southern Atlantic trade brought outlying regions of the world into contact with Europe *without* those regions' investing significant quantities of valuable metals, which European mercantilists understood narrowly as "capital," in money and wages. The trade concentrated precious metals and multiplied financial strength in Europe to the point that Britain and other countries could eventually afford the expensive outlays of coin and notes required to pay cash wages on a daily, weekly, or monthly basis, long before manufacturers could accumulate currency returns from the labors of their employees on their own accounts.

African clientage based on textiles and Brazilian slavery based on credit and drawing heavily on a local, noncash provisioning sector both hastened Europe's conversion to wage-labor relations by yielding slaves, bullion, and commodities without investing money in wages. The quantitative contribution of southern Atlantic slaving to the vast and complex transformation in Europe was not great, since slave trading was in its essence marginal, a highly risky noncash adjunct of much larger and more fully commercial systems operating within Europe and between Europe and the Americas. But slave trading's limited contribution came from the gold and silver it returned from mercantile credit extended abroad through it, for long centuries before Europe itself relied extensively on wage relations of production at home: mercantilistic slaving, and surely other forms of trade in that era also, concentrated in Europe the bullion reserves that later financed further transformations in technology and productive relations there.

The mercantilist tone of the eighteenth-century Portuguese empire, even after industrialization was well advanced in Britain, highlights the particular roles that Africa, the slave trade, and slavery in the New World played in the rise of capitalism, or in the industrial revolution, in northwestern Europe. If "capitalism" was the distinctive feature of the unsettlingly new forms of social and economic organization that emerged in Britain at that time, then the place to seek the origins of its distinctive features was in the accumulation of "capital"—which meant first and foremost credit, later invested in technology, and finally the shift from labor relations based on unpaid apprenticeships, land ownership, and family ties to ties between strangers hinging on the payment of a wage in "cash." This accumulation of capital—not just in the hands of a few industrialists, but rather, a pool of liquid wealth infusing an entire economy centered on the British Isles and expanding to adjacent parts of Europe and portions of North America—in turn took the form of an expanded supply of money, at first mainly gold and silver coins, but later also paper instruments of credit. A long-term shortage of the bullion needed to support growth in commerce and credit, starting in the fourteenth-century Mediterranean,[58] had first sent fifteenth-century Portuguese mariners coasting along West African shores in search of gold. The same hunger for noble metals still drove Portuguese and British merchants of the eighteenth century, as they sought slaves in Africa and silver and gold in South America. African slaves became the medium through which merchants peripheral to the main commercial flows of their time were able, at high risk, to convert goods that were of relatively low currency value in Europe into currency credits and ultimately into specie.

From the perspective of funding European investment in capitalist means of production and wage labor relations, the advantage of selling goods in Africa lay not in the miniscule quantities that merchants could sell there, but rather in the eventual high-specie yield of what the Africans bought. The conversion to capitalism implied an enormous rate of saving at home, and hence of postponed consumption, except as increased supplies of money and credit could finance current needs. Any lessening of pressure on the lower classes, who were forced to bear the burden of foreign consumption at home, could be critical to maintaining this process and the political survival of the classes in control of it. Trade within the bullion zone, which most emphatically included Asia as well as some of the American colonies and most of Europe, simply transferred specie and credits from one part of the far-flung world economy to another, without increasing its overall stock of gold and silver. Trade with Asia, worst of all, tended to consume precious metals and thus to diminish the supply of them available for circulation in Europe and America.

Trade with Africa, which was almost alone in the eighteenth century in not being within the sphere of bullion-based currencies, had exactly the opposite effect. Africa required very low investments of prized shiny metals and was in fact a net exporter of gold, as it has remained throughout its history. It was also a market where traders could acquire slaves convertible into American gold and silver without prior investment of significant quantities of specie. The shell, copper, cloth, and salt currencies of western central Africa, like the cloth, copper, shell, and iron currencies of West Africa, all complemented Europe's quest for precious metals and allowed the exchanges of complementing values that underwrote distinct forms of expanded commerce and economic "development" in the two areas, in the northern hemisphere partly in high-energy technology, but in the tropics mostly in intensified hierarchical relations of human production, largely slavery.

58. John Day, "The Great Bullion Famine of the Fifteenth Century," *Past and Present* 79 (1978): 3–54.

But the process was ultimately one and the same in Africa and Europe: commercialization. Parties in both cases constructed new productive relations through endowing scarce imported assets with exchange value. African lords spread hierarchies of all sorts—political, clientage, and slave— by lending textiles, consuming alcohol, and displaying other rare imports. Europeans circulated their metallic coins and paper currencies representing hoarded bullion to bind workers to factories through wages. Wealthy Africans advanced goods and commodity-currencies first and accepted service and slaves later, while European entrepreneurs demanded labor up front and then compensated workers later with money. Both sides aimed to retain their most valued assets—people in Africa and gold in Europe— even though both also had to invest a portion of their treasure in order, they hoped, to reap more of what they prized later.

To the extent that the African trade enabled European merchants to dispose of surpluses, defective goods, or wares with low marginal currency costs in Africa—that is, to dump goods valueless anywhere in the currency-based world economy—exporters in Europe limited potential cash losses to the wages and overhead costs of transporting them to Africa. Even these residual monetary expenses could be reduced further by allowing ships' officers and crews to take their compensation in goods to be traded for slaves. Africa's position outside the bullion currency zones centered on Europe made the opportunity cost *in specie* of doing business there extremely low, whatever values merchants imputed in currencies of account to the goods they sold or to the transportation costs connected with their ventures.

Slavery in the New World similarly constituted a non-bullion-based form of investment, since delivery of African slaves to the Portuguese or Spanish colonies of South America produced, ideally, bullion itself, or in practice often cotton, coffee, cocoa, sugar, hides, or tobacco, all readily salable for currency credits or specie in Europe. The American colonies served as a permanent debtor zone to Europe, as the amounts they constantly owed for slave labor and for supplies from Europe revealed. All European forms of currency, in theory, fled the colonies, to be replaced by other tokens of value, consumption goods and labor imported from Europe or via European merchants. The Americans may have turned to Africa as a source of workers after the decline of native American populations available for impressment, as a common demographic hypothesis offered to explain New World slavery accurately emphasizes, but slave labor relations arose in part because slavery allowed economic expansion without significant investments of specie. Slavery persisted because every time a planter or a miner bought an African, he transferred most of his currency credits or bullion to a merchant who sped them back to Europe. Americans had too few notes or specie left to pay their workers in cash. New World slave relations remained cheap to maintain without investment of specie or currency in a widely circulating wage medium so long as the slave trade lasted, since bewildered new slaves submitted to outright force more readily than would their acculturated native-born progeny. Thus, from the point of view of financing eighteenth-century capitalism, slavery and the slave trade extended Europe's reach in Africa and the New World beyond the scale permitted by expenditures of scarce gold and silver, freeing currencies for investment in technology, plant, and equipment and for circulation as wages among industrial workers in Europe.

Everyone abroad, except, of course, for the slaves, eagerly accepted European credit because it allowed accumulation of wealth in the varying forms specific to each local political economy: human capital originally in Africa, trade goods of any sort in the trading sectors, even elements of landed wealth in the plantation zones of Brazil (though there paradoxically defended by the production, with slave labor, of agricultural commodities to exchange for currency credits) and among Portuguese physiocrats who put their profits into titles of nobility and landed estates at home. None of these conflicted with the countervailing flows of specie into industrial and financial capital in Britain. Each party gained, though only in its own terms, by lending assets which were lower valued in its own sector to adjacent sectors where the same assets had higher worth or gave access to more highly prized forms of wealth. Thus Europe and America on the whole tended to dump surplus goods on Africa—third-rate tobacco, spoiled wines, rums too harsh for the taste of drinkers at home, second-rate arms that munitions makers could produce when peace destroyed markets for better weapons in Europe, cheaper grades of textiles, used bedsheets, and soft iron—though, to be sure, the volume of trade in such items frequently supported deliberate large-scale fabrication of these inferior wares in the longer run. Africans, on the other hand, welcomed the same goods in the context of cementing their relations with other lineages and with their overlords, and they perceived parallel advantages in ridding themselves of rebellious youths or of more dependent mouths than they could feed, in return for fertile young women and political status. Each asset increased in value as it passed through the sequence of political economies. The slaves, who had only their own lives to treasure, absorbed the costs in social, political, and economic extinction, but caused economic loss to their owners only when they expired physically.

The history of southern Atlantic slaving also illuminates the conundrum of whether merchant capital enabled its holders and lenders to promote revolutionary or conservative effects, whether goods and credit enabled their possessors to accomplish radical changes in their own political economies or, rather, allowed them to consolidate the *anciens régimes*.[59] Credit did both, of course, depending on which segments of the broader system it entered and on the points in their long and changing histories at which its consequences are assessed. It permitted the greatest changes in the least commercialized sectors. But its truly revolutionary effects there arose mainly during earlier phases of the influx of credit, with reactionary consequences following later, when the heirs of the mercantile revolutionaries turned to defend their revolution as later beneficiaries from the industrial phase of world capitalist economic growth mounted new challenges.

The old African kings welcomed foreign traders to enhance their positions in politics based on segmentary forms of rule, they surely thought, but in expanding and centralizing these federal polities by military means they also transformed them and prompted lower nobility and eventually even rank upstarts much more dependent on foreign capital than they to complete the transformation of African political systems toward the merchant principalities of the commercialized areas of western central African slaving. People in the primarily commercial segments of the continuum, like diaspora trading communities near the Loango Coast and on the middle reaches of the Zaire, used increased credit and wealth mainly to expand and intensify existing forms of social relations and exchange, though not without guilt and other strains of the kind the Bobangi experienced. Luso-Africans in Angola gradually abandoned late medieval warfare and became merchants who handled guns more as merchandise than as weapons. Merchant capital turned Brazilian patrons of local clients and owners of only incipiently slave-based plantations from hunting Indians to buying Africans at the end of the sixteenth century and thus supported an entire new social formation based on classically purchased slave labor.

But once any of these revolutionaries had brought a region within the orbit of commerce around the Atlantic basin, their successors—lords, traders, and slaveowners alike—used further credit conservatively, often to defend themselves against later and more expansive phases of the ongoing capitalist transformation in Europe. African merchant princes, with Kasanje as the archetype, borrowed from early merchants to consolidate debt-based polities and then fended off later traders with more assets who wished to replace the services of African brokers with direct investments of their own in the east. African traders who settled isolated diaspora communities amidst villages of farmers gradually became patrons of autonomous groups of slaves at the centers of entire societies, masters poised to eclipse the strength of the remaining lineages and aristocrats of the old

59. Here the discusion is inspired by Elizabeth Fox-Genovese and Eugene D. Genovese, *The Fruits of Merchant Capital* (New York: Oxford University Press, 1983).

order. Against wealthier capitalists from Portugal Luso-Africans protected themselves with slaves, marriage alliances with African trading partners, and commercial wealth invested in the trading systems of the African interior. Brazilian slaveowners by the nineteenth century were buying slaves on credit to preserve a place in a global economy rapidly converting to wage and contract labor and debt peonage, and they finally yielded only when the prices of their slaves, and hence also the mortgage value of their property, dropped below the costs of continuing to defend slavery. Nineteenth-century Luso-Africans in Angola fought off the first liberal industrializers from Portugal and their initiatives toward client and wage-labor systems in the colony with gains they made from the last illegal merchant-capital-supported slaving in the first half of the nineteenth century. Merchant capital over and again served reactionary ends in the hands of heirs of revolutionaries.

As eighteenth-century mercantilism and slaving helped to move northern Europe toward industrial capitalism, European banks and manufacturers were simultaneously expanding the scale on which outlying participants in the world economy could employ merchant credit and wage relations of production for themselves. Advancing technology and growing financial sophistication in Europe provided the wealth necessary to spread loans more widely throughout the world and eventually to make them directly in currency credits rather than only in trade goods, to circulate the currencies necessary to impose taxes and to create other debts payable in cash abroad, and to substitute envelopes containing coins and banknotes for food rations, clothing, and chits at a company store. In other terms, Europe by the nineteenth century had accumulated enough wealth, through mercantilism and in many other ways, to substitute direct seizure of land and labor abroad for the credit that it had earlier employed to stimulate production under local ownership. Simultaneously, the same advances had also reduced many of the risks and costs that had formerly made it safer to invest more valuable forms of assets only at home. These innovations reached the southern Atlantic slave trade when Britain began to buy directly into Brazil, the wealthiest of Portugal's colonies, in the mid-nineteenth century, while Portugal herself, thus displaced from America, made plans to launch a parallel but much more modest intervention in Angola just a few years later.

These structural changes over time, viewed first as events internal to each sector, made each link in the chain of credit more dependent on borrowing from, or lending to, the links adjacent. Secondly, each advanced from the function it had performed when it had joined the consolidating world system to that of the next sector nearer the commercialized center. Over the century and a half between roughly 1700 and 1850, Britain thus led the parade in converting from mercantile to industrial capitalism, from sending finished goods abroad on credit to financing production of raw materials all around the world. Portugal moved haltingly from a dependent form of mercantilism, largely reliant on foreign capital, to the precarious beginnings of domestic capital formation and a neomercantilism focused on carefully protected markets in overseas colonies. Brazil, despite its continuing dependence on foreign capital, strained to supplement its functions as a passive market for finished goods and slaves with immigrant wage labor and with simple fabrications of its own.[60]

The Luso-Africans of Angola gradually converted their wealth in slaves to trade goods, and they depended less and less on credit from abroad and more on commercial assets of their own. African kings changed from slave-trading to distributing goods as creditors of their subjects. The lineages of Africa, initially the quintessential reproducers of people, gradually yielded to patrons and slaveowners who bought followers rather than breeding them. Since increasing reliance on abstract financial capital defined the continuum linking peripheries to the center, credit borrowed from outsiders enabled obscure upstarts to advance themselves locally by drawing their sector as a whole one step further into the exchange economy. The net effect in western central Africa was to commercialize the old political economies, thus paralleling the simultaneous shift to merchant capitalism in Europe but on the basis of currencies that traders in the Atlantic viewed primarily as commodities.

Reviewing these structural changes in spatial terms, one may trace displacements of the location of each function outward along the continuum as the center grew in wealth and size. To take only the example of slavery, centers of slave production formed and reformed in progressively more remote locations as commercial capital flooded through each outlying region and into the ones beyond it. Southern Portugal and the adjacent Atlantic islands had been the destinations of most slaves in the fifteenth and sixteenth centuries. Brazil took most of the slaves in the seventeenth- and eighteenth-century trade of the southern Atlantic. Finally, western central Africa itself emerged as the last growth point for slave production after the ending of the Atlantic trade in the 1850s. Within central Africa slavery moved inland at about the same time from the Portuguese colony of Angola into the independent territories farther in the interior. Slave trading always supported each growing zone of slave production, and the geography of the trade moved too, with the emergence of successive slave systems. It receded from fifteenth- and sixteenth-century Europe and the Mediterranean, first into the southern Atlantic phase during the mercantilist era, and finally to the internal African trade characteristic of the age

60. Luiz Felipe de Alencastro, "Prolétaires et esclaves: immigrés portugais et captifs africains à Rio de Janeiro, 1850–1872," *Cahiers du C.R.I.A.R.* (Centre des recherches ibériques et ibéro-américaines de l'Université de Rouen), no. 4 (1984): 119–56.

of early industrialism in Europe. Ownership of the slaves in transit in the southern Atlantic drifted in the opposite direction, toward the center, as wealth grew in Europe, as administrative controls intensified, as technologies improved, and as risks declined: from African producers who had themselves driven slaves right down to the Atlantic coast in the seventeenth century, to Luso-Africans who held them all the way to Brazil for most of the eighteenth century, then to Brazilians after the 1770s, and finally to displaced Portuguese by the nineteenth century. Lisbon merchants themselves would by then have bought into the trade's human cargoes if they had had the means. Only London bankers stood aside.

With the seizure of Africa by colonial rulers in the 1880s and 1890s came still another phase in these trends, underway for centuries. Slavery and the slave trade, which could retreat geographically no farther, disappeared beneath the increased outflow of European capital, sufficient by then, if only barely so, to reach directly out to Africa to impress poorly paid African wage-workers, to buy agricultural commodities inexpensively from partially self-supporting peasants, and to stimulate migrant labor with cash taxes, but not to pay a cash wage sufficient to support the families of the laborers contributing to the colonial economy. Colonial rulers abolished African slavery in the process, amidst violence similar to that to which upstart and indebted African brokers of borrowed trade goods had resorted since their first forcible displacements of overextended old regimes that were too strong in other sorts of productive relations to be bought out directly.[61] It was a process of "primitive accumulation," like the one familiar in Europe but evident also in the western central African slaving frontier since the first Kongo kings had sold off their reserves of criminals and captives and had begun to push their borders violently off to the east.[62] The trade in slaves had resulted, as European demand for labor enabled warriors to dispose of dying captives and to consolidate new regimes based on debt clientage. It had continued as merchant princes fighting in many ways to stay in power had gained strength from goods borrowed from Luso-African traders, who were themselves fending off the claims of creditors in Portugal. But the end of the trade, at last, eliminated all of these intermediaries and brought much African labor directly within the European currency sphere. Slaving and slavers, whatever their locations, disappeared late in the nineteenth century, abolished as the accumulation of capital in Europe allowed industrialists and financiers there to abandon

61. See the forthcoming Suzanne Miers and Richard Roberts, eds., *The End of Slavery in Africa* (Madison: University of Wisconsin Press, 1988).

62. The violence of the initial stages of overextended integration of new areas into a world capitalist economy was evident also along the Upper Nile during the nineteenth century: Janet Ewald, "Soldiers, Traders, and Slaves: The Political Economy of the Upper Nile Valley System in the Nineteenth Century" (Paper presented to the Southeastern Regional Seminar in African Studies, Charlottesville, Va., 1984).

the violence and unpaid slaves that had contributed to their wealth, employ low-paid migrant and contract workers, and buy inexpensive peasant produce for cash.

The morbidity and mortality of colonial central Africa's plantations, forced labor camps, rural villages, migrant workers' barracks, and mine camps were significantly less than the deaths of slaving, even in the poorer rural areas. The declining trend in mortality underway throughout the history of the eighteenth-century trade thus continued, though it remained high enough to alarm sympathetic Europeans accustomed to the expensive modern standards of health and life expectancy taken for granted at the center. Africa, despite the substantial achievements of colonial health services, thus remained on the periphery of the world economy, lacking the wealth to afford costly advanced medical technology and medical welfare systems like those in industrialized portions of the world. A modern echo of the old economics of mortality thus conditioned Europe's investment in colonial Africa to the extent that capitalist employers did not cover the full social costs of their labor force. Wages and migrancy had eliminated ownership of labor and thus the equivalent of the "slave risk" that earlier merchants had merely reduced by passing that risk along to others. Modern African workers bore the costs of sickness and death alone.

Appendices
Glossaries
Works Cited
Index

Appendix A: Comparative Estimates of Basic Labor Rations

Average caloric requirements for inactive men, women, and children, taken together, could be as low as 1,625 per day in warm climates; modern Angolans received 2,215 calories in 1960–61 and Congolese 2,650.[1] This caloric range translates into about 0.5 to 0.85 kilograms of unmilled grain, or something very close to what seems to have been a worldwide standard, though much less than what the slaves were meant to eat, without taking account of the dietary imbalance or nutritional inadequacies of a diet consisting largely of carbohydrate. The mixture of one kilogram of beans and about twice as much manioc flour that the Portuguese and Brazilians provided slaves in the southern Atlantic would have yielded about 3,300 calories per day, far more than these estimated adult daily requirements.[2]

An unsystematic and far from thorough survey of literature on diets of the past conveys the impression of a fairly uniform theoretical standard of approximately one kilogram of carbohydrate as the minimum daily ration for a working adult male. The limitations of a crude calculation of diet by prescribed weights of starch are too obvious to require more than passing acknowledgement here. Nutritional balance and the physiological abilities of the body to utilize the nutrients provided are, of course, critical to health.[3] Moreover, workers who fed themselves doubtless supplemented this theoretical standard in a great variety of ways, and such workers included many New World slaves, whose diets are known mainly from rations, given them by masters, that perhaps amounted only to supplements, meals taken while at work away from the slaves' home food supplies and preparation, in a situation similar to what must have been the practice in the Angolan sulfur and gold mines. Further, dependent laborers who ate exclusively rations supplied to them by masters of slaves or of ships, by military quartermasters, or

1. See Table IV, p. 15, in Clark and Haswell, *Economics of Subsistence Agriculture* et passim.

2. Based on Lisanti, *Negócios coloniais,* 1:dv, n.5. Lisanti also calculated a caloric value for provisions given a shipment of Mina slaves in Rio in 1715 and found that it amounted to between 483 and 644 calories per day, or about one-third of the 1,500 regarded as minimal. His calculations depended on an assumption that the slaves were held, and fed, for 15–20 days.

3. Kenneth F. Kiple, *The Caribbean Slave: A Biological History* (New York: Cambridge University Press, 1984), is the most sophisticated discussion of these points applied to slave populations. Also see Richard Sutch, "The Care and Feeding of Slaves," in Paul A. David et al., *Reckoning with Slavery* (New York: Oxford University Press, 1976), pp. 231–301.

by the bosses of work gangs certainly received less in practice than what the rules prescribed. The theoretical ration in the Angolan slave trade, as the discussion in the text makes clear, frequently fell short of legal requirements.

Nonetheless, information on diets elsewhere in the premodern world makes it clear that slaves on ships in the southern Atlantic were meant to receive something close to a diet believed adequate for soldiers, day laborers, and other humble folk. In the utter absence of more detailed information on the food actually consumed, readers will make their own assumptions about whether ship captains in the eighteenth-century southern Atlantic violated the proclaimed standard to greater or lesser degrees than those responsible for feeding slaves and other workers elsewhere.[4]

Precedents throughout the Portuguese empire varied enormously but often converged on the usual approximate kilogram of starch per day. Calculations made in sixteenth-century Portugal for annual wheat allowances were equivalent to 1.15 to 1.33 kilograms per day.[5] The accepted standard for slaves in early eighteenth-century Brazil was one *alqueire* per month—that is, 0.86 kilograms per day.[6] Later in the eighteenth century, the annual consumption by a slave was reported as 20 *alqueires* per year, a substantially higher daily figure of 1.43 kilograms.[7] However, the bread ration allotted soldiers in the Mina garrison in the sixteenth century, to be made from 1/10 *alqueire*—exactly the same standard implicit in the practice of the Angolan slave trade—was a more ample 1.96 kilograms per day; the troops also received wine, two liters of cooking oil and vinegar per month, and honey, plus such fresh fruits, vegetables, chickens, and so on as they could acquire for themselves.[8]

Closer to home, in Angola, the mid-eighteenth-century adult male laborers requiring half an *exeque* of manioc flour per month received the equivalent of 1.03 kilos of carbohydrate daily.[9] The doubling of rations to a full *exeque* of manioc

4. The text of Chapter 11 presents my own opinion. For a more fully documented and argued statement of the position, see Joseph C. Miller, "Overcrowded and Undernourished: The Techniques and Consequences of Tight-Packing in the Portuguese Southern Atlantic Slave Trade" (Paper presented to the Colloque International sur la Traite des Noirs, Nantes, 1985), condensed in *Actes du Colloque international sur la Traite des Noirs (Nantes, 1985)*, 2 vols., Société Française d'Histoire d'Outre-mer and Centre de Recherche sur l'Histoire du Monde Atlantique (forthcoming 1988). A full version is also in preparation.

5. A. C. de C. M. Saunders, *A Social History of Black Slaves and Freedmen in Portugal, 1441–1555* (London: Cambridge University Press, 1982), p. 98.

6. Amaral Lapa, *Bahia e a carreira da India*, p. 175, citing A. F. Brandão, *Diálogos das grandezas do Brasil* (1618), ed. R. Garcia (Salvador: Imprensa Nacional, 1956).

7. José da Silva Lisboa to Dr. Domingos Vandelli, 18 Oct. 1781, *Annaes da Biblioteca nacional do Rio de Janeiro* 32 (1910): 503.

8. Vogt, *Portuguese Rule on the Gold Coast*, pp. 49–50, using the Lisbon *alqueire* of 8.4 liters, and assuming wheat at 72 lbs./*alqueire*.

9. Da Cunha, 21 Dec. 1753, AHU, Angola cx. 25. The standard taken here—the Lisbon *alqueire* specified by Peçanha, 18 June 1783, AHU, Angola cx. 40—would generate a conversion as follows: 2×34.05 (that is, the Brazilian *alqueire* of 56.75 lbs. reduced to its Lisbon equivalent at a ratio of 8.4:14) lbs./*alqueire* = 30.95 kg/mo., or 1.03 kg/day. Use of the smaller Lisbon *alqueire*, 60% of the Brazilian measure, in Angola may explain the apparent discrepancy between Peçanha's specification of 4 (Lisbon) *alqueires* to the *exeque* and a statement in Cadornega, *História geral*, 1:16, giving the volume of flour reaching Luanda in canoes as of the 1680s in terms of *exeques* and *alqueires* that work out to only 2

flour (or its equivalent in beans or other carbohydrate) for impressed African labor in the colony proposed in the late 1760s would have brought a laborer's consumption above two kilograms of manioc flour per day.[10] The recurring tenth of a *cazonguel* of manioc flour per day allotted workers on the proposed canal from the Kwanza River to Luanda in 1816 amounted to 1.55 kilos per day, plus 0.38 kilograms of beans, for an ample total of nearly two kilos.[11] The provisions for thirty-three workers and bearers in the Mundombe sulphur mines south of Benguela work out to a figure closer to the standard: 0.77 kilos of *farinha* per day, plus 0.48 kilos of beans, or a total ration of 1.25 kilos per day (as well as 7 cc *gerebita*, or a bit over 2 fluid ounces).[12]

Elsewhere in Africa, adherence to the standard kilo/day ration was routine. Slaves in the West African Sudan received just that from Muslim African traders and masters. Philip D. Curtin calculated the annual diet for a person in eighteenth-century Senegambia as approximately 0.4 tons of millet, that is, something just over a kilogram per day. Christian Africans at the same time consumed 0.857 kilograms of millet per day, plus 0.245 kilograms of meat.[13] In the Sokoto Caliphate in the nineteenth century, slavers figured the subsistence ration of grain as the same kilogram each day.[14]

The prevailing standard reappeared later in colonial Africa, adopted by the European rulers. Rations were one kilo per day for the French early in the twentieth century in West Africa.[15] Sena Sugar Company workers in interwar Mozambique received 0.85 kilos per day of maize and 0.16 kilos of beans per day. The Portuguese Estado Novo labor code provided for the same 0.8 to 1.0 kilogram of basic cereals each day, though workers may actually have received somewhat less.[16] The Germans gave porters in East Africa somewhat less: fifty pounds of food (or approximately one porter load) for a thirty- to forty-day trek, or about two-thirds of a kilo per day.[17] Contract laborers in Angola in the 1940s fared much worse than others, receiving only 0.5 kilogram of maize or cassava flour per day, plus the usual tiny amounts of dried fish and palm oil.[18]

---

alqueires/exeque. Cadornega's 2 *alqueires,* if Brazilian ones, would roughly equal the 4 Lisbon *alqueires* specified by Peçanha. Cf. Rau, "*Livro de Razão,*" p. 48n, who may thus misapply the Brazilian 14-liter measure to a Lisbon official's affairs in Angola in the 1680s–90s.

10. Sousa Coutinho *portaria,* 7 Dec. 1770, published in *Arquivos de Angola* 1, no. 2 (1933): n.p.

11. Memória sobre o encanamento do Rio Coanza, 1816, AHU, Angola cx. 64. The *cazonguel* was the local Angolan equivalent of the *alqueire.* The Lisbon volume is used in the calculation.

12. Rebelo, *Relações,* pp. 171–73.

13. Curtin, *Economic Change,* p. 169.

14. Hogendorn, "Slave Acquisition and Delivery," p. 484.

15. Richard Roberts and Martin A. Klein, "The Banamba Slave Exodus of 1905 and the Decline of Slavery in the Western Sudan," *Journal of African History* 21, no. 3 (1980): 375–94. The concrete example cited, however, was one of underfeeding.

16. Leroy Vail and Landeg White, *Capitalism and Colonialism in Mozambique: A Study of Quelimane District* (London: Heinemann, 1980), pp. 220–25, 326, 329–30.

17. Helge Kjekshus, *Ecology Control and Economic Development in East African History: The Case of Tanganyika, 1850–1950* (London: Heinemann, 1977), p. 140.

18. Gervase Clarence-Smith, "Capital Accumulation and Class Formation in Angola," in Birmingham and Martin, *History of Central Africa,* 2:193.

Among slave populations in the New World, two distinct sets of figures appear, the one near the world kilogram standard and the other about twice as much, though still below rations prescribed for the Angolan slave trade. British planters in the Caribbean generally supplied only about one pint of meal per day, and that worked out to approximately one kilogram (0.85 kg manioc, or 0.86 kg corn, or 1.08 kg rice or beans).[19] Detailed figures show a single pint per day of maize, wheat, rice, or cassava prescribed in the British Leeward Islands at the end of the eighteenth century but over 2 pints (1 qt.) of unground maize or rice (1.72–2.16 kg), roughly 3 pints per day of unground wheat flour, or a weekly 56 pounds of potatoes or yams (almost exactly the Brazilian *alqueire,* equivalent to 3.64 kg, but an undried form of starch including water, not weighed in maize, rice, or manioc flour), plus small amounts of fish or salted provisions, for slaves in the Jamaican workhouse and as the standard in the Bahamas.[20] These rations, too, were very much in the range of those standard in the Angolan slave trade. It may be that the lower figure reflects diet supplementation and the higher the entire food consumption of the recipients.

In the Old South U. B. Phillips long ago reported the standard as one quart per day (2 pts.) of cornmeal, plus a half pound of salt pork and whatever the slaves' gardens yielded in season, thus equivalent to the higher of the two figures for the Caribbean.[21] The calculations in Fogel and Engerman's *Time on the Cross* for the period just before the Civil War reduced the conventional estimate for corn to 507 pounds per year (0.63 kg/day) but added 489 pounds (0.61 kg/day) of other carbohydrates to a diet much more varied (and nutritious) than previous writers had assumed.[22] Their total was the equivalent of 1.24 kilos per day for the average North American slave, about two-thirds of what had been believed. From the probing discussion that followed publication of the Fogel and Engerman study came a detailed recalculation of their figures, yielding 636 pounds of corn annually (0.79 kg/day) but only 291 pounds of other carbohydrates (0.36 kg/day), for a slightly lower total of 1.15 kilos per day.[23] Both figures fall reasonably close, if on the high side, to the common kilogram standard, though well below custom in the southern Atlantic. Planters elsewhere in the Americas made the calculation in

19. Kiple, "Historical Dimensions," p. 6, and the useful table and sophisticated discussion in idem, *Caribbean Slave,* pp. 78–79 ff.; Robert Dirks, "Resource Fluctuations and Competitive Transformations in West Indian Slave Societies," in Charles A. Laughlin, Jr., and Ivan D. Brady, eds., *Extinction and Survival in Human Populations* (New York: Columbia University Press, 1978), p. 132.

20. Sheridan, *Doctors and Slaves,* pp. 169–73.

21. U. B. Phillips, "Slavery in the Old South," as reprinted in Peter I. Rose, ed., *Americans from Africa* (New York: Atherton, 1970), 1:119; cf. Sutch "Care and Feeding of Slaves," p. 235, for a summary of other similar estimates.

22. Robert W. Fogel and Stanley L. Engerman, *Time on the Cross: The Economics of American Negro Slavery* (Boston: Little-Brown, 1974), 1:109–11. But see the extensive subsequent debate, referred to in Kenneth F. Kiple and Virginia Himmelsteib King, *Another Dimension to the Black Diaspora: Diet, Disease, and Racism* (London: Cambridge University Press, 1981), pp. 79–95.

23. Sutch, "Care and Feeding of Slaves," pp. 235, 259–60, and Table 1 (pp. 262–63), et passim.

terms of hills of manioc or some other form of planted area not readily convertible to kilograms.[24]

Elsewhere in the world, Christian slaves in Muslim North Africa received less, a single 1½-pound (0.68 kg) loaf of bread per day.[25] According to Braudel, European urban populations in the seventeenth and eighteenth centuries consumed fewer cereals—about half a kilo per day—as part of a much more varied diet, though French peasants ate the standard kilo. "Eating consists of a lifetime of consuming bread, more bread, and gruel," as he described their diet, and his point applies also to most slave populations.[26] A modern "well-fed peasant" in the Tonkin Delta would consume the usual kilo of rice per day, but a rice-eating farmer in India actually had only 0.56 kilograms of carbohydrates in 1940.

Among other slavers in the Atlantic, slave ships loading in Senegambia in 1718 reported their ration for slaves as one kilogram per day, exclusive of meat.[27] Robert Stein seems to estimate a rather higher 1⅔ kilo of food per day for slaves in the eighteenth-century French trade, but he assumes a standard crossing of only fifty-six days to reach that figure.[28] A middle passage of eighty to one hundred days, the actual average,[29] would bring the French basic cereal allotment almost in line with the common kilo-per-day ration. Quantities of food recommended at Nantes in the 1780s seem to have been only one-half kilo per day, and data for the British trade in the late eighteenth century convert to a similar 0.6 kilos per diem.[30]

The Brazilian and Portuguese standard, three to four times higher, may thus have been less realistic than other European prescriptions for slave diet, but even wholesale evasions of the law would leave room for the impression that they may have fed their slaves more amply. The Cacheu ship from Upper Guinea, which loaded 400 *alqueires* of rice "for the slaves" (plus other provisions assumed to have been for the crew), would have carried 1.96 kilos per day per slave for the 210 slaves landed later in Brazil, on the basis of a thirty-day crossing (assumed) and 5 percent mortality (also assumed), though a longer crossing would have reduced the daily allotment.[31] A Portuguese ship trading off the Mozambique coast early in the nineteenth century appears to have carried about 0.73 kilos of *milho*, rice, and beans (together) for each slave.[32]

---

24. Gabriel Debien, "La question des vivres pour les esclaves des Antilles françaises aux XVIIe et XVIIIe siècles," *Anuario del Instituto de antropología del Estado Carabobo* (Caracas) 7–8 (1970–71): 144; Amaral Lapa, *Bahia e a carreira da India*, p. 170.

25. William D. Phillips, Jr., *Slavery from Roman Times to the Early Transatlantic Trade* (Minneapolis: University of Minnesota Press, 1985), p. 70.

26. Fernand Braudel, *The Structures of Everyday Life: The Limits of the Possible* (New York: Harper and Row, 1979), pp. 132, 151, 170.

27. Curtin, *Economic Change,* p. 169.

28. Stein, *French Slave Trade,* p. 96.

29. Per Klein's data, *Middle Passage,* p. 192.

30. Boudriot, "Etude sur la navire négrier"; Richardson, "Costs of Survival."

31. Antonio Carreira, *O tráfico português de escravos na costa oriental africana nos começos do século XIX (estudo de um caso)* (Lisbon: Junta de Investigações do Ultramar, 1979), pp. 16, 35, 37. Brazilian *alqueires*; using the Lisbon measure would give a figure of 0.44.

32. Despezas que nos Felipe Damazio de Aguiar e Francisco José Gomes fizemos co a

Crew rations in the Atlantic slave trade may have run significantly less than those laid in for the slaves.[33] Crewmen were the first to be deprived when rations ran short, and they are known to have stolen food from the supplies reserved for the slaves.

---

curveta N. S^n da Oliveira, Cacheu, 24 Jan. 1774, BAPP, 140, no. 38 (with thanks to Dauril Alden).

33. In general, see Edward Reynolds, *Stand the Storm: A History of the Atlantic Slave Trade* (New York: Allison and Busby, 1985), p. 49, who gives 3 lbs. of bread (biscuit?) per week, or only 0.2 kg/day, plus an equivalent weight of salt meat.

Appendix B: Estimate of Mortality among Slaves Awaiting Sale in the New World

Scattered imprecise indications of mortality among slaves awaiting sale in the New World seem to suggest generally falling death rates over the history of the trade. The Cabildo of Rio de Janeiro had noted, on 18 September 1721, the city's urgent need for a cemetery adequate to bury the bodies of the many new (and also settled) slaves dying in the city during a period of serious epidemics among the increasing cargoes of Angolan slaves reaching the city.[1] The Rio Santa Casa da Misericórdia became the burial grounds for such slaves, and over a century later, by the last months of the legal slave trade in 1830, according to Dr. Joseph François Xavier Sigaud, physician to the emperor of Brazil, Rio slave dealers were interring 700 to 800 new slaves there each month, or at a rate of some 9,000 per year, some 300 per 1,000 per annum, about the same level of mortality as prevailed aboard the slave ships toward the end of their crossing.[2]

One may convert losses of the magnitude suggested by Sigaud late in the history of the trade to a biweekly percentage of 1.2 percent. On the assumption that slaves generally remained in the hands of dealers for about a fortnight before sale, other reports suggest a mortality rate that had declined through time to about that level. A proposal of 1810 to deliver slaves to Pará estimated that 10 percent of the landed captives would die before they could be sold, or about the same loss of 1.2 percent in two weeks.[3] Two Maranhão Company ships that had left Angola at a time of growing drought had lost 4.7 percent in 1768 (Pará) and 4.9 percent (Maranhão) in 1765, but other ships from Luanda in 1762 and from Benguela during the rainy 1770s had fatalities of only 1.3 percent each; another ship in 1763 had suffered high mortality at sea and may have lost another 11.8 percent in Pará before it completed sale of its cargo.[4] A mid-eighteenth-century proposal had, probably excessively, budgeted 10 percent losses after landing but before sale in Brazil.[5] Earlier, only 1 of 112 (Mina) slaves reaching Rio in 1715 died in the

1. Conselho Ultramarino to Aires de Saldanha de Albuquerque, 27 May 1722, *Publicações do Arquivo Nacional* (Rio de Janeiro), pp. 190–91 (with thanks to Dauril Alden for the reference).

2. Joseph François Xavier Sigaud, *Discurso sobre a statistica medica do Brasil* (Rio de Janeiro: Seignot-Plancher, 1832), p. 13. See Karasch, *Slave Life,* for extensive and revealing notes on death and dying among Rio slaves after 1800.

3. Rebelo, *Relações,* pp. 88–89.

4. Carreira, "Companhias pombalinas de navegação," pp. 366, 373–77.

5. "Relação sobre escravatura," n.d. (ca. 1760s), AHU, Angola maço 10 (D.O.).

fifteen to twenty days they were held before sale, but 4 of 26 of a group of unhealthy Mina slaves (15.7%) died before sale in 1726.[6] Much earlier still, five ships reaching Brazil in 1625 had experienced unusually high mortality at sea (48.1%) and had then lost 10.8 percent of the survivors after landing.[7]

The data from Spanish ports seem to confirm higher seventeenth-century mortality in the slave pens. Deaths may have dropped below 2 percent or so there by the end of the eighteenth century, but the evidence for the last years of the trade illuminates only epidemic years.[8] According to the records of the South Seas Company in the 1714–18 period, 5.8 percent of the *asiento* slaves it delivered at Cartagena died before sale.[9] At Buenos Aires during the period of epidemics from the 1710s to the 1730s, deaths in the first fifteen days after landing ran about 2.5 to 2.7 percent, with the exception of one disastrously sick cargo from Angola that raised the overall loss to 4.6 percent. Losses at Buenos Aires reportedly rose to 29.6 percent between 1730 and 1736, again during a time of drought and epidemics in Angola. Total deaths before sale (an unknown period of time) for a different sample of ships in the 1715–19 period were 14.1 percent but averaged only 10.7 percent if one excludes the one ship with extraordinarily high losses.[10] Of 1,472 slaves from Bonny and Calabar delivered by the English at Montevideo late in the eighteenth century and then transferred to Buenos Aires before sale, 23.4 percent died, in this sample also after voyages that experienced high mortality.[11]

In the Caribbean, the standard estimate of mortality between landing and sale appears to have been about 4 to 5 percent in the late eighteenth century.[12] In the nineteenth century, Humboldt put losses in Cuba during the "hot months" also at 4 percent.[13]

6. Lisanti, *Negócios coloniais,* 1:dv; 3:88.
7. Mattoso, *Etre esclave au Brésil,* p. 52.
8. Chandler, *Health and Slavery,* pp. 50–51, states the point as a general proposition for Cartagena.
9. Palmer, *Human Cargoes,* p. 120.
10. Ibid., pp. 116–17, 120, but cf. Scheuss de Studer, *Trata de negros,* p. 227, for much lower losses aboard (some of?) the same ships in the 1730s, in a range of 0.9%–3.8%, and 2.0% overall.
11. Scheuss de Studer, *Trata de negros,* pp. 275–76.
12. Mannix and Cowley, *Black Cargoes,* p. 123; Chandler, *Health Conditions,* pp. 50–51, 262.
13. Personal reference frrom Kenneth Kiple.

Appendix C: Principal Authors of Documentation Cited

Name	Title/Position and Dates
Aguiar, Conde do	minister for colonies, c. 1813
Albuquerque, Paulo Caetano de	governor, Angola, 1726–32
Albuquerque e Tovar, Manoel de	governor, Angola, 1819–21
Almeida, João António de	merchant, Lisbon, c. 1825
Almeida, José Maria Doutel d'	governor, Benguela, c. 1810
Almeida e Souza, António de	petitioner, c. 1720s
Almeida e Vasconcelos, Manoel	governor, Angola, 1790–97
Alvares de Mello, João	*ouvidor geral*, c. 1798
Alvellos Leiria, João de	governor, Benguela, c. 1814–15
Alves, Joaquim Gomes	merchant, Lisbon, c. 1825
Anjos, António Lopes	merchant, Benguela, c. 1825
Araujo, Anna Luiza de	petitioner, c. 1791
Arauss, Jacob Pedro	contractor, India, c. 1772
Ataide, Marçal Pedro da Cunha	*capitão de mar e guerra*, c. 1817
Avelino Dias, Christovão	governor, Angola, 1823–24
Avellar, Manoel Gomes de	*ouvidor geral*, c. 1732
Ayres, Francisco Miguel	petitioner?, c. 1749
Azevedo, Domingos de Araujo e	merchant, c. 1799
Bandeira, José Alvares	merchant, Luanda, c. 1767
Barboza e Moura, Francisco da Costa	member, Conselho Ultramarino, Lisbon, c. 1744
Barboza Mourais, Francisco	*ouvidor*, c. 1721–22
Barreto, Coronel Francisco Lobo	petitioner, c. 1740
Bastos Viana	merchant, Lisbon?, 1757
Beça, Jeronimo Caetano de Barros Araujo de	*juiz de fora (interino)*, Benguela, c. 1796
Beltrão, Pedro	*tenente regente*, Pungo Andongo, c. 1794
Bezerra, Francisco Antonio Pita (e Alpoim e Castro)	*capitão de infantaria*, c. 1796
Botelho de Vasconcelos, Alexandre José	governor, Benguela, c. 1796
Braga, Jacinto Dias	contractor, 1742–48
Cabral, Francisco Xavier de Sousa	Treasury minister?, c. 1823

Name	*Title/Position and Dates*
Câmara, José Gonçalo de	governor, Angola, 1779–82
Campos, José Pereira	trader, petitioner, c. 1816
Campos Rego, António de	*provedor,* c.1753
Carvalho da Costa, Joseph	*mestre de campo,* interim governor, Angola, c. 1725–26
Castelobranco, Nicolao de Abreu	governor, Angola, 1824–29
Castro, Manoel Patricio Correa de	deputy, Portuguese Cortes, c. 1823
Castro Barboza, Joaquim Manoel Garcia de	*ouvidor,* c. 1781
Coelho de Carvalho, António de Albuquerque ·	governor, Angola, 1722–25
Cordeiro, João Paulo	merchant, Lisbon, c. 1823–26
Correa da Silva, Francisco Infante de Sequeira e	governor, Benguela, c. 1803
Correa de Araujo, Félix	*juiz de fora, juiz da Alfandega, ouvidor,* c. 1803
Coutinho, Francisco Inocêncio de Sousa: *see* Sousa Coutinho	
Coutinho da Silva, Euzebio Queiroz	*ouvidor geral,* c. 1814
Cruz, Manoel da (e Socio)	merchant, c. 1818
da Cunha, D. António de Alvares	governor, Angola, 1753–58
Cunha e Souza, Manoel Pinto da	*provedor da Fazenda Real,* c. 1767–70
Dantas Lima, Manoel	*vigário geral,* c. 1799
Dias, João Oliveira	petitioner, c. 1807
Dias da Silva, Domingos	contractor, 1766–72
Domingues, Marsal	petitioner, c. 1755
Faria de Mello, Antonio de	petitioner, c. 1744
Faria e Mello, Adriano de	c. 1732
Ferreira, Guilherme João	petitioner, c. 1799
Ferreira, João Alvares	petitioner, c. 1762
Ferreira, Vicente	appointee?, c. 1742
Ferreira Dias, Joseph Antonio	petitioner, c. 1789
Ferreira Diniz, Joseph António	merchant, petitioner, Benguela, c. 1789
Figueiredo (e Alarcão), Henrique de	governor, Angola, 1717–22
Fogaça, Antonio Gomes	trader, c. 1819
Fonseca Coutinho, Anselmo	merchant, petitioner, *coronel,* c. 1799
Fonseca Coutinho, António da	trader, c. 1739
Fonseca Coutinho, Manoel da	*capitão-mor,* Ambaca, c. 1790
Forjaz, Manoel Pereira	governor, Angola, 1607–11
Franco, Francisco Jozé	*escrivão,* Cassange, c. 1739
Freitas de Noronha, Lourenço de	c. 1735
Fronteira, José Pinheiro de Moraes	petitioner, c. 1782
Furtado, Luiz Candido Cordeiro Pinheiro	*tenente coronel, brigadeiro* of the military engineers, c. 1783–1806

Name	Title/Position and Dates
Godinho, Francisco de Sousa Guerra de Araujo	*desembargador,* c. 1804
Gomes, Antonio Marques	contractor, c. 1735
Gomes, Francisco de Paula	trader, Luanda, c. 1825–26
Gomes, Francisco Manoel	resident of Lisbon, c. 1715
Guimarães, Francisco José Gomes	merchant, Lisbon, c. 1823
Guimarães, João da Silva	merchant, c. 1799
Homem e Magalhães, Pedro José	governor, Benguela, c. 1785–86
Honorato da Costa, Francisco	director, Cassange, 1790s–1810s
Lamas, José Gonçalves	petitioner, c. 1737
Lavradio, Conde de	viceroy, Brazil, 1769–79
Leitão, Joseph Correa	lt. col., militia, c. 1732
Leitão, Manoel Correa	trader, c. 1750s
Lencastre, D. António de	governor, Angola, 1772–79
de Lima, João Joseph	trader, c. 1762
Lisboa, Francisco and Manoel	contractors, c. 1718–24
Loureiro, Domingos Lopes	merchant, petitioner, c. 1766
Loureiro, Paulo José	director, Cassange, c. 1791
Magalhães, João Jacques de	governor, Angola, 1738–48
Marinho, Manoel de Faria	petitioner, c. 1798
Marques de Graça, Jozé Joaquim	governor, Benguela, c. 1816
Martins, Belchior Clemente Domingos	accused smuggler, c. 1774
Mello, Boaventura José de	priest, petitioner, c. 1806–7
Mello, José de	petitioner, trader, c. 1816
de Mello, Miguel António	governor, Angola, 1797–1802
Mello, Rafael de Souza Correa e	*juiz de fora,* Benguela, c. 1786
Mello e Alvim, Manoel d'Abreu de	governor, Benguela, c. 1817
Mello e Castro, Martinho de	minister for colonies, 1770–92
Meneses, Rodrigo Cesar de	governor, Angola, 1733–38
Menezes, Francisco Mattozo de	*capitão-mor,* Ambaca, c. 1778
Mesquita, António José Pimentel de Castro e	governor, Benguela, c. 1781
Miranda de Vasconcelos, Dr. Joseph	*provedor da Fazenda,* c. 1739–40
Moçâmedes, Barão de	governor, Angola, 1784–90
Motta Feo e Torres, Luiz da	governor, Angola, 1816–19
Noronha, D. Fernanco António Soares de	governor, Angola, 1802–6
Oeyras, Conde de (also Pombal, Marques de)	chief minister, Portugal, 1750–77
Oliveira, Joaquim Aurelio de	governor, Benguela, c. 1828–29
Oliveira Barboza, João de	governor, Angola, 1810–16
Ornellas, Francisco Paim da Câmara	governor, Benguela, c. 1792–95
Peçanha, Francisco Xavier do Lobão	*ouvidor,* c. 1783–85
Pereira, Fernando Joseph da Cunha	?, c. 1748
Pereira, Henrique Martins	trader, merchant, c. 1820s

Name	Title/Position and Dates
Pereira, José António	merchant, c. 1804–6
Pereira, José Soares da Sylva	*provedor,* Benguela, c. 1814
Pereira da Costa, Francisco	*provedor da Fazenda,* c. 1727
Pilarte da Silva, João	trader?, c. 1770
Pinto, Joaquim Correia	petitioner, c. 1812
Pitta, Francisco Antonio	*capitão comissário da conquista,* c. 1793
Pombal, Marques de (also Oeyras, Conde de)	chief minister, Portugal, 1750–77
Portella, Bernardo Nunes	merchant, c. 1791–95
Quinhões, António Guedes	governor, Benguela, c. 1821
Rialho, Vicente Roiz	*capitão-mor,* Ambaca, c. 1800
Ribeiro, Manoel da Silva	petitioner, c. 1778
Ribeyro, Paulo	merchant, Luanda, c. 1731–32
da Rocha, Joaquim José	merchant, Rio, c. 1820
da Rocha, Manoel Monteyro	contractor, 1730–36
Roza Coutinho, Joseph da	contractor, c. 1715
Saldanha da Gama, António de	governor, Angola, 1807–10
Santa Cecelia, Padre José de	priest, c. 1747
Santa Comba Dão, Barão de	governor, Angola, 1829–34
Silva, João Victo da	petitioner, c. 1762
Silva, Joaquim José da	*capitão-mor/regente,* Ambaca, c. 1795
Silva, Manoel da	petitioner, c. 1730s
Silva, Manoel da	petitioner, c. 1778–84
Silva Lisboa, António da	*juiz de fora,* Benguela, c. 1791
Simões, Maria da Conceição	petitioner, c. 1767
Simões da Silva, Custódio	petitioner, c. 1762
Sousa, Fernão de	governor, Angola, 1624–30
Sousa, José Severino de	petitioner, c. 1819–20
Sousa Coutinho, Francisco Inocêncio	governor, Angola, 1764–72
Sousa Coutinho, Rodrigo	minister for colonies, 1796–1803
Souto, Francisco Roque	*capitão-mor,* c. 1739–45
Souza Magalhães, António Maximo de	commissioned explorer, c. 1773–84
Tavora, Francisco da	governor, Angola, 1669–76
Torres, Estevão Martins	contract administrator, 1748–54
Torres, José de	contractor, 1748–54
Torres, Manoel Barboza e	contractor, 1748–54
Valente, António José	*capitão-tenente,* c. 1791
Vasconcelos, D. António de	governor, Angola, 1754–60
Vasconcelos e Souza	resident of Benguela, c. 1812
Vega, Manoel Soares	?, c. 1744
Veiga, Francisco Chagas	director, Cassange, c. 1793
Vicente, Antonio	merchant, c. 1819
Vidal, Manoel Bernardo	governor, Angola, 1837–39

Name	*Title/Position and Dates*
Vieira, José Ignacio Vaz	merchant, Rio, c. 1820
Vieira, José Maria	*capitão-mor de guerra,* c. 1821
Xavier, Francisco	*capitão-mor,* Ambaca, c. 1739–40
Xavier, Joaquim	*capitão-mor,* Pungo Andongo, c. 1790s

Glossary of Foreign Terms
Used in the Text

aguardente   Generic term for brandies and other highly distilled spirits, generally implying better quality than the Brazilian *gerebitas*.

almude   Unit of liquid measure, approximately 20 liters. (See also *barril, canada, pipa, tonel.*)

alqueire   Unit of dry measure, the Portuguese term for the local Angolan *cazonguel* (officially 13.8 liters). (See also *exeque.*)

arqueação   Rated capacity of a ship for carrying slaves.

arratel   Unit of weight, 0.459 kilograms, the pound (or *libra*). (See also *arroba.*)

arroba   Unit of weight equal to approximately 15 kilograms. (See also *arratel.*)

asiento   Spanish contract authorizing deliveries of slaves to Spanish colonies in the New World.

aviado   Portuguese term equivalent to *funante*, or trading agent.

(de) bando   Phrase referring to a slave ship authorized by government proclamation (*bando*) to load slaves as a general common freight carrier.

banzo   The "bundle" of goods worth a standard slave, especially at Luanda.

barril   "Barrel," a unit of liquid measure, approximately 85 liters. (See also *almude, canada, pipa, tonel.*)

beirame   Also *birama*. Standard length of trade textile, approximately that required to wrap an adult, i.e., about 5 meters or less.

cabeça   "Head," used in the Portuguese trade to refer to an individual slave, particularly later in the eighteenth century.

cachaça   Brazilian term for the cane brandies known in Angola as *gerebita*.

canada   Unit of liquid measure, approximately 1.4 liters. (See also *almude, barril, pipa, tonel.*)

cazonguel	Angolan unit of dry volume, equivalent to the *alqueire*, approximately 14 liters.
comissário	Commission agent, the basic type of commercial agent for conducting business from Lisbon through the colonies. (Also *comissário volante* if a nonresident agent.)
conduta	See *libambo*.
conquista	Portuguese designation for the "conquered" lands of their colony, in Angola between the lower Kwanza and the Dande rivers.
côvado	Unit of length, probably about 2/3 meter, or 3 *palmos*. (See also *dedo, palmo, vara*.)
cria	Literally, a young animal, but also applied to an infant child of a slave, especially an untaxed category of slave children too young to walk (*crias de peito*). Also *crias de pé*.
cruzado	Portuguese currency, worth $400 *réis,* circulating particularly in Brazil.
cuberta(s)	(Covered) deck(s) of a ship.
dedo	A "finger" (measure of length) of some seven centimeters (?), a subdivision of the *palmo* (span). (See also *côvado, palmo, vara*.)
degradado	A person in penal exile, usually sent from Lisbon or Brazil to Angola for a term of years. Such persons were often, while there, part of the Luso-African community.
direitos	Duties or taxes, in Angola those owed on slaves exported. There were two categories: "old duties" (*direitos velhos*) and "new duties" (*direitos novos*).
(de) efeitos próprios	Phrase referring to ships that owned the slaves they carried from Angola to Brazil. Cf. (*de*) *bando*.
exeque	A measure of dry volume used at Luanda, approximately 56 liters.
farinha	Flour, nearly always manioc.
feijão	Beans, of many varieties (pl. *feijões*).
feira	An interior marketplace, so designated by the Portuguese government in Angola as an officially recognized center for exchange between the Atlantic and African sectors, mostly around the borders of the colony. Cf. *pumbo*.
fiador	Guarantor; giver of a bond guaranteeing payment of a debt on behalf of another.
folhinha	Imported textile, approximately one meter on a side.
frasqueira	A measure of liquid volume, one-sixteenth of the large *pipa* casks in which cane brandies were distributed in Angola.

fretado	Freight (general common) carrier, applied to a ship carrying slaves for shore-based merchants at Luanda or elsewhere. Same as *(de) bando*.
frete	Freight charge on a sailing vessel.
funante	A local trader, usually free, not a slave, sent by Luanda merchants to the interior to trade for slaves. Cf. *aviado*.
garrafa	Unit of liquid measure, a demijohn of approximately 5 liters.
gerebita	Brazilian cane brandies, often of very high proof, basic to the trade in slaves. Sometimes also *geribita*.
guia	Passes, issued to traders taking goods from Luanda to the interior of Angola; these documents functioned as bills of lading confirming ownership and value of the goods.
kibuka	See *libambo*.
ladino	A slave acculturated to Portuguese, or Luso-African, colonial life; usually skilled and valuable.
lançado	West African (Senegambian) term for a Euro-African trader.
lemba	Commerical trading "cult" inland from Loango.
letra	Bill of exchange or a note of debt. Subtypes included bills representing privileged claims to the slave duties (*letras dos direitos*), ordinary unsecured bills (*letras de risco*), and so on.
libambo	A "chain" or coffle of slaves, in the area east of Luanda; *kibuka* in Kongo, *conduta* in Portuguese.
livrança	A personal note of indebtedness, an IOU, circulating frequently among merchants in Luanda.
mafouk	Trade minister responsible for Europeans' dealings in the African economy, a term used on the Loango Coast, roughly signifying "great borrower." Also *mambouk* at Loango and *sekulu* in the central highlands.
mambouk	See *mafouk*.
mani	Title of the kings of Kongo.
milho	"Corn" or grain, sometimes specifically sorghum or millet.
moleque	Slave youth or child.
morador	A local resident of Angola or its environs, usually implying a Luso-African "settler" in contrast with officials from Lisbon.
mubire	A trader from the Vili kingdom of Loango, known as such in the regions near Angola.
musumba	Capital of the Lunda empire.

mwaant yaav	Ruler of the Lunda empire.
Mwene Puto	Kongo (and western central African) term for the Portuguese king, and by extension the Portuguese colonial administration.
ndembu	Title of southern Kongo warlords and slave traders, and source of the ethnonym for Africans living on the headwaters of the Bengo, Dande, and Lukala rivers.
ndua	A poison oath administered at Kasanje.
nzimbu	Small marine shell fished from the waters of Luanda Bay and circulated as currency in and around the colony of Angola.
palmo	Span (a measure of length), approximately 18–23 centimeters. (See also *côvado, dedo, vara.*)
pardo	A person of mixed blood, a mulatto.
pataca	Brazilian silver coin worth 320 *réis*.
patrão mor	Harbor master.
peça	"Piece," used to refer to the prime male adult slave in the Portuguese trade, the standard according to which all slaves were valued before the later eighteenth century.
pipa	Cask, approximately 500 liters' capacity, used in the Portuguese and Brazilian trade. (See also *almude, barril, canada, tonel.*)
pombeiro	Caravan leader; petty trader in the interior.
porão	Hold (of a ship).
praça	(1) Space for shipping a slave aboard a vessel leaving Luanda; often bought and sold. (2) The commercial center—in a narrow sense the open square around which firms and warehouses were arranged and in a broad sense the merchants interacting in this space—of a city.
preferência	A tax (of uncertain status) on slaves loaded at Luanda.
presidio	Government military fortification in Angola; including Ambaca, Caconda, Encoje, and Pungo Andongo, among others.
procurador	Legal representative; holder of another's power of attorney (*procuração*).
pumbo	A trading locale, within the African economy. Cf. *feira*.
quintal	A slave "pen" or barracoon (pl. *quintais*).
regente	Civilian official in charge of a district in Angola, a position employed increasingly in the nineteenth century.
réis	The Portuguese currency of account during the eighteenth century; also counted in *mil-réis*

	(1,000 *réis,* written 1$000, with the $ marking the thousands). From *rei* (king) or *real* (royal).
reviro	Illegal payment of slaves purchased with credit from one importer to a different customer, a favorite smuggling strategy of the Luso-Africans.
risco dos escravos	The "slave risk," referring to the high propensity of the slaves to die and thus cause financial loss to their owner.
sekulu	See *mafouk.*
sertão	The "backlands," generally referring to the remote interior of the colony of Angola (pl. *sertões*).
soba	An African petty squire under the domination of the Portuguese military authorities in Angola.
sobrados	Elegant, two-storied townhouses.
sociedade	Joint-partnership company, the main form of commercial combination in eighteenth-century Angola.
sustentos	Daily food-provision charges levied by merchants managing slaves for other owners.
tanga	Loincloth.
terreiro público	The public grain market in Luanda.
tipoia	The hammock, or litter, supported by slaves, in which traders rode along the trails of the interior.
tonel	Huge water cask (pl. *toneis*), and a unit of liquid volume. (See also *almude, barril, canada, pipa.*)
tonelada	The standard volume capacity measure used in Portuguese shipping, of variable size.
tumbeiro	Term employed to refer to slave ships, implying "floating tomb."
vara	Unit of length, approximately 5.5 meters. (See also *côvado, dedo, palmo.*)

Glossary of Portuguese Terms Used in the Notes

alvará	Decree law.
apontamentos	Notes.
auto	An official "act," a legally certified determination of a proceeding (of evaluation, inquiry, etc.).
avaliação	An official evaluation or determination of value for legal purposes (taxation, suits, etc.); the act certifying the established value was the *auto de avaliação*.
aviso	Official notice, warning.
bando	Public proclamation, issued by the government and posted or called to the attention of the general public. Ships sailing (*de*) *bando* (or *fretado*) at Luanda posted such a notice to advertise their availability to owners of slaves wishing shipping space to Brazil (cf. (*de*) *efeitos próprios*).
brigadeiro	Brigadier (general).
caixa	Box of unbound documents in the Lisbon Arquivo Histórico Ultramarino (abbreviated *cx.*).
Câmara	See Senado da Câmara.
capitão comissário de conquista	Commissioned captain of an expedition.
capitão de mar e guerra	Navy commander.
capitão-mor	Captain major in command of a military district in the colony of Angola.
carta regia	A royal letter of instruction.
certidão	A certification, or authentication, of fact or legal evidence.
códice	Codex of bound documents, usually in the Lisbon Arquivo Histórico Ultramarino (abbreviated *cód.*).
Conselho Ultramarino	Lisbon advisory council to the king for overseas affairs.
consulta	An official opinion, usually of the Conselho Ultramarino (Overseas Council, Libon) but also of other constituted advisory bodies (e.g., the Junta do Comércio, or Lisbon Chamber of

	Commerce), advising the king as to the action he should take on a matter. The council was thus "consulted" by the Crown.
desembargador	Appeals court judge (Portugal).
devassa	A hearing or inquest in which official testimony was taken from witnesses in regard to government investigations. The "act" recording such testimony was the *auto da devassa.*
edital	Bulletin of or notice of government decision.
Erário Real	Royal Treasury, as reformed under Pombal.
escrivão	Scribe, more generally a secretary (of government marketplaces and other institutions).
Fazenda Real	Royal Treasury. See also Junta da Fazenda.
juiz de defuntos e auzentes	Probate judge, responsible for assembling and assessing the estates of deceased persons and distributing the assets to creditors and heirs. He also held the position of *juiz dos orfãos* (responsible for orphans' claims to deceased parents' assets).
juiz de fora	The royally appointed local judge in towns throughout the Portuguese empire.
Junta da Fazenda	Royal Treasury Board in Angola. See also Fazenda Real.
Junta do Comércio (Luanda)	Luanda Board of Trade, created in 1764 (replacing an earlier Junta Commercial, created in 1761).
Junta do Comércio (Lisbon)	Lisbon Board of Trade.
lata	Shelf, a location designation used in the Instituto Histórico e Geográfico Brasileiro (Rio de Janeiro).
macete	A sub-*maço,* a subdivision of the following.
maço	An unbound set of papers ("mass") in the Lisbon Arquivo Histórico Ultramarino.
mappa	A summary report in chart format (not a cartographic map).
memória	"Memorial," any sort of advisory report circulating within the Portuguese colonial administration.
mestre de campo	Head of colonial militia.
ouvidor (geral)	Crown judge, sitting in Luanda.
papeis avulsos	Miscellaneous (loose) documents in the Lisbon Arquivo Histórico Ultramarino, arranged in *caixas* and *maços.*
parecer	An official opinion submitted by an individual government functionary to the Crown, stating how an issue "appeared" to him.
Parte não oficial	Unofficial portion of a government publication.

petição	Petition; one form in which a Portuguese subject requested the favor of the Court. (See also *requerimento*).
portaria	A government order, or instruction, issued usually by the colonial governor.
processo	"Process," or legal proceeding, usually criminal.
provedor	Inspector, especially in Angola, of the Royal Treasury (Fazenda Real).
provisão	Also *provizão*. Document making a government appointment or giving an official instruction.
regente	Regent; civilian governor of colonial district.
regimento	Instructions defining the responsibilities of an office, or the competence of an institution, in the Portuguese imperial administration.
relação	"Relation," report.
relatório	A "report" submitted to a Portuguese government official.
representação	Representation of an opinion or position.
requerimento	The usual form in which Portuguese petitioned ("required of") the Crown, usually for appointment to an office, but also for confirmation of the applicability of existing law to their personal circumstances.
Senado da Câmara	Luanda municipal council.
tenente	Lieutenant.
vigário geral	Vicar general.

Works Cited

Abreu, Alexo de. *Tratado de las siete enfermedades*. Lisbon: Pedro Craesbeeck, 1623.

Abreu, José Rodrigues de. *Luz de cirurgiones embarcadissos*. Lisbon: Antonio Pedrozo Galvam, 1711.

Aguiar, [Manuel] Pinto de. Intro. *Aspectos da economia colonial*. Salvador: Livraria Progresso Editora, 1957. Also see "Discurso preliminar. . . ."

Albuquerque Felner. See Felner, Alfredo de Albuquerque.

Alden, Dauril. "Late Colonial Brazil, 1750–1808: Demographic, Economic, and Political Aspects." In Leslie Bethell, ed., *The Cambridge History of Latin America*, 2:601–60. Cambridge: Cambridge University Press, 1984.

Alden, Dauril. "Manoel Luis Vieira: An Entrepreneur in Rio de Janeiro during Brazil's Eighteenth-Century Agricultural Renaissance," *Hispanic American Historical Review* 39, no. 4 (1959): pp. 521–37.

Alden, Dauril. " 'Rogues, Vagabonds, Sturdy Beggars' and Other Undesirables: The Practice of Banishment in the Portuguese Empire." Unpublished paper, University of Washington, Seattle, 1981.

Alden, Dauril. *Royal Government in Colonial Brazil*. Berkeley and Los Angeles: University of California Press, 1968.

Alden, Dauril. "Vicissitudes of Trade in the Portuguese Atlantic Empire during the First Half of the Eighteenth Century: A Review Article." *Americas* 32, no. 2 (1975): 282–91.

Alden, Dauril, and Joseph C. Miller. "Unwanted Cargoes: The Origins and Dissemination of Smallpox via the Slave Trade from Africa to Brazil, c. 1560–c. 1830." In Kenneth F. Kiple, ed., *The African Exchange: Toward a Biological History of the Black People,* pp. 35–109. Durham, N.C.: Duke University Press, 1988. Revised as "Out of Africa: The Slave Trade and the Transmission of Smallpox to Brazil, ca. 1560–ca. 1830." *Journal of Interdisciplinary History* 18, no. 1 (1987): 195–224.

Alencastro, Luiz Felipe de. "Prolétaires et esclaves: immigrés portugais et captifs africains à Rio de Janeiro, 1850–1872." *Cahiers du C.R.I.A.R. (Centre des recherches ibériques et ibéro-américaines de l'Université de Rouen)*, no. 4 (1984): 119–56.

Alencastro, Luis-Felipe de. "La traite nègriére et l'unité nationale brésilienne." *Revue française d'histoire d'outre-mer* 66, 3–4 (nos. 244–45) (1979): 395–419.

Alexandre, Valentim. "O liberalismo português e as colónias de Africa, 1820–1839." *Análise social* 16, 1–2 (nos. 61–62) (1980): 319–40.

Alexandre, Valentim. *Origins do colonialismo português moderno*. Lisbon: Sá da Costa, 1979.

Allan, William. *The African Husbandsman*. Rev. ed. Edinburgh: Oliver and Boyd, 1965.

Almeida, Manoel Lopes de, ed. *Notícias históricas de Portugal e Brasil*. Coimbra: n.p., 1961.

Alpers, Edward A. *Ivory and Slaves in East Central Africa: Changing Patterns of International Trade to the Later Nineteenth Century*. London: Heinemann, 1975.

Alpers, Edward A. "The Story of Swema: Female Vulnerability in Nineteenth-Century East Africa." In Robertson and Klein, *Women and Slavery in Africa*, pp. 185–219.

Amaral, Ilídio do. "Descrição da Luanda oitocentista, vista através de uma planta do ano de 1755." *Garcia de Orta* 9, no. 3 (1961): 409–20. Also published as a *separata*.

Amaral, Ilídio do. *Luanda (estudo de geografia urbana)*. Lisbon: Junta de Investigações do Ultramar, 1968. (*Memórias*, 2ª série, no. 53.)

Amaral Lapa, José Robert do. *Bahia e a carreira da India*. São Paulo: Companhia Editora Nacional, 1968.

Andrews, George Reid. *The Afro-Argentines of Buenos Aires, 1800–1900*. Madison: University of Wisconsin Press, 1980.

"Angola no fim do século XVIII: Documentos." *Boletim da Sociedade de geografia de Lisboa* 6, no. 5 (1886): 284–304.

Annaes do Conselho Ultramarino (parte não oficial). (Lisbon: Imprensa nacional, 1867), sér. 1 (1854–58).

Anstey, Roger T. *The Atlantic Slave Trade and British Abolition, 1760–1810*. London: Macmillan, 1975.

Arquivo das colónias (Lisbon, Ministério das Colónias), 1917–19, 1929–30.

Arquivos de Angola (Luanda, 1933–).

Arruda, José Jobson de Andrade. *O Brasil no comércio colonial*. São Paulo: Editora Ática, 1980.

Arruda, José Jobson de Andrade. "O Brasil no comércio colonial (1796–1808): Contribuição ao estudo quantitativo da economia colonial." Ph.D. diss., Universidade de São Paulo, 1972.

Azeredo, José Pinto de. *Ensaios sobre algumas enfermidades d'Angola*. Lisbon: Regia Oficina Typografica, 1799.

Azevedo, R. Ávila de. "Princípios de uma economia de fixação em África (século XVIII)." *Actas do V Colóquio internacional de estudos luso-brasileiros* (Coimbra, 1963), 1:121–31.

Bal, Willy. "Portugais *pombeiro*, commerçant ambulant du 'sertão'." *Annali dell'Istituto Universitario Orientalis* (Naples) 7 (1965): 123–61.

Balbi, Adrien. *Essai statistique sur le royaume de Portugal et d'Algarve*. 2 vols. Paris: Rey et Gravier, 1822.

Barba, Enrique M. "Sobre el contrabando de la Colonia del Sacramento (siglo XVIII)." *Investigaciones y ensayos* (Buenos Aires) 28 (1980): 57–76.

Bathily, Abdoulaye. "La traite atlantique des esclaves et ses effets économiques et sociaux en Afrique: le cas du Galam, royaume de l'hinterland sénégambien au dix-huitième siècle." *Journal of African History* 27, no. 2 (1986): 269–93.

Bauss, Rudy. "General Observations of Bullion Movements in the Portuguese Empire, 1785–1815." Unpublished paper, ca. 1978.

Bauss, Rudy. "A Legacy of British Free Trade Policies: The End of the Trade and Commerce between India and the Portuguese Empire, 1780–1830." Unpublished paper, ca. 1981.

Bauss, Rudy. "A Preliminary Examination of the British Role in the Destruction of the Lusitanian and Indian Cotton Manufacturers and the Cessation of Trade between the Luso-Brazilian Empire and India: 1780–1830." Unpublished paper, ca. 1979.

Bauss, Rudolph William. "Rio de Janeiro: The Rise of Late Colonial Brazil's Dominant Emporium, 1777–1808." Ph.D. diss., Tulane University, 1977.

Bauss, Rudy. "Rio Grande do Sul in the Portuguese Empire: The Formative Years, 1777–1808." *Americas* 39, no. 4 (1983): 519–35.

Beach, David. "The Shona Economy: Branches of Production." In Robin Palmer and Neil Parsons, eds., *The Roots of Rural Poverty in Central and Southern Africa*, pp. 37–65. London: Heinemann, 1977.

Bean, Richard N. *The British Trans-Atlantic Slave Trade, 1650–1775.* New York: Arno Press, 1975.

Becker, Charles, and Victor Martin. "Kayor and Baol: Senegalese Kingdoms and the Slave Trade in the Eighteenth Century." In Inikori, *Forced Migration*, pp. 100–125.

Bender, Gerald J. *Angola under the Portuguese: The Myth and the Reality.* Berkeley and Los Angeles: University of California Press, 1978.

Berg, Gerald M. "The Sacred Musket: Tactics, Technology, and Power in Eighteenth-Century Madagascar." *Comparative Studies in Society and History* 27, no. 2 (1985): 261–79.

Bethell, Leslie. *The Abolition of the Brazilian Slave Trade: Britain, Brazil, and the Slave Trade Question, 1807–1869.* Cambridge: Cambridge University Press, 1970.

Birmingham, David. *Central Africa to 1870.* Cambridge: Cambridge University Press, 1981.

Birmingham, David. "The Coffee Barons of Cazengo." *Journal of African History* 19, no. 4 (1978): 523–38.

Birmingham, David. "Early African Trade in Angola and Its Hinterland." In Gray and Birmingham, *Pre-Colonial African Trade*, pp. 163–73.

Birmingham, David. *Trade and Conflict in Angola: The Mbundu and Their Neighbours under the Influence of the Portuguese, 1483–1790.* Oxford: Clarendon Press, 1966.

Birmingham, David, and Phyllis Martin, eds. *History of Central Africa.* 2 vols. London: Longmans, 1983.

Boletim do Arquivo histórico colonial (Lisbon), vol. 1 (1950).

Boletim do Conselho Ultramarino (legislação antiga). 2 vols. Lisbon: Imprensa Nacional, 1867–.

Bomtempo, José Maria. *Compendios de medicina pratica.* Rio de Janeiro: Regia Officina Typografica, 1815.

Bomtempo, José Maria. *Trabalhos medicos oferecidos a Magestade do Senhor D. Pedro I, Imperador do Brasil.* Rio de Janeiro: Typographia Nacional, [1825].

Bontinck, F. "Derrota de Benguella para o sertão: critique d'authenticité." *Bulletin de l'Académie royale des sciences d'outre-mer* (Brussels) 3 (1977): 279–300.

Bontinck, F. "Le voyage des pombeiros: essai de réinterpretation." *Cultures au Zaïre et en Afrique* 5 (1974): 39–70.

Boogaart, Ernst van den, and Pieter C. Emmer. "The Dutch Participation in the Atlantic Slave Trade, 1595–1650." In Gemery and Hogendorn, *Uncommon Market,* pp. 353–75.

Botelho, Sebastião Xavier. *Escravatura: benefícios que podem provir ás nossas possessões d'Africa da prohibicão daquelle tráfico.* Lisbon: Typographia de José B. Morando, 1840.

Boudriot, Jean. "Etude sur le navire négrier." Paper presented to the Colloque International sur la Traite des Noirs, Nantes, 1985.

Bowdich, T. Edward. *An Account of the Discoveries of the Portuguese in the Interior of Angola and Mozambique.* London: J. Booth, 1824; reprinted New York: AMS Press, 1980.

Boxer, Charles R. *The Golden Age of Brazil, 1695–1750.* Berkeley and Los Angeles: University of California Press, 1962.

Boxer, Charles R. *The Portuguese Seaborne Empire, 1415–1825.* New York: Knopf, 1969.

Boxer, Charles R. *Portuguese Society in the Tropics.* Madison: University of Wisconsin Press, 1965.

Boxer, Charles R. *Salvador de Sá and the Struggle for Brazil and Angola, 1602–1686.* London: University of London Press, 1952.

Brásio, António. "Descripção dos governos dos Ill.^{mos} e Ex.^{mos} Snr.^{es} António de Vasconcellos, e D. Francisco Innocencio de Souza Coutinho." *Studia* 41–42 (1979): 205–25.

Brásio, António. "O inimigo dos antigos colonos e missionários de África." *Portugal em Africa* 1 (1944): 215–29. Reprinted in *História e missiologia: inéditos e esparsos,* pp. 735–49. Luanda: Instituto de Investigação Científica de Angola, 1973.

Brásio, António, ed. *Monumenta missionaria africana: Africa occidental (Série I).* Vols. 1–11 Lisbon: Agência Geral do Ultramar, 1952–72. Vols. 12–14. Lisbon: Academia Portuguesa de História, 1981. 1984–85.

Braudel, Fernand. *The Structures of Everyday Life: The Limits of the Possible.* Vol. 1 of *Civilization and Capitalism, 15th–18th Century.* Trans. and rev. Siân Reynolds. New York: Harper and Row, 1982.

Breen, Timothy H., and Stephen Innes. *"Myne Owne Ground": Race and Freedom on Virginia's Eastern Shore, 1640–1676.* New York: Oxford University Press, 1980.

Broadhead, Susan. "Beyond Decline: The Kingdom of Kongo in the Eighteenth and Nineteenth Centuries." *International Journal of African Historical Studies* 12, no. 4 (1979): 615–50.

Broadhead, Susan Herlin. "Luso-Kongolese Armed Conflict in Northern Angola: An Historical Perspective." *Etudes d'histoire africaine* (forthcoming).

Broadhead, Susan Herlin. "Slave Wives, Free Sisters: Bakongo Women and Slavery, c. 1700–1850." In Robertson and Klein, *Women and Slavery in Africa,* pp. 160–81.

Broadhead, Susan Herlin. "Trade and Politics on the Congo Coast: 1770–1870." Ph.D. diss., Boston University, 1971.

Brooks, George E., Jr., "A Nhara of the Guinea-Bissau Region: Mãe Aurélia Correa." In Robertson and Klein, *Women and Slavery in Africa,* pp. 295–319.

Brooks, George E., Jr. "The *Signares* of Saint-Louis and Gorée: Women Entrepreneurs in Eighteenth-Century Senegal." In Nancy J. Hafkin and Edna G. Bay, eds., *Women in Africa: Studies in Social and Economic Change,* pp. 19–44. Stanford: Stanford University Press, 1976.

Brown, Larissa V. "Internal Commerce in a Colonial Economy: Rio de Janeiro and Its Hinterland, 1790–1822." Ph.D. diss., University of Virginia, 1985.

Buescu, Mircea. *300 anos de inflação.* Rio de Janeiro: APEC, 1973.

Cadornega, António de Oliveira de. *História geral das guerras angolanas (1680).* Ed. José Matias Delgado. 3 vols. Lisbon: Agência Geral das Colónias, 1940.

Caldas, Jozé Antonio. "Notícia geral de toda esta capitania da Bahia desde o seu descobrimento até o prezente anno de 1759." *Revista do Instituto geográphico e histórico da Bahia* 57 (1931): 287–321.

Caldwell, John C. Comment on Manning, "The Enslavement of Africans: A Demographic Model." *Canadian Journal of African Studies* 16, no. 1 (1982): 127–30.

Caldwell, John C., ed. *Population Growth and Socio-Economic Change in West Africa.* New York: Columbia University Press, 1975.

Cameron, Verney Lovett. *Across Africa.* New York: Harper and Brothers, 1877.

Campbell, Gwyn R. "Madagascar and the Slave Trade, 1810–1895." *Journal of African History* 22, no. 2 (1981): 203–27.

Campbell, Gwyn R. "The Monetary and Financial Crisis of the Merina Empire, 1810–1826." *South African Journal of Economic History* 1, no. 1 (1986): 99–118.

Campbell, Gwyn R. "The Role of the London Missionary Society in the Rise of The Merina Empire 1810–1861." Ph.D. diss., University College, Swansea, 1985.

Campos, Fernando. "A data da morte da Rainha Jinga D. Verónica I." *Africa* (São Paulo), no. 4 (1981): 79–103, and no. 5 (1982): 72–104.

Cannecattim, Bernardo Maria de. *Collecção de observações grammaticaes sobre a lingua Bunda ou Angolense e Diccionario da lingua Congueza.* Lisbon: Impressão Regia, 1805; 2d ed., Lisbon: Imprensa Nacional, 1854.

Cannecattim, Bernardo Maria de. *Diccionario da lingua bunda ou angolense, explicada na lingua portugueza e latina.* Lisbon: Impressão Regia, 1804.

Capela, José. *O vinho para o preto.* Porto: Afrontamento, 1973.

Capello, H., and R. Ivens. *From Benguella to the Territory of Yacca.* Trans. A. Elwes. 2 vols. London: S. Low, Marston, Searle, and Rivington, 1882.

Cardoso, Manuel da Costa Lobo. *Subsídios para a história de Luanda.* Luanda: Edição do Museu de Angola, 1954.

.Carnaxide, António de Sousa Pedroso. *O Brasil na administração pombalina (economia e política externa).* São Paulo: Companhia Editora Nacional, 1940.

Carreira, António. "As companhias pombalinas de navegação, comércio, e tráfico de escravos entre a costa africana e o nordeste brasileiro." *Boletim cultural da Guiné portuguesa* 22 (nos. 89–90) (1967): 5–88; 23 (nos. 91–92) (1968): 301–454; 24 (no. 93) (1969): 59–188; 24 (no. 94) (1969): 284–474. Also published in book form under the same title, *As companhias pombalinas de navegação . . .* (Lisbon, 1969). New, revised edition: *As companhias pombalinas de Grão-Pará e Maranhão e Pernambuco e Paraíba* (Lisbon: Presença, 1983).

Carreira, António. *Notas sobre o tráfico português de escravos.* Lisbon: Universidade Nova de Lisboa, 1978; 2d ed. rev., 1983.

Carreira, António. *O tráfico português de escravos na costa oriental africana nos começos do século XIX (estudo de um caso).* (Centro de Estudos de Antropologia Cultural, Estudos de Antropologia Cultural, no. 12.) Lisbon: Junta de Investigações Científicas do Ultramar, 1979.

Carreira, António. "Tratos e resgates dos Portugueses nos Rios de Guiné e Ilhas de Cabo Verde nos começos do século XVIII." *Revista de história económica e social* 2 (1978): 91–103.

Carter, Henry R. *Yellow Fever: An Epidemiological and Historical Study of Its Place of Origin.* Baltimore: Williams and Wilkins, 1931.

Carvalho, Henrique Augusto Dias de. *Ethnographia e história tradicional dos povos da Lunda.* Lisbon: Imprensa Nacional, 1890.

Cascudo, Luis da Camara. *História da alimentação no Brasil.* 2 vols. São Paulo: Companhia Editora Nacional, 1967–68.

Cascudo, Luis da Camara. *Prelúdio da cachaça: etnografia, história e sociologia da aguardente no Brasil.* (Coleção Canavieira no 1.) Rio de Janeiro: Instituto do Açúcar e do Alcool, 1968.

Castro e Almeida, Eduardo. *Inventario dos documentos relativos ao Brasil existentes no Archivo de Marinha e Ultramar.* 8 vols. Rio de Janeiro: Biblioteca Nacional, 1936.

Cavazzi de Montecucculo, João António. *Descrião histórica dos três reinos de Congo, Matamba e Angola.* Trans. and ed. Graciano Maria de Luguzzano. 2 vols. Lisbon: Junta de Investigações do Ultramar, 1965.

Chandler, David L. *Health and Slavery in Colonial Colombia.* New York: Arno Press, 1981.

Chandler, David L. "Health Conditions in the Slave Trade of Colonial New Granada." In Robert B. Toplin, ed., *Slavery and Race Relations in Latin America,* pp. 51–88. Westport, Conn.: Greenwood Press, 1974.

Chaunu, Hugette, and Pierre Chaunu. *Séville et l'Atlantique (1594–1650).* 8 vols. Paris: A. Colin for the Institute des Hautes Etudes de l'Amérique Latine, 1955–59.

Childs, Gladwyn M. "The Kingdom of Wambu (Huambo): A Tentative Chronology." *Journal of African History* 5, no. 3 (1964): 367–79.

Childs, Gladwyn M. *Umbundu Kinship and Character.* London: Oxford University Press, International African Institute, 1949.

Clarence-Smith, Gervase. "Capital Accumulation and Class Formation in Angola." In Birmingham and Martin, *History of Central Africa,* 2:163–99.

Clarence-Smith, Gervase. "Capitalist Penetration among the Nyaneka of Southern Angola, 1760s to 1920s." *African Studies* 37, no. 2 (1978): 163–76.

Clarence-Smith, Gervase. "The Farmer-Herders of Southern Angola and Northern Namibia, 1840s to 1920s." In Heimer, *Formation of Angolan Society* (forthcoming).

Clarence-Smith, Gervase. "The Portuguese Contribution to the Cuban Slave and Coolie Trades in the Nineteenth Century." *Slavery and Abolition* 5, no. 1 (1984): 25–33.

Clarence-Smith, Gervase. *Slaves, Peasants, and Capitalists in Southern Angola, 1840–1926.* New York: Cambridge University Press, 1979.

Clarence-Smith, Gervase. *The Third Portuguese Empire, 1825–1975: A Study in Economic Imperialism.* Manchester: Manchester University Press, 1985.

Clarence-Smith, Gervase, and Richard Moorsom. "Underdevelopment and Class Formation in Ovamboland, 1845–1915." *Journal of African History* 16, no. 3 (1975): 365–82.

Clark, Colin, and Margaret Haswell. *The Economics of Subsistence Agriculture.* New York: St. Martin's Press, 1967.

Cohn, Raymond L., and Richard A. Jensen. "The Determinants of Slave Mortality Rates on the Middle Passage." *Explorations in Economic History* 19, no. 3 (1982): 269–82.

Collecção chronologica de leis extravagantes. See Freitas, Joaquim Ignacio de, ed.

Conrad, Robert Edgar. *Children of God's Fire: A Documentary History of Black Slavery in Brazil.* Princeton: Princeton University Press, 1983.

Conrad, Robert Edgar. *World of Sorrow: The African Slave Trade to Brazil.* Baton Rouge: Louisiana State University Press, 1986.

Conselho Ultramarino (Lisbon). See its *Annaes, Boletim.*

Coquery-Vidrovitch, Catherine. "Research on the African Mode of Production." In Martin A. Klein and G. Wesley Johnson, eds., *Perspectives on the African Past,* pp. 33–54. Boston: Little, Brown, 1972.

Cordell, Dennis D. *Dar Al-Kuti and the Last Years of the Trans-Saharan Slave Trade.* Madison: University of Wisconsin Press, 1985.

Corrêa, Elias Alexandre da Silva. *História de Angola.* Intro. and notes by Dr. Manuel Múrias. 2 vols. Lisbon: Editorial Ática, 1937.

Cosme, Dr. Francisco Damião. See Pina, Luis de, ed., "Tractado das queixas endemicas."

Costa, Emilia Viotti da. "The Portuguese-African Slave Trade: A Lesson in Colonialism." *Latin American Perspectives* 12, no. 1 (no. 46) (1985): 41–61.

Coughtry, Jay. *The Notorious Triangle: Rhode Island and the African Slave Trade, 1700–1807.* Philadelphia: Temple University Press, 1981.

Couto, Carlos. *Os capitães-mores em Angola no século XVIII (subsídios para o estudo da sua actuação).* Luanda: Instituto de Investigação Científica de Angola, 1972.

Couto, Carlos. "O pacto colonial e a interferência brasileira no domínio das relações econômicas entre Angola e o Reino no séc. XVIII." *Estudos históricos* (Marília) 10 (1971): 21–32.

Couto, Carlos. "Regimento do governo subalterno de Benguela." *Studia* 45 (1981): 285–94.

Couto, Carlos. *O zimbo na historiografia angolana.* Luanda: Instituto de Investigação Científica de Angola, 1973.

Craton, Michael. "Death, Disease, and Medicine on Jamaican Slave Plantations: The Example of Worthy Park, 1767–1838." *Histoire sociale / Social History* 9 (no. 18) (1976): 237–55.

Craton, Michael. *Sinews of Empire: A Short History of British Slavery.* Garden City, N.Y.: Anchor Press, 1974.

Curtin, Philip D. "Africa and the Wider Monetary World, 1250–1850." In John F. Richards, ed., *Precious Metals in the Later Medieval and Early Modern Worlds,* pp. 231–68. Durham, N.C.: Carolina Academic Press, 1982.

Curtin, Philip D., ed. *Africa Remembered: Narratives by West Africans from the Era of the Slave Trade*. Madison: University of Wisconsin Press, 1967.

Curtin, Philip D. *The Atlantic Slave Trade: A Census*. Madison: University of Wisconsin Press, 1969.

Curtin, Philip D. *Cross-Cultural Trade in World History*. New York: Cambridge University Press, 1984.

Curtin, Philip D. *Economic Change in Pre-Colonial Africa: Senegambia in the Era of the Slave Trade*. Madison: University of Wisconsin Press, 1975.

Curtin, Philip D. *The Image of Africa: British Ideas and Action, 1780–1850*. Madison: University of Wisconsin Press, 1964.

Curtin, Philip D., Steven Feierman, Leonard Thompson, and Jan Vansina. *African History*. Boston: Little, Brown, 1978.

Daaku, Kwame Yeboa. *Trade and Politics on the Gold Coast, 1600–1720: A Study of the African Reaction to European Trade*. Oxford: Clarendon Press, 1970.

Daget, Serge. "À Vieux-Calabar, en 1825: l'éxpedition du *Chârles* (ou de l'*Eugène*) comme élément du modèle de la traite négrière illégale." In *Etudes africaines offertes à Henri Brunschwig*, pp. 117–33. Paris: Editions de l'Ecole des Hautes Etudes en Sciences Sociales, 1982.

Davies, K. G. *The Royal African Company*. London: Longmans Green, 1957.

Day, John. "The Great Bullion Famine of the Fifteenth Century." *Past and Present* 79 (1978): 3–54.

Debien, Gabriel. "Le journal de traite de la *Licorne* au Mozambique, 1787–1788." In *Etudes africaines offertes à Henri Brunschwig*, pp. 91–116. Paris: Editions de l'Ecole des Hautes Etudes en Sciences Sociales, 1982.

Debien, Gabriel. "La question des vivres pour les esclaves des Antilles françaises aux XVIIe et XVIIIe siècles." *Anuario del Instituto de antropologia del Estado Carabobo* (Caracas) 7–8 (1970–71): 131–73.

Debien, Gabriel. "La traite nantaise vue par un Nantais." In "Documents sur la traite (XVIIe–XIXe siècles)," *Enquêtes et documents* (Centre de Recherches sur l'Histoire de la France Atlantique) 2 (1972): 203–12.

Delgado, Ralph. *Ao sul do Cuanza (ocupação e aproveitamento do antigo reino de Benguela)*. Lisbon: n.p., 1944.

Delgado, Ralph. *A famosa e histórica Benguela: catálogo dos governadores (1779–1940)*. Lisbon: Edições Cosmos, 1940.

Delgado, Ralph. "O governo de Sousa Coutinho em Angola." *Studia* 6 (1960): 19–56; 7 (1961): 49–86; 10 (1962): 7–48.

Delgado, Ralph. *O reino de Benguela: do descobrimento à criação do govêrno subalterno*. Lisbon: Imprensa Beleza, 1945.

Dias, Gastão Sousa. *Relações de Angola*. Coimbra: Imprensa da Universidade, 1934.

Dias, Gastão Sousa, ed. "Uma viagem a Cassange nos meados do século XVIII." *Boletim da Sociedade de geografia de Lisboa* 56, nos. 1–2 (1938): 3–30.

Dias, Jill R. "Famine and Disease in the History of Angola, c. 1830–1930." *Journal of African History* 22, no. 3 (1981): 349–78.

Dias, Jill R. "Uma questão de identidade: respostas intelectuais às transformações económicas no seio da elite crioula da Angola portuguesa entre 1870 e 1930." *Revista internacional de estudos africanos* 1 (1983): 61–94.

Dias, Jill R. "A sociedade colonial de Angola e o liberalismo português, c. 1820–1850." In *O liberalismo na península Ibérica na primeira metade do século XIX*, 1:267–86. Lisbon: Sá da Costa, 1982.

Diniz, José de Oliveira Ferreira. *Populações indígenas de Angola*. Coimbra: Imprensa da Universidade, 1918.

Diop, Marie-Louise. "Le sous-peuplement de l'Afrique noire." *Bulletin de l'Institut fondemental de l'Afrique noire*, sér. B, 40, no. 4 (1978): 718–862.

"Directorio para o Capitão Chagas com o estabelecimento da nova Regulação do Commercio," 22 Aug. 1792. *Arquivos de Angola* 1, no. 6 (1936): doc. 6.

Dirks, Robert. "Resource Fluctuations and Competitive Transformations in West Indian Slave Societies." In Charles D. Laughlin, Jr., and Ivan D. Brady, eds., *Extinction and Survival in Human Populations*, pp. 122–80. New York: Columbia University Press, 1978.

Dirks, Robert. "Slaves' Holiday." *Natural History* 84, no. 10 (1975): 82–91.

Dirks, Robert. "Social Responses during Severe Food Shortages and Famine." *Current Anthropology* 21, no. 1 (1980): 21–44.

"Discurso preliminar, histórico, introductivo, com natureza de descripção económica da comarca e cidade de Bahia. . . ." *Anais da Biblioteca nacional do Rio de Janeiro* 27 (1905): 281–348. Also in [Manuel] Pinto de Aguiar, intro., *Aspectos da economia colonial*. Salvador: Livraria Progresso Editora, 1957.

Donnan, Elizabeth. *Documents Illustrative of the History of the Slave Trade to America*. 4 vols. Washington: Carnegie Institution of Washington, 1930–35.

Douglas, Mary. "Primitive Rationing: A Study in Controlled Exchange." In Raymond Firth, ed., *Themes in Economic Anthropology*, pp. 119–47. London: Tavistock, 1967.

Douglas, Mary, and Baron Isherwood. *The World of Goods: Towards an Anthropology of Consumption*. New York: Basic Books, 1979.

Douville, Jean-Baptiste. *Voyage au Congo et dans l'intérieur de l'Afrique équinoxiale—fait dans les années 1828, 1829 et 1830*. 3 vols. Paris: J. Renouard, 1832.

Duncan, T. Bentley. *Atlantic Islands: Madeira, the Azores and the Cape Verdes in Seventeenth-Century Commerce and Navigation*. Chicago: University of Chicago Press, 1972.

du Toit, Brian M. "Man and Cannabis in Africa: A Study of Diffusion." *African Economic History* 1 (1976): 17–35.

Ekholm, Kajsa. "External Exchange and the Transformation of Central African Social Systems." In Jonathan Friedman and Michael J. Rowlands, eds., *The Evolution of Social Systems*, pp. 115–36. Pittsburgh: University of Pittsburgh Press, 1978.

Ekholm, Kajsa. *Power and Prestige: The Rise and Fall of the Old Kongo Kingdom*. Uppsala: Skriv Service AB, 1972.

Elbl, C. Ivana. "The Portuguese Trade with West Africa, 1440–1521." Ph.D. diss., University of Toronto, 1986.

Eltis, David. "The British Contribution to the Nineteenth-Century Trans-Atlantic Slave Trade." *Economic History Review* 32, no. 2 (1979): 211–27.

Eltis, David. "The British Trans-Atlantic Slave Trade after 1807." *Maritime History* 4, no. 1 (1974): 1–11.

Eltis, David. "Fluctuations in the Age and Sex Ratios of Slaves in the Nineteenth-Century Transatlantic Slave Traffic." *Slavery and Abolition* 7, no. 3 (1986): 257–72.

Eltis, David. "Free and Coerced Transatlantic Migrations: Some Comparisons." *American Historical Review* 88, no. 2 (1983): 251–80.

Eltis, David. "The Transatlantic Slave Trade, 1821–1843." Ph.D. diss., University of Rochester, 1978.

Eltis, David. Draft appendix on mortality to *Economic Growth and the Ending of the Transatlantic Slave Trade*. New York: Oxford University Press, 1987. (Appendix D, pp. 265–69, in the published book.)

Esaguy, Augusto d'. *Breve notícia sobre a escola medica de Luanda*. Lisbon, 1951. *Separata* from *Imprensa médica* (Faculdade de Medicina—Lisbon).

Esaguy, Augusto d'. *Notulas para a história da medicina de Angola (Documentos)*. Lisbon: Editorial Império, 1952. Reprint of "Três documentos inéditos para a história da medicina de Angola." *Imprensa médica* (Faculdade de Medicina—Lisbon) 16, no. 1 (1952): 15–19.

Esparteiro, António Marques. *Dicionário ilustrado de marinha*. Lisbon: Clássica Editora Livraria, 1962.

Estermann, Carlos. *The Ethnography of Southwestern Angola*. Trans. and ed. Gordon D. Gibson. 2 vols. New York: Africana, 1976–79.

Ewald, Janet. "Soldiers, Traders, and Slaves: The Political Economy of the Upper Nile Valley System in the Nineteenth Century." Paper presented to the Southeastern Regional Seminar in African Studies, Charlottesville, Va., 1984.

Fage, John D. "The Effect of the Export Slave Trade on African Populations." In R. P. Moss and R.J.A.R. Rathbone, eds., *The Population Factor in African Studies*, pp. 15–23. London: University of London Press, 1975.

Fage, John D. "Slaves and Society in Western Africa, c. 1445–c. 1700." *Journal of African History* 21, no. 3 (1980): 289–310.

Falcon, Francisco José Calazans. *A época pombalina: política econômica e monarquia ilustrada*. São Paulo: Editora Ática, 1982.

Felner, Alfredo de Albuquerque. *Angola: apontamentos sôbre e colonização dos plan-altos e litoral do sul de Angola*. 3 vols. Lisbon: Agência Geral das Colónias, 1940.

Felner, Alfredo de Albuquerque. *Angola: apontamentos sôbre a ocupação e início do estabelecimento dos portugueses no Congo, Angola e Benguela (extraídos de documentos históricos)*. Coimbra: Imprensa da Universidade, 1933.

Feo Cardoso (de Castello Branco e Torres), João Carlos. See Torres.

Fernandes de Oliveira, Mário António. *Alguns aspectos da administração de Angola em época de reformas (1834–1851)*. Lisbon: Universidade Nova de Lisboa, 1981.

Fernandes de Oliveira, Mário António, comp. *Angolana (Documentação sobre Angola)*. 3 vols. to date. Luanda: Instituto de Investigação Científica de Angola, 1968–.

Ferrez, Gilberto. "Diário anônimo de uma viagem às costas d'África e às Índias Espanholas (1702–1703)." *Revista do Instituto histórico e geográfico brasileiro* 267 (April–June 1965): 3–42.

Ferry, Robert J. "Encomienda, African Slavery, and Agriculture in Seventeenth-

Century Caracas." *Hispanic American Historical Review* 61, no. 4 (1981): 609–35.

Filesi, Teobaldo, and I. Villapadierna. *La "Missio Antiqua" dei Cappuccini nel Congo (1645–1835)*. Rome: Istituto Storico dei Cappuccini, 1978.

Fisher, H.E.S. *The Portugal Trade: A Study of Anglo-Portuguese Commerce, 1700–1770*. London: Methuen, 1971.

Flory, Rae Jean. "Bahian Society in the Mid-Colonial Period: The Sugar Planters, Tobacco Growers, Merchants, and Artisans of Salvador and the Recôncavo, 1680–1725." Ph.D. diss., University of Texas, 1978.

Fogel, Robert W., and Stanley L. Engerman. *Time on the Cross: The Economics of American Negro Slavery*. 2 vols. Boston: Little-Brown, 1974.

Forde, Daryll. *Marriage and the Family among the Yakö in South-Eastern Nigeria*. London: Percy Humphries, 1951.

Fouchard, Jean. *Les marrons de la liberté*. Paris: Editions de l'Ecole, 1972.

Fouchard, Jean. "The Slave Trade and the Peopling of Santo Domingo, 1764–1793." In UNESCO, *The African Slave Trade from the Fifteenth to the Nineteenth Century*, pp. 270–88. Paris: UNESCO, 1979.

Fox-Genovese, Elizabeth, and Eugene D. Genovese. *The Fruits of Merchant Capital*. New York: Oxford University Press, 1983.

Freeman, Peter H., et al. *Cape Verde: Assessment of the Agricultural Sector*. McLean, Va.: General Research Corp., 1978.

Freitas, Joaquim Ignacio de, ed. *Collecção chronologica de leis extravagantes: posteriores á nova compilação das ordenações do Reino, publicadas em 1603*. 6 vols. in 5. Coimbra: Real Imprensa da Universidade, 1819.

Freitas, Octavio de. *Doenças africanas no Brasil*. São Paulo: Editora Nacional, 1935.

Gaulme, François. "Un document sur le Ngoyo et ses voisins en 1784; l' 'Observation sur la navigation et le commerce de la côte d'Angole' du comte de Capellis." *Revue française d'histoire d'outre-mer* 64, 3 (no. 236) (1977): 350–75.

Gemery, Henry A., and Jan S. Hogendorn. "The Atlantic Slave Trade: A Tentative Economic Model." *Journal of African History* 15, no. 2 (1974): pp. 223–46.

Gemery, Henry A., and Jan S. Hogendorn. "Technological Change, Slavery, and the Slave Trade." In Clive Dewey and A. G. Hopkins, eds., *The Imperial Impact: Studies in the Economic History of Africa and India*, pp. 243–58. London: Athlone Press, 1978.

Gemery, Henry A., and Jan S. Hogendorn, eds. *The Uncommon Market: Essays in the Economic History of the Atlantic Slave Trade*. New York: Academic Press, 1979.

Gibson, Gordon D., Thomas J. Larson, and Cecilia R. McGurk. *The Kavango Peoples*. Studien zur Kulturkunde, Bd. 56. Wiesbaden: Franz Steiner Verlag, 1981.

Glasgow, Tom, Jr. "Sixteenth-Century English Seamen Meet a New Enemy—the Shipworm." *American Neptune* 27, no. 3 (1967): 177–84.

Goodyear, James D. "The Slave Trade, Public Health, and Yellow Fever: The Image of Africa in Brazil." Paper presented to the annual meeting of the American Historical Association, Washington, D.C., 1982.

Goodyear, James D. "A Preliminary Epidemiology of the Bahian Slave Trade, 1780–1810." Unpublished paper, 1981.

Goulart, Maurício. *Escravidão africana no Brasil: das origens á extinção do tráfico.* São Paulo: Livraria Martins, 1949.

Graça, Joaquim Rodrigues. "Viagem feita de Loanda com destino às cabeceiras do Rio Sena, ou aonde for mais conveniente pelo interior do continente, de que as tribus são senhores, principada em 24 de abril de 1845." *Annaes do Conselho Ultramarino* (parte não oficial), sér. 1 (1854–58): 101–14, 117–29, 133–46. Republished as "Expedição ao Muatayanvua." *Boletim da Sociedade de geografia de Lisboa* 9, nos. 8–9 (1890): 365–468. Also excerpted in *Boletim oficial de Angola* (1855) and in *Arquivos de Angola,* sér. 2, 2, nos. 9–10 (1945): 225–39.

Grant, Andrew. *History of Brazil.* London: H. Colburn, 1809.

Gray, Richard, and David Birmingham, eds. *Pre-Colonial African Trade.* London: Oxford University Press, 1970.

Greenfield, Sidney M. "Entrepreneurship and Dynasty Building in the Portuguese Empire in the Seventeenth Century: The Career of Salvador Correia de Sá e Benevides." In Sidney M. Greenfield, Arnold Strickon, and Robert T. Aubey, eds., *Entrepreneurs in Cultural Context,* pp. 21–63. Albuquerque: University of New Mexico Press, 1979.

Guerra, Francisco. "Aleixo de Abreu (1568–1630), Author of the Earliest Book on Tropical Medicine, Describing Amoebiasis, Malaria, Typhoid Fever, Scurvy, Yellow Fever, Dracontiasis, Trichuriasis, and Tungiasis in 1623." *Journal of Tropical Medicine and Hygiene* 71, no. 3 (1968): 55–69.

Guerra, Francisco. "Medicine in Dutch Brazil, 1624–1654." In E. van den Boogaart, H. R. Hoetink, and J. P. Whitehead, eds., *Johan Maurits van Nassau-Siegen, 1604–1679, A Humanist Prince in Europe and Brazil: Essays on the Occasion of the Tercentenary of His Death,* pp. 472–93. The Hague: Johan Maurits van Nassau Stichting, 1979.

Hair, P.E.H. "The Enslavement of Koelle's Informants." *Journal of African History* 6, no. 2 (1965): 193–203.

Hall, John R. "World-System Holism and Colonial Brazilian Agriculture: A Critical Case Analysis." *Latin American Research Review* 19, no. 2 (1984): 43–69.

Hanson, Carl A. *Economy and Society in Baroque Portugal, 1668–1703.* Minneapolis: University of Minnesota Press, 1981.

Harms, Robert W. *Games against Nature: An Eco-Cultural History of the Nunu of Equatorial Africa.* New York: Cambridge University Press, 1987.

Harms, Robert W. "The Genesis of the Commercial Economy along the Middle Zaire River." *Enquêtes et documents d'histoire africaine* 4 (1980): 101–13.

Harms, Robert W. *River of Wealth, River of Sorrow: The Central Zaire Basin in the Era of the Slave and Ivory Trade, 1500–1891.* New Haven: Yale University Press, 1981.

Hartwig, Gerald W. "Social Consequences of Epidemic Diseases: The Nineteenth Century in Eastern Africa." In Gerald W. Hartwig and K. David Patterson, eds., *Disease in African History: An Introductory Survey and Case Studies,* pp. 25–45. Durham, N.C.: Duke University Press, 1978.

Heimer, Franz-Wilhelm, ed. *The Formation of Angolan Society.* Forthcoming.

Heintze, Beatrix. "Angola nas garras do tráfico de escravos: as guerras do Ndongo (1611–1630)." *Revista internacional de estudos africanos* 1 (1984): 11–59.

Heintze, Beatrix. "The Angolan Vassal Tributes of the Seventeenth Century." *Revista de história económica e social* 6 (1980): 57–78.

Heintze, Beatrix. "Das Ende des unabhängigen Staates Ndongo (Angola)." *Paideuma* 27 (1981): 197–273.

Heintze, Beatrix. *Fontes para a história de Angola do século XVII*. Wiesbaden: Franz Steiner Verlag, 1985.

Heintze, Beatrix. "Historical Notes on the Kisama of Angola." *Journal of African History* 13, no. 3 (1972): 407–18.

Heintze, Beatrix. "Luso-African Feudalism in Angola? The Vassal Treaties of the Sixteenth to the Eighteenth Century." *Revista portuguesa de história* 18 (1980): 111–31.

Heintze, Beatrix. "Der portugiesisch-afrikanische Vasallenvertrag in Angola im 17. Jahrhundert." *Paideuma* 25 (1979): 195–223.

Heintze, Beatrix. "Die portugiesische Besiedlungs- und Wirtschaftspolitik in Angola, 1570–1607." *Aufsätze zur portugiesischen Kulturgeschichte* 17 (1981–82): 200–219.

Herbert, Eugenia W. "Portuguese Adaptation to Trade Patterns: Guinea to Angola (1443–1640)." *African Studies Review* 17, no. 2 (1974): 411–23.

Herbert, Eugenia W. *Red Gold of Africa: Copper in Precolonial History and Culture*. Madison: University of Wisconsin Press, 1984.

Heusch, Luc de. *Le roi ivre (ou l'origine de l'état)*. Paris: Gallimard, 1972.

Heywood, Linda. "Production, Trade, and Power: The Politics of Labor in the Central Highlands of Angola, 1850–1930." Ph.D. diss., Columbia University, 1984.

Heywood, Linda, and John Thornton. "Demography, Production, and Labor: Central Angola, 1890–1950." In Dennis D. Cordell and Joel W. Gregory, eds., *African Population and Capitalism: Historical Perspectives*, pp. 241–54. Boulder, Colo.: Westview Press, 1987.

Hilton, Anne (Wilson). *The Kingdom of Kongo*. Oxford: Clarendon Press, 1985.

Hilton, Anne (Wilson). "Political and Social Change in the Kingdom of Kongo to the Late Nineteenth Century." In Heimer, *Formation of Angolan Society* (forthcoming).

Hitchcock, R. K. "The Traditional Response to Drought in Botswana." In Madalon T. Hinchey, ed., *Proceedings of the Symposium on Drought in Botswana*, pp. 91–97. Hanover, N.H.: Clark University Press, 1979.

Hoeppli, R. *Parasitic Diseases in Africa and the Western Hemisphere: Early Documentation and Transmission by the Slave Trade*. Basel: Verlag für Recht und Gesellschaft AF, 1969.

Hogendorn, Jan S. "The Economics of the African Slave Trade" (review-essay). *Journal of American History* 70, no. 4 (1984): 854–61.

Hogendorn, Jan S. "Slave Acquisition and Delivery in Precolonial Hausaland." In Raymond E. Dumett and Ben K. Schwartz, eds., *West African Culture Dynamics*, pp. 477–93. The Hague: Mouton, 1980.

Hogendorn, Jan S., and Marion Johnson. *The Shell Money of the Slave Trade*. New York: Cambridge University Press, 1986.

Hoover, Jeffrey J. "The Seduction of Ruwej: Reconstructing Ruund History (The Nuclear Lunda: Zaire, Angola, Zambia)." Ph.D. diss., Yale University, 1978.

Hoppe, Fritz. *A Africa oriental portuguesa no tempo do Marquês de Pombal (1750–1777)*. Lisbon: Agência Geral do Ultramar, 1970.

Horton, Robin. "Stateless Societies in the History of West Africa." In J.F.A. Ajayi and Michael Crowder, eds., *History of West Africa*, 2d ed., pp. 72–113. New York: Columbia University Press, 1971.

Inikori, Joseph E. "The Import of Firearms into West Africa, 1750–1807: A Quantitative Analysis." *Journal of African History* 18, no. 3 (1977): 339–68.

Inikori, Joseph E. "Introduction," in idem, ed., *Forced Migration*, pp. 13–60.

Inikori, Joseph E., ed. *Forced Migration: The Impact of the Export Slave Trade on African Societies*. London: Hutchinson, 1981.

Isaacman, Allen F. *Mozambique: The Africanization of a European Institution: The Zambesi Prazos, 1750–1902*. Madison: University of Wisconsin Press, 1972.

Janzen, John. *Lemba, 1650–1930: A Drum of Affliction in Africa and the New World*. New York: Garland, 1982.

Johnson, Harold B., Jr. "A Preliminary Inquiry into Money, Prices, and Wages in Rio de Janeiro, 1763–1823." In Dauril Alden, ed., *Colonial Roots of Modern Brazil*, pp. 231–83. Berkeley and Los Angeles: University of California Press, 1973.

Johnson, Marion. "Art and Patronage in Ashanti." Unpublished paper, n.d.

Johnson, Marion. "The Atlantic Slave Trade and the Economy of West Africa." In Roger Anstey and P.E.H. Hair, eds., *Liverpool, the African Slave Trade, and Abolition*, pp. 14–38. Liverpool: Historic Society of Lancashire and Cheshire, 1976.

Johnson, Marion. "Cloth Strip Currencies." Paper presented to the Annual Meeting of the African Studies Association, Houston, 1977.

Johnson, Marion. "Elephants' Teeth in the Age of Elegance." Unpublished paper, n.d.

Johnson, Marion. "The Ounce in Eighteenth-Century West African Trade." *Journal of African History* 7, no. 2 (1966): 197–214.

Johnson, Marion. "Technology, Competition, and African Crafts." In Clive Dewey and A. G. Hopkins, eds., *The Imperial Impact: Studies in the Economic History of Africa and India*, pp. 259–69. London: Athlone Press, 1978.

Johnson, Marion. "To Barter for Slaves." Unpublished paper, n.d.

Jordan, Winthrop D. *White over Black: American Attitudes toward the Negro, 1550–1812*. Chapel Hill: University of North Carolina Press, 1968.

Karasch, Mary C. "The Brazilian Slavers and the Illegal Slave Trade, 1836–1851." M.A. thesis, University of Wisconsin—Madison, 1967.

Karasch, Mary C. *Slave Life in Rio de Janeiro, 1808–1850*. Princeton: Princeton University Press, 1987.

Kea, Raymond. "Firearms and Warfare on the Gold and Slave Coasts from the Sixteenth to the Nineteenth Centuries." *Journal of African History* 12, no. 2 (1971): 185–213.

Kea, Ray A. *Settlement, Trade, and Polities in the Seventeenth-Century Gold Coast*. Baltimore: Johns Hopkins University Press, 1982.

Kiple, Kenneth F. *Blacks in Colonial Cuba, 1774–1899*. Gainesville: University Presses of Florida, 1976.

Kiple, Kenneth F. *The Caribbean Slave: A Biological History*. New York: Cambridge University Press, 1984.

Kiple, Kenneth F. "Historical Dimensions of Disease in the Plantation Economies." Paper presented to the Seminar on Health, Welfare, and Development in Latin America and the Caribbean, Ontario Cooperative Program in Latin Caribbean Studies, Windsor, Ont., 1980.

Kiple, Kenneth F., and Virginia Himmelsteib King. *Another Dimension to the Black Diaspora: Diet, Disease, and Racism.* New York: Cambridge University Press, 1981.

Kjekshus, Helge. *Ecology Control and Economic Development in East African History: The Case of Tanganyika, 1850–1950.* London: Heinemann, 1977.

Klein, Herbert S. *The Middle Passage: Comparative Studies in the Atlantic Slave Trade.* Princeton: Princeton University Press, 1978.

Klein, Martin A. "Women in Slavery in the Western Sudan." In Robertson and Klein, *Women and Slavery in Africa,* pp. 67–92.

Kodi, Muzong Wanda. "A Pre-Colonial History of the Pende People (Republic of Zaire) from 1620 to 1900." 2 vols. Ph.D. diss., Northwestern University, 1976.

Kuper, Adam. "Lineage Theory: A Critical Retrospect." *Annual Review of Anthropology* 11 (1982): 71–95.

Lacerda, José Maria de. "Observações sobre a viagem da costa d'Angola á Costa de Moçambique." *Annaes marítimos e coloniaes* (parte não oficial) 5 (1844): 188–214.

Lacerda, Paulo Martins Pinheiro de. "Noticia da campanha, e paiz do Mosul, que conquistou o Sargento Mór Paulo Martins Pinheiro de Lacerda, no anno de 1790, até principio do anno de 1791." *Annaes marítimos e coloniaes* (parte não oficial), sér. 6, no. 4 (1846): 127–33.

Lacerda, Paulo Martins Pinheiro de. "Noticia da cidade de S. Filippe de Benguella e dos costumes dos gentios habitantes daquelle sertão." *Annaes marítimos e coloniaes* (parte não oficial), sér. 5, no. 12 (1845): 486–91.

Lacerda e Almeida, Franciso José Maria de. *Travessia da África.* Lisbon: Agência Geral das Colónias, 1936.

Lane, Frédéric C. "Progrès technologiques et productivité dans les transports maritimes de la fin du Moyen Âge au début des temps modernes." *Revue historique,* 98ᵉ année, 51, no. 510 (1974): 277–302.

Lang, James. *Portuguese Brazil: The King's Plantation.* New York: Academic Press, 1979.

Larson, Thomas J. "The Significance of Rainmaking for the Mbukushu." *African Studies* 25, no. 1 (1966): 23–36.

La Rue, G. Michael. "Khabir 'Ali at Home in Kubayh: A Brief Biography of a Dar Fur Caravan Leader." *African Economic History* 13 (1984): 56–83.

Latham, A.J.H. "Currency, Credit, and Capitalism on the Cross River in the Precolonial Era." *Journal of African History* 12, no. 4 (1971): 599–605.

Latham, A.J.H. *Old Calabar, 1600–1891: The Impact of the International Economy upon a Traditional Society.* Oxford: Clarendon Press, 1973.

Laughlin, Charles D., Jr., and Ivan A. Brady. "Introduction: Diaphasis and Change in Human Populations." In Laughlin and Brady, eds., *Extinction and Survival in Human Populations,* pp. 1–48. New York: Columbia University Press, 1978.

Leitão, Manoel Correia. See Dias, Gastão Sousa, ed., "Uma viagem a Cassange."

Leitão, Humberto, and José Vicente Lopes. *Dicionârio da linguagem de marinha antiga e atual.* Lisbon: Centro de Estudos Ultramarinos, 1963.

Leite, Glacyra Lazzari. "Pernambuco dentro do império português: o setor de exportação—final do século XVIII e início do século XIX." *Anais de história* 9 (1977): 52–53.

Leynseele, P. van. "Les transformations des systèmes de production et d'échanges de populations ripuaires du Haut-Zaire." *African Economic History* 7 (1979): 117–29.

Lima, José Joaquim Lopes de. *Ensaios sobre a statistica das possessões portuguezas.* Vol. 3. Lisbon: Imprensa Nacional, 1846.

Lisanti, Luis, ed. *Negócios coloniais (uma correspondência comercial do século XVIII).* 5 vols. São Paulo: Visão Editorial, 1973.

Lisboa, José da Silva. See Silva Lisboa, *Princípios de direito mercantil.*

Livingstone, David. *Missionary Travels and Researches in South Africa.* London: J. Murray, 1857.

Lobo, Eulália Maria Lahmeyer. "O comércio atlântico e a comunidade de mercadores no Rio de Janeiro e em Charleston no século XVIII." *Revista de história* (São Paulo), no. 101 (1975): 49–106.

Lobo, Eulália Maria Lahmeyer. "Economia do Rio de Janeiro nos séculos XVIII e XIX." In Paulo Neuhaus, ed., *Economia brasileira: uma visão histórica,* pp. 123–59. Rio de Janeiro: Editora Campus, 1980.

Lockhart, James, and Stuart B. Schwartz. *Early Latin America: A History of Colonial Spanish America and Brazil.* New York: Cambridge University Press, 1983.

Lopes, Edmundo Correia. *Escravatura (subsídios para a sua história).* Lisbon: Agência Geral das Colónias, 1944.

Lovejoy, Paul E. *Transformations in Slavery: A History of Slavery in Africa.* New York: Cambridge University Press, 1983.

Lovejoy, Paul E. "The Volume of the Atlantic Slave Trade: A Synthesis." *Journal of African History* 23, no. 4 (1982): 473–502.

Lovejoy, Paul E., and Steven Baier. "The Desert-Side Economy of the Central Sudan." *International Journal of African Historical Studies* 8, no. 4 (1975): 551–81.

Luccock, John. *Notes on Rio de Janeiro and the Southern Parts of Brazil, 1808–1818.* London: S. Leigh, 1820.

Lugar, Catherine. "The Merchant Community of Salvador, Bahia, 1780–1830." Ph.D. diss., State University of New York, Stony Brook, 1980.

McCaskie, T. C. "Accumulation, Wealth, and Belief in Asante History." *Africa* 53, no. 1 (1983): 23–43.

MacCormack, Carole P. "Slaves, Slave Owners, and Slave Dealers: Sherbro Coast and Hinterland." In Robertson and Klein, *Women and Slavery in Africa,* pp. 271–94.

McCulloch, Merran. *The Ovimbundu of Angola.* Ethnographic Survey of Africa, West Central Africa, no. 2. London: International African Institute, 1952.

McEvedy, Colin, and Richard Jones. *Atlas of World Population History.* Harmondsworth: Penguin Books, 1978.

MacGaffey, Wyatt. "The Closing of the Frontier in Lower Congo, 1885–1921." Paper presented at the annual meetings of the African Studies Association, New Orleans, 1985.

MacGaffey, Wyatt. "Cultural Roots of Kongo Prophetism." *History of Religion* 17, no. 2 (1977): 177–93.

MacGaffey, Wyatt. "Kongo and the King of the Americans." *Journal of Modern African Studies* 6, no. 2 (1968): 171–81.

MacGaffey, Wyatt. "Lineage Structure, Marriage, and the Family amongst the Central Bantu." *Journal of African History* 24, no. 2 (1983): 173–87.

MacGaffey, Wyatt. *Modern Kongo Prophets: Religion in a Plural Society.* Bloomington: Indiana University Press, 1983.

MacGaffey, Wyatt. "The West in Congolese Experience." In Philip D. Curtin, ed., *Africa and the West: Intellectual Responses to European Culture*, pp. 49–74. Madison: University of Wisconsin Press, 1972.

Maesen, A. "Les Holo du Kwango." *Reflets du Monde* 9 (1956): 31–44.

Maestri Filho, Mário José. *A agricultura africana nos séculos XVI e XVII no litoral angolano.* Porto Alegre: Instituto de Filosofia e Ciências Humanas, Universidade Federal do Rio Grande do Sul, 1978.

Magyar, László. *Reisen in Süd-Afrika in den Jahren 1849 bis 1857.* Trans. Johann Hunfalvy. Pest and Leipzig: Lauffer and Stolp, 1859.

Mainga, Mutumba. *Bulozi under the Luyana Kings: Political Evolution and State Formation in Pre-Colonial Zambia.* London: Longmans, 1973.

Manchester, Alan K. *British Preëminence in Brazil: Its Rise and Decline: A Study in European Expansion.* Chapel Hill: University of North Carolina Press, 1933.

Manning, Patrick. "The Enslavement of Africans: A Demographic Model." *Canadian Journal of African Studies* 15, no. 3 (1981): 499–526.

Manning, Patrick. "The Impact of Slave Trade Exports on the Population of the Western Coast of Africa, 1700–1850." Paper presented to the Colloque International sur la Traite des Noirs, Nantes, 1985.

Mannix, Daniel P., and Malcolm Cowley. *Black Cargoes: A History of the Atlantic Slave Trade, 1518–1865.* New York: Viking Press, 1962.

Maret, Pierre de. "L'évolution monétaire du Shaba Central entre le 7^c et le 18^c siècle." *African Economic History* 10 (1981): 117–49.

Martin, Phyllis M. "Cabinda and Cabindans: Some Aspects of an African Maritime Society." In Jeffrey C. Stone, ed., *Africa and the Sea*, pp. 80–96. Aberdeen: Aberdeen African Studies Group, 1985.

Martin, Phyllis M. *The External Trade of the Loango Coast, 1576–1870.* Oxford: Clarendon Press, 1972.

Martin, Phyllis M. "Family Strategies in Nineteenth-Century Cabinda." *Journal of African History* 28, no. 1 (1987): 65–86.

Martin, Phyllis M. "The Making of Cabindan Society, Seventeenth to Nineteenth Century." In Heimer, *Formation of Angolan Society* (forthcoming).

Martin, Phyllis M. "The Trade of Loango in the Seventeenth and Eighteenth Centuries." In Gray and Birmingham, *Pre-Colonial African Trade*, pp. 138–61.

Martins Filho, Amilcar, and Roberto B. Martins. "Slavery in a Nonexport Economy: Nineteenth-Century Minas Gerais Revisited." *Hispanic American Historical Review* 63, no. 3 (1983): 537–68. With comments by Robert W. Slenes, pp. 569–81; Warren Dean, pp. 582–84; and Stanley L. Engerman and Eugene D. Genovese, pp. 585–90.

Matos, Raymundo José da Cunha. *Compêndio histórico das possessões de Portugal na Africa*. Rio de Janeiro: Arquivo Nacional, 1963.

Matthews, Timothy I. "The Historical Tradition of the Peoples of the Gwembe Valley, Middle Zambezi." Ph.D. diss., University of London, 1976.

Mattoso, Katia M. de Queirós. *Être esclave au Brésil XVIe–XIXe siècle*. Paris: Hachette, 1979.

Mauro, Frédéric. "L'Atlantique portugais et les esclaves (1570–1670)." *Revista da Faculdade de letras* (Universidade de Lisboa) 22, no. 2 (1956): 5–52.

Mauro, Frédéric. *Le Portugal et l'Atlantique au XVIIe siècle, 1570–1670*. Paris: S.E.V.P.E.N., 1960.

Maxwell, Kenneth R. *Conflicts and Conspiracies: Portugal and Brazil, 1750–1808*. New York: Cambridge University Press, 1973.

Mayer, Brantz. *Captain Canot, An African Slaver*. New York: Arno Press, 1968.

Meillassoux, Claude. "Female Slavery." In Robertson and Klein, *Women and Slavery in Africa*, pp. 49–66.

Meillassoux, Claude. "The Role of Slavery in the Economic and Social History of Sahelo-Sudanic Africa." (Trans. R. J. Gavin.) In Inikori, *Forced Migration*, pp. 74–99.

Mello, José Antonio Gonçalves de. *João Fernandes Vieira, Mestre de Campo do terço de infantaria do Pernambuco*. Recife: Universidade do Recife, 1956.

Mello, Gov. D. Miguel António de. "Angola no começo do século." *Boletim da Sociedade de geografia de Lisboa* 5 (1885): 548–64.

Mello, Gov. D. Miguel António de, et al. "Angola no fim do século." See "Angola no fim do século XVIII."

Mendes, Luiz António de Oliveira. *Memória a respeito dos escravos e tráfico da escravatura entre a costa d'Africa e o Brazil*. Ed. José Capela. Porto: Escorpião, 1977. Also published as "Discurso academico ao programma . . . ," *Memórias económicas da Academia real das sciencias de Lisboa* 4 (1812): 1–64, and under "Literatura portuguesa," in *O investigador portuguez em Inglaterra* 8, nos. 29–31 (1813): 1–18, 212–22, 417–26; 9, no. 1 (1814): 12–34. Another version published in Carreira, "Companhias pombalinas," *Boletim cultural da Guiné portuguesa* 24 (no. 94) (1969): 406–70.

Metcalf, George. "Gold, Assortments, and the Trade Ounce: Fante Merchants and the Problem of Supply and Demand in the 1770s." *Journal of African History* 28, no. 1 (1987): 27–41.

Miers, Suzanne, and Richard Roberts, eds. *The End of Slavery in Africa*. Madison: University of Wisconsin Press, 1988.

Miller, Joseph C. "Capitalism and Slaving: The Financial and Commercial Organization of the Angolan Slave Trade, According to the Accounts of António Coelho Guerreiro (1684–1692)." *International Journal of African Historical Studies* 17, no. 1 (1984): 1–56.

Miller, Joseph C. "Central and Southern Angola." In Heimer, *Formation of Angolan Society* (forthcoming).

Miller, Joseph C. "Cokwe Expansion, 1850–1900." Occasional Paper, no. 1; 2d ed. rev. Madison: African Studies Program, University of Wisconsin, 1974.

Miller, Joseph C. "Cokwe Trade and Conquest." In Gray and Birmingham, *Pre-Colonial African Trade,* pp. 175–201.

Miller, Joseph C. "The Formation and Transformation of the Mbundu States from the Sixteenth to the Eighteenth Centuries." In Heimer, *Formation of Angolan Society* (forthcoming).

Miller, Joseph C. "Imports at Luanda, Angola: 1785–1823." In Gerhard Liese-gang, Helma Pasch, and Adam Jones, eds., *Figuring African Trade: Proceedings of the Symposium on the Quantification and Structure of the Import and Export and Long-Distance Trade of Africa in the Nineteenth Century (c. 1800–1913)* (St. Augustin, 3–6 January 1983), pp. 165–246. Kölner Beiträge zur Afrikanistik, no. 11. Berlin: Dietrich Reimer Verlag, 1986.

Miller, Joseph C. *Kings and Kinsmen: Early Mbundu States in Angola.* Oxford: Clarendon Press, 1976.

Miller, Joseph C. "Kings, Lists, and History in Kasanje." *History in Africa* 6 (1979): 51–96.

Miller, Joseph C. "Legal Portuguese Slaving from Angola: Some Preliminary In-dications of Volume and Direction, 1760–1830." *Revue française d'histoire d'outre-mer* 62, 1–2 (nos. 226–27) (1975): 135–76. Republished as *La traite des Noirs par l'Atlantique: nouvelles approaches / The Atlantic Slave Trade: New Approaches* (Paris: Société française d'histoire d'outre-mer, 1976).

Miller, Joseph C. "Lineages, Ideology, and the History of Slavery in Western Central Africa." In Paul E. Lovejoy, ed., *The Ideology of Slavery in Africa,* pp. 40–71. Beverly Hills: Sage Publications, 1981.

Miller, Joseph C. "Listening for the African Past." In Miller, ed., *The African Past Speaks: Essays on Oral Tradition and History,* pp. 1–59. Folkestone, Eng.: Wm. Dawson and Sons, 1980; Hamden, Conn.: Archon Books, 1980.

Miller, Joseph C. "Mortality in the Atlantic Slave Trade: Statistical Evidence on Causality." *Journal of Interdisciplinary History* 11, no. 3 (1981): 385–434.

Miller, Joseph C. "Nzinga of Matamba in a New Perspective." *Journal of African History* 16, no. 2 (1975): 201–16.

Miller, Joseph C. "Overcrowded and Undernourished: The Techniques and Con-sequences of Tight-Packing in the Portuguese Southern Atlantic Slave Trade." Paper presented to the Colloque International sur la Traite des Noirs, Nantes, 1985.

Miller, Joseph C. "The Paradoxes of Impoverishment in the Atlantic Zone." In Birmingham and Martin, *History of Central Africa,* 1:118–59.

Miller, Joseph C. "The Portuguese Slave Trade in the Southern Atlantic, 1780–1830." Seminar paper, Institute of Commonwealth Studies, University of London, 1974.

Miller, Joseph C. "Quantities and Currencies: Bargaining for Slaves on the Fringes of the World Capitalist Economy" (forthcoming).

Miller, Joseph C. "The Significance of Drought, Disease, and Famine in the Agriculturally Marginal Zones of West-Central Africa." *Journal of African History* 23, no. 1 (1982): 17–61.

Miller, Joseph C. "Slave Prices in the Portuguese Southern Atlantic, 1600–1830." In Paul E. Lovejoy, ed., *Africans in Bondage: Studies in Slavery and the Slave Trade*, pp. 43–77. Madison: African Studies Program, University of Wisconsin, 1986.

Miller, Joseph C. "Slaves, Slavers, and Social Change in Nineteenth-Century Kasanje," In Franz-Wilhelm Heimer, ed., *Social Change in Angola*, pp. 9–29. Munich: Weltforum Verlag, 1973.

Miller, Joseph C. "Sources and Knowledge of the Slave Trade in the Southern Atlantic." Paper presented to the Western Branch of the American Historical Association, La Jolla, Calif., 1976.

Miller, Joseph C., and John K. Thornton. "The Chronicle as Source, History, and Hagiography: The 'Catálogo dos Governadores de Angola.'" *Paideuma* 33 (1987): pp. 359–89.

Mintz, Sidney W. "The So-Called World System: Local Initiative and Local Response." *Dialectical Anthropology* 2, no. 4 (1977): 253–70.

Molinari, Diégo Luis. *La trata de negros: datos para su estudio en el Río de la Plata*. 2d ed. Colección de textos y documentos relativos a la Historia Económica Argentina y Americana, vol. 2. Buenos Aires: Facultad de Ciencias económicas, Universidad de Buenos Aires, 1944.

Morão, Simão Pinheiro, João Ferreyra de Rosa, and Miguel Dias Pimenta. *Morão, Rosa, e Pimenta: Notícia dos três primeiros livros em vernáculo sôbre a medicina no Brasil*. Historical introductions, interpretations, and notes by E. Duarte; critical studies by Gilberto Osório de Andrade. Pernambuco: Arquivo Público Estadual, 1956.

Moreira, E. D. Macarthy. "O caso das presas espanholas." *Revista do Instituto de filosofia e ciências humanas da Universidade federal do Rio Grande do Sul* (1974), pp. 185–205.

Moreira, José Joaquim. "Memoria sobre as molestias endémicas da costa occidental d'Africa." *Jornal da Sociedade das sciências médicas de Lisboa* 15, no. 1 (1842): 121–52.

Mouser, Bruce L. "Women Slavers of Guinea-Conakry." In Robertson and Klein, *Women and Slavery in Africa*, pp. 320–39.

N'Dua, Edouard. "L'Installation des Tutshokwe dans l'Empire Lunda, 1850–1903." Mémoire de licence, Histoire, Université Lovanium de Kinshasa, 1971.

Neale, Caroline. "The Idea of Progress in the Revision of African History, 1960–1970." In Bogumil Jewsiewicki and David Newbury, eds., *African Historiographies: What History for Which Africa?*, pp. 112–22. Beverly Hills: Sage, 1986.

Neves, António Rodrigues. *Memoria da expedição à Cassange commandado pelo Major Graduado Franciso de Salles Ferreira em 1850*. Lisbon: Imprensa Silviana, 1854.

Neves, Maria Tereza Amado. *D. Francisco Inocêncio de Sousa Coutinho: aspecto moral da sua acção em Angola*. I Congresso da História da Expansão Portuguesa no Mundo. Lisbon: Sociedade Nacional de Tipografia, 1938.

Nicholson, Sharon E. "Climate, Drought, and Famine in Africa." In Art Hansen and Della E. McMillan, eds., *Food in Sub-Saharan Africa,* pp. 107–28. Boulder, Colo.: Lynne Rienner Publishers, 1986.

North, Douglas C. "Sources of Productivity Change in Ocean Shipping, 1600–1850." *Journal of Political Economy* 76, no. 5 (1968): 953–70.

Northrup, David. "African Mortality in the Suppression of the Slave Trade: The Case of the Bight of Biafra." *Journal of Interdisciplinary History* 9, no. 1 (1978): 47–64.

Northrup, David. *Trade without Rulers: Pre-Colonial Economic Development in South-Eastern Nigeria.* Oxford: Clarendon Press, 1978.

Novais, Fernando A. *Portugal e Brasil na crise do antigo sistema colonial (1777–1808).* São Paulo: Editorial HUCITEC, 1979.

Nunes Dias, Manuel. *A Companhia Geral do Grão Pará e Maranhão (1755–1778).* São Paulo: Universidade de São Paulo, 1971.

Oliveira Marques, A. H. de. *History of Portugal.* 2 vols. New York: Columbia University Press, 1972.

Omboni, Tito. *Viaggi nell'Africa occidentale.* Milano: Civelli, 1845.

Orde-Morton, F. W. "Growth and Innovation: The Bahian Sugar Industry, 1790–1860." *Canadian Journal of Latin American Studies* 5, no. 10 (1980): 37–54.

Oroge, E. Adeniyi. "Iwofa: An Historical Survey of the Yoruba Institution of Indenture." *African Economic History* 14 (1985): 75–106.

Owen, Capt. William F. *Narrative of Voyages to Explore the Shores of Africa, Arabia, and Madagascar. . . .* 2 vols. London: Richard Bentley, 1833.

Packard, Randall M. *Chiefship and Cosmology: An Historical Study of Political Competition.* Bloomington: Indiana University Press, 1981.

Palmer, Colin. *Human Cargoes: The British Slave Trade to Spanish America, 1700–1739.* Urbana: University of Illinois Press, 1981.

Pantaleão, Olga. "Aspectos do comércio dos domínios portuguêses no período de 1808 a 1821." *Revista de história* (São Paulo), no. 41 (1960): 99–100.

Papstein, Robert J. "The Upper Zambezi: A History of the Luvale People, 1000–1900." Ph.D. diss., University of California, Los Angeles, 1978.

Pardo, Anne W. "A Comparative Study of the Portuguese Colonies of Angola and Brazil and Their Interdependence from 1648 to 1825." Ph.D. diss., Boston University, 1977.

Patterson, Orlando. *Slavery and Social Death: A Comparative Study.* Cambridge: Harvard University Press, 1982.

Phillips, Ulrich B. "Slavery in the Old South." In Peter I. Rose, ed., *Americans from Africa,* 1:117–30. New York: Atherton, 1970.

Phillips, William D., Jr. *Slavery from Roman Times to the Early Transatlantic Trade.* Minneapolis: University of Minnesota Press, 1985.

Piersen, William D. "White Cannibals, Black Martyrs: Fear, Depression, and Religious Faith as Causes of Suicide among New Slaves." *Journal of Negro History* 62, no. 2 (1977): 147–50.

Pina, Luís de. "Notas para a história médica nacional ultramarina: a água de Inglaterra em Angola." *Jornal do médico* 1 (1940): 5–6.

Pina, Luís de, ed. "Tractado das queixas endemicas, e mais fataes nesta Conquista (Dr. Francisco Damião Cosme, Luanda, 1770)." *Studia* 20–22 (1967): 119–268.

Pinto, Virgílio B. Noya. *O ouro brasileiro e o comércio anglo-português (uma contribuição aos estudos da economia atlântica no século XVIII)*. São Paulo: Nacional, 1979.

Plancquaert, M. *Les Yaka: essai d'histoire*. 2d ed. Brussels: Musée Royale d l'Afrique Centrale, 1971.

Pluchon, Pierre. *La route des esclaves: négriers et bois d'ébène au XVIIIe siècle*. Paris: Hachette, 1980.

Polanyi, Karl. "Sortings and 'Ounce Trade' in the West African Slave Trade." *Journal of African History* 5, no. 3 (1964): 381–93.

Pole, L. M. "Decline or Survival? Iron Production in West Africa from the Seventeenth to the Twentieth Centuries." *Journal of African History* 23, no. 4 (1982): 503–13.

"População de Angola (1779)." *Arquivo das Colónias* 3, no. 16 (1918): 175–76.

"População de Angola (1778)." *Arquivo das Colónias* 3, no. 16 (1918): 177–78.

Postma, Johannes. "The Dimension of the Dutch Slave Trade from Western Africa." *Journal of African History* 13, no. 2 (1972): 237–48.

Postma, Johannes. "The Dutch Slave Trade: A Quantitative Assessment." *Revue française d'histoire d'outre-mer* 62, 1–2 (nos. 226–27) (1975): 232–44.

Postma, Johannes. "Mortality in the Dutch Slave Trade, 1675–1795." In Gemery and Hogendorn, *Uncommon Market*, pp. 239–60.

Postma, Johannes. "The Origin of African Slaves: The Dutch Activities on the Guinea Coast, 1675–1795." In Stanley L. Engerman and Eugene D. Genovese, eds., *Race and Slavery in the Western Hemisphere: Quantitative Studies*, pp. 33–49. Princeton: Princeton University Press, 1975.

Price, Richard, ed. *Maroon Societies: Rebel Slave Communities in the Americas*. New York: Anchor Press, 1973; 2d ed., Baltimore: Johns Hopkins University Press, 1979.

Prins, Gwyn. *The Hidden Hippopotamus: Reappraisal in African History: The Early Colonial Experience in Western Zambia*. New York: Cambridge University Press, 1980.

Pruitt, William. "An Independent People: A History of the Sala Mpasu of Zaire and Their Neighbors." Ph.D. diss., Northwestern University, 1973.

Rau, Virginia. *O "Livro de Razão" de António Coelho Guerreiro*. Lisbon: DIAMANG, 1956.

Rawley, James A. *The Transatlantic Slave Trade: A History*. New York: Norton, 1981.

Rebelo, Manoel dos Anjos da Silva. *Relações entre Angola e Brasil (1808–1830)*. Lisbon: Agência Geral do Ultramar, 1970.

Redinha, José. "Subsídio para a história e cultura da mandioca entre os povos do Nordeste de Angola." *Boletim do Instituto de investigação científica de Angola* 5, no. 1 (1968): 95–108.

Reefe, Thomas Q. *The Rainbow and the Kings: A History of the Luba Empire to 1891*. Berkeley and Los Angeles: University of California Press, 1981.

Reefe, Thomas Q. "The Societies of the Eastern Savanna." In Birmingham and Martin, *History of Central Africa*, 1:160–204.

Rego, António da Silva. *O Ultramar português no século XVIII*. Lisbon: Agência Geral do Ultramar, 1967.

Reynolds, Edward. *Stand the Storm: A History of the Atlantic Slave Trade.* New York: Allison and Busby, 1985.

Ribeiro, Leonidio. *Medicina no Brasil.* Rio de Janeiro: Imprensa Nacional, 1940.

Ribeiro Júnior, José. "Alguns aspectos do tráfico escravo para o Nordeste Brasileiro no século XVIII." In *Anais do VI Simpósio nacional dos professores universitários de história* (Goiâna, 1971), pp. 385–404. São Paulo, 1973.

Ribeiro Júnior, José. *Colonização e monopólio no nordeste brasileiro: a Companhia geral de Pernambuco e Paraíba (1759–1780).* São Paulo: Editorial HUCITEC, 1976.

Richards, W. A. "The Import of Firearms into West Africa in the Eighteenth Century." *Journal of African History* 21, no. 1 (1980): 43–59.

Richardson, David. "The Costs of Survival: The Treatment of Slaves in the Middle Passage and the Profitability of the Eighteenth-Century British Slave Trade." Paper presented at the Colloque International sur la Traite des Noirs, Nantes, 1985.

Richardson, David. "West African Consumption Patterns and Their Influence in the Eighteenth-Century English Slave Trade." In Gemery and Hogendorn, *Uncommon Market,* pp. 303–30.

Roberts, Andrew D. *A History of Zambia.* New York: Africana, 1976.

Roberts, Richard. "Production and Reproduction of Warrior States: Segu Bambara and Segu Tokolor, c. 1712–1890." *International Journal of African Historical Studies* 13, no. 3 (1980): 389–419.

Roberts, Richard, and Martin A. Klein. "The Banamba Slave Exodus of 1905 and the Decline of Slavery in the Western Sudan." *Journal of African History* 21, no. 3 (1980): 375–94.

Robertson, Claire C., and Martin A. Klein, eds. *Women and Slavery in Africa.* Madison: University of Wisconsin Press, 1983.

Rodney, Walter. "African Slavery and Other Forms of Social Oppression on the Upper Guinea Coast in the Context of the Atlantic Slave-Trade." *Journal of African History* 7, no. 3 (1966): 431–43.

Rodney, Walter. "Gold and Slaves on the Gold Coast." *Transactions of the Historical Society of Ghana* 10 (1969): 13–28.

Ross, Robert. *Cape of Torments: Slavery and Resistance in South Africa.* London: Routledge and Kegan Paul, 1983.

Ross, Robert. "Ethnic Identity, Demographic Crises, and Xhosa-Khoikhoi Interaction." *History in Africa* 7 (1980): 259–71.

Ruela Pombo, Pᵉ. "Angola—medicina indígena: Caderno que trata dos paus, ervas, raízes, cascas e óleos vegetais e animais, que serviam em Angola para curar certas e terminadas doenças escrito pelo Sargento-Mór Afonso Mendes." *Diogo Cão* (Lisbon, 1935), no. 4, pp. 105–12; no. 5, pp. 149–50.

Russell-Wood, A.J.R. "Colonial Brazil: The Gold Cycle, c. 1690–1750." In Leslie Bethell, ed., *Cambridge History of Latin America,* 2:547–600. Cambridge: Cambridge University Press, 1984.

Ryder, A.F.C. *Benin and the Europeans, 1485–1897.* New York: Humanities Press, 1969.

Sahlins, Marshall. *Stone-Age Economics.* Chicago: Aldine-Atherton, 1972.

Saldanha da Gama, António de. *Memoria historica e politica sobre o commércio da escravatura entregue no dia 2 de novembro de 1816 ao Conde Capo d'Istria ministro do Imperador da Russia*. Lisbon: Imprensa Nacional, 1880.

Saldanha da Gama, António de. *Memoria sobre as colonias de Portugal situadas na costa occidental d'Africa, mandada ao governor pelo antigo governador e capitão-general do reino de Angola . . . em 1814*. Paris: Tipographia de Casimir, 1839.

Salles Ferreira, Francisco de. *Do tabaco em Angola*. Lisbon: Typ. Luso-Hespanhola, 1877.

Salles Ferreira, Francisco de. *Minas em Angola: memória histórica*. Lisbon: n.p., 1896.

Salvador, José Gonçalves. *Os Cristãos-novos e o comércio no Atlântico meridional (com enfoque nas capitanias do sul, 1530–1680)*. São Paulo: Livraria Pioneira Editora, 1978.

Salvador, José Gonçalves. *Os magnatas do tráfico negreiro (séculos XVI e XVII)*. São Paulo: Livraria Pioneira Editora, 1981.

Sandoval, Candido de Almeida. "Noticia do sertão do Balundo (1837)." *Annaes do Conselho Ultramarino* (parte não oficial), sér. 1 (1858): 519–21.

Santos, Corcino Medeiros dos. "O comércio do porto do Rio de Janeiro com o de Lisboa de 1763 a 1808." Ph.D. diss., Marília, 1973.

Santos, Corcino Medeiros dos. *Relações comerciais do Rio de Janeiro com Lisboa (1763–1808)*. Rio de Janeiro: Tempo Brasileiro, 1980.

Santos, Corcino Medeiros dos. "Relações de Angola com o Rio de Janeiro (1736–1808)." *Estudos históricos* (Marília) 12 (1973): 7–68.

Santos, João Marinho dos. "Angola na governação dos Felipes: uma perspectiva económica e social." *Revista de história económica e social* 3 (1979): 53–76.

Santos, Maria Emília Madeira dos. "Perspectiva do comércio sertanejo do Bié na segunda metade do século XIX." *Studia* 45 (1981): 65–129.

Santos, Maria Emília Madeira dos. *Viagens e apontamentos de um portuense em África*. Coimbra: Biblioteca Geral da Universidade de Coimbra, 1986.

Santos Filho, Lycurgo de Castro. *História geral da medicina brasileira*. 2 vols. São Paulo: Editorial HUCITEC, 1977.

Santos Filho, Lycurgo de Castro. *Pequena história da medicina brasileira*. São Paulo: Universidade de São Paulo, 1966.

Saunders, A. C. de C. M. *A Social History of Black Slaves and Freedmen in Portugal, 1441–1555*. London: Cambridge University Press, 1982.

Schecter, Robert E. "History and Historiography on a Frontier of Lunda Expansion: The Origins and Early Development of the Kanongesha." Ph.D. diss., University of Wisconsin, 1976.

Scheuss de Studer, Elena F. S. *La trata de negros en el Río de la Plata durante el siglo xviii*. Buenos Aires: Universidad de Buenos Aires, 1958.

Schotte, Dr. Johan Peter A. *A Treatise on the Synochus Atrabiliosa, a Contagious Fever Which Raged in Senegal in the Year 1778*. London: M. Scott, 1782.

Schwartz, Stuart B. "Colonial Brazil, c. 1580–c. 1750: Plantations and Peripheries." In Leslie Bethell, ed., *Cambridge History of Latin America*, 2:422–99. Cambridge: Cambridge University Press, 1984.

Schwartz, Stuart B. "Indian Labor and New World Plantations: European Demands and Indian Responses in Northeastern Brazil." *American Historical Review* 83, no. 1 (1978): 43–79.

Schwartz, Stuart B. *Sugar Plantations in the Formation of Brazilian Society.* New York: Cambridge University Press, 1985.

Scott, Henry Harold. "The Slave Trade and Disease." In Henry Harold Scott, *A History of Tropical Medicine,* 2:982–1010. London: E. Arnold, 1939.

Serrano, Carlos. *Os senhores da terra e os homens do mar.* São Paulo: FLHC/USP, 1983.

Serrano, Carlos. "O poder político no Reino Ngoyo: um estudo sociológico." *Africa* (São Paulo) 4 (1981): 129–30.

Serrão, Joel, ed. *Dicionário de história de Portugal.* 4 vols. Lisbon: Iniciativas Editoriais, 1963–71.

Sheridan, Richard B. "The Commercial and Financial Organization of the British Slave Trade, 1750–1807." *Economic History Review* 11, no. 2 (1958): 249–63.

Sheridan, Richard B. *Doctors and Slaves: A Medical and Demographic History of Slavery in the British West Indies, 1680–1834.* New York: Cambridge University Press, 1985.

Sideri, Sandro. *Trade and Power: Informal Colonialism in Anglo-Portuguese Relations.* Rotterdam: Rotterdam University Press, 1970.

Sigaud, Joseph François Xavier. *Discurso sobre a statistica medica do Brasil.* Rio de Janeiro: Seignot-Plancher, 1832.

Sigaud, Joseph François Xavier. *Du climat et des maladies du Brésil: ou statistique médicale de cet empire.* Paris: Fortin, Masson et Cie, 1844.

Silva, José Justino de Andrade e. *Collecção chronologica de legislação portugueza.* 10 vols. Lisbon: Imprensa Nacional, 1859.

Silva Corrêa, Elias Alexandre da. See Corrêa.

Silva Lisboa, José da. Letter to Dr. Domingos Vandelli, 18 October 1781. *Annaes da Biblioteca nacional do Rio de Janeiro* 32 (1910): 494–506.

Silva Lisboa, José da. *Princípios de direito mercantil e leis de marinha.* Lisbon: Impressão Regia, 1815–19; reprinted Rio de Janeiro: Serviço de Documentação do M.N.I., 1963.

Simon, William Joel. "Scientific Expeditions in the Portuguese Overseas Territories, 1783–1808: The Role of Lisbon in the Intellectual-Scientific Community of the Late Eighteenth Century." Ph.D. diss., City University of New York, 1974.

Smith, David Grant. "The Mercantile Class of Portugal and Brazil in the Seventeenth Century: A Socioeconomic Study of the Merchants of Lisbon and Bahia, 1620–1690." Ph.D. diss., University of Texas, 1975.

Socolow, Susan Migden. *The Merchants of Buenos Aires, 1778–1810: Family and Commerce.* London: Cambridge University Press, 1978.

Spix, Johann Baptist von, and C.F.P. von Martius. *Viagem pelo Brasil, 1817–1820.* 3 vols. São Paulo: Editôra da Universidade de São Paulo, 1976. (Trans. by Lúcia Furquim Lahmeyer of *Reise in Brasilien.* . . . 3 vols. Munich: M. Lindauer, 1823–31.)

Stamm, Anne. "La société créole à Saint-Paul de Loanda dans les années 1836–1848." *Revue française d'histoire d'outre-mer* 59, 4 (no. 217) (1977): 578–610.

Stein, Robert. *The French Slave Trade in the Eighteenth Century: An Old Regime Business.* Madison: University of Wisconsin Press, 1979.

Stitt, E. R. "Our Disease Inheritance from Slavery." *United States Naval Medical Bulletin* 26, no. 4 (1928): 801–17.

Suret-Canale, Jean. "Refléxions sur quelques problèmes d'histoire de l'Afrique." *La Pensée,* no. 212 (May 1980): 94–112.

Sutch, Richard. "Care and Feeding of Slaves." In Paul A. David, Herbert G. Gutman, Peter Temin, and Gavin Wright, *Reckoning With Slavery,* pp. 231–301. New York: Oxford University Press, 1976.

Tams, Georg. *Visit to the Portuguese Possessions in South-Western Africa.* (Trans. H. Evans Lloyd.) 2 vols. London: T. C. Newby, 1845; reprinted New York: Negro Universities Press, 1969.

Taunay, Affonso Escragnolle de. *Subsídios para a história do tráfico africano no Brasil.* São Paulo: Anais do Museu Paulista, 1941.

Taussig, Michael T. *The Devil and Commodity Fetishism in South America.* Chapel Hill: University of North Carolina Press, 1980.

Taylor, William B. *Drinking, Homicide, and Rebellion in Colonial Mexican Villages.* Stanford: Stanford University Press, 1979.

Teixeira, Alexandre da Silva, and José da Silva Costa. "Relação da viagem que fiz deste cidade de Benguella para as terras de Lovar no anno de mil setecentos noventa e quatro." *Arquivos de Angola* 1, no. 4 (1935): doc. X. Also published in Felner, *Angola,* 1:236–37.

Teixeira, Waldemar Jorge Gomes. "Subsídios para a história da medicina portuguesa em Angola." *Boletim do Instituto de Angola,* nos. 30–32 (1968): 5–26.

Theal, George McCall. *Records of the Cape Colony from February 1793.* 9 vols. London: Printed for the Government of the Cape Colony, 1897–1903.

Thornton, John K. "Art of War in Angola." *Comparative Studies in Society and History.* Forthcoming.

Thornton, John K. "The Chronology and Causes of Lunda Expansion to the West, 1700–1852." *Zambia Journal of History* 1 (1981): 1–14.

Thornton, John K. "The Demographic Effect of the Slave Trade on Western Africa, 1500–1850." In *African Historical Demography: II,* pp. 691–720. Edinburgh: Centre of African Studies, 1981.

Thornton, John K. "Demography and History in the Kingdom of Kongo, 1550–1750." *Journal of African History* 18, no. 4 (1977): 507–30.

Thornton, John K. "Early Kongo-Portuguese Relations: A New Interpretation." *History in Africa* 8 (1981): 183–204.

Thornton, John K. "The Kingdom of Kongo, *ca.* 1390–1678: The Development of an African Social Formation." *Cahiers d'études africaines* 22, 3–4 (nos. 87–88) (1982): 325–42.

Thornton, John K. *The Kingdom of Kongo: Civil War and Transition, 1641–1718.* Madison: University of Wisconsin Press, 1983.

Thornton, John K. "The Kingdom of Kongo in the Era of the Civil Wars, 1641–1718." Ph.D. diss., University of California, Los Angeles, 1979.

Thornton, John K. "The Slave Trade in Eighteenth-Century Angola: Effects on Demographic Structures." *Canadian Journal of African Studies* 14, no. 3 (1980): 417–27.

Torres, João Carlos Feo Cardoso de Castello Branco e. *Memórias contendo a biographia do vice almirante Luis da Motta Feo e Torres, a História dos governadores e capitaens generaes de Angola desde 1575 até 1825, e a Descripcão geographica e politica dos reinos de Angola e Benguella*. Paris: Fantin, 1825.

Tosh, John. *Clan Leaders and Colonial Chiefs in Lango*. Oxford: Clarendon Press, 1978.

Tuckey, Captain J. K. *Narrative of an Expedition to Explore the River Zaire*. . . . London: John Murray, 1818.

Urquhart, Alvin W. *Patterns of Settlement and Subsistence in Southwestern Angola*. Washington: National Academy of Sciences, National Research Council, 1963.

Vail, H. Leroy, ed. *The Creation of Tribalism in South and Central Africa: Studies in the Political Economy of Ideology*. London: James Currey, forthcoming.

Vail, Leroy, and Landeg White. *Capitalism and Colonialism in Mozambique: A Study of Quelimane District*. London: Heinemann, 1980.

Vansina, Jan. "The Bells of Kings." *Journal of African History* 10, no. 2 (1969): 187–97.

Vansina, Jan. *The Children of Woot: A History of the Kuba Peoples*. Madison: University of Wisconsin Press, 1978.

Vansina, Jan. "Equatorial Africa and Angola: Migrations and the Emergence of the First States." In D. T. Niane, ed., *Africa from the Twelfth to the Sixteenth Century*, pp. 551–77. Vol. 4 of *General History of Africa*. Paris: UNESCO, 1984.

Vansina, Jan. *Kingdoms of the Savanna*. Madison: University of Wisconsin, 1966.

Vansina, Jan. "Knowledge and Perceptions of the African Past." In Bogumil Jewsiewicki and David Newbury, eds., *African Historiographies: What History for Which Africa?*, pp. 28–41. Beverly Hills: Sage, 1986.

Vansina, Jan. "Lignage, idéologie, et histoire en Afrique equatoriale." *Enquêtes et documents d'histoire africaine* 4 (1980): 133–55.

Vansina, Jan. "The Peoples of the Forest." In Birmingham and Martin, *History of Central Africa*, 1:75–117.

Vansina, Jan. "Probing the Past of the Lower Kwilu Peoples (Zaire)." *Paideuma* 19–20 (1973–74): 332–64.

Vansina, Jan. *The Tio Kingdom of the Middle Congo, 1880–1892*. London: Oxford University Press, for the International African Institute, 1973.

Vansina, Jan. "Towards a History of Lost Corners in the World." *Economic History Review* 35, no. 2 (1982): 165–78.

Vansina, Jan, et al. *Introduction à l'ethnographie du Congo*. Kinshasa/Lubumbashi/Kisangani: Editions Universitaires du Congo, [ca. 1965].

Vasconcelos, Alexandre José Botelho de. "Descripção da Capitania de Benguella, suas provincias, povos, rios mais caudelosos, minas de ferro, e enxofre, e outras particularidades que tem, mais consideraveis (1799)." *Annaes marítimos e coloniaes* (parte não oficial) 4, no. 4 (1844): 147–61.

Vellut, Jean-Luc. "Africa central do oeste, em vésperas da partilha colonial: um esboço histórico do séc. XIX." *Africa* (São Paulo) 3 (1980): 73–120.

Vellut, Jean-Luc. "Diversification de l'économie de cueillette: miel et cire dans les sociétés de la forêt claire d'Afrique centrale (c. 1750–1950)." *African Economic History* 7 (1979): 93–112.

Vellut, Jean-Luc. "Les grands tournants dans l'histoire de l'est du Kwanza du XIXe siècle." *Revista do Departamento de biblioteconomia e história* (da Fundação Universidade do Rio Grande do Sul) 1, no. 2 (1979): 93–111.

Vellut, Jean-Luc. "Notes de cours: histoire de l'Afrique Centrale." Unpublished lecture notes, Université de Louvain, 1977–78.

Vellut, Jean-Luc. "Notes sur le Lunda et la frontière luso-africaine (1700–1900)." *Etudes d'histoire africaine* 3 (1972): 61–166.

Vellut, Jean-Luc. "Relations internationales du Moyen-Kwango et de l'Angola dans la deuxième moitié du XVIIIe siècle." *Etudes d'histoire africaine* 1 (1970): 75–135.

Vellut, Jean-Luc. "Le Royaume de Cassange et les réseaux luso-africains (ca. 1750–1810)." *Cahiers d'études africaines* 15, 1 (no. 57) (1975): 117–36.

Venâncio, José Carlos. "A economia de Luanda e hinterland no século XVIII: um estudo de etnologia histórica." Dissertação inaugeral, Universidade de Johannes Gutenberg em Mogúncia, 1983.

Venâncio, José Carlos. "Espaço e dinâmica populacional em Luanda no século XVIII." *Revista de história económica e social* 14 (1984): 67–89.

Verger, Pierre. *Flux et reflux de la traite des nègres entre le golfe de Bénin et Bahia de Todos os Santos du XVIIe au XIXe siècle.* Paris: Mouton, 1968. (Trans. by Evelyn Crawford as *Trade Relations between the Bight of Benin and Bahia from the Seventeenth to the Nineteenth Century.* Ibadan: Ibadan University Press, 1976.)

Vianna, Hélio. "Um humanitário alvará de 1813, sôbre o tráfico de africanos em navios portuguêses." *Revista do Instituto histórico e geográfico brasileiro* 256 (1962): 79–88.

Villalobos, Sergio R. *Comercio y contrabando en el Rio de la Plata y Chile, 1700–1811.* Buenos Aires: Editorial de la Universidad de Buenos Aires (EUBEBA), 1965.

Villiers, Patrick. *Traite des Noirs et navires négriers au XVIIIe siècle.* Grenoble: Editions des 4 Seigneurs, 1982; new ed., Grenoble: J. P. Debbane, 1985.

Vogt, John. *Portuguese Rule on the Gold Coast, 1489–1682.* Athens: University of Georgia Press, 1979.

Wallerstein, Immanuel. *The Modern World System.* 2 vols. to date. New York: Academic Press, 1974, 1980.

Walter, Dr. Jaime. "A propósito de uma doença de Angola de há mais de três séculos: doença do bicho ou maculo." *Boletim clínico e estatistico do Hospital do ultramar* 7 (1957): 47–68.

Walton, Gary M. "Obstacles to Technical Diffusion in Ocean Shipping, 1675–1775." *Explorations in Economic History* 8, no. 2 (1970–71): 123–40.

Walton, Gary M. "Sources of Productivity Change in American Colonial Shipping, 1675–1775." *Economic History Review* 20, no. 1 (1967): 67–78.

Walton, Gary M. "Trade Routes, Ownership Proportions, and American Colonial Shipping Characteristics." In *Les routes de l'Atlantique,* pp. 471–502. Travaux, Colloque international d'histoire maritime, 9th, Seville, 1967. Seville, 1968.

Westbury, Susan. "Analyzing a Regional Slave Trade: The West Indies and Virginia, 1698–1775." *Slavery and Abolition* 7, no. 3 (1986): 241–56.

Wilks, Ivor. "Land, Labour, Capital, and the Forest Kingdom of Asante: A Model of Early Change." In J. Friedman and M. J. Rowlands, eds., *The Evolution of Social Systems,* pp. 487–534. Pittsburgh: University of Pittsburgh Press, 1978.

Williams, David M. "Abolition and the Re-deployment of the Slave Fleet, 1807–11." *Journal of Transport History* 2, no. 2 (1983): 103–15.

Wilson, Anne. "The Kongo Kingdom to the Mid-Seventeenth Century." Ph.D. diss., University of London, 1977.

Wilson, Anne. "Long-Distance Trade and the Luba Lomami Empire." *Journal of African History* 13, no. 4 (1972): 575–89.

Wolf, Eric R. *Europe and the People without History.* Berkeley and Los Angeles: University of California Press, 1982.

Worden, Nigel. *Slavery in Dutch South Africa.* Cambridge: Cambridge University Press, 1985.

Yoder, John C. "A People on the Edge of Empires: A History of the Kanyok of Central Zaire." Ph.D. diss., Northwestern University, 1977.

Index

abolition, of maritime slave trade, 268, 373, 374, 432; Brazilian responses to, 526–30, 636ff; British pressures for, 350, 506–8ff, 510–11, 517, 522, 526, 635, 636ff, 642–43; economic alternatives in Angola, 269, 529, 638, 643–49; Portuguese adjustments to, 432, 636ff. *See also* ivory; population, "bubble"; wax

accounting techniques: Portuguese, 303–6, 540; without literacy, 64, 69, 303–4

adelos, 389

adultery, 164

affinity. *See* marriage

Afonso I (*mani* Kongo), 107–8

age structure: of African populations, 160–64; of slaves, 387–88. *See also* children; slaves, youthfulness

agoa da Inglaterra, 435*n*

agriculture, in Africa, 39, 79, 136; seasonal cycle of, 14, 120, 157; shifting cultivation, 157; trade in products of, 54–55. *See also* bananas; beans; maize; manioc; millet; pulses; sorghums; yams

agricultural "renaissance", in Brazil, 436, 491–92ff, 570, 598ff, 610–11. *See also* coffee; cotton; sugar

agro-pastoralism, 18–19, 30, 46; and slave exporting, 147, 222–23

aguardente. See brandies

Albuquerque, Gov. Paulo Caetano de, 551

Albuquerque e Tovar, Gov. Manoel de, 649

alcohol (imported), alcoholism, 83–84, 136, 682

alfandega. See customs house

Alima River, 219, 225

Almada, Gov. D. Lourenço, 548

Almeida e Vasconcelos, Gov. Manoel, 618, 620–24, 625–26, 681

alqueire, 415–17

alvará. See decree

Amazon River, mentioned, 447, 448–49

Ambaca: commercial rivalries in, 264, 585; Luso-Africans in, 251, 255, 257, 264, 267, 280, 523, 582, 584, 618, 620, 622, 644, 648; mentioned, 195, 213, 249, 266, 627

Ambaquistas, 644

Ambo (people). *See* Ovambo

Ambriz, 229, 432, 518, 519ff, 528, 529–30, 641, 642, 646

Ambuila, battle of, 133, 142, 151, 247*n*

Americans. *See* United States

Amerindians, 116, 449–50, 457, 674–75, 686, 688

Amsterdam, 77, 86

Angola (Portuguese colony): abandonment of, 598–633, and Brazilian independence, 526–28, 638–39; caravan trade in, 195, 264ff; convicts in, 117, 247, 250ff, 261; creation of, 110; currency in, 558, 596; economic diversification in, 604, 634, 638, 643–49, 670; fiscal system of, 541–42; forced labor in, 159, 161, 264–73, 281, 560, 647–49, 670; general location of, 34; government functionaries in, 248; labor shortages in, 529, 647–49; military expeditions of, 98, 141–43, 150, 152, 273ff, 602, 615, 617–18, 622–23, 631–32; military forces in, 541, 543, 550, 558, 585*n*, 588; origin of name, 33; population of, 159–66, 266ff; mentioned, 98. *See also* abolition, economic alternatives; *capitães-mores;*

DEMCO